D0367495

CALIFORNIA
WINE COUNTRY

PHILIP GOLDSMITH & MICHAEL CERVIN

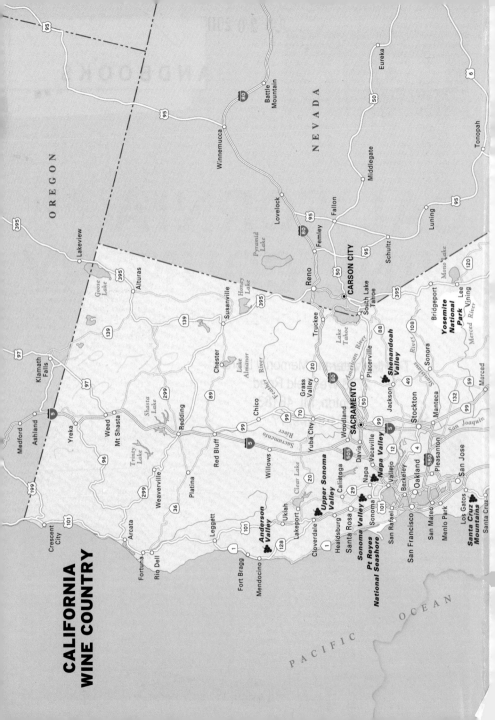

CALIFORNIA
WINE COUNTRY

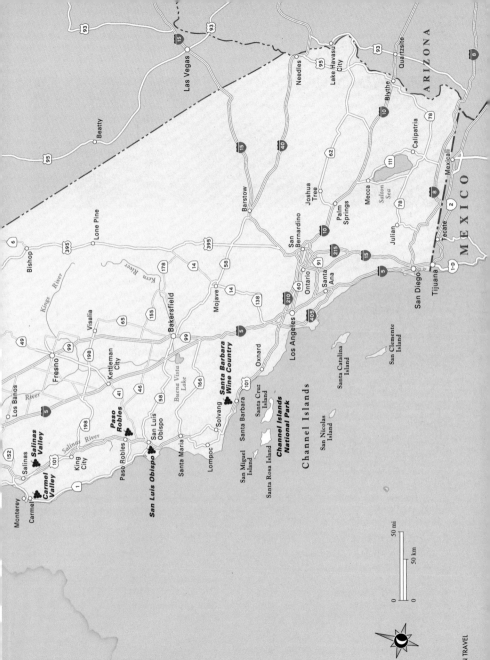

Contents

Discover California Wine Country

You're relaxing on a winery terrace, with a glass of glorious cabernet in hand, fragrant lavender wafting in the warm air. The golden glow of the late afternoon sun casts long shadows in the endless green corduroy of the vineyards. It's the end of another perfect summer day in California Wine Country.

It's hard not to dream of living here. You wouldn't be the first. Over the centuries, people from all over the world have been lured by the lush forests, tall mountains, abundant rivers, warm valleys, and dramatic coastline of California. The state's remarkable attraction as a land of golden opportunity has also created a wine landscape like no other — a rich historical, cultural, and agricultural tapestry that continues to grow and evolve even in the 21st century.

Back in the 1800s, early winemakers chose this geographically diverse and largely unpopulated area of the state to grow grapes — a testament to the favorable soils and micro-climates here. Over the years, each California wine region has developed a distinctive taste and personality of its own. Though it only produces about four percent of the state's wine, Napa puts on one of the greatest wine shows on earth, with ever-more-elaborate wineries and world-class restaurants. In neighboring Sonoma, wineries coexist with quirky small towns and vast expanses of forest, grassland, and wetland. Founded during

the gold rush, many vineyards in the Sierra Foothills have a Wild West feel. And newer wine regions in the Santa Cruz Mountains and along the Central Coast have become refuges for maverick farmers, risk-taking winemakers, and independent business owners. Such a varied geography, population, and character give rise to just about every kind of food and wine imaginable – all the more for wine-lovers and gourmands alike to enjoy.

Before your head starts spinning thinking of all the wine you'll be tasting, keep in mind that California also offers an array of opportunities for peace and relaxation. Take a long, slow drive on quiet country roads that showcase stunning redwoods, an eternity of rolling hills, the satisfying symmetry of vineyards, and sunny, vibrant mustard flowers. Soak in restoration at natural hot springs. Or wiggle your toes in the wet sand at the edge of the Pacific.

From the hard-won decadence of the wine elites to the rustic charms of the latest start-ups, there's sure to be a place in California Wine Country that will fire your imagination and feed your dreams.

Planning Your Trip

▶ WHERE TO GO

Napa Valley

This *is* California Wine Country, as far as many people are concerned—arguably the most important winemaking region in the state, with a name recognized around the world. Some 15 distinct appellations are home to hundreds of wineries, ranging from historic names that make millions of cases of wine per year down to modest wineries turning out some of California's best cabernet sauvignons. It can be expensive and crowded in Napa, yet it's not hard to find pockets of rural tranquility if you venture off the beaten path.

Southern Sonoma

Although it now lives in the cultural shadow of the Napa Valley, this is ground zero not only for California's modern wine industry but for California itself. The notable town of Sonoma is at peace with itself, worn out from the tumultuous series of events more than 150 years ago that gave birth to the state. Life is more laid-back (and cheaper) than in Napa, yet there are still plenty of cultural, culinary, and outdoor attractions, alongside the first-class wines, from the sleepy town of Glen Ellen to the cool flatlands of Los Carneros.

Northern Sonoma

In northern Sonoma, scenery and wines from the multitude of hills and small valleys often have little in common other than their addresses. The cool, lush Russian River Valley has forests, rivers, small farms, and some of the best pinot noir and chardonnay in California. The warmer Dry Creek Valley and Alexander Valley are home to big red wines from small family-owned wineries. Bordering all three regions is the fascinating town of Healdsburg, a mix of the upscale and down-home.

Mendocino County

Mendocino is refreshingly rural and laid-back,

Wild mustard blankets a Napa Valley vineyard in February.

but with a growing reputation for sophisticated wines. In the isolated Anderson Valley, the population is barely into four figures and old-timers in sleepy towns like Boonville still speak an obscure local lingo from a century ago. Scattered among the farms and forests are quirky family wineries and world-class producers of pinot noir, sparkling wines, and gewürztraminer. Across the hills in Eastern Mendocino, the varied landscape and warmer weather give rise to a wider range of red and white wines, including the Coro blends, from organic wineries around the county seat of Ukiah and Hopland farther south.

Sierra Foothills

The gold rush of 1849 lasted only a few years, but the new rush to become the next great California wine destination continues. El Dorado, Amador and Calaveras Counties comprise the Foothills region, with the best known wine coming out of the Shenandoah Valley in Amador. Zinfandel is king here, with historic vines from the late 1880s still producing juice, but barbera and syrah are coming on strong. Bold reds, along with a smattering of whites, most notably viognier, draw wine lovers to historic Old West towns like Murphys and Fair Play.

The Santa Cruz Mountains

The Santa Cruz Mountains stretch from the hot western fringes of Silicon Valley up to elevations of over 3,000 feet before sloping gently down toward the ocean. Historic and moneyed towns like Los Gatos and Saratoga anchor wineries on the eastern slopes, producing some of the state's best chardonnay and cabernet sauvignon. The western slopes are prime pinot noir territory, where small pockets of vineyards mingle with groves of ancient redwoods and acres of parkland. Where the mountains meet the sea, the city of Santa Cruz is more summer beach town than wine destination, with the distinction of the only roller coaster within walking distance of a tasting room.

Monterey, Carmel, and the Santa Lucia Highlands

The Santa Lucia Highlands have become one of the most respected growing areas for pinot noir and chardonnay grapes; many Napa

a vineyard in the green hills of San Luis Obispo

and Sonoma producers routinely buy fruit there. Carmel Valley and Monterey vineyards keep up with 40,000 acres of grapes and perhaps the most scenic backdrop for wine-tasting in the state, including Cannery Row overlooking the bay and charming Carmel-by-the-Sea.

San Luis Obispo and Paso Robles

Slow-paced San Luis Obispo beckons with a beautiful downtown fronted by Higuera Street, an ideal spot for creek-side dining and strolling. Make a short day trip to Paso Robles, the hub of the most exciting wine industry area in all of California, with access to more than 200 wineries that have made their home along the languid and scenic Highway 46.

Santa Barbara Wine Country

Sandwiched between the sparkling Pacific and the rugged mountains, Santa Barbara is the quintessential California getaway. Small towns with intimate wine-tasting venues punctuate the surrounding region. Quaint Solvang features sights that explore Danish heritage and a multitude of tasty Danish bakeries and restaurants. Santa Ynez and Los Olivos boast scenic wine roads and excellent wineries; and in Santa Maria, you can visit the beautiful Mission La Purisima Concepcion de Maria Santisima.

▶ WHEN TO GO

Summer and fall are the most popular seasons for wine-tasting, and for good reason. This is when the weather is at its best and the wineries are at their most active, laying out lavish food and wine events, preparing for harvest, and releasing new vintages.

The problem is, everyone seems to be here at this time of year. Hotel prices surge, traffic clogs the roads, and getting a restaurant reservation is like a game of roulette. Weekends can be particularly bad. Tourist traffic swells with day-trippers, turning a weekend getaway into a weekend in purgatory. Visiting midweek at this time of year

fall grape leaves, Sebastiani Vineyards

can make a huge difference. If you're wine-tasting along the coast, be aware of "June gloom," with the marine layer of fog covering the area until as late as 4 P.M.

In the fall (October-December), things quiet down a little bit, hotel rates drop, and the weather is pleasant as the vineyards turn glorious hues of red and gold.

Winter is the wettest but also the quietest period, when wineries can be blissfully devoid of visitors, enabling plenty of time with tasting-room staff.

In spring (March-May), it's warm, not hot, and the skies are clear. The landscape is a fresh, vivid green after the winter rains. It's a good time to visit Wine Country ahead of the summer crowds.

▶ BEFORE YOU GO

Transportation

Almost everyone gets around by car in California. You might be able to park the car to explore some of the bigger towns by foot for the day, visiting urban tasting rooms, shops, and sights. Ultimately, however, you'll need two wheels or four to fully appreciate California Wine Country.

There's one obvious problem—drinking and driving (or cycling) are not the best combination. If you're wine-tasting, designate a driver for each day (or the duration of the trip), or book daylong tours either in a car with a driver or as part of a group in a small bus. If you must taste and drive, master the discipline of spitting out wine in the tasting room.

As you plan an itinerary, be aware that driving times can be slower than you expect. Average speeds can be very slow on rural roads, especially on mountain roads and in busy areas during rush hour. Distances between wineries and summer heat can also make biking more exhausting than you might think, so plan accordingly.

What to Take

Despite its sunny reputation, California's weather can be unpredictable—especially along the coast. The key to staying comfortable is to wear layers of clothing that can be shed along the way. Put some layers back on in the evening, as temperatures can drop sharply after dark, particularly in the fall.

Sunscreen, hats, and sunglasses are essential, especially with alcohol thrown into the mix to accelerate dehydration. Take casual clothing and good walking shoes for tramping up to picnic spots or through vineyards. Hiking boots and binoculars are helpful for exploring the mountain and forest trails.

Very few restaurants require anything more than smart casual attire, so unless you're planning to eat at the more upscale establishments, it's fine to leave cocktail dresses and sport coats behind.

Explore California Wine Country

▶ BEST OF NAPA AND SONOMA

This weeklong tour will give a taste of the diversity that Napa and Sonoma Valleys offer, mixing in wineries, sights, and outdoor activities. Driving is the best way to get around, but you could also rent a bike in Sonoma or Healdsburg to explore some of the local attractions.

Day 1

In the city of Napa, grab some breakfast at one of the many eateries in the Oxbow Public Market and get your first taste of gourmet Wine Country food. Drive north on the Silverado Trail, stopping first at the spectacular Persian palace Darioush. Continue north to the organic champion Robert Sinskey Vineyards, where food is as much a part of the visitor experience as wine. A few miles farther north, stop at the sparkling wine specialist Mumm and explore its photography galleries before chilling with a glass of bubbly on the terrace overlooking the Napa Valley. If you time it right, the sun might be starting to set over the western hills. Continue to Calistoga for a creek-side dinner at the Calistoga Inn.

Day 2

After a hearty breakfast at the cozy Café Sarafornia, learn more about Calistoga's colorful Victorian history at the Sharpsteen Museum. Buy picnic supplies in town before heading south for a tour of the caves at the nearby Schramsberg Vineyards, a champagne house with its own unique Victorian history. Alternatively you could experience some fake Tuscan history with a tour of the spectacular Castello di Amorosa.

Continue south to Bothe-Napa Valley State Park for a short hike through the redwoods, followed by a picnic under the trees. Drive farther south to St. Helena, stopping off for one of the cooking demonstrations at the Culinary Institute of America if you have time.

From St. Helena, take the scenic drive up Spring Mountain Road to the very top to experience the sweeping views and wonderful mountain wines of Pride Mountain Vineyards. Continue west and spend the night down in Sonoma Valley.

Day 3

Take a fun, motorized tour around the Benziger Family Winery vineyards in Glen Ellen, one of the few biodynamic wineries in California. After tasting some of their classic Sonoma cabernets, head for nearby Figone Olive Oil Company just south of Glen Ellen to taste some diverse olive oils.

After lunch at one of the many great restaurants in Glen Ellen, hike around the scenic Jack London State Historic Park, once part of the Victorian author's giant ranch and now full of fascinating ruins. Those with enough energy can expend plenty of it in Sugarloaf Ridge State Park on the other side of the valley, where redwoods and sunny ridges offer ample outdoor choices and spectacular views.

End the day tasting reserve wines on the peaceful patio overlooking the valley at Chateau St. Jean.

the view from Domaine Carneros

Day 4

Browse the shops and sights around the historic Sonoma Plaza, perhaps tasting some crisp chardonnay at the Charles Creek Vineyards tasting room or on the patio of the Roche Winery tasting room. If you have time, consider exploring some of the historic wineries nearby, including Sebastiani Vineyards and Gundlach Bundschu.

Have lunch in Sonoma before heading south to Carneros for a pre-booked afternoon Discovery Tour at the artistic wonderland of The di Rosa Preserve. Finish your afternoon relaxing on the terrace at the château-like Domaine Carneros, sampling some of the fine sparkling wines, or visit the modern, minimalist tasting room of neighboring Cuvaison Estate to sample classic chardonnay and pinot noir while overlooking the vineyards. Inspired by the wines, make the short drive back up to Sonoma to dine at one of the town's many superb restaurants.

Day 5

Drive north through the Sonoma Valley, stopping at tiny Loxton Cellars to taste the wonderful syrah and, if owner Chris Loxton has the time, take a short tour of the vineyards. Contrasting the modest winemaking operation at Loxton, a little farther north is the splendor of the Ledson Winery.

Continue up-valley to Santa Rosa and then head west into the Russian River Valley for a change of scenery and a change of wines. After lunching in the tiny town of Graton, head up to Iron Horse Vineyards for some afternoon champagne overlooking the rural scenery.

Drive north to the funky riverside town of Guerneville and, if you have time, continue up to the Armstrong Redwoods State Reserve for a late afternoon hike in the cool shade of the majestic redwoods. Choose from cheap and cheerful or gourmet dining options in Guerneville, perhaps ending the day at one of the colorful local bars.

Day 6

With a breakfast from Guerneville's River Inn Grill preparing you for a busy day, head east to Korbel Champagne Cellars for a tour of the historic winery. Stop at the Korbel

VARIETAL TOURS

If you're a fan of a particular type of wine, it's worth planning a trip to the wineries that specialize in it.

CLASSIC CABERNETS

- **Stags Leap District** makes beautifully structured cabernets.

- **Shafer Vineyards** is tucked away in its own private canyon, where you might be lucky enough to taste its Hillside Select cabernet.

- **Stag's Leap Wine Cellars** is home to the vineyards that beat the best in the world in the famous Paris tasting of 1976.

- **Beaulieu Vineyard** offers bigger, bolder cabernets, laced with the Rutherford appellation's distinct flavor of "Rutherford dust."

- **Rubicon Estate Winery,** puts on the best winery show in the Napa Valley, courtesy of owner and filmmaker Francis Ford Coppola.

- **Pride Mountain Vineyards** showcases both panoramic views and the taste of their elegant cabernet.

- **Beckmen Vineyards** in the Santa Ynez Valley crafts excellent cabs from biodynamic grapes.

- **Eberle Winery** in Paso Robles has consistently made sultry reserve cabernets for decades.

- **Heller Estate Vineyards** in the Carmel Valley makes organic cabs that will surprise you with their complexity and depth.

- **Cedarville Vineyard,** in El Dorado County, makes competitive cabs at a competitive price.

THE PLEASURES OF PINOT

- **Domaine Carneros** is known for its flagship Avant Garde pinot noir.

- **Landmark Vineyards** produces the highly regarded Kastania and Grand Detour pinot noirs, sourced from coastal vineyards.

- **Siduri Wines** offers cult-favorite pinots from just about every major growing region on the West Coast.

- **Dutton Goldfield Winery** is one of the Russian River Valley's best pinot vineyards.

- **Hartford Family Winery** offers highly praised pinots in a beautiful location near the Russian River.

- **Davis Bynum** features vineyard-designate pinot noirs in an old hop kiln building.

- **Talbott Vineyards** succeeds with several iterations of world-class pinot noir in Monterey.

- **Pessagno Winery** crafts seductive pinot noir in the Santa Lucia Highlands.

- **Flying Goat Cellars** succeeds in Santa Maria with pure pinot noir fruit not masked by heavy oak.

- **Tantara Winery** crafts eight different versions of upper-end pinot noirs using indigenous yeasts and basket presses in their small facility in Santa Maria.

- **Presidio Winery** samples Burgundian style pinot noir farms in their Solvang tasting room.

ZINFANDEL: CALIFORNIA'S SIGNATURE GRAPE

- **Jeff Runquist Wines** in the Shenandoah Valley crafts robust, hefty zinfandels worthy of its heritage.

- **Newsome-Harlow Wines** in Murphys makes a voracious zinfandel named after the Donner party.

- **Hunt Cellars** in Paso Robles produces a zin so smooth that you'll fall in love with wine all over again.

- **Saucelito Canyon Vineyard,** located in San Luis Obispo, has vineyard plantings from the 1880s that still produce fruit.

- **Ridge Vineyards** is one of the best-known makers of the underappreciated classic Northern California zinfandel.

- **Beauregard Vineyards** in Santa Cruz uses wild yeast to make their zinfandel.

- **Gundlach Bundschu Winery** makes a terrific limited edition version of zin in Sonoma.

- **Ravenswood Vineyards** makes over a dozen iterations of the zinfandel grape.

- **Mayo Family Winery** produces a zinfandel port that's luscious, sweet, and addictive.

- **Frog's Leap Winery** produces an organically farmed zinfandel worth sampling.

- **Caymus Vineyards** has a little-known zinfandel that's sold only at their Napa winery.

Northern California's Napa Valley, with new spring growth on older vines

Armstrong Woods in Guerneville

deli to pack a picnic, then continue along the river to spend an hour or two lounging at Sunset Beach or Steelhead Beach along the Russian River.

Gather up the energy to continue up the Westside Road to visit some of the region's best pinot noir producers, including Thomas George Estates and C. Donatiello Winery, perhaps stopping off at Hop Kiln Winery along the way to see the giant kilns that once dried hops for beer making. Finish up in the pretty town of Healdsburg, where there are ample dining, lodging, and entertainment options.

Day 7

Explore the many downtown tasting rooms of Healdsburg, then drive or bike into the nearby Dry Creek Valley to visit some small wineries that produce some big zinfandels. Ridge Vineyards has an environmentally friendly winery building that is as organic as its wines, and the Timber Crest Collective is home to a handful of small innovative wine producers.

If you're on four wheels rather than two, cross over into neighboring Alexander Valley, where cabernet is king. Visit Alexander Valley Vineyards, one of the most historic in the valley, and drive to the far northern end of the valley to visit the historic Asti Winery, once home to the Italian-Swiss Colony and now home to Souverain.

Finish the day with a pizza and local wine at Diavola Pizzeria & Salumeria, perhaps taking home some locally made salami as an unusual Wine Country gift.

► BEST OF SANTA BARBARA AND THE CENTRAL COAST

These five days of bliss will get you to many of the high points on the Central Coast. This itinerary is not designed for a leisurely pace, but offers the best overview of what the region has to offer, including its wines.

Day 1

Start in Santa Barbara with breakfast at Renaud's Patisserie for the best croissants in town. From there head over to the Old Mission Santa Barbara. Meander down to the County Courthouse and get your photo op at the clock tower with its expansive views of red-tile roofs, the ocean, the mountains, and downtown. Since you're near State Street, walk through El Paseo, the historic and quintessential Santa Barbara street with its meandering path, Spanish architecture, bougainvillea, and fountains. While there sample the wines at the Wine Cask Tasting Room, which features small boutique wines.

Head to the waterfront and experience syrah and sauvignon blanc at Kunin Wines and Westerly Vineyards, housed in the same tasting room. Get your seafood fix with lunch at Brophy Brothers with views of the marina. After lunch, visit Santa Barbara Winery, the oldest winery in the county. Plan for dinner tonight at Opal for a good introduction to the local culinary scene.

Day 2

Get up early and drive Highway 150 north heading to Solvang. Along the way, check out Knapp's Castle for great views of the ocean and the Santa Ynez Valley. Once in Solvang, stop at Mortensen's for local pastries and coffee. Explore the Solvang Antique Center and the Elverhøj Museum of History and

colorful Santa Barbara countryside

Solvang is a picturesque Danish village.

Art. Visit Mandolina winery for California wines with an Italian flare, then walk down the street to sample Grenache blanc and pinot noir at D'Alfonso-Curran.

Stop at Mission Santa Inés on your way to Los Olivos (a five-minute drive). Have lunch at Patrick's Side Street Café, then taste killer syrah and viognier at Carina Cellars and Stolpman Vineyards.

Heading back toward Solvang, consider a stop at the Quicksilver Miniature Horse Farm on Alamo Pintado Road to see the miniature horses. Take advantage of the nightly wine and cheese offering at Hadsten House, and stay the night there as well. After dinner soak in the hot tub or swim in the pool.

Day 3

Start your day by heading out to Highway 101 to Santa Maria, but not before seeing the ostriches at Ostrich Land. For an uncomplicated and traditional breakfast, go to Pappy's Restaurant.

Start wine-tasting with Kenneth Volk Vineyards, making sure to sample their negrette and cabernet pfeiffer. From there, check out Cottonwood Canyon, and head back to Santa Maria for lunch at Chef Ricks.

It's a bit of a drive, but Guadalupe/Nipomo Dunes are worth it. You'll be amazed at the other-worldly nature of this beach. A brief drive will get you to Pali Wine Company for grenache and pinot noir and, since they are open later, swing by McKeon Phillips Winery for cabernet sauvignon.

Check into the Santa Maria Inn, but head to the Far Western Tavern in Guadalupe for a dinner of steaks grilled over red oak.

Day 4

Head out on Highway 101, stopping in Avila Beach for a late breakfast near the water at the Custom House, then stroll the pier. By mid-morning Wood Winery opens and you can sample wines right on the boardwalk.

A walkway among Nipomo Dunes leads to the beach on a foggy day.

Drive on toward San Luis Obispo, stopping by Salisbury Vineyards, right off Highway 101 for a little zinfandel and art appreciation. Once you arrive in SLO, explore Higuera Street, checking out the shops and Bubblegum Alley. Cross the creek to visit Mission San Luis Obispo before lunching creek-side at Novo.

For afternoon wine-tasting, make the short drive to Tolosa Winery and their hip, modern tasting room for merlot and viognier, then Per Bacco Cellars for classy pinot noir.

Check in to the Madonna Inn, then head to the Gold Rush Steakhouse for a terrific steak dinner while lounging in their signature pink booths. End the evening with some dancing—or a soak in the hot tub.

Day 5

It's only a 30-minute drive to Paso Robles. Swing by House of Bagels for a breakfast sandwich, then head to Hunt Cellars for luscious plush wines. Take Vineyard Drive north toward Halter Ranch for cabernet and viognier.

After a leisurely drive on Adelaida Drive through the backcountry of Paso, you'll reach downtown. Lunch at Berry Hill Bistro or Artisan, near the town square, before dropping by Edward Sellers for killer Rhône-style wines. Stroll through City Park, take a peek in the Paso Robles Historical Museum, and visit Pianetta Winery for blended wines in a historical setting. Stay at the Paso Robles Inn, which is close to several dining options.

▶ ROMANTIC WEEKENDS

What better way to spend a long weekend than by experiencing the best eating, drinking, and pampering that Wine Country has to offer? These long weekends showcase both the diversity and the hedonism of California's wine regions.

Napa and Sonoma

DAY 1

Get acquainted with the Napa Valley, its history, and its wines at the Napa Valley Museum just outside Yountville before toasting your arrival in Wine Country with so luxuriously rich blanc de noirs champagne at nearby Domaine Chandon. Have lunch at the winery's renowned restaurant, then take a tour or simply explore the sculpture-filled gardens.

In the evening, head down to the old red-brick Napa Mill on the river in downtown Napa for a classic Wine Country dinner on the patio at the charming French bistro Angèle, followed by an after-dinner cocktail

and dancing at Silo's jazz and blues bar right next door.

DAY 2

Drive south into Carneros to The di Rosa Preserve to see some whimsical contemporary art at the Gatehouse Gallery. In advance of your trip, make an appointment for one of the morning tours of all the galleries and gardens, home to one of California's biggest collections of contemporary art.

Afterward, head across the road to the palatial Domaine Carneros and contemplate art with a glass of fruity brut rosé champagne and hors d'oeuvres on the terrace overlooking the vineyards, or in front of a blazing fire on a chilly winter day.

Drive a little farther west to Sonoma and enjoy a light gourmet lunch before spending the afternoon exploring the sights and boutiques around pretty Sonoma Plaza, perhaps even taking a stroll past flower-filled front

the winery terrace at Domaine Chandon

FREE TOURS AND TASTINGS

Wine-tasting can be expensive – but it doesn't have to be. Although free wine is getting harder to come by, a handful of wineries still offer free tasting as part of a tour. In Napa this includes **Frog's Leap** (which also offers free organic produce if you're lucky), **Caymus Vineyards, Mayacamas Vineyards,** and **Reverie Vineyard & Winery** on Diamond Mountain. Free tasting without a tour is available at **V. Sattui Winery,** though you'll have to endure crowds most of the year.

At **Goosecross Cellars,** for the $10 Napa-standard tasting fee you can also enroll in the educational and entertaining Wine Basics class offered on the winery lawn every Saturday morning during the summer, which includes a couple of tastings.

In Paso Robles **Eberle Winery** has always offered complimentary tastings, and around Paso Robles many tasting fees are still only $5. In the Sierra Foothills, the majority of wineries still provide complimentary tastings, though the wineries in **Murphys** all have tasting fees in the $5 range, with the exception of **Indian Rock,** which is free. **Lava Cap Winery** in El Dorado County offers free tours and **Sobon Estate** in the Shenandoah Valley has a free self-guided tour of one of the oldest wineries in the state.

Another way to save money is to go coupon hunting. Drop in to the local chamber of commerce or any other tourist information center; they sometimes have vouchers for free tastings at various wineries hidden among the piles of free brochures and magazines. Or, browse a few of the free magazines, like *The Vine* and *Wine Country This Week,* available at wineries and information centers: The winery ads often include offers for free or two-for-one tastings. And don't forget to contact the local winery associations as they can give you the most up-to-date information on what tasting fees are going for in that area. In Calaveras County the visitor center offers the **VIP Card,** which is free just for signing up and will get you discounts at many of the wineries around Murphys. In Santa Barbara, the **Axxess Book** (www.sbaxxess.com) is a coupon book which costs $30, but allows a number of

two-for-one wine tastings, discounts at area restaurants, golf and local sights.

Similarly, if you have the chance, trawl the websites of the wineries you want to visit and see if they have printable vouchers for discount tasting (Beringer, for example, nearly always has two-for-one coupons). Or check out NapaValley.com and WineCountry.com, which often have pages dedicated to discounts and promotions. Even social networking sites like Facebook and Twitter, or review sites like Yelp, often offer two-for-one tasting coupons from wineries with an online presence.

Talk to the concierge or owner wherever you're staying. Many hotels and inns arrange free or discount tastings for their guests at local wineries, or at least have a few vouchers they can give you.

If you can't avoid paying to taste the wines at a favorite winery, check if the cost of the tasting can be deducted from any wine purchases you make, which is fairly standard in Paso Robles and throughout the Sierra Foothills. Many wineries offer this courtesy. As a last resort, tag along with a local wine club member: All club members at wineries taste for free and that extends to their guests.

V. Sattui Winery

guarding the tasting rooms at Sebastiani Vineyards

yards to the Sebastiani winery to taste some of its more unusual Italian-varietal wines.

In the evening, enjoy a glass of wine while watching the plaza's wildlife—from ducks to humans—at the Ledson Hotel before driving north for dinner in Glen Ellen at the cozy and romantic bistro Saffron. If you're in the mood for some nighttime stargazing, drive east from Glen Ellen up into the dark Mayacamas Mountains on Trinity Road, then descend back into the Napa Valley via the Oakville Grade.

DAY 3
Begin the day with breakfast or brunch at the classy Bardessono restaurant in Yountville. If it's not too late in the morning, drive north to the winery that has come to symbolize the Napa Valley like no other—the Robert Mondavi Winery. Take one of the regular tours to see the best of the sprawling mission-style buildings and taste some classic Napa wines.

Continue north to the V. Sattui Winery, just outside St. Helena, to buy a cheap, fruity bottle of gamay rouge and picnic supplies (including a corkscrew) before continuing north to the Bothe-Napa Valley State Park, where you can be in the redwoods within minutes and find a perfect picnic spot.

After a relaxing lunch, and perhaps a short hike to appreciate some of the park's valley views, it's time for some pampering, Calistoga-style. Drive north to the famous spa town for your appointment for a couple's restorative mud bath at the Lincoln Avenue Spa. Since it's a wine-themed weekend, choose the antioxidant-laden mud containing wine, grapeseed oil, and green tea.

Later in the afternoon, head south from Calistoga along the rural Silverado Trail to Rutherford and the Mumm Napa Valley winery, where there's usually a fascinating exhibition of art or photography that can be enjoyed with a glass of bubbly in hand.

Stay in Rutherford or return later in the evening for the culinary highlight: a sunset dinner overlooking the valley at the Auberge du

dinner on the terrace at Auberge du Soleil

Soleil resort, high up in the hills. Book well in advance to secure a table on the terrace.

Santa Barbara Wine Country

Santa Barbara practically defines romantic getaway. The ocean spreads out before you and there are vineyards, mountains, excellent restaurants, and shopping, all with a Spanish adobe backdrop.

DAY 1

Begin in the city of Santa Barbara where the sapphire blue of the Pacific will lull you into a relaxed state of mind. An early morning walk along Leadbetter Beach is invigorating and provides a likely chance you'll see dolphins. Begin with breakfast at Via Maestra 42 for a light, flavorful breakfast. You're near the mission, so stop in if you like, but definitely visit the rose garden across the street to experience the scents of 1,000 different varieties.

Amble down State Street and poke around the shops, ducking into El Paseo, the lovely meandering street that symbolizes Santa Barbara with its colorful tile work, bursts of bougainvillea, and many fountains. Stop at the County Courthouse and go to the clock tower for stunning views of the city. Often times it's not crowded so you might have the place to yourself.

Have lunch at Arts & Letters Café, where not only will you see beautiful art in the gallery, but the intimate back courtyard is perfect for a quiet romantic meal. Next head to the waterfront and rent tandem bikes to take you past the zoo. After returning the bikes, taste wine at Municipal Winemakers, and maybe Santa Barbara Winery if you have time.

Check into The Upham Hotel, then dine at the 12-table restaurant Julienne.

DAY 2

Drive up the San Marcos Pass for breakfast at the secluded Cold Spring Tavern, long a locals favorite for a secret rendezvous. Next, head towards Rancho Oso stables for an hour horseback ride in the backcountry where you might spot bald eagles.

Drive towards Solvang and stop at El Rancho Market Place to pick up picnic fixings to bring to Rusack Vineyards in beautiful Ballard Canyon, where you can wine taste first, then enjoy your lunch under the old oak trees that flank the deck.

After lunch, head to Los Olivos and check out the heady scents of lavender at Clairmont Farms and maybe pick up lavender scented bath salts and bath gel for later. Swing by Carhartt winery which ends up being romantic simply because it's so small and cute. Walk down the street for an olive oil–tasting at Global Gardens.

With all the ole factory bliss it's time to be pampered with a spa treatment at the Champagne Spa at Fess Parker's Wine Country Inn. Relaxed, check into the Ballard Inn for a romantic night and have dinner at their in-house restaurant. At twilight, take

Ballard Inn & Restaurant

a brief walk around Ballard and absorb the scents of a small town.

DAY 3

Start the day by getting high in a glider from Windhaven Glider Rides and soar over wine country. After the exhilaration, head into Solvang and park the car; you won't need it. There are several windmills in town, which make perfect backdrops for a photo.

Visit the Hans Christian Andersen Museum, where you'll learn about his love for a woman, which is what drove much of his writing. Next wander to Ingeborg's for real Danish chocolates. You'll be near the Solvang Antique Center and who knows, you may feel like buying a present for that special someone.

Head over to The Red Viking for lunch in one of the oldest buildings in Solvang.

Now it's time for some fruit of the vine. Sort This Out Cellars will get you moody with their 1950s Rat Pack vibe. Next head over to the husband and wife winemaking team of D'Alfonso-Curran Wine Group for terrific wines in a sleek environment. There are many shops to poke your head into if something strikes you, but don't miss Jule Hus, where the festive Christmas decorations will surely make you smile.

In late afternoon, the beautiful gardens and views over the old orchards at Mission Santa Inés look beautiful in the amber light. Check into the Solvang Gardens Lodge for a unique room to call your own, then walk across the street to have dinner at Root 246. Back at the lodge, if you feel like taking a stroll, walk south towards the Santa Ynez River to get away from the city lights and stargaze.

NAPA VALLEY

Mention California wines and most people will think of Napa. There's no escaping it—the Napa Valley is regarded as the center of everything wine in California, no matter how Sonoma, Santa Barbara, or Mendocino might jump up and down for attention.

The oft-mentioned Paris tasting of 1976, which pitted the valley's wines in a blind tasting against France's best, put the Napa Valley—and California—firmly on the international wine map: Napa Valley wines won both the red and white tasting, while other Californian wines placed in the top five. The Napa Valley then led the premium wine revolution in the 1980s and saw the building of some of California's most ostentatious wineries in the last two decades, most recently a grandiose castle near Calistoga and, coming soon, a Frank

Gehry–designed winery near St. Helena. This little valley is now home to more than a quarter of all the wineries in California, despite the fact that it accounts for only about 5 percent of all the wine made in the state. The statistics speak for themselves—the Napa Valley turns out some of the best wine in California.

Natural beauty, colorful history, some of the biggest names in world wine, and $100 bottles of cabernet all serve to draw hordes of visitors—almost 5 million a year at last count. They in turn are entertained by top chefs, luxury pampering, and lavish winery shows like nowhere else in the world.

It can all seem a bit like a giant wine theme park at times, especially when lining up at yet another ticket booth to empty your wallet for the privilege of being herded around another

HIGHLIGHTS

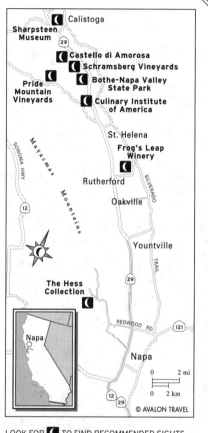

◖ The Hess Collection: Located in the mountains above Napa, this part gallery, part winery brings new meaning to the expression "the art of wine making" (page 44).

◖ Frog's Leap Winery: Revel in the laid-back vibe at this organic winery. In addition to good wine, there's an organic garden, and it's one of the few places left in the valley where tasting is free (page 78).

◖ Pride Mountain Vineyards: Straddling the Napa and Sonoma border, this mountain-top winery has some of the best views in the valley and some of the best mountain wines (page 96).

◖ Culinary Institute of America: The West Coast's next star chefs are born inside this fortresslike former winery, and you can get a taste of their training at regular cooking demonstrations (page 98).

◖ Bothe-Napa Valley State Park: Take a break and stroll back in time through the redwoods in this gem of a park (page 100).

◖ Schramsberg Vineyards: If you plan to visit just one champagne cellar, why not make it the most historic one in the valley? Take a tour through the spooky cellars once visited by Robert Louis Stevenson (page 112).

◖ Castello di Amorosa: Just down the road from the Victorian splendor of Schramsberg, step back even further in time and visit this astonishing replica of a medieval castle. They make wine here too (page 113).

◖ Sharpsteen Museum: Learn about Calistoga's early days at this quirky little museum. It's right next to one of the original

LOOK FOR ◖ TO FIND RECOMMENDED SIGHTS, ACTIVITIES, DINING, AND LODGING.

cottages from the first-ever hot springs resort in the town (page 118).

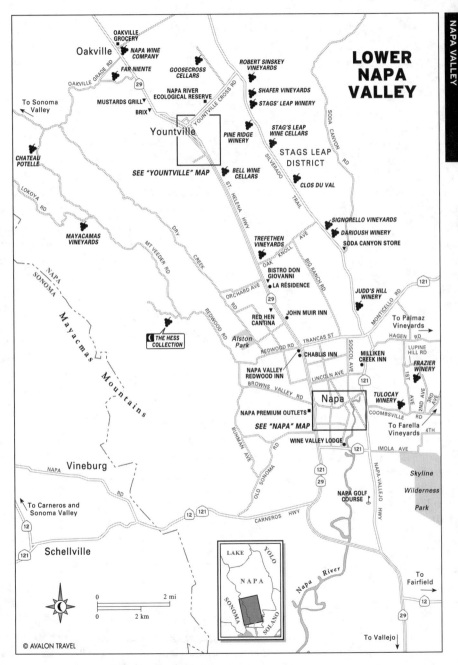

LOWER NAPA VALLEY

Oakville

OAKVILLE GROCERY
OAKVILLE GROCERY
NAPA WINE COMPANY
FAR NIENTE
GOOSECROSS CELLARS
NAPA RIVER ECOLOGICAL RESERVE
MUSTARDS GRILL
BRIX
Yountville
PINE RIDGE WINERY
SEE "YOUNTVILLE" MAP
BELL WINE CELLARS

ROBERT SINSKEY VINEYARDS
SHAFER VINEYARDS
STAGS' LEAP WINERY
STAG'S LEAP WINE CELLARS
STAGS LEAP DISTRICT
CLOS DU VAL

To Sonoma Valley

CHATEAU POTELLE
LOKOYA RD
MAYACAMAS VINEYARDS

DRY CREEK
MT VEEDER RD
REDWOOD RD
THE HESS COLLECTION
Alston Park
RED HEN CANTINA
NAPA VALLEY REDWOOD INN
CHABLIS INN
NAPA PREMIUM OUTLETS
SEE "NAPA" MAP
WINE VALLEY LODGE

TREFETHEN VINEYARDS
OAK KNOLL AVE
BISTRO DON GIOVANNI
LA RÉSIDENCE
ORCHARD AVE
JOHN MUIR INN
TRANCAS ST
REDWOOD RD
BROWNS VALLEY RD
Napa

SIGNORELLO VINEYARDS
DARIOUSH WINERY
SODA CANYON STORE
JUDD'S HILL WINERY
To Palmaz Vineyards
HAGEN RD
MILLIKEN CREEK INN
LUPINE HILL RD
FRAZIER WINERY
LINCOLN AVE
TULOCAY WINERY
COOMBSVILLE
To Farella Vineyards
IMOLA AVE

Mayacmas Mountains

NAPA SONOMA COUNTY

NAPA
To Sonoma Valley

Vineburg
To Carneros and Sonoma Valley
Schellville
CARNEROS HWY
BUHMAN AVE
OLD SONOMA RD
NAPA GOLF COURSE
Skyline Wilderness Park

0 2 mi
0 2 km

LAKE
YOLO
NAPA
SONOMA
SOLANO
Napa River

To Fairfield
To Vallejo

© AVALON TRAVEL

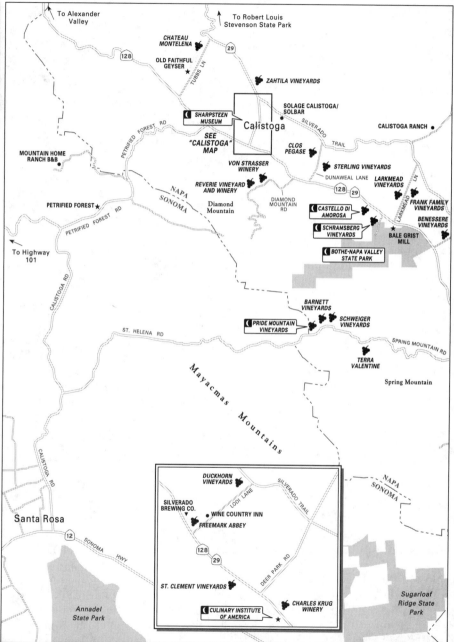

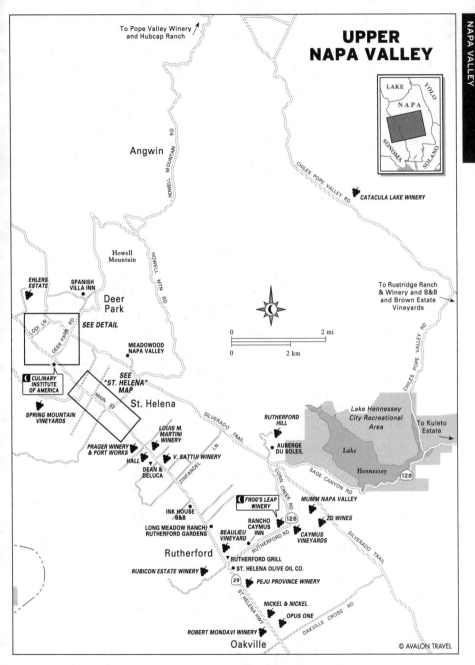

UPPER NAPA VALLEY

To Pope Valley Winery
and Hubcap Ranch

Angwin

HOWELL MOUNTAIN RD

CHILES POPE VALLEY RD

CATACULA LAKE WINERY

Howell Mountain

HOWELL MTN RD

EHLERS ESTATE

SPANISH VILLA INN

Deer Park

To Rustridge Ranch & Winery and B&B and Brown Estate Vineyards

LODI LN

DEER PARK RD

SEE DETAIL

MEADOWOOD NAPA VALLEY

0   2 mi

0   2 km

CHILES POPE VALLEY RD

CULINARY INSTITUTE OF AMERICA

SEE "ST. HELENA" MAP

MAIN ST

St. Helena

SPRING MOUNTAIN VINEYARDS

SILVERADO TRAIL

RUTHERFORD HILL

Lake Hennessey City Recreational Area

To Kuleto Estate

LOUIS M. MARTINI WINERY

AUBERGE DU SOLEIL

Lake Hennessey

PRAGER WINERY & PORT WORKS

HALL

V. SATTUI WINERY

DEAN & DELUCA

ZINFANDEL LN

CONN CREEK RD

SAGE CANYON RD

128

MUMM NAPA VALLEY

FROG'S LEAP WINERY

INK HOUSE B&B

RANCHO CAYMUS INN

128

ZD WINES

LONG MEADOW RANCH/ RUTHERFORD GARDENS

BEAULIEU VINEYARD

RUTHERFORD RD

CAYMUS VINEYARDS

SILVERADO TRAIL

Rutherford

RUTHERFORD GRILL

ST. HELENA OLIVE OIL CO.

RUBICON ESTATE WINERY

29

PEJU PROVINCE WINERY

ST HELENA HWY

NICKEL & NICKEL

OPUS ONE

OAKVILLE CROSS RD

ROBERT MONDAVI WINERY

Oakville

© AVALON TRAVEL

LAKE YOLO

NAPA

SONOMA   SOLANO

winery by guides who are probably as bored as they look. It's not a great stretch to imagine that one day there will be giant gates at either end of the valley where all-inclusive passes will be sold to the "Greatest Wine Show on Earth" (the Sonoma Valley would be the parking lot if some competitive types had their way).

The diversity of literally hundreds of wineries—big and small, glamorous and rustic—is one of Napa Valley's big draws. Art lovers could easily spend an entire vacation visiting the many wineries with art or sculpture displays. Photosensitive souls can hunt down all the cool, dark, underground wine caves. Architecture buffs will have a field day at some of the more outlandish facilities, ranging from medieval to avant-garde.

And that's before even considering wine itself. The valley is home to boutique wineries making just a few hundred cases of wine a year and to corporate behemoths turning out millions. The multitude of microclimates has given rise to a patchwork of 15 (and counting) distinct appellations, or AVAs, where just about every major type of grape can be grown. Although this is a red wine–lover's paradise, there's a wine made here for almost every palate.

The valley's diversity extends well beyond wine: At one end of the valley are the hot springs and spas of Calistoga, while Napa at the other end contains some big-city entertainment. In between, nature offers plenty of diversions from wine, and restaurants turn out delicacies that would put many in world capitals to shame.

The locals are remarkably sanguine about the endless stream of visitors clogging their valley. Clearly, they are wise enough not to discourage the hands that ultimately feed them. But they also get to experience the beauty and diversity of the valley, the quality of the food, and the strong sense of community when the rest of us have long since gone home.

And, of course, they get to toast their good fortune with some of the best wines in the world.

ORIENTATION

The Napa Valley, including Carneros, is roughly 35 miles long, with two main roads running up each side of the valley and about half a dozen roads traversing the 2–4 miles between them. As far as the world's major wine-making regions go, this is baby sized, so don't be intimidated.

Just north of Carneros is the city of **Napa** itself, the biggest settlement in the valley, home to many of the workers who keep the wine industry humming. It's not the most attractive city and has traditionally been bypassed by tourists speeding to the big-name wineries and trendy towns farther north, but Napa has been making an effort to cash in on its Victorian history, riverside setting, and namesake valley.

From Napa, the two main valley roads begin. The St. Helena Highway—more commonly known as Highway 29—is the well-beaten path up the valley. It passes the town of **Yountville,** dominated by increasingly upscale shops, restaurants, and hotels, then whistles past sleepy **Rutherford** before hitting what has become almost the spiritual heart of the valley, **St. Helena.** St. Helena and the surrounding big-name wineries are the main draw in this part of the valley, and rural tranquility quickly returns as Highway 29 continues north to the narrow top of the valley, where sleepy **Calistoga** attracts tourists to its up-and-coming wineries and volcanic hot springs.

Calistoga is also where the other main valley road, the Silverado Trail, ends. Named for a silver mine that it once served north of Calistoga, it runs from Napa along the foot of the eastern hills and is the shortcut used to get up and down the valley in the summer when the other side of the valley is clogged. This undulating, winding two-lane road remains almost eerily quiet at times and feels like it's in another valley altogether. It's a road along which smaller wineries turn out some of the best wines in the valley, with little of the hoopla of the big showoffs farther west. It's also a road down which serious wine lovers might prefer to travel, sampling famous cabernet sauvignons in the Stags Leap or Rutherford appellations before heading up into the hills to some hidden gems on Howell Mountain or in the rural Chiles Valley.

NAPA'S SILLY-MONEY WINES

At the Napa Valley Wine Auction in 2008, six bottles of 1992 Screaming Eagle sold for $500,000. They were magnums, but that still works out to more than $40,000 per bottle or about $7,000 per glass. Granted, the auction is a charity event and therefore encourages big spending for a good cause, but there are probably no other wines that would be bid so high, whatever the occasion.

Make that *few* other wines. There were 10 magnums of Harlan Estate wine that sold for $340,000. And then there was an eight-magnum vertical of Bryant Family Vineyards wine that sold for $290,000 and six bottles plus one Methuselah (6 liters) of the latest vintage from Dalla Valle that went for a mere $200,000. Just those four lots illustrate the power of Napa's so-called cult wines to open the wallets of both serious collectors and those simply with more money than they know what to do with.

The cult wine phenomenon started in the early 1990s and reached a crescendo during the dot-com boom years, when a lot of people really did have more money than they knew what to do with. They bought the beautifully made, limited-production Napa Valley cabernets, like those from Screaming Eagle and Harlan Estate, probably as much to gain the cachet of owning something so rare as to resell for a profit a few years later. As with any rare commodity, lots of bidders will push up the price.

The dot-com bubble burst, but the cult wine bubble never really did. Retailers report that sales of such silly-money wines remain as solid as their prices. There's no doubting that they are good wines, made by some of the best winemakers and sourced from some of the best vineyards. Whether they're worth hundreds of dollars or more is a question often asked — though it's ultimately irrelevant, because there are plenty of people still willing to pay and to wait years to get on the exclusive mailing lists to even get a chance to pay.

A little more troubling is that the term "cult wine" is now bandied about a little too casually. It is commonly used as a marketing tool or for bragging rights, so it's no surprise that calling even the Screaming Eagles of the world a cult wine these days is as likely to elicit a roll of the eyes as an opening of the wallet.

THE WINES

The Napa Valley probably has more microclimates and soil types along its 35-mile length than any other valley in the Wine Country. The climates and the soils drew the attention of wine-loving European settlers in the 1800s, and the seeds of the modern day wine industry were sown.

As you drive from the city of Napa north to Calistoga in the middle of summer, the temperature can rise by up to 20 degrees. Although the northern end of the valley is significantly hotter than the southern end, throughout the length of the valley there are dozens of unique microclimates created by small hills on the valley floor as well as the canyons and slopes of the mountains that define its eastern and western sides.

In addition, geologists have identified a staggering 33 different types of soil in the valley, laid down over millions of years by volcanoes, rivers, and the earth's shifting crust. The combined soils and microclimates create a patchwork of growing conditions that could keep winemakers happy for centuries more, and that is why there are so many distinct, recognized growing regions within the Napa Valley.

The Napa Valley north of Carneros is predominantly a red wine–growing region, thanks primarily to a warm climate that ensures the most popular red grape varietals can easily ripen and attain the sugar levels needed to make the big, powerful wines for which the valley is known. White grapes and some red varietals like pinot noir can get by in cooler climates because they generally reach their desired ripeness more easily while retaining high enough acid levels desired by winemakers.

The one red grape for which Napa is most famous is cabernet sauvignon. There were about 45,000 acres of vineyards planted in Napa County in 2008, about three-quarters of which were planted with red grape varietals, according to the U.S. Department of Agriculture. Just over half that red grape acreage was cabernet, which means that one varietal accounts for 40 percent of all the vineyards in Napa County (about 19,000 acres). The figure is probably closer to 50 percent of all the vineyards in the Napa Valley north of Carneros, where pinot noir and chardonnay are the more dominant varietals.

That's not to say that other wines are not important here; far from it. The Napa Valley is where some of California's most distinctive chardonnay and sauvignon blanc are produced, together with increasing amounts of syrah, sangiovese, and many other minor varietals. But cabernet always has dominated the vineyards and probably always will, with chardonnay a distant second in terms of vineyard acreage, followed closely by merlot.

Most of the big Napa Valley wineries own vineyards all over the valley. They and smaller wineries also often buy fruit from other growers outside Napa Valley, so white wine drinkers need not despair—there will usually be plenty of whites on offer, even at wineries in the big-cab appellations like Rutherford and Stags Leap. But ultimately this is a valley dominated by cabernet and chardonnay, and those looking for more unusual types of wine will want to choose the wineries they visit carefully.

PLANNING YOUR TIME

So how can visitors make sense of all those wineries and avoid all the crowds? Many visitors seem to follow a similar pattern, never making it much farther north than St. Helena and sticking to the western side of the valley. If you can avoid that pattern, you're halfway to lowering your blood pressure.

The other key to enjoying the valley rather than being frustrated by it is plenty of planning. There's so much to do and so many wineries to visit that anyone simply turning up without a plan, however vague, will end up with a headache even before drinking too much wine in the sun.

Research the type of wine that wineries specialize in before choosing which to visit, especially if you're not a big red wine drinker. This is, after all, the land of endless cabernet sauvignon, but it is also a land where plenty of stunning white wines, including champagne, are made. And if you are a big cabernet drinker, this can be the place to learn much more about the king of wines—how and why a Spring Mountain cabernet is different from a Stags Leap cabernet, for example.

Alternatively, pick a theme not related to wine for a day of touring. Wineries in Napa have distinguish themselves from their competitors to attract increasingly jaded visitors, a form of Wine Country evolution. Some rely on the reputation of their wines, others on art, caves, car collections, architecture, gardens, tours—the list is endless.

When the crowds get to be too much, simply head for the hills, where healthy doses of nature help make the hidden wineries in the Mount Veeder, Spring Mountain, and Chiles Valley appellations that much more enjoyable. Even the sleepy Coombsville area right outside the city of Napa has plenty to offer.

If possible, avoid the peak season that runs roughly July–October. It brings peak crowds, particularly on weekends; peak hotel prices; and peak daytime temperatures. April–June is perhaps the best time to visit, when the wet winter season is finally drying out, the temperatures mild, the creeks flowing, the hills green, and the vineyards full of vivid yellow wild mustard.

TOURS

One way to visit wineries without having to worry about traffic, drinking, or cooking an expensive wine in a sun-baked car is to take a daylong organized wine tour. Someone else does the driving, you can drink until you can no longer stand, and any precious wine purchases will get transported back to your hotel probably in better shape than you.

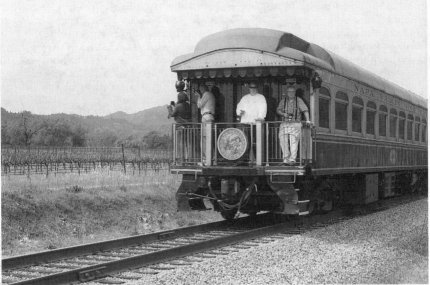

© PHILIP GOLDSMITH

Wine, dine, and see the valley on the Wine Train.

Another advantage is that the local tour guides are knowledgeable about the valley, the wineries, and often about wines as well, making an organized tour an option worth considering if you have no idea where to start.

There are two tour companies, each offering different experiences. The **Napa Winery Shuttle** (707/257-1950, www.wineshuttle .com) is basically a hop-on, hop-off minibus that picks up at any of a long list of local hotels at about 10 A.M. (though they can often pick up at any hotel not on the list) and runs among 10 wineries between Oakville and St. Helena, plus a couple of Yountville restaurants for those who want a sit-down lunch. Those wineries represent a good cross section of the valley and include a handful of smaller producers, a champagne house, and some of the big names, including Mondavi, Niebaum-Coppola, and Beaulieu Vineyard. Visit as many or as few as you like during the day for $75 per person.

Beau Wine Tours (707/257-0887 or 800/387-2328, www.beauwinetours.com) is more of a custom touring company and is often the owner of the limos seen parked at some of the bigger wineries. Rent a chauffeured car, SUV, or limousine for 3–14 people for $55–135 an hour plus tax, tip, and (depending on gas prices) a fuel surcharge, and plan your own itinerary. Note that the size of the stretch limos and vans means they sometimes cannot visit smaller wineries at all, or only by prior arrangement. Beau Wine Tours has plenty of knowledge of the valley, however, and can offer lots of advice. It also offers private, preplanned, daylong tours starting and finishing in either the Napa Valley or San Francisco from $99.

NAPA VALLEY WINE TRAIN

The age of the steam trains that first brought the masses to the valley's Victorian spas and early wineries has long gone, but a modest reminder remains in the Napa Valley Wine Train (1275 McKinstry St., Napa, 707/253-2111 or 800/427-4124, www.winetrain.com). It has been kept alive by providing what the valley does best—good food and wine. The train runs 20 miles from downtown

Napa up to St. Helena and back, and reservations are essential.

The idea of being cooped up on a glorious fall day watching the vineyards and wineries through the windows of a restored Pullman rail car might not seem appealing, but it's better than it sounds. The only problem is that it eats into your day. Think of it as taking a four-hour lunch or dinner at a gourmet, if slightly unusual, restaurant with entertainment often thrown in for free. The food is beautifully prepared, the wine first-class, and the restaurant dripping with brass and mahogany. There are no comparisons to Amtrak here.

Lunch and dinner trips are offered daily, as well as a brunch excursion on weekends. The basic fare of $50 gets you on the train, but food is extra. Those additional rates range from $45 for the Gourmet Express lunch menu up to $75 for a four-course dinner with specially paired wines, with plenty of dining options in between. In reviving the old rail cars, the Wine Train also revived the old railroad class system too—each car caters to a different class of diner, so you won't be jealously eyeing your neighbor's five-course spread when you've already polished off your three courses.

GETTING THERE

There were far more ways to get to the Napa Valley a century ago, when trains and riverboats brought the visitors and goods that made the valley so successful. The car has long since become the main transportation mode, though the more adventurous can still get here on public transportation.

By Car

The Napa Valley is almost the same driving distance from three major international airports—Oakland, San Francisco, and Sacramento. Driving from the airports to the city of Napa itself will take 1–2 hours, depending on traffic; from downtown San Francisco or Oakland, it's closer to an hour of driving time.

The most direct route from Oakland and Sacramento is on I-80 (west from Sacramento, east from Oakland). Exit at Marine World Parkway (Highway 37), then take Highway 29 north into Napa and beyond. From Sacramento, a slightly more direct route is to exit at Jameson Canyon Road (U.S. 12), a little farther north of American Canyon. This also heads west and meets Highway 29 at the Napa airport.

From the San Francisco airport and city (especially downtown), it takes about the same amount of time to drive across the Bay Bridge to I-80 and north to Napa as it does to go the prettier route through Marin. This route crosses the Golden Gate Bridge on U.S. 101 to Marin County, past Novato, then west on Highway 37, which links with U.S. 121 through Carneros, past the turnoff to the Sonoma Valley, and eventually to Highway 29 just south of Napa.

The Napa Valley is also easily accessible from other parts of the Wine Country, thanks to the numerous roads that cross the Mayacamas Mountains down the western side of the valley.

From the Sonoma Valley, just north of Glen Ellen, Trinity Road winds its way east into the mountains, becoming Dry Creek Road in the Mount Veeder appellation, before coming down into the Napa Valley to Oakville as the Oakville Grade. Farther north in the Sonoma Valley, just east of Santa Rosa, Calistoga Road heads to the hills and eventually to Calistoga, or you can turn off on St. Helena Road after about three miles to cross into the Napa Valley down through the Spring Mountain appellation and into St. Helena.

From the Russian River Valley, just north of Santa Rosa, take Mark West Springs Road east, eventually turning onto Porter Creek Road, which leads down into Calistoga. And from the Alexander Valley, U.S. 128 runs south through Knights Valley to Calistoga.

Try not to be in a rush if you take these routes, because they are narrow, winding, and slow, but a lot of fun if time is not of the essence.

By Boat and Bus

The most unusual way to get to the valley without driving, short of an epic bicycle ride, is on the **Baylink Ferry** from San Francisco via Vallejo. The speedy catamarans leave San Francisco's Ferry Building about every hour 7 A.M.–10 P.M. during the week and every couple of hours 9 A.M.–10 P.M. on weekends for the 55-minute crossing to Vallejo, which is about 12 miles south of Napa. The one-way fare is $13. For a detailed seasonal schedule, contact Baylink Ferries (707/643-3779 or 877/643-3779, www.baylinkferry.com).

From the Vallejo ferry terminal, route 10 of Napa Valley's **VINE** bus service runs directly to downtown Napa about every hour until 8 P.M. during the week, every two hours until 6:50 P.M. on Saturday, and just four times a day on Sunday, with the first bus leaving at 10:15 A.M. and the last at 5:30 P.M. It's about a 65-minute journey to Napa (except for a few times of the day when the bus makes stops) and is a bargain at $2.15. Route 10 also continues to the valley through Yountville and St. Helena to Calistoga; check the schedule for details on this route. For more information on schedules and routes contact VINE (707/255-7631 or 800/696-6443, www.napavalleyvine.net).

Taking the ferry and bus to the valley and then renting a bike in downtown Napa, St. Helena, or Calistoga for a couple of days would certainly make for a memorable Wine Country experience, but it might not be for the impatient.

GETTING AROUND
By Car

Seemingly everyone drives to the Napa Valley, so you'd think everything would be geared up for the cars transporting those 5 million annual visitors to this part of the world. Wrong! This is essentially agricultural land that its custodians battle to protect, so the mighty vine and strict planning laws limit all sorts of development—including, evidently, road widening.

The 28-mile drive from Napa to Calistoga up Highway 29 can take less than 45 minutes in the middle of a winter day. Try that same drive on a summer weekend or a weekday during the evening rush hour and it might take close to double that. The sheer volume of traffic is really what slows things down, especially with so much traffic coming and going from the multitude of wineries and the traffic bottleneck of St Helena's Main Street.

Heading north on Highway 29, you can be lulled into a false sense of security as you zip towards St. Helena, only to hit a wall of traffic about a mile south of the town caused by traffic lights that seem to meter only a dozen cars at a time onto Main Street. Heading south from St. Helena from mid-afternoon until evening on many days, your average speed is likely to be less than 20 mph until well after Rutherford. The mid-valley traffic situation is not helped by the countless turnoffs for wineries from Rutherford to St. Helena that also slow traffic. Make your life easier and use the empty center lane of the road to turn left into wineries or when turning left out of wineries to merge into traffic. That's what it's there for.

The almost constant traffic jams on Highway 29 are also a reason to discover the Silverado Trail, running north–south on the other side of the valley. There might be the occasional slowdown caused by a valley visitor unfamiliar with its dips and bends or who is simply lost. Usually, however, this is the domain of merciless local speed demons zipping up and down the valley at 60 mph, a feat usually possible even when the road through St. Helena across the valley is at a standstill. Many locals will use the Silverado to bypass St. Helena altogether, cutting back to Highway 29 when necessary using one of the many small cross-valley roads.

Napa is the only city in the valley to have made an effort to ease traffic flows, with its brief stretch of smooth-flowing freeway and frustrating yet effective one-way system downtown. The irony, of course, is that so many valley visitors bypass the city for destinations up-valley, so traffic is usually light anyway.

By Bike

Picking the right route at the right time of the day and exploring a section of the valley by bike can be one of the most enjoyable ways to experience the Wine Country. Whether you plan a long bike ride up the Silverado Trail or a short hop around a handful of Rutherford-area wineries, there are a handful of established places to rent well-maintained bicycles in St. Helena, Calistoga and Napa. All know the area from a biker's perspective and so will have plenty of suggestions on routes from easy rides of a few miles to epic loops through some of the best mountain appellations. Helmets, locks, bottle cages, and puncture repair kits are always included with rentals. It's also worth asking about free roadside assistance should you get a flat.

St. Helena Cyclery (116 Main St., St. Helena, 707/963-7736, www.sthelena cyclery.com, 9:30 A.M.–5:30 P.M. Mon.–Sat., 10 A.M.–5 P.M. Sun.) rents basic hybrid bikes for $10 per hour or $35 per day and more advanced road bikes from $65 per day but only takes reservations for groups of 10 or more wanting road bikes. Check the website for coupons and other specials. **Calistoga Bike Shop** (1318 Lincoln Ave., Calistoga, 707/942-9687 or 866/942-2453, www.calistogabikeshop .com, 10 A.M.–6 P.M. daily) does take reservations and rents hybrids for $35 per day and both road and mountain bikes from $45 per day. **Napa River Velo** (680 Main St., Napa, 707/258-8729, www.naparivervelo.com, 10 A.M.–6 P.M. Mon.–Sat., 10 A.M.–5 P.M. Sun.) is on the river side of the new Riverside Plaza development near the Napa Mill and rents bikes in the city of Napa for $35–75 per day, depending on whether you want a basic hybrid or a fancy road or mountain bike. Also in the city of Napa, Napa Valley Bike Tours (6795 Washington St., Building B, Yountville, 800/707-2453, www.napavalleybiketours.com) offers rentals by the day along with its all-inclusive tours and might also drop off and pick up its bikes at your hotel.

Touring on a bike is easy in almost every part of the valley thanks to the flat landscape (on the valley floor, at least) and the proximity of all the wineries. The only place you might want to avoid is the stretch of Highway 29 between Oakville and St. Helena, which is the scene of regular car accidents—probably caused by inattentive, lost, or simply drunk visitors. It's also such a busy stretch of road that you might not want the hassle of car-dodging anyway.

The best stretches of valley to explore on a bike include the Silverado Trail in the Stags Leap District, where big-name wineries like Clos du Val, Pine Ridge, Shafer, Stag's Leap, and Robert Sinskey are all along a three-mile stretch of winding road. Just beware the speed demons on the Trail. Other easy rides include many of the cross-valley roads, which sometimes have fewer wineries per mile but also have far less traffic. Biking the Rutherford Road from Highway 29 to the Silverado Trail, for example, takes in Beaulieu, Frog's Leap, and Caymus. Then a few hundred yards down the Silverado Trail are Mumm and ZD.

The Coombsville area east of the city of Napa is also worth exploring on bike, not only because it has relatively quiet and flat roads but also because of its proximity to the hotels and amenities of the city. You could leave your hotel after breakfast, visit a couple of small wineries and have a relaxing picnic, then be back in Napa by mid-afternoon.

A couple of companies can do all the work and planning for your bike tour. All you need to do is show up and pedal. To plan an entire vacation centered around biking in the valley, try **Getaway Adventures** (2228 Northpoint Pkwy., Santa Rosa, 707/568-3040 or 800/499-2453, www.getawayadventures.com), which offers day, weekend, and weeklong all-inclusive packages, including hotel, meals, bike, tour guide, and shuttle van. Weekend packages are $899–1,000, and 4–6-day packages run $1,299–2,499, with prices depending on both luxury and the number of days. Tours are usually offered once a month and take in the Napa Valley and parts of northern Sonoma. The day trips cost $149 and include the bike, helmet, water, lunch, and a guided tour of about five wineries in the Calistoga area.

Napa Valley Bike Tours (6795 Washington St., Building B, Yountville, 800/707-2453, www.napavalleybiketours.com), based at the other end of the valley, offers three- and four-day all-inclusive packages that stay within Napa Valley. The two-night, three-day Romantic Getaway packages are $705–840, depending on accommodations and time of the week (weekends are more expensive), and the longer packages start at $800. Day tours are also offered at $139–149 for the day, lunch and group tour guide included. If the sight of all the lovely straight rows of vines snaking up and down hills with pristine dirt between them appeals to your inner mountain biker, there's even a day trip offered that takes you biking through the vineyards of Bouchaine Winery in Carneros for $150. Plain old bike rentals to go it alone start at $24 for two hours or $35 per day for hybrids. The company also offers free delivery and pickup of two or more bikes to hotels and B&Bs south of St. Helena.

Napa and Vicinity

Many people bypass Napa, heading up to the middle of the valley to start their wine-tasting day, but there's plenty happening this far south as well. Napa is filled with tasting rooms, and the city is bordered by one of the best mountain appellations in the valley as well as the newest valley appellation, both home to historic and modern wineries, small and large.

Just north of the city of Napa is one of the newest of the Napa Valley's 14 appellations, **Oak Knoll.** As in the Yountville appellation farther north, the climate is a blend of the cooler weather in Carneros, south of Napa, and the hotter mid-valley temperatures. Just about every major grape varietal is grown here, though the appellation is probably best known for whites such as chardonnay and sauvignon blanc. Being such a new appellation it does not yet have much name recognition, so don't expect to see many wines with Oak Knoll identified on the label.

West of the Oak Knoll appellation is the **Mount Veeder** appellation, stretching all the way from Napa up the middle of the valley on the slopes of the Mayacamas Mountains to the highest ridges and the Sonoma County line. Compared to Spring Mountain and Diamond Mountain subappellations further north on the slopes of the same mountain range, Mount Veeder wines have a leaner, more mineral edge to them. The thin volcanic soils provide little nourishment for the struggling vines, and the region is far enough south to feel the cooling effects of the bay. The conditions result in elegant, age-worthy cabernets with good acidity and an earthiness lacking from mountain appellations farther north. Syrah and zinfandel are also grown on the mountain slopes and produce wines with a distinct sense of place.

Just a few miles east of the city itself, meanwhile, is an area that could become the next official AVA in the valley—Coombsville. Small in terms of vineyard acreage (under 1,000 acres) and the number of wineries, it is nevertheless starting to turn out some noteworthy wines as distinct as any in the valley thanks to a patchwork of different soils and microclimates, from sun-soaked hillsides to cool, breezy lowlands. It is an ideal place to grow both bordeaux varietals as well as cooler-climate varietals like pinot noir and riesling. The cabernets and merlots made have a more restrained, Old World style than those from warmer up-valley vineyards, so lovers of big, burly Napa Valley wines might be disappointed.

WINE-TASTING
Tasting Rooms in Napa

You could spend a whole day, or even two, sampling wines from the dozen tasting rooms in the city of Napa itself—a process that's made a lot cheaper with the **Taste Napa Downtown wine-tasting card.** Available at any of the 10 participating tasting rooms and shops, the

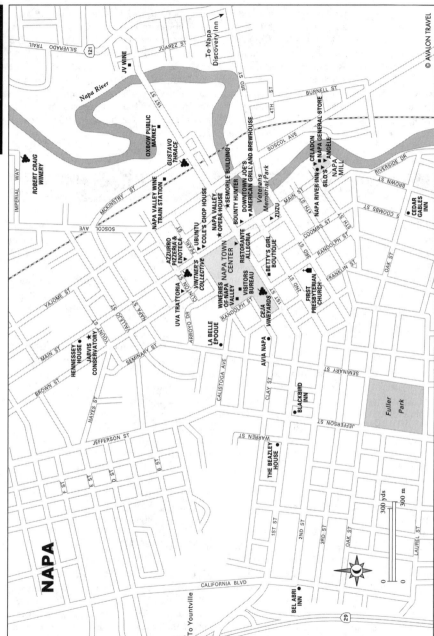

© AVALON TRAVEL

NAPA

card costs only $20 and is valid at all the bigger tasting rooms and many stores that offer wine tasting, including JV Wine, Bounty Hunter, and the Napa General Store—and gets you initial tastes for only $0.10.

Without the card, tasting prices range from a couple of dollars up to $25 at the larger collectives (though you can keep the quality Riedel tasting glass at the Vintner's Collective). The three main tasting rooms are the only places to taste the wine of some of the valley's smallest wineries, and the winemakers themselves will sometimes be pouring the wines on weekends.

WINERIES OF NAPA VALLEY

One of the most central participating tasting venues is the café-style Wineries of Napa Valley (1285 Napa Town Center, 707/253-9450 or 800/328-7815, www.napavintages.com, 11 A.M.–6 P.M. Mon.–Thurs., 10 A.M.–7:30 P.M. Fri.–Sat., 10 A.M.–6 P.M. Sun.) in the Napa Town Center shopping mall on 1st Street. Managed by Goosecross Cellars, it is also the outpost of a half-dozen other small valley producers, including Burgess Cellars and Ilona, both of which make some good wines from the Howell Mountain appellation. You can also buy wine by the glass here and take advantage of the free wireless Internet access.

CEJA VINEYARDS

A stone's throw away is Napa's newest downtown tasting room, the public outpost of Carneros-based Ceja Vineyards (1248 1st St., 707/226-6445, www.cejavineyards.com, noon–6 P.M. Sun.–Fri., noon–11 P.M. Sat.). The large space is part wine-tasting bar and part art and entertainment venue, featuring a rotating display of works from local Hispanic artists and free salsa lessons on Saturday evenings. Both reflect the Mexican roots of the Ceja family, the eldest generation of which epitomized the American dream as children of immigrant farm workers who worked their way to becoming vineyard owners and finally winery owners in less than three decades. At least one member of the extended Ceja family is likely to be behind the bar to tell the story. Ceja makes only 5,000 cases of wine a year, but all the major varietals are represented from Ceja's cool-climate vineyards in Carneros and further west near Petaluma. The Carneros Chardonnay and Pinot Noir, along with the bargain-priced red blend Vino de Casa, are among the standouts. The white house blend has the flavor and price to be a great summer picnic wine. If you're looking for a Saturday night of entertainment, have an early dinner and head over to Ceja for happy hour (5:30–7:30 P.M.). A few glasses of wine will quickly remove you inhibitions for the salsa and freestyle dancing to follow.

GUSTAVO THRACE

Just across McKinstry Street from the Oxbow Public Market is the spacious tasting room of GustavoThrace (1021 McKinstry St., 707/257-6796, www.gustavothrace.com, 11 A.M.–5:30 P.M. daily), another boutique Napa Valley winery established in the 1990s by Mexican American winemaker Gustavo Brambila, a Napa Valley wine veteran who started his storied career as the Chateau Montelena assistant winemaker in the 1970s, and his business partner, Thrace Bromberger. If you're lucky, at least one of them is likely to be in the tasting room to recommend some wines to taste and places to visit. If not, you can't go wrong with any of the cabernets, the spicy barbera, the powerful petite sirah, or the clean and crisp sauvignon blanc. Also check out the two proprietary red blends, Tessera and the bargain-priced 3rd Bottle.

VINTNER'S COLLECTIVE

The biggest tasting room is the Vintner's Collective in the historic stone Pfeiffer Building (1245 Main St. at Clinton St., 707/255-7150, www.vintnerscollective.com, 11 A.M.–6 P.M. daily, tasting $25). A house of ill repute during its Victorian youth, it is now the public face of 15 different wineries and winemakers, most notably the zinfandel specialist D-Cubed; Gregory Graham, a winemaker with a résumé that reads like a who's who of Napa wineries; the pinot noir specialist Ancien Wines; and the single-vineyard wines of Chiarello Family Vineyards, founded by the chef behind St. Helena's Tra Vigne restaurant. The regular tasting includes a flight of five wines, while the more expensive tasting adds four more-expensive wines. Parking is free, although limited.

ROBERT CRAIG WINERY

Fans of mountain-grown cabernet sauvignon should make an appointment for a tasting at Robert Craig Winery (625 Imperial Way, 707/252-2250, www.robertcraigwine.com, 10 A.M.–4:30 P.M. Mon.–Sat., tasting $20), which is a little off the beaten path in Napa yet still only a short drive (or long walk) from the Oxbow Market or downtown area. Craig got his start in the wine industry by buying a vineyard on nearby Mount Veeder in the late 1970s (it was later bought by Donald Hess, founder of the Hess Collection), and since those early days his focus has been on mountain-grown cabernets. Tasting Robert Craig wines from Mount Veeder, Howell Mountain, and Spring Mountain alongside the more approachable Affinity proprietary blend sourced from lower-elevation vineyards illustrates the astounding difference in characteristics that each mountain appellation creates—differences that are more obvious than those between cabernets from different valley floor appellations, for example. Mountain-grown cabernets are not for the faint-hearted, and the wines aren't cheap, but even at $50–70 per bottle, any cabernet lover would be hard-pressed not to leave with at least one.

Coombsville Wineries

The rolling hills and country lanes to the east of the city of Napa are home to an increasing number of small wineries that coexist alongside horse farms, sheep pasture, and the giant Napa Valley Country Club. In a valley of big wineries and big traffic jams, exploring this area by car or on a bike is a welcome respite from the more hectic parts of the valley. Due to local planning codes, all the wineries in this area require an appointment.

FRAZIER WINERY

At the end of a small paved road nestled among rolling hills, Frazier (70 Rapp Ln., Napa, 707/255-3444, www.frazierwinery.com, tours by appointment 10 A.M.–4 P.M. Mon.–Sat.) is one of the larger wineries in this area yet is still small by Napa Valley standards. It makes about 3,000 cases of mainly cabernet sauvignon and merlot that consistently seem to receive good ratings from the major wine magazines and are worth a visit to Coombsville to try.

Founder and former airline pilot Bill Frazier moved here in the early 1980s and by the end of the decade had caught the wine bug and planted merlot and cabernet on his small estate, becoming a pioneer in this cooler part of the valley, which had yet to become a major wine-producing area, let alone a place where cabernet was grown. After selling the grapes for a few years, the estate vineyard was expanded and Frazier started to make his own wine at customer crush facilities before converting an old barn on the estate into his own winery in 2000. The winery remains very much a family affair with several of Bill's children helping run the operation today. You're more than likely to have a Frazier as your tour guide if you visit.

The flagship wine is a powerful and complex reserve cabernet sauvignon called Memento that is made in very limited quantities and only in the best vintages. It has been favorably compared to some of the top cult cabernets in the valley, although at over $100 per bottle it might not be in everyone's price range. The equally intense nonreserve cabernet wins almost as much acclaim and is half the price. The merlot has a lot in common with merlots from Carneros, having more subtle and earthy characteristics compared to some of the fruit bombs made up-valley. All three can usually be tasted from either bottle or barrel, accompanied by cheeses and chocolate, on the appointment-only tour of the winery and caves.

The slightly cheaper Lupine Hill label cabernet and merlot accounts for about half the winery's output and is made from the juice deemed not quite good enough for the Frazier label. The style is a little more fruit-forward and approachable, and the price is more palatable. There are no white wines made here, although Frazier recently planted a new vineyard to chardonnay, so expect that to be added to the portfolio in the coming years.

FARELLA VINEYARD

Tom Farella has been a grape grower in this part of the Napa Valley for decades, so to say he knows Coombsville fruit well is perhaps an understatement. He still sells most of his estate fruit to other wineries, but also makes about 1,200 cases of his own wines a year under the Farella and Farella-Park labels, with a more varied portfolio than many small producers. The small winery (4111 Redwood Rd., Napa, 707/255-1144, www.hesscollection.com, by appointment 10 A.M.–5:30 P.M. daily, tasting $10 Mon.–Fri., $10–30 weekends) is nestled in the trees at the end of a long driveway cutting through the vineyards and, depending on the time of year, Tom's personalized tour might involve a walk through the vineyards or a tasting of some barrel samples.

Very reasonably priced estate cabernet sauvignon, merlot, and syrah account for about half the production here, but the standouts are the 19 Block Cuvee ($36) and 2008 Sauvignon Blanc ($19).

PALMAZ VINEYARDS

With a 100,000-square-foot four-story cave system extending underground and complete with its own elevators and a computerized carousel of giant fermentation tanks, this winery could be in a James Bond movie. It's actually the home of Palmaz Vineyards (4029 Hagen Rd., Napa, 707/226-5587, www.palmaz vineyards.com, tours and tasting by appointment only, $60) and was hailed as an architectural and engineering marvel when it was completed in 2009 after a reported eight years of construction costing $20 million. This is not just a wine aging cave like so many others in the Napa Valley; it's a huge gravity-flow winery facility built entirely underground with its own water treatment plant and the world's largest reinforced underground structure at its center. Only in the Napa Valley could you have a reproduction of a medieval castle at one end of the valley and an underground castle at the other.

In 1997 the Palmaz family bought the historic Cedar Knoll Winery, founded by Henry Hagen in 1881 but abandoned since Prohibition, and began work on creating a modern winery operation funded by the sale of the lifesaving coronary stent technology developed by Dr. Julio Palmaz during his long medical research career. Estate vineyards were replanted, and plans were drawn up to build the underground winery, taking advantage of the cool temperatures underground and the less stringent planning rules for caves in Napa County.

The resulting structure is certainly impressive. The wines are also pretty impressive, and most can be tasted as part of the pricey, appointment-only tour that takes place with a family member and includes small bites of gourmet food to pair with the wines. Book well in advance because every tour is private, so only a handful of visitors can visit each week.

About 7,000 cases of wine are made here each year (although the winery has a far larger capacity). Most is cabernet sauvignon that costs upwards of $100 per bottle. Typical of Coombsville cabernets, it is a more Old World style with more elegance and less sheer power than cabernets from elsewhere in the Napa Valley. A very Burgundian style of chardonnay is also made here with less buttery oak and more crispness than many in Napa Valley. If you're lucky, you might also get to taste the very limited production riesling, sourced from a cool spot in the nearby Oak Knoll district, and the wonderfully aromatic Muscat Canelli dessert wine.

TULOCAY WINERY

Bill Cadman has been making wines in this part of the world under the Tulocay label since 1975 and previously worked at some of the biggest wineries in the valley, making him one of the Napa Valley's modern pioneers and his winery the oldest in Coombsville. Yet he still manages to fly under the radar in this valley of superstar winemakers and super egos, quietly going about his business making a few hundred cases each of chardonnay, cabernet sauvignon, syrah, and pinot noir from locally grown grapes as well as a big, bold merlot and monster zinfandel from further afield in the Sierra Foothills. This is a refreshingly downhome winery operation.

Tulocay (1426 Coombsville Rd., Napa, 707/255-4064, www.tulocay.com, tasting by appointment) is perhaps best known for its elegant, age-worthy pinot noir and both a traditional (for Napa, at least) barrel-fermented chardonnay and a unoaked, stainless steel fermented version. Both are sourced from the nearby Haynes vineyard. Bill also makes two cabernets, one from the nearby Rancho Sarco vineyard and one a blend from vineyards further up-valley. Taste both with him under the oak trees at his tasting table and you'll better understand what makes this part of the Napa Valley such a unique spot for growing cabernet. You'll also likely hear plenty of local history and gossip.

Bill's more recent claim to fame has been as a spoiler to attempts by local wineries to have the area designated an AVA called Tulocay, a name that is derived from an 8,000-acre parcel of land called Rancho Tulocay that was granted to a local land manager by the Mexican government in 1841 (Tulocay is said to have been a Native American word for "red clay earth"). Cadman's use of the Tulocay label for his wines made from grapes outside the region would have fallen foul of labeling laws if the AVA was granted, and that conflict caused the federal government to scrap the application in 2008. Local wineries have since reapplied to have the area designated an AVA under the Coombsville name instead.

Oak Knoll Area Wineries
JUDD'S HILL
With the founder of Whitehall Lane Winery behind the scenes and a novel business plan, this small winery at the southern end of the Silverado Trail is beginning to make a big reputation. Judd's Hill (2332 Silverado Trail, Napa, 707/255-2332, www.juddshill .com, 10 A.M.–4 P.M. daily, appointments recommended) is named for Judd Finkelstein, the ukulele-playing son of Art Finkelstein, who was one of the founding partners of St. Helena's Whitehall Lane Winery. After selling the Whitehall business in the late 1980s, Art established Judd's Hill, and it has since become a thoroughly family affair. His wife, Bunnie, together with Judd and his wife, Holly, all take active roles, with Art and Judd the resident winemakers.

Only 3,000 cases of wine are made here, but the portfolio has grown rapidly in recent years. An approachable, complex cabernet sauvignon remains the mainstay and accounts for about half the production and many rave reviews. The flagship wine is a cabernet sourced from the hillside estate vineyards and exhibiting dusty tannins and a long finish. A few hundred cases of a rich, juicy petite sirah from Lodi-area vineyards are produced, along with a rustic Napa Valley syrah and a light, elegant pinot noir from the vineyards around the winery. Judd's Hill also makes a proprietary red blend called Magic, so named because Judd not only works his magic on wines and the ukulele but also on audiences as an amateur magician.

Tasting at the small modern visitors center, completed in 2006, gives a chance to talk to the winemaker about the wines and learn more about the other side of the business. As well as a producer of its own wines, Judd's Hill is also a micro-crush facility that enables small producers and wine enthusiasts to make as little as one barrel of wine using the winery's equipment. Walking around the barrel room, it quickly becomes evident that there are more barrels of other producers' wines than there are of Judd's Hill wines, but Judd still knows what's in just about every barrel whether it's his or not.

DARIOUSH
This Persian palace rising from the vineyard flatlands just north of Napa is one of the more unusual recent additions to Napa Valley's ever-colorful architectural mash-up. Darioush and

© JAMES GATELEY

Darioush Winery

Shahpar Khaledi came to the United States from Iran in the 1970s, and after a stint making cartloads of money in the grocery business, they set about creating their dream winery. They made their first wines in 1997; the palatial visitors center, with its unique mix of Persian and contemporary architecture, opened in 2004.

Darioush (4240 Silverado Trail, Napa, 707/257-2345, www.darioush.com, 10:30 A.M.–5 P.M. daily, tasting $25) is a hard-to-miss winery, thanks in part to the 16 giant sandstone pillars, each topped with a double-headed bull, that take the place of more traditional trees in front of the main entrance. The theme is continued in the luxurious interior, where carved sandstone looks like it's straight from the set of *Raiders of the Lost Ark,* but it still manages to blend seamlessly with designer furnishings, architectural lighting, and stainless steel trim. If you have to wait for the crowds to thin out at the glass-topped tasting bar, take a seat on what looks like (and probably is) a Le Corbusier leather sofa.

About half the winery's total production

of 10,000 cases is the Signature cabernet sauvignon, a luxurious wine made with all five bordeaux varietals. Other wines include, appropriately, a shiraz—the grape is named for the Shiraz region of Iran, where it was once believed to have originated (recent DNA analysis disproved this); coincidentally, Shiraz is also where the Khaledis grew up. Merlot, chardonnay, and viognier round out the wines sourced from the winery's 75 acres of Napa Valley vineyards. Darioush also makes a small amount of pinot noir from the Russian River Valley.

SIGNORELLO VINEYARDS

Originally a grower of predominantly white grapes, Signorello (4500 Silverado Trail, Napa, 707/255-5990, www.signorellovineyards.com, general tastings 10:30 A.M.–5 P.M. daily by appointment) started making its own wine in the mid-1980s and by the early 1990s had planted red grapes and started making the bordeaux-style wines that it is best known for today. Visiting here is a nice reassurance that small wineries can still thrive in the big-time Napa Valley even without attaining cult status.

The estate cabernet sauvignon now dominates the winery's 5,000-case annual production, but limited-production estate chardonnay and syrah are also made, together with some highly rated pinot noir from the Las Amigas vineyard in Carneros, and zinfandel from hotter vineyards up near Calistoga. The winery is set back from the road on a hill with an idyllic view from its sunny poolside patio, making it a pleasant enough stop on a daily tasting schedule.

The best way to experience the winery, its wines, and the wonderful patio, however, is through the various food-related tastings offered every day. The appointment-only Enoteca Experience is a 1.5 hour tour and tasting offered twice a day (11 A.M. and 2:30 P.M., $65) that includes gourmet appetizers paired with various Signorello wines that vary by the season. On Saturdays and Sundays April–October there are other foodie options, most recently Kobe beef and Cabernet ($55) and Pizza Sundays ($35). Check the website for current food and wine activities.

TREFETHEN VINEYARDS

One of the southernmost of Napa Valley's historic 19th-century wineries lies just a stone's throw from Highway 29 and is worth the short detour even if you're heading for the more famous wineries further north. Trefethen (1160 Oak Knoll Ave., Napa, 707/255-7700, www .trefethen.com, 10 A.M.–4:30 P.M. daily) is one of the oldest wineries in the valley, and unusually for the valley, is made entirely of wood. Originally called the Eshcol winery, it was built by a couple of well-to-do Napa bankers in the 1880s and designed by the legendary Victorian winery designer Hamden McIntyre—the man behind many other historic valley winery buildings, including Far Niente and Greystone.

Like most of the big Victorian wineries, Eshcol originally used a gravity-flow wine-making system on its three floors, a minimalist approach now increasingly fashionable in modern wineries. The Trefethen family bought the place in 1968 and still owns it today. It was also briefly used by Domaine Chandon to produce sparkling wine while the champagne house built its current home near Yountville.

The old Eshcol name graces the approach road to the winery and a cheaper range of wines not sold at the winery, but the building, with its large brick patio and pretty gardens (including a 100-year-old cork-oak tree), is lovingly preserved and appears on the National Register of Historic Places. The original wine-making equipment is long gone, and wines are made in an adjacent modern facility. The historic structure is primarily used for barrel storage and hospitality, yet it's still worth taking the appointment-only tour offered each morning to see the upper levels in all their musty wooden glory. Otherwise you can get a peek at the solid redwood beams and trusses from one of the barrel rooms open to the public on the ground floor, right next to the cozy tasting room.

Trefethen is perhaps best known for its chardonnay, which grows well in the slightly cooler southern end of the valley. It also makes a good dry riesling, a decent cabernet sauvignon, and a host of other wines. Tasting four of the estate wines costs $10. Double your money and you can taste some of the reserve wines in the wood-paneled Wine Library. All told, the winery now makes about 65,000 cases of wine a year.

The Trefethen family was the driving force behind the decade-long quest to have Oak Knoll designated as an official AVA in the Napa Valley—the title was finally bestowed in 2004.

Mount Veeder Wineries
◖ THE HESS COLLECTION

The art is probably going to be more memorable than the wines at this mountain estate (4111 Redwood Rd., Napa, 707/255-1144, www .hesscollection.com, 10 A.M.–5:30 P.M. daily, tasting $10 Mon.–Fri., $10–30 weekends) just

15 minutes from downtown Napa and right next door to the Christian Brothers' Mont LaSalle Novitiate. That's not to say the art of wine-making has not been perfected here. It certainly has, but the soaring four-story gallery linking the two historic stone winery buildings is the biggest draw. It houses part of the private contemporary art collection of winery founder and Swiss entrepreneur Donald Hess.

Most of the contemporary paintings and sculptures are by lesser-known European artists discovered by Hess through his artistic grapevine, though works by some big names like Francis Bacon and Frank Stella are also there. While lost in the art, it would be easy to forget this is a winery but for a couple of large windows looking from the gallery onto the inner workings of the winery itself, one framing a bottling line that could be called a piece of industrial art.

There are no organized tours, so take yourself on a free iPod-guided tour of the gallery and also the cool dark barrel room off the lobby, which is open to visitors and offers a glimpse at the inside of one of the original winery buildings. A winery was built here in 1903 and later sold to Christian Brothers in 1930. Hess secured a 99-year lease on the property in the 1980s and rebuilt the winery to produce wine from the mountain vineyards he had started planting in the 1970s.

Hess now owns about 300 acres of vineyards in the Mount Veeder appellation that provide the core of the Hess Collection wines, augmented by hundreds more acres elsewhere in the Napa Valley and farther south in Monterey County that provide grapes for the cheaper Hess Estate and Hess Select labels.

A few of the Hess Collection wines, including the cabernet and chardonnay, are the only ones usually available to taste, but on weekends you might be treated to impromptu tastings of some of the rest of the huge portfolio here, including perhaps the beautifully structured Mountain Cuvée red blend or even some of the Peter Lehman wines from South Australia that are distributed in the United States by Hess and sold at the winery.

MAYACAMAS VINEYARDS

Down the road from Chateau Potelle is tiny Lokoya Road, leading to the historic stone winery of Mayacamas Vineyards (1155 Lokoya Rd., Napa, 707/224-4030, www.mayacamas.com, tasting and tours by appointment 8 A.M.–4 P.M. Mon.–Fri. only), which dates from the 1880s but was abandoned soon after. It was bought in 1941 by Jack Taylor, who brought the winery back to life and named it after the Mayacamas Mountains it stands on. He is said to have issued stock and paid dividends of winery picnics and chardonnay, a concept that might not fly so well in today's cash-driven world.

The current owners, Robert and Elinor Travers, bought the winery in 1968 and now produce an earthy and concentrated cabernet sauvignon with great aging potential as well as a crisp, oak-free chardonnay that will also mellow with a couple of years of aging. Those two wines account for the bulk of the 4,000-case production. Mayacamas also produces smaller quantities of outstanding sauvignon blanc, merlot, and (unusually for this appellation) pinot noir from its mountain vineyards. Rising up to 2,400 feet, the vineyards are some of the highest in the region, giving the wines a cool mountain character that few other Napa Valley wineries can match.

SIGHTS
Napa River Front District

The most obvious result of Napa's efforts at revitalization can be seen in the historic commercial area along Main Street, both north and south of the downtown area. The cultural anchor of the River Front District is the recently restored **Napa Valley Opera House** (1030 Main St., 707/226-7372, www.napa valleyoperahouse.com). La Scala it isn't, but the 1880 Italianate building is a reminder of Napa's Victorian boom times. The opera house is one of a handful of pre-1890 buildings scattered around downtown. In fact, Napa has more buildings that survived the 1906 earthquake than any other city or town in this part of the Wine Country. At one end of the spectrum is the fabulous Gothic Victorian **First**

NAPA VALLEY

© PHILIP GOLDSMITH

Napa's Italianate opera house now hosts theater, not opera.

Presbyterian Church (1333 3rd St., 707/224-8693, www.fpcnapa.org) at 3rd and Randolph Streets, built in 1875, and at the other is the 1888 **Semorile Building** (975 1st St.), just around the corner from the opera house and now home to the Bounty Hunter restaurant. An easy-to-follow walking tour of Napa's historic buildings is available from the Napa Valley Conference & Visitors Bureau.

Farther south, right at the end of Main Street, is the southern anchor of the River Front District, the restored **Napa Mill** (www.historicnapamill.com). This riverside complex in a redbrick Victorian building used to be where steamships docked before the automobile age. It now houses upscale restaurants and shops, including the Napa General Store. The Riverbend Performance Plaza here hosts free music and art shows on weekends.

ENTERTAINMENT

There's usually something going on in the bars and restaurants along bustling Main Street in downtown Napa's River Front District,

especially on the **Third Thursday Night on the Riverfront** each month, when many places stay open until 9 P.M. with accompanying music and other events. In general, however, Napa is not a city with much active nightlife, and there are only a handful of small venues that cater to live entertainment, mainly of the jazz variety.

A popular casual jazz venue is **Uva Trattoria** (1040 Clinton St. at Brown St., Napa, 707/255-6646, www.uvatrattoria.com, lunch and dinner weekdays, dinner weekends, dinner entrées $14–26)—not a bad place to eat either. There is music from the Leo Cavanaugh Trio and the big-band sound of the Gentlemen of Jazz (6:30–9 P.M. Wed.–Sat.), together with some occasional visiting artists, mainly on Saturday nights. Another Napa eatery with live music is **Downtown Joe's** brewery and grill (902 Main St. at 2nd St., 707/258-2337, www.downtownjoes.com). Music is varied and ranges from rockabilly to Latin to jazz.

At the Napa Mill complex, **Silo's** (530 Main St., 707/251-5833, www.silosjazzclub.com, 5–10 P.M. Wed.–Thurs., 5 P.M.–midnight Sat.–Sun.) has become as popular for evening wine tasting or a predinner drink as it has for its live jazz and blues, featured almost every night. Cover charges vary from free to $25 depending on the band. Wines on the decent wine list have far lower markups than at most local restaurants, and there is also a small food menu of appetizers, pizza, and desserts.

Napa might not be the center of the valley's wine scene, but it is the cultural center. The **Napa Valley Opera House** (1030 Main St., Napa, 707/226-7372, www.napavalleyoperahouse.com) is home to just about every performance art except opera. It is the base of the **Napa Valley Repertory Theater** (707/251-9126, www.naparep.com), which usually presents about four programs each season, and schedules its own wide range of music, dance, and theater throughout the year. Call for more information, or check the website for a schedule of programs.

The first Saturday of every month is Opera Night at Napa's **Jarvis Conservatory** (1711

Main St., Napa, 707/255-5445, www.jarvis
conservatory.com), a few blocks north of the
opera house, opposite the grounds of a rather
bleak-looking high school. It's a casual night
of entertainment provided by local Bay Area
singers accompanied by the conservatory's musicians, a bit like a greatest hits of opera. The
$15 ticket price includes wine and snacks dur-
ing the intermission, and the entertainment
usually starts at 8 P.M.

SHOPPING

The city of Napa is a slightly schizophrenic
place as far as shopping goes, having to cater to
its large working-class population, downtown
office workers, and visitors alike. Many locals
frequent the car-friendly big box stores and
supermarkets that line Trancas Street north of
downtown Napa. Many visitors make a beeline for the outlet mall west of downtown next
to Highway 29. Food-loving locals and visitors alike frequent the Oxbow Public Market
east of downtown. That leaves the downtown
area itself feeling like a ghost town for much
of the week and downtown merchants struggling for business.

The situation was not helped by the 2009
recession and the scrapping of an ambitious
downtown redevelopment plan that left the
area in limbo for years. By early 2010 there
were dozens of empty storefronts in the downtown area. Even a free trolley service that for
seven years linked all these disparate parts of
the city was scrapped in 2009 because rider-
ship was so low and local businesses no longer
wanted to give it financial support. As a
result, a car, bike, or good pair of legs will be
needed to visit the handful of shopping locations worth visiting.

Head across the freeway on 1st Street from
downtown and it's hard to miss the **Napa
Premium Outlets,** a typical modern outlet
mall with 50 stores that include Ann Taylor,
Timberland, J Crew, Bennetton, and Izod
(629 Factory Stores Dr., right off Highway
29, 707/226-9876, www.premiumoutlets
.com, all stores 10 A.M.–8 P.M. Mon.–Thurs.,
10 A.M.–9 P.M. Fri.–Sat., 10 A.M.–6 P.M. Sun.).

Despite its lack of Wine Country charm and
distinctly suburban feel, this is about as vibrant as the shopping experience gets in the
city of Napa.

The anchor development for downtown
Napa is the **Napa Town Center**, a rather
forlorn-looking 1980s open-air shopping center that is now home to a motley collection
of unremarkable chain and local stores. It is,
however, home to the Napa Valley Conference
& Visitors Bureau and the Wineries of Napa
Valley tasting room, so you might find yourself
walking through it anyway.

There are still some quirky local shops in
the downtown area that continued to thrive
through the downturn, however. One of the
more original is the women's vintage clothing store **Betty's Girl Boutique** (1239 1st St.,
707/254-7560, 11 A.M.–6 P.M. daily except
Wed. and Sun.), on 1st Street opposite the shopping center and far more original than most of
the clothing stores you'll find downtown.

Continue east on 1st Street and cross the
river to the Oxbow Public Market (644 1st
St.), a food mecca that is also home to the
charming antique and gift store **Heritage
Culinary Artifacts** (610 1st St., Stall 14,
707/224-2101, www.heritageartifacts.com,
9 A.M.–7 P.M. Mon.–Sat., 9 A.M.–6 P.M. Sun.).
Some of the culinary treasures from around
the world are so unusual that you might be
tempted despite their high price tags. Continue
east on 1st Street to one of the best wine shops
in town, **JV Wine** (301 1st St., 707/253-2624,
www.jvwine.com, 8 A.M.–9 P.M. Mon.–Sat.,
9 A.M.–8 P.M. Sun.). It's a Napa institution that
sells a huge selection of wine and beer and can
ship wine to states that allow it. It also offers
afternoon tasting of wine every Friday for $5,
and takes part in the Taste Napa Downtown
wine-tasting card program.

Although it's a short walk from downtown,
the best place to find a gift in Napa is probably the **Napa General Store** (540 Main
St., Napa, 707/259-0762, www.napageneral
store.com, 8 A.M.–5 P.M. daily) in the redbrick
Napa Mill complex. Alongside the café and
wine bar, the store sells a huge range of Wine

NAPA VALLEY FESTIVALS AND EVENTS

JANUARY-APRIL

The year in the Napa Valley kicks off with the **Napa Valley Mustard Festival,** a celebration of food and wine in the valley that lasts from the end of January to early April, roughly coinciding with the blazing yellow flowers of wild mustard that brighten up the otherwise bare, leafless vineyards.

The festival is as much about drumming up business for valley businesses during the tourism off-season as raising dollars for local charities. There are countless events throughout the two months in towns up and down the valley, most notably **Mustard, Mud, and Music** in Calistoga on the first Saturday in March; and the **Taste of Yountville,** usually held on the third Saturday of March. All are essentially big street parties featuring local restaurants, entertainment, wineries, and stores. For more information and tickets for these events and others during the Mustard Festival, contact the festival organizers in Yountville (707/938-1133, www.mustardfestival.org).

MAY

It might seem strange to have a wine festival in the Napa Valley, a place where wine seems to be celebrated every day of the year. But the **Napa Valley Wine Festival,** held in early May in Yountville, has a higher purpose than simply indulgence – it raises money for local schools. Some 50 wineries pour their wines to accompany food from countless valley restaurants, making it the best place to sample the wines of the valley without spending hours in a car. Tickets ($35-45) and information can be obtained from the festival sponsor, Napa Valley Unified Education Foundation (707/253-3563, www.nvef.org).

JUNE

Summer begins with big blowout sales at the **Napa Valley Wine Auction,** usually a three-day event over the first weekend in June. The annual charity event brings together the valley's biggest wine names and some very big wallets to wine, dine, and bid sometimes crazy prices for barrels and bottles of wine, all for a worthy cause. Most of the pricey tickets are sold by invitation only, and the few available to the general public usually sell out early in the year. Contact the Napa Valley Vintners

Country products including cookbooks and cooking supplies, specialty foods, wine accessories, soaps from the Napa Soap Company, and even some furniture, all with some link to the Napa Valley. If you're looking for a Napa gift for anyone, this should be your first stop.

RECREATION
Skyline Wilderness Park

Most people don't associate Napa Valley with serious mountain biking, but just outside the city of Napa is Skyline Wilderness Park (707/252-0481, www.skylinepark.org, 8 A.M.–7 P.M.), which hosted the U.S. round of the Mountain Bike World Cup three years in a row in the late 1990s. It's not the prettiest park in the valley—that distinction goes to Bothe-Napa Valley State Park near St. Helena—but

it does offer 16 miles of trails for bikers, hikers, and horseback riders through its 850 acres of meadows and woodland. Spring is probably the best time to come, when the meadows are full of wildflowers doing their thing before the dry season turns the grassland to golden brown.

The park is reached from downtown Napa on Imola Avenue. The day-use fee is $5, and be sure to pick up a map when you arrive because the trail system is more complex than most. Hikers should look out for bikers and horses—all users share all the trails.

Mountain bikers wanting to try their skills on the world cup route should ride from near the park's entrance for about a mile up Lake Marie Road before turning right onto the murderous ascent of Passini Road and then descending on the rocky, sometimes steep single-track of the Bayleaf Trail. The next stage

for more information (707/963-3388, www .napavintners.com/auctions).

JULY-SEPTEMBER

The **Robert Mondavi Summer Music Festival** (888/769-5299, www.robertmondaviwinery .com) in July and August has become a summer institution in the Napa Valley and features big-name rock, jazz, blues, and Latin music artists (Julio Iglesias, Tears for Fears, Aimee Mann, and India.Arie, for example). The outdoor concerts are held Saturday evenings on the Robert Mondavi winery grounds, usually from the beginning of July through mid-August. Tickets cost $60-115 depending on the concert.

The celebration of music continues in August with the monthlong **Music in the Vineyards** (707/258-5559, www.napavalleymusic .com) series of chamber music concerts. The festival kicks off in early August and features a concert every couple of days at wineries and other venues up and down the valley.

Downtown Napa is also host to a couple of other annual fairs. The **Napa Town & Country Fair** in August at the Napa Valley Expo Fairgrounds (www.napavalleyexpo.com) is a kid-friendly arts, crafts, and (of course) culinary celebration, though distinct from the free **Annual Napa Wine and Crafts Faire** (call 707/257-0322 for information) that takes over streets in downtown Napa in early September.

OCTOBER

Not to be left out of the music action, Calistoga throws a big blues party in October. **Calistoga Downtown Blues** (866/306-5588, www.calistogajazz.com) includes local and national blues artists playing on stages set up along Lincoln Avenue. This being Wine Country, wine tasting is a big part of the fun too. It's free to attend, though the wine tasting and the biggest evening events require tickets.

NOVEMBER-DECEMBER

The valley's wine caves are great for aging wine but also have pretty good acoustics, as you can discover at one of the weekend **Carols in the Caves** concerts from late November through December. Visit www.cavemusic .net or call 707/224-4222 for more information on the wineries hosting the concerts.

of the cup was the Manzanita Trail, reached by climbing back up Lake Marie Road to the fig tree. The undulating two-mile trail was described as one of the best single-tracks on the cup circuit.

Disc golf offers some less traditional exercise. You might know it as Frisbee golf, but the Professional Disc Golf Association would prefer you use the D word instead. It is played exactly as you might think, like golf but throwing a Frisbee instead of hitting a little white ball. There is an 18-hole course, and (in case you don't always travel with one) Frisbees (sorry, discs) are available at the entrance kiosk, along with course maps. The dress rules are a little more relaxed than on most traditional golf courses—no collared shirts or fancy shoes are required. In fact, you don't even have to wear shirts or shoes.

Those who'd prefer to expend less energy can find **picnic areas** near the park entrance and about 2.5 miles up the Lake Marie Road at the lake itself.

Alston Park

Untouched by either vineyards or development, Alston Park instead has sweeping views of both from the western fringe of the city of Napa. The park is off Dry Creek Road, reached by driving west from Highway 29 from either Redwood Road or Trower Avenue. There's no entrance fee, and the park is open dawn to dusk, although the only map is on an information board.

It's not on quite the same scale as Skyline but still offers plenty of picnicking, hiking, and biking possibilities in its 150 acres of rolling hills and meadows and along five miles

MORE THAN JUST HOT AIR

Hot-air balloons have become so synonymous with the Napa Valley that locals barely even blink when they float overhead in the early morning. There are still plenty of people willing to pay to get up before dawn for this unique adrenaline rush followed by a serene aerial view of the valley and its spectacular wineries, though perhaps fewer than in recent years; mergers between ballooning companies have reduced the number offering rides to less than half a dozen.

Most are farther south in the valley, especially around Yountville, but a couple farther north can float the bleary-eyed over some of the volcanic scenery at the northern end of the valley. Early-morning winds tend to be southerly, so pick a company that launches north of any place you really want to see from the air, but also bear in mind that balloons generally don't float far – often only a few miles over the course of a flight.

The drill is more or less the same for any ballooning adventure, whatever the company: get up before the sun rises and its rays start to generate unstable warm air that balloon pilots hate; get to a prearranged pickup point by 6-7 A.M. (depending on the season), usually a hotel or restaurant near the launch site (some companies will also collect customers staying locally); drive to the launch site and watch, sometimes take part in, the inflation of the balloon; then finally take off with the roar of the burners for an hour-long, silent drift at elevations ranging from treetop to several thousand feet, depending on the conditions. Brunch usually follows, either at a local restaurant or alfresco in a meadow, and the whole experience usually lasts about four hours.

Plenty of variables, however, can make a balloon trip less than perfect. The obvious one is the weather, which can either cancel a trip outright (fog, rain, and high winds especially), or, in the case of more localized fog, the launch site might be moved to somewhere where the skies are clearer, sometimes even outside the valley.

Some companies will do a "double hop," leaving those unfortunate enough to be assigned to the second hop, or flight, of the day following behind the balloons in a van to the landing spot before finally getting a flight. The drawback of the second flight (apart from the feeling of having woken up early for nothing) is that air currents can die down after the sun rises and the balloon might not float very far. Ask if a double hop is planned – they tend to be more common during the busy summer and fall seasons. If it is, insist on hopping on board with the first group.

Ask how big the basket is and how many groggy souls will be crammed in with you. Some companies limit riders to eight or even four people; others take up to 16 per flight. For a large premium, most also offer the option of a private flight for two.

Farthest north in the valley is **Calistoga Balloons** (888/995-7700, www.calistogaballoons.com, $225), which launches from the Calistoga area and offers brunch afterward at the Hydro Grill in town. **Napa Valley Aloft** (www.napavalleyaloft.com) owns three Yountville-area ballooning companies with three different prices, and can be visited in the Vintage 1870 Marketplace building in Yountville. One of the three is **Above the West Ballooning** (800/627-2759, $295), which offers a free shuttle from anywhere in the valley, guarantees no more than four people to a basket, and in summer has its postflight brunch alfresco in a vineyard. The cheapest is **Balloon Aviation** (800/367-6272, $225), which has no shuttle but still guarantees no double hops.

The **Bonaventura Balloon Company** (707/944-2822 or 800/359-6272, www.bonaventuraballoons.com, $215-250) offers flights in the northern half of the valley and a variety of brunch options, from the most expensive at the Meadowood Resort to a cheaper picnic option. Also check the website for special rates. **Balloons Above the Valley** (707/253-2222 or 800/464-6824, www.balloonrides.com, $230) usually launches from near the Domaine Chandon winery in Yountville and offers a private brunch after the flight. It also sometimes has good online deals, including no-frills flights that are shorter, foodless, and cheaper.

of trails. There are picnic tables and a canine common where dogs can be let off the leash—a rarity in the relatively dog-unfriendly valley. Just avoid the park during the middle of hot summer days unless you're training for a desert trek, because there are few trees and little shade.

Golf

The southern end of the valley is where all the biggest and most exclusive golf courses are, many of them not open to the public. Among those that are, the biggest is the 18-hole **Napa Golf Course** (2295 Streblow Dr., Napa, 707/255-4333, www.playnapa.com, call for tee times) at Kennedy Park a couple of miles south of downtown on Soscol Avenue, which eventually becomes the Napa-Vallejo Highway. The 6,500-yard, par-72 championship course costs $25–35 to play during the week for nonresidents and $34–46 on weekends. Rates vary depending on time of day. It has a driving range, practice putting greens, and a fully stocked golf shop.

ACCOMMODATIONS

Although it feels a little removed from all the wine action in the valley, and is not the most attractive Wine Country town in this part of the world, the city of Napa provides the widest choice of accommodation options. Many major chain hotels can be found here (including some recent upscale additions) as well as cheap independent motels, Victorian B&Bs, and a couple of modern boutique hotels. Best of all, rooms are generally cheaper here than anywhere else in the valley, especially at the low end of the market.

Another advantage of staying in Napa, particularly if you're not a cabernet sauvignon fan, is its proximity to the Carneros region, the land of pinot noir and chardonnay. It's just a 15-minute drive south to many wineries in the eastern half of Los Carneros, or a 15-minute drive north to some of the Napa Valley's best cabernet producers. And for those traveling to or from Oakland or San Francisco, Napa has the shortest drive time

of any of the valley's towns—a full 45 minutes closer to San Francisco than Calistoga, for example.

The city is also home to a good selection of restaurants, most within a short walk of most downtown hotels and B&Bs. Indeed, if you don't want to drive to dinner and still have the choice of more than a handful of restaurants, then Napa is the probably the best place to stay in the valley.

Under $100

There are more lodging options at the low end of the price spectrum in and around Napa than anywhere else in the valley. The **Wine Valley Lodge** (200 S. Coombs St., Napa, 707/224-7911, www.winevalleylodge.com) is a simple, clean, and bargain-priced independent motel let down only by its location about a mile south of downtown Napa, putting it just out of walking distance to most good restaurants and shops. It is just off Imola Avenue, however, which provides a quick connection to Highway 29 and wineries to the north and south. The guest rooms are simply but tastefully furnished, though with the ubiquitous motel-standard floral bedspreads made of some sort of synthetic material that feels like it could stop a bullet. All have TVs, air-conditioning, and private bathrooms with showers, and cost $50–80 midweek, depending on the season, and $80–130 on weekends.

A little north of downtown Napa is **Napa Valley Redwood Inn** (3380 Solano Ave., off Redwood Rd., Napa, 707/257-6111, www.napavalleyredwoodinn.com). Some big-hotel touches (newspapers, free high-speed Internet access, HBO, a decent-sized outdoor pool) sweeten the appeal of the otherwise small and well-worn motel-style rooms. Its location right next to the St. Helena Highway (Highway 29) puts it in easy reach of wineries but also means there's some traffic noise to contend with, and you must drive to reach local restaurants in Napa and Yountville. A new mall across the street, Redwood Plaza, at least puts decent coffee within easy reach, and nothing is too unbearable considering the rates are as low as

$80–90 midweek and $80–150 on weekends, depending on the season.

Right next door to the Redwood Inn is the **Chablis Inn** (3360 Solano Ave., off Redwood Rd., Napa, 707/257-1944 or 800/443-3490, www.chablisinn.com). It's a bit more upscale than its neighbor but is still a glorified motel with prices that squeak in at just under $100 midweek for the basic rooms (with the bulletproof bedspreads). The deluxe rooms are only $20 more per night and a little more luxurious, with comforters, CD players, and whirlpool tubs in the bathrooms. Weekend rates are considerably higher, starting at $140 per night.

Across town and a little off the beaten track is the **Napa Discovery Inn** (500 Silverado Trail, 707/253-0892, www. napadiscovery inn.com), a small and relatively clean motel with a decent list of amenities and rooms starting at $85 midweek, rising to almost $200 on summer weekends. It's in a quiet part of town but not really close to any major attractions, so you'll definitely need a car if you plan to stay here.

$100-200

For just a few dollars more a night than the nearby motels you could stay in, the more hotel-like **John Muir Inn** (1998 Trower Ave., Napa, 707/257-7220 or 800/522-8999, www .johnmuirnapa.com) is a sprawling building just off Highway 29 on the northern edge of Napa. The bland building is nothing much to look at, but it has nice gardens and plenty of clean and comfortable rooms that are a step up from most motel rooms. Standard amenities include Internet access, air-conditioning, and enough room for a desk. Some have refrigerators and microwaves or full kitchenettes, and three of the deluxe king rooms have whirlpool tubs. Standard rooms start at $140–210 per night midweek, depending on the season, and $170–220 on weekends. Deluxe rooms are usually only $10 more per night. As with most inns and hotels, a free continental breakfast is included, but guests can instead choose a money-off voucher for breakfast or brunch at the neighboring Marie Callender's restaurant.

Napa's first and still most unique boutique hotel, the **Napa River Inn** (500 Main St., Napa, 707/251-8500 or 877/251-8500, www .napariverinn.com) has perhaps the best location in the city at the historic redbrick Napa Mill, a small riverside food and entertainment complex only a 10-minute walk to more shops and restaurants in downtown Napa. The 66 guest rooms are spread among three buildings—two are part of the historic mill itself and one (the Embarcadero building) was built in 1997. All rooms are furnished in an eclectic mix of contemporary and either Victorian or nautical style, many with fireplaces, balconies, or views, though the views vary wildly from a parking lot to the river, which still bears some scars of recent flood-control construction work. Staying here is not as pricey as the location and luxury might suggest. Smallish standard rooms cost $180–200 midweek and only about $20 more on weekends. The most expensive deluxe rooms in the historic buildings are double that, though there are plenty of options in between. The larger rooms tend to be in the main historic building.

The Napa Mill itself has everything a hotel guest might need: Choose between two of the city's best restaurants (Celadon and Angèle) for dinner. In the morning, after the hotel breakfast from Sweetie Pies bakery, buy picnic supplies at the Napa General Store and book an evening spa treatment before setting off for a day of wine tasting.

Giving the Napa River Inn a run for its money is the **Avia Napa** (1450 1st St., 707/224-3900 or 866/644-2824, www.aviahotels.com) hotel, which opened in 2009 in a brand new building on 1st Street, bringing some much-needed modern energy to the tired downtown accommodation and architecture scene. Touted as a boutique hotel, it is actually a new addition to a rapidly expanding national chain of affordable and stylish hotels, featuring lots of polished wood, crisp linens, and modern amenities from iPod docks to massive plasma-screen TVs. Some aspects of the service will not be up to the same levels of more established or expensive local hotels, but the location and quality of amenities are hard to beat for the price. The smallest king rooms with walk-in showers start at $130 midweek in the spring, rising to $280 on a busy summer weekend, but as with most chains there are often discounts available. Prices increase about $30 per night with every additional luxury room feature, such as soaking tubs, balconies, fireplaces, and views.

The choice of Victorian B&Bs in Napa can be a bit bewildering. One establishment that has some of the cheaper rates and plenty of room options is **Hennessey House** (1727 Main St., Napa, 707/226-3774, www .hennesseyhouse.com), about six blocks north of downtown Napa. The only downside to the location is the particularly ugly high school across the road. Six rooms in the main Queen Anne–style Victorian house cost $139–239, depending on season, all with private bathrooms and some with four-poster beds and claw-foot tubs. Four larger, more ornate rooms, with fireplaces, whirlpool tubs, and CD players, are in the Carriage House and cost $189–299. The full gourmet breakfast is enough to soak up plenty of wine during those morning wine tastings, and the sauna is a place to relax tasting-weary feet at the end of a winter day. Allergy sufferers be warned: The resident cat has free rein of the common areas.

Anyone fed up with Victorian frills should check out the **(Blackbird Inn** (1755 1st St., 707/226-2450 or 888/567-9811, www .blackbirdinnnapa.com), an arts and crafts–style shingled house dating from the 1920s with furnishings to match the era's relatively clean and simple lines. It's just a few blocks from downtown Napa, right opposite the West Coast home of *Wine Spectator* magazine, making it probably the most conveniently located B&B in Napa. The teddy bears on each bed are a trademark of the Four Sisters group, which owns this and a handful of other small Wine Country inns—although there's no corporate feel to the place. The only disadvantage is that there are no owners living there to take care of any late-night problems, but there are advantages too. Unusually for a B&B, there

are TVs in every room with DVD players (the walls supposedly have some decent sound-proofing, unlike those at many B&Bs) and free wireless Internet access in addition to the more common fireplaces and whirlpool tubs in some rooms. Rates range from $145 midweek to $185 on weekends for the smallest room, though most are in the $200–285 range.

Just a couple of blocks from the Blackbird Inn and touted as Napa's first B&B when it opened in the 1980s, **The Beazley House** (1910 1st St., Napa, 707/257-1649 or 800/559-1649, www.beazleyhouse.com), with its own feline resident, is in another squat shingled mansion, this one dating from 1906 and adorned with rather garish blue-and-white canopies over the windows. Rooms contain the usual mix of what look like your great-grandmother's best furnishings. The five guest rooms in the main house have private bathrooms, though only one of the five has a claw-foot tub, and cost $180–260. The other five rooms are in the Carriage House and are more luxurious, with whirlpool tubs, fireplaces, individual air-conditioning, and views of the lush garden; they cost $255–340.

Despite being somewhat marooned right next to the freeway opposite the outlet stores, the **Bel Abri Inn** (837 California Blvd., off 1st St. at Hwy. 29, Napa, 877/561-6000, www .belabri.net) offers good value for money and convenience but is not the most stylish accommodation in the city. The clean, modern building is furnished in a faux French country style and has 15 rooms, including a few with patios or fireplaces, starting at $140 in winter and about $50 per night higher in winter. Midweek and weekend prices are usually the same, but there is the usual two-night minimum at the weekend. In terms of amenities and services it lies somewhere between a motel and a hotel, but it does offer a few luxury touches like concierge service and an evening wine and cheese tasting. Downtown Napa is a little too far to walk comfortably, but it is only a few minutes' drive.

Over $200

Arguably one of the finest Victorian B&Bs

in Napa is **La Belle Époque** (1386 Calistoga Ave., Napa, 707/257-2161 or 800/238-8070, www.labelleepoque.com), a glorious Queen Anne–style mansion built in 1893 with an antique-stuffed interior that looks like the movie set for an Agatha Christie mystery. The six guest rooms are all unique, most with stained-glass windows, some with canopy beds, and others with fireplaces or whirlpool tubs. Standard amenities include TVs with VCRs, high-speed Internet access, and CD players, and all guests are invited to evening wine receptions featuring wines from local wineries or from the inn's own big wine cellar. All this pampering and history, plus a very central yet tranquil location, comes at a cost. Rates range from $180 for a couple of the rooms midweek in midwinter up to $275–329 on summer weekends. Two suites in a separate Victorian house across the street go for $199–439 more.

Like a set for a real-life game of Clue, the sprawling mansion that is home to the **Cedar Gables Inn** (486 Coombs St. at Oak St., Napa, 800/309-7969, www.cedargablesinn.com) might have you wondering if you'll bump into Colonel Mustard in the study. Built in 1892 by a renowned English architect, the huge Tudor-style mansion covered in cedar shingles was one of the grandest houses in Napa County in its heyday and the site of many lavish balls and gatherings. Today the labyrinth of stairways, passages, and secret doors is home to a lavish B&B with nine guest rooms, all exquisitely furnished with Victorian finery. All have private bathrooms, four have fireplaces, and four have whirlpool tubs. Other amenities include free wireless Internet access and a gourmet breakfast befitting the surroundings. They range in price $209–359. The Inn has an ideal location in a peaceful residential neighborhood about a 10-minute walk to downtown Napa and a similar distance from the restaurants at the Napa Mill.

Less chintz and more privacy than at most B&Bs are part of a stay at **La Résidence** (4066 Howard Ln., Napa, 707/253-0337 or 800/253-9203, www.laresidence.com), on the northern edge of the city. It's actually more of a luxury country inn, with 25 guest rooms

contained in four buildings set on two acres of wooded grounds with a hot tub and a small heated pool. In early 2006 the property was bought by the owners of Hall Winery, who plan to upgrade and possibly expand the hotel, but meanwhile it's business as usual. The smallest and cheapest rooms ($175–235, depending on the season) are in the main mansion house, dating from 1870 and furnished with queen beds, original antiques, CD players, and TVs. Readers report that the plumbing in the old house can be temperamental, but all the bathrooms are nicely modernized. Larger rooms in the more modern French Barn building ($225–275) have a touch of French country style, plus balconies or patios and working fireplaces. The newest and biggest rooms ($300–350) are in the new Cellar House, with LCD TVs, wet bars, and giant bathrooms added to the already long list of amenities. A couple of unique suites are similarly luxurious. Although the inn is nowhere near downtown Napa, it does offer easy access to the rest of the valley and is virtually next door to the excellent Bistro Don Giovanni. There is free wireless Internet access, a gourmet breakfast, and a casual reception every evening featuring wines from Hall Winery.

There are luxurious resorts in the valley with views, others with wooded privacy, some with vineyards, but the **Milliken Creek Inn** (1815 Silverado Trail, Napa, 707/255-1197 or 888/622-5775, www.millikencreekinn.com) has another twist—its riverside setting, understated mix of Victorian and colonial Asian furnishings, relaxing earth tones, and the sense of exclusivity that comes from having just 12 guest rooms to share the lush gardens and fountains.

Relax on the lawn by the riverbank or lounge in the room in front of a fireplace or on a private deck and have yourself a peaceful Zen experience. All rooms come with full entertainment systems, luxurious linens, and wireless Internet access. The cheapest are the two Milliken rooms at $275–650, depending on the season and the time of the week. The premium rooms, starting at $450 a night (and

© PHILIP GOLDSMITH

The Napa Mill complex is a food and entertainment hub along Napa's waterfront.

going up to $775), include extras ranging from Jacuzzis and canopied beds to plasma-screen TVs and expansive private decks.

Worth noting is that the inn is a gratuity-free zone, but as a reminder that nothing is free in the Napa valley, a 12 percent service fee is added to your bill each day. Unless you want to complain and have the fee removed or reduced (and feel like a grinch), be sure to make full use of the helpful staff and the evening wine tastings to get your money's worth.

FOOD
River Front District and Downtown

"Global comfort food" is how the culinary creations at **Celadon** (500 Main St., Napa, 707/254-9690, www.celadonnapa.com, lunch Mon.–Fri., dinner daily, dinner entrées $16–34) have been described, and the surroundings in the historic Napa Mill buildings are equally comfortable. The shabby-chic exterior and huge sheltered patio give way to a pure bistro-chic interior, the perfect match

for the internationally influenced Californian menu. The wine list offers about the same balance of California and the rest of the world.

At the other end of the mill is the pocket of Francophone charm **(Angèle** (540 Main St., Napa, 707/252-8115, www.angele restaurant.com, lunch and dinner daily, dinner entrées $18–36). The rustic interior and canopied riverside patio are perfectly romantic settings for the classic French bistro food that has won plaudits from critics. Adding to its sophistication is an outstanding Californian and French wine list that includes about a dozen wines available by the half-bottle.

Sandwiched between Celadon and Angèle, the Napa General Store is home to the **General Café** (540 Main St., 707/259-0762, breakfast and lunch daily, www.napageneralstore.com, entrées $8–14), serving a wide range of Asian-inspired entrées as well as sandwiches and pizza from the wood-fired oven. There are a handful of tables in the store, but the main draw is the riverside patio. The accompanying wine bar is open until 6 P.M. and is an ideal place to whet your dinner appetite with a glass of bubbly by overlooking the river.

Cole's Chop House (1122 Main St., Napa, 707/224-6328, dinner daily, entrées $18–46) is the baby brother to Celadon, offering a slightly less refined but equally well-designed (though short) menu featuring steakhouse dishes, from oysters to well-aged beef, in a classic steakhouse setting rich with dark wood and contrasting white tablecloths. It doesn't quite stack up to the best steakhouses up-valley, but it is a credible alternative if you crave a hunk of meat in downtown Napa.

Those craving some hearty Italian food have several choices. **Ristorante Allegria** (1026 1st St., 707/254-8006, www.ristoranteallegria .com, lunch and dinner daily, dinner entrées $14–28) is a cozy, leafy oasis tucked into a corner of the rather desolate First Street Plaza and is housed in a historic Italianate bank building that creates an air of Old World elegance. The restaurant is far larger than the exterior suggests, however, and can get noisy inside, so reserving a table on the small patio bordering the plaza is recommended. There's nothing terribly inventive about the menu, and the dining experience is not quite up to par with some of the more famous Italian restaurants up-valley, but with reasonable prices, a huge wine list, and competent cooking, it's a solid choice.

Uva Trattoria (1040 Clinton St. at Brown St., Napa, 707/255-6646, www.uvatrattoria .com) has become a Napa institution for its rustic Italian food and lively bar and as one of the few live music venues in the city.

The River Front District is the main food center in downtown Napa, and one of its most inventive establishments is █ **Bounty Hunter** (975 1st St., off Main St., Napa, 707/226-3976 or 800/943-9463, www.bounty hunterwinebar.com, lunch and dinner daily, plates and entrées $6–18), a wine shop, tasting bar, and (most recently) casual restaurant serving small plates to help the wine go down. The setting, in a historic brick-walled Victorian building with knotty wood floors, a copper ceiling, and wine barrels for table bases, is as relaxed as the comfort food served. It includes

gumbo, the beer-can chicken (a Cajun-spiced chicken impaled on a Tecate beer can), and chili. Alternatively, just order some cheese and settle down at the wine bar with one of the 400 wines sold here (40 by the glass) or a tasting flight. Since it's a wine shop too, you'll pay retail prices for wines bought with a meal, and there'll be plenty of advice available from the fun-loving staff.

The best pizza in town can be found at **Azzurro Pizzeria & Enoteca** (1260 Main St., Napa, 707/255-5552, www.azzurropizzeria .com, lunch and dinner daily, pizzas $13–16), which earned a loyal local following at its former modest location on Second Street before moving to its current fancier digs in 2008. The thin-crust pizzas from the wood-fired oven are some of the best in this part of the world—not surprising considering the founder of this popular restaurant honed his pizza skills at the famous Tra Vigne restaurant in St. Helena. The menu includes classic Italian starters, salads, and a handful of pasta dishes alongside the dozen or so pizzas, and there are plenty of choices for vegetarians. The wine list is dominated by thoughtfully chosen Napa and Sonoma wines, yet another sign that this is a no-nonsense and hassle-free dining experience favored by locals.

With the amount of critical praise heaped on **ZuZu** (829 Main St. at 2nd St., Napa, 707/224-8555, www.zuzunapa.com, lunch weekdays, dinner daily, plates $5–13), you'd think it was competing with French Laundry for title of the valley's best restaurant. Thankfully, it's a refreshingly down-to-earth tapas bar that's a great place to end a stressful day of touring without having to worry about reservations or the bill. The cozy interior with its exposed brick, beams, and tile is the perfect setting for the Spanish-inspired small plates, none of which (except the Moroccan glazed lamb chops) costs over $10. Lunch is only served during the week, when it's a popular local hangout.

Downtown Joe's American Grill and Brewhouse (902 Main St., 707/258-2337, lunch and dinner daily, breakfast weekends, dinner entrées $9–21) is a hopping alternative to the swanky restaurants and endless wine of the Napa Valley. Sure, it has a wine list (a short one), but most people come here for the more than half-dozen microbrews with the usual comical microbrew names, like Tantric India Pale Ale and Catherine the Great Imperial Stout. The menu is pretty standard if slightly pricey grill fare, but there's also a cheaper pizza and pub grub menu. There is live music in the evening Thursday–Sunday.

Throw all preconceptions of vegetarian restaurants out of your mind when you visit **C Ubuntu** (1140 Main St., 707/251-5656, lunch weekends, dinner Mon.–Sun., dinner entrées $9–16). The upstairs yoga studio might suggest this place is a little "granola," but the restaurant has garnered rave reviews and a Michelin star, and there is barely a chunk of tofu to be seen in the sleek Zen-like interior. Cofounder and executive chef Jeremy Fox had a philosophy of celebrating locally grown produce rather than actively shunning meat, and with such an abundance of vegetables in the Napa Valley (including from Ubuntu's own nearby farm) he has plenty to work with. The main dishes on the seasonal menu are small, but most are under $15, so buying a handful to share at the table is the best bet. Their richness and sophistication, however, should satisfy even the most ardent meat eaters. The well-thought-out international wine list is, naturally, dominated by wines from organic or biodynamic vineyards, although the options are on the pricey side. In early 2010 both Jeremy Fox and pastry chef Deanie Fox left Ubuntu, and it remains to be seen how the restaurant will fare without them.

Oxbow Public Market

A one-stop shop for anyone looking for a quick fix of Napa Valley cuisine, the Oxbow Public Market (610 1st St., Napa, www.oxbowpublicmarket.com) showcases local and artisanal food suppliers in a farm stand–like setting. All the tenants in the market are generally open at least 10 A.M.–7 P.M. weekdays

and 10 A.M.–6 P.M. on weekends, but many are open later, as noted below.

Some of the restaurants that anchor the new development include outposts of St. Helena's gourmet burger joint **Gott's Roadside Tray Gourmet** (10:30 A.M.–9 P.M. daily)—formerly Taylor's Automatic Refresher—together with popular bakery and café **Model Bakery** (7 A.M.–7 P.M. daily). Another interesting addition to the Napa food scene that has proven to be very popular is **Pica Pica,** said to be one of the first restaurants in California to offer Venezuelan street cuisine, which is known for its unique combinations of sweet and savory flavors, such as shredded skirt steak with black beans, cheese, and sweet plantains. The specialty dish is *arepas,* a corn flour-based flatbread filled with your choice of almost a dozen savory fillings and grilled to a crisp. Two other bread options are also offered, and all cost $8–9. The kitchen is open until 8 P.M. Monday–Thursday, until 9 P.M. Friday-Saturday, and until 5 P.M. Sunday.

Almost next to Pica Pica is the **Folio Enoteca & Wine Bar,** which serves Mediterranean-inspired food that complements the many Californian and international wines available to buy or taste. The only problem, if you want a more substantial meal, can be finding somewhere to sit at one of the few tables or the four-seat bar. The best options are the mouth-watering panini or pita sandwiches, which can be ordered to go and cost $8–10.

Restaurants are only half the story at Oxbow, however. One of the biggest draws is the cornucopia of Napa Valley food, from organic ice cream and olive oil to cheese and meats. **Five Dot Ranch** sells every cut of grass-fed beef and every other meat imaginable, while the **Oxbow Cheese Market** is a pungent tribute to local artisanal cheese makers. There's also an outpost of Sonoma's **Olive Press** and more meats at the charcuterie **The Fatted Calf** at the side of the market on McKinstry Street. Finish shopping or dining with a delectable organic dessert from **Three Twins Ice Cream** or with one of everyone's favorite treats from **Kara's Cupcakes,** which is hard to miss at the front of the main market building thanks to its giant pink menu board.

Vicinity of Napa

A few miles north of downtown Napa is the popular Italian restaurant **Bistro Don Giovanni** (4110 Howard Ln., next to Hwy. 29, Napa, 707/224-3300, lunch and dinner daily, dinner entrées $14–28). It's hard to miss on the east side of Highway 29 (though you might miss the turn for Howard Lane) and is a favorite of locals looking for moderately priced Italian bistro food with a bit of Californian flair, all in a relaxed and vibrant setting. On a warm summer night, ask for a table on the huge bustling outdoor patio. Anything from the wood-fired oven is worth trying here, especially the pizzas and oven-roasted fish. The wine list is dominated by Napa and Sonoma, but there's a good choice from the mother country too, and an unusually wide selection by the half-bottle.

If the relentless Wine Country–themed activities and food gets to be a bit too much, you can escape it all at the **Red Hen Cantina** (4175 Solano Ave., 707/255-8125, most dishes under $12), a colorful and sometimes raucous Mexican bar and restaurant right off Highway 29. Just look for the giant red hen on the roof of the building; it used to grace a nearby barn containing an antique store. The food is by no means gourmet, and the bar can get packed, but if you stick to basics on the menu like enchiladas or a burrito, have a margarita or two, and sit out on the patio, you'll have an experience that is refreshingly devoid of Wine Country pretension.

Picnic Supplies

If you're in Napa and heading to the hills for lunch, the **Napa General Store** (540 Main St., 707/259-0762) in the Napa Mill complex is about as gourmet as you can get for takeout food in the town. You'll have to battle your way past all the other nonfood trinkets and gifts it sells, though. At the **Oxbow Public Market** (610 1st St., Napa, www.oxbowpublic market.com) there are plenty of options for take-out food, from Pica Pica's Venezuelan food to gourmet sandwiches from the Model Bakery or Fatted Calf charcuterie.

Just south of the Darioush winery is the **Soda Canyon Store** (4006 Silverado Trail, at Soda Canyon Rd., Napa, 707/252-0285), just about the only decent place to buy deli food, cheeses, and wine along the Silverado Trail.

Farmers Markets

Downtown Napa might not instantly bring to mind bucolic country farms, but farm-fresh produce (and craft stalls) can be found at **Napa Downtown Market** May–October, on Tuesday and Saturday mornings until noon in the parking lot of the Wine Train just down McKinstry Street from the Oxbow Public Market.

Music, chef's demonstrations, wine tasting, and food from local restaurants fill several blocks of downtown Napa one evening a week during the summer as part of the **Napa Chef's Market** (at 1st St. and Napa Town Center, 707/257-0322, 5–9 P.M. Thurs. Memorial Day–early Aug.). It's like a mini Taste of Napa event and a fun predinner diversion, especially if you have bored kids in tow.

INFORMATION AND SERVICES

First stop for any visitors without a plan—whether staying in Napa, heading up to Calistoga, or simply doing some on-line research—should be the **Napa Valley Conference & Visitors Bureau** (1310 Napa Town Center, 707/226-7459, www.napa valley.com, 9 A.M.–5 P.M. daily). The staff know the valley like the backs of their hands and can usually rustle up some useful printed information.

The nearby **Napa Chamber of Commerce** (1556 1st St., Napa, 707/226-7455, www .napachamber.com, 8:30 A.M.–5 P.M. Mon.–Wed. and Fri., 10:30 A.M.–5 P.M. Thurs.) sells packages of information from maps to directories and touring guides, although you might be able to find some of the same information for free at the visitors bureau.

Yountville and Vicinity

The appellations in the southern half of the Napa Valley encompass some of the best cabernet-growing regions in California. They can also be cool enough for growing many other varietals, both red and white, most notably in the **Yountville** appellation, where chardonnay, sangiovese, zinfandel, sauvignon blanc, and even some pinot noir seem to thrive. Although wines from the Yountville AVA are certainly worthy of the Napa Valley pedigree, there is no one particular trait for which they are known. Indeed, you rarely see the Yountville name mentioned on bottles, and the appellation certainly lacks the cachet of the hilly region to its east.

The **Stags Leap District** appellation on the eastern side of the valley along the Silverado Trail is perhaps one of the most recognizable Napa AVAs to wine lovers, particularly red wine lovers. This fairly cool, hilly 1,300 acres of land rising up to the mountain crags (across which the legendary stag leapt to escape its hunters) is without doubt the land of cabernet sauvignon, and few other varietals get a look in. The cabernets have been famously described by the founder of Stag's Leap Wine Cellars as "an iron fist in a velvet glove," and they certainly have a gentle elegance that belies their sometimes astonishing aging potential. The combination of volcanic soils and cool air channeled between the handful of knolls that make up the district are thought to play a role in making this such a good place to create some of Napa Valley's best cabernets. Despite the fame of the Stags Leap District, most wineries here are refreshingly low-key.

North of Yountville is the **Oakville** appellation, warmer and home to some of the most famous cabernet sauvignon vineyards and wineries, including Robert Mondavi and Far Niente. Although this is where the land of big bold Napa cabernets begins in the valley, the appellation also turns out some excellent sauvignon blanc and chardonnay. Oakville is often compared to Rutherford just to its north,

and both appellations have very similar growing conditions and a similarly long list of famous wineries stretching back to the 1800s. Both also turn out rich, meaty cabernets that have helped give Napa Valley its reputation for powerhouse wines. Oakville just does it with slightly less fanfare than its more famous neighbor, Rutherford.

WINE-TASTING
Yountville Wineries
DOMAINE CHANDON

The first big French champagne house to come to California was Moët-Hennessy in 1973, and its Domaine Chandon winery (1 California Dr., off Hwy. 29, Yountville, 707/944-2280, www.domainechandon.com, 10 A.M.–6 P.M. daily, tasting $18–22) is still one of the most impressive wineries in terms of architecture and landscaping. The buildings blend into the hillside beneath towering trees next to a giant (if slightly murky) pond and are almost invisible from the road. It's not the sort of modesty that one expects from such a big glamorous operation producing several hundred thousand cases of sparkling and still wines each year; the surroundings are more earth-mother than youthful bling.

Once across the bridge and into the cavernous reception, skip the PR presentations and head upstairs to the spacious tasting bar and salon, with its cozy club-like atmosphere and doors out onto a leafy terrace and lawn area. Art is everywhere, both inside and out in the gardens, and you can buy pieces from some of the ever-changing exhibitions. The basic half-hour tour, which costs $12, takes in all stages of champagne making but runs only once daily at 11:30 A.M. For an additional $18 you can combine the tour with a tasting of both still and sparkling wines.

The tastings alone start at $18, free glass included, for the Classic flight that includes the popular bone-dry Riche and some lower-end bubblies. At the other end of the tasting

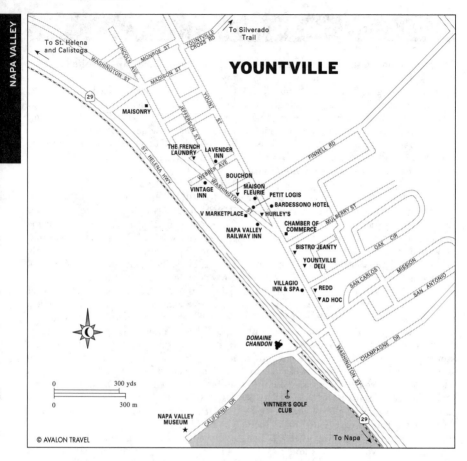

YOUNTVILLE

spectrum is the Prestige flight ($22), which includes the more expensive vintage brut and Étoile sparklers that are bottle-aged for years to give them a rich, toasty aroma.

If you plan to take home a bottle or two, some of the reserve wines offer perhaps the best bargains, with far more complexity than the nonreserve wines for not much more money. Domaine Chandon also makes still wines from the three most important champagne grapes—pinot noir, chardonnay, and petit meunier. They're a little overpriced but worth trying if champagne is not your thing. All can be tasted as part of the Varietal flight ($15).

Unless you are into some serious champagne, however, pick the Classic tasting flight and kick back on the terrace with one of the tasty, if meager, appetizers. The terrace and the sometimes energetic atmosphere are as much reasons to come here as the champagne. Another big draw is the acclaimed restaurant, Étoile, which is as unashamedly high-end and stylish as the champagnes with which it shares the name. Gold cards and restrained elegance are the themes at this destination eatery—there is no written dress code, but you'll have a hard time getting beyond the concierge if you're wearing shorts.

GOOSECROSS CELLARS

Anyone lamenting that everything wine-related in the Napa Valley costs too much should head on over to Goosecross (1119 State Ln., Yountville, 707/944-1986 or 800/276-9210, www.goosecross.com, 10 A.M.–4:30 P.M. daily, tasting $10) on a Saturday morning for the fun, informative, and free Wine Basics class (10:30 A.M. Sat., reservations essential). The hour-long session is held on a shady lawn and pitched at just the right level for novices and wine buffs alike to learn some fascinating facts (and myths) about wines and the best ways to savor them. Of course, there are a couple of wines to taste as part of the education.

The cozy Goosecross tasting room itself is squeezed in next to the barrels and offers all 10 wines that this family-owned winery makes, including the standout Howell Mountain cabernet sauvignon, the juicy syrah sourced from vineyards in southern California, and the crisp but fruity Napa Valley chardonnay. The flag-ship wine is the Aeros, a powerfully flavored red blend made only in the best vintages. From the minimal metal winged label this is clearly a special wine, and chances are you won't be able to taste it because only a couple of hundred cases are made of each vintage. It's worth looking out for, nevertheless.

In total, Goosecross produces only about 9,000 cases of wine, making it one of the valley's smaller wineries that is open to the public. The laid-back family vibe is refreshing, especially considering its location in the heart of the Napa Valley, and if you can't get to the Wine Basics class, the standard tasting fee here is only $10, which is half what you'd pay at most nearby wineries.

BELL WINE CELLARS

It's not surprising that a former assistant wine-maker at Rutherford's Beaulieu Vineyard now makes his own critically acclaimed cabernet sauvignon from Rutherford-area vineyards. Anthony Bell established Bell Wine Cellars (6200 Washington St., Yountville, 707/944-1673, www.bellwine.com, tastings daily by appointment, tasting $15) in the early 1990s,

first making wine at other wineries before buying the former Plam Vineyards winery near Yountville in 1998. Since then, new partners have provided an injection of money, and the winery has started to expand, all the while keeping its reputation for outstanding cabernet.

The cab from Baritelle Vineyards in Rutherford, Bell's signature wine since 1991, is famous for being the valley's first-ever single-vineyard cabernet made from just one clone of the vine. Clone 6 cabernet is one of a handful of cabs made here that together account for the majority of the 10,000-case production. True cabernet lovers might want to splurge on the $75 clonal tasting, which includes cheese and a chance to try to distinguish the characteristics of four wines each made from a distinct clone of cabernet, including the clone 6 version.

Bell has also made a name for his syrah, sourced from the Sierra Foothills, and offers a couple of reasonably price red blends, including a classic cabernet-based claret that understandably sells out fast considering its quality and modest $30 price. Whites are represented by Yountville chardonnay and several sauvignon blancs from vineyards in Lake County and Bell's native South Africa. The appointment-only tastings offer the chance to talk to people who really know their wines.

Stags Leap Wineries
THE STAGS LEAP DUO

A trip down the Silverado Trail would not be complete without visiting at least one of the two wineries that share the name of one of the best-known Napa appellations—one that helped put California on the international wine map in the 1970s.

If you're wondering how two unrelated wineries can use such a well-known name in this age of fiercely guarded trademarks, it will be no surprise to learn there was a lengthy legal battle involved. These neighbors fought over the use of the Stags Leap name as it became associated with world-class wines in the 1970s and 1980s, and the case was finally settled in

The Stags Leap district, home of blockbuster Cabernets

1985 when the court ruled that the term Stags Leap referred simply to a geographical area, and each winery agreed to let the other use it (each also kept the apostrophe in a different position). Not long after the dust had settled, Stags Leap became an official appellation with no apostrophe in its name at all. Confused? You should be!

The more famous of the duo is **Stag's Leap Wine Cellars** (5766 Silverado Trail, Napa, 707/261-6422 or 866/422-7523, www .cask23.com, 10 A.M.–4:30 P.M. daily), which made the cabernet sauvignon that beat out the best French bordeaux in the now-famous 1976 blind tasting in Paris, and followed it up with another win in the anniversary tasting 30 years later in 2006. It still makes outstanding single-vineyard cabernet from that same SLV vineyard as well as the older Fay vineyard next to it. Such renowned wines command high prices, none more so than the Cask 23 cabernet, which uses the best grapes from both vineyards.

These three estate cabernets, together with an equally impressive chardonnay, can be tasted for $30. Non-estate wines from other Napa vineyards offer a cheaper tasting option ($15) and might include the excellent Artemis cabernet, which has some Fay vineyard grapes in it; the merlot; or the sauvignon blanc (you might also be able to steal a taste of these nonestate wines if you indulge in the more expensive tasting option). Appointment-only tours ($40) take in the pristine-looking cave system and its fascinating Foucault pendulum (for measuring the earth's rotation), and they conclude with the estate tasting.

Although a magnet for serious wine enthusiasts, and a fairly large producer (about 50,000 cases, including the cheaper Hawks Crest label), this family-run winery exudes an unassuming and friendly atmosphere, making it far less intimidating for the casual day-tripper than many of the valley's other big names. The small tasting room is off to the left of the main winery building and can get crowded, so plan to get here early.

Farther north on the Silverado Trail, down a long driveway lined with ancient walnut trees, is the first winery to bear the area's name, **Stags' Leap Winery** (6150 Silverado Trail, Napa, 707/944-1303 or 800/640-5327, www .stagsleap.com). Its wines might be less famous than those of the other Stag's Leap, but its history and setting are far more impressive. The winery was founded in 1893, taking its name from the old Native American legend of a stag that evaded hunters by leaping across the craggy cliffs towering above the winery. The Victorian splendor remains fully intact today.

In 1909 the winery's original owner sold out and the stone Manor House went through many incarnations, including a hotel and a navy camp, before being abandoned in 1953. It wasn't until 1970 that it was brought back to life as a winery and the vineyard was replanted to include cabernet sauvignon, merlot, and petite sirah, alongside some of the original sirah vines, said to be some of the earliest plantings of that grape in the United States. Those three varietals still dominate the winery's production of about 60,000 cases today.

Perhaps the most noteworthy wines are the

inky, full-bodied petite sirah (spelled "petite syrah" here) and the proprietary Ne Cede Malis, a true Rhône-style field blend dominated by petite sirah that gets its name from the Latin phrase "Don't give in to misfortune," the motto of winery founder Horace Chase.

Since 1997 the winery has been owned by multinational Fosters Wine Estates, but the Victorian splendor of the manor house and tranquility of the lush surroundings far from the valley crowds certainly don't hint at corporate ownership. Few people realize it's open to the public, but appointment-only tours (10:30 A.M. and 2:30 P.M.) are available during the week for a limited number of people. They fill up fast, so book early. The tours take in the Manor House, wine-making facilities, and wonderful gardens including the apothecary, full of medicinal plants, and the sensory garden, devoted to flavorful and aromatic plants. Tie a visit here in with a tour of Shafer Vineyards, which shares the same driveway off the Silverado Trail.

CLOS DU VAL

Although it has long since become a well-known Stags Leap District winery, Clos Du Val (5330 Silverado Trail, Napa, 707/259-2200 or 800/993-9463, www.closduval.com, 10 A.M.–5 P.M. daily, tasting $10–20) is said to have come about thanks to a Frenchman sticking his arm out of a moving car window. The Frenchman was Bernard Portet, and he was searching for a patch of land on which to create a winery to rival the best in Bordeaux, where he grew up and learned his wine-making skills. In 1970, on that fateful road trip through the valley, he settled on this prime 120-acre chunk of Napa Valley because, he said, the cooler air signified it could produce wines of a more reserved, French style than the hotter appellations du jour of Rutherford and Oakville. The winery was established by Portet and American business partner John Goelet in 1972 and later purchased more land down in Carneros.

The winery has always produced wines to rival some of the best of Bordeaux, though the rather plain, concrete winery building itself seems to take more inspiration from 1970s design aesthetics than a Bordeaux château. It looks best in the summer when its walls are softened by ivy and the pretty gardens are in bloom. The showmanship here is definitely in the wines rather than the buildings or interior.

Almost half the 80,000 cases of wine made here each year are cabernet sauvignon, and this is the wine Clos Du Val is best known for. The generic Napa cabernet is good, but the Stags Leap estate cabernet is outstanding and comes from the vineyard right outside the winery door. Chardonnay is the other large-production wine in the portfolio and comes from the Carneros vineyard, as does a pinot noir. Another estate wine worth trying is the white bordeaux blend of semillon and sauvignon blanc called Ariadne.

There's plenty to do here other than taste wine, from a self-guided tour around the demonstration vineyard that illustrates all the different trellis systems used in vineyards (the tour provides an accompanying explanation) to playing a game of *pétanque,* the French version of boccie. Tours are available by appointment only.

PINE RIDGE WINERY

Nestled in a small dell with its trademark ridge of pine trees above is another of the Stags Leap District's big cabernet houses, established by Gary Andrus in 1980. He has since expanded the winery to 65,000 cases and increased his vineyard holdings to about 200 acres throughout the valley, helping make Pine Ridge (5901 Silverado Trail, Napa, 707/252-9777 or 800/575-9777, www.pineridgewinery.com, 10:30 A.M.–4:30 P.M. daily, tasting $15 or $25, tours by appointment $25, barrel tasting $30) one of the few wineries to make highly rated wines from most of Napa's finest cabernet appellations—Stags Leap, Rutherford, Oakville, and Howell Mountain. The flagship is the Andrus Reserve, a bordeaux-style blend made with grapes from almost all those appellations.

The smallish tasting room is virtually devoid of merchandise, putting the wines firmly center stage as long as a tour bus has not just disgorged its passengers. The regular tasting option ($15) covers the white wines and cheaper reds, and might include a Carneros- or Rutherford-sourced chardonnay, viognier, merlot, or cabernet franc. The reserve and some of the cabernets can only be tried with the more expensive tasting option ($25) or as part of the appointment-only barrel tasting in the Hillside Room, offered three times a day for $30.

Tours of the vineyard and aging caves, followed by a barrel tasting with cheese accompaniment, are offered three times a day by appointment (10 A.M., noon, and 2 P.M., $25), and there's a small picnic area under the trees above the winery.

SHAFER VINEYARDS

Tasting wine at Shafer (6154 Silverado Trail, Napa, 707/944-2877, www.shafervineyards .com, sales 9 A.M.–4 P.M. weekdays, tasting by appointment 10 A.M. and 2 P.M. weekdays, $45) is about as close as many visitors might get to one of Napa's much-hyped cult wines without forking over hundreds of dollars for the rare bottles that do make it beyond the waiting lists. Schafer's limited-production Hillside Select cabernet sauvignon is regularly compared to the highly extracted wines from small producers like Screaming Eagle, Harlan Estate, and Bryant Family that are critically acclaimed and rare enough to command their cult status. About 2,000 cases of Hillside Select are made each year, out of about 32,000 for the winery as a whole.

The secrets to success here are the rocky hillside vineyards behind the modest winery, which produce limited quantities of powerfully flavored grapes that go into the Hillside Select cabernet. Some of these grapes also make it into the lower-priced but equally plush cabernet, supplemented by grapes from vineyards farther south that also provide fruit for the acclaimed syrah (called Relentless) and merlot. Shafer's chardonnay is sourced from the winery's Carneros vineyards. A small vineyard on the hillside behind the winery is planted to sangiovese, which provides the fruit for the limited-production Firebreak blend of sangiovese and cabernet.

An informative sit-down discussion and tasting is offered twice a day on weekdays by appointment only, but the $45 price tag is a bit steep considering a tour of the facility is no longer included. The price could be worthwhile if the Hillside Select is available for tasting, but sometimes it has already sold out for the year. The consolation is that an excellent cabernet port that is only available at the winery usually is available for tasting. Visitors will also probably meet John Shafer's canine grape tester, Tucker, and perhaps John himself.

Space is limited to 10 people and demand is high, so booking weeks in advance is sometimes necessary, as is a tolerance of the serious oenophiles who tend to flock here. There's no sign for the winery on Silverado Trail, so look for the cluster of property numbers at the end of the private road almost opposite the entrance to Silverado Vineyards.

ROBERT SINSKEY VINEYARDS

It might be part of the elite group of Stags Leap wineries, but the reputation of Robert Sinskey Vineyards (6320 Silverado Trail, Napa, 707/944-9090 or 800/869-2030, www.robert sinskey.com, 10 A.M.–4:30 P.M. daily, tasting $25–50) was built on wines from Carneros. It is now at the forefront of the organic and biodynamic movement in the valley and is almost as well known for its culinary reputation as its wines. Founder Robert Sinskey planted his first vineyard on land in Carneros and for many years sold the grapes to the neighboring Acacia winery. When Acacia changed hands, Sinskey embarked on his own wine-making odyssey, buying more Carneros land and eventually a five-acre parcel in Stags Leap on which he built his winery in the late 1980s. His son, Rob Sinskey, eventually took over running the business, and the winery now produces about 25,000 cases of wine per year.

The elegant stone and redwood winery with its lofty cathedral-like tasting area is a feast for the senses in many different ways. Visitors are greeted by a field of lavender, an organic

© PHILIP GOLDSMITH

the gardens at Robert Sinskey Vineyards

beyond the kitchen hosts the white wine bar, and food from the kitchen is often part of the fun, but you can also bring your own picnic to eat with a glass of Sinskey wine. Even at the tasting bar there are always morsels of food to accompany the wines, to illustrate the food-friendliness of the wines and perhaps to make the relatively high tasting fees easier to swallow. Better value is the $30 appointment-only cave and cellar tour, which ends with a similar tasting.

The wine that Robert Sinskey Vineyards is best known for is pinot noir, and there are three versions, all from Carneros—two from single vineyards and a slightly cheaper blend. Carneros vineyards are also the source of the merlot, cabernet, and cabernet franc that go into the elegant, bordeaux-like Vineyard Reserve, a wine that tastes like it should cost far more than its sub-$40 price tag (which is why it usually sells out fast). Sinskey also makes some nice white pinots, including an unoaked pinot blanc and a heady Alsace blend of pinot gris, pinot blanc, riesling, and gewürztraminer called Abraxas. The Stags Leap District is represented by the estate cabernet sauvignon, which is every bit as good as wines from Sinskey's neighbors.

Oakville Wineries
NAPA WINE COMPANY
The modest Cellar Door tasting room of the Napa Wine Company (7830 Hwy. 29, Oakville, 707/944-1710 or 800/848-9630, www.cultwinecentral.com, 10 A.M.–4:30 P.M. daily, tasting $20), just across the road from the Oakville Grocery, does not suggest that this is a huge wine-making and grape-growing operation. The tasting room is a cooperative of 25 small wineries, all of which use the Napa Wine Company's custom crush facilities to make their wines. In fact, the venture makes more than 1.5 million cases of wine for wineries ranging from tiny boutiques making a few hundred cases up to some of the giants of the valley that would probably prefer that people didn't know they outsource some production.

Between all those jobs, the Napa Wine

vegetable garden, and parking lot arbors covered in aromatic jasmine. The spacious tasting bar and demonstration kitchen are in the slender, tall main room that's reminiscent of a cathedral nave.

As early as 1991 the winery started championing organic growing practices, and now all 170 acres of its vineyards (most in Carneros) are certified organic, making Sinskey the second-largest organic farmer in the Napa Valley (the largest is the Napa Wine Company). The next step was biodynamic certification, which the winery finally obtained in 2007 (and explains the photos of sheep in vineyards you will see around the winery). Organic farming principles were embraced by Rob Sinskey's wife, Maria, who is a well-known chef and author of one of the better Napa Valley cookbooks, *The Vineyard Kitchen.*

In fact, food is as important as wine here. The demonstration kitchen at the back of the tasting room is a key stop on the culinary tour ($50) offered by appointment daily at 11 A.M. On summer weekends, the sheltered terrace

THE TALE OF THE MISSING VINTAGES

If you decide to splurge at Napa Valley wineries to taste some older library vintages, be aware that some wineries have unexpected gaps in their collections. A huge fire in 2005 at the giant Wines Central warehouse on Mare Island near Vallejo, just south of Napa, wiped out an estimated 6 million bottles of California wines that were stored there. Both current vintages and rare library collections belonging to more than 90 wineries were destroyed. Many Napa Valley wineries, both large and small, were affected, and it's sad now to see gaping holes in the lineup of older vintages at some of them today. Long Meadow Ranch, for example, lost its entire library collection going back to 1994.

Smaller wineries that stored all their wines at the warehouse were particularly hurt, and some lost almost an entire year of sales. Even larger wineries will take a long-term financial hit due to their inability to fulfill future orders from restaurants and other buyers. But for everyone, the loss is more than financial — older vintages are essential for winemakers to assess how their wines age, enabling them to adjust blends or other aspects of the wine-making process.

What makes it harder to swallow for those affected is that the fire is believed to have been started deliberately. Federal prosecutors alleged that the man trusted with running the business and safeguarding the wines started the fire in the warehouse to hide evidence that he'd been illegally selling his clients' wines. In 2009 he pleaded guilty as part of a plea agreement with prosecutors.

Company manages to make about 10,000 cases of its own wine as well, including a highly regarded cabernet sauvignon. It manages all this wine-making using equipment bought from the wine conglomerate Heublein in 1993, including what used to be the white-wine production facility for the Inglenook Winery. But wine making is just part of its business. Grape growing has been the foundation on which the wine business was built. The Pelissa family has been supplying grapes to wineries in the valley for three generations and owns more than 600 acres in the Oakville and Yountville appellations, all now farmed organically.

Some of the small wineries represented in the tasting room have links to some major valley figures like Karen MacNeil Fife, the Beckstoffer family, and David Abreu. Other wineries here are simply small or medium-sized family affairs, making a stop here the best way to taste some outstanding Napa Valley wines made without the usual Napa Valley fanfare.

OPUS ONE

Only serious wine lovers need go out of their way to visit Opus One (7900 Hwy. 29, Oakville, 707/944-9442, www.opusone winery.com, 10 A.M.–4 P.M. daily, tours 10:30 A.M., tasting $30), the monolithic tribute to red bordeaux that was formed in 1979 by Robert Mondavi and the late legendary French winemaker Baron Philippe de Rothschild, head of famed Château Mouton-Rothschild in France. In a valley filled with ever more bold architectural statements, the building housing this grand winery is still one of the most fascinating and looks like it will stand the architectural test of time.

This is a proudly appointment-only winery. The concierge escort to the tasting room and $30 tasting fee to taste just the single type of wine made here are reminders that Opus One was California's very first ultrapremium winery. It still tries hard to retain that edge with its attitude and its wines, including among the best cabernet in the valley. It's not a place for those easily intimidated by posh exclusivity. The tasting fee is made easier to swallow because it buys you virtually an entire glass of the current vintage of the signature wine, which retails for $160 a bottle, and gets you access to the rooftop terrace with its fantastic views.

© JAIME PHARR/123RF.COM

Opus One winery

Opus One also makes a cheaper nonvintage cabernet called Overture that sells for about a third that price, not that you'll see much evidence of it at the winery.

The hour-long appointment-only tour ($35) is well worth taking if you can get a reservation. It takes in some of the striking features and technology of the building. Completed in 1991, the winery is a half-buried architectural tribute to the contemporary and old-school heritages (and wines) of the two founders, and from afar it resembles a giant limestone spaceship landed in the vineyards. Inside, antique European furniture blends with minimalist design touches and state-of-the-art wine-making elements like the giant semicircular barrel-aging room. Despite the opulence, this is a relatively small winery by Napa standards, making about 35,000 cases of wine a year.

FAR NIENTE

One of the most highly regarded wineries in the valley opened to the public only in 2004, but the appointment-only tour and

tasting is among the best in the valley, not least because Far Niente (1350 Acacia Dr., off the Oakville Grade, Oakville, 707/944-2861, www.farniente.com, tours by appointment 11 A.M.–3 P.M. daily, $50) makes only two highly regarded (and expensive) wines—cabernet sauvignon and chardonnay—so the tasting of five wines will always include some older library vintages. Despite the $50 price tag, the tour is extremely popular and booking in advance during the summer is essential.

Far Niente was established as a winery in the late 1800s, and the name is Italian for "without a care," which was appropriate considering the place was abandoned before Prohibition in 1919. Oklahoma businessman Gil Nickel bought the elegant old stone buildings in 1979 and has since transformed the winery into a Napa wine-making powerhouse (he also established the nearby Nickel & Nickel winery). Far Niente now produces just over 30,000 cases of wine per year, around a third of it cabernet from the Oakville appellation, and is known for its consistently high ratings from critics.

Among the highlights of the tour are a walk through the aging caves under the main house, which have been extended into a 40,000-square-foot labyrinth over the decades, and a chance to see Nickel's classic cars in the Carriage House, many of which he raced at some point, including a rare prototype Ferrari known as the Yellow Beast. Those lucky enough to visit in April and May will also see some of the 8,000 azaleas in bloom in the 13 acres of gardens with a sweeping view of the valley.

NICKEL & NICKEL

Almost opposite the lavish Mondavi winery is the rather quaint Victorian farmstead of Nickel & Nickel (8164 Hwy. 29, Oakville, 707/967-9600, www.nickelandnickel.com, tasting and tours by appointment 10 A.M.–3 P.M. Mon.–Fri., 10 A.M.–2 P.M. weekends, $40), sister winery to Far Niente just down the road. Gil Nickel, of Far Niente fame, founded the winery in the mid-1990s to make 100 percent varietal wines (made entirely from one type of grape rather than containing small percentages of blending grapes that never get mentioned on the bottle). Many of the buildings in the complex date from the late 1800s, but there is also a cunningly disguised state-of-the-art winery hidden in the huge barn built recently using Victorian building methods. The barn sits atop a huge underground barrel room with vaulted ceilings that would make any Victorian engineer proud.

The collection of beautifully restored cottages and barns and the centerpiece 1884 Sullenger House opened to the public in 2003 and can be seen on the appointment-only tour, a sedate and classy affair that culminates in the tasting of five of the wines. The winery now makes about 30,000 cases of wine a year, and all of them are vineyard-designate from just about every Napa Valley appellation as well as the Russian River and Dry Creek Valleys in Sonoma. There are more than 10 different cabernet sauvignons, for example. Sadly, tasting them all is out of the question, but you can often try four as part of the Terroir Tour

© PHILIP GOLDSMITH

Behind the Victorian charms of Nickel & Nickel is a state-of-the-art winery.

tasting. Although cabernet dominates the production, there are some outstanding chardonnays from Napa Valley and the Russian River Valley made in varying styles, as well as syrah, merlot, and zinfandel.

ROBERT MONDAVI WINERY

This sprawling mission-style complex with its distinctive giant archway and bell tower is considered by some to be the temple of modern Napa wine-making, with the late Robert Mondavi the high priest. Others are of the opinion that it's a classic example of the over-commercialization of the Napa wine industry— and judging by the crowds and limos that throng the winery, they have a point.

The winery (7801 Hwy. 29, Oakville, 707/226-1395 or 888/766-6328, www.robert mondaviwinery.com, 10 A.M.–5 P.M. daily) was once the crown jewel of the Robert Mondavi Corporation, which started life as the more modest winery Mondavi established in the 1960s, ushering in the valley's modern-day wine industry. Decades later, after swallowing many California and international wineries, the Mondavi Corporation was acquired by the multinational giant Constellation Brands and has since shed some of its former acquisitions, most notably Arrowood in the Sonoma Valley. The core brands remain, however, including the Woodbridge winery in central California, which makes vast quantities of cheaper wines, and the share of the exclusive Opus One winery just down the road. Annual production for all the Mondavi labels is measured in the millions of cases rather than the thousands, but the best Napa Valley wines that can be tasted at the winery account for only a fraction of that total.

At the time it was built in 1966, this was the first new winery in the valley since Prohibition, and as Robert Mondavi grew his business, he blazed a trail down which many of the valley's more recently established wineries have followed. Some go so far as to credit Mondavi with helping create the modern Napa Valley wine industry. Although the Mondavi family accumulated an enviable portfolio of vineyards

over the decades, many critics believe the quality of the wines has never lived up to the hype, particularly after the company went public in the 1990s to fund its massive expansion.

Touring the impressive grounds and buildings and learning about their history and about wine-making are certainly the highlights of visiting the winery and give the wines a lot to live up to. Despite the naysayers (and there are plenty), the wines are still rather special, particularly if you stick to the classic cabernet, chardonnay, and sauvignon blanc on which Mondavi has historically focused. Opportunities to taste more wines are somewhat limited.

The comprehensive $25 tour of the vineyards and winery includes a tasting of three wines and is offered by appointment on the hour 10 A.M.–4 P.M. You can usually sign up for a same-day tour at the reception desk. The number of other tours is quite bewildering, numbering almost a dozen in the summer, so check the website for options. Highlights include the Twilight Tour, which is perfect for the end of a hot summer day, and the Wine Basics tasting, which is a bargain at $15 for wine tasting "beginners."

Without a tour the tasting options are limited to $5–15 per wine in the Le Marche tasting room or $30 for a flight of four reserve wines in the To Kalon Room. Of course, if the modern-day Napa Valley that Mondavi helped create has already bankrupted you, it's always free to wander around the courtyard to admire the architecture and views, and imagine a time in the 1960s when this was virtually the only winery in the area.

SIGHTS

More about the history of Napa and the entire valley can be found at the **Napa Valley Museum** (55 Presidents Circle, off California Dr., Yountville, 707/944-0500, www.napa valleymuseum.org, 10 A.M.–5 P.M. Wed.–Mon., adults $5, children under age 7 free). It usually has a fascinating mix of exhibits exploring the valley's natural and cultural heritage, from the modern wine industry back to Native American life, together with an interactive high-tech exhibit on the science of wine making. From the St. Helena Highway (Highway 29) north of Napa, take the Veteran's Home exit and head west on California Drive.

SHOPPING

Yountville, population about 3,500, is the little Napa Valley town that has become a big draw for diners and shoppers, with more restaurants per capita than seemingly any other place in the valley. Most of the action is in and around the giant brick **V Marketplace** building (6525 Washington St., Yountville, 707/944-2451, 10 A.M.–5:30 P.M. daily) that was once a winery and distillery. It was built in 1870 by German immigrant Gottlieb Groezinger, who made most of his fortune decades earlier in the California gold rush.

His huge winery was left abandoned following Prohibition, and just over a century after it was built, the giant building was transformed from a temple of wine to a temple of consumerism. Groezinger might turn in his grave if he saw it today, but not every shopping center can boast of being on the National Register of Historic Places.

The building has been tastefully restored inside, with the exposed brick and giant wooden beams lending an air of sophistication to the 36 generally unsophisticated little boutique shops selling everything from clothes and accessories to toys, art, and the usual Wine Country gifts.

Most of the stores clearly thrive on tourist dollars, but it's still fun to get lost for half an hour exploring the nooks and crannies of the three floors. Some of the more memorable shops include **Cravings,** on the ground floor near the back entrance, which sells some gourmet food that could be useful for a picnic as well as some interesting gourmet cookware; **Domain Home & Garden** and **Gami's Scandia Imports,** which both sell fun items for the home and garden; and **Napa Style,** just off the courtyard, which is a home chef's cornucopia and a slightly overdone homage

Maisonry pairs wine with art.

to local celebrity chef Michael Chiarello—it's a challenge to find any item sold here that is not in some way branded with his name (a few steps away you can even eat at his newest restaurant, Bottega). Just across the courtyard is the **V Wine Cellar,** a decent and fairly large wine shop that sells a lot of local and international wines and has occasional tastings.

Arts and crafts lovers should cross Washington Street to the rather undistinguished and equally touristy **Beard Plaza,** which is where some of the town's galleries can be found, including **RAS Galleries** (707/944-9211), which features contemporary ceramic, glass, and sculpture artists.

A short walk away at the northern end of Washington Street, art and design meets wine tasting at one of the most unique shopping experiences in the valley, **Maisonry** (6711 Washington St., 707/944-0889, 10 A.M.–6 P.M. Sun.–Wed., 10 A.M.–8 P.M. Thurs., 10 A.M.–10 P.M. Fri.–Sat.). Housed in a historic Victorian-era stone house, the concept for Maisonry is to be a living gallery, where the work of both contemporary and classical artists and designers is part of the decor and also happens to be for sale. The reality is that it can be a little intimidating stepping into such a rarefied atmosphere with its immaculately dressed staff, but just pretend you have several thousand dollars to blow and you'll quickly feel relaxed poking around the imaginative and beautifully made home furnishings and design pieces. There are a few reasonable priced items that would make good souvenirs of the Napa Valley, from antique wine bottles to Native American arrows, and the beautifully designed garden is a relaxing refuge in which to taste the many wines on offer.

RECREATION
Napa River Ecological Reserve

A small patch of land next to the river in Yountville has been saved from the vineyards, and it's now a great place to see wildlife other than the flocks of tourists more commonly sighted in these parts. Almost 150 types of bird and 40 types of butterfly call this peaceful 70-acre patch of the valley home. The reserve has no specific hours but is probably best avoided during the rainy season (December–April) when it can be too wet to be accessible.

The small paved parking lot is on the north side of Yountville Cross Road, about halfway between Highway 29 and the Silverado Trail just west of the small bridge over the river. There's just one trail, about a mile long, that dives into woodland, crosses the river (only possible during the dry summer and fall months), and eventually loops back on itself, but not before affording a unique view of the valley's native wildlife and plant life.

Golf

Just south of the Domaine Chandon winery is the nine-hole, 2,800-yard **Vintner's Golf Club** (7901 Solano Ave., off California Dr., Yountville, 707/944-1992, www.vintnersgolfclub.com, call for tee times). Fees for nonresidents range from $25 midweek to $35 weekends for nine holes, and up to $45 to play 18 holes.

ACCOMMODATIONS

The small town of Yountville, just eight miles north of Napa, halfway to St. Helena, not only has an impressive number of restaurants and shops but also a lot of hotel rooms for its size. Being right next to Highway 29 and a major cross-valley road, it is within easy reach of just about every valley winery.

Those advantages make the town both blessed and cursed, however. Easy access and plentiful services make it a great base from which to explore the valley, but Yountville also attracts hordes of visitors during the day and suffers from almost constant traffic noise near Highway 29, destroying much of the rural charm and often making it feel more like a suburban mall than a historic town of 3,000 residents. You might wonder where all the locals actually are—they tend to emerge at night after the shops close.

For years, the character of Yountville could best be described as Mediterranean pastiche, but as the Napa Valley continues to reinvent itself and go upmarket, Yountville's character has changed, and several new contemporary high-end hotels have opened or were slated to open as this edition went to press.

Under $150

The Orient Express it is not, but this is the only place in the valley where you can sleep on a train. Sort of. The nine railcars and cabooses that constitute the affordable **Napa Valley Railway Inn** (6523 Washington St., Yountville, 707/944-2000) took their last trip many decades ago and are now fitted out with king or queen beds, air-conditioning, skylights, flat-screen TVs, and private bathrooms, making surprisingly comfortable accommodations right in the middle of Yountville (ranging $125–185, depending on the season and the time of week). The downside is that they are stranded in the middle of a sea of blacktop that is the parking lot for the V Marketplace (no problem parking here), and the inn is only staffed during daylight hours with just an emergency number for any nighttime mishaps. The odd-numbered red rooms have nice views of vineyards and the hills beyond, if you can overlook the large parking lot and Highway 29. The blue rooms are a bit quieter and back onto a smaller parking lot and downtown Yountville. There's enough tall greenery planted to offer some privacy from late-night parkers, but it's still wise to remember to draw the curtains when it gets dark.

$150-200

In the heart of Yountville is the **☾ Maison Fleurie** (6529 Yount St., Yountville, 707/944-2056 or 800/788-0369, www.maisonfleurie napa.com), which also does its best to be more French than Californian. The old ivy-covered stone-and-brick buildings around a pretty courtyard certainly evoke the French countryside, as do the vineyards almost across the street (if you ignore the contemporary Bardessono Hotel that sprouted up next to the vines). Inside the cozy lobby and the 15 guest rooms the French country theme continues, though it tends to go a little over the top with the flowery fabrics and faux antiques. Cozy is also the word used by the hotel to describe its smallest and cheapest rooms—the Cozy Double is just 80 square feet. They start at $140 and at that price sell out quickly despite their diminutive floor space. If you do get one, plan on spending time outside by the small pool to prevent claustrophobia. The biggest rooms ($235–300) are in the adjoining Carriage House and Bakery buildings and include fireplaces, views, and spa tubs in some.

The French theme continues (in name, at least) at the tiny **Petit Logis** (6527 Yount St., Yountville, 877/944-2332, www.petit logis.com), tucked away in a one-story building next to Maison Fleurie. The five rooms in a row of former shops have their own outside entrances and are decorated in fairly minimal but comfortable France-meets–New England country style. They include private bathrooms with whirlpool tubs ($150–200 per night midweek, depending on the season; $215–275 on weekends). Rates are $20 more with breakfast, but the extra is worth paying because the inn smartly defers to the cooking skills of Pacific Blues across the street—far better than picking over the less-than-impressive breakfast options at many other inns in the valley.

Over $200

The Yountville area has more than its fair share of upscale lodgings, many of which seem to be competing for conference and meeting business. That roughly translates to some slightly unjustified prices for the average visitor. Two that are probably more worth the top dollar they charge than most are Villagio Inn & Spa and Vintage Inn, large resort-style properties on either side of the V Marketplace shopping center that are spacious, luxurious, and far more service-oriented than lower-priced inns. The concierges are actually able to get reservations at the best local restaurants when your own attempts might fail.

The **Vintage Inn** (6541 Washington St., Yountville, 707/944-1112 or 800/351-1133, www.vintageinn.com) has a French theme and is the smaller and more attractive of the two, with rooms arranged around gardens, fountains, and pools. The **Villagio Inn & Spa** (6481 Washington St., 707/944-8877 or 800/351-1133, www.villagio.com) has Tuscan-themed decor and similar amenities, plus an on-site spa (that can also be used by Vintage Inn guests), but it is in a cluster of buildings that looks like an extension of the neighboring apartment complex despite the faux Roman gardens. Neither Euro-theme is terribly convincing, but both inns have very similar spacious rooms with fireplaces, sunken tubs, and a small outdoor patio or balcony. Rates are identical at both properties and are determined in part by position. A ground-floor exterior room starts at $340 midweek ($555 on weekends) and the price increases for courtyard rooms, peaking with the giant suites ($505–1,295).

The teddy bears on the beds are a feature of the small chain of hotels owned by Four Sisters Inns, which owns the **Lavender Inn** (2020 Webber St., Yountville, 707/944-1388 or 800/522-4140, www.lavendernapa.com). The nine spacious rooms here are themed in

French country style, though with a little more of a contemporary feel, and cost $225–300 per night. All have fireplaces, and a few have private hot tubs and patios to take in the smell of the lavender gardens on warm summer nights. Guests can use the pool at Maison Fleurie down the road.

If you're looking for some contemporary luxury with plenty of green cred, the sprawling **Bardessono Hotel** (6526 Yount St., 707/204-6000, www.bardessono.com) is the newest member of the Napa Valley's growing collection of super-resorts catering to those with money to burn for the ultimate in pampering. The 62-room hotel is one of only a few worldwide to be LEED-Platinum certified, thanks to a laundry-list of nature-friendly design and operational features, but its much-touted environmental credibility is dented somewhat when you consider the fact that part of the vineyard farmed by the Bardessono family for three generations was ripped out to build the place. Arranged around multiple courtyards with its own meandering streams, it resembles a contemporary luxury condo development more than a traditional hotel, but the amenities and services are what you'd expect when every room is a suite and costs upward of $600 per night—massive TVs, private patios, fireplaces, outdoor showers, giant Jacuzzi tubs, countless spa treatments, and the finest linens money can buy.

FOOD

Anchored by The French Laundry, Yountville has become something of a restaurant mecca in the Napa Valley in recent years as the town continues to transform itself and move further upmarket. Several old stalwarts have closed, including the much-loved breakfast spot Gordon's, the Napa Valley Grille, and Compadres Mexican restaurant, while new upscale dining places have opened, including one at the new super-resort Bardessono as well as Bottega, the flagship restaurant of celebrity chef Michael Chiarello. Much of the new action on the restaurant scene is likely to take place at the northern end of Yountville

© PHILIP GOLDSMITH

The French Laundry offers memorable meals for a memorable price.

on Washington Street, however, where there has been significant redevelopment. As this edition went to press, rumors suggested both the former Napa Valley Grille site and redeveloped property on the former PJ Steak site were being eyed by other well-known chefs, and the new Hotel Luna right next door was poised to open its upscale Italian restaurant, Cantinetta Piero. Even the venerable Gordon's opposite the Hotel Luna could reopen, according to locals.

Downtown Yountville

Good luck trying to get a reservation at ◖ **The French Laundry** (6640 Washington St., Yountville, 707/944-2380, dinner daily, lunch Fri.–Sun.). The famous restaurant is usually booked up two months in advance thanks to its world renown, limited seating, and strict reservations system. Reservations can only be made two months in advance, and such is the demand that all the slots for the two evening seatings two months hence are usually snapped up the first morning they are made available. This is the case for much of the year, particularly on weekend nights and despite the astronomical price tag, so either be prepared to hit redial for the best part of a morning or persuade your hotel to make a reservation for you. If you are one of the lucky few to get in, you'll probably remember the seven- or nine-course prix fixe dinner as your best meal all year, but you'll want to forget the $250 price in a hurry. If you can't get a reservation, you can at least see some of the ingredients growing in the restaurant's own organic vegetable garden just across the street.

Touched by the same magic, however, is French Laundry's little cousin down the road, **Bouchon** (6534 Washington St., Yountville, 707/944-8037, lunch and dinner daily until 12:30 A.M., entrées $16–33), a French bistro. There's a little more bustle here than at the similar Bistro Jeanty nearby, perhaps because of the French Laundry connection or proximity to Yountville's thriving downtown scene (if there is such a place as downtown Yountville), but the brief menu still evokes a relaxed Parisian

© PHILIP GOLDSMITH

a hidden courtyard for two near the Bouchon bakery in Yountville

hole, helped by a smattering of French wines on the otherwise Napa-dominated list.

A few doors down the street is the down-to-earth **Hurley's** (6518 Washington St., Yountville, 707/944-2345, lunch and dinner daily, entrées $10–28). It might lack the Gallic charm of some of its neighbors, but the spacious restaurant with a large, heated patio has won a loyal following for its Mediterranean-inspired food prepared by renowned Valley chef Bob Hurley. It also stays open far later than other local restaurants, serving from a smaller bar menu 9 P.M.–midnight daily.

The name ◖ **Ad Hoc** (6476 Washington St., Yountville, 707/944-2487, early dinner Thurs.–Mon., prix fixe menu $49). was reportedly chosen because owner Thomas Keller wanted only a temporary name while he worked out this restaurant's style. The name has stuck, the style has settled at rustic family style, and the popularity has soared. That's probably due to the Keller name—the same Thomas Keller who is behind French Laundry and Bouchon just up the road. The four-course menu changes nightly, and you'll get no choices, but considering the quality of the rustic seasonal fare, that's not necessarily a bad thing. The only certainty is that there'll be either soup or salad followed by a meat or fish main course, a cheese course, and dessert. The casual family-style dining suits the food better than the wine. The wine list is suitably endowed with moderately priced Californian and international wines, but markups are higher than is usual in this part of the wine world, and glasses are simple tumblers rather than stemware, which makes the prices even more egregious. Reservations are not quite as hard to get as at the Laundry, but don't expect to walk in and get a table most evenings either.

Next door to Ad Hoc is the sleek modern home of **Redd** (6480 Washington St., Yountville, 707/944-2222, www.redd napavalley.com, lunch Mon.–Sat., dinner daily, dinner entrées $20–32), a critically acclaimed restaurant opened in 2005 by renowned Bay Area chef Richard Reddington, who made a name for himself at Auberge du Soleil before turning his attention across the valley to Yountville. The minimalist contemporary dining room oozes with luxurious fabrics, fixtures, and furniture, a style that is mirrored by the modern American cooking that has been compared favorably to the food at French Laundry. If you're in the mood to splurge, the $70 five-course taster menu will leave you with a lasting memory of the Napa Valley.

A visit to the classy restaurant at super-resort **Bardessono** (6526 Yount St., 707/204-6030, www.bardessono.com, breakfast and dinner daily, lunch weekdays, breakfast dishes $5–20) needn't break the bank if you plump for its best-value meal—breakfast. Dinner prices are at the high end even for pricey Yountville, but for breakfast it is a great place to start the day with a small menu of classic dishes from a full cooked breakfast to simple coffee and pastries served inside or out.

Along St. Helena Highway (Highway 29)

One of the first big roadside restaurants north of Napa is **Brix** (7377 St. Helena Hwy., Yountville, 707/944-2749, lunch and dinner daily, entrées $12–31), a cavernous place with a little bit of an expense-account atmosphere but that serves some interesting Asian-American food—somewhat of a rarity in the valley. A standout feature of the restaurant is the big patio overlooking vineyards.

Mustards Grill (7399 St. Helena Hwy., Yountville, 707/944-2424, lunch and dinner daily, dinner entrées $17–26) is considered the king of the valley grills, having been around for over 25 years and having seen many more fashionable restaurants in the valley come and go. Such longevity and fame, however, have also put it firmly on the tourist map, as illustrated by the line waiting for tables on busy weekends. It might not look like much from the outside and resembles a fancy roadhouse on the inside, but unlike the Napa Valley Grille and the Rutherford Grill that are both now part of a chain, Mustards is a thoroughly Napa Valley affair, run by Cindy Pawlcyn, who also owns a couple of unique restaurants in St. Helena. It has spawned a cookbook and grows many of its own vegetables in its garden, as only a Napa restaurant could. The menu is filled with the sort of rich roasted and grilled meats that scream for a powerful Napa cabernet sauvignon, of which there are several dozen on the international wine list.

Picnic Supplies

In Yountville, the **Bouchon Bakery** (6528 Washington St., Yountville, 707/944-2253), opposite the V Marketplace, has a limited selection of very good sandwiches for under $10, as well as fresh bread and some sweeter bakery delights (try the macaroons). Right at the back of the **Napa Style** store, itself at the back of the V Marketplace, a small deli offers gourmet made-to-order sandwiches, although they tend to be on the pricey side. A limited selection of soft drinks is also available. Locals are usually to be found ordering lunch at the **Yountville Deli**, which is on the north side of the Yountville Ranch Market (6498 Washington St., 707/944-2002, 6 A.M.–10 P.M. daily, deli 6 A.M.–3 P.M.

© PHILIP GOLDSMITH

The Oakville Grocery is one of the Napa Valley's best picnic stops.

daily). A full range of sandwiches is available in the deli for $6–8, and the market itself has everything else you might need for a picnic, from bread and cheese to beverages, including plenty of half bottles of local wine.

Farther up the St. Helena Highway (Highway 29) is the hard-to-miss **Oakville Grocery** (7856 St. Helena Hwy., Oakville, 707/944-8802, 7 A.M.–5 P.M. Mon.–Thurs., 7 A.M.–6 P.M. Fri.–Sat., 8 A.M.–5 P.M. Sun.). Just look for the line of cars parked at the side of the road next to a rather underwhelming-looking building with only a giant vintage Coca-Cola sign on one wall to brighten it up. Although it lacks the modern glamour of its spin-offs in Healdsburg and Palo Alto, this original is one of the best picnic supply stops in the valley (some say in the entire country) and has certainly stood the test of time.

Farmers Market

Those who really want to assemble a picnic from scratch might want to pick through **Yountville's farmers market,** which operates May–October in the giant V Marketplace parking lot (where else?) 4 P.M.– dusk Wednesday.

INFORMATION AND SERVICES

The tiny **Yountville Chamber of Commerce** (6484 Washington St., Suite F, Yountville, 707/944-0904, www .yountville.com, 10 A.M.–5 P.M. daily) is awash with guides, leaflets, magazines, and advice about the local area. The concierge desk at the **V Marketplace** shopping center is also worth stopping at for some local tips and information.

Rutherford

This is a part of the valley where the weather starts to get seriously warm in the summer and the cabernets get seriously muscular. In fact, 71 percent of the vineyards in this appellation are planted to cabernet sauvignon, and the area was home to some of the pioneering wineries in the Napa Valley.

Like Oakville, Rutherford is a big appellation that spans the width of the valley. Some critics suggest there is not a great deal of difference between the two neighboring appellations—both have similar soils and weather, and both are capable of producing rich, muscular cabernets with exceptional balance. How Rutherford earned the bigger name over the years for cabernets might be partly due to the historic and influential wineries that made wine here, such as Inglenook and Beaulieu. Indeed, it was Beaulieu's famous winemaker, André Tchelistcheff, who made the connection between the distinctive soils of the region and their influence on the characteristics of the equally distinctive wines. "It takes Rutherford dust to grow great cabernet," he famously said.

You might also often hear the term "Rutherford Bench," a section of the AVA down the western side of the valley that is not benchland in the traditional sense and was never granted its own appellation status. It has become an oft-used marketing term nonetheless, normally used to suggest the best part of the Rutherford region.

WINE-TASTING
Rutherford Wineries
PEJU PROVINCE WINERY

The slightly overstated French provincial architecture here hints at the roots of owner Anthony Peju, who arrived in the Napa Valley in the 1980s from his homeland of Azerbaijan by way of France, England, and Los Angeles. He was initially a grape grower in the valley, selling fruit to other valley winemakers before finally making his own wine. He also inadvertently helped smaller winemakers in the late 1980s by successfully suing Napa County when it tried to prevent him from selling wine out of his garage before his new winery had been completed. He won, thanks to a state law that allows a grower to sell his product where it is grown, and his victory subtly redefined what the term "winery" actually meant.

Peju's winery (8466 Hwy. 29, Rutherford, 707/963-3600 or 800/446-7358, www.peju .com, 10 A.M.–6 P.M. daily, tasting $10), with its manicured gardens, koi pond, curiously shaped trees, and lofty tasting room in a tower replete with giant stained-glass window, was finally completed in 1990, and the result is like a French country estate viewed through a hallucinogenic haze. It now produces about 35,000 cases of wine, and for years there has been talk of increasing this dramatically, but that has yet to happen. The trees lining the driveway make this an easy winery to spot from a distance, and their curved trunks are slowly but surely being trained to form arches over the road.

Apart from the curious trees, Peju is perhaps best known for its cabernet franc, but that's one wine that's usually not available for tasting due to its almost cultlike status. It sells out within months of its release each year, but Peju eventually plans to expand production and offer both reserve and vineyard-designate cabernet franc in the tasting room. Instead, visitors can taste the equally outstanding estate cabernet sauvignon and the unusual Provence table wine, a dark rosé blend of almost all the other varietals Peju grows—merlot, cabernet franc, and syrah, plus the white colombard and sauvignon blanc. Those varietals, together with zinfandel, are also available as separate wines, many sold only through the winery.

Peju is open later than most in the area, but during particularly crowded times you might find getting into the tasting room involves a bit of a wait. Once inside, however, the tasting fee is low for Napa Valley standards, and there might be some additional entertainment

TAKING TOURS TO ANOTHER LEVEL

There are already cable cars and castles, modern art and historic architecture, Hollywood connections and classic car collections. What could possibly upstage such a diverse collection of attractions in this giant theme park of viticultural egotism and hedonism?

One candidate is a six-wheel-drive vintage Swiss military vehicle called a Pinzgauer, which looks like no other vehicle in the valley. It is the transport of choice at **Long Meadow Ranch,** a tranquil ranch and winery high up in the Mayacamas range above Rutherford, which is itself unlike any other winery you're likely to visit in the bustle of Napa Valley.

Visiting the 650-acre ranch and tasting the grass-fed beef, olive oil, and wines does not come cheap, but for a change of pace it might be worth the price. The trip from Rutherford up the narrow mountain roads in the open-sided Pinzgauer is rather like going on a safari – one that provides a refreshing escape from the Napa Valley zoo.

Once at the ranch, it no longer feels like the Napa Valley. The stress of Highway 29 traffic is just a distant memory. Horses munch contentedly in the paddock, the smell of sagebrush wafts through the crisp air (perhaps mingling with a hint of manure), and only the rows of vines struggling up distant mountainsides are a reminder that this is still Wine Country.

Ted Hall, a former management consultant who grew up on a farm in Pennsylvania, bought the historic ranch in 1989 and has since transformed it into a farming and ranching business that could probably keep restaurants up and down the valley supplied with ingredients all year long. Grass-fed beef, eggs, vegetables, and fruit are all part of the organic bounty. The ranch also breeds and sells horses, cattle, and the occasional rooster, so you might be able to pick up an unusual souvenir. This being Wine Country, however, it is olive oil and wine that visitors learn most about on the tours.

Vineyards were planted up here as far back as the late 1800s, by some accounts, and today there are about 25 acres of vines farmed at the ranch, producing about 5,000 cases of wine. The cabernet sauvignon has taken its place alongside some of the best in the valley in recent years and is a softer, earthier style of wine more reminiscent of bordeaux than the wines made on the hotter valley floor. A sauvignon blanc is the only white wine produced. Sangiovese was added to the portfolio in 2000, though it is made in such limited quantities that it usually sells out within a few months of being released in early summer. The couple of acres of merlot grapes planted in the late 1990s go into the proprietary Ranch House Red blend, a relative bargain at under $20 a bottle.

The olive oil history goes back just as far. A grove of some 200 olive trees dating from about 1870 was discovered shortly after Hall

by the "Yodelmeister," a uniquely talented tasting room server.

◖ FROG'S LEAP WINERY

Unlike many of his haughty neighbors, owner John Williams injects some fun into the often staid Napa wine scene, from the name of the winery and its classy black-and-white deco-style wine labels to a wine called Leapfrogmilch (a blend of riesling and chardonnay, and a perfect picnic wine) and the ever-present winery motto "Time's fun when you're having flies."

Frog's Leap (8815 Conn Creek Rd., off Silverado Trail, Rutherford, 707/963-4704 or 800/959-4704, www.frogsleap .com, 10 A.M.–4 P.M. Mon.–Sat., last tasting at 3:30 P.M., free tours at 10:30 A.M. and 2:30 P.M.) was formed by Williams and partner Larry Turley in 1981 near St. Helena on a former frog farm that once supplied the little amphibians' legs to restaurants throughout California. The winery's name was also a take on Stags Leap, that famous winery farther south where Williams was once winemaker. It was not until 1994, when the partnership ended, that Williams moved the winery to

bought the land; it had been overgrown by a forest of taller trees. The grove has since been brought back to productive life and is the source of the flagship oil, Prato Lungo. Another 2,000 olive trees were planted, and the ranch is now home to one of only two oil presses in the Napa Valley.

Sustainable farming is the byword here, as the huge piles of compost suggest. Even the winery building is a model of sustainable practices. Walls are made from compressed earth dug out during construction of the caves, and all power is provided by solar panels.

Tasting the wines, olive oil, and perhaps some local cheese and beef is the culmination of the various tours offered at Long Meadow Ranch. A Pinzgauer ferries visitors up ever-narrower mountain roads to the ranch, passing vineyards, olive orchards, and meadows (sit on the right side on the way up for the best views of the valley below). The safari-like excursion continues up into vineyards and olive groves, where principles of grape and olive growing and organic farming practices are explained, before returning to the winery building for a look at the olive press and barrel-aging caves, and the all-important tasting.

The cheapest tour lasts about two hours, costs $35, and is offered every Saturday at 11 A.M. during the summer. During the week, daily tours cost $50 but are slightly longer, and the tasting at the end includes more

oils and wines. There's also a self-propelled tour – following a hiking trail around the ranch to work up an appetite for the tasting. For $150, you can taste just about everything the ranch produces with a gourmet picnic after the main tour.

All the tours are appointment-only and are limited to 10 people, which is the seating capacity of the Pinzgauer. That means they book up fast during the summer but also ensures they are always fairly intimate and relaxing.

The ranch has an organic outpost down on the valley floor called **Rutherford Gardens** (1796 St. Helena Hwy., Rutherford, just opposite Grgich Hills winery), from where all the tours begin. Ted Hall bought a six-acre parcel of land next to Highway 29 and, instead of planting vines like all his neighbors, turned it into an organic fruit and vegetable farm. Produce is sold to local restaurants, at the St. Helena farmers market, and at the farm stand that's open Saturdays May–October.

Whether you have a tour booked or not, take a few minutes to wander around the gardens for an aromatic and mouthwatering reminder that there's more to Napa Valley than grapes – and, perhaps, to snag a spot at the secluded picnic table hidden under the giant fig tree.

For more information about the tours and to book a spot, contact Long Meadow Ranch (707/963-4555, www.longmeadowranch.com) at least 48 hours in advance.

Rutherford and restored the huge red barn that was home to the Adamson winery 100 years before.

Williams has used organic farming practices all along, and Frog's Leap is now regarded as a champion of organic practices in the valley. It also has a big organic vegetable and fruit garden, and visitors can usually help themselves to produce. The red barn is still the landmark to look out for, not least because there are precious few signs identifying the winery from the road, but it is no longer the main destination for visitors. In 2006 the winery opened a new

tasting and hospitality building on what was once a huge expanse of grass beloved by picnickers. Thankfully the spacious lounge-like interior and wrap-around veranda of the new building are just as relaxing for tasting wine as soft grass, although the modernity is not quite in keeping with the rustic ramshackle charm of the older buildings and gardens.

No appointment is needed to visit the winery, and you can often taste the wine of the day for free (and perhaps some freshly harvested produce in the box by the main door). Regular tastings for $15 offer four wines and a few morsels to eat, all served inside or out. The best reason to visit, however, is for one of the free tours offered twice daily by appointment only. They highlight the organic farming principles for which the winery is famous and end with a free tasting.

Almost half the 60,000 cases of wine made here each year are the excellent and well-priced sauvignon blanc, but Frog's Leap is also known for its cabernet sauvignon, zinfandel, and the flagship Rutherford, a bordeaux-style red blend that highlights the unique fruit-meets-earth characteristics of Rutherford appellation wines. The portfolio also includes merlot, chardonnay, syrah, and a wine called (appropriately enough) Pink, which is another fun and cheap picnic wine.

CAYMUS VINEYARDS

This is a great example of how wineries on this side of the valley turn out some of the best wines with little fanfare. The Caymus family has been farming in the valley for more than 100 years but was ahead of the modern wine rush when they ripped up their prune orchards to plant vines in the early 1970s.

Since then, Caymus (8700 Conn Creek Rd., Rutherford, 707/967-3010, www.caymus.com, tasting by appointment 10 A.M.–4 P.M. daily, $25) gained a reputation under the ownership of the late Charlie Wagner for producing one of the best Napa cabernets, the Special Selection, made with the best grapes from the estate vineyard in Rutherford. It garners regular praise from all the major critics and is usually on the tasting flight at the sit-down, appointment-only tasting. The other well-known Caymus wine, now made by Charlie's son, Chuck, is a nonreserve cabernet that is equally impressive and half the price. A less-well-known wine, but one to look out for nonetheless, is the outstanding zinfandel that is sold only at the winery.

Don't come expecting a flashy Napa-style spectacle for the money. This is definitely a winery tasting experience for those serious about their wines, but gardening aficionados will also get a kick from the pretty surroundings.

BEAULIEU VINEYARD

A giant ivy-clad winery building that looks as dominant as any in the Napa Valley is a reminder of the huge role Beaulieu Vineyard (BV, 1960 Hwy. 29, Rutherford, 707/967-5200, www.bvwines.com, tastings and tours 10 A.M.–5 P.M. daily) played in the modern Californian wine industry. Founded in 1900 by Frenchman Georges de Latour, BV was one of the few wineries to maintain production during Prohibition. After repeal, Latour brought a young wine expert over from France to help him refine his wines and ensure they would not spoil while being shipped to the East Coast markets. That man was the late André Tchelistcheff, a Russian émigré who ended up transforming the way wine was made in California while he was winemaker at Beaulieu 1938–1973.

Tchelistcheff helped modernize the winemaking process and improved vineyard management at Beaulieu, introducing new principles of cellar hygiene, improving fermentation techniques, and even introducing those giant wind machines you still see in the valley today that are designed to prevent frost damage to vines. Where he led, others followed. BV wines were soon winning awards, and the quality of the valley's other wines drastically improved as Tchelistcheff's methods became commonplace. He is said to have coined the term "Rutherford dust" for the area's soils, an expression still used today by critics who claim to be able to taste the soil's characteristics in the wines.

The winery has long since passed into the hands of multinational wine conglomerates (it is currently owned by Diageo) and now makes well over 1 million cases of wine per year, although the best Napa Valley wines available here represent only a fraction of the total. BV is perhaps best known for its powerful, dusty cabernet sauvignons, in particular the flagship Georges Latour Private Reserve and the more approachable Tapestry blend, plus the cheaper nonreserve Rutherford. It also makes a full range of other red and white wines from its Napa Valley vineyards, four of which can be sampled on the red-only or white-only tasting menu.

The best option, however, are the two cabernet-focused tasting options. One includes some clonal bottlings and the Tapestry blend ($20) and the other is a horizontal or vertical $30 tasting of the single-vineyard reserves, including the Latour, that is offered in the impressive new reserve tasting room, which has rich stonework, subdued lighting, and a marble-topped tasting bar that does a good job of conveying the appropriate degree of gravitas for wines that helped put California on the world wine map. A tasting of some of BV's best cabernets is also part of the $40 appointment-only tour of the historic winery and its cellars.

RUTHERFORD HILL

One of the best merlots for the price and certainly the best winery picnic grounds in the valley can be found at Rutherford Hill Winery (200 Rutherford Hill Rd., off Silverado Trail, Rutherford, 707/963-1871, www.rutherford hill.com, 10 A.M.–5 P.M. daily, tasting $15–30), housed in a giant barnlike redwood building just a mile up the hill from the Silverado Trail (and neighboring the Auberge du Soleil resort). The winery was created in the early 1970s, and the Rutherford Hill name dates from 1975, when a group of investors bought the winery. It changed hands again the mid-1990s, but the decades-long reputation for making excellent and consistent merlot has remained. That varietal now accounts for about three-quarters of the approximately 100,000 cases of wine made here.

Rutherford Hill also makes small quantities of a lot of other wines that never seem to garner quite the same praise as the merlot. They include cabernet sauvignon and a couple of chardonnays, syrah, and sangiovese, all from Napa Valley vineyards.

A chilled bottle of sauvignon blanc or rosé of merlot are perhaps the best wines to grab for a picnic in one of the two oak-shaded picnic grounds, both of which offer tantalizing glimpses through the trees of the valley far below. The view also takes in the rooftops

© PHILIP GOLDSMITH

Rutherford Hill Winery makes some fine merlot and is a great spot for a picnic.

of the exclusive Auberge du Soleil resort just down the hill, so even if you can't afford to stay there, you can at least see what some of the fuss is about.

In the 1980s the winery carved out some of the most extensive aging caves in the valley, with more than a mile of tunnels that can store about 8,000 barrels of wine. They can be seen as part of the short tour offered three times a day at 11:30 A.M., 1:30 P.M., and 3:30 P.M. for $5 on top of the regular tasting fees.

RUBICON ESTATE WINERY

When a fabled Hollywood director buys one of the most storied of the historic Napa Valley wineries, it's somewhat inevitable that the result would be one of the most ostentatious winery shows in the valley. And so it is at Rubicon Estate (1991 Hwy. 29, Rutherford, 707/968-1100, www.rubiconestate.com, 10 A.M.–5 P.M. daily, tour only $25, tasting and tour $25–50), where stretch limos idle in the parking lot and an eager group of valets relieve visitors of their cars before they are sent down the red carpet to the historic ivy-clad stone mansion nestled at the foot of the scenic hills.

Try to ignore the pergolas and fountains outside—they are modern additions that add a bit of film-set drama to the otherwise beautiful mansion. Instead, take your small green visitor's passport inside the mansion house and sign up for the next hour-long Legacy Tour to learn more about the winery's colorful history and explore the new storage caves, or sidle up to the bar in the cavernous tasting room for a taste of five wines (possibly more if the entertaining pourers are in a jovial mood). Both the tour and tasting are included in the $25 entrance fee, which everyone (except valley residents) must pay just to get beyond the gatehouse. It's a policy that might prevent a surplus of gawkers, but it doesn't seem to prevent huge crowds flocking here on the busiest days.

While waiting for the tour to start, you can browse the small museum that highlights the history of the former Inglenook Estate, which Francis Ford Coppola and his wife, Eleanor, bought in sections between 1975 (a year after *The Godfather II* was released) and 1994 and have since transformed into a huge tourist and wine-making presence in the valley. With this being part Hollywood production, there's also plenty of ego-massaging museum space devoted to the Coppolas themselves, including the film careers of Francis, Eleanor, and their children Sofia and Roman.

The Inglenook Estate was established in 1871 by the son-in-law of George Yount, the first white settler in Napa Valley, who is also credited with planting the first vineyard in the valley in 1838. Inglenook, its vineyard, and some surrounding land were bought in 1879 by Alaskan fur trader Gustave Niebaum, who set about becoming a serious wine producer, albeit as more of a hobby than a business. Niebaum died in 1908, but the winery and its mission to make world-class wines lived on in fits and starts in the hands of Niebaum's widow, friends, and relatives (including Niebaum's great-nephew, renowned valley winemaker John Daniel), until it was sold to United Vintners in 1964, which eventually became Heublein in 1969.

What the Coppolas bought in 1975 was not actually the Inglenook winery operation but part of the estate's land and Niebaum's mansion. Nevertheless, a new winery was born in 1978 and called Niebaum-Coppola in homage to Gustave Niebaum and his pursuit of wine perfection. Legendary winemaker André Tchelistcheff helped the Coppolas create their first wine, called Rubicon, a powerful bordeaux blend that is still made today. The entire Inglenook Estate was eventually reunited almost 20 years later when the Coppolas bought much of the rest of the Inglenook winery and its vineyards from Heublein in 1994 (one of the Inglenook production facilities was sold to the Napa Wine Company in Oakville).

Despite its grand surroundings and history, Rubicon Estate makes a modest 35,000 cases of estate wines, including the flagship Rubicon and its white equivalent, called Blancaneaux. Other wines from the Rutherford estate vineyards include the Edizione Pennino zinfandel, named after Coppola's maternal grandmother; the blockbuster Cask cabernet sauvignon; an aromatic cabernet franc; and an unusual sparkling wine called Sofia blanc de blancs, which is made using pinot blanc, muscat, and sauvignon blanc, giving it a richer fruit flavor than traditional sparklers (there's no mention of whether the wine's character matches Sofia Coppola's). The cheaper Captains Reserve wines, available only at the winery, account for about a third of the production and are sourced from other Napa Valley vineyards. They include a Carneros pinot noir, a crisp sauvignon blanc from the Pope Valley, and merlot with a dash of petite sirah added to the blend.

If you like the wines, you can get more than a taste at the small wine bar down the end of the long passage to the left of the entrance. In addition to wines by the glass, the bar offers coffee and some food-friendly appetizers that can be enjoyed at one of the cozy tables under the vaulted ceilings of the cellar or on the sunny patio.

The Coppola name is also attached to many other cheaper wine labels, however, and those are the focus at a winery the Coppolas bought in 2005 near Geyserville in the Alexander Valley. Production of Coppola-branded wines amounts to about 750,000 cases a year, with the Rubicon Estate representing the cream of the crop.

MUMM NAPA VALLEY

A late starter among the French champagne houses to set up in California, Mumm Napa (8445 Silverado Trail, Rutherford, 707/967-7700, www.mummcuveenapa.com, 10 A.M.–5 P.M. daily, tasting $5–25) was established in 1985 by France's G. H. Mumm and Seagram, though it has been owned by several other multinationals since then, including Allied Domecq and currently Pernod Ricard. There is definitely a corporate air about the operations here, but not really more so than many other large valley wineries. The unassuming redwood winery building, completed on the Silverado Trail in 1988, is certainly lower key than you would expect for a winery

that makes about 200,000 cases of sparkling wine and owns more than 50 vineyards all over Carneros and the Napa Valley.

The wines range from the classic and reasonably priced Brut Prestige, a dry blend of pinot noir and chardonnay, up to the more fruit-forward and expensive DVX, which comes in white and rosé styles. Mumm also makes a winery-only pinot gris still wine, which is perfect for a picnic but tends to sell out quickly.

Like all the big champagne houses in the valley, Mumm puts on quite a show for visitors, but the tasting options are by the glass and can prove to be pricey. The upside is that you can relax on the big terrace overlooking the vineyards and have someone bring your bubbly of choice, whether you want to spend just $5 or splurge $15 for the best as you watch the sun set on a balmy summer evening. Be prepared to wait on holiday weekends or at other busy times because lines often snake out the door. A seat is not essential; you can stroll over to the small art gallery, glass in hand, to see the permanent collection of about 30 original Ansel Adams prints as well as other photography exhibits that change several times a year. Large windows in the gallery give tantalizing views of the barrel and triage rooms below.

Those who prefer to learn more about what they are drinking and seeing should take the informative (and free) tour, which runs on the hour from 10 A.M. until 3 P.M. and illustrates the art and science behind the bubbles. Private tours are available by appointment.

ZD WINES

People leave all sorts of professions to establish wineries, though perhaps one of the more unusual is the rocket engineering business that Gino Zepponi (the Z in the name) and Norman de Leuze (the D) left to concentrate on the winery they had started as a hobby in Carneros in 1969. By the time they had put ZD on the map as a producer of high-quality chardonnay and pinot noir, wine-making was a full-time job. Their winery moved to its current location in Rutherford in 1979. It's an unassuming winery and tasting room that offers a relaxing change of pace in the often frenetic valley along with a chance to actually have a meaningful conversation about wine with the staff. The basic fee of $10 for tasting some consistently good wines is also a refreshing change from the many pricier, hit-and-miss tasting-room experiences elsewhere in the valley.

ZD is now owned by the De Lueze family and still makes outstanding chardonnay and pinot from its Carneros vineyards, including reserves. Those two varietals still account for the majority of the 30,000 cases made each year but have been joined by a rich cabernet sauvignon from other Napa appellations along with a reserve cabernet from ZD's own three acres of vineyards in Rutherford. All are available in the tasting room and can also be tried at the $20 wine-and-cheese pairing offered every Saturday morning by appointment. Tours of the winery, including a barrel tasting, are also available by appointment for $25, but the better touring option is the $30 ecotour that takes visitors out into an organic cabernet vineyard to discuss the principles of Wine Country organic farming.

Taking pricey Napa cabernet to the extreme, ZD also makes limited quantities of its Abacus wine each year from a blend of all its previous vintages of reserve cabernet, starting from 1992. In 2010, Abacus XII was released, containing 17 former vintages. The idea is to combine the best aspects of aged wine with the fruit of more youthful wine. You'll have to pay upwards of $450 per bottle to find out if it succeeds, however, because Abacus is not available for tasting (8383 Silverado Trail, Napa, 800/487-7757, www.zdwines.com, 10 A.M.–4:30 P.M. daily, regular tasting $10, reserve $15).

SHOPPING

Yountville and St. Helena have done a pretty good job of sucking the retailing life from elsewhere in the mid-valley area, with the exception of the **St. Helena Olive Oil Company** (8576 St. Helena Hwy. S., Rutherford, 707/967-1003 or 800/939-9880, www.sholiveoil.com, 10 A.M.–5 P.M. daily), which is orphaned a few miles south of its namesake town in Rutherford. Don't be put off by the modest storefront while tooling up the road toward St. Helena. This place has a cavernous interior and sells far more than olive oils. In fact, almost every condiment a gourmet cook might need (and some they never knew they needed) is probably here, from balsamic vinegar to honey by way of strange concoctions like apricot pepper and stone-ground cabernet mustard. Take a break from wine tasting and try some of the 20 or so olive oils lined up on the counter. Then end the break and wash the oils down with more wine at the tasting counter of **Off the Map Wines** (tasting fee $10), which represents more than a dozen of the valley's small high-end wine producers.

ACCOMMODATIONS

High up in the eastern hills of the valley, bathed in afternoon sun and buzzing with the sound of the golf carts used to ferry guests around, is **Auberge du Soleil** (180 Rutherford Hill Rd., Rutherford, 707/963-1211 or 800/348-5406, www.aubergedusoleil.com), or the Inn of the Sun, one of the valley's most luxurious resorts, famous for being the hangout of the rich, the famous, and lucky honeymooners. This is a place totally at ease with itself, where the decor plays a relaxed second fiddle to the stunning location rather than competing with it. Terra-cotta tiles, natural woods, fireplaces, leather, and earth tones hint at some French country style, but it's the views from almost everywhere that dominate. Work out in the gym with views, eat with views at the acclaimed restaurant, swim with views, or step out of your room's French doors onto a balcony with views. Just be prepared to pay dearly for those views, the amenities, and the exclusivity of the whole place. Whether they're worth the money is open to debate, but Auberge regularly shows up on lists of the world's top hotels, and its rates have climbed significantly in recent years, suggesting there is no shortage of people willing to empty their bank accounts for the privilege of staying here.

There are 50 rooms and suites in cottages spread throughout the 33 lush acres of this former olive grove, and all have the word *view* in their descriptions. The cheapest and smallest are the Hilltop View rooms ($575 in winter, $725–750 summer–fall) in the main building upstairs from the restaurant and bar, though they "may be inappropriate for light sleepers," the resort suggests. Slightly larger rooms in better locations start at $625, and the mammoth suites that are the size of a typical apartment run $1,150–1,625 per night.

Slightly more down-to-earth than Auberge in terms of price, altitude, and attitude is the cozy **Rancho Caymus Inn** (1140 Rutherford Rd., Rutherford, 707/963-1777 or 800/845-1777, www.ranchocaymus.com). Wood beams and floors, adobe walls, and quirky design elements, including hand-dyed South American rugs and carved headboards, give this 26-room Spanish-style inn a rustic hand-crafted charm. Modern amenities are somewhat lacking, but the rooms all have private bathrooms, small patios overlooking the lush gardens, wet bars and refrigerators, and a separate seating area that make them more like junior suites. All but the smallest Caymus Suites have fireplaces. Some of the more expensive suites also have whirlpool tubs. Rates for the Caymus Suites start at $155 midweek in winter and reach $260 per night on fall weekends. The larger Rancho Suites run $185–310 per night and the Master Suites are $215–410 a night.

FOOD

If a special occasion requires a special restaurant (and French Laundry is not answering the phone), there's probably no better place in this part of the valley than **(Auberge du Soleil**

(180 Rutherford Hill Rd., off Silverado Trail, Rutherford, 707/967-3111 or 800/348-5406, reservations required, lunch and dinner daily, four-course prix fixe $105, chef's tasting six-course prix fixe $125). You don't need to be a guest to see why this resort restaurant has been wowing diners with its menu and stunning views of the valley since 1981. The wow factor is still as strong as ever and might make you want to stay at the resort on your next visit (after saving up, that is).

The exquisitely prepared French-Californian food is not as expensive as you'd think—the $105 set price buys you a four-course dinner with plenty of choices for every course (although that doesn't include wine, of course). Just make sure you choose a fine day, and try to get a table out on the terrace for the best views, especially at sunset. And casual as it might be, this is still a fancy restaurant, so don't turn up in baggy shorts and flip-flops.

For some more down-to-earth dining, often without the need for a reservation, the **Rutherford Grill** (1180 Rutherford Rd., next to Beaulieu Vineyard's winery, Rutherford, 707/963-1792, lunch and dinner daily, dinner entrées $15–40) offers traditional steakhouse fare in a slightly corporate setting that hints at the fact that it is owned by the Houston's restaurant chain. Nevertheless, it has become one of the most popular steakhouses among Napa Valley residents and is a great place for a reliably cooked and aged steak to pair with a well-aged Rutherford cabernet. This is not the place to go for cutting-edge California cuisine, but it is the place for a classic steak dinner. There's also a nice shady patio, although it's a little too close to the road to be classified as peaceful.

St. Helena and Vicinity

St. Helena has been the center of the valley's wine industry from the very beginning. George Crane first planted grapes in the area in 1861, followed by Charles Krug a few years later. With the new wine industry springing up all around, the town grew rapidly and was incorporated in 1876, only a few years after Napa and many years before Calistoga in 1885.

St. Helena's history has been inextricably linked to the valley's wine industry ever since. Calistoga to the north had its spas to draw visitors, and Napa to the south became a thriving commercial port city, gateway to the valley, but to a certain extent St. Helena has always been a tourist town. Wealthy weekenders came here to wine and dine in the early 1900s, an influx of European immigrants created the thriving Italian and French heritage, and the town was the epicenter of the valley's bootlegging industry during Prohibition, making the St. Helena Highway (Highway 29, to locals) almost as busy in the 1930s as it is today.

This might be a town with the dubious distinction of having a name used disparagingly as a verb—"St. Helena–ization" being the process of a historic pretty town selling its soul to tourism—but it also boasts active civic leaders who fight hard against overdevelopment in an attempt to keep some semblance of the town's historic and rural charm intact.

The Wines

As the Napa Valley gets narrower farther north and the mountains ever more sheltering, the weather gets hotter. The **St. Helena** appellation includes the narrowest point of the valley and also some of the biggest and most historic winery names, like Beringer, Charles Krug, and Louis Martini. The heat and rich alluvial soils are responsible for wines that help give the Napa Valley its name for rich and highly extracted wines. You'll know a St. Helena cabernet when you taste one—big, bold, and powerful.

West of St. Helena, up the slopes of the Mayacamas mountains, is the **Spring Mountain** appellation, an area with almost as

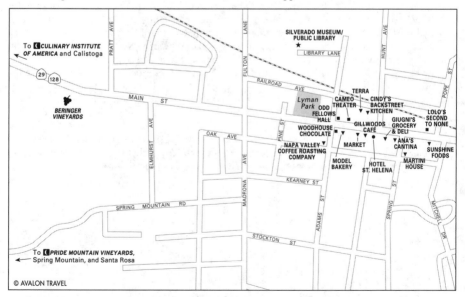

© AVALON TRAVEL

much wine-making history as the valley floor below. The region gets its name from the many springs and creeks—there's actually not a peak called Spring Mountain. The mountain wineries here make cabernet sauvignon and merlot with uncommon density and power. White wines are less common but include sauvignon blanc with a classic mountain minerality. As with many mountain-grown wines, however, the reds can be less approachable when young than those from the valley floor, but they tend to be more consistent year to year and usually only need a few years of aging to reach their full potential.

WINE TASTING
St. Helena Wineries
V. SATTUI WINERY

To say this place gets crowded in the summer is like saying the Napa Valley is an undiscovered wine region. Sattui (1111 White Ln., St. Helena, 707/963-7774, www.vsattui.com, 9 A.M.–6 P.M. daily spring–fall, 9 A.M.–5 P.M. winter) has become a victim of its own success, and can resemble a supermarket the night before Thanksgiving as hordes descend on the

pretty winery for its extensive deli and even more extensive list of well-priced wines. This is picnic central (and often party central) in this part of the valley, though after eating enough free deli samples, you might not need to buy picnic supplies. The pungent smell of the dozens of cheeses and countless other gourmet foods fills the tasting room of the stone winery building, while on summer weekends hardly an inch of grass is visible outside in the two-acre picnic area as tour buses disgorge their stumbling passengers.

The reason for its popularity is simple—this is the only place in the valley where you can buy good food and cheap wines, then plop yourself down on the grass right outside to eat and drink. You just have to ignore the constant drone of traffic from the main road and the shrieks of drunken visitors. It's also one of only three wineries in the entire valley with an exemption to a planning law banning wineries from hosting weddings or wedding receptions, so don't be surprised to see the occasional bride.

V. Sattui is an old wine-making business, but the winery itself is not that old. Vittorio Sattui started making wine in San Francisco

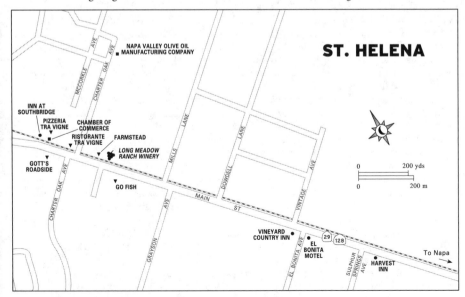

in the late 1800s using grapes from St. Helena vineyards. It wasn't until 1975 that a winery was built here by great-grandson Daryl Sattui, and its combination of cheap wines and a well-stocked delicatessen was an instant hit. As the winery became swamped in the 1990s, Sattui embarked on a new venture to fulfill his dreams of creating a Tuscan wonderland and high-end wines. Opened in 2007, his Castello di Amorosa near Calistoga is a tranquil contrast from V. Sattui and should be the destination for those wanting to taste the best Sattui wines.

The V. Sattui operation now makes about 45,000 cases of wine each year, with many bottles costing less than $20, and has won several "Winery of the Year" awards from the State Fair. You will not find any reviews from magazine critics, however, because Sattui wines cannot be bought at any wine shop. The entire production is sold at the winery and through the Sattui wine clubs, making this one of the most successful direct-to-consumer wineries in California. The huge portfolio includes a host of great picnic wines, like the popular Gamay Rouge rosé (both still and sparkling forms), a dry riesling, and a tangy sangiovese. Cabernet sauvignon in both blended and vineyard-designate styles is what the winery is perhaps best known for. All can be tasted for a modest $5 (which also adds to the popularity), but despite the size of the tasting bar you might have to wait a while for space to open up.

Also worth trying are the dessert wines, including delicious madeira and juicy muscat. Buy a case of any wine and you instantly become a member of the Cellar Club, which has its own tasting bar. The winery also has some of the longest opening hours in the valley, making it an ideal stop if you're an early riser or late eater.

HALL

This is the classy public face of one of Napa Valley's rising stars and has been snapping up prime vineyards since it was established in Rutherford in 1995 by entrepreneurs Kathryn and Craig Hall. By 2006 the Halls were the third-largest land owners in the valley, and the Hall winery (401 St. Helena Hwy. S., St. Helena, 707/967-2626 or 866/667-4255, www .hallwines.com, 10 A.M.–5:30 P.M. daily, tasting $15–25) is set to become the talk of the valley in a couple of years when a new winery, designed by Frank Gehry and local architect John Lail, is finally completed.

Behind the modest tasting room is the former Napa Valley Cooperative Winery, a warehouse-like facility built around an old stone winery dating from 1885. The original winery is an important piece of valley history that will be uncovered and form the centerpiece of the new winery complex. The trademark Gehry flourishes had to be toned down before approval was granted by the city of St. Helena in early 2006, but it will still be a unique, modern addition to the architectural mash-up of the Napa Valley winery scene.

Once the new winery is completed, production of Hall wines will probably increase from the current 25,000 cases to take full advantage of the growing portfolio of vineyards in the Napa and Alexander Valleys. Until then, the relaxed tasting room is in what looks like a shabby-chic cottage-style building with a large shaded patio. But as you approach the entrance with its bright red awning, don't be fooled by the peeling paint on the exterior—it was hand-painted to look shabby-chic and is just another artistic addition to the many sculptures in the grounds from the Halls' private collection.

The Halls have another winery, the exclusive Hall-Rutherford, in the hills above Auberge du Soleil across the valley, which is open to the public by appointment only and is where a high-end cabernet sauvignon is made from the Sacrashe estate vineyard. You might be lucky enough to taste this along with more reasonably priced Hall wines, including cabernet sauvignon, merlot, and sauvignon blanc.

LOUIS M. MARTINI WINERY

The hulking winery of Louis M. Martini (254 St. Helena Hwy., St. Helena, 707/968-3362, www.louismartini.com, 10 A.M.–6 P.M. daily, tasting $15–30) just north of V. Sattui is another piece of Napa's wine-making history, established here after the repeal of Prohibition in the 1930s by Louis Martini, an Italian immigrant who had been making wine at his small family winery and later at a larger facility in the Central Valley. Shortly after setting up in the Napa Valley he also bought 240 acres of vineyards in the Mayacamas Mountains above the Sonoma Valley. That Monte Rosso vineyard has been responsible for Martini's best wines ever since.

The winery was family owned right up to 2002, when it was bought by the even bigger family wine business, the giant E&J Gallo, and became Gallo's first Napa Valley outpost. Gallo pumped millions into upgrading the rather tired old winery, and by all accounts the wines have improved as a result. This is very much a winery for red wine drinkers—the two white wines made here don't generally feature on the tasting menu, although you might get a free taste of the muscat and gewürztraminer blend during the summer.

The 300,000 cases of wine made here each year are dominated by various iterations of cabernet sauvignon, from appellation-specific bottlings to vineyard-specific and right down to lot-specific. The few other noncabernet wines on the list include a petite sirah and meritage blend that is arguably better value and more approachable than some of the cabs. Many of the best wines come from the Monte Rosso vineyard, including cabernets, a zinfandel, and a syrah. Several vintages of the Monte Rosso cabernet are usually featured on the priciest of the tasting menus. A sheltered patio has tables and chairs for those who want to linger, and Martini is open at least half an hour later than most neighboring wineries, making it a good last stop.

PRAGER WINERY & PORT WORKS

Right opposite the entrance to Martini is the little wooden sign and driveway leading to Prager Winery (1281 Lewelling Ln., St. Helena, 707/963-7678 or 800/969-7678, www .pragerport.com, 10 A.M.–4:30 P.M. daily, tasting $15), a funky, family-owned port producer

that is a refreshing change from the commercial atmosphere of most wineries in the area. The closest you'll find to a winery museum here is the Web Window, a masterpiece of spiderweb engineering that's supposedly been untouched since 1979.

The Prager family makes a few regular wines here (a couple are usually included in the tasting), but most of the 3,500-case annual production is an unusual selection of ports and late-harvest dessert wines, including a fruity white port made from chardonnay and the more usual vintage and tawny ports made predominantly with cabernet sauvignon and petite sirah grapes. Bring a cigar to enjoy with port out in the garden.

BERINGER VINEYARDS

The oldest continuously operated winery in Napa Valley is now a huge tourist attraction that often contributes to St. Helena's summer traffic jams, though it is still worth a visit (ideally midweek, when it's a bit quieter) for its significance in the valley's wine history and for some outstanding reserve wines.

Beringer Vineyards (2000 Main St., St. Helena, 707/963-7115, www.beringer.com, 10 A.M.–6 P.M. daily summer, 10 A.M.–5 P.M. daily fall–spring) was started by a couple of German brothers, Jacob and Frederick Beringer, who already knew a bit about wine-making by the time they reached California. Jacob arrived first, working briefly for Charles Krug before he bought land nearby. By 1878 his winery was said to be making 100,000 gallons of wine a year (about 45,000 cases by today's measure), and he was eventually joined by his brother, who built the lavish and ornate Rhine House to remind him of home.

The winery operated through Prohibition and shortly after repeal was making an astonishing 200,000 gallons of wine a year. It was good wine too: Beringer is one of a handful of historic wineries in the valley (others include Inglenook, Beaulieu, and Larkmead) credited with helping modernize the wine industry after Prohibition by introducing European-style production techniques and quality control

The Rhine House at Beringer Vineyards is a reminder of the winery's German roots.

rather than making cheap bulk wines. The entire estate was placed on the National Register of Historic Places in 2001.

Successive corporate owners have poured millions into restoring both the property and the reputation of the winery. Most recently its current owner, Fosters Wine Estates, restored and upgraded the Rhine House, making it an even more impressive location to taste some of Beringer's best wines. Overall the winery is a huge operation, making several million cases of wine each year (at a modern facility over the road) under numerous labels, but it owns many prime vineyards and is still known for turning out some of the best and most consistent premium wines in California, most notably its Private Reserve chardonnay and cabernet sauvignon, which are both beloved by well-known U.S. wine critics.

Beringer was the first Napa winery to offer reserve wine tasting, back in the 1980s, and continues the tradition in the Rhine House, where $25 buys you a flight of any four wines from the dozen usually on the menu, including some outstanding single-vineyard cabernets as well as the Private Reserve cabernet and chardonnay that are considered among the best in the Napa Valley. You can also make an appointment for a more civilized and relaxing reserve tasting on the porch of the Rhine House surrounded by greenery for the same price. The regular tasting in the old winery building up the hill costs just $10 for one of several themed flights of wine, but the atmosphere is far less enjoyable than the wood-paneled and stained-glass charm of the Rhine House unless you draw a particularly entertaining and generous pourer.

The half dozen different tours at Beringer are also well worth experiencing, offering plenty of wine education, history, and a tasting for not much more than a tasting alone would cost. They are generally offered four times a day. Check the website for exact times. The two best are the Taste of Beringer Tour ($20), which has a wine-making focus and takes in vineyards, the 19th-century hand-dug caves, and a tasting; and the Rhine House tour ($25), a must for history buffs that includes a sit-down tasting. Reservations are strongly recommended for these tours, particularly in the summer, but you might be able to buy tickets on the same day during quieter times of the year. The shorter Family Tour takes you deep inside the old stone winery and caves, finishing with a tasting of a couple of wines, and is a bargain at $15 (no reservations are taken, so come early to buy tickets for a later tour that day).

The popularity of the winery along with the ticket booths adjacent to the parking lot tend to make the place feel more like a wine theme park in the summer, but the grounds are expansive enough that you can escape the worst of the crowds and take a self-guided stroll around the Rhine House and gardens to get a sense of how grand the estate must have been in its heyday. In the summer you might also be able to help yourself to the succulent fruit from the numerous peach trees growing near the parking lot.

CHARLES KRUG WINERY

It's probably fitting that the winery founded by the grandfather of the Napa Valley wine industry, Charles Krug, was also the winery that helped start the modern-day wine dynasty of the Mondavis. Krug arrived in California in the heady days after the gold rush and fell in with the likes of Agoston Haraszthy, credited with being the first serious winemaker in the state. He planted his first vineyard in the Sonoma Valley in the 1850s next to Haraszthy's ranch and was soon making wine for friends and acquaintances in the Napa Valley, including George Yount (father of Yountville) and Edward Bale (who built the nearby Bale Grist Mill). He eventually sold up in Sonoma and moved to the winery's present-day location in the 1860s, using the land belonging to his new wife, Carolina Bale, to set up the valley's first large-scale winery.

Krug made a lot of wine there, and he made quite a reputation for himself as both a winemaker and a pillar of the local community. When he died in 1892, his winery was run by his business associate, local banker James Moffit, who maintained its reputation before Prohibition sent it reeling.

Enter the Mondavis. In 1943, the Krug winery was saved from its post-repeal life as a bulk wine producer when Cesare Mondavi bought it and built a new family wine business around it, creating one of the leading wineries in the valley. After his death in 1959, however, there was a bitter feud between his two sons, Robert and Peter, that resulted in Robert establishing his own separate winery (which has since become an empire), while Peter's side of the family held on to and still controls the Charles Krug business.

With a history like that, it's hardly surprising that parts of the Charles Krug Winery (2800 Main St., St. Helena, 707/967-2200 or 800/682-5784, www.charleskrug.com, 10:30 A.M.–5 P.M. daily, tasting $10–20) are historical landmarks, including the stately old Carriage House and giant redwood cellar building. At some point the tasting room will move to the restored winery, but until then the experience of visiting a winery so steeped in history can be a little anticlimactic because the tasting room is in a small cottage standing in the shadows of the historic structures and ancient trees. That cottage has a bit of history itself, however. It is said to have been the first dedicated tasting room in the valley when it was built in the 1950s. Once inside, the wines rather than the surroundings are very much the focus.

The winery owns more than 800 acres of vineyards throughout Napa and produces about 80,000 cases of wine, including just about every major varietal but specializing in cabernet sauvignon. The wines have never achieved the critical acclaim of those from the other Mondavi-related winery further south, but recent replanting in the vineyards should eventually pay dividends. Krug does produce a handful of approachable and well-priced wines, however, including a sauvignon blanc and a rosé (both great summer picnic wines), a Russian River pinot noir, and one of the better value Napa Valley cabernets you'll find in this area. Hardcore cabernet lovers should focus on the reserve tasting, however,

the Victorian home of St. Clement Vineyards, the smaller, sister winery to neighboring Beringer

© PHILIP GOLDSMITH

which includes some of the vineyard-specific and small-lots wines, as well as the flagship Voltz blend.

ST. CLEMENT VINEYARDS

After passing the big boys of Napa wine like Beringer, Krug, and Markham, it's hard not to miss the quaint turreted Victorian house perched on the side of the hill west of the main road. That is St. Clement (2867 St. Helena Hwy. N., St. Helena, 800/331-8266, www .stclement.com, 10 A.M.–5 P.M. daily, tasting $10–25), a small winery that used to be Spring Mountain Winery before those owners moved their operation farther up the hill in the 1970s and sold this place.

It is now owned by Fosters Wine Estates, making it the little sister to Beringer Vineyards just down the road. The winery is as small as its home suggests, making about 25,000 cases of wine per year, three-quarters of which is cabernet sauvignon and the flag-ship Orropas red meritage blend (a backwards spelling of Sapporo, the Japanese company

that owned the winery until 1999). The two tasting rooms in the mansion itself can feel a little cramped and are not terribly representa-tive of the charm of the Victorian estate, but for $25 you can taste some of the excellent single-vineyard and library wines in the old winery building behind the house, a far more relaxed setting.

The old winery and stone cellars under the house, where its original owner used to make wine, can also be seen as part of the appoint-ment-only tour offered twice a day. There's also a pretty porch overlooking the valley, though traffic noise is ever-present. Nevertheless, it's a good place to enjoy the company of the win-ery cat along with a bottle of the rosé wine called La Vache, which is a steal and perfect for picnics.

FREEMARK ABBEY

Despite the name, there is no religious connec-tion with the weathered stone barn sandwiched between a brewpub and an unremarkable group of small office buildings. Freemark

Abbey (3022 St. Helena Hwy. N., St. Helena, 800/963-9698, www.freemarkabbey.com, 10 A.M.–5 P.M. daily, regular tasting $10, reds only $20) instead got its current identity in the 1940s from the nickname of Albert "Abbey" Ahern and the names of partners Charles Freeman ("Free") and Markquand Foster ("Mark"), who bought the former Lombarda Winery and its stone building, which date from 1899.

That wine-making era lasted only 20 years, however. After a brief stint as a candle factory and a restaurant, the place once again became a winery in 1967 when it was bought by a new set of partners. Today, Freemark Abbey is probably best known for its cabernet sauvignon, from the generic Napa Valley version to a couple of vineyard-designates, including the flagship from the Bosche Vineyard near Rutherford.

Plenty of other wines are available to try in one of the more relaxing and spacious tasting rooms in the valley, though it's in the decidedly unhistoric building next to the winery. The portfolio includes merlot, sangiovese, chardonnay, and viognier, which may or may not be on the five-wine tasting menu. Cabernet lovers should consider the red-only tasting option, which offers a chance to compare some of the single-vineyard cabernet sauvignons along with the cabernet franc.

DUCKHORN VINEYARDS

Adjacent to Freemark Abbey is Lodi Lane, which cuts across the valley to the Silverado Trail and the impressive farmhouse-style home of Duckhorn (1000 Lodi Ln. at Silverado Trail, St. Helena, 888/354-8885, www.duckhorn .com, 10 A.M.–4 P.M. daily, tasting $15–25), a winery known for some outstanding merlot and cabernet sauvignon. Those two wines were the first to be made when the winery was established in the mid-1970s, and they still account for most of the 50,000 cases of wine made each year. Sauvignon blanc is the only white wine in the portfolio. Duckhorn also makes about 10,000 cases of its Paraduxx wine, a proprietary blend of zinfandel, cabernet, and merlot, and they built a custom Paraduxx winery to

the south near Yountville that opened at the end of 2005.

The stylish entrance lounge of the winery and the big circular tasting bar beyond, surrounded by neatly arranged tables and chairs, resemble an upscale club or restaurant so it's no surprise that trying the wines can be pricey. But the personal service, quality wines, and peaceful veranda overlooking the vineyards make the tasting experience far more relaxing and fulfilling than at some other wineries.

Although you can visit the winery whenever you want, tastings require an appointment. During the week it's usually possible to get on the list right away, but for weekends it's best to call ahead. The flight of four wines in the basic tasting includes both Napa Valley–designated wines, while the more expensive Enhanced tasting includes estate wines from the Howell Mountain and St. Helena appellations. More of the estate wines, including the best merlots, can be tasted with food pairings following a tour for an additional $10.

EHLERS ESTATE

Moderate wine consumption might be good for the heart, according to some researchers. Moderate consumption of Ehlers Estate wines is most certainly good for hearts in general. The historic stone Ehlers Estate winery (3222 Ehlers Ln., St. Helena, 707/963-5972, www .ehlersestate.com, 9:30 A.M.–4:30 P.M. Tues.– Sat. by appointment, tasting $25–45), just north of St. Helena, is owned by the Leducq Foundation, a French charity that funds cardiovascular research at high-profile medical schools around the world including Harvard, Columbia, and the University of California at San Diego. Visiting such a nonprofit enterprise is a refreshing idea in a valley known more for unashamed hedonism.

The winery was established in 1886 by Bernard Ehlers but lasted only until Prohibition. It languished until the 1960s, when the first of a series of well-intentioned owners brought the estate back to life as a winery under various names for the next two decades. French businessman Jean Leducq and his wife, Sylviane, bought part of the estate in the late 1980s and continued acquiring other parts as they became available. In 2001 they bought the winery building, thus reuniting the entire 42-acre estate for the first time since Prohibition. (Jean died the following year.) Since then, the beautiful stone building has been enhanced by a tasteful architectural makeover and now sits peacefully among the vines in the middle of the valley.

Unlike many valley wineries, Ehlers Estate makes only estate wines from the surrounding organic and biodynamic vineyards, many of which have been replanted over the past decade. About 10,000 cases of wine are made now, including a worthy cabernet sauvignon, merlot, and sauvignon blanc, but that will undoubtedly increase. One thing that won't change: a portion of the sales generated by the winery go to the Leducq Foundation to support its research programs. Tasting is by appointment only, and the best option is to sign up for one of the twice-daily tours of the vineyard and winery followed by a sit-down tasting accompanied appetizers and perhaps the company of winemaker, Kevin Morrisey.

BENESSERE VINEYARDS

The family that established Benessere (1010 Big Tree Rd., St. Helena, 707/963-5853, www .benesserevineyards.com, 10 A.M.–5 P.M. daily, tasting $15) in 1994 does not publicize the fact that the winery used to be owned by **Charles Shaw**, a name that will forever be associated with the Two-Buck Chuck phenomenon of cheap and cheerful wines. Shaw owned the winery from the early 1970s but eventually sold up when he and his wife divorced. The brand was bought by the Bronco Wine Company, which now churns out those cheap wines, but the winery property itself and 42 acres of neglected vineyards were eventually bought by John and Ellen Benish in the early 1990s.

They have since transformed it into a producer of increasingly well regarded Italian varietal wines with the help of some expert Italian wine-making consultants. The lively and light Italian wines here are a nice diversion from the more intense cabernet and chardonnay that dominate the scene in this part of the Napa Valley, and the winery itself is at the end of a small road far off the beaten path of the St. Helena Highway (Highway 29), surrounded by aromatic gardens and guarded by a hefty Newfoundland dog.

Sangiovese and zinfandel dominate the 5,000-case production, but Benessere also makes a small amount of pinot grigio, a unique and picnic-friendly sparkling muscat, and some unique blended reds that incorporate both French and Italian varietals. The flagship wine is called Phenomenon and is a rich blend of sangiovese, cabernet sauvignon, syrah, and merlot. The Sorridente is a blend of cabernet, merlot and aglianico, a dark and powerfully flavored grape normally grown in southern Italy. An appointment for tasting is technically necessary, but calling ahead by even an hour is usually fine during the week.

Spring Mountain Wineries

Exploring this lesser-known appellation makes an interesting diversion from St. Helena and is a beautiful drive. From Highway 29, turn onto Madrona Road, and Spring Mountain Road is three blocks further on the right. Alternatively, just south of Beringer Vineyards, Elmhurst Road also leads to Spring Mountain Road. From there the road follows a creek as it climbs steeply through redwoods and oak trees, past terraced mountain vineyards and orchards, to the many small wineries that often have stunning views of the valley far below.

If you're on a schedule, be sure to leave plenty of time to visit wineries up here because the drive is slow and quickly becomes frustrating (and potentially dangerous) if you're in a hurry. Allow at least a half hour to drive one way from St. Helena to Pride Mountain Vineyards, for example. All the wineries on Spring Mountain are appointment-only (thanks to a county ordinance that aims to prevent the small road becoming too busy), but with the exception of Pride you can usually secure an appointment a day or two ahead.

SPRING MOUNTAIN VINEYARDS

Not far out of St. Helena is one of the oldest Spring Mountain wineries, one that is almost as famous for its Hollywood connection as for its history and wines. It was established in the 1880s as the Miravalle estate by businessman Tiburcio Parrot, who also constructed the ostentatious Victorian mansion that is said to have been inspired by the Rhine House built down the hill by his friends the Beringer brothers.

The estate became Spring Mountain Vineyards (2805 Spring Mountain Rd., St. Helena, 877/769-4637 or 707/967-4188, www .springmtn.com, tour and tasting $25) when it was bought in the 1970s by Michael Robbins. He built a modern winery on the grounds, but his wines were somewhat forgotten when the grounds and mansion became better known as the set for the 1980s television soap opera *Falcon Crest*. Although Robbins tried to cash in by releasing wines under the Falcon Crest label, the winery never regained its former glory and eventually went bankrupt in 1990.

It has since been brought spectacularly back to life after it was bought in 1992 by a Swiss banker, Jaqui Safra, who bought several surrounding vineyards (including part of the historic La Perla vineyard) and built a new winery. The winery reopened to the public in 2003 after Safra's investments had paid off and the quality of the wines, along with the glory of the estate, had been restored. Spring Mountain's vineyards stretch from the valley floor almost to the top of Spring Mountain, giving the winery a huge variety of soils and microclimates to work with. It is perhaps best known for its sauvignon blanc and cabernet sauvignon, in particular the meritage blend called Elivette, which is both predominantly cabernet and gets consistently high ratings. The winery also makes a Spring Mountain syrah that has won plenty of critical praise in recent years, and thanks to a cool spot in the mountain vineyards it also grows and produces a few hundred cases of pinot noir, a wine not normally made this far north in the valley.

Tours of the beautiful grounds and some of the historic buildings, including the famous Miravalle mansion and caves, are offered just once a day by appointment at 2 P.M. Tours are followed by a tasting of four wines, though there's also a tasting-only option offered four times a day, and the fee can be applied to any purchase.

TERRA VALENTINE

One man's remarkable stone folly of a building is reason alone to visit this winery, which was established in 1999 on the former Yverdon Vineyards property. Yverdon itself was founded in the 1970s by a reclusive eccentric, Fred Aves, who built himself a Gothic-style drystone and concrete winery replete with stained-glass windows (which he made as well), statues, and curious features like fish-shaped doorknobs and a sculpted spiral staircase. Any home improvement aficionado will be in awe of his handiwork.

Terra Valentine (3787 Spring Mountain Rd., St. Helena, 707/967-8340, www.terra valentine.com, open daily, tour and tasting $30) still makes wine in the building and is known mainly for its cabernet sauvignon, which accounts for much of the 7,000-case annual production, and the best cabernet is the flagship bottling from the Wurtele vineyard. It also makes a Russian River Valley pinot noir and a couple of limited-production wines, including a sangiovese-and-cabernet blend called Amore.

Appointment-only tours are offered twice a day (10:30 A.M. and 2:30 P.M.); they can be on the short side depending on the time of year but are worth it to see the fabulous building and for the sit-down tasting of wines paired with cheese and chocolate.

SCHWEIGER VINEYARDS

Toward the top of the hill on the right is another of Spring Mountain's small makers of highly regarded cabernet sauvignon and another with spectacular views from its vineyards. Schweiger (4015 Spring Mountain Rd., St. Helena, 707/963-4882 or 877/963-4882, www.schweigervineyards.com, tours and tasting by appointment 10 A.M.–3:30 P.M.

daily, $10) used to sell its fruit to other wineries in the Napa Valley but started making its own wines in the mid-1990s, gradually increasing production to the current level of about 5,000 cases and building a new winery along the way.

Winemaker Andy Schweiger used to ply his trade at Chateau St. Jean in the Sonoma Valley and Cain Vineyards near St. Helena before he started making wine for his family's label. He is also the winemaker for several of Napa Valley's smallest boutique wineries.

The vast majority of the wine is cabernet, but Schweiger also makes small amounts of merlot and chardonnay, all from the estate vineyards at about 2,000 feet in elevation, and a nice sauvignon blanc from a vineyard over the hill in the Sonoma Valley. The flagship wine is the reserve cabernet, called Dedication, which competes with the best from Spring Mountain. Another perennial favorite is the cabernet port, which is made in true nonvintage style by blending wines dating back more than a decade.

BARNETT VINEYARDS

It's a long and winding driveway leading to Barnett Vineyards (4070 Spring Mountain Rd., St. Helena, 707/963-7075, www.barnett vineyards.com, by appointment 10 A.M.– 4:30 P.M. daily, $35) from the main road, but the reward is worth the few wrong turns you might take along the way. This appointment-only boutique winery, established by the Barnett family in the late 1980s, takes care to keep guests to a minimum to ensure the wines and the tranquility of the panoramic Napa Valley view can be enjoyed in all their glory. It's one of the best views from a vineyard you'll find in this part of the world.

A visit to the winery starts at the tasting bar, tucked away in a corner of the cool dark barrel room, where most of the half-dozen wines are usually available to taste. Spring Mountain vineyards account for about half the 5,000-case production here and are the source of Barnett's cabernet and merlot, both of which exhibit the classic concentration and robust tannins of Spring Mountain fruit. The

tangy chardonnay is sourced from the famous Sangiacomo Vineyard in southern Sonoma, and the pinot noir comes from the cool Green Valley appellation in the Russian River Valley, but it often sells out within six months of its release. Another wine that sells out fast despite its $125 price tag, probably due to the glowing reviews it gets almost every year, is the flagship Rattlesnake Hill cabernet, sourced from vines on a small knoll above the winery at 2,400 feet elevation.

If the weather is cooperating, guests can often continue tasting the wines and learn more about the winery and its vineyards on one of the two small decks perched at the end of rocky paths among the terraced vineyards. You feel a little like a mountain goat traversing the terraces, and heels are not recommended. A wood-burning pizza oven on the top deck might one day be pressed into action for hungry visitors, but until then the panoramic views across the Napa Valley and the almost uncanny silence are perfect accompaniments to the outstanding wines.

(PRIDE MOUNTAIN VINEYARDS

When you reach the line on the road that marks the border of Napa and Sonoma Counties, you're as far up Spring Mountain as you can go and just outside the estate of Pride Mountain (4026 Spring Mountain Rd., St. Helena, 707/963-4949, www.pridewines .com, by appointment 10 A.M.–3:30 P.M. Mon. and Wed.–Sat., tasting $10), a winery that has been receiving wine reviews almost as lofty as its location 2,000 feet up in the Mayacamas Mountains. The former Summit Ranch was bought by the Pride family in the late 1980s and has since grown to make about 15,000 cases of wines per year, most notably some powerful and intense examples of cabernet sauvignon and merlot that account for about two-thirds of the winery's production. Other wines that regularly score over 90 points with the critics include an aromatic cabernet franc, chardonnay, and viognier. Many Pride wines sell out quickly, particularly the limited-production reserves.

Grapes have been grown here since 1870, by some accounts, and the size of the burned-out shell of the old Summit winery building, constructed in 1890, suggests that a fair amount of wine was produced until Prohibition ended the party. The 80 acres of vineyards that Pride owns straddle the Sonoma-Napa border on these mountain ridges that afford panoramic views over the two valleys and beyond. Some wines are made from Napa grapes, others from both Napa and Sonoma grapes—the winery has to take great care to keep Napa and Sonoma grapes separate during harvest to ensure it doesn't put Sonoma grapes in a bottle that's designated Napa (or vice versa) and fall afoul of the strict labeling laws.

The views and wines are best sampled on the tour and tasting ($15) offered once a day at 10 A.M., for which you must book well in advance even at relatively quiet times of the year. Appointment-only tastings are offered the rest of the day and cost only $10, a relative bargain considering the quality of the wines that generally cost upwards of $50 a bottle and the attentive, often entertaining service. Visitors can also book picnic tables and eat at what is probably the highest picnic ground in Wine Country. With views across the vineyards to distant mountains there's definitely a feeling of being on top of the world.

SIGHTS

Much of St. Helena's Victorian heyday is on display on Main Street (mainly between Hunt and Adams Streets), in the residential area stretching a few blocks west and just one block east on Railroad Avenue. Even the unusual street lamps on Main Street are antiques, dating from 1915.

At **1302 Main Street** (at Hunt Street), a brass inlay in the sidewalk is the only sign that the wonderfully named Wonderful Drug Store had its home for half a century in this building constructed in 1891 by local businessman Daniel Hunt (as a sign of the times, the building is now home to a plus-size clothing store and a real estate agent).

North up that block is the retro-looking **Cameo Cinema** (1340 Main St., www.cameocinema.com), the latest in a long line of theaters to inhabit the 1913 building with its pressed-steel ceilings and classy deco exterior, both now complemented by state-of-the-art seating, sound, and projection.

At the end of that block is the former **Odd Fellows Hall** (1350 Main St.), built in 1885 as Lodge 167 of the Independent Order of Odd Fellows, the social fraternity established in 1810 in England. The building is said to have a sealed granite memorial stone containing a time capsule of articles from the era. It was also once home to the neighboring **Steves Hardware,** itself founded in 1878.

Almost opposite at 1351 Main Street is what used to be the **Bank of St. Helena,** established and built in the 1880s by a group of local winemakers, including Charles Krug. A lot of the original interior features and stone walls are still evident, though the building, until recently the 1351 Lounge, is now an olive oil store. Farther south is another 1880s building (this one made of wood) that is home to the **Hotel St. Helena** (1305–1309 Main St.).

Silverado Museum

One of the Valley's most famous literary visitors, the Scottish writer Robert Louis Stevenson, spent his honeymoon in the valley just as St. Helena's Victorian building boom was getting under way in 1880. His life and visit is celebrated in the compact Silverado Museum (1490 Library Ln., off Adams St., 707/963-3757, www.silveradomuseum.org, noon–4 P.M. Wed.–Sun., free), right next to the small library a few blocks from Main Street.

There are more than 9,000 of Stevenson's personal artifacts on display, including original manuscripts of some of his many books. The most famous in these parts is *The Silverado Squatters*, published in 1883, which chronicles his Napa Valley travels and meetings with early wine industry pioneers. Stevenson is probably best known elsewhere in the world for some of his other books, including *Treasure Island* and *The Strange Case of Dr. Jekyll and Mr. Hyde.*

Bale Grist Mill

About two miles north of St. Helena is one of the more unusual sights in a valley dominated by the wine industry, the Bale Grist Mill (3801 St. Helena Hwy. N., 707/942-4575, mill grounds open 10 A.M.–5 P.M. daily, tours 11:30 A.M. and 1, 2:30, and 3:30 P.M. Sat.–Sun., $3). The small rickety-looking redwood mill building with its oversized, 36-foot-high waterwheel is now part of a small State Historic Park. It was built in 1846 by Edward Bale on a tiny part of the 10,000 acres of land he was granted by the Mexican government as thanks for his role as surgeon-in-chief for the Mexican army in California (it also probably helped that he had married the niece of the army's regional commander, General Mariano Vallejo, a few years earlier).

He bartered away chunks of his land for money and services to help build both this mill and a separate sawmill not far away. It originally had a 20-foot waterwheel, but a later owner made a few power upgrades, adding the bigger wheel and iron cogs in the 1850s, a few years after Bale died. This was all before the age of wine, so the mill became a big part of valley life, and people from far and wide brought their grist (grain) to be milled here.

The weekend-only tours shed more light on both the man and the milling. The wheel turns sporadically these days, subject to the vagaries of its age and park budget cuts. When it is operating (usually only during the summer), there is usually some "run of the mill" flour for sale, ground between the giant millstones that literally weigh a ton. If it's not operating, the only real reason to visit (unless you're a water mill junkie) is the setting. The mill itself and a handful of picnic tables are reached from the parking lot along a quarter-mile trail that ends looping back to the main road, so traffic noise and the rather sad state of the mill building itself make for a bit of an anticlimax. Instead, turn left before reaching the mill to take the pretty mile-long hike through the madrone woods, past the remains of the valley's first church and the old Pioneer Cemetery, and into neighboring Bothe-Napa Valley State Park.

ENTERTAINMENT

(Culinary Institute of America

The Napa Valley takes food very seriously, so it's fitting that the West Coast outpost of the CIA is housed in one of the grandest old winery buildings in California, the fortresslike former Greystone Winery just north of downtown St. Helena (2555 Main St., St. Helena, 707/967-2320). Built in 1890, it later found fame as the Christian Brothers winery until a new corporate owner put it up for sale in the late 1980s. The institute bought the building in 1992 and spent $15 million renovating it to its former glory. It still makes some wine under the Greystone label from a small estate vineyard nearby.

Chefs and sommeliers are busy being trained behind the imposing stone walls, but you don't need the dedication they have to learn a secret or two from the Napa Valley's top chefs. Hour-long cooking demonstrations are open to the public (reservations 707/967-2320, 10:30 A.M. and 1:30 P.M. weekends, $15) and include a tasting of the finished dish, so the fee makes it worthwhile, especially at lunchtime. Don't expect to go more than once over a weekend, though, because the same demonstration is given on both days.

A small exhibit just beyond the huge, carved redwood entrance doors illustrates the history of the Greystone Winery with some of the original Christian Brothers barrels, casks, and brandy-making stills. Most intriguing of all is a display of more than a thousand corkscrews, some of them hundreds of years old and miniature marvels of engineering, all collected by Brother Timothy, a wine chemist and renowned winemaker at Christian Brothers 1935–1989.

Nightlife

It might seem like this part of the valley goes to sleep after the restaurants have closed down for the evening, and sadly that's more or less true. The popular 1351 Lounge, a little piece of cocktail heaven in St. Helena, closed in 2005 and was turned into an olive oil store. It was one more small step in the "St. Helena–ization" of St. Helena.

Now the job of keeping the locals lubricated at night falls to the casual hangout **Ana's Cantina** (1205 Main St., 707/963-4921). It's a Mexican restaurant by day and a bar by night, when beer and margaritas are the drinks of choice, and pool, karaoke, and live weekend music provide the entertainment, usually until 1 A.M. Although the bartenders know how to mix some good cocktails, this falls just shy of being a dive bar, so don't expect to see much, if any, of the usual "Wine Country" ambience.

Having to drive for an evening's entertainment is by no means perfect, but the best live music options in the valley are down in the city of Napa, at Silo's jazz club and Uva Trattoria, or eight miles up the road in Calistoga at the Calistoga Brewery.

SHOPPING

It's hardly surprising in a valley that was built on the guilty pleasures of consumption that shopping is a close third to eating and drinking for many visitors. St. Helena is dominated by small boutiques that tend to cater to tourists—locals head south to the big-box stores around Napa or Santa Rosa for any significant shopping. Nevertheless, St. Helena is by far the best place for shopaholics to get their fix in the Napa Valley.

The short stretch of Main Street in downtown St. Helena is quick and easy to explore, with an eclectic mix of shops that draw crowds and help create some horrendous traffic jams as visitors look for parking. Countless gift shops sell everything from soap to wine trinkets; some of the more eclectic gifts are to be found at **Findings** (1269 Main St., 707/963-6000, www.findingsnapavalley.org, 10 A.M.–6 P.M. daily). Fashionable St. Helena dogs must shop for gifts and clothes at **Fideaux** (1312 Main St., 707/967-9935, 10 A.M.–5 P.M. daily), which sells the latest fashions for Fido as well as other pricey pet-related paraphernalia. Down the southern end of Main Street next to the gas station is **Lolo's Second to None** (1120 Main St., 707/963-7972, www.lolosconsignment.com, 10:30 A.M.–5:30 P.M. Tues.–Sat., 10:30 A.M.–4 P.M. Sun.–Mon.), a consignment store stuffed with St. Helena's version of pre-owned junk, from designer labels to collectible crockery.

High-end contemporary art and design is gradually supplanting the more traditional Wine Country paraphernalia in the valley, as illustrated by two eclectic galleries that opened right next to each other in 2009 in the historic Independent Order of Odd Fellows building on Main Street. The **Martin Showroom** (1350 Main St., 707/967-8787, www.martinshowroom.com, 10 A.M.–6 P.M. Mon.–Sat., noon–4 P.M. Sun.) is a showcase for designer Erin Martin, who fashions contemporary pieces with a rustic or industrial chic from natural and reclaimed materials. While you may not take home a $15,000 table or bronze statue as a souvenir of the Wine Country, there is nonetheless plenty of inspiration on offer from the works of Erin and a handful of other artists and designers represented here, along with plenty of more affordable, whimsical items for sale, from jewelry to housewares. Right next door is the St. Helena outpost of the **I Wolk Gallery** (1354 Main St., 707/963-8800, www.iwolkgallery.com, 10 A.M.–5:30 P.M. daily), which is represented at four locations in the Napa Valley, including Maisonary in Yountville and at the Auberge du Soleil resort. Unlike the Martin showroom, this is a more traditional gallery with rotating exhibitions of contemporary works from Bay Area artists and sculptors.

Probably the valley's best kitchen store, the **Spice Islands Marketplace** (2555 Main St., St. Helena, 707/967-2309, 10 A.M.–6 P.M. daily) in the Culinary Institute of America supplies all those trainee chefs and sommeliers (and you) with the best culinary equipment, spices, and other essentials from around the world. It is also the place to go to pick up a cookbook memento of the Wine Country. It carries thousands of wine bibles and cookbooks, including every Napa Valley title under the sun. Some might even be signed by the authors, if they teach a course here.

Foodies might drool on entering the only West Coast outpost of New York's super-deli **Dean & Deluca** (607 St. Helena Hwy. S., 707/967-9980, www.deandeluca.com, 7 A.M.–7 P.M. Sun.–Thurs., 7 A.M.–8 P.M. Fri.–Sat.), just south of downtown St. Helena. This being the Wine Country, of course, it stocks some 1,400 wines plus countless local cheeses, meats, and produce, all alongside the already unmatched selection of gourmet foods from around the world.

Chocoholics might get a sugar rush just by looking at the neat rows of dozens of handmade bonbons at **Woodhouse Chocolate** (1367 Main St., 707/963-8413 or 800/966-3468, www.woodhousechocolate.com, 10:30 A.M.–5:30 P.M. daily). It's a good old-fashioned chocolatier with interior decorations as sumptuous as the confectionery made by Tracy Wood Anderson, a former pastry chef. Indulging is not as expensive as you'd think, particularly in this valley of pricey wine tasting. For less than a flight of wines at a local winery, you can walk out of here with a small box of chocolate bliss.

The best olive oil in town is undoubtedly at the **Napa Valley Olive Oil Manufacturing Company,** though it no longer presses its oils here (835 Charter Oak Ave., St. Helena, 707/963-4173, 9 A.M.–5:30 P.M. daily). Despite being in the heart of the valley's food scene, it retains a decidedly small-time family feeling, selling its organic oils and thoroughly Italian deli items out of a colorful and chaotic small barnlike store.

RECREATION
◖ Bothe-Napa Valley State Park

This is the most accessible place up-valley to escape anything wine-related and also the inside of the car, just a few miles north of St. Helena and right off the main highway (3801 St. Helena Hwy. N., 707/942-4575, sunrise–sunset, $8 day-use fee). Proximity to the wineries and shops of St. Helena makes the park a popular picnic spot, but most people packing a lunch don't venture far beyond the shady picnic area just beyond the parking lot near the Pioneer Cemetery (and the road). They miss the best reason to come here,

which is to experience the relative wilderness that's so close to the beaten path and home to some of the most easterly stands of coastal redwood trees.

Most of the best hiking trails start from the **Redwood Trail,** which runs from the main parking lot through the cool redwood forest along Ritchey Creek for just over a mile before meeting the **Ritchey Canyon Trail.** That trail more or less follows the creek for about another mile to the site of an old homestead, an ideal destination for adventurous picnickers.

More strenuous hikes start from the Redwood Trail and climb steeply into the heat to some rewarding lookout points. The closest is Coyote Peak, accessed via the **Coyote Peak Trail** and just under a mile from the creek. From the lookout spur, the trail continues to the **South Fork Trail.** Turn right here to head back down to the creek for a loop of about four miles, or go left to climb again to another lookout. These trails are not for the faint-hearted, especially in the summer when it can get very hot, so don't underestimate the dehydrating power of too many glasses of wine.

Mountain bikers (or anyone on a Wine Country bike tour tired of dodging weaving rental cars) also have a few miles of trails to explore here, but only those that start north of the creek near the campground. Those same trails are also open for horseback riding, offered during the spring and summer by the **Triple Creek Horse Outfit** (reservations 707/887-8700, www.triplecreekhorseoutfit .com) for those without their own steed; a one-hour ride costs $60.

Golf

There are a couple of nine-hole golf courses up-valley, but serious golfers should head south to the Napa area, where all the valley's 18-hole courses are.

The **Meadowood Country Club & Resort** (900 Meadowood Ln., off Silverado Trail, St. Helena, 707/963-3646, www.meadowood .com) has a nine-hole par-62 course open only to guests or guests of guests of this exclusive 250-acre hideaway.

ACCOMMODATIONS

This part of the valley has a far wider range of accommodations than Calistoga, but at far higher prices, justified perhaps by the convenient location in the middle of the valley, the pretty Main Street, the thriving restaurant scene, or maybe because, in world-famous St. Helena, they can get away with it.

Prices are all relative, of course. The cheapest accommodations in this area might be pricier than the low end in either Napa or Calistoga, but don't expect that extra money to buy more luxury. The low end of this scale is the same as the low end on any other scale, where rooms will generally be clean and comfortable but not as luxurious as their price might suggest. At the other end of the scale are some truly luxurious rooms but at prices that might make you choke on a glass of cabernet, especially on summer weekends.

Under $150

The 1940s-era **El Bonita Motel** (195 Main St., St. Helena, 707/963-3216 or 800/541-3284, www.elbonita.com), with its retro neon sign, is not the most glamorous place to stay in St. Helena but is one of the cheaper options and still pretty fancy for a motel. The cheapest rooms are laid out around a small pool but suffer from less privacy and more road noise than the pricier Homestead and Garden rooms set further back on the property. All contain modern but fairly sparse furnishings and include air-conditioning and microwave ovens. Rates for the Poolside rooms start at $90 on winter weekdays and go as high as $269 on summer and fall weekends ($209 during the week). The Garden and Homestead rooms are quieter but less of a bargain, with rates starting at $120 during winter weeks and rising to $269 on peak-season weekends.

$150-250

The **Hotel St. Helena** (1309 Main St., St. Helena, 707/963-4388 or 888/478-4355, www .hotelsthelena.net) is about as central as can be, down a little alley off Main Street right in the middle of town. The old Victorian building is full of original features and stuffed with knick-knacks, including a lot of dolls. The 18 guest rooms get some of the same treatment (minus the dolls), with brass beds, a smattering of antiques, plush carpeting and fabrics, but limited modern touches—air-conditioning is included, but you'll have to ask for a TV. You might also have to tolerate some less charming Victorian traits such as temperamental plumbing and poor sound insulation. The four smallest and cheapest rooms share a bathroom and run $105 midweek, $195 weekends. The best deals are the North Wing rooms, which are still on the small side but have private bathrooms and start at $145 midweek, $235 weekends. The larger Windsor rooms start at $165 midweek, $275 weekends, and the single suite starts at $250 midweek, $375 weekends.

Right next to El Bonita Motel is the **Vineyard Country Inn** (201 Main St., St. Helena, 707/963-1000, www.vineyardcountry inn.com), a combination of hotel and motel with 21 spacious suites that all cost the same, ranging from a relative bargain of $185 in winter months to less of a bargain at $325 during peak summer and fall seasons. All are in a main two-story building or several cottages around the pool and pleasant brick patios— just be sure to ask for a room away from the main road, which is noisy enough to render the balconies of some suites next to useless. All suites have either two queens or one king bed, vaulted or beamed ceilings, fireplaces, refrigerators, and comfortable but unexceptional country-style furniture.

One of the more reasonably priced B&Bs in the area is **Ink House** (1575 S. St. Helena Hwy., St. Helena, 707/963-3890, www .inkhouse.com), an 1884 Victorian just south of the town with an unusual observatory room perched on top of the roof where guests can sip wine and watch the world (and the wine train) go by. The common areas are chock-full of unusual antiques, from the grand piano and pipe organ to the stained glass in the observatory. The six bedrooms continue the theme and have been lovingly decorated with a mix of antiques, and most have a view of either hills or vineyards. Standard queen rooms start at $175, and larger rooms with king beds start at $225. Midweek discounts are usually offered during the winter. Rates include a full gourmet champagne breakfast each morning, wine and appetizers each evening, and Winery VIP tasting passes.

For some true peace and quiet, skip the valley floor and head for the hills. Northeast of St. Helena near the small community of Deer Park is secluded **Spanish Villa Inn** (474 Glass Mountain Rd., St. Helena, 707/963-7483, www.napavalleyspanishvilla.com), a small Mediterranean-style B&B set in several acres of beautifully tended grounds with boccie and croquet courts as well as roses galore. The six rooms and two suites start at $150 during the winter (sometimes there's a 20 percent discount during slow weeks) and $199 during the summer. All have private bathrooms and unusual touches like hand-painted sinks, plantation-style shutters, and carved headboards but, alas, an overabundance of floral prints. Downstairs rooms open onto a patio overlooking the garden, while one of the upstairs suites has its own balcony.

Over $250

On the southern edge of St. Helena, hidden from the road behind a thicket of trees, is the mock-Tudor mansion of the **Harvest Inn** (1 Main St., St. Helena, 707/963-9463 or 800/950-8466, www.harvestinn.com), set in eight acres of lush gardens shaded by mature trees. The place is crammed with stylish antiques, fancy brickwork, and other often-surreal English country features. There's nothing surreal about the luxury of the 74 rooms and suites, however: All have CD players and VCRs, featherbeds, and minibars; some have their own private terrace or views of neighboring vineyards. The smallest queen and king rooms cost from about $250 midweek during the winter and $315 in the summer. The priciest deluxe rooms with vineyard views start at $400 in the winter and $435 in the summer. Add about $50 to those rates for weekend nights. There are some good deals

during the winter at more reasonable rates. The more expensive Vineyard rooms are furthest from the main road, and many have vineyard views. The Fountain rooms are the newest and were opened in 2005 around a new conference center.

The **Inn at Southbridge** (1020 Main St., St. Helena, 800/520-6800, www.innat southbridge.com) doesn't even try to pretend it's in the middle of Wine Country and instead offers luxurious urban sophistication with barely a hint of faux Tuscan decor or Victorian antiques, all in a refreshingly modern building opposite the Taylor's Automatic Refresher diner. The 20 spacious rooms have vaulted ceilings, understated modern furniture, DVD players, down comforters, and high-speed Internet access. A few also have fireplaces and balconies with a view of either the highway or vineyards. They start at $275 midweek in winter ($350 weekends), though there are often deals that take the rate closer to $200 midweek. Summer rates start at $325 midweek for the cheapest king rooms ($425 weekends) and shoot up to more than $500 for the suite. In the same complex of buildings is the bargain Pizzeria Tra Vigne, and right next door is the Napa Valley Health Spa, with a fitness center and heated outdoor pool (both free for inn guests) and a full-service luxury spa.

Its location surrounded by vineyards a few miles north of St. Helena makes the **Wine Country Inn** (1152 Lodi Ln., St. Helena, 707/963-7077 or 888/465-4608, www.wine countryinn.com) a slightly cheaper alternative to some of the other luxury resorts out in the wilds. This family-run establishment offers an unusual down-home atmosphere, good amenities, and a decent breakfast. Rooms are decorated with a mix of modern and rustic; CD players and handmade quilts enhance the sometimes unremarkable furniture. You'll either love the combination or wonder why you're paying so much for a riot of flowery fabric. Splurge on a room with a view, though, and there'll be no questioning it. The cheapest rooms start at $194, but rooms with views or a private patio cost about $275–405 for most of the year, increasing about $30 during the harvest season (Aug.–Oct.). Small suites with added features like balconies with a view, whirlpool tubs, and double-headed showers cost $315–450 most of the year. There are five luxury cottages with 800 square feet of lounging space starting at $465 a night.

The luxurious **Meadowood Napa Valley** (900 Meadowood Ln., off Silverado Trail, St. Helena, 707/963-3646 or 800/458-8080, www.meadowood.com) resort is a bit past its prime and facing increasing competition in this astronomical price bracket, but it's still worth considering if you're planning to splurge, not least because of its spectacular setting on 250 lush acres in the hills above the Silverado Trail. The rooms are in 20 country-style lodges spread around the grounds and range from simple two-room studios ($475–575, depending on the season) up to spacious suites ($675–2,500). All have fireplaces, beamed ceilings, private decks or terraces, and every conceivable luxury trapping. For those who actually venture out of the rooms, there are plenty of distractions, including miles of hiking trails, two swimming pools surrounded by vast expanses of lawn, tennis courts, a nine-hole golf course, and croquet. And to make sure visitors never have to venture down into the valley, there's a small spa, wine-tasting events, and two highly regarded restaurants on-site.

Camping

The Napa Valley might be touted by every marketing brochure as a bank-breaking hedonistic playground, but it actually has a couple of remarkably good campgrounds where two people can stay for less than it would cost them to taste wine at most of the nearby wineries. So forget about matching a Napa cabernet with the latest in-season gourmet produce—instead see how it goes with s'mores around a campfire under a warm summer night sky.

You can light your fire and unpack the marshmallows just a few miles north of St. Helena in the leafy **Bothe-Napa Valley State Park** (3801 St. Helena Hwy., 707/942-4575). There are 50 sites, 42 of which can

accommodate RVs up to 31 feet long (though there are no hookups). The other eight sites are tent-only, and all cost $35 per night. Sites can be reserved through Reserve America (www.reserveamerica.com or 800/444-7275) April–October, and the rest of the year they are available on a first-come, first-served basis. Most sites offer some shade beneath oak and madrone trees, and there's a swimming pool in which to cool off, as well as flush toilets, hot showers, and that all-important fire ring at every site. The park itself stretches up into the hills and offers miles of hiking trails through the redwoods along the creek or up into the sun for some great views.

Further north in Calistoga is a slightly less appealing camping location at the **Napa County Fairgrounds** (1435 Oak St., Calistoga, 707/942-5221). It's ostensibly an RV park with 78 sites, 32 with sewer hookup ($33 per night) and the other 46 with only water and electricity ($30). Tent campers are corralled onto a grassy area with 20 tent-only sites ($20). Showers and a restroom are provided, but for most other amenities you'll have to head to downtown Calistoga.

FOOD

There's an ongoing tug-of-war between up-valley and down-valley restaurants for the limited tourist food dollars, and the balance seems to shift almost every time one restaurant closes and a new one opens—both common occurrences in the Napa Valley. St. Helena's ever-changing restaurant scene with its big-name chefs continues to do battle with towns down south, competing with Yountville for the title of Napa Valley's culinary epicenter.

Californian

The lush gardens, waterfalls, and twinkling lights outside might make it seem like a curious Zen center or fancy private house, but **☐ Martini House** (1245 Spring St. at Oak St., 707/963-2233, www.martinihouse.com, dinner entrées $17–35, prix fixe $63 or $109 with wine pairing) is actually another popular venture by super-restaurateur Pat Kuleto that celebrates the valley's wine-making and Native American heritages. That roughly translates to some beautifully designed dishes prepared by chef Todd Humphries, who has a tendency to go foraging in the local woods for some of the ingredients (or so we're told), like the wild mushrooms used in the restaurant's popular mushroom soup. The wine list is suitably stocked with cult classics, but this place has become such a classic itself that it is usually tough to get a reservation, even though it recently lost its Michelin star. The curious craftsman-style house just off Main Street is worth a look, however. It was built by an opera singer turned bootlegger named Walter Martini, and Kuleto seems to have spared no expense restoring it. If you have no reservation but want to sample the namesake martinis, head downstairs to the cellar bar. You can also order food downstairs, but the rustic atmosphere is not as enjoyable as the main restaurant upstairs.

A couple of restaurants are worth discovering on Railroad Avenue, just a block east of Main Street but a world away from the bustle. The eponymous owner of (Cindy's Backstreet Kitchen (1327 Railroad Ave. at Hunt St., 707/963-1200, www.cindysbackstreetkitchen .com, lunch and dinner daily, dinner entrées $15–26) is Cindy Pawlcyn, the woman behind the ever-popular Mustards Grill in Yountville. She has created a charming hole-in-the-wall here with a side entrance that makes it feel like you're walking into someone's house. The quiet patio is a hive of activity at lunchtime. The menu goes for the same homey charm, with large plates including meatloaf, wood-oven duck, and *steak frites*. The small plates and sandwiches for lunch can be ordered to go.

A few doors from Cindy's in the historic stone Hatchery Building is **Terra** (1345 Railroad Ave., 707/963-8931, www.terras restaurant.com, dinner Wed.–Mon., entrées $20–36), a romantic restaurant that competes with the best restaurants in the valley (with its food and spin-off cookbook) thanks to chef Hiro Stone, who won the prestigious James Beard Foundation award for Best Chef in California. The menu is French and Californian

with Asian flourishes, and might include such eclectic creations as sake-marinated Alaskan black cod with shrimp dumplings. The prices, however, are on the high side, befitting the Michelin star awarded to Terra every year since 2007, but are by no means astronomical. The best value (assuming you are hungry) is the seasonal four-course tasting menu for $65.

When three partners with résumés that read like the greatest hits of Bay Area restaurants got together in 2002 to create **Market** (1347 Main St., St. Helena, 707/963-3799, www.market sthelena.com, lunch and dinner daily, dinner entrées $12–24), the result could well have been another quality Napa Valley dining experience ending with an astronomical bill. That's certainly what the stone walls, Victorian bar, and elegant tables might suggest. Instead, the prices and atmosphere are very down-to-earth, and jaded locals have grown to love the place. The American bistro–style food is sophisticated yet familiar, with dishes like pan-roasted crispy chicken sharing the menu with mac and cheese made, of course, with the best artisanal cheeses. The wine list manages to keep a lid on prices, with none of the wide selection more than $14 above retail, beating even the corkage fee of most local restaurants. The lunch menu is even more of a bargain, with most of the gourmet sandwiches and salads under $15. All are also available to go, providing an instant gourmet picnic.

In a sleek modern building with a giant outdoor patio on the southern edge of St. Helena is the most recent of Cindy Pawlcyn's culinary adventures, **Go Fish** (641 Main St., St. Helena, 707/963-0700, www.gofishrestaurant.com, lunch and dinner daily, dinner entrées $17–30, sushi $5–20). You can have your meal battered, fried, grilled, or raw, but the only caveat is that it has to be fish. There are a couple of nonfish items on the menu, but the biggest draw here is the daily fresh fish listed on the board that can be cooked and sauced any way you want— the wood-fired grill offers the most tempting choice in many cases. Or let the kitchen make the choice with the "Fish Our Way" menu option, a little cheaper because it includes the sides. An accompanying raw bar offers oysters and clams, and the small sushi bar has the rest of the raw options covered.

Almost opposite Go Fish is **Farmstead** (738 Main St., St. Helena, 707/963-9181, dinner daily, entrées $15–26), which takes the idea of farm-fresh to a new level. Opened in 2010, it is the newest venture from Long Meadow Ranch, a winery and farm based in the hills above Rutherford that supplies many of the ingredients, including vegetables, herbs, olive oil, eggs, and grass-fed beef (a specialty). The rustic restaurant is housed in the barn of the former Whiting Nursery, where salvaged farm equipment and even old tree stumps have found new life as fixtures, fittings, and furnishings. Even the booths are covered in leather sourced from the Ranch's cattle. The former executive chef of the Rutherford Grill brings just the right balance of sophistication and familiarity to the simple menu, and if none of the well-priced wines in the varied California-heavy wine list appeals, the restaurant imposes only a $2 charitable donation to open a bottle of your own. To escape the echo-chamber noise in the barn, ask for one of the coveted tables on the outdoor patio surrounded by fruit trees.

Italian

Tra Vigne (1050 Charter Oak Ave., 707/963-4444, www.travignerestaurant.com, lunch and dinner daily, dinner entrées $16–29) is a rarity in the valley—a restaurant that has been around since the early 1990s without ever really changing its formula (it has changed chefs a few times, however). This is a thoroughly Italian place with a classic Italian-American menu, lots of cool stone and terracotta tile, and a wonderful enclosed leafy patio straight out of Tuscany. The wine list reflects the California-inspired Italian menu, with a good selection of local and Italian wines to go with the exquisite pizzas, pastas, and dinner entrées prepared with the usual high-quality local ingredients. As well as a cookbook, Tra Vigne has spawned a deli, wine bar, and pizzeria in St. Helena.

If getting a reservation at Tra Vigne is a problem, there are still plenty of ways to experience its winning formula, thanks to its numerous offspring. One is **Pizzeria Tra Vigne** (1016 Main St., 707/967-9999, lunch and dinner until 9 P.M. Sun.–Thurs., until 9:30 P.M. Fri. and Sat., pizzas $13–20), which, like any adolescent, has had many incarnations over the years, but always the same parent. This being Napa, the pizzas have some unusual and exotic toppings on the perfect thin crusts, and are best enjoyed on the patio. Look for the giant tomato outside the front door opposite the entrance to the Merryvale winery—left over from the restaurant's previous incarnation as Pizzeria Tomatina. There is no corkage fee here, so bring your own wine, or choose from more than two dozen local wines by the glass or bottle.

Casual Dining

Although St. Helena's food scene is constantly changing, there is one place that the term "institution" could apply to, and that's the half-century-old **Gott's Roadside**, formerly Taylor's Automatic Refresher (933 Main St., 707/963-3486, www.gottsroadside.com, lunch and dinner until 10 P.M. daily spring–fall, until 9 P.M. daily in winter, $3–13). This unmistakable old diner just south of downtown is home of the ahi burger and other diner delights, many given a Wine Country gourmet twist but also with prices that have been given a Wine Country lift. A big grassy picnic area with plenty of tables gives a little respite from the traffic, or perch on a stool at the counter. It's a unique experience, but after dropping $30 or more for lunch for two people in the summer, and waiting in a long line for the restrooms, you might wish you'd gone to a more traditional restaurant with more traditional air-conditioning and facilities. New outposts of Taylor's that are more civilized have opened in Napa and San Francisco, but this is the original and still the best if you want some old-school kid-friendly outdoor fun.

The **Model Bakery** (1357 Main St., 707/963-8192, www.themodelbakery.com, 7 A.M.–6 P.M. Tues.–Sat., 7 A.M.–4 P.M. Sun., lunch items

$4–10) is known for baking some of the best bread in the valley and is the latest incarnation of a bakery that has existed here since the 1920s. It's a great place for quick and easy lunches, including gourmet sandwiches, salads, and pizza cooked in the same brick ovens as the bread. Most can be ordered to go, but you might also be lucky enough to snag one of the few tables dotted around the black-and-white tiled floor like strategically placed chess pieces.

For the best breakfasts and no-nonsense lunches in St. Helena, head to **Gillwoods Café** (1313 Main St., 707/963-1788, 7 A.M.–3 P.M. daily, most dishes $8–12). It's a friendly, no-frills diner popular with locals and perfect for some good old fashioned hearty food to prepare you for a day of exploring or to help you recover from yesterday's overconsumption of wine.

If quick refreshment is all you need to keep going, the **Napa Valley Coffee Roasting Company** (1400 Oak Ave., 707/963-4491, www.napavalleycoffee.com, 7 A.M.–6 P.M. weekdays, 7:30 A.M.–6 P.M. weekends) offers some peace and quiet on its patio a block from Main Street.

A couple of miles north of St. Helena is the **Silverado Brewing Company** (3020 St. Helena Hwy. N., 707/967-9876, www.sthelenabrewing company.com, dinner daily, entrées $7–18), sprawling right next to the historic stone winery of Freemark Abbey. The menu won't win awards for originality, but it uses quality local produce and is generally well priced. The main attraction here is the beer, which is complemented by an unexpectedly generous wine list. Relaxing on a warm evening on the patio with a cool India pale ale helps you understand how the old Wine Country cliché came about: "it takes good beer to make good wine."

Picnic Supplies

The ease of finding picnic food in this part of the valley is matched only by the ease of finding a place to eat it, whether at the countless wineries with big and small patches of grass or among the redwoods in the Bothe-Napa Valley State Park.

Several of St. Helena's restaurants offer almost all their lunch menu items to go, including **Cindy's Backstreet Kitchen, Market,** and the **Model Bakery.** But even then they cannot compete with the gourmet paradise of **Dean & Deluca** (607 St. Helena Hwy. S., 707/967-9980). Just don't lose track of time while browsing the food you never knew existed. A cheaper and altogether quirkier place to buy sandwiches is the old-fashioned deli counter at **Giugni's Grocery & Deli** (1227 Main St., St. Helena, 707/963-3421), an old St. Helena institution that's chock-full of fascinating family memorabilia. Be sure to ask for some Giugni juice, a trademark marinade that's delicious. Those planning to build their own sandwich can also battle through the crowds to the well-stocked deli at the **V. Sattui Winery** (1111 White Ln., St. Helena, 707/963-7774, www.vsattui.com, 9 A.M.–6 P.M. daily spring–fall, 9 A.M.–5 P.M. daily winter).

And don't shun the ugly strip mall home of **Sunshine Foods** (1115 Main St., 707/963-7070, 7:30 A.M.–8:30 P.M. daily), next to the Wells Fargo bank at the southern end of the downtown zone. It's a quality grocery store with a remarkably broad range of deli sandwiches and salads, wines, and even freshly made sushi.

Farmers Market

The place to buy local produce direct from the farmers is the **St. Helena Farmers Market,** held 7:30 A.M.–noon every Friday, May–October, at Crane Park, west of Main Street via Sulphur Springs Road or Mills Lane.

INFORMATION AND SERVICES

Just about every brochure, free magazine, and coupon can be found at the **St. Helena Chamber of Commerce** (1010 Main St., 707/963-4456 or 800/799-6456, www.sthelena .com, 10 A.M.–5 P.M. Mon.–Fri.) at the southern end of Main Street.

Those who need to look up some obscure wine fact on the fly should head to the small wine annex of the modest **St. Helena Public Library** (1492 Library Ln., off Adams St.,

707/963-5244, open daily), a few blocks off Main Street, though it's not nearly as comprehensive as the Sonoma County Wine Library in Healdsburg. Just across the street from Library Lane, on the 2nd floor of the modern office building, is the **Napa Vintners Association** (707/963-3388, www.napa vintners.com). You can usually pop in to buy one of the excellent maps it publishes of the valley and its wineries.

If you're in town for a few days, the local *St. Helena Star* newspapers are worth picking up at any local café, as much for the latest Wine Country gossip as for information about local events and some entertaining wine-related columns.

Calistoga

No other town in the Napa Valley retains a sense of its pioneer Victorian roots more than Calistoga, with the remaining stretch of its old boardwalk and Victorian storefronts framed by views in all directions of mountains and forests. Replace the cars and paving with horses and mud, and things would probably look much like they did a hundred years ago when the spa town was at its peak, drawing visitors from far and wide to its natural hot springs and mud baths.

The town was built on mud, literally and figuratively. San Francisco businessman Sam Brannan bought up thousands of acres of land here in the 1850s, drawn by the development potential of the hot springs. He opened a very profitable general store in the late 1850s (now a historic landmark at 203 Wapoo Ave.) followed by his lavish Hot Springs Resort in 1868. He was also instrumental in bringing the railroad this far up the valley to transport visitors to his new resort, making the town a destination for

© PHILIP GOLDSMITH

Calistoga is the northern frontier of the Napa Valley, where life goes a little slower.

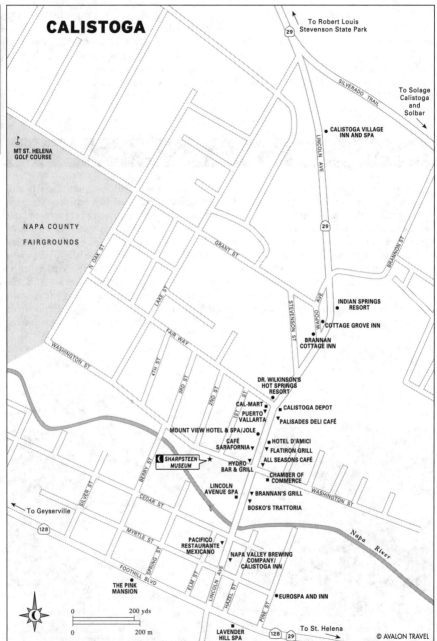

the masses and gateway to Sonoma and Lake Counties to the north.

What Brannan is perhaps best known for, however, is an alcohol-induced slip of the tongue. Legend has it that in a speech promoting his resort he planned to say that it would become known as the "Saratoga of California," referring to the famous New York spa town, but his words instead came out as "the Calistoga of Sarafornia."

Calistoga's modern fortunes have been mixed, and the town has struggled in recent years to keep pace with the frenetic development activity further south in the Napa Valley. Some well-known restaurants have closed, and the eastern edge of downtown looks rather forlorn and neglected, a situation that is supposed to be remedied at some point by the city's redevelopment plan. Whatever ends up being built, Calistoga will likely never lose its relaxed, homely feeling.

The Wines

Many visitors never really explore the wineries this far north in the valley, and they are missing out. Not only are the crowds thinner up here (and the food cheaper), but the area was a historic hub of wine-making in the valley. There's still plenty of wine-making action at both small boutique wineries and grand architectural palaces. The area's latest claim to fame is the impressive Tuscan castle built by valley son Daryl Sattui just south of Calistoga.

Although the Calistoga area was one of the first places that grapes were grown in the Napa Valley, it has been one of the last to be granted its own subappellation status. Chateau Montelena led the charge to get the Calistoga AVA officially designated, and the process took far longer than anticipated, but finally, in December 2009, after six years, the "Battle of Calistoga" was won, and the area became the 15th AVA in the Napa Valley. One reason it took so long is that a nearby winery called Calistoga Cellars does not use grapes from the region in its wine, so would be unable to continue using the word "Calistoga" on its labels. It tried and failed to get an exception to the labeling rule, and must now either change its name or start buying local grapes.

On the western slopes, home of the historic Schramsberg winery and the pseudo-historic Castello di Amorosa, is the **Diamond Mountain** AVA. It was designated in 2001 as the first subappellation in the northern part of the Napa Valley. Winemakers there are already making a name for Diamond Mountain wines as they learn to tame and soften the powerful tannins of the mountain grapes to create increasingly impressive and intense wines with trademark hints of dark chocolate.

Not many white-wine grapes are grown on Diamond Mountain, but on the valley floor, in the Calistoga AVA, whites are common and as impressive as anywhere else in the valley, while the reds have an intensity and power indicative of the warm climate this far up-valley. Indeed, Calistoga temperatures in the summer are often a good 20 degrees warmer than down in Carneros, and nights are not nearly as cold, creating ripening conditions closer to those in Sonoma's Alexander Valley than in some parts of the Napa Valley.

WINE-TASTING
Calistoga Area Wineries
FRANK FAMILY VINEYARDS

The imposing sandstone building of the historic Larkmead Winery (1091 Larkmead Ln., Calistoga, 707/942-0859 or 800/574-9463, www.frankfamilyvineyards.com, 10 A.M.–5 P.M. daily, tasting $10) a few miles south of Calistoga has had a more colorful history than most, finding fame for still wines and sparkling wines as well as surviving many identities and a big fire in 2000. In its current incarnation it is now perhaps as well known for an unpretentious and slightly quirky tasting experience as for its wines.

The Larkmead area was christened by Lillie Hitchcock Coit (memorialized by San Francisco's Coit Tower) in the 1870s for the many larks in the area, and a winery was first established here in 1884. It was not until the wine-making operation found fame under the ownership of the Italian-Swiss Salima family that the big stone winery building was constructed in 1906, and Larkmead went on to be known for making some of the valley's best wines in huge quantities, right up until 1940 when Felix Salima died.

After changing ownership several times, Larkmead was bought by the Solari family in 1948, and the winery building was sold so they could concentrate on managing the hundreds of acres of vineyards. Kornell Champagne Cellars bought the building, and went on to become one of the biggest producers of sparkling wines in the valley. At one point Kornell made close to 80,000 cases of mainly sweeter, German-style bubbly before bankruptcy ended its run in the early 1990s.

The most recent incarnation of the winery has also had its ups and downs. In the early 1990s, the Rombauer family (a name familiar to food lovers for Irma Rombauer's book *The Joy of Cooking*) bought the winery in partnership with Hollywood executive Rich Frank. Both partners made wine there and ran a custom crush business for small wineries up and down the valley—until a disastrous warehouse fire in 2000 destroyed an estimated 85,000 barrels of stored wine, wiping out the entire stock of many of those clients.

Now the winery makes about 15,000 cases of Frank Family Vineyards still and sparkling wines. The increasing emphasis is on still wines, particularly cabernet sauvignon from Rutherford-area vineyards and chardonnay from Carneros. Sparkling wine remains an important part of the portfolio, however, and a dry blanc de blancs and blanc de noirs are offered as the first part of the tasting in the new tasting room that opened in 2008 in the original craftsman bungalow on the property. Free tours are offered twice a day for most of the year, except when the winemakers are particularly busy around bottling or crush time. If there are no tours, while away some time in the shady picnic area behind the winery.

LARKMEAD VINEYARDS

When Larry and Polly Solari bought the historic Larkmead Winery in 1948, keeping the vineyard and quickly selling the old stone winery building (now the home of Frank Family Vineyards across the road), they could not have imagined that more than half a century later their daughter would be producing critically acclaimed wines at a brand-new winery. For decades the Solaris were known more as grape growers than winemakers, but in the past few decades Kate Solari Baker and Cameron Baker have been quietly perfecting wines sourced from their 110 acres of vineyards just on the other side of Larkmead Lane.

Until the smart new Larkmead Vineyards (1100 Larkmead Ln., Calistoga, 707/942-0167, www.larkmead.com, 10 A.M.–3 P.M. daily, tasting $30) winery building became functional in 2005 (it was completed in 2006), the wines were made at the Napa Wine Company in Oakville with the help of experienced winemakers Paul Hobbs and Andy Smith. With new winemakers and a new winery, Larkmead has gone from strength to strength in recent years and won particular praise for its opulent and elegant cabernets made in a classic European style. Anyone wondering just how good the red wines from the new Calistoga AVA can be should give these a try.

Larkmead still sells about two-thirds of its fruit to other winemakers but keeps the cream of the crop for the 8,000 cases of wine it makes each year, almost half of which is accounted for by the opulent estate cabernet sauvignon that critic Robert Parker seems to like, judging by some recent reviews. The bordeaux-like blends are just as impressive. They include the merlot-dominated Firebelle Meritage, a powerfully flavored wine named for the nickname given to Lillie Hitchcock Coit, who christened the Larkmead area back in the 1800s, and the cheaper 60/40, which is a more straightforward blend of cabernet sauvignon (60 percent) and merlot. All three are usually available to taste, along with a crisp sauvignon blanc. The two flagship wines, Salon and the Solari Reserve, are made in such small quantities that almost the entire production goes to wine club members, a canny move that maintains the exclusivity of Larkmead wines.

The cottage-style winery surrounded by aromatic native plants is modest by Napa Valley standards, a sign that it is more serious about wines than tourists. It's also usually pretty quiet during the week, and that's when it's possible to get a tasting appointment with just a few hours' notice. If you're the only visitors, you might also be treated to a quick tour of the wine-making facilities.

STERLING VINEYARDS

When it opened in 1973, this contemporary, monastery-like winery, perched high on a wooded knoll rising straight from the valley floor just south of Calistoga, was hailed as one of the most spectacular wineries in the valley by some and lambasted by others. Sterling Vineyards (1111 Dunaweal Ln., Calistoga, 707/942-3345 or 800/726-6136, www.sterling vineyards.com, 10:30 A.M.–5 P.M. daily, visitor fee $25–40) remains one of the most striking to this day, with whitewashed walls and bell towers that look like they're straight from a Greek travel brochure—hard to miss driving north on Highway 29 into Calistoga.

Such an unusual building, with its aerial gondola whisking visitors 300 feet up to the winery, was bound to become a serious tourist attraction, and so it has. At first glance the gondola, ticket booths, and giant parking lot make it feel more like an out-of-season ski resort than a winery, but once at the top of the hill it's all about wine and views.

Sterling was established in the late 1960s by executives Peter Newton and Michael Stone, who owned the Sterling Paper Company that gave the winery its name. Newton even added some sounds of his homeland by shipping over the bells rescued from the old St. Dunstan's Church in London, which was destroyed during World War II.

Since then, Sterling has built up its production and vineyards. It now makes about 400,000 cases of wine per year and has more than 1,200 acres of vineyards in just about every Napa appellation, from Los Carneros, where it owns the Winery Lake vineyard in the Di Rosa Preserve (source of some highly rated pinot noir and chardonnay), to high up in the Diamond Mountain appellation (source of grapes for some powerhouse cabernet sauvignon). Its growth was helped by the deep pockets of the multinational corporations that have owned the winery since the late 1970s, most recently Diageo.

Once visitors have paid the $25 to get up the hill, everything is pretty much free, including a fun self-guided tour of the winery on elevated walkways, the views, and a sit-down tasting of five wines either inside or out on the patio (weather permitting). It's a unique experience, but one that involves more walking that at most wineries. Those more interested in the wines than the views should opt for one of the pricier tasting options that includes the limited release and single-vineyard wines for which Sterling is better known (those fees can be put toward a purchase). The only thing sometimes missing is the sort of personal service found at smaller wineries, so you might have to persevere to get any detailed information from the staff about what you're drinking.

CLOS PEGASE

Sterling might be easy to spot perched atop its nearby hill, but just down the road, Clos Pegase (1060 Dunaweal Ln., Calistoga, 707/942-4981, www.clospegase.com, 10:30 A.M.–5 P.M. daily, tasting $15) is truly hard to miss. If the giant pink-and-yellow boxy creation reminds you partly of the whimsical home appliances in your local Target store and partly of a 1980s shopping mall, there's good reason. Clos Pegase was designed in the 1980s by postmodernist architect Michael Graves, better known to most consumers these days as the designer of cheerful teakettles, toasters, and other household paraphernalia.

Graves won a competition sponsored by the San Francisco Museum of Modern Art to design a "temple to wine and art" for entertaining owner Jan Schrem's wine-making passion and displaying his sizable art collection. The original design, which included a giant statue of the winged horse Pegasus, after which the winery is named, had to be toned down, but

© PHILIP GOLDSMITH

Clos Pegase, modern architecture amid the vines

the resulting building, completed in 1987, is still pretty garish against the bucolic backdrop. It could be mistaken for the Napa outpost of a modern art museum; giant sculptures lurk around every corner, and postmodern design touches grace almost every part of the building. It's a place that's a lot easier to admire up close than from afar.

Look for art and sculpture, both ancient and modern, by Kandinsky, Ernst, Moore, and other big names during one of the free tours offered here at 11:30 A.M. and 2 P.M. Despite the fact that the tour tends to be pitched more toward the less artistically inclined among us, it's really the only way to fully appreciate the winery, its art, and the building's ancient Greek design influences. The tour also takes in the fermentation room and maze of caves burrowed into the hillside behind the winery—nothing particularly notable compared to the arty stuff, but fun nonetheless.

Schrem, who made his fortune in the publishing business, also bought hundreds of acres of vineyards in the Calistoga area and down

in Carneros. Much of the fruit is sold to other winemakers, and only about a third goes into the 40,000 cases of wine made each year at Clos Pegase, from the high-end Homage reserves down to a local cabernet sauvignon and some reasonably priced, approachable pinot noir, merlot, and chardonnay from Carneros.

◖ SCHRAMSBERG VINEYARDS

If you plan to visit just one of the valley's big champagne makers, the historic Schramsberg winery (1400 Schramsberg Rd., via Peterson Dr. off Hwy. 29, Calistoga, 707/942-4558 or 800/877-3623, www.schramsberg.com, 10 A.M.–4 P.M. daily, tour and tasting $40) should be high on the list. The winery was established high on the wooded slopes of Diamond Mountain in 1862 by German immigrant Jacob Schram, who had soon made such a name for himself as a maker of high-quality wines that he was paid a visit by a vacationing Robert Louis Stevenson in 1880, a visit memorialized in Stevenson's book *Silverado Squatters*.

In those days, Schram made still wines mainly from German grape varietals, and the winery pretty much died with Schram in 1905. Its fame as a sparkling winemaker didn't begin until the 1960s, when the Davies family bought the rundown property. Rather than compete with the makers of sweeter sparkling wines like the nearby Kornell winery (long since gone) and Korbell in the Russian River Valley, the new owners opted to make drier wines from traditional French champagne grapes—a risk, considering the American palette was more accustomed to sweet white zin than bone-dry champagnes at the time.

The Davies's 1965 blanc de blancs was the first American-made champagne to use chardonnay grapes. The 1969 vintage was served to President Richard Nixon and Chinese Premier Zhou Enlai in Beijing in 1972 for a toast to the normalization of diplomatic relations. In fact, the sales room is full of photos and menus from various White House events at which Schramsberg wines have been served.

Today Schramsberg makes about 45,000 cases of wines, ranging from that historic blanc de blancs and a rich, creamy blanc de noirs up to its flagship J. Schram wine, regarded as one of the best Californian champagnes. To taste them, however, you must sign up for one of the appointment-only tours of the winery, which include a visit to the Victorian mansion, a trip into the spooky bottle-lined caves that date from the late 1800s, and a lesson on the art of champagne making, all culminating in a sit-down tasting. The price is on the high side, but the setting, the history, and the quality of the wines you taste make it worthwhile.

If the wines taste complex, that could be because the grapes come from 67 different vineyards in four California counties, with many in Carneros and the Anderson Valley in Mendocino. The hotter estate vineyard around the winery was replanted mainly to cabernet sauvignon in the late 1990s, and Schramsberg now makes a cabernet (the 2001 vintage was the first release) under the J. Davies label.

Even if you cannot book yourself on a tour, it's worth a quick detour from Highway 29 up the perilously narrow wooded road (with almost invisible speed bumps) just to see the mansion and the ornate gardens that are like a Victorian oasis hidden in the forest. You can also buy any of the wines and look at the old photos in the sales room, which is open all day.

◖ CASTELLO DI AMOROSA

Daryl Sattui's Tuscan wonderland, Castello di Amorosa (4045 N. St. Helena Hwy., Calistoga, 707/942-8200, www.castellodiamorosa.com, tours 9:30 A.M.–4:30 P.M. Mon.–Fri., 9:30 A.M.–5 P.M. weekends, tasting $16–26, two-hour tour and tasting $31, no children under age 5), is a sight for the eyes. Surrounded by such a fantastic structure, it's easy to forget that this is also a working winery. At the back of the castle and in a neighboring building designed to resemble a Tuscan farmhouse, there's a state-of-the-art gravity-flow winery where Sattui creates limited-production Italian-inspired wines from his Diamond Mountain vineyards together with a handful of acres in Mendocino's Anderson Valley and elsewhere in the Napa Valley. Current production is a modest 10,000 cases.

The 38 acres of vineyards planted to cabernet sauvignon, sangiovese, merlot, and primitivo (a relative of zinfandel) around the castle produce intensely flavored red wines typical of Diamond Mountain, but some also with the typical tannic bite that can take a few years to mellow in the bottle. They include the excellent-value Il Brigante, a blend of cabernet, merlot, and sangiovese that's a bit like a baby super-Tuscan but with a baby price to go with it. Its big sister is the supple and opulent super-Tuscan blend called La Castellana, named for the traditional lady of the castle. The flagship Diamond Mountain wine is Il Barone, a powerhouse mountain cabernet. Other reds include well-priced and limited-production sangiovese and merlot. The highlights of the white wines are the Mendocino gewürztraminers, made in both a slightly sweet (dolcino) and bone-dry style. Other whites include several chardonnays and the classic Italian white wine, pinot grigio.

In terms of both the wines produced and

© PHILIP GOLDSMITH

Castello di Amorosa brings some outlandish Tuscan heritage to the Napa Valley.

the number of visitors, Sattui plans to make Castello di Amorosa a far more exclusive experience than his crowded V. Sattui winery. There has been talk of setting some limits on the number of people allowed up the driveway to the castle, but judging by summer crowds, that has not yet happened. Those crowds do mean it's worth calling ahead, particularly on busy weekends, to reserve a spot on a tour and ensure you're able to experience Daryl Sattui's kingdom of wine.

REVERIE VINEYARD & WINERY

At the end of the long driveway off Diamond Mountain Road, Reverie (1520 Diamond Mountain Rd., Calistoga, 707/942-6800 or 800/738-3743, www.reveriewine.com, by appointment 10 A.M.–4 P.M. daily) shares a hidden sun-drenched valley surrounded by terraced vineyards that are key to its success as well as the success of the neighboring wineries that share this little part of wine-growing heaven. Reverie released its first wine in 1995 and now produces about 2,500 cases of mainly

bordeaux-style red wines, together with small amounts of a delicious cabernet franc, from its 40 acres of rocky mountain vineyards, with the help of consultant winemaker Ted Lemon, better known for his sought-after Littorai pinot noir and chardonnay wines.

These big ripe reds with muscular tannins are classic Diamond Mountain wines, enhanced (at least mentally) by the alfresco tasting experience under towering redwood trees. With help from a different winemaker, Reverie also makes small quantities of crisp, nonmalolactic chardonnay from Diamond Mountain fruit, and a sauvignon blanc sourced from vineyards down in the valley, both under the Daydream label. Of all the wines, however, it's hard not to go home with a bottle of the fun proprietary red blend called AsKiken, named after winery founder (and former PR guru) Norm Kiken.

A quick tour of the small low-key winery followed by a tasting in the caves or under the redwoods can easily be arranged by calling first. There's no real tour schedule—if someone's

A MAGIC KINGDOM OF WINE

Whether or not you think a replica medieval castle in the Napa Valley is just a bit over the top (and there are many in the valley who do), it's hard not to be impressed when the fairytale turrets and massive stone walls rear into view as you round a curve on the steep driveway. The product of one man's dream, **Castello di Amorosa** finally opened in 2007, some 14 years and a reported $30 million after the painstaking construction began. As its Italian name implies, this castle was a labor of love.

Despite its rather unfortunate symbolism to critics of the Disneyfication of the Napa Valley, Castello di Amorosa is in many ways no different from other lavish structures that have been built in the valley over the centuries by eccentric winemakers honoring their family roots or simply realizing grand ambitions. The trend started in the 1880s when the Beringer brothers painstakingly recreated an ornate Gothic mansion modeled on their German home. In the following 120 years the valley has become host to extravagant buildings inspired by architecture in Greece (Sterling Vineyards), Persia (Darioush), France and Italy (countless wineries), as well as some fascinating modern interpretations of classic structures like Opus One and Clos Pegase. Many of those architectural imposters created quite a stir when first completed, but all have now settled into the valley's cultural and architectural blend. The Castello simply adds a touch more Tuscany to the mix – 121,000 square feet of Tuscany, to be precise.

This latest Napa winemaker to build his dream is Daryl Sattui, a fourth-generation Italian American winemaker and medieval history buff who had already made a name for himself in the valley with the highly successful V. Sattui winery in St. Helena. His monumental castle is an architectural mash-up, built in just over a decade to resemble the various additions that were commonly made to castles over centuries.

It's not based on any particular castle in Tuscany but was inspired by features of many, distilled into a final design by Sattui himself.

Cross the dry moat on the drawbridge, enter through the iron gates into the stone passageway, and sign up for the two-hour tour and tasting ($31–68, no children under 5) to get the most from a visit here. The basic wine-tasting option ($16–26) gives you barely a hint at the history lessons that lie in the towers rising four stories above and passageways that plunge four stories below. First stop on the tour is the Great Hall, a two-story marvel of frescos, coffered ceilings, and stone walls fit for any wine-fueled banquet. The cloistered main courtyard beyond, with its tiny chapel and colorful planters, could be out of almost any ancient French or Italian village. The towers offer strategic views over the valley and even have chutes to pour hot oil on the advancing hordes below.

The best parts of the castle, though, are underground. A warren of cool, damp passageways descend to catacombs and vaulted cellars, including the breathtaking, 130-foot-long main barrel room with its vast cross-vaulted ceiling. There's even a dungeon, stocked with some particularly heinous torture instruments – including an original iron maiden, which looks rather like an upright mummy case but is lined with spikes to impale hapless victims inside. Next door is an aptly named pit of despair, into which victims were thrown to starve to death with only the company of rats.

Everything was painstakingly recreated using traditional materials and a small army of artisans. Every piece of iron, from the elaborate gates and dragon-head sconces down to the nails in the massive wooden doors, was hand-forged in Italy, where the antique bricks and tiles were also sourced. Much of the stone used in the walls was quarried locally, and the pieces were hand-shaped onsite to fit together like a giant three-dimensional jigsaw.

there, they will probably be happy to show you around, although in recent years Reverie has suspended its tours during the winter months, so call before you plan your itinerary.

VON STRASSER WINERY

To get to Reverie, the driveway off Diamond Mountain Road first passes the unobtrusivez home of the Von Strasser winery (1510 Diamond Mountain Rd., Calistoga, 707/942-0930, www.vonstrasser.com, 10:30 A.M.–4:30 P.M. daily, tour and tasting $20), established in 1990 by Rudy von Strasser, who was instrumental in putting Diamond Mountain on the wine map. He spearheaded the alliance of local growers that finally succeeded in having Diamond Mountain declared its own subappellation within Napa Valley in 2001, after almost a decade of trying.

Von Strasser offers plenty of memorable examples of what can be done with Diamond Mountain grapes. It makes a selection of intense, vineyard-designate cabernet sauvignons from its own estate and adjacent vineyards, together with a chardonnay and a few hundred cases of the appellation's only zinfandel. Total production of about 9,000 cases makes it one of the largest of Diamond Mountain's handful of wineries.

The Estate Vineyard cabernet is the wine that Von Strasser is probably best known for, balancing powerful tannins with equally powerful fruit, resulting in high ratings from critics almost every year. This and a couple of other cabernets are usually available to taste by appointment as part of a flight of five wines at the low-key tasting room. Also ask about tours of the winery, and you might be lucky enough to have Rudy as your tour guide.

ZAHTILA VINEYARDS

Across the valley from Diamond Mountain, where the Silverado Trail meets Highway 29 just east of Calistoga, is a little cluster of modest buildings belonging to this family-owned boutique winery. Zahtila (2250 Lake County Hwy., Calistoga, 707/942-9251, www.zahtila vineyards.com, 10 A.M.–5 P.M. daily, tasting

$10) makes some fine cabernet sauvignon and zinfandel. Its relaxed atmosphere and smooth-drinking wines offer a nice change of pace (and price) from the Napa Valley crush. Staff in the cozy tasting room are also a mine of information about other small local wineries. Just don't trip over the chewed toys left lying around by the friendly winery dog.

The specialty here is zinfandel, which is grown in the small Oat Hill Vineyard next to the winery, planted in the 1970s by the previous owners. Most of the fruit, however, is bought from other growers for its 2,000 cases of wine. Cabernet sauvignon comes from the Rutherford and Calistoga areas and goes into the rich, smooth Napa cabernet and flagship Beckstoffer cabernet. Additional zinfandel is bought from the Russian River Valley and sometimes the Dry Creek Valley. Chardonnay was added to the portfolio in recent years and is sourced from vineyards near St. Helena.

CHATEAU MONTELENA

This beautiful French- and Chinese-inspired Chateau Montelena (1429 Tubbs Ln., Calistoga, 707/942-5105, www.montelena .com, 9:30 A.M.–4 P.M. daily, tours 9:45 A.M. Tues., Thurs., and Sun., $40; tasting $20 or $40) wine estate will forever be remembered for putting Napa Valley on the map when its 1973-vintage chardonnay trounced the best French white burgundies at the famous 1976 Paris tasting. The winery is by no means resting on its past achievements, however, and is still a top Napa winemaker today. Yet even before the Paris tasting it had quite a colorful history.

Chateau Montelena dates back to the 1880s, when Alfred Tubbs (after whom Tubbs Lane is named) bought land and built the imposing stone château, eventually naming it after Mount St. Helena, which looms in the distance. The winery prospered until Prohibition, after which it made limited amounts of wine and sold grapes to other growers before the estate was broken up in the 1950s.

The giant five-acre Jade Lake and Chinese flourishes like the lacquered bridges and pavilions were added by Yort Wing Frank, who bought a chunk of the estate in 1958 for a bit of retirement fun. Serious wine-making didn't start again until just over a decade later, when the château and original vineyards were re-united by James Barrett and partner Leland Paschich, signaling the start of Chateau Montelena's modern-day wine-making heritage. In an ironic twist to the story of a winery that humiliated some of the finest French wine châteaus in the 1970s, Chateau Montelena was destined to be acquired by the Bordeaux wine château Cos d'Estournel in 2008, but the deal fell through and left the Barrett family still firmly in charge.

James' son, Bo Barrett, has been Montelena's winemaker since 1982 and was famously portrayed as a long-haired renegade in the semifictitious 2008 movie *Bottle Shock,* about the 1976 Paris tasting. Not surprisingly, there is a "behind the scenes" tour offered three times a week that includes a tasting of the latest vintage of chardonnay and a movie souvenir; check the website for times.

Soft, plush cabernet sauvignon is now just as acclaimed as the rich chardonnay at Montelena, and together they account for the bulk of the 35,000-case production. An excellent estate zinfandel is also made, and all are usually available to taste. Cabernet fans can also try a vertical Library tasting of the age-worthy but pricey estate cabernet in the intimate stone-walled Estate Room. Reservations for this twice-daily sit-down tasting are essential.

The Eastern Mountains Wineries

The oak-studded peaks and valleys hidden in the Vaca Mountains on the eastern side of Napa Valley offer a relaxing diversion and a total change of pace. Grapes have been grown here for more than 100 years, and the area was ripe for a new wave of viticultural development until the valley's biggest growers recently turned their attention farther north to Lake County, where land is cheaper and the promise greater.

Nevertheless, there are still some great wines made in these hills, most notably in the Chiles Valley appellation, where zinfandel and sauvignon blanc enjoy the warmer growing conditions, and on Howell Mountain, where cabernet sauvignon reigns supreme in the thin volcanic soils.

The Chiles Valley offers the best touring possibilities and is easy to reach. Take Highway 128 (Sage Canyon Road) up into the hills from the Silverado Trail at Rutherford, past Lake Hennessey, and go either left or right at the junction. Both roads lead to the valley. Just be sure to leave plenty of time to drive there and back on the mountain roads and to take lunch because there's very little apart from farmland and vineyards up there.

CATACULA LAKE WINERY

Turn left at the Lake Hennessey junction onto Chiles Pope Valley Road and continue for about six miles into the Chiles Valley to this former summer camp. The first vintage from Catacula Lake (4105 Chiles Pope Valley Rd., St. Helena, 707/965-1104, by appointment daily, tasting $5) was in 1999, and it now makes about 5,000 cases of wine per year, including some increasingly good zinfandel and sauvignon blanc, at bargain prices.

Considering so few wines are made here, none costing more than $20 a bottle, the $5 fee for the appointment-only tasting might seem a little steep, but a couple of library wines are thrown in, and there's also sometimes a two-for-one tasting offer on the winery's website. The peaceful setting next to the lake with an outdoor patio and picnic area also makes it a worthwhile outlay.

RUSTRIDGE RANCH & WINERY

About three miles from Lake Hennessey on Chiles Pope Valley Road, turn right onto Lower Chiles Valley Road to get to this very rustic part-winery, part-ranch, where thoroughbred horses are just as important as wine. Tastings at RustRidge (2910 Lower Chiles Valley Rd., St. Helena, 707/965-9353, www.rustridge.com, 10 A.M.–4 P.M. daily, tour and tasting $20) are held in an old cattle barn that now houses the winery workings, and a visit here is as much about smelling the horses as the wine.

About 55 of the ranch's 440 acres are planted with grapes, and the winery makes about 2,000 cases of zinfandel, both barrel- and tank-fermented chardonnay, cabernet sauvignon, and sauvignon blanc. The rest of the fruit is sold to other wineries. Tours and tastings are offered every day by appointment only, but with life up here so relaxed, all that's usually required is a call to check that someone's home.

BROWN ESTATE VINEYARDS

At the far southern end of the Chiles Valley appellation is a relative newcomer to the wine business, but one that is already making a name for its zinfandels.

The Brown family bought the land as a vacation home in 1981, and by 1990 had planted 40 acres of vineyards on the former Victorian homestead. The Browns sold their fruit to other wineries until 1996, when they made their first zinfandel vintage. It was lauded by critics, as were many of the subsequent vintages. Since then Brown (3233 Sage Canyon Rd., St. Helena, 707/963-2435, www.brown estate.com, open to Wine Club members only) has added chardonnay to the mix and blasted a 6,500-square-foot cave complex out of the hillside behind the winery.

Brown makes about 4,000 cases of predominantly zinfandel but also small quantities of cabernet sauvignon and chardonnay from the estate vineyards, though it still sells some fruit to other local wineries.

KULETO ESTATE

When one of the Bay Area's most successful restaurateurs turns his hand to wine-making, you can be sure the resulting winery is going to be quite a destination. Pat Kuleto's hillside estate does not disappoint, from the secret gate code given to visitors who make an appointment to the Tuscan-style house, Villa Cucina, with its infinity pool framing a view of Lake Hennessey and the valley beyond.

Kuleto is the man behind such swank San Francisco restaurants as Boulevard and Farallon as well as the popular Martini House down the hill in St. Helena. The Kuleto Estate winery (2470 Sage Canyon Rd., St. Helena, 707/302-2200, www.kuletoestate.com, tours by appointment at 10:30 and 11:45 A.M. and 1 and 2:30 P.M. daily, $35), completed in 2002, will likely be just as successful if recent ratings are any indication, particularly as Kuleto works his culinary contacts to get his wines on the lists of some of the country's top restaurants.

The 90 acres of vineyards planted on the twists and turns of these 800 acres of former grazing land are planted predominantly to cabernet sauvignon and sangiovese, with small blocks of zinfandel, syrah, pinot noir, and chardonnay. Production is about 8,000 cases now but will undoubtedly grow if the success of Kuleto's other ventures is anything to go by.

Tours of the diverse vineyards and modern winery, together with a comprehensive tasting of wines with cheeses, are available four times a day by appointment. And as you enter the gate code and drive onto the estate, you can imagine for a fleeting moment that you've arrived at your own personal Wine Country estate.

SIGHTS
◖ Sharpsteen Museum

The quirky little Sharpsteen Museum (1311 Washington St., Calistoga, 707/942-5911, www.sharpsteen-museum.org, 11 A.M.–4 P.M. daily, donations requested) was donated to the city in the 1970s by its creators, Ben and Bernice Sharpsteen, and depicts up-valley life from the days of the Wappo people to the early 1900s. Its main claim to fame is a beautifully painted diorama depicting Calistoga in its hot springs heyday, but it also has some more traditional exhibits, many no doubt enhanced by the skills of Ben Sharpsteen, who was an Academy Award–winning animator.

Next door is one of the frilly little cottages built by Sam Brannan in the 1860s for his groundbreaking Hot Springs Resort in Calistoga. It was moved here in the 1970s, leaving only one of Brannan's cottages where it was built—at the Brannan Cottage Inn on Wapoo Avenue.

© PHILIP GOLDSMITH

An ornate Victorian cottage that was once part of Sam Brannan's original Calistoga spa resort is now part of the Sharpsteen Museum.

© SUSAN LEONARD/123RF.COM

Old Faithful Geyser

Old Faithful Geyser

Although it may not really be worth the time or money, visitors continue to flock to Calistoga's Old Faithful Geyser (1299 Tubbs Ln., Calistoga, 707/942-6463, www.oldfaithful geyser.com, 9 A.M.–6 P.M. daily spring–fall, 9 A.M.–5 P.M. daily winter, adults $10, children $3), one of only three geysers in the world reliable enough to get the "Old Faithful" moniker. There must be something hypnotic about the thought of watching water shoot 60 feet or more into the air that keeps people coming. Or perhaps it's the free mud bath into which you can unwittingly sink if you get too close to the edge of the pools. Just hope you don't get there right after an eruption has finished, or it could be as long as a 45-minute wait until the next one (the gap between eruptions varies depending on the season, so check the website for the latest updates). Still, that's time enough to open your faithful old wallet for some overpriced and tacky Old Faithful gifts. Even the famous fainting goats near the entrance seem bored by all the fuss and rarely faint on cue, as their "genetic defect" is supposed to guarantee.

Petrified Forest

Another natural attraction nearby that illustrates the area's volcanic past but with far more scenic value (though no goats) is the Petrified Forest (follow the signs to Santa Rosa, 707/942-6667, 9 A.M.–7 P.M. daily summer, 9 A.M.–5 P.M. daily winter, $8), a couple of miles up Petrified Forest Road from Calistoga. Like the Geyser down the hill, the experience feels very homespun with little in the way of glossy corporate tourist facilities. You also might start wondering what you paid for, because the short trails meander through what seem like recently fallen redwood trees. In fact, they were long ago turned to stone at such a microscopic level that they still look almost like real wood rather than the fossils they are. In the distance looms Mount St. Helena, believed to have been the source of the volcanic eruption that buried the trees millions of years ago and started the long petrification process. Guided tours are available on weekends at 11 A.M., and there are plenty of chunks of petrified wood for sale in the wonderfully tacky visitors center under a very old oak tree (no one knows how old, but probably over 600 years).

Pope Valley

Sleepy Pope Valley is the unlikely setting for California Historic Landmark No. 939. Even more unlikely is that California would designate a collection of thousands of hubcaps strung from posts, fences, and trees as a historic landmark. But such is the importance of this strange collection to the state's eclectic folk-art scene (or so someone thought) that the **Hubcap Ranch,** created by Emanuel "Litto" Damonte from the 1950s to his death in 1985, was given its lofty status, and Litto was immortalized as the Pope Valley Hubcap King.

It is still a private ranch, so don't expect any Wine Country–style tours, though you're welcome to leave a hubcap from the rental car or your own to ensure the collection keeps growing. The ranch's dogs seem to love trying to

Donations are always welcome at the Hubcap Ranch.

© PHILIP GOLDSMITH

scare visitors, so don't be surprised when they hurl their snarling bodies at the fence behind the landmark plaque.

Litto's grandson, Mike Damonte, has kept up the folk-art tradition that his grandfather inadvertently started when he hung lost hubcaps on his fence in case their hapless owners wanted them back. The growing collection proved to be a magnet, and soon neighbors and anonymous visitors were leaving hubcaps rather than taking them. Now, half a century later, there are, it is said, about 5,000 of the things glinting in the sun, from lavish chrome 1960s trim to the present-day plastic wannabes.

Hubcap Ranch is easy to get to and easy to spot. From the Silverado Trail, head up Deer Park Road, through the small college town of Angwin, and down through the forest to the auto-repair shop, junkyard, and general store that constitute downtown Pope Valley. At that intersection, turn left onto Pope Valley Road. From the Catacula Lake Winery, continue east along Chiles Pope Valley Road, then bear right at the general store. Hubcap Ranch is about two miles farther, at 6654 Pope Valley Road just past the Pope Valley Winery, though you certainly won't need to look for the number on a mailbox.

While you're in the area, the **Pope Valley Winery** (6613 Pope Valley Rd., 707/965-1246, www.popevalleywinery.com, 11 A.M.–5 P.M. Thurs.–Sun., call ahead Mon.–Tues., free tasting) is worth a stop, despite its sprawling scrappy-looking setting. The original three-story winery building was built in 1909 and operated as the Sam Haus Winery until 1959. Since then a variety of owners have tried to make a go of it in this remote location, the latest being a group of valley residents who bought the old buildings in 1998 and now make about 4,000 cases of mainly red wines from the 80 acres of Pope Valley vineyards, including zinfandel, cabernet sauvignon, and sangiovese.

ENTERTAINMENT

For the sleepiest and most mellow town in the Napa Valley, Calistoga has some of the best nightlife. This is still Wine Country, however, so don't expect too much beyond live local bands and the ability to buy a beer after 11 P.M. The **Hydro Bar & Grill** (1403 Lincoln Ave., 707/942-9777) sometimes hosts local live music on weekend nights, and the **Napa Valley Brewing Company** at the Calistoga Inn (1250 Lincoln Ave., 707/942-4101, www.calistoga inn.com) offers live jazz or blues every night of the week on the creek-side patio during the summer and often on weekends in the winter. There's also a popular open mike night on Wednesday and themed music on most other weekday nights hosted by the house DJ. More information is available online or by phone from the Calistoga Inn.

SHOPPING

Like many things in Calistoga, shopping is a little more down-to-earth here than elsewhere in the valley. Sure, there are plenty of gift shops, but there's a decidedly artisanal feel to most of them, like the **American Indian Trading Company** (1407 Lincoln Ave., next to the Hydro Bar & Grill, 707/942-9330, 10 A.M.–6 P.M. daily), which sells arts, crafts, and jewelry from Native American tribes all over the country, including a few local groups. On Highway 29 just south of Lincoln Avenue is **Calistoga Pottery** (1001 Foothill Blvd., 707/942-0216, 9 A.M.–5 P.M. daily), another good place to buy something original from local artists who have supplied some of the valley's biggest wineries and restaurants with their stoneware.

At the eastern end of Lincoln Avenue is the historic **Calistoga Depot** (1458 Lincoln Ave.), the second-oldest remaining railroad depot in the country, built by Sam Brannan in 1868 and crucial to the early success of Calistoga's Victorian spas. It is now home to a handful of funky little stores, some of them in six old railroad cars parked on the tracks that lead to nowhere. **Calistoga Wine Stop** (707/942-5556, 10 A.M.–6 P.M. daily) is in the main depot building and has a good selection of wines from both Napa and Sonoma, including a few rarities.

Wine aficionados will also probably enjoy sniffing around the small **Enoteca Wine Shop** (1348 Lincoln Ave., 707/942-1117, 11:30 A.M.–5:30 P.M. daily), which specializes in smaller (sometimes cult) producers of wines from California and beyond. Another fascinating wine shop, one that prides itself on selling hard-to-find boutique California wines, is the **Wine Garage** (1020 Foothill Blvd., Calistoga, 707/942-5332, 11 A.M.–6:30 P.M. Mon.–Sat., 11 A.M.–4:30 P.M. Sun.) on Foothill Boulevard just south of Lincoln Avenue. Owner Todd Miller travels throughout the lesser-known wine regions of Northern California trying and buying wines from small wineries, loading them onto his truck, and bringing them back to the shop. No bottle costs over $25, and many are under $15—a refreshing change in a valley of big wine names and big prices.

If your visit to Calistoga is too brief to get immersed in a mud bath, you can buy a jar of the stuff to take home with you at **Mudd Hens** (1348 Lincoln Ave., 707/942-0210, www.muddhens.com, 10:30 A.M.–6 P.M. Sun.–Thurs., 10:30 A.M.–9 P.M. Fri.–Sat.). In addition to the (rather expensive) Calistoga mud, you'll find countless other body-care related products, from teas to potions.

RECREATION
Robert Louis Stevenson State Park

By far the best views in the valley, and perhaps the entire Wine Country, are from the top of Napa's highest peak, Mount St. Helena, which is at the northern end of the valley in the park named for the mountain's most famous Victorian visitor.

Stevenson honeymooned in a cabin here after traveling from his native Scotland to marry Fanny Osbourne, the woman he met at an artists' retreat. The area had just been abandoned by silver miners following the rapid rise and fall of the **Silverado mine** in the 1870s, after which the Silverado Trail is named, along with Stevenson's account of his brief stay in the valley, *Silverado Squatters*.

The happy couple's cabin is long gone,

marked only by a small monument partway up the five-mile trail to the summit. Look out for two big dirt parking lots on either side of the road about eight miles north of Calistoga on Highway 29. The **Mount St. Helena Trail** starts from the western lot and has virtually no shade, together with some particularly steep sections—it climbs about 2,000 feet in five miles to the 4,339-foot summit of the mountain—so hiking it in the middle of a hot summer day is not recommended. On the clearest days, usually in spring, the 360-degree views stretch for more than 100 miles, and in winter there is often a dusting of snow near the peak. Those not so determined to get to the summit can take a spur off the main trail at about the 3.5-mile point to the 4,000-foot South Peak, which has impressive views of the valley.

The eastern parking lot marks the start of the **Table Rock Trail,** a shorter and less strenuous 2.2-mile trail that climbs out of the woodland and past volcanic rock outcroppings to a ridge overlooking the flat moonscape known as Table Rock and the entire valley to the south. The more adventurous can connect to the **Palisades Trail,** which crosses Table Rock and eventually meets the Oat Hill Mine Road leading down into the valley, though it turns the hike into a daylong expedition and ends miles from the parking lot.

Calistoga Spas

During his stay here in 1880, Robert Louis Stevenson observed that Calistoga "seems to repose on a mere film above a boiling, subterranean lake." That mineral-laden boiling water fueled the growth of one of the biggest spa destinations in California. Railroad baron Samuel Brannan first cashed in on the endless hot water supply in 1862 with his Hot Springs Resort, and by the late 1860s the new railroad was bringing the fashionable and well-heeled from San Francisco to immerse themselves.

The emphasis of the dozens of spas these days has broadened to include everything from restorative volcanic mud to mineral soaks, wraps, and facials. The clientele has

LEAVE WINE (AND CLOTHES) BEHIND

Put away the camera, forget about wineries, leave your cynicism behind, and take off all your clothes (if you want to) at the historic and decidedly alternative **Harbin Hot Springs,** about a half hour north of Calistoga, beyond Mount St. Helena in rural Lake County (Harbin Springs Rd., off Big Canyon Rd., Middletown, 707/987-2477 or 800/622-2477, www.harbin.org).

In some sense, this place could be described as a hot springs resort. It has the natural springs and the history of its Calistoga spa cousins to the south, dating from the late 1800s when the sick and infirm sought out the natural waters here. A more accurate description these days, however, would be a New Age ecoresort still running on 1960s flower power. It's a place where you're far more likely to hear about the joy of finding a higher state of consciousness than the joy of savoring the best cabernet in Napa. That's if you hear anything. In some parts of the resort, even a whisper will elicit gentle but firm rebukes that might conjure up fears of some bizarre karmic retribution. It also has a bit of a reputation for being a pickup joint, both gay and straight, which makes you wonder how one hooks up in silence.

Nevertheless, there's enough on offer within the 1,200 acres to please even a wine-soaked cynic – from hiking trails in the hills to the series of indoor-outdoor hot and cold pools among the trees; from the organic food store to the communal kitchen. Best of all is the endless flow of free classes and workshops ranging from dance and yoga to meditation and massage. Harbin is perhaps best known for its Watsu massage – a form of Shiatsu massage performed while you float in a pool.

Nearly all the activities are free after paying a day-use fee of $25 (weekdays) or $35 (weekends), though at least one person in your party will need to buy a $10 trial membership to the nonprofit organization that runs Harbin. If you only want to sunbathe naked (or clothed) for half a day or take a yoga class, the six-hour fee is $5-10 less. Check the website for a full schedule of events and classes.

Another reason to come here is for the wide range of accommodations. They range from dorm rooms ($35-50, bring your own towels and bedding) and basic rooms with shared baths ($60-140) up to rooms with full baths (from $130 midweek, $190 weekends) and three cottages tucked away in the woods ($170-190 midweek, $230-260 weekends). The most bizarre rooms are in a space-age domed complex perched on a hillside that look as though they were designed by an architect on acid. The double rooms with wacky windows and shared bathrooms cost from $110 midweek and $150 weekends. Camping in the meadows is also an option and is free with the day-use fee ($25-35), though no fires or camping stoves are allowed, so you'll be eating in one of the on-site vegetarian restaurants or using the communal kitchen.

also broadened to include the less well-heeled, drawn by the straightforward, no-nonsense spa treatments here that dispense with the more luxurious frills offered by the bigger Napa Valley and Sonoma super-resorts. Don't go expecting glamorous establishments straight out of a glossy magazine spread—some of the places look like decidedly unglamorous motels in need of some restorative work themselves.

The region's Wappo people were the first to discover the unlikely pleasure of soaking in the local mud (one wonders who first had the idea and why). These days the mud is usually a mixture of dark volcanic ash, peat (for buoyancy), and hot mineral water that suspends your body, relaxes muscles, and draws out impurities in the skin, all accompanied by a rather off-putting sulfurous smell. A 10–15-minute soak is usually followed by a rinse in crystal-clear mineral water and a steam wrap with or without piped music. Aromatherapies, massages, and other hedonistic treatments can be added afterward but will quickly run up the price. Those worried about lying in someone else's impurities can take comfort from the claims that the mud is regularly flushed with fresh spring water. There is evidently such a thing as "clean" mud.

Wherever and whatever the treatment, remember that the heat can rapidly dehydrate your body, so lay off the wine beforehand and don't plan to hike to the top of Mount St. Helena afterward. Reservations are usually needed, but you might luck out just by walking in, especially midweek. Most spas are also open late, making them an ideal way to wrap up a long day of touring (pun intended).

On the site of Brannan's original resort is the **Indian Springs Resort** (1712 Lincoln Ave., 707/942-4913, www.indianspringscalistoga .com, 9 A.M.–8 P.M. daily), which specializes in 100 percent volcanic mud bath treatments ($85), using the volcanic ash from its 16 acres of land, and mineral baths ($70). It also has what is said to be California's oldest continuously operating swimming pool, an Olympic-sized version built in 1913 and fed by warm spring water. In fact, you can usually see the puffs of steam from the natural hot springs on-site. Spa customers can lounge by the pool as long as they want, though it can get crowded and the water is a little too warm for any serious swimming.

Another muddy Calistoga institution announced by its big, red neon sign is the funky **Dr. Wilkinson's Hot Springs** (1507 Lincoln Ave., 707/942-4102, www.drwilkinson.com, 8:30 A.M.–3:45 P.M. daily), founded by an eccentric chiropractor in the 1950s who developed his own secret recipe for the mud that his children still guard closely today. "The Works," a 1.5-hour pampering with mud bath, facial, mineral soak, and blanket wrap, costs $89. For $40 more, you can finish with a 30-minute massage, and there are plenty of other competitively priced packages available.

The **Lincoln Avenue Spa** (1339 Lincoln Ave., 707/942-5296, www.lincoln avenuespa.com, 10 A.M.–6 P.M. Sun.–Thurs., 10 A.M.–8 P.M. Fri.–Sat.) offers couples the chance to float in twin tubs of mud in a private room ($85). There is a choice of four types of mud, including an Ayurvedic herbal mud and an antioxidant-laden wine mud containing wine, grape seed oil, and green tea. It also offers salt scrubs, with or without accompanying mud, and a full range of massages and facials. No jokes about spa treatments breaking the bank here—this spa is in an impregnable-looking stone building that was a Victorian-era bank.

At the **Lavender Hill Spa** (1015 Foothill Blvd., 707/942-4495, www.lavenderhillspa .com, 9 A.M.–9 P.M. daily) the mud is used only once before being discarded and is an international affair, containing Calistoga volcanic ash, French sea kelp, Dead Sea salt, and the trademark lavender oil. Like most treatments here, the mud bath ($85) is available for singles or couples. For the same price there is also a Thai milk bath with sea kelp and some fruity essential oils that is part of a whole range of other Thai-inspired massages and facials, all in a relaxing gardenlike setting.

There is an equally diverse selection of ways to immerse yourself **Mount View Spa** (1457 Lincoln Ave., 707/942-5789 or 800/816-6877, www.mountviewhotel.com, 9 A.M.–9 P.M. daily) in the namesake hotel, including mineral mud baths, aromatherapy baths and saunas, mud- and seaweed-wraps, massages, and facial treatments in perhaps the classiest setting in Calistoga. The mineral mud baths ($70, couples $80) and wraps might contain grape seeds, aromatherapy essences, as well as Moor mud added to the water. Massages start at $99, and the huge selection culminates with a three-hour $360 extravaganza called the Head to Toe package, which includes a mineral bath, body polish, Swedish massage, and facial. The hotel's pool can also be used by spa customers.

ACCOMMODATIONS

Calistoga is one of the cheapest places in the valley for most purchases, from food and gas to a place to stay. This is still Wine Country, however, so "cheap" is a relative term, and prices have risen faster than the valley average in the past few years. Calistoga might finally be cashing in on its charms, or at least cashing in on the fact that a fancy new resort, Solage, opened in 2007 and promises to bring a flood of new tourist dollars to town.

Some of the Victorian B&Bs strung along the Highway 29 and Foothill Boulevard seem downright reasonable during the week, but rates can almost double on summer weekends, much like everywhere else in the valley. The best bargains are probably the numerous spa resorts that offer slightly less elegant motel-style rooms for slightly more reasonable prices. All generally offer free continental breakfast, though with some you might be left wondering which continent manages to function on such meager morning sustenance.

Whatever the accommodation, remember that this end of the valley is the hottest, and sleeping without air-conditioning in the height of summer can be a challenge. As in the rest of the valley, there is also a penalty to pay for wanting to stay during a weekend, when rates are often 50 percent higher than midweek and a two-night minimum is pretty standard. And that's if you can find a room. As always, book plenty of time in advance from July through October.

Under $100

To use the term "bargain" to describe the **C** **Calistoga Inn** (1250 Lincoln Ave., Calistoga, 707/942-4101, www.calistogainn .com) might be a bit of an overstatement, but this no-nonsense inn right on the creek in the center of town does offer some of the cheapest, if not the most luxurious, accommodations in town. The 18 rooms are Spartan compared to those of the Victorian inns in the surrounding blocks—no air-conditioning, no televisions, shared bathrooms (but an in-room sink), a dose of street or restaurant noise, and often not enough room to swing a proverbial cat. Still, they are clean, comfortable, even stylish in their minimalist way, and cost from only $69 a night midweek year-round—that's about as cheap as it gets in Calistoga. On summer weekends the price shoots up to $119, making the basic rooms far less of a bargain, though

there is no minimum-stay requirement. One of Calistoga's better restaurants and a microbrewery are right downstairs, making for a night of good food, entertainment, and (hopefully) sleep, all in a charming Victorian package.

A more rustic accommodation option is at the **Mountain Home Ranch** (3400 Mountain Home Ranch Rd., off Petrified Forest Rd., Calistoga, 707/942-6616, www.mountain homeranch.com), up in the hills about a 10-minute drive from Calistoga. This is a down-home family B&B and working ranch with rooms in the main house and separate cottages that are more practical than stylish. The cheapest, with a shared bathroom, squeak in at just under $100 March–November (less during the winter), while regular rooms with private bathrooms are just over $100 during the high season and $80 during the winter. The two- and three-room cabins scattered among the oak trees start at $140 for double occupancy, though there's an additional $20 charge per person for more than two guests. They are fairly cheap and private but a little run-down and by no means luxurious. Part of the charm of the ranch, however, is its peaceful rural setting. Hiking trails lead from the accommodations to the farm and down to a creek—just be sure to get directions because the trail is not obvious. It's a great place for outdoorsy types who don't want the hassles of camping and for families with adventurous kids.

Within walking distance of downtown Calistoga is motel row, the eastern stretch of Lincoln Avenue where the chains and cheapies are located. One of the best of the cheap options is the **Calistoga Village Inn and Spa** (1880 Lincoln Ave., Calistoga, 707/942-0991, www.greatspa.com), which has a variety of rooms starting at $75 midweek and $95 on the weekends. All are decorated in the style of Anywhere, USA, with the ubiquitous flowery synthetic bedspreads and plain furniture, though they also have air-conditioning and pools, two essential extras for hot Calistoga summers. An on-site spa offers 60-minute massages for $165 plus tax.

$100-200

This is the price range into which many of Calistoga's spas and B&Bs fall. One of the best values is the Calistoga institution **Dr. Wilkinson's Hot Springs Resort** (1507 Lincoln Ave., Calistoga, 707/942-4102, www.drwilkinson.com). Best known for its mud baths, the doctor also has 42 basic rooms just a few steps from all the shops and restaurants of Lincoln Avenue. From the outside this looks like a 1950s motel, but the rooms have a little more going for them, with modern and tasteful (if slightly sparse) furnishings, including comfortable beds, air-conditioning, and fairly standard motel levels of equipment. Don't expect luxury at this price, although the charm of the lively resort more than compensates. The cheapest rooms are arranged around the courtyard or pool and cost from $149 midweek during the winter up to $235 on summer weekends. A small neighboring Victorian cottage houses some more expensive rooms that run $279–299, though there's little in the way of additional creature comforts to justify the higher prices.

Also at the low end of the price range is the **EuroSpa and Inn** (1202 Pine St., Calistoga, 707/942-6829, www.eurospa.com), a motel-style establishment on a peaceful residential street just a block from Lincoln Avenue. Rooms in the small bungalows arranged around a central parking lot are fairly tastefully furnished and come with a long list of standard features including whirlpool tubs, air-conditioning, gas stoves (certainly not needed in summer), Internet access, and refrigerators. They start at $140 midweek during the summer and $200 on weekends, and go up to $190 midweek ($260 weekends) for the largest rooms with two beds. Winter rates are generally 20 percent lower. Being on the edge of town, the inn's pool looks onto vineyards and is where the continental breakfast is usually served in summer.

Staying in a little piece of history is cheaper than you might think at the **Brannan Cottage Inn** (109 Wapoo Ave., Calistoga, 707/942-4200, www.brannancottageinn.com). The Victorian cottage with its white picket fence is the only cottage from Sam Brannan's original Calistoga resort that still stands where it was built, on a quiet street just off Calistoga's main drag. It is now on the National Register of Historic Places and contains six rooms furnished in tasteful and restrained Victorian style, all with air-conditioning, private bathrooms, views of the pretty gardens, and a private entrance from the wraparound porch. The smallest room with a four-poster bed costs $185 midweek and $210 weekends. The biggest room, an upstairs mini-suite, costs $230 midweek and $255 weekends. Knock about $30 off those prices during the winter.

One of the biggest old buildings in downtown Calistoga (though that's not saying much) is home to the **Mount View Hotel** (1457 Lincoln Ave., Calistoga, 707/942-6877 or 800/816-6877, www.mountviewhotel.com), which brings a bit of urban style within walking distance of almost everything Calistoga has to offer. The cheapest queen and king rooms ($199 weekdays, $249 weekends during the high season) can be a bit on the small side, but all 29 rooms and suites have a slightly eclectic mix of modern furnishings with Victorian antique and art deco touches harking back to the hotel's 1920s and 1930s heyday. The list of standard features is impressive for Calistoga and stretches to CD players in some rooms and free wireless Internet access. The more expensive suites ($329 midweek, $429 on weekends during the high season) have claw-foot tubs and wet bars, and the pricier suites have balconies overlooking the street. Best of all are the three separate cottages, each with its own small outdoor redwood deck and hot tub, though expect to pay upward of $400 a night during the summer. The hotel used to be home to one of Calistoga's best restaurants, Stomp, but that closed in 2006 and was replaced by a more modest wine and tapas bar called BarVino.

If you're able to get a reservation for one of the four rooms at the **Hotel d'Amici** (1436 Lincoln Ave., Calistoga, 707/942-1007, www.hoteldamici.com), consider yourself lucky. The charming hotel above the Flatiron Grill offers spacious and comfortable junior suites in the heart of Calistoga for very reasonable rates, which makes it very popular. The two smaller suites at the back of the hotel are the cheapest, with official rates starting at $185 per night but often available for $40 less midweek in winter. The larger suites at the front of the building have fireplaces and share a balcony looking over Lincoln Avenue. They start at about $200 off-season and go up to about $300 on summer weekends. All the rooms are decorated in simple, clean style and offer private bathrooms with soaking tubs, down comforters, cable television, and a bottle of Rutherford Grove wine (the Pestoni family owns both the winery and the hotel). A continental breakfast appears as if by magic outside the door every morning, but the lack of on-site staff can make late-night arrivals challenging. Be sure to keep the confirmation letter for the code to get into the hotel.

Over $200

Hats off to the owners of **The Pink Mansion** (1415 Foothill Blvd., Calistoga, 707/942-0558 or 800/238-7465, www.pinkmansion .com) for not even attempting to come up with a clever name for their bright pink Victorian pile, which dates from 1875. The honest name is matched by some unique features that were added by the last person to live there full-time, the eclectic Alma Simic—like the small heated pool in what looks like a Victorian parlor. She's the one who painted the house pink in the 1930s, the color it has been ever since. The woodsy surroundings, quaint but not overly frilly furnishings, and features like claw-foot tubs and air-conditioning make this one of the pricier establishments along this stretch of road, however. The smallest rooms start at $225 a night, and the gargantuan and luxurious Master Suite, dripping with period features and exotic woods, goes for $345. At $245, the Wine Suite is perhaps the best value, with a fireplace, private garden entrance, and separate sitting area.

One of the prettiest spa resorts in Calistoga with among the most tastefully decorated rooms and a giant spring-fed pool is **Indian Springs** (1712 Lincoln Ave., Calistoga, 707/942-4913, www.indianspringscalistoga .com). The cheapest rooms are in the two-story mission-style lodge building, which used to be a neighboring hotel but was bought and renovated by Indian Springs in 2005. They start at $185 midweek in winter, rising to $225 midweek in the summer. Weekend rates are $50–75 higher. The 1940s-era cottages that the resort is best known for are on the pricey side, but are made more palatable by the plank flooring, kitchenettes, and barbecues on their back porches. At one end of the spectrum are Sam's Bungalows, named for Sam Brannan, who set up his Victorian-era resort on the land that Indian Springs now occupies. They start at $285 during the summer (Jul.–Oct.) and on winter weekends but are only $195 midweek in winter. The palm-lined driveway is surrounded by the cozy one- and two-bedroom Palm Row cottages that start at $410 during the summer ($215 midweek in winter) and are probably the best bargains, with their separate sitting area with a sofa-bed. Ask for numbers 16 or 17—they back onto open fields for some extra isolation. Both the Sam's and Palm Row bungalows share front porches and a wall with the neighboring unit, but the more expensive Colbert bungalows are totally detached and can comfortably sleep four. They cost $355 during the summer ($225 midweek in winter).

As its name suggests, the **Cottage Grove Inn** (1711 Lincoln Ave., Calistoga, 707/942-8400 or 800/799-2284, www.cottagegrove .com) is actually 16 private cottages strung along a small road under a pretty grove of old elm trees on the edge of Calistoga. The cottages were built in 1996 and offer some modernity along a strip dominated by older motels. Despite their individual names, all 16 are furnished in a similar Mediterranean style with vaulted ceilings, beautiful antique wood floors, and a long list of luxury features including a double Jacuzzi tub, CD and DVD player, fireplace, and front porch on which to sit, sip, and watch the world go by. The price for such personal space and luxury starts at $295 midweek and $360 on weekends during the summer and runs $250–295 the rest of the year.

Calistoga was chosen to host the first resort created by Solage Hotels, a new brand from the exclusive Auberge Resorts chain that owns the staggeringly expensive Auberge du Soleil down in Rutherford. Opened in 2007, **Solage Calistoga** (755 Silverado Trail, Calistoga, 866/942-7442, www.solagecalistoga.com) is best thought of as a baby Auberge, offering stylish contemporary accommodation for far less money. Being Calistoga, there's also a spa, but this one shares the resort's chic, modern style, although you'll pay extra to use it if you're not a hotel guest. Touted as the Napa Valley first "affordable" resort, Solage is clearly targeted at a younger, more urban crowd than places like Auberge and Meadowood. Fashionable materials like polished concrete, pebbled floors in the steam showers, and plenty of dark wood complement the abundant technology in every room, from flat-screen TVs and CD players to wireless Internet access and iPod docks. A couple of cruiser bikes are parked outside each room; they're not touring quality, but they'll certainly get you into downtown Calistoga, a half mile away, and maybe to a few nearby wineries. Arriving here can be a little underwhelming because the trees planted here have yet to grow large enough to create a feeling of an oasis on what is otherwise a rather featureless patch of land bordering a trailer park, but once you're settled in this self-contained resort it's easy to forget the world outside. "Affordable" is a relative term for the resort, however. It's certainly affordable compared to Auberge du Soleil, but it's the top end of the scale for sleepy Calistoga. The 89 studio-style rooms have winter rates starting at $395–495, rising to $495–595 in summer. Suites will set you back $725–895 depending on the season and day.

Nearby is another member of the exclusive Auberge chain of resorts, this one hidden away on a wooded hillside with super-resort prices to match the glorious setting. The **Calistoga Ranch** (580 Lommel Rd., off Silverado Trail, Calistoga, 707/254-2800, www.calistogaranch.com) is like a collection of exclusive lodges with a country-club atmosphere. Guests are relieved of their cars upon entering and whisked off up the hill to their rooms in golf carts. The accommodations consist of a series of rooms joined by a deck, with every conceivable luxury bell and whistle, from indoor-outdoor fireplaces and showers to plasma-screen TVs and wet bars. The smallest are 600 square feet, about double the average hotel room size and also double the average price around here, starting at $550 in winter and $750 in the peak fall season. Expect to pay more for views of any kind, and for one of the apartment-sized one-bedroom lodges (starting at $790 without hot tub, $890 with). For those who can bear to leave their luxury hideaways, there's the exclusive Bathhouse spa (treatments $75–260), outdoor pool, classes and seminars, and miles of hiking trails around the grounds.

FOOD

Calistoga is often overlooked in the valley's food scene, eclipsed by the culinary destinations of Yountville and St. Helena. High-end restaurants have struggled to survive here, as illustrated by the seemingly endless stream of restaurants that have tried, and failed, to make money in the town's fancy Mount View Hotel. Even the venerable Wappo Bistro, a favorite of many valley residents and frequent visitors, could not survive the 2009 recession. The new Solage resort, which opened in 2007, could bring back some much-needed culinary cachet to this part of the valley as well as some much-needed big spenders. Meanwhile, there remains a diverse selection of mid-priced bistros and grills that should satisfy all but the pickiest diners.

Breakfast

The old-fashioned **Café Sarafornia** (1413 Lincoln Ave., 707/942-0555, www.cafe sarafornia.com, 7 A.M.–2:30 P.M. daily, entrées $6–13), named for the famous verbal blunder by the town's founder, Sam Brannan, is the favorite destination of locals, serving down-home, no-nonsense breakfast and brunch at the bar, booths, or tables. It also sells sandwiches to go ($8–10).

Fine Dining

The latest tenant to try to make a go of it in the Mount View Hotel is **JoLe** (1457 Lincoln Ave., 707/942-5938, www.jolesrestaurant.com, dinner Wed.–Mon., small plates $6–20), where the emphasis is on small plates of locally-sourced, Mediterranean-inspired food in a contemporary setting. Select two or three dishes per person, such as sea scallops and sweetbreads with a parsnip puree or roasted quail with fingerling potatoes and Italian black cabbage, or try the four-course tasting menu. The list of local and international wines is well priced, and all but the most expensive wines are available by the glass and by the Pichet, which is about a half bottle.

Walking past the **⟨** **Calistoga Inn** (1250 Lincoln Ave., 707/942-4101, www.calistogainn.com, dinner and lunch daily, dinner entrées $15–28) on a cool dark winter evening, it's tempting to go into the restaurant just for the cozy rustic atmosphere exuded through its Victorian windows. During the warmer months the draw is the creek-side patio, but all year the cuisine would probably best be described as reliable bistro-style comfort food. Next door to the restaurant is an equally relaxed pub that's home to the **Napa Valley Brewing Company,** founded in 1989 and said to be the first brewery established in the valley since Prohibition. The inn also usually has some sort of evening entertainment, from open mike nights to jazz.

The menu at the **All Seasons Café** (1400 Lincoln Ave., 707/942-9111, lunch 11:30 A.M.–2:30 P.M., dinner 5–9 P.M. Tues.–Sun., dinner entrées $17–27) is, as the name suggests, inspired by local produce currently in season, and the sophisticated dishes attract food lovers from all over the valley, though recent reports suggest quality has slipped a bit. The small wine list at the table is just a sampling of the hundreds of labels available in the wine store

at the back of the main restaurant. Buy a bottle to take home, or pay the $15 corkage fee to drink it at the table, saving plenty on the usual markup for wines.

Bosko's Trattoria (1364 Lincoln Ave., 707/942-9088, www.boskos.com, 11:30 A.M.–10 P.M. daily, dinner entrées $10–18) is another Calistoga institution with a reputation for its Italian comfort food as solid as the stone building it calls home. The simple salads, some of the valley's best pastas, and wood-fired pizzas served in the homey surroundings all cost less than $16, and there's a good selection of delicious, well-stuffed panini sandwiches for less than $9.

At the eastern edge of town is the trendy **Solbar** (755 Silverado Trail, 707/226-0850, breakfast, lunch, and dinner daily, lounge menu available until 11 P.M., dinner entrées $18–30, small plates $11–15), part of the luxurious Solage Calistoga resort. It was already an increasingly popular outdoor dining destination up-valley after opening in 2007, and that was before it was awarded a Michelin star in 2009. The sleek and contemporary indoor dining room is a fine backdrop for the innovative cuisine with Asian and Latin influences, like grilled salmon with coconut rice, bok choy, and pickled ginger, or the chili-rubbed pork-cheek tacos, but the spacious outdoor patio with its floating fireplace is the biggest draw in summer and fall. With a couple of appetizers and a bottle of wine on a warm summer night there's no better place for some up-valley people-watching and stargazing.

Grills

Brannan's Grill (1374 Lincoln Ave., 707/942-2233, lunch and dinner daily, dinner entrées $19–35) brought the big-time Napa food scene right to the heart of Calistoga when it opened in 1998, though its reputation is said to have slipped a bit in recent years. White tablecloths, the 19th-century dark-wood bar, and the giant murals of the valley's past lend an air of elegance to accompany the pricey all-American menu, which usually includes two or three steaks. The wine list offers a smattering of choices from Oregon, Europe, and Australia alongside Napa and Sonoma regulars. Lunch or brunch ($7–12) is a cheaper way to experience the sumptuous interior.

A few doors down the road is Brannan's sister restaurant, **Flatiron Grill** (1440 Lincoln Ave., 707/942-1220, lunch weekends, dinner daily, dinner entrées $12–26), which is an altogether cheaper dining option. In terms of both the food and decor it's a bit like a baby Brannan's, serving slightly less sophisticated food from the grill in stylish, but not quite as elegant, surroundings.

Mexican

Traditional Mexican food can be found at the spacious **Pacifico Restaurante Mexicano** (1237 Lincoln Ave., 707/942-4400, lunch and dinner daily, dinner entrées $13–18), including some regional specialties and weekend brunches. Those who prefer more of a hole-in-the-wall Mexican experience should walk to the other end of Lincoln Avenue to **Puerto Vallarta** (1473 Lincoln Ave., 707/942-6563, lunch and dinner until 9 P.M. daily, $5–10), right next to the supermarket. The traditional food comes with equally traditional plastic surroundings both inside and out on the patio leading to the entrance.

The roomy, exposed-brick interior of the **Hydro Bar & Grill** (1403 Lincoln Ave., 707/942-9777, dinner entrées $9–15) hints at its other life as a live-music venue, but it's also a place to get quick meals at the bar, ranging from traditional burgers to Mexican-themed small plates ($4–10), together with plenty of microbrews. It stays open well after most other restaurants have closed.

Picnic Supplies

Although Calistoga's Palisades Market has long since closed, The Depot is now home to its offspring, the **Palisades Deli Café** (1458 Lincoln Ave., 707/942-0145, 7 A.M.–6 P.M. daily). In addition to coffee and other café staples, it sells a range of cold and hot sandwiches to eat in or take out ($6–9), including a decadent tri-tip sandwich. Just across the road is the less glamorous **Cal Mart** supermarket (1491 Lincoln Ave., 707/942-4545, 7 A.M.–9 P.M. daily), which sells even cheaper deli sandwiches, though it has a more limited selection.

Nicola's Delicatessan (1369 Lincoln Ave., breakfast and lunch daily) in the middle of the town also offers a good range of typical deli sandwiches ($5–8) that can be ordered to go. Another alternative is to drop in to **Café Sarafornia** (1413 Lincoln Ave., 707/942-0555) a block away to pick up one of its sandwiches, or for a gourmet alternative you could go to **Bosko's Trattoria** (1364 Lincoln Ave., 707/942-9088) and order a panini to go.

Farmers Market

The **Calistoga Farmers Market** (Lincoln Ave. at Washington St.), which sells crafts as well as produce, is held 8:30 A.M.–noon on Saturday June–September.

INFORMATION AND SERVICES

The **Calistoga Chamber of Commerce** (1133 Washington St., 707/942-6333, www.calistogafun.com, 9 A.M.–5 P.M. daily) has just about every brochure and flyer for the Calistoga area and much of the rest of the Napa Valley, as well as helpful staff on hand to answer any questions.

SOUTHERN SONOMA

Southern Sonoma is one of those places that doctors should send the hypertensive, because there's something about the place that makes your blood pressure drop. The Sonoma Valley and neighboring Carneros region are just so laid-back and slow-going that even finding parking is unnervingly easy, and sitting in what passes as rush-hour traffic here will barely get you tapping your fingers.

Apparently it has always been a pretty good, stress-free life in these parts. Mother Nature might mix things up a bit with the occasional fire or earthquake, but she also provides hot springs, redwood forests, burbling streams, fertile soils, and a friendly climate. In terms of climate, scenery, and growing conditions, the Sonoma Valley is a mini Napa Valley, but it has been spared the same level of development by some favorable rolls of the historical dice.

In a sense, southern Sonoma is fairly close to paradise: a place where wine, history, scenery, and some of the best California produce combine in an area small enough to tour in a day or two. A visitor can spend the morning sipping splendid wine and be strolling through historic Victorian splendor by the afternoon, or might traverse a muddy mountain one hour and spend the next relaxing in a spa covered in therapeutic mud. There are few other parts of the Wine County as compact yet packed with opportunity.

Hundreds of years ago, these same natural attributes attracted numerous Native American tribes, who lived peacefully side by side without the turf battles common elsewhere. Even

© SONOMA COUNTY TOURISM BUREAU

HIGHLIGHTS

◖ **Gundlach Bundschu Winery:** Witness Shakespeare or Mozart performed on a summer day at the outdoor amphitheater of this historic winery (page 139).

◖ **Benziger Family Winery:** See Benziger's biodynamic vineyards from a tractor-drawn tram, the most entertaining tour in the valley (page 144).

◖ **Chateau St. Jean:** It's worth it to pay a little extra for the reserve tasting and learn about wine while relaxing on the patio overlooking the valley (page 149).

◖ **Sonoma Plaza:** Spend an afternoon exploring the eclectic shops and historic sites of the notable Sonoma Plaza (page 154).

◖ **Sonoma Mission:** The last Californian mission has been immaculately restored, and its museum sheds light on the important role it played in the region's history (page 155).

◖ **Sugarloaf Ridge State Park:** Meander down the short nature trail or hike to the top of Bald Mountain for the best valley views (page 160).

◖ **Jack London State Historic Park:** Scenic hiking trails surround the former residence of the valley's prolific author and adventurer, Jack London (page 161).

◖ **Domaine Carneros:** Take a private tour and learn how champagne is made, all with a glass of bubbly in hand (page 176).

◖ **Cline Cellars:** Enter an oasis of green at this historic winery next to a natural spring and explore all of California's missions in miniature (page 181).

◖ **The di Rosa Preserve:** Enter a wonderland of art and leave the Wine Country behind (page 185).

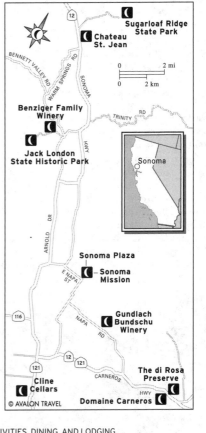

LOOK FOR ◖ TO FIND RECOMMENDED SIGHTS, ACTIVITIES, DINING, AND LODGING.

author Jack London sensed something intoxicating in the air. He relocated from Oakland to put down deep roots in the Sonoma Valley, transforming himself from working-class hero to gentleman farmer and landowner. The main characters in his 1913 novel *Valley of the Moon* spend months wandering up and down California in search of their nirvana, the Sonoma Valley.

The lucky locals have worked hard against the odds to keep their valley and flatlands so inviting. In the 1960s, they fought off a plan developed by car-crazed California to drive a freeway down the middle of Sonoma Valley. Instead it was built through the middle of Santa Rosa to the west. While fame and freeways brought the heaving masses to Napa and northern Sonoma, the valley became the land that development forgot.

By 1980 there was a grand total of two sets of traffic lights—and there aren't many more now. One of the busiest intersections in the valley, on the south side of Sonoma plaza, is still very politely controlled by four simple stop signs. The valley's modern custodians are still a potent force, even defending a few local chickens in the downtown Sonoma threatened with resettlement. Such is the passion here to keep the "slow" in this place the locals call Slownoma.

Can the valley keep its identity amid modern population and development pressures? It's trying hard, but is swimming against the tide of tourism. Wineries and hotels are being mopped up by bigger and bigger conglomerates. The succulent local food is transforming into ever more expensive "cuisine." An average family home in the valley now costs more than $1.5 million. Visit quickly before Napa hops over the mountains, pushes up the prices, and ends the mellow fun.

In the long term, there's more hope for Carneros, simply because there is no "there" there. The vineyards that are slowly covering any remaining pastureland (that is, the land that's not already underwater) are effectively spiking future development. Chances are that nothing much will change here

anytime soon—except perhaps that rush-hour traffic on the two-lane roads may worsen as more people visit or move to the Napa and Sonoma Valleys.

PLANNING YOUR TIME

The Sonoma Valley and Carneros are two of the easiest parts of Wine Country to visit, each having just one main road running its entire length. A visit to Carneros can be slightly harder to plan due to the lack of major towns, but it's easy enough to stop there for a few hours on the way to or from Sonoma and Napa.

Within the 17-mile-long Sonoma Valley, the wineries, shops, and hotels are generally centered around the towns of **Glen Ellen** and neighboring **Kenwood,** and Sonoma itself. Without a well-planned strategy, it can be time-consuming to try to visit wineries at both the northern and southern ends of the valley, especially when the Sonoma Highway (Highway 12) slows down with northbound rush-hour traffic in the afternoon.

If you do find yourself traveling slower than you like on Highway 12, it's worth heading a few miles west at Glen Ellen or Boyes Hot Springs to pick up Arnold Drive, an alternative north-south route in the valley. It runs mainly through residential areas, but sticking to the 30 mph speed limit on this quiet road might be more relaxing than being tailgated on Highway 12. It runs right down to the junction with Highway 121 in **Carneros.**

It can easily take a full day to visit about five wineries around Sonoma and Kenwood, or in Carneros, and still have enough time for lunch without getting indigestion. An alternative strategy might be to pick four or five wineries that specialize in a particular wine. Or spend a full day exploring the shops and historic sights of Sonoma while tasting wine at several dedicated tasting rooms on the Sonoma Plaza. There are also four wineries just outside downtown.

If you do plan to visit wineries throughout the valley, get an early start. Their busiest times are mid–late afternoon, especially for the wineries around Kenwood that most visitors only get to toward the end of the day. Most wineries are open at 10 A.M. (a few from 11 A.M.) and close between 4:30 and 6 P.M., depending on the season.

Wineries along the Carneros Highway (Highway 121) are generally clustered at the eastern and western ends of Carneros. Those at the western end include Viansa, Gloria Ferrer, and Cline, on the way from San Francisco to Sonoma. Those farther east are more spread out and generally lie between the road to Sonoma (Napa Road or Highway 12) and the city of Napa. They include Artesa, Mahoney, and Bouchaine.

For some reason very few wineries have any sizable trees in their parking lots, preferring instead to plant trees that either look stunted or have minimal leaf cover. Consequently there's usually no shade, and for the nine months of the year that the sun shines, parked cars quickly heat up to the temperature of an oven. Take a cooler if you plan a picnic or want to prevent that $100 bottle of wine from trying to become vinegar.

Compared to the Napa Valley, wine tasting in the Sonoma Valley is refreshingly cheap. Most wineries charge a tasting fee of either $5 or $10, perhaps more for tasting the more expensive reserve wines. It's a refreshing change from the Napa Valley, where $25 tasting experiences have become the norm. As in many other parts of the Wine Country, the tasting fee can sometimes be recouped when you buy one or more bottles of wine.

GETTING THERE

A century ago there were more ways to get to Sonoma than there are today—by ferry, train, stagecoach, automobile, or plane. The train is long gone, ferries come nowhere near, the tiny local airports have no scheduled services, and there is no direct bus service to Sonoma, just some local connections to Santa Rosa and Petaluma—all of which leaves the car with a monopoly.

Getting there by car, however, is straightforward. From San Francisco the most traveled route is via U.S. 101, Highway 37,

and Highway 121, which leads to the heart of Carneros and to the junction of Highway 12 to Sonoma and the Sonoma Valley. The drive from the bridge to Sonoma takes just under an hour, longer if you have to navigate San Francisco local traffic.

To avoid Sonoma and go straight to Glen Ellen, go straight on Arnold Drive at the junction and gas station about five miles after joining Highway 121. It is a slower road but avoids heavy traffic and leads to the heart of Glen Ellen.

Other routes to the area from the north and east include Highway 12 east into the valley from U.S. 101 at Santa Rosa, or Highway 37 west from I-80 at Vallejo to the junction of Highway 121. Be warned that Highway 121 through Carneros is infamous for nasty accidents due to its unexpected bends and dips, dawdling tourists, and high volume of commuter (in other words, speeding) traffic.

GETTING AROUND

Once again, the car is how most people get around Carneros and the Sonoma Valley. The only real alternative to the tiring car-to-winery-to-car relay is a tiring bike ride. Rent a **bicycle** in either Glen Ellen or Sonoma and stick to the wineries in those areas to avoid long distances, summer heat, and tipsy drivers. Cruising around the empty flatlands of Carneros on two wheels is a rewarding way to get off the beaten track and visit less-crowded wineries, but only for those with the stamina for long distances.

Some hotels and B&Bs have their own bicycles for rent. Otherwise, two shops rent bikes and supply tour maps. **Sonoma Valley Cyclery** (20093 Broadway, Sonoma, 707/935-3377, 10 A.M.–6 P.M. Mon.–Sat., 10 A.M.–4 P.M. Sun.) rents bikes for $25 per day. For $10 more it offers a self-guided tour from the shop to local Sonoma wineries or a 35-mile roundtrip trek to some Carneros wineries. The area around Sonoma is perfect for exploring by bike. If you're staying downtown, park the car, rent a bike, and visit the historic downtown sites as well as the

Ravenswood, Buena Vista, and Gundlach Bundschu wineries that are within a mile or two of the plaza.

There is no physical address for the **Goodtime Touring Company** (707/938-0453 or 888/525-0453), but it will deliver bikes to your hotel. It rents basic bikes for $25 per day, road bikes for $40, and tandems for $45. The closest thing to biking luxury (short of having someone else pedal) is Goodtime's half-day guided tour of Sonoma-area or Kenwood-area wineries, which includes a gourmet lunch and wine-tasting fees. Those tours are $135 and start at 10:30 A.M.

Sonoma Valley

They must feed the ducks of Sonoma Plaza something special to make them stick around the car-choked plaza rather than flying a few miles north to the serenity of the valley, even with the nice new plaza ponds completed in 2006. Getting out of Sonoma, as fascinating and historic as it is, is the only way to really get an idea of what valley residents are fighting to preserve.

The road north out of Sonoma passes fast-food outlets and a strip mall, about as close to urban sprawl as there is. In keeping with the valley's laid-back nature, it's a spaced-out, relaxed sort of sprawl linking Sonoma and three spring towns: Boyes Hot Springs, Fetters Hot Springs, and Agua Caliente, all of which look like they could do with a rejuvenating spa treatment themselves.

The towns end abruptly, and the serene valley lies ahead. Plum, walnut, and peach orchards once shared the valley with cows that must have thought they'd died and gone to heaven to be grazing here. Now the mighty vine has taken over the valley floor. There's really little else but green things along the Sonoma Highway, except the loose-knit community of **Kenwood** (with the valley's cheapest gas) and, at the border of Santa Rosa, the retirement community of Oakmont.

Slightly off the main road southeast of Kenwood, the town of **Glen Ellen** is a Wine Country town with plenty of fancy restaurants and inns hidden in the surrounding woods yet still with the valley's nice laid-back vibe. It's truly a one-street town, with a curious dogleg halfway down the main street that is the real center of it all—not that there's all that much happening. It has managed to remain quaint without succumbing to the fake frills that so many other old towns in the United States get wrapped in. One of the biggest buildings is an auto shop, a sign that real life still takes place in this part of the valley.

The Wines

The volcanic soils of the hot mountainsides and the rich alluvial plains of the valley floor make Sonoma an ideal place to grow a plethora of grape varietals, a fact the missionaries and immigrants of the 1800s quickly discovered. The valley doesn't have quite the number of different growing conditions and soils of the larger Napa Valley, but winemakers maintain that its wines can be just as good.

In many ways the Sonoma Valley and Napa Valley are more alike than different. Both have productive mountain growing regions, both are proportionally similar, face the same direction, and are affected by the same wind and rain patterns. The fact that Sonoma's early head start in winemaking in the mid-1800s petered out by the early 1900s seems to have had more to do with chance and bad business decisions by the early pioneers like Agoston Haraszthy. The larger Napa Valley wineries established in the late 1800s gained more commercial traction, perhaps due to the greater availability of land. Once a critical mass of winemaking had been reached, there was no turning back.

Climate-wise, the Sonoma Valley has three distinct appellations. The **Sonoma Valley** AVA is the largest and includes some or all of

SOUTHERN SONOMA

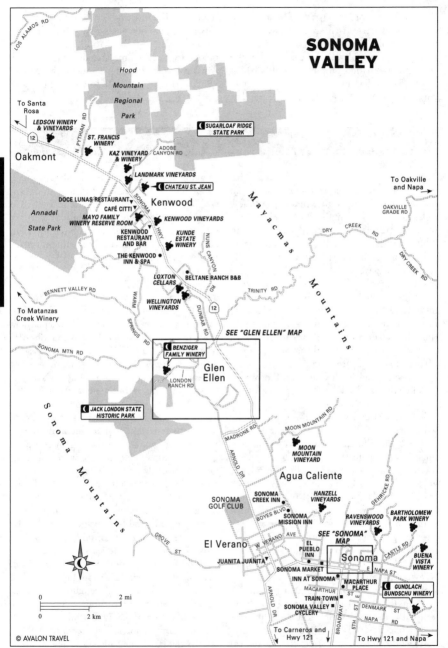

SONOMA VALLEY

LOS ALAMOS RD

Hood Mountain Regional Park

To Santa Rosa

LEDSON WINERY & VINEYARDS

ST. FRANCIS WINERY

N PYTHIAN RD

KAZ VINEYARD & WINERY

Oakmont

SUGARLOAF RIDGE STATE PARK

ADOBE CANYON RD

LANDMARK VINEYARDS

CHATEAU ST. JEAN

To Oakville and Napa

OAKVILLE GRADE RD

DOCE LUNAS RESTAURANT

CAFÉ CITTI

MAYO FAMILY WINERY RESERVE ROOM

Kenwood

KENWOOD VINEYARDS

Annadel State Park

KENWOOD RESTAURANT AND BAR

KUNDE ESTATE WINERY

THE KENWOOD INN & SPA

M a y a c m a s   M o u n t a i n s

DRY   CREEK   RD

DRY CREEK RD

LOXTON CELLARS

BELTANE RANCH B&B

NUNS CANYON RD

BENNETT VALLEY RD

WELLINGTON VINEYARDS

TRINITY RD

To Matanzas Creek Winery

WARM   SPRINGS   RD

DUNBAR RD

12

SONOMA MTN RD

SEE "GLEN ELLEN" MAP

BENZIGER FAMILY WINERY

Glen Ellen

LONDON RANCH RD

S o n o m a

JACK LONDON STATE HISTORIC PARK

MADRONE RD

MOON MOUNTAIN RD

M o u n t a i n s

MOON MOUNTAIN VINEYARD

ARNOLD DR

Agua Caliente

GEHRICKE RD

SONOMA GOLF CLUB

SONOMA CREEK INN

HANZELL VINEYARDS

RAVENSWOOD VINEYARDS

BARTHOLOMEW PARK WINERY

BOYES BLVD

SONOMA MISSION INN

GROVE   ST

W VERANO   AVE

SEE "SONOMA" MAP

CASTLE RD

El Verano

EL PUEBLO INN

Sonoma

BUENA VISTA WINERY

JUANITA JUANITA

SONOMA MARKET

E   NAPA ST

INN AT SONOMA

MACARTHUR PLACE

GUNDLACH BUNDSCHU WINERY

MACARTHUR   ST

TRAIN TOWN

SONOMA VALLEY CYCLERY

BROADWAY

5TH   ST   E

DENMARK   ST

NAPA   RD

ARNOLD DR

To Carneros and Hwy 121

To Hwy 121 and Napa

0   2 mi

0   2 km

© AVALON TRAVEL

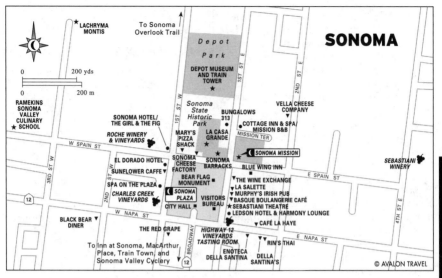

the other two. It stretches from the top of the valley near Santa Rosa all the way down to the bay, bordered by 3,000-foot-high mountains on each side and encompassing 116,000 acres of land and about 13,000 acres of vineyards (compare that to the Napa Valley's 35,000 acres of vineyards).

The valley acts like a giant funnel, channeling cooler air (and sometimes fog) up from the bay, leaving the mountainsides to bask in warm sunshine. Zinfandel loves the higher, hotter elevations, while cabernet and merlot ripen well on hillsides and the warmer north end of the valley. Pinot noir, chardonnay, and other white varietals prefer the slightly cooler valley floor, especially farther south toward Carneros.

The 800 acres of vineyards in the cooler and rockier **Sonoma Mountain** appellation just up the hill from Glen Ellen vary widely depending on their exposure, but the region is known mostly for its cabernet, although chardonnay, pinot noir, and other white varietals are also grown here.

The newest appellation is **Bennett Valley,** created in 2003, which stretches northeast from the Sonoma Mountains toward Santa Rosa and only just overlaps with Sonoma

Valley. Its 700 acres of vineyards are primarily planted with merlot and chardonnay and generally have rocky, volcanic-based soils. A gap in the low mountains west of the Bennett Valley lets ocean air and fog through and keeps growing conditions cool compared to the Sonoma Valley and the mountains.

WINE-TASTING
Sonoma Wineries
BARTHOLOMEW PARK WINERY
There seems to be a history competition between Bart Park (1000 Vineyard Ln., Sonoma, 707/935-9511, www.bartpark.com, 11 A.M.–4:30 P.M. daily, tasting $5), as it's known, and the neighboring Buena Vista Winery. Both have links to the Sonoma wine pioneer Agoston Haraszthy, and both are equally entitled to brag about it since they share what used to be Haraszthy's land. While Buena Vista has the original press house and caves from Haraszthy's winery, Bart Park has the site of Haraszthy's Romanesque home (a reproduction now stands there and is open on Wednesdays and weekends) and most of the vineyard land. Neither of the two wine-making operations that exist today has been operating very long.

Since Haraszthy's day, Bart Park has been home to a cat-loving widower, a home for "delinquent women," a hospital, and finally the home of the Bartholomew family, which bought it in the 1940s and soon started making wine again under Haraszthy's defunct Buena Vista label. They later sold the winery and the Buena Vista name, keeping a large chunk of the vineyards and creating the Hacienda Winery, which they operated until their deaths. In 1994 it became the Bartholomew Park Winery and is now owned by the nearby Gundlach Bundschu Winery and operated as a boutique sibling.

Bart Park's colorful history is detailed in a small but packed museum housed in the old hospital building, along with the small tasting room where you can taste the estate chardonnay, cabernet sauvignon, and merlot, as well as several wines from other vineyards around Sonoma. Only 4,000 cases are produced a year, though for such limited-production wines, they're not too expensive.

The real charm of Bart Park, however, has nothing to do with history or wine. The winery sits in some glorious open space, including what remains of the formal gardens of an old mansion that was burned down (reportedly by the delinquent women) and the small garden of the reproduction Haraszthy home. You can wander freely throughout as if it's your own private garden and find great shaded picnic spots with sweeping views of the valley. Miles of hiking trails start from the winery and wind up the nearby hillsides. Where they start is not obvious, however, so ask someone in the winery for directions.

BUENA VISTA WINERY

Buena Vista (18000 Old Winery Rd., Sonoma, 800/926-1266, www.buenavistacarneros.com, 10 a.m.–5 p.m., tasting $10) boasts that it was California's first premium winery, but the claim sounds more grandiose than it actually is. Today's Buena Vista sits on some of the land used by the original Buena Vista Winery, established by Agoston Haraszthy in 1858. Among the old winery structures that remain are the original hand-dug caves (now unsafe

BATTLE OF THE CHICKENS

They are sometimes there, but officially they're not. The saga of the Sonoma Plaza chickens perfectly illustrates Sonoma's enduring small-town quirkiness in the face of the creeping invasion of expensive hotels, restaurants, and other newcomers.

At one point there were more than 100 chickens scratching out a living in the plaza, and they had plenty of local fans who appreciated the hick character they brought to the city. Letters to local newspapers told newcomers to "go home" if they didn't like the chickens. A city plan to cull the birds and keep their numbers to a more manageable 40 was met with squawks of protest from supporters.

"You'd see them crossing on the crosswalk. I think they learned from watching people," a reporter at the Sonoma Index-Tribune newspaper recalls. There was even one that regularly laid eggs in a plaza crafts store.

In 2000, however, the roosters were implicated in several pecking and scratching attacks on small children, marking the beginning of the end for the chicken population. In May that year, citing safety and liability issues, the city council voted to evict the chickens from the plaza and resettle them at local farms, a move that prompted a "roost-in" protest by 100 chicken lovers in front of City Hall.

There was an attempt to reintroduce some friendlier breeds of chicken later that year, together with an "egg patrol" to ensure their numbers didn't get out of hand, but four of them quickly fell foul of local dogs, and the rest were rounded up and whisked off to safety.

Now there are officially no chickens, just the plaza's friendly duck population to occasionally hold up traffic. But a small group of unofficial chickens can sometimes be seen scratching around City Hall, especially at night, perhaps trying to undermine the council that sent them packing years ago.

and closed), the original champagne cellar, and the old stone press-house, which is today the visitors center and helps the site qualify as a California Historic Landmark.

The original Buena Vista Winery did not survive Prohibition, however, and the current winery is a modern incarnation. One could also argue that Haraszthy's original Buena Vista Winery wasn't actually the first premium winery in California. It all depends on the definition of premium.

The winery has been owned by various multinational conglomerates for decades (the current owner is Ascentia Wine Estates) and is a thoroughly commercial operation (as it was in Haraszthy's day), producing half a million cases of wine a year and attracting an estimated 120,000 visitors. Despite the fact that it gets very crowded in the summer, the leafy complex of stone buildings is still worth visiting for its historical importance. The plentiful hillside picnic tables are well shaded, though none of them offer much privacy on summer weekends when the winery tends to be swamped by busloads of visitors.

Although Buena Vista is in the Sonoma Valley, its 1,000 acres of vineyards are now about seven miles south in the Carneros area, apart from a few acres used for demonstrations and tours. The mid-priced Carneros estate wines include pinot noir, cabernet, merlot, chardonnay, and a newly released syrah that are all pretty good value for money. The flagship Ramal Vineyard wines are available only at the winery and include cabernet, pinot noir, and chardonnay.

C GUNDLACH BUNDSCHU WINERY

Not many wineries in California can boast that they won awards for their wines almost 100 years ago, but GunBun (2000 Denmark St., Sonoma, 707/938-5277, www.gunbun. com, 11 A.M.–4:30 P.M. daily, tasting $5–10), as it's known, is one of them. The 19 Gundlach Bundschu wines entered into the 1915 Panama-Pacific International Exhibition in San Francisco all won medals, and the winery today focuses on squeezing the highest

quality wines possible out of its estate vineyards without buying grapes from anywhere else. The other aspect of the estate that makes this winery worth visiting are the ample outdoor picnicking and entertainment opportunities in a peaceful part of the valley.

Grapes have been grown in the winery's Rhinefarm vineyard since they were first planted in 1858 by Bavarian-born Jacob Gundlach, a pioneer of the early California wine industry who is credited with planting Sonoma County's first riesling vines. He was joined in the business by his son-in-law, Charles Bundschu, in 1868, and the next generation of Gundlachs and Bundschus established the Gundlach Bundschu Wine Company in the early 1900s. Wine production was stopped during Prohibition and was restarted in 1973 by Jim Bundschu, Gundlach's great-great-grandson, who runs the winery today with his son Jeff.

Today the 300 acres of Rhinefarm vineyards principally grow cabernet sauvignon, merlot, pinot noir, chardonnay, and gewürztraminer, together with some zinfandel, tempranillo, and a few other minor varietals. The winery's emphasis is on red bordeaux- and burgundy-style wines, and the cabernets and merlots tend to have plenty of tannic backbone. Some of the cheaper wines are available only from the winery and include the nonvintage Bearitage red blend and the unusual Kleinberger, an aromatic, fruity German wine.

The tasting room is housed in one of the original stone winery buildings, which can feel cramped when full of visitors—but the fun atmosphere makes it more bearable. Browse the historical memorabilia, including old wine posters from the 1800s. A short walk away is the 430-foot-long hillside cave, which is often part of the seasonal tours offered once daily (Thurs.–Mon., $20). The focus of the tours changes with the seasons, however, so check to see what you'll be seeing when you make a reservation. In winter it might be the cave and in summer the wine-making facilities. In all cases, the price includes a sit-down tasting. During the summer months, on Friday or

THE HUNGARIAN CONNECTION

Although German and Italian families founded some of the oldest wineries still operating in this part of Sonoma, it was a Hungarian immigrant named **Agoston Haraszthy** who became the area's first big commercial winemaker, and in doing so he helped change the face of the Californian wine industry.

Within a decade of arriving in the state, he had established the pioneering Buena Vista Winery in the Sonoma Valley and was producing some of the best wines in the United States. A decade later he was gone. While his contribution to California's wine industry was important, it was not quite as important as might be suggested by some of the accolades heaped upon him over the centuries.

Haraszthy is often called the Father of California Viticulture, for example, despite the fact that by the time he started bottling wine at Buena Vista the state was already producing about 240,000 gallons of the stuff. He is also sometimes credited with introducing the ubiquitous zinfandel grape to California, but there is some evidence that it arrived in the state even before he did.

One thing that is safe to say is that Haraszthy helped introduce European grapes and European-style commercial wine production to an industry still dependent on its missionary roots. He also had an entrepreneur's sense of self-promotion, which might explain his larger-than-life image.

His wine odyssey started in Wisconsin, of all places. He arrived there from Hungary and helped create what is now Sauk City, but the harsh Wisconsin winter quickly killed the vines he tried to cultivate. In 1849, like modern-day snowbirds, he headed west to the kinder, gentler climate of Southern California.

In San Diego, Haraszthy entered politics as a state legislator, and a combination of political and agricultural aspirations gradually drew him north. The 560-acre plot of land he bought in the Sonoma Valley in 1856 was quickly planted with many European grape varietals, and soon the Buena Vista Winery, with its hand-dug caves, boasted the largest vineyard in the United States and was producing award-winning wines.

He also reportedly helped plant vineyards for other Sonoma families that became (and still are) big names in the wine industry themselves, including Krug, Gundlach, and Bundschu.

By the 1860s, Haraszthy was combining his political and viticultural interests, promoting Californian wine across the country and getting state funding to travel around Europe to study wine-making techniques.

He returned in 1862 with thousands of vine cuttings collected in almost every European country, from Spain to Turkey. Among them are believed to be the cabernet sauvignon, pinot noir, sauvignon blanc, riesling, and semillon varieties that have become mainstays of the California wine industry.

Exactly what he brought back is open to debate, however, since cataloguing and naming conventions in those days were unreliable. Some of those well-known grapes might also have stealthily arrived in California long before, and many others that he brought back never took hold.

Haraszthy's downfall was as sudden as his success. In 1863, facing financial problems, he sold his wine business to the Buena Vista Viticultural Society, a conglomerate in which he held almost half the shares, and took a management position. But within three years he was accused of mismanagement and Enron-style fraud in an attempt to create the biggest winemaker in California; in 1866 he quit.

What happened after this is still a bit of a mystery. Haraszthy left California in 1868 to run a sugar plantation in Nicaragua, but he disappeared in the rain forest and is believed to have been killed by a crocodile.

It's hard not to raise a glass to an immigrant who, in the space of 25 years, had been the co-founder of a Wisconsin town, a businessman, a politician, and a crocodile's meal. But as you raise that glass of mass-produced Sonoma Valley red wine, also consider that it might not taste quite the same (or be as cheap) if not for Agoston Haraszthy.

Saturday mornings, GunBun also offers a tour of the estate vineyards in a quirky former Swiss military vehicle called a Pinzgauer, followed by a tasting of some of the best Estate wines.

GunBun also provides a shady patio, a picnicking area at the top of Towles' Hill overlooking the valley, and even a grassy amphitheater where you can see performances of Shakespeare or Mozart during the summer. Overall it has one of the nicest outdoor spaces of any winery in the valley. Check the website for event schedules or just pack a picnic before visiting.

SEBASTIANI VINEYARDS & WINERY

A visit to Sonoma would not be complete without a trip to the Sebastiani winery (389 4th St. E., Sonoma, 707/933-3230 or 800/888-5532, ext. 3230, www.sebastiani.com, 10 A.M.–5 P.M. daily, tasting $10–15), founded by one of the city's most important benefactors and philanthropists, Samuele Sebastiani. It's the only large winery within walking distance of the Sonoma Plaza and has both wines and a history worth exploring.

Samuele Sebastiani arrived in Sonoma from northern Italy in 1895 and worked in local stone quarries before gathering enough money to buy an old winery in 1904. The business grew rapidly and was one of only 10 wineries that stayed open during Prohibition, when it made sacramental and medicinal wines as well as a fortune for Samuele. He spent money lavishly around town, building the Sebastiani Theater on the plaza and countless other commercial and residential buildings, most of which survive today in some form or another.

Samuele's son August took over the business in 1934 and transformed Sebastiani into a huge wine empire before his death in 1980. The winery was then managed by August's son, Sam Sebastiani, but a family dispute forced him out in the 1980s, and he went on to establish the Viansa winery in Carneros with his wife (this fact is airbrushed out of the official winery history). For many years the Sebastiani winery was run by August's daughter, Mary Ann Sebastiani Cuneo, but in late 2008 the family ties came to an end with the sale of the winery and most of its vineyards to the Foley Wine Group.

Sebastiani pioneered the sale of cheap and cheerful half-gallon bottles of wine in the 1970s and developed a slew of additional wine brands in the 1980s, eventually producing a mind-boggling 8 million cases (96 million bottles) of wine per year. With the new millennium came a new strategy to focus only on premium Sebastiani-labeled wines, and all the other brands were sold off in 2001, reducing production to less than 200,000 cases.

The flagship wine is the Cherryblock cabernet sauvignon, sourced from an old vineyard near the winery, but the best value is another proprietary wine called Secolo, a bordeaux blend first made in 2001 to celebrate the winery's 100th anniversary. Both regularly garner 90-plus-point ratings from wine critics, but the Secolo is half the price of the $75 Cherryblock. Most of the other wines come from vineyards throughout Sonoma County and are reds, including merlot, pinot noir, zinfandel, and cabernet, together with a barbera that reflects Sebastiani's Italian heritage. One standout is the Alexander Valley cabernet sauvignon. The only white offered, in both vineyard-designate and Sonoma County versions, is a chardonnay. Several wines are available exclusively at the winery, including a Napa Valley cabernet, the Italian-style red blend Dolcino Rosso, and Eye of the Swan, a pinot noir–based wine with a pale pink color that reminded August Sebastiani (who was an avid amateur ornithologist) of the eyes of a black swan.

The cool, vaulted visitors center is chock-full of Italian-themed gifts but is on a scale that can feel slightly impersonal, with more of a corporate than a family atmosphere. It's worth taking one of the three daily historical tours of the cellars and old stone buildings to see some of the original wine-making equipment from the early 1900s and learn more about the history of the winery and its family. Alternatively you can hop on a trolley and see some of the oldest family vineyards together with key Sebastiani buildings in Sonoma. Complimentary tours are given daily at 11 A.M., 1 P.M., and 3 P.M.

SOUTHERN SONOMA

© SONOMA COUNTY TOURISM BUREAU

Ravenswood Vineyards

Other tours and seminars are available by appointment.

RAVENSWOOD VINEYARDS

"To err is human but to zin is divine" is just one of the many droll mottos you'll find at the tasting room of this fun and friendly zinfandel specialist a few blocks north of downtown Sonoma. To use a wine industry pun, visiting here is a barrel of laughs; you're as likely to leave with a zin-inspired bumper sticker as a bottle of the jammy wine.

Bordeaux-style wines were the original inspiration of founder, Joel Peterson, but in the 1970s he discovered the joys of zinfandel and instead of heading down the path of Old World subtlety he ended up in the new world of powerhouse reds. Ravenswood (18701 Gehricke Rd., Sonoma, 707/933-2332 or 888/669-4679, www.ravenswood-wine.com, 10 A.M.–4:30 P.M. daily, tasting $10–15) now makes about a half million cases of wine a year, some three-quarters of which is accounted for by more than a dozen different zinfandels.

If you're a zinfandel fan or just after a bit of wine-tasting fun, this will be heaven. The vineyard-designate zins at Ravenswood exhibit the full range of flavors and styles that the humble zinfandel is capable of producing, from the full-throttle fruitiness of Dry Creek and Amador County zins to the more subtle spiciness of cooler-climate versions from Mendocino and the Russian River Valley. In case none of those help you see the light, there's always the Zen of Zin, a zinfandel-dominated field blend that might help you on your journey of discovery.

Despite being known for zinfandel, Ravenswood also makes some remarkably good Rhône-style wines with the same rustic appeal as the zinfandels, from the peppery Sonoma County carignane to the bold, syrah-dominated blend called Icon. The most expensive wines are the vineyard designates, which include plenty of zinfandels but also cabernet sauvignon, merlot, and the flagship Pickberry meritage, a lush yet elegant blend of cabernet sauvignon, merlot, and cabernet franc from the slopes of Sonoma

Mountain and so named because the vineyard owner's kids used to pick blackberries there.

It's worth opting for the pricier tasting, which includes many of the best single-vineyard wines. If you're up early enough, the daily tour at 10:30 A.M. ($15) is an entertaining start to the day and usually includes tasting of barrel samples. As Ravenswood grew and was eventually bought by Constellation Brands in 2001, the winemaking operations were moved to a more modern facility further south, but the rustic old stone winery with its patios, picnic tables, and pretty gardens still has plenty of atmosphere today, and Joel Peterson is still very much in charge.

Plaza Tasting Rooms
ROCHE WINERY & VINEYARDS

A homey 1940s craftsman-style cottage just off the Sonoma Plaza with flower-filled gardens and street-front outdoor tasting patio is the new tasting location of the Carneros-based winery Roche Winery & Vineyards (122 W. Spain St., Sonoma, 707/935-7115, www .rochewinery.com, 11 A.M.–6:30 P.M. daily, free tasting). The winery opened its tasting room here in 2009 after the family sold its existing winery in Carneros and embarked on the development of a new facility on the 500-acre estate it retained in the area. The wines are all sourced from the estate vineyards and include several pinot noirs and some nice chardonnays (including a unique late-harvest version) as well as syrah and merlot. Taste them indoors or outdoors while sitting at a patio table watching the street life go by.

HIGHWAY 12 VINEYARDS & WINERY

At the southeast corner of the Plaza next to the Ledson Hotel is the tasting room for the latest venture of Michael Sebastiani, member of Sonoma's famed Sebastiani winemaking clan and former winemaker at Viansa, Highway 12 Vineyards & Winery (498 1st St. E., 707/939-1012, www.highway12winery .com, 10:30 A.M.–5:30 P.M. daily). Along with partners Paul Giusto and Doug Offenbacher, Sebastiani has helped propel Highway

12 from humble beginnings in 2003 to a producer of several thousand cases of highly regarded and well-priced wines, dominated by cabernet blends and chardonnays. As the name implies, Highway 12 makes wines from vineyards along the highway that runs through the Sonoma Valley and Carneros. The bulk of the wines are sourced from just three vineyards, including Serres Ranch at the southern end of the Sonoma valley and the famed Sangiacomo Family vineyard on the border of Carneros. Highlights include both the chardonnays, which are made in a plush, full-bodied style. Among the reds, the most interesting wines are the blends, from the traditional Bordeaux blend to the La Piazza blend of sangiovese, primitivo, and zinfandel.

CHARLES CREEK VINEYARDS

Outstanding chardonnays, and a large cow sculpture made entirely of wine corks, are the specialties of Charles Creek Vineyards (483 1st St. W., 707/935-3848, www.charlescreek.com, 11 A.M.–6 P.M. daily, tasting $5) at its small storefront tasting room and gallery space on the west side of the plaza. The winery was established in 2002 by Bill Brinton, a descendent of tractor pioneer John Deere, after many years as a grape grower on his Sonoma Mountain estate. It now makes about 12,000 cases of mainly chardonnay and cabernet sauvignon from vineyards across Sonoma and Napa, including the renowned Sangiacomo Vineyard just south of Sonoma and Dutton Ranch in the Russian River Valley. Fruit from both features strongly in many of the chardonnays, including the bright and tangy Las Patolitas ("little ducks") and the mellower La Sorpresa ("the surprise"). The flagship chardonnay is Las Abuelas ("the grandmothers"), a lightly oaked and intensely flavored wine sourced from various Carneros vineyards with far more spring in its step than its name would suggest. The several cabernets are also subtly different blends from famous-name vineyards all over Napa, many of them in mountain appellations that give the wines intensity and earthiness. The En Casa label of wines, which includes cabernet and a syrah, offer the best vales at under $25 a bottle, but none of the wines cost more than $40.

Wineries by Appointment

Many of the wineries open to the public in the Sonoma Valley are those of big producers that can attract big crowds. For a more personal (and free) experience of some valley wines, call ahead to visit one of these historic, appointment-only wineries on the eastern mountain slopes of the valley.

MOON MOUNTAIN VINEYARD

Moon Mountain Vineyard (1700 Moon Mountain Dr., Sonoma, 707/996-5870, tour and tasting $20) is high up in the Mayacamas Mountains on a site that has been planted with vines since the 1800s. The winery's current 74 acres of organic vineyards grow bordeaux varietals for its cabernet sauvignon, sauvignon blanc, and cabernet franc wines, as well as grapes for its dense, concentrated zinfandel. The drive up to the winery is pretty, and if you have the time you can hike up to the top of the estate for some spectacular views of the valley.

HANZELL VINEYARDS

Hanzell Vineyards (18596 Lomita Ave., Sonoma, 707/996-3860), just north of Sonoma, was established in 1948 by industrialist James D. Zellerbach and is today renowned for its luxury-priced but limited-production chardonnays and pinot noirs that regularly score over 90 points in reviews. The secret to its success are its very own Hanzell clones of both pinot and chardonnay. In fact, the pinot noir vineyard on the mountain slopes is said to be the oldest in California. A new winery was recently opened, enabling Hanzell to double its existing production to 7,000 cases a year from its 42 acres of estate vineyards. The tour and tasting fee is pricey for Sonoma ($45) but buys a very personalized experience, including a jaunt into the vineyards, a tour of the winery and caves, and a sit-down tasting.

Glen Ellen Wineries
◖ BENZIGER FAMILY WINERY

With vines poking out from the hillside grass, free-range cockerels crowing, and its collection of rustic wooden buildings hidden among the trees, the mountainside Benziger Family winery (1883 London Ranch Rd., Glen Ellen, 888/490-2739, www.benziger .com, 10 A.M.–5 P.M. daily, regular tasting $10, reserves and estate wines $15) seems like an old family farm rather than a commercial wine business. In some ways it is. The Benziger family came from New York in the 1980s to this former hippie ranch and transformed it into the valley's only biodynamic winery while managing to keep three generations of Benzigers happy on its 800 acres. Some 30 Benziger folk now call this land their home, many of them working in the winery.

Biodynamic farming principles go beyond organic. Instead of simply ensuring no harmful chemicals pollute the land, biodynamic principles attempt to recreate the natural interactions among all aspects of the environment, from earth to sky. The overgrown look of the vineyards is deliberate (they are cover crops, in biodynamic terms), as are the 30 acres of woods and wetlands. The colorful Insectory is a garden in the middle of the vineyards planted with native flowers to attract dynamic pest-fighting insects. Cows and sheep help mow the grasses and fertilize the land, but the more entertaining (and nonnative) peacocks had to be fenced in because they were playing havoc with the vines. Benziger, along with a handful of Mendocino wineries, was ahead of the curve, and biodynamic principles are now catching on across Wine Country.

All the wildlife and more can be seen on an entertaining 45-minute tractor-drawn tram tour that winds through the vineyards, giving information on vines, local nature, and biodynamic principles before delivering visitors to the wine-making facility and hillside storage cave. It's the best tour in the valley for the money (only $15) and culminates with a basic tasting back at the winery. Tours are offered four times daily, but the tram isn't big, so in

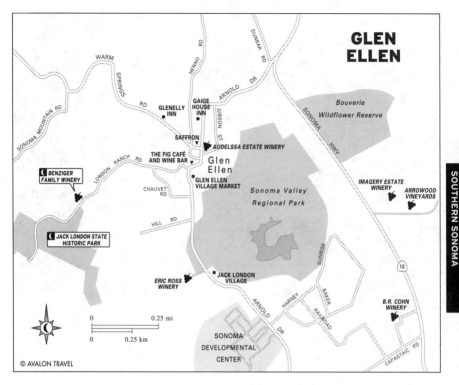

GLEN ELLEN

(Map labels)
WARM SPRINGS RD
SONOMA MOUNTAIN RD
HENNO RD
DUNBAR RD
ARNOLD DR
GIBSON ST
GLENELLY INN
GAIGE HOUSE INN
SAFFRON
THE FIG CAFÉ AND WINE BAR
AUDELSSA ESTATE WINERY
Glen Ellen
BENZIGER FAMILY WINERY
LONDON RANCH RD
CHAUVET RD
GLEN ELLEN VILLAGE MARKET
Bouverie Wildflower Reserve
SONOMA HWY
Sonoma Valley Regional Park
IMAGERY ESTATE WINERY
ARROWOOD VINEYARDS
HILL RD
JACK LONDON STATE HISTORIC PARK
ERIC ROSS WINERY
JACK LONDON VILLAGE
SUNRISE
ARNOLD DR
HARVEY
BAKER
RAILROAD
12
B.R. COHN WINERY
0   0.25 mi
0   0.25 km
SONOMA DEVELOPMENTAL CENTER
CAPASTAIC RD
© AVALON TRAVEL

SOUTHERN SONOMA

the summer you should buy a same-day ticket as far in advance as possible. Call the winery for the seasonal schedule. If you only want to taste the wines, the best option is the $15 reserve tasting that includes many of the best biodynamic wines.

Almost two-thirds of the 45 biodynamic acres at Benziger is planted with cabernet sauvignon, taking advantage of the natural sun trap created by the surrounding hillsides. Other Bordeaux varietals are also planted, plus some zinfandel and sauvignon blanc. The Sonoma Mountain estate wines are biodynamic and are priced from about $25 and up. The Family and Reserve ranges of wines, together with some more pricey vineyard designates, are made with grapes from vineyards all over Sonoma and Northern California, including a couple of interesting clone-specific pinot noirs from Los Carneros. Most can be tried in the spacious but sometimes crowded tasting room. Benziger's Imagery brand of small-lot wines, with its unique label art, has its own home in the nearby Imagery Winery.

B. R. COHN WINERY

If you're a cabernet lover, then you have something in common with Bruce Cohn, founder and owner of B. R. Cohn winery (15000 Sonoma Hwy., Glen Ellen, 800/330-4064, www.brcohn.com, 10 A.M.–5 P.M. Mon.–Thurs., 10 A.M.–6 P.M. Fri.–Sun., tours by appointment, tasting $10–15). He is so fond of cabernet that he has planted all 100 acres on a former dairy with cabernet sauvignon. His Olive Hill vineyard has its own microclimate warmed by an underground geothermal aquifer (the same one that feeds the valley's hot springs) and shielded from cool air by Sonoma Mountain.

Cohn used to sell his grapes to other wineries

Benziger vineyards

© SONOMA COUNTY TOURISM BUREAU

in the valley, but started bottling under his own label after an Olive Hill vineyard wine produced by the Gundlach Bundschu Winery was chosen to accompany President Reagan on a trip to China in the 1980s. In the early days, Cohn received advice and help from famed winemaker Charlie Wagner at Napa's Caymus Winery. The rest, as they say, is history.

Cohn buys chardonnay from Carneros vineyards together with merlot, zinfandel, and syrah from elsewhere in Sonoma for some of his other wines, including an interesting syrah-cabernet blend that incorporates some Olive Hill vineyard fruit. Also look out for Moose, a huge black bulldog-Labrador cross, in the winery and on the label of a bold red blend.

The olive trees surrounding the buildings and lining the driveway give the vineyard not only its name but also some award-winning olive oil that is available in the tasting room. The French picholine olive trees are relatively young by olive standards—only 140 years old—and the eight acres around the winery form the largest picholine orchard in the valley.

The estate oil is 100 percent picholine, and various blended oils are also available, together with some unusual vinegars, such as raspberry champagne vinegar and cabernet vinegar. Many can be tasted at the winery.

As you walk from the parking lot up to the tasting room, you might also hear Doobie Brothers songs wafting over the patio, giving away Bruce Cohn's other profession as the manager of the Doobies since the early 1970s and some other bands in the 1980s, including Bruce Hornsby and Night Ranger. The music connection continues to this day—the winery hosts an annual fall music festival charity event featuring members of the Doobies plus countless other rock and country musicians.

IMAGERY ESTATE WINERY

The world's largest collection of wine label art by some well-known contemporary artists (including Sol LeWitt and Terry Winters) is one reason to visit Imagery (14335 Sonoma Hwy., Glen Ellen, 707/935-4515 or 877/550-4278, www.imagerywinery.com, 10 A.M.–4:30 P.M.

daily fall–spring, 10 A.M.–4:30 P.M. Mon.–Fri., 10 A.M.–5:30 P.M. Sat.–Sun. summer, tasting $10). Another is the wide variety of small-lot wines that are available only at the winery itself. Imagery was established as a boutique offshoot of the Benziger Family Winery in the 1980s when art labels were catching on and winemaker Joe Benziger met the art director at nearby Sonoma State University, Bob Nugent. That relationship helped spawn the Imagery brand and the unique labels.

Artists have free rein apart from two rules: There can be no nudity on the label (for legal reasons), and every label has to include an image, however abstract or small, of the Greek Parthenon, a small replica of which stands on a hillside at parent winery Benziger and was evidently the site of some wild parties before the Benziger family bought the ranch in the 1980s. The Parthenon is also now the symbol for Imagery, and a Greek theme seems to have been worked into almost every aspect of the winery.

Nugent, who has painted some of the labels himself, is now curator of the collection, charged with finding new up-and-coming artists. Benziger focuses on creating unusual wines from vineyards on the 20-acre estate and other vineyards throughout Sonoma, including Ash Creek, which is the highest-altitude vineyard in Sonoma County. Imagery produces fewer than 8,000 cases of wine per year. The Artist Series includes sangiovese, barbera, malbec, petite sirah, viognier, and a white burgundy, while the Vineyard Collection includes more traditional wines like cabernet sauvignon, merlot, and zinfandel. Most are priced $20–40.

MATANZAS CREEK WINERY

It's worth the 10-minute drive up scenic Bennett Valley Road (off Warm Springs Road) from Glen Ellen to visit Matanzas Creek (6097 Bennett Valley Rd., Santa Rosa, 707/528-6464 or 800/590-6464, www.matanzascreek.com, 10 A.M.–4:30 P.M. daily, tasting $5), especially in May and June when the lavender is in full bloom and is quite a sight (and smell) to behold. The winery is in Sonoma's newest appellation,

nestled at the foot of the hills surrounded by woods, flower-filled gardens, and the largest planting of lavender in California. Like the fields outside, the tasting room is filled with the scent of lavender in the form of soaps, oils, cut stems, and all sort of other aromatic products for pampering and cooking.

The former dairy became a winery in 1977, although the current barnlike winery building was built in 1985. Former owners Sandra and Bill MacIver led the application to get the Bennett Valley classified as its own appellation, and in December 2003 it became the 13th AVA in Sonoma County, encompassing only four wineries (including Matanzas Creek) and 850 acres of vines.

The winery's own 280 acres of Bennett Valley vineyards are planted with chardonnay, merlot, cabernet sauvignon, sauvignon blanc, and syrah, all benefiting from cooling influences of the ocean air that never really makes it over the mountains into the Sonoma Valley. More grapes are now brought in from elsewhere in Sonoma and Mendocino Counties as the new owner, Kendall-Jackson, ramps up production to 60,000 cases per year. All the estate's grape varietals are represented in the wines, but the winery is particularly well known for its chardonnays and limited-production merlots.

Tours are available by appointment twice a day, and printed guides to the surrounding flower and lavender gardens are available in the tasting room. Although no food is sold at the winery, this is a great place for a picnic accompanied by a bottle of Matanzas rosé or sauvignon blanc. The lavender is harvested each year right before the winery holds its annual Wine & Lavender event, usually on the last Saturday in June. Tickets for the wine, food, and lavender party are $75 and should be booked in advance.

AUDELSSA ESTATE WINERY

The former tasting room of Navillus Birney was revamped in 2007 to reflect the winery's merger the previous year with another local family winery, Audelssa Estate. The small downtown space now resembles more of an upscale café, with neat rows of tables and a tasting menu that includes morsels of food as well as wine.

The Audelssa Estate Winery (13647 Arnold Dr., Glen Ellen, 707/933-8514, www.audelssa .com, 11 A.M.–5 P.M. Thurs.–Mon., tasting $15) is a small family-run operation started in the late 1990s that now makes a modest 3,000 cases of wine per year, sourced predominantly from its highly regarded mountain vineyards on the other side of the Sonoma Valley. Since the early 1990s the Schaefer family has farmed a steep 120-acre vineyard known as Mountain Terraces near the top of the Mayacamas Mountains on the eastern side of Sonoma Valley, and the fruit has become much sought-after as some of the best in Sonoma.

Like many growers with quality vineyards, the family eventually chose to make its own wines from a small portion of the vineyard. The result was an impressive collection of accolades from national wine critics for its cabernet sauvignon, syrah-based blends, and a bordeaux blend called Summit, all exhibiting the intensity that's unique to mountain-grown fruit. Originally called Schaefer Sonoma Vineyards, the winery was forced to change its name to avoid confusion with Napa Valley's Schafer Vineyards. Dan Schaefer came up with the word Audelssa, using parts of his three daughters' names.

There are plenty of tasting options, but be aware that the tasting room is closed midweek and is small, so there might be standing room only on busy days. Despite those drawbacks and a tasting fee on the high side for this part of the valley, the intimate atmosphere and outstanding wines make it a worthwhile stop.

ERIC ROSS WINERY

You can almost imagine author Jack London himself relaxing with a book in the cozy tasting room of the Eric Ross winery (14300 Arnold Dr., Glen Ellen, 707/939-8525, www.ericross .com, 11 A.M.–5 P.M. Thurs.–Mon., tasting $5), across the street from the Jack London Village complex. The bright red–painted rustic building throngs with visitors on summer weekends, but during the week you'll likely have the comfy leather sofa inside to yourself. On winter days the fireplace makes it all the more homey; just imagine a few artfully crammed bookcases, and this could be Jack London's living room.

The metal-topped corner tasting bar almost seems like an afterthought, but it's where all the action is to be found. The Eric Ross winery was created in the mid-1990s by two photographers, Eric Luse and John Story Ross, both of whom had come to know wine and the Wine Country very well through their assignments on the two main San Francisco daily newspapers. Their previous careers explain the abundance of photographs on display in the tasting room. The winery itself is located in Marin, but this is the winery's only tasting room and the place to sample the range of pinot noirs, chardonnays, zinfandels, and other wines, all sourced from Russian River Valley vineyards.

The pinots in particular are worth trying, and there are usually two or three available to taste, each from a different vineyard and each with a distinct character featuring classic Russian River complexity and smoothness. The syrah and zinfandel also offer some of the same cool-climate elegance and a refreshing alternative to more exuberant examples from the warmer Sonoma Valley at other wineries. One of the more unique offerings is the white Rhône-style Marsanne-Roussanne, a full-bodied white that balances wonderful aromatics with a refreshing acidity. The winery recently added a nice cabernet sauvignon sourced from a valley vineyard near Glen Ellen to its portfolio. All the wines are made in limited quantities; total production at Eric Ross is only about 3,000 cases per year.

LOXTON CELLARS

Although it's officially an appointment-only winery, visiting Loxton Cellars (11466 Dunbar Rd., Glen Ellen, 707/935-7221, www.loxtoncellars .com, 11 A.M.–5 P.M. daily, free tasting) is usually as easy as checking to see if the sign is out on the road at the end of the driveway. If it is, then someone's home to pour some wines on the makeshift tasting bar set up in the corner of the spotless, warehouse-style barrel room. Visiting here is as unpretentious an experience as you can have in a valley that is already pretty laid-back.

Owner and winemaker Chris Loxton used to be assistant winemaker at neighboring Wellington Vineyards and had plenty of experience before that in his native Australia, so he knows Sonoma well and knows how to make distinctive red wines. He focuses mainly on syrah and zinfandel made from both Sonoma Valley and Russian River Valley grapes, including a shiraz from Australian vine clones, an earthy syrah from hillside fruit, a robust syrah port, and a dry rosé syrah. More recently he added cabernet sauvignon and a cabernet-shiraz blend—a sure sign that there's an Aussie at work.

Loxton owns no vineyards, instead working through lease agreements with established growers and helping them manage the vineyards. With just 2,000 cases made each year, the small-lot wines from quality vineyards offer outstanding value for money with most costing $20–30 a bottle. Call ahead and arrange a personal tour of the vineyards and winery from Chris himself to gain more insight into the wines and his winemaking style.

Kenwood Area Wineries
KUNDE ESTATE WINERY

The Kunde Estate (9825 Sonoma Hwy., Kenwood, 707/833-5501, www.kunde.com, 10:30 A.M.–4:30 P.M. daily, tasting $10–20) sprawls across 2,000 acres of valley land, making it the largest family-owned winery in the west and providing enough space for a whopping 800 acres of estate vineyards where 20 varietals of grape are grown from the valley floor up to elevations of 1,000 feet on the terraced hillsides. In fact, the winery has enough vineyards, and varied enough growing conditions, to make only estate wines and still have enough fruit left to sell to neighboring wineries.

Grapes have been grown here by the Kunde family since 1904, when Louis Kunde acquired the historic Wildwood Vineyard, which was first planted in 1879 by some of the valley's wine pioneers. There is still a patch of zinfandel vines

dating from 1882 happily growing here, grapes from which go into the limited-production Century Vines zinfandel.

The current incarnation of the winery was built in the late 1980s to resemble a giant version of an old dairy barn that stood nearby and is run by the fourth wine-making generation of the family. Kunde makes fine examples of just about every wine that can be made from Sonoma Valley grapes, though it is perhaps best known for its zinfandel, cabernet sauvignon, and vineyard-designate chardonnays. It also makes a few unusual wines among its bargain-priced Tasting Room series, available only at the winery, including a fruity gewürztraminer, a strawberry-laced grenache rosé (both perfect picnic wines), and an intriguing blend of cabernet and zinfandel called Bob's Red. There are plenty of good picnic wines to complements an alfresco lunch in shady lakeside picnic area.

The spacious tasting room rarely seems crowded, but the best tasting option here is in the Kinneybrook Room, where you can taste the more expensive Grand Estate reserve wines along with a small cheese plate while relaxing in one of the leather club chairs. Free tours of the aging caves stretching half a mile under the hillside behind the winery are offered on the hour Friday–Sunday. Groups of six or more can also go on one of many appointment-only tours to see parts of the huge estate. Contact the winery for more information.

◖ CHATEAU ST. JEAN

If you were to build your own personal château in the Sonoma Valley, you couldn't pick a much better location than this. A long driveway through the vineyards leads up to Chateau St. Jean (8555 Sonoma Hwy., Kenwood, 707/833-4134, www.chateaustjean.com, 10 A.M.–5 P.M. daily, tasting $10–15), a white turreted mansion at the foot of the mountains. The walk from the parking lot to the tasting rooms leads through a manicured formal garden, and on the other side of the reserve tasting room is a patio and expanse of lawn overlooking the valley and its vineyards.

The winery itself was once a private residence

SOUTHERN SONOMA

surrounded by walnut groves, built as a palatial summer home by a family of Michigan mining barons in the 1920s. The château was acquired by a group of investors who opened it as a winery in 1975. The winery pioneered the production of vineyard-designate wines in Sonoma in the 1970s and now has almost a dozen in its portfolio, including several pinot noirs and chardonnays, a pinot blanc, a fumé blanc, and a syrah. Grapes for all the wines are sourced from vineyards all over Sonoma County, including the Russian River Valley and Los Carneros, but 80 acres of estate vineyards around the château are planted principally with chardonnay.

Although St. Jean is best known for its white wines (which include multiple chardonnays, viognier, gewürztraminer, pinot blanc, riesling, and fumé blanc), it also has its share of big reds, including Cinq Cepages, a Bordeaux-style red blend of five varietals—some grown in a tiny vineyard perched on a steep slope above the winery—that is always rated highly by critics. Other red wines are Sonoma County cabernet sauvignon, merlot, and pinot noir, as well as some powerhouse reserve and estate versions priced $50–100. The Reserve malbec in particular is worth trying just for its heady aroma of blueberries. Tasting-room staff love to boast that this is the only California winery (as of 2006) that has had five wines in the *Wine Spectator* Top 100 in one year (1996).

The spacious main tasting room has a small deli and countless Wine Country gifts, but it's worth spending a little extra to taste wines in the more comfortable and intimate reserve tasting room, especially in summer when its sun-drenched patios and petanque courts are open. Upstairs from the reserve tasting room, there's a small gallery featuring the work of local artists. An educational Terroir Tour gives some insight into growing grapes, making wine, and then tasting wine. St. Jean also offers VIP reserve tasting in a private room and an hour-long sensory analysis class—just some of the additional educational courses and tours offered.

KAZ VINEYARD & WINERY
This is the one winery in the valley where

The crazy world of Kaz Winery lurks in this modest barn.

it's guaranteed that the owner will be pouring the wine in the tasting room. Kaz (a.k.a. Richard Kasmier) is also as close as you'll get to a renegade winemaker, producing just 1,000 cases per year of bizarrely named wine blends and ports, some dominated by relatively rare grapes for California, such as the red alicante bouschet and lenoir, which is a varietal more commonly found in Texas or in tiny amounts in some California blends. The wines will not be to everyone's taste, but it's unlikely that you won't find at least one that tickles your fancy.

Kaz also grows syrah, cabernet franc, chardonnay, and dechaunac in his 2.5-acre organic vineyard (he once grew an unimaginable 15 varietals on five acres) and buys other grapes from neighboring wineries. A winery motto, "No harm in experimenting," ensures that many blends will change each year, though some are pretty much constant, including the ZAM (zinfandel, alicante, mourvèdre), Sangiofranc (sangiovese and cabernet franc), and Mainliner (100 percent lenoir). For added interest, all the wine labels are vintage photos hand-colored by Kaz's wife, Sandi.

Kaz Vineyard (233 Adobe Canyon Rd., Kenwood, 707/833-2536, www.kazwinery.com, 11 A.M.–5 P.M. Fri.–Mon. or by appointment, tasting $5) is open Friday–Monday only and is four driveways up the road from Landmark Vineyards on the left (drive slowly because it's easy to miss). The tiny tasting room doubles as a barrel storage area, and it doesn't take many people to fill it up, but Kaz keeps the crowd entertained and you'll quickly get to know everyone around you. The unmarked door at the back of the tasting room opens onto a small garden with just enough room for a private picnic.

LANDMARK VINEYARDS

Landmark (101 Adobe Canyon Rd., Kenwood, 707/833-1144, www.landmarkwine.com, 10 A.M.–4:30 P.M. daily, tasting $5–15) was one of the first California wineries to make only chardonnay, though it has since expanded to pinot noir and most recently syrah, all made using grapes from the 11 acres of

SOUTHERN SONOMA

Enjoy a game of bocce ball while sipping wine at Landmark winery.

estate vineyards and others sourced from all over California.

Chardonnay still accounts for the majority of the 25,000-case production, and the wines range in price from the $28 Overlook chardonnay up to the most expensive Lorenzo Reserve and Damaris Reserve, named after the winery's founder, Damaris Deere Ethridge, the great-granddaughter of John Deere (inventor of the steel plow and a name now associated with tractors). Another well-regarded Sonoma County chardonnay producer, Charles Creek Vineyards, also has some Deere family heritage. There must be something in the genes.

The red wines at Landmark include the single-vineyard Kanzler pinot, the Grand Detour (named after John Deere's home town in Michigan), and the limited-production Steel Plough syrah, named for John Deer's first farming invention. Like the chardonnays, all three reds are generally well-liked by critics.

A large mural behind the tasting bar livens up an otherwise drab room, but the best aspects of the Spanish-style buildings are outside. The large shady courtyard outside the tasting room leads to a fountain and gardens with a view straight over the vineyards to Sugarloaf Mountain in the distance. A few picnic tables are available, as is a free boccie ball court to test how straight you can throw after a few glasses of wine.

MAYO FAMILY WINERY RESERVE ROOM

Forgo a picnic and instead try to get a lunch-time reservation at this tasting room with a resident chef. Seven wines are served with seven different small appetizers exquisitely prepared by the chef and served at tables in the small, intimate Mayo Family winery reserve tasting room (9200 Sonoma Hwy., Kenwood, 707/833-5504, 10:30 A.M.–6:30 P.M. daily). Instead of traditional wine tasting with crackers or perhaps breadsticks at the bar, this is a thoroughly gourmet affair with seasonal morsels such as seared scallops with oyster mushrooms and applesauce-braised short ribs paired with red and white wines from Mayo's Russian River and Sonoma Valley vineyards. The "meal" ends with a delectable dessert paired with Mayo's zinfandel port. The $35 tasting fee is easier to swallow considering the food and wine education you'll receive, and especially if you treat the tasting as a lunch substitute.

Mayo Family Winery was established in the early 1990s by Diane and Henry Mayo and is now run by their son, Jeff. From the beginning, the Mayo's goal was to make small quantities of vineyard-specific wines. They own small vineyards in the Sonoma Valley and Russian River Valley and over the years have sourced fruit from other vineyards in those two areas. Since their current winery opened in 2000, production has ramped up to about 10,000 cases of about 30 different wines, although not all will be available year-round. Most of the production is sold direct to consumers, so reviews in magazines are rare, but the success of the winery is a testament to the popularity of its wines.

Mayo is perhaps best known for its zinfandels and Rhône-varietal wines like syrah and carignane sourced from Russian River Valley vineyards, but it also makes some nice

Bordeaux-style red blends and several white wines sourced from nearby vineyards, including a gewürztraminer from the Kunde estate that has a hint of sweetness. If the Reserve Room tasting is too much to bite off, many of the Mayo wines can be sampled in a more traditional environment at the winery's main tasting room (13101 Arnold Dr., 707/938-9401, 10:30 A.M.–6:30 P.M. daily, tasting $6–12), which is open later than most, just down the road near Glen Ellen.

LEDSON WINERY & VINEYARDS

It's worth driving almost all the way to the top of the valley just to see "the Castle," as it's known to locals—a description that at first was meant more in a derogatory sense but has now been embraced by the Ledson winery (7335 Sonoma Hwy., Kenwood, 707/537-3810, www.ledson.com, 10 A.M.–5 P.M. daily, tasting $15–25). This is about as ostentatious as the Sonoma Valley gets, and it's still a far cry from the palaces (and actual castles) in the Napa Valley.

Steve Ledson made his money in the local contracting business and set about building this 16,000-square-foot Gothic dream home to get back to his childhood roots of farming and ranching in the Sonoma Valley (and it's literally a dream home—Ledson says its design came to him in dreams). By the time it was finished in 1999 he had decided that it was attracting a little too much attention for his family, so he turned it into a winery and hospitality property and continued to live near Sonoma, where he has another vineyard.

Enter through the grand front door, pass the sweeping staircase, polished oak accents, and marble fireplaces, and you almost feel like you're walking onto the set of some Wine Country soap opera. There are no fewer than six tasting bars in various rooms, together with a small marketplace stocked with wines and a pungent selection of cheeses, sandwiches, and other picnic supplies. You can picnic on the grounds in the shade of a giant oak tree, although there's limited space and you can only eat food bought at the winery itself.

SOUTHERN SONOMA

© SONOMA COUNTY TOURISM BUREAU

Ledson Winery, known locally as "the Castle"

The house is surrounded by 17 acres of merlot vineyards, but Ledson also owns about 20 acres of zinfandel near his home just south of Sonoma and thousands of acres in Mendocino County, where he grows chardonnay, pinot noir, and syrah. In addition, he sources grapes from all over the Wine Country to make a huge portfolio of red and white wines, all of which are available only from the winery and the exclusive Ledson Hotel on Sonoma Plaza. There's no need to bother selling them anywhere else, because the entire 35,000-case output of the winery is sold directly to visitors and the winery's club members.

Almost every grape varietal is represented in the portfolio, including the estate merlot; cabernet sauvignon from Northern Sonoma; chardonnay, pinot grigio, and pinot noir from the Russian River Valley; Rhône varietals from Sonoma and Mendocino; and the unusual orange muscat from the Monterey area that's worth tasting. It's a case of pick your poison—there's bound to be a wine to please everyone—but the highlights include

the estate merlot, both the Russian River and Carneros chardonnays, and the red meritage blends.

ST. FRANCIS WINERY & VINEYARDS

Named to honor the Franciscan monks who are widely credited with planting California's first wine grapes, St. Francis (100 Pythian Rd., Santa Rosa, 800/543-7713, www.stfranciswine.com, 10 A.M.–5 P.M. daily, tasting $10–15) is a place for red-wine lovers, and particularly merlot fans. Merlot grapes have been grown here since the winery was established in 1971, and St. Francis was one of the first California wineries to bottle merlot as a stand-alone wine rather than as part of a Bordeaux-style blend.

The winery has expanded from the original, historic 100-acre Behler Ranch vineyard and now has more than 600 acres of vineyards in the Sonoma Valley and Russian River Valley that supply grapes for its chardonnay, cabernet, merlot, zinfandel, and syrah wines. They include the Nun's Canyon vineyard high up in the Mayacamas Mountains, which produces some of St. Francis's best cabernets and merlots. All the reserve wines are from single vineyards, while the cheaper Sonoma County wines include grapes from multiple vineyards.

The spacious tasting room is one of the best-designed in the valley, not surprising considering the mission-style winery complex was opened in 2001, making it one of the newer rooms in the valley. Windows running the length of the room look out onto the vineyards and mountains, and you can easily escape into the garden if it gets too crowded.

Tasting the reserve wines costs $15, though for $20 more the winery throws in some food at the appointment-only food and wine pairing session with appetizers from the winery's chef, Todd Muir.

FAMILY WINERIES

Perhaps the cheapest wine-induced buzz in the Sonoma Valley can be had at Family Wineries (9380 Sonoma Hwy., Kenwood, 888/433-6555, www.familywines.com, 10:30 A.M.–5 P.M. daily, tasting $5), a cooperative tasting room on a busy Kenwood corner. Four wineries are featured, and there are usually plenty of tastes for the regular tasting fee, including a very varied selection of pinot noirs and chardonnays. All the wineries represented are small family-owned affairs, and on weekends some of the winemakers themselves often do the pouring.

David Noyes Wines is a producer of mainly pinot noir, chardonnay, and zinfandel sourced from some well-known vineyards in the Dry Creek and Russian River Valleys and made using spare production capacity at some equally well-known wineries. In some respects it's a virtual winery, except David clearly knows his vines and wines, having started his winemaking career at Ridge Vineyards and having helped the Kunde family establish the Kunde Estate Winery in the late 1980s. He started his own label in 2001 and now also works as part of the wine-making team at nearby Wellington Vineyards.

The Macrae Family Winery also specializes in Russian River Valley pinot noir and chardonnay, but also has some full-throttle reds in its portfolio, including merlot and cabernet sauvignon sourced from the Stagecoach Vineyard on the slopes of Napa Valley's Atlas Peak appellation. S. L. Cellars is a small producer of pinot noir and chardonnay sourced from the Carneros and Russian River Valley regions, but it also makes a Brut sparkling wine as well as a Syrah from Dry Creek Valley. Another winery represented at the tasting room is Collier Falls Vineyards, which is based in the Dry Creek Valley and produces a few thousand cases a year of zinfandel, cabernet sauvignon, primitivo, and petite sirah from its estate vineyards.

SIGHTS

Sonoma is not the only Wine Country town with a rich history stretching back hundreds of years, but it holds the distinction of being ground zero both for the turbulent events that led to the creation of the state of California in the 1840s and for the beginnings of California's booming wine industry. Many of the most important buildings from that active period in the mid-1800s are still standing, making Sonoma one of the most historically alive Wine Country towns in Northern California.

◖ Sonoma Plaza

Sonoma Plaza (Spain St. between 2nd St. and 4th St., 707/996-1090), the eight-acre square that over the past 180 years has seen religious uprisings, revolution, fires, and now large numbers of tourists, is at the center of the region's history and is the heart and soul of the valley. Fascinating shops and boutiques selling everything from designer clothes to African handicrafts fill the streets around the plaza, along with galleries and some of the valley's best restaurants, many of them in historic buildings that date from the 1800s.

Sonoma Plaza was created in 1835 by General Vallejo for troop maneuvers and for a long time was little more than a muddy patch of grazing land surrounded by a picket fence. It is now the largest town square in California, and despite being thoroughly gentrified and besieged by cars, still maintains a sense of grace that only somewhere with such a rich history can pull off.

© PHILIP GOLDSMITH

Sonoma City Hall was built to look the same from every direction.

An excellent self-guided walking tour of the plaza's many Victorian-era buildings is buried between the endless pages of advertisements in the free *Sonoma Valley Guide,* copies of which are usually in the **Sonoma Valley Visitors Bureau** on the plaza.

A few yards north of the visitors bureau is the **Bear Flag Monument,** a bronze statue that is roughly where the flag was raised by settlers in 1846 heralding the eventual creation of the State of California and the demise of Mexican rule. Smack in the middle of the plaza is **Sonoma City Hall,** built from locally quarried stone with four identical sides—to give equal importance to traders on all four sides of the plaza, so the legend goes. Like most civil construction projects today, the building project came in late and way over its budgeted cost of $15,000, delayed by stonemason strikes and the ballooning price of materials following the 1906 San Francisco earthquake. It took five years to build and was finally completed in 1909.

Almost opposite the mission entrance on Spain Street, the wobbly-looking adobe building with a long first-floor veranda is the **Blue Wing Inn,** a gold rush–era saloon and stagecoach stop that is thought to be one of the oldest unaltered buildings in the city and the oldest hotel north of San Francisco. It is now a private residence.

◖ Sonoma Mission

The north side of the plaza was the first to be developed in the early days of Sonoma and is where the oldest buildings can be found, many now part of the Sonoma State Historic Park. The **Mission San Francisco Solano de Sonoma** (corner of 1st St. and E. Spain St., 707/938-9560, 10 A.M.–5 P.M. Fri.–Wed., $3), established in 1823, was the last of California's 21 missions but had a short religious life. Its land and buildings were seized by the Mexican government in 1834 along with all the other missions on the West Coast. By the end of the 1800s, Sonoma's once-proud mission had suffered the ignominy of being used as hay barn and a winery, and of having a saloon built right in front of it.

© PHILIP GOLDSMITH

Sonoma's historic mission, the last of the Spanish missions built in California

Enter the unlikely figure of newspaper magnate William Randolph Hearst, who helped provide funding that enabled a preservation society to buy the mission in 1903 for $5,000. Restoration didn't start until 1911, however, by which time various collapses had left the building in ruins. The reconstructed building open to the public today has a large cross on the roof where an old bell tower used to be but is otherwise largely the same as the original. The $3 entrance fee buys access to a small museum and the large dusty courtyard full of giant prickly pear cactus plants said to be as old as the mission itself. Just don't touch the cacti or you'll be pulling tiny hairlike spikes out of your hands for the rest of the day.

The Vallejo Connections

Many of the historic sights in Sonoma that date from the turbulent mid-1800s were built for or by General Mariano Vallejo, the Mexican army commander who later became an important state politician.

Across 1st Street from the mission is the two-story adobe **Sonoma Barracks** building (10 A.M.–5 P.M. Fri.–Wed., $3), which was constructed in stages between 1834 and 1841 by Native American slaves captured by the same Mexican army it eventually housed. In 1860 it was converted to a winery by General Vallejo (many plaza buildings saw service as wine cellars or wineries over the years) and in the late 1800s became a store with an ornate Victorian facade tacked on the front. It was partly restored in the 1930s and was used for private residences and offices until being bought by the state in 1958 and fully restored. The small museum housed there today contains artifacts from its military history. The courtyard was once the scene of grisly staged animal fights.

Next to the barracks is the old **Toscano Hotel,** which was built in the 1850s. Just across the small square behind the 1940s building that contains the Sonoma Cheese Factory is the site of Vallejo's first home, **La Casa Grande,** built in 1840 and where Vallejo was arrested by the Bear Flag party in

1846. The house itself burned down long ago, and just the two-story, adobe-brick servants quarters remain.

Vallejo's next home, built in 1850, reflected his new status as a state senator and is on 20 acres of parkland about a 10-minute walk west of the plaza on Spain Street at 3rd Street West. Vallejo called this new home **Lachryma Montis,** Latin for "tear of the mountain," the name given by Native Americans to a nearby spring that once supplied much of the town's water. The Mission, Barracks, and Lachryma Montis are all part of the Sonoma State Historic Park (707/938-9560).

In a display of excess that would put many of today's movie stars to shame, Vallejo spent $150,000 (in 1850 dollars) to build and decorate the ornate Gothic-style Victorian house, construct numerous summer houses, and plant the huge 250-acre estate where he lived until his death in 1890. Even the wood-framed **Swiss Chalet** next to the house, originally used to store the estate's fruit (and, of course, used as a winery), was built from materials imported from Europe. Today it is a visitors center and museum (10 A.M.–5 P.M. Fri.–Wed., $3). The house itself is open during museum hours and is still full of Vallejo's decadent marble fireplaces, rosewood furniture, chandeliers, and frilly lace.

The Sebastiani Theatre

Not only was California born in Sonoma, but so was California theater. What was believed to be California's first theatrical presentation, Benjamin Webster's *The Golden Farmer,* was put on by American soldiers in an old adobe storehouse converted to a theater in 1849.

Today, a theater of the silver screen era is one of the most prominent buildings on the plaza. The Sebastiani Theatre (476 1st St. E., 707/996-2020, www.sebastianitheatre.com), built to replace the burned-down Don Theatre, was funded by Samuele Sebastiani, city benefactor and founder of the eponymous winery. It opened its doors in April 1934 with the film *Fugitive Lovers* and today hosts films or live entertainment almost every night.

© PHILIP GOLDSMITH

SOUTHERN SONOMA

The Sebastiani Theatre dominates Sonoma's plaza just like the Sebastiani family has dominated the town's wine-making history.

Depot Museum and Train Town

The scale-model trains that haul passengers around a 1.25-mile track at the Train Town amusement park in Sonoma are the only reminders of the once-thriving railroad that brought visitors to Sonoma Valley.

The first stretch of the original Sonoma Valley Railroad opened in 1879 and ran from Vineburg just south of Sonoma to Wingo, three miles south of present-day Schellville, where it connected with boats to San Francisco. It was soon extended down to San Pablo Bay and north to Sonoma Plaza. From the plaza it followed Spain Street and turned right on present-day Highway 12, running all the way up the valley to Glen Ellen.

Back in 1890, taking the ferry and train from San Francisco's Ferry Building to Sonoma took about two hours, not much longer than it takes by car now. But the rising popularity of cars in the early 1900s and the opening of the Golden Gate Bridge in 1937 eventually led to the demise of the region's railroads.

FIGHTING FIRE WITH WINE

On a breezy day in September 1911, a stove exploded in a cobbler's shop on the east side of Sonoma Plaza, setting off what the *Sonoma Index-Tribune* newspaper described as a "disasterous fire" that was eventually extinguished with the help of a quick-thinking wine merchant.

The town's fire truck and 100 firefighters were quickly on the scene of the original fire, but were soon overwhelmed when changing winds spread the flames to buildings up and down the street and, at one point, set fire to the grass on the plaza.

When the roof of Agostino Pinelli's wine cellars on Spain Street caught fire and he saw the fire truck was too far away to help, he and some firefighters connected a hose and pump to a 1,000-gallon tank of his wine and, as reported by the *Index-Tribune*, "A powerful stream of red wine was directed on the burning wine cellar."

Although the fire eventually destroyed most of the other buildings on 1st Street East, Pinelli's red wine was credited with helping firefighters prevent the fire from spreading to even more buildings on the south side of the plaza.

The Pinelli building is still standing today on 1st Street East near Spain Street. It was built in 1891 from local stone quarried by the Pinelli family, which also helped Samuele Sebastiani get his start in the quarrying business before he went on to establish the Sebastiani Winery. Today, the building is home to offices and shops, including (rather appropriately) the **Sonoma Wine Shop** (412 1st St. E., Sonoma, 707/996-1230, 11 A.M.–6 P.M. daily).

More about the history of the Sonoma railroads can be found at the small Depot Museum (270 1st St. W., 1–4:30 P.M. Wed.–Sun., 707/938-1762, free admission), a block north of the plaza. The museum is an exact replica of the original railroad depot, which burned down in 1976, and is surrounded by Depot Park, popular with the city's drunks except on Friday when the farmers market takes over.

Riding the only trains left in town requires a visit to the brightly painted station of Train Town (20264 Broadway, 707/938-3912, www.traintown.com). The strange and often crowded combination of amusement park, model railway, and petting zoo is open 10 A.M.–5 P.M. daily June–Labor Day, and 10 A.M.–5 P.M. Friday–Sunday only for the rest of the year. The fare is $4.75 for all ages, but adults should be warned that the mandatory stop at the petting zoo at the halfway point can be a little tedious. The amusement park rides, which include a Ferris wheel and vintage carousel, each cost $2.50.

ENTERTAINMENT AND EVENTS

The Sonoma Valley is as much about olives as wine during the winter when the annual **Sonoma Valley Olive Festival** (www.olivefestival.com) is in full swing. The festival kicks off with the Blessing of the Olives at Sonoma's mission and the Olive Harvest Tasting in early December, then runs through February. Check the website for a full list of the 30 or more events, including plenty of fun cooking demonstrations organized at wineries, restaurants, and outdoors to celebrate the oily fruit. Many are free, but the biggest events usually require tickets, available at the Sonoma Valley Visitors Bureau on Sonoma Plaza.

Late May through June is lavender season in the Sonoma Valley, and the aromatic purple flower is celebrated with the annual **Lavender Festival** (usually the third weekend in June, 707/523-4411, www.sonomalavender.com, $5 per car) next to the Chateau St. Jean winery in Kenwood. Learn about growing countless varieties of lavender, how to use the oil, and even how to cook with lavender. There's also a lavender festival held in early June at the Matanzas Creek Winery near Glen Ellen.

Shakespeare in Sonoma celebrates the town's theatrical heritage and its great summer weather July–September with Sunday-evening performances of Shakespeare's plays put on by the local Avalon Players group in the outdoor amphitheater at the Gundlach Bundschu Winery. Tickets cost $15–20. For more information, contact the Avalon Players (707/996-3264, www.sonomashakespeare.com).

If the silver screen is more your thing, August brings the annual **Wine Country Film Festival** to the historic Sebastiani Theatre on Sonoma Plaza and several valley wineries. Film screenings are usually accompanied by a range of other Wine Country events during the month, all involving plenty of food and wine. For a schedule of events and ticket prices, visit www.winecountryfilmfest.com.

Among the big wine events in the valley during the year is the annual **Passport to Sonoma Valley,** usually held on the third weekend in May, when 40 wineries up and down the valley throw themed parties with free food, wine, and entertainment for those lucky enough to have a festival passport. They can be bought ahead of time for either the whole weekend or just one day from the Sonoma Valley Vintners & Growers Alliance (707/935-0803, www.sonomavalleywine.com). Some passports might also be available from select wineries on the day.

Earlier in the year is the **Savor Sonoma Valley** event (707/431-1137, www.heart ofthevalley.com), hosted by the Heart of Sonoma Valley Association, usually the third weekend in March at wineries around Glen Ellen and Kenwood.

Ramekins Sonoma Valley Culinary School

The Napa Valley has the famous Culinary Institute of America, but the Sonoma Valley, not to be outdone, has its own renowned culinary school in Ramekins (450 W. Spain St., Sonoma, 707/933-0450, www.ramekins.com), just four blocks from the plaza and voted 2005 Cooking School of the Year by the International Association of Culinary Professionals.

Ramekins has far more in the way of a hands-on cooking experience for casual visitors than the CIA over in St. Helena, including classes and demonstrations, sometimes by well-known chefs, that don't cost much more

than a meal at many local restaurants, making the evening classes a fun alternative to eating a meal that someone else prepared. Check the website for a constantly updated schedule.

RECREATION
Annadel State Park

Redwoods, oaks, meadows, and a large well-stocked lake make 5,000-acre Annadel State Park (6201 Channel Dr., Santa Rosa, 707/539-3911, sunrise–sunset, $6 per car) one of the most diverse of Sonoma Valley's parks. It's easily accessible from both Santa Rosa and Kenwood. Most trails start from Channel Drive, which is reached by driving north from Kenwood on Highway 12; just before the road becomes four lanes, turn left on Melita Road, then left on Montgomery Drive, and left on Channel Drive.

The rocky trails that make Annadel a bone-jarring ride for mountain bikers today also give away its previous life as an important source of

More than 35 miles of hiking, biking, and horseback-riding trails weave through Annadel State Park.

obsidian for Native American tools and rock for cobblestones for cities up and down the West Coast in the early 1900s. There's still some evidence of quarrying on many of the trails, including the aptly named Cobblestone Trail, which used to be the route of a tramway carrying rock down the hill to the railroad.

Mountain bikers love the fact that most of the trails are either single-track or double-track and strewn with rocks for a bit of added fear. This is probably not the best place for novice bikers to find their wheels, but it offers some of the best midlevel mountain biking in the Bay Area, with plenty of technical trails and an elevation gain and drop of about 1,000 feet for most loops.

Popular downhills include the Lawndale Trail from Ledson Marsh, a smooth, fast single-track through the forest; the Upper Steve's Trail and Marsh Trail loop; and the rockier Orchard and Cobblestone Trails (including the Orchard Loop). Lake Ilsanjo is pretty much the center of the park and a good start and end point for many biking loops, although it can be relatively crowded on summer weekends. The best way to reach it from the main parking lot is to ride up the Warren Richardson fire road, saving the single-track for going downhill.

An alternative entrance that avoids the fee and is popular with mountain bikers is on Lawndale Road. From Highway 12, take a left just north of the Landmark Winery; the un-marked dirt parking lot is on the right about a mile down the road. Farther up Lawndale Road, forking off to the right, is Schultz Road, leading to the Schultz Trailhead. It's better to bike up the Schultz Trail and come down Lawndale.

The best time to go **hiking** in Annadel is spring or early summer when the wildflowers are in full bloom in the meadows around Lake Ilsanjo, named after two former land-owners, Ilsa and Joe Coney. (Dogs are not allowed on any major trails in any of the state parks.) The two-mile trek from the parking lot up the Warren Richardson Trail to the lake gives a good cross section of the park's flora, starting in a forest of redwoods and Douglas fir and climbing up through oaks to the relatively flat area around the lake where miles of other trails converge.

Lower Steve's Trail, which branches off and then rejoins the Richardson trail, is one of the few trails off-limits to bikes and therefore worth taking if you've been harassed by speeding bikers. Allow about four hours to make the round-trip and explore the lake area.

The Cobblestone Trail to Rough Go Trail is an alternative but rockier and longer ascent to the lake, and one on which you're more likely to meet bikers hurtling down the hill or some of the park's wild turkeys ambling across your path. At the lake there are picnic areas and restrooms, plus access to the rest of the trail network.

Fishing at the lake is also popular, with black bass and bluegill the most common catch. The Park Service suggests the purple plastic worm as the best bait for bass, and garden worms or grubs are favored by bluegills. Anyone over 16 must have a California fishing license.

◖ Sugarloaf Ridge State Park

2,700-acre Sugarloaf Ridge State Park (2605 Adobe Canyon Rd., Kenwood, 707/833-5712, $8) is perfect for either a quick fix of shady redwood forests or for hikes to some of the best views, both terrestrial and extraterrestrial, in the valley. It's about a 10-minute drive up Adobe Canyon Road from the Landmark Winery, putting it within easy reach of the valley floor for picnics and short day hikes. The park is open from sunrise until about two hours after sunset, but hours change depending on the time of year. Call to check times. It also has the only campground in the valley.

The somewhat barren hillside near the entrance is deceiving. From winter to early summer, a 25-foot waterfall tumbles just a few hundred yards from the parking lot along the Canyon Trail, and the 0.75-mile-long shady Creekside Nature Trail runs from the picnic area.

The big **hiking** draw is the seven-mile round-trip slog up to the summit of 2,729-foot Bald Mountain, rewarded by spectacular 360-degree views of the North Bay. It starts off on paved fire roads, but the paving soon ends as the trail climbs 1,500 feet in about three miles with no shade at all, so take a hat and plenty of water in the summer. From the summit, the Grey Pine Trail offers an alternative route downhill, and on the way up there's a short detour to the peak of neighboring Red Mountain.

To get 12 inches closer to the sun, there's an equally long and hot hike from the parking lot to the 2,730-foot summit of Hood Mountain, which actually lies in neighboring Hood Mountain Regional Park. The dirt parking lot for the Goodspeed Trailhead is on the left of Adobe Canyon Road next to a stand of redwood trees just before the road starts climbing steeply.

From the lot, the trail crosses and follows Bear Creek through the forest, eventually crossing the creek again and steepening for the next three miles into exposed grass and scrubland. Eventually it reaches a ridge where you can bear left for the sweeping views west from the Gunsight Rock Overlook, or turn right and trek the remaining half mile up to the Hood Mountain summit. Allow at least five hours round-trip. During fire season (June–Oct.) the trail is closed about halfway up but is still a good place to go for a picnic.

Sugarloaf is also home to the **Robert Ferguson Observatory** (707/833-6979, www.rfo.org, $3 for night viewing, under age 18 free, daytime solar viewing free), the largest observatory open to the general public on the West Coast. It's just a short walk from the main parking lot. Check the website or call for a schedule of daytime solar viewing and regular stargazing through 8-, 14-, and 24-inch telescopes. There are usually at least two public day- and night-viewing sessions per month, plus regular astronomy classes throughout the year. Ask about the huge 40-inch refractor telescope, which opened in 2005.

◖ Jack London State Historic Park

The 800-acre Jack London State Historic Park (2400 London Ranch Rd., Glen Ellen, 707/938-5216, 10 A.M.–5 P.M. daily, $8 per car) is a short distance past the Benziger Family Winery and offers a unique combination of scenic hiking and self-guided history tours around the buildings that once belonged to one of the valley's best-known authors, Jack London.

From the entrance kiosk, turn left to visit the **House of Happy Walls** (10 A.M.–5 P.M. daily, free), the former residence of Jack London's widow, Charmian, and now a museum about the author's life. From there it's only a half-mile walk on a paved trail to London's grave and the ruins of the spectacular **Wolf House,** his 17,000-square-foot dream home that burned down accidentally just before it was completed in 1913. There was speculation that it was arson, but modern-day investigators conducted a forensic arson investigation in 1995 and concluded the fire was probably caused by spontaneous combustion of rags soaked in highly flammable turpentine and linseed oil used during construction. Today, only the monumentally thick stone walls remain in the dappled shade of the surrounding redwoods,

the ruins of Jack London's imposing Wolf House, which mysteriously burned down in 1913 just days before being completed

SOUTHERN SONOMA

© PHILIP GOLDSMITH

but in the House of Happy Walls there's a model of just how impressive the house would have looked had it not met such a fiery fate.

The parking lot for the miles of **hiking** trails is to the right after the entrance. From there, the Beauty Ranch Trail winds around the buildings on London's former ranch, including the cottage where he wrote many of his later books and died at a youthful 40 years old. Many of the other buildings once belonged to the 19th-century Kohler and Frohling winery, including a barn, an old distillery building, and the ruins of the winery itself. Others, like the piggery known as the Pig Palace, were built by London himself.

From the Beauty Ranch Trail, the Lake Trail goes uphill past the vineyards and through the redwoods for about half a mile to the forest-fringed lake created by London, where there are picnic spots and restrooms.

From there, explore the oak woods and meadows on a series of looping trails, or take the long Mountain Trail to the park summit next to Sonoma Mountain. That hike is about seven miles round-trip but can be lengthened by taking loops off the main trail. Another long hike is the Ridge Trail, which leaves the Mountain Trail and twists through forests and clearings with sweeping views before reaching the connecting Vineyard Trail leading back to the lake.

Mountain biking is allowed on all the trails in the park except the Cowan Meadow, Fallen Bridge, and Quarry Trails, plus a few around the lake. You might see a member of the Benziger family from the winery down the road hurtling by, but be aware that all trails are shared with hikers and some with horses. The Ridge Trail loop is recommended over the Mountain Trail to the summit, which is a steep uphill and perilously rocky downhill.

Sonoma Overlook Trail

Nowhere is the spirit of Slow-noma better represented than in this three-mile trail just north of Sonoma Plaza that winds through woods and meadows to the top of Schocken Hill, with fine views over the town below. The site almost became home to another Wine Country resort in 1999, but residents banded together to ensure it was instead preserved as a city-owned open space.

Grab picnic supplies and head for the trailhead near the entrance to the Mountain Cemetery on West 1st Street about a half mile north of the plaza beyond Depot Park. Within an hour you'll feel like you're in the middle of nowhere. Dogs, bikes, and smoking are not allowed on the trail.

In spring, the **Sonoma Ecology Center** (707/996-0712, www.sonomaecologycenter .org) offers docent-led weekend hikes along the trail to identify the abundant spring wildflowers and other natural highlights. Contact the center for more information.

Golf

An alternative to hiking miles up a hot dusty trail is to meander around a lush golf course never far from a glass of crisp chardonnay.

The grande dame of the valley golf scene is the **Fairmont Sonoma Mission Inn Golf Club** (17700 Arnold Dr., Sonoma, 707/996-0300), opened in 1928 and planned by the original investors to rival the famous Del Monte course in Monterey. The 18-hole, par-72 course is on 170 acres bordered by the Sonoma Mountains and vineyards. Only club members and guests at the neighboring Fairmont Sonoma Mission Inn can play here, however.

The closest public course is in Petaluma, a 15-minute drive from Sonoma, at the **Adobe Creek Golf Club** (1901 Frates Rd., Petaluma, 707/765-3000, www.adobecreek.com). The 18-hole, par-72 links course has tee rates from $20 midweek afternoons up to $60 on the weekends, and rents clubs and carts. Be sure to check the website for last-minute discounted greens fees that can save you up to half off the regular fee.

Horseback Riding

Rides of 1–3 hours, together with more expensive private rides that include lunch, are available in Sugarloaf Ridge and Jack London State Parks through the **Triple Creek Horse**

Outfit (707/887-8700, www.triplecreekhorse outfit.com). Rates start from $60 for one hour, and groups don't usually exceed six riders. Reservations must be made in advance, and rides are limited to those over eight years old and weighing less than 220 pounds. Wear appropriate footwear, and arrive at the stable (located at the end of the main parking lots in both parks) about a half hour before your date with the horse. Rides in Sugarloaf State Park are offered year-round, and on the half dozen nights during the summer when the moon is full there are two-hour rides offered at dusk for $90. In Jack London State Park, the ride takes you past some of Jack London's favorite haunts.

Sonoma Valley Spas

Aware that local Native American tribes had long talked about the healing properties of Sonoma Valley's numerous hot springs, Captain Henry Boyes spent two years drilling all over his property at the southern end of the valley in search of them. In 1895 he hit what would turn out to be liquid gold—a 112°F gusher that ushered in decades of prosperity for the valley's hotel owners.

Within a few months, another source of the hot water had been tapped by the owner of the neighboring Agua Caliente Springs Hotel. By 1900 thousands of visitors were bathing in the new hot mineral baths every year, and developers saw the potential for mass tourism, especially with the increasing popularity of the new railroad that ran from San Pablo Bay to Sonoma and up to Glen Ellen.

Soon the Boyes Springs mineral baths and the Agua Caliente Springs Hotel were transformed into first-class resorts. By 1910 many other hotels and resorts had opened, including Fetters Hot Springs and Verano Springs, complete with vaudeville shows, dances, and concerts. The *Sonoma Index-Tribune* newspaper reported that 23,000 people came in on the railroads for the Fourth of July weekend in 1916, close to the peak of the resort boom. Just seven years earlier there had been no one to witness the annual Fourth of July parade except local residents.

Boyes Hot Springs Hotel (along with several other resorts) burned down in a huge valley fire in September 1923, and an exclusive new resort, the **Sonoma Mission Inn** (100 Boyes Blvd., Sonoma, 707/938-9000, www.fairmont.com/ sonoma), with its mission-style architectural touches, opened on the site in 1927.

Today, the inn is the only spa hotel in the valley with its own natural source of hot mineral water. Even if you're not a guest at the Fairmont-owned hotel, basic spa packages are available for $49–89, depending on how many extra salon pamperings are added on. The basic spa includes an exfoliating shower, warm and hot mineral baths, and herbal steam room and sauna, interspersed with various cold showers and baths. Various add-on massages, stone treatments, and mud baths are also available to purify and relax you (until you see the bill).

The **Kenwood Inn & Spa** (10400 Sonoma Hwy., Kenwood, 707/833-1293 or 800/353-6966, www.kenwoodinn.com/spa.php) might not have its own source of mineral water, but its Caudalie Vinotherapie Spa makes full use of the surrounding vineyards, and it was voted one of the top resort spas in the United States by readers of *Condé Nast Traveler* in 2009. The wraps, baths, and other treatments use vine and grape seed extracts to purify body and mind. Some might make you feel like a grape yourself, such as the wine barrel bath that exfoliates using bubbling water enriched with crushed grape seeds, skin, stalks, and pulp. For non–hotel guests there's a $35 day-use fee on top of the regular fees, which range from $70 for 20 minutes in a wine barrel to almost $200 for longer massages and facials. Complete packages incorporating body treatments, massages, and facial treatments (plus lunch) cost upward of $300.

Just south of the Sonoma Plaza, the **Garden Spa** at the luxurious MacArthur Place inn is a good place for some luxury pampering with a list of spa treatments that could cause you to tense up with indecision (29 E. MacArthur St., Sonoma, 707/933-3193, www.macarthurplace .com/spa.php). Facials, wraps, and massages featuring all sorts of therapeutic herb, flower, and vegetable extracts and essential oils start at $120, with longer treatments incorporating mineral baths starting at $225. Couples can get their treatments together, and all spa guests also have full use of the inn's tranquil outdoor pool and fitness center.

ACCOMMODATIONS

Anyone expecting cheap and cheerful accommodation over the hills from overpriced Napa Valley establishments will be sadly disappointed. The cheapest place to sleep in the valley is with Mother Nature in a campground. The second cheapest is more than $100 per night.

Like the wine made here, the Sonoma Valley is increasingly marketed as a luxury destination with luxury bells and whistles that command premium prices. The pressure to keep the small-town feel of Sonoma doesn't help either, ensuring that most hotels and inns stay small and planning hurdles remain high, thus limiting the number of rooms available. As in Napa, many places here sell a Wine Country lifestyle that mixes Mediterranean with Victorian influences, but there are some new options that throw a little more contemporary inspiration into the mix.

Apart from a few big resort or chain hotels, the accommodation scene in Sonoma Valley is one of small, usually independent establishments with a handful of rooms. The smaller the hotel or inn, the more likely there is to be a two-night minimum over weekends, especially during the busiest summer and early fall months. Cancellation policies might also be less than flexible. The peak hotel season is generally from the end of May through October, roughly corresponding to the best weather in the region.

The closest place for true bargain-priced accommodations is along the U.S. 101 freeway corridor across the Sonoma Mountains, where most of the chain motels can be found. Stay around Petaluma or in the Rohnert Park and Santa Rosa areas, and it's only a 10–15-minute drive into the valley.

Under $150

The ◖ **Sonoma Hotel** (110 W. Spain St., Sonoma, 707/996-2996 or 800/468-6016, www.sonomahotel.com) is one of the rare bargains in the valley, offering some of the cheapest rooms and a superb location in a historic building right on Sonoma Plaza next to the highly rated Girl & the Fig restaurant. Even the four cheapest rooms ($99–110 depending on the season) have views of something worthwhile, though don't expect luxury. The rooms are small, dark, and sparsely (though tastefully) furnished, but for this price in this location there's really nothing to complain about. More expensive rooms and junior suites get more light and floor space, plus some additional French country–style furniture, and cost $140–220 in winter, $150–245 in summer. In keeping with the price and the hotel's heritage (the building dates from 1880), there are few amenities, and you're likely to hear your neighbor's nighttime antics. Also be warned that the bathroom for one of the cheapest rooms (room 34), although private, is out in the hallway past the friendly ghost.

El Pueblo Inn (896 W. Napa St., 707/996-3651 or 800/900-8844, www.elpuebloinn .com) is actually more of an upscale motel but offers a lot of rooms for a modest price and is just a 10-minute walk from the plaza. It's also one of the few places with no weekend minimum-stay requirements. The cheaper Adobe rooms all have air-conditioning and are $89–149 in winter, $150–219 the rest of the year, while two-room suites are available for as little as $150. Although they still hint at the 1950s motel rooms they once were, they now open onto a courtyard rather than a parking lot. The larger, more luxurious Sonoma rooms, added during a 2001 reconstruction, feel more hotel-like, with DVD players and high ceilings, but generally cost $20–30 more per night. All rooms have access to the small outdoor pool and landscaped gardens.

Most B&Bs in this area tend toward plenty of Victorian frills, but the **Sonoma Chalet** (18935 5th St. W., Sonoma, 707/938-3129 or 800/938-3129, www.sonomachalet.com)

goes beyond the chintz to a fabulously over-the-top Swiss Family Robinson–meets–Wild West theme, with its alpine murals, dark wood accents, antiques, and colorful fabrics. There are four individually decorated rooms in the main Swiss-style farmhouse: The two cheapest ($125) share a bathroom, while the larger of the other two ($160–180) has a fireplace and balcony. Several small cottages on the three acres of wooded grounds have claw-foot tubs and wood-burning stoves and cost from $185 per night. The leafy location on the edge of Sonoma is peaceful but a fairly long walk to most of Sonoma's shops and restaurants.

Although located in the relative no-man's land of Boyes Hot Springs just north of Sonoma, the **Sonoma Creek Inn** (239 Boyes Blvd., 888/712-1289 or 707/939-9463, www.sonomacreekinn.com) is one of the cheapest nonchain hotels in the valley, with rooms starting at $89–159 midweek, depending on the season, and $139–199 weekends. In this price range it's more common to see IKEA furniture, but the furnishings here are delightfully quirky, and some look like spoils from local antique stores. The 15 rooms are small and laid out in motel style; all are clean and have air-conditioning, and some have tiny private patios.

$150-250

The Chapel Suite with its vaulted ceilings and skylight above the bed is one of the more unusual rooms at the **Cottage Inn & Spa** and the neighboring **Mission B&B** (310 1st St. E., 707/996-0719 or 800/944-1490, www.cottageinnandspa.com), just a block north of Sonoma Plaza. This self-styled "micro resort" with its mission-style architectural flourishes is an oasis of calm and style, with a wide range of rooms for all tastes and wallets. The cheapest are the plain but comfortable Courtyard rooms ($150–220 per night midweek, $25 more on weekends), but for not much more money some of the quirky junior suites like the Chapel Suite ($225–365) come into play, many with private patios and fireplaces. The South Suite ($225–355) has a double-sided fireplace, the Vineyard View Suite ($300–440) is over

700 square feet of cathedral ceilings and panoramic views, while the three-room North Suite ($300–415) includes a full kitchen.

Just a bit further up the street and a step up on the luxury scale is the five-room B&B **Bungalows 313** (313 1st St. E., 707/996-8091, www.bungalows313.com). As the name implies, this is a cozy collection of bungalows around a peaceful courtyard fountain. Each suite is decorated in Italian country style with modern luxuries like sumptuous linens, an LCD television, and a DVD player. All are spacious, with seating areas, a kitchen or kitchenette, and private patio, yet all are unique in some way. One has a fireplace, another a jetted tub, and the largest is 1,200 square feet. Prices vary wildly from season to season, starting at $160–275 midweek in the winter and jumping to $239–379 in late summer. Weekend rates are $210–469. Beware of the 14-day cancellation policy.

A teddy bear slumbering on the bed greets everyone staying at the **Inn at Sonoma** (630 Broadway, Sonoma, 888/568-9818 or 707/939-1340, www.innatsonoma.com). It is one of Sonoma's newest hotels, and what it lacks in historic charm it makes up for in functionality, price, and convenience, being only a few blocks from the plaza. The 19 guest rooms are furnished in slightly pastiche, flowery Wine Country style but have a full range of modern amenities, including fireplaces, DVD players, and luxury bathrooms. The smallest Quaint Queen rooms are $205–270 per night. The larger queen and king rooms that cost $215–300 per night also have small patios.

A historic inn dating from 1843 is now home to the newly renovated **El Dorado Hotel** (405 1st St. W., Sonoma, 707/996-3220, www.eldoradosonoma.com), offering stylish 21st-century accommodations for not much more money than a pricey Wine Country motel. The lobby exudes the style of a classy boutique hotel but the luxurious spaciousness of the lounges doesn't quite make it upstairs to the 23 smallish guest rooms. They are instead decorated with simple modern furnishings and earth tones that give a nod to the hotel's mission-era history. A decent list of amenities includes CD players, flat-screen televisions, and wireless Internet access but doesn't stretch to bathtubs—only showers—or room service. The courtyard swimming pool looks nice but is somewhat pointless unless you like to swim or sunbathe just yards from diners spilling onto the patio from the hotel's bar and restaurant. Still, for $155–175 per night midweek, depending on the season ($20 more on weekends and for the four bungalow rooms), and a location right on the plaza, it's hard to complain. All have a view of some sort from their small balconies—the best overlook the plaza, although they suffer from some associated street noise.

The two dachshunds and Nutmeg, the cat, help provide the welcome at the ◖ **Glenelly Inn** (5131 Warm Springs Rd., Glen Ellen, 707/996-6720, www.glenelly.com), a B&B tucked away behind Glen Ellen in a former railroad inn. The seven guest rooms and suites with private bathrooms are relative bargains for such a historic B&B, costing $119–229 per night. All are decorated in cottage style with plenty of floral prints and are relatively small except for the Valley of the Moon room, which has a wood-burning stove. There are also two small cottages for $269–299 per night with private porches and whirlpool tubs. As with most well-priced historic B&Bs, the soundproofing is minimal, none of the basic rooms has a television, and most have no air-conditioning. Breakfast is served outside in the pretty gardens during the summer, and there's also an outdoor hot tub.

Also near Glen Ellen, the **Beltane Ranch B&B** (11775 Sonoma Hwy., Glen Ellen, 707/996-6501, www.beltaneranch.com) looks like a little piece of the Deep South landed in the vineyards. The Victorian-era house with its New Orleans–style wraparound veranda and lush gardens sits in the middle of the valley at the end of a long driveway, far from the madding crowds of Highway 12. The five tastefully furnished, white-paneled rooms ($150–240 per night) evoke a bygone era without going over the top, and all open onto the veranda.

The ranch is actually 1,600 acres of vineyards, pasture, and woods at the bottom of the Mayacamas Mountains, with miles of hiking trails and a tennis court for guests.

$250-350

MacArthur Place (29 E. MacArthur St., Sonoma, 707/938-2929 or 800/722-1866, www.macarthurplace.com) touts itself as a historic Victorian inn. What it doesn't tell you is that by expanding and transforming itself into an exclusive seven-acre spa resort in 1997 it came to resemble more of a luxury executive-housing development. Nevertheless, the cookie-cutter faux-Victorian cottages and landscaped gardens that now fan out from the original 1850s building provide 64 luxurious and spacious guest rooms, making it one of the larger hotels in Sonoma. High season rates start at $349–399 for the queen rooms and rise to $650–699 for the garden spa suites. All rooms are sumptuously furnished in a cottage style that makes it seem more like a luxurious B&B, and all have the usual modern conveniences for this price range. Other amenities include an outdoor pool, free DVD library, breakfast, evening cheese and wine, and the onsite steakhouse and martini bar, Saddles. Suites and cottages also come with a fireplace and decadent hydrotherapy tub. Try to avoid the rooms on the south side of the complex that overlook the neighboring high school or those bordering the street to the west.

An alternative to the big-name luxury resorts in the valley is the luxuriously appointed and fantastically Zen **Gaige House Inn** (13540 Arnold Dr., Glen Ellen, 707/935-0237 or 800/935-0237, www.gaige.com), where the serene setting is complemented by contemporary Asian-inspired furnishings, gourmet breakfasts, a big outdoor pool, and indulgent spa treatments to help soften the financial blow. The cheapest of the 23 rooms and suites in the main Victorian house start at $260 midweek and $360 weekends during the summer, and as the price increases the features include fireplaces and small private Japanese Zen gardens. The more expensive suites include fireplaces and truly indulgent bathrooms, while the Creekside rooms add a private patio overlooking the Calabazas Creek to the package. Vaulting into the next price category are stunning, Asian-minimalist spa suites added in late 2004, each with its own freestanding granite soaking tub, sliding glass walls, and contemporary furnishings. They cost from $460 per night.

Over $350

The **Ledson Hotel** (480 1st St. E. on Sonoma Plaza, Sonoma, 707/996-9779, www.ledson hotel.com), a sibling to the Ledson Winery up the valley, made the Hot List of *Condé Nast Traveler* magazine in its first full year of operation, 2004. The Victorian-style brick building looks as old as the plaza itself, despite the fact it was built in this century. The six ornately decorated guest rooms ($350–395) are all named after previous generations of owner Steve Ledson's family, and all are on the second floor. Three have balconies looking onto the plaza, and all include just about every luxury feature possible, from state-of-the-art entertainment systems and high-speed Internet access to marble bathrooms with whirlpool tubs. Unusually for a hotel in this category, there is no dedicated reception area; guests either check in while sipping wine at the bar downstairs in the Harmony Club restaurant or slip in through a side door.

At the other end of the scale to the intimate Ledson Hotel is the 228-room **Sonoma Mission Inn** (100 Boyes Blvd., Sonoma, 707/938-9000, www.fairmont.com/sonoma), which dates from 1927 and is now owned by Fairmont Hotels. It is luxurious, even by Fairmont standards. The well-heeled are drawn by the 40,000-square-foot full-service spa, use of the exclusive Sonoma golf club next door, and one of the best (and most expensive) restaurants in the valley, Santé. Many of the rooms have tiled floors and plantation-style wooden shutters to complement their colonial-style furnishings, some have fireplaces, and they generally cost from $300 in the summer. The 60 suites, including the newest Mission suites, are priced upward of $500. Despite the exclusivity, the in-room amenities are typical of chain hotels, albeit a high-end chain.

Cottages

For a more private getaway, or for groups of more than two people, there are a lot of cottages available for rent in the valley, many owned by wineries. Although most charge an extra small fee for more than two people, they usually have full kitchens and still work out cheaper than booking multiple hotel rooms. Even with only one or two occupants, some cottages cost less than some mid-priced hotels or B&Bs.

Some of the wineries listed earlier in this chapter that have rental properties on their grounds or nearby include **Sebastiani Vineyards & Winery** in Sonoma, the **Kaz Winery** near Kenwood, and **Landmark Vineyards** next door to Kaz. A couple of the local inns also have rental management companies, including the **Glenelly Inn,** with some 10 local cottages on its books, and the **Gaige House Inn,** which manages several local properties, including one on the **Andelssa Estate Winery** estate.

Camping

With cheap rooms at a premium in the valley and not a drop of rain falling for about five months of the year, camping starts to look attractive, especially when the campground also happens to be just 10 minutes from many wineries and a stone's throw from some of the best hiking trails in the area.

The year-round **Sugarloaf Ridge State Park** campground (2605 Adobe Canyon Rd., Kenwood) is the only one in the valley and has a lot going for it if you can stand the summer heat (it does get cooler at night). It's a somewhat typical state park campground, with a small ring road serving the 49 mostly shady sites for tents and small RVs (up to 27 feet), drinking water, restrooms, fire pits, and picnic tables.

Sites 1–11 and 26–28 back onto a small creek, across which is the start of a popular hiking trail. Most of the rest of the sites are at the foot of a hill and get the most shade, although none can be described as truly secluded. Year-round reservations can be made through www.reserveamerica.com or by calling 800/444-7275. Fees are $30 year-round.

FOOD

Sonoma's food scene has gradually been transformed over the years from rustic to stylish, but many of the most successful establishments are still small and relaxed, retaining a degree of intimacy. The key to a restaurant's longevity here seems to be honesty, modesty, and reasonable prices.

There's a strong European theme to food in the valley, but ingredients will likely be fresh and local. Expect to see menus change throughout the year as vegetables, fish, and meats come in and out of season. Sonoma itself offers a huge variety of places to eat, from cheap to chic, while most of the other notable restaurants are up-valley, in and around the scenic little town of Glen Ellen.

Downtown Sonoma

Ask any of the valley's winemakers where they like to eat and the list will likely include

© PHILIP GOLDSMITH

Good food is never far away in Wine Country.

the family-owned Italian trattoria ☾ **Della Santina's** (133 E. Napa St., 707/935-0576, lunch and dinner daily, dinner entrées $12–18). The big outdoor patio and the simple Italian country food garner consistently good reviews, so reservations are usually essential despite the casual atmosphere. Prices for the pastas, daily fish, and spit-roasted meats run $10–18, and if the excellent local wine list does not satisfy, there's a $12 corkage fee, lower than the $20 charged by many other restaurants. Right next door to the restaurant is the wine bar and wine shop **Enoteca Della Santina** (127 East Napa St., 707/938-4200, Wed.–Thurs. 2–10 P.M., Fri. 2–11 P.M., Sat. noon–11 P.M., Sun. and Tues. 4–10 P.M., closed Mon.), which serves 30 Californian and international wines by the glass accompanied by appetizers at its copper-topped bar. It's a great place for a predinner drink while you wait for your table at a nearby restaurant or a late glass of port to end your day.

If a table is hard to come by at Della Santina or you simply fancy some Thai food, right next door with an equally nice outdoor patio space is the popular **Rin's Thai** (139 E. Napa St., 707/938-1462, lunch and dinner Tues.–Sun., dinner entrées $10–14). Fresh local ingredients feature strongly in the classic Thai dishes that include curries, noodles, and Thai-style barbequed meats, and the elegant Zen interior of the old Victorian house and the pretty patio are far from the usual hole-in-the-wall atmosphere of Thai restaurants. Rin's also offers takeout and delivery (minimum $35) for those craving some gang dang (spicy red curry) or tom yum (spicy and sour soup) in their hotel rooms.

Almost opposite Della Santina is another trusted and well-loved restaurant, ☾ **Café La Haye** (140 E. Napa St., 707/935-5994, dinner Tues.–Sat., entrées $17–30). Local ingredients are the backbone of the simple yet polished dishes like house-smoked wild salmon ($8), pan-roasted Wolfe Ranch quail ($25), and a daily risotto ($18), while the wine list is dominated by smaller wineries from all over Sonoma and farther afield. The uncluttered, split-level dining room is small, so either book well in advance or be prepared to sit at the bar in front of the tiny kitchen. The café is part of La Haye Art Center, which contains studios and the work of several local artists.

The Girl & the Fig (110 W. Spain St., 707/938-3634, www.thegirlandthefig.com, lunch and dinner daily, brunch 10 A.M.–3 P.M. Sun., dinner entrées $17–25) is somewhat of a valley institution, having moved to the Sonoma Hotel on the plaza from its previous home in Glen Ellen, spawning a cookbook and also a wine bar in its old Glen Ellen digs. The French country menu includes main courses like free-range chicken and seafood stew, Sonoma rabbit and *steak frites,* an excellent cheese menu, and delicious salads, including the signature arugula, goat cheese, pancetta, and grilled fig salad. The Thursday evening Plat du Jour menu is a bargain at $32 for three courses, or $40 including a three-wine flight or paired wines. To match the Provençal cuisine, the wine list focuses on Rhône varietals, with many from local Sonoma producers. There's not a cabernet to be seen. The restaurant usually closes at 10 P.M., but a smaller brasserie menu is also offered until 11 P.M. on Friday and Saturday.

Hearty Portuguese food in rustic, Mediterranean-inspired surroundings are the hallmarks of **La Salette,** just off the plaza (452 1st St. E., Suite H, 707/938-1927, lunch and dinner daily, dinner entrées $16–26). The menu reflects Portugal's seafaring colonial history, with traditional dishes such as the Portuguese national soup, *caldo verde* ($7), complementing international influences like pan-roasted Mozambique prawns, and the filling Brazilian stew *feijoada completa.* The wine list includes a wide range of both local and Portuguese wines, plus a dozen madeiras and 19 ports.

Every Wine Country town worth its salt seems to have a restaurant started by an alum of the French Laundry in Napa Valley's Yountville. Sonoma's arrived in 2005 when the sleek **El Dorado Kitchen** (405 1st St. W., 707/996-3030, lunch and dinner daily, dinner entrées $20–30) opened in the historic namesake hotel that itself had undergone a transformative renovation. Seasonal farm-fresh fish and meat dishes are given modern twists in keeping with the sleek surroundings that make this a unique addition to the Sonoma dining scene. Many consider this one of the top restaurants in Sonoma, and executive chef Justin Everett, a former sous-chef at French Laundry, has become something of a celebrity in cooking circles. Inside the restaurant is all cool dark wood and slate minimalism, while outside by the pool the casual dining scene is more Miami than Sonoma and is one of the nicest locations for Sunday brunch in town.

It's not the best place for a relaxed dinner, but for wine, light evening food, and outstanding people-watching opportunities, the **Ledson Hotel & Harmony Lounge** (480 1st St. E., 707/996-9779, 11 A.M.–9:30 P.M. daily, $6–14) on the plaza can't be beat, with a beautifully detailed and ornate (but faux) Victorian-style dining room that spills out onto the sidewalk. Small plates of internationally inspired food, ranging from fries to dishes like tropical lobster salad and beef tenderloin carpaccio, can be washed down with Ledson wines that are available only here and at the winery itself.

Pay attention after ordering anything at the **Basque Boulangerie Café** (460 1st St. E., Sonoma, 707/935-7687, 7 A.M.–6 P.M. daily), because customer names are only called once when food is ready. The line to order often snakes out the door at lunchtime, but it usually moves fast. The wide selection of soups, salads, and sandwiches can also be bought to go, which is handy because table space inside and out is usually scarce.

There are more seating options at the colorful **Sunflower Caffe** (421 1st St. W., 707/996-6645, 7 A.M.–5 P.M. daily) across the plaza. It sells a fairly basic selection of cheap beverages and sandwiches, but the real gem is a big patio hidden down the side passageway at the back of the neighboring historic adobe home of Captain Salvador Vallejo (brother of General Vallejo), an oasis of greenery with plenty of tables.

Glen Ellen and Kenwood

The intimate and cozy **Saffron** (13648 Arnold Dr., Glen Ellen, 707/938-4844, dinner

Tues.–Sat., entrées $16–25) describes its daily menu as "eclectic," but the emphasis is firmly on Sonoma with a hint of Spain. Main course options might include saffron-laced paella alongside roasted pork with winter vegetables. The wine list is certainly eclectic, with both Californian, Spanish, and other international wines together with an unusual selection of beers.

Some of the most reasonably priced food in the valley, together with free corkage all the time, can be found just down the street at **The Fig Café and Wine Bar** (13690 Arnold Dr., Glen Ellen, 707/938-2130, dinner daily, brunch weekends, dinner entrées $12–20). It is the North Valley offshoot of the popular The Girl & the Fig restaurant in Sonoma and serves up some of the same fig-accented French dishes in its colorful tiled dining room. The emphasis here is on lighter (and cheaper) food: thin-crust pizzas (including one with figs), sandwiches, and main courses like braised pot roast. The Sonoma-dominated wine list is also more compact, but markups are modest enough that you might not even decide to take advantage of the free corkage—a generous policy, but one that's slightly curious for a wine bar.

Eating outdoors right next to the vineyards is one of the attractions of the **Kenwood Restaurant and Bar** (9900 Sonoma Hwy., 707/833-6326, lunch and early dinner Wed.–Sun., dinner entrées $15–28). The simple country decor inside is pleasant enough, but the outdoor patio that's open during the summer is one of the most idyllic places to eat in this part of the valley, overlooking vineyards and surrounded by flowers. The small plates and main courses are simple and unpretentious combinations of local ingredients like goat cheese with red beets and grilled lamb chops with mushroom ravioli. The wine list is also dominated by locals and includes wines from almost every valley winery as well as the rest of Sonoma, plus a few bottles from Napa, France, and Italy for good measure.

One of the more unusual menus in this part of the world can be found at the quirky **Doce Lunas Restaurant** (8910 Sonoma Hwy.,

Kenwood, 707/833-4000, lunch and dinner Wed.–Sun., dinner entrées $16–21). The small menu is farm-fresh Californian with plenty of Asian and European influences, representing the heritage and globe-trotting culinary career of chef and co-owner Alex Purroy and his wife Jackie. Dishes like Nakayama Katsu can be found alongside more traditional steak au poivre and the signature dessert sticky toffee pudding. The location doubles as an antique store, creating an eclectic atmosphere that is made all the more quirky by the random plates on display as homage to the places all over the world where Alex has cooked. The four tables outside on the peaceful patio are perfect for summer evening dining.

Casual Valley Dining

Sonoma's Italian heritage is not only represented by fancy trattorias. **Mary's Pizza Shack,** founded by Italian New Yorker Mary Fazio in 1959, has been around longer than many other Sonoma restaurants and now has 15 branches throughout the North Bay. It might now be a chain, but you will at least be eating in the town where it all started. The traditional or build-your-own pizzas (starting at $12 for a medium) are consistently good, and there's a big selection of traditional pasta dishes ($11–15), including spaghetti with baseball-sized meatballs. Local branches are on the plaza (8 W. Spain St., 707/938-8300) and in Boyes Hot Springs (18636 Sonoma Hwy., 707/938-3600). Both are open for lunch and dinner daily.

Some inventive red (with tomato sauce) and white (no tomato sauce) pizzas at **The Red Grape** (529 1st St. W., Sonoma, 707/996-4103, lunch and dinner daily) include a pear, gorgonzola, and hazelnut pizza ($12), and another using local Sonoma Sausage Company meat ($12). There are plenty of less inspiring, but cheap, pizza and pasta options, and it's worth looking for a seat on the patio. The restaurant is named after a type of particularly sweet tomato.

For a monster burrito to soak up excess wine or to refuel after a long bike ride, try the roadside Mexican diner **Juanita Juanita** (19114

Arnold Dr., 707/935-3981, 11 A.M.–8 P.M. daily, entrées $6–12, cash only) on the west side of Arnold Drive just north of Sonoma. Although it isn't the cheapest Mexican food in Sonoma, it has come to be known as some of the best in this part of Sonoma County, and the ramshackle building with a patio is as colorful as the food. Choose one of the favorites listed on the menu, like the Jerk in a Blanket chicken, and you can't go wrong. Some of the food can be mind-blowingly spicy. Indeed, the menu warns: "Food isn't properly seasoned unless it's painful to eat."

With no microbreweries in this part of Sonoma, the next place to find beer is **Murphy's Irish Pub** (464 1st St., 707/935-0660, 11 A.M.–11 P.M. daily, 11 A.M.–midnight Fri.–Sat.) just off the plaza behind the Basque Boulangerie. It's one of the few places in the valley where beer trumps wine and live music, usually of the Irish variety, gets people dancing four nights a week. The food includes pub standards like fish-and-chips, shepherd's pie, and Irish stew, as well as sandwiches and a kids' menu. Nothing comes in over $18, and many dishes are under $10. Unfortunately, the pub also stays true to its Irish roots with its beer selection, which includes international favorites but little in the way of Northern Californian brews.

If you have a bear of an appetite but a bare wallet, head for the friendly, no-nonsense **Black Bear Diner** (201 W. Napa St., 707/935-6800, breakfast, lunch, and dinner daily, dinner entrées $7–17) a few blocks from the plaza. The portions are huge, from the Hungry Bear breakfast to the steaks and other comfort foods at dinner, all of which include salads and sides. The causal, fun atmosphere is family friendly too, offering entertainment for kids and discounts for seniors.

Up-valley in Kenwood, **Café Citti** (9049 Sonoma Hwy., Kenwood, 707/833-2690, lunch and early dinner daily) is a roadside cottage known for its rustic Northern Italian food, particularly the moderately priced rotisserie chicken dishes and risottos. The tasty focaccia sandwiches and pizzas also make it a popular lunch stop for winery workers in the area. Buy food for a picnic, or hang out on the patio with a tumbler of the cheap and tasty house wine.

Just south of Glen Ellen in Jack London Village you can buy gourmet soups, salads, sandwiches, and entrées at **Olive & Vine** (14301 Arnold Dr., No. 3, 707/996-9150). Owner and chef Catherine Driggers has cooked at numerous local wineries and restaurants, so don't be surprised to find luxurious picnic options like parmesan basil picnic chicken with fresh peach chutney on the seasonal menu. The cavernous room has a few tables inside, but the best place to eat is the big shady deck out back overlooking Sonoma Creek, where you might be able to pick some wild plums during summer.

Picnic Supplies

The Sonoma Valley is like one giant picnic ground. Many of the wineries have large open spaces or picnic tables, and the more adventurous can drive or hike into one of the many parks in the valley, such as the outlook above Sonoma, Jack London State Park, or up into the western hills in Sugarloaf State Park.

Many wineries now offer a limited selection of deli-style food in their visitors centers or gift stores, but some offer more than most, including the **Ledson Winery,** with its pungent selection of cheeses, and **Chateau St. Jean** in Kenwood.

Good bread can usually be found at most delis, though many places run out by lunchtime. Two bakeries supply most of the valley's bread, both centrally located. The **Basque Boulangerie Café** (460 1st St. E., Sonoma, 707/935-7687, 7 A.M.–6 P.M. daily) on the plaza sells not only sandwiches and salads to go ($5–8) but also freshly baked breads. It is one of the leading suppliers of bread to grocery stores in the area. The other big local bread supplier is **Artisan Bakers** (720 W. Napa St., 707/939-1765, 7 A.M.–4:30 P.M. Mon.–Sat., 7 A.M.–2 P.M. Sun.), in a nondescript building about half a mile from the plaza. It also sells a picnic-worthy selection of sandwiches, salads, and pizza.

Three good cheese shops are around the

SOUTHERN SONOMA

plaza. On the north side is the **Sonoma Cheese Factory** (2 Spain St., 800/535-2855, 8:30 A.M.–5:30 P.M. daily), which is easy to spot: just look for the ugliest building, a brutal 1940s edifice that stands in stark contrast to the Victorian character of the rest of the plaza. It is the home of Sonoma Jack cheese and also sells other strangely flavored cheeses (which, thankfully, you can usually taste first) as well as a limited selection of salads and fancy sandwiches. A less-crowded place to buy cheese is the historic **Vella Cheese Company** (315 2nd St. E., 707/938-3232 or 800/848-0505, 9:30 A.M.–6 P.M. Mon.–Sat.), a block north of the plaza in a former brewery building. It's the latest incarnation of the cheese store opened in the 1930s by Thomas Vella.

Other places to stock up on some delicious gourmet sandwiches for well-traveled roads include the **Vineburg Deli & Grocery** (997 Napa Rd., 707/938-3306, 6 A.M.–6 P.M. daily) just south of Sonoma not far from the Gundlach Bundschu Winery. At the north end of the valley are **Olive & Vine** (14301 Arnold Dr., No. 3, 707/996-9150) and **Café Citti** (9049 Sonoma Hwy., 707/833-2690), both of which sell a big selection of picnic-ready food in addition to being great sit-down dining destinations.

Perhaps the easiest option for getting everything in one place is to visit one of the valley's excellent general grocery stores. The **Sonoma Market** (500 W. Napa St., 707/996-3411), not far from the plaza, and the **Glen Ellen Village Market** (13751 Arnold Dr., Glen Ellen, 707/996-6728) are both owned by the same partners and sell a wide variety of basics, including a decent local wine selection. Each has an extensive deli that includes hot and cold foods, sandwiches, and a salad bar. Both are open 6 A.M.–9 P.M. daily.

Fresh Produce

A well-known Californian oil producer with ties to the Sonoma Valley, the **Figone Olive Oil Company** (9580 Sonoma Hwy., Kenwood, 707/282-9092) has been in the family olive oil business since the early 1990s and has become well known in the state's burgeoning olive oil industry. Figone's makes its own oils from olive groves in the Central Valley and Sonoma Valley and also presses oil for some other well-known oil suppliers, including winemaker Bruce Cohen here in the Sonoma Valley. The B. R. Cohen oils are sold in the tasting room along with Figone's own oils, some in hand-marked bottles. There are usually several oils to taste (for free) against a backdrop of the shiny equipment (some of it hand-me-downs from the Figone's Italian cousins) in the glass-walled olive press room.

Seasonal produce from the organic Oak Hill Farm and some fabulous freshly cut flowers are sold in an old dairy barn known simply as the **Red Barn Store** (15101 Sonoma Hwy., Glen Ellen, 707/996-6643, 10 A.M.–6 P.M. Wed.–Sun. April–Christmas), off Highway 12 just north of Madrone Road near Glen Ellen.

The Sonoma Valley's prolific farmers congregate at the **farmers market** in Depot Park, a block north of the plaza on 1st Street West, every Friday morning year-round. April–October there's an additional market in front of city hall on Tuesday evenings, 5:30 P.M.–dusk.

INFORMATION AND SERVICES

First stop for visitors to the Sonoma Valley should be the **Sonoma Valley Visitors Bureau** (453 1st St. E., Sonoma, 707/996-1090, www.sonomavalley.com, 9 A.M.–5 P.M. Mon.–Sat., 10 A.M.–5 P.M. Sun.) in the Carnegie Library building in the middle of the plaza right next to city hall and across from the Sebastiani Theatre. It publishes a free valley guide, and its staff is happy to dispense all sorts of local information for nothing more than an entry in the visitors book. There's a branch of the visitors bureau just through the gates of the Viansa Winery in Carneros.

If you're staying in the valley, be sure to pick up a copy of the *Sonoma Index-Tribune* newspaper, which has been published for more than 100 years and now comes out twice a week. It is full of local news, gossip, event information, and reviews.

For wine-related information, including events at individual wineries, check the website of the **Sonoma County Wineries Association** (www.sonomawine.com), which represents all of Sonoma's wineries, including those in the valley. The **Heart of Sonoma Valley Association** (www.heartofthevalley.com) represents only those wineries around Glen Ellen and Kenwood and organizes plenty of local events throughout the year.

Los Carneros

Replace the vineyards with grass, throw in a few more cows, and the Carneros area would probably look a lot like it did 100 years ago. *Carneros* is Spanish for sheep or ram, and grazing was the mainstay of the region for hundreds of years. In fact, it has more of a Wild West feel to it than most of the Wine Country and was home to the annual Sonoma Rodeo until 1950. These days it's car and bike racing at the Infineon Raceway that draws adrenalin addicts, but even here the area's bovine history is celebrated by the snarling supercharged cow that sits atop the giant raceway billboard.

In addition to the grazing land that used to dominate the Carneros area, there were also fruit orchards growing every type of soft fruit. The first vineyards were thought to have been planted in the 1830s, and by the end of the 1800s the advent of the ferries and railroad had made Carneros a veritable fruit and wine basket.

Phylloxera and Prohibition wiped out the small wine industry in Carneros in the early 1900s, and it didn't get back on its feet again until the 1960s. By then the fruit growers had moved elsewhere, and the march of the vineyards across the pastureland began.

Today, the western part of Carneros primarily resembles grazing land, and huge marshes still merge at the edge of the bay with the low-lying flatlands. Drive east and the low rolling hills are now covered with vineyards as far as the eye can see, a sign that cows will probably not return anytime soon.

The Wines

The 39,000-acre Los Carneros appellation borders San Pablo Bay and straddles the county line dividing Napa and Sonoma Counties, though the majority of its vineyards are actually on the Sonoma side of that line. Hence it's included in this chapter and not in the Napa Valley chapter, although both regions claim it as their own. The cool winds that blow off the bay and the murky cloud cover that often takes half the morning to burn off in the summer help make this one of the coolest appellations in California, ideal for growing pinot noir, chardonnay, and other grapes with a flavor profile that makes crisp, aromatic, and well-balanced wines.

Not surprisingly, those two varietals fill 85 percent of the vineyards, but more winemakers are now discovering that very distinctive wines can be made from syrah and merlot grapes grown here. Carneros is about as cool as it can be for merlot to ripen completely, and the resulting wines have a greater structure and subtlety than their hot-climate cousins.

Despite its cool, damp appearance, Carneros actually gets less annual rainfall than any other part of Napa or Sonoma County. In addition, the fertile-looking topsoil is usually only a few feet deep and sits on top of a layer of dense cold clay that is unforgiving to vines and forces them to put more energy into producing fruit than leaves.

There are far fewer wineries in the Carneros region than its size might suggest. Its prized cool growing conditions mean that most of the vineyards seen from the road are either owned by, or sell their grapes to, wineries based outside the area. Those that are open range from international champagne houses to tiny family-owned businesses where you're more likely to experience informative (and occasionally free)

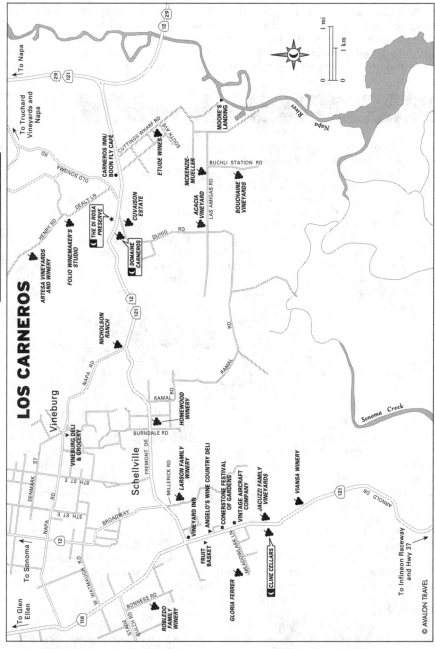

SOUTHERN SONOMA

LOS CARNEROS

To Napa

To Truchard Vineyards and Napa

OLD SONOMA RD

HENRY RD

DEALY LN

ARTESA VINEYARDS AND WINERY

FOLIO WINEMAKER'S STUDIO

THE DI ROSA PRESERVE

CARNEROS INN/ BOON FLY CAFE

CUTTINGS WHARF RD

SOUTH AVE

ETUDE WINES

MOORE'S LANDING

CUVAISON ESTATE

DOMAINE CARNEROS

DUHIG RD

MCKENZIE-MUELLER

ACACIA VINEYARD

LAS AMIGAS RD

BUCHLI STATION RD

BOUCHAINE VINEYARDS

Napa River

1 mi

1 km

NICHOLSON RANCH

NAPA RD

RAMAL RD

RAMAL RD

Sonoma Creek

Vineburg

VINEBURG DELI & GROCERY

BURNDALE RD

HOMEWOOD WINERY

FREMONT DR

Schellville

DENMARK ST

8TH ST E

5TH ST E

BROADWAY

NAPA RD

MILLERICK RD

LARSON FAMILY WINERY

VINEYARD INN

ANGELO'S WINE COUNTRY DELI

CORNERSTONE FESTIVAL OF GARDENS

VINTAGE AIRCRAFT COMPANY

JACUZZI FAMILY VINEYARDS

VIANSA WINERY

FRUIT BASKET

MEADOWLARK LN

GLORIA FERRER

CLINE CELLARS

ARNOLD DR

121

To Infineon Raceway and Hwy 37

To Sonoma

12

To Glen Ellen

116

W WATMAUGH RD

STAGE GULCH RD

BONNESS RD

ROBLEDO FAMILY WINERY

To Napa

29

121

12

29

12

121

© AVALON TRAVEL

tasting sessions that used to be the norm in Napa and Sonoma but are, alas, no more.

Finding some of the wineries can be a test, best taken when sober. Plenty of big white signs mark the vineyard owners, but they're of absolutely no help in actually finding a winery, so a sharp eye is needed to spot the tiny signs tied to trees and posts. Most of the bigger wineries are fairly obvious from the main road, however, and there are few back roads on which to get lost.

WINE-TASTING
Eastern Carneros Wineries
ARTESA VINEYARDS & WINERY

A sure sign of how close this part of Carneros is to the Napa Valley, both geographically and culturally, is the marriage of wine, art, and design at Artesa (1345 Henry Rd., Napa, 707/224-1668, www.artesawinery.com, 10 A.M.–5 P.M. daily, tasting $10–20), an outpost of the historic Spanish sparkling wine producer Codorníu. The grass-covered winery was designed by Barcelona architect Domingo Triay to blend in with the surrounding land, and to a certain extent he succeeded: Driving up tiny Henry Road through the vineyards, the only sign of the winery's presence is that one of the low hills happens to be peculiarly square-shaped.

Art is everywhere, from the sculptures and reflecting pools around the parking lot up to the gallery-like interior of the winery, and much of it was created by the winery's artist-in-residence, Gordon Huether, who also has his own gallery in Napa. The airy tasting room has a spacious indoor seating area and large (if breezy) patio overlooking the Carneros vineyards, and a small museum gives some history of champagne making and the Codorníu family.

Like those of most Carneros wineries, Artesa's 350 acres of vineyards are planted primarily with chardonnay and pinot noir, and the wine list reflects this. The winery also makes cabernet sauvignon, merlot, and syrah from Napa and Sonoma County grapes. Despite being owned by one of the world's great producers of cava sparkling wines, however, Artesa doesn't make any sparkling wine here, although it does offer tasting of some from Spain.

There are several tasting options in the sleek tasting room with its adjoining patio overlooking the vineyards. You can try the lower tiers of wines or the limited releases. Alternatively, a horizontal tasting of pinots from both Carneros and the Russian River Valley illustrates the subtle differences inherent to the wines from each region. Overall, however, the tasting options don't quite match the architectural and artistic scope of the winery, but tours are offered at 11 A.M. and 2 P.M. daily ($20). Perusing the art is free.

FOLIO WINEMAKER'S STUDIO

Just down the road from the fake hill of Artesa, in a homey yet modern farmhouse, is a tasting room that can be either inspiring or intimidating, depending on your mood. Folio (1285 Dealy Ln., Napa, 707/256-2757, www. folio winestudio.com, noon–5 P.M. Mon.–Tues., 11 A.M.–5 P.M. Fri.–Sun., tasting $10–20) is the home of no less than 35 different wines under seven different labels, all linked through some sort of family tie to the founder of Folio Fine Wine Partners, Michael Mondavi, who was long considered the less successful of the three children of famed winemaker Robert Mondavi. His son, Rob, is winemaker for many of the labels, which include one named for his wife, Isabel.

The seven different labels account for about 35,000 cases of wine per year, which might sound like a lot but is actually only an average 1,000 cases per wine. To complicate things further, however, there are three additional wine brands you can taste here that use the Folio facility to produce their "custom crush" wines. The result is a dizzying array of wines on the tasting menu, many with names that offer no clue as to their style or origins. They are organized by varietal, which might sound helpful, except it means you might end up tasting a Carneros pinot alongside one from Oregon. Be sure to question the server thoroughly before deciding which of the wines to taste. That will help ensure you're less intimidated and more inspired by one of the more diverse tasting line-ups in Carneros.

If you can afford it, go for the more expensive "artisan" tasting, which includes pinots from some of the best West Coast pinot growing regions and a nice selection of old-vine zinfandels. If it's a quiet day and the weather's nice, then also be sure to make a beeline for the verandah at the back of the house through the door to the right of the main tasting bar. Piped music aside, it's a peaceful and cozy space overlooking a small secluded vineyard. Bring your own food and buy a bottle of rosé at the bar for a relaxing lunch.

◖ DOMAINE CARNEROS
The French heritage of one of California's premier champagne houses is obvious when you see the ornate château and its formal gardens on a low hill next to the main road. The Domaine Carneros estate (1240 Duhig Rd., Napa, 707/257-0101, www.domainecarneros.com, 10 A.M.–6 P.M. daily, tasting $15) was built in the style of the 18th-century Chateau de la Marquetterie, home of one of the winery's principal founders, Champagne Taittinger. The sweeping staircase leading from the parking lot and the palatial interior leave no doubt about the winery's fancy French pedigree. It all feels a little over-the-top, particularly when contrasted with the rustic, windswept Carneros landscape on a foggy day. With some sun on a less crowded day, however, it can feel almost magical. Be warned, however: Less crowded days in the middle of summer can be rare.

When it opened in 1990 it was the first Carneros winery devoted to champagne production and now produces more than 40,000 cases per year of sparkling wines, including a regular brut, brut rosé, and the flagship Le Rêve blanc de blancs that is made from 100 percent chardonnay and considered one of California's top champagnes. The most interesting sparkler, however, is the LD (late-disgorged) brut, which has an extra creaminess and crispness that comes from leaving the lees in the bottle for longer before it is disgorged, essentially slowing down the bottle-aging process.

Domaine Carneros, a taste of French glamour in Carneros

In 2003, Domaine Carneros achieved another first when it opened the first Carneros wine-making facility dedicated to pinot noir production right behind the château. The solar-powered facility was designed to look like a carriage house to fit with the château theme. It produces about 15,000 cases of the winery's three pinot noirs. All the Domaine Carneros wines are made using grapes from the 300 acres of organically farmed vineyards around the winery.

There are three informative tours per day (11 A.M., 1 P.M., and 3 P.M.) that let visitors peer into the squeaky-clean, modern production and bottling areas after first sitting through a rather tiring PR-laden DVD presentation. At $25 per person, the tours offer the best value because they include a tasting of four wines along the way and you get to keep the tasting glass. Alternatively, one can simply chill on the huge terrace overlooking the vineyards and let the bubbles do their work, perhaps with some caviar or a cheese plate to help the wines go down. The tasting flight of three sparkling wines (including the Le Rêve flagship) or all three pinots is $15. Wines by the glass start at $6 and come with a few morsels to eat.

CUVAISON ESTATE

Right opposite the entrance to Domaine Carneros and its fancy French architectural excesses is the modern and minimalist home of Cuvaison (1221 Duhig Rd., Napa, 707/942-2455, www.cuvaison.com, 10 A.M.–5 P.M. daily, tasting $15), a winery that (rather ironically) takes its name from an old French term describing the part of the winemaking process that gives red wine its color. Cuvaison lets nature do the talking with an airy and contemporary concrete, wood, and glass indoor-outdoor tasting lounge from which you can almost reach out and touch the vines.

Also unlike its neighbor, Cuvaison is a bubble-free zone, and the portfolio of still wines here reflects the history of the winery. It was founded in the late 1960s at the northern end of Napa Valley near Calistoga (where the winery's second tasting room is located), but changed ownership in the 1970s and underwent a dramatic expansion, buying up hundreds of acres of land in Carneros, where the bulk of its estate vineyards and this tasting room are located today. In the late 1990s a prime vineyard on nearby Mount Veeder was bought, making Napa Valley cabernet as important a part of the portfolio as the Carneros-grown pinot, chardonnay, merlot, and syrah.

Although the tasting room only opened in 2009, the winemaking facility across the parking lot was up and running five years earlier, and a few years before that a new winemaker and new management arrived on the scene. By all accounts, this makeover of Cuvaison over the last decade had a big impact on the quality of the wines. The chardonnays and pinots here are as good as any in the area, particularly the pricier single-block versions, and they regularly get high ratings from the critics (chardonnay accounts for about two thirds of the winery's annual production of 60,000 cases). The syrah and merlot are also nicely made and offer a change from the usual Carneros varietals.

The real treat, however, is the Mount Veeder cabernet sauvignon, which is about as far from a fruit-bomb as a Napa cabernet can get. This is very much an Old World style of cabernet, with a balance, concentration, and structure typical of wines made from mountain-grown fruit.

Although Cuvaison advertises this tasting room as appointment-only, there's usually no problem rolling up unannounced. It's worth calling ahead if you can, however, because it can get crowded at certain times of the day.

BOUCHAINE VINEYARDS

Before turning in to the palatial grounds of Domaine Carneros, continue on Duhig Road for about a mile into the flatlands, turn left on Las Amigas Road, and then right on Buchli Station Road to get to this historic spot out on the scenic flatlands of Carneros close to the bay.

The current Bouchaine winery (1075 Buchli Station Rd., Napa, 707/252-9065, www.bouchaine.com, 10:30 A.M.–4 P.M. daily, tasting $15–30) was established in 1981, but there has been a winery on the site since 1934, when the Garetto Winery was established, and grapes were first grown here way back in 1899. Not much remains of the old winery following a 1990s renovation, although the old redwood tanks were recycled to create the sidings of some of the current buildings. The cozy tasting room is refreshingly free of Wine Country paraphernalia, and for a little more money you can taste the wines with cheese and olives on the veranda overlooking the vineyards with San Pablo Bay in the distance.

The winery's picnic area, however, is reserved for its club members and those who preorder a "Table for Two" picnic lunch, which includes a wine tasting, freshly prepared food, and a bottle of wine. At $75 for two people, it's as good a way to have lunch as any in Carneros, particularly if the sun is out. The lunch option is offered May–October and must be booked at least a day in advance. Bouchaine is also a popular stop for bikers who relish the quiet, straight, and flat roads of the area.

Bouchaine grows pinot noir, chardonnay, and a small amount of pinot gris in its 90 acres of Carneros vineyards and also sources grapes from neighboring vineyards for the 30,000 cases of wine produced annually. Pinot noir and chardonnay account for much of the production and include the pricey estate versions, blends from multiple Carneros vineyards, and some limited-production Bacchus Collection wines. The cheaper Buchli Station–labeled wines are generally not sourced from the Carneros region, however.

The estate wines are certainly good, but some of the more interesting wines are in the Bacchus Collection. They include the popular Chene d'Argent, a crisp and fruity chardonnay made with no oak contact at all, and a light, flowery pinot meunier, a varietal that is normally used as a blending grape in champagne production. There's also a spicy syrah sourced from northern Sonoma vineyards and a good gewürztraminer from Mendocino's Anderson Valley.

The appointment-only tour of the winery is worth taking just to see the old concrete open-top fermenters that are used instead of more modern stainless steel to ferment the pinot noirs.

HOMEWOOD WINERY

Just a mile or so from the grandeur and glitz of Domaine Carneros, halfway down tiny Burndale Road, is the down-home atmosphere of Homewood Winery (23120 Burndale Rd., Sonoma, 707/996-6353, www.homewood winery.com, 10 A.M.–4 P.M. daily, free tasting), where owner and winemaker Dave Homewood produces just 3,000 cases of reasonably priced wines from grapes he buys all over Napa, Sonoma, and often far beyond. A couple of acres of pinot noir right outside the tasting room were recent additions and started producing wines for the 2005 vintage.

The focus here is on small batches of a variety of mainly red wines like zinfandel, merlot, syrah, and bordeaux-style red blends sourced from vineyards elsewhere in Sonoma and Napa. There are also some excellent Napa and Carneros chardonnays available, and a couple of bottlings of pinot noir sourced from a neighboring Carneros vineyard. Most wines are very reasonably priced, with the best bang for the buck being the Flying Whizzbangers, a zinfandel-dominated red blend.

The staff will happily spend an hour or more with visitors in the tiny tasting room explaining the wines, conducting some vertical tastings, and teaching some tasting tricks, like how to identify the oak used in the barrels. That is, if no big groups arrive; otherwise the small indoor tasting area can quickly get claustrophobic, and it's best to spill out onto the back porch "lounge" if it's open. Be sure to check out the olive oils also sold at the winery.

Wineries by Appointment

Tucked away off the well-beaten path of the Carneros Highway are some notable appointment-only wineries that give more opportunities to discover some hot wines from the cool Carneros region.

MCKENZIE-MUELLER

The McKenzie-Mueller winery (2530 Las

Amigas Rd., Napa, 707/252-0186, www
.mckenziemueller.com) is the family-run
operation of Napa Valley wine veterans Bob
and Karen Mueller. From their 50 acres of estate vineyards they produce only 2,500 cases
of wine, encompassing many varietals, including merlot, pinot noir, and cabernet sauvignon.
Standouts include a steel-fermented pinot grigio and an aromatic cabernet franc, which is
made with fruit from both Carneros and Napa
Valley's Oak Knoll appellation. A large proportion of the vineyard grapes are sold to other
wineries. The winery is on Las Amigas Road
at the junction with Buchli Road, just up the
road from Bouchaine.

ACACIA VINEYARD

Just down Las Amigas Road from McKenzie-
Mueller is Acacia Vineyard (2750 Las Amigas
Rd., Napa, 707/226-9991 or 877/226-1700,
www.acaciavineyard.com, by appointment
10 A.M.–4 P.M. Mon.–Sat., noon–4 P.M.
Sun.), a much larger winery that has produced
pinot and chardonnay wines since 1979 and
now owns 150 acres of local vineyards. The
rather inelegantly named but powerful-tasting
Marsh chardonnay is worth buying just for
the fact that proceeds support the restoration
of the nearby Napa-Sonoma Marsh. Acacia is
on Las Amigas Road near the junction with
Duhig Road.

ETUDE WINES

At the eastern end of Carneros close to Napa
is Etude Wines (1250 Cuttings Wharf Rd.,
Napa, 707/257-5300, www.etudewines.com),
which is well known for its refined but pricey
Carneros pinot noir. It also produces pinot blanc
and pinot gris from local Carneros vineyards
together with some Napa Valley merlot and cabernet. The winery is owned by the multinational
Fosters Wine Estates and offers tastings by
appointment 10 A.M.–4:30 P.M. daily.

The highly acclaimed wines made by
Truchard Vineyards (3234 Old Sonoma Rd.,
Napa, 707/253-7153, www.truchardvineyards
.com) come from its huge 270-acre Carneros
vineyard, where 10 varietals are grown,

including cabernet, tempranillo, and zinfandel grapes that reflect the vineyard's location
near the border with the warmer Napa Valley.
Truchard sell most of its estate grapes to other
wineries, using around 20 percent to make
its 15,000 cases of premium limited-release
wines, the best of which are the elegant syrah
and pinot noir. A tour and $15 tasting also
provides the chance to see the winery's 100-
year-old barn.

Western Carneros Wineries
NICHOLSON RANCH

Though just outside the Los Carneros appellation boundary by literally a few yards (it's
technically in the Sonoma Valley appellation),
the mission-style Nicholson Ranch winery
(4200 Napa Rd., Sonoma, 707/938-8822,
www.nicholsonranch.com, 10 A.M.–6 P.M.
daily, tasting $10) is perched on a small
hill above the intersection of the Carneros
Highway and Napa Road, putting it on the
route of most visitors to Carneros or anyone
heading to or from Napa beyond.

The winery, opened in 2003, was built by
the Nicholson family on land where Socrates
Nicholson, a first-generation Greek immigrant, had spent decades raising the other
major Carneros agricultural product: cows.
His daughter and her husband are the brains
behind the winery, and dotted around the
hillsides are Greek flourishes that hint at the
family's heritage, including a small temple
near the visitor parking lot.

Nicholson Ranch is predominantly a pinot
and chardonnay producer, and those two varietals account for much of the 10,000 cases
of wine made each year. The chardonnays,
and in particular the flagship Cuvée Natalie,
garner some good reviews from critics, and bottle prices are generally reasonable. The winery
also makes small quantities of syrah and merlot from local vineyards, both of which exhibit
the classic aromas and restraint of cool-climate
wines. Tasting is $10, but you can usually
sample two or three vintages of some of the five
chardonnays and four pinot noirs available, all
worth trying. For just $5 more, you can take an

A roadside sign in Carneros extols the virtues of the humble grape.

appointment-only tour of the winery caves and winemaking facilities with a couple of extra tastes thrown in along the way.

The bright and spacious tasting room oozes sophistication, with limestone floors and a cherrywood central tasting bar topped with granite. Cheap gifts are nowhere to be seen, but a modest selection of picnic supplies are sold, including a cheese plate that can be paired with one of the half bottles of chardonnay available to create a nice lunch for two. There are tables on the veranda overlooking the surrounding hills and a grassy area next to the pond for those days when the weather's cooperating. The tasting room is open later than most in the area, even in winter, so those on a hectic schedule should make this their last winery of the day.

LARSON FAMILY WINERY
To get to this historic patch of land, you must turn off Highway 121 and head towards the wetlands, down a small country road almost as far as dry land will take you. Only the whimsical, hand-painted signs along the way suggest there's civilization at the end of the road. The Larson Family Winery (23355 Millerick Rd., Sonoma, 707/938-3031, www .larsonfamilywinery.com, 10 A.M.–5 P.M. daily, tasting $5) is situated next to Sonoma Creek at the edge of the San Pablo Bay, near what was once call Wingo, where steamships from San Francisco docked in the mid-1800s and disgorged their Sonoma-bound passengers. It's a pretty part of the world, but being surrounded by wetlands has its disadvantages. The area is prone to flooding during winter rains, and summer days can be a bit chilly this close to the water.

A 100-acre plot of land and farmhouse were bought in 1899 by Michael Millerick, the great-grandfather of winery owner Tom Larson. The Millerick Ranch found local fame for decades as the site of the Sonoma Rodeo until, in the 1970s, it succumbed to the steady advance of vineyards across Carneros.

The Larson family has been a big player in the Carneros wine scene ever since. The Larson

Family Winery rose, phoenix-like, from the financial ashes of the Sonoma Creek Winery, which filed for bankruptcy in 2003 some 25 years after it was formed by Tom and his father. The Sonoma Creek brand and inventory was eventually sold and the creditors paid off, leaving Tom Larson free to start on his latest winemaking venture.

Today, the winery produces about 4,000 cases of wine from its 70 acres of Carneros vineyards, as well as a far larger amount under contract for the new owners of the Sonoma Creek brand. Despite the relatively small production of Larson wines, the portfolio is large and dominated by cool-climate Carneros wines including pinot noir, barrel-aged chardonnay, and a gewürztraminer. Standouts among the reds include an unusual (and cheap) house blend of cabernet, merlot, and pinot noir, a petite sirah made using fruit from both Sonoma and Amador County in the warm Sierra Foothills, and an award-winning estate cabernet sauvignon, which is one of the only wines sealed with a cork rather than cheaper screw-caps. The small production does mean that some wines might be sold out by late summer, however.

You won't find Larson wines on many reviewers' lists, but part of the fun of visiting here is the unique location and the down-home family-farm atmosphere that'll be a hit with kids and provide a refreshing contrast to the fancier wineries all around. The winery tasting room is in an old redwood barn with a small enclosure of goats and sheep right opposite and usually a couple of the winery dogs, Pete, Bubba and Sonny, lounging nearby. You might also be lucky enough to see the pet llama.

There's also a regulation-sized boccie ball court and a grassy picnic and play area behind the tasting room to enjoy a bite to eat with a bottle of Larson's Wingo White, a tantalizing blend of chardonnay, sauvignon blanc, and gewürztraminer. Jeep tours of the surrounding vineyards and wetlands are also sometimes available through an unaffiliated company—just look for the bright green Jeep in the parking lot.

◖ CLINE CELLARS

Originally established across the bay in Contra Costa County, Cline (24737 Hwy. 121, Sonoma, 707/940-4000 or 800/546-2070, www.clinecellars.com, 10 A.M.–6 P.M. daily, free tasting) has come to thrive in southern Sonoma much like the lush, spring-fed garden oasis it calls home. The winery moved here in 1991 and brought its East Bay emphasis on Rhône varietals, planting syrah, viognier, marsanne, and roussanne instead of the more usual Carneros varietals, pinot noir and chardonnay. Cline is now one of Sonoma's biggest makers of Rhône-style wines and produces about 200,000 cases of wine a year from vineyards all over the Bay Area.

Despite being a relatively new member of the winery set in Carneros, Cline sits on some historic land. The tasting room is in a modest farmhouse with wraparound porch that dates from 1850. It sits on land that was once the site of a Miwok Indian village and later used by Father Altimira as a forward camp while investigating a site for what would become the Sonoma mission. Natural springs feed the three ponds and help sustain the giant willow trees, magnolias, and colorful flower beds surrounding small patches of lawn that are ideal for picnics. The tasting room contains a small deli, and the wines include several picnic-friendly options, including a light and fruity blend of chardonnay and pinot grigio and a dry mourvèdre rosé.

The winery's colorful history comes alive in the three tours offered daily at 11 A.M., 1 P.M., and 3 P.M. Celebrating the site's history as a temporary Spanish mission, the California Missions Museum is located in a barn right behind the tasting room and displays intricately detailed scale models of every single Californian Mission, from the first in San Diego to the last just north of here in Sonoma. They were created by two German cabinetmakers for the 1939 World's Fair in San Francisco and all bought by the Cline family in 1998 to keep the collection together.

The wines are a pleasant change from the Carneros staples of pinot and chardonnay, and most are pleasantly priced at $20 or less. Standouts among the whites include a full-bodied yet dry blend of marsanne and roussanne, two traditional varietals from France's Rhône region, and the fun, fruity chardonnay–pinot grigio blend. All the red Rhône varietals sourced from Cline's East Bay vineyards are worth tasting, particularly the Cashmere, a velvety blend of grenache, mourvèdre, and syrah; a bright and flavorful carignane; and a dark, brooding mourvèdre. The Sonoma wines include some nice examples of cool-climate syrah and zinfandel, the best of which are the single-vineyard versions that cost $1 each to taste.

JACUZZI FAMILY VINEYARDS

Right across the road from Cline Cellars is another Cline family venture in the form of a giant Tuscan farmhouse, an homage to the family's Italian heritage. Jacuzzi Family Vineyards (24737 Arnold Dr., Sonoma, 707/940-4031, www.jacuzziwines.com, 10 A.M.–5:30 P.M. daily, free tasting) was opened in mid-2007 and is modeled after the Jacuzzi family home in Italy—the same Jacuzzi family that invented the eponymous bubbling bathtubs. In that sense it could be considered as another Carneros producer of bubbly.

Valeriano Jacuzzi, the grandfather of Fred Cline, immigrated to the United States in 1907 and eventually found his way to California, where he established an aeronautical engineering firm with his brothers—hence the giant airplane propeller on display in the main courtyard. Over the decades, that same company went from making aircraft to water pumps and filters, and eventually invented various hydrotherapy devices that morphed into the prototype Jacuzzi bathtubs in the 1960s. During the Depression, Valeriano also planted a vineyard in Contra Costa County, the same vineyard that is the source of Cline's Ancient Vine Rhône varietals today.

The Cline connection with Jacuzzi is not heavily publicized at the winery (and neither is the Jacuzzi connection to bathtubs), but Jacuzzi-label wines were being made for several years before the winery opened and are sourced from Cline family vineyards across Sonoma. They include the classic Italian varietals nebbiolo, primitivo, and pinot grigio as well as the more common varietals in this part of the world like chardonnay, pinot noir, and merlot. The flagship red wine is named after Valeriano and is the winery's version of a super-Tuscan blend, albeit one incorporating the rather unusual combination of cabernet, malbec, barbera, and merlot. The flagship white is named after Valeriano's wife, Giuseppina, and is a mellow example of a Carneros chardonnay.

Jacuzzi is also the new home of Sonoma olive oil producer **The Olive Press** (www.theolivepress.com), which used to be based up in Glen Ellen. Its small tasting room is on the right as you enter the winery (for wine, turn left) and is the place to discover that olive oils can be as diverse in taste as wines. A small tasting bar usually features oils ranging from a light and grassy taste up to a rich, mellow one, with flavors generally determined by the olives used and where they're grown (sound similar to wine-grape lore?). The Olive Press is also a functioning production center, processing olives from growers across Northern California, and it sells a full range of oil-related gifts, from cookbooks and oil containers to soaps.

From a distance, the giant stone structure surrounded by lush gardens containing mature fig and olive trees looks distinctly marooned on the windswept Carneros flats. Up close, however, the imposing building with its huge courtyard overlooking the wetlands is impressive and another example of just how much money is sloshing around this part of the Wine Country. Thankfully visitors will not have to slosh around much of their own money, because tasting is free, although that could change once the winery becomes better known and a regular stop for tour buses. Some parts of the winery were still being completed as this edition went to press, so check the website for information about tours.

ROBLEDO FAMILY WINERY

If you ever wondered about the fate of the laborers who hand-pick the grapes throughout

CHAMPAGNE CENTRAL

The French fiercely guard the word *Champagne*, and over the last few decades they have forced much of the rest of the world to accept that a sparkling wine can only be called Champagne if it comes from the Champagne region of France, just east of Paris. Their hardest won battle was with the United States, and it wasn't until 2006 that the U.S. government agreed to prevent American wineries from using traditional French regional names like Burgundy and Champagne on their labels.

The agreement was part of broader trade talks, but there was a small catch for the French: American wineries already using the term *Champagne* on their labels could continue to use it. Most Californian wineries, however, have long stuck to the term *sparkling wine* to describe their bubbly and *méthode champenoise* to describe how it's made.

Champagne-style wines have popped up all over the world over the centuries, from the sophisticated cava wines of Spain that have been made for hundreds of years to the more recent rise of sparkling wines in California, where Carneros is the center of it all.

In the 1980s and 1990s, the world's top producers of cava and champagne saw the potential of Carneros to produce world-class sparkling wines, and many set up shop in the area. The two biggest cava makers in Spain, Freixenet and Codorníu, are represented by the Carneros wineries Gloria Ferrer and Artesa, while Domain Carneros is the American outpost of champagne house Taittinger.

The local wineries of many other big French champagne houses, including Mumm, Krug, and Moët & Chandon, might be located in the nearby Napa Valley, but all grow a large proportion of their champagne grapes in Carneros.

The cool climate of Carneros is ideally suited for growing the two most important champagne grape varietals, chardonnay and pinot noir. Brisk winds and overcast summer mornings might not be the best conditions for touring with the top down, but a taste of some crisp local champagne more than makes up for the morning chill.

the Wine Country, a visit to this winery will provide one answer. In the 1970s, Mexican immigrant Reynaldo Robledo was one of those laborers working in local vineyards, a job that was the beginning of his path to realizing the American Dream. He eventually formed a successful vineyard management company and finally created his dream winery, making his first commercial vintage in 1998.

The Robledo Family winery (21901 Bonness Rd., Sonoma, 707/939-6903, www.robledo familywinery.com, by appointment 10 A.M.–5 P.M. Mon.–Sat., 11 A.M.–4 P.M. Sun., tasting $5–10) is a low-key affair down a sleepy, semirural residential street off Highway 116 (Arnold Drive) just north of the busy junction with Highway 121. Despite the lack of architectural flourishes of the big wineries nearby, the small tasting area with a giant oak communal table at its center is located in the barrel room, providing a wonderfully cool and intimate atmosphere in which to sample the wines surrounded by towering racks of barrels. You're also likely to be served by one of the Robledo family, so be sure to ask about the story of Reynaldo.

Grapes for the merlot, pinot noir, and chardonnay come from Robledo's three separate estate vineyards in Carneros, totaling 30 acres. There's also the chance to try cabernet sauvignon and sauvignon blanc from Robledo's Oak Ranch vineyard in the much warmer Lake County region north of the Napa Valley—not wines that are often found on tasting menus in this part of the world. Production is about 20,000 cases a year, making this a small winery by local standards but fairly large considering its family roots.

GLORIA FERRER

At one end of Carneros is Artesa, the California outpost of one of the giants of cava production in Spain. At the other end is Gloria Ferrer (23555 Carneros Hwy., Sonoma, 707/933-1917, www.gloriaferrer.com, 10 A.M.–5 P.M. daily), representing the other global Spanish bubbly producer, Freixenet, now the largest sparkling wine producer in the world. The fact that both these Spanish companies joined the largest French champagne houses in Carneros over the years is simply further testament to the ideal growing conditions here for the chardonnay and pinot noir grapes used to make classic sparkling wines.

Gloria is the wife of José Ferrer, latest in a long line of Ferrers to have made Spanish champagnes, and they opened their little piece of Spain here in 1986. The winery is styled much like a Spanish farmhouse, with stucco walls, tiled floors, and a large terrace that has sweeping views south over San Pablo Bay and far beyond. It can get crowded, but if you can snag a terrace table and it's not too foggy, there are few better places in Carneros to enjoy an early evening aperitif.

It now has the largest selection of champagnes in Carneros, priced from a modest $20 for the classic Brut or lively and aromatic Va de Vi up to $50 for the flagship Carneros Cuvée in a distinctly curvaceous bottle that matches its smooth elegance. In addition to the champagnes, the winery also makes an increasing quantity of still wines. There are four pinot noirs, including several highly regarded single-vineyard versions, as well as several chardonnays and small quantities of both syrah and merlot. In all, more than 100,000 cases of wine are now made here from almost 400 acres of Carneros vineyards.

The informative daily tours ($10) take in the long, cool cellars in the hillside behind the winery and are as good a lesson in how to make champagne as you'll find at any other sparkling wine producer (call for times). Alternatively you can relax on the terrace with your choice of wine. The set up is more wine bar than tasting room—buy a glass of champagne, prices of which range $5–10 per glass, or taste the still wines in generous two-ounce pours for $2–3 each.

The visitors center shop is not only the place to buy wines but also to pick up all sorts of edibles, from picnic supplies and Spanish cooking ingredients to cookbooks and striking, pop art–inspired posters for some of the wines. You can also bring your own food, although you'll have to buy some wine if you want to eat it here and be happy sitting at a table—the only patch of picnic-worthy grass is essentially in the parking lot next to the entrance steps, a hectic position likely to give you indigestion.

VIANSA WINERY & ITALIAN MARKETPLACE

When a family dispute forced Sam Sebastiani out of his family's historic winery in Sonoma in the mid-1980s, he and wife, Vicki, founded their own operation down in Carneros and used a contraction of their own names (Vicki and Sam) to christen it. The Viansa winery (25200 Arnold Dr., Sonoma, 800/995-4740, www.viansa.com, 10 A.M.–5 P.M. daily, tasting $5–10) and

Tuscan themes are everywhere at Viansa.

its pretty gardens are perched on a windswept knoll overlooking the wetlands of Carneros, and the Italian heritage of its founders is obvious from the Tuscan-style architecture of the terracotta–roofed villa and from the 55,000 cases of Cal-Ital wines made there each year.

Although the winery was sold in 2004 shortly after Sam and Vicki divorced and the new owners have struggled, Viansa remains as popular as ever, with its 15,000 dedicated wine club members swallowing up much of the wine production and the giant parking lot regularly filled to overflowing with cars and tour buses.

Cabernet sauvignon, merlot, and chardonnay are about the only non-Italian wines you'll find here. The long tasting menu is instead filled with red Italian varietals like sangiovese, barbera, dolcetto, nebbiolo, and freisa, and whites including pinot grigio, arneis, and vernaccia. Most of those grapes are grown in Viansa's own estate vineyards and elsewhere in Sonoma.

If you've never heard of most of those grapes, the $5 tasting of four wines will be a good introduction. The premier tasting option ($10) includes reserve cabernet sauvignon and the Samuele cabernet franc, named for the founder of the Sebastiani wine-making heritage in Sonoma.

As your mouth waters from the crisp, food-friendly reds and whites, the vast array of deli foods also sold in the tasting room will seem all the more appealing. (As it is such a popular destination for busloads of visitors, however, you might end up feeling more like a Mediterranean sardine yourself.) Many of the wines are also a perfect accompaniment (and price) for a picnic, and you can buy most by the glass from the tasting bar.

The neighboring 90-acre wetlands built by Viansa with the bay in the distance make a fine view from the numerous picnic tables on the long terrace, marred only by the constant drone of traffic and the sometimes-brisk winds. In the spring (Feb.–May), two-hour **wetland tours** are offered every other Sunday for $15, or for $25 with lunch. Call the winery for more

details and reservations. Tours of the winery itself are offered twice a day at 11 A.M. and 2 P.M. and are free with the $5 tasting fee.

MACROSTIE WINERY & VINEYARDS
Just south of Sonoma, MacRostie (21481 8th St. E., Sonoma, 707/996-4480, www.macrostiewinery.com) makes 20,000 cases of highly regarded and elegantly understated chardonnay, pinot noir, and syrah from vineyards all over Carneros, including Steve MacRostie's own local Wildcat Mountain vineyard, a windswept hillside that he first planted in 1998. The winery is open for tastings 11 A.M.–4:30 P.M. Saturday, or call for an appointment Monday–Friday.

SIGHTS
◖ The di Rosa Preserve
When writer Rene di Rosa sought rural tranquility in 1960 and bought some old grazing land in Carneros, locals might have thought they were as likely to see cows walking on water as the eventual creation of the biggest collection of Northern Californian contemporary art and one of the largest regional art collections in the country. Thirty years later, they saw both.

The di Rosa Preserve (5200 Carneros Hwy./Hwy. 121, Napa, 707/226-5991, www.dirosaart.org) opened to the public in 1997 and now has more than 2,000 works on display throughout its 217 acres, including a colorful cow that has floated on the 35-acre lake since 1989, although it occasionally tips over.

When he bought the land, di Rosa restored a turreted former winery building as his residence and eventually planted 250 acres of vineyards on the land where grapes were once grown until disease and Prohibition killed the wine industry. The art first came from local artists, often through barter arrangements, and di Rosa eventually sold off the vineyards to focus purely on his passion for collecting art.

The Winery Lake vineyards are now owned by Sterling Vineyards (the Winery Lake name can be seen on some of Sterling's premium merlot, pinot noir, and chardonnay wines), and the old winery building is now one of the four indoor galleries on the grounds of the preserve.

Di Rosa himself lives in an apartment above the neighboring tractor shed and still actively collects art from up-and-coming artists all over the Bay Area to add to the huge collection of works that date from the 1950s. Visiting the preserve is to enter an eclectic, artistic wonderland, where giant sculptures march up into the hills, a car hangs from a tree, and every indoor space is crammed with photographs, paintings, and video installations of sometimes mind-bending strangeness. Even nature seems to do its part to maintain the sense of whimsy as the preserve's 85 peacocks (including two albinos) strut, screech, and occasionally crash-land around the galleries.

Don't expect labels to help make sense of the art because there are none, just a numbered catalog in each gallery. This is to ensure viewers approach each piece with no preconceptions. The only aspects that tie everything together are the Bay Area and di Rosa's love of maximal art over minimal. "The Bay Area is the pond in which I fish," he says. "The artists I like use the familiar as a hook to lead you into new realms. The best artists are like shamans who can take us to deeper truths."

The preserve is on the north side of the Carneros Highway (Highway 121) almost opposite the Domaine Carneros winery. Look for the two-dimensional sheep on the hillside. There are three tours you can take to see some or all of the collection, but they are only offered Wednesday–Saturday, so plan accordingly. You might be able to sign up for one of the tours on the day, but chances are you'll need a reservation, especially on Saturday. The one-hour introductory tour ($10) covers the main gallery and residence at 11 A.M. all year and additionally at noon during the summer. The 2.5-hour Discovery Tour (2 P.M. Wed.–Sat. year-round and also at 10 A.M. Wed.–Sat. summer, $15) is similar to the introductory tour but gives visitors more time to peruse the art and sculptures in the main galley, house, and surrounding lawns. The 2.5-hour Art & Meadow Tour ($15) takes in the main gallery and the acres of

gardens teeming with sculptures but is only offered on Saturday at 10 A.M. during the summer months. For reservations call 707/226-5991 or visit www.dirosaart.org.

Some key pieces from the collection are on display at the Gatehouse Gallery, which can be visited free and without a reservation 9:30 A.M.–3 P.M. Wednesday–Friday and is still worth the time if you cannot get on a tour.

Cornerstone Sonoma

It's hard to classify this sprawling collection of shops, studios, cafés, tasting rooms, and gardens, but Cornerstone Sonoma (23570 Arnold Dr., Sonoma, 707/933-3010, www.cornerstone gardens.com, 10 A.M.–5 P.M. daily summer, gardens 10 A.M.–4 P.M. daily summer) should certainly be on the list of any architecture or gardening enthusiast. The centerpiece of Cornerstone is a nine-acre plot of land that's a showcase for several dozen well-known landscape architects, each of whom designed and planted separate plots. The result is a fascinating blend of traditional and contemporary gardens that make art and sculpture out of plants. Sadly the giant Monterey pine tree covered in blue plastic balls by Claude Cormier, which for years stood like a giant advertisement for Cornerstone, had to be removed before it fell down, but it has since been replaced by a smaller ball-covered tree. Tickets and a map for a self-guided tour of the gardens cost $9, but the price drops to $4 December–mid-March, when it's more often than not likely to rain.

To get to the entrance to the gardens, you have to navigate through an ever-growing collection of fancy shops, restaurants, and most recently, tasting rooms. The growing retail presence is no doubt a necessary moneymaker, and the landscaped outdoor spaces along with some unique shops make it far more pleasant than your average Wine Country retail experience. The downside is that it sometimes feels more like a crowded shopping center than a celebration of the outdoors, particularly if several tour buses have just disgorged their hungry passengers in search of sustenance.

The **Sonoma Valley Visitors Bureau** has

a useful outpost here and is a first stop for many visitors to the region. **Sage Fine Foods & Provisions** is one of the best places in Carneros to pick up picnic supplies and sandwiches, and it also has a few tables inside and outside in the shade that can be relaxing if it's a fairly quiet day. The most fascinating of the shops and studios include **Artefact Design & Salvage,** which sells antiques and whimsical home and garden accessories made from salvaged materials (bar stools with a giant railroad springs in place of legs, for example) and **A New Leaf Gallery,** which is the showcase for some diverse sculptures from dozens of international artists.

In the last few years, tasting rooms have also found homes here. The current winery tenants include the irreverent **Roshambo,** tucked away around the corner from the entrance. This is currently the only place to sample Roshambo's broad selection of wines since it was forced to sell its contemporary Russian River Valley winery in late 2006 after overreaching with an ambitious expansion. A new winery is planned in the Dry Creek Valley, but as of press time there was no news about when it might open. Next to the visitors center is the often-packed tasting room of the **Larson Family Winery.** If you have the time, however, it's more enjoyable to visit the Larson Family's actual winery just a 10-minute drive away. Almost opposite the Larson outpost is the cavernous, contemporary space of the **Grange Sonoma** tasting room collective, which features wines from six Sonoma boutique wineries (Wed.–Mon., tasting $10). The sheer scale and starkness of the interior can feel a little unnerving if you're the only visitor, but there is some warmth to be found in the friendliness of the proprietor and staff, and in the sun at one of the outside tables near the entrance.

EVENTS

Both big and small wineries open their doors during the **April in Carneros** event, usually held on the third weekend in April. Just visit one of the participating wineries for a ticket ($40), which gets you a glass and access to special tastings and events at all the other wineries, including many that are not usually open to the public. Later in the year there's a similar event called **Holiday in Carneros,** usually held on the weekend before Thanksgiving. For a list of wineries and more information about the events, visit www.carneroswineries.org.

RECREATION
Infineon Raceway

Sleepy Carneros is the unlikely setting for one of the busiest racetracks in the country, the Infineon Raceway (29355 Arnold Dr., Sonoma, 800/870-7223), which usually has some sort of motorized vehicle racing round its two miles of track 340 days of the year. Born in 1968, the track is now part of the circuit for major national motor-sport events, including **NASCAR** in June (when the area is choked with traffic and best avoided in the late afternoon, when everyone leaves). The raceway is on the way from San Francisco at the turnoff for Sonoma and Napa, hidden behind the hill at the intersection of Highways 37 and 121. It's not hard to find—just watch for the turbo-charged cow atop the giant raceway billboard at the junction. The entrance is a few hundred yards north on Highway 121. A full list of events at the raceway can be found on their website (www.infineonraceway.com).

Those who prefer a more hands-on approach to motor-sports can try out the track through the **Russell Racing School** (800/733-0345, www.espnrussellracing.com), which is based at the raceway and offers driving, go-karting, and racing courses, most starting at about $500 for the day. Anyone worried about missing out on the Wine Country experience can buy a pricey Speed and Spa multiday package that includes racing instruction, a local hotel room, and spa services to soak out the smell of burned rubber.

Tubbs Island

When the tide comes in, large swaths of lower Carneros disappear underwater, so it's not surprising that the only hike in the area is through the wetlands at Tubbs Island, part of the San

Pablo Bay National Wildlife Refuge. The path is on solid ground, so waders are not required, but it does get muddy in the winter. The eight-mile loop, open to hikers and bikers, is a dirt road that runs through farmland before reaching the edge of the bay and marshes.

It offers little in the way of memorable scenery or strenuous exercise, so the main reason to go is for the wildlife. Legions of migrating wetland birds call the tidal marshes home, particularly in the cold and wet winter months. Even in the slightly warmer summer months there are hawks, pelicans, and plenty of other interesting critters to see, including several endangered species, making the often bracing wind worth enduring.

The Tubbs Island gravel parking lot, where the trail begins, is on the south side of Highway 37, about 0.5 miles past the traffic lights at the junction with Highway 121 to Sonoma. Leaving the parking lot, you have to drive east almost all the way to Vallejo before you can turn around, so plan accordingly. For more information on the refuge, its wildlife, and the ongoing restoration projects, contact the Vallejo headquarters of the San Pablo Bay National Wildlife Refuge at 707/769-4200.

Flying

Elsewhere in the Wine Country, balloons might be the traditional way to see Wine Country from above, but Carneros has an altogether more adventurous way to take to the air. The **Vintage Aircraft Company** (23982 Arnold Dr., 707/938-2444, www.vintageaircraft.com, Thurs.–Mon.) offers rides in its fascinating collection of old planes, which include biplanes and a World War II–era training aircraft.

Simply pick your adrenaline level for the biplane flights, and the FAA-certified pilots can oblige. For a modest rush pick the 20-minute Scenic ride over the vineyards and mountains of the Sonoma Valley ($175, $270 for two people) or double the flying time (and price) for a trip out to the ocean. To really get the adrenaline pumping, try the Aerobatic ride

© PHILIP GOLDSMITH

Experience a different kind of barrel roll in one of the Vintage Aircraft Company's old planes.

with a few loops and rolls thrown in for fun for an additional $50. Longer trips of 35–40 minutes are also offered, with or without aerobatics, down to San Francisco, over the Napa Valley, or to the Pacific coast, starting at $300. Appointments are usually needed for the flight, but on weekends you might get lucky just by walking in.

The Vintage Aircraft Company's home is the Sonoma Country Airport, a thriving base for vintage aircraft restoration and flights. You'll probably see an old plane or two parked close to the Carneros Highway as you drive by.

ACCOMMODATIONS

As the drive through the endless vineyards and fields of Carneros might suggest, there's not much in the way of lodging in this part of Wine Country. Carneros thinks of Sonoma as its main town, and that's where most of the "local" hotels can be found. There are, however, a couple of options at opposite ends of the price spectrum for those looking for either an out-of-the-way bargain or some out-of-this-world luxury.

$100-200

The recently refurbished **Vineyard Inn** (23000 Arnold Dr., Sonoma, 707/938-2350 or 800/359-4667, www.vineyardinnsonoma.com) is one of the best values in southern Sonoma. The Spanish-style former motel has 17 modern and comfortable rooms that cost from $159 per night just minutes from some of the biggest wineries in Carneros. The standard queen rooms are the cheapest, and the list of standard amenities includes private baths, satellite television, wireless Internet access, air-conditioning, breakfast, and use of the very small outdoor pool. The vineyard rooms in separate bungalows start at $249 midweek and have more space and additional features that include DVD players and fireplaces. Some rooms also have Jacuzzi tubs. There are also a handful of two-room suites and deluxe rooms starting at $269. One drawback is the inn's location at one of the busiest intersections in Carneros, which makes some of the cheaper rooms at the front of the building a bit

noisy. Other than the constant traffic and a gas station opposite, there's not much else around, so you'll have to drive to dinner; Sonoma plaza is only about 10 minutes away.

Over $200

The **Carneros Inn** (4048 Sonoma Hwy., Napa, 707/299-4900, www.thecarnerosinn.com) is a new development of 86 individual cottages surrounded by vineyards at the eastern end of Carneros, providing a dose of contemporary luxury on a 27-acre site that used to be a trailer park. As you drive past the place on the Sonoma-Napa Highway (U.S. 121), the tall, stark walls resemble those of a prison, but on the other side of those walls is a luxury planned community with its own manicured streets, a town square, and some privately owned three-bedroom houses that share the spa, infinity pool, vineyard views, and other amenities with the resort cottages. Not surprisingly, there's a hefty price to pay in the Wine Country for a personal cottage that's bigger than some apartments and boasts cherrywood floors, a plasma TV, a fireplace, an alfresco shower, and a private garden. The cheapest places start at $480 per night. The price rockets past $600 for a vineyard view and up to almost four figures for the 10 walled compounds they call suites. The popularity of the place also means that rates change very little with the seasons, although you might find some special deals in winter. One of the on-site restaurants is the highly regarded and remarkably cheap (for the inn, at least) Boon Fly Café, serving breakfasts that will make you feel instantly at home. The inn is only about a 10-minute drive from downtown Napa or Sonoma, but the often cool and breezy Carneros weather can make the cottage fireplaces and down comforters essential features even in the middle of summer.

FOOD

The bright red exterior of the █ **Boon Fly Café** (4048 Sonoma Hwy., Napa, 707/299-4870, breakfast, lunch, and dinner daily, dinner entrées $10–20) brightens up the gray prison-like walls of the Carneros Inn on the

Sonoma-Napa Highway. The food is rustic and full of fresh ingredients like those that might have been eaten by a local known as Boon Fly who used to farm the surrounding land. Breakfast and brunch are the fortes here and are priced low enough to make you want to fill up for the day, but it's also worth making a road stop in the evening to sample the flatbread pizzas or simple but elegant main courses, which are equally well priced.

Look for the sign to the Napa River Resorts a little farther east from Boon Fly and take Cuttings Wharf Road as far south as it will go, making sure you go left at the confusing fork in the road. There are no resorts at the river these days, but there is a popular juke-joint next to the boat ramp called **Moore's Landing** (6 Cuttings Wharf Rd., Napa, 707/253-7038, breakfast and lunch weekends, lunch Wed.–Fri., dinner Fri.–Sat., entrées $8–14). It serves American-Mexican comfort food to boaters, anglers, and the occasional stray winery visitor and has an idyllic deck right next to the river. The winter hours tend to be erratic, so call first.

Picnic Supplies

Carneros is often chilly and windy compared to the Napa and Sonoma Valleys just to the north and so might not be the most inviting part of Wine Country for a picnic, but there are plenty of places to stop for supplies if the weather's nice or you're en route to warmer climes.

Angelo's Wine Country Deli (23400 Arnold Dr., 707/938-3688, 9 A.M.–5 P.M. daily), almost opposite the entrance to the Gloria Ferrer winery, is renowned for its smoked meats but also sells a wide range of other deli food and has become a bit of a Carneros institution. Despite being small, the store is hard to miss—there's a large model of a cow on its roof.

Just up the road is the **Fruit Basket** (24101 Arnold Dr., 707/938-4332, 7 A.M.–7 P.M. daily), which looks a little like a shack in the middle of its dusty parking lot but is actually a comprehensive open-air market and one of the best places to buy local in-season fruit and vegetables along with almost every other grocery staple, including bread, cheese, and a good selection of wine by the half-bottle. There's a second Fruit Basket on U.S. 12 in Boyes Hot Springs.

If you fancy a picnic without the hassle of finding the food yourself, give **Bouchaine Vineyards** (1075 Buchli Station Rd., Napa, 707/252-9065, www.bouchaine.com, 10:30 A.M.–4 P.M. daily) a call the day before and order one of its "Table for Two" picnic lunches. For $95, the winery includes a free wine tasting for two (worth $10), freshly prepared sandwiches and other treats, and a bottle of wine that can all be enjoyed at the scenic picnic area next to the winery.

At the other end of Carneros a popular picnic stop is the **Viansa Winery** (25200 Arnold Dr., Sonoma, 800/995-4740, www.viansa .com, 10 A.M.–5 P.M. daily), which sells a broad range of Italian-themed deli foods and sandwiches in its tasting room. There are some nice spots around the tasting room to eat, but when the winery gets crowded in the summer months, you'd do better to flee to somewhere more peaceful.

NORTHERN SONOMA

There's probably no other wine-producing region in California that has as much to offer as northern Sonoma. Famed Victorian horticulturist Luther Burbank called this part of Sonoma the "chosen spot of all this earth as far as Nature is concerned," and he was pretty well traveled. For a man who tinkered with plants, this was paradise.

This is also a place where living off the land has always been, and still is, a way of life. That land provides some of California's best wine and food and countless recreational possibilities. You can mix wine with almost anything outdoors here: kayaking, mountain hikes, apple picking, camping, fishing, lounging on a sandy beach, flying, or even a safari.

That's not to say that all is peace and rural tranquility; the freeway that was carved through the region in the 1960s has brought with it the kind of suburban sprawl and rush-hour traffic that sucked the soul out of the largest city, Santa Rosa. But while Santa Rosa continues to bulge outward, it doesn't take much to get back to the land and step back in time. Less than a half hour away, deep in the woods, are towns like Guerneville and Occidental that still retain some feeling of the frontier towns they once were, even as they become overrun in the summer by an unlikely mix of urbanites, hippies, bikers, and ranchers who all seem to coexist happily for a few months.

The whole area is slowly being dragged upmarket as the burgeoning Bay Area population seeks out bigger backyards. At the southernmost edge of this part of the Wine Country, Sebastopol is starting to resemble a hip San

HIGHLIGHTS

◖ Hop Kiln Winery: The towering hop kilns are so well preserved that this small winery could almost produce beer in addition to its unusual range of well-priced wines (page 200).

◖ Korbel Champagne Cellars: In a forest clearing in Victorian times, two Czech brothers started making wine, and the historic stone winery still makes sparkling wine fit for presidents and plebeians alike (page 201).

◖ Iron Horse Vineyards: An unassuming barn off the beaten track is home to some of the Russian River Valley's best sparkling wines and a view to die for (page 202).

◖ Luther Burbank Home & Gardens: Learn about the Victorian horticulturist who created hundreds of new plants in his greenhouses, and see many of those plants in the historic gardens (page 206).

◖ Armstrong Redwoods State Reserve: Take a break from the car and the heat on a short hike through the cool, damp redwood forest in this historic park (page 210).

◖ The Russian River: Rent a canoe for a day and drift through the trees on the Russian River, stopping at some of the many secluded beaches (page 211).

◖ Ridge Vineyards: This is a sister winery to its more famous sibling in the Santa Cruz Mountains. The building, made of rice-straw bales, takes the principle of organic wines to a whole new level (page 228).

◖ Michel-Schlumberger: Producing some of the best cabernet in a valley dominated by zinfandel, this winery is housed in a beautiful mission revival building tucked away down a scenic canyon (page 229).

◖ Raven Performing Arts Theater: Visit this historic theater for performance art, a movie, or simply a quick lunch, and support the artists that help keep Healdsburg real (page 238).

◖ Alexander Valley Vineyards: Incorporating part of the homestead of the valley's first settler, Cyrus Alexander, the grounds of this winery are peppered with historic buildings (page 257).

© AVALON TRAVEL

LOOK FOR ◖ TO FIND RECOMMENDED SIGHTS, ACTIVITIES, DINING, AND LODGING.

Francisco neighborhood. Property prices everywhere are soaring, slowing down the mechanisms of change that have continually transformed the land since European immigrants first arrived here in the 1800s and carved out a life for themselves in the soil and forests.

Winemakers still produce wines to rival the best in the world, but as the cost of doing so rises, the conglomerates are beginning to take over, much as they've already done in the Napa and Sonoma Valleys. You increasingly have to be big to survive in the wine world here, and many new winemakers are looking farther north in Mendocino and Lake Counties for a chance to get in on the action.

Nevertheless, there's still plenty of life left in the northern Sonoma scene, with an amazing diversity of wine, scenery, and activities. There might be trouble in paradise, but it's still paradise to visit.

PLANNING YOUR TIME

Parts of northern Sonoma are easy to get around, others are not. The **Russian River Valley** is definitely in the "not" category. This sprawling appellation encompasses forests and mountains, hills and dales, and has the navigational inconvenience of a large river cutting almost straight through the middle of it. A map is essential, as is a bit of planning to ensure you spend more time in wineries than backtracking on the roads. The Russian River Wine Road publishes one of the best maps, which can usually be found free at wineries.

The **Dry Creek** and **Alexander Valleys** are relatively straightforward to navigate by comparison, with most of the wineries strung along a few long, relatively straight roads. These valleys are almost like miniature Sonoma or Napa Valleys as far as climate, shape, and scenery, and it's easy to get a good feel for the area in a day or even a half day.

The three main appellations are like night and day when it comes to wine, which makes planning a wine route either exciting or daunting. Sample some velvety Alexander Valley cabernets, for example, before crossing into the Dry Creek Valley and tasting the subtly

different cabernets there. Or try the warm-climate chardonnays in the Alexander Valley, then head down Westside Road to try some leaner, cool-climate versions in the Russian River Valley.

Alternatively, try to find your favorite Dry Creek zinfandel from the hundreds on offer in the valley, or hunt out the next big pinot noir in the Russian River Valley.

If all the possibilities just seem too overwhelming, there's always the option of staying in **Healdsburg,** which has enough tasting rooms to satisfy the most fussy wine drinker, as well as plenty of shops and restaurants to occupy those less curious about the region's wines. Healdsburg is also the most central town in the region, and the large number of good hotels and restaurants make it an almost essential staging post for any trip to this part of the world.

As in other parts of the Wine Country, wineries generally open late and close early, so don't expect to get started until late morning, and plan to be finished touring by about 5 P.M., closer to 4 P.M. during the winter. Unlike the rest of Sonoma and Napa, free tasting is still fairly commonplace but is getting increasingly less so. Even when there is a fee for tasting regular or reserve wines, it will be far more palatable than in some other parts of Wine Country.

And of course, non-wine-related activities also abound. Check out the burgeoning Santa Rosa Arts District, or the multitude of hiking options in wilderness areas such as Armstrong Redwoods State Reserve.

GETTING THERE

The railroad came and left this part of Sonoma before most of us were even born, leaving the car and sporadic bus services as the only real options for getting around.

U.S. 101, which runs down the center of this region, might be a bit of an eyesore as it snakes up otherwise picturesque valleys leaving strip malls in its wake, but it's a pretty convenient way to get places fast. The drive time from San Francisco up the freeway to almost every major Russian River Valley town is usually not much more than an hour, to Healdsburg and beyond about an hour and a half.

From the freeway, Highway 116 (West) runs up through Sebastopol to Guerneville. In the Santa Rosa area, River Road runs west to Forestville, though it tends to get choked during rush hour. The Healdsburg Avenue exit leads straight into downtown Healdsburg, and the Westside Road exit is the entry to the Dry Creek Valley and Russian River regions. The next four exits serve Dry Creek and Alexander Valleys before the freeway reaches Cloverdale and then heads into the hills towards Hopland and Mendocino.

Although most people come to this part of the Wine Country by car, there are other transport options. Both Santa Rosa and Sebastopol are well served by **Golden Gate Transit** (415/923-2000 or 707/541-2000, www.golden gatetransit.org), which runs scheduled bus service to and from San Francisco hourly for much of the day. From Santa Rosa, **Sonoma County Transit** (707/576-7433 or 800/345-7433, www.sctransit.com) runs regular services to Healdsburg, Geyserville, and Guerneville. From Sebastopol there's service to Guerneville through Graton and Forestville. Things are so spread out in the Russian River Valley, however, that once you arrive there by bus you'll still need some mode of transport to see anything.

GETTING AROUND

The Russian River Valley is roughly square in shape, with an arm stretching from its northwestern corner up to Healdsburg. The major towns are Guerneville, in the northwest corner of the square, Sebastopol on the southern edge, Occidental on the western edge, and Santa Rosa on the eastern side. In the middle is a patchwork of farmland and vineyards, together with the hamlets of Graton and Forestville. Highway 116, also called the Gravenstein Highway, is the main road running north–south through them.

Wineries are spread mainly along Eastside and Westside Roads, which both run on either side of the river from Healdsburg down toward Guerneville, and throughout the patchwork in the middle of the area.

Many of the region's food and lodging options lie in Healdsburg and around the edge of this Russian River square. Unlike in the Dry Creek and Alexander Valleys farther north, roads here tend to meander as they follow the river and hills, often making driving times longer than anticipated.

By comparison, the Dry Creek Valley could be navigated with your eyes shut. Just two roads run the length of the valley, and the wineries are roughly spread out along them, making it the easiest part of northern Sonoma to visit in a day, even without a map.

Along the other side of the freeway is the longer and wider Alexander Valley. Even here, the wineries are concentrated along Geyserville Avenue on the western side of the valley and along Highway 128 on the eastern side.

Of course, driving is not the only way to get around. Wine Country would not be complete without cycling. The compact, flat Dry Creek Valley and relatively flat Westside Road from Healdsburg down into the Russian River Valley are two of the most bikeable routes. The Alexander Valley is also relatively flat, but distances between wineries are greater. In all areas, temperatures get high in the summer, so plenty of water is essential.

The best place to rent bikes is in Healdsburg, where there are several options. The friendly folks at **Spoke Folk Cyclery** in Healdsburg (201 Center St., 707/433-7171, www.spokefolk .com) can set you up on decent touring bikes for $30 per day. Nice road bikes and tandems cost from $50. They'll send you on your way with maps for biking routes that range from leisurely 12-mile loops in Dry Creek Valley to 40-mile adventures down to Guerneville. At the other end of town next to the Old Roma Station winery complex, **Wine Country Bikes** rents bikes from $33 for basic hybrids up to $55 for road bikes (61 Front St., 707/473-0610 or 866/922-4537, www.winecountrybikes.com). It also has plenty of options for organized tours, including a day tour of local organic farms and wineries during the spring and summer ($129) and a longer day tour for more avid bikers, which takes in scenery and wineries in both the Dry Creek and Russian River Valleys on its 45-mile loop ($149).

Russian River Valley

The Russian River Valley is one of Sonoma's largest and most diverse geographic regions. It covers about 150 square miles of forest, orchards, vineyards, and pastureland from trendy Sebastopol in the south to chic Healdsburg in the north and from the suburban freeway sprawl in the east to rural Occidental in the west. Running right through it is the mighty Russian River, shaping the climate, scenery, and recreational opportunities in the region.

The Russian River Valley attracted immigrants in the late 1800s to exploit its vast forests, and many of the towns that exist today were established as logging or railroad outposts. Once the redwood forests had been largely cleared, it was sheep ranches, cattle pasture, orchards, and even hop farms that took over the land. The Gravenstein apple, now an endangered piece of local agricultural history, was embraced as the region's very own, though its roots remain somewhat ambiguous.

It wasn't until the 1980s, when the cool growing climate was recognized as ideal for the increasingly fashionable pinot noir and chardonnay grapes, that the area's wine industry took off, and the Russian River Valley has long since been recognized as one of the best cool grape-growing regions in California. This is not an easy part of Wine Country to explore compared to relatively self-contained valleys elsewhere in Sonoma, however. Roads wind through forests, over hills, and along the snaking river, making wineries sometimes hard to find. Large parts of the region are rural, dotted with small communities like **Forestville** and **Graton,** which hide their already small populations very well in the surrounding hills and woods.

The center of the action is **Guerneville** and neighboring **Monte Rio,** both slightly faded Victorian resort towns that are transformed each summer into a surreal scene of leather-clad bikers and plaid-clad outdoorsmen, hipsters, and hippies. Guerneville is something of a gay mecca and party town, and the rustic resorts and bars often pulsate with the beat of dance music and drunken hordes on summer evenings.

The eastern and western edges of the appellation could not be more of a contrast. The suburban sprawl of **Santa Rosa** is just outside the eastern boundary of the appellation and is almost a poster child for how not to grow a city. It is by far the biggest city in the region—a place where culture meets characterless malls—but a far cry from the peaceful and remote Bohemian Highway running along the appellation's western edge, where the picture-postcard town of **Occidental** exists in the midst of dense forests.

The Wines

Almost a third of all the grapes grown in Sonoma County come from the Russian River Valley, but there's the potential for it to be a far higher proportion. Only 12,000 acres, or about 10 percent, of the 125,000 acres in the valley are actually planted with vineyards. The rest is still pasture, forest, and the occasional town.

The river and the valley it carved through the coastal mountain ranges over millennia provide the region with the unique climate that is perfect for growing grapes that like cool conditions. There's enough strong sunlight each day to ensure the grapes ripen, but the air remains cool, often downright chilly at night, and keeps a lid on the fruit's sugar levels.

Pinot noir and chardonnay are the dominant varietals in this part of the Wine Country, but zinfandel is almost as important, and the resulting wines have a subtlety that is often lacking in the brawny zins from the warmer valleys to the north. Growers are also having increasing success with syrah and some other Rhône varietals, while gewürztraminer is also starting to make more of an appearance. The ubiquitous cabernet sauvignon and merlot are largely absent, however, except on the warmest eastern hills of the region.

The cool layer of damp marine air from

NORTHERN SONOMA

NORTHERN SONOMA

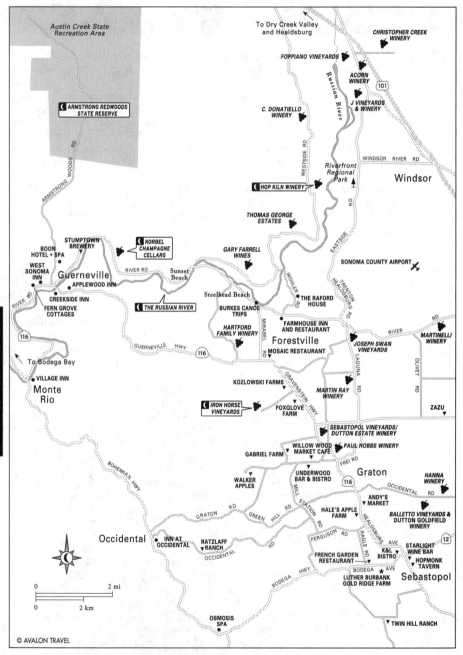

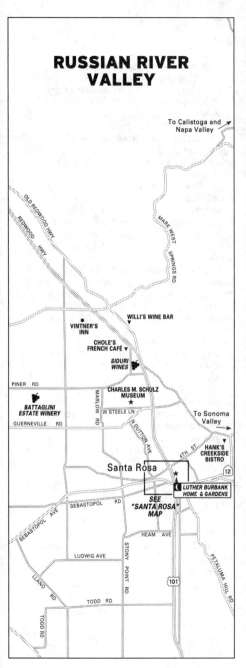

RUSSIAN RIVER VALLEY

To Calistoga and
Napa Valley

MARK WEST SPRINGS RD

OLD REDWOOD HWY

REDWOOD HWY

WILLI'S WINE BAR

VINTNER'S INN

CHOLE'S FRENCH CAFÉ

SIDURI WINES

PINER RD

CHARLES M. SCHULZ MUSEUM

MARLOW RD

BATTAGLINI ESTATE WINERY

W STEELE LN

GUERNEVILLE RD

To Sonoma Valley

N DUTTON AVE

4TH ST

HANK'S CREEKSIDE BISTRO

Santa Rosa

12

LUTHER BURBANK HOME & GARDENS

SEE "SANTA ROSA" MAP

SEBASTOPOL AVE

SEBASTOPOL RD

HEAM AVE

STONY POINT RD

LUDWIG AVE

LLANO RD

PETALUMA HILL RD

101

TODD RD

TODD RD

the Pacific Ocean just a few miles west is the region's natural air-conditioner and was a big factor in the granting of the Russian River Valley's AVA status in 1983. Marine fog rolls down the river valley during the summer, snaking into gullies and canyons and keeping the temperature here lower than any other inland portion of Sonoma County. As the ripening process slows, the fruit can gain in complexity and retain enough acidity to keep the wines interesting. Grapes are usually harvested several weeks later here than in some hotter Sonoma regions.

The river is also responsible for the area's unique soils, depositing deep, well-drained sandy and gravelly sediments over million of years. The combination of relatively cool microclimates, no summer rain, and a patchwork of soils is a grape-grower's dream and a reason there are so many styles of pinot made here.

Within the southwest corner of the Russian River appellation, closest to the ocean, is the even cooler Green Valley AVA. This is just about as cool as a climate can be and still ripen grapes, and it is the source of some of Sonoma's best pinot noir.

WINE-TASTING

Many of the Russian River wineries are south of Healdsburg down the meandering Westside Road, which has been dubbed the Rodeo Drive of Pinot Noir due to the number of high-end pinot producers strung along it. Once Westside Road reaches River Road, a map is an essential tool to find the hidden gems around Forestville, Graton, and beyond.

FOPPIANO VINEYARDS

The first major winery south of Healdsburg on the Old Redwood Highway is also one of the few historic wineries that continued to operate right through Prohibition. Foppiano Vineyards (12707 Old Redwood Hwy., Healdsburg, 707/433-7272, www.foppiano.com, 10 A.M.–4:30 P.M. daily, free tasting) remains a family-owned affair, producing about 40,000 cases of wine a year under a couple of labels.

Giovanni Foppiano founded the winery in 1896, and the fourth generation of Foppianos

THE GRAVENSTEIN HIGHWAY

Although almost every imaginable fruit and vegetable seems to be grown in Sonoma, the most celebrated crop in the Russian River Valley (apart from grapes) is perhaps the apple, and in particular the small yellow and red Gravenstein with its strong aroma and taste.

Highway 116, which runs through Sebastopol and Graton, is also called the Gravenstein Highway for the large number of orchards it used to pass. The orchards are now disappearing, along with the Gravenstein apple itself, as growers favor bigger and more easily transported varieties of apple like Fuji and golden delicious.

At one point apple orchards covered 14,000 acres of Sonoma County, but by 2005 there were only about 3,000 acres left, and Gravensteins accounted for only one-third of that total. Slow Food Russian River, the local chapter of the Slow Food movement, is now campaigning to raise the profile of this humble little apple among consumers, retailers, and restaurants to slow any further decline.

Nothing specifically links the Gravenstein apple to this area – it is actually believed to have originated in Germany. It just happens to grow particularly well here and has been doing so for almost 200 years.

The Gravenstein is the earliest-ripening apple in the region, so look for it starting in late July. Other apple varieties tend to ripen August–December. Farms offering apples and other seasonal produce are generally clustered around Sebastopol and Graton. Many are open only during the summer and fall.

In Graton they include **Foxglove Farms** (5280 Gravenstein Hwy. N., 707/887-2759, Thurs.-Tues. July-Oct.), **Kozlowski Farms** (5566 Gravenstein Hwy. N., 707/887-1587, daily year-round), **Gabriel Farm** (3175 Sullivan Rd., just off Graton Rd., 707/829-0617, Sun.-Fri. Sept.-Oct.), and **Walker Apples** (10955 Upp Rd., off Graton Rd., daily Aug.-mid-Nov.), which sells a staggering 27 varieties of apple. Just south of Sebastopol on Pleasant Hill Road is **Twin Hill Ranch** (1689 Pleasant Hill Rd., 707/823-2815, Mon.-Sat. year-round), and halfway between Sebastopol and Occidental is **Ratzlaff Ranch** (13128 Occidental Rd., Sebastopol, 707/823-0538, Sun.-Fri. year-round), which grows Gravensteins along with other apples and pears.

Between Sebastopol and Graton on the Gravenstein Highway you will also likely find a bountiful supply of apples at the big roadside produce store called **Andy's Market** (1691 Gravenstein Hwy. N., Sebastopol, 707/823-8661, 8:30 A.M.-8 P.M. daily). Just south of Andy's on the other side of the road is the farm stand for local grower **Hale's Apple Farm** (1526 Gravenstein Hwy. N., Sebastopol, 707/823-4613, 9 A.M.-5 P.M. daily).

More information about all the fruits and vegetables grown here and the farms that sell them is available from **Sonoma Country Farm Trails** (707/571-8288, www.farmtrails .org). You might also see the free *Farm Trails* map and guide at wineries and farms in the region.

today runs the business and its 200 acres of estate vineyards. You could well bump into one of the two Louis Foppianos in the cozy tasting room that shares the parking lot with barns and other winery buildings.

Today, Foppiano is best known for its powerful, inky petite sirah, which accounts for about a third of the winery's total production. Other wines include pinot noir, cabernet sauvignon, and merlot from Russian River Valley grapes, plus sangiovese and zinfandel sourced from vineyards elsewhere in Northern Sonoma.

Unusually, most are aged in American oak barrels that impart a stronger tannic punch than the French oak more commonly used by Russian River wineries. The tannins will mellow over time, but those who are impatient should try the softer Reserve petite sirah, which is the only Foppiano wine aged in French oak. White wines including sauvignon blanc and chardonnay are sold under the cheaper Riverside label.

Although there are no official tours, visitors are free to wander off into the vineyards on a self-guided tour, leaflets for which can be found in the tasting room.

J VINEYARDS & WINERY

Just south of Foppiano, the giant parking lot shared with the neighboring Rodney Strong Winery can be a magnet for busloads of tourists, but there's a relative oasis and some delicious food to be found inside the sleek and modern J Winery (11447 Old Redwood Hwy., Healdsburg, 707/431-3646, www.jwine.com, 11 A.M.–5 P.M. daily, food and wine tastings $20–60).

Food pairings are part of the tasting experience here—a unique but expensive proposition. At the main tasting bar, $20 buys generous pours of five wines from the lengthy menu of red, white, sparkling, and dessert wines. If the spacious tasting room is overrun, a common occurrence on weekends, the more exclusive Bubble Room (four seatings per day Fri.–Sun.) takes the tasting experience (and the price) up a notch with comfy seating, table service, heartier food samples, and the chance to taste more expensive sparkling and single-vineyard wines. Each of the six wines (two red, two white, and two sparkling) is paired with food, such as pinot noir with pan-seared Alaskan halibut, or viognier with French mussel soup. Despite its $60 cost, the Bubble Room is popular, and the six-course menu is pretty filling, so it's best to make reservations during the summer. If it's already booked up, there's a similarly structured but slightly less indulgent tasting menu available on the outdoor terrace Thursday–Monday during the summer.

J specializes in sparkling wines and pinot noir from the Russian River Valley. Its portfolio of bubbly includes a late-disgorged brut and the flagship Vintage Brut, which is the signature wine here. It was the only wine that owner Judy Jordan made when she started the winery in 1986. The sparkling wine-making process is the focus of the appointment-only tours that finish with a food and wine tasting.

About half the 65,000-case production here is still wine and includes chardonnay, pinot gris,

and three excellent pinot noirs, of which the best is arguably the limited-production Nicole's Vineyard version. There are also a couple of limited-production winery-only wines, including a Russian River Valley zinfandel and viognier from the Alexander Valley.

C. DONATIELLO WINERY

The wine's not bad, but a visit to C. Donatiello (4035 Westside Rd., Healdsburg, 707/431-4442 or 800/433-8296, www.cdonatiello.com, 11 A.M.–5 P.M. daily, tasting $7–12) might well have you raving about aromas of a different kind—those from the wonderfully scented culinary and medicinal herb gardens that surround the rustic redwood winery buildings in a maze of terraces. There's probably a medicinal cure for a hangover in there somewhere.

The winery was established in the early 1980s by investment banker and philanthropist William R. Hambrecht, and for many years it was run as the Belvedere Winery. In 2008, wine industry executive Christopher Donatiello took over the facilities and, with backing from Hambrecht, transformed the winery into a smaller and leaner operation producing about 10,000 cases of high-end pinot noir and chardonnay from local Russian River Valley vineyards. The relaxing, contemporary tasting room and shady patio overlooking the estate are in keeping with the quality of the wines. Hambrecht, meanwhile, continues to operate the smaller **Bradford Mountain Winery** (707/431-4433, www.bradfordmountain .com), tucked behind C. Donatiello. It makes a wide range of wines from Russian River and Dry Creek vineyards, and is open for tasting by appointment at the weekends.

Most of the production at C. Donatiello is accounted for by the blended Russian River Valley pinot and chardonnay, which retail for about $40 and $25, respectively. From that starting point, the prices and accolade increase with the single-vineyard and single-clone versions of the wines. The best values are arguably the mid-priced Maddies Vineyard bottlings, sourced from the vineyard right in front of the winery.

NORTHERN SONOMA

© PHILIP GOLDSMITH

Hops, not grapes, were once processed in the building that's now Hop Kiln Winery.

◖ HOP KILN WINERY

A few miles south of Healdsburg is one of Sonoma's best-preserved old hop kilns, a towering wooden building where hops were once dried before being used to make beer. The hop vines of Sonoma have long since been replaced by grapevines, but the Hop Kiln Winery (6050 Westside Rd., Healdsburg, 707/433-6491, www.hopkilnwinery.com, 10 A.M.–5 P.M. daily, tasting $5) has kept much of the cavernous interior of the 1905-era building intact, including the old stone drying ovens.

Belying its giant home, the winery itself is a fairly small operation, producing about 12,000 cases a year of reasonably priced zinfandel, cabernet sauvignon, chardonnay, and some interesting blends.

King of the cheaper wines is Big Red, which is as big as its name suggests—a rambunctious blend of zinfandel, cabernet, and syrah. A Thousand Flowers is a more delicate white blend of chardonnay, gewürztraminer, and riesling. The once-common Napa gamay red grape is also represented under its more accurate name of valdiguié. Very few wineries still make it, and it's an acquired taste.

There are plenty of picnic tables around the building, including some next to a rather murky pond. The winery stocks a host of vinegars, oils, and mustards, but not much in the way of more filling picnic fare, so you'll have to bring your own.

THOMAS GEORGE ESTATES

Opened in 2009 in the former Davis Bynum winery, Thomas George Estates (8075 Westside Rd., Healdsburg, 707/431-8031, www.thomasgeorgeestates.com, 11 A.M.–5 P.M. daily, tasting $5) has brought some Canadian blood and new ideas to the Westside Road scene.

Bynum originally established a winery here in the 1970s in a former hop kiln and worked with many of the region's pinot pioneers as the area became established. Among the secrets to his success were the agreements he made to buy grapes from some of the best growers in the area. Thomas George Estates will still buy grapes from some well-known local growers as they ramp up production to a planned 15,000 cases, but they also bought a couple of additional vineyards in the Russian River Valley to complement the estate Baker Vineyard that was acquired from Bynum.

Several different pinots and chardonnays are poured in the tasting room alongside zinfandels from Dry Creek and a Sonoma Valley viognier. In early 2010, as this edition went to press, the winery completed construction of new caves and what promised to be a nice picnic area, which promise to make the visitor experience as much about the hillside surroundings as the wine.

GARY FARRELL WINES

The last winery on Westside Road before it reaches River Road, Gary Farrell Wines (10701 Westside Rd., Healdsburg, 707/473-2900, www.garyfarrellwines.com, 10 A.M.–4 P.M. daily, tasting $10–15), is also one of the newest. The spacious tasting room at the end of a long driveway (easy to miss when driving east) was completed in 2001, and its huge picture window overlooks some of the Russian River vineyards from which some acclaimed chardonnay and pinot noir are made.

Gary Farrell set up the winery in the 1980s to pursue his pinot passion. Since 2004, it's been owned by multinational wine companies (first Allied Domecq, now Ascentia Wine Estates), but retains a low-key atmosphere. Farrell is currently working on a pet pinot project, Alysian Wines, in nearby Forestville (that winery is not open to the public).

Most of the wines made here are pinots and chardonnays, both appellation-specific versions from the Russian River Valley and beyond to the pricier vineyard-specific bottling sourced from some well-known local vineyards that are part of the more expensive Limited Release tasting. Those two varietals account for more than half the 17,000-case annual production. Don't overlook the beautifully structured cabernet sauvignon and zinfandel, however, which all have the same understated elegance.

◖ KORBEL CHAMPAGNE CELLARS

This is one of the most impressive of the 19th-century wineries in Sonoma—a collection of solid, imposing stone and brick buildings at the edge of redwood forests. If you're a fan of sparkling wines, it's a place worth visiting—it might not have the acclaim of top producers like Iron Horse, but Korbel (13250 River Rd., Guerneville, 707/824-7000, www.korbel.com, daily 10 A.M.–5 P.M. summer, 10 A.M.–4:30 P.M. winter, free tasting) offers perhaps the best value for money among sparkling wine producers.

Three Korbel brothers, immigrants from the Bohemia region of what is now the Czech Republic, founded the winery in 1882 after making their money in the local redwood lumber business. Today, the winery makes close to 1.7 million cases of the fizzy stuff a year in a dizzying array of styles. It has also added some respectable table wines to its portfolio, as well as brandy and port, all of which can only be bought at the winery.

The Korbel family connection is long gone, but Korbel wines remain the tipple of both presidents and plebeians alike. The champagne has been poured at five presidential inaugurations, and is claimed to be the most popular premium champagne in the United States.

From the bone-dry top-of-the-line Le Premier to the sweeter Sec, Korbel's 10 or so champagnes are eminently affordable, as are the cabernet, pinot noir, chardonnay, and zinfandel table wines, and even the barrel-aged port. After the tasting room bubbles have gone to your head, the prices look even better. It's hard to leave without at least a couple of bottles.

How the bubbles get into the wine and how the Korbel brothers got into the wine business are both covered in an entertaining tour offered five times a day—buy tickets in the little shack at the opposite end of the parking lot from the tasting room. A tour of the sweet old rose garden is offered twice a day, Tuesday–Sunday mid-April–mid-October, and after all that touring you can lounge on the deck of the small delicatessen, shaded by redwood trees with a gourmet sandwich and even a beer.

NORTHERN SONOMA

HARTFORD FAMILY WINERY

A little off the beaten track about a mile up Martinelli Road and surrounded by lush gardens and redwood forest is the big white barnlike winery and mansion of this pinot noir and chardonnay specialist. Hartford (8075 Martinelli Rd., Forestville, 707/887-1756 or 800/588-0234, www.hartfordwines.com, 10 A.M.–4:30 P.M. daily, tasting $5) makes about 20,000 cases of some serious point-scoring regional and single-vineyard wines from the Sonoma Coast, Russian River Valley, Carneros, and (unusually) Marin County to the south.

Although it is touted as a down-home family winery, you're forgiven for thinking it's too big, smart, and formal for the average family. That's because part-owner Don Hartford married into the Kendall-Jackson wine empire.

The portfolio of wines is very compact, however, comprising only pinot noir, chardonnay, and zinfandel, all from cool-climate vineyards and all well worth tasting. Chances are that many of the best vineyard-designate chardonnays and pinots made under the Hartford Court label will be sold out, but you're still likely to find a few winners on the tasting list. The slightly cheaper Hartford-labeled wines are well worth trying and include four zinfandels from some of the oldest vineyards in the Russian River region.

SEBASTOPOL VINEYARDS/ DUTTON ESTATE WINERY

The modest tasting room (8757 Green Valley Rd., Sebastopol, 707/829-9463, www.sebastopolvineyards.com, 10 A.M.–5 P.M. daily, tasting $10–15) of the Dutton family, just off Highway 116, barely hints at the renown of their Dutton Ranch in the Green Valley AVA for producing highly rated, limited-production wines.

Dutton Ranch is not a single vineyard but a collection of 10 vineyards and a few apple orchards totaling more than 1,300 acres, all farmed by the family and supplying grapes to wineries across the region. Indeed, most of the grapes are sold to other wineries, but enough are used in the two wineries in this region to bear the Dutton name. Joe

Dutton produces about 10,000 cases of wine under the premium Dutton Estate label and slightly cheaper Sebastopol Vineyards label. (His brother Steve is a partner in the nearby Dutton-Goldfield Winery.)

Chardonnay, pinot noir, and syrah are the only wines made here, but there are lots of different versions of them made from specific vineyards and sometimes specific blocks within a vineyard. Discovering some of the nuances of the tiny Green Valley subappellation with the more expensive vineyard-specific wines entails a higher tasting fee, but there is also a wine and cheese pairing offered for $20.

◖ IRON HORSE VINEYARDS

One of the southernmost wineries in the Green Valley appellation, Iron Horse Vineyards (9786 Ross Station Rd., Sebastopol, 707/887-1507, www.ironhorsevineyards.com, 10 A.M.–3:30 P.M. daily, tasting $10), is also well off the beaten track down Ross Station Road (off Highway 116), a one-lane road that winds

a bottle of Benchmark wine from Iron Horse Vineyards

© IRON HORSE VINEYARDS

through orchards, over a creek, and (perhaps) past some wild turkeys before climbing up the palm-lined driveway to the winery.

The rustic simplicity of the barnlike building and its indoor-outdoor tasting bar belies the pedigree of the sparkling wines made here—they have been served to presidents and won numerous accolades from wine critics over the past 30 years. Tours are offered by appointment weekdays only, but with such panoramic views over the valley from right behind the tasting area, you might be content just to sit back and relax in the bucolic setting.

Today the winery is still run by the Sterling family that built it in the 1970s and makes about 20,000 cases of sparkling wines a year, most priced at $30 and up. They include the ever-popular Wedding Cuvée and a series of late-disgorged wines, including the flagship Brut LD, which are bottle-aged for four or more years in contact with the lees to give them a rich aroma and flavor. All the grapes for the sparkling wines are sourced from the winery's vineyards in the surrounding Green Valley AVA, the coolest part of an already cool Russian River Valley appellation.

It's an ideal place to grow chardonnay and pinot noir, both of which Iron Horse also bottles as outstanding still wines that are worth tasting. Try the unoaked chardonnay—one of the best examples of this new breed of food-friendly chardonnays. A wide range of mainly red wines are also made from the winery's T-bar-T vineyard in the warmer Alexander Valley, including a juicy sangiovese and a petite verdot, normally a blending grape but also capable of producing a plush wine in its own right. Worth noting is that Iron Horse closes far earlier than most in the area and is a five-minute drive off the main road, so get there early.

MARTINELLI WINERY

One of the most noteworthy zinfandels made in the Russian River Valley comes from the Jackass Vineyard of Martinelli Winery (3360 River Rd., Windsor, 707/525-0570 or 800/346-1627, www.martinelliwinery.com, 10 A.M.–5 P.M. daily, tasting $5), planted in the 1800s and still going. That notable vineyard's name has absolutely no historical significance, instead referring to the sort of farmer who would consider farming such a steep and rugged slope.

The Martinellis have been a fixture here since the early 1900s as grape and apple growers. In fact, apples can be found alongside the wines and other gourmet food in the rather chaotic winery gift shop inside the big red barn, a former hop barn. (This Martinelli apple-and-wine clan is, however, unrelated to the Martinelli clan that supplies cheap apple cider to your local supermarket.)

The family only started making wines in the late 1980s from their vineyards and only got noticed more recently when it hired renowned consultant winemaker Helen Turley to tame the Jackass vineyard. Since then the accolades have poured in for the wines, particularly the powerhouse Jackass zinfandel together with several syrahs and chardonnays from Russian River Valley vineyards.

Not much of the popular, if expensive, Jackass zin is made each year, however, so chances are it will have sold out. There are plenty of other wines to try in the huge portfolio. So many different wines are made here that it's hard to believe total production is only about 10,000 cases. The portfolio of pinot noir stretches to more than a half-dozen wines, most sourced from the Russian River Valley or Green Valley and most being big, earthy, and full-bodied affairs. Others worth tasting include an off-dry, exotically flavored gewürztraminer and an intensely aromatic muscat, both unusual wines for this area.

HANNA WINERY

From humble beginnings in the 1970s, Hanna (5353 Occidental Rd., Santa Rosa, 707/575-3371, www.hannawinery.com, 10 A.M.–4 P.M. daily, tasting $5) has grown to become one of the larger privately owned wineries in northern Sonoma, making 35,000 cases of wine at its modest Home Ranch winery here in the Russian River Valley and set to grow even larger following the completion of a

NORTHERN SONOMA

new 100,000-case winery at its Alexander Valley location (9280 Hwy. 128, Healdsburg, 707/431-4314).

Hanna's specialty is crisp, steel-fermented sauvignon blanc that is usually a hit with critics, but it has a full portfolio of wines from the 250 acres of vineyards it owns around its two winery locations and high up in the Mayacamas Mountains at its Bismark Ranch vineyards above Sonoma Valley—claimed to be the highest-elevation vineyard in Sonoma.

The Bismark red wines, including cabernet sauvignon, nebbiolo, and zinfandel, are powerful and often highly rated by critics. At the other end of the scale is the fruity rosé made from petite sirah and zinfandel, an ideal accompaniment to a picnic on the pretty patio overlooking the vineyards.

BALLETTO VINEYARDS & DUTTON GOLDFIELD WINERY

An industrial-looking modern building is an unlikely setting for two wineries with deep roots in the grape-growing business in the Russian River Valley. Both only recently started making wines from their renowned vineyards, and together they offer a remarkable range of Russian River Valley wines in terms of both price and style in their new tasting room.

The Balletto family (5700 Occidental Rd., Santa Rosa, 707/568-2455, www.ballettovineyards.com, 10 A.M.–4:30 P.M. Mon.–Fri., 10 A.M.–5 P.M. Sat.–Sun., tasting $5) started out as fruit growers in the 1970s, then became grape growers, and finally began making small quantities of wines from their four Russian River Valley vineyards in 2001. The new winery was completed in 2006 and now produces a modest 5,000 cases of Balletto wines, although higher production is planned. Pinot noir and pinot gris account for much of the output, with zinfandel and chardonnay making up the balance. All are decent enough and made all the more palatable by their reasonable prices—the pinot noir is the most expensive at $25. The best of the four are undoubtedly the two reds.

The vineyards are also home to the Dutton-Goldfield Winery (tasting room at 3100 Gravenstein Hwy. N., 707/827-3600, daily 10 A.M.–4:30 P.M., tasting $10), which makes limited-production wines positioned at the other end of the price spectrum. Founded in 1998 by Dan Goldfield, a well-known winemaker, and Steve Dutton, a member of the family that farms the renowned vineyards of Dutton Ranch, the winery produces about 5,000 cases of high-end wines that garner some glowing reviews.

Pinot noir accounts for most of the production, both a blended Russian River Valley version and several exquisite single-vineyard bottlings that are made in such limited quantities and win such stellar reviews that they usually sell out fast. Chardonnay, zinfandel, and syrah make up the balance of the production. The syrah and zinfandel, in particular, are elegant and earthy cool-climate examples of the varietals and well worth trying.

MARTIN RAY WINERY

Although housed in the oldest continually operating winery in Sonoma and named after one of California's pioneering modern winemakers, the Martin Ray Winery (2191 Laguna Rd., Santa Rosa, 707/823-2404, www.martinraywinery.com, 11 A.M.–5 P.M. daily summer, 11 A.M.–4 P.M. daily winter, tasting free or $5) is actually a relatively modern operation with few links to the site's historic past or the man after whom it is named. Nonetheless, it makes some good wines from mountain fruit and has some fascinating historic features and heritage that make it worth visiting.

The winery itself dates back to the late 1800s. Current owner Courtney Benham acquired the property in 2003. He had already bought the rights to the Martin Ray name a decade earlier and set about reintroducing it more than 100 miles from where Ray originally found fame, in the Santa Cruz Mountains.

The winery today makes several hundred thousand cases of wine, a size that's evident from the huge warehouses and water tower on the site. The wines cover just about every major varietal and growing region in northern

California, with an emphasis on mountain fruit. From a historic and quality perspective the most interesting are the expensive reserve cabernet sauvignons from vineyards in the Santa Cruz Mountains, Martin Ray's old stomping ground, and Diamond Mountain in the Napa Valley. Both are intensely flavored mountain wines, each with the distinctive character of its region. They're worth paying the modest reserve tasting fee to try. The best pinot noir in the lineup, from the Russian River Valley, is also a reserve wine. The cheaper nonreserve Martin Ray wines include a nice Russian River chardonnay and Mendocino pinot gris along with a series of less unique wines from Napa Valley vineyards.

Cheaper wines sold under the Angeline label account for the vast majority of total production here and are good value but not in the same league as the reserves. Most fun is the fruity one-liter jug wine, a blend of tempranillo, syrah, and cabernet sauvignon that costs just $15.

Wineries by Appointment

Tucked away inside an anonymous unit in the middle of an industrial estate on the northern edge of Santa Rosa, **Siduri Wines** (980 Airway Ct., Suite C, Santa Rosa, 707/578-3882, www .siduri.com, by appointment 10 A.M.–3 P.M. daily) has quietly carved out a huge reputation for its single-vineyard pinot noirs sourced from just about every great pinot-growing region on the West Coast. Owners Adam and Dianna Lee have followed a dream of making their favorite wine fervently, since they first left their native Texas in their twenties. After years gaining experience working for small wineries, they leased their first acre of vineyards, made their first 100 cases of wine in 1994 and, through a chance meeting with critic Robert Parker, won what would be the first of countless stellar ratings.

The key to Siduri's success is buying fruit from some of the best pinot growers and best vineyards in California and Oregon. The portfolio runs to more than 15 single-vineyard pinots sourced from the Willamette Valley in Oregon all the way down to the Santa Rita Hills near Santa Barbara. Anywhere from a few hundred to 1,000 cases are made of each wine, but all are richly extracted and regarded as among the cream of West Coast pinots. The big news is when Siduri *doesn't* receive a 90-plus point rating for one of its wines, which generally cost $30–50 per bottle. Visiting the winery is a refreshing change from Wine Country chintz—in such an industrial setting you can't help but focus solely on what's under your nose, which might well be one of the keys to Siduri's success. That and perhaps the fact that the winery is named after the Babylonian goddess of wine.

The setting does make finding Siduri challenging, however. From Piner Road just west of U.S. 101 go north on Airway Drive, into what looks like (and is) a light industrial area. The first road on the right is Airway Court, and Siduri is in the warehouse right at the end of the street, through the gates, on the right.

Another winery renowned for Russian River pinot but with a far longer history is **Joseph Swan Vineyards** (2916 Laguna Rd., Forestville, 707/573-3747, www.swanwinery .com, 11 A.M.–4:30 P.M. Sat.–Sun., by appointment weekdays). Joseph Swan got into the wine-making game when he bought a run-down farm in Forestville in the late 1960s with a plan to grow grapes and make wine during his retirement. He went about it with such a perfectionist passion and with so many good wine-making connections, however, that he became one of a small group of pinot pioneers in the Russian River Valley—a group that helped put the region firmly on the world pinot noir stage. Today his son-in-law continues Swan's legacy, producing beautifully crafted single-vineyard pinots as well as an excellent-value Russian River Valley blend called Cuvée de Trois, which usually sells out fast. Also worth trying are the equally elegant single-vineyard zinfandels. The small, rustic winery tasting room is off the beaten path, down tiny Trenton Road at the northern end of Laguna Road, and is open without an appointment on weekends, by appointment only during the week.

From Healdsburg via Argentina to Graton might seem like a tortuous route for a winemaker, but the founder of **Paul Hobbs Winery** (3355 Gravenstein Hwy. N., Sebastopol, 707/824-9879, www.paulhobbswinery.com) picked up some valuable wine-making experience along the way from Simi Winery near Healdsburg and Vina Cobos winery in Mendoza, Argentina, before establishing his wine label in 1991. As he built up his vineyard holdings during the 1990s, his wines were made at other Sonoma wineries, including Kunde; a dedicated facility in Graton was opened in 2003. Now Hobbs makes highly rated, vineyard-designate chardonnay and pinot noir from Russian River vineyards, and a cabernet sauvignon using Napa fruit. Prices of the wines, like their ratings, are high.

Acorn Winery (12040 Old Redwood Hwy., down a gravel driveway just south of Limerick Ln., Healdsburg, 707/433-6440, www.acorn winery.com), with its modest tasting bar in the corner of Bill and Betsy Nachbauer's garage, couldn't be further from the wine-making behemoths of Rodney Strong and Foppiano nearby. The Nachbauers are former corporate lawyers who bought their 26 acres of vineyards here in 1990 and started making their own wine six years later using equipment at other wineries but barrel aging (and tasting) in their garage. Production now is about 3,000 cases a year and a thoroughly Italian affair. Wines include zinfandel, sangiovese, dolcetto, and field blends including Medley, a blend of 15 varietals that redefines the term "complex." Being popular, however, most of the wines sell out fast each year.

Most Italian wine families in northern Sonoma can trace their roots back over a century, but Giuseppe Battaglini and family arrived in the 1950s with the same dream of recreating his memories of the Italian Wine Country right here in Sonoma. **Battaglini Estate Winery** (2948 Piner Rd., Santa Rosa, 707/578-4091, www.battagliniwines.com) has the advantage of owning vineyards planted by one of those early Italian immigrant families in the 1880s that supply grapes for the intensely flavored zinfandel and petite sirah wines. A more recent planting of chardonnay brought total production up to about 2,100 cases. It's all very much a family affair, and visitors will probably bump into a Battaglini family member in the tasting room in a small barn.

SIGHTS

The Russian River Valley is full of beautiful natural sights, from rivers to fir-covered mountains, but most of the cultural sights in the region are clustered around Santa Rosa, which has made a big effort in the last decade to nurture a small but growing arts scene. In the 1990s, the city designated a large chunk of the downtown area as the **Santa Rosa Arts District** in an effort to encourage investment in public art and institutions. The district is bounded by College Avenue to the north, Sonoma Avenue to the south, and Railroad Square to the west, and it incorporates the best cultural and historic sites (listed below) along with a growing collection of public murals and sculptures, with more planned. It is by no means a tourist-friendly district because everything of interest is so spread out. More information and a map of the current and planned art-related locations can be found at the City of Santa Rosa website (ci.santa-rosa.ca.us/departments/recreationandparks/programs/artsandculture/artsdistrict).

◖ Luther Burbank Home & Gardens

Apples and pears, grapes and hops, plums and peaches—as Sonoma County's rich agricultural history suggests, pretty much anything will grow here. Pioneering horticulturist Luther Burbank recognized this when he made Sonoma County his home in 1875. Burbank's cross-breeding experiments at his Santa Rosa and Sebastopol greenhouses are credited with creating more than 800 new strains of flowers, fruits, trees, and other plants over his 50-year science career, including the big white Shasta daisy, a spineless cactus, the blight-resistant Burbank potato, and the plumcot, a cross between an apricot and a plum.

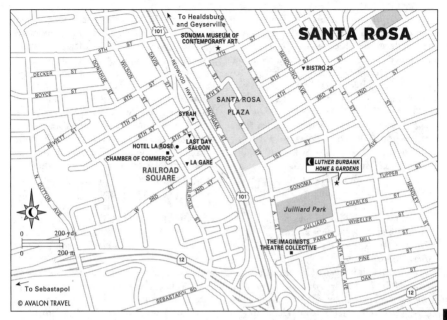

He was well connected in scientific circles of the time, counting Thomas Edison and Henry Ford, among others, as friends. Ford sent him the first tractor off the company's production line as a gift in 1918.

A Santa Rosa promotional brochure in the 1920s described him as "California's best citizen," and borrowed one of his many famous Sonoma quotes: "I would rather own a piece of land the size of a good healthy house lot in Sonoma County than an entire farm anywhere else on earth." Burbank's own healthy house lot, where he lived until 1906, is preserved along with a small greenhouse and the gardens as part of the 1.6-acre State Historic Park in Santa Rosa (on the 200 block of Santa Rosa Ave. at Sonoma Ave., just across the street from City Hall, 707/524-5445, www.luther burbank.org).

The gardens contain many of Burbank's horticultural creations and are open 8 A.M.– sunset every day. The museum and greenhouse (10 A.M.–4 P.M. Tues.–Sun. Apr.–Oct., $4) include some of his tools and explain the significance of his work. Guided tours are available during the summer months.

Also open about a half mile west of downtown Sebastopol is the 15-acre **Gold Ridge Experiment Farm** (7781 Bodega Ave., Sebastopol, 707/829-6711, open daily year-round, cottage open Wed. 9 A.M.–noon), where Burbank did many of his horticultural experiments and where there is now a historic collection of some of his creations. The replica cottage (the original was destroyed in 1906) and gardens have a rather unflattering modern setting in the middle of a retirement community. Take a self-guided hike or join a docent-lead tour (by appointment year-round).

Railroad Square

There's a hopping restaurant, shopping, and entertainment scene around the historic Railroad Square district in Santa Rosa, encompassing 3rd, 4th, and 5th Streets downtown, just west of the freeway. The center of the Railroad Square district is the **Northwestern Pacific Railroad Depot,** a small stone station house built in 1904 to replace an earlier wooden structure that burned down. Like many of the basalt stone buildings in the surrounding blocks, the depot is as solid as it looks and withstood the 1906 earthquake that leveled much of downtown Santa Rosa.

Its claim to fame was acting as a backdrop in the Alfred Hitchcock film *Shadow of a Doubt,* and it is now home to the **Santa Rosa Convention & Visitors Bureau** (9 4th St., Santa Rosa, 707/577-8674 or 800/404-7673, 9 A.M.–5 P.M. Mon.–Sat., 11 A.M.–5 P.M. Sun.).

Pick up a historic walking map from the visitors bureau to see some of the other historic buildings made from the locally quarried basalt stone. The buildings now house dozens of **antique stores, jewelry stores,** and other boutiques; 4th Street is particularly rich in historical storefronts.

Old Towne Jewelers (125 4th St., Santa Rosa, 707/577-8813, 10 A.M.–5:30 P.M. Mon.–Sat.) specializes in glamorous vintage jewelry and watches from Victorian and Edwardian to mid-century and 21st century periods. **Whistlestop Antiques** (130 4th St., Santa Rosa, 707/542-9474, 10 A.M.–5:30 P.M. Mon.–Sat., 11 A.M.–5 P.M. Sun.) is a collective of dozens of antique dealers worth visiting not least because of its antique home—a 1911 brick-and-steel building that won the city's first merit award for historical preservation.

Over the road, **Gado Gado** (129 4th St., Santa Rosa, 707/525-8244, 11 A.M.–6 P.M. daily) is an ethnic wonderland of Asian and African antiques and Asian-inspired home furnishings, all imported by the owners themselves. The retail business is just part of the story—a few blocks away is the company's huge warehouse, chock-full of everything from giant Indonesian gazebos to tiny Buddhas.

Museums

Santa Rosa has only a modest number of cultural attractions, but being the biggest city in Sonoma County does mean it's the rightful home of the **Sonoma County Museum** (425 7th St., Santa Rosa, 707/579-1500, www.sonomacountymuseum.org, 11 A.M.–5 P.M. Tues.–Sun.,

$5). Located in the city's historic former main post office building, the museum includes permanent exhibits of historic artifacts and photos that help tell the story of the county alongside temporary local art and photography exhibits. There's also an unlikely collection of art from the world-famous artists Christo and Jeanne-Claude that was donated to the museum in 2001 by their longtime assistant Tom Golden, who's from nearby Freestone.

In 2005, the Sonoma County Museum and the **Sonoma Museum of Contemporary Art** decided to merge after determining the city could not sustain two separate institutions. The MOCA, as it was known, was relatively small but claimed to be the only museum between San Francisco and Portland, Oregon, dedicated to contemporary art. Over the coming years the Sonoma County Museum will open additional gallery space to try to cram in some of the former MOCA exhibits, eventually creating a more balanced art and history museum.

The **Charles M. Schulz Museum** (2301 Hardies Ln., off W. Steele Ln., 707/579-4452, www.schulzmuseum.org, 11 A.M.–5 P.M. weekdays, 10 A.M.–5 P.M. weekends summer, 11 A.M.–5 P.M. Mon. and Wed.–Fri., 10 A.M.–5 P.M. weekends fall–spring, adults $10, kids $5), just north of downtown Santa Rosa, is dedicated to the Peanuts creator, who lived in the city until his death in 2000. Exhibits of original cartoons by Schulz and his peers are on display alongside Snoopy-related art and other dog-related exhibits. The gift shop, of course, sells every conceivable Snoopy toy as well.

ENTERTAINMENT

Santa Rosa's entertainment scene is somewhat dispersed, but the city does have a well-established local theater group. **The Imaginists Theatre Collective** (461 Sebastopol Ave., Santa Rosa, 707/528-7554, www.theimaginists.org) puts on an eclectic series of original and imaginative plays year-round at a small theater once home to an auto-repair shop. The evening performances are usually concentrated in a two-week stretch each month. Check the website for a performance schedule.

One of the most popular live music venues in the city is the **Last Day Saloon** in the Railroad Square area (120 5th St., Santa Rosa, 707/545-2343, www.lastdaysaloon.com, bar and restaurant Thurs.–Sat. until late, and other times when a show is scheduled). It's a fairly big and somewhat grungy venue with a decent bar and basic restaurant at the front, but most people come here for the DJs or the live music—generally rock and blues with some fairly big-name bands sometimes appearing. It also boasts the biggest dance floor of any venue in the area, which is not saying much. Check the website for upcoming shows and other events.

Guerneville and Sebastopol are two other local towns to go for some late-night fun. Guerneville and its environs have probably the most diverse entertainment scene in the Russian River Valley, befitting the eclectic population that swells in the summer with an influx of both gay and straight revelers. Sebastopol's action is a little more mainstream.

Much of Guerneville's nightlife caters to the gay scene with a curious mix of rustic bars enhanced with Day-Glo furnishings, all open late (and a few open unusually early too) and all along a three-block stretch of Main Street downtown. **The Rainbow Cattle Company** (16220 Main St., 707/869-0206, 6 A.M.–2 A.M. daily) is one of the oldest, with a big outdoor patio and legendary quarts of Long Island iced tea to get patrons in the mood. The poolside bar at the **Russian River Resort** (16390 4th St., 707/869-0691, www.russianriverresort .com, from 11 A.M. daily), also known as the Triple-R, is a popular drinking location for the gay masses and has some form of entertainment on weekend nights during the summer and Friday nights during the winter.

A few miles east of Guerneville and almost an institution in the area is the **Rio Nido Roadhouse** (14540 Canyon 2 Rd., off River Rd., Rio Nido, 707/869-0821 www.rionido roadhouse.com), which combines a rustic bar, restaurant, and poolside entertainment. Here you can lounge on a lawn next to bikers and aging hippies, surrounded by redwoods while soaking up the alcohol and the last rays of sun while tucking in to some freshly barbecued ribs and listening to a local blues band. It can be quite a trip, even for Guerneville. Bands play most weekend evenings throughout the year, and the pool is open Memorial Day–Labor Day.

About 15 minutes west on Highway 116, Monte Rio is a sort of miniature Guerneville on acid, a self-proclaimed Vacation Wonderland with more going on than its scrappy cluster of downtown buildings suggests.

Hard to miss is the brightly painted, neon-signed hump of the **Rio Theater** (20396 Bohemian Hwy., at Hwy. 116, Monte Rio, 707/865-0913, www.riotheater.com, daily summer, Wed.–Sun. winter), an old World War II–era Quonset hut, one of 170,000 churned out for emergency housing and warehousing in the 1940s. The theater now shows a program of current films that would put any big-city independent theater to shame. The weekend matinees ($6) start late afternoon, and the main daily show time is 7 P.M. in winter, 7:30 P.M. in summer ($8). Check the website or call the theater for the regularly changing schedules.

If you think a movie theater satiates the cultural requirements of tiny Monte Rio, think again. Monte Rio is also home to an active nonprofit theater group, the **Pegasus Theater Company,** established in 1998 by some veteran regional actors. It puts on plays and readings during the year, most from well-known playwrights (except the holiday variety show). Each runs for about six weeks at the 90-seat Pegasus Theater (20347 Hwy. 116, Monte Rio, 707/522-9043, www.pegasustheater.com).

Live local bands, DJ dance nights, and the occasional open-mike night are the main forms of entertainment at the **Hopmonk Tavern** (230 Petaluma Ave., 707/829-7300, www.hopmonk .com, daily until late) in Sebastopol. There's something going on nearly every night, particularly in summer when the dance action can also sometimes spill out onto the patio. Check the website for upcoming events. Covers for live bands range $5–30, and most come on around 8 P.M. There's also a late-night menu for anyone looking for some food to wash down the microbrews made here.

Redwoods are almost as common as vines in the Russian River Valley.

RECREATION
◖ Armstrong Redwoods State Reserve

This 805-acre reserve is just a few miles up Armstrong Woods Road from the center of Guerneville and is, as its name suggests, home to some neck-twistingly tall redwoods. The shady and damp forest provides welcome relief from the summer heat and is now the largest remaining old-growth redwood forest in Sonoma.

Some of its trees survived the region's vast 19th-century logging operations and were ironically saved by a lumberman—Colonel James Armstrong—who bought the land in the 1870s to preserve the last tracts of the very same forest he profited from.

Visitors with little time or energy can make a short trek on groomed paths from one of the three parking lots to some fine redwood specimens, including the 308-foot-tall Armstrong Tree, which is believed to be about 1,400 years old. If craning your neck is too strenuous, relax at one of the picnic tables scattered among the trees.

The more adventurous can choose from any number of longer hikes up out of the redwoods to the oak and madrone forests on the ridges higher up and continue on into the Austin Creek State Recreation Area, which is north of the reserve.

One such hike is a relatively quick loop (2.2 miles) that illustrates the wide range of vegetation and microclimates. The **East Ridge Trail** climbs steeply from just behind the visitors center up to a warm ridge that ducks in and out of the sun before descending back into the redwoods (head down the hill at the first sign-posted trail junction, or the hike will become a half-day ordeal). Once back in the redwoods it's an easy walk down the road or the **Pioneer Trail** back to the visitors center.

Another moderate loop is the 2.3-mile **Pool Ridge Trail,** which climbs 500 feet up a series of switchbacks before looping back down into the forest.

The reserve is open sunrise to sunset, and there's a $8 day-use fee for cars. Alternatively, park at the visitors center (17000 Armstrong Woods Rd., Guerneville, 707/869-2958, 11 A.M.–3 P.M. weekdays, 10 A.M.–4 P.M. Sat.–Sun.) and walk in on the road or a trail to avoid the fee. Dogs and bikes are not allowed on any trails. For more information, call 707/869-2015.

Riverfront Regional Park

About three miles south of J Vineyards on Eastside Road, this park is the perfect retreat to stretch your legs or sit in the shade of a redwood grove next to the parking lot and enjoy a picnic. The former gravel-mining operation here left behind a series of small lakes that look very inviting on a hot summer day but are strictly off-limits to swimmers. Several miles of trails around the 300-acre park give plenty of chances to see the wildlife on and around the lakes, however, and fishing for bass in the lakes is allowed with a current license. A new picnic area opened at the end of 2007 (along with permanent restroom facilities) about a half mile from the main parking lot. Just beyond that is the Russian River, where you can swim if you're brave enough. There's no official river access and no real beach, but it's easy enough to get down to the water if you're desperate to cool off. The park is open sunrise to sunset, and there's a $6 day-use fee.

The Russian River

With the Russian River gently snaking through the vineyards and forests towards the sea, it's not surprising that canoeing and kayaking are popular summer activities here. The river flow is relatively smooth this far downstream, even in the winter when the water is higher and faster, so don't expect any adrenaline-pumping rapids. Do expect to have to slather on the sunscreen on a hot summer day, however, and not to care if you tip over and take an unexpected dip in the river.

The least strenuous way to experience the river's meandering pace is to rent a canoe at **Burkes Canoe Trips** (8600 River Rd., Forestville, 707/887-1222, www.burkescanoe trips.com, May–Sept., $60 per day). Paddle or simply float 10 miles downriver, stopping at the many secluded beaches along the way, to Guerneville, where courtesy shuttles run back to base every half hour all day long.

For a slightly more strenuous option involving real "sit on top" touring kayaks rather than the glorified aluminum cans that most places rent, go to **Russian River Outfitters** (behind the old railway depot building on Moscow Rd., 707/865-9080), farther downstream in the old logging town of Duncans Mills, about five miles west of Guerneville. From here it is six miles to the ocean at Jenner, where a shuttle can pick you up by prior arrangement, or simply paddle upstream to the beach at Monte Rio and back.

Single kayaks cost from $55 for a half day and doubles from $75. This less-populated section of the river downstream from Guerneville is where you're less likely to see garbage and old tires, and more likely to see some of the river's wildlife, including otters, herons, and an occasional turtle sunning itself.

Kayaks and canoes can be rented for a day or more from **Kings Sport & Tackle** in

© ROBERT JANOVER

Take a dip in the cool Russian River on a hot summer day.

NORTHERN SONOMA

NORTHERN SONOMA FESTIVALS AND EVENTS

Whatever the time of year, there's always some sort of festival or wine-related event going on in this part of the world.

JANUARY

Wineries have to think of something to bring in customers in the depths of winter. Hence the **Winter Wineland** event (707/433-4335, www.wineroad.com), held around the middle of the month. More than 100 of the region's wineries take part. For the ticket price of $40–50, visitors get the VIP treatment and samples of limited-release wines. There's even a special designated-driver ticket price of $10.

MARCH

The region's annual **Barrel Tasting** (707/433-4335, www.wineroad.com), held on the first two weekends of the month, is a great excuse to visit as many wineries as possible in a day and sample wines straight from the barrel, whether you're interested in buying wine futures or not. Tickets are $20 in advance, $30 at the door.

APRIL

The **Passport to Dry Creek Valley,** held on the last weekend of the month, gets visitors into almost every winery in the valley, even those usually open by appointment only. Every one of them has some sort of theme for the weekend and puts on quite a party, with plenty of food and, of course, wine. The mock passports are stamped at every winery, though numbers are limited so book early. Contact the Winegrowers of Dry Creek Valley (707/433-3031, www.wdcv.com) for more information.

MAY

At the end of the month, on Memorial Day weekend, Healdsburg's antique sellers set up shop on the plaza for the one-day **Healdsburg Antique Fair** (707/433-6935, www.healdsburg .org). May is also the month that farmers markets all over Northern Sonoma dust off the stalls and start their summer season, which lasts through October or November.

JUNE

Before wine there was the Wild West, which is celebrated every year at the **Russian River**

Guerneville (16258 Main St., 707/869-2156, www.guernevillesport.com, open daily). Single kayaks cost $30 per day, doubles are $50, and aluminum canoes cost $55. From Guerneville's Johnson's Beach, it's four miles to Monte Rio downstream or eight miles to Forestville upstream. Make it a round-trip or pay $15 for the store to send a shuttle for pickup or drop-off (9 A.M.–2 P.M. only).

Fishing for the river's bass, bluegill, catfish, and winter salmon is also popular from a rented canoe or one of the many beaches, though a California fishing license is required. Two-day and longer licenses can be bought at Kings Sport & Tackle in Guerneville (which also rents fishing equipment) and most other tackle shops in the area. Also ask about the myriad rules and regulations. Barbed hooks cannot be used, for example, and only artificial lures (no bait) are allowed during the summer.

Ballooning

Taking to the air in Wine Country usually means ballooning, which entails getting up before the crack of dawn (balloons typically take off not long after sunrise), spending several hundred dollars, waiting around as the balloon is set up, and having little idea of which way it will drift once it does get airborne. Almost everyone thinks the reward, however, is worth it, as the initial adrenaline surge from lifting off yields to a sense of relaxation from being in a still and silent world thousands of feet above the stress of daily life. The aerial views of vineyards, mountains, rivers, forests, and the distant ocean are even more impressive than in less scenically diverse

Rodeo (707/865-9854), held the first weekend of the month at the Duncans Mills Rodeo, a 15-minute drive west of Guerneville. Over in Healdsburg, the beginning of June marks the beginning of the annual **Healdsburg Jazz Festival** (www.healdsburgjazzfestival.com), a weeklong series of concerts at venues around the city.

AUGUST

They named a highway after this apple, so why not have a festival in its honor as well? The **Gravenstein Apple Fair** (800/207-9464, www.farmtrails.org) in Sebastopol is held around the middle of the month at the town's Ragle Ranch Park. It celebrates the increasingly rare little apple that is still grown in orchards along the nearby Gravenstein Highway. The event includes music, crafts, and plenty of apple-flavored fun.

SEPTEMBER

The big blowout wine event of the year is the **Sonoma Wine Country Weekend** (800/939-7666, www.sonomawinecountryweekend.com), a three-day wine, food, and arts extravaganza held during the beginning of the month at the region's wineries. The main event is the **Taste of Sonoma County,** which is usually held at a winery near Healdsburg.

Celebrate the end of summer on the beach in Guerneville at the **Russian River Jazz and Blues Festival,** usually held the weekend after Labor Day. Top jazz musicians, fine wine, late summer sun, and the option of simply floating on the river all combine to make a unique experience. Tickets for the weekend event are available starting in April from the festival organizers (510/869-1595, www.omega events.com).

NOVEMBER

With all the creative names for food and wine events apparently exhausted for the year, this month's reason to eat and drink to excess is called simply **A Food & Wine Affair.** Many of the region's wineries match their wines with all sorts of food on the first weekend of the month. All you have to do is get from one winery to another. Tickets ($40-60) and information are available from the Russian River Wine Road (707/433-4335, www.wineroad.com).

Napa. Flights usually last about an hour, but expect the whole experience, including a post-flight brunch, to take up about half a day. Also expect to have to make reservations up to a month in advance during the summer and be held to a strict cancellation policy.

Wine Country Balloons (707/538-7359 or 800/759-5638, www.balloontours.com, $225 pp) usually flies from the Sonoma County airport near Santa Rosa and meets passengers at a nearby restaurant. **Up and Away** (707/836-0171 or 800/711-2998, www.up-away.com, $235 pp) also meets passengers at the Sonoma County airport, though balloons may take off elsewhere, depending on the weather. Both companies' balloons fly year-round and usually carry 6–8 people, though private flights can also be arranged for a lot more money.

Golf

Stroll among the redwoods without donning hiking boots at the **Northwood Golf Club** in Monte Rio, just west of Guerneville (19400 Hwy. 116, Monte Rio, 707/865-1116). The historic par-36, nine-hole course was conceived by members of the exclusive gentlemen's retreat Bohemian Grove, just across the road, designed by famous course architect Alistair McKenzie (who also designed the Augusta National course), and completed in 1928. Weekend greens fees start at $28 for nine holes, $43 for 18.

Spas

This spa destination in the Russian River Valley is as alternative as its remote location on the Bohemian Highway just south of Occidental suggests. The mud baths at **Osmosis** (209 Bohemian Hwy., Occidental, 707/823-8231,

RUSSIAN RIVER BEACHES

It can get hot in this part of Sonoma in the summer – too hot for even a chilled chardonnay to take the edge off. Luckily, the cool waters of the Russian River are always only a short drive away, though perhaps best experienced without being inebriated.

Native Americans had a good name for the river – Long Snake – and as it snakes its way down the Alexander Valley, loops around Fitch Mountain in Healdsburg, then barrels past Guerneville to the ocean, there are ample opportunities to take a dip.

As summer temperatures soar and the water level falls, the river is relatively calm and benign compared to the swift torrent it can become in the winter and spring, fed by the rains and melting snow hundreds of miles away in the mountains. Don't be fooled, though: It's still fairly cold with plenty of hidden obstacles underwater.

The dozens of small beaches exposed as the water level falls in the summer are technically public land, but getting to them usually involves crossing private or restricted areas. That puts many out of reach unless you're floating down the river in a canoe – the best way to experience some summer river fun.

It is still possible to get to some key beaches from the road, however.

In the Alexander Valley west of Geyserville on Highway 128 is the **Geyserville Bridge,** with space for a few cars to park off the side of the road at both ends. The easiest way down to the river is a short trail at the southwest end of the bridge that leads down to a gravelly beach area and stretches for quite a ways downstream.

A better place for swimming in the area is **Memorial Beach** at the southern end of Healdsburg, just across the Memorial Bridge. This is a more family-friendly beach with a swimming lagoon and concession stands for renting canoes. There's a $5 fee for parking in the lot, which can fill up quickly in the summer. Finding free parking anywhere near the beach is usually tough. The best alternative is to park on 1st Street in Healdsburg and walk back over the bridge.

As the river snakes its way down toward Guerneville the beaches become less plentiful and some of the visitors less modest. Don't be surprised at the occasional nude sunbather, especially at some of the more secluded sunning spots.

The historic **Wohler Bridge** on Wohler Road (just off the southern end of the Westside Rd.) has a small parking lot and boat ramp at the west side of the bridge and some limited parking along the road. Walk back to the other side of the bridge, hop over the steel gate, and follow the gravel trail for about a half mile, past the Water Agency yard and bearing right at a small fork until you reach the meadow and generally sandy beach just beyond. This is a popular beach with nude sunbathers and has recently gained a reputation as a gay cruising area.

Continue southeast on Wohler Road, past the Raford House B&B, and turn right on River Road. About one mile further, on the right, is the entrance to **Steelhead Beach** ($5 day-use fee). The large parking lot and boat ramp at the main beach hint at the spot's popularity for fishing and canoeing. A couple of trails heading east from the parking area lead to a more secluded stretch of beach that is better for swimming.

Farther along River Road, just west of the junction with Westside Road, is **Sunset Beach** (also known as Hacienda Beach), a popular spot with locals but easy to miss. Look for tiny Sunset Avenue off the south side of River Road next to a cluster of old wooden buildings. Parking on Sunset is illegal unless you live there, but there's usually plenty of space on the wide shoulder along River Road. At the first bend on Sunset Avenue there's a dusty trail off to the right leading down to a wide, gravelly beach and a good swimming hole. From there you can walk further downstream to additional, more secluded beaches.

Another good family beach is **Johnson's Beach** in the middle of Guerneville, just a few hundred yards off Main Street, where a makeshift dam is set up each summer to create a lagoon for swimming or paddling around in a rented canoe. It's crowded in summer, but the big parking lot is free, the food plentiful, and the atmosphere fun. The beach is also the site of the town's Fourth of July bash and the annual Jazz on the River festival.

www.osmosis.com, 9 A.M.–8 P.M. daily) are of the dry variety, in which hundreds of enzymes are mixed with rice bran and ground-up evergreen leaves to ferment the impurities out of the skin.

ACCOMMODATIONS

The main city in these parts is Santa Rosa, and it has perhaps more rooms than any other town, although mostly in chain hotels. But the bohemian resort town of Guerneville and the surrounding area offer the widest range of accommodations, from so-called river resorts that have seen better days to some classier and reasonably priced inns and B&Bs.

As usual, camping is by far the cheapest option, and there's plenty of the great outdoors to choose from, including the wilds of the backcountry and the relative comforts of the grounds of some of those resorts along the river.

Under $100

The **Creekside Inn** (16180 Neely Rd., Guerneville, 707/869-3623, www.creekside inn.com) is indeed right beside the creek otherwise known as the Russian River. It is just a few minutes' stroll to Guerneville's main street but also even closer to noisy Highway 116. Nevertheless, the rooms in the main house are cheap, starting at $98 for those with rather plain furnishings and increasing to $175 for the more sumptuously decorated suites with their own decks that can sleep four. The several acres of grounds include a pool and eight cottages, from studios to two-bedrooms, starting at $130 per night, and a handful of new solar-powered Nature Suites starting at $200 per night that come with fully equipped kitchens and can sleep four.

Rather like a funky Guerneville version of an 1830s resort, **Fern Grove Cottages** (16650 Hwy. 116, Guerneville, 707/869-8105, www .ferngrove.com) offers equal measures of tranquility and activity among the redwoods at the far western end of town. The collection of well-spaced cottages includes studio, one-bedroom, and two-bedroom accommodations starting at less than $90 per night during the

week, $110 per night on weekends, plus some twists including wet bars, hot tubs, and fireplaces. They are relative bargains, though the somewhat sparse decor is a reminder that they were built in the 1920s as a cheap family resort. On-site amenities include a pool, a bar, and a giant picnic area that's a hive of activity in the summer.

$100-200

Another refreshing change from the rustic nature of many cheap lodging options in the area is the **West Sonoma Inn** (14100 Brookside Ln., Guerneville, 707/869-2470 or 800/551-1881, www.westsonomainn.com). The 36-room self-styled resort and spa is surprisingly cheap considering its relatively central location in Guerneville and the modern decor and amenities that include down comforters, fireplaces in most rooms, luxury bathrooms, and nice views. It would almost fit in to the chic Healdsburg scene. The cheapest are the two Vineyard rooms and two Creekside rooms ($109–169). The best value is the Deluxe Vineyard or Courtyard rooms ($119–179), which are more spacious and have either panoramic views or a cozy fireplace. More expensive suites range in price $139–299.

In a pretty part of the valley en route to Armstrong Redwoods State Reserve is a new hotel that adds some much needed style to the Guerneville accommodation scene, the **Boon Hotel + Spa** (14711 Armstrong Woods Rd., Guerneville, 707/869-2721, www.boonhotels .com). The new owners have transformed a tired old resort into a sleek modern hotel with 14 rooms furnished in contemporary style. Many of the rooms have fireplaces and decks, and all are appointed with luxury fixtures, high-end electronics, and quality linens, including bath robes that are ideal to wear while sipping a cocktail beside the solar-heated saline pool and hot tub. Downtown Guerneville is about a half mile away, which is easily walkable but best navigated using one of the hotel's cruiser bikes that can be rented for a modest daily or half-daily fee. The cheapest junior queen rooms without fireplaces or decks are $145–195. Rooms with a private deck cost $10–15 more, and rooms with both a fireplace and a deck start at $165–225, rising to $230–290 for the biggest king suites that can sleep four.

A few miles west of Guerneville in Monte Rio is the **Village Inn** (20822 River Blvd., off Bohemian Hwy., Monte Rio, 707/865-2304, www.villageinn-ca.com), a tastefully restored Victorian home set in the redwoods on the south bank of the river not far from the infamous Bohemian Grove, an exclusive country club for America's elite and powerful. All 11 rooms have private bathrooms and a view of something, whether trees or the river. The bargains here are the three queen studios in the main inn (all $180), which have comfy club chairs and views of the river from their private balconies. The cheapest rooms are in the separate lodge and start at $125, while the most expensive deluxe king studio ($215) has a big private deck overlooking the river. Amenities include TVs and VCRs, wireless Internet access, and minifridges so you can chill a bottle of Russian River chardonnay to enjoy on the balcony.

Standing sentinel at a sharp bend in Wohler Road just half a mile south of Wohler Bridge is the historic ◖ **Raford House** (10630 Wohler Rd., Healdsburg, 707/887-9573 or 800/887-9503, www.rafordhouse.com), once part of a huge hop-growing estate in its Victorian heyday but now a charming hotel with verandahs overlooking acres of vineyards. All six rooms have private bathrooms and are decorated in a tasteful and fairly restrained Victorian style. The smallest of the six are $150–180, while the biggest rooms ($205 and up) have their own fireplaces. The largest of all, the Bridal Room, has a private covered porch overlooking the valley. Rooms at the front of the house have the best views. Standard amenities include a CD player–radio, wireless Internet access, and an evening wine reception.

One of the larger nonchain hotels in Santa Rosa is the **Hotel La Rose** (308 Wilson St., Santa Rosa, 707/579-3200 or 800/527-6738, www.hotellarose.com), an imposing basalt stone building that's part of the historic Railroad Square development downtown, within walking

distance of many of the city's sights and restaurants. The 49 guest rooms in the main building and Carriage House across the street (built in 1985) cater to the tourist and business crowd alike and so are well equipped and businesslike with minimal frills on the Victorian-style decor. Standard rooms start at about $130 in winter, $150 in summer, and top-floor rooms in both buildings are the most interesting, with either vaulted or sloping ceilings.

Over $200

A bit like staying on a French country wine estate, the **Vintners Inn** (4350 Barnes Rd., Santa Rosa, 707/575-7350 or 800/421-2584, www.vintnersinn.com) sprawls amid 50 acres of manicured gardens and vineyards just a few miles north of Santa Rosa. It's ideally located for exploring the Russian River Valley, and quick access to the freeway (River Road exit) gives easy access to Healdsburg and beyond (though also some freeway noise). All 44 rooms and suites are cozy and luxurious, some with fireplaces and all with either balconies or patios. Rates start at $195 for the patio rooms and just over $300 for the junior suites but rise rapidly in the summer and on weekends to $330–420. Breakfast is always included in the room rates, but on weekends you could also indulge with a sumptuous brunch at the Inn's renowned **John Ash & Co.** restaurant, one of the eateries credited with starting the Californian "Wine Country cuisine" style of cooking that so many other restaurants now mimic.

A little off the beaten track is the neat former railroad town of Occidental, and just off the main road on the edge of the forest is a delightfully rambling Victorian homestead that is now the ◖ **Inn at Occidental** (3657 Church St., Occidental, 707/874-1047, www.innatoccidental .com), a quirky yet luxurious bed-and-breakfast. None of the 16 whimsical rooms and suites are alike, although all have fireplaces and are stuffed with odd pieces of folk art, as are many of the inn's common areas. Rates drop close to $200 for a few of the smaller rooms during winter, but most usually cost $250–350.

A little piece of the Mediterranean landed in

the redwoods just south of Guerneville in the form of the **Applewood Inn** (13555 Hwy. 116, Guerneville, 707/869-9093 or 800/555-8509, www.applewoodinn.com). Three salmon-pink villas are nestled around a manicured central courtyard, the oldest of which is the 1922 Belden House with the cheapest (and smallest) rooms, starting at just under $200. The more modern Piccola Casa and Gate House, built since 1996, both contain the bigger and more expensive rooms, costing over $300. At those prices, the tranquil surroundings, swimming pool, in-room luxuries, and available spa therapies are to be expected. The big building at one end of the courtyard houses an outstanding restaurant offering classy Mediterranean-influenced Californian food and an extensive local-wine list. Alternatively, order a gourmet picnic basket for $50 and head for the hills.

Just a stone's throw from the Russian River, tucked away in the woods just off busy River Road, is the **Farmhouse Inn and Restaurant** (7871 River Rd., Forestville, 707/887-3300 or 800/464-6642, www.farmhouseinn.com),

© SONOMA COUNTY TOURISM BUREAU

the Farmhouse Inn

which has recently undergone a complete renovation and expansion to take it further up-market than it already was. Brightly painted cottages nestled among the trees house the 10 cheapest rooms with rates that start at just under $300 for the smallest (rooms 3 and 5) and rise to $345–575 for the largest suite or luxury king rooms with their own fireplaces and saunas or steam showers. A new barn was added on the site in 2007 containing seven more luxurious guest rooms that start at $525 and include every amenity you could imagine, from radiant heating and fireplaces to steam showers and jetted tubs. The restaurant is considered one of the best in the Wine Country.

Camping

There are plenty of resort campgrounds along the Russian River, but many cater to summer crowds and RVs and usually charge a premium price for the extensive services and facilities they offer. In all cases, reservations are essential during the busy summer months.

One of the more reasonable is **Burkes Canoe Trips** (8600 River Rd., Forestville, 707/887-1222), hidden in the redwoods right next to the river (and the road) just north of Forestville. The full-service campground, open May–October, has 60 sites for tents or RVs for $10 per person per night. This is also a popular place to rent canoes. The year-round **Hilton Park Family Campground** (10750 River Rd., Forestville, 707/887-9206, www.hiltonpark campground.com) is one of the smaller of the riverside resort campgrounds, with 49 open or secluded sites for tents ($35 per night, $40 for the premium riverside sites) and small RVs ($45), all in a lush, woodsy setting. There are also eight "camping cottages" that just about sleep two people and have space for a tent outside, but cost a relatively steep $65 per night.

The more scenic campgrounds are generally off the beaten track—well off the beaten track in the case of the primitive but scenic creek-side campgrounds high up in the **Austin Creek State Recreation Area.** The road up into the park through Armstrong Redwoods State Reserve ends at the **Bullfrog Pond**

NORTHERN SONOMA

Campground, with 23 sites ($15), toilets, and drinking water. No vehicles over 20 feet long are allowed into the park, so the camping experience here is relatively free of humming RVs.

From Bullfrog Pond it's about a three-mile hike to the **Tom King Trail** and **Gilliam Creek Trail** primitive campgrounds, and about four miles to **Manning Flat** campground. A water purifier or filter is essential if you want to drink the creek water, which you probably will in the summer when it can get very hot. The required backcountry camping permits ($15 on a first-come, first-served basis), together with maps, can be picked up at the Armstrong Redwoods park office (17000 Armstrong Woods Rd., Guerneville, 707/869-2958, 11 A.M.–3 P.M. weekdays, 10 A.M.–4 P.M. Sat.–Sun.) on the way up into the Austin Creek area.

FOOD

The food scene in the Russian River Valley is one of the most varied in northern Sonoma, as would be expected from a place that is effectively the produce basket of Northern California.

It certainly has its share of pricey, stylish establishments, particularly in the many inns hidden away in the woods. But since it's a down-to-earth, outdoorsy sort of place, there are also plenty of cheap and homey establishments where the lack of an uptight reservation system can make the experience instantly relaxing.

Guerneville

Being the hub of the region, Guerneville should be the first stop for those desperate for a quick and easy meal. There might be a bit of a wait in the busy summer months, particularly on festival weekends, but there are plenty of places to cater to the ravenous hordes.

This is not a five-star resort town, so don't expect five-star restaurants. Instead, most places are the caliber of the landmark **River Inn Grill** (16141 Main St., 707/869-0481, breakfast and lunch 8 A.M.–2 P.M. daily, breakfast $6–$13, lunch entrées $9–13). Its cozy booths, acres of Formica, hunks of ham, and piles of pancakes seem right out of a 1950s movie.

A California town would not be complete without its cheap Mexican restaurant, and one of Guerneville's most popular is the spacious **Taqueria la Tapatia** (16632 Main St., 707/869-1821, lunch and dinner daily, $5–12) serving decent quality food at the western end of town. More daring Mexican food connoisseurs might want to check if Guerneville's taco truck is parked in front of the Safeway parking lot for a more authentic street food experience. Right next door to the Taqueria is **Spliffs Organic Espresso** (16626 River Rd., 707/869-2230). Only in alternative Guerneville can hemp, organics, and coffee be inspiration for a name (and a big sign), though don't expect anything more potent than caffeine in the coffee.

Coffee, sandwiches, and other snacks are also available at the **Coffee Bazaar** (14045 Armstrong Woods Rd., 707/869-9706, 6 A.M.–8 P.M. daily), just around the corner from Main Street. The cool cavernous hangout is about as laid-back as things get in this part of the world, and there's a fascinating little used bookstore to browse through right next door.

With a modern, minimalist interior that looks like it belongs more to the trendy Healdsburg restaurant scene than in rustic old Guerneville, **Boon Eat & Drink** (16248 Main St., 707/869-0780, dinner and lunch Thurs.–Mon., dinner entrées $14–25) is a popular new bistro related to the nearby (and equally hip) Boon Hotel, where some of the vegetables are grown. It checks all the right boxes of a modern Wine Country bistro—organic, sustainable, and locally-produced ingredients prepared in imaginative small plates and main dishes with international influences. The small wine list is dominated by Russian River wines from small local producers.

One of the few saviors of beer drinkers in this part of Wine Country is the **Stumptown Brewery and Smokehouse** just east of Guerneville in Rio Nido (15045 River Rd., 707/869-0705, lunch and dinner Wed.–Sun.), which serves juicy ribs, brisket, and sandwiches for less than $15. Its heady microbrews, like Red Rocket and Racer 5, will get you drunk as fast as their names suggest and are best enjoyed while chilling on the giant deck out back.

Just south of Guerneville things get classier and more romantic at the **Applewood Inn** (13555 Hwy. 116, 707/869-9093 or 800/555-8509, www.appplewoodinn.com, dinner Tues.–Sat., entrées $24–34). Seasonal dishes like braised rabbit with olives and Humboldt Fog cheese are inspired by local produce and classic French cooking. As would be expected, the wine list is a who's who of local growers and regularly wins *Wine Spectator*'s Award of Excellence.

Monte Rio and Duncans Mills

About a 15-mile drive west of Guerneville in the two-block hamlet of Duncans Mills is the **Cape Fear Café** (25191 Hwy. 116, Duncans Mills, 707/865-9246, breakfast and lunch daily, dinner Fri.–Wed., dinner entrées $16–24), where Sonoma seafood meets Southern soul food. Many dishes in this cozy restaurant have a Cajun twist, and the grits make it worth an early morning drive for breakfast or a weekend brunch.

A scenic place to grab a bite halfway between Guerneville and Duncans Mills is the **Village Inn Restaurant** (20822 River Blvd., off Bohemian Hwy., Monte Rio, 707/865-2304, dinner Wed.–Sun., entrées $14–25) in Monte Rio. The beautifully restored building and its dining patio peek out from the redwoods onto the banks of the river. Most of the bistro-style main courses are well under $20 and can be washed down with wine from the award-winning list.

Forestville

You would not expect world-class food to find a home out in the woods east of Guerneville, but that's fast becoming the reputation of the restaurant at the luxurious **Farmhouse Inn and Restaurant** (7871 River Rd., 707/887-3300 or 800/464-6642, www.farmhouseinn.com, dinner Thurs.–Mon., dinner entrées $28–42). Chef Steve Litke, a proponent of the Slow Food movement, lets the veritable treasure trove of local produce do the talking here, with dishes like oven-roasted bluenose sea bass, or roasted red kuri squash and mascarpone ravioli. With main courses averaging $30 or more and a

cheese cart to die for, however, this slow food will quickly empty your wallet. The exception is the three-course prix fixe menu that is often offered on Sunday and Monday nights for a more modest $45.

Behind a modest storefront in sleepy Forestville, the **Mosaic Restaurant & Wine Lounge** (6675 Front St., 707/887-7503, lunch and dinner daily, dinner entrées $21–34) has energized the local food scene since it opened in 2005. The decor is rustic chic, with concrete floors, brick walls, and plenty of dark wood that is a perfect foil for the exuberant modern food, like the signature coffee-crusted filet mignon with chocolate-cabernet sauce and mashed potatoes. There are also simpler dishes executed with the same flair and a wine list that includes plenty of reasonably priced local wines. If you're just after more modest sustenance or a quiet drink, head to the cozy wine bar nook at the back of the restaurant. One look at the leafy patio, however, and you might be ready to make a dinner reservation.

Graton

Halfway between Forestville and Sebastopol is the tiny rural town of Graton, home to some big names in Russian River Valley dining. The best known is the **Underwood Bar & Bistro** (9113 Graton Rd., just west of Hwy. 116, 707/823-7023, lunch Tues.–Sat., dinner Tues.–Sun., dinner entrées $19–27), where lots of dark wood, plush red booths, and a nickel-plated bar add some unique luxury beyond the rustic exterior. The Mediterranean-inspired bistro menu features tapas plates (the oysters are popular) and hearty main dishes like Catalan fish stew and Moroccan-spiced lamb. There's a late-night tapas menu served after 10 P.M. on weekend nights.

Across the road (and sharing the same owners) is a rustic local gathering spot that doubles as a country store, the **Willow Wood Market Café** (9020 Graton Rd., 707/823-0233, 8 A.M.–9 P.M. Mon.–Sat., brunch and lunch Sun.). The well-priced breakfast, lunch, and light dinner menu is always popular with locals, and the polenta ($11–15) is legendary in these parts. It is becoming a victim of its own success, however, with lines that snake out the door on the busiest lunchtimes, although the back patio provides a bit more space. On a Sunday morning, this is where those in the know come for a brunch of Willow Wood Monte Cristo washed down with a mimosa.

Sebastopol

Sebastopol is chock-full of places to eat, though many of them cater to Bay Area urban commuters and don't particularly stand out. A few are worth navigating the town's one-way street system to visit, however.

Wine is the main attraction at the **Starlight Wine Bar** (6761 Sebastopol Ave./Hwy. 12, 707/823-1943, dinner Tues.–Sun., dinner entrées $10–29), inside a 1950s Southern Pacific railroad car now permanently stationed at the Gravenstein Station mall. The many small plates of tapas or cheese might be enough to satisfy as you explore the fascinating and reasonably priced wine list from the comfort of a booth. More filling fare comes in the form of pizzas and southern-influence comfort food like gumbo or chicken pot pie. If you think this gloriously restored railroad relic resembles a movie set, you will not be surprised to learn that the co-owners of the restaurant are former Hollywood visual effects artists.

If something more filling is needed, the popular **K&L Bistro** (119 S. Main St., 707/823-6614, lunch Mon.–Sat., dinner Mon.–Sun., dinner entrées $13–26) serves classic French-style bistro food, including French fries that are probably the best in the region. Equally suited to the relaxed, if slightly cramped, setting is K&L's famous mac and cheese, which can be ordered either as a main dish or a side.

On the western edge of town, the **French Garden Restaurant** (8050 Bodega Ave., 707/824-2030, lunch and dinner Wed.–Sun., entrées $25, three-course prix fixe $28 Sun. only) offers some French sophistication in an unlikely setting. The appeal here is the simple, beautifully crafted Mediterranean-inspired food that takes full advantage of the wide range of produce grown on a neighboring 16-acre

farm run by the restaurant owners. The ambience in the main dining room is as awkward as the faux-Renaissance building, which formerly housed a family-style Italian restaurant, might suggest. Outdoors on the large patio is the best place to ask for a table, or you can order some of the filling appetizers from the full menu in the cozy bar warmed by a large fireplace. Sunday Brunch here is accompanied by a farm stand selling much of the same produce used in the restaurant.

The comfort food goes very well with the microbrews in the classy dining room or on the patio of the **Hopmonk Tavern** (230 Petaluma Ave., 707/829-7300, lunch and dinner daily, dinner entrées $10–19). The menu is filled with the greatest hits of pubs, such as meatloaf, fish-and-chips, grilled chicken, and burgers, but the main draws are entertainment and beer, both in-house and domestic brews. The entertainment ranges from open-mike nights to DJs and live music. There's also a late-night menu. If you go for the New York steak from the menu, there's a modest wine list with plenty of middle-of-the-road wines at reasonable prices to help wash it down.

Occidental

At first glance, picture-postcard Occidental would seem to be the sort of town teeming with celebrated chefs ready to turn its sleepy Victorian charm into the next big food destination. Instead, the rural counterculture is alive and well here and so, evidently, is the Italian culture. There are almost as many Italian restaurants here as organic-labeled eateries and services (organic housecleaning, anyone?).

Find mountains of cheap Italian comfort food and surroundings in need of some updating at **Negri's** (3700 Bohemian Hwy., 707/823-5301, lunch and dinner daily, entrées $9–15). Specialties include the "world-famous" homemade ravioli, made from an old family recipe, alongside plenty of other pasta, chicken, and fried seafood dishes.

Similar family-style food with pizza thrown into the mix can be found in the homey dining room of the historic **Union Hotel** (3731 Main

St., 707/874-3444, lunch and dinner daily, dinner entrées $12–20), which curiously also offers free overnight RV parking with dinner.

A breath of garlic-free fresh air is provided by the tiny French-inspired **Bistro des Copains** (3782 Bohemian Hwy., 707/874-2436, dinner daily, entrées $19–23). Classic bistro dishes include pan-seared halibut on a potato pancake with cherry tomato beurre blanc or braised cloverdale rabbit in mustard sauce with butter noodles, while a wood-fired oven ensure pizzas, breads, and roasted meats turn out perfect. The wine list is dominated by Russian River Valley and Sonoma Coast wines, including more than a dozen pinot noirs, and if you bring your own bottle of Sonoma wine on Tuesday, the normal $15 corkage fee is waived.

Santa Rosa

With vast expanses of Napa and Sonoma Counties to explore, there are few reasons to head into Santa Rosa. One reason, however, is the city's burgeoning restaurant scene, in particular French restaurants, which might eventually persuade people to linger for longer downtown.

Some of the best restaurants are around the historic Railroad Square development near downtown. The location was obviously an inspiration when naming **La Gare** (208 Wilson St., 707/528-4355, dinner Wed.–Sun., entrées $19–44), which serves simple but sophisticated French-Swiss food, including some lavish steaks, in an old-school setting of starched white tablecloths (the French influence) and mountain ambience (from Switzerland). It was established in 1979, and such longevity is rare for a Sonoma restaurant, which means it must be doing something right.

As the French grape varietal syrah becomes more popular in Northern California, it seems only fitting that the French-American restaurant **Syrah** (205 5th St., 707/568-4002, lunch and dinner Tues.–Sat., dinner entrées $17–34) found its roots and is now a popular fixture with an impressive cheese menu. Not surprisingly, syrah and shiraz dominate the red wine portion of the wine list, but there are plenty

of other California and international wines to choose from, all well-priced.

One of the most popular new restaurants on the Santa Rosa scene is **Bistro 29** (620 5th St., 707/546-2929, lunch Fri., dinner Tues.–Sat., dinner entrées $19–26). The food is inspired by Breton regional cuisine from northwestern France (29 is the number of the Département, or district, called Finistère in Brittany) and includes dishes like *fromage blanc* buckwheat gnocchi à la Bretonne, sautéed Alaskan Halibut with cauliflower-lobster risotto, and old French standbys like cassoulet and *steak frites*. The modern decor hints at French country style, and the wine list also gives a nod to French regional wines with choices from Bandol, the Rhône, the Loire, and Languedoc complementing the extensive Northern Californian options. Ask about the three-course prix fixe dinner menu ($29) that is offered midweek.

During the day, the schizophrenic **Hank's Creekside Bistro** (2800 4th St., at Farmer's Ln., 707/575-8839, breakfast and lunch daily) belongs to all-American Hank, who flips burgers and pancakes and pours coffee in a rustic diner-style atmosphere.

A favorite if slightly out-of-the-way breakfast and lunch spot for locals is **Chloe's French Café** (3883 Airway Dr., Suite 145, 707/528-3095, breakfast and lunch Mon.–Fri., sandwiches $7–9) tucked into an anonymous unit at the back of a medical building on the northern edge of the city. It has a plain-looking commercial café interior, but the gourmet cold and grilled sandwiches made from fresh local ingredients are what draw legions of fans. Chloe is not the owner but the name the Pisan family gave to their trusty old Citroën truck that they shipped over from France.

Also just north of Santa Rosa, **Willi's Wine Bar** (4404 Old Redwood Hwy., just south of River Rd., 707/526-3096, lunch Tues.–Sat., dinner daily, $7–15) is another player in the burgeoning small-plate scene, where sipping wine or cocktails is as much a part of the fun as eating. Willi's shares the same owners as Willi's Seafood and Raw Bar in Healdsburg and has a relaxed New Age ambience that creates a perfect backdrop for the globally inspired small dishes, few of which are over $10. There are so many dishes to choose from that they almost outnumber the wines.

What was once the much-loved Willowside Café reopened in 2002 as **ZaZu** (3535 Guerneville Rd., Santa Rosa, 707/523-4814, dinner Wed.–Sun., brunch weekends, dinner entrées $16–25), a stylish, compact roadhouse about three miles east of Graton that serves California-inspired northern Italian cuisine. Enjoy familiar seasonal dishes with special touches, like flat-iron steak with Point Reyes blue cheese ravioli, at copper-topped tables overlooking the vineyards.

Picnic Supplies

There is no shortage of supermarkets, including organic ones, in most of the region's towns, but a few smaller stores are worth searching out for more unusual options.

The **Korbel Delicatessen** (13250 River Rd., Guerneville, 707/824-7313, 10 A.M.–4:30 P.M. daily fall–spring, 10 A.M.–5 P.M. daily summer), right next door to the winery's tasting room, makes fat sandwiches and gourmet salads to go. Eat on the small deck outside or head off into the wilds.

The **Kozlowski Farms** store in Forestville (5566 Hwy. 116, 707/887-1587, www .kozlowskifarms.com, 9 A.M.–5 P.M. daily), hidden down a driveway a few yards north of Ross Station Road, has a deli and offers a different kind of tasting—the countless jams, jellies, sauces, and chutneys it makes. A little further toward Sebastopol is the barnlike **Andy's Market** (1691 Hwy. 116, Sebastopol, 707/823-8661, 8 A.M.–8 P.M. daily), which is part organic produce market and part grocery store. In addition to the piles of fresh produce, the market sells breads, cheeses, olives, and sandwiches. In late summer it's the place to find countless varieties of local apples, and throughout the summer you'll often find a barbeque fired up outside.

The **Duncan's Mills Wine and Cheese Company** (25179 Hwy. 116, 707/865-0565, noon–6 P.M. Wed.–Mon. summer, noon–6 P.M.

Fri.–Mon. winter) is the first little building on the north side of the road from Guerneville, next to the cows, and offers not only a great selection of local wines (with regular tastings) but also an equally impressive selection of local cheeses.

And in Guerneville, almost thumbing its nose at neighboring 24-hour Safeway, is the little organic grocery store **Food for Humans** (1st St. at Mill St., 707/869-3612, 9 A.M.–8 P.M. daily), an eminently better place to buy produce.

In Santa Rosa, head to **Chloe's French Café** (3883 Airway Dr., Suite 145, 707/528-3095, breakfast and lunch Mon.–Fri., sandwiches $7–9) just north of downtown for gourmet sandwiches to go. In the heart of the downtown area, **Arrigoni's Deli** (701 4th St., Santa Rosa, 707/545-1297, 7 A.M.–4:30 P.M. Mon.–Fri., 7 A.M.–3:30 P.M. Sat., sandwiches $7–10) has a good selection if sandwiches and other deli items needed for a gourmet picnic.

There is also no shortage of tranquil places to have a picnic, from the beaches of the Russian River to the shade of the redwoods at the Armstrong Redwoods State Reserve just north of Guerneville. Or head to one of the many picnic-friendly wineries and pick up a bottle of wine to go with lunch. Some of the better picnicking wineries include Davis Bynum, Hop Kiln, and Foppiano.

Farmers Markets

With so many small towns in this agricultural region, there's a farmers market almost every day of the week, usually from Memorial Day to Labor Day. On Fridays (4 P.M.–dusk June–Oct.) it's **Occidental**'s turn, downtown in front of the Howard Station Café. **Sebastopol's** farmers market is held on Sunday morning (until 1:30 P.M. Apr.–Nov.) at the Downtown Plaza, and **Duncan's Mills** has its own on Saturday (11 A.M.–3 P.M. May–Oct.) behind the Blue Heron Restaurant on Steelhead Boulevard.

Santa Rosa has two farmers markets worth checking out. The **Santa Rosa Downtown Market** includes chef demonstrations and other entertainment alongside farm stands. It is held on 4th Street from Mendocino Avenue to E Street on Wednesday evenings 5–8:30 P.M., Memorial Day–Labor Day. The more traditional **Santa Rosa Farmers Market,** without the fun and games, can be found on Wednesday and Saturday mornings, 8:30 A.M.–noon, in the parking lot of the Veterans Building at 1351 Maple Avenue just south of the downtown area.

INFORMATION AND SERVICES

The most important tool for visiting the Russian River Valley is the excellent free map published by the **Russian River Wine Road** (707/433-4335 or 800/723-6336, www.wine road.com), an organization representing wineries and other businesses throughout northern Sonoma that is based in Healdsburg. The map is pretty easy to find at all major wineries and covers all the major roads in the Russian River Valley and up into the Dry Creek and Alexander Valleys.

More detailed and specific information about the Russian River Valley can be found in the free guide published by the **Russian River Valley**

Winegrowers Association (707/521-2534, www.rrvw.org), also widely available. Neither organization has offices open to the public.

Maps and other information about the region are available at the drop-in office of the **Russian River Chamber of Commerce** in the center of Guerneville (16209 1st St., at the old bridge, 707/869-9000 or 877/644-9001, www .russianriver.com, 10 A.M.–5 P.M. Mon.–Sat., 10 A.M.–3 P.M. Sun.). There's also an outpost at the Korbel winery in the old station house that is now the ticket office.

In downtown Santa Rosa, the **Santa Rosa Convention & Visitors Bureau** (9 4th St., Santa Rosa, 800/404-7673, www.taste santarosa.com, 9 A.M.–5 P.M. Mon.–Sat., 10 A.M.–5 P.M. Sun.) offers countless maps and brochures about accommodation, food, and wine, and activities in the city and surrounding regions.

Also worth noting is that there are virtually no gas stations west of Sebastopol and Guerneville, so fill up in Forestville or Sebastopol if you plan to venture out to the coast.

Dry Creek Valley

This compact valley is perhaps one of the easiest parts of northern Sonoma to visit in a day, and certainly one of the easiest to get around by car or bike.

At its southern end is the Victorian town of **Healdsburg,** with plenty of Wine Country frills but still relatively crowd-free even on summer weekends. It also has a staggering number of downtown tasting rooms, so many in fact that you can't help but wonder whether they'll all survive. You could tour northern Sonoma wines, never venturing more than a few blocks from the plaza, but that would mean missing out on the rustic charms of places like the Dry Creek Valley.

Although Healdsburg is the only place to shop, stay, or eat, getting out of the town is essential if you plan to experience the area. At its hot northern end, the Dry Creek Valley

is dominated by the huge Lake Sonoma Recreation Area, which offers some of the best outdoor recreation opportunities in Sonoma County. Between Healdsburg and the lake, there are vineyards, barns, and small wineries full of character, many run by eccentric characters.

Although the wine industry got an early start here when French and later Italian immigrants planted grapes in the late 1800s, Prohibition killed everything off, and for much of the 20th century the valley was full of plum and pear orchards. It was not until the early 1970s that grape growing started to pick up again, and the 7,000 acres of prune orchards that once filled the valley with their bounty shriveling in the hot sun are now long gone.

During that agricultural transition, little else apparently changed in the valley, and the

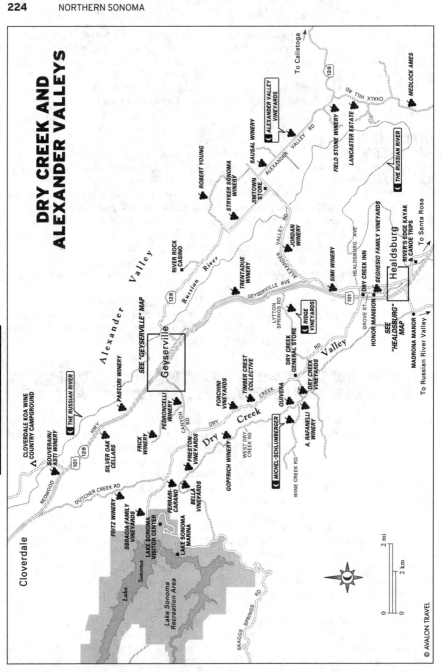

DRY CREEK AND ALEXANDER VALLEYS

© PHILIP GOLDSMITH

rural charm in the Dry Creek Valley

only development seems to have been winery related. Just two main roads run up the valley, on either side of Dry Creek itself: West Dry Creek Road and the original Dry Creek Road, which eventually becomes Skaggs Springs Road and heads off over the coastal hills to the ocean. Apart from a couple of roads traversing the valley and cutting through the eastern hills to the freeway and Alexander Valley beyond, that's about it.

Development did significantly change one thing: the valley's eponymous creek. Dry Creek used to dry up to nothing more than a few puddles by the end of the summer, like the many smaller creeks running down the valley sides still do today. Since the dam that created Lake Sonoma was completed in the 1980s, however, Dry Creek has become wet year-round.

The Wines

Dry Creek is perhaps best known for its zinfandels, which can sometimes take on an overbearing, jammy style in the hotter parts of the valley. But zinfandel vines do not dominate the valley as much as the wine's prevalence

might suggest and account for only about a quarter of the almost 10,000 acres of vineyards in the Dry Creek AVA. That's a big total acreage for such a small and narrow valley, especially when you consider the sprawling Russian River Valley AVA to the south only contains a few thousand acres more.

About 4,000 acres in the Dry Creek Valley are planted with cabernet sauvignon and merlot, particularly on the cooler western hillsides around places like the renowned Bradford Mountain. The hotter valley floor with its richer, alluvial soils grows excellent sauvignon blanc and, increasingly, semillon. Other varietals hint at the valley's French and Italian heritage, with syrah and petite sirah coexisting with small amounts of sangiovese and carignane.

The ideal mix of growing conditions for so many grape varietals results from the two ranges of low mountains that flank the valley—the 1,500-foot coastal hills on the valley's western side and the lower hills on the eastern side that separate it from the Alexander Valley. These hillsides have thousands of acres of benchland and canyons where growers can usually find just the right degree of heat needed for ideal ripening of most grape varietals. The hills also shield the valley from direct influence of the cold coastal air, yet just enough cool air and fog is funneled up from the Russian River Valley to prevent things from getting too hot and sticky, particularly at night.

At the far northern end of the valley, on the hot rocky ridges overlooking Lake Sonoma, is the aptly named Rockpile AVA, established in 2002. Don't expect to be visiting wineries here, though, because there are none. In fact, there are few paved roads. The 200 acres of vineyards are planted predominantly with zinfandel and cabernet, producing intensely flavored wines for the few wineries lucky enough to own land here.

WINE-TASTING
Dry Creek Valley Wineries

This part of the world offers perhaps the most eclectic mix of wineries, from rustic homespun operations of families that have been making wine for generations to the splashier newcomers reflecting the increasing popularity of the Dry Creek Valley as a major wine destination. Most wineries (even some newcomers) are fairly small and many still offer some sort of free tasting, although more are now charging a modest fee for a basic tasting, usually $5. Nearly all the wineries also have some sort of outdoor space for picnics.

FRITZ WINERY

Fritz (24691 Dutcher Creek Rd., Cloverdale, 707/894-3389 or 800/418-9463, www.fritz winery.com, 10:30 A.M.–4:30 P.M. daily, tasting $10) has recently started to focus on producing only single-vineyard wines rather than regional blends. The estate and other Dry Creek Valley vineyards provide grapes for zinfandel, sauvignon blanc, and cabernet, including a rich cabernet from the tiny Rockpile appellation just north of here. The Russian River wines include chardonnay and pinot noir, both of which have become as highly regarded as some of the Dry Creek wines. Don't miss the two tasty Vino Valpredo–labeled proprietary blends—one a

cabernet and zinfandel blend and the other sauvignon blanc and chardonnay.

The winery building itself, buried in a hillside north of the Frick Winery (with which it's sometimes confused), owes its *Jetsons*-like styling in part to the energy crisis of the late 1970s when it was built by Jay and Barbara Fritz. The patio and domed tasting room are above two levels of winery workings deep underground, so no pumps, coolers, or air-conditioning were needed, saving power and adding to its modern-day green credentials.

SBRAGIA FAMILY VINEYARDS

This northernmost winery in the valley, with sweeping views south, couldn't help but be a success thanks to some useful family connections. Sbragia Family Vineyards (9990 Dry Creek Rd., Geyserville, 707/473-2992, www. sbragia.com, 11 A.M.–5 P.M. daily, tasting $5–10) was created by Adam Sbragia and his father, Ed, who also happens to be the winemaker at Beringer Vineyards in the Napa Valley, where he produces some of Napa's greatest cabernets.

Ed's skill at creating highly extracted yet elegant wines, together with his connections to some of the best growers in Sonoma and Napa, gave his latest family venture quite a leg up. All the wines made here are single-vineyard versions from both the family's own vineyards and other growers.

Much of the wine is sourced from estate vineyards in the Dry Creek Valley and includes a merlot and a highly rated chardonnay from the 20-acre Home Ranch vineyard in the southeast part of the valley. The Gino's Vineyard zinfandel is a quintessentially spicy and jammy Dry Creek zin from the vineyard named after Ed's grandfather, and the cabernet sauvignon comes from the benchland Andolsen Vineyard owned by the family's doctor.

The Sbragias also make some limited-production wines from elsewhere in Sonoma and Napa using grapes sourced from renowned vineyards. There's an intense cabernet from Monte Rosso vineyard atop the Mayacamas Mountains above Sonoma Valley, for example, and a powerfully flavored chardonnay from Gamble Ranch in the Napa Valley. More outstanding vineyard sources are constantly being added to the portfolio, mainly cabernet in the Napa Valley, where Ed still has his day job at Beringer. They include the Rancho del Oso vineyard on Howell Mountain and the Wall vineyard on Mount Veeder, both in the Napa Valley. All the cabernets can be tasted for $10 at the winery, or choose from three of five wines for the cheaper tasting option.

FERRARI-CARANO
VINEYARDS AND WINERY

Ferrari-Carano (8761 Dry Creek Rd., Healdsburg, 707/433-6700 or 800/831-0381www.ferraricarano.com, 10 A.M.–5 P.M. daily, tasting $5–15) might sound like it was established by one of the old Italian wine-making families of northern Sonoma, but this is actually the flagship winery of a hospitality empire built up by the Carano family in the last 40 years. Sister businesses include the Eldorado Hotel and Casino in Reno and the Vintners Inn in Santa Rosa.

Despite its lack of historic pedigree, the pink Italianate mansion known as Villa Fiore (which translates to House of Flowers, a fitting name when the spring bulbs are in full bloom) and the acres of manicured gardens evoke a grandiose past, albeit one that's a little out of sync with the rustic charm of most Dry Creek wineries. Equally grandiose is the huge vaulted cellar that can house up to 1,500 barrels of aging wine down the grand stairs from the main tasting room. As you wander in the lush gardens, be careful not to trample any of the flower beds, or you might meet the same fate as a wild boar that once did and is now memorialized by a statue outside the tasting room.

The 160,000 cases of wine made each year are sourced from the 1,200 acres of vineyards that Carano owns throughout Sonoma, including its rapidly growing Alexander Valley mountain estate. They include a whole raft of highly rated single-vineyard chardonnays and a wide range of reds from single varietals to blends including the Bordeaux-style Tresor blend. There are also two decadent dessert wines,

© GEORGE ROSE

chateau at Ferrari-Carano Winery

including the Eldorado Noir, made from black muscat.

Those are among the best wines that can be tasted downstairs (for a price) in the Enoteca Lounge, a sumptuous den opened in 2006 that is effectively the winery's reserve tasting room. It provides respite from the bustling, Mediterranean-style main tasting room and the somewhat unexceptional wines poured there. Among the best of the cheaper lineup are the fumé blanc and an unusual blend of sangiovese, cabernet sauvignon, and malbec called Siena.

FRICK WINERY

Proceeds from the sale of a '57 Chevy helped get Bill Frick started in the wine business in 1976 near Santa Cruz. He moved to this small hillside winery at the end of sleepy Walling Road at the far northern end of Dry Creek Valley in the late 1980s.

The six acres of estate vineyards at Frick Winery (23072 Walling Rd., off Canyon Rd. or Dutcher Creek Rd., Geyserville, 707/857-1980, www.frickwinery.com, free tasting) are mainly planted to Rhône varietals, and owner Bill Frick is perhaps Dry Creek's most ardent Rhône Ranger. The 3,000 cases of wine produced each year include syrah, viognier, cinsault, and C-Squared, which is a blend of cinsault and carignane. More unusual still is the Grenache Blanc, a white version of this varietal that is rarely seen in California.

The cottage tasting room is open noon–4:30 P.M. weekends, but by appointment only during the week.

J. PEDRONCELLI WINERY

It no longer sells jug wines like it did up to the 1950s, but Pedroncelli (1220 Canyon Rd., Geyserville, 707/857-3531 or 800/836-3894, www.pedroncelli.com, 10 A.M.–4:30 P.M. daily) still produces some very approachable wines for the masses at the slightly ramshackle cluster of buildings on Canyon Road. None of the wines sell for more than $25 and most are under $15, making this a good place to buy a picnic wine or stock up with some everyday drinkers.

The winery has been a family affair since

John Pedroncelli bought the rundown former Canota winery and 90 acres of vineyards in 1927. The 75,000-case production includes zinfandel, chardonnay, sangiovese, petite sirah, and cabernet sauvignon, all made in the style of robust, easy-drinking table wines. Nearly all the wines are sourced from Dry Creek Valley vineyards with one notable exception—a Russian River Valley pinot noir that's pretty good for its modest price.

Some more unusual wines include vintage port and a zinfandel rosé that is bone-dry compared to its distant cousin, the nasty "white zin" found at supermarkets. Zinfandel is something of a specialty here, and the portfolio includes the Mother Clone zin, sourced from clones of Victorian-era vines.

In addition to the cheap wines, a boccie ball court, a nice picnic area, and regular exhibitions by local artists make this an entertaining place to visit.

FORCHINI VINEYARDS & WINERY

The Forchini winery (5141 Dry Creek Rd., Healdsburg, 707/431-8886, www.forchini .com, 11 A.M.–4:30 P.M. Fri.–Sun., tasting $5) has a charming homey character that makes you feel like a privileged guest.

The 3,000 cases of wine made each year use only about a quarter of the fruit from the family's 90 acres of vineyards; the rest is sold to other winemakers. The well-balanced Dry Creek cabernet sauvignon is, unusually, blended with 10 percent carignane; the zinfandel is a typically intense Dry Creek style; and the Russian River vineyards are represented by a big, rich chardonnay and a more reserved pinot noir. The cheap and cheerful Papa Nonno blend, made in the style of easy-drinking Tuscan table wine, is primarily zinfandel and makes a great picnic wine.

The small tasting room in the main house is open weekends only (or by appointment during the week) and has a small deck next to the cabernet vines lining the driveway.

◖ RIDGE VINEYARDS

Not just the wines here but the entire

building is organic. The new barrel and tasting rooms at Ridge (650 Lytton Springs Rd., Healdsburg, 707/433-7721, www.ridgewine .com, 11 A.M.–4 P.M. weekdays, 11 A.M.–5 P.M. Sat.–Sun., tasting $5) were constructed using only sustainable materials, although the contemporary design and solid feeling of the building barely hint at just how unusual the building materials actually were. The thick walls of the winery are made of rice-straw bales and a natural plaster, both chosen for their superior insulating properties. In fact, the building was the largest commercial straw-bale building when it was completed in 2003. Recycled lumber was used for the framing, flooring, and siding, and even the facing on the tasting room bar is made of pieces of old oak fermentation tanks. To cap it all off, 400 solar panels on the roof provide most of the winery's power.

The building is new, but Ridge has been active in the region for more than 30 years. It started buying grapes from the surrounding vineyards in 1972 and eventually acquired the former Lytton Springs winery property and its vineyards in 1991 to add to many other vineyards it owned throughout Northern and Central California.

Ridge is the king of zin, some years making more than 13 different versions that account for the majority of its 85,000-case annual production. Two-thirds of the zinfandel vineyards are in northern Sonoma, which makes the Lytton Springs outpost the company's Zinfandel Central, though it also makes syrah, petite sirah, and grenache. Even those who are not partial to zinfandel are likely to find at least a couple of wines to like here.

Ridge has another winery in the Santa Cruz Mountains that is more famous for its outstanding cabernet and chardonnay, and some of those wines can often be tasted here too.

DRY CREEK VINEYARDS

Built in 1973 not far from Dry Creek itself, this ivy-clad winery was the first to be built in the valley since the repeal of Prohibition. Although it is by no means the oldest in the valley and is far more commercial than

most neighbors, the Dry Creek winery (3770 Lambert Bridge Rd., Healdsburg, 707/433-1000 or 800/864-9463, www.drycreek vineyard.com, 10:30 A.M.–4:30 P.M. daily, tasting $5) has, without doubt, played an important role in transforming the valley from prune orchards to vineyards. What it lacks in homey charm it makes up for by producing some of the best white wines in the valley.

Owner David Stare planted the valley's first sauvignon blanc vines and is now a cheerleader for the varietal. Unusually for the Dry Creek Valley, the flagship wine here is the fumé blanc, although zinfandels like the Heritage Clone are still well worth tasting. Together those two wines account for almost half the winery's annual production of 120,000 cases. A full range of other reds and whites are also made from grapes grown in the estate vineyards and throughout Sonoma, including cabernet sauvignon, chenin blanc, a meritage blend, and even a zinfandel grappa.

The nautical theme on all the wine labels and in the cavernous tasting room hints at Stare's other passion, sailing. Grab a bottle of the bargain-priced Regatta white blend or Chenin blanc and relax at a picnic table on the shady, grassed picnic area while planning the rest of your day.

◖ MICHEL-SCHLUMBERGER

In a beautiful mission-revival building surrounding a tranquil courtyard, Michel-Schlumberger (4155 Wine Creek Rd., off W. Dry Creek Rd., Healdsburg, 707/433-7427 or 800/447-3060, www.michelschlumberger.com, tour and tasting $15–30) is tucked away up Wine Creek Canyon and surrounded by 100 acres of undulating benchland vineyards that create a multitude of different growing conditions, from the cool heights of nearby Bradford Mountain down to the hotter canyon floor.

Unusually for the Dry Creek Valley, zinfandel is notably absent from the wine portfolio here, but that's for good reason, according to the winemaker. Good zins come from old vines, he says, and Schlumberger currently has only young zinfandel vines. The cooler

NORTHERN SONOMA

© SONOMA COUNTY TOURISM BUREAU

Bella Vineyards

hillsides do, however, favor cabernet sauvignon, merlot, pinot blanc, chardonnay, and pinot noir. The cabernets, particularly the Reserve, are outstanding illustrations that the Dry Creek Valley is good for growing more than just zinfandel. Some young-vine zinfandel does sometimes make it into the plush and popular Maison Rouge blend, however.

The cheaper wines in the portfolio are sourced from Schlumberger's 90 acres of vineyards outside the valley, including a syrah and various components of the Maison Rouge. All told, the winery produces about 20,000 cases of wine per year. Tours of the winery and vineyards followed by a wine tasting are offered twice a day by appointment at 11 A.M. and 2 P.M. for $15. Longer tours into the vineyards to learn about organic farming principles followed by an outdoor tasting are offered at 10:30 A.M. Thursday–Saturday for $30.

QUIVIRA VINEYARDS

Although the winery is named after a mythical place where Spanish explorers expected to

find untold riches in the 1500s, there's nothing mythical about the qualities of the vineyard-designate zinfandels and the flavorful sauvignon blanc made by biodynamic Quivira (4900 W. Dry Creek Rd., Healdsburg, 800/292-8339, www.quivirawine.com, 11 A.M.–5 P.M. daily, tasting $5, tours $15).

Those wines are Quivira's specialties, but it also makes several Rhône-style wines, including a syrah, a mourvèdre, and the highly regarded Steelhead Red blend, taking total production to about 25,000 cases annually. Quivira is also one of the few Sonoma wineries to have its vineyards certified biodynamic, and its green credentials were given a further boost in 2006 with the addition of vast array of solar panels on the winery roof that provide all its electricity.

Tours are by appointment only.

BELLA VINEYARDS

This rising star of the Dry Creek Valley was founded in the mid-1990s just up the road from Preston Vineyards as a grape supplier to other wineries, but owners Scott and Lynn Adams soon decided to start making wine themselves and have since expanded their vineyard holdings in the Dry Creek Valley and neighboring Alexander Valley. Bella (9711 W. Dry Creek Rd., Healdsburg, 707/473-9171 or 866/572-3552, www.bellawinery.com, 11 A.M.–4:30 P.M. daily, tasting $5) is now known as a producer of outstanding single-vineyard zinfandels and syrahs.

The best zinfandels are sourced from old vines in each of Bella's three vineyards, including the robust and complex Lily Hill zinfandel from the vineyard around the winery. There's also a sweet late-harvest zinfandel and a limited-production Rhône-style blend of zinfandel, syrah, and grenache called the Hillside Cuvée.

Syrah was a fairly recent addition to the portfolio, and in addition to a version made from both Dry Creek and Alexander Valley grapes, there are two very distinctive but limited-production single-vineyard versions. The best is the smoky and dense Big River Ranch syrah. Even more site-specific versions of zinfandel and syrah were released in 2007 from specific vineyard blocks.

The farm-like setting of the winery overlooking the valley is pretty enough, but the pristine caves completed in 2004 with vines growing literally right above the entrance add a touch of class to the tasting experience. Tasting wines underneath a vineyard certainly is a cool summer diversion at this hot northern end of the valley.

PRESTON VINEYARDS

Dry Creek's ubiquitous zinfandel falls way down the list of interesting wines at Lou Preston's idiosyncratic establishment. Like Fritz, this is another of Dry Creek's incredible shrinking wineries. Founded in the mid-1970s, the annual production at Preston (9282 W. Dry Creek Rd., Healdsburg, 707/433-3372, www.preston vineyards.com, 11 A.M.–4:30 P.M. daily, tasting $5) eventually grew to 30,000 cases in the late 1980s but is now down to about 8,000.

This is probably to allow Lou and wife Susan to pursue their other varied Wine Country passions, from bread making (there's a commercial bakery on-site) to olive-oil production from the small olive grove at the winery, and even an annual boccie tournament on the winery's two boccie ball courts. The selection of locally-produced foods here rivals that in some delis and makes this an ideal place to buy everything you need for an impromptu picnic next to the boccie courts in the company of the winery cats.

The organic wines are just as varied. Zinfandel is produced here, but the list is dominated by Rhône varietals, including a highly regarded petite sirah, syrah, cinsault, carignane, mourvèdre, and an unusual blend of syrah and petite sirah (called, naturally enough, Syrah Sirah). Also worth trying are the spicy barbera, the grassy sauvignon blanc, and the cheery Guadagni Red jug wine, a robust blend of zinfandel, malvoisie, and carignane made in tribute to the Guadagni family, which established some of the best of Preston's 110 acres of vineyards in the late 1800s.

TIMBER CREST COLLECTIVE

The distinctive red barn up the hill next to Dry Creek Road marks the location of a collective wine-making facility, shared by some of the valley's best small wineries, Timber Crest Farms (4791 Dry Creek Rd., Healdsburg, 11 A.M.–4:30 P.M. daily). The driveway is marked by a well-populated signpost next to the road. Four wineries make wines and have modest tasting rooms here—in some cases just a counter propped on barrels. Tasting is more about the wine and the unpretentious vibe than the surroundings. Indeed, the wineries are small enough that it's likely to be the winemakers themselves doing the pouring.

After decades of making wine for other valley wineries, Rick Hutchinson started his own **Amphora Winery** (707/431-7767, www .amphorawines.com) in 1997 in a small barn just down the hill from Michel-Schlumberger and recently moved his operation across the valley to this site. He makes a little over 2,000 cases of vineyard-designate zinfandel, cabernet, syrah, merlot, and petite sirah. Pottery is Hutchinson's other passion, in particular the creation of the amphorae that inspired the winery's name and appear on the wine labels.

Another long-time Dry Creek producer, Fred Peterson, moved his winery here in 2006 after 20 years making his wines up-valley, and his son has now taken over most of the wine-making duties. The **Peterson Winery** (707/431-7568, www.petersonwinery.com, tasting 11 A.M.–4:30 P.M. Sat.–Sun., weekdays by appointment) makes small lots of about a dozen different wines, with total production around 5,000 cases annually. There are several very good and well-priced zinfandels, but it is some of the more unusual (and unusually named) blends that stand out here, including a powerful cabernet-syrah blend called Shinbone and a cheap and cheerful Rhône blend called Zero Manipulation. You also can't go wrong with any of the single-vineyard wines (cabernet, syrah, and zinfandel) sourced from Fred's Bradford Mountain vineyard in the southwest corner of the valley.

The **Papapietro Perry Winery** (707/433-0422, www.papapietro-perry.com, tasting $5) was formed by two former San Francisco newspaper men, Ben Papapietro and Bruce Perry, in 1998 and has established quite a reputation for its more than half dozen pinot noirs sourced from Russian River Valley and Anderson Valley vineyards along with a more recent addition to the portfolio, a trio of zinfandels—two from nearby Dry Creek vineyards and one from the Russian River Valley. Although not all the vineyard- and clone-specific pinots are likely to be available to taste, there will still be a dizzying array of wines for any pinot or zin lover to taste.

The fourth winery at Timber Crest is a relative newcomer to this area. **Kokomo Winery** (707/433-0200, www.kokomowines.com) is the brainchild of Eric Miller, originally from Kokomo, Indiana, who makes a varied portfolio of elegant, understated wines with the help of longtime local grower Randy Peters. The Dry Creek wines include zinfandel, cabernet sauvignon, sauvignon blanc, and syrah. There are also a couple of pinot noirs, a chardonnay, and a malbec made

using fruit from a vineyard to the south that straddles the Russian River Valley and Chalk Hill appellations.

SEGHESIO FAMILY VINEYARDS

Another of the old Italian family wineries that helped define the northern Sonoma wine industry over the past hundred years is about a 20-minute walk (or five-minute drive) from Healdsburg Plaza in a building dating from the 1890s. Although it is not surrounded by bucolic vineyards and fields, the ample gardens at Seghesio (14730 Grove St., Healdsburg, 707/433-3579, www.seghesio.com, 10 A.M.–5 P.M. daily, tasting $5) make it the best place to picnic and play a game of boccie within easy reach of the plaza.

Although the winery is now in a leafy residential area rather than farmland, it remains very much a family affair, run by the grandchildren of founder Edoardo Seghesio, who arrived in the region from Italy in 1886, planted his first vines in 1895, and established the winery in 1902. The wines are very much Italian as well, sourced from 400 acres of vineyards throughout the Russian River, Alexander, and Dry Creek Valleys.

About half the winery's 80,000-case production is just one wine—the excellent and bargain-priced Sonoma County zinfandel. Even with so much made, however, it often sells out after receiving its almost-standard rave reviews in the press. At the opposite end of the zin scale are the limited-production and ageworthy San Lorenzo and Cortina zinfandels as well as one from the tiny Rockpile appellation at the northern end of the Dry Creek Valley.

Sangiovese is the other dominant varietal here and an important component in Omaggio, a blend of cabernet and sangiovese that is Seghesio's version of a super-Tuscan. The limited-production Venom is sourced from the oldest sangiovese vines in the United States and named for the rattlesnakes that thrive in the hilltop vineyard. Also represented are the Italian varietals barbera and the unusual arneis, a grape that has roots in the same Piedmont region of Italy as the Seghesios.

The best way to experience the varied portfolio of wines here is with a wine and food pairing ($35) that is offered by appointment several times a day for most of the year except in winter. Five wines are served with Cal-Ital appetizers like fettuccine primavera with prosciutto and braised chicken with black olives and porcini mushrooms at one of the winery's giant redwood-topped banquet tables.

Wineries by Appointment
A. RAFANELLI WINERY
Up a long driveway off West Dry Creek Road, just south of Wine Creek Road, is where the fourth generation of Rafanellis now makes its limited-production wines at the A. Rafanelli Winery (4685 W. Dry Creek Rd., 707/433-1385). An intense zinfandel accounts for more than half the 11,000-case annual production, and the rest is cabernet and merlot sourced from the hillside vineyards. All the wines have attained an almost cultlike status, so the winery tends to attract those serious about their zins. The views from the vegetable garden next to the old redwood barn are also pretty spectacular, which along with the difficulty getting an appointment only adds to the slightly exclusive atmosphere.

GÖPFRICH ESTATE VINEYARD AND WINERY
There is more than the family's German heritage to the Göpfrich Estate Vineyard and Winery (7462 W. Dry Creek Rd., 707/433-1645). In addition to limited-production cabernet, zinfandel, and syrah wines from the Dry Creek estate, Göpfrich also sells limited quantities of fragrant, late-harvest German white wines including riesling, huxelrebe, and silvaner from its sister winery in the Rheinhessen region of Germany.

Healdsburg Tasting Rooms
Being located at the junction of the three most important northern Sonoma appellations makes Healdsburg a good jumping-off point to visit them all. Westside Road heads down into the Russian River Valley, Dry Creek Road to

its namesake's valley, and Healdsburg Avenue heads north into the Alexander Valley.

But it's just as easy to ditch the car and sample wines from those appellations and many more in the numerous downtown tasting rooms and wineries, all within walking distance from the plaza. There are more wineries represented here than most people can comfortably visit in a day and more than in any other Wine Country town. They might lack the rustic, rural charm of wineries surrounded by vineyards, but visiting these urban tasting rooms at least saves you from having to hop in and out of a hot car all day.

All opening times listed below are for the summer months through October. In winter, many tasting rooms close an hour earlier.

LA CREMA
One of the first tasting rooms you come to on entering Healdsburg from the south is this fancy new outpost of a well-established Russian River Valley winery. La Crema (235 Healdsburg Ave., 707/431-9400, www.lacrema.com, 10:30 A.M.–5:30 P.M. daily, tasting $5) has long since been absorbed into the Kendall-Jackson wine empire and turns out huge volumes of sometimes mediocre wine but still makes some nice examples of cool-climate pinot noir and chardonnay.

Look for the wines from the Russian River Valley, which tend to be better (and more expensive) than those from the larger Sonoma Coast region. La Crema also makes some nice pinot from other cool-climate appellations including Los Carneros and the Anderson Valley in Mendocino. The flagship wines are the limited-production pinot and chardonnay made under the Nine Barrel label, but they are not usually available to taste.

Instead the free tasting menu rotates through the La Crema portfolio, changing regularly but usually including a couple of the Russian River wines along with the cheaper Sonoma Coast versions.

THUMBPRINT CELLARS
Touting itself as a "micro-winery," Thumbprint

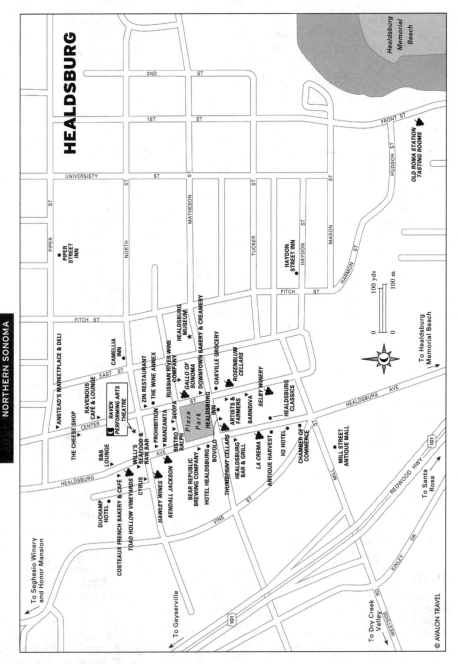

HEALDSBURG

Healdsburg Memorial Beach

100 yds

100 m

To Healdsburg Memorial Beach

To Seghesio Winery and Honor Mansion

To Geyserville

To Dry Creek Valley

To Santa Rosa

© AVALON TRAVEL

(102 Matheson St., 707/433-2393, www
.thumbprintcellars.com, 11 A.M.–6 P.M. Sun.–
Thurs., 11 A.M.–7 P.M. Fri.–Sat., tasting $5–10)
was started as a hobby for winemaker Scott
Lindstrom-Dake in the late 1990s and has rapidly grown to become a member of the boutique
brigade. It now makes more than 3,000 cases
of mainly warmer-climate, fruit-forward wines
from the Alexander and Dry Creek Valleys and
further north in Lake County.

The small, relaxed tasting room has a vibe
that's about as far from the corporate airs of
Kendall-Jackson around the corner as you can
get. Try the Threesome—a sexy blend of cabernet franc, cabernet sauvignon, and syrah—or
any of the other lush red wines that include
syrah, zinfandel, and cabernet sauvignon.
The Russian River pinot noir is one of the few
cooler-climate wines but just as approachable as
the others. The lone white wine is a sauvignon
blanc from Lake County, and it is a veritable
flavor explosion.

Both Scott and his wife are vegetarians and
make all their wines without animal-based
fining agents, so they're fit not only for vegetarians but also vegans. You might also pick up
some interesting ideas for pairing wines with
vegetarian food.

TOAD HOLLOW VINEYARDS
The toad in this hollow is actually owner Todd
Williams, the half brother of comedian Robin,
who has sported the amphibious nickname
since his youth. This downtown tasting room
is the only public face of the Russian River Valley
winery where you can taste its unusual selection of red, white, rosé, and sparkling wines at
the gnarled redwood bar.

Toad Hollow (409A Healdsburg Ave.,
707/431-8667, www.toadhollow.com,
10:30 A.M.–5:30 P.M. daily, free tasting) is best
known for its oak-free chardonnay, sourced
from the 103 acres of estate vineyards, but also
makes estate pinot noir and merlot, a Central
Coast zinfandel, and one or two unique (and
uniquely named) wines, including the popular
Eyes of the Toad, a bone-dry pinot noir rosé,
and a cheaper red blend called Erik's the Red,

which is made from a staggering 15 different
types of grape. The two sparkling wines are not
local, however, but imported from France.

If the wines don't entertain, their colorful
labels, painted by San Francisco artist Maureen
Erickson, might. Serious wines sport a very
conservative-looking toad while the fun wines
see the toad in party mood.

HAWLEY WINES
John Hawley certainly knows the area, having
been a winemaker at the giant Clos du Bois and
Kendall Jackson wineries since he started his
wine-making career in the 1970s. In the mid
1990s he started making small quantities of
wine under his own label, and along with help
from his sons has since expanded his portfolio to about a dozen varietals sourced from a
wide variety of northern Sonoma vineyards,
including the family's own estate on Bradford
Mountain in the Dry Creek Valley.

From overseeing the production of a several
million cases of wine at Kendal Jackson, he now
focuses on making a few hundred cases of each
of his own wines today. Hawley's Russian River
wines include pinot noir and chardonnay. Wines
from the estate vineyard in the Dry Creek Valley
include an acclaimed barrel-fermented viognier,
a classic Dry Creek zinfandel, and a merlot from
the Bradford Mountain estate that usually sells
out fast. Two cabernet sauvignons are also
made, one from Dry Creek fruit and one from
Alexander Valley fruit.

Hawley (36 North St., 707/473-9500, www
.hawleywine.com, 11 A.M.–6 P.M. daily, tasting $5) completed a new wine-making facility
just a few miles away in 2000. This new downtown tasting room opened in late 2009 and is
as much a showcase for the family's wines as for
its resident artist, Dana Hawley. Her striking
figurative work and impressionist paintings of
vineyards and other Northern California landscapes add a splash of color and class to the
elegant tasting room.

ROSENBLUM CELLARS
Although the winery itself is in industrial
Alameda just across the bay from San Francisco,

NORTHERN SONOMA

Rosenblum (250 Center St., 707/431-1169, www.rosenblumcellars.com, 11 A.M.–6 P.M. daily, tasting $5–8) is best known for its big, bold, highly praised zinfandels sourced from vineyards in the Dry Creek Valley and Rockpile appellations, hence the tasting room in Healdsburg next to the Oakville Grocery.

Zinfandels might dominate the 100,000-case annual output, but Rosenblum also makes a lot of other wines from vineyards all over California. These include some rich muscat dessert wines and the fun Coat du Bone blends sold under the Chateau La Paws label—a tribute to the veterinarian roots of founder Dr. Kent Rosenblum.

The tasting room is through a vine-draped pergola just a few yards down Center Street from the Oakville Grocery and shares its space with a small art gallery.

SELBY WINERY

Down Center Street from Rosenblum and almost opposite the police department is the tiny tasting room of the Selby Winery (215 Center St., 707/431-1288, www.selbywinery.com, 11 A.M.–5:30 P.M. daily, tasting free or $5), which has its production facility in a nearby warehouse.

The 10,000 cases of wine Selby makes each year come from vineyards all over Sonoma, with an emphasis on the nearby Russian River Valley, Alexander Valley, and Dry Creek Valley. The Russian River Valley chardonnay is perhaps the best wine here and one that regularly wins praise from the critics. The reserve chardonnay has even been served at the White House.

Other wines include a Russian River pinot noir, a couple of nicely structured syrahs, including a dry syrah rosé, and some nice zinfandels, including a juicy port. Most of the red bordeaux varietals are also in the winery's large portfolio, including a nice malbec from the nearby Chalk Hill appellation.

All can be tasted free in the relaxed and usually very quiet tasting room, where you're as likely to see a few locals hanging out as you are visitors. There's a nominal charge for trying the reserve wines.

GALLO OF SONOMA

It might be part of the largest privately owned wine company in California, and the largest landowner in Sonoma County, but Gallo of Sonoma (320 Center St., 866/942-9463, www.gallosonoma.com, 11 A.M.–5 P.M. Sun.–Wed., 10 A.M.–6 P.M. Thurs.–Sat., tasting $5–15) has a remarkably modest, café-style tasting room on the plaza that only opened in 2002.

Also remarkable is the fact that this is the only place that the public can taste Gallo's best wines, made under the Gallo of Sonoma label. None of the countless historic wineries acquired by Gallo over the years, including the nearby Frei Brothers winery in the Dry Creek Valley, are open to the public. A local supermarket is the place to pick up some of Gallo's 57 other labels of cheap and cheerful brands.

The premium wines poured here include the full range of reds, including the Italian varietals barbera and sangiovese. Whites are represented by chardonnay and pinot gris, and some of the wines, most notably the cabernet and chardonnay, are available in more expensive vineyard-specific and estate forms.

The stalwart Sonoma County cabernet and chardonnay are consistently highly rated and a good price. And with so many wines to taste, Gallo has created a series of fun and educational tasting flights that range in price from nothing to $15.

You can do a horizontal tasting (sample wines of the same varietal from different vineyards or regions), a vertical tasting (different vintages of the same wine), a cabernet tasting, and even an oak tasting that compares white wines that have had different oak treatments, from barrel fermentation to no oak contact. Or you can simply pick three of the single-vineyard wines and watch the world go by on the plaza.

KENDALL-JACKSON

If Gallo is the largest landowner in Sonoma County, then the Kendall-Jackson (337 Healdsburg Ave., Healdsburg, 707/433-7102, www.kj.com, 10 A.M.–5 P.M. daily, tasting $5–15) empire can boast the county's highest acreage of vineyards.

© SONOMA COUNTY TOURISM BUREAU

Kendall-Jackson

The Healdsburg tasting room of this Sonoma wine titan is a cavernous but chintzy place that offers tastes of some of the bewildering array of wines for $5, including not only Kendall-Jackson wines but also some from the numerous other wineries the company owns in California and Australia. Tasting the reasonably priced reserves and other high-end wines costs $15.

If there is a specific wine not available for tasting here, it might be offered at the main visitors center (5007 Fulton Rd., Healdsburg, 707/571-7500, 10 A.M.–5 P.M. daily), a French-style château next to U.S. 101 at the Fulton Road exit, a short drive south of Healdsburg. Before you go to either tasting room, visit the winery's website, where there's often a coupon that can be printed for a free tasting.

OLD ROMA STATION

A dozen small wineries have tasting rooms in the Old Roma Station (Front St. and Hudson St., Healdsburg, www.oldromastation.com), an old complex of warehouses on the southern edge of town right across from the Russian River, a pleasant 10-minute walk from the plaza. This was once home to the Roma Winery, a Victorian-era winery that shipped fortified wines by rail from its own station before the trains were halted by Prohibition. After finding various uses throughout the rest of the 20th century, the complex was renovated a few years ago and is once again home to wineries, often referred to by locals as the Front Street Wineries. Most offer tasting every day, but some are appointment-only, and a few are closed for a few days midweek. Whatever time you visit, however, you're sure to taste some unique wines from unique wineries, the most notable of which are listed below.

The tiny tasting room of the boutique **Camellia Cellars** (57 Front St., Healdsburg, 707/433-1290, www.camelliacellars.com, 11 A.M.–6 P.M. daily) makes less than 2,000 cases per year of sangiovese, cabernet, and its super-Tuscan Proprietor's Blend.

Dry Creek zinfandels and cabernets are the specialties of **Pezzi King Vineyards**

(707/431-9388, www.pezziking.com, tasting by appointment). It makes a half dozen zins, including several nice single-vineyard and old-vines versions sourced from the estate vineyard. The estate zinfandel and cabernet sauvignon are standouts, along with a nice Russian River Valley chardonnay.

Sapphire Hill Vineyards (707/431-1888, www.sapphirehill.com, 11 A.M.–4:30 P.M. Thurs.–Mon.) produces several thousand cases of Russian River Valley chardonnay, syrah, pinot noir, and four single-vineyard zinfandels, including a late-harvest version. The best value is a juicy blend of syrah and zinfandel called Harlot. Also ask about the infamous limited-release zinfandel called VineAgra that is only available in (you guessed it) magnums rather than those regular-sized bottles.

J. Keverson Winery (707/484-3083, www.jkeverson.com, 11 A.M.–5 P.M. Thurs.–Mon.) makes a couple of very good Dry Creek and Russian River zinfandels, but is also well known for its Carneros chardonnays. Also worth trying is a light and vibrant sangiovese from Mendocino.

SIGHTS

Healdsburg is one of the more appealing Wine Country towns, with the right mix of history, modernity, shops, and wine, and a population (11,000) that's large enough to prevent the town's economy from lurching too far in favor of wine tourism.

There is still plenty of Wine Country paraphernalia here, however, and there are often-voiced concerns that the town is being "St. Helena-ized," but it remains decidedly less frenetic than that smaller Napa Valley town. This could be partly thanks to some of its active cultural counterweights, including the loose collective of local artists called Stark Raving Beautiful, who have the motto "Help Make Healdsburg Weird" and a desire to prevent the town from becoming a "bourgeois play-land."

The town has a history as storied as any other in the region. It was established in the mid-1800s by an enterprising former gold miner from Ohio, Harmon Heald, who eventually bought enough parcels of land to lay out the town around a Spanish-style plaza and sell plots to other businessmen. He bought the land from Captain Henry Fitch, who was granted most of the surrounding area by the Mexican government and whose name lives on in Fitch Mountain, the small hump at the bend in the Russian River just east of the town.

Healdsburg was incorporated in 1867 and boomed after the railroad arrived in 1871. The modest-looking **Healdsburg Museum & Historical Society** (221 Matheson St. at Fitch St., 707/431-3325, www.healdsburgmuseum.org, 11 A.M.–4 P.M. Wed.–Sun., free), a few blocks from the plaza, is a treasure trove of information and photos illustrating the town's Victorian heyday and its Native American roots. Serious history buffs can pore through oral histories, official records, and newspapers going back to the 1860s.

Ask for a pamphlet about historic homes and visit some of the many Victorian buildings around town. The library itself is in one of Healdsburg's most notable neoclassical buildings, and the **Healdsburg Plaza** has been constantly reinvented since it was created in 1873.

The plaza was donated to the city by Harmon Heald in the 1850s. Most of the mature trees in the plaza today were planted between 1897 and 1900, including Canary date palms, orange and lemon trees, and a rare dawn redwood from China that is deciduous.

The last addition of note is the pavilion on the east side of the plaza, which was built in 1986 and resembles (in postmodernist style) the gazebo that had stood on the plaza a century earlier.

ENTERTAINMENT
◖ Raven Performing Arts Theater

Hats off to Healdsburg's fiercely independent Raven Performing Arts Theater (115 North St., 707/433-6335, www.raventheater.org) for keeping it real in the middle of Wine Country.

Believe it or not, there are four movie theaters squeezed into the **Raven Film Center** (415 Center St., 707/522-0330, www.sr

© PHILIP GOLDSMITH

The independent Raven Theater helps keep Healdsburg real.

entertainmentgrp.com) behind this historic building (though one is about the size of an average living room), so there's usually a combination of mainstream, independent, and documentary films showing 3–5 times every day (entrance on Center St., admission $9, matinees $6). For a more unique Wine Country movie experience, opt for a Hollywood & Vine ticket, which costs $11.50 but includes snacks and a glass of wine that you can drink at your leisure.

The theater is owned by a performing arts cooperative, ensuring an eclectic mix of live performances, most of which revolve around music, from Broadway musicals to jazz, classical, and rock. Local artists feature as strongly as national and international acts, particularly in the occasional theater productions put on by local groups and ensembles. Check the website for a full calendar of events or stop by the theater a block away from the plaza to check the listings and catch a movie.

Nightlife

A couple of local hangouts keep the bar scene in Healdsburg real too, staying open all day, every day until 2 A.M. Both **John & Zeke's Bar & Grill** (111 Plaza St., 707/433-3735) and the **B&B Lounge** (420 Healdsburg Ave., 707/433-5960) have a no-nonsense attitude and grumpy bartenders, and they shun Wine Country frills for good old-fashioned barroom entertainment like jukeboxes, pool, and darts. The B&B is more popular with locals and slightly less of a dive.

At the other end of the drinking spectrum are places like **Barndiva** (231 Center St., Healdsburg, 707/431-0100) and **Willi's Wine Bar** (4404 Old Redwood Hwy., just south of River Rd., 707/526-3096), where cocktails are often the drink of choice, the Hawaiian shirt is the clothing of choice, and the entertainment revolves around fancy food and people-watching. Both have nice patios outside that are the best places to nurse a drink on a warm summer evening.

A novel addition to the upscale Healdsburg bar scene, **Prohibition** (340 Healdsburg Ave, 707/473-9463, 11 A.M.–9 P.M. daily) opened in early 2010. As the name suggests, it's a bar that celebrates the secret speakeasy joints that flourished in the area during prohibition in the 1920s. Pass through a secret door in a corner phone booth at the back of a harmless-looking shop selling wine-related knick-knacks and enter a world of exposed brick, wood, and leather where it's not home-brewed hooch but cocktails and fine wines from small, high-end local producers that is served. The wine bar was the idea of the owner of the local Grape Leaf Inn who fondly remembers his grandfather's stories about running a real Prohibition-era speakeasy.

As Healdsburg slowly goes upscale, jazz is fast becoming the evening music of choice. The poster child for upscale, the swank **Hotel Healdsburg** (25 Matheson St., 707/431-2800) usually has some sort of live jazz in its lobby on Friday and Saturday evenings from 7 P.M. during the summer.

The best place to escape the Wine Country scene and nurse a cold beer at a small hole-in-the-wall bar is, ironically, right among the wineries of Dry Creek Valley. The **Dry Creek**

Bar (3495 Dry Creek Rd., at Lambert Bridge Rd., 707/433-4171) at the Dry Creek General Store is open daily from 3 P.M. Grab a beer, sit outside, and watch the wine tasters drive by. Closing time varies and usually depends on how many people are left propping up the bar.

SHOPPING

Wine is about all you'll be buying in most of the Dry Creek Valley, except in Healdsburg, a town of boutiques and antiques. Most of the treasures have long gone and many of the old antique stores have gone too as rents increased, but it's still fun to rummage through the handful of stores that remain along Healdsburg Avenue just south of the plaza.

The barnlike antiques cooperative **Healdsburg Classics** (226 Healdsburg Ave., 707/433-4315, 10 A.M.–5 P.M. daily) features the wares of more than 20 small dealers and is fun to rummage around in. There's another antiques cooperative a short distance away at the **Mill Street Antique Mall** (44 Mill St., just off Healdsburg Ave., 707/433-8409, 11 A.M.–5 P.M. daily). It boasts more than 20,000 square feet of floor space that is home to numerous local dealers and craftspeople.

Possibly the best place in town to buy a unique gift is **Artists & Farmers** (237 Center St., 707/431-7404, 10 A.M.–5 P.M. Mon.–Fri., 10 A.M.–6 P.M. Sat.–Sun.), a cavernous space in what used to be part of the town's opera house that is part studio and part marketplace, featuring artistic gifts and home furnishings together with unusual foods and fresh-cut flowers. It is a spin-off of the Barndiva restaurant next door, and it sells some of the same locally sourced foods as well as glasses and dishes used at the restaurant. It's far from just a cynical marketing exercise for Barndiva, however, and has developed more of a showcase of weird and wonderful artistic creations from local and global artisans. Wine Country clichés are nowhere to be seen among the products, and prices of many of the unique creations are not as expensive as the hipper-than-thou atmosphere suggests.

Other shopping highlights include the

Russian River Wine Company (132 Plaza St., 707/433-0490, 11 A.M.–4 P.M. Tues.–Fri., 11 A.M.–6 P.M. Sat.), which sells wine from all over the area, not just the Russian River, and specializes in smaller producers. The space also doubles as the Healdsburg tasting room of **Sunce Winery,** a small Russian River Valley winery that specializes in small-lot wines from the region, most notably some lean chardonnays and a rich, age-worthy Meritage red blend. Right next door is the cool tranquil space of the **Plaza Arts Center** (130 Plaza St., 707/431-1970), which showcases varied, mainly contemporary art from its local-resident artists, one of whom will likely be staffing the front desk.

There are several other wine shops in town, perhaps the most novel of which is **The Wine Annex** (340 Center St., 707/433-6488, 11 A.M.–7 P.M. daily), a combination tasting room and retail store. Behind the long tasting bar are dozens of wines on tap from all over California, and a few from elsewhere in the world. From the regularly changing tasting menu you can buy everything from one-ounce tastes of individual wines ($1–6, depending on the retail price of the wine) to a larger taste or an entire glass. If you find something you like, you can buy a bottle safe in the knowledge that you probably won't find a cheaper price. The Wine Annex is an outpost of the popular Santa Rosa wine shop, The Bottle Barn, which is widely known for its discount prices and regular generous sales.

RECREATION
Lake Sonoma Recreation Area

When the Army Corps of Engineers completed the Warm Springs Dam at the northern end of Dry Creek Valley in 1983, the resulting lake not only made Dry Creek's name obsolete by providing a year-round source of water but also became one of the best regional recreation areas.

Controversially, Lake Sonoma flooded some sacred sites of the Pomo people, now represented in a small exhibition in the **Milt Brandt Visitor Center** (3333 Skaggs Springs

Lake Sonoma is a camping and boating mecca.

Rd., Geyserville, 707/433-9483, 8:30 A.M.–5:30 P.M. daily), right at the end of Dry Creek Road. Despite protests during the drawn-out planning stages in the 1970s, the flood control, water supply, and recreation advantages created by the dam won the day, and it was finally completed more than 20 years after first getting approval.

The 17,000 acres of hot oak-studded hills of the Lake Sonoma Recreation Area have more than 40 miles of trails for hikers, bikers, and riders, the region's best bass fishing, and plenty of open water (about 2,700 surface acres, to be precise) for swimming and boating.

The main access points to the lake and trails are Stewarts Point Road, just south of the bridge; Rockpile Road, north of the bridge; and the grassy **Yorty Creek Recreation Area** (from S. Cloverdale Blvd., turn left on W. Brookside Rd., left on Foothill Rd., and right onto Hot Springs Rd.), which is on the eastern side of lake and is accessible from Cloverdale.

A couple of the easier and more accessible hiking trails start at the South Lake Trailhead (on Stewarts Point Rd. about 0.5 miles south from its junction with Skaggs Springs Rd., just before the marina turnoff). From there it's a quick jaunt up the hill to the **Overlook,** with great views of the lake. Or take the **South Lake Trail** for a longer hike, ducking in and out of groves of madrone and pine along the way. At about two miles, head right; it's then about 0.75 miles down to the Quicksilver campground, where you can duck into the lake for a swim, if you come prepared. Alternatively, go left and stay on the South Lake Trail for as long as you want. Other trails start at another trailhead across the bridge off Rockpile Road. A trail map is available at the visitors center.

Mountain bikers will have to be content with just one loop on the **Half-a-Canoe Trail,** which starts at the No Name Flat Trailhead, about 1.5 miles north of the bridge on the left. The loop is about 4.5 miles of mostly fire road with a short section of single-track.

You might notice that it gets hotter as you drive up Dry Creek Valley. Temperatures around the lake regularly top 100°F in the summer, so take plenty of water, whatever you do (the lake water is not drinkable). Other natural hazards include the occasional rattlesnake, disease-carrying ticks, and poison oak. You might be lucky enough to see the odd jackrabbit, a wild pig, or a rare peregrine falcon.

Fishing

The **Congressman Don Clausen Fish Hatchery** (behind the recreation area visitors center) was built to beef up the steelhead, chinook, and coho salmon populations in the Russian River and its tributaries and to mitigate some of the detrimental effects caused by construction of the Warm Springs and nearby Coyote Valley Dams. Tours are offered during the January–April spawning season (call 707/433-9483 for information). The main fishing draw on the lake is the healthy stock of largemouth bass, which love the submerged trees that were left in the Dry Creek arm of the lake when it was flooded.

The bass record stands at just over 15 pounds, though most reportedly weigh less than 10 pounds. There are also smallmouth bass, catfish, crappies, sunfish, perch, and numerous other species, including some landlocked steelhead.

When the water is clearest, during the summer, sight fishing is possible in the shallower waters close to the shore, as is bank fishing, particularly at the Yorty Creek Recreation Area. The lake is primarily a boat-fishing lake, however, and boats can be rented at the **Lake Sonoma Marina** (100 Marina Dr., 707/433-2200, $25–45 per hour for fishing boats, depending on the season, or $70–90 per hour for larger powerboats), just off Stewarts Point Road about 0.5 miles south of Skaggs Springs Road.

On the Water

There are three places to launch boats on Lake Sonoma—a trailer ramp at the Lake Sonoma Marina ($10 to launch), a big public ramp just across the bridge ($3), and a car-top launch area at Yorty Creek ($3). Check with a ranger for the boating rules. If fishing or high-octane boating doesn't appeal, paddleboats can also be rented at the marina.

Unless you're fortunate to be camping at one of the hike-in or boat-in campsites, there are not many places with decent shoreline access for swimming on the lake, however. The only official swimming beach is at the Yorty Creek Recreation Area.

Further south, in Healdsburg, the Russian River provides a few water-related recreation opportunities. On the south side of town, just beyond the Old Roma Station complex and over the bridge, is **Memorial Beach,** a stretch of sandy and rocky shoreline along the river with a swimming area and concession for canoe rental. Parking at the beach costs $5, but the lot is often so crowded that a better option is to park on the other side of the bridge in a residential area and walk back to the beach. Alternatively, it's about a 15-minute walk from downtown Healdsburg.

During the summer (generally May–Oct.), canoes or kayaks can be rented at Memorial Beach from **River's Edge Kayak & Canoe Trips** (13840 Healdsburg Ave., 707/433-7247, www.riversedgekayakandcanoe.com). Prices are $10–15 per hour, or you can sign up for a half-day or full-day river adventure through Alexander Valley.

The best aspect of renting a kayak or canoe for even a couple of hours is the access to more beaches. Paddle upstream under the railroad bridge toward the small hump of Fitch Mountain, and you'll find a whole host of little beaches and swimming holes. The public is allowed on all the beaches along the Russian River that fall below the winter high-water mark—basically every beach you see during the summer.

Golf

Touting itself as a Wine Country golf course, the **Tayman Park Golf Course** (927 S. Fitch Mountain Rd., Healdsburg, 707/433-4275, www.taymanparkgolfcourse.com) is actually in a Healdsburg residential area, a five-minute drive from downtown, but it does have some nice views west toward Dry Creek and the Russian River Valley. It's a nine-hole course that can also be played as an 18-hole par-68 course.

Green fees are $14–24 for nine holes, depending on the time of the week, and $18–31 for 18 holes. Golf-cart rental starts at $9. Drive east on Matheson Street from Healdsburg Plaza; the road becomes Fitch Mountain Road and heads up the hill to the club.

ACCOMMODATIONS

Take one look at the expanses of vineyards and hills dotted with the occasional winery and it's clear that the Dry Creek Valley is not a part of the world that's chock-full of hotels. Pretty much every accommodation option is in the town of Healdsburg, where Victorian frills still dominate the scene, though some contemporary style has recently crept in. As would be expected in a premium Wine Country destination town, prices are not low, regardless of style.

Under $150

Few options exist for those on a budget other than chain hotels and motels. Cheaper lodging is available to the north in the Alexander Valley and south in the Russian River Valley, but the town of Healdsburg itself seems to work hard to retain its sense of exclusivity.

One of the better among the chain lodging options is the **Dry Creek Inn** (198 Dry Creek Rd., Healdsburg, 707/433-0300, www.drycreekinn.com), a Best Western property less than one mile from the plaza but perilously close to the freeway at the Dry Creek Road exit. The hotel underwent a renovation in 2006, and most of the comfortable but ultimately plain rooms start at around $125, even in peak season. Amenities that include free wireless Internet access, a large pool, and a free tasting coupon for Simi winery make the stay a little more bearable.

$150-250

This could be classified as the Victorian frills price category, into which fall the many small family-owned inns and B&Bs in often historic houses. There might be some inflexibilities inherent to such small establishments (check whether smoking or pets are allowed, for example, and ask about the sometimes-strict cancellation policies), but the advantage is that the owners usually know the area like the backs of their hands and can offer great local insights and, of course, a great local breakfast.

One of the relative bargains in a crowded local field of frilly B&Bs is the **Camellia Inn** (211 North St., Healdsburg, 707/433-8182 or 800/727-8182, www.camelliainn.com). Flowers abound on the walls and fabrics inside the elegant 1869 house and in the gardens, which contain more than 50 varieties of camellia, some planted by renowned horticulturist Luther Burbank, who was a friend of the original owners. Unusually for a small B&B, there is air-conditioning in all rooms as well as a small swimming pool. Four of the nine guest rooms have gas fireplaces. Rates start at $129–149 for the tiny budget room but jump to $199–249 for the queen rooms and the single suite. The Lewand family owns both the inn and the **Camellia Cellars** winery, which has a tasting room not far away on Front Street. Wine shows up in the Victorian parlor most evenings, and you can chat with the innkeeper and winemaker himself, Ray Lewand.

There's a little more chintz on show at the ◖ **Haydon Street Inn** (321 Haydon St., Healdsburg, 707/433-5228 or 800/528-3703, www.haydon.com) on a quiet residential street about a 10-minute walk from the plaza. The Queen Anne–style house was built in 1912 as a private residence and briefly used as a convent before becoming a B&B in the 1980s. The six rooms in the main house cost $190–290, and all have private baths (across the hallway in the case of the Blue Room). Two additional deluxe rooms are in a separate cottage on the manicured grounds and cost upward of $300 depending on the season.

Other standouts in the crowded Victorian B&B scene include six-room **Calderwood Inn** (25 W. Grant St., Healdsburg, 707/431-1110 or 800/600-5444, www.calderwoodinn.com), not far from the Seghesio Family Winery. The Queen Anne Victorian boasts gardens that were laid out by famed horticulturalist Luther Burbank and has a beautifully (and tastefully) restored interior, right down to the reproduction Victorian wallpaper. The spacious rooms all have garden views and cost $210–300 depending on the season.

Filling a gaping hole for reasonably priced, Victorian frill–free accommodation is the hip **H2 Hotel** (219 Healdsburg Ave., 707/922-5251, www.h2hotel.com), which opened in 2010 just down the block from its sister establishment, the Hotel Healdsburg. As seems to be the norm for trendy new hotels, the green credentials of the sleek new building are impeccable, from the undulating grass-covered "living" roof to the solar heating and water collection system and right down to the furniture in each room, made from reclaimed wood or sustainable bamboo. The hotel was on the verge of opening as this edition went to press, so full details were not available, but it promises a rustic yet modern aesthetic with balconies or private patios for the 36 rooms and suites and an impressive list of luxury features, from high-definition TVs to custom organic bathroom amenities. Complementary bike rentals, a fireside lounge and bar, and a new restaurant are also promised. Rates for the hotel's opening summer started at $195–215 midweek and from just under $300 on weekends. Expect winter rates to be about $50 lower.

The town of Healdsburg might have a surplus of historic Victorian houses, but the (C) **Madrona Manor** (1001 Westside Rd., Healdsburg, 707/433-4231 or 800/258-4003, www.madronamanor.com), just outside the town at the southern end of the Dry Creek Valley appellation, puts them all in the shade. This enormous pile of Victorian opulence is the centerpiece of an eight-acre hilltop estate dating from the 1880s and is on the National Register of Historic places. Not surprisingly, the Manor's movie-set looks make it a very popular wedding location, and they also attracted the attention of director Francis Ford Coppola, who bought the estate in 2006.

The elegantly furnished rooms and common areas contain plenty of genuine and reproduction antiques as well as most amenities, except for televisions, which is probably fine since no children under 12 can stay here anyway. Any

bored adults can watch the fire burn or the sun set from the private decks of some of the 21 rooms and suites that are spread among five buildings.

Room rates are not as high as the opulence suggests, but with such high-profile new ownership of the Manor they could rise in the coming years. Summer rates start at $210–250 for the cheapest rooms in the Carriage House and manor house itself and rise to more than $350 for the suites. Winter rates are sometimes as low as $180. If the romantic setting, landscaped grounds, and swimming pool aren't enough to keep guests from ever leaving during their stay, then the manor's renowned restaurant might be. It serves the sumptuous breakfast included in the rate and a stylish, though pricey, dinner (on the big porch in the summer) with an outstanding wine list that leans heavily on the local appellations.

Over $250

In this price range, Victorian frills start to yield to more contemporary style, nowhere more so than at the (C) **Hotel Healdsburg** (25 Matheson St., Healdsburg, 707/431-2800, www.hotelhealdsburg.com), the centerpiece of the decidedly un-Victorian hunk of modern architecture that dominates the western side of the plaza. Strategically placed design elements and luxurious furnishings successfully soften the angular concrete minimalism of the interior, both in the rooms and the starkly minimalist lobby area. Such Manhattan style doesn't come cheap, however, even in sleepy Healdsburg. The smallest of the 49 rooms start at about $275, though they include the usual luxury amenities, including an iPod dock, a walk-in shower, and high-speed Internet. Add a tub and a few more square feet, and the rate jumps to more than $350. All guests have access to the tranquil outdoor pool and small fitness room, while the minimally named **The Spa** offers a wide range of spa treatments and massages for $110 and up. Downstairs is the pricey and equally contemporary restaurant, the **Dry Creek Kitchen.** A similar modern aesthetic at a lower price is offered by the hotel's new sister property just down the road, the H2 Hotel.

Slightly more reasonable rates but a slightly less contemporary feel can be found at the **Healdsburg Inn on the Plaza** (112 Matheson St., Healdsburg, 707/433-6991 or 800/431-8663, www.healdsburginn.com). The inn is part of the Four Sisters hotel chain and was recently renovated, so comfort and a reasonable level of amenities are guaranteed (as well as the signature teddy bear on each bed). All rooms have nice bathrooms, bay windows or balconies, and simple modern decor that blends with the original features of the Victorian building to create a sort of contemporary-lite character. Rates for the standard rooms start at $275, rising to more than $325 for some of the larger rooms. Afternoon cookies and wine are usually on offer, and the inn will also lend you bikes, although being right on the plaza you might not need them.

Even more luxury, tranquility, and contemporary style can be found at the even more expensive **DuChamp Hotel** (421 Foss St., Healdsburg, 707/431-1300 or 800/431-9341, www.duchamphotel.com), a short walk from the plaza and voted one of the top 25 hot new hotels by *Condé Nast Traveler* in 2001. Where the Hotel Healdsburg sometimes feels like it's trying a bit too hard to be hip, the DuChamp feels effortlessly chic, from the low-key minimalism of the six pool- and creek-side villas starting from $350–425. There's every luxury amenity you can imagine and a few you can't, such as a 50-foot lap pool, private terraces, and its private-label champagne (made by Iron Horse Vineyards). Private tastings can also be arranged at the nearby DuChamp Estate Winery (which makes only syrah).

A few Victorians offer some healthy competition to the high-end modern newcomers, not least the **Honor Mansion** (14891 Grove St., Healdsburg, 707/433-4277 or 800/554-4667, www.honormansion.com). At this gloriously indulgent establishment the unusual antiques and period architectural features do the talking without an excess of applied frills, giving some rooms at the self-styled "resort inn" an almost artistic feel. The 13 rooms and suites don't come cheap ($230–600) but do come with all amenities, including CD players and VCRs, as well as some fun features ranging from double-headed showers and ornate four-poster beds to private patios and giant fireplaces. There's even a two-story suite inside an old Victorian water tower. The three acres of verdant grounds contain a swimming pool, a koi pond, boccie and tennis courts, and a croquet lawn. The two- or three-course breakfast can be enjoyed out on the dining patio, weather permitting.

Camping

Lake Sonoma Recreation Area, at the northern end of Dry Creek Valley, is a tent-camping mecca, especially if you have a boat. There are more than 100 hike-in or boat-in primitive campsites along its 50 miles of shoreline, most of them on the Warm Springs arm of the lake. The most easily accessible on foot are the Island View or Quicksilver campgrounds, though the heat and terrain make the 2.5-mile hikes to them fairly strenuous during the summer months.

Most of the campgrounds are small, with an average of about 10 tent sites. None have drinking water, but all have fire rings and chemical toilets. Apart from the usual wildlife warnings (look out for rattlesnakes and ticks that carry Lyme disease), visitors should also keep an eye out for feral pigs, descendants of domestic pigs brought by early white settlers.

Also worth noting: Some campsites are located on lake areas designated for waterskiing, and the constant drone of power boats and Jet Skis can spoil an otherwise idyllic scene. More peace and quiet can be found near parts of the lake designated as wake-free zones (marked on the free map available at the visitors center). Island View is the quieter of the two most accessible hike-in campgrounds.

Reservations cost $14 during the summer months (877/444-6777, www.reserveusa.com). Even with a reservation, all backcountry campers must first get a permit from the hard-to-miss **visitors center** (3333 Skaggs Springs Rd., Geyserville, 707/433-9483), which also has trail maps. More information about the campsites is also available at the Army Corps website (www.spn.usace.army.mil/lakesonoma/index.htm).

For car campers, there's just one developed drive-in campground: **Liberty Glen** (877/444-6777, www.reserveusa.com). About a mile across the bridge from the visitors center, it has 95 sites for tents and RVs (no electrical hookups) that cost $10. Worth noting is that during the summer the gates to the site are closed to cars at 10 P.M., so don't plan on any late-night reveling.

FOOD

With Dry Creek largely devoid of shops and restaurants, it is left to Healdsburg to supply

BEER BEFORE WINE

It's hard to imagine a time before vineyards in Sonoma, but another type of vine was once the mainstay of the agricultural economy in the Russian River Valley. From Sebastopol to Healdsburg and up into Mendocino, hop vines rather than grapevines once lined the roads and covered the hillsides. All that is left to remind us now are the tall hop kilns that rear up over the landscape from Guerneville to Hopland, some long since converted into wineries.

The conditions were perfect here for hop growing. Rich alluvial soils and the cooling influence of the fog favored the hop vines just like they favor chardonnay and pinot noir grapevines today. Hops were first planted in the region around 1880, and by 1930 almost 3 million pounds were harvested each year. That's enough to make more than 100 million gallons of beer, by some estimates.

The small green fruit, resembling a miniature pine cone, was harvested, dried (or "toasted") in the giant kilns, and used in the making of beer. A resin-like substance from the hops called lupolin is what gives beer its distinctive bitter taste.

Market forces, disease, and (ironically) a mechanical invention by a local hop grower all spelled doom for the local hop industry. After World War II, demand and prices for hops plummeted as the public started to prefer less bitter beer (call it the Budweiser effect). Adding to growers' misery, downy mildew started to thrive in the damp, foggy air and infected the soils in the 1950s, killing vast tracts of hops.

The final nail in the hop growers' coffin was the invention of an automated hop harvesting machine in the 1940s by Santa Rosa grower Florian Dauenhauer. It quickly made the small, hand-harvested growing lots that were common in Sonoma far less economical. Growers sought out bigger plots of land elsewhere in California and the Pacific Northwest that could be machine-harvested, and by the 1960s the Sonoma hop industry was dead.

All that is left of the beer-related industry in northern Sonoma these days is a handful of brewpubs, many of them now buying hops from the Pacific Northwest or further afield. In Healdsburg, the **Bear Republic Brewing Company** (345 Healdsburg Ave., Healdsburg, 707/433-2337, www.bearrepublic.com) is right behind the Hotel Healdsburg and has a quiet, sunny outdoor patio. In Guerneville, the **Stumptown Brewery** (15045 River Rd., Guerneville, 707/869-0705, www.stumptown.com) offers such potent-sounding microbrews as Red Rocket and Death and Taxes.

Over in Santa Rosa, the **Third Street Ale Works** (610 3rd St., Santa Rosa, 707/523-3060, www.thirdstreetaleworks.com) challenges drinkers to get their mouths around names like Drunken Weasel Dunkelweizen and Goat Rock Doppelbock. A few blocks away is the **Russian River Brewing Company** (725 4th St., Santa Rosa, 707/545-2337, www.russianriverbrewing.com), which was actually founded by a winery (Korbel) in 1997 but now goes it alone, brewing dozens of ales and lagers with names that probably sound funnier when drunk, like Hop 2 It, Pliny the Elder, and Blind Pig IPA. Down in Sebastopol the beer legacy is kept alive by the **Hopmonk Tavern** (230 Petaluma Ave., Sebastopol, 707/823-7837, www.hopmonk.com) and its modest portfolio of four brews.

most of the food. In keeping with the town's breezy atmosphere, the culinary scene is also fairly relaxed. Restaurants generally never seem to be trying as hard as in some other Wine Country destination towns.

There are a few exceptions, and well-known regional chefs have had their eye on the place for some time. Some big-name establishments have taken hold here, like Manzanita, with input from Bizou in San Francisco, but they lack the big-city attitude (and, reportedly, the polished big-city service). Dinner reservations, though usually not needed, are nearly always recommended, especially in summer.

Fine Dining

The dining destination in Healdsburg and indeed most of the Northern Sonoma these days is **Cyrus** (29 North St., Healdsburg, 707/433-3311, dinner daily spring–fall, Thurs.–Mon. winter, 5–8 courses $102–130). The intimate restaurant with its vaulted ceilings and dark-suited waitstaff has been flatteringly compared to the famous French Laundry in Yountville for its contemporary and elegant food, fixed-price menus, and collection of Michelin stars. It has a more relaxed atmosphere, however, and diners actually get a choice for each of the courses from a small selection on the menu, a flexible system that still allows the kitchen to focus its efforts on a handful of dishes. Main-course choices might include Thai marinated lobster with avocado or mango roulade of lamb with porcini mushrooms and sangiovese sauce. Matching a wine to such simple yet sophisticated dishes is made more challenging by a wine list that runs to many hundreds of different Californian and international options, so be sure to make use of the reportedly excellent sommelier. For a cheaper dining option with fewer frills (and a greater chance of getting a seat) head to the small bar area, where many of the appetizers and entrées on the regular menu can be ordered separately along with a half dozen different caviars. Seats at the bar are on a first-come, first-served basis.

It's no surprise that almost half the wines available at **Zin Restaurant** (344 Center St., Healdsburg, 707/473-0946, lunch Mon.–Fri., dinner daily, dinner entrées $14–28) are zinfandels. More surprising is that chef Jeff Mall manages to match many of the dishes on the menu to one style of the wine or another, highlighting just how flexible the humble zinfandel grape really is. Of course, you don't need to be a zinfandel lover to enjoy the postindustrial interior, with its concrete walls and exposed beams, or the elegantly understated but exquisitely executed dishes made with seasonal local produce. Wines from all northern Sonoma regions are represented, and in addition to the reasonably priced main courses there are cheaper blue plate specials on many days of the week, depending on what's available down on the farm.

Bistro Ralph (109 Plaza St., Healdsburg, 707/433-1380, lunch and dinner Mon.–Sat., dinner entrées $15–29) is everything a cozy local bistro should be, with whitewashed brick walls, white-clothed tables, and giant plates of cheap fries. Owner Ralph Tingle kicked off Healdsburg's culinary resurgence with this bistro in the early 1990s, and it still serves sophisticated Cal-Ital food in a relaxed, if cramped, environment right across from the leafy plaza. Dinner can get pricey, but lunch remains a relative bargain.

The big red barn housing **Barndiva** (231 Center St., Healdsburg, opposite the police station, 707/431-0100, lunch and dinner Wed.–Sun., dinner entrées $12–40) looks very Wine Country from the outside but inside is more Manhattan. This being a rural part of the world, the clientele doesn't quite match the contemporary interior, but it's still a fun and unusual scene, albeit one that sometimes gets a bit full of itself. Barndiva opened in 2004 and bills itself primarily as a cocktail lounge, though one that also serves stylish Asian-influenced food and a huge selection of wine from a menu that is best examined while sober. The dinner menu is arranged according to mood, the wines by their flavor profile, so it takes a while to decide whether you're in a spicy, passionate mood or are feeling light and clean. Service is reportedly a bit spotty, perhaps because the waitstaff are as confused as diners about the menu.

Another newcomer to the small-plate phenomenon is **Willi's Seafood and Raw Bar** (403 Healdsburg Ave., Healdsburg, 707/433-9191, lunch and dinner daily, small plates $8–13), a few blocks north of the plaza. This is a sister establishment to the popular Willi's Wine Bar just south of Healdsburg and suffers from the same pleasant problem—there are just too many of the small plates of food to choose from. Most are under $10, so just try them all if you're peckish. This is also the place to experiment with food and wine pairing, particularly as most wines are available by the glass or half bottle. Although the decoration in the dining room is straight from Cuba, the inspiration for the food seems to come from all over the world.

An unassuming house opposite a strip mall a block from the plaza is home to the flagship of perhaps one of Healdsburg's most successful restaurant partnerships, Joyanne and John Pezzolo. Their ◖ **Ravenous Café & Lounge** (420 Center St., Healdsburg, 707/431-1302, lunch and dinner Wed.–Sun., dinner entrées $11–25) was moved here from its previous pint-sized location next to the Raven Theater (they transformed that former space into an equally successful lunch spot, Ravenette). Inside, the Ravenous Café feels as homey as the exterior suggests and serves generous portions of sophisticated bistro food from the ever-changing menu, though the trademark Ravenous Burger is always on the menu. On summer evenings, the tranquil garden dining space is as much the star of the restaurant as the food.

If you want a Victorian setting for dinner, there is probably no better option than the restaurant at **Madrona Manor** (1001 Westside Rd., Healdsburg, 707/433-4321, dinner Wed.–Sun., entrées $17–30) just outside Healdsburg. Eating here is as much about the sumptuous five-room Victorian setting and candlelit table decorations as the food, though the very expensive and stylish modern cuisine gets rave reviews.

Casual Dining
Although most of Healdsburg's many bistros serve very reasonably priced lunches, there are plenty of even cheaper places to grab a quick bite. At the back of the Plaza Farms market hall and offering a unique take on casual Italian dining is **Bovolo** (106 Matheson St., 707/431-2962, 9 A.M.–4 P.M. Mon.–Thurs., 9 A.M.–8 P.M. Fri.–Sat., 9 A.M.–6 P.M. Sun.). The self-serve style restaurant was created by the chefs behind Santa Rosa's successful ZaZu and features a smorgasbord of Italian treats, from wood-fired pizza and cured salamis to gelato and cheap carafes of house wine, all made from local ingredients. The restaurant gets its name from the Italian for a type of snail, a symbol for the "slow food" movement that encourages people to grow, prepare, and enjoy their own creations at a leisurely pace rather than eat and run. That's no doubt why you have to order and carry your own food to your own table, although the patio on a summer day is reason enough to linger.

Unpretentious and delicious Italian small plates, pizza and pastas along with a energetic yet intimate vibe have made **Scopa** (109A Plaza St., 707/433-5282, dinner Tues.–Sun., antipasti dishes $5–10, entrées $13–17) wildly popular since it was opened in 2008 by the former chef of Geyserville's award-winning Santi restaurant. Antipasti dishes like grilled calamari and Venetian-style sardines won't necessarily win awards for inventiveness but have won accolades for perfect execution and very reasonable prices. Main courses include pizzas, pastas, and simple meat dishes that exude the same rustic yet gourmet quality, and the wine list offers just as many regional Italian wines as northern Sonoma options. Being so popular makes securing one of the tables wedged into the long, narrow industrial-looking space a challenge, however, so consider eating at the small bar instead.

A block from the plaza is the younger sister to the successful Ravenous Café, **Ravenette** (117 North St., 707/431-1770, dinner Fri.–Sat.). The eight-table café with leopard-print seats and barely enough room to swing a cat is in the annex of the Raven Theater and serves seasonal food as eclectic as its location and decor suggests.

At the other end of the casual dining spectrum from the likes of Ravenette and Scopa is the spacious **Healdsburg Bar & Grill** (245 Healdsburg Ave., Healdsburg, 707/433-3333, lunch and dinner daily), with as many tables inside its saloon-style interior as outside on its shady patio. As its name and the giant outdoor barbecues suggest, this is paradise for lovers of big hunks of char-grilled meat, and they form the basis of the classic pub menu. There's a half decent wine list too.

There's more saloon-style dining and food just around the corner at the **Bear Republic Brewing Company** (345 Healdsburg Ave., Healdsburg, 707/433-2337, lunch and dinner daily), right behind the Hotel Healdsburg. The many microbrews are the main attraction, however, and can be enjoyed right in the shadow of stainless steel brewing tanks on the patio outside.

The southwest corner of Healdsburg's plaza is dominated by the bustling **Oakville Grocery** (124 Matheson St., Healdsburg, 707/433-3200, 8 A.M.–6 P.M. daily). Go there for deli food with that added Wine Country flair (and price) to stock up for a picnic or to eat at one of the shaded tables on the large patio overlooking the plaza.

Adding some European flair to the deli scene is the **Costeaux French Bakery & Café** (417 Healdsburg Ave., Healdsburg, 707/433-1913, 7 A.M.–4 P.M. Mon.–Thurs., 7 A.M.–5 P.M. Fri–Sat., 7 A.M.–1 P.M. Sun.). It sells the usual crusty bread and other bakery fare together with some tasty breakfasts and deli lunches that can be enjoyed on the big patio next to the sidewalk, a few blocks north of the plaza and considerably calmer than Oakville's. It also offers a light dinner and wine on Friday and Saturday evenings. Filling breakfasts and decadent pastries are the specialty of the **Downtown Bakery & Creamery** on the south side of the plaza (308A Center St., 707/431-2719, 7 A.M.–5:30 P.M. Mon.–Sat., 7 A.M.–4 P.M. Sun.).

Picnic Supplies

The **Oakville Grocery** (124 Matheson St., Healdsburg, 707/433-3200) is also picnic central, and it has just about everything, including wine, needed for either a gourmet alfresco feast or just some simple bread and cheese. Don't forget the sandwiches and bread available at the **Costeaux French Bakery** (417 Healdsburg Ave., Healdsburg, 707/433-1913, 7 A.M.–5 P.M. Tues.–Sat., 7 A.M.–4 P.M. Sun.).

Artisanal cheeses from all over the world, together with bread and other potential picnic fare, is available nearby at **The Cheese Shop** (423 Center St., 707/433-4998, 11 A.M.–6 P.M. Mon.–Tues. and Thurs.–Sat.). Also ask about cheese tastings and guest lectures by local cheese makers.

If you're heading up to the Alexander Valley or Dry Creek Valley, **Big John's Market** (1345 Healdsburg Ave., just north of W. Dry Creek Rd., 707/433-0336, 8 A.M.–8 P.M. daily), a bakery, deli, and grocery store all in one, is on the way.

Once in the Dry Creek Valley there's really only one place to buy food, and that's the **Dry Creek General Store** (3495 Dry

NORTHERN SONOMA

The Dry Creek General Store is the only place to buy a beer and sandwich in the valley.

Creek Rd., at Lambert Bridge Rd., 707/433-4171, 6 A.M.–6 P.M. Mon.–Sat., 7 A.M.–6 P.M. Sun.), which has existed in some form or another since the 1880s and continues to supply modern-day picnickers and peckish winery employees with deli sandwiches and groceries. Locals also like to hang out at the neighboring **Dry Creek Bar** (3495 Dry Creek Rd., 707/431-1543) to sip a cool beer while contemplating the wine business. The bar opens at 3 P.M. Monday–Thursday and noon Friday–Sunday, and usually closes whenever the last person falls off a stool.

Farmers Market

If you're after something really fresh, the **Healdsburg Farmers Market** is held 9 A.M.–noon Saturday mornings May–November in the parking lot of the Plaza Park (North St. and Vine St.), a few blocks west of the plaza itself. Those in the know say it's one of the best farmers markets in this part of Sonoma. On Tuesday evenings from June through October (4–7 P.M.) the market sets up on the main plaza downtown.

INFORMATION AND SERVICES

Comprehensive information about the wines and the winemakers of the Dry Creek Valley is available from the **Winegrowers of Dry Creek Valley** (www.wdcv.com, 707/433-3031). The association does a sterling job of ensuring the area's wineries get national attention and organizes the sell-out Passport Weekend event, a two-day party involving nearly all the valley's wineries on the last weekend in April.

Wine buffs can do even more research at the Healdsburg Public Library, which houses **Sonoma County's Wine Library** (Piper St. and Center St., 707/433-3772, Mon.–Sat.), a small annex crammed with every conceivable wine book, including plenty on local and California wine history.

More information about Healdsburg and its amenities can be found at the **Healdsburg Chamber of Commerce & Visitors Bureau** (217 Healdsburg Ave., 707/433-6935, www.healdsburg.com, 9 A.M.–5 P.M. weekdays, 9 A.M.–3 P.M. Sat., 10 A.M.–2 P.M. Sun.), a few blocks south of the plaza.

Alexander Valley

Most people speeding north on the freeway might glimpse vineyards as they cruise past the Alexander Valley. Some might even stop to visit some of the valley's biggest wineries that are close to off-ramps. Finding the true character of this part of the Wine Country and many of its smaller wineries requires a little more time navigating U.S. 128, however. The road runs from Geyserville through some rather alarming 90-degree bends and down into the rustic Chalk Hill and Knights Valley appellations. From there it's only a short drive to Calistoga at the northern end of the Napa Valley.

The 20-mile-long Alexander Valley stretches from Healdsburg in the south to the cow town of Cloverdale in the north. In between there is only one town of note: the hamlet of **Geyserville,** which for years has been destined

to become the next big Wine Country resort town, only to stubbornly remain its old sleepy self.

Geyserville wasn't always so quiet. Back in the late 1800s the nearby geysers drew visitors from far and wide, and the resulting influx of money helped build the town's grand Victorian homes. Now the only signs of the area's underground hot water supply are the clouds of steam sometimes visible from the 19 geothermal plants in the hills east of Geyserville (an area known simply as The Geysers). The area is one of the world's largest geothermal energy sources.

As with many other parts of the Wine Country, this valley was once dominated by cattle pasture and fruit orchards. The cows still hold sway around **Cloverdale** and farther north, where dairies are still more common than wineries, but the vineyards are spreading. Cloverdale marks the end of Northern California's most famous wine regions and the beginning of the new frontier of wine-making in Mendocino County. The Anderson Valley and Hopland are only short drives from Cloverdale but a world apart.

How many Wine Country visitors will venture north beyond Napa and Sonoma is yet to be seen, but Cloverdale optimistically opened its Wine and Visitors Center in 2000, clearly anticipating a northward shift in wine-making attitudes and winery visitors.

The Wines

The Alexander Valley is the northernmost appellation in Sonoma and also one of the hottest, despite the fact that the Russian River flood plain is wide enough to allow some of the more persistent fog to creep this far north on summer nights. Summer temperatures in Geyserville can often be 10 degrees higher than in Healdsburg just a few miles south. Cloverdale is hotter still.

With the ripening power of the sun and heat, together with the rich alluvial soils deposited by the Russian River over millions of years, it's relatively easy to guess what style of wine can be made here—big and opulent. Indeed, Alexander Valley cabernets have a softness and suppleness that they attain in few other places. There was good reason why the cabernet specialist Silver Oak Cellars chose this valley in 1993 for its first vineyard and winery outside the Napa Valley.

Sometimes the wines can get a little too soft and undistinguished. In general, however, Alexander Valley cabernets are characterized by soft tannins and lush fruit with hints of dark chocolate, making them perhaps the easiest drinking in California, if not necessarily the most complex or long-lived.

Other varietals grown here include chardonnay, which ripens easily to make rich and flavorful wines, along with merlot, zinfandel, and increasing quantities of syrah and sangiovese.

The appellation expanded in 1990 to include the vineyards creeping up the hillsides, particularly on the eastern side of the valley where the mountains climb to more than 2,500 feet. As growers experiment with the cooler hillside vineyards, subtler styles of wine are being created than the blockbusters from the fertile, sun-drenched valley floor.

At the southern end of Alexander Valley, east of Santa Rosa, is the Chalk Hill appellation, which derives its name from soils that contain chalk-like volcanic ash, similar to those at the northern end of the Napa Valley. It's directly in the path of the cooler Russian River Valley air and is mostly contained within the easternmost part of the Russian River appellation. The few wineries here are perhaps best known for some tangy chardonnays.

Sandwiched between the eastern parts of Chalk Hill and Alexander Valley, with the border of Napa County to the west, is the Knights Valley appellation, a primarily grape-growing region with just a couple of small wineries.

Millions of years ago the Russian River ran down the Alexander Valley, through Knights Valley, and into the Napa Valley, depositing

NORTHERN SONOMA

© PHILIP GOLDSMITH

Navigating the Alexander Valley is a cinch.

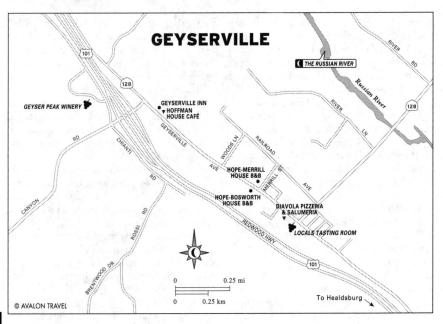

gravelly soils ideal for growing grapes. Knights Valley soils are also part volcanic, deposited during the volcanic eruptions that eventually changed the course of the river westward to its present-day path past Healdsburg and Guerneville to the ocean.

Completely shielded from the cool ocean air, Knights Valley is the hottest of Sonoma's appellations, providing ideal conditions for sauvignon blanc and cabernet sauvignon. Look for the Knights Valley appellation in the wines from Napa Valley's Beringer Vineyards, which owns about half the vineyards here.

WINE-TASTING

From the north end of the valley at the historic Asti winery, home of Italian-Swiss Colony (no longer open to the public), the Alexander Valley stretches southeast, past Healdsburg down to the Chalk Hill Road.

Most major wineries are on Geyserville Avenue, which runs parallel to the freeway between Healdsburg and Cloverdale, and on Highway 128, which runs southeast from Geyserville.

PASTORI

One of the northernmost wineries open to the public is also one of the quirkiest and among the smallest in the valley. The primitive, cinderblock tasting room of Pastori (23189 Geyserville Ave., Cloverdale, 707/857-3418, open whenever there's someone there, usually 9 A.M.–5 P.M. daily, free tasting), squeezed into one of the old warehouses at the side of the road, is a throwback to the old days of wine making when locals would come and fill up their jugs for a couple of bucks.

Frank Pastori is one of Sonoma's old-timers, and his family has been making wine here since the early 1900s. If the tasting room is open at all (it seems to have no regular hours) he's likely to be the only one there and will happily spin yarns about the good old days of wine making and perhaps try to convince you that white wine is "not real wine."

He offers good old prices for his zinfandel wine and port, and jug wines (bring your own jug). Don't expect much more than basic table wines, but do expect an unusual Wine Country experience.

SOUVERAIN

Souverain (26150 Asti Post Office Rd., Cloverdale, 707/265-5490 or 866/557-4970, www.souverain.com, 10 A.M.–5 P.M. daily, tasting $5–15) was originally a Napa Valley winery when it was established in 1944, but it moved to the Alexander Valley when its founder sold to the Pillsbury food company in 1973 and became known as Souverain Cellars, and later as Chateau Souverain when the next owner, Nestlé, came along in the 1980s. Half a century later, it has its original name back.

It may have an unsettled history, but there's nothing unsettled about the wines, which include consistently high-scoring Alexander Valley cabernet and merlot together with chardonnay, sauvignon blanc, viognier, syrah, and zinfandel. Some grapes are sourced in the Dry Creek Valley and elsewhere in Sonoma County.

All told, Souverain produces about 300,000 cases of wine, more than a third of which is cabernet and chardonnay. Winemaker Ed Killian also keeps the best grapes for the Winemaker Reserve cabernet, merlot, and chardonnay wines, available only at the winery and well priced considering their reserve status. Wines from another Fosters brand, the cheap and cheerful Cellar No. 8, are also made here and available to taste.

Perhaps the best reason to trek this far north in the Alexander Valley, however, is to see the parts of the historic Asti property, home of the Italian-Swiss Colony that was established in the late 1800s and was once the biggest winery in California before Prohibition ended its run. The tour ($15) takes in the original winery building, since retrofitted for modern production; the huge barrel room; and the old Victorian villa on the bank of the Russian River that was once home to the founder of the Colony, Andrea Sbarboro.

SILVER OAK CELLARS

On just the other side of the freeway from Pastori is a temple for red-wine lovers, the Sonoma outpost of Silver Oak (24625 Chianti Rd., Geyserville, 800/273-8809, www.silveroak.com, 9 A.M.–4 P.M. Mon.–Sat., appointment-only tours at 1:30 P.M. Mon.–Fri., tasting $10), which makes just one wine—cabernet sauvignon. If you like cabernet, you'll undoubtedly like Silver Oak's powerful, velvety version that some say has an unusual aroma from being aged for years only in American oak barrels. You might not like the price, however.

The 50,000 cases made here are produced from the winery's 200 acres of vineyards in the Alexander Valley, Russian River Valley, and Chalk Hill appellations. A further 10,000 cases of cabernet are made at Silver Oak's original Oakville winery in the Napa Valley, which was recently rebuilt after a fire destroyed the facility in 2006.

The Alexander Valley winery was established in the early 1990s more than a decade after the Napa Winery. Both facilities have legions of die-hard fans that line up each year to buy the new release, despite its ready availability, a testament to the loyalty of Silver Oak crowd and the quality of the wine. Some less adoring fans, however, think this cult status makes the wines more expensive than they perhaps deserve to be.

The Alexander Valley cabernet is $70 per bottle, and the Napa version is over $100. Not surprisingly, there's a $10 tasting fee, although you can keep the glass. Another option for $10 is to take the tour offered weekdays only at 1:30, which culminates in a tasting of both Silver Oak wines and a Napa Valley merlot from sister winery Twomey (but no free glass). You might also be able to taste the more moderately priced port that's only available at the winery.

GEYSER PEAK WINERY

Just down Chianti Road from Silver Oak is the giant ivy-clad home of one of the region's biggest wineries. Geyser Peak (22281 Chianti Rd., Geyserville, 707/857-2500 or 800/255-9463, www.geyserpeakwinery.com, 10 A.M.–5 P.M. daily) turns out hundreds of thousands of cases of mediocre wines and a few very good ones.

There has been a winery on the site since 1880, but the Geyser Peak name dates from 1911.

Through the 1980s it was a bulk wine producer, making up to 1 million cases of cheap wines per year, and only became known for premium wine in the late 1990s; it proudly boasts being named Best U.S. Wine Producer at the 2003 International Wine & Spirit Competition. For more than a decade Geyser Peak has been owned by various big corporations and was most recently acquired in 2008 by Ascentia Wine Estates.

A dizzying selection of wines makes up the 350,000-case production, including cabernet, merlot, zinfandel, shiraz, sauvignon blanc, and chardonnay, nearly all available as regular, reserve, and vineyard-designate wines. Expect to see more than two dozen wines on the tasting list. The cheaper wines in particular can be good value, but the winery is perhaps best known for its concentrated Alexander Valley cabernets and red blends that compared well with some of the best in the valley. One of the more unusual wines worth trying (although it's an acquired taste) is the Alexander Valley tannat, a varietal more commonly seen in Uruguay and southwestern France.

The giant tasting room is big enough to cope with the vast number of wines and crowds but has an understandably corporate vibe, and you won't necessarily learn much about the wines from the inexperienced staff. Five of the lower-end wines can be tasted for $5, while four of

THE ITALIAN CONNECTION

It is not by chance or climate alone that there is a preponderance of Italian names among the wineries of the Dry Creek and Alexander Valleys. In the 1880s an Italian immigrant named Andrea Sbarboro, a financier by trade, had the bright idea of starting a sort of grape-growing cooperative, or colony, to provide worthwhile work and lodging to the many other Italians arriving by the boatload in San Francisco.

He and his financial backers, including several Swiss businessmen, bought about 1,500 acres of land just south of Cloverdale and called the place Asti, after the town in the Piedmont region of Italy that was (and still is) famous for its wines. The Italian-Swiss Agricultural Colony, later shortened to Italian-Swiss Colony, was born.

The idea was that workers recruited to work there contributed a small portion of their salary each month in exchange for food and lodging, and to buy shares in the venture, thus making some money for Sbarboro and giving workers a sense of ownership.

Things didn't go quite to plan. Workers were suspicious of Sbarboro's financial intentions and didn't want to share the risk. The falling price of grapes soon meant the colony had to build its own winery to remain viable.

But the colony and its winery eventually became a huge success. By the turn of the 20th century it was both profitable and said to be the biggest producer of table wine in California. By 1910 it was making more than 14 million gallons of wine per year.

Early generations of many local wine families came to work at the colony. Edoardo and Angela Seghesio met there, and Ed went on to create the Seghesio Family Vineyards in the early 1900s, for example. Ferrari, Martini, and Rossi are other Italian names once associated with the colony that have been influential in the local wine world over the last century.

Pietro Rossi was Sbarboro's first winemaker, and the Rossi family bought the winery during Prohibition, keeping it alive as the Asti Grape Products Company before reentering the commercial wine business after repeal. It was eventually sold in the 1940s, and after changing hands a few more times it was finally bought by Fosters Wine Estates in 1988.

The old winery at Asti has been well preserved even after Fosters invested in new wine-making equipment for its Souverain and Cellar No. 8 brands that are made there today. After being closed to the public for over a decade, Fosters reopened the winery to the public in 2009 and now offers daily tours that allow visitors to see once again the grandeur of the old buildings and grounds along the bank of the Russian River.

the better single-vineyard wines can be tried upstairs in the more relaxing reserve tasting room overlooking the barrel room for $10.

TRENTADUE WINERY
In keeping with the Tuscan heritage of the founding family, Trentadue (19170 Geyserville Ave., Geyserville, 707/433-3104 or 888/332-3032, www.trentadue.com, 10 A.M.–5 P.M. daily, tasting free or $5) was one of the first wineries in this region to grow sangiovese grapes and now produces a cluster of sangiovese-based wines. The flagship La Storia Cuvée 32 wine (*trentadue* is Italian for the number 32) is a super-Tuscan style blend of sangiovese, merlot, and cabernet. Sangiovese even makes its way into the Old Patch Red blend, named for a 100-year-old block of zinfandel vines.

Trentadue also makes some of the best-value wines in the valley. The limited-production La Storia wines regularly score over 90 points in the press yet start at well under $30. The cheaper Trentadue wines are rarely over $20. Many of the wines are produced in small lots, however, so they sell out quickly.

About one-fifth of the winery's 20,000-case production is merlot, but sauvignon blanc, viognier, zinfandel, cabernet, and mourvèdre are also made here. You can also taste a flight of the red and white ports in the Mediterranean-style tasting room for the same price as the reserve wine tasting.

JORDAN VINEYARD AND WINERY
While Judy Jordan focuses on bubbly and pinot noir at the J Winery in the Russian River appellation, father Tom crafts rich cabernet sauvignon and chardonnay at this château-style winery just north of Healdsburg, making about 90,000 cases of supremely drinkable wine.

The beautifully manicured Jordan Vineyard estate (1474 Alexander Valley Rd., Healdsburg, 707/431-5250 or 800/654-1213, www.jordan winery.com, open daily for sales, tours and tastings by appointment only 11 A.M. Mon.–Sat. fall–spring, Mon.–Sun. summer, tasting $20, tour tasting $30) is perhaps the most picturesque winery setting in the valley and is best

appreciated on the hour-long tour that culminates in a tasting of wines and the estate olive oil together with some tasty morsels of food. Cabernet lovers might want to opt for the library tasting, which includes current releases of red and white wines along with several older vintages of the estate cabernet sauvignon, accompanied by a cheese plate.

Two-thirds of the production at Jordan is the cabernet, which has a style typical of the Alexander Valley's soft and fruit-forward red wines, and the rest is a crisp chardonnay from the Russian River Valley.

SIMI WINERY
Brothers Pietro and Giuseppe Simi came from Tuscany in the 1860s and set themselves up as winemakers and traders in San Francisco before moving to the current site of Simi Winery (16275 Healdsburg Ave., Healdsburg, 800/746-4880, www.simiwinery.com, 10 A.M.–5 P.M. daily, tasting $5–10), just north of Healdsburg, in 1881.

Back then the winery was called Montepulciano, after the Simis' Tuscan homeland. The Simi name was adopted after the repeal of Prohibition, but by the 1970s the family connection had ended and the winery was bought by a subsidiary of multinational conglomerate Constellation Brands in the 1990s.

In its heyday, the winery boasted Sonoma's first public tasting room—a 25,000-gallon redwood tank set up at the side of the road by Isabelle Simi Haigh, the second-generation owner of the winery. It was evidently a roaring success, but the current tasting room is a more modern affair inside the historic stone cellar building, which dates from the late 1800s.

The winery is best known for its chardonnay, sourced from the 120 acres of Russian River Valley vineyards, and its cabernets, from 600 acres of Alexander Valley vineyards. Those two varietals alone account for more than two-thirds of the 300,000-case annual production, and both garner consistently good reviews. Other wines in the portfolio include sauvignon blanc and merlot sourced from a variety of vineyards in Sonoma County.

Tastings are $5, for reserve wines $10, and $3

extra buys an informative tour of the gardens, which include a stand of redwood trees planted by Isabelle Simi. Tours followed by a tasting are offered twice daily at 11 A.M. and 2 P.M.

STRYKER SONOMA WINERY
The name is appropriate considering the new Stryker Sonoma winery (5110 Hwy. 128, Geyserville, 707/433-1944 or 800/433-1944, www.strykersonoma.com, 10:30 A.M.–5 P.M. daily, tasting free or $5–10) is housed in one of the most striking buildings in the Alexander Valley, a contemporary glass, wood, and concrete structure that won an architectural award when it was completed in 2002.

The huge glass-walled tasting room overlooks 26 acres of estate vineyards that provide some of the grapes for the 8,000 cases of wine made each year—mainly cabernet, merlot, zinfandel, and chardonnay plus some interesting blends.

The cabernets are the standouts and range from the intense version from the Monte Rosso vineyard high in the Mayacamas Mountains further south to the plush estate version, which is a fine example of an Alexander Valley cab. There are also other cabernets from the Knights Valley and Dry Creek valley. Many are only available in the tasting room.

There is an even more bewildering array of zinfandels from up and down Sonoma, including an estate version and a couple of bright, cool-climate zins from Russian River Valley vineyards. One of the more unusual red wines to try, however, is the inky and pungent Petite Verdot, normally used as a blending grape in Bordeaux-style wines.

The portfolio of whites is tiny, by contrast, but includes a couple of nice Russian River chardonnays and a chardonnay-semillon blend with an enticing mix of citrus and tropical fruit flavors. There are usually four of the cheaper wines to taste free, but flights of the pricier single-vineyard zinfandels, cabernets and blends will cost $5–10 to taste.

SAUSAL WINERY
One of the more rural and relaxed wineries in the valley, Sausal (7370 Hwy. 128, Healdsburg,

Sausal Winery

707/433-2285 or 800/500-2285, www.sausal winery.com, 10 A.M.–4 P.M. daily, free tasting) is perfect for a picnic. Some of the first zinfandel vines planted in the valley are part of the winery's 120 acres of vineyards. Sausal takes full advantage of them: The bulk of the 10,000 cases of wine made here each year is zinfandel, and much of that is made using grapes from these old vines. The resulting Century Vines zinfandel is arguably the best wine in the portfolio.

Other wines range from the affordable Private Reserve zin down to cheap, summer-drinking Cellar Cats Red, named for the winery's two feline residents and perfect for a picnic in the shade of the old oak trees on the grounds.

This is still the Alexander Valley, however, so a rich, age-worthy cabernet sauvignon gets a look in too. The sangiovese that goes into the robust Sogni d'Oro blend along with zinfandel is a nod to the Italian heritage of the current owners of the winery, who are third-generation relatives of some of the valley's pioneering winemakers. Leo Demostene, son of a first-generation Italian immigrant, bought this former prune and pear farm in the 1950s and started making bulk wine after working for many years at Abele Ferrari's historic Soda Rock Winery and marrying Ferrari's daughter, Rose.

ROBERT YOUNG ESTATE WINERY

Chardonnay dominates among the 14 varietals grown on the 320 acres of Alexander Valley vineyards owned by the Robert Young winery (4960 Red Winery Rd., Geyserville, 707/4331-4811, www.ryew.com, 10 A.M.–4:30 P.M. daily, tasting $5), and a rich, full-bodied version of this varietal is what the winery is best known for. In fact, there is a Robert Young clone of the chardonnay grape. Much of the rest of the estate is planted with merlot and cabernet, both of which go into the flagship Scion blend. Only about 4 percent of the grapes are used to make the 4,000 or so cases of wine; the rest are sold to other wineries.

The Young family first settled this part of the world in 1858, but it was Robert Young who planted grapes here in the 1960s, slowly transforming what had been prune orchards

and grazing land into hundreds of acres of vineyards, planting the very first cabernet sauvignon vines in the valley in 1963, and chardonnay in 1967. Robert died in 2009 at the ripe old age of 91, but there are still plenty of other Youngs who call the beautiful estate home, including Fred Young, who established the wine-making operations, and Jim Young, who is the vineyard manager.

◖ ALEXANDER VALLEY VINEYARDS

It shares the name of the historic valley for good reason. In the 1960s the founders of the winery bought a large chunk of the original homestead once owned by Cyrus Alexander, the mountain man who became a ranch manager and finally a landowner credited with planting the valley's first vineyards in 1846.

Whether Alexander ever made wine from those grapes is not known, but today's vineyards provide the grapes for the 100,000 cases of mainly red wines that Alexander Valley Vineyards (8644 Hwy. 128, Healdsburg, 800/888-7209, www.avvwine.com, 10 A.M.–5 P.M. daily, free tasting) produces. About half that volume is cabernet and merlot, with another quarter accounted for by chardonnay and the two decadent zinfandel blends, Sin Zin and Redemption Zin.

Other varietals include chardonnay, pinot noir, sangiovese, syrah, and viognier, together with some interesting red blends, including the flagship wine called Cyrus, a Bordeaux-style wine honoring the winery's namesake.

Historical sites pepper the current estate, including a wooden schoolhouse built by Alexander in 1853 and the Alexander family gravesite up the hill behind the winery. Educational tours of the expansive wine caves are also available by appointment.

FIELD STONE WINERY

Built from stones unearthed during construction in 1977, the small Field Stone winery (10075 Hwy. 128, Healdsburg, 707/433-7266 or 800/544-7273, www.fieldstonewinery .com, 10 A.M.–5 P.M. daily, tasting $5), cut into a dusty valley hillside, was one of the first of a wave of modern underground wineries built in the Wine Country, but it had a tumultuous early life.

Wallace Johnson, a former mayor of Berkeley, founded the winery to test his newly invented mechanical grape-harvesting system, but he died just two years later. The winery then passed to his daughter, Katrina, and son-in-law, the Reverend John Staten, giving it a unique claim of being the first (and perhaps only) winery managed by a Presbyterian minister.

Grapes from the 50 acres of estate vineyards, together with some from the Russian River Valley and Mendocino, go into the 10,000 cases of wine made each year. Reds include cabernet, merlot, sangiovese, and the winery's signature, petite sirah. Whites include a limited-production viognier, sauvignon blanc, chardonnay, and gewürztraminer. Some of the proceeds from the sale of the Convivio line of lower-priced wines are donated to a local clinic serving farm workers.

Oak trees shade two small picnic areas outside the small tasting room, sometimes shared with the local wild turkeys, and staff might be willing to take you on an impromptu tour if it's not too busy.

LOCALS TASTING ROOM
Opened in 2003, this charming tasting room cooperative on Geyserville's main street pours wines from 10 of northern Sonoma's boutique wineries. It is a broad mix of wineries representing wines from as far south as the Central Coast up to Mendocino and most points between. Locals (Geyserville Ave. at Hwy. 128, 707/857-4900, www.tastelocalwine.com, 11 A.M.–6 P.M. daily, free tasting) also has its own wine club incorporating most of the wineries represented here, making it one of the more varied and worthwhile clubs to join.

They include the Russian River region's **Eric Ross** winery as well as several small Dry Creek Valle producers that include **Peterson Winery, Martin Family Vineyards,** and **Ramazzotti Wines,** the Mendocino syrah specialist **Saracina,** and **Laurel Glen Vineyards,** which makes a couple of nice mountain-grown

cabernets as well as several versions of malbec sourced from vineyards thousands of miles away in Argentina's famous Mendoza region.

Wineries by Appointment
LANCASTER ESTATE
You might miss the turnoff from Highway 128 to Chalk Hill Road, but you won't miss the striking modern gates of the Lancaster Estate (15001 Chalk Hill Rd., Healdsburg, 707/433-8178 or 800/799-8444, www.lancaster-estate.com). This small but exclusive maker of cabernet sauvignon offers a free tour of the vineyards, state-of-the-art wine-making facility, and caves before retiring to what seems like a private salon for tastings of the Bordeaux-style red wines, which range from the limited production Nicole's Vineyard blend to the flagship Lancaster Estate cabernet.

MEDLOCK AMES
Make sure to get detailed directions to Medlock Ames (13414 Chalk Hill Rd., Healdsburg, 707/431-8845, www.medlockames.com), about a mile off the Chalk Hill Road down what seems like an endless dirt driveway. Take a wrong turn and you might end up in a neighbor's driveway. Take the right turn and you'll find the striking new stone and steel winery building surrounded by manicured lawns, organic vineyards, and perhaps some stray wildlife. Medlock Ames was started by two thirty-something friends with money to invest and a passion for the Wine Country lifestyle. Newly minted winemaker Ames Morrison and moneyed business partner Chris Medlock James have produced limited production merlot, cabernet, and chardonnay from the 55 acres of organic vineyard since 1999. The current 5,000-case production could eventually reach 20,000 cases, as revealed by an informal tour of the huge but still relatively empty barrel room.

SIGHTS
Cloverdale Historical Museum
The modest Cloverdale Historical Museum (215 N. Cloverdale Blvd., Cloverdale, 707/894-

2067, 11 A.M.–3 P.M. Fri.–Sun. Nov.–Feb., 11 A.M.–3 P.M. Thurs.–Mon. Mar.–Oct., free) is actually the meticulously restored Gothic revival-style Gould-Shaw Victorian house and headquarters for the nonprofit Cloverdale Historical Society.

The house itself is one of the oldest dwellings still standing in Cloverdale, and almost everything in it, from the iron crib to the pump organ, is from the same era, donated or borrowed from other historic homes in the area. It also houses the society's research center, with archives going back to the late 1800s, and you can pick up a guide for a short walking tour of some of the other historic Victorian homes in the town.

ENTERTAINMENT

If you can ignore the ugly concrete scar it creates halfway up the otherwise unspoiled hillside, the **River Rock Casino** (3250 Hwy. 128, Geyserville, 707/857-2777, www.riverrock casino.com, open 24 hours) provides one of the more unusual recreational opportunities in the county. That is, if you call winning or losing money recreation.

The casino is jointly owned by a Nevada gaming company and the Dry Creek Band of the Pomo Indian tribe, which has suffered at the hands of white people since the first settlers arrived in the 1800s. The Pomo tribe's 85-acre Dry Creek Rancheria, on which the casino is built, is a far cry from the vast territory of mountains and valleys in the region they used to call home.

The casino has sweeping sunset views over the vineyards of the Alexander Valley, as well as the usual array of modern amenities to help visitors part with their money, including restaurants, bars, 1,600 slot machines, and 16 tables. It's also easy to find—the entrance is right off Highway 128 about three miles south of the bridge over the river, just past the red barn on the left.

RECREATION
On the Water

Although most opportunities to float on the river are focused south of Healdsburg, the stretch of Russian River between Cloverdale and Healdsburg is long, straight, and probably one of the easiest to navigate. It's also a pretty route through the vineyards.

River's Edge Kayak & Canoe Trips (13840 Healdsburg Ave., 707/433-7247, www.rivers edgekayakandcanoe.com, Apr.–Oct. only), at the bridge in Healdsburg, offers a whole host of options for trips starting from either the top of the valley near Asti or halfway down and floating downstream to the beach in Healdsburg or beyond. There are a few rough patches of water but nothing worse than feeble Class I rapids. Later in the summer it will probably be a totally smooth float downstream.

The full day trips are 11–15 miles, which usually takes 4–6 hours and gives plenty of time for stopping at swimming holes along the way. The shorter trips are about half that. In all cases the price includes the rental of the kayak ($55 per day) or canoe ($85 per day) and a free shuttle ride upriver to start the adventure. Double kayaks are $85 per day. For a few extra dollars you can buy one of the packages that include everything from lunch to sunscreen.

Kayaks and canoes can also be rented on an hourly basis ($10–15) from the company's concession stand at Healdsburg's Memorial Beach at the eastern end of the bridge.

Safari West

Cruising around the Alexander Valley in a rental car might not exactly bring to mind the savannas of Africa, unless you happen upon this little animal oasis of cheetahs, zebras, and giraffes that happily laze away in the sun just over the hill from many of Chalk Hill's wineries.

The Chalk Hill appellation is the unlikely setting for the 400-acre Safari West wildlife preserve (on Porter Creek Rd. at Franz Valley Rd., 707/579-2551 or 800/616-2695, www .safariwest.com), home to a wide variety of endangered species from around the world, including many from central Africa. Whether the weather in Africa is similar to northern

Sonoma is somewhat irrelevant considering the apparent happiness of the animals.

This is not a zoo or safari in the regular sense of the word, however. Instead, it started out in the late 1980s as a private ranch and preserve dedicated to saving endangered species from around the world. Humans were only admitted in 1993.

Seeing the magnificent beasts requires a reservation for one of the three-hour tours that set off three times a day (twice a day in winter) on a customized old jeep. They cost $68 for adults, $30 for kids under 12. The more adventurous might consider sleeping overnight in one of the luxurious tent cabins ($225–245 for two people, each extra guest $25) or cottages ($300 for two people). Lunch and dinner are available at the on-site café; wine is served, but antelope steaks are not.

Because it's a working preserve, visitors get easy access to the wildlife experts who work there and who are happy to reel off fascinating facts about the animals. This little corner of wild Africa in Sonoma also provides a welcome escape from the wilds of Wine Country tourism.

ACCOMMODATIONS

The Alexander Valley has more places to stay than its rural setting and tiny towns might suggest. Most of the B&Bs are clustered up at the far northern end of the valley in the quiet cow town of Cloverdale, but there are a few worthwhile places to consider around Geyserville to the south.

Under $100

With all the B&Bs in the valley costing well over $100, it is once again left to the motels to accommodate those with tight budgets or an aversion to Victorian inns. The biggest concentration of motels (all totally unexceptional) in this area is just off the freeway on Cloverdale Boulevard (take the Citrus Fair Dr. exit) and includes the **Cloverdale Oaks Motel** (123 S. Cloverdale Blvd., 707/894-2404) and the **Garden Motel** (611 N. Cloverdale Blvd., 707/894-2594). Best

Western and Holiday Inn also have properties in the area.

$100–200

At the lowest end of the price range is the conveniently located **Geyserville Inn** (21714 Geyserville Ave., Geyserville, 707/857-4343 or 877/857-4343, www.geyservilleinn.com), a modern two-floor building resembling an upscale motel at the northern edge of Geyserville. Request an east-facing room to get a view of the vineyards and mountains rather than the freeway, which is a little too close for comfort. The smaller of the 38 rather plain guest rooms start at $110–119. The larger rooms, all of which have a fireplace and most of which have a balcony or patio, go for $149–249. Next door is the homey **Hoffman House Café,** which serves breakfast and lunch every day.

Driving through Geyserville, it's easy to miss two bargain B&Bs among the homes along the main road, but slow down and the historic elegance of the two Victorian-style **Hope Inns** (21253 Geyserville Ave., Geyserville, 707/857-3356 or 800/825-4233, www.hope–inns.com) becomes more obvious. The richly decorated interiors were restored in painstaking detail by the Hope family in the 1980s, and they put many of the historic Healdsburg B&Bs to shame.

There are eight guest rooms ($150–290) in the **Hope-Merrill House,** an 1870 Eastlake-style Victorian that features silk-screened wallpapers, coffered ceilings, and original woodwork. This is where the dining room (where breakfast is served), pool, and registration desk are located. Across the street is the Queen Anne–style **Hope-Bosworth House,** which has four guest rooms ($150–200) featuring the more restrained furnishings of that period. Only one room, the sumptuous Sterling Suite in the Hope-Merrill House, has a television, though others have some features that more than compensate, from fireplaces and chaise longues to whirlpool and claw-foot tubs. Free wireless Internet access was recently added.

The huge brick fireplace in the lobby of

the **Old Crocker Inn** (1126 Old Crocker Inn Rd., Cloverdale, 707/894-4000 or 800/716-2007, www.oldcrockerinn.com), just south of Cloverdale, gives a hint of the Wild West roots of this charming lodge. It was built in the early 20th century by railway magnate Charles Crocker, founder of the Central Pacific Railroad, as a grand summer house, and the current owners have recreated the rustic character that it must originally have had—an odd blend of the Wild West and Victoriana.

The biggest guest room is the namesake Crocker room ($155–295), with a massive mahogany four-poster. The other four guest rooms ($130–185) in the main lodge building are named after Crocker's railroad partners. There are also three small cottages ($130–215), two of them able to comfortably sleep four people. All the rooms have old and modern features alike, including claw-foot tubs, gas fireplaces, TVs, and Internet access. The peaceful five-acre property also has an outdoor pool and feels like it's far from the madding crowds of the Wine Country. The complimentary gourmet breakfast is served in the lodge's spacious dining room.

Camping

The valley's main campground is the **Cloverdale KOA Wine Country Campground** (1166 Asti Ridge Rd., across the River Rd. bridge from Geyserville Ave., 707/894-3337) next to the hamlet of Asti. It might be part of the KOA chain, but it is a clean, easily accessible, and family-friendly option when the sites at nearby Lake Sonoma in the Dry Creek Valley are full. It also has a well-stocked fishing pond, bicycles for rent, and a big swimming pool.

There are 47 tent sites that cost from $35, and over 100 RV sites from $55. Reserve at 800/368-4558 or online (www.winecountrykoa.com). The rustic little one- and two-room **Kamping Kabins** ($72–82) might also be an alternative if the local B&Bs are full, though you have to supply your own bedding. Better still are the so-called **Lodges** dotted around the hillside. Each is like a luxury

mini cabin with one bedroom plus a futon sofa, a full kitchen, and a barbeque outside (but no linens or towels). They cost from $175 and will comfortably sleep four with no extra charge.

Those with an aversion to developed campsites would do better to head 20 minutes west to Lake Sonoma in the Dry Creek Valley, where there are dozens of more primitive campsites, including many hike-in or boat-in sites.

FOOD

Most valley dining options are in nearby Healdsburg, but there are some notable exceptions. With the closure in 2010 of the renowned Taverna Santi in the center of Geyserville, the job of keeping the Italian food flame alive in the town was handed off to the less luxurious but no less delicious sister restaurant **Diavola Pizzeria & Salumeria** (21021 Geyserville Ave., 707/814-0111, www.diavolapizzeria.com, lunch and dinner daily, pizzas and antipasti $13–16, dinner entrées $18–24). This is very much a restaurant for meat eaters, specializing in house-cured salamis and wood-fired pizzas, but also crafting a dozen or so antipasti plates of seasonal Italian-inspired food served on rustic copper-topped tables in a historic brick-walled building. The list of two dozen wines has as many Italian wines as local wines.

A little farther north on Geyserville Avenue is the **Hoffman House Café** (21712 Geyserville Ave., Geyserville, 707/857-3264, until 2 P.M. daily), with a big outdoor patio and a reputation for great brunches. It also sells gourmet boxed lunches, ideal for picnics.

For more food on the go, and some of the best picnic supplies around, the bright yellow and green **Jimtown Store** (6706 Hwy. 128 at Alexander Valley Rd., Healdsburg, 707/433-1212, 7:30 A.M.–5 P.M. daily), with its bright-red vintage pickup truck parked outside, is a valley fixture and seems to sell a bit of everything, including its own label wine. The boxed lunches alone are worth a detour and include a fat gourmet baguette sandwich, cookies, salad, and fruit, all for less than $11.

Jimtown Store owner Carrie poses with her beloved dog.

INFORMATION AND SERVICES

More information about this area's wines together with a comprehensive winery map can be found on the **Alexander Valley Winegrowers Association** website (www.alexandervalley.org).

More information about the history and businesses of Cloverdale and Geyserville can be obtained from their respective chambers of commerce. The **Geyserville Chamber of Commerce** (707/857-3745, www.geyserville cc.com) is not open to the public but has an excellent website. The **Cloverdale Chamber of Commerce** (105 N. Cloverdale Blvd., 707/894-4470, www.cloverdale.net) also contains the **North Coast Wine & Visitors Center** (9 A.M.–5 P.M. weekdays, 10 A.M.–4 P.M. weekends), which has maps, guides, and discount vouchers for anyone planning to explore northern Sonoma and Mendocino wineries.

MENDOCINO COUNTY

"Another time, another place" is the tag line conjured up by the Mendocino marketing folks. But it's more than a marketing pitch. It's a reality. There are only a few towns here—and some have populations outnumbered by the local sheep and cattle. Even U.S. 101, which exists as a wide and fast freeway through most of Sonoma, puts on the brakes as it crosses the hills from Cloverdale into Mendocino—a symbolic and literal reminder that residents here live life at a slower pace.

Mendocino does three things very well: scenery, agriculture, and hippy. It's a beautiful part of the world. From the rugged coastline to the inland redwood forests and craggy mountains, there's still barely any sign of human encroachment. Since adventurous immigrants first entered the region in the mid-1800s and

stole it from the contented Native American tribes, Mendocino has been an agricultural wonderland, blessed as it is with numerous microclimates in which to grow almost any crop, including grapes. The region's remoteness and scarcity of population were also big draws for the counterculture movement in the 1970s, with urban refugees fleeing burgeoning Bay Area capitalism to set up communes among the Mendocino hills.

The counterculture spawned an earth-friendly vibe that still exists in Mendocino. In most other wine regions, the term "cash crop" refers to grapes or high-end edibles. In Mendocino, it may refer to an illegal crop that is smoked. Much of the marijuana growing for which Mendocino was once known has moved north to Humboldt

MENDOCINO COUNTY

HIGHLIGHTS

◖ **Navarro Vineyards:** Broaden your wine palate, practice your pronunciation, and enjoy one of the best picnic spots in the Anderson Valley (page 272).

◖ **Roederer Estate:** In keeping with its Mendocino location, even this maker of the ultimate bubbly bling manages to feel homey and welcoming (page 274).

◖ **Anderson Valley Brewing Company:** It's been around longer than many valley wineries and offers a fun alternative to wine tasting on a hot day (page 277).

◖ **Parducci Wine Cellars:** A dizzying array of well-priced wines, a colorful history, and a dedication to the environment make Parducci a worthwhile detour (page 287).

◖ **Graziano Family of Wines:** More than two dozen different wines, including many Italian varietals, make this tiny tasting room a convenient place to explore the world of Mendocino wines (page 292).

◖ **Solar Living Center:** If saving the planet can be this much fun, it's a wonder more people don't kick the oil habit (page 299).

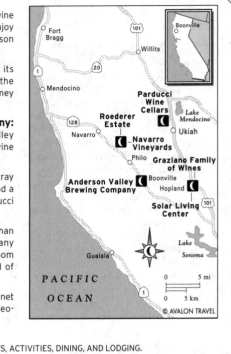

LOOK FOR ◖ TO FIND RECOMMENDED SIGHTS, ACTIVITIES, DINING, AND LODGING.

County, but the hills of central and northern Mendocino still get plenty of attention from federal drug enforcers. Local radio stations often report current locations of Drug Enforcement Agency helicopters during the summer and fall marijuana-growing season—another sign of the splendid, anti-establishment isolation that many residents still cling to as the rest of the world steadily encroaches.

While the rest of California's Wine Country wheeled out the PR bandwagon to publicize its increasing organic farming practices, Mendocino has been quietly leveraging its earth-friendly, counterculture credentials for decades to become the organic capital of

California Wine Country. In 2008, about 28 percent of the more than 16,000 acres of vineyards in the county were certified organic or biodynamic, by far the highest percentage of any Californian county. Biodynamic farming is all the rage now, and you're as likely to hear the term "fish-friendly" as you are "solar-powered."

But Mendocino's modesty and quiet determination to save the planet won't necessarily bring home the bacon, a problem that is now being addressed with increasing fervor by local winery associations. For more than 100 years, Mendocino has been the agricultural cash cow of Northern California, a place where crops are grown for someone to process and

Mendocino coast sunset

© PETER DANIELS/123RF.COM

sell elsewhere. Now Mendocino wants to keep some of that cash for itself, and it's ramping up its solar-powered PR machine.

Fetzer Vineyards was, for a decade or more, the power behind that machine, putting Mendocino on the map by its sheer size. Now that it is owned by a multinational corporation, its ability to promote Mendocino has dwindled somewhat. The Anderson Valley, meanwhile, was discovered as a prime pinot noir growing region, and the trickle of new wineries that arrived in the 1980s and 1990s has started to swell, creating enough momentum to stir a few old-timers off their rockers in sleepy Boonville.

Eastern Mendocino still struggles with its identity, despite being home to the county's largest city, Ukiah. Its patchwork of appellations and growing conditions are suited to just too many grape varietals for its own good, and as a result there's no particular wine for which it is known. The ingenious Coro Mendocino regional wine program seeks to fix this conundrum and has generated some much-needed publicity.

Chances are it will be only a matter of time before the viticultural allure of the Anderson Valley spills over the eastern hills and combines with the sustainable farming movement to give winemaking a boost, bringing more winemakers and visitors up the slow road from Sonoma. But if they come, Mendocino runs the risk that many a child of the counterculture could start to crave life from another time and end up moving to another place.

PLANNING YOUR TIME

There are as many ways to see and do this part of Wine Country as there are alternative lifestyles in Mendocino. **Hopland** is generally considered the gateway to Mendocino's Wine Country, and is an ideal place to visit for a day if you're already staying somewhere in Northern Sonoma. Less than an hour north of Healdsburg, Hopland's tasting rooms and restaurants are mostly within walking distance of each other. The proximity of Hopland to points south and the lower price of its hotel rooms makes it a worthy base to explore Northern Sonoma.

To immerse yourself more fully in the Eastern Mendocino wine scene, consider basing yourself in **Ukiah,** where there are plenty of cheap rooms and restaurants. Ukiah and Redwood Valley wineries are only a 10- or 15-minute drive from the city, and Hopland is just 20 minutes south. It would be easy to fill a weekend touring the area. From Ukiah, the Anderson Valley is less than an hour's drive west, and experiencing both eastern and western Mendocino culture is an interesting, mind-expanding exercise.

The best way to experience the **Anderson Valley,** however, is to spend at least one night there, giving two days to enjoy the wineries and natural beauty. From the valley, you can also continue west to get a taste of the scenic Mendocino coast. Day-tripping into the valley from Northern Sonoma is possible if you are prepared for a lot of driving on some challenging roads. From Healdsburg, for example, it's at least a 1.5-hour drive to Boonville, much of it on two-lane roads. Many people arrange a day trip into the Anderson Valley if they are already on the coast visiting the town of Mendocino. Boonville is only about 30 miles from U.S. 1, or 40 miles from Mendocino, and many of the wineries around Philo are far closer.

GETTING THERE AND AROUND

Eastern Mendocino is better known to many people as a series of rest stops on busy U.S. 101, while the Anderson Valley revels in its remoteness. Wherever you decide to go, you'll be sitting in the car a while.

The Anderson Valley has always been hard to reach. Early settlers had to cross the mountains of California's Coastal Range to get here from the Russian River Valley, or navigate the treacherous coastal highway to come in from the west. It's really not much easier today. Sickness-inducing rises, dips, and curves are still ever-present; pick up some Dramamine before setting out.

The main route for most travelers coming from Sonoma is via U.S. 128, which leaves U.S. 101 at Cloverdale and heads west into the warm oak woodland of the hills. It's only about 25 miles from Cloverdale to Boonville, but the drive can take more than an hour. From U.S. 101 in Ukiah you can cut across the hills on U.S. 253 to Boonville, an even more scenic—and more hair-raising—route that's only about 17 miles but will still take about an hour. From San Francisco, count on about a 2.5- to 3-hour drive to Boonville via U.S. 101 and 128, assuming no traffic problems—a risky assumption.

An alternate, more scenic route into the valley is from the coastal U.S. 1, either via U.S. 128 from just north of Elk or on tiny Mountain View Road just north of Albion. Getting to and driving on the coastal highway can, however, be frustratingly slow, so if you decide to go the scenic route, expect the trip from San Francisco to take 4–5 hours.

The Eastern Mendocino wine town of Hopland is only about 13 miles beyond the northern Alexander Valley on U.S. 101. The freeway becomes Highway 1 as you pass Cloverdale, narrowing as it passes through the hills, so the drive will take about a half hour. The Mendocino County seat of Ukiah is about 15 miles further up the road and the Redwood Valley wineries a few miles beyond that, although once off the main road, finding those small wineries in the maze of rural roads can take some time and good map-reading skills.

Driving is the only way to get to this part of the Wine Country, and it is the only way to get around, too. There's only one major road running down the 20-mile-long Anderson Valley, from Boonville to the coast, and that's U.S. 128. Pretty much everything to see is within a half-mile of it, and most wineries are right on the road. The valley can essentially be divided into two halves, with Philo more or less halfway between the only other two towns, Navarro about seven miles northwest and Boonville about six miles southeast.

Anderson Valley

The history of the Anderson Valley reads much like that of Northern California. In the 1800s, white settlers, drawn by new opportunities in California and the gold rush, displaced native American tribes that had lived off the land for centuries. The settlers found ample forests of redwoods that could be logged to supply building materials for California's boom and plenty of fertile land for farming.

There is one important difference, however,

between the Anderson Valley and its more famous counterparts in Sonoma and Napa, which is its distance from the Bay Area. This remoteness not only delayed development of the agricultural industry but, to this day, is perhaps the biggest single factor influencing the valley's distinct culture. Urban life never took hold here. Ironically, this remoteness was said to have been what attracted the first settlers to the valley—Walter Anderson and his family.

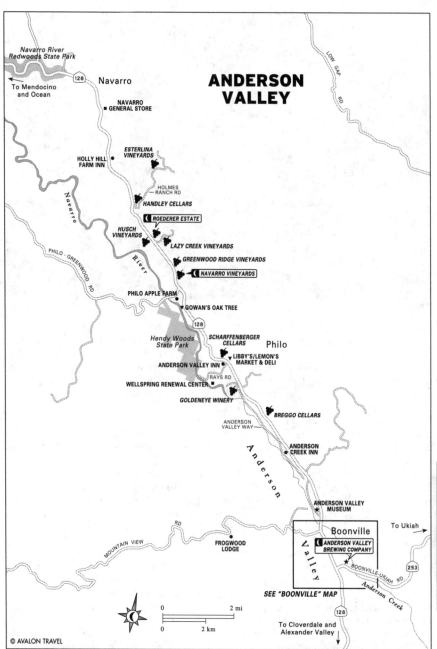

ANDERSON VALLEY

Navarro River Redwoods State Park

To Mendocino and Ocean

Navarro

128

NAVARRO GENERAL STORE

ESTERLINA VINEYARDS

HOLLY HILL FARM INN

HOLMES RANCH RD

HANDLEY CELLARS

ROEDERER ESTATE

HUSCH VINEYARDS

Navarro River

PHILO - GREENWOOD ROAD

LAZY CREEK VINEYARDS

GREENWOOD RIDGE VINEYARDS

NAVARRO VINEYARDS

PHILO APPLE FARM

GOWAN'S OAK TREE

128

Hendy Woods State Park

SCHARFFENBERGER CELLARS

Philo

LIBBY'S/LEMON'S MARKET & DELI

ANDERSON VALLEY INN

RAYS RD

WELLSPRING RENEWAL CENTER

GOLDENEYE WINERY

BREGGO CELLARS

ANDERSON VALLEY WAY

ANDERSON CREEK INN

Anderson

LOW GAP RD

ANDERSON VALLEY MUSEUM

To Ukiah

Boonville

MOUNTAIN VIEW RD

FROGWOOD LODGE

ANDERSON VALLEY BREWING COMPANY

Valley

SEE "BOONVILLE" MAP

BOONVILLE-UKIAH RD

253

Anderson Creek

128

To Cloverdale and Alexander Valley

0   2 mi
0   2 km

© AVALON TRAVEL

MENDOCINO COUNTY

Anderson Valley

The Andersons didn't arrive in the valley until the 1850s and were followed by only a trickle of other settlers. A handful of large farms were established, supplying livestock and produce to local lumber mills in the valley and on the coast. Tradesmen arrived to service the small but growing population and the few travelers heading to the coast, including William Boone, after whom the town of Boonville is named.

Though the population swelled to over 1,000, the valley's geographic isolation acted as a cap on further growth and also allowed residents to start developing a unique, isolationist culture, including their own form of local dialect called Boontling. The splendid isolation drew hippies and other urban escapees in the 1960s and 1970s, ensuring that the valley's counterculture would thrive. The brief threat of urbanization came with the growth frenzy of the 1970s, but new zoning laws in subsequent decades have more or less put a halt on any major future development.

Today the valley's residents number about 1,200, just a couple of hundred more than at the beginning of the 1900s. The population of hippies, farmers, and urban refugees love their little valley and have come to grudgingly accept that tourism is here to stay. It will stay firmly on their terms, however.

The Wines

Winemaking got off to a slow start in the Anderson Valley. As Eastern Mendocino farms started supplying grapes to the growing number of Napa and Sonoma wineries in the late 1800s, the wine industry in the Anderson Valley was limited to a few European immigrants making wines for themselves to drink. In addition to the remoteness of the valley, which hindered transport of products to the big Bay Area markets, the relatively cool weather made ripening early varietals of grapes difficult. Most of the early settlers in the valley were from the Midwest, a region that had no culture of winemaking or wine drinking.

The arrival of Italian settlers in the 1890s and early 1900s was a catalyst for winemaking in the valley. They brought knowledge of winemaking and of the best place to grow grapes—above the fog on the sunnier hillsides, particularly Greenwood Ridge. Winemaking was just starting to grow when Prohibition brought it to a screeching halt. After Prohibition, the momentum was never regained. Grapes were still grown in the valley, but most were sold to wineries in Sonoma. The next growth spurt in the wine industry didn't begin until the 1960s, when the boom in the wider California wine industry filtered into the valley, helped, in the 1970s, by a viticulture survey that identified the Anderson Valley as one of the most promising areas for grape growing. What began as a trickle, started by modern pioneers Donald Edmeades and Tony Husch, who bonded their respective wineries in the early 1970s, soon turned into a rush.

In 1983 the valley was granted American Viticultural Area (AVA) status, and by the end of the 1980s the region's cool growing conditions had been identified by sparkling wine producers as some of the best in California for pinot noir and chardonnay, the two main champagne varietals. One champagne house, Roederer Estate, planted those two varietals so rapidly in the late 1980s and into the 1990s that it was almost single-handedly responsible for much of the growth in the valley's vineyard acreage at that time.

The valley is classified as a Region II climate, one of the coolest, ideal for making dry and well-balanced wines. Marine fog keeps valley nights cool, but the further east you go toward Boonville the less of an influence it has. Four grape varietals that thrive in this climate dominate the valley's vineyards: pinot noir, chardonnay, gewürztraminer and riesling.

Anderson Valley gewürztraminers and rieslings, in particular, have earned a reputation as some of the most elegant and aromatic in the state. Pinot noir and chardonnay grapes were for a long time grown primarily for sparkling wine production, resulting in some of California's best champagnes but not necessarily the best still wines. Recently, still wines have received more attention from local winemakers. Since the late 1990s, new vine clones and improved winemaking techniques have resulted in a pinot renaissance, attracting yet more wineries (and visitors) and further boosting vineyard acreage. Of the approximately 2,400 acres of vineyards in the Anderson Valley, about half are now planted to pinot.

Few other varietals will ripen down near the valley floor. But at higher elevations, above the fog line, it's a different story; so different that in 1997 a cluster of the hilltop ridges south of the valley and a few at its western end were granted their own status as an AVA called Mendocino Ridges. At these sunnier, higher elevations, zinfandel is one of the most common varietals and makes a more reserved style of wine far removed from the jammy, overblown zins typical from hotter parts of the state.

WINE-TASTING
GOLDENEYE WINERY
The small duck's head on the label of Goldeneye's wines is a hint at the pedigree

COURTESY OF VISIT MENDOCINO COUNTY, INC.

MENDOCINO COUNTY

Goldeneye patio

BOONVILLE + LINGO = BOONTLING

Just as London has its cockney slang and Louisiana has its Cajun dialect, sleepy Boonville at one time developed its own minor local lingo, known as Boontling. As with many local dialects around the world, Boontling was born of isolation, independence, and a distrust of outsiders, all features of Anderson Valley farm life in the late 1800s when the colorful language developed.

Linguistic experts have documented as many as 1,300 different Boontling words and phrases that came about in a manner typical of most dialects, from a combination of local mother tongues (in this case English, Scottish, Irish, Spanish, and Native American), mispronunciation, and a healthy dose of local folklore.

Many words have their roots in old British or Irish slang and others are loosely based on the sounds of Spanish or Native American terms. What makes Boontling so fascinating, however, is not only the tiny number of people who ever spoke it but also the incorporation of so many bizarre local characters into the vocabulary. They give Boontling an almost homey feel.

There was once a valley resident named Jeff, for example, who became known for having blazing fires at home, which gave rise to the Boontling term *Jeffer*, meaning large fire.

Then there was the unfortunate buck-toothed valley doctor who was the inspiration for the Boontling term *shoveltooth,* meaning doctor. And a local hunter nicknamed Zeese (for his initials, Z.C.) was known for making particularly strong coffee and was immortalized in the Boontling term for coffee.

As the valley gradually became less isolated, with the advent of better roads and motor vehicles, so Boontling started to die out. Today it seems to be invoked more for tourism purposes than for any meaningful communication. Hang around some older residents, however, and you might hear a conversation peppered with the occasional Boontling term.

To learn more about Boontling, visit the Anderson Valley Museum (12340 Hwy. 128, just north of Boonville, 707/995-3207, www .andersonvalleymuseum.org, 1-4 P.M. Fri.-Sun., Feb.-Nov., donation requested) or try to find a copy of the book *Boontling: An American Lingo* by Charles Adams, which is stocked in several Boonville stores and includes an extensive Boontling dictionary. Meanwhile, here are some particularly relevant terms:

- **aplenty bahl frattey horn** – really great wine
- **applehead** – girlfriend

of this relative newcomer in the Anderson Valley. Owners Dan and Margaret Duckhorn established Goldeneye (9200 Hwy. 128, Philo, 707/895-3202, www.goldeneyewinery .com, 11 A.M.–4 P.M. daily, tasting $5–10) in 1997 to make pinot noir that complements the portfolio of other wines from their Duckhorn Winery in Napa Valley. The name Goldeneye was chosen for a type of duck that flies over the region on its migration every year—not for the James Bond movie—and images of ducks are omnipresent, from the fabrics to the paintings on the walls of the homey, Craftsman-style tasting room in the stylishly modernized 1930s farmhouse. It's hard to miss the winery from the road—the white picket fence is more New England than Old Mendocino.

Pinot noir is the only wine made here, but it is made very well and garners the same sort of critical praise as some of the Duckhorn Napa Valley wines. Since being established in 1997, Goldeneye has progressively bought more land in the Anderson Valley and now owns about 150 acres of vineyards, including the original 80-acre Confluence vineyards behind the winery itself. Production is now about 10,000 cases.

The cheapest Goldeneye wine is the Anderson Valley pinot, a blend of grapes from all four vineyards. It has the complexity

- **bahl** – good
- **Boont** – Boonville or anything about Boonville
- **Boonter** – a resident of Boonville
- **the Briney** – the Pacific Ocean
- **bucky walter** – a telephone
- **Charlie walker** – a photographer
- **chiggurl** – food
- **chucklehead** – an ignorant person
- **codgy** – old
- **Deep Enders** – residents of Navarro at the western end of the Anderson valley
- **frattey** – wine
- **frattey shams** – grape vines
- **ganno** – an apple
- **gorm** – to eat, food
- **gorm sale** – a restaurant
- **harp** – to talk
- **hewtle** – hotel

- **higgs** – money
- **higher'n a billy** – drunk
- **high gittin** – drunkenness
- **highpockety** – wealthy
- **hoot** – laugh
- **horn** – a drink or cup
- **horner** – a bar
- **ling** – a language
- **ose-draggy** – very tired
- **plenty** – very
- **Poleeko** – the town of Philo
- **pothead** – an unattractive girl
- **rosy** – red wine
- **seep** – port wine or to sip
- **sol** – the sun
- **steinber** – beer
- **wee** – small
- **zeese** – coffee

and full-bodied gravitas you'd expect from a wine that regularly rates over 90 points and costs over $50. Goldeneye also makes several single-vineyard pinots that are regarded as some of California's best, but these tend to sell out within months of release. Also available to taste at the winery is the cheaper pinot noir made under the Migration label, which is altogether lighter and fruitier than the Goldeneye-label wines but an excellent value.

Goldeneye is one of the few wineries to charge for tasting in the valley—a sign that it takes its wines seriously, perhaps a bit too seriously. For the modest price it does throw in a few morsels of food and a rather nice picnic area for marinating in the slow pace of Anderson Valley life.

TOULOUSE VINEYARDS

Even in this valley that redefines laid back, Toulouse Vineyards (8001 Hwy. 128, Philo, 707/895-2828, www.toulousevineyards.com, 11 A.M.–5 P.M. daily, free tasting) is one of the more laid back wineries you'll encounter. The owners live here and are usually pouring their delicious pinot, reisling, and gewürztraminer wines in the winery barn tasting bar with their many dogs. Their wines have garnered increasingly positive reviews from the national press since they were first released in 2005.

Toulouse Vineyards was established in the late 1990s as a retirement project for long-time Bay Area residents Vern and Maxine. For years it sold pinot noir grapes to other wine makers and several high-end wineries still source fruit from Toulouse, including several locally and Sonoma's MacPhail Family Wines (James MacPhail is also reportedly a consultant winemaker for Toulouse).

With the 2002 vintage, Vern decided to start keeping some of his fruit to make his own wines, and after expanding his vineyard holdings, he now bottles about 3,000 cases of mainly pinot noir (including a rose) and reisling, both grown on the estate, as well as smaller amounts of gewürztraminer and pinot gris sourced from other vineyards in the area. The name of the winery comes from a particularly large breed of goose; some of the goose-related puns might not hit the mark, but the wines do.

SCHARFFENBERGER CELLARS

You might be more familiar with the Scharffenberger name from gourmet dark chocolate, but it also adorns the label of some gourmet sparkling wines made in the Anderson Valley. Both winery (8501 Hwy. 128, Philo, 707/895-2957, www.scharffenbergercellars .com, 11 A.M.–5 P.M. daily, tasting $3) and chocolate empire were established by John Scharffenberger—the winery in the 1980s and the Scharffen Berger chocolate business in the mid-1990s, after he sold the winery. John Scharffenberger still lives in Mendocino County, and he's still exploring the frontiers of gourmet food.

The winery was founded in 1981 and quickly became a major sparkling wine producer as it grew its vineyard holdings in the region, helped by the financial muscle of French champagne house Champagnes Pommery & Lanson, which bought the winery in the late 1980s (and was later itself bought by the Moët Hennessy empire). Scharffenberger got completely out of the wine business a few years later, and the winery was renamed Pacific Echo Vineyards, an awful name that was thankfully scrapped when the current owners, Champagne Louis Roederer,

acquired the winery in 2004. An earlier licensing agreement allowed the Scharffenberger name to once again adorn the bottles.

The focus remains on sparkling wines from Mendocino County. The excellent-value brut is a dry yet creamy nonvintage bubbly made from both pinot noir and chardonnay—it accounts for the majority of the 26,000 cases of wine made here each year. The extra dry champagne is, rather confusingly, slightly sweeter than the brut, with a satisfying toastiness that makes it a great aperitif. Small quantities of pinot noir and chardonnay are also available at the winery only and are made in classic Mendocino style—the chardonnay with a refreshing crispness and the pinot in a more full-bodied style with the stuff for some moderate aging.

The modest selection of wines feels right at home in the cozy tasting room, tucked at the back of a cottage adorned with local art and photography, and relaxing, wraparound veranda.

◖ NAVARRO VINEYARDS

Navarro Vineyards (5601 Hwy. 128, Philo, 707/895-3686, www.navarrowine.com, 10 A.M.–6 P.M. daily, free tasting) is fast becoming to the Anderson Valley what V. Sattui is to Napa—the destination winery that attracts crowds of loyal customers, weekenders, and picnickers to taste its huge selection of relatively cheap wines. As is the case with Sattui, you won't necessarily find the best local wines here, but you are bound to find something you like and have a good time trying, assuming you don't mind summer crowds.

Navarro is one of the oldest wineries in the Anderson Valley, with a rustic yet airy (by Anderson Valley standards, at least) tasting room. It was established in the early 1970s by Ted Bennett and Deborah Cahn and is still family-owned. It was a large winery when it started and has doubled production capacity to about 45,000 cases today, mostly Mendocino-sourced wines but also some made with grapes from elsewhere in California. The portfolio stretches to more than 15 wines, which means no more than a few thousand cases of any one

COURTESY OF VISIT MENDOCINO COUNTY, INC.

Navarro Vineyards

wine are produced. It also means it can take the best part of an hour to taste them all, so choose just a handful from the tasting list or risk an early hangover.

As well as the Anderson Valley staples of pinot and chardonnay, the winery is a champion of Alsace-region wines. It is particularly known for gewürztraminer, and there are usually a couple of wonderfully aromatic, dry examples to taste. A similarly aromatic white blend called edelzwicker is almost worth buying for the name alone, while one of the most unusual white Alsace wines Navarro makes is the muscat blanc, a dry version of an exotic-smelling wine that's usually made in a far sweeter style. The chardonnays and pinots tend to be fairly light wines with a modest complexity that is easy to miss. Zinfandel and a red blend called Navarrouge are the weightier reds, while the rieslings and dry muscat are blessed with some of the most exotic aromas.

With many of the wines selling for less than $20 a bottle, and the availability of nonalcoholic red and white grape juice, this is an ideal place to buy picnicking wines, particularly if you come prepared with food and can snag one of the half-dozen picnic tables on the shaded lawn. Alternatively, just buy a chilled bottle of the fruity rosé and enjoy it on the large deck overlooking the vineyards or down on the grass. Tours of the vineyards and winery are offered twice a day year-round and reservations can be made online.

GREENWOOD RIDGE VINEYARDS

The winery (5501 Hwy. 128, Philo, 707/895-2002, www.greenwoodridge.com, 10 A.M.–5 P.M. daily, free tasting) takes its name from the nearby vineyard planted by Tony Husch (founder of Husch Vineyards) in the early 1970s and bought by Allan Green shortly after. Green bonded his own winery in 1980 and built the funky octagonal winery building, which was designed by an associate of Frank Lloyd Wright and made from a giant, storm-felled redwood tree.

The eponymous vineyard is now the main source of grapes for the 7,000 cases of wine

COURTESY OF VISIT MENDOCINO COUNTY, INC.

The octagonal tasting room at Greenwood was designed by Aaron G. Green, father of owner/winemaker Allan Green.

made at Greenwood each year, including pinot noir, sauvignon blanc, and cool-climate versions of merlot and cabernet sauvignon that are worth tasting. Also usually available to taste is a full-throttle zinfandel from Sonoma County and a zinfandel-dominated red blend called Home Run Red, in honor of the winery's baseball team, the Greenwood Ridge Dragons.

Greenwood Ridge has kept production small over the years but has always retained a sense of ambition. Organic farming has been augmented by energy independence, in the form of solar panels and biodiesel fuel. The octagonal tasting room is spacious, and the views from the deck over the winery's lake and colorful gardens, filled with Asian-inspired features, are impressive. And every year the winery hosts the annual California Wine Tasting Championships on the last weekend in July (free for pre-registered visitors), briefly making Greenwood Ridge the center of the action in the Anderson Valley.

◖ ROEDERER ESTATE

From the outside it's hard to tell that Roederer Estate (4501 Hwy. 128, Philo, 707/895-2288, www.roedererestate.com, 11 A.M.–5 P.M. daily, tasting $6) is owned by the French champagne house that makes Cristal, the ultimate in bubbly bling. The rustic redwood winery buildings are more in keeping with the region's rural heritage than high society, but the sparkling wine made here is regarded as some of the best in California. Like many of the big French champagne houses, Champagne Louis Roederer started scouting for a California location back in the 1980s. Unlike the others, it settled on the Anderson Valley rather than Napa or Sonoma, a testament to the cool growing conditions that are ideal for the two key champagne grapes— pinot noir and chardonnay—and the classic Roederer style of lean but complex wines.

Roederer bottled its first Anderson Valley sparkling wine in the late 1980s. It now owns almost 600 acres of vineyards in the valley and makes more than 70,000 cases of wine a year.

Most of the production is accounted for by the nonvintage brut, which consistently garners rave reviews for its crisp, well-defined flavors and an elegant creaminess that suggests a price far higher than it actually costs ($23).

A small quantity of slightly sweeter and fruitier brut rosé is also made, but the flagship wine is the limited-production L'Ermitage, a vintage champagne that is only made in those years the fruit is deemed to be worthy. The brut always seems to be compared favorably with sparklers from the other top producers in California, but for comparisons to the complexity, long finish, and aging potential of L'Ermitage the critics often reach for the names of the top producers back in the mother country, France. Consider it as close to Cristal as a California sparkling wine can probably get.

The staggering amount of work that goes into making L'Ermitage, requiring the involvement of four master blenders, is explained in the tasting room—a location that has the same sense of restrained elegance as the wines and a rather tasty view over the lawn to the valley beyond. The tasting room is also the only place to try and buy the big, bold limited-production pinot noir and the extra dry sparkling wine, which has a hint more sweetness than the bone-dry brut. The tasting comes at a price, modest by California standards but by far the highest in the Anderson Valley. Savor the bubbles as long as you can to get your money's worth.

HUSCH VINEYARDS

Possibly the most interesting tasting rooms you'll experience can be found at the oldest winery (4400 Hwy. 128, Philo, 800/554-8724, www.huschvineyards.com, 10 A.M.–5 P.M. daily, until 6 P.M. in summer, free tasting) in the Anderson Valley. Tony and Gretchen Husch started planting grapes here in the late 1960s, making them the first to do so since Prohibition, and their winery was bonded in 1971, beating Navarro to the title of "oldest" by a couple of years. The tiny tasting room looks like it was here long before—a rustic, shingled former pony barn that's now smothered by colorful plants and contains a tasting

bar that can host no more than about four visitors. Luckily the doors on each side of the room are usually wide open to the surrounding gardens and deck.

Tony Husch eventually sold the winery, and it has been owned by the Oswald family for almost three decades; there's a friendly, family air to the place. In contrast to the humble tasting room, the portfolio of wines is anything but modest: The winery produces about 40,000 cases of 18 wines sourced from either the Anderson Valley or other Mendocino appellations. Only a handful of wines are distributed nationally—the best are saved for winery visitors, who can taste six wines for free.

Standouts include the rose-scented dry gewürztraminer and the Anderson Valley pinot noirs, including the complex and spicy Reserve, which incorporates fruit from the original vineyard planted by Tony Husch back in the 1960s. The two cabernet sauvignons are also worth trying and are typical of the more restrained, less fruit-forward cabs that Mendocino is known for.

Among the other wines available are a couple of worthy chardonnays, a very popular zinfandel (chances are it'll be sold out), and a handful of bargains—the rustic carignane; the $11 Mojo Red, an unusual but fun blend of cabernet sauvignon and carignane; and the La Blanc, a white blend with a hint of aromatic muscat that makes it quite possibly the best picnic wine in the valley for under $10.

HANDLEY CELLARS

The usual Wine Country interior theme gets a jolt at Handley (3151 Hwy. 128, Philo, 707/895-3876 or 800/733-3151, www.handleycellars .com, 10 A.M.–5 P.M. daily, until 6 P.M. in summer, free tasting), where you can prop yourself on the dark wood of the antique London pub bar, glass of wine in hand, and admire the international folk art that fills the room. It's the only place in the valley that offers such a collision of eras and styles, although the combination of Victorian splendor and ethnic art in the otherwise sparse, Craftsman-style room tends to feel a little disingenuous. Nonetheless, it's hard not to explore the displays and end up leaving with a Native American rug or Bolivian "fiber bug" rather than a bottle of wine.

That's not to say the wines are not worthy. Owner Milla Handley not only collects art from around the world but also makes the wines from the family's vineyards (in Mendocino and the Dry Creek Valley in northern Sonoma) and has been doing so since the early 1980s. Hallmarks here are reliability and reasonable prices. Only a few of the dozen or so bottles made here cost over $20, and wines run the gamut of Mendocino varietals, with the estate chardonnay and pinot noir accounting for the biggest share of the 15,000-case production. The pinot is made in the lighter, brighter style typical of cheaper Anderson Valley pinots, with plenty of enticing strawberry and cherry aromas. The chardonnay is on the sweeter side but with a good acidity to provide some balance.

Both are usually available on the tasting list of four reds and four whites, along with bargain-priced Ranch House Red and Water Tower White, two blends that are unique every year but always easy drinkers. Rounding out the red tasting list might be one of the three rich zinfandels and the spicy syrah, while the whites tasting list might include Anderson Valley stalwarts like gewürztraminer and riesling or some more unusual varietals for the region such as sauvignon blanc, pinot gris, or a creamy viognier from Dry Creek.

The large courtyard to the side of the tasting room is a tranquil place to enjoy a glass of wine away from the ethnic explosion of the tasting room, but it's a little too lacking in privacy to be an ideal picnic spot. Instead, try to visit on the first weekend of the month, when you'll get the chance to try some Asian- or South American–inspired food, which Handley pairs with one of its wines.

BREGGO CELLARS
Surprisingly, this is the only winery (11001 Hwy. 128, Boonville, 707/895-9589, www .breggo.com, 11 A.M.–5 P.M. daily,, free tasting) in the Anderson Valley named after a Boontling expression—you'd think more would take advantage of the unique lingo of the local dialect. *Breggo* is Boontling for "sheep," and the winery was so named because the 200-acre patch of land was a sheep farm before it was bought by Doug and Ana Stewart in 2000. They have plans to plant vineyards and establish a traditional estate winery; for now, they've renovated the pretty craftsman-style cottage and built a modest winery, making wines from other valley vineyards.

The Stewarts buy fruit from some of the best-known vineyards in the valley and make about 2,000 cases of wine a year. With outstanding fruit and the help of a consulting winemaker, Breggo has already made quite a name for its pinots. They range from the bright and silky Anderson Valley version, at a fairly standard Anderson Valley pinot price, to the brawny Savoy Vineyard Pinot Noir, which has an opulence and intensity befitting its more expensive price tag.

Breggo also makes a fine gewürztraminer and remarkably floral pinot gris, together with a rosé made from pinot and syrah that is a contender for the valley's best picnic wine. Try it at one of the handful of picnic tables outside the cozy tasting room.

Wineries by Appointment
LAZY CREEK VINEYARDS
Lazy Creek Vineyards (4741 Hwy. 128, Philo, 707/895-3623, www.lazycreekvineyards.com, tasting room Fri.–Mon. 10:30 A.M.–4:30 P.M.) might officially be an appointment-only winery, but if the gate just off Highway 128 is open (and it usually is, especially on the weekend), then there's probably someone home and ready to welcome visitors at the colorful cottage hidden away up a long dirt driveway. The Chandler family owns this modest, 2,500-case boutique winery, first bonded in the early 1970s, and it feels very much like a family affair. Josh is usually the generous host at the small tasting area in the barrel room, but Mary Beth, the children, and the dogs and other assorted animals are never far away. The portfolio of wines is small, but all are outstanding, justifying their price at the upper end of the Anderson valley range.

Whites include a gewürztraminer that's possibly one of the driest examples in the valley yet still packs in the classic aromas and flavors. There's also a juicy pinot blanc that's worth trying. Reds here are big and chewy. The inky, concentrated pinot noir is from some of the oldest pinot vines in the valley and made in a dark, earthy Burgundian style that will age well, and there's also a dry pinot rosé that's probably one for the dinner table rather than the picnic table. Josh started making a syrah in 2004, and it, too, has the earthy, almost chewy characteristics found in his pinot, making it much closer to a Rhône-style wine than many warmer-climate Californian syrahs, which are often best described as "jammy." Another white Alsace varietal, pinot blanc, was released in 2005.

ESTERLINA VINEYARDS

Esterlina Vineyards (1200 Holmes Ranch Rd., Philo, 707/895-2920, www.esterlinavineyards .com) is almost as famous in wine circles for being the sole owner of a wine appellation as it is for turning out sought-after pinots and rieslings. The Sterling family, owners of Esterlina, bought the tiny Cole Ranch AVA in 1999 from John Cole, who, decades earlier, had persevered to have a 250-acre patch of chilly land on his ranch designated an appellation unto itself.

Such are the unique conditions of Cole Ranch that Esterlina keeps most of these grapes for itself. As well as making outstanding pinot noir (which usually sells out fast) and both an unctuously sweet and a tangy dry riesling, it also makes worthy examples of cool-climate cabernet sauvignon and merlot that will appeal to bordeaux lovers. Visiting Esterlina is a lesson in small-town Anderson Valley hospitality, but one requiring faith and good eyes to spot the tiny signs on the way up the long, dirt road. The setting is rustic, the views (and the generous pours) inspirational, and the hosts friendly. It's hard not to leave without a couple of bottles.

SIGHTS
𝕔 Anderson Valley Brewing Company

For anyone who prefers beer over wine, this is not so much a sight as a sight for sore eyes. The brewery (17700 Hwy. 253, at Hwy. 128,

COURTESY OF VISIT MENDOCINO COUNTY, INC.

MENDOCINO COUNTY

Anderson Valley Brewing Company

Boonville, 707/895-2337, www.avbc.com, 11–6 P.M. daily, until 7 P.M. Fri.) started out in what is now the Highpockety Ox saloon in downtown Boonville, but in 2000 it moved to a new, custom-built facility a short distance away, confirming the commercial success of its beers. The new brewery also enabled it to expand production significantly, using giant copper kettles from Germany. They can be seen on the tours of the brewery that are offered twice a day, at 1:30 P.M. and 3 P.M. The $5 price of the tour can be redeemed against a purchase of $10 or more. If you can't make a tour, you can still sample some of the 10 different beers, which range from seasonal beers like Summer Solstice, through light ales, including the popular Boont Amber, to darker ales like the rich Dark Porter. Bring a picnic and enjoy a beer in the garden, or see if you can simultaneously drink beer and throw a Frisbee on the disc golf course ($5 per person, redeemable with purchases). Just don't leave without finding out why the packaging features a bear with antlers. (Spoiler alert: What do you get when you cross a bear and a deer? A beer!)

Anderson Valley Museum

This one-room museum (12340 Hwy. 128, just north of Boonville, 707/995-3207, www .andersonvalleymuseum.org, 1–4 P.M. Fri.– Sun., Feb.–Nov., donation requested), in an old Victorian school building known affectionately as the Little Red Schoolhouse, is only open a few days a week, but if you're in the area and have a half-hour to spare, it's worth browsing for a few minutes—if for no other reason than to learn a little Boontling. The Anderson Valley Historical Society has put together a pretty comprehensive set of exhibits, using artifacts and personal stories to give a good overview of the valley's rich history, from the Pomo Indians to its agricultural heyday.

EVENTS

Popular events tend to fill every hotel and B&B in the valley, so if you plan to visit on an event weekend, be sure to book well in advance. The valley's major events usually take place

at local wineries or the Mendocino County Fairgrounds, right on Highway 128 at the southern end of Boonville.

The event year kicks off in February with the **International Alsace Varietals Festival,** organized by the Anderson Valley Winegrowers Association (707/895-9463, www.avwines .com) and held the second weekend of the month at one of the valley wineries. Despite its rather inelegant name, the festival is a chance for the valley's wineries to show off just how elegant the aromatic Alsatian wines are in this part of the world. Visitors can also try to learn how to pronounce wines with names like edelzwicker and gewürztraminer.

In May, the Anderson Valley Brewing Company sponsors the **Boonville Beer Festival,** held at the Mendocino County Fairgrounds on the first Saturday of the month—probably the only day of the year that beer drinking eclipses wine sipping in the valley. More than 50 microbreweries from around California and up to Washington are represented, including all of Mendocino's finest, and the event takes on a party atmosphere, with live music and plenty of barbeque smoke. For more information about ticket prices and outlets, contact the Anderson Valley Brewing Company (707/895-2337, www.avbc.com).

Later on in May, wine once again takes center stage at the annual **Pinot Noir Festival,** organized by the Anderson Valley Winegrowers Association (707/895-9463, www.avwines .com) and usually held the third weekend of the month. Winemaker dinners and seminars culminate in the grand tasting at one of the valley's wineries on Saturday. The tasting is a ticket-only event, but on Sunday many of the valley's other wineries roll out the red carpet with free music, food, and tours.

At the end of June, the Anderson Valley briefly becomes the center of the world music scene when the **World Music Festival** (www .snwmf.com) takes over the fairgrounds and much of the rest of the valley. If you hope to simply have a relaxing weekend and taste some wine, this is definitely not the weekend to come to the valley. If you're a big fan of almost

WAR ON THE PALACES, PEACE TO THE COTTAGES

Boonville's local newspaper, the *Anderson Valley Advertiser*, is a small-town triumph in this day and age. Under the reign of editor Bruce Anderson, who bought the weekly in 1984, it became famous in Northern California and, briefly, nationally as a sort of community *National Enquirer*, skewering local politicians, businesspeople, and environmentalists in colorful, ranting stories with sometimes dubious credibility. Anderson's rabble-rousing credo was captured by the newspaper motto (and socialist battle cry), "War on the Palaces, Peace to the Cottages," and it apparently generated plenty of interest, if not money. The paper sold many more copies each week than there are residents of the Anderson Valley.

Anderson's blunt, combative style made many enemies. He's said to have survived in business for so long in part because the newspaper's circulation was still too small for people to care much and because his pockets were too shallow for anyone to consider a libel suit against him. He sold the newspaper in 2004, but his planned new publishing venture in Oregon didn't work out and he bought it back in 2007, once again installing himself as the outspoken and entertaining editor.

His family's legacy will also live on in the eponymous valley thanks to the novel *Boonville*, published to modest critical acclaim in 2001 by Bruce's nephew, Robert Mailer Anderson. The story of a Florida yuppie's existential crisis that brings him to Boonville gives the younger Anderson his own opportunities to poke fun at local hippies and rednecks, though in a slightly less incendiary style than his uncle.

The *Advertiser* is still a good read, addressing lofty subjects of global importance alongside tales of daily struggles in the valley, all the while never missing the chance to stick it to The Man. Rather than killing the newspaper off, the Internet has enabled the *Advertiser* to take small-town Mendocino global and a few minutes perusing the site (www.theava.com) will get you in the right state of mind for a visit to this part of the world.

---

any type of international music and don't mind existing cheek-by-jowl with a mind-boggling array of cultures on a hot, dusty field, this is the place to be. The festival is so popular that the organizers set up a huge campground next to the fairgrounds.

In July, when tranquility has once again returned to the valley, wine lovers can investigate the **California Wine Tasting Championships,** held every year in the scenic gardens of Greenwood Ridge Vineyards (707/895-2002, www.greenwoodridge.com) on the last weekend of the month. Spectators get in free to enjoy the food, wine, and music. For a modest ticket price, novices and professionals can enter the singles or doubles tasting competitions and test their skill at identifying wines.

Fall is apple harvest time in the Anderson Valley, and as good a place as any to sample the bounty is the **Mendocino County Fair and Apple Show** (707/895-3011, www .mendocountyfair.com), held at the fairgrounds the weekend after Labor Day. It's a good old-fashioned agricultural fair, with apples galore plus local wines, arts and crafts, livestock shows, and fairground rides. It's the most kid-friendly festival of the year.

RECREATION
Hendy Woods State Park

Almost as famous for its one-time hermit as for its towering redwoods, Hendy Woods (18599 Philo-Greenwood Rd., 707/895-3141, www .parks.ca.gov, sunrise–sunset, $8 parking) is a natural jewel in the Anderson Valley. The damp, shady groves of ancient trees are a particularly stark contrast to the grassland and dry oak woodland that surround them. Indeed, the park entrance barely hints at what lies within.

The 845-acre park is named for Joshua Hendy, an English immigrant who, ironically, built the first redwood lumber mill in

California, in the mid-1800s. He later established a sawmill on the Navarro River (and an ironworks near San Francisco), but he vowed never to touch the ancient groves of trees that survive today. After his death in 1891, much of the surrounding forestland was cleared, as demand for lumber soared with the Bay Area building boom. The park was established in the 1950s to protect what was left.

It's easy to understand why someone wanting to escape from society would make the dark, remote forest their home. For more than a decade in the 1960s and 1970s, Pitro Zalenko did just that. He became known as the Hendy Hermit, surviving off the land (and neighboring farms) and living a life of solitude in the woods. Several of his "huts" (actually more like piles of branches), including one in a hollowed-out stump, can be seen alongside the Hermit Hut Trail. The most popular destinations in the park, however, are the two groves of old-growth redwoods—the 80-acre **Big Hendy** grove and the 20-acre **Little Hendy.**

A 1.5-mile-long series of trails loop through Big Hendy from near the day-use area and include the half-mile, self-guided **Discovery Trail** that continues via the Upper Loop and Back Loop trails around the rest of the grove. Make sure you have a trail map because signage on the trails is almost nonexistent. You can also hike via the **Eagle Trail** from the day-use area to Little Hendy, although the quickest way to see it is to park at the entrance kiosk to the park and go from there. The **Hermit Hut Trail** climbs up from the day-use area, through redwoods and into mixed forest. For a longer hike (about three miles), stay on this trail and link up with the **Azalea Trail** that descends down to Little Hendy before taking the Eagle Trail back to the day-use area.

If all that hiking sounds too strenuous, the handful of picnic tables on the oak-dotted grassland of the day-use area are as good a place as any to relax with a bottle of wine and some sandwiches. To get to the park, turn onto the Philo-Greenwood Road (about a half-mile west of the Gowan's Oak Tree farm stand), cross the river, and the entrance is on the left.

ACCOMMODATIONS

The Anderson Valley has a worrying lack of rooms. As the valley's wineries and summer events grow more popular, finding a room in peak season can be next to impossible. Just hope there's not a wedding in town, too. The valley is a popular place to get married, and a single wedding party can book almost every room in the valley for an entire weekend. The long, winding drive makes staying outside the valley a less than attractive option if you plan any meaningful exploration. Book well in advance. A two-night minimum on summer weekends (May–October) is the norm. Rooms in the valley often lack more modern amenities such as TVs, hairdryers, or CD players. You might not even get a phone. It's another way the Anderson Valley welcomes tourists on its own terms, not yours.

Camping is a more viable option here than in other nearby wine regions. The main campground is smack in the middle of the valley, has plenty of sites and plenty of clean showers, and stays comfortably warm and fog-free during the summer.

$100-150

The **Anderson Valley Inn** (8480 Hwy. 128, Philo, 707/895-3325, www.avinn.com, $75 winter, $120 summer) is one of the more charming B&Bs in the Philo area and also one of the cheapest. The four standard rooms with private bathrooms are furnished with country-style antiques, quilts, and down comforters. There are also a couple of two-bedroom suites ($130–180) with kitchenettes that sleep four. The lack of hotel amenities (not even phones) is more than made up for by the pretty garden, hearty breakfasts, and proximity to the valley's biggest wineries—but you'll have to drive to dinner.

$150-200

The **Holly Hill Farm Inn** (2151 Hwy. 128, at mile marker 16.16, Philo, 707/895-2269, www.hollyhillfarminn.com) in Philo is off the beaten path on 12 rural acres at the western end of the valley, but offers a luxury lacking in most other B&Bs. The main guesthouse has two bedrooms that can be booked separately (one queen, one king, each $180 a night), so you might have to share the grand piano or 130 channels of satellite television in the spacious living area.

The ◖ **Boonville Hotel** (14050 Hwy. 128, Boonville, 707/895-2210, www.boonvillehotel .com) has witnessed the comings and goings in the Anderson Valley for almost 150 years. Its exterior looks every bit the Victorian stagecoach stop it once was, but inside, its historic features have been complemented by clean, modern decor, creating an effortlessly chic ambience in both the common areas and the ten rooms. Chic, however, comes at a price: the cheapest rooms start at $125 a night, with most at $185. A couple of small suites with private balconies ($250 a night) at the front of the building suffer from street noise, which can be surprisingly loud for such a small town. The best bang for your buck are the Creekside Suite and Studio (each $295 a night) with separate seating areas, private entrances, and their own little yards. The spacious bar is always inviting, as is the acclaimed restaurant (except when closed on Tuesday and Wednesday) and the gorgeous garden. It's also just steps from just about everything there is to eat, drink, and do in Boonville.

Part B&B, part fruit farm, and part culinary school, the ◖ **Philo Apple Farm** (18501 Greenwood Rd., Philo, 707/895-2333, www .philoapplefarm.com, $175 weekdays, $250 weekends) is one of the most interesting places you can stay in the valley and, despite being relatively expensive, it offers perhaps the best value for money. Three guest cottages look like small boats marooned in a sea of apple trees. Beyond their colorful doors are spacious one-room cabins with simple country furnishings. The Red Door cottage has an alfresco shower, the Green Door cottage, a wood-burning stove. Outside, each has a porch where you can sit and watch the apples grow in the surrounding organic orchard. A fourth room, the Room with a View, is a bright, sunny space upstairs in the main house, with its own private entrance and orchard views. Downstairs, the dining room opens onto the lush gardens, a perfect place to start the day with breakfast. The nearby swimming hole is a bonus.

There's a catch, however. Weekend nights at the Apple Farm can be booked up to a year in advance thanks to the weekend-long, all-inclusive cooking class offered by the innkeeper and former restaurant owner Sally Schmitt and her daughter Karen. The reason the class is wildly popular is because of the restaurant that Sally and her husband used to own—the French Laundry in Yountville. For $625 per person, people hope some of their culinary success might wash off on them. If you're not able to get a room (and sometimes they are available on short notice), you can still sample some Schmitt family hospitality at the Boonville Hotel, run by Sally's son, chef Jon Schmitt.

Serene doesn't even begin to describe the setting for the cottages of **The Other Place** (address and directions given upon reservation, 707/895-3979, www.sheepdung.com), brought to you by the same folks who dreamed up the name Sheep Dung Ranch for their first hospitality venture on these hundreds of acres of ranch land. The dog-friendly Sheep Dung Ranch morphed into two separate sets of accommodations, this one in the hills above Boonville. The cottages were all recently built and take full advantage of panoramic, pastoral views across the 500 acres of land that is their backyard. Hiking opportunities are almost endless, and there's a large swimming pond not far from the cottages. Dogs are even allowed in that, too.

All are set up as fully functioning vacation homes, with well-stocked kitchens, luxury bathrooms, and those technological rarities in the Anderson Valley—televisions and CD players. The Oaks is a rustic one-bedroom studio and the Buckeye is a full one-bedroom. Both sleep two people (and two dogs) in luxury and cost $190 midweek and $250 on weekends. The two-bedroom Breezeway cottage, a converted agricultural building, sleeps four (plus four dogs) and costs $275 a night midweek and $350 on weekends. Worth noting, there are three-night weekend minimums in some months during the summer, and payment must be made by good old-fashioned check or cash (no credit cards).

Retreats

The number of retreats and spiritual centers in the Anderson Valley is yet another sign that this is a part of the world in which to unwind and escape the stimuli of modern life. Retreat centers are generally geared toward hosting large groups, up to a hundred people, and are often spiritual in nature, but anyone can stay at them. Probably the best-known retreat in the valley is the **Wellspring Renewal Center** (18450 Rays Rd., Philo, 707/895-3893, www .wellspringrenewal.org), set on 50 acres next to the Navarro River near Philo. The former resort is now a nonprofit that bills itself as a setting for the renewal of the human spirit. Miles of hiking trails, a swimming beach on the river, and plenty of peace and quiet are the biggest attractions. You can take or leave the many programs and classes on offer. There are a handful of houses that sleep a dozen or more people, but the best lodging options are the handful of housekeeping cabins that include a small kitchenette ($70 for one guest, $20 per additional guest) and the rustic cabins near the river that are just as billed—rustic two-room cabins with a bed, electricity, and a fireplace, but very little else. You have to bring your own bedding and towels, and prepare for a short trek to the shared bathhouse, but for $73 a night for two people to stay under the redwoods, it's a sacrifice that might be worth making.

Camping

The Anderson Valley's anti-establishment history suggests anyone should simply be able to pitch a tent anywhere. Doing so might indeed result in an interesting experience. Unless you know the surrounding hills like the back of your hand, however, it's not recommended. There are plenty of official camping options in the valley, and being able to pitch a tent is one surefire way to have a place to stay for the night. Just be sure to bring mosquito repellent because the campgrounds are all close to the river.

The biggest and most convenient campground is at **Hendy Woods State Park** (18599 Philo-Greenwood Rd., Philo, 707/895-3141, reservations 800/444-7275, www.reserve america.com, $35) near Philo. The park entrance is just over the bridge from one of the best local swimming holes on the Navarro River and only a few minutes' drive to many wineries. There are actually two neighboring campgrounds, Azalea and Wildcat, with a total of 92 sites for tents and RVs up to 27 or 35 feet. All are well shaded, but during the summer it gets very hot during the day and stays pretty warm at night.

This is not the cheapest campground, but its location in the heart of the valley and its amenities are worth paying for. There are water spigots every hundred yards, and the clean, relatively modern bathroom blocks provide flush toilets and coin-operated showers. Miles of trails crisscross the 100-acre park, and it's only a short hike from the campgrounds to the two main groves of old-growth redwoods, Big Hendy and Little Hendy, as well as to the picnic tables and river access of the park's day-use area. Campgrounds are open March–October, and reservations are recommended during the summer. To get to the park, turn off Highway 128 onto the Philo-Greenwood Road about three miles west of Philo, cross the river, and the park entrance is on the left.

Further west is the smaller, more primitive Paul M. Dimmick Campground in the heart of the **Navarro River Redwoods State Park** (Hwy. 128, 707/937-5804, www.parks.ca.gov, $25), about 10 miles west of Navarro in the cool, dark "redwood tunnel" that runs almost to the coast. Stock up on supplies in Philo or Navarro beforehand, and take a few extra layers of clothing—it can get cool here at night in the summer. The campground, just off the main highway, has 25 shady sites among the redwoods for tents and RVs up to 30 feet, but the only amenities are vault toilets. Drinking water is only available in the summer. The campground is open year-round in theory, but it sometimes closes during the winter if the nearby river runs too high. During the summer, however, the river is the biggest draw for swimmers—and in the fall, for both kayakers and anglers. Sites cannot be reserved, so arrive early to stake your spot.

FOOD

Boonville shares the honor, along with Hopland further east, of having possibly the most restaurants per capita in Wine Country. It's not that they have a huge number of places to eat, just more than one would expect for towns with only a few hundred inhabitants. Boonville, like Hopland, has always been a place that travelers have stopped en route to somewhere else, giving rise to hotels and eateries where normally there might be none. Recently, however, it has become a destination itself, and a viable location for an even larger number of restaurants. Outside Boonville, the food scene is still nonexistent but for a few delis and markets to supply wayward travelers and the valley's sparse population.

Becoming a Wine Country destination has also had the effect of upping the quality of food available. "Focaccia" was probably a word rarely heard before the winos arrived en masse. Although many places still retain a humble air, the one constant among all the valley food outlets is organic ingredients. You'll find far less crowing about organic this and organic that on menus or marketing material, because organic is simply a way of life here.

Boonville

Locals would probably consider the restaurant at the **Boonville Hotel** (14050 Hwy. 128,

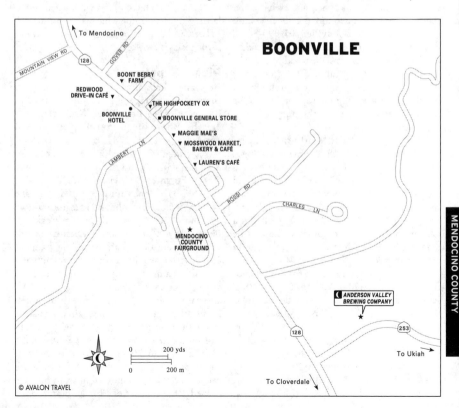

Boonville, 707/895-2210, wine bar open daily, dinner Thurs.–Mon., entrées $16–25) the most highpockety in town (to use a Boontling expression), and it's the only place where reservations are both taken and recommended on summer weekend evenings when valley visitors rub shoulders with the local winegrowers. Minimalist modern flourishes and a sunny outdoor patio give the historic hotel's restaurant a decidedly trendy, big-city atmosphere. The menu includes many classic bistro favorites like steak (grass-fed meat, of course) and also plenty of other seasonal dishes that unpretentiously meld local ingredients with international influences. It's not too surprising that the food is as good as it is—the parents of chef and hotel owner Jon Schmitt established the famous French Laundry in the Napa Valley.

A more eclectic atmosphere and even less pretentious food can be found at **Lauren's Café** (14211 Hwy. 128, Boonville, 707/895-3869, dinner Tues.–Sat., entrées $8–13), a casual hangout and restaurant. Weekend live music, dancing, and a pool table are as important here as the local wines and home-style, Mexican-influenced food. You might even be lucky enough to be there the night of some dance lessons.

The tiny **Mosswood Market, Café and Bakery** (14111 Hwy. 128, Boonville, 707/895-3635, breakfast and lunch Mon.–Sat., entrées $4–10) is a relative newcomer in Boonville and an ideal place for a quick breakfast of freshly made pastries and coffee or a lunch of homemade soup, focaccia sandwiches, quiche, or a seasonal salad. If you're lucky, you might be able to snag one of the two small tables out on the boardwalk.

Other options for quick and easy sustenance include the **Boonville General Store** (17810 Farrer Ln., at Hwy. 128, Boonville, 707/895-9477, 8 A.M.–3 P.M. Mon.–Fri., 8:30 A.M.–3 P.M. Sat.–Sun.), which sells breakfast, coffee, and Boonville's best deli sandwiches, which can be eaten at the handful of tables outside. The **Redwood Drive-In Café** (13980 Hwy. 128, Boonville, 707/895-3441, 6 A.M.–8 P.M. Mon.–Thurs., 6 A.M.–9 P.M. Fri.–Sun.) also has a few booths indoors and some outdoor seating, if you don't mind traffic from the gas station next door. Like any good roadhouse, it serves no-nonsense diner food, including huge breakfasts and burgers from the crack of dawn to late at night, and is a favorite among local early-morning coffee drinkers.

Philo

Outside Boonville the food choices are as sparse as the population. Only the little hamlet of Philo has a decent place to rest your wine-weary legs and eat, at the Mexican restaurant **Libby's** (8651 Hwy. 128, Philo, 707/895-2646, lunch and dinner Tues.–Sat., entrées $7–12). Don't be put off by the unadorned interior and rather plain exterior storefront—it serves perhaps the best basic Mexican food in the valley, from tacos to mole-drenched enchiladas. Skip the skimpy wine selection and stick to beer, and don't expect lightning-fast service if the place is crowded.

Picnic Supplies

In a valley that's all about the great outdoors, there is no shortage of places to pick up picnic supplies. In Boonville, the best choices are the **Boonville General Store** (17810 Farrer Ln. at Hwy. 128, Boonville, 707/895-9477, 8 A.M.–3 P.M. Mon.–Fri., Sat.–Sun. 8:30 A.M.–3 P.M.) and the quirky little **Boont Berry Farm** (13981 Hwy. 128, Boonville, 707/895-3576, open until 6 P.M. daily). The General Store is larger but is less a grocery store and more a café and deli, selling breakfast, pizza, and some of Boonville's best deli sandwiches. Boont Berry Farm is a hippy hangout at the western end of town that's not actually a farm but a modest organic deli, bakery, and grocery store, very much reflecting the valley's alternative culture. This should be the first stop for both vegetarians and the plain curious.

Further west, Philo has its own grocery store and deli, **Lemon's Market & Deli** (8651 Hwy. 128, Philo, 707/895-3552, 8 A.M.–8 P.M. Mon.–Sat., 9 A.M.–7 P.M. Sun.). Just like the one-block town, it's not a big store but has gained a big reputation (for its meats, both fresh and cured, and as the place to pick up abalone during the fleeting season). Not far away, under a vast, spreading oak tree, is the valley institution **Gowan's Oak Tree** (6600 Hwy. 128, Philo, 707/895-3353, 8 A.M.–5:30 P.M. daily). Part farm stand and part grocery store, it has been serving travelers en route to the coast since the 1930s and sells far more fresh, seasonal produce than its diminutive size suggests. It is perhaps best known for local apples and delicious, unpasteurized apple cider, but you're also likely to see more types of pears, squash, and other vegetables than you ever imagined existed.

At the western end of the valley, just before the road dives into the dark coastal redwood forest, the **Navarro General Store** (231 Wendling St., off Hwy. 128, Navarro, 707/895-9445) is the last place to stock up on food as well as camping and fishing supplies before the Mendocino coast. The food selection is limited, but there's a small deli counter and on summer weekends a big, smoky barbeque in the parking lot under the redwoods.

Fresh Produce

The Anderson Valley's plentiful bounty (of the legal variety) is never hard to find. In Boonville, **Boont Berry Farm** (13981 Hwy. 128, Boonville, 707/895-3576, open until 6 P.M. daily) often has plenty of fresh local produce, and near Philo, **Gowan's Oak Tree** (6600 Hwy. 128, Philo, 707/895-3353, 8 A.M.–5:30 P.M. daily) seems to be the outlet of choice for local farms and is well-stocked with produce year-round.

Gowan's specializes in apples, for which the Anderson Valley is almost as well known as wine. The ultimate apple outlet in the valley, however, is the **Philo Apple Farm** (18501 Greenwood Rd., Philo, 707/895-2333), just before the bridge on the Philo-Greenwood

Road off Highway 128. Over 80 varieties are grown here, including some rarities, together with plenty of other fruits and vegetables. The best time to visit is during apple season: August–November. Other times of the year, you'll have to make do with all sorts of apple-related jams, chutneys, and cider at a small farm stand just inside the main gate. It operates on an honor system; make sure you have cash. While you're there, take a stroll around the lush, aromatic gardens.

A surefire way to pick up local seasonal produce is at the valley's main **farmers market** (14050 Hwy. 128, 9:30 A.M.–noon Sat., May–Oct.) which is as colorful and diverse as the residents of the valley. It is held in the parking lot of the Boonville Hotel.

INFORMATION AND SERVICES

When in Boonville, pick up a copy of the weekly **Anderson Valley Advertiser,** a newspaper that has garnered fame far beyond the valley's borders for its quirky and literary contributors. Other publications that are usually available at local markets and most wineries include the quarterly **Mendocino Travelers Guide,** which lists events and attractions throughout the county. Much of the information about the valley is to be found online. **The Anderson Valley Chamber of Commerce** (www.andersonvalleychamber.com) has a website with details of all the main retailers and events, but more information on local goings-on can be found at the independent website **www.andersonvalley.org,** which is run by a valley resident. For more specific wine-related information, the **Anderson Valley Winegrowers Association** (www.avwines.com) has a useful website with details about all its member wineries and the region's wine-making history.

Eastern Mendocino

Eastern Mendocino, in the upper reaches of the Russian River Valley, had a huge geographical advantage over the Anderson Valley in the 1800s: easier access to Sonoma and the San Francisco Bay. With no mountains to cross and a river to aid in transport, the area quickly tapped into the agricultural boom—and the resulting immigration boom—that gripped Sonoma County in the mid-1800s.

The fertile river valley quickly became covered in orchards, pastureland, and vineyards of hops and wine grapes to help supply the burgeoning populations further south. The local Native American people, who called themselves "Yokaya," or "people of the deep valley," succumbed to the inevitable displacement as the valley was settled, leaving behind only their name. Its spelling was changed to Ukiah, which became the name of the county seat.

The status of the region as agricultural supplier to Sonoma also became a milestone. Although Mendocino was flush with Italian immigrants who knew how to manage vineyards and make wine, the grapes were more often than not sold to wineries elsewhere or made into cheap jug wines. As a result, Mendocino became an important grape-growing region but not a widely recognized wine-producing region, a pattern still evident today. Eastern Mendocino accounts for about two-thirds of the 16,000 acres of vineyard acreage in Mendocino County, yet is home to just a couple of dozen wineries.

A big factor in the eventual rise of Mendocino as a serious winemaking region in the late 20th century was the juggernaut of **Fetzer Vineyards,** possibly one of the most successful winery ventures in California and certainly the most successful in Mendocino. Established in the 1950s, the winery planted hundreds of acres of vineyards in eastern Mendocino over the subsequent decades, was instrumental in getting several regional appellations approved, and helped transform sleepy Hopland into the wine destination it is today.

Fetzer was sold to the multinational Brown-Forman group in the early 1990s, and the winery's lavish hospitality facilities near Hopland were closed in 2006, but many members of the extended Fetzer family, flush with buyout cash, have established new wineries in the region, continuing the family's legacy. Without the support and marketing clout that Fetzer gave (and still gives) this region, many of today's small Mendocino wineries might not exist.

While the wine industry struggled, Mendocino became famous for a new wave of immigrants, the urban refugees and hippies of the counterculture. The earth-friendly culture they imported is still evident today and helped spur the organic farming practices that Mendocino has become famous for, both in the wine industry and in the wider agricultural sector.

The Wines

For much of its history, eastern Mendocino never got much recognition for the grapes it supplied to wineries further south or the bulk wines it shipped in anonymous bottles to markets far away. Some critics have argued that this part of Mendocino doesn't deserve recognition because the wines lack individuality and a true sense of place. However, the level of innovation shown by wine growers experimenting with unusual Italian and Rhône varietals, and the long commitment to organic farming practices—something that other wine regions only recently implemented—make this area as noteworthy a contributor to California's wine heritage as any other.

There's no specific varietal for which this area is particularly known. If you were to pick a type of wine that is made particularly well here, however, it would probably be one of the Rhône varietals—syrah or grenache, for example. Some wineries specialize in nothing but Rhône-style wines. Redwood Valley zinfandels are also fairly distinctive, taking on an earthier profile in the cooler climate.

It's hard to pin down a type of wine to this area because of the patchwork of appellations and growing regions, an indication that there's no one particular set of growing conditions unique to the region. Each appellation is also small, some ridiculously so, which means few have gained the sort of fame that appellations have in the Napa Valley, for example.

The Redwood Valley AVA north of Ukiah is the biggest and arguably the best known, as much due to the influence of Fetzer's hundreds of acres of vineyards as for the small wineries that operate there today. At the other end of the spectrum is the McDowell Valley AVA, the playground of just one winery—McDowell Valley Vineyards—but source of some good Rhône varietals.

Beyond the few gems, you're as likely to be wowed by low prices and organic credentials as by taste sensations. That's perhaps why the Mendocino Winegrowers Alliance has kicked up its marketing effort in recent years, aware that the Anderson Valley has started to steal the Mendocino limelight. One of the most successful new marketing drives has been the Coro Mendocino collaboration, which has helped small and large wineries in the region to create a wine unique to the region. And just to prove the Fetzer factor continues to influence the wine industry here, the Coro program was the brainchild of Paul Dolan, former president of Fetzer Vineyards.

WINE-TASTING
Ukiah Area Wineries
◖ PARDUCCI WINE CELLARS

Parducci (501 Parducci Rd., Ukiah, 707/463-5350, www.mendocinowinecompany.com, 10 A.M.–5 P.M. daily, $5–10 tasting fee) is a winery returning from the brink, both of bankruptcy and of being known for bland, mass-produced wines. It still targets the lower end of the wine spectrum, but the sheer quantity of different wines on offer in the tasting room, the winery's history, and the lofty environmental goals of its new owners, the Mendocino Wine Company, make it worth tracking down on the northern edge of Ukiah.

COURTESY OF VISIT MENDOCINO COUNTY, INC.

downtown Ukiah

MENDOCINO COUNTY

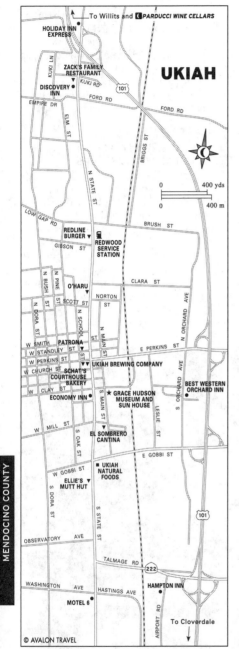

To Willits and **PARDUCCI WINE CELLARS**

UKIAH

HOLIDAY INN EXPRESS

ZACK'S FAMILY RESTAURANT

DISCOVERY INN

KUKI RD

FORD RD

FORD RD

EMPIRE DR

N DICK

ELM ST

BRIGGS ST

N STATE ST

0   400 yds
0   400 m

LOW GAP RD

BRUSH ST

REDLINE BURGER

REDWOOD SERVICE STATION

GIBSON ST

CLARA ST

O'HARU

NORTON ST

N BUSH ST

N PINE ST

SCOTT ST

N DORA ST

N SCHOOL ST

N ORCHARD AVE

W SMITH

PATRONA

N MAIN ST

E PERKINS ST

W STANDLEY ST

W PERKINS ST

W CHURCH ST

UKIAH BREWING COMPANY

SCHAT'S BAKERY

COURTHOUSE

S ORCHARD AVE

BEST WESTERN ORCHARD INN

W CLAY

ECONOMY INN

GRACE HUDSON MUSEUM AND SUN HOUSE

S MAIN ST

LESLIE ST

EL SOMBRERO CANTINA

S OAK ST

E GOBBI ST

W GOBBI ST

UKIAH NATURAL FOODS

ELLIE'S MUTT HUT

S DORA ST

OBSERVATORY AVE

S STATE ST

TALMAGE RD

222

WASHINGTON AVE

HASTINGS AVE

HAMPTON INN

MOTEL 6

AIRPORT RD

To Cloverdale

© AVALON TRAVEL

The winery's long Italian heritage began in the early 20th century, when Adolph Parducci bought vineyards near Ukiah and eventually bonded his winery in 1932. By the end of the 1930s, Parducci was making more than 100,000 gallons of wine a year, selling much of it on the East Coast but also to the growing local market. The Parducci family continued to expand the winery, planting more vineyards and eventually topping production of 100,000 cases a year in the early 1970s, just as the first crop of wineries over the hills in the Anderson Valley were getting started. That's when things started to unravel. The family sold the winery to an investment company, but it remained under family management until the early 1990s, when the partnership, and some of the investment company's other businesses, started to go sour.

After changing hands several times in the 1990s, the winery was bought in 2004 by the Mendocino Wine Company, a partnership between the Thornhill family, who were local grape growers, and Paul Dolan, the former president of Fetzer Vineyards just down the road. Since the acquisition they have focused on improving the quality of Parducci's rather lackluster selection of wines. Production has been slashed to a mere 180,000 cases a year (down from about a half million), new vines are being planted with an increasing emphasis on Italian varietals, and the existing 400 acres of vineyards are now either certified organic, "fish friendly," biodynamic, or all three. Topping off the environmental credentials, the winery also became the first in the United States to be certified as carbon neutral in 2007—perhaps not as hard as it might sound when it has 400 acres of carbon dioxide–consuming vines to help out.

The history of the winery has been somewhat obliterated over the decades, and the dark, intimate tasting room feels more like a 1970s ranch house than a slice of old Italy. The modern and airy private tasting area opposite is more inviting, as is the patio outside, but by the time you've tried wines from the seven-plus labels made here you might not care. The

Parducci tasting room

history is still very much evident just up the hill where, behind the walls of a nondescript warehouse, stand lines of massive old redwood fermenting tanks that are still in use today. In fact, the winery boasts 480,000 gallons of redwood storage capacity at the winery, more than any other winery on the planet. If you are there on a quiet day, the tasting room staff will happily direct you to take a peek.

With so many wines on offer, the tasting menu is helpfully organized not only by brand and varietal, but also by the style of the wine—fresh, smooth, juicy, bold, and sweet, for example. The Parducci-label wines focus on Italian varietals, with chardonnay, cabernet sauvignon, and pinot noir thrown in for good measure. The style is relatively simple and fruit-forward, in part due to the use of redwood tanks rather than oak barrels in the winemaking process. The price is always cheap, with most coming in at under $15 a bottle except for the Signature organic wines, which are about $30. Some higher-end wines are made under the Sketchbook label, and include a pinot,

cabernet, and merlot aged in both French and American oak. In between are all the fun labels, including Big Yellow (as in taxi), Zig Zag Zin, and Tusk'n Red, all puns intended. Also usually on offer is the winery's Coro blend, which might be the only attraction for more serious wine connoisseurs, although some new limited-production wines are also planned under the Paul Dolan label.

BARRA OF MENDOCINO

You'd be forgiven for thinking that Barra of Mendocino (7051 N. State St., Redwood Valley, 707/485-0322, www.redwoodvalleycellars .com, 10 A.M.–5 P.M. daily, free tasting, tours by appointment) was some sort of evangelical church built in the 1970s. The pointy, circular building next to the freeway a few miles north of Ukiah certainly looks like a church, complete with large parking lot out front. In fact, it's more of a temple to wine, built in 1972 by the now-defunct Weibel Champagne Cellars and said to have been designed to mimic an upside-down champagne glass (the shallow

COURTESY OF VISIT MENDOCINO COUNTY, INC.

Barra of Mendocino tasting room

type). The stem of the glass was represented by a spire on the roof, but that is no more. After peaking in the 1980s, Weibel sank under debt and sold the winery in the mid-1990s to the Barra family and Braren Pauli Winery, who then ran their respective wineries along with a custom crush business all under one roof.

That roof, with massive arching beams, covers a single 5,000-square-foot room that certainly feels rather church-like but is the most impressive venue for a tasting room in the region. The only worshipping going on here is of wines at the long curved tasting bar along the far wall, although sun worshippers will appreciate the gardens and large lawn behind the tasting room.

Charlie Barra has been growing grapes in the Redwood Valley for more than a half century, and his organic winery is best known for its pinot noir, which accounts for about half the 20,000-case annual production. There are two different labels of wine—Barra of Mendocino, which is usually available to taste, and the cheaper Girasole label. Despite the quantity made, the pinot usually sells out quickly, so you might not be able to taste it at all.

Barra's other wines from the Redwood Valley appellation are certainly worth trying, however, and offer excellent value for their $15–20 price. They include a surprisingly complex, limited-production cabernet, a rich sangiovese that sometimes includes a little zinfandel or petite sirah blended into it. Both those varietals are also bottled separately, with the petite sirah having the most intense and powerful flavors. The reds dominate the lineup, but there are a couple of whites usually available to taste as well, most notably a tangy pinot blanc.

Although there might be some Braren Pauli wines to taste, they won't be there for long. Barra bought out the Paulis in early 2007 and their partnership dissolved, leaving Barra of Mendocino as the only winery represented in the tasting room.

FREY VINEYARDS

The Frey family started growing grapes organically on their Redwood Valley ranch in the 1960s and quickly made a name for high-quality fruit, so much so that they eventually went into the winemaking business themselves. Since then the winery (14000 Tomki Rd., Redwood Valley, 707/485-5177, www .freywine.com, free tasting by appointment only) has become a champion of organic wines in Mendocino—an area already the center of organic growing—and was the first California winery to be certified organic. Not satisfied with simply being organic, the winery went on to become certified as biodynamic in the late 1990s. Now all its estate wines are biodynamic, and none contain sulphite preservatives or have been in contact with egg-white-based fining agents, making them big sellers among vegans and vegetarians around the country but not necessarily giving them a long shelf life.

Sulphites are blamed for allergic reactions and headaches, among other ailments, but most winemakers argue that minimal doses cannot be detected in taste tests and are needed to keep wines from oxidizing and going bad after bottling. Winemaker Paul Frey would beg to differ.

Today, Frey makes about 60,000 cases of organic and biodynamic wines covering the full spectrum of varietals, including almost 20,000 cases of the nonvintage Natural Red, a robust blend of carignane, zinfandel, and syrah that is probably the best deal at $8 a bottle. Most can be tasted up on the ranch by appointment only, and it's worth making the effort. The wines are not generally showered with accolades by critics, but the warm hospitality and informal atmosphere will make you appreciate the passion behind organic farming just a little bit more.

Hopland Area Wineries
JERIKO ESTATE

When the giant Fetzer Winery near Hopland was sold to the international wine conglomerate Brown-Forman in the early 1990s, the Fetzer family siblings took their gains and scattered throughout the region, to resurface years later (after noncompete agreements had expired) in various new wine ventures. One

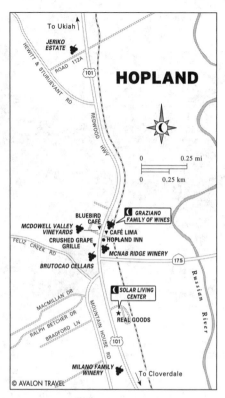

of them, Daniel Fetzer, founded Jeriko Estate (12141 Hewlitt and Sturtevant Rds., just off Hwy. 101, Hopland, 707/744-1140, www .jerikoestate.com, 10 A.M.–5 P.M. daily Apr.–Oct., 11 A.M.–4 P.M. Nov.–Mar., free tasting, tours by appointment) in the late 1990s, just north of Hopland, and built an impressive Tuscan-themed estate and winery around an already impressive Mediterranean-style villa, built 100 years earlier by a retired San Francisco judge. The name comes from an alternative spelling of the biblical city of Jericho, said to be the birthplace of modern agriculture.

The sound of inquisitive goats from the wooded hillside will probably greet you when you first get out of the car, but once inside the winery the atmosphere is more sleek and modern than rustic. What used to be an old

COURTESY OF VISIT MENDOCINO COUNTY, INC.

Jeriko Estate

tractor barn has been transformed into an enormous tasting area with a wall of glass offering views into the barrel room. The winery makes about 15,000 cases a year of nine varietals, all sourced from the organic vineyards surrounding the winery. They tend to be on the pricier end of the Mendocino scale but include particularly good merlot, pinot noir, and sangiovese. You might also be able to taste the limited-production Natural Blonde wines, one of Linda Fetzer's pet projects.

Despite describing itself as a "boutique" winery, Jeriko has the capacity to make up to 25,000 cases of wine a year. Despite its relatively large size for this area, it has a somewhat small winery feel and at times the sheep and goats seem to outnumber visitors by a healthy margin, leaving the picnic area next to the tasting room deserted.

◖ GRAZIANO FAMILY OF WINES

For such a modest little tasting room at the end of the boardwalk, Graziano (13251 S. Hwy. 101, Suite 3, Hopland, 707/744-8466, www

.grazianofamilyofwines.com, 10 A.M.–5 P.M. daily, free tasting) offers a bewildering array of wines to try. There are more than 25 different wines made under four labels, a result of Greg Graziano's position as a good old-fashioned *négociant*—a wine merchant who buys grapes or juice to create his own wines, something he's been doing for more than 40 years. Greg's grandfather, Vincenzo, first started growing grapes here in 1918, and the Italian heritage is well represented in the 20,000 cases of wine made by Graziano each year.

A dozen wines fall under the Graziano label, including five zinfandels, four of them from single vineyards in the Redwood Valley AVA that provide a very zinful education. When tasted one after another, they illustrate the full range of flavor profiles that can be coaxed out of zin, from cool-climate hints of smoke and pepper to the warmer-climate prunelike ripeness. The Rhône varietals carignane, grenache, and petite sirah, together with two whites (chenin blanc and sauvignon blanc) and the Coro Italian blend round out the portfolio.

Two of the other labels, Monte Volpe and Enotria, are dominated by Italian varietals, many of which you won't find anywhere else in Mendocino and a few you won't find anywhere else in the country. Steadfastness will be needed to sample all the wines, but the result will be quite an education on Italian varietals.

The Monte Volpe wines focus on Tuscan varietals and include three sangioveses, together with some unique Italian varietals. Graziano's is the only U.S. producer of montepulciano, a varietal widely planted in Italy but little known outside the mother country. It makes a wine of inky darkness that packs quite a tannic punch. The Peppolino is a blend of montepulciano, sangiovese, and the powerfully flavored Sicilian varietal nero d'avola. If big, tannic reds are not your thing, try the pinot grigio, which is as good as any in California, or the tocai Friulano, an aromatic, fruity delight.

Enotria wines are all made with varietals that hail from Italy's Piemonte region and include dolcetto, barbera, and nebbiolo, the key grape in Italy's famous barolo wines and one that Graziano describes as pinot noir's "twin brother from a different mother." Perhaps the most interesting wine in this lineup is the arneis, a dry, beautifully scented wine that's rarely found outside Italy.

This being Mendocino, of course, pinot noir has to make an appearance, and Graziano devotes his St. Gregory label to all things pinot. In addition to a worthy and well-priced Mendocino pinot noir (and its Reserve sibling), there is a pinot meunier, made from a grape normally used for blending, and a pinotage, a soft and appealing wine with more of a flavor punch than pinot noir, made from a varietal created in South Africa by crossing pinot noir and cinsault. Last but not least, Graziano is one of the makers of the Mendocino Coro blend, so be sure to give that a try.

McNAB RIDGE WINERY

After John Parducci was forced out of managing his family's winery near Ukiah in the early 1990s, most people expected him to retire. Instead he proved that winemaking is truly in his family's blood, and a few years later he and some business partners bought the McNab Ranch and winery (13441 S. Hwy. 101, Hopland, 707/744-1986, www.mcnabridge .com, 10 A.M.–5 P.M. daily, free tasting) just down the road in Ukiah. The winery is located in McNab Valley, so named for the Scottish homesteader Alexander McNab, who settled there in the 1860s. John Parducci was joined in the venture by his grandson, Richard, and the two of them now make about 6,000 cases of wines a year from McNab's Mendocino vineyards.

This tasting room in Hopland is a relatively recent addition, located in the modern Lawson Station building. Inside, the enormous space tries to hide its modern bones. The subdued lighting, dark maroon walls, and the imposing replica of a mahogany Victorian bar with an antique cash register evoke a splendid Victorian parlor and provide a cool respite if the sun is blazing down outside.

McNab's is also one of a handful of California wineries that champions the pinotage grape (as does Graziano a few blocks away), and the spicy wine has some unmistakable aromas of strawberries and raspberries. McNab's version of Coro is also particularly distinctive for the small amount of pinotage added to the blend. Several of the other reds in McNab's portfolio are also worth trying, including the petite sirah and the Redwood Valley zinfandels. The whites include some relative rarities, such as a fragrant colombard, as well as good examples of tried-and-trusted varietals like chardonnay and a particularly light and crisp sauvignon blanc.

Zinfandel lovers will also want to get to know Zinzilla, a monster zin that gives new meaning to the term "jammy" and certainly offers plenty of bang for the buck, if not much in the way of complexity. The chocolate drops on the tasting bar are almost a match for Zinzilla, but they are a better complement to the zinfandel mistelle, a sweet dessert wine made by adding brandy to fermenting grape juice. Taste it before and after eating the chocolate—it actually tastes better after.

SINGING THE PRAISES OF MENDOCINO

Mention the Anderson Valley and almost anyone with knowledge of California wines will think of pinot noir, much the same way Napa is known as the land of cabernet and Carneros the land of bubbles. But the rest of Mendocino still lives in the shadow of the Anderson Valley and doesn't really have a type of wine to call its own.

The problem is partly historic – since the early 20th century Mendocino has been the Bay Area's fruit basket, supplying agricultural products (including grapes) anonymously to other parts of California. Not helping matters is the fact that so many different grape varietals grow well in the patchwork of hills and valleys here. Eastern Mendocino turns out some fine zinfandels, but that varietal was long ago adopted by the entire state of California. It's also the source of some good Rhône-style wines, Italian wines, and traditional Bordeaux varietals like cabernet and merlot, but there's no single grape or style of wine that makes you think "Mendocino!"

Marketing types and winemakers have been increasing their efforts in recent years to fix the identity crisis. One of the most successful projects to date has been the **Coro Mendocino** program to create a uniquely Mendocino wine (www.coro mendocino.com).

The term Coro comes from the Latin "from many into one" (or more simply "chorus"), and since the first vintage of Coro wine was released in 2004 an increasing number of Mendocino wineries have jumped on the bandwagon, each following a set of guidelines to make a blended wine that's more about place, or terroir, than any particular kind of grape.

Coro Mendocino is loosely based on the *appellation d'origine contrôlée* system in France, which establishes rules for winemaking methods within certain geographical areas and is responsible for the labeling of French wines as, for example, Bordeaux or Cotes du Rhône. Coro was the brainchild of winemaker Dennis Patton and Paul Dolan, the former president of Hopland-based Fetzer Vineyards – a company that has already done much to get Mendocino recognized as a serious wine-making region in the last couple of decades through its sheer size and marketing clout.

They and other Mendocino winemakers worked to create detailed guidelines by which all the Coro wines must be made. Zinfandel must make up 40-70 percent of the final blend. Other varietals that can be included are bar-

McDOWELL VALLEY VINEYARDS

Among all the historic buildings in Hopland, the tasting room of McDowell (13380 S. Hwy. 101, Hopland, 707/744-8911, www.mcdowell syrah.com, 11 A.M.–5 P.M. daily, free tasting) stands out perhaps the most. The century-old redwood storefront is straight out of the Wild West. All that's missing are the swinging saloon doors. The building was, in fact, reputedly once a saloon, both of booze and ill-repute. Today the only alcohol served in the creaky old building with its knotty wooden floors is wine, while assorted wine-related gifts have replaced the personal services once said to have been on offer here.

There's no Lone Ranger left in town, but McDowell has long been known as the region's Rhône Ranger. The winery was established in 1970 when the Keehn family bought land in the McDowell Valley and planted the Rhône varietals syrah and Grenache, alongside some older vines said to date from the early 1900s. They later expanded their plantings to more than 17 different varietals, but that didn't last long. Although McDowell was one of the first wineries to sell Rhône-style wines in California and had its very own McDowell Valley AVA (granted by the Bureau of Alcohol, Tobacco, and Firearms in the early 1980s), it struggled to make money. In the early 1990s the winery was sold to a vineyard management company, but the family retained the vineyards and continued to supply grapes to the winery, beginning a partnership that continues to this day.

Around the same time, McDowell pared

bera, carignane, charbono, grenache, dolcetto, primitivo, petite sirah, and syrah, but none of them can exceed the percentage of zinfandel. Winemakers are also allowed to include 10 percent of any other varietal they choose, but in reality few actually do. Naturally, all the grapes have to come from Mendocino.

There are plenty of other rules, too, dictating everything from acidity and alcohol content (a very broad range of 12.5-16 percent) to how long wines must be aged in barrels and bottles before release and even the price – $35 a bottle. The guidelines seem pretty specific, but still allow plenty of leeway for individual wineries to create a unique wine that reflects their particular area of specialization. In creating the Coro program, Mendocino became the first place in the United States to establish such regional winemaking parameters.

To ensure a Coro wine is worthy of promoting Mendocino, a panel of five local winemakers must first judge the blends, allowing winemakers to make adjustments if necessary, before they're allowed to be graced by the Coro label. The blind-tasting panels occasionally throw some curveballs – in a few cases a winemaker has actually rejected his own blend without

knowing so until the identities of the wines were revealed.

All the different Coro wines, regardless of the winery, use the same basic label design, with the only distinction being a small image of the winery's logo and the winemaker's signature. Even a specific bottle size and shape is laid out in the guidelines. The final wines, however, are very different.

Eight wineries made a Coro blend for the inaugural 2001 vintage, from the giant Fetzer Vineyards down to tiny Golden Vineyards. By the time the 2006 vintage was released in mid-2009, there were 11 wineries on board. Italian wine specialist Graziano Family Wines makes a Coro blend that includes three classic Italian varietals: sangiovese, barbera, and dolcetto. The Rhone-style wine specialist McDowell Valley Vineyards blends syrah and petite sirah with zinfandel in its Coro wine. McNab Ridge adds a little pinotage to the mix.

Tasting each winery's Coro blend is one of the unique aspects of touring this part of Mendocino. All are different enough that you might not necessarily come away with a firm idea of what a "Mendocino" wine really is, but you'll at least have tasted some nice wines.

down its portfolio to once again focus on Rhône varietals. Today it makes about 15,000 cases of wine, and some 300 of the 500 acres of vineyards in the McDowell valley are syrah, grenache, and viognier. The winery is perhaps best known for its spicy, supple shiraz and a dark, brooding syrah, but one of the most interesting (and popular) wines is the grenache noir, a very approachable yet complex blend of grenache, syrah, petite sirah, and zinfandel. There's also a dry grenache rosé, a vibrant wine that's cheap enough for picnics but serious enough to accompany a wide range of Asian food, and the winery's version of a Coro Mendocino blend.

The two whites usually available to taste are a couple of viogniers, one light and cheap, the other a more luscious wine brimming with tropical

fruit aromas and flavors. The most luscious wine of all is the port, one of the few in Wine Country that's made using the traditional Portuguese varietals of touriga and souzao. And with McDowell being a Rhône Ranger, there's a splash of syrah added to the blend for good measure.

BRUTOCAO CELLARS

School's permanently out in Hopland, or at least it is in the town's old 1920s schoolhouse, which is now a place of food and alcohol-fueled fun. The old school building is now home to a coffee shop, a couple of restaurants, and a giant tasting room (13500 S. Hwy. 101, in the old schoolhouse, Hopland, 707/744-1664, www.brutocaocellars.com, 10 A.M.–5 P.M. daily, free tasting) with a less-than-subtle Venetian

outdoor dining at Brutocao Cellars' restaurant, The Crushed Grape

COURTESY OF VISIT MENDOCINO COUNTY, INC.

theme, including a giant mural of Venice's Saint Mark's Plaza behind the long tasting bar. The theme doesn't quite gel with the 1920s building and the rather generic Wine Country gifts on offer, but the sheer amount of space and views out to the busy bocce courts help deflect attention from the clash of styles.

The Italian theme is a reminder of the Venetian roots of the Brutocao family, which got into the wine business through marriage to a local farming family many decades ago. They started growing grapes in the area in the 1940s and started making wine in the early 1990s. Grape growing is still an important part of the business, and the 13,000 cases of wine made each year use only a fraction of the fruit from the 500 acres of vineyards owned by the Brutocaos. Their success helped finance the purchase in 1997 of Hopland's old schoolhouse, which graduated its last pupils back in the 1960s. The Crushed Grape and Lion's Den restaurants next to the tasting room are also Brutocao ventures, and the six regulation-sized bocce courts are open to all comers, although an active league

program takes precedence during the week. A helpful brochure outlining the game's rules is available in the tasting room.

Not surprisingly given the family's roots, Italian varietals feature prominently and include a dolcetto, primitivo, and barbera, but the best of the bunch is a beautifully structured blend of all three of those varietals, plus sangiovese, called Quadriga. Despite its Italian roots, the bulk of Brutocao's wines are more traditional varietals. Standouts include the Hopland Ranches zinfandel, a powerful yet restrained example of cool-climate zin, a very age-worthy cabernet, and a velvety syrah, all from local vineyards. Among the limited selection of whites, the crisp, steel-fermented sauvignon blanc stands out, but the two chardonnays are also nicely made and, like all the wines, nicely priced.

MILANO FAMILY WINERY

Just south of Hopland is what could be the local zoo but is actually the Milano Family Winery (14594 S. Hwy. 101, Hopland, 707/744-1396, www.milanowinery.com,

10 A.M.–5 P.M. daily, free tasting), where goats, geese, tortoises, and llamas share the limelight with both wine and the rustic former hop kiln that is home to the winery one of only a few remaining in Mendocino. Inside, the quirkiness continues as wines with names like Recall Red (a bargain-priced red blend), Sunshine (a light, fruity white), Risqué Rosé, and Big Ass Red (easy to guess the style of that one) are lined up in the simple but homey tasting room.

There was actually a big old fight over the Big Ass label in 2006. Milano had been granted a license to use the Big Ass name from the trademark owner, a Californian brewer, and got a little ticked when another California winery started using the same name without a license for some of its private-label wines. The case was kicked around the courts, generating lawsuits and countersuits, until both wineries settled their differences and agreed to each license and use the trademark.

Milano does a roaring trade in these and other fun and cheap wines but also makes plenty of more serious, powerhouse reds from traditional Rhône grape varietals. Standouts include the lush carignane and the rich syrah, which is sourced from McDowell's vineyards nearby. There are also usually a couple of late-harvest dessert wines to try.

SIGHTS
Grace Hudson Museum and Sun House

Artist Grace Carpenter Hudson and her ethnologist husband, John Hudson, built this charming craftsman-style redwood home (431 S. Main St., Ukiah, 707/467-2836, www .gracehudsonmuseum.org, 10 A.M.–4:30 P.M. Wed.–Sat., noon–4:30 P.M. Sun., $4) in 1911, just a few miles from the Potter Valley where Grace grew up. Her training as a painter and a deep interest in the local Pomo Indian culture started her career as a prolific painter and chronicler of Native American culture.

By the time of her death in 1937, she had completed almost 700 oil paintings and earned herself the nickname of "the painter lady."

COURTESY OF VISIT MENDOCINO COUNTY, INC.

the Sun House, Grace Carpenter Hudson's 1912 Craftsman-style redwood bungalow

MENDOCINO COUNTY

COURTESY OF VISIT MENDOCINO COUNTY, INC.

The City of Ten Thousand Buddhas is the largest Buddhist center in the United States

Docent-led tours throughout the day highlight some of those paintings together with various artifacts collected by the Hudsons over the years—as well as some of the quirky design elements of the house, such as hand-stenciled wallpaper. Grace and John were true bohemians long before Mendocino's modern alternative-lifestyle culture began in the 1960s. Their eclectic possessions give a fascinating glimpse into both Edwardian culture and regional history.

The addition of the Ivan B. and Elvira Hart Wing in 2001 vastly expanded the exhibit space at the museum and allowed the museum to exhibit more of Grace's paintings and the 30,000 artifacts the Hudsons collected over the decades. Probably the most important of those are the Pomo Indian baskets, which illustrate what has become something of a lost art. The galleries also host a number of temporary art and photography exhibits from local artists, highlighting the diversity of ethnic cultures in California. Outside the house and museum are several acres of landscaped gardens that offer a few secluded and shaded nooks for picnics.

City of Ten Thousand Buddhas

Just east of Ukiah, the small town of Talmage is home to a serene, 480-acre "city" (Talmage and East Side Rds., Talmage, 707/462-0939, www.cttbusa.org, 8 A.M.–6 P.M. daily), established in 1976 on the site of a former state hospital as part of the Dharma Realm Buddhist Association by the Venerable Master Hsuan Hua. It's a fascinating cultural window into the Buddhist way of life, and in keeping with Buddhist traditions, anyone is welcome. Enter under the three-arched Mountain Gate (the arches represent morality, concentration, and wisdom), sign in at the administration building, and explore the landscaped grounds and temples. The doors of the City are always open, and the monks regard it as a sanctuary for people of all religions.

The Ten Thousand Buddhas can be found literally around the walls of the ornate **Jeweled Hall of Ten Thousand Buddhas.** The center of the Hall is dominated by a giant statue of Guanyin Bodhisattva, with a thousand hands and a thousand eyes to better save all living

COURTESY OF VISIT MENDOCINO COUNTY, INC.

The Solar Living Center provides professional solar training and sustainability courses.

beings, according to Buddhist teachings. Each of the 10,000 small Buddhas were said to have been cast and carved by The Master himself over the course of 10 years. Although the exterior of the building still resembles the school gymnasium it once was, the monks transformed the interior into a sanctuary. Services at the Hall are open to all visitors and can be a mesmerizing way to forget the stresses of modern life.

The City is also one of the largest Buddhist communities in the West. It is home to the Dharma Realm Buddhist University, an elementary school, a monastery, and a cheerful restaurant called **Jyun Kang** (which means "to your health," noon–3 P.M. Wed.–Mon.), serving locally-grown pure vegetarian food free of MSG, meat, seafood, poultry, eggs, and pungent vegetables like onions, garlic, chives, and scallions.

◖ Solar Living Center

Only in Mendocino could a store devoted to off-grid lifestyles evolve into an educational alternative-lifestyle institute known the world over for promoting solar power and green living. The Real Goods Trading Company started out as a modest establishment in the town of Willets, north of Ukiah, in the late 1970s, selling some of the first commercial solar panels to the children of the counterculture. Real Goods is now owned by global green powerhouse Gaiam, but the spin-off Solar Living Center (13771 S. Hwy. 101, Hopland, 707/744-2017, www.solarliving .org, 10 A.M.–6 P.M. daily, free), established in 1998 just south of Hopland, is part of the nonprofit Solar Living Institute, which has lofty goals to change the way people live.

Visiting the 12-acre site is like stepping into the future, where life as we know it has long ceased to be sustainable. The parking lot includes hookups to recharge electric vehicles as well as a biodiesel fueling station. The curved pathway up to the center is alive with native plants and solar-powered water features, and the center itself is set around a shady circular courtyard surrounded by all manner of alternative-energy gizmos to play with. You almost expect everyone working there to be sporting long beards, hemp robes, and secret handshakes. Thankfully they're a pretty normal bunch of folks, albeit fiercely dedicated to green living.

The large store sells everything from bumper stickers for your Prius to giant arrays of the latest solar panels for your roof. In some ways it's more than just a green-living store and offers an insight into just how easy it can be to do your bit to save energy and prevent pollution. Many of the objects and implements are so mundane that they'll have you wondering why they're in such a store, but eventually it becomes clear. A normal insulated coffee mug that you can buy almost anywhere is more than a simple convenience, for example. It prevents you from wasting energy reheating a cold beverage. Other items are just plain fun, like the mini solar devices you can use to recharge cellphones or iPods.

The goal of the institute is ultimately to educate consumers on the importance of sustainable living and alternative sources of energy—to help the world "kick the oil habit." There are self-guided tours around the center's green living exhibits and the gardens, which represent a microcosm of the world's varied landscapes and vegetation (much of it edible) and make a few green statements. Don't miss the world's first solar-powered carousel, or the memorial car grove, where plants have taken over the rusting hulks of old 1960s gas-guzzlers. Guided tours (11 A.M. and 3 P.M. Fri.–Sun. Feb.–Nov., $3 suggested donation) of the site are offered and take about 50 minutes. More than 200 seminars and workshops are offered throughout the year, both here and at other California locations (see www.solarliving.org for details). They range from technical photovoltaic seminars to workshops on green building methods, recycling, and organic gardening.

EVENTS

Food and wine are the focus of events in this rural part of the world. Despite being a little off the beaten path, it is still Wine Country, after all. Like similar events in Northern Sonoma, the **Hopland Passport Weekend**
(www.hoplandpassport.com, first weekend in May and last weekend in Oct., tickets $35) is a chance for wineries in the area to throw a party. Tickets allow visitors to see as many wineries as they can over the weekend and sample wines, together with themed food and entertainment. There are fifteen wineries in the Hopland area, and a free shuttle runs among them on Saturdays. Two such weekends are held during the year when the weather is at its best.

Not to be outdone, Redwood Valley holds its own show-and-tell weekend, the **Taste of Redwood Valley** (www.atasteofredwoodvalley.com) over Father's Day weekend in June. You can taste the wines of a dozen local wineries at a special winemakers dinner ($55) or sample food, wines, and entertainment at each of the wineries during the weekend ($25). The area is not quite as compact and tour-friendly as Hopland, however, so make sure you have a designated driver.

Ukiah has a thriving community scene, and the culinary highlight of the year is the annual **Taste of Downtown** (707/462-4705, www.ukiahchamber.com, contact the Chamber of Commerce for the exact date, tickets $25–30), held on a Friday evening in early June. In addition to wine and beer tastings, local shops and musicians get in on the action.

RECREATION
Natural Springs

If you need a day off from wine tasting, you could combine a visit to Montgomery Woods with a dip in the warm pools of the **Orr Hot Springs Resort** (13201 Orr Springs Rd., Ukiah, 707/462-6277, day-use fee $25, reservation required). The experience is not for the shy, however, because this is a clothing-optional resort and bathing suits rarely make an appearance. The warm spring water feeds a bathhouse and several communal tubs. There's also a sauna and steam room, and a small spring-fed swimming pool, all surrounded by colorful gardens, a collection of low-slung, rustic redwood buildings, and mountain wilderness. Overnight stays in private rooms, cottages, or the resort's campsite are also available, as are half-hour massages. Be sure to stock up with personal luxuries before you leave Ukiah on the long and winding road because there is no store here.

A little more upscale (but not much) is the **Vichy Springs Resort** (2605 Vichy Springs Rd., Ukiah, 707/462-9515, www.vichysprings .com, day-use fee $50, two hours for $30) just east of Ukiah. It was established in the mid-1800s to take advantage of the naturally carbonated, warm mineral spring that runs through the grounds, and over the past century it has attracted a veritable who's-who of celebrities, from presidents and politicians to actors and literary luminaries like Mark Twain and Jack London. The waters are said to have a curative effect discovered by indigenous people centuries ago. Whether or not that's true, the surroundings are certainly relaxing and offer miles of hiking trails, including a half-hour hike to a waterfall with a natural plunge pool that's almost worth the price of the two-hour-use fee.

Back at the resort, the spring water is channeled into what's best described as a bathhouse, and also a small pool that's heated to a warmer temperature than the spring water's natural 90 degrees—refreshing on a hot summer day but less so in the middle of winter (it's the reason this is not a "hot" springs resort). In addition to the mineral pools, there's an 80-foot swimming pool that's open May–October, with water that is treated using odorless ozone instead of chlorine. Unlike Orr Hot Springs, clothing is a requirement at Vichy, but if you didn't pack a bathing suit you can rent them for $2. Overnight accommodation is also available.

Golf

Farmland, vineyards, hills, and redwoods tend to dominate the land in this part of Mendocino, so golf courses are few and far between. The only one of note is the **Ukiah Municipal Golf Course** (599 Park Blvd., Ukiah, 707/467-2832, www.ukiahgolf.com), an 18-hole par-70 course that is probably best known for its undulating greens, which make precision more important

than distance. Green fees range from $22 on a midweek afternoon to $30 for a regular weekend day.

ACCOMMODATIONS

Eastern Mendocino remains a less popular destination than most other parts of Northern California's Wine Country, despite its growing recognition as a world-class wine region. Although that makes it worth visiting before the number of wineries grows and the crowds inevitably increase years from now, it also results in some challenges if you plan to spend the night. Most of the accommodation options are national motel and cheap hotel chains in Ukiah geared toward travelers heading up the California coast on Highway 101. Other options tend to be targeted more at the backpackers that Mendocino has always attracted, so there are plenty of camping options. In between, there is precious little.

Booking early is not quite as important in this part of the world as it is in Napa or Sonoma. The best place to stay, if you can, is Hopland, because it is only a little more than a half-hour drive from many parts of northern Sonoma's Wine Country and even closer to the Redwood Valley near Ukiah. As such, it provides a relatively cheap base for a weekend spent exploring not only the local Mendocino wineries but also the Alexander Valley and Dry Creek Valley. The problem is that there are only a couple of dozen rooms in the whole town, so you'll need to plan ahead.

Ukiah-Area Motels

Ukiah is either blessed or cursed with more motels than a city this size probably needs. All the major chains are represented here as well as a handful of independent operators, and all are clustered around just a few freeway off-ramps or down the main drag in Ukiah, State Street. Easy as they are to access from the freeway, none of them are really within walking distance of the restaurants downtown, so driving is usually the only option if you plan to wine and dine at night. If you do drive to dinner, it's more important than ever that you choose a designated driver—there's usually a high-profile police presence on State Street.

The biggest chains are also the priciest and the most modern, usually with a decent-size swimming pool and a "continental breakfast" that stretches the term "breakfast" just a little. Rates are similar at all of them, starting at about $90 a night for a standard room and rising to $140 a night on summer weekends. They include the **Best Western Orchard Inn** (555 S. Orchard Ave., 707/462-1514), **Holiday Inn Express** (1720 N. State St., 707/462-5745), and the slightly more expensive **Hampton Inn** (1160 Airport Park Blvd., 707/462-6555), which can cost up to $180 a night in the summer.

Many of the smaller chains are strung along State Street and offer slightly cheaper accommodations in older, less well-equipped rooms. Rates in all of them start at around $50 a night for two people but can climb to around $100 a night on summer weekends. They include the relatively modern **Motel 6** (1208 S. State St., 707/468-5404), **Days Inn** (950 N. State St., 707/462-7584), and **Economy Inn** (406 S. State Street, 707/462-8611).

There are also a number of independent motels on State Street, the largest and best known of which is the **Discovery Inn** (1340 N. State St., 707/462-8873), a sprawling complex at the northern end of Ukiah (close to the Holiday Inn). It drives home the point with plenty of mountain-style decor, from carved redwood animal sculptures to rock-covered walls. Underneath all the kitsch is a well-equipped motel with all the same amenities as the larger chains (if not quite as squeaky clean) with the bonus of having probably the largest outdoor swimming pool in Ukiah. Rates at the Discovery Inn are similar to the Best Western and Holiday Inn, starting at around $80 for a double and rising to around $140 a night on peak weekends, but its quirky character and plentiful amenities make it a more attractive option for the money.

Under $150

Given its long history and location in the heart of tiny but thriving Hopland, the **◖ Hopland Inn** (13401 S. Hwy. 101, Hopland, 707/744-1890 or 800/266-1891, www.hoplandinn .com) is a rare bargain for Wine Country accommodations. You won't get many cutting-edge conveniences or modern design, but the warm, lived-in feeling of the Victorian building and communal spaces that seem stuck in time make a refreshing change from the often bland, pastiche Wine Country decor in hotels further south. The Hopland Inn is hard to miss in this three-block town. It was built in 1890 to provide lodgings for farmers and businessmen traveling from the Bay Area to Oregon and Washington; today there are 21 rooms, including a couple of suites, which range in price from $80 (off-season, midweek) to $140 a night. Cheaper deals are sometimes available in winter, but the hotel completely closes every January. A recent renovation spruced the place up and added a few more modern touches (wireless Internet access and air conditioning in all rooms), but half the rooms are still without televisions, perhaps due to the limited sound insulation in such an old building. Given the large, comfy bar and excellent organic restaurant, chances are you won't spend much time in the room anyway.

Only no-nonsense Mendocino could be home to a back-to-nature resort that manages to be an invigorating escape from modern life without being intimidating to meat-eating, Starbucks-sipping suburbanites. **Orr Hot Springs** (13201 Orr Springs Rd., Ukiah, 707/462-6277) is in the hills about 13 miles west of Ukiah and walks that fine line largely thanks to its remote, serene location and a fiercely loyal tribe of relatively young devotees that are as much hip as hippy. The biggest attractions here are the natural hot springs that feed the many soaking tubs and pools. Clothing is optional, and most opt to do without while soaking, but there is generally a little more modesty around the rest of the site. The shy would be well-advised to bring a robe.

The water from the springs flows constantly through the tubs and into the creek, so none of it needs to be chlorinated, but as a result of the lack of water treatment, no soap or shampoo is allowed in the showers or bathrooms.

Indeed, the atmosphere is decidedly rustic, as would be expected of a place that used to cater to the Victorian loggers who largely cleared the surrounding hills of their redwoods in the late 1800s. Just down the road is the Montgomery Woods State Reserve, which contains impressive old-growth redwoods that were spared the axe.

Lodging options at Orr are varied and include dorms, private rooms, cottages, and camping. The best options are the private rooms that cost from $135 midweek up to $155. Some have private bathrooms; others share bathrooms with one other room. There's also a well-equipped, 24-hour communal kitchen (which can get rather crowded at times), but if you plan to prepare your own meals, be sure to bring enough food (and any of life's little luxuries you might want overnight) because there's nowhere to buy anything closer than Ukiah, which is a 30-minute drive away.

The dozen motels that ring Ukiah dominate the town's lodging scene, but one B&B is alive and well and offers a charming Victorian alternative to the soulless chains. **Sanford House** (306 S. Pine St., Ukiah, 707/462-1653, www.sanfordhouse.com) is also in a far better location than any motel—just a few blocks from Ukiah's small downtown, and in walking distance to the best restaurants and cafés. The turreted, Queen Anne–style house was built in 1904 by a state legislator of the same name and still contains many of the original features, along with five guest rooms, each maintaining the Victorian theme with queen beds, private bathroom, air conditioning, wireless Internet access, and, of course, a far better breakfast than you'd ever get at a motel. Rates start at $95 midweek for single occupancy, while double occupancy rates start at $175 a night.

$150-250

The destination hotel in eastern Mendocino is **Vichy Springs** (2605 Vichy Springs Rd., Ukiah, 707/462-9515, www.vichysprings.com), a small, historic resort just east of Ukiah that combines a rustic charm that is typical Mendocino with prices more typical of Napa or Sonoma. The resort dates from the mid-1800s and has attracted a constant stream of the famous and not-so-famous to its baths and pools, which are filled by a naturally carbonated warm mineral spring. Other attractions include an 80-foot swimming pool and miles of hiking trails on the resort's hundreds of acres of land.

The basic Mountain View rooms are the cheapest at $195 a night (double occupancy), while the Creekside rooms and modest Applewood Suites start at $245 and Cottages run upward of $300 a night. Prices vary little by season, and discounts also seem to be relatively rare, so you'll be paying around the same in winter, when the pool is closed, as in summer, which is certainly the better season to take advantage of the hiking trails and refreshing pools. For the money, the amenities might seem a little sparse—this is not a luxury hotel by any means—but its location and history are pretty unique, and a filling breakfast is included.

Camping

With guaranteed warm weather during the summer months, camping in this part of the world is probably a more viable option than in other parts of Wine Country. The biggest and best campgrounds are found around **Lake Mendocino** just north of Ukiah. All are developed grounds with running water, toilets, and, in a couple of cases, showers, and all are within spitting distance of the lake itself, which provides plenty of recreational opportunities. All the sites also accept RVs up to 35 feet long, have fire rings and picnic tables, and are at least partly shaded. They might not be the most rustic or peaceful camping areas, but the scenic surroundings make up for it.

At the northern end of the lake, the **Ky-En** (meaning "duck" in Pomo, $20–22) campground is adjacent to the main visitor center and boat ramp, and accessed off Highway 20 and Marina Drive. It has 101 sites divided into two sections, with around 30 sites on the south side of Marina Drive closest to the lake and the remainder on the hillside on the other side of the road. The **Bu-Shay** (meaning "deer," #20) campground is accessed from the Inlet Road, a few miles beyond Marina Drive on Highway 20 just after the bridge. It's the biggest campground on the lake, with 164 sites, including several group camping areas. Both have coin-operated showers and flush toilets. Farther south, accessed from Mendocino Drive off Highway 101, is the smaller **Che-Ka-Ka** (meaning "quail," $16) campsite, with about 20 sites for tents or RVs. There are no showers here, and the sites are a little way up the hill from the lake.

To reserve spaces at any of the sites, visit www.reserveamerica.com and search for Lake Mendocino. Alternatively, you can book sites through the Army Corps of Engineers (877/444-6777, www.spn.usace.army.mil/mendocino).

Further south from the lake and just east of Ukiah is the **Cow Mountain Recreation Area** (contact Ukiah office of the Bureau of Land Management, 707/468-4000, www.blm.gov/ca/st/en/fo/ukiah/cowmtn.html) named for the longhorn cattle that once grazed the 50,000 acres now under the control of the Bureau of Land Management. There are a number of small primitive campsites here, but the downside is that the recreation area has more than 100 miles of dirt roads that are very popular with off-road bikers and drivers. Off-road vehicles are confined to the southern part of the recreation area, so those sites, which include **Red Mountain Campground,** are best avoided unless you happen to have dirt bikes in tow. The northern part of the land is geared more toward horse and foot traffic, mountain biking, and, in the fall, hunting, so it is generally quieter. The main campsite in this area is the **Mayacamas Campground,** but even this has only six sites with vault toilets. There's no running water and little in the way of shade, so it gets very hot in the summer.

Access to Cow Mountain is via the Talmage Road (off Highway 101 near Ukiah) to Talmage, then right on Eastside Road, then left on Mill Creek Road. The northern part of the area is a few miles farther, and the southern part about seven miles away. Given the primitive nature of the campgrounds and their remote location, there's no camping fee.

A more unusual camping experience can be found at **Orr Hot Springs** (13201 Orr Springs Rd., Ukiah, 707/462-6277, $45 midweek, $50 weekend), a rustic spa resort in the hills west of Ukiah. A dozen or so creekside sites are located right next to the rambling resort buildings. The camping fee also includes use of the spa facilities.

FOOD

Of the two main towns in this part of Mendocino's Wine Country, Ukiah has the most restaurants and the most diverse choices, catering to the city's equally diverse blue- and white-collar population. The best are clustered downtown around the courthouse, but there are many others strung north and south on State Street in the various anonymous strip malls, including just about every fast food chain you can think of. Hopland, by contrast, seems to have more than its fair share of high-quality restaurants for such a small town, and all are within a few blocks of one another.

Ukiah

The **Ukiah Brewing Company** (102 S. State St. on the corner of Perkins St., Ukiah, 707/468-5898, www.ukiahbrewingco.com, lunch and dinner daily, dinner entrées $16–32) is not just any old brewpub. This is earth-friendly Mendocino, after all. The cozy saloon-style restaurant and bar was certified as California's first (and the nation's second) organic restaurant in 2005, meaning that it goes further than most establishments that simply use "organic ingredients" in their dishes. Everything here, from the organically raised meat and vegetables down to the salt and pepper and even the cleaning products used in the kitchen, come from federally certified organic suppliers. Naturally, the many microbrews on offer here are also certified organic.

The food is typical of pub fare but well made, flavorful, and suited to the surroundings of dark wood and exposed brick. The lunch menu includes burgers and burritos, while the backbone of the dinner menu is steak, pasta, chicken, and a couple of vegetarian options. There is a short list of Mendocino wines here, but the brews take center stage.

Line up a row of tasting glasses to try all five of the beers made here (most of which are not sold anywhere else). They range from crisp pilsner to increasingly dark ales to the rich Coop's Stout that should keep Guinness drinkers happy. The pub is also a venue for local bands on weekend nights, when there's a cover charge after about 9 p.m. (and when the restaurant stops serving food).

More of a Wine Country vibe can be found at **Patrona** (130 W. Standley St., Ukiah, 707/462-9181, dinner Tues.–Sat., entrées $13–22, tapas $8–12), a bistro with perhaps the best wine list in Ukiah. Soothing colors, exposed brick, and well-spaced tables create a relaxed setting for the Italian-inspired dishes, with a touch of Wine Country sophistication and Mendocino ingredients. In addition to traditional entrées, the menu usually includes about a half-dozen tapas plates. The wine list is dominated by Mendocino wineries, with a smattering of Sonoma Central Coast and international wines but absolutely nothing from Napa Valley, perhaps because most Napa wines would not fit in the very reasonable $20–40 price range of most on the list here.

Better known as a take-out lunch spot for workers at the County Courthouse across the street, **Schat's Courthouse Bakery** (113 W. Perkins St., Ukiah, 707/462-1670, www.schats .com, breakfast and lunch Mon.–Sat., under $7) nevertheless has plenty of tables for breakfast- and lunchgoers who are not in a hurry. The bakery is owned by a family that must have flour in their blood—various branches of the Schats still run bakeries in the Netherlands (location for the family's roots) as well as in Cloverdale and Bishop in California. This out-post is relatively new but has quickly become part of Ukiah's fabric. The breakfast and lunch menu is the main draw.

If you feel the need to eat something other than American comfort food or Californian cuisine, there's a surprisingly good little sushi restaurant in Ukiah, beloved of many in the local wine industry, called **O'Haru** (570 N. State St., Ukiah, 707/462-4762, lunch and dinner Mon.–Sat., sushi $2–3, dinner entrées $6–12). In addition to the full menu of freshly prepared sushi and sashimi, there's a selection of dinner combinations, most seafood-based but a couple with meat. The lunch menu includes take-out box lunches for $5, ideal for a picnic with a bottle of Riesling or Rose.

Ellie's Mutt Hut and Vegetarian Café (732 S. State St., Ukiah, 707/468-5376) is a funky little place that, despite its name, does serve meat, including the hot dogs for which it's well known (and hence the "Mutt" in its name). There are, of course, plenty of vegetarian items on the reasonably priced, café-style menu, and a handful of tables inside and out. Alternatively, you can order food to go.

Hopland

Almost opposite the Hopland Brewery, the **Bluebird Café** (13340 S. Hwy. 101, Hopland, 707/744-1633, breakfast and lunch daily, din-ner Fri.–Sun., entrées $4–13) retains its 1960s family diner vibe in a building dating from 1870. It also continues to serve huge portions of classic diner fare that it's become relatively famous for, including perhaps the best all-American breakfasts in Mendocino. This is also a place for burger aficionados, with patties made from almost every species of ani-mal you can imagine, including buffalo and ostrich. You can also order food from here while enjoying a beer in the brewery across the road and if you're lucky it will be deliv-ered to you.

Italy is the main influence on the lunch and dinner menu of the **Crushed Grape Grille** (13500 S. Hwy. 101, Hopland, 707/744-2020, lunch and dinner Mon.–Sat., brunch Sun., dinner entrées $13–20), next to the Brutocao Cellars tasting room in the old schoolhouse building. The wood-fired oven is the defining feature, and the food is relatively straightfor-ward Italian fare, as is the atmosphere, with a rather unsubtle Italianate theme stamped on the otherwise plain surroundings. If possible, get a table out on the spacious deck overlooking the bocce courts. Best bets include anything out of that oven, including pizzas and oven-grilled steaks and ribs. The wine list is basic and, not surprisingly, dominated by Brutocao Cellars wines.

If a quick lunch is all you need and the thought of filling up on the massive portions at the Bluebird Café is too daunting, the tiny **Café Lima** (13275 S. Hwy. 101, Hopland, 707/744-1441) is your best choice. Its range of organic, made-to-order pannini sandwiches cost $7–9 and can either be made to go or enjoyed at the handful of tables inside and out on the boardwalk, just a few doors from the Graziano tasting room.

Picnic Supplies

If you're looking for sandwiches and baked goods to go in Ukiah, make a beeline for **Schat's Courthouse Bakery** (113 W. Perkins St., Ukiah, 707/462-1670) and join the line with lawyers, judges, and administrators from the county courthouse across the street. Most sandwiches cost less than $6, and there's usually freshly made bread and plenty of assorted pies available, too. Another option that might appeal more to vegetarians is to order food to go at **Ellie's Mutt Hut and Vegetarian Café** (732 S. State St., Ukiah, 707/468-5376) a half mile south, while Japanese food lovers might want to pick up a box lunch at **O'Haru** (570 N. State St., Ukiah, 707/462-4762), a few blocks north of the courthouse square.

If you'd prefer to create your own alfresco meal, the best grocery store in Ukiah is undoubtedly the **Ukiah Natural Foods Co-op** (721 S. State St., Ukiah, 707/462-4778, daily), in an anonymous strip mall just south of downtown. The store promotes local suppliers of organic food and has an espresso bar serving both coffee and plenty of non-caffeinated beverages like smoothies and juices. About the only thing you won't find here is meat, but carnivores can always skip across the road to Safeway.

In Hopland the options are more limited, and the best bet is to order a sandwich at the **Café Lima** (13275 S. Hwy. 101, Hopland, 707/744-1441), buy a bottle of wine at Graziano a few doors down, and head into the hills.

Fresh Produce

If you want to get your hands on some of Mendocino's famous organic bounty, Ukiah has a couple of **farmers markets** during the week in summer. The Saturday market (Alex Thomas Plaza, 8:30 A.M.–noon May–Oct., 9:30 A.M.–noon Nov.–Apr.) is the largest of them, and the largest farmers market in Mendocino County. It was also the first in California to be certified (back in 1977), a guarantee that you'll actually be buying directly from the farmer or grower. It's held at Alex Thomas Plaza, which is at Clay and School Streets, just a block west of State and three blocks south of the courthouse. A smaller market is held in the same location on Tuesdays (3–6 P.M. June–Oct.).

Year-round, you can also buy seasonal produce from local growers as well as other organic food at the **Ukiah Natural Foods Co-op** (721 S. State St., Ukiah, 707/462-4778, daily).

INFORMATION AND SERVICES

First stop in this part of Mendocino should be the **Ukiah Chamber of Commerce** (200 S. School St., Ukiah, 707/462-4705, www.ukiah chamber.com), a few minutes off the freeway in downtown Ukiah. The chamber is on the ground floor of a small office building, and down the hallway to the left you'll see racks brimming with every conceivable Mendocino magazine, brochure, map, and leaflet. If you need more specific information, stick your head into the office and ask for help during normal office hours. Wine-related information, including regional wine history and maps of the area, can be found on the website of the **Mendocino Winegrape and Wine Commission** (www .mendowine.com).

SIERRA FOOTHILLS

Gold has always been integral to the fabric of the Sierra Foothills. It was gold that initially brought throngs of people here in the 1850s seeking to stake their claims and make their fortunes. Today, people still flock to the Foothills in search of new discoveries. And perhaps the most surprising of those discoveries is the quality of the local wine.

Set in rugged, rolling pine-covered hills, the counties of El Dorado, Amador, and Calaveras are best known for historic Old West towns, such as Placerville, Sutter Creek, Jackson, and Murphys. "Charming" and "quaint" are the words most often used to describe these towns, some a mere whisper of their former glory, others nearly pristine from their gold rush days. Visitors wander main streets only a few blocks long and browse historic storefronts from the late 1800s, many with their original doors and windows. These are historic timepieces, silent witnesses to California's coming of age when people from across the globe contracted gold fever. Popular activities in the Foothills include cavern and mine tours, and outdoor recreation like river rafting and golf. But wine tasting is now moving quickly to the top of that list.

The foothills of the Sierra Nevada Mountain range are just an hour's drive east of Sacramento and less than two hours from Napa; just an hour from Lake Tahoe, and about three hours from Yosemite. Therein lies part of the allure; the Foothills are easy to reach, easy to get around, and haven't yet been discovered by crowds of tourists that frequent California's other wine regions.

That may be changing, as the profile of

© MICHAEL CERVIN

SIERRA FOOTHILLS

HIGHLIGHTS

◖ Miraflores Winery: Though you are in El Dorado County, the winery and tasting room will make you feel like you are in Italy (page 315).

◖ Rafting the American River: Class 3 and 4 rapids on the south fork of the American River get you outdoors and squarely in the middle of the beauty of the Foothills (page 322).

◖ Cooper Vineyards: The Cooper family has been farming in the Shenandoah Valley for over 100 years and that knowledge translates into some of the best wines coming out of Amador County (page 328).

◖ Sutter Gold Mine: Delving a mile underground at this working mine will give you an inkling of what it was like for the miners who drilled for gold 150 years ago (page 330).

◖ Lavender Ridge Vineyard: Taste Rhône wines, paired with an international selection of cheeses, inside a historic building in the heart of Murphys (page 339).

◖ Moaning Cavern: When you stand at the bottom of one of the largest natural caverns in California, you realize that the Statue of Liberty can fit inside with room to spare. You can also go cave spelunking under

the earth and fly on the zip lines above it (page 342).

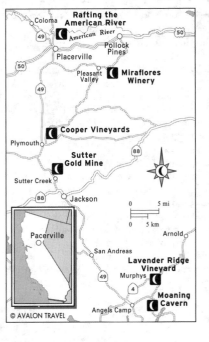

LOOK FOR ◖ TO FIND RECOMMENDED SIGHTS, ACTIVITIES, DINING, AND LODGING.

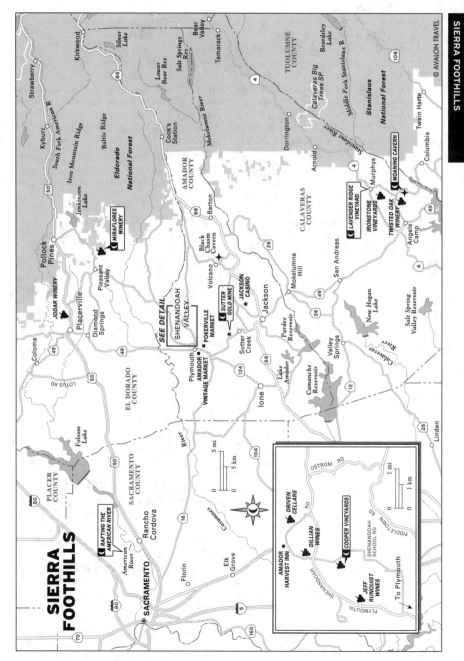

© AVALON TRAVEL

SIERRA FOOTHILLS

local wineries and the grape growers increase. They're realizing how to work with their fruit to maximize the quality of their wines. What were once "mom and pop" wineries are increasingly influenced by an influx of big money to develop state of the art production facilities. Some may decry this particular element of progress, but the wines overall have improved with greater competition and better technology. And small family-owned wineries still exist: At many local tasting rooms, the owners or winemakers will happily pour you a glass themselves.

As a judge at the Amador and El Dorado County Fair commercial wine competitions, I've witnessed the exponential growth of the wine industry as well as the new sophistication of the wines. More and more, wines produced from Napa to Paso Robles use fruit grown right here in the Foothills, a testament to the quality of the grapes.

Wine tasting in the Foothills is a great experience not only because of the picturesque hills and the historical backdrop, but also because of the exceptional value of the wines. You are guaranteed to leave with a case or two.

HISTORY

For some reason, the myth that Sutter Creek was ground zero for the discovery of gold in California still persists. The 1848 gold discovery was actually at Sutter's Mill in Coloma, El Dorado County. With the massive influx of people to the region in search of gold in the 1850s, enterprising men and women planted vineyards to make wine to sell to the miners. In many instances formerly drinkable water from the streams and rivers became heavily polluted by the mining operations; therefore cheap wine was often consumed more than water. California's gold rush began to fade by 1853 and the 49ers, most of whom now had no money, moved to San Francisco to seek their fortunes. Few wanted to live in the remote Foothills once the gold was gone. That mass exodus weakened one wine region, but spawned the growth of another: Napa.

A handful of wineries survived through the turn of the 20th century until Prohibition effectively killed off commercial wine making, leading to the early demise of the Foothills wine region. The local wine industry was resurrected in the early 1970s. Much of the farm and ranch land had been over-farmed, leaving top soil of dubious value, where little seemed to grow. Long-time ranchers looking for viable new crops looked back on their history and wondered, why not plant grapes? And the grapes thrived. The descendants of the first families to plant grapes over 100 years ago work the land today, with a newfound respect for their heritage.

PLANNING YOUR TIME

You can use any of the major towns here as a base from which to explore the whole region, be that Placerville in El Dorado County, Sutter Creek in Amador County, or Murphys in Calaveras County. Drive time, for example, from Murphys to Placerville is less than an hour. Most people explore the area by driving north or south on Highway 49. Highway 49 is a designated historic highway that connects with major east-west highways like Highway 50, which runs from Lake Tahoe to Sacramento. State Route 99, which also runs north-south, most notably from Central Valley cities like Bakersfield and Fresno, makes an easy drive as well. Route 12 near Lodi takes you right into Sutter Creek and Jackson in Amador County, and Highway 4 runs directly into Murphys.

Over a three-day weekend, it's easy to spend one day in each of these main towns and get a reasonable Foothills experience. Ideally, two days in each county is best, not only to visit the wineries, but also walk the towns, explore the caves, and get outdoors. Traffic increases during the summer months, though by comparison to other California wine regions, the Foothills is the least crowded. But bear in mind that Highway 49 is a two-lane road, as are many of the other roads in the area, meaning it can take time to get from point to point. Most of locals drive at the speed limit or just under; there is no need to rush in the Foothills.

The Foothills are hot in the summer months,

ONE-DAY WINE TOUR: THE SIERRA FOOTHILLS

Make the most of the Foothills by visiting all three counties. If you are heading south, begin in El Dorado County with **Jodar Vineyards & Winery,** near Placerville, for sangiovese and great views. A 20-minute drive will get you to Fair Play; make an appointment in advance at **Cedarville Vineyard** for a personal tasting with the winemaker. Their cabernet sauvignon is the best in the county.

Another 20-minute drive takes you directly into the Shenandoah Valley. Pre-order a picnic lunch from **Amador Vintage Market,** then bring that to **Cooper Vineyards** and pair it with their amazing barbera and viognier.

Stop by **Jeff Runquist Wines** on the way out of the valley for killer petite sirah and make your way to Murphys, about 30 minutes south. Swing by **Lavender Ridge Winery** first so you can get a little cheese with your grenache blanc and mourvèdre, then walk a few yards to **Newsome-Harlow Wines** to finish off the day with bold zinfandels and a nice Muscat blanc.

You've earned dinner, so walk to **Alchemy Market & Café,** then spend the night at the **Dunbar House.** You'll wake up to a fabulous breakfast, a perfect ending to a trip in the Foothills.

---

typically in the high 90s, and cold in the winter, with a dusting of snow at higher elevations, in places like Fair Play and Murphys. This is a thick, heavy, wet snow that burns off in a matter of hours or days, referred to as "concrete snow," by locals. The fall and spring, with milder weather, are the best times to visit. Because these are small communities, it's not uncommon for businesses to have seasonal hours, or to open later or close earlier than listed times. If foot traffic is slow, some wineries and shops will simply lock the door and leave as much as an hour prior to their official closing times.

El Dorado County

More than five dozen wineries sprang up in El Dorado County after gold was discovered at Coloma in 1848, a mere eight miles from the county's major town, Placerville. By the end of the Civil War, the region was one of the largest wine producing areas in all of California. But the wines faded as the gold faded, and the industry sat dormant for the most part until new plantings began in the early 1970s.

Today, agriculture continues to define El Dorado County. Apple orchards, berry patches, and tree farms support places like Camino, Apple Hill, and Fair Play with a wealth of fresh fruits and vegetables. And the wine industry is enjoying a resurgence: While there are still fewer acres of grapes planted here currently than there were in the late 1880s, the area is producing some exceptional wines. The elevation of the region ranges from 1,200 to 3,500 feet above sea level, which aids in the acidity levels of the grapes, creating more complexity. About 50 different varieties are planted throughout El Dorado County including the usual suspects like zinfandel, the best-known red; as well as syrah, barbera, cabernet sauvignon; and the most ubiquitous white, viognier; followed by chardonnay and pinot gris. But there are also oddball varieties such as charbono, refosco, and vermentino.

In keeping with the area's Wild West feel, the largest town in the county, Placerville, is affectionately known as Hangtown; there were three confirmed hangings at a tree near 305 Main Street (now a closed brick building).

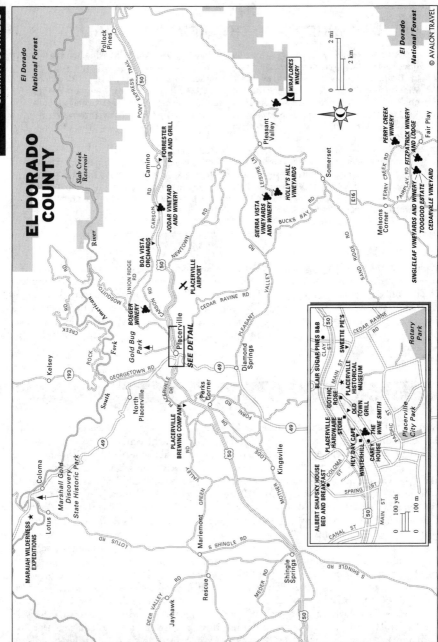

EL DORADO COUNTY

© AVALON TRAVEL

Although three fires in 1856 wiped out most of the town, a few old stone and brick buildings survive to this day, and the town does what it can to preserve the Old West quality for visitors. The town looks much as it did at the turn of the 20th century, despite an influx of trendy restaurants and shops that cater to visitors from the San Francisco Bay Area. You get to know Placerville by walking its downtown: it's slow going as people meander in and out of the shops and the tasting rooms, taking time for leisurely meals and idle conversation.

To visit wineries, caves, mines, and other sights beyond downtown Placerville, you'll need to drive to Camino (5 minutes east of downtown, with wineries widely dispersed) and Fair Play (30 minutes south of downtown, with wineries heavily concentrated). Services are also available in larger communities east of Placerville, like Folsom and El Dorado Hills, which have their roots more in the sprawl of the Sacramento suburbs than the gold rush.

WINE-TASTING

Most wineries in the Placerville and Fair Play areas do not charge a tasting fee…yet. Any tasting fees listed are for reserve wines, meaning that standard tasting lists are complimentary, unless otherwise noted.

Placerville
THE WINE SMITH

It's not a winery, but The Wine Smith (346 Main St., Placerville, 530/622-0516, www .thewinesmith.com, 11 A.M.–closing Mon.– Sat., noon–closing Sun., tasting $6) should be your first stop for a day of El Dorado wine-tasting. Maybe they won't know your name when you walk in the door, but this friendly wine store located right downtown is known as "the Cheers of Placerville." Take a seat at the small bar or on the narrow outdoor patio. You'll find mainly Foothills wines here to taste, including whites, reds, and dessert wines from predominantly small wineries with no tasting room, but also wines from Napa and even Santa Barbara. They also pour eight beers on tap and have a

stagecoach rides in Placerville

© MICHAEL CERVIN

dozen more in bottles, both foreign and domestic. Their multiple wine clubs incorporate wines from throughout the Foothills. They offer cheese and salami plates as well. It's no wonder that many people stop in and find it hard to leave.

BOEGER WINERY
As you enter the grounds of Boeger Winery (1709 Carson Rd., 530/622-8094, www .boegerwinery.com, 10 A.M.–5 P.M. daily, reserve tasting $10), you're struck by the beautiful green vines set on rolling hills against the ochre-colored earth. The fantastic scenery draws many visitors: Mature trees shade several picnic benches with views of the landscaped gardens and vineyards. The Italian-themed tasting room is spacious enough to hold large groups. You can taste six wines for free, so mix it up with whites and reds. Their sauvignon blanc and Riesling are both very nice. For reds there is the classic jammy zinfandel; barbera; cabernet sauvignon; and one of the best blends, Real Deal Red, made from four different grapes. All of their wines,

with the exception of Walker petite sirah and Walker zinfandel, are estate, including the pinot noir. The back deck has wonderful views of the surrounding mountains.

LAVA CAP WINERY
Started in 1981, Lava Cap Winery (2221 Fruitridge Rd., 800/475-0175, www.lavacap .com, 11 A.M.–5 P.M. daily, reserve tasting $5) has won many wine competitions, becoming one of the best known wineries in the area as a result. You'll notice the medals and ribbons dangling from the ceiling in the otherwise unimpressive tasting room. They are one of the largest producers in the area, making about 20 different wines. Try their calling-card petite sirah, the chardonnay (one of the best from El Dorado County), and the very good viognier. Cabernet sauvignon, merlot, pinot noir, zinfandel, barbera, and grenache are also available, along with several blended wines. The outdoor deck offers wonderful views. Occasional 30-minute tours are available on weekends; call ahead for their schedule.

the view from the deck at Lava Cap Winery

© MICHAEL CERVIN

© MICHAEL CERVIN

Miraflores Winery is patterned after a Tuscan villa.

MIRAFLORES WINERY

With 40 acres under vine, Miraflores Winery (2120 Four Springs Trail, Placerville, 530/647-8505, www.mirafloreswinery.com, 10 A.M.–5 P.M. daily) produces a wide range of wines including muscat canelli, viognier, petite sirah, and syrah. Some of their standouts are pinot grigio, dry syrah rose, an excellent barbera, and, of course, zinfandel. They are also making a dynamite mourvèdre I tasted in barrel. Their brand new Tuscan tasting room is exceptional: the solid cross timbers were pulled from the Oakland Ferry building, and the stone floors are actual stone, not stained concrete. They offer monthly cooking classes and a slew of special events.

JODAR VINEYARDS AND WINERY

Jodar Vineyards and Winery (3405 Carson Ct., Placerville, 530/644-3474, www.jodar winery.com, 11 A.M.–5 P.M. daily) makes an excellent sangiovese that's delicate and soft. They also produce chardonnay, petite sirah, pinot gris, and a delightful, mild cabernet sauvignon.

Most of the wines are 100 percent varieties and a vast majority of their fruit is estate. Fruit that is not estate is purchased from within the Foothills. Their tasting room is small and unpretentious, with a compact bar and few furnishings. The best views are from a grassy area in front of the entrance, where you can see Blakely Lake and the surrounding pines. They offer a food pairing every weekend.

MADROÑA

Named after the madrone tree in the middle of the vineyard, Madroña (2560 High Hill Rd., Camino, 530/644-5948, www.madrona vineyards.com, 11 A.M.–5 P.M. daily, reserve tasting $5) produces wines made from fruit grown on the estate, including a very good merlot and nebbiolo; chardonnay, zinfandel, and malbec are also available. A majority of their wines are under $20. Second-generation owners Maggie and Paul Bush are very hands-on, and offer a number of events throughout the year, including blending seminars, new wine release parties, and music and art weekends.

Environmentalists will be pleased to know that the entire operation runs on solar power.

SIERRA VISTA VINEYARDS AND WINERY

The aptly named Sierra Vista Vineyards and Winery (4560 Cabernet Way, Placerville, 800/946-3916, www.sierravistawinery.com, 10 A.M.–5 P.M. daily) look out to the often snow-covered Sierra Nevada Mountains in the near distance. Their flagship wine, Flour de Montagne, is a Châteauneuf-du-Pape–style blend of syrah, grenache, mourvèdre, and cinsault; it's soft and mild, not a tannic bruiser. Also notable is the spicy, medium-bodied Red Rock Ridge syrah. Pine trees and seasonal flowers ring the shaded grassy picnic area.

HOLLY'S HILL VINEYARDS

Located next to Sierra Vista, Holly's Hill Vineyards (3680 Leisure Ln., Placerville, 530/344-0227, www.hollyshill.com, 10 A.M.–5 P.M. daily) emphasizes Rhône wines like viognier, roussanne, and grenache noir. Their viognier is excellent, as is their flagship wine, El Dorado Patriarche, a blend of mourvèdre, syrah, grenache, and counoise. They always offer at least one library wine—something six or more years old—and, of course, the ubiquitous zinfandel. The small, unadorned tasting room has lovely views of Mt. Aukum, one of the tallest peaks in the area. You might prefer to lounge on the deck to take in the views of the tree-covered mountains.

Fair Play

Located 30 minutes south of Placerville, down Cedar Ravine Road, Fair Play is officially recognized as a distinct AVA (American Viticulture Area). It's become a popular wine in part because it's surrounded by pine trees and rolling mountains. Lodgings and restaurants in Fair Play are few, so most people base themselves in Placerville and visit Fair Play as a day trip.

SINGLELEAF VINEYARDS AND WINERY

No-frills Singleleaf Vineyards and Winery

© MICHAEL CERVIN

Mountain driving in Fair Play comes with hazards.

(7480 Fair Play Rd., Fair Play, 530/620-3545, www.singleleaf.com, 11 A.M.–5 P.M. Wed.–Sun.) is a labor of love for owner Scott Miller, who spent over two years clearing the property, planting the vineyards, and building the winery, which opened to the public in 1993. All of that hard work has resulted in a terrific, nicely balanced barbera, a crisp non-oaked chardonnay, and silky viognier. Zinfandel, malbec, and ports are also available for tasting.

FITZPATRICK WINERY AND LODGE

In the 1980s, Fitzpatrick Winery and Lodge (7740 Fair Play Rd., Fair Play, 530/620-3248, www.fitzpatrickwinery.com, 11 A.M.–5 P.M. Thurs.–Mon.) was the first winery to implement organic farming before it became popular. Owner Brian Fitzpatrick is a farmer at heart; it shows in his passion for the grapes, and in the diversity of wines here, from a very nice rose and petite sirah to several well done dessert and port wines, nearly every one under

$20. Located inside the lodge, the tasting room also serves a few bottled Irish beers and Irish cheeses. Be sure to check out the great views from the massive deck.

TOOGOOD ESTATE WINERY

The wine caves built into the hillside at Toogood Estate Winery (7280 Fair Play Rd., Fair Play, 530/620-1910, www.toogoodwinery .com, 11 A.M.–5:30 P.M. daily, tasting $5) are pretty cool, figuratively and literally. They're not historic caves from the gold rush days—they're constructed out of shotcrete—but they make an interesting tasting room. Toogood produces a very nice petite verdot as a stand-alone varietal. Their cabernet franc and nine-year old tawny port are also good. They also produce viognier, primitivo syrah, and pinot noir.

LATCHAM VINEYARDS

Founder Frank Latcham started Latcham Vineyards (2860 Omo Ranch Rd., Somerset, 800/750-5591, www.latcham.com, 11 A.M.–5 P.M. Thurs.–Mon., by appt. Tues.–Wed.) back in 1981 as a retirement project after he left the San Francisco Bay Area. It quickly grew into a full-fledged business. An old chicken coop houses the tasting room—it's as unpretentious as it sounds, with pressboard walls. Current owner John Latcham, Frank's son, used to work on his tractor in this building, and there are still oil stains on the concrete floor. They make a very good cabernet franc and barbera; but their best wine is the reserve zinfandel, a big jammy wine with hefty tannins and acidity. They also make both a stainless steel chardonnay and a traditional oak and butter version, along with pinot grigio and port. There's a small fenced picnic area under a lone oak tree.

WINDWALKER VINEYARD

Windwalker Vineyard (7360 Perry Creek Rd., Fair Play, www.windwalkervineyard .com, 11 A.M.–5 P.M. daily) makes 29 different wines—more than anyone else in the county—and buys fruit from 22 different growers. After a succession of owners and about 10,000 cases,

their wines are better than ever. Their cabernet franc, merlot, zinfandel (from 50–70 year old vines), and viognier are all noteworthy. Many

APPLE HILL: ORCHARDS AND FARMERS MARKETS

The Apple Hill area, just five miles east of downtown Placerville, right off Highway 50, is an area ripe with orchards, vineyards, and even Christmas tree farms. It's become a great place for a family day trip. Pick your own fruit or purchase local fruit at seasonal roadside stands.

Stop by the roadside market at **Boa Vista Orchards** (2952 Carson Rd., Placerville, www.boavista.com, 530/622-5522, 9 A.M.–5 P.M. daily), one of the few large ranches open year-round. Picnic tables out front offer a nice place to enjoy their wares, which include fruits, nuts, jams, jellies, apple butter, and even fresh baked turnovers and pies made with their fruit.

Ten-acre farm **Pine O Mine** (2620 Carson Rd., Placerville, 530/344-0288, 8 A.M.–6 P.M. daily) makes an ideal family outing. It is one of the few places where you can still pick your own fruit: In the summer months, fill up your pail with blueberries and strawberries; in the fall, pick apples off the trees and cut pumpkins right off the vine. Barbecue is often available on weekends.

El Dorado County also offers several farmers markets. The **Placerville market** (Main St. and Cedar Ravine, 530/622-1900, www.eldoradofarmersmarket.com, 8 A.M.–noon Sat. May–Oct.) is located downtown. You'll find not only fresh fruits and veggies, but flowers and fresh baked breads, preserves, and pies, all local. There are also two markets in **El Dorado Hills** (530/622-1900, www.eldoradofarmers market.com; El Dorado Hills Blvd. and Harvard Way: 8 A.M.–noon Thurs. June–Sept.; El Dorado Hills Blvd. at Highway 50: 9 A.M.–1 P.M. Sun. June–Oct.), about 20 miles west of Placerville.

of the wines are produced in small lots, a few hundred cases of each, and they sell quickly. Winemaker James Taff started out making wine at home, got married on the deck in front of the tasting room, and today he owns the place.

CEDARVILLE VINEYARD

Cedarville Vineyard (6320 Marestail Rd., Fair Play, 530/620-9463, www.cedarvillevineyard.com, by appointment only) is one of the best wineries in all of El Dorado County, with the best cabernet sauvignon around and a superior viognier. After stints at Cakebread Winery in Napa and Smith & Hook in Monterey, owner Jonathan Lachs approaches wine-making with power and finesse. All fruits are farmed organically and hand harvested prior to crushing. Jonathan or his wife Mary will give you their personal attention; Cedarville is open by appointment.

PERRY CREEK WINERY

Perry Creek Winery (7400 Perry Creek Rd., Fair Play, 530/620-5175, www.perrycreek.com, 11 A.M.–5 P.M. daily) is best known for their Zinman zinfandel, an inexpensive and very pleasing wine, which accounts for half of their annual production. Using mainly estate fruit (they buy chardonnay grapes), they produce a decent roster of wines including a nice, viscous viognier and a strawberry-laden rose, as well as syrah, cabernet, and barbera. They pour six-ounce wines by the glass, and stock a full deli case, which, along with the grassy area and covered porch, makes this a good spot for a picnic. Perry Creek is the largest producer of wines in the Fair Play AVA at only 15,000 cases—which gives you an idea of how small the region actually is. With advance scheduling, occasional tours are offered on weekends.

SIGHTS
Placerville Historical Museum

Located right downtown, the Placerville Historical Museum (524 Main St., 530/626-0773, 11 A.M.–4 P.M. Wed.–Sun., free) is housed in the oldest standing building on Main Street, which dates back to 1852. The

The Placerville Historical Museum is housed in the oldest building in Placerville.

© MICHAEL CERVIN

COLORFUL CHARACTERS OF THE GOLD RUSH

During the California gold rush tens of thousands of people descended into the Sierra Foothills to make their fortune in gold, silver, or by providing lodging and services – virtually anything, as long as it made money. Inevitably, certain key figures emerged during this tumultuous period. One of the key personalities was **Black Bart,** the gentleman robber. His real name was Charles E. Bolton, a respected San Francisco citizen who committed 28 robberies against Wells Fargo stagecoaches before he was finally arrested. He never took the personal belongings of the stagecoach passengers, only the bank loot, and it was said he was personable, even polite, when committing his crimes. He was known to have stayed at the **Murphys Historic Hotel** and you can stay in the room he once occupied.

The name **John Sutter** will always be linked with the discovery of gold, though Sutter himself did not discover it, John Marshall did. But the gold was found at **Sutter's Mill,** a sawmill on the banks of the American River in Coloma. Originally from Switzerland, Sutter was never a good businessman and racked up debts throughout most of his life. Generous and kind, he was often taken advantage of by the unscrupulous people he hired. He was granted 50,000 acres of land where the American River and the Sacramento River meet. He crafted a town nearby that he called New Helvetia, what we now know as Sacramento. He fought for California statehood, worked with Russia to secure Fort Ross, and gave aid to immigrants in the area. His name is nearly everywhere in the Foothills. He was broke when he died in 1880.

The most singularly well known personality of the gold rush however was **Mark Twain,** who migrated from San Francisco to the Foothills in the early 1860s and wrote about the mining life. While visiting friends in **Angels Camp** he heard a story about a frog jumping contest and how one frog lost because someone had fed the frog buckshot. Twain then penned "The Celebrated Jumping Frog of Calaveras County," which a magazine published, and Twain became a media sensation and eventually an American icon.

small two-story museum displays early photographs of the period furniture, glass bottles, and even a piece of the hangman's tree that made Placerville's reputation. The exterior and interior brick- and stonework are outstanding examples of how buildings were constructed during the gold rush.

Gold Bug Mine

Located in Gold Bug Park, five minutes north of downtown Placerville, Gold Bug Mine (2635 Gold Bug Ln., 530/642-5207, www.goldbug park.org, 10 A.M.–4 P.M. daily Apr.–Oct., noon–4 P.M. Sat.–Sun. Nov.–Mar., adults $5, children 10–17 $3, children 3–9 $2) is one of the few mining sites where you can still see how a real mine and stamp mill run. About 12,000 mines operated throughout California during the heyday of the gold rush. Gold Bug Mine first opened in 1888, although the nearby

creek was mined for gold as early as 1848. Self-guided tours take you nearly 360 feet deep into the mountain. The mine is well lit: You can see chisel marks on the rock walls, as well as veins of quartz and what looks like gold. The tunnel is rugged and coarse; all visitors are required to wear a hard hat. The mine is 56 degrees year-round, making it a great spot to hang out during the hot summer months. Located just above the mine is a replica of a 1900s stamp mill, sitting on the site of the original. Stamp mills were used to crush hard rocks to extract the valuable minerals inside. There's also an interesting collection of minerals from around the world on display.

Marshall Gold Discovery State Historic Park

John Marshall discovered gold on January 24, 1848, a date that irrevocably changed

California. Visit the place where it all began at the Marshall Gold Discovery State Historic Park (State Hwy. 49, Coloma, 530/622-3470, www.parks.ca.gov, 8 A.M.–7 P.M. daily summer, 8 A.M.–5 P.M. daily Labor Day–Memorial Day, closed on major holidays). The 280-acre park, which hugs the American River along State Highway 49, north of Placerville, contains the actual old town of Coloma. Its buildings include an old jail, the post office in use since the 1850s, the original Catholic church, and replicas of John Marshall's cabin and Sutter's Mill (not on its original site, which was on the banks of the river). The blacksmith shop is staffed by volunteer blacksmiths who demonstrate the use of a hammer on an anvil, in spite of the intense heat from the forge, and tell stories of the gold rush days. The **Gold Discovery Museum and Visitor Center** (310 Back St., Coloma, 530/622-3470, www.parks.ca.gov, 10 A.M.–3 P.M. Tues.–Sun., $8) has maps of the area as well as displays on mining, and runs half a dozen short films about the area, the original indigenous community, and the impact that the discovery of gold had on the state. There are three picnic sites, but no camping is allowed inside the park.

ENTERTAINMENT AND EVENTS
Live Music
The cozy atmosphere at **Powell's Steamer** (425 Main St., Placerville, 530/626-1091, www.powellssteamer.com, Mon.–Thurs. 11 A.M.–10 P.M., Fri.–Sat. 11 A.M.–11 P.M., Sun. noon–10 P.M.) is conducive to the music. Live bands play folk, rock, and blues on Thursday and Saturday. Sunday afternoons are jazz time, with a trio jamming laid back cords. Wednesday and Friday are karaoke nights. In addition to food, the bar features 24 draft beers, bottled beer, and wines by the glass.

Both a coffee bar and a performance space, **Cozmic Cafe** (594 Main St., Placerville, 530/642-8481, www.ourcoz.com, 7:30 A.M.–6 P.M. Sun.–Wed., 7:30 A.M.–8 P.M.

Thurs.–Sat.) features local bands Friday–Sunday nights. Concerts usually start at 8 P.M.; the average cost is about $8. If you're feeling brave, try the free open mic night at 7:30 P.M. every Thursday during the summer months. The space itself has an interesting history: It was built in 1897 as a bottling room for the soda works factory below it. An authentic, historic mine in the back of the building was once used to store ice, butter, vegetables, and so on. Today, you can sip your drink in the mine's chiseled-out remains, which go 150 feet back into the earth.

Bars and Brew Pubs
Every town needs a dive bar and Placerville has **Liars Bench** (255 Main St., 530/622-0494, daily 8 A.M.–1 A.M.). The long narrow space is mainly populated by locals eager for conversation. At the far end of the tight room is a pool table and in between is a long wood bar. It's not too much to look at but it is pure dive and the drinks are reasonably priced.

Placerville Brewing Company (155 Placerville Dr., 530/295-9166, www.placerville brewing.com, 11 A.M.–9 P.M. Wed.–Mon., $15) is less bar and more family place. Yes, they brew up about 12 different beers on tap and seasonal ones, but it feels more like a nice coffee shop than a brewery. They also have games and toys for the kids in the back. If you didn't see the fermentation tanks behind the large plate glass windows, you would never know it's a microbrewery. The strong blond, golden ale, and stout are the best bets, but if you can't decide, get the sampler: eight beers for nine bucks. Yes, there's food: Beer battered fish and chips are a favorite.

Festivals and Events
The **El Dorado County Fair** (100 Placerville Dr., 530/631-5860, www.eldoradocounty fair.org, adults $8; children 7–12 and seniors 60 and up $6; children under 6 and military in uniform free) runs the third week of June each year. It's one of the largest gatherings in the Sierra Foothills, attracting 65,000 people. The four-day event has a packed

schedule: Expect live bands, a wine competition, minerals and gems, quilts, book signings by local authors, and, of course, lots of animals and agriculture.

The **Fair Play Wine Festival** (www.fairplay wine.com, first weekend in June, $25) is a great opportunity to explore the Fair Play AVA, with all of the wineries open at the same time (which is not the case the rest of the year). It started in 1984 with just 3 wineries, but today has expanded to about 15. It's a day of open houses where each winery offers something different, including food, music, wine specials, and barrel tastings.

SHOPPING

Modern shopping malls are available in nearby Folsom and El Dorado Hills, but Placerville's Main Street offers shopping with a historic twist.

The **Gold Country Artists Gallery** (379 Main St., Placerville, 530/642-2944, www. goldcountryartistsgallery.com, 11 A.M.–5 P.M. daily) is a two story co-op, with about 45 local artists showcasing everything from traditional oil painting to plein air, pottery, photography, ceramics, jewelry, and even sculpture. It's a low-key vibe where you can wander and browse without feeling pressured to buy.

At the **Black Oak Antiques Mall** (460 Main St., Placerville, 530/295-1761, 10 A.M.–5 P.M. daily) you'll find seven different vendors located inside one building, including country antiques, lamp restorers (for many of the original lamps and shades in the area), and clock and watch repair and sales. The vendors are a small collection of local people specializing in mainly restorative works.

When is a hardware store not just another hardware store? When it's **Placerville Hardware** (441 Main St., Placerville, 530/622-1151, 8 A.M.–6 P.M. Mon.–Sat., 9 A.M.–5 P.M. Sun.), originally built in 1852, and the oldest continuously operated hardware store west of the Mississippi. The floors are original hardwood and the rolling ladders are from the 1860s. Some of the original built-

ins for the hardware are also still in use. You can find almost anything here: both plastic and metal gold mining pans, hunting knives, even sunglasses.

Winterhill (321 Main St., 530/626-6369, www.winterhillfarms.com, 10 A.M.–6 P.M. Mon.–Sat., 11 A.M.–5 P.M. Sun.) is packed with specialty olive oils from local farmers. They only sell extra virgin oils from the current harvest; there are usually nine oils for sampling, with varieties like basil, Meyer lemon, and Persian lime. Local jams, jellies, and chutneys, with flavors like garlic thyme and raspberry jalapeno, are also available for tasting and sale. Park yourself at the tasting bar, dipping little pieces of bread into the wonderfully flavorful oil.

If you are in the mood for mischief, step into the **Gothic Rose** (484 Main St., Placerville, 530/259-0703, www.gothicroseantiques.com, 11 A.M.–5 P.M. Thurs.–Sun.). You'll find dark and macabre clothing, daggers, potion bottles, and skull jewelry. It's definitely a change of pace from gold mines and wineries.

There's a sort of spiritual overtone at **Empress** (582 Main St., Placerville, 530/621-4030, 11 A.M.–5 P.M. Thurs.–Sun.), which offers gypsy wear, belly dance outfits, and lingerie. Think funky, flowy dresses and sheer skirts. You'll also find incense, henna tattoo kits, and candles.

The **Placerville Clothing Company** (327 Main St., Placerville, 530/626-3554, 10 A.M.–5 P.M. Mon.–Sat., 10 A.M.–6 P.M. Sun.) has clothing for men and women, with both summer and winter clothing from the likes of Patagonia, Royal Robbins, and Tommy Bahama.

As the name suggests, **The Bookery** (326 Main St., Placerville, 530/626-6454, www .gothicroseantiques.com, 10 A.M.–5:30 P.M. Mon.–Thurs., 10 A.M.–7 P.M. Fri.–Sat., 10 A.M.–4 P.M. Sun.) has books stacked everywhere, even on the floor; watch your step. The helpful staff can locate most anything you need. Jackie the dog is less helpful; though, she occasionally wanders the store as well.

© MICHAEL CERVIN

rafting the American River

SPORTS AND RECREATION
◀ Rafting the American River

Gold was first discovered on the American River, but chances are you won't find any on your rafting trip. You will, however, experience the smell of pine trees and crisp clean fresh water from the Sierra Nevada snowmelt. After heavy snows, the river can develop class 4 rapids. But since the river is wide and fairly shallow, you can also enjoy a leisurely float. Trips can be as short as half a day and as long as a week; many are family oriented and make a great group activity.

Whitewater Connection (7237 Hwy. 49, Coloma, 800/336-7238, www.whitewater connection.com) offers one- and two-day rafting trips through the south fork of the American River, beginning eight miles north of Placerville and running through Coloma. Class 3 rapids are typical. Half-day trips start at $94.

Mariah Wilderness Expeditions (7170 Hwy. 49, Coloma, 800/462-7424, www.mariah rafting.com) offers one- and two-day rafting trips as well, but also half day trips for those

who can't afford too much time. They have been in business since 1982 so they know the river well. Prices start at $65 per person and kids as young as four can participate.

Golf

Don't be alarmed by the cemetery you pass when entering **Bass Lake Golf Course** (3000 Alexandrite Dr., Rescue, 530/677-4653, www .basslakegolfcourse.com, green fees $25–34), unless your game is really bad. This 18-hole, par 72 course has a beautiful tree line at the far end of the 30 stall driving range. There's also a pro shop and grill on site. From the 10th tee you can see Sacramento. The golf course is located 11 miles west of Placerville in the small residential community of Rescue.

Built into the hills, **Apple Mountain Golf Resort** (3455 Carson Rd., Camino, 530/647-7400, www.applemountaingolfresort.com, green fees $49–69) is hands-down gorgeous, surrounded by pristine landscaping and plenty of pine trees. Alpacas are available as beasts of burden to carry your clubs. They're easygoing,

© MICHAEL CERVIN

Alpacas haul your clubs at Apple Mountain Golf Resort.

docile animals—and they won't judge your shots either. Because it's a hilly course, alpacas are far superior to golf carts. Be sure to request them in advance. The course is in Apple Hill, five miles east of Placerville.

ACCOMMODATIONS
$100-200

Two massive sycamore trees flank the entrance of (**Albert Shafsky House Bed & Breakfast** (2942 Coloma St., Placerville, 530/642-2776, www.shafsky.com, $140–180 d), which offers three bedrooms in a 1902 Victorian. Inside, the warm wood wainscoting pares nicely with the warm yellow walls. The bedrooms are large enough for comfort and small enough to be cozy. Breakfast is served at 9 A.M. The Shafsky Eggs Benedict is typical of their fine food: scrambled eggs on a muffin topped with sautéed veggies, feta cheese, and lemon olive oil marinated tomatoes. Enjoy your coffee inside in one of the craftsman chairs, or outside in the side garden. The rooms are fully decorated each with a theme, and two of them

have bathtubs. There's a communal area with a TV, but it's rarely used. The house is close enough to walk to downtown. Also appealing is Lillie, the house's resident mini-dachshund, who will charm even the hardest of hearts.

Built by lumber man James Blair in 1901, **Blair Sugar Pines B&B** (2985 Clay St., Placerville, 530/626-9006, www.blair sugarpine.com, $130–160 d) is a testament to his love of wood and amazing woodwork, from beautiful built-ins to ornate doors. It's likely that Blair and Shafsky knew each other, since their homes were built one year and a few blocks apart. The coastal redwood the Blairs planted outside the dining room is still thriving. There's ample outdoor space for relaxation and wine and cheese in the evenings. It's only two blocks to Placerville's Main Street.

The historic **Cary House** (300 Main St., Placerville, 530/622-4271, www.caryhouse .com, $138–149 d) claims Mark Twain, Bette Davis, and Burt Reynolds as former guests. Period furniture and a nice display of historical artifacts in the lobby enhance the atmosphere,

SIERRA FOOTHILLS

© MICHAEL CERVIN

The lake is part of the draw at Eden Vale Inn.

but most notable is the 1926 elevator, which still works. Many of the 40 rooms feature kitchenettes. Each room has an entryway and a second bedroom. Take your coffee outside on the second floor balcony, where presidential contender Horace Greely made a stump speech in 1872. He didn't win.

If you are looking for a nice standard hotel, the **Best Western-Placerville Inn** (6850 Greenleaf Dr., 530/622-9100, $130–160 d) has 105 rooms on three floors and easy access to Highway 50. They are pet-friendly and have a pool, hot tub, and small fitness room. Continental breakfast and Wi-Fi are included. It's a five-minute drive to downtown Placerville.

The 《 **Fitzpatrick Lodge** (7740 Fair Play Rd., Fair Play, 800/245-9166, www.fitzpatrick winery.com, $115–150 d) is a white fir lodge on a vineyard hill overlooking Fair Play, 30 minutes south of downtown Placerville. The best room is the Log Suite, with exposed fir walls, a private deck, and lots of space. Breakfasts are made to order; their signature meal is sherry-

poached eggs topped with salmon and spinach. It's quiet here; There are no phones or televisions in the rooms, although there is a communal TV upstairs. Other amenities include a lap pool, Wi-Fi, and plenty of Fitzpatrick port wines to sample.

$200-300

You're transported to a lush green paradise at the aptly named 《 **Eden Vale Inn** (1780 Springvale Rd., Placerville, 530/621-0901, www.edenvaleinn.com). This old horse barn located near Shingle Springs (about 15 minutes west of downtown Placerville) has been converted into an upscale, modern-yet-rustic retreat using European styling and sophisticated computerized lighting. There is an elegant functionality to the rooms—equal parts calming and energetic. Three of the five rooms have hot tubs outside on private decks. The secluded location adds to the appeal: Wander along footpaths amid dense verdant foliage, or go swimming or rowing on the little lake. Take breakfast (with fresh fruit, baked goods, and an entrée) on the outside deck, surrounded by great views of all the greenery.

FOOD
Mexican

Yes, **Casa Ramos** (6840 Green Leaf Dr., Placerville, 530/622-2303, www.casaramos.net, 11 A.M.–9 P.M. Sun.–Thurs., 11 A.M.–10 P.M. Fri.–Sat., $15) is part of a restaurant chain, but they do Mexican food well. From the festive painted chairs to the carved tables, the ambience is all about high-octane color. The portions are ample and the food is well prepared: Try burritos, tacos, or the best smelling fajitas, all with lots of chips and salsa. The margaritas are pretty good, and they have Mexican beers too.

Cascada's (384 Main St., 530/344-7757, 11 A.M.–8 P.M. Sun.–Thurs., 11 A.M.–9 P.M. Fri.–Sat., $17) has a more upscale feel, with a popular bar serving mixed drinks flanking one wall. The food is proper Mexican, with fresh spices and ingredients. Begin with the chipotle spinach and artichoke dip, followed by an entrée like the Puerco con Frambuesa, pork sautéed in a chipotle raspberry sauce. There are a handful of vegetarian options as well, including the classic chile relleno.

American

It gets loud at **Hey Day Café** (325 Main St., 530/626-9700, Placerville, www.heyday cafe.com, 11 A.M.–9 P.M. Wed.–Thurs., 11 A.M.–10 P.M. Fri.–Sat., 11 A.M.–8 P.M. Sun., $20), an upscale hot spot crowded with locals who come for the comfortable space and the great food: pizzas and salads are superior and entrees like seared ahi and filet mignon. The respectable wine list features wines from the Foothills, with some California and foreign wines as well.

One of the only restaurants in the Apple Hill area, **The Forester Pub and Grill** (4110 Carson Rd., Camino, 530/644-1818, noon–9 P.M. daily, $15) gets busy, especially on weekends. The eclectic menu presents burgers, tuna melts, and pork chops alongside with Hungarian goulash and Weiner schnitzel. One of their signature dishes is the chicken and dumplings with red cabbage, with a dumpling that's crisp like a biscuit. Dine inside next to the bar or out on the back patio. Entertainment includes horseshoes, pool table, jukebox, and video games.

Italian

At **Bocconato Trattoria** (7915 Fair Play Rd., Somerset, 530/620-2493, www.bocconato .com, noon–9 P.M. Fri.–Sun., 5–9 P.M. Mon. and Thurs., $20), chef Giovanni Gaudio cooks according to his whims, so the menu is always a surprise. This is free-form dining, always fresh, prepared just for you: You might stumble on lamb carpaccio, olive oil cake, ribs, or pasta (no substitutions, please!). It's on the way to Fair Play.

Chinese

New owners have taken over **Wonderful Chinese** (4570 Pleasant Valley Rd., Fair Play, 530/647-8111, 11:30 A.M.–9 P.M. Tues.–Sun., $10), creating a large menu that features traditional Hunan and Szechuan dishes, with plenty of vegetarian options. The blue-grey walls and Asian accents don't seem to match, but the food is quite good. Their most popular dish is the General Chicken, a sweet, spicy, and crunchy chicken with chow mein noodles. Lunch specials include a small salad and egg flower soup. Dinners may include clay pots with garlic eggplant or seafood tofu. The restaurant seems out of place in its strip-mall location on the way to Fair Play, but it's a great change of pace.

Cheap Eats

The unpretentious but dependable **Train Station Coffee Shop** (4274 Motherlode Dr., Shingle Springs, 530/677-6287, 6 A.M.–2 P.M. daily, $10) is a family diner located 10 miles west of Placerville. You'll find tuna melts, Rubens, patty melts, and chili dogs, and they put sliced black olives in their potato salad for a twist. They have a large selection of breakfasts too.

The classic **Old Town Grill** (444 Main St., Placerville, 530/622-2631, 11 A.M.–3 P.M. Wed.–Mon., $8) does food right: all made to order. Affable owner John Sanders can usually be found behind the grill, chatting with the locals while he works. Expect burgers and sandwiches: Try the sloppy but very tasty buffalo burger, or the vegetarian earth burger.

You might not even notice the **Gold Vine Grill** (6028 Grizzly Flat Rd., Fair Play, 530/626-4042, www.goldvinegrill.com, 5–9 P.M. Wed.–Sun., 11:30 A.M.–2:30 P.M. Fri.–Sun., $15) in a tiny, corner strip mall in Fair Play. This local hangout is homey and comfortable, with wood floors and soft burgundy walls. The food is all about comfort as well, with steak, chops, burgers, paninis, and salads.

Breakfast

Housed in a circa 1865 home that once belonged to the sheriff of Hangtown, **Sweetie Pie's** (577 Main St., Placerville, 530/642-0128, www.sweetiepies.biz, Mon.–Fri. 6:30 A.M.–3 P.M., Sat. 7 A.M.–3 P.M., Sun. 7 A.M.–1 P.M., $10) has been serving up immensely popular breakfasts for over 20 years. They make a mean Hollandaise sauce and terrific olallieberry muffins. Get there early on weekends—it's packed by 9 A.M. They offer lunch as well, and outdoor patio seating.

Zachery Jacques (1821 Pleasant Valley Rd., Placerville, 530/626-8045, breakfast 8 A.M.–noon Sat.–Sun., dinner 4:30 P.M.–close Wed.–Sun., $20) is a great breakfast stop, about 20 minutes from downtown Placerville, heading south toward Fair Play. Brunch options are very French: veal sausage with eggs and rosemary bread, duck confit with eggs, or sautéed salmon and eggs. The interior is French county casual as well, all yellow and blue.

Sweets

At **Zia's** (312 Main St., Placerville, 530/642-9427, www.ziasgelato.com, 8 A.M.–9 P.M. Mon.–Thurs., 8 A.M.–10 P.M. Fri.–Sat., 9 A.M.–9 P.M. Sun., $5) you'll find a dozen different gelatos, all made with local ingredients. They're thick and creamy but not too sweet. Intriguing flavors like Viennese coffee, lemon honey, and cantaloupe rotate weekly. There are also espresso drinks and pastries.

INFORMATION AND SERVICES

For an overview of the county, www.visit-eldorado.com provides lots of links. For wines, both areas have their own dedicated sites: Fair Play at www.fairplaywine.com and the broader county at www.eldoradowines.org.

The Sierra Foothills regions are welcoming and helpful and if you call, a person will answer, not a recording. In Placerville visit the **El Dorado County Tourist Authority** (542 Main St., 800/457-6279, 9 A.M.–5 P.M. Mon.–Fri., 11 A.M.–3 P.M. Sat.–Sun.) for maps and brochures. There are multiple two-hour free parking lots along Main Street.

If you have an **emergency,** call 911 immediately. The **Placerville Police Department** (730 Main St., 530/642-5210, www.cityofplacerville.org) is located in downtown Placerville. The **Marshall Medical Center** (1100 Marshall Way, 530/622-1441, www.marshallmedical.org) in Placerville has served the surrounding communities since 1959 and offers a full range of services.

GETTING THERE AND AROUND

Placerville sits at the intersection of Highway 50 (which runs east-west) and Highway 49 (north-south), making it the most easily accessed town in gold country. From Sacramento, there is one bus commuter line (www.erdoradotransit.com) that will take you to Placerville and back. **Amtrak** (www.amtrak.com) also offers curbside bus service from Sacramento to Placerville.

Within the county, **El Dorado Transit** (www.eldoradotransit.com) operates bus routes with one-way fares starting at $1.50. **Dial-A-Ride** (530/642-3696, www.erdorado transit.com) is a shared commuter service for disabled and senior citizens, with fares beginning at $3. If you're in need of taxi services try the **Lightening Cab Co.** (530/626-8000) or **Extreme Taxi** (530/626-8294).

The Sierra Foothills' closest major airports are San Francisco (SFO), Oakland (OAK), and Sacramento (SMF). Commuters can reach the Foothills via Stockton (SCK) and Modesto (MOD) airports.

Amador County

Of all the Sierra Foothills regions, Amador County is perhaps the most associated with Gold Country. It has the most gold rush towns, with historic buildings restored and still intact. Sutter Creek is the best known and most pristine, but there are several blink-and-you'll-miss-them towns neatly lined up on Highway 49. The landscape shifts as you move into the Shenandoah Valley: The elevation gently drops, the pine trees give way to sweet grasses on the now-rolling hills, and the temperatures cool. These conditions, along with the rich soils, are ideal for growing grapes.

Amador County's long history with wine dates back to the mid 1850s when the Mission vines were first planted, using cuttings that the Spanish brought up from Mexico. The first winery was established in 1856; its building still stands at the current Sobon Estate winery. While prohibition took its toll on wineries in El Dorado and Calaveras counties, Amador County winemakers survived due to a law that allowed them to make up to 200 gallons at home for personal use. Much later, Amador was the first county in the Foothills to welcome a major player. Sutter Home from Napa bought property here, which confirmed the area as an up-and-coming wine region. Today, wine remains the driving economic factor in the county, with the Shenandoah Valley wine region growing rapidly. Larger producers have discovered the potential of the rich soil, and small family operations still thrive.

Heading south from El Dorado County into Amador you hit Plymouth, and just to the east is the Shenandoah Valley wine region and the smallest remaining gold town, Fiddletown. After a few miles there is Drytown, Amador City, then Sutter Creek, and west of Sutter Creek, Ione, and finally the larger county seat of Jackson with its big box stores, casino, and movie theaters.

In the Valley, there are two main roads where the majority of wineries are located:

Shenandoah Road, which houses many of the tasting rooms, and Steiner Road, which breaks off from this road and forms a loop, taking you back to where you began. All in all, the Shenandoah Valley is simple and easy to navigate and most of the tasting rooms are within close proximity to each other.

WINE-TASTING

Any tasting fees listed are for reserve wines; standard tasting lists are complimentary, unless otherwise noted.

JEFF RUNQUIST WINES

Jeff Runquist Wines (10776 Shenandoah Rd., Plymouth, 209/245-6282, www.jeff runquistwines.com, 11 A.M.–5 P.M. Fri.–Sun.) makes big beefy wines that are not for the faint of heart. All are reds: well-balanced and oh so fun to drink. Jeff's best wine is his barbera. Although he makes zinfandel, the predominant

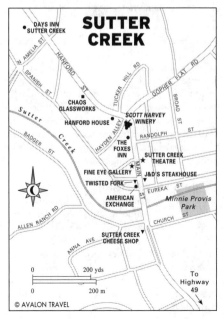

OLD VINES, NEW LIFE

"Old vine" is a designation that is often found on wine bottles to denote grapes harvested from particularly old vines, mainly zinfandel, from the Foothills to Napa and Sonoma. However, there is no official legal designation for the term; therefore vines that are as young as 25 years old can be considered old vine, though in fact they are not. Anything planted prior to 1900 is indeed old vine and the Sierra Foothills has its share of old vine wines with grapes still sacrificing their fruit over 130 years later.

It is well known that the first grapes planted in California were generically called mission grapes and were sunk into the ground when the Spanish Missionaries set up shop along the coastal route. They were originally vine cuttings brought over from Spain in the 1500s into Mexico, when Mexico was part of the Spanish Empire. The Spanish padres needed grapes for use in sacramental wine, but what exactly they planted is unknown. There are very few acres of authentic mission plantings in the state, but they do still exist, most from the early 1800s. **Deaver Vineyards** in the **Shenandoah Valley** has true mission vines that are nearly five feet tall.

It is believed that zinfandel was in the ground as early as 1820, though there is no definitive proof of that. What is true is that zinfandel had already been planted by the time Abraham Lincoln was president. Some grape cuttings were planted in the ground of the Sierra Foothills by the Swiss, Italians, and Germans. In **Amador County** the Eschen Vineyard is still producing fruit planted in 1865, as is the Grandpere Vineyard planted in 1869 and the 1881 Deaver Vineyards.

Wine country in the Sierra Foothills benefitted from its isolation from the rest of the state: Planted vineyards in the region, both mission and zinfandel, largely avoided the devastation caused by the phylloxera louse at the end of the nineteenth century which harmed Napa and Sonoma. Because of this, there are some exceptionally old vines still alive. Does this mean that older fruit is better? Well, that's something you need to decide for yourself. However, it is fun knowing that the wine you're currently drinking comes from vines that have been producing fruit for well over a century.

wine in the region, he believes that barbera is better suited to the area; one sip and you might become a convert too. Other good options include petite sirah, syrah, sangiovese, cabernet sauvignon, and a Carneros pinot noir. No white wines are allowed at the rustic, wraparound bar inside the spacious but simply adorned tasting room.

◖ COOPER VINEYARDS

A stop at Cooper Vineyards (21365 Shenandoah School Rd., Plymouth, 209/245-6181, www .cooperwines.com, 11 A.M.–4:45 P.M. Thurs.– Mon.) will give you an appreciation for how good Amador County wines can be. The Cooper family came to the Shenandoah Valley at the turn of the 20th century. They made their living planting wheat, fruit, and walnuts before getting into the wine game in

2002. Today, their wines are uniformly some of the best coming out of the Sierra Foothills, especially their barbera, the vines of which are right outside the front door. Many other wineries use Cooper's barbera fruit to make their own.

DRIVEN CELLARS

Someone at Driven Cellars (12595 Steiner Rd., Plymouth, 209/245-4545, www.drivencellars .com, 10 A.M.–5 P.M. Fri.–Mon.) has a thing for fast cars and easy wines. As you ascend to the top of the hill on the way into the vineyard, you'll see cars—lots of cars, some restored like a 1940 Ford, or a 100-year old Mack truck, some still on blocks awaiting restoration, parked along the road. But don't let the cars distract you from your goal: the modest tasting room, where wines like pinot grigio, sangiovese, syrah, primitivo, and zinfandel shine. The cars may pique your interest, but it's the wines you'll remember.

DILLIAN WINES
Tom Dillian, who runs Dillian Wines (12138 Steiner Rd., Plymouth, 209/245-3444, 11 A.M.–4:30 P.M. Fri.–Sun.), is a soft spoken man who makes terrific wine. Unfortunately, he doesn't make very much, so it routinely sells out. But when the juice is flowing, it's worth a trip. This is a family operation: Photos of several generations of Dillians decorate the tasting room, and the walnut trees and lilacs outside were planted by Tom's grandparents in the 1920s. Dillian's best wines are zinfandel, barbera, and syrah. He also makes sauvignon blanc, Semillon, a few dessert wines, and a red Italian blend of sangiovese and barbera called Vino Nostro.

SOBON ESTATE
Sobon Estate (12300 Steiner Rd., 209/245-4455, www.sobonwine.com 9:30 A.M.–5 P.M. daily, reserve tasting $5) is on the site of the very

first commercial winery in Amador County. The original winery, which dates back to 1856, is no longer functioning as such, but is open for self-guided tours. The bottling room of the old winery was converted into the current tasting room; the only thing that has changed in the last 20 years is the floor. Sobon is best known for a trio of zinfandels from vineyards planted in 1910, 1923, and 1928, and also produces a very nice roussanne and syrah. Since this winery is the farthest out on Steiner Road, you may want to start your winery tour here, then work your way back into Plymouth.

VINO NOCETO
The wines at Vino Noceto (11011 Dickson Rd., Plymouth, 209/245-6556, www.noceto.com, 11 A.M.–4 P.M. Mon.–Fri., 11 A.M.–5 P.M. Sat.–Sun.), located just off Shenandoah Road, are primarily Italian, with seven different iterations of sangiovese. They also produce pinot grigio, barbera, a lovely old-vine zinfandel, and an estate olive oil. The tasting room is simple and functional, with three long tables that host

When visiting Vino Noceto, you need to inquire about the dog head.

the crowds that swell on weekends. You'll notice a large fiberglass dog head in the parking lot, something purchased at an auction and believed to be the most photographed dog in the county. (Once you see it, you'll know why.)

DEAVER VINEYARDS

Deaver Vineyards (12455 Steiner Rd., Plymouth, 209/245-4099, www.deaver vineyard.com, 10:30 A.M.–5 P.M. daily) is one of the older wineries in the Shenandoah Valley. Their Old Vine Zinfandel is truly that, made from vines that are about 140 years old but still give up their berries. They also have Mission grapes on site that they use to make Angelica, a dessert wine popular with the Spanish padres. They also make syrah, sauvignon blanc, and nearly a dozen ports. The tasting room is adjacent to a picnic area near a small lake where Canadian geese strut around. Wine by the glass is $5–7.

SCOTT HARVEY WINERY

Scott Harvey has expanded his portfolio, producing wine in Napa and Mendocino, but Scott Harvey Winery (21 Eureka St., Sutter Creek, 209/267-0122, www.scottharveywines .com, noon–5 P.M. Thurs.–Sun.) remains a fixture in Amador County, beautifully showcasing the region's grapes. The handsome tasting room, all sophistication and dark wood, fronts Main Street in downtown Sutter Creek. Try the Foothills syrah, barbera, and zinfandel, or even some non-Amador wines like Riesling and port.

SIGHTS
◖ Sutter Gold Mine

At Sutter Gold Mine (13660 Hwy. 49, 866/762-2837, www.suttergold.com, 10 A.M.–4 P.M. daily, longer hours in summer, adults and children 13 years and up $17.50, children 3–12 $11.50, gold-panning $5), you'll learn how dangerous mining was during the gold rush and still is today; this is an actual working mine. Their hour-long tram tours descend into the cold earth on a wide, carved road—some 1,500 feet into the mountain. Along the way,

Sutter Gold Mine will plunge you 1,500 feet below the earth.

© MICHAEL CERVIN

you'll see original mining equipment once used to search for gold. Back on the surface, you can visit a gold panning site and learn how to pan for gold. (The bag of dirt they sell comes with little flecks of gold, perfect for kids to discover on their own.) By doing the actual panning and knowing the miners stood in the streams panning for hours, you realize how exhausting it must have been. You can also picnic (bring your own food) by the original Highway 49 gold road, where the miners once hauled out their loot.

Black Chasm Cavern

You can also tour Black Chasm Cavern (15701 Volcano Pioneer Rd., Volcano, 866/762-2837, www.caverntours.com, 10 A.M.–4 P.M. daily, adults $14.75, children 3–12 $7.50), a natural cavern filled with stalactites, stalagmites, flowstones, and helictite, all back-lit for maximum appreciation. The 50-minute guided walking tour takes you down and up and down stairs leading to various chambers. The formations are nearly poetic, some soft and smooth and others jagged and sharp, all made over the course of thousands of years. End your visit at the large visitor center and gift shop. The cavern is located in Volcano, a 13-mile drive up Sutter Creek Road, which follows the actual Sutter Creek heading northeast.

ENTERTAINMENT AND EVENTS
Nightlife

Nightlife in Sutter Creek centers around the **American Exchange Hotel** (53 Main St., Sutter Creek, 800/892-2276). Local resident Harry Jordan belts out tunes from the 1960s and 1970s in the banquet room on Friday nights, 5–9 P.M. He's a damn fine singer, with an infectious enthusiasm that quickly wins over the crowd. You can also head downstairs to the basement to enjoy **The Annex,** a bar with two pool tables, two dart boards, a jukebox, and live music or a DJ Friday–Saturday nights. Expect a local crowd that might get rowdy.

If you're missing the one-armed bandit, head to the **Jackson Rancheria Casino** (12222

© MICHAEL CERVIN

the Jackson Rancheria Casino

New York Ranch Rd., Jackson, 800/822-9466, www.jacksoncasino.com, open 24 hours/day), which features over 1,500 slot machines (including about 400 penny slots), as well as poker and other table games. Smoking is allowed in the casino, so beware if you're sensitive to smoke. They also have a hotel, large RV park, restaurant, and even Peet's coffee on the premises. From the Shenandoah Valley, head south on Highway 49, then east on Highway 88.

Festivals and Events

For 23 years, people have flocked to the **Sutter Creek Duck Races** (Minnie Provis Park, 50 Church St., 8 A.M.–5 P.M. on last Sat. in Apr.). Contestants adopt rubber ducks (for $5 each) and let them loose in the Sutter Creek. The individual races last about 10 minutes each, depending on the prior year's snowfall and currents in the creek. The big prize? Bragging rights. There are three heats, then a final race. There's also live entertainment, food, games and over $5,000 in cash and prizes. All proceeds go to raise money for Amador County charities.

Sutter Creek gets all decked out in green boughs for the **Sutter Creek Christmas Open House** (Dec. 3–4). There's a communal lighting of the Christmas tree, carolers stroll Main Street, and stores stay open late and serve hot cocoa and wine. It's about as Norman Rockwell as you can get.

SHOPPING
Sutter Creek

Stroll in Sutter Creek to enjoy the best example of an original gold rush town. Most of Main Street's two blocks of stores are in original buildings, with authentic doors and windows.

With an eclectic mix of artists from as close as Amador and as far away as Israel, **Fine Eye Gallery** (71 Main St., Sutter Creek, 209/267-0571, www.fineeye.com, 10:30 A.M.–5:30 P.M. daily) is by far the best gallery in Sutter Creek. Expect the unconventional: Watches, furniture, arts, and crafts all display a unique knack for looking like nothing you've ever seen before.

Gallery 10 (15 Eureka St., Sutter Creek, 209/267-0203, www.gallery10suttercreek.com,

Sutter Creek is packed with original 1850s buildings.

© MICHAEL CERVIN

11 A.M.–5 P.M. Thurs.–Mon.) features a small but eclectic collection of local artists' photography, pottery, oil painting, jewelry, glass, and even greeting cards.

Artisans blow glass right on the premises of **Chaos Glassworks** (121 Hanford St., Sutter Creek, 209/267-9317, www.chaosglassworks .com, noon–7 P.M. Wed.–Fri., 10 A.M.–7 P.M. Sat., 10 A.M.–6 P.M. Sun.); it's fun to stop in just to watch. It's also worth exploring two floors filled with a variety of one-of-a-kind glasswork: vases, paperweights, bowls, and lamps.

Open for almost 40 years, **Lizzie Ann's Books & Gifts** (59 Main St., Sutter Creek, 209/267-5680, 10 A.M.–5 P.M. daily) probably has the best selection of historical books on the Sierra Nevada region, along with a diverse selection of paperbacks and kids books. They also sell antiques, dishes (mainly teacups), and other knick-knacks. The building itself is a bit of an antique, built in 1858.

Romancin' The Range (38 Main St., Sutter Creek, 209/267-9137, 11 A.M.–5 P.M. Wed.–Mon.) stocks trendy western wear mainly for women and girls. There are lots of sheer flowy dresses, vests, studded boots, and tops, all with an upscale cowgirl feel.

Jackson Historic District
Jackson is right off Highway 49, 10 minutes south of Sutter Creek. There are some great shops along the compact, two-block historic district.

Small but mighty, **The Biggest Little Kitchen Store** (215 N. Main St., Jackson, 209/223-0264, www.biggestlittlekitchenstore .com, 9 A.M.–5 P.M. daily) is dedicated to home and hearth, with copper cookware, plenty of cookbooks, and a big selection of pepper grinders. The staff is wise in the cooking arts.

The Real Deal Antiques (104 Main St., Jackson, 209/257-1954, 11 A.M.–5 P.M. Thurs.–Mon.) has been in the antiques game for 30 years, specializing in furniture—sideboards, old wash stands, and the like—at very affordable prices.

The aptly named **Antiques Downstairs** (3 Main St., Jackson, 209/223-2420, 11 A.M.–5 P.M. daily) is located below street-level, in what was once the garage for an automobile dealership up top. Fifteen dealers are represented with items for all tastes, from reproductions to actual antiques.

Book lovers will love the old-school **Hein and Company** (204 Main St., Jackson, 209/223-9076, 9 A.M.–7 P.M. Mon.–Fri., 10 A.M.–7 P.M. Sat., 11 A.M.–6 P.M. Sun.). Its two stories are loaded with books—old hardbacks, rare and out of print books, and plenty of paperbacks on every subject—all very well-organized. Worn chairs offer a comfortable spot for browsing, and free coffee and tea is always available. Dive into the $1.50-paperbacks room upstairs, or browse the DVDs and video games downstairs.

ACCOMMODATIONS
Amador County has a selection of both traditional chain hotels and bed-and-breakfasts, which tend to be a bit more expensive than the other two counties.

Under $100
The **Day's Inn** (271 Hanford St., Sutter Creek, 209/267-9177, www.daysinn.com, $95 d) is uncomplicated lodging. The rooms are clean and the staff is very helpful. Guests can use the running track and Olympic-size swimming pool at the high school just up the hill. There's a simple continental breakfast and free Wi-Fi.

$100-200
C Hanford House (61 Hanford St., Sutter Creek, 800/871-5839, www.hanfordhouse .com, $149–239 d) offers both small-town charm and upscale style. The main brick building takes a traditional approach, with period furniture and decor, including rotating local art. The suites, located in an old converted house next door, are modern and sleek. Coffee, warm scones, and the morning paper are delivered to your room in the morning. Breakfast features fresh eggs produced by the chickens on-site, and local wines and cheeses are served at 5 P.M. Pet-friendly and ADA rooms are available, as are DVDs and Wi-Fi.

The **C Amador Harvest Inn** (12455 Steiner Rd., Plymouth, 209/245-5512, www

.amadorharvestinn.com, $150–170 d) offers a quiet country feel right in the heart of the Shenandoah Valley, in walking distance to half a dozen wineries. There are four upstairs rooms and the downstairs has a kitchen, living room with a TV, and reading room with a fireplace. The spacious Zinfandel room includes a small reading area. Breakfasts (served about 9 A.M.) include fresh baked scones, fresh fruit, and eggs; gluten-free options are also available. From the patio, you can watch the mists rise off the lake. A two-night stay is required on weekends.

Located in Amador City, between Plymouth and Sutter Creek, the **Imperial Hotel** (14202 Hwy. 49, Amador City, 209/267-9172, www.imperialamador.com, $135–145 d) was built in 1879 and operated as a hotel until 1927, when it was shuttered for 40 years; locals still recall playing hide-and-seek in the abandoned building. Today, this six-room hotel has new life, but retains its historic charm, with the original hardwood floors and some of the original brick walls. There's a quaint reading room

upstairs, leading out to the balcony looking out over tiny Amador City. There are no TVs and no phones, but there is Wi-Fi. They offer an exceptional midweek package: dinner and a room for $150. There is a full bar and restaurant downstairs.

The no frills **American Exchange Hotel** (53 Main St., Sutter Creek, 800/892-2276, www.americanexchangehotel.com, $105–165 d) also offers a great sense of history: It has operated continuously since it was built in 1860, right in the center of Sutter Creek. Ten nicely appointed rooms occupy the second floor, each with their own TVs and baths. The third floor offers 15 smaller, less expensive rooms with shared bathrooms. Amenities include Wi-Fi, a small coin-free laundry area, and a parking lot where horses were parked prior to automobiles.

Renovated in 2010, the pet-friendly **Shenandoah Inn** (17674 Village Dr., Plymouth, 800/542-4549, www.theshenandoahinn.com, $120–160 d) is quiet and conveniently located close to the Shenandoah Valley. The rooms in

The Amador Harvest Inn sits in the middle of the Shenandoah Valley.

the back, near the pool, offer views of the soft, oak-studded hills. All rooms have coffee makers; some have refrigerators and microwaves.

$200-300

Built in the late 1850s, **The Foxes Inn** (77 Main St., Sutter Creek, 800/987-3344, www.foxesinn.com, $219–289 d) offers seven rooms and suites furnished with unbelievable antiques and fireplaces. The homemade breakfasts feature fresh local fruit, and are delivered right to your room. All rooms have CD, DVD, and VHS players. Some feature claw-foot bathtubs, and better yet, the bath towels are the softest you will encounter.

FOOD
Wine Country Cuisine

It's a little surprising to find a high-caliber restaurant like **Taste** (9402 Main St., Plymouth, 209/245-3463, www.restauranttaste.com, 5 P.M.–close Thurs.–Mon., $25) amid the burger joints and funky old diners in Plymouth. Chef Mark Berkner has amassed

a slew of awards for his thoughtful approach to seasonal cuisine, which results in a rotating menu featuring the likes of Alaskan cod, foie gras, and Colorado rack of lamb. This is a true destination restaurant with such a loyal following that reservations are nearly mandatory.

The dining room at the **Imperial Hotel** (14202 Hwy. 49, Amador City, 209/267-9172, www.imperialamador.com, 5 P.M.–close Tues.–Sun., noon–2 P.M. Sat.–Sun., $20) dates back to the 1880s. One wall shows off the original brick, but the others are painted to create a yellow mottled look. The bar is all original as well. Their signature dish is duck breast with a spicy raspberry chile port reduction, which perfectly melds the sweet port, hot chile, and berry flavors. Their pumpkin ravioli with sage cream sauce and crispy garlic is also a favorite. Weekends get busy, so reservations are advisable.

The ◖ **Union Pub** (21375 Consolation St., Volcano, 209/296-7711, www.volcanounion.com, 3–9 P.M. Fri., noon–9 P.M. Sat.–Sun.,

Taste in Plymouth has become a wine country destination restaurant.

© MICHAEL CERVIN

5–8 P.M. Mon., $15) is an out of the way place in the tiny town of Volcano. Chef Mark Berkner has devised a stellar menu with lots of interesting twists. Try their signature starter: five surprisingly large duck legs with an orange glaze; they are so tender the meat nearly falls off the bone. Another good option is the fresh fish: The salmon is flavorful, served up with white beans and cilantro. The dining room achieves a classy but laid-back pub atmosphere, with a game room, where you can play darts or shoot pool, and an outdoor patio.

Italian

The potent blend of pastas and garlic make **The Twisted Fork** (53 Main St., Sutter Creek, 209/267-5211, 11 A.M.–8:30 P.M. Tues.–Sun., $15) a great stop. Try not to fill up on the addictive pesto bread dip; save some room for old-school Italian entrées, like spaghetti and house-made meatballs and fettuccini. There are meat and fish dishes too.

Steakhouses

Loud, boisterous, and blue collar, **J&D's Steakhouse** (36 Main St., Sutter Creek, 209/267-0535, 4–9 P.M. Wed.–Mon., $22) is the local meat and potatoes place. Start with the coconut shrimp, elevated by a raspberry-mint–cayenne pepper sauce. Chicken, seafood, and salads are available, but the order of the day is right in the name of the restaurant: steak. The top sirloin is a long-time favorite, served with herbed peppercorn sauce and caramelized onions and garlic mashers.

Mexican

Tambien Mexican Kitchen (250 French Bar Rd., Jackson, 209/257-1122, www .tambienmexican.com, 11 A.M.–2 P.M. Tues., 11 A.M.–8 P.M. Wed.–Sat., $9) is a great spot for fresh, flavorful Mexican food. Their best dish is their enchilada Ranchera, with earthy Yucatán pulled pork. The salsa bar offers eight salsas, including their own creation, Rockin' Red, a mildly spicy thick red sauce. There are traditional Mexican beers as well as foreign and domestic. If you're in a hurry, try the drive-thru.

Breakfast

For over 50 years **Mel & Faye's Diner** (31 Hwy. 49, Jackson, 209/223-0853, 5 A.M.–10 P.M. daily, $10) has been serving up dependable breakfasts in large portions. You'll usually find locals filling up the counter seats facing the open kitchen. There's also a bar, separate from the main dining room, with a big-screen TV.

The **Backroads Coffee House** (75 Main St., Sutter Creek, 209/267-0440, 7:30 A.M.–3 P.M. daily, $8) is a homey little breakfast place. In addition to coffee and tea they provide basic breakfast foods, including bagel sandwiches, muffins, and quiche. The selection is limited but it will do the trick.

Picnic Supplies

The **Amador Vintage Market** (9393 Main St., Plymouth, 209/245-3663, amadorvintage market.com, 10 A.M.–6 P.M. Wed.–Sun., $8) has the look and feel of an old-time market, but it's all new. Deli options include sandwiches with black forest ham and fontina cheese and curried chicken salad. This is a great place to pre-order a box lunch for a Wine Country picnic feast. They also have a selection of local wines as well as espresso drinks.

Veer left as you enter the **Pokerville Market** (18170 Hwy. 49, Plymouth, 209/245-6986, 8 A.M.–8 P.M. daily) to find their deli case and bakery. Sandwiches to go ($5.99) make for an inexpensive picnic.

There are always new cheeses to discover at the **Sutter Creek Cheese Shoppe** (33B Main St., Sutter Creek, 209/267-5457, 11 A.M.–5 P.M. daily). Cheese monger Kathy Dawson keeps the selections fresh, rotating in two new cheeses each week, with cow, goat, and sheep cheeses from domestic producers and across the globe.

Farmers Markets

The **Amador Farmers Market** is really two markets. Saturday's market in Sutter Creek (52 Eureka St., 209/419-2503, 8–11 A.M. Sat., June–Oct.) is pretty small, with less than a dozen vendors; but you will find fresh veggies, eggs, olive oils, and honey, as well as live

© MICHAEL CERVIN

picnicking along Sutter Creek

music. The larger version is Sunday in Jackson (Busi Municipal parking lot at Hwys. 49 and 88, 209/419-2503, 10 A.M.–1 P.M. Sun., May–Oct.), with a more varied selection and larger crowds.

INFORMATION AND SERVICES

The **Sutter Creek Visitor Center** (71 Main St., 209/267-1344, www.suttercreek.org, 11 A.M.–2 P.M. Sun.–Wed., 10 A.M.–5 P.M. Thurs.–Sat.) not only has a plethora of information, but the walls are lined with historic photos of the old days. It's located in downtown.

GETTING THERE AND AROUND

You can reach Sutter Creek, the Shenandoah Valley, and Jackson easily by traveling north-south on Highway 49, or via Lake Tahoe to the east or Highway 99 near Stockton off Highway 88. These are all two-lane roads, so allow extra time to reach your destination.

The **Amador Regional Transit System** (11400 American Legion Dr., Jackson, 209/267-9395, www.amadortransit.com) has limited service between Jackson and Sutter Creek, and Jackson and the wine area near Plymouth. Bus service runs Monday–Friday only; an all-day pass is $3. There are no commercial buses that will take you to Sutter Creek or Jackson from outside of the county.

Taxis in the region are as scarce as the gold was. **Amador Pioneer Cab Co.** (105 Main St., Jackson, 209/223-3355) is one of the few to serve Sutter Creek and Jackson.

The Sierra Foothills' closest major airports are San Francisco (SFO), Oakland (OAK), and Sacramento (SMF). Commuters can reach the Foothills via Stockton (SCK) and Modesto (MOD) airports.

SIERRA FOOTHILLS

Calaveras County

Mark Twain's short story, "The Celebrated Jumping Frog of Calaveras County" put the county on the map in 1865. Today, it may be the best wine region you've never heard of. The local wine industry is centered around the small town of Murphys, which is also the best place to stop for wine tasting. Brothers Daniel and John Murphy came here in 1848 to make it rich off gold and became goods traders to mine the money out of the pockets of those who did the panning. Murphys' designated historic district consists of a lot of stone and brick buildings, built in response to a fire that almost destroyed the town. Summers are packed with people who come to enjoy Murphys' small town charms, and maybe taste a little wine.

While there are a few wineries along Highway 4 heading into Murphys, most of the tasting rooms are in town along a single road: Main Street. For the quintessential Wine Country experience, you'll want to drive along the highway and enjoy the scenic vineyards. Other Calaveras County towns, like Angels Camp, Vallecito, and Bear Valley, are perhaps better known for mountain skiing than winemaking. To reach them, continue east on Highway 4. It's worth noting that during the slower months of January and February, the "unofficial" day for stores in Murphys to close is Tuesday, even though many businesses state that they are open daily.

WINE-TASTING
Murphys
NEWSOME-HARLOW WINES

At Newsome-Harlow Wines (403 Main St., Murphys, 209/728-9817, www.nhvino.com, noon–5 P.M. Mon.–Thurs., 11 A.M.–5:30 P.M. Fri.–Sun., tasting $5), winemaker Scott Klamm's sensibility leans toward big and bold, but with enough balance to make his wines easy and drinkable, from the subtle and clean muscat blanc, to the hefty Donner Party zinfandel (a survivor of the Donner party married one of the Murphys brothers), to the utterly plush petite sirah. Newsome-Harlow

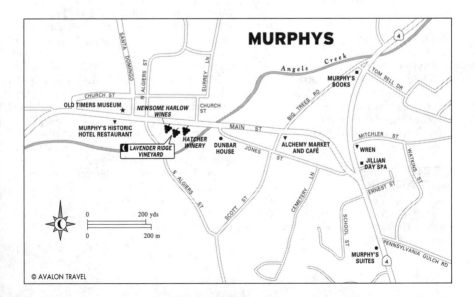

© MICHAEL CERVIN

Hatcher Winery's tasting room feels like an old mine.

© MICHAEL CERVIN

Lavender Ridge Vineyard makes some of the best Rhône wines in Murphys.

purchases most of its grapes from local farmers using sustainable practices. The tasting lounge is at the back of a courtyard off Main Street. It's simple and uncluttered, sort of like a nice hotel lobby.

HATCHER WINERY

Popular Hatcher Winery (419 Main St., Murphys, 209/605-7111, www.hatcher wine.com, 11 A.M.–5 P.M. Fri.–Sun., tasting $3) is located on Main Street too—well actually underneath it. Once you walk down a few steps and enter through the wooden door, you'll feel like you're in one of the local mine caves: There are low ceilings, candles on the rock walls, and a long wood tasting bar. Winemaker Matt Hatcher's best wines are his cabernet franc, petite sirah, and zinfandel; the pinot grigio, grenache, malbec, and port wine are also worth a taste.

◖ LAVENDER RIDGE VINEYARD

Housed in a historic stone building, Lavender Ridge Vineyard (425A Main St., Murphys,

PROHIBITION: PROBLEMS AND POTENTIAL

The Volstead Act, passed by Congress and enacted in 1919 and better known as Prohibition, officially signaled the end of the wine industry in California. However, some wineries, like Sobon Estate in Amador County, then called D'Agostini Winery, were able to keep their doors open by making wine for sacramental purposes for a few churches. Though Prohibition outlawed the sale and transport of alcohol, it allowed any home winemaker to produce 200 gallons of wine per year for home use. Since there was little oversight of this exemption, many home winemakers made a lot more than 200 gallons and sold it to their neighbors, to restaurants and bars, and to travelers coming through town.

Since the Foothills were in such remote locations for the time, they were difficult to find and even more difficult for federal agents to raid. Thus, bootleg booze did reasonably well. As prohibition reached the Foothills, grape plantings in El Dorado and Calaveras counties declined. But mysteriously, grape acreage in Amador County surged. Saloons in the Foothills

that appeared on county maps simply changed their names to avoid detection by federal authorities. Many maps drawn in the 1920s and 1930s where saloons were known to exist were labeled as "fish markets" or unmarked altogether. And home winemakers were known to have produced well over 200 gallons of wine, selling much of it on the side. The remote wineries in the Foothills also had the ability to funnel their wines over the Sierra Nevada Mountains and into Nevada, where towns like Carson City and Reno anxiously awaited the next arrival of wine from California.

Prohibition alone did not truly kill the wine industry; it merely slowed the growth. The other decisive factor was the Great Depression, which drove down grape prices and many Sierra Foothills wineries were forced to shut their doors or simply abandon their parcels and the vines went dormant. Had wineries not dealt with a 13-year moratorium, a country in financial crisis, and a new fondness for extremely cheap bathtub gin and dubious other alcohols, there's no telling where the industry would be today.

209/728-2441, www.lavendarridgevineyard.com, 11 A.M.–5 P.M. daily, tasting $5) is a must stop for any Rhône wine lover, with some of the best Rhône wines in the area. You'll also find viognier, roussanne, grenache blanc, mourvèdre, syrah, and petite sirah, all unfiltered. In addition to wine, they offer about 30 cheeses from around the world; a cheese pairing is included with the tasting fee. The property's namesake lavender is for sale as well.

MUIR'S LEGACY

The great grandson of the legendary John Muir, who was instrumental in the formation of the National Park Service and the Sierra Club, is the owner of Muir's Legacy (219 Main St., Murphys, 209/728-0500, www.muirslegacy.com, 11 A.M.–5 P.M. Sun.–Thurs., 11 A.M.–6 P.M. Fri.–Sat., tasting $10). Muir's

certified organic vineyards produce about 4,000 cases of wine each year. Try the chardonnay, pinot noir, and Bordeaux blend; they also pour merlot and primitivo. The tasting room expands out to an outdoor deck. They sell wines by the glass and platters of cheese, crackers, and prosciutto—perfect for a bite to eat. A portion of the proceeds helps support one of John Muir's eternal loves: Yosemite National Park.

Outside Murphys
IRONSTONE VINEYARDS

Just three miles west of Murphys proper, Ironstone Vineyards (1894 Six Mile Rd., Murphys, 209/728-1251, www.ironstonevineyards.com, 10 A.M.–5 P.M. daily, reserve tasting $6) is the largest winery in the area, both in terms of wine production and their huge facility. You can't help but be impressed by the sheer scope of the complex, with caves below the tasting room, replicas of mining equipment, beautiful landscaped gardens, walkways, picnic areas, and even an outdoor amphitheater that hosts acts like Faith Hill, Pat Benatar, and ZZ Top. The Heritage Museum onsite focuses on mining history; its most notable exhibit is a 44-pound gold nugget. The beautiful landscaping includes over half a million daffodils in season. With all that, who needs wine? Who am I kidding: Their standard-list wines (priced at $10) include a nice verdelho and cabernet franc. Their reserve list showcases an excellent chardonnay, Meritage blend, and port. Tours are available Monday–Friday at 1:30 P.M. and Saturday–Sunday at 11:30 A.M. and 1:30 P.M.

INDIAN ROCK

Indian Rock (1154 Pennsylvania Gulch Rd., Murphys, 209/728-8514, www.indianrock vineyards.com, noon–5 P.M. Fri.–Sun.) sits quietly off by itself, across Highway 4 and away from the frenetic downtown scene in Murphys. With large picnic tables and a trout-filled pond, this is a great family spot. The narrow tasting room has a copper topped bar that looks out on the vineyards. Indian Rock has a large portfolio, but produces less than 3,000 cases; wines are for sale only in the tasting room and a few restaurants in Murphys. Priced under $20, these wines are a great value, with an amazing line-up that includes their reserve chardonnay, cabernet sauvignon, tawny port, pinot noir, and Angelica.

TWISTED OAK WINERY

Want to get twisted? Twisted Oak Winery (4280 Red Hill Rd., Vallecito, 209/736-9080, www.twistedoak.com, 10:30 A.M.–5:30 P.M. daily, tasting $5) is a must-stop for wine with an attitude. Launched in 2003, this winery takes its philosophical cues more from Monty Python than viticulture: Rubber chickens line the trees heading to the tasting room and random road signs warn of adults running with a bottle of wine. Given the offbeat approach, you may be surprised

© MICHAEL CERVIN

Making the drive to Twisted Oak Winery, you know you're in for something!

to discover that they actually make really good wine, focusing on Spanish and Mediterranean varieties like tempranillo, verdelho, and garnacha (the original Spanish grape, not the better known French version). The Spaniard is their flagship wine, an excellent blend of tempranillo, graciano, and garnacha. Syrah, viognier, and petite sirah round out their offerings. The winery is located in Vallecito, a tiny town just east of Murphys. Although they have a second tasting room on Main Street in Murphys, it's better to visit here—how can you pass up the rubber chickens? You can also see the real twisted oak tree that gives the winery its name.

SIGHTS
Old Timers Museum

The Old Timers Museum (470 Main St., Murphys, 209/728-1160, noon–4 P.M. Fri.–Mon., free, contributions are welcome) is well worth a stop. The building dates to 1856, but the museum started in 1958 as local people began to donate old items collected over their lifetimes: historic photos, old guns, an old bar, bibles, books, even an 1843 Steinway piano. This collection of dropped-off history offers a series of snapshots of days gone by. It's an all-volunteer operation. They sells books and historical accounts of the area to help offset costs.

Moaning Cavern

Moaning Cavern (5350 Moaning Cave Rd., Vallecito, 866/762-2837, www.moaningcavern.com; 9 A.M.–6 P.M. daily in summer, shorter hours rest of the year; walking tour $14.75 adults, $7.50 children 3–12; adventure trip $76) is the largest cavern in the Foothills, large enough that the entire Statue of Liberty could fit inside. The Cavern, 165 feet deep, is accessed two ways: by walking down a 264-step iron spiral staircase or rappelling down the rock walls. Remember that after you walk down, you'll also have to walk back up. For those who want to experience the cavern as cleanly as possible, there's a 45-minute guided tour.

Spelunking is also available for the more adventurous, who don't mind getting their hands dirty. Caving is arduous and challenging both physically and mentally: You'll be crawling on your hands and knees, amid rock, mud, and water. Along the way you'll encounter the Meat Grinder, a place where you need to twist and contort on your back, then on your stomach to fit through a small opening, only to then find yourself on top of a precariously placed rock. Then there's the Pancake Room, two slabs of flat rock where you'll need to flatten yourself, head turned to the side, and shimmy between the mammoth stones, pulling yourself along using toe holds and finger holds. You need to work with the rock in order to reach your goal; working in harmony with natural forces clearly greater than yourself is almost a spiritual experience. You'll emerge from the depths of the earth tired, but exhilarated.

Gold Cliff Mine

Gold Cliff Mine (Angels Camp, 866/762-2837, www.goldcliffmine.com, $99, tours

The zip lines at Moaning Cavern let you race.

© MICHAEL CERVIN

by reservation only) will give you an idea of what life for the miners was actually like. You'll gear up in overalls and hardhat for the three-hour tour descending into the earth. It's not an arduous tour, but it requires effort and concentration. At one point, you'll also shimmy along slanted rock, gripping on to a rope to descend to old shafts filled with water. At another, as you're scrunched down by flat rock overhead, your guide will turn off the lights and illuminate the space with a single candle. At the end of the tour, you're rewarded with the realization that your daily existence is incomparably easier than that of the miners of old.

ENTERTAINMENT AND EVENTS

Main Street closes to traffic for one of the biggest events in the county, **Irish Days** (Main St., Murphys, 209/728-8471, www.murphys irishdays.com, 10 A.M.–5 P.M. on the third Sat. in Mar., free), which pays homage to the Murphys brothers who were, you guessed it,

Irish. There's a parade, bagpipes, activities for kids, live entertainment, food, and Irish beer.

Although Mark Twain's short story about the jumping frogs of Calaveras County was published in 1865, the first **Jumping Frog Jubilee** (2465 Gun Club Rd., Angels Camp, 209/736-2561, www.frogtown.org, held the third weekend in May) frog jump didn't occur until 1928. It has continued ever since. Today, it's part of the Calaveras County Fair. Contenders hope to be commemorated on Angels Camp's walk of fame, not unlike the one on Hollywood Boulevard, which celebrates the winning frogs.

SHOPPING

Enter a world of cool olfactory bliss at **The Spice Tin** (457 N. Algiers St., Murphys, 209/728-8225, www.thespicetin.com, 11 A.M.–5 P.M. daily), set back from Main Street. The shop carries some 150 spices, salts, and rubs, in both jars and individually packaged in less expensive 2–4 ounce bags. You'll find spices from the world over, from sweet

© MICHAEL CERVIN

The frog-jumping contest is one of the largest events in Calaveras County.

Hungarian paprika to saffron to a pumpkin pie spice blend.

Spice is nice, but **Tea an' Tiques** (419 Main St., Murphys, 209/728-8240, 11 A.M.–5 P.M. daily) is the stop for over 150 teas, mainly loose leaf, and all manner of tea related gifts, including beautifully crafted and hand-painted tea pots, with matching tea cups, saucers, and spoons. Some tea sets are Victoriana; others are more whimsical.

Feeling adventurous? Stock up at the **Sierra Nevada Adventure Company** (448 Main St., Murphys, 209/728-9133, 10 A.M.–6 P.M. daily), which sells backpacks, hiking boots, heavy-duty sandals, hats, sunglasses, and travel guidebooks.

Calm and quiet **Murphys Books** (178 Big Trees Rd., Murphys, 209/728-9207, 11 A.M.–6 P.M. Mon.–Sat.) has housed a general selection of books on most subjects for almost 20 years.

Upscale resale shop **Next!** (220 Big Pines Rd., Murphys, 209/728-2274, 10 A.M.–5 P.M. daily) has a very nice collection of rotating items that includes furniture and house wares. You'll also find complete China sets and even exercise equipment. The longer the items sit on the shelf, the lower the prices go, so you can score some great deals.

There's a lot of talent on the walls of **The Art Gallery In Murphys** (432 Main St., Murphys, 209/728-8640, 11 A.M.–4 P.M. Fri.–Sun.), owned by husband and wife artists George Durkee and Sharon Strong, who show their own work exclusively. Sharon Strong works on masks and installation pieces, while George Durkee uses oil on canvas in rich, vivid colors with many scenes of the area.

SPORTS AND RECREATION

Burn off the calories as you drink with **Get On Your Mark** (209/890-6244, www.geton yourmark.com, $75), which hosts 3- to 4-hour cycling tours of Wine Country. You'll visit 3–4 wineries and enjoy wine-tasting and lunch. The groups are small, no more than 15 people.

If you've ever wondered what it's like to soar

above the earth, here's your chance to find out: **California Zip Lines** (5350 Moaning Cave Rd., Vallecito, 866/762-2837, www .caverntours.com, 9 A.M.–6 P.M. daily, $39) will propel you across the treetops, 90 feet in the air, at speeds near 40 miles an hour. You'll sit in a harness attached to a cable. Try the cannonball position or go "superman style," leaping out into the air. The launch platform is 30 feet high, with the landing platform 1,500 feet away; the whole trip takes about 45 seconds. It's frightening and exhilarating all at once. The scariest part is waiting to go as the anticipation builds. Cast your fear aside and you'll have a blast. It's in the blink-and-you'll-miss-it town of Vallecito, on Highway 4, just a few miles before you arrive at Murphys.

Golf

At the base of the Foothills in the tiny town of Copperopolis, **Saddle Creek Golf Resort** (1001 Saddle Creek Dr., Copperopolis, 800/611-7722, www.saddlecreek.com, green fees $45–99) is an 18-hole Carter Morrish–designed championship course. It's a relatively flat course, with views to the low hills. The resort offers a value-added green fee which includes breakfast or lunch; call for specific details.

The greens at **Forest Meadows Golf Course** (633 Forest Meadows Dr., Murphys, 209/728-3439, www.forestmeadowsgolf.com, green fees $26–49) are ringed by pine trees and redwoods. It's an 18-hole par 60 course designed by Robert Trent Jones II, shorter than most with par 3s and only one par 5. There's a golf shop, putting green chipping area, and grill on site.

ACCOMMODATIONS
$100-200

The ambience is authentic at **Murphy's Historic Hotel** (457 Main St., Murphys, 209/728-3444, www.murphyshotel.com, $109–119 d), built in 1856. Each of the nine original rooms is named for a celebrity who visited the hotel, including Mark Twain, John Jacob Astor (who went down with the Titanic), John Wayne, Black Bart, and Susan B. Anthony. The small rooms are close to

Murphys Historic Hotel has been operating since the 1850s.

their original size, with tiny sinks tucked into the corner and shared bathrooms down the narrow hallways. There are no TVs, phones, alarm clocks, or coffee makers in the rooms, and no air-conditioning either (talk about authentic!). But you can sleep in the same bed as Ulysses S. Grant (and discover that you're probably taller).

A lot of families stay at **Murphys Suites** (134 Hwy. 4, Murphys, 877/728-2121, www.murphyssuites.com, $129–179 d), which offers 70 one- and two-bedroom suites. Amenities include a fitness room, sauna, outdoor swimming pool and hot tub, coin-operated laundry, in-room coffee makers, fridges, and microwaves. There's no Wi-Fi, but there are two computers in the lobby. Pre-packaged muffins and coffee are delivered to your room in the morning.

Clean and inexpensive, **Murphys Inn Motel** (78 Main St., Murphys, 888/796-1800, www.centralsierralodging.com, $129–140 d) is a five-minute walk to downtown Murphys. The 37 rooms all have two queen beds, in-room

coffee, refrigerators, and microwaves. There's a tiny exercise room and a seasonal outdoor swimming pool. There's no Wi-Fi but there is a communal computer in the lobby.

$200-300

The attention to detail makes all the difference at the **(Dunbar House, 1880** (271 Jones St., Murphys, 800/692-6066, www.dunbarhouse.com, $225–300 d), a four-diamond B&B set back from Main Street in a lush garden. Fountains at the front and the rear of the property mean you'll hear the calming sound of running water wherever you go. You're welcomed to your room with an appetizer plate, fresh-baked cookies, and complimentary bottle of local wine, beer, and bottled water. In the parlor, there's always hot tea; and sherry and port are at the ready in the dining room. Two rooms downstairs and two upstairs offer privacy as well as two-person Jacuzzi tubs, towel warmers, and gas-burning fireplaces. Two of the rooms have private seating areas on the

© MICHAEL CERVIN

The Dunbar House, 1880 is one of the best B&Bs in Murphys.

porch, overlooking the gardens. Herbs grown on-site are used in 35 different breakfast creations. Breakfasts are served at 9 A.M.; coffee is delivered to your door at about 7:30 A.M. to get things started.

Over $300

Querencia (4383 Sheep Ranch Rd., Murphys, 209/728-9520, www.querencia.ws, $275–400 d) is only four miles outside of downtown, but truly a world away. It's perched on a hill with some of the best views in the entire Foothills region. This is the dream home of Mike and Mary Jo MacFarlane and is filled with custom details, including unique art work, iron work, and tile. Other unusual details include reinforced bulging walls—similar in architectural style to Antoni Gaudi—to a hidden wine cellar for private meals. There are no phones, but there is a funky phone booth. There are two large bedrooms upstairs and two smaller ones downstairs, each with fireplaces, TVs, DVD players, and refrigerators. Accommodations are only offered Friday–Sunday. Breakfasts are included.

FOOD
American

Everything is made from scratch at ◖ **Alchemy Market & Café** (191 Main St., Murphys, 209/728-0700, www.alchemy market.com, Mon.–Tues. 11 A.M.–8 P.M., Thurs.–Fri. 11 A.M.– 8 P.M., Sat.–Sun. 10:30 A.M. –8 P.M., $15), and it shows. Chef Jason Wright's food is universally delicate, from the panko-breaded sand dab tacos and mushroom and artichoke pizzas to the wonderful Greek ahi salad. There's a long list of wines by the glass, with no corkage charged for local wines; there are also 75 varieties of beer.

Murphys Grill (380 Main St., Murphys, 209/728-8800, Thurs.–Tues. 11:30 A.M.– 3:30 P.M. and 5:30 P.M.–9 P.M., $15) has been turning out consistently good food for years. Try the prime rib salad with thin sliced meat, layered on a bed of lettuce with papaya, green apples, and strawberries, all drizzled with a housemade vinaigrette (Yes, it works). Other perennial favorites include the Cobb salad, reuben sandwich, and crab cakes. The outdoor seating fronting Main Street is popular;

a small bar and tables inside are available as well. The local art hanging on the walls rotates monthly.

℃ Murphys Historic Hotel (457 Main St., Murphys, 209/728-3444, daily 7 A.M.–9 P.M., $20) offers the most eclectic menu in town. You'll find pasta, seafood, fried chicken, and traditional sandwiches and salads on the menu alongside lumpia, escargot, and grilled alligator (Yes, you heard that right: alligator). One of the best options is the tender lamb shank, served with an exceptional polenta. For dessert, try the bread pudding, cinnamon-raisin bread glazed with a whiskey sauce.

Breakfast

Aria Bakery and Espresso Cafe (458 Main St., Murphys, 209/738-9250, 6 A.M.–4 P.M. Wed.–Sun., $5) opens early to satisfy caffeine cravings with coffee, cappuccino, and espresso. The bakery case is filled with croissants, bagels, muffins, scones, and occasionally quiche. They also bake their own breads, with specialties like artichoke Parmesan and polenta wheat. There are only a few cramped tables inside and out front; consider walking over to enjoy your coffee and Danish by the creek.

Pizza

You'll find just about every topping available, at Murphys favorite **Pizza Plus** (178 Big Trees Rd., Murphys, 209/728-8666, 4–9 P.M. Sun.–Mon., 11 A.M.–9 P.M. Tues.–Sat., $15), including feta cheese, cashews, and artichokes. Expect standard pizza-place decor, plastic tables and chairs, a worn interior, and a few arcade games. They also have a small salad bar, but the pizza's the main draw.

Cheap Eats

Sit outside on the patio for a calm, leisurely meal at **Wren Café** (64 Mitchler Rd., Murphys, 209/728-9736, 11 A.M.–5 P.M. Tues.–Sat., $9), located just outside the historic area. The menu includes half a dozen salads, like curried chicken salad, and sandwiches, such as grilled eggplant with caramelized onions and mozzarella. Try the Mexican meatloaf, which is soft

turkey mixed with a chipotle honey sauce, served in a flour tortilla. They also bake their own desserts and incredible sugar cookies: thin, crispy and loaded with butter.

Deli Nini's (403 Main St., Murphys, 209/728-9200, 11 A.M.–5 P.M. Wed.–Mon., $8) is best known for their very sloppy but tasty meatball sandwich. Other sandwiches use salami, provolone, basil, and focaccia. There are hot dogs and grilled cheese for the kids. The small dining room gets very warm on hot days, so most people hang out in front and eat at the stand up tables.

Dependable **El Jardin** (484 E. Hwy. 4, Murphys, 209/728-8300, 11 A.M.–9 P.M. daily, $9) makes a wide variety of Mexican food. Try the combination meal: one, two, or three items, like tamales, fish tacos, or burritos, that you can mix and match, served with rice and beans. Avoid the margaritas: too much like a lime Tang without the bang.

Farmers Markets

The only farmers market (1100 S. Main St., Angels Camp, 209/559-9995, 5 P.M.–dusk Fri. June–Oct.) in Calaveras County is located at Utica Park in Angels Camp on Friday evenings. Forty vendors bring fresh vegetables, baked breads, olive oils, and honey.

INFORMATION AND SERVICES

It's worth stopping at **The Calaveras Visitors Bureau** (1192 S. Main St., Angels Camp, 800/225-3764, www.gocalaveras.com, 9 A.M.–5 P.M. Mon.–Fri., 10 A.M.–5 P.M. Sat., 11 A.M.–4 P.M. Sun.) just to get their VIP (Visitor Incentive Program) deal. You receive a discount card, honored at local businesses that display the VIP logo, including wineries, restaurants, and shops. Note that its located in Angels Camp, not Murphys, as you might expect.

The *Calaveras Enterprise* (www.calaverasenterprise.com) publishes twice weekly on Tuesday and Friday (Friday has a larger arts and entertainment section). It is widely available. The website www.thepinetree.net covers

© MICHAEL CERVIN

Murphys Community Park is the perfect spot to relax.

the area as well with daily updates to politics and local activities.

GETTING THERE AND AROUND

Accessed by Highway 49, Murphys is off Highway 4 to the east. Traveling north-south, you can reach Murphys off Highway 49, or if you're farther west on Highway 99 or state Highway 5, you can take Highway 4 east directly into Murphys.

Within the county, **Calaveras Transit** (209/754-4450, www.calaverastransit.org) operates bus lines between Murphys and surrounding communities. Transfers are free; one-way tickets cost $2 and an all-day pass is $4. There are no commercial buses that will take you to Murphys from outside the county. To get a cab in Murphys, call **Murphy's Cab Company** (209/559-8777).

The Sierra Foothills' closest major airports are San Francisco (SFO), Oakland (OAK), and Sacramento (SMF). Commuters can reach the Foothills via Stockton (SCK) and Modesto (MOD) airports. Rhe Calaveras County Airport (3600 Carol Kennedy Dr., 209/736-2501, www .calaveras.ca.us) located in San Andreas, just north of Murphys, can accommodate private aircraft.

THE SANTA CRUZ MOUNTAINS

Santa Cruz has carved out a unique identity in California's cultural landscape. It has some of Northern California's best redwood forests to satisfy outdoor junkies, fabulous beaches to the west, a progressive college campus, and plenty of Silicon Valley money to the east, resulting in a curious cultural blend of capitalists, hippies, mountain folk, free thinkers, and surfer dudes.

And then there's the wine: True oenophiles know that the Santa Cruz Mountains are steeped in just as much wine-making history—and turn out wines just as well-respected—as the more famous appellations to the north. Clinging to the eastern and western slopes of the Santa Cruz Mountains are a few hundred acres of vineyards. Some face east and others west, some at high elevations and others at lower altitudes, some warm and others exposed to chilling ocean winds. It all creates a patchwork of growing conditions ideal for a wide variety of grapes. The notoriously finicky pinot noir grape thinks much of the land is heaven, and there are fine growing areas for chardonnay, cabernet sauvignon, and other grapes, too.

Small mountain wineries happily craft limited-production wines with a greater sense of place than many in other appellations. A limited supply of local mountain grapes often means making wine from regions farther south along the Central Coast, giving visitors the chance to compare great wines like pinot noir and chardonnay from prime coastal growing regions in both Northern and Southern California. Thanks to a few particularly

© VICKI & CHUCK ROGERS

SANTA CRUZ MOUNTAINS

HIGHLIGHTS

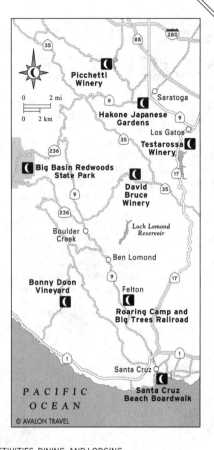

◖ Picchetti Winery: This rustic, historic winery is set amid hiking trails in the hills above Silicon Valley. Just watch out for the energetic peacocks (page 356).

◖ Testarossa Winery: It's a pretty walk from downtown Los Gatos to this pinot specialist on the hilltop, housed in a former Jesuit Novitiate (page 359).

◖ Hakone Japanese Gardens: Discover a little piece of Zen in the already serene hills above Saratoga (page 361).

◖ David Bruce Winery: Perched on a mountain ridgeline, this is the winery that helped put Santa Cruz pinot noir on the map (page 370).

◖ Roaring Camp and Big Trees Railroad: Though crowded in the summer, the old steam trains of Roaring Camp are a unique way to experience the area's redwood forests (page 373).

◖ Big Basin Redwoods State Park: Experience the mountain forests firsthand with a half-day hike, or simply visit the Nature Lodge and stroll the short Redwood Trail (page 374).

◖ Bonny Doon Vineyard: It's a little out of the way, but a lot of fun and home to a staggering range of unusual varietal wines (page 382).

◖ Santa Cruz Beach Boardwalk: This seedy but fun combination of sun, sea, sand, and thrill rides is a great family attraction (page 385).

LOOK FOR ◖ TO FIND RECOMMENDED SIGHTS, ACTIVITIES, DINING, AND LODGING.

famous wines, the region is well and truly on the wine map.

THE WINES

The Santa Cruz region is one of the oldest grape-growing regions in Northern California. It got a head start on the more famous Napa and Sonoma regions for two reasons: It was the earliest area to be tamed by the missionaries, and the wines could be easily transported over land to the thirsty cities of San Francisco and Oakland. Early Napa and Sonoma wineries, by contrast, had to ship wines across the bay to San Francisco.

Heavy logging in the 1800s cleared large swaths of the forested mountainsides, making way for agriculture and viticulture. By the early 1900s, there were thousands of acres of vineyards to serve the burgeoning Bay Area population, but the boom abruptly ended.

The increasing success of the wine industry in Napa and Sonoma, where flat valleys were easier to farm, combined with the double whammy of the phylloxera infestation and Prohibition, all but wiped out the once-flourishing wine business in the Santa Cruz Mountains. By the 1940s, only a handful of small wineries remained and virtually no intact vineyards. Nevertheless, the mountain wine industry hung on and is flourishing again, albeit in an altogether more compact and specialized form than in its Victorian heyday.

Today there are only about 300 acres of vineyards in the Santa Cruz appellation, though hundreds more surround its fringes. The small acreage, together with low yields of fruit from the rocky mountain soil, means that nearly every winery in this region has to use grapes from elsewhere in California to make commercial quantities of wine. The nearby Monterey and Central Coast regions are some of the most common sources.

Some estate wines carry the Santa Cruz Mountains designation, mainly pinot noir, cabernet sauvignon, and chardonnay—the three main varietals grown here. As the geography suggests, they tend to have an earthy, sometimes austere flavor, compared to wines from

ONE-DAY WINE TOUR: SANTA CRUZ MOUNTAINS

Santa Cruz wineries are spread out and therefore a bit of driving is involved. Staring in Los Gatos, aim for **Testarossa Winery** first for their stunning pinot noirs, chardonnay, and syrah in their historic old-stone tasting room. Then amble to **Byington Vineyard & Winery** a rather ostentatious winery built as a family home, but with sweeping views to the ocean. There you can sample rose while pondering how you could make enough money to buy a place like this.

Next, head to **Hallcrest Vineyards,** which has a cozy tasting room dating from the 1940s when it was built by a San Francisco lawyer, making this one of the oldest wineries in the mountains. Sample the pinot noir and their wonderful merlot. Have lunch at the wacky and over the top **Ciao Bella Act II** in Ben Lomond, where the staff will probably spontaneously perform a musical number on stage.

After lunch make your way to **Big Basin Redwoods State Park** to stand in awe at the majestic trees before you and reflect on how great a day of wine-tasting can be. Finish your day at Santa Cruz's best-known winery, **Ridge Winery,** for cabernet and zinfandel. The views are certainly more breathtaking outside than from the modest tasting room.

the hotter Napa and Sonoma Counties. Cooler weather is one reason, but the poor soil is another big factor in the unique taste of the area's wines. Mountain soils tend to be thin and rocky to begin with, and the more than 50 inches of rain that fall here every year has washed out much of the goodness over the millennia, leaving infertile yet mineral-rich earth.

The chardonnay in particular is a total contrast to some of the buttery fruit bombs farther north, but even the cabernet sauvignon grown on the hottest ridgelines can have a mineral,

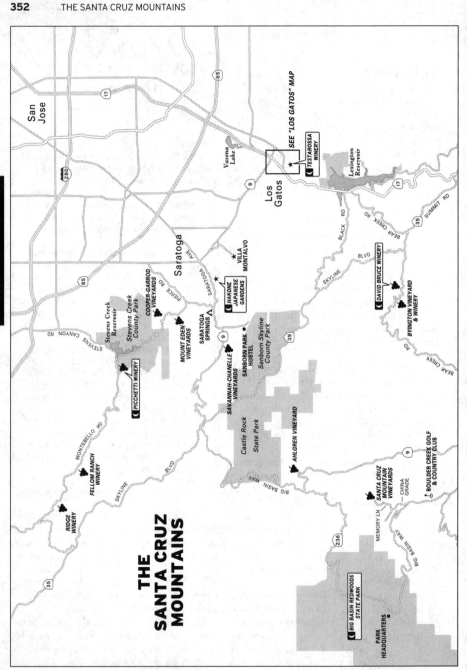

THE SANTA CRUZ MOUNTAINS

San Jose

Saratoga

Los Gatos

SEE "LOS GATOS" MAP

TESTAROSSA WINERY

Lexington Reservoir

Vasona Lake

Villa Montalvo

HAKONE JAPANESE GARDENS

Stevens Creek Reservoir

Stevens Creek County Park

COOPER-GARROD VINEYARDS

MOUNT EDEN VINEYARDS

SARATOGA SPRINGS

PICCHETTI WINERY

SAVANNAH-CHANELLE VINEYARDS

SANBORN PARK HOSTEL

Sanborn Skyline County Park

DAVID BRUCE WINERY

BYINGTON VINEYARD & WINERY

Castle Rock State Park

AHLGREN VINEYARD

FELLOM RANCH WINERY

RIDGE WINERY

BOULDER CREEK GOLF & COUNTRY CLUB

SANTA CRUZ MOUNTAIN VINEYARDS

CHINA GRADE

MEMORY LN

BIG BASIN REDWOODS STATE PARK

PARK HEADQUARTERS

SKYLINE BLVD

MONTEBELLO RD

STEVENS CANYON RD

PIERCE RD

SARATOGA AVE

BIG BASIN WAY

BLACK RD

BEAR CREEK RD

SUMMIT RD

SANTA CRUZ MOUNTAINS

almost angular taste, just like the rocky surroundings. Palates more used to the plump Napa or Sonoma wines might find it hard going in these mountains. In this case, stick to the pinot noir, a varietal that finds life as comfortable here as in Carneros or the Russian River Valley. Zinfandel also does well and is a varietal that ripens easily even up in the mountains, though it's still sparsely planted.

PLANNING YOUR TIME

Exploring the Santa Cruz Mountains, you might begin to realize why the area doesn't show up on nearly as many radar screens as do Napa and Sonoma. In fact, you might wish you *had* radar to help navigate the often widely spaced wineries that leave little in the way of signage to indicate where they actually are.

Even when there are signs, you might be concentrating more on trying not to fly off the narrow mountain road as another hairpin bend approaches. But when you do eventually find the wineries, you'll have a rewarding and often intimate experience. Just don't come expecting the sort of Wine Country frills found in the towns and large wineries of Napa and Sonoma—this area is all about small producers making serious wine surrounded by some seriously impressive scenery.

Many of these Santa Cruz wineries are clustered on the eastern slopes of the mountains around **Los Gatos** and **Saratoga.** They are generally closer together (though no less easy to find) than those on the west-facing slopes of the mountains leading down toward the city of **Santa Cruz.**

Forget about hopping from winery to winery, trying to cover them all in one hectic day. Instead, accustom yourself to slow but scenic mountain roads and let the great outdoors lure you out of the car (and lower your blood pressure). Driving from Saratoga up over the mountains to Santa Cruz can take up to two hours, depending on the route, even without stopping. Throw in a few wineries and a bit of outdoor exercise en route, and it can easily turn into a half- or full-day trip.

Virtually all wine events for the Santa Cruz Mountains region are organized by the Santa Cruz Mountains Winegrowers Association (831/685-8463, www.scmwa.com), including the notable **Wineries Passport Program** ($40 admission, but all tasting is free), which runs on four weekends during the year (usually the third Saturday of January, April, July, and November) and is the only way to visit many small wineries not otherwise open to the public. Plan wisely so you don't spend the whole day driving the mountain roads.

The association also organizes other annual events, including the **Vintners' Festival** ($30 in advance, $35 at the door), an arts, music, wine, and food celebration on the first and second weekends in June, and recently started the **Pinot Paradise** ($55 in advance) event in March, which sells out fast given this wine's newfound popularity.

One factor to consider if planning a trip to the Santa Cruz Mountains is that many of the smaller wineries tend to be closed during much of the week, opening only on weekends.

Los Gatos and Saratoga

To the east are the suburbs of San Jose and Santa Clara. To the west are mountains, canyons, and redwood forests. And straddling the divide are towns like Los Gatos and Saratoga that, in many respects, have more in common with parts of Sonoma and Napa than with their neighboring cities. Expensive restaurants, boutique shopping, Victorian history,

and million-dollar homes are the norm here, made all the more desirable by their proximity to the lush mountains visible from almost every vantage point.

The mountains, not the wine industry, gave these towns their start, and the wealthy helped shape them. As loggers cleared the mountains, the eastern mountain towns sprang up to serve the lumber industry. Once the trees had served their purpose, the area became a summer playground for the San Francisco elite. Today, the area is still a destination for the rich, as local real estate prices and the Ferrari dealership in Los Gatos illustrate. The same natural beauty that helped start these towns also prevented further development, as the mountains acted as a natural buffer to the spreading suburbs.

That's not to say development hasn't encroached on agricultural land. Many of the wineries in the hills north of Saratoga share the landscape with ostentatious McMansions, as bland as the scenery is beautiful. But the land is not under the same development pressure as is the case closer to the suburbia of San Jose, where a few historic wineries still cling to life in a sea of concrete. Nevertheless, some of the rural charm that makes many wineries in Napa and Sonoma so individual is missing.

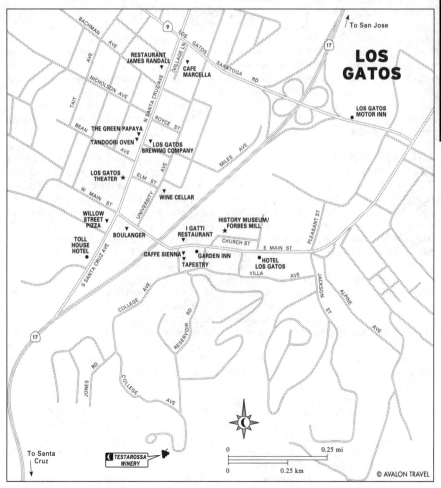

The Wines

The eastern side of the mountains, along the ridgeline and down into Saratoga and Los Gatos (at the border of the Santa Clara AVA), is largely shielded from the cold ocean wind and fog. This is where much of the cabernet sauvignon tends to be planted, so it can fully ripen in the longer hours of sunshine and warmer temperatures. Chardonnay is also common in this area, and one of California's best chardonnay producers, Mount Eden Vineyards, is remarkably close to Saratoga, with private residences nipping at its borders.

Although the Santa Cruz Mountains AVA is home to relatively small wineries, tasting fees have become more common. Most wineries in this area now charge, but there are still some that offer freebies. Winery opening hours also tend to reflect the lack of tourist traffic in the area. Some wineries are only open weekends, others for limited hours or by appointment only. All tend to be open an hour later in the summer.

WINE-TASTING

◖ PICCHETTI WINERY

This historic and rustic Picchetti Winery (13100 Monte Bello Rd., Cupertino, 408/741-1310, www.picchetti.com, 11 A.M.–5 P.M. daily, tasting $5), in a handful of old barns about a half mile up Monte Bello Road, is one of only a few still surviving in some form or another from the area's pre-Prohibition wine heyday. Picchetti was first established in the 1890s by Italian immigrant Vincent Picchetti, and managed to survive Prohibition by replanting much of the original vineyard with fruit trees and raising livestock, only to fall victim to slumping profits in the 1960s when the winery was sold.

It was leased in 1998 from the Mid-Peninsula Open Space District—its caretaker since the 1960s—and wine production started again after the necessary equipment upgrades. Now it makes about 9,000 cases of wine. Some, including a nice (but expensive) cabernet sauvignon, are estate wines from vineyards near the winery, but most are from other vineyards elsewhere in the Santa Cruz Mountains as well as the Central Coast and even Sonoma.

The land is still owned by and located in the Mid-Peninsula Open Space District, and there are plenty of hiking trails heading off into the wooded hills also managed by the District around the winery. A trail map is usually available right near the parking lot. There are a handful of picnic tables, and the huge expanse of grass makes it very kid-friendly—just watch out for the many amorous and hungry peacocks often seen (and heard) strutting around the area.

RIDGE WINERY

Ridge Winery (17100 Monte Bello Rd., Cupertino, 408/867-3233, www.ridgewine.com, 11 A.M.–5 P.M. weekends, until 4 P.M. in winter, tasting $5) is about a 3.5-mile drive up twisting Monte Bello Road from Picchetti, but it feels like driving to the top of the world—the views east across San Jose and the bay are spectacular. Ridge is one of the biggest names in Santa Cruz, thanks to the almost cult-like following for the cabernet sauvignon sourced from its ridgetop Monte Bello vineyard right above the modest redwood winery building. Take a picnic and get there early to claim one of the couple of tables, because the view is certainly more breathtaking outside than from the modest tasting room.

Grapes were first grown here in the 1880s by Oseo Perrone, but those original vineyards, like many others in the region, were abandoned during Prohibition. The current 80-acre Monte Bello vineyard was first planted in the 1960s and rises from an elevation of 1,300 feet up to 2,600 feet (you pass some on the drive up here). It now provides grapes for Ridge's famous cabernet, considered by some to be one of California's best, and one of the wines that helped put California on the map in the famous Paris tasting of 1976. The Monte Bello vineyard is also the source for Ridge's acclaimed chardonnay, considered one of the best in the Santa Cruz Mountains and often compared to the equally revered chardonnay made by neighboring Mount Eden from vineyards along the same mountain ridge.

Ridge also makes some equally good cabernet

Ridge Winery

and chardonnay from grapes grown elsewhere in the Santa Cruz Mountains, and both are a more palatable price. To confuse matters, Ridge also owns the former Lytton Springs winery up in the Dry Creek Valley and hundreds of acres of vineyards in Sonoma County, so its portfolio of wines stretches far beyond the cabernet, chardonnay, and small quantities of zinfandel made here. Many of these, together with the Santa Cruz Mountains wines, can be tasted on weekends when the tasting room is open, though public tasting of the Monte Bello wines is limited to a couple of special pre-release weekend events in March and May. Call the winery for more information.

MOUNT EDEN VINEYARDS
Another post-Prohibition success story, Mount Eden Vineyards (22020 Mt. Eden Rd., Saratoga, 888/865-9463, www.mount eden.com, by appointment only, free tour) was established in the 1940s by the controversial wine industry figure Martin Ray, known for producing some phenomenal wines and for

his attempts to reform the industry's wine labeling practices, which won him as many enemies as friends. After getting legally tangled with investment partners, Ray was forced to sell the winery, and it was bought by another group of investors that renamed it Mount Eden in 1972.

Since then, Mount Eden has gained a reputation for producing one of the best Santa Cruz Mountains chardonnays from its vineyards on the ridgeline. Indeed, some critics have called it the best chardonnay in California. The winery also makes a chardonnay using grapes from several vineyards in the Edna Valley, about a hundred miles south, and the contrast between the two is a fascinating example of just how different chardonnay can be depending on where the grapes are grown and how they're handled.

The estate chardonnay is intensely flavored with a steely mineral edge, a style designed to mellow with age for up to a decade, an unusual length of time for a Californian white wine. The version from the warmer, more fertile

Edna Valley has more of the tropical fruit flavors and creaminess that people normally associate with Californian chardonnay.

Mount Eden's other wines, including an estate cabernet sauvignon and pinot noir, are less highly regarded but still some of the best examples in this region. The pinot in particular has been receiving some rave reviews in recent years, and the vines were grafted from plants said to have been brought to California from famous Burgundian vineyards in France. Total production is about 15,000 cases, about half of which is the Central Coast chardonnay.

The winery can only be visited by appointment, but it is a worthwhile trip to make, not only for the wines but also for the view east across the sprawl of Silicon Valley and the sight of the multimillion-dollar homes that have sprung up in the hills over the last decade. Tours need to be booked about a week in advance and are offered only on weekdays during regular business hours.

COOPER-GARROD VINEYARDS

The stables and their distinct aroma right near the entrance to Cooper-Garrod Vineyards (22645 Garrod Rd., off Mt. Eden Rd., Saratoga, 408/867-7116, www.cgv.com, noon–5 P.M. Mon.–Fri., 11 A.M.–5 P.M. Sat.–Sun., tasting $5) give away the ranching roots of this small winery. The land was bought in the late 1800s by the Garrod family and planted with fruit orchards right up until the 1970s, when the last apricot and plum trees were pulled out to make way for vines. The Cooper name entered the equation through marriage in the 1940s.

About 3,000 cases of wine are now made from the 28 acres of vineyards. The tasting room is the old Fruit House, where those apricots and prunes were once stored, and it certainly gives the feeling of being on a farm. The best wines include some fine estate chardonnay and an aromatic cabernet franc sourced from vines said to be related to those brought from France at the turn of the 20th century. The newest vineyard, planted in 1999, provides grapes from syrah, merlot, and viognier, with the syrah perhaps the best of the

lot. Three wines can be tasted free, more for a small fee and for an additional $5 you get to keep the glass.

The ranching heritage is not entirely forgotten, either. The **Garrod Farms Riding Stable** (408/867-9527, call for reservations) offers horseback rides by appointment on weekend afternoons in the nearby hills, followed by a private tasting at the winery.

SAVANNAH-CHANELLE VINEYARDS

The tasting room at Savannah-Chanelle Vineyards (23600 Congress Springs Rd./Hwy. 9, Saratoga, 408/741-2934, www.savannah chanelle.com, 11 A.M.–5 P.M. daily, tasting $10), in a big redwood barn dating from 1910 a few miles west of Saratoga on Highway 9, is one of the few open to the public in this area, and perhaps the easiest to miss. Going up the hill from Saratoga, the driveway is a hidden hairpin turn on the left about a half-mile beyond the Saratoga Springs campground. Coming down the steep hill from the mountains, the driveway is easy to spot but also easy to fly by if you're going too fast.

The winery makes a huge number of different wines, most from vineyards outside the Santa Cruz region, but is perhaps best known for its pinot noir. Seven different versions of pinot account for about 80 percent of the 10,000 cases of wine made here and include several single-vineyard wines. Grapes come from vineyards in some of California's best pinot regions, including the Santa Lucia Highlands down near Monterey, farther south along the Central Coast, the Russian River Valley, and in Marin County up north. The winery's first estate-grown pinot noir (the 2002 vintage) was released in 2005, and future releases should be worth checking out considering the vast experience the winery now has with that pinot.

The only estate wines up until 2004 were the few hundred cases of zinfandel and cabernet franc, both from vineyards with links back to the original winery on this site, Ville de Monmartre, founded by French immigrant Pierre Pourroy in the 1890s. After several post-Prohibition owners, the winery was bought by current owners, the Ballard family, who named it after their daughters, Savannah and Chanel. The current spelling is said to have resulted from the less-than-enthusiastic reaction to the use of the word "Chanel" by a certain French couture house.

【 TESTAROSSA WINERY

It's a pretty half-mile walk (or five-minute drive) from downtown Los Gatos up the College Avenue hill to the old Jesuit Novitiate that now houses Testarossa Winery (300-A College Ave., Los Gatos, 408/354-6150, www .testarossa.com, 11 A.M.–5 P.M. daily, tasting $10), a rapidly growing pinot noir specialist. Don't go expecting to taste many Santa Cruz pinot noirs: Instead, Testarossa makes pinot from almost every other important growing region along the Central Coast of California, as far south as Santa Barbara, and only added pinot from the Santa Cruz Mountains appellation with the 2004 vintage.

At last count, there were about a dozen single-vineyard pinots from pretty much every major pinot-growing region in the state. The only acclaimed pinot appellation missing seems to be Los Carneros. The Russian River Valley, together with Central Coast and Santa Barbara appellations including the Santa Lucia Highlands, Santa Rita Hills, and Santa Maria Valley, are all represented, so it's no wonder that Testarossa wines frequently end up on critics' lists of top California pinots. There's also a dizzying array of chardonnays from vineyards up and down California, though none from the Santa Cruz Mountains. A couple of syrahs were added more recently and, like the rest of the wines, have received some favorable reviews. All told, the winery makes about 15,000 cases of wine a year and production is growing rapidly.

The wines are pricey even by Santa Cruz standards, with most of the limited-production, single-vineyard wines costing upwards of $60 (if they're even available) and even the blended Palazzio versions costing close to $40 a bottle. Their consistently high ratings, however, mean

they should be on the tasting list of any pinot or chardonnay lover. Cheaper wines are made under the Novitiate label, harking back to the small winemaking operation that the Jesuits once had. A small display about the history of the Novitiate and its winemaking legacy can be seen in the historic cave that leads to the big, modern tasting room.

CINNABAR VINEYARDS & WINERY

Cinnabar Vineyards & Winery (14612 Big Basin Way, Saratoga, 408/741-5858, www .cinnabarwine.com, 11 A.M.–5 P.M. daily, tasting $5–10) has long been a member of the elite group of mountain wineries around here, but its tasting room in downtown Saratoga, next to the Saratoga Oaks Lodge, only opened in 2007. Until then, the winery that's located a few miles up the hill was only open to the public for rare special events.

Named after the natural mineral that medieval alchemists believed could turn cheap metals into gold and silver, Cinnabar was founded in the early 1980s by a research engineer at the nearby Stanford Research Institute. The best wines are the cabernet sauvignon, chardonnay, and pinot noir from the Santa Cruz Mountain vineyards, some or all of which can be tasted as part of the more expensive advance tasting flight.

The bulk of Cinnabar's portfolio is made up of wines from the Central Coast region of California—including well-priced pinot noir, chardonnay, and the proprietary Mercury Rising red and white blends, all of which cost less than $20 a bottle. There are also sometimes some more unusual wines to try in the tasting room, such as the light and fruity red wine made from Valdiguié grapes, which has similar characteristics to the cheap and cheerful Beaujolais.

SIGHTS

Los Gatos and Saratoga are two of the most historically fascinating towns in Silicon Valley, largely thanks to the neighboring mountains that shaped the industrial and agricultural history of the region. Some of that history has been preserved, though there are some exceptions. Most notably, the Old Town of Los Gatos is now more accurately the New Old Town, after the shopping center that grew up in the old Victorian University Avenue School was "remodeled" by the enterprising city in the late 1990s (at least it wasn't renamed Ye Olde Town).

Los Gatos sits on what was once the main gateway from the coast at Santa Cruz to the Bay Area (a route down which Highway 17 now runs). Early Spanish pioneers from the Santa Cruz mission used it as a shortcut to San Francisco and, legend has it, coined the area's original name, La Rinconada de Los Gatos (little corner of the cats), from the large number of mountain lions seen drinking at what is now Los Gatos Creek.

With the supply route established, industry flourished in both Los Gatos and Saratoga, helped along by the gold rush supply business in the mid-1800s. Logging in the mountains during the late 1800s was followed by fledgling vineyards and other agriculture on the freshly cleared mountainsides. Where there are now subdivisions and McMansions stretching toward San Jose, there were once hundreds of acres of prunes, apricots, and other fruit orchards.

Los Gatos Creek

You can now walk along Los Gatos Creek without fear of mountain lions on **Los Gatos Creek Trail.** The trail runs from **Lexington Reservoir,** a popular boating and fishing lake south of town, north past Vasona Lake (another popular summer fun spot) to **Los Gatos Creek County Park** and beyond. Sadly, it also runs within earshot of a freeway for much of its length. Access the trail at East Main Street just before it crosses the freeway to West Main Street (look for the sign near Caffé Siena) and head south for a mile to the reservoir. Alternatively, go north a few yards to Church Street and see the site of the old **Forbes Mill,** built in 1854 by Scottish entrepreneur James Forbes to cash in on the demand from hungry gold miners for flour. It

was the first commercial building here and the catalyst for the eventual creation of the town, though only one wall remains today.

In the small storage annex built for the mill in 1880 is the **History Museum of Los Gatos** (75 Church St., at E. Main St., 408/395-7375, www.museumsoflosgatos.org, noon–4 P.M. Wed.–Sun., $2 donation). Exhibits cover local history and related history of the surrounding region, including the history of the Ohlone Native Americans who once called the area home.

Historic Los Gatos

From the history museum at the Forbes Mill, head across the freeway on Main Street to visit several of Los Gatos's finest historic buildings, including the modest 1902 **Opera House** (140 W. Main St.); the ornate renaissance revival **First National Bank** (W. Main St. at N. Santa Cruz Ave.) dating from 1920; the art deco **Bank of Italy** (160–170 W. Main St.) from the 1930s; and the 1891 **La Canada Building** (1–17 N. Santa Cruz Ave.), with its circular bay window and pointy-roofed turret. These buildings are all part of a short walking tour, maps of which are available from the Los Gatos Chamber of Commerce.

Turn the corner from historic Main Street onto North Santa Cruz Avenue and you're suddenly thrust very much into the 21st century. Boutiques, restaurants, and an increasing number of chain shops (to the dismay of locals) line the half dozen blocks down to the Los Gatos-Saratoga Road. Look for the art deco **Los Gatos Theater** (41 N. Santa Cruz Ave., 408/395-0203), which dates from 1915 and was remodeled in 1929, and the hard-to-miss **Coggeshall Mansion** (115 N. Santa Cruz Ave.), a turreted Victorian house said to be haunted and now home to an unexceptional seafood and steak restaurant.

Historic Saratoga

About the time James Forbes was grinding his flour in Los Gatos, the town that would become Saratoga was growing around a mountain pass tollgate on what is now Big Basin

Way. The tollgate settlement was later named McCartysville after the man who drew up the first town plan and sold off lots for as little as $10 (now those lots would sell for about 100,000 times that). The town's current name didn't come about until 1865, when a mineral spring in the hills above the town inspired the residents to copy the name of the famous upstate New York spa town of Saratoga.

Some of the town's history told through memorabilia and stories is on display in the tiny, one-room **Saratoga Museum** (20450 Saratoga-Los Gatos Rd., just south of Big Basin Way, Saratoga, 408/867-4311, noon A.M.–4 P.M. Fri.–Sun.), in an old storefront in the modest, roadside Saratoga Historical Park.

Villa Montalvo Arts Center

In its heyday, Saratoga became a magnet for wealthy San Franciscans looking to escape that city's summer fog, including Senator James Phelan, who built Villa Montalvo (15400 Montalvo Rd., off Los Gatos-Saratoga Rd., Saratoga, 408/961-5800, www.montalvo arts.org, 8 A.M.–7 P.M. Mon.–Thurs. and 9 A.M.–5 P.M. Fri.–Sat. Apr.–Sept., shorter hours rest of year, free) up in the hills in 1912. He created an impressive oasis that puts modern mansions in the area to shame (including those in the rather tony neighborhood leading up to the grounds).

The classic, Mediterranean-style villa stands regally at the top of a long, formal lawn with mountains rising spectacularly behind it. The formal gardens of the arboretum are all around, with hidden grottos and trails to explore. Longer hiking trails radiate out from the mansion throughout the 175 acres of land, winding up the hill to a lookout point and down the hill to the creek. The 1.5-mile nature trail on the hillside behind the mansion is particularly worth exploring. The house and its gardens are open to the public every day and a trail map is available from outside the box office to the left of the villa.

To get to the Villa you enter through the main gates at the top of Montalvo Road and first pass a rather less impressive building that's home to the thriving Montalvo Arts Center, which offers residencies for artists, plus regular art and sculpture shows. As one of Silicon Valley's most popular concert venues, the Montalvo also attracts big-name musicians, from rock to classical. There's a concert virtually every weekend of the year (on two or three nights a week during summer) either in the Villa or the Carriage House Theater, or outside on the lawn or in the huge open-air amphitheater. Contact the Arts Center (408/961-5858, www .montalvoarts.org) for a schedule or pick one up at the box office next to the Villa. If you do attend an event, book a restaurant well in advance if you plan to eat in Saratoga before a concert. A free shuttle runs from nearby West Valley College (14000 Fruitvale Ave., off Saratoga Ave., Saratoga) on concert nights, when parking at the villa is limited.

Once through the gates at Villa Montalvo, you'll be on a one-way road that threads through the gardens, past the Villa itself and multiple parking lots, and after leaving the grounds it spits you out seemingly in the middle of nowhere. To get back to Saratoga, turn left and then left again once you get to the main Saratoga-Los Gatos Road.

Hakone Japanese Gardens

Shortly after Phelan settled down in his summer retreat, San Francisco art patrons Oliver and Isabel Stine bought 18 acres of land above Saratoga for their own summer home. Regular trips to Japan led them to gradually transform the hillside into what is now the Hakone Japanese Gardens (21000 Big Basin Way, Saratoga, 408/741-4994, www.hakone.com, until 5 P.M. daily, $5), up a steep driveway just west of Saratoga village. This is actually one of a number of Japanese gardens built in the area during the early 20th century, inspired by the mountain scenery. Only this and one private garden remain.

The idea of crowds of visitors wandering around these very Zen gardens might not seem to be very Zen, but there are still plenty of peaceful spots to be found among the maples, pavilions, and ponds, which are said to be the oldest residential Japanese gardens in the western hemisphere. It is actually a series of separate gardens rising up the hillside with spectacular views. The Kizuna-En bamboo garden is designed to represent Saratoga and its sister city in Japan, Muko-Shi. The classic, gravelly Zen Garden is designed for meditation, the lush Hill and Pond Garden for strolling, and the mossy, damp Tea Garden for soothing away your worries before witnessing the arcane and fascinating Japanese tea ceremony.

EVENTS

The big annual blowout in Los Gatos is the **Fiesta de Artes** art and wine festival(www .lgfiesta.org), usually held in the second weekend of August along Main Street and at the Town Plaza. Many local wineries and restaurants take part in this sweaty street fair along with local arts and crafts vendors and live music.

In July and August, Los Gatos hosts the free **Jazz on the Plaza** (www.jazzontheplazz .com) six concerts on consecutive Wednesday evenings at the Town Plaza.

The summer also flushes out the thespians in the **Los Gatos Shakespeare Festival.** The outdoor performances are held on several evenings a week during July at Oak Meadow Park on the corner of Blossom Hill Road and University Avenue. Ticket prices and the schedule are usually posted in the spring. Contact the Festival Theatre Ensemble for more information or tickets (408/996-0635, www.festival theatreensemble.org).

Saratoga has its annual shindig in September, usually the evening of the third Saturday: the **Celebrate Saratoga** event downtown on Big Basin Way features local restaurants, wineries, and entertainment.

Many wineries in the area, including some not normally open to the public, take part in the four **Passport Weekends** organized by the Santa Cruz Mountains Winegrowers Association (831/685-8463, www.scmwa .com) and held on the third Saturday of January, April, July, and November. Tickets

(actually small passports you get stamped at each winery) cost $40 and allow you to tour the wineries, taste the wines, and talk to winemakers. Plan the day well, however, because the distances between mountain wineries can eat up the time.

ACCOMMODATIONS

Although lacking the sort of cozy B&Bs that dominate the accommodation scene up in the Santa Cruz Mountains and along the coast, the warmer eastern hills and slopes of this part of the Wine Country around Los Gatos and Saratoga have plenty of no-nonsense and well-priced places to stay, all on the doorstep of both urban sophistication and woodsy wilderness.

The two towns are on a quiet periphery of the Silicon Valley sprawl yet only a 20-minute drive to San Jose (traffic permitting). As a result, many hotels, however cheap, are often popular with visiting business travelers looking to escape the nearby urban and suburban bustle. Midweek rooms might therefore be a little harder to come by (even in the middle of winter), but weekend rooms, by contrast, might be more plentiful—the opposite of the pattern in much of the rest of Wine Country. The room rates are more uniform, with fewer, if any, weekend or summer price spikes compared to, say, the city of Santa Cruz.

Under $100

Considering the amount of rain that falls in these mountains during the winter, camping is out of the question between November and May for all but the hardiest souls. Perhaps the best value hotel-style accommodation in the area is at the **Los Gatos Motor Inn** (55 Los Gatos-Saratoga Rd., Los Gatos, 408/356-9191, www.losgatosmotorinn.com). It's a 10- or 15-minute walk to most of the action in downtown Los Gatos and has the ubiquitous synthetic motel-style bedspreads, but for under $90 a night, who's complaining? Rooms can actually be as cheap as $80, rising to $120 for the largest suites. Air-conditioning and free Internet access keep life bearable and the leafy, green surroundings create a pleasant setting.

It's also right off Highway 17, making it a modestly priced base from which to explore the entire mountain region.

$100-150

When Joe DiMaggio and Marilyn Monroe stayed here in the 1950s, the **Garden Inn** (46 E. Main St., Los Gatos, 408/354-6446 or 866/868-8383, www.gardeninn.us) in downtown Los Gatos was probably one of the swankiest joints in the then-sleepy village. Now the stars of Silicon Valley are more likely to visit the swanky car dealership next door to pick up their Rolls, Bentley, or Aston Martin. The inn shows its age a bit, but downtown location and price outweigh any decorative disadvantages of the unexciting but comfortable and well-equipped rooms arranged around the quiet courtyard and patio area. Rates start at $100 year-round for the basic rooms, rising to $120–160 for executive suites, equipped like a home away from home. Cheaper rates, especially for the suites, might be available on the website.

The **Saratoga Oaks Lodge** (14626 Big Basin Way/Hwy. 9, Saratoga, 408/867-3307 or 888/867-3588, www.saratogaoakslodge.com) is not far from the site of a former tollgate on the main road a few blocks from downtown Saratoga. The tolls to stay in this modern, airy hotel today are pretty good deals. The most basic queen and king rooms start at $100 a night, though the more luxurious and secluded rooms and suites in cottages up the hill among the trademark oaks cost $170–215. All the rooms are modern, with refrigerators and microwaves; some rooms have fireplaces and steam baths.

Over $150

The **◖ Inn at Saratoga** (20645 4th St., Saratoga, 408/867-5020, www.innatsaratoga.com) is a stone's throw from just about everything Saratoga has to offer, yet seemingly in the middle of nowhere in its quiet, creekside setting. The decor inside is neutral, both in terms of color and any great sense of design, leaving Mother Nature to put on

the main show outside the big windows or balconies in every room. The creek, neighboring Wildwood Park, and abundant patios and other outdoor nooks create a sense of tranquility, complemented by a broad range of amenities and services, including free Internet access, exercise room, VCRs and refrigerators in every room, and evening wine receptions. Rates start at $180 for standard queen or king rooms during the winter (request a creek view) and quickly rise to $260 for junior suites and $380 for the mammoth full suites. Summer rates can be pricier, with standard rooms often costing over $200 a night due to the popularity of summer events at nearby Villa Montalvo and Mountain Winery.

Two hotels vie for both high-end business and discerning private travelers in downtown Los Gatos, both offering central locations, quality restaurants, and modern luxury. The **Toll House Hotel** (140 S. Santa Cruz Ave., Los Gatos, 408/395-7070 or 800/238-6111, www.tollhousehotel.com, winter $170–190 d, summer $190–230d) is the least attractive of the two from the outside but is smack in the middle of the downtown action and underwent an extensive renovation in 2004, which equipped its rooms with luxuries like featherbeds, DVD and CD players, and free high-speed Internet access. Guests can use the nearby Los Gatos Athletic Club or eat on the huge patio of the hotel's Three Degrees restaurant. Choose from standard rooms or bigger Select rooms with patio or balcony; discounts are often available if you book online and pre-pay. Suites have accommodated the likes of Ray Charles and the Doobie Brothers over the years.

The **◖ Hotel Los Gatos** (210 E. Main St., Los Gatos, 408/335-1700 or 866/335-1700, www.hotellosgatos.com) is the more modern of the two buildings, a faux-Mediterranean pile built around patios and a small pool on the edge of the downtown area (and opposite the local high school). The 72 rooms sport more contemporary, edgy furnishings than those at the Toll House but have the same high level of amenities, and the hotel is also home to Kuleto's Restaurant, a destination in its own right. Rates start at $170 for standard rooms if booked online (nondiscounted rates are often over $200) and jump to $200 and higher for the suites, many of which have fireplaces and balconies or patios. Packages that include treatments at the on-site Preston Wynne Spa are also available.

Camping

The closest place to camp near civilization is at **Saratoga Springs** (22801 Big Basin Way, Saratoga, 408/867-3016, www .saratoga-springs.com; tent $25/night, $150/week; RV $32/night, $199/week), the creekside site of a former Victorian resort just a few miles up Big Basin Road (Hwy. 9) from Saratoga. For total wilderness, head farther into the mountains, because this campground is geared up for family fun, with a video arcade, playground, laundry facility, swimming pool, and weekly rates available. Of the 42 sites, about half are for RVs, with full hookups, and half are for tents only and up to six people. All rates are for two people only; $5 extra for each additional person; maximum six people.

Only a mile up Sanborn Road from Big Basin Road and Saratoga Springs is **Sanborn-Skyline County Park** (16055 Sanborn Rd., off Hwy. 9, Saratoga, information 408/867-9959, reservations 408/355-2201 or www.gooutside andplay.org), a 3,600-acre park that climbs up the eastern slopes of the mountains. It is home to the Sanborn Park Hostel and plenty of campsites, with showers and restrooms. Kids will enjoy a short nature trail and science center. Nine sites for RVs up to 30 feet long with hookups are available year-round (reservations required). The 33 tent sites are set up in a wooded area overlooking the park's huge meadow and are open late March–October. They are technically walk-in sites, but most are only a few hundred yards from the parking lot, and handcarts are provided to help schlep camping gear from the car up the hill.

Hardcore campers will probably prefer the more primitive hike-in campsites in **Castle Rock State Park** (15000 Skyline Blvd., Los Gatos, information 408/867-2952, $10/night),

a 3,600-acre wilderness strung along the crest of the mountains just a few minutes' drive from the hubbub of Silicon Valley. From the main overnight parking lot on Skyline Boulevard (Hwy. 35, 2.5 miles south of Hwy. 9), the Castle Rock Trail Camp is about a 2.5-mile hike along the Saratoga Gap Trail and is the bigger of the two, with 19 sites sheltered by oak and madrone trees. It's also the highest elevation at about 2,400 feet, so it can get chilly at night.

The smaller Waterman Trail Gap campground is about a four-mile hike beyond, at a slightly lower elevation in redwood forest along the Skyline to the Sea Trail. There is a parking lot far closer, at the junction of Highways 9 and 236 just north of Big Basin Redwoods State Park, but no overnight parking is allowed there. Both campgrounds have vault toilets and drinking water, but campfires are only allowed at Castle Rock, and even then only outside peak fire season. Reservations (call 831/338-8861) are required at Waterman Trail Gap and are recommended at the Castle Rock Trail campground, particularly in summer.

FOOD

There are some classy dining options in the Los Gatos and Saratoga area, where some of the South Bay's best restaurants cater to the moneyed crowds of Silicon Valley. Of the two towns, Los Gatos has more in the way of cheap and cheerful places to eat, particularly along Santa Cruz Avenue. Hardcore foodies might prefer Saratoga.

Downtown Los Gatos

Modest digs are often a sign that bistros are going to be unpretentious and worth visiting, and this is certainly the case with **I Gatti** (25 E. Main St., Los Gatos, 408/399-5180, lunch Mon.–Sat., dinner daily, dinner entrées $15–32), on Main Street just east of the freeway overpass. The bistro is small but comfortable, thanks to well-spaced tables and warm earth tones throughout, and it cooks up some interesting modern twists on Italian comfort food without losing sight of solid Italian traditions.

A little more experimental with its bistro fare is **C Tapestry** (11 College Ave., Los Gatos, 408/395-2808, lunch Tues.–Sat, dinner Tues.–Sun., large plates $19–35), in a little craftsman cottage just off Main Street. It offers both small, appetizer-sized plates and large plates of true California fusion food, taking fresh, California ingredients and creative inspiration from all over the world (often from Asia). Sometimes it works, other times it's too complicated for its own good. The smallish wine list is equally international in its inspiration.

Replacing the popular Café Marcella at the far end of North Santa Cruz Avenue, **Cin-Cin Wine Bar** (368 Village Ln., Los Gatos, 408/354-8006, dinner Mon.–Sat., entrées $15–27, appetizers $4–14) had a big act to follow when it opened in 2008 and by all accounts it has done a pretty good job. It serves fairly good (but pricey), Mediterranean-inspired bistro food in the main dining room, but the lounge area is most popular as a place to kick back with appetizers and some wine or a cocktail, especially during the happy hour, 4–6 P.M. Wines from the international list include a few local offerings and all are available by the bottle, glass, or as a taste. Some imaginative tasting flights are also offered for $15.

Taking the cooking and price up a notch is the nearby **Restaurant James Randall** (303 N. Santa Cruz Ave., Los Gatos, 408/395-4441, dinner Tues.–Sat., entrées $18–35) near the end of the main Santa Cruz Avenue drag. The cozy little bistro has a few tables on the front patio next to the herb garden, but the homey interior is perhaps more appealing. Its fireplace, oriental rugs, and artwork make it feel rather like someone's tasteful living room. The food is classic Californian bistro fare with Asian influences enhancing the fresh, seasonal ingredients. The wine list covers most of California but is a little light on the Santa Cruz region.

Those looking for a romantic but unintimidating place to eat should try the **Wine Cellar**

(50 University Ave., Los Gatos, 408/354-4808, lunch and dinner daily, dinner entrées $20–42). It's underneath a Borders bookstore and there are no white tablecloths or other fancy trappings to be seen, but the basement setting and warm, earthy decor create a relaxed, cozy atmosphere in keeping with the modern American bistro food. There's also outdoor seating at ground level under a vast old oak tree. Serious fondue lovers should avoid the cheesy dip here and head to La Fondue in Saratoga instead. The wine list is dominated by California wines but there are a few offerings from Santa Cruz.

Vietnam meets California at the cozy **Green Papaya** (137 N. Santa Cruz Ave., Los Gatos, 408/395-9115, lunch and dinner Tues.–Sun., dinner entrées $13–25). This is no generic noodle house, more a classy Asian bistro with prices to match. Try the signature green papaya salad or one of the clay pot dishes, classic Vietnamese with Californian flair. Or try more American dishes with an Asian slant like the rib-eye steak with fragrant basmati rice.

If South Asian food is more what you're after, look a couple of doors down the street, where the **Tandoori Oven** (133 N. Santa Cruz Ave., Los Gatos, 408/395-1784, lunch and dinner daily, $6–13) is just what a casual Indian restaurant should be—cheap, spicy, and with a menu chock-full of double-voweled dishes from Northern India. For something more American, try one of the wraps made with tasty naan bread.

Pub grub and microbrews are the all-American draws at the **Los Gatos Brewing Company** (130G N. Santa Cruz Ave., entrance at back of building, Los Gatos, 408/395-9929, lunch and dinner daily, breakfast Sat.–Sun.). The simple pub menu of burgers, pizzas, and pastas is reasonably priced ($5–15) and the best option if you want to eat here, although there is also a more adventurous dinner menu of steaks and other grilled meats that push the $25 mark. The lofty, cavernous space with exposed brick walls and beams develops quite an atmosphere on busy weekend nights and is pretty popular during the weekday-evening happy hours.

Pizza lovers should head to **Willow Street** (20 S. Santa Cruz Ave., Los Gatos, 408/354-5566, Sun.–Thurs. 11:30 A.M.–9:30 P.M., Fri.–Sat. 11:30 A.M.–10 P.M.), with a big outdoor patio overlooking the plaza. Pizzas from the wood-fired oven, burgers, steaks, and daily specials are not usually much more than $15, many less than that.

A quick and cheap Mexican fix is never more than a few blocks away thanks to several colorful Los Gatos locations of **Andalé Mexican Restaurant** (6 and 21 N. Santa Cruz Ave., Los Gatos, 408/395-8997, lunch and dinner daily, breakfast weekends, under $12).

Downtown Saratoga

The Basin (14572 Big Basin Way, Saratoga, 408/867-1906, dinner daily, entrées $16–30) thrives in the Saratoga restaurant field, having carved out a popular niche with its earth-friendly menu that draws strongly on fresh organic or wild local ingredients, including hormone- and chemical-free meats and locally-caught fish. Dishes are fairly typical gourmet Californian bistro food with plenty of Mediterranean influences, a perfect accompaniment to the romantic yet relaxed dining room and small patio. The modest wine list is international in scope, but the Santa Cruz region is fairly well represented by a handful of wines.

Huddled together on the same few blocks at the edge of the village are some of Saratoga's best (and most expensive) restaurants. The **Plumed Horse** (14555 Big Basin Way, Saratoga, 408/867-4711, dinner Mon.–Sat., entrées $30–42) is the grandfather of them all, serving stylish, traditional haute cuisine since 1952 in its contemporary yet stately surroundings with a wine list endorsed by *Wine Spectator* magazine. It has become a destination restaurant for the well-heeled of Silicon Valley and is often compared favorably to some of the best restaurants in Napa and Sonoma, so expect to part with a lot of money to eat here. The **Crazy Horse** attached lounge has occasional live music and a much cheaper bistro menu of small plates and salads

($7–15), together with a big wine list and plenty of fruity cocktails.

White tablecloths, French influence, and exquisite food presentation can also be found at **Sent Sovi** (14583 Big Basin Way, Saratoga, 408/867-3110, dinner Tues.–Sun., entrées $26–38) a little way up the road. They must be doing something right with the sophisticated, contemporary food and intimate, romantic atmosphere, because it's evidently a favorite spot for couples to get engaged. Check out the weekly prix-fixe menu that offers three courses and two wine pairings for only $45 and your wallet will thank you.

Fondue never really goes out of style, which is just as well because **La Fondue** (14550 Big Basin Way, Saratoga, 408/867-3332, dinner daily, $30–50 a person) adds some levity to Saratoga's increasingly serious, upscale dining scene. The dark interior is a fantasyland of castles, lairs, and medieval chambers where diners loom over pots of bubbling cheeses and sauces like time-traveling sorcerers. There are a staggering number of combinations of cheeses, sauces, exotic meats, and vegetables to choose from, not to mention chocolate fondue for dessert. Because eating the vast volumes of food takes many hours, there are usually only two sittings a night, so reserving a table a couple of weeks in advance is essential, though you might luck out on the night. Worth noting is that on Monday–Wednesday there is no corkage fee, so bring your own wine.

The casual, rambling café █ **Blue Rock Shoot** (14523 Big Basin Way, Saratoga, 408/872-0309, Sun.–Thurs. 7 A.M.–11 P.M., Fri.–Sat. 7 A.M.–midnight) is in a hillside house that is hard not to feel instantly at home in, thanks to its rustic atmosphere and countless private nooks upstairs, downstairs, and outside. Buy cheap coffee, beer, wine, pizza, or sandwiches on the main floor, then get lost somewhere inside with a good book. Live music (with cover charge) on Friday and Saturday nights showcases local musicians and livens up the otherwise mellow atmosphere.

Picnic Supplies

Quick lunches, sandwiches, and other deli foods perfect for a picnic can be found at **LeBoulanger** (145 W. Main St., Los Gatos, 408/395-1344) on the plaza. There's usually plenty of seating inside and outside.

Farmers Markets

Build your own meal from scratch with ingredients from the **Los Gatos Farmers' Market** (408/353-4293) every Sunday morning next to the Town Park Plaza. It operates all year and is probably one of the few farmers markets to have its own oyster bar. The **Saratoga Farmers' Market** (14000 Fruitvale Ave., 800/806-3276) is a little east of the downtown area in the parking lot of West Valley College and is held on Saturday mornings almost year-round, closing only for a few weeks at the end of the year.

INFORMATION AND SERVICES

On this side of the mountains, the **Los Gatos Chamber of Commerce** (349 N. Santa Cruz Ave., 408/354-9300, www.losgatoschamber .com) is the source of information, listings, and guides for the busy town. Similar information is available for Saratoga from the **Saratoga Chamber of Commerce** (14460 Big Basin Way, 408/867-0753, www.saratogachamber .org) in Saratoga village.

The weekly newspapers, usually available in cafés and on the street, are worth picking up for up-to-date event and entertainment listings. *Metro* is the weekly paper for Los Gatos, Saratoga, and other Silicon Valley towns, though its territory also stretches to Santa Cruz. The *Los Gatos Weekly Times* is a more news-oriented weekly but also has some listings.

GETTING THERE AND AROUND

Access to Saratoga and Los Gatos area wineries from the north is via I-280, a pretty and remarkably traffic-free freeway that runs along the eastern edge of the coastal mountains from San Francisco down to San Jose (reached from San Francisco International airport via I-380).

From I-280, take Highway 85 south at Cupertino and exit on Saratoga Avenue to reach Saratoga village at Big Basin Way (Highway 9), or continue on to Highway 17, taking that road west for one junction to the Los Gatos exit. Turn left at the top of the offramp and cross back over the freeway to get to one end of downtown Los Gatos at East Main Street, or head north from the freeway and turn left at the lights onto Santa Cruz Avenue to get to the other end. It's about four miles between Los Gatos and Saratoga along the Los Gatos-Saratoga Road via Monte Sereno.

Highway 85 also links to U.S. 101 when coming from the south, and those coming from San Jose and the East Bay can get straight onto Highway 17 from I-880.

Parking in Los Gatos and Saratoga is usually a relatively simple affair, which is lucky because a car really is the best means of getting around in this area. Some of the wineries north of Saratoga can prove tricky to find when navigating the winding roads through the hills and woods. Pay close attention to directions and geographical features on any map, as many of the roads will not be clearly named when you reach a junction.

SANTA CRUZ MOUNTAINS

San Lorenzo Valley

The heart of the Santa Cruz Mountains is actually a valley, the San Lorenzo Valley, which leads southwest down to the ocean at Santa Cruz. To the east, Skyline Boulevard runs along the ridgeline, high enough that it's possible to see both the ocean and the bay peeking through the trees at certain points.

From Skyline Boulevard, it's easy to see how the giant Big Basin Redwoods State Park got its name. The top portion of the San Lorenzo Valley really does look like a giant basin when viewed from the ridge above, one that is brimming with dark green redwood forests surrounded by sharp, parched ridgelines.

Down in the San Lorenzo Valley it still feels like you're in the mountains. Small, one-street former logging towns like **Boulder Creek** and **Ben Lomond** lie against a backdrop of forested mountain slopes. It's the sort of place where Bigfoot sightings are common, if some residents are to be believed. At the other end of the valley is the small town of **Felton,** which is closer to Santa Cruz, and, although still very much in mountain territory, has a bit more of an urban feel. All these mountain towns have an eclectic culture born of the waves of development over the centuries, from early loggers to Victorian resorts, bible camps, and a more recent influx of artists.

The Wines

The western slopes of the mountains tend to be planted more to chardonnay and pinot noir, though other varieties like syrah are now gaining ground. Wherever they are grown, grapes only just ripen here. Any cooler and the winemaker's job would be even harder than it already is.

During the summer, a sunny day in the mountains can rapidly turn into a fog-shrouded afternoon as the cool marine air rushes up the western slopes of the mountains and spills over the eastern ridge, often burning off before it has a chance to descend into the warm Silicon Valley. Most of the vineyards are at the higher elevations of the western slopes, areas that the fog takes longer to reach and remain warmer for longer. Chardonnay needs the warmth to ripen, though pinot noir can be happy up high or slightly lower down the slopes.

Closer to the ocean, the lower elevations can be so cool that growing vines is a struggle. The Ben Lomond sub-appellation covers many of these lower slopes, and, despite its large geographical size, (38,000 acres) it contains very few vineyards, so don't expect to see it named on many bottles.

WINE-TASTING

As is the case farther east, most wineries offer free tasting, but their opening hours vary considerably, so bear that in mind when planning a tour.

AHLGREN VINEYARD

Hewlett and Packard famously started their business in a Silicon Valley garage, and so did the Ahlgrens back in the 1970s, moving to a custom-built winery in the hills only when their garage winemaking operation started to outgrow its suburban location.

The Ahlgren Vineyard (20320 Hwy. 9, Boulder Creek, 831/338-6071, www.ahlgren vineyard.com, noon–4 P.M. Sat., free tasting) winery now has a bit more space, though it is still a delightfully homespun operation tucked under the cabin-style home in the hills. Production has grown to about 2,000 cases a year, all made with grapes bought from vineyards locally and as far away as Paso Robles and Livermore. Considering so few cases are made, the portfolio holds a remarkable number of wines.

The most notable wines come from the local Bates Ranch Vineyard and include cabernet sauvignon, cabernet franc, and extremely limited-production merlot. Another cluster comes from vineyards down near Monterey, including a chardonnay, syrah, and pinot noir.

Being such a tiny operation run literally out

ORGANIC WITH VOODOO

Organic farming is relatively common these days, especially in environmentally-conscious California, and a good proportion of wineries follow some if not all of the organic farming techniques required to become certified organic. An increasing number of wineries are taking things a step further and dabble in the world of biodynamic farming, described by one organic winemaker in the Sonoma Valley as "organic with voodoo."

Biodynamic farming has its roots in the early 1900s teachings of an Austrian philosopher and scientist, Rudolf Steiner, who believed there was a spiritual connection between the environment and the wider cosmos that had to be preserved. The spiritual element is what baffles many people, but on a practical level biodynamic farming has a little less voodoo than it first appears.

Where organic farming focuses on ensuring specific physical activities like fertilizing and pest control are done in an environmentally friendly way, biodynamic farming requires that the entire farm be considered a living system, kept in perfect natural balance and connected to all the natural rhythms of the earth.

To be certified organic by state and federal regulators, wineries cannot use certain things like synthetic pesticides and fertilizers, plastic containers and plastic corks, and certain wine additives (organic wine-making principles are actually surprisingly tolerant of many other slightly unnatural practices). Biodynamic principles require altogether more proactive actions and are certified only by a nongovernmental body, the Demeter Association. Certain composts, for example, have to be made using specific natural ingredients and applied to the soil at certain times of the year, plants must be planted in line with the rhythm of the sun and moon, and all plants and animals, from crops to weeds, livestock to insects, must be treated as one living, integrated ecosystem.

It's a bit like stepping back in time hundreds of years to an age before modern farming techniques were developed, an age when farmers had to work with whatever nature provided and crop rotation was considered the height of farming technology.

From a winemaking point of view, biodynamics is appealing because it is the only way that wines can be guaranteed to express the true, unadulterated natural characteristics of the land on which the grapes are grown, otherwise known as terroir.

Many organic wineries already use some biodynamic principles in some of their vineyards and are happy to leave it at that. After all, few wine buyers understand what goes into biodynamic wines, so the cost and approximate two-year time span it usually takes to have a winery certified biodynamic is often not worth it from a marketing standpoint. In the long run, however, it has been shown that a successful biodynamic farm or winery can actually save money by letting nature do much of the work of tending to the vines. Some also argue that biodynamic wine tastes better, though that's a more subjective test.

One of the champions of biodynamic farming in Northern California's Wine Country is Benziger Family Winery in the Sonoma Valley, which has been certified biodynamic since 1994. Many Mendocino wineries that have long treated organic practices as second nature are also either certified biodynamic or well on their way. In the Napa Valley an increasing number of wineries are obtaining biodynamic certification, too, including Frog's Leap Winery and Robert Sinskey Vineyards. Perhaps the biggest endorsement comes from the trailblazing founder of Bonny Doon Vineyards, Randall Grahm, who has embraced biodynamic principles in California and at his big new Pacific Rim winery in the Pacific Northwest and has become an ardent advocate for biodynamic principles.

More information on biodynamic farming can be found at the **Demeter Association** (541/998-5691, www.demeter-usa .org) in Oregon and the Michigan-based **Biodynamic Farming and Gardening Association** (888/757-2742, www.biodynamics .com).

of an oversized garage it's hardly surprising that the winery is only open Saturday afternoons. But it's a unique experience very much in keeping with the low-key atmosphere of Santa Cruz winemakers.

HALLCREST VINEYARDS

Most wineries in these mountains farm organically, but Hallcrest Vineyards (379 Felton Empire Rd., Felton, 831/335-4441, www .hallcrestvineyards.com, noon–5 P.M. daily, tasting $5) takes organic a step further into the production process and makes a range of cheaper wines under the Organic Wine Works label that are even free of sulfites, the preservatives added to wines in tiny amounts to prevent them from spoiling too quickly.

Those wines are not quite up to the standard of the regular Hallcrest label, which graces several vineyard-designate pinot noirs, a chardonnay, and a cabernet sauvignon blend, all from Santa Cruz appellation vineyards. These can usually be tasted side by side with the organic wines, most of which cost under $20 a bottle but none of which are from the Santa Cruz area, probably because grapes are too expensive to grow here for wines not made for longevity.

Like the rest of the winery, the cozy tasting room with its picnicking deck dates from the 1940s when it was built by a San Francisco lawyer, Chaffee Hall, making this one of the oldest wineries in the mountains. Tucked away in a residential neighborhood, the winery continued to operate under various owners until the Schumacher family bought it in 1987 and restored the Hallcrest name. They now make about 10,000 cases of organic wines and 5,000 cases of the Hallcrest label.

The tasting room overlooks the site of Hall's original vineyard that was planted in 1941 with riesling and cabernet sauvignon and was replanted more recently with the same clone of riesling and four different clones of pinot noir, far better suited to this climate than cabernet. The pretty grounds with plenty of grassy picnic spots can be further explored on an appointment-only tour.

◖ DAVID BRUCE WINERY

Regarded as the king of pinot noir in these mountains, David Bruce founded his winery (21439 Bear Creek Rd., Los Gatos, 408/354-4214 or 800/397-9972, www.david brucewinery.com, noon–5 P.M. Thurs.–Fri., 11 A.M.–5 P.M. Sat.–Sun., tasting free, $5 reserve tasting) on top of the world in 1964, supplementing his main profession as a dermatologist after being inspired by the wines of Martin Ray (now Mount Eden).

He has been somewhat of a pioneer since then, credited with being one of the first winemakers in the 1960s to make both a white zinfandel (later turned into a huge commercial success by Sutter Home) and a late-harvest zin that critics didn't quite know what to make of. He also planted some Rhône grape varietals like grenache long before most other wineries in California.

But his pinot noir is what won him the most fame and accolades over the years. Seven pinots are now made alongside cabernet sauvignon, chardonnay, syrah, sangiovese, and petite sirah. Not surprisingly, pinot noir accounts for about two-thirds of the 60,000 cases of wine made here each year.

As is the case with most wineries on the wild slopes of the mountains, the estate vineyards here at about 2,200 feet are tiny, covering just 16 acres. More than half of these acres are planted to pinot noir, which goes into the limited-production flagship wine. Another Santa Cruz–designated wine is made using some estate grapes and fruit from other small vineyards nearby.

If you hit the winery on the right day, you might be able to taste a Santa Cruz pinot noir beside versions from one or both of the other two great pinot-growing regions in Northern California—the Russian River Valley and Carneros. Other wines usually available to taste include the highly regarded chardonnay from the estate and other Santa Cruz vineyards, and a cabernet sauvignon from the hotter Santa Clara appellation farther east. The surroundings and views easily compensate for the less exciting modern winery building and modest tasting room.

SANTA CRUZ MOUNTAINS

© BYINGTON VINEYARD & WINERY

Byington Vineyard & Winery

BYINGTON VINEYARD & WINERY

Just beyond David Bruce on Bear Creek Road, the ostentatious Byington Vineyard & Winery (21850 Bear Creek Rd., off Hwy. 17, Los Gatos, 408/354-1111, www.byington.com, 11 A.M.–5 P.M. daily, tasting $5, tour $10) has sweeping views to the ocean. It was built in the late 1980s in a style that's part chateau, part McMansion. It now makes about 20,000 cases of wine a year from its modest estate vineyard and a chunk of land down near Paso Robles on the Central Coast.

Pinot noir and chardonnay dominate the production, both made in three styles using grapes from the estate, the Central Coast, or further north in Sonoma. There is also a cabernet sauvignon worth trying from the renowned Bates Ranch nearby in the mountains, and a red blend called Alliage, made predominantly with Sonoma grapes. The winery's general manager, Frank Ashton, also makes his own wine here under the Downhill label and occasionally it is poured alongside the Byington wines. Worth tasting in the Downhill portfolio

are a chardonnay from the nearby Martin Ray vineyard and a couple of barberas sourced from the Sierra Foothills.

This is also one of the few Santa Cruz wineries big enough to cater to large gatherings and does a roaring trade in weddings and meetings. The Byingtons evidently want individuals to have fun here, too. There are picnic tables, balls for the bocce court, and they even go so far as to offer barbeques—bring your own tools.

BURRELL SCHOOL VINEYARDS

It's hard to miss Burrell School Vineyards (24060 Summit Rd., Los Gatos, 408/353-6290, www.burrellschool.com, 11 A.M.–5 P.M. Thurs.–Sun., tasting $5), a little red schoolhouse building perched above Summit Road, home to this producer of some fine mountain wines. The schoolhouse itself dates from the 1890s and had the distinction of being the first in the district to get both a flagpole and a bell, which features prominently on the Burrell School wine labels. The tasting room is upstairs in the old carriage house next door and is just as charming. Picture windows and the spacious deck outside offer views over a chardonnay vineyard to the tree-covered mountains beyond, almost all the way to the ocean. You might be tempted to head a half-mile up the road to the Summit Market to pick up some food and take advantage of the serene spot.

Owners Dave and Ann Moulton started their winery here in 1973 and now make about 5,000 cases of predominantly red wines. Most notable are the elegant estate cabernet franc and syrah, both sourced from a vineyard a few miles away above Lexington Reservoir. Just as good are the pinot noir and chardonnay that come from vineyards right behind the winery and exhibit all the classic hallmarks of mountain wines. There's also a cabernet sauvignon and merlot from the Santa Cruz Mountains, together with a jammy zinfandel from Amador County.

For such a small winery, Burrell has a huge portfolio of wines, all of which have amusing schoolhouse subtitles. The flagship wine is Valedictorian, "Head of the Class," a powerhouse blend of cabernet sauvignon, merlot, and cabernet franc that is a lesson in how well the Santa Cruz Mountains can do Bordeaux-style blends.

REGALE WINERY AND VINEYARDS

In stark contrast to the rustic home of Burrell School Vineyards is the ostentatious Tuscan-style villa of the Regale Winery (24040 Summit Rd., Los Gatos, 408/353-2500, www .regalewine.com, noon–5:30 p.m. by appointment on weekends only, tasting $10–15), which opened in 2009 to offer a wine tasting experience that would be more at home in the Napa Valley than the sleepy Santa Cruz Mountains, with pricey wines, manicured gardens, olive groves, an outdoor tasting bar, bocce ball courts, and pairings of pizzas and bread from the wood-fired oven.

It is clear that no expense was spared during construction and therefore perhaps no surprise to learn that the man behind Regale, Larry Schaadt, is a former real estate developer turned winemaker. Except for a very good, but limited production pinot noir made from the small estate vineyards behind the villa, the wines here are sourced from vineyards all over the Wine Country, from the Central coast to northern Sonoma and the Sierra Foothills. Among the more interesting wines are the elegant Bordeaux blend Ovation, which uses grapes from the little known Carmel Valley appellation just south of the Santa Cruz area; an aromatic cabernet franc from the Napa Valley; and a juicy barbera from El Dorado Country in the Sierra Foothills. Annual production is about 4000 cases.

There are two tasting flights offers (with reservations only), the more expensive of which focuses on pinots and cabernets. Both include bites of whatever delicious snack just came out of the wood-fired oven drenched in the estate olive oil. Alternatively you can bring your own picnic to enjoy in the gardens as long as you buy a bottle of Regale wine to go with it.

Visiting such a fancy ridge-top winery is certainly a unique experience for this part of the Wine Country, although it remains to be seen how popular a destination it will become considering the wine prices (most well over $40 a bottle) and the slightly off-beat location. Regale is currently open weekends only, but it could open more frequently in the future so be sure to check.

BARGETTO WINERY

By just a few years, Bargetto (3535 N. Main St., Soquel, 831/475-2258, www.bargetto.com, noon–5 p.m. daily, free tasting) is the oldest operating winery in the Santa Cruz Mountains, though technically it's just outside the appellation's boundary. Italian immigrants Philip and John Bargetto first started making wine before Prohibition and resumed commercial production in 1933 after repeal. The third generation of Bargettos now runs the winery, and it has grown to make about 25,000 cases of wine a year.

The bulk of Bargetto's wines are sourced from its 50-acre Regan Vineyard east of the winery and include pinot noir, chardonnay,

© SANTA CRUZ COUNTY CVC/PAUL SCHRAUB

wine tasting at Bargetto Winery, Soquel

merlot, and a handful of Italian wines, including a highly regarded pinot grigio, dolcetto, and the pricey La Vita blend of three Italian grapes. Most of the wines are reasonably priced at under $20 a bottle and do not suffer from the over-oaking or over-extraction typical of many other cheap chardonnays or pinots. Most can be tasted for free in the rustic tasting room or outdoors on a pretty tasting patio overlooking a creek. The La Vita and some library wines will cost $5 to taste.

Most fun of all are the unusual mead wines made from fermented honey. They're not listed on the tasting sheet, but the staff are happy to let you try them. Despite having upwards of 10 percent residual sugar, the mead does not taste as sickly sweet as you might think. In fact, it has some rather wine-like aromas that come from the different types of honey used. A little more of an acquired taste are the fruit wines, which are essentially mead with small quantities of raspberries, apricots, or olallieberries added. All the mead wines are bottled under the Chaucer's label and are a fun alternative to grape-based dessert wines. Tours are also available by appointment.

To get to the winery take Soquel Avenue south from the Soquel-San Jose Road, then turn left on North Main Street.

SIGHTS
❰ Roaring Camp and Big Trees Railroad

For a taste of the redwood forests and mountain scenery without struggling up and down rocky trails, let an old steam train do the puffing and wheezing as it hauls passengers up and down the valley.

The narrow-gauge railroad of the Roaring Camp and Big Trees Railroad (Graham Hill Rd., off Hwy. 9, Felton, 831/335-4484, www.roaringcamp.com) once transported logs from the first sawmill established west of the Mississippi in 1842. The settlement was named Roaring Camp for the alcohol-fueled excesses of its residents. Steam trains (adults $21.50, children $15.50) now run over old-fashioned wooden trestle bridges in a loop up Bear Mountain, through towering stands of the redwoods that were saved from the Roaring Camp axes. During the winter there is just one train a day on weekends only (12:30 P.M.), but more on some holiday weekends; in spring and fall there are three trains on weekend days and one on weekdays (at 11 A.M.), and in the summer (mid-June–Aug.) there are three trains on weekdays and four on weekends starting at 11 A.M. Judging by the size of the parking lot, it can get as busy as Grand Central Station during rush hour.

Roaring Camp Railroad also runs the **Santa Cruz, Big Trees, and Pacific Railway,** a less glamorous diesel-powered train that runs from Felton down the San Lorenzo gorge to the Santa Cruz Beach Boardwalk. If you're in Santa Cruz, hop on the **Redwood Express** for a stress-free way to enjoy a picnic up in redwood country. And if you're already among the redwoods and want to visit Santa Cruz, avoid the hassle of parking and traffic, pack the sunscreen, and take the **Suntan Special.** It's an hour-long spectacular train ride from the redwoods to the beach.

© SANTA CRUZ COUNTY CVC/DENIS JOCKMANS

Roaring Camp and Big Trees Railroad, Felton

Trains (adults $23.50, children $18.50) run daily June–late August and on weekends in spring and fall, leaving the Beach Boardwalk daily at 12:30 and 4:30 P.M., and departing Roaring Camp at 10:30 A.M. and 2:30 P.M. There is no service from January to Memorial Day.

Bigfoot Discovery Museum

Where there are mountains and forests you can be sure there'll be Bigfoot sightings, and it's no different here in the Santa Cruz Mountains, despite ever-advancing urbanization. The last alleged sighting of a giant, shaggy Pacific Coast Bigfoot was as recent at 2004, and the species (for want of a better word) is celebrated at the Bigfoot Discovery Museum (5497 Hwy. 9, Felton, 831/335-4478, www.bigfoot discoveryproject.com, 11 A.M.–6 P.M. Wed.–Sun. in summer; 1–6 P.M. Wed.–Fri. and 11 A.M.–6 P.M. Sat.–Sun. in winter, donation requested), housed in a modest collection of huts next to the main road in Felton.

The photos, artifacts, and other information gathered here about worldwide Bigfoot sightings is the culmination of a life of amateur research by Michael Rugg, who has lived in the area since the 1950s and is as passionate about Bigfoot as he is about his countless arts-and-crafts pursuits.

Whether Bigfoot will ever be discovered by science is open to debate, though the fact that a previously unknown species of monkey was found in the jungles of southern Africa in 2005 certainly suggests it's still possible, at least in theory. The truth is out there, somewhere deep in the forests of the Santa Cruz Mountains.

RECREATION
Big Basin Redwoods State Park

This was California's first state park (21600 Big Basin Way in Boulder Creek, Hwy. 236 off Hwy. 9 about 12 miles west of Saratoga, 831/338-8860, 9 A.M.–5 P.M. daily, $10 day-use fee), established in 1902 thanks to the efforts of the Sempervirens Club. These early conservationists managed to save 3,800 acres of

...ably in **Big Basin Redwoods State Park** ...600 Big Basin Way, off Hwy. 9, Boulder ...ek, 831/338-8860), California's oldest state ...k, containing towering redwoods and tow...ng views from its loftiest points.

The camping options are almost endless. ...e 146 campsites ($35) include 31 for RVs up ...27 feet long (no hookups) and 74 tent-only ...es. There are also a handful of hike-in trail ...mps throughout the park, two group camp-...es, horse camps, and hike and bike camps. ...he main camping area has restrooms, show-...s, and a small grocery store. The park gets ...ery popular with backpackers and Bay Area ...veekenders during the summer, so make res-...rvations early through Reserve America (www ...reserveamerica.com or 800/444-7275).

Families or the tentless might consider one ...f Big Basin's 41 tent cabins (800/444-7275, www.bigbasintentcabins.com, $75), canvas-roofed huts that sleep up to four people and sit on their own little campsites with picnic tables and fire rings. Bring your own sleeping bag or rent linens from the concession that runs the cabins. Despite being glorified campsites, the tent cabins have a two-night weekend minimum during the summer.

Toward Santa Cruz is the smaller (but equally pretty and packed with redwoods) **Henry Cowell Redwoods State Park** (101 N. Big Trees Park Rd., off Hwy. 9, Felton, 831/438-2396). The ...ntrance to the campground is on Graham Hill ...oad (off Hwy. 9) on the other side of the park ...rom the headquarters. There are 112 campsites ...35) for tents or RVs (no hookups), plus showers ...d restrooms. Unlike Big Basin, this camp-...ound is closed during the winter (Jan.–Mar.). ...eserve sites the rest of the year through Reserve ...merica (www.reserveamerica.com or 800/444-...75). Anyone not feeling energetic enough to ...e the miles of trails in this and Big Basin ...k can take an easy 15-minute hike from the ...mpground to an observation deck with views ...anta Cruz and the ocean.

...OD

...aurants in the San Lorenzo Valley have a ...hings in common, like the fact that most

are along Highway 9 and have a typically rusti... feel to the food and the interiors. But if you'r... anticipating big slabs of meat fit for a lumber... jack, you're in for a few surprises, courtesy ... the more sophisticated artist community tha... thrives in the woods.

Boulder Creek

The **Boulder Creek Brewing Company** (1304... Hwy. 9, Boulder Creek, 831/338-7782, lunc... and dinner daily) has the sort of hearty men... needed to fuel long hikes in nearby Big Basi... Redwoods State Park. Load up on carbs an... protein with the burgers, pizzas, burritos, an... pastas, or order a bulging sandwich to go for... mountain picnic. Wash it all down with one... the dozen or so microbrews that range from th... crisp Summer Wheat beer to the thick, da... Black Dragon Stout. The flagship beer is t... aptly named Redwood Ale, an amber ale th... packs in the malty hop flavors without bitt... ness. The brewery is regarded as the best in th... part of the world, better even than what's ... offer down in Santa Cruz (it reportedly boug... much of the equipment from the now-defu... Santa Cruz Brewing Company). The dec... however, is more questionable.

Ben Lomond

They might not have redwoods in Bavaria, ... that didn't stop German native Dieter Sei... from recreating a cozy Bavarian meat shack ... the middle of Ben Lomond, the **Tyrolean I**... (9600 Hwy. 9, Ben Lomond, 831/336-51... dinner Tues.–Sun., lunch Sun., dinner ... trées $15–27). Dieter will have you doing ... polka while waiting for the bratwurst, sau... kraut, and countless other less-pronouncea... German staples. There seems to be some s... of beer festival going on every month, idea... you happen to need an excuse to down a h... gallon of hefeweizen in Wine Country ... don't mind crowds.

If German kitsch is not your style, h... about some Italian kitsch? Ben Lomond ... that too at **Ciao Bella Act II** (9217 H... 9, Ben Lomond, 831/336-8547, www.... bellaactii.com, breakfast and dinner da...

Big Basin Redwoods State Park

old-growth redwoods from the axes that cleared most of the other mountain slopes, and the park has since expanded to encompass 18,000 acres of forest and chaparral stretching from 2,000 feet up in the mountains down to the Pacific coast.

This wild area was once the domain of grizzly bears, but now the biggest animals found here (though you rarely see them) are mountain lions, coyotes, and foxes. Deer are usually more visible, as are the raccoons and hundreds of bird species. More than 80 miles of trails offer a bewildering array of ways for hikers and bikers to see the animals, forest, flowers, and waterfalls. Mountain bikes are only allowed on fire roads, however, not on any of the tempting single-track.

Be sure to pick up a map at the **visitors center** in the park headquarters. Also ask about the free guided hikes and wildflower walks offered at certain times of the year, and be sure to check out the small Nature Lodge museum near the park headquarters to learn more about the park and its natural history.

The easiest hike, more of a stroll, is the half-mile jaunt around the **Redwood Trail** loop

close to the park headquarters. It's the quickest way to see the famous trees, including the tallest of them all, the 329-foot-tall Mother of the Forest, but you won't experience the wilderness that the park is known for.

All other trails head deep into the park, so you'll have to double back if you don't have more than a couple of hours to spare. Good half-day hikes include the **Meteor Trail** to the park's best lookout, Ocean View Point at 1,600 feet (though you'll see nothing but clouds if it's foggy). From the park headquarters, head north on the Skyline to the Sea Trail, through the redwoods along Opal Creek and past the historic Maddocks Cabin site (turn back here if you're short on time) before turning left at the two-mile point up the Meteor Trail, which climbs steeply to a fire road. Turn left on the fire road and the lookout point is only a few hundred yards farther. It's about 5.5 miles to the lookout and back.

Longer hikes include the 12-mile slog to three spectacular waterfalls: **Berry Creek Falls**, 70 feet of vertical water framed by lush ferns

SANTA CRUZ MOUNTAINS

and forest; freefalling **Silver Falls;** and the **Golden Falls** cascading over sandstone rock. Take the Skyline to the Sea Trail west from the park headquarters up over the ridge and down to the creek, following it until you round a bend and can't miss the Berry Creek Falls. At this point, head north on the **Berry Creek Falls Trail** to the other two waterfalls, sticking your head into the path of the cascading Silver Falls water if you're overheating. Either return the same way or, just north of Golden Falls past the Sunset camp, take a right on the **Sunset Trail** to loop back toward park headquarters.

That **Skyline to the Sea Trail,** a jumping-off point for so many other trails in the park, is itself a great 11-mile hike all the way down to the ocean at Waddell Beach. Either have someone pick you up at the end, or camp at one of the trail camps along the way.

Henry Cowell Redwoods State Park

At the other end of the San Lorenzo Valley is Big Basin's little brother, Henry Cowell

Henry Cowell Redwoods State Park

Redwoods State Park (101 N. Big Trees Park Rd., Felton, 831/335-4598, $10 day-use fee), with equally impressive redwoods and 20 miles of hiking trails set in the San Lorenzo River canyon. Park headquarters are off Highway 9, just south of Felton, and there are numerous trailheads along Highway 9 farther south and at the campground, which is accessed from Graham Hill Road just south of Felton.

As at Big Basin, there's a short **Redwood Trail** loop from the park headquarters for instant big-tree gratification, but it's worth continuing along the **River Trail** for a longer hike into the middle of the park, linking with other trails that could keep you occupied all day. Worth noting is that the **Santa Cruz, Big Trees, and Pacific Railway** runs right through the middle of the park from Felton along the river on its way down to Santa Cruz, an ideal way to experience the park for those without the time, inclination, or wet-weather gear to explore it on foot.

ACCOMMODATIONS

To describe the San Lorenzo Valley as "rustic" is a bit of an understatement, which means that, despite the natural beauty of the area, there is little in the way of luxury when it comes to accommodations. The majority of places to stay are cabin or motel style, many built a half century ago with furnishings that seem to be from the same era. Even the handful of B&Bs are by no means luxurious, so if it's pampering you're after, it's probably best to head down from the mountains to Santa Cruz or Saratoga.

Under $100

The **Brookdale Inn and Spa** (11570 Hwy. 9, Brookdale, 831/338-1300, www.brookdale innandspa.com, from $60 midweek and $80 on weekends in winter, $80–100 in summer) has a storied history, playing host to film stars and politicians (including president Herbert Hoover) during its heyday in the 1930s and 1940s. Now it's a bit of a faded star and was still undergoing extensive renovations as this edition went to press, so check the status before booking a room. It is a fascinating and

cheap place to stay up in the redwoods, not least because of the mountain brook running right through the middle of the main dining room, a sight that has to be seen to be believed (although the food is not worth experiencing). Suites and cottages are $130 a night, and are a better option if you can afford them. Any strange sounds you hear during the night could either be your neighbors on the other side of the thin walls or the ghosts said to haunt the lodge, including a nine-year-old girl who drowned in the dining room brook in the 1970s.

The **Ben Lomond Econo Lodge** (9733 Hwy. 9, Ben Lomond, 831/336-2292, www.stay intheredwoods.com, from $80 in winter, from $100 in summer, more on weekends) is a slightly shabby, unremarkable place, but its location surrounded by redwoods and a creek is pretty remarkable for a motel. It actually looks a bit like a motel plucked from beside a freeway offramp and dropped into the middle of a forest. In addition to the scenic surroundings, its prices, a decent-size outdoor pool, and its location just a short walk from the few blocks that constitute downtown Ben Lomond more than make up for the rather sparse interior comforts. There's also a two-bed cabin with a kitchen that costs $150–250 depending on season and time of the week.

$100-200

The mountains tend to be the domain of rustic inns and resorts, but there are a couple of cozy B&Bs worth investigating.

In a more central mountain location is the **Fairview Manor** (245 Fairview Ave., off Hwy. 9, Ben Lomond, 831/336-3355, www.fairview manor.com, $140–160). The five rooms, all with private bathrooms, are by no means luxurious but are nicely furnished, clean, and include a full breakfast. This is a great price for the location in the redwoods next to the San Lorenzo River in Ben Lomond.

Jaye's Timberlane Resort (8705 Hwy. 9, Ben Lomond, 831/336-5479, www.jayes timberlane.com, $80–160) is a resort in the rustic rather than the pampering sense of the word, featuring 10 simple cabins set among seven acres of redwoods and tarmac. The cabins themselves

have either one or two bedrooms, ... and a small kitchen. Furnishings h... ter days and the walls are plain wo... do get a TV and a fireplace to stay w... ter (though it won't help at all in t... when you might be wishing for air-con... You won't be knocking together a f... dinner to go with your favorite Sa... pinot, or luxuriating in a foaming, ... bath, but, for the price and locatio... middle of the redwoods, these comp... dwellings are a pretty good deal.

More upscale but usually with m... ited availability are the 1-, 2-, and 3-be... condos at the **Boulder Creek Go... Country Club** (16901 Big Basin Hwy., B... Creek, 831/338-2111, www.bouldercre... .com, from $125). There are countless ... ages available that incorporate golf, tennis... many other sporting activities. Contact th... sort for more information. Golfers will b... paradise with the par-65 course set among... redwoods, but the club is also convenient f... all the other outdoor and wine-related activi... ties the mountains have to offer and is set i... beautiful location.

Over $300

At the other end of the B&B scale is the ... ish **C Felton Crest Inn** (780 El Solyo H... Dr., Felton, 831/335-4011 or 800/474... www.feltoncrest.com), on a quiet, priva... off the main highway. Four sumptuou... nished rooms, each on a separate flo... down comforters, TVs and VCRs, a... of towering trees. A couple rooms e... with jetted tubs and private decks. ... the main deck or in hammocks amo... woods, or head down one of the ... that leads into neighboring Henry ... Park. Such tranquility and luxu... price—from $200 for the bottom... up to $399 for the penthouse or... with vaulted ceilings.

Camping

In the middle of the Santa C... are some of the Bay Area's bes...

dinner entrées $12–28). This is part restaurant, part Broadway musical, and completely wacky. The classic Italian comfort food is decent enough but that's more or less where the Italian connection ends. Everything screams roadhouse on acid in the land of Oz, right from when you drive up to the riotous exterior and park in a space "Reserved for Elvis" to the jaw-dropping moment the waitstaff get up on stage to perform an impromptu Broadway rendition. It's loud but a lot of fun (much of it for adult eyes and ears only) and a bonus is the outdoor seating area surrounded by redwoods.

Felton

Head down the road for reasonably priced family-style Italian food in more traditional surroundings at **Mama Mia's Ristorante Italiano** (6231 Graham Hill Rd., off Hwy. 9, Felton, 831/335-4414, dinner daily, entrées $14–22). It's the original restaurant in a small South Bay chain and still turns out down-home Italian pizza, pasta, and meat dishes on checkered tablecloths, earning a loyal following from Boulder Creek to Santa Cruz.

A giant oak tree sheltering the garden and patio was the inspiration behind the name of **Oak Tree Ristorante** (5447 Hwy. 9, Felton, 831/335-5551, dinner daily, lunch and breakfast on weekends, dinner entrées $14–22), an Italian bistro that replaced the popular La Bruschetta in 2009. Simple southern-Italian dishes, including freshly-made pastas and locally-sourced meat, fish, and vegetables, are prepared with style and flair by owner and chef, Sebastian Nobile, who was also the chef at La Bruschetta for many years. Try to get a table out on the big brick patio under the oak tree for a classy alfresco Wine Country dining experience.

INFORMATION AND SERVICES

For all wine-related information, turn first to the **Santa Cruz Mountains Winegrowers Association** (831/685-8463, www.scmwa .com), which has information about all the region's wines and wineries on a free map, usually available in winery tasting rooms. The website has information about the regular wine events the association arranges, including the Passport weekends, often the only way to visit some of the smaller wineries not listed in this chapter. Some of the non-wine-related listings on the website tend to be a little out of date, so take them with a pinch of salt, but the map is an essential tool for exploring the widely spaced wineries in the mountains.

For more information about the various state parks up in the mountains, visit the **California State Parks** website (www.parks.ca.gov).

GETTING THERE AND AROUND

Anyone planning to visit wineries in the Santa Cruz Mountains should really only consider driving, since most wineries are in the middle of nowhere and accessible only by car. Even intrepid bike riders will quickly give up on any ideas of biking between wineries once the distances and inclines become clearer, and when they've experienced the speed of the traffic on the treacherous mountain roads. It is true that Highway 9 is a popular biking route for local riders and offers plenty of fueling stops along the way, but it is not for the faint of heart.

The mountain wineries can be accessed from Highway 9, which runs between Santa Cruz and Saratoga, via the San Lorenzo Valley towns of Felton, Ben Lomond, and Boulder Creek. Alternatively, Highway 17 slices through the mountains and provides access to the handful of wineries north and south via Summit Road, a few miles southwest of Los Gatos.

Travel south on Summit Road past the Burrell School and neighboring wineries, turning right on what becomes the Old San Jose Road toward Soquel, which takes you past some more wineries as it heads down through woodland and farmland to the coast and Highway 1 at Soquel, just east of Santa Cruz. Go north on Summit Road for faster access to the David Bruce Winery and Byington Vineyard before descending on Bear Creek Road to Boulder Creek. Summit Road also links up with Skyline Boulevard, which runs along the ridgeline of the mountains above

Los Gatos and Saratoga, eventually intersecting with Highway 9.

Although distances between towns in the mountains are not huge (and gas stations are common in the San Lorenzo Valley), some of the roads can be tortuously slow, especially the southern end of Skyline Boulevard and Highway 9 as it climbs from Saratoga up to the ridge. Signage is also spotty in some areas, so you might have to trust your sense of direction. Make sure you pick up the winery map provided by the Santa Cruz Mountains Winegrowers Association, available in most winery tasting rooms. It offers detailed local direction to wineries listed here and many more open on the Passport Weekends.

Santa Cruz

The seaside surf town of Santa Cruz is a fascinating mix of sleaze, students, and staid middle-class culture that only a historic university city on the edge of the wealthy Bay Area could be. It attracts millions of visitors every year in search of a hedonistic beach lifestyle and boardwalk entertainment, and the city's main beach is still the center of action, if not the prettiest part of town. Away from the sand, the city of 55,000 feels more like a small suburban town, sprawling lazily around the San Lorenzo River with only the area around Pacific Avenue lending any sense of a lively downtown.

The seed of modern-day Santa Cruz was the mission, established here in the late 1700s, around which a small trading post built up. The trading post eventually became a port serving the mountain lumber business and trades associated with the gold rush, before the pleasures of the climate and location were recognized by the newly mobile Victorian society. Santa Cruz was quickly transformed into the resort town it is today as tourism overtook the dwindling logging and fishing industries.

Despite its religious and Victorian heritage, Santa Cruz became famous in the 1960s for being a low-key counterculture town, attracting surfers and the fringes of the San Francisco hippie scene. The city is home to the most progressive campus of the University of California, established here in 1965, and a city council that has been equally progressive, regularly taking a position on international political situations and passing socially conscious legislation, including a minimum wage that is almost double that required under state law.

More recently, Silicon Valley types, lured by relatively cheap property and the pleasant summer climate, moved in. As money gains influence, the laid-back vibe of Santa Cruz is increasingly being challenged with new rules and regulations to bring order to what many perceive as chaos. The city introduced a stringent law to ban aggressive panhandling, and the signs posted at regular intervals along Pacific Avenue downtown list plenty of other activities now deemed antisocial that could get you in trouble. The city's downtown has undergone a modest redevelopment boom, spurred by the damage inflicted by the Loma Prieta earthquake in 1989. Inevitably this has brought more chain stores and restaurants downtown, but the city still maintains a healthy number of independent businesses to keep the alternative vibe alive.

Santa Cruz is also one of the best surfing spots in Northern California, and riding the waves along the city's beaches has been a pastime since the 1930s when the sport was introduced from Southern California. Some world-class surfing events are held here each year, including the O'Neill Cold Water Classic every fall, and there's usually a cluster of surfers bobbing just off Cowell Beach, come rain or shine.

WINE-TASTING
Downtown Tasting Rooms
In the height of summer, when tourists throng

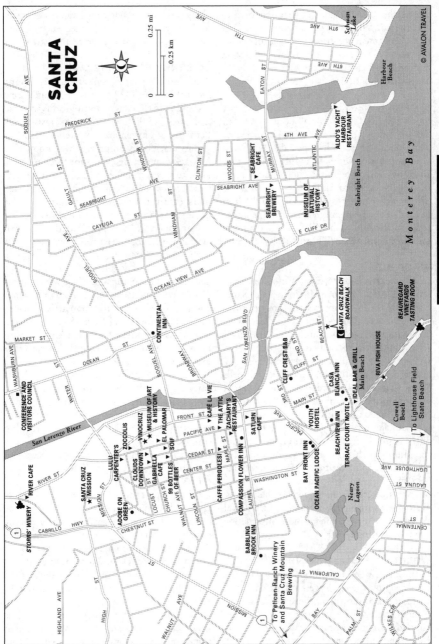

SANTA CRUZ MOUNTAINS

© AVALON TRAVEL

SANTA CRUZ

- 0.25 mi
- 0.25 km

Schwan Lake

7TH AVE

6TH AVE

Harbour Beach

FREDERICK ST

4TH AVE

ALDO'S YACHT HARBOUR RESTAURANT

WINDSOR ST

CLINTON ST

WOODS ST

MURRAY ST

ATLANTIC AVE

SEABRIGHT CAFE

SEABRIGHT AVE

SEABRIGHT BREWERY

MUSEUM OF NATURAL HISTORY

E CLIFF DR

Seabright Beach

SOQUEL AVE

GAULT ST

SEABRIGHT AVE

CAYUGA ST

WINDHAM ST

Monterey Bay

OCEAN VIEW AVE

SAN LORENZO BLVD

MARKET ST

CONTINENTAL INN

BROADWAY

SANTA CRUZ BEACH BOARDWALK

BEAUREGARD VINEYARDS TASTING ROOM

WASHBURN AVE

OCEAN ST

WATER ST

CONFERENCE AND VISITORS COUNCIL

San Lorenzo River

3RD AVE

2ND ST

CLIFF CREST B&B

CLIFF ST

BEACH ST

RIVA FISH HOUSE

CASA BLANCA INN

IDEAL BAR & GRILL
Main Beach

To Lighthouse Field State Beach

Cowell Beach

STORRS' WINERY

RIVER CAFE

RIVER ST

LULU CARPENTER'S

ZOCCOLIS

VINOCRUZ

MUSEUM OF ART & HISTORY

EL PALOMAR

CAFE LA VIE

SOIF

THE ATTIC

ZACHARY'S RESTAURANT

SATURN CAFE

MAIN ST

PACIFIC AVE

YOUTH HOSTEL

BEACHVIEW INN

TERRACE COURT MOTEL

SANTA CRUZ MISSION

MISSION ST

ADOBE ON GREEN

CLOUDS DOWNTOWN

GABRIELLA CAFE

99 BOTTLES OF BEER

FRONT ST

CEDAR ST

MAPLE ST

CAFFE PERGOLESI

CHURCH ST

LOCUST ST

CENTER ST

WALNUT AVE

LINCOLN ST

COMPASSION FLOWER INN

WASHINGTON ST

BAY FRONT INN

OCEAN PACIFIC LODGE

LAUREL ST

Neary Lagoon

LIGHTHOUSE AVE

LAGUNA ST

CABRILLO HWY

ADOBE ON GREEN

CHESTNUT ST

BABBLING BROOK INN

CALIFORNIA ST

CENTENNIAL ST

HIGHLAND AVE

HIGH ST

WALNUT AVE

To Pelican Ranch Winery and Santa Cruz Mountain Brewing

MISSION ST

BAY ST

PALM ST

WILKES CIR

the beaches and the smell of fried fish permeates the air, Santa Cruz might not feel much like a wine town, but there are a handful of tasting rooms in the city that pour local wines—a reminder that there's a great wine region up in the nearby mountains.

STORRS WINERY

Storrs Winery (303 Potrero St., off River St., Santa Cruz, 831/458-5030, www.storrswine .com, noon–5 p.m. daily) specializes in Santa Cruz appellation wines, including chardonnay, zinfandel, and pinot noir, but also makes fruity riesling and gewürztraminer from the warmer Salinas Valley to the south—about 10,000 cases in total. The tasting room is near the center of town in the Old Sash Mill, a former lumber mill now home to small businesses and cafés.

VINOCRUZ

In the heart of downtown, VinoCruz (725 Front St. #101, entrance off Cooper St., Santa Cruz, 831/426-8466, www.vinocruz.com, 11 a.m.–7 p.m. Mon.–Thurs., 11 a.m.–8 p.m. Fri.–Sat., noon–6 p.m. Sun.) is technically a wine shop, but its specialty is selling Santa Cruz wines, and local winemakers regularly hold special tastings here. In fact, VinoCruz only sells Santa Cruz wines, representing 60 different wineries in the sleek, modern space next to the Museum of Art & History. You won't get the same ambiance as tasting at a winery, but many of the region's smaller wineries are not open to the public so this is one place you might be able to taste some rarities. Tasting events are held on most weekends and sometimes involve the winemakers or winery owners themselves. Tasting fees vary but are usually $5–10. Contact the store or check online for more information about upcoming events.

Westside Tasting Rooms

In the last few years a new gourmet ghetto has developed on the city's west side, a couple of miles from downtown and close to the Natural Bridges State Beach. As manufacturers moved out and warehouses became vacant, new food outlets and independent fashion stores moved in

along with tasting rooms for a number of wineries, a brewery, and even a distillery, all creating a vibrant new food, wine, and retail district.

◖ BONNY DOON VINEYARD

The highest profile tenant here is Bonny Doon Vineyard (328 Ingalls St., Santa Cruz, 831/425-4518, www.bonnydoonvineyard .com, noon–5:00 p.m. Wed.–Sun., tasting $5). Perhaps one of the most irreverent wineries in California, Bonny Doon is as well known for its wacky marketing as it is for the staggering array of wines it makes, and has recreated the sort of wacky-woodsy atmosphere that existed in its former mountain tasting room inside the giant steel warehouse it now inhabits.

Founder and "president for life" Randall Grahm has trailblazed a path (often a very wide path) along which the rest of the California industry has usually followed, from his recent adoption of screwcaps on some wines to his distinctive wine labels. Over the years he has commissioned labels from pop artists including Chuck House and Ralph Steadman, who is perhaps best known for the illustrations in Hunter S. Thompson's drug-fueled epic *Fear and Loathing in Las Vegas*.

Known as a hippie boutique winery in its early days in the 1980s, Bonny Doon grew to become a behemoth, churning out over 400,000 cases of mainly cheap and cheerful (and fun) wines and, some argued, turning into one of the corporate giants that the winery likes to mock. But Grahm once again confounded the critics in 2006 when he sold off its two biggest brands, Big House and Cardinal Zin, to focus on higher-end organic and biodynamic wines. At the same time, he established a separate business for his Pacific Rim wines that is based in Washington. After the "doonsizing," annual production at Bonny Doon is now back down to about 40,000 cases, and Grahm is once again set to turn the industry on its head with his devotion to all things biodynamic.

Beyond all the marketing fun are some serious wines. Grahm is very much a Europhile when it comes to wines and has become known as Santa

© SANTA CRUZ COUNTY CVC/PAUL SCHRAUB

wine-tasting at Bonny Doon Vineyard

Cruz's Rhône Ranger. He planted a bewildering array of poetically named Rhône grape varietals over the last few decades and makes wines with bizarre-sounding names that win praise not only for their quality but also their bargain prices. The winery has few vineyards in the Santa Cruz appellation, however. Most are farther south in the Central Coast region.

Try Le Pousseur, a powerful syrah blend; the fruity Il Fiasco sangiovese from the Monterey area; the Madiran Heart of Darkness, made with the French regional grape tannat that few people in France have probably heard of; or the peppery Clos de Gilroy, made from grenache grown in the region just south of here that's better known for its garlic. In all, there are usually more than 20 wines available for tasting.

Randall Grahm teamed up with fellow biodynamic afficionados and well-known local chefs Charlie Parker and David Kinch to create the **Cellar Door Café,** a popular eatery within the cavernous Bonny Doon tasting room that possesses the same combination of quality, value,

and creativity as the winery. The Café only offers a daily, fixed-price menu for $35 or small plates for $5–25. For those who want the full wine and food experience, however, $50 will buy you a private sit-down tasting in a private "pod" (actually the inside of a giant wine cask) as a steady supply of Charlie Parker's food is brought out to accompany Bonny Doon wines.

There are several other Santa Cruz wineries with tasting rooms in the complex, all going about their business with far less fanfare than Bonny Doon, yet well worth visiting for their wines alone.

PELICAN RANCH WINERY

The Pelican Ranch Winery (402 Ingalls St., Ste. 21, Santa Cruz, 831/426-6911, www.pelican ranch.com, noon–5 P.M. Fri.–Sun.) makes a handful of moderately priced, single-vineyard chardonnays from the Santa Cruz Mountains up to the Dry Creek Valley, as well as a half-dozen pinot noirs, several from the Santa Cruz region. Also worth tasting is a Russian River Valley zinfandel and a juicy Rhône-style red blend. Pelican Ranch has always been an urban winery since it was established in 1997 and moved here in 2003. It makes only about 1,000 cases of wine a year.

SANTA CRUZ MOUNTAIN VINEYARD

Next door to Bonny Doon is the new location of Santa Cruz Mountain Vineyard (334-A Ingalls St., Santa Cruz, 831/426-6209, www .santacruzmountainvineyard.com, noon–5 P.M. Fri.–Sun.), which moved its winemaking operations from Boulder Creek in 2008 after 30 years of making wine up in the mountains. The winery still makes a pinot from part of the old Jarvis Vineyard that it bought back in the 1970s, but it is now known as much for Rhône varietals, including a syrah sourced from mountain vineyards together with a petite syrah and grenache from vineyards in the McDowell Valley in Mendocino.

The petite syrah has been labeled by what the winery says is its correct name: durif. DNA testing over the years has shown that much of what is called petite syrah in California is actually one of three different grape varietals, so the name durif is not likely to take off until the genetic confusion is sorted out. A more recent addition to the portfolio are a cabernet sauvignon sourced from a warm vineyard on the eastern slopes of the Santa Cruz Mountains along with a merlot from a vineyard on the cooler western slopes.

SANTA CRUZ MOUNTAIN BREWING COMPANY

It doesn't exactly qualify as a winery, but the Santa Cruz Mountain Brewing Company (402 Ingalls St., Santa Cruz, 831/425-4900, www.santacruzmountainbrewing.com, noon– 10:00 P.M. daily) does have a tasting room in its brewery behind Kelly's French Bakery in the Swift Street Courtyard complex. In addition to tasting the range of organic amber and pale ales, you can simply hang out in the brewery's bar in the middle of the warehouses and drink to your heart's content or fill up your own bottles for later. The popular Happy Hour is Friday 5–6 P.M.

© SANTA CRUZ MOUNTAIN BREWING COMPANY

Santa Cruz Mountain Brewing Company

BEAUREGARD VINEYARDS

The much-loved former tasting room of Bonny Doon Vineyard, a rustic cottage under towering redwood and pine trees on the western slopes above Santa Cruz, is now the new home of local winery Beauregard Vineyards (10 Pine Flat Rd., Bonny Doon, 831/425-7777, www .beauregardvineyards.com, 11 A.M.–5 P.M. Wed.–Mon., tasting $5), which moved here in 2008 from its previous location stranded at the end of the Santa Cruz pier.

The winery is a product of a father and son team. Jim Beauregard has been making wines in the Santa Cruz Mountains for decades and spearheaded the drive to establish the surrounding Ben Lomond AVA. He and his son, Ryan, formed Beauregard Vineyards in the late 1990s, building on several generations of family involvement in local winemaking. The bulk of the estate vineyards are in the Bonny Doon area not far from the tasting room, including Beauregard Ranch, which was originally bought by Jim's grandfather, Amos Beauregard, in the 1940s.

The winery is perhaps best known for its crisp single-vineyard chardonnays and pinot noirs sourced from its local mountain vineyards. Those same vineyards also provide grapes for a zinfandel, syrah, and merlot. In fact Beauregard's portfolio of wines offers arguably the best education on the characteristics and diversity of Santa Cruz Mountain wines, enhanced by the classic mountain scenery (still recovering from fire damage). Visiting here is as much about experiencing the mountains as it is about tasting the mountain wines.

SIGHTS
◖ Santa Cruz Beach Boardwalk

It may have turned 100 years old in 2007 and have tamer rides compared to some bigger and more modern theme parks, but the Santa Cruz Beach Boardwalk (400 Beach St., 831/423-5590, www.beachboardwalk .com, daily late Mar.–early Sept., weekends and holidays the rest of the year) is about the most fun adrenaline junkies can have on a trip

© SANTA CRUZ COUNTY CVC/BEACH BOARDWALK

Santa Cruz Beach Boardwalk

SANTA CRUZ MOUNTAINS

BEACH BLUBBER

The Santa Cruz Beach Boardwalk might not conjure up images of deserted California coastline where animals can freely frolic, but just a few miles north the human influence wanes and nature reclaims the coast. At **Año Nuevo State Park** nature reclaims it in a big way.

The park is home to a large colony of northern elephant seals, monsters more of the beach than the deep that can weigh up to 2.5 tons and grow up to 16 feet long. In December every year they haul their blubbery masses out of the water, not so much to frolic as simply to wallow on the rocks and sand in preparation for the breeding season.

Immobile as they might look, get too close to an irritable male and you might discover that they have quite good acceleration, though little stamina for a chase. Be aware that it's illegal, however, to harass them, and you shouldn't get closer than 25 feet. During breeding season mid-December–end of March, docent-led tours (800/444-4445, call for reservations) are the only way to get near the breeding colony.

Although the seals live most of the rest of the year in the water, they do come ashore to molt. Watching them roll and flap around on land you can see why their terrestrial excursions are rare and fairly brief. The giant, mature males of the species, with their long, trunk-like snouts, molt July–August, smaller females and juveniles April–May, and younger males somewhere in between.

With the huge numbers of these blubber torpedos that haul out onto the beach it's also hard to believe that elephant seals were once hunted almost to extinction. By the end of the 1800s only 50-100 were believed to be left, and they were down in Mexico. By the mid-1990s an estimated 2,000 pups were born in California, and there were about 2,000 seals in the Año Nuevo colony. If you're here in the breeding season, you might just be witnessing several thousand tons of elephant seals strutting their stuff.

to Wine Country, short of a bungee jump out of a balloon over the Napa Valley.

Unfortunately, the city has not realized the full potential of the rest of the beachfront site. The road that runs along the beach in front of the boardwalk is a seedy-looking mix of cheap fast-food restaurants, shabby motels, and acres of crumbling parking lots. Ignore the mess out front and head through the gates to the boardwalk—it's a different world.

The half-mile-long stretch of former beach boardwalk (it's now asphalt) along the city's main swimming beach is the West Coast's answer to Atlantic City or Coney Island. It has more than 30 rides, some that hark back to its Victorian beginning, others that will keep kids entertained for hours, and still more that have the potential to rearrange your internal organs. Cruising the boardwalk and inhaling the aromas of greasy seaside fast food are free but the rides are not, though they are thankfully cheap and cost $3–5. To make a day of it, buy an unlimited-ride wristband for $30.

There are a dozen rides for kids, including the **Charles Looff Carousel** ($3), a candy-colored piece of spinning history with a 342-pipe organ and 70 handmade horses dating from 1911. Charles's son, Arthur Looff, was the man behind the **Giant Dipper** roller coaster ($5), a soaring wooden structure built in 1924. It might lack the inverted thrills of modern coasters but it has a certain stomach-churning Victorian ambience (and great views from the top) that has kept it rolling for more than 80 years. Both Looff rides are registered as National Historic Landmarks.

The **Hurricane** is a compact, twisting steel rollercoaster opened in 1992 that offers two minutes of even greater twists and turns, creating forces of up to 4.5G that seem to never let up. There's talk that it might be replaced by a new coaster sometime soon.

Those in search of more G-force fun should check out the newest attraction, the **Double Shot** ($5), and we're not talking tequila. It's certainly a descriptive name—riders rocket up a 125-foot-high tower, hang at the top a while to appreciate the views, then plummet back to earth. Drinking tequila beforehand is not recommended.

If a Hurricane is not enough, there are other stormy rides to batter and twirl you around, including **Cyclone, Whirlwind,** and the upside-down experience of the **Typhoon.** There are many more opportunities to be flung around in mechanical contraptions plus plenty more sedate amusements like miniature golf and the nearby **Boardwalk Bowl** (115 Cliff St., 831/426-3324, www.boardwalkbowl.com, 9 A.M.–close daily year-round).

For more information on all the rides and arcade games on the boardwalk, together with a full list of events throughout the year both outdoors and in the **Cocoanut Grove** casino and ballroom, visit www.beachboardwalk.com or call 831/426-7433.

Santa Cruz Mission State Historic Park

The history of Santa Cruz has been punctuated by earthquakes that literally reshaped the city over the last 200 years. The mission that gave the city its name and its start, **Misión de Exaltación de la Santa Cruz** (144 School St., 831/425-5849), was built in 1794, but eventually succumbed to the shaking ground and no longer exists. Despite its importance, its influence was quickly overshadowed by the Spanish colony of Branciforte, which was built across the San Lorenzo River in 1797 and quickly turned into a den of iniquity that proved more of a lure for the Ohlone Native Americans than religion did.

Today, a half-scale replica, built in the 1930s, stands near the site of the original mission. It's a short walk from downtown. Behind the mission replica, on School Street, there is an old adobe building dating from 1791 that housed people working at the mission. It somehow survived the earthquakes and has been restored by the State Park Service as a small museum detailing the history of Santa Cruz; it is the main attraction at the small park open on weekends (10 A.M.–4 P.M. Thurs.–Sat.).

Historic Districts

Earthquakes destroyed the original mission, and more recently the 1989 Loma Prieta earthquake damaged large swaths of other parts of the city that dated from the post-mission period, especially some of the famed Victorian homes. In fact, one of the town's three National Register Historic Districts was de-listed in 1991 due to the loss of so many old buildings downtown, particularly along Pacific Avenue.

The two other historic districts are still largely intact and have enough to keep any Victorian fanatic happy. At the **Mission Hill Historic District,** on the site of the old Branciforte settlement, and downtown along both **Walnut Avenue** (between Center St. and Rincon St.) and **Ocean View Avenue** (south of Broadway St.), gabled Queen Anne–style homes rub shoulders with ornate Italianate or Gothic revival buildings, many built with money from the logging industry that fueled a citywide building boom in the mid- to late 1800s. Pick up information about historic walking tours from the Santa Cruz County Conference and Visitors Bureau (303 Water St., Ste. 100, 831/425-1234 or 800/833-3494).

Museums

The **Santa Cruz Museum of Art and History** (705 Front St., at Copper St., Santa Cruz, 831/429-1964, www.santacruzmah .org, 11 A.M.–5 P.M. Tues.–Sun., $5) in the McPherson Center was established in 1996 by the merger of the city's history museum and art museum (another result of the 1989 earthquake) and is now housed in a sleek, modern building. Permanent exhibits include *Where the Redwoods Meet the Sea,* which highlights the history of Santa Cruz County from the Native Americans to present-day industries. There are always several temporary exhibits of art, photography, or history. There's free admission on the first Friday of every month.

The modest **Santa Cruz Surfing Museum** (701 W. Cliff Dr., Santa Cruz, 831/420-6289, www.santacruzsurfingmuseum.org, 10 A.M.–5 P.M. Wed.–Mon. in summer, noon–4 P.M. Thurs.–Mon. the rest of the

Santa Cruz Surfing Museum

year) packs more than 70 years of local surfing history into the Mark Abbott Memorial Lighthouse at Lighthouse Point on West Cliff Drive. See the giant redwood surfboards used in the early days of surfing and a modern board that was attacked by a shark, plus hundreds of photos and memorabilia from a century of wave riding. The museum is right across from the famous Steamers Lane surfing spot.

The surfing museum is affiliated with the **Santa Cruz Museum of Natural History** (1305 E. Cliff Dr., Santa Cruz, 831/420-6115, www.santacruzmuseums.org, 10 A.M.–5 P.M. Tues.–Sun. in summer, 10 A.M.–5 P.M. Tues.–Sat. the rest of the year, $2.50) located on a bluff above the ocean on the other side of town. Kid-friendly exhibits explore the history of the region and its first people, the Ohlone. Or stick your hands into the Tidepool Touch Tank, just one of the museum's nature and wildlife exhibits.

EVENTS

Santa Cruz is hopping with events all year long, about which more information can be found at the Santa Cruz Conference and Visitors Council (303 Water St., 831/425-1234 or 800/833-3494, www.santacruzca.org). On the last Saturday of February, the **Annual Clam Chowder Cook-Off** (831/420-5273, tasting kits $8) is held on the Beach Boardwalk and you can be the judge, too.

The free **Jazz on the Wharf** is held on a Sunday in early March (usually the first weekend). The Santa Cruz Wharf plays host to several other annual events, including **Woodies on the Wharf** in late June, a celebration of classic surf wagons; and **Halloween on the Wharf** on the obvious date.

Big names play at the **Santa Cruz Blues Festival** (www.santacruzbluesfestival.com, $75–110) on Memorial Day weekend; tickets usually sell out fast. Despite the name, it is held a few miles south of the city at the Aptos Village Park. Alternatively, visit the **Boulder Creek Art, Wine, and Music Festival** up in the mountains, where local blues and jazz bands will provide the entertainment to accompany your culinary indulgences in the redwoods. Contact the Boulder Creek Business Association (www.bcba.net) to check if the event is still happening—in 2010 the state highway agency shut it down because it involves consumption of alcohol on a state road, Highway 9. But there are hopes it may be revived in the future.

On the first weekend in August, the **Cabrillo Music, Art, and Wine Festival** (Church St., 831/426-6966) is the city's outdoor food, wine, and entertainment summer blowout, held on Church Street outside the Civic Auditorium.

Surfing is a big draw all year, and the Steamers Lane surf break off Lighthouse Field State Beach is the usual venue. The world's largest **Kayak Surf Festival** is held every year at Steamers Lane in mid-March, and late May brings the longboarders out at the **Annual Longboard Club Invitational**, the oldest and longest-running surfing event on the West Coast, organized by the Santa Cruz Longboard Union. The world-class surfing event, **O'Neill Cold Water Classic** (www.oneillcwc.asglive.com), is held in mid-

SANTA CRUZ MOUNTAINS

October, ironically the time of year that the sea is warmest in these parts.

RECREATION
Santa Cruz Beaches

Visiting one of the city's beaches is a must, whether on a crowded summer weekend when bodies can be packed like sardines on the shore, or in winter when a few lone surfers brave the ocean chill. Be warned that even in the summer the sea feels like it could induce mild hypothermia. You'll quickly understand why surfers wear wetsuits year-round.

The city's **Main Beach,** the long stretch of sand right in front of the Beach Boardwalk, gets the most crowded in summer with an influx of families and local teens. This is the best people-watching beach. Slightly quieter, though not by much, is **Cowell Beach,** on the other side of the wharf from Main Beach. This is where novice surfers tend to congregate. For some more impressive surfing action, head southwest to **Lighthouse Field State Beach,** off West Cliff Drive. The headlands overlook the renowned Steamers Lane surf break, which tends to pick up the most steam in the winter months.

Right at the end of West Cliff Drive is the beautiful cove of **Natural Bridges State Beach** (2531 W. Cliff Dr., $10 parking), famous for both its natural sandstone arch and for the more than 100,000 monarch butterflies that overwinter here between October and February before embarking on their long spring migration of up to 2,000 miles. On cold, wet days the butterflies huddle together, forming colorful clumps that hang from the eucalyptus trees along a trail that leads around the **Monarch Butterfly Natural Preserve** (831/423-4609). Docent-led tours are offered on weekends when the butterflies are in town. There are events to celebrate the arrival and departure of the butterflies—the Welcome Back Monarchs day is on the second Sunday of October, and the Migration Festival is on the second Saturday of February. (Those folks in Santa Cruz certainly know how to party.) Down near the

A sailboarder and kitesurfer head to shore after a long day's fun.

SANTA CRUZ MOUNTAINS

© SANTA CRUZ COUNTY CVC/DIANNE DERIN

Surf Santa Cruz.

shore there are hundreds of tide pools to explore at low tide, as well as the ever-present seals, sea lions, and seabirds.

This being a counterculture city, there has to be at least one clothing-optional beach, and it's a few blocks south of Natural Bridges. Look for access down to the tiny **2222 Beach** right opposite the house at 2222 West Cliff Drive near Auburn Avenue.

Many of the quieter beaches frequented more by locals are southeast of Main Beach and the wharf, across the mouth of the San Lorenzo River and accessed from East Cliff Drive. **Twin Lakes State Park** actually encompasses three beaches that locals call Seabright, Harbor, and Schwan Lake. **Seabright Beach** is perhaps the prettiest and most easily accessible from downtown. It is between the mouth of the San Lorenzo River and the harbor entrance. **Harbor Beach** on the other side of the harbor entrance is smaller but with plenty of restaurants and cafés along its edge, and farther east is a stretch of beach in front of **Schwan Lake**, a good bird-watching spot.

Wilder Ranch State Park

A couple of miles north of Santa Cruz on the coast road, Wilder Ranch State Park (1401 Coast Rd. on the west side of Hwy. 1 north of Santa Cruz, 831/423-9703 or 831/426-0505, $10 day-use fee) boasts 7,000 acres of forest, chaparral, marshes, and meadows together with 34 miles of hiking and biking trails. This is more than simply a hiking destination, however. It was once a working ranch and still is to a certain extent. The land was bought by dairy farmer D. D. Wilder in 1871 but was also the site of the rancho that once supplied food to the mission in Santa Cruz.

Victorian farmhouses, several barns, and an old adobe said to be roofed with tiles from the long-gone mission have been restored and are now central to the living history events and demonstrations that go on year-round. There are still about 900 acres of agricultural land in the park (brussels sprouts anyone?), some of it still plowed using horses, as shown by docents dressed in period costume who also demonstrate many other Victorian farming practices.

If the hard farm life is too exhausting, go for a stroll out to the bluffs overlooking the sea, or duck through the tunnel under Highway 1 and start hiking for the hills.

ACCOMMODATIONS

The city of Santa Cruz has about as much in common with rustic mountain wineries as seawater has with a fine pinot noir. Santa Cruz became a beach resort town in the late 1800s and has never looked back, which means there are plenty of hotels and B&Bs to accommodate the hordes of summer tourists and surfers that still throng the beaches and boardwalk today.

Expect the usual price manipulation typical of hotels in tourist destinations—a jump in rates during the summer plus sometimes unreasonable minimum-stay and cancellation requirements. Be sure to check all the details when you book.

If Santa Cruz is booked up or simply too brash for your taste, there are some notable places to stay a little farther to the north or south.

Hostels

Serious bargain hunters or those who have blown their travel budget on cases of wine might want to check out the **Santa Cruz Youth Hostel** (321 Main St., Santa Cruz, 831/423-8304, www.hi-santacruz.org, dorms $22–25, private rooms starting at $55–60). It's everything a hostel should be: clean, cheap (add $3 temporary membership fee for nonmembers), centrally located, and with a bit of history to boot. The dorm-style rooms plus a couple of family rooms are in the Victorian Carmelita Cottages, built to house sea captains awaiting their next vessel. Reservations are essential in the summer, and there's a small fee for parking.

Under $100

Other bargain-price accommodations tend to be of the motel variety. Just about every chain is represented, and there are dozens of independents that range from seedy to comfortable. This being a resort town, however, bargain price is a relative term and prices can top $100 in the summer for less-than-luxurious rooms. One amenity that thankfully is not really needed in the summer is air-conditioning. Cool ocean breezes do the job just as well.

A central location a few blocks from the

"SEABIRD INVASION HITS COASTAL HOMES"

So screamed the headline of the *Santa Cruz Sentinel* on August 18, 1961. The previous night's event will go down in the annals of Santa Cruz's strange history (annals that are, by now, bulging) – a nighttime invasion of swarms of suicidal seabirds that slammed into houses and cars while vomiting the remains of anchovies, sending terrified residents running indoors and leaving the stench of rotting fish on the streets in the morning.

It is thought that swarms of sooty shearwaters that had happily been gorging on anchovies were startled and rose in a giant flock, became disoriented in the thick, dark ocean fog that regularly envelops the coastline, and flew toward the nearest light they saw, which happened to be the streetlights, house lights, and car headlights along the northern Santa Cruz Bay shoreline. Pity the poor residents who then came outside to investigate the thud of birds against their windows only to have even more birds fly straight toward the beams of their flashlights.

As if the event itself wasn't strange enough, it occurred just two years before Alfred Hitchcock released his film *The Birds*. Hitchcock reportedly had a copy of the story sent to him, and it may well have inspired the scenes of menacing birds attacking terrified residents when *The Birds* was filmed in Bodega Bay, just north of San Francisco. The Santa Cruz seabird incident did not, however, inspire Hitchcock's movie outright; it was already in the making, based on a Daphne DuMaurier novel.

beach and some low prices for the 38 rooms make the motel-style **Bay Front Inn** (325 Pacific Ave., Santa Cruz, 831/423-8564, www.bayfrontinnsc.com, $70–90 weekdays, $90–110 weekends and summer) a pretty good value in the crowded motel scene. Suites are available for less of a bargain at $225. Don't expect luxury at this price.

The **Beachview Inn** (50 Front St., Santa Cruz, 831/426-3575 or 800/946-0614, www.beach-viewinn.com) is even closer to the ocean, with views of the beach over the rooftops of neighboring buildings, and just a little pricier. Rates range from $60 for the smaller motel-style rooms with one bed up to $110 for the larger rooms with two beds, some with whirlpool tubs. Summer rates are $80–190 a night. All rooms have cable TV and air-conditioning.

The **Continental Inn** (414 Ocean St., Santa Cruz, 831/429-1221 or 800/343-6941, www.continentalinn.net) is on motel row in Santa Cruz, a little off the beaten track but still only about six blocks from the boardwalk and downtown area. The rooms are clean and fairly well equipped for a glorified motel, with some big-hotel amenities like free high-speed Internet access, irons, and hair dryers. Rates start at $75 in winter and $95 in summer for the queen rooms and run up to $160 for suites. Summer weekend rates can be up to $220 a night.

$100-150

In this crowded price bracket, **The Adobe on Green Street** (103 Green St., Santa Cruz, 831/469-9866, www.adobeongreen.com) stands out above other B&Bs thanks to its simple, well-appointed rooms, privacy, and the tranquil garden setting of the Victorian cottage, just a few blocks from many of the city's best shops and restaurants. If you're lucky enough to get one of the four charming rooms, however, you might opt to stay in and watch a DVD instead, or relax in the main living room that you'll probably have to yourself. The cheapest Mission room with a tub (but no shower in the bathroom) starts at $119 midweek, $189 on weekends in winter and

$149–189 in summer. The other three rooms, including the 300-square-foot Lookout room, are up to $30 more. Discounts are often available online.

The relatively modern **Ocean Pacific Lodge** (301 Pacific Ave., Santa Cruz, 831/457-1234 or 800/995-0289, www.theoceanpacificlodge.com) is about halfway between the beach and the action on Pacific Avenue and is perhaps the best value in Santa Cruz. The 57 rooms are clean and thankfully devoid of much of the appalling decor seen in many older motels but are still not luxurious by any means, although you do get free wireless Internet access. The cheapest start at $80 a night off-season and just over $100 a night during the summer, rising to $140–200 for larger rooms and suites.

The **Terrace Court Motel** (125 Beach St., Santa Cruz, 831/423-3031, www.terracecourt.com) is right opposite the beach above a row of shops but stretches back up the hill on several terraces, creating a lot of ocean-view rooms. There are also a handful of rooms and suites around the small pool up the hill. It boasts the same owners since the 1950s and is something of a Santa Cruz institution, although this also means the rooms are showing their age a bit. It's not cheap, either, but most rooms have kitchens and there are some nice common areas outdoors, including a charcoal grill for summer barbeques. Poolside rooms start at $120 in the winter and rise to $160 in the summer. Ocean-view rooms are $130–200 a night.

$150-250

The **Casa Blanca Inn** (101 Main St., at Beach St., Santa Cruz, 831/423-1570 or 800/644-1570, www.casablanca-santacruz.com, $85–375 off-season, $175–425 high season) has 39 rooms ranging from spacious and uniquely furnished to gussied-up motel rooms, all in a prime oceanfront location. Amenities include microwaves and refrigerators, fireplaces, and whirlpool tubs in some rooms, and ocean views in all but six of the rooms. Rates are as varied as the rooms themselves. The inn incorporates the 1918 Cerf Mansion, which contains some of the better rooms.

The **Cliff Crest Bed and Breakfast Inn** (407 Cliff St., Santa Cruz, 831/427-2609, www.cliffcrestinn.com, $145–195 off-season, $195–245 high season) is an Easter egg–blue Queen Anne Victorian up the hill a few blocks from the beach and boardwalk. The five rooms are all tastefully decorated with antiques that the owners, an artist and chemical engineer, collected over the years. The smallest Pineapple and Apricot rooms might leave you feeling a bit claustrophobic, but they are the cheapest. Some midweek specials are often available in the winter.

Touting itself as the biggest and oldest B&B in Santa Cruz, the (**Babbling Brook Inn** (1025 Laurel St., Santa Cruz, 831/427-2437 or 800/866-1131, www.babblingbrookinn .com) is also one of the most unusual places to stay in the city. The rustic buildings surround a log cabin that incorporates foundations from a grist mill built here in the 1700s and a tannery that dated from the 1870s, all set in an acre of lush gardens through which the namesake brook really does babble, assuming traffic noise doesn't drown it out. Most of the 13 well-equipped rooms are named after historic artists and have fireplaces, whirlpool tubs, featherbeds, and sofas. The cheapest (and smallest) include the elegant Contessa room ($159–209, depending on season), named after the Countess Florenzo de Chandler, who bought the property in 1924 and made a few additions. Other rooms start at $179–259 a night, including a generous breakfast.

Romantics who want to escape the bustle of Santa Cruz could head a few miles east to Capitola where the **Inn at Depot Hill** (250 Monterey Ave., Capitola, 831/462-3376 or 800/572-2632, www.innatdepothill.com) offers some of the area's most luxurious and intimate accommodations. The upscale B&B is in a former railroad depot, where eight rooms have been transformed into geographic time capsules that transport guests to old England, France, Holland, Italy, and Japan without leaving behind any modern amenities like whirlpool tubs, stereos, or TVs behind. The English cottage decor of the Stratford-on-Avon room

offers one of the cheapest getaways at $190–260. Other rooms run $240–360 a night, though winter midweek specials can sometimes push the rates to under $200.

Over $250

Injecting some much-needed 21st Century style into the tired Santa Cruz accommodation scene, The Joie de Vivre hotel chain managed to turn a drab 1960s ocean-front hotel into the stylish and modern **Dream Inn** (175 W. Cliff Dr., Santa Cruz, 831/426-4330, www .dreaminnsantacruz.com). The 165 rooms and suites combine modern luxury amenities like flat screen TVs, Wi-Fi, and rainwater shower heads with some mid-century retro styling and panoramic views from balconies overlooking the pool deck, Cowell Beach, and the ocean. Such luxury in a prime location next to the wharf doesn't come cheap, especially in peak season, but for ocean-view luxury it's not outrageously priced. Midweek rates in winter start at $199 for the basic deluxe rooms and $249 for the suites. Add about $50 to those rates for weekends, and an additional $100 in the peak summer season. The high-rise "cloud" rooms will also generally cost an additional $30.

FOOD

Santa Cruz is a big city by Wine Country standards and consequently has a thriving restaurant scene, but one that tends to favor the student population more than high rollers. Many upscale restaurants have tried and failed to gain traction with the laid-back residents who seem to prefer low-key and well-known eateries rather than upscale upstarts. A lively café scene thrives off the student population, and if you can't decide what to eat, head for tree-lined Pacific Avenue, which is the commercial center of the city.

Beachfront Dining

Casablanca Restaurant (101 Main St., at Beach St., Santa Cruz, 831/426-9063, dinner daily, entrées $16–33) has a tough time living up to one of the best restaurant views in the city but manages it with aplomb. The setting overlooking the ocean and wharf from its perch in the eponymous hotel is romantic, and the food is classic seasonal Californian cuisine, although the focus is more on steak and seafood than anything more adventurous. Topping it off is an exhaustive wine list blessed by *Wine Spectator.*

The wharf itself is home to a handful of seafood restaurants, the most reliable and least tacky of which is the **Riva Fish House** (31 Municipal Wharf, Santa Cruz, 831/429-1223, lunch and dinner daily, entrées $12–25, cash only). The layout of the sleek interior ensures everyone gets a piece of the wonderful ocean view, but it's still worth waiting a while for a window seat. Meanwhile, perch yourself at the long bar and soak up the atmosphere and view, with some oysters washed down with a bloody Mary to whet your appetite for the classic seafood dishes to come. Stick to the basics on the menu and you won't be disappointed.

Seafood with a contemporary twist and comfort foods made with local organic produce are the specialty of **Aquarius** (175 W. Cliff Dr., Santa Cruz, 831/460-5012, breakfast, lunch, and dinner daily, dinner entrées $17–37) just north of the wharf in the sleek and hip Dream Inn. Dishes like roasted Halibut with mussels, chorizo, and organic potato can be found alongside imaginatively presented classics like fish and chips and steak on the dinner menu. Alternatively a cocktail and appetizer might be all you need as you soak up the ambiance of the sleek space while watching the sun set over the Pacific.

If the sun's shining, leave the downtown crowds behind and indulge in seafood, listening to the waves and the clanking of boat rigging, at **Aldo's Harbor Restaurant** (616 Atlantic Ave., off Seabright, Santa Cruz, 831/426-3736, breakfast and lunch daily, dinner during the summer months only, dinner entrées $12–18). The former fish shack is now a popular restaurant perched above the water at the entrance to the Santa Cruz Yacht Harbor. Seafood is the starring feature whatever the time of day, from the seafood scramble at breakfast (washed down with

famously strong coffee) to a seasonal local catch at lunch or dinner. Get here in time and you can watch the sun set over a cool beer and bowl of calamari as the water laps beneath the deck.

On the other side of the harbor from Aldo's, about a five-minute drive from downtown, is the popular **Crow's Nest** (2218 E. Cliff Dr., Santa Cruz, 831/476-4560, lunch and dinner daily, dinner entrées $15–22), a sprawling, rustic restaurant that has been a dining and drinking destination for locals since the 1970s. The food is basic surf'n'turf plus some pastas that are well prepared but will not win any awards for creativity. The biggest draws for locals and tourists alike are the location and the entertainment. Every table, inside and out, has a view of the ocean or harbor, and from some you can almost reach out and touch the beach. Most nights of the week there is also live music, ranging from jazz to rock, making this a popular evening drinking destination.

Downtown Santa Cruz

Everything is cozy charm at the star of the small Santa Cruz bistro scene, **◖ Gabriella Café** (910 Cedar St., at Church St., Santa Cruz, 831/457-1677, lunch and dinner daily, brunch weekends, dinner entrées $18–29). Flowers bloom outside the modest mission-style cottage, white-clothed tables are squeezed into every nook, and a hand-scribbled menu features a modest selection of simple but beautifully executed, Italian-inspired dishes (including thin, crispy pizza) incorporating seasonal produce from local organic farms. The wine list is equally well stocked with local productions from the Monterey and Santa Cruz regions. Prices are on the high side for Santa Cruz, however, and service can be reportedly slow, but the ambience and quality of the food still make it worth a visit.

It's surprising so close to Wine Country that it took so long for a wine bar to find success in the Santa Cruz restaurant scene, but **Soif** (105 Walnut Ave., Santa Cruz, 831/423-2020, www.soifwine.com, dinner daily, small plates $4–10, entrées $10–25) seems to have hit the right note to satisfy wine lovers and counts Bonny Doon's Randall Grahm among its many fans. There's a bewildering list of several hundred different wines from around the world, more than 50 available by the glass, and the modest menu of small and large plates of modern American food is almost a second thought. The best option here is to graze, sharing some small plates of food or the cheese platter over a bottle of wine. Everything here is reasonably priced, and markup on the wine is virtually nonexistent thanks to the neighboring wine shop where all the wines can be bought retail. It is open the same hours as the wine bar. The only disappointment is that Soif doesn't do more to champion Santa Cruz region wines, which are not very well represented on the mainly international wine list.

Santa Cruz meets South Beach at **Clouds Downtown** (110 Church St., Santa Cruz, 831/429-2000, lunch and diner daily, dinner entrées $13–23). This popular bar and restaurant with a sleek red exterior that's more LA or Miami than Santa Cruz can be a bit of a scene but is a draw, for both the cocktail crowd as well as diners who can tolerate high decibels, for the menu of surf and turf dressed up with Asian-inspired finery.

Highly praised Mexican food in a slightly more luxurious setting than the average taqueria is served at **El Palomar** (1336 Pacific Ave., Santa Cruz, 831/425-7575, lunch and dinner daily, dinner entrées $12–27) in the beautifully restored Palomar Inn Hotel downtown on the main drag. The hotel has long since gone residential, but the restaurant occupies the sunny atrium patio and former lobby, a spectacular space with an ornate, arching ceiling and huge fireplaces. At the back of the restaurant is a bar that's open late and a taco bar that's ideal for a quick meal to go.

The place to go downtown for breakfast is **Zachary's Restaurant** (819 Pacific Ave., Santa Cruz., 831/427-0646, breakfast until 2:30 P.M. Tues.–Sun.), a funky Santa Cruz institution at the western end of Pacific Avenue. The lines snaking out of the door on weekends are a testament to the appeal of brunch here.

Try Mike's Mess, a plateful of eggs scrambled with all sorts of good stuff and topped with cheese, sour cream, and tomatoes.

A convenient place to grab food to go is the downtown deli and diner **Zoccolis** (1534 Pacific Ave., 831/423-1711, until 6 P.M. daily). None of the gourmet sandwiches and daily pasta dishes cost more than $10 and there are nearly 20 different salads to choose from.

Day or night, the vegetarian universe is spinning downtown at Santa Cruz's spacey **☑ Saturn Café** (145 Laurel St., Santa Cruz, 831/429-8505, 11 A.M.–3 A.M. Mon.–Fri., 10 A.M.–3 A.M. Sat.–Sun., most items under $10). Have a lunchtime burger with choice of veggie or vegan patty and all the usual fixings, a midnight sandwich named after one of our neighboring planets, or an afternoon snack from the cheap eats menu for less than the cost of parking downtown. The fries are frequently voted the best in the city.

The **River Café** (415 River St., Santa Cruz, 831/420-1280, 6:30 A.M.–6 P.M. Mon.–Sat., 10 A.M.–3 P.M. Sun.) is part artisan cheese shop and part tiny eatery. Bring your own wine and sit on the outside patio for a late lunch of salad and a plate of some of the dozens of sheep, cow, and goat cheeses, or simply stock up for a picnic in the mountains.

Breakfasts are well worth the sometimes lengthy weekend line at the popular and homey **Seabreeze Café** (542 Seabright Ave., Santa Cruz, 831/427-9713, breakfast and early lunch daily, under $10, no credit cards!) in Santa Cruz's Seabright district near the harbor. For under $10, meat eaters and vegetarians alike can fill up for the day. Check the board for delicious daily specials.

Cafés

Santa Cruz is serious about its coffee and has a thriving café scene. Being a big student town, however, many of the city's more popular cafés are often filled with laptop-toting throngs voraciously consuming the free Wi-Fi more than the global coffees on offer, made using the best machines in the business.

Billing itself as the "oldest" coffee shop in

Santa Cruz, the charming **Caffe Pergolesi** (418 Cedar St., Santa Cruz, 831/426-1775, 7 A.M.–11 P.M. daily) really means no other café is located in an older building. The Perg, as it is known, has taken over an ornate 1886 Victorian on the corner of Cedar and Elm Streets where it serves countless teas, coffees, beer, pastries, and sandwiches. Find a nook in one of the four main interior rooms or the sprawling outside deck to surf the Internet or simply people-watch. This is a place better known for its hipster student scene and alcoholic happy hour than for the best coffee in town.

Many of Santa Cruz's downtown cafés sell light meals (plus good, earth-friendly coffee) and are generally strung along the parallel Pacific Avenue and Cedar Street, plus some of the cross streets. Most also offer free wireless Internet access. The **Santa Cruz Coffee Roasting Company** (1330 Pacific Ave., 831/459-0100, www.santacruz coffee.com, Mon.–Thurs. 6 A.M.–10 P.M., Fri. 6 A.M.–11 P.M., Sat. 6:30 A.M.–11 P.M.) is the grandfather of the local coffee scene and was instrumental in establishing the international fair-trade coffee business. **Caffe Bene** (1101 Cedar St., 831/425-0441, caffebene.com, Mon.–Fri. 6:30 A.M.–6P.M., Sat. 8 A.M.–6P.M.) is more relaxed than some of the trendier local cafés and serves what some consider to be the finest coffee in Santa Cruz.

Lulu Carpenter's (1545 Pacific Ave., 831/429-9804) is in an atmospheric building with bare brick walls at the quiet end of Pacific Avenue. It is also said to have some of the best (and most expensive) coffee in town and there's a small patio at the back of the store if you need some peace and quiet. It's also open until 11 P.M. if you crave a late-night espresso and dessert. There's another, more spacious outpost of LuLu in an octagonal-shaped former archive building at the Museum of Art and History (118 Cooper St., 831/429-5858) a few blocks away.

Coffee meets music and art at **The Abbey** (350 Mission St., www.abbeylounge .org, Mon.–Fri. 7 A.M.–8 P.M., Sat. –Sun.

8:30 A.M.–10:30 P.M.), which is operated as a non-profit venue by the neighboring Vintage Faith Church, a short walk from the downtown area. It is one of the more laid-back and eclectic places in town to grab a coffee, with a chaotic mixture of antique and modern furniture, contemporary art, and an artsy clientele. On weekend nights it is open until 10 P.M. and hosts an equally eclectic mixture of live music. Check the website for current listings.

Brewpubs

Because Santa Cruz is a big student and party town, there are plenty of temples to beer, all open daily until late. The most bewildering array (including 40 on tap) are at the aptly named **99 Bottles of Beer on the Wall** (110 Walnut Ave., Santa Cruz, 831/459-9999). Drink all 99 (not necessarily in a day) and win a T-shirt. They range from local brews to international beers, although none are brewed onsite—this isn't a traditional brewpub, more of an international pub. The full menu offers typical pub fare, including some fine burgers and sandwiches ($8–11).

With the closure of the Santa Cruz Brewing Company a few years ago, the granddaddy of the Santa Cruz brewing scene is now the **Seabright Brewery** (519 Seabright Ave., Santa Cruz, 831/426-2739, 11:30 A.M.– 11:30 P.M. daily), which has been hopping for about 20 years a mile south of the downtown area. Its home is a characterless and slightly grubby 1980s building, but the outdoor patio facing Murray Street saves it, providing a great place to kick back with some of the brewery's eight beers, including several pale and amber ales, together with pretty good pub grub ranging from sandwiches and burgers to flatiron steak. Live music on weekend nights usually extends the opening hours until well after midnight.

At the other end of Santa Cruz, the **Santa Cruz Mountain Brewing Company** (402 Ingalls St., Ste. 27, Santa Cruz, 831/425-4900, www.santacruzmountainbrewing.com, noon–10 P.M. Fri.–Sun.) has a tasting room in its brewery, behind Kelly's French Bakery in the Swift Street Courtyard complex on the Westside.

INFORMATION AND SERVICES

Information about both the city and county of Santa Cruz is available at the **Santa Cruz County Conference and Visitors Council** (303 Water St., 831/425-1234 or 800/833-3494, www.santacruzca.org, 9 A.M.–4 P.M. Mon.–Fri., 11 A.M.–4 P.M. Sat.–Sun.), a little off the beaten path in Santa Cruz. There's useful city information in its free visitor guide, as well as information about sights and wineries further afield in the county. Also worth checking out for more detailed information about Santa Cruz itself is the City of Santa Cruz website maintained by **Santa Cruz City Hall** (www.ci.santacruz.ca.us).

The weekly newspapers, usually available in cafés and on the street, are worth picking up on either side of the mountains for up-to-date event and entertainment listings. *Good Times* covers Santa Cruz and up into the mountains, and *Metro* is the weekly paper for Los Gatos, Saratoga, and other Silicon Valley towns, though its territory also stretches to Santa Cruz. The *Los Gatos Weekly Times* is a more news-oriented weekly but also has listings.

GETTING THERE

Driving to Santa Cruz from either San Francisco to the north or San Jose to the east involves navigating through or around the mountains, and will likely take longer than the mileage might suggest. If you're in Saratoga, Highway 9 is going to be by far the quickest route, slow as it might feel, and it meets Highway 1 in Santa Cruz just a few blocks from the mission just up the hill from the downtown area.

From San Francisco and points north, the slow and pretty route is on the Pacific Coast Highway (Highway 1), but faster routes use Highway 17, which runs past Los Gatos and through Scotts Valley. This is the main road across the mountains, but it's by no means quick. It twists and turns like any mountain road and is often clogged with rush-hour traffic, beach traffic, or traffic backed up by one of the regular rain-induced spinouts in winter.

From the south, Highway 1 also heads straight into Santa Cruz and can be picked up easily from U.S. 101 just north of Salinas.

Greyhound (425 Front St., 831/423-1800) offers daily bus service from San Francisco or Los Angeles via either San Jose or Monterey.

GETTING AROUND

Biking as a means of winery touring might be out of the question in the mountains, but in the city of Santa Cruz you might be wishing you had a bike when searching for parking downtown or at the beach, especially in summer—or when you discover just how efficient the parking and traffic cops are.

The bicycle is king in earth-friendly Santa Cruz, and it seems to be the main mode of transport for the students at the University of California at Santa Cruz. If you're in Santa Cruz for a few days, leave the car at the hotel and rent bikes (and locks). It need not be as strenuous as it sounds.

Try out an electric bike from **Electric Sierra Rentals** (302 Pacific Ave., at W. Cliff Dr. a few blocks from the wharf, 831/425-1593 or 877/372-8773, www.electricrecbikes.com). There are electric versions of mountain bikes, beach cruisers, and tandems starting at $10 an hour or from $35 a day. They have a range of about 20 miles, making them perfect for puttering around town, but speed demons take note—you won't get more than 20 miles per hour out of them. Electric Sierra Rentals also rents more traditional human-powered bikes for $25 a day.

On crowded summer weekends you can usually find free parking at the County Government Center (701 Ocean St.), and hop on the **Santa Cruz Beach Shuttle,** which runs about every half hour during daylight hours down to the wharf and boardwalk and back.

MONTEREY, CARMEL, AND THE SANTA LUCIA HIGHLANDS

It would be easy to suggest that if John Steinbeck hadn't written novels like *Cannery Row, East of Eden,* and *Tortilla Flat* about the Monterey Bay region, it might never have come into prominence. Steinbeck's novels, many of them set against the backdrop of Monterey's wildly differing geography, opened the door to one of California's best agricultural areas.

Today, Monterey is best known for the bay itself, a hidden wonderland of sea life, which is now visible for everyone to see at the renowned Monterey Bay Aquarium. It's also popular for its rugged and wild coastline, ripe with outdoor activities like kayaking, biking, and hiking. Cannery Row, the signature street Steinbeck's novel made famous, is one of the most visited streets in the entire country, its blue-collar past still evident in its architecture, even though

these days it's a huge tourist attraction. Nearby Carmel, in contrast, was founded by artists and wealthy landowners who carved out an idyllic village gently descending to white-sand beaches. The homes, all individual and unique, express their owner's passions and interests. There are no planned urban developments here; the community focus is on maintaining Carmel's seaside charm.

But the area is not just Cannery Row, lettuce fields, and otters. There's also the wine. In Carmel Valley, not far from the village of Carmel, the inland heat allows for cabernet sauvignon and merlot grapes to grow, facilitating the continuing success of a handful of wineries. Moving farther inland, you'll reach the Santa Lucia Highlands, a bench of nearly flat land at the base of the Santa Lucia mountain range.

© MICHAEL CERVIN

HIGHLIGHTS

◖ **Monterey Bay Aquarium:** There is no better place to see the hidden beauty of the Monterey Bay than at the aquarium, which not only sits above the bay, but in it. From otters to sharks, tuna to anchovies, this place has it all (page 404).

◖ *Bella Monterey Bay:* Experience Monterey Bay on a sailing yacht that seats only six people. Intimate, exhilarating, and relaxing, this is the de facto way to see the bay (page 408).

◖ **Lover's Point Park:** This stunning piece of land, jutting out into the Pacific Ocean is not just for lovers, but for anyone who loves the beauty of the Monterey coastline. Part grassy picnic area, part rock climbing, and part beach, this park has something for everybody (page 409).

◖ **Talbott Vineyards:** Talbott has long been the standard-bearer of high quality pinot noir and chardonnay from Monterey County (page 419).

◖ **Point Lobos State Reserve:** In the sunshine, in the rain, it doesn't matter as long as you're at Lobos. This state park commands killer views of the ocean and up and down the coast along unspoiled rocks weathered by time and flanked by pine trees (page 420).

◖ **San Carlos Borromeo de Carmelo Mission:** The largest and most beautiful of the 21 missions in the California chain, the Carmel Mission boasts an ornate chapel and the very first library in California (page 421).

◖ **Carmel Art Association:** Carmel has always been an artist's enclave, but no where is the genuine talent of the Carmel art scene better represented than at this 1920s converted residence filled with a diversity of local art work (page 421).

◖ **Wrath Wines:** Wrath's Rhone-style wines are balanced, layered, and seductive (page 431).

◖ **Pinnacles National Monument:** It's Monterey, only different. Gone are the ocean views and in its place are wild, volcanic formations jutting up in the parched earth. This magnificent spot offers both easy and hard hikes (page 432).

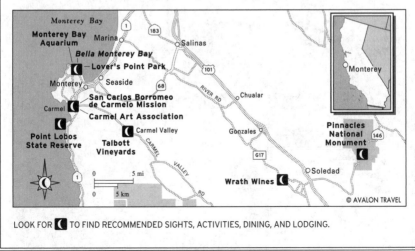

LOOK FOR ◖ TO FIND RECOMMENDED SIGHTS, ACTIVITIES, DINING, AND LODGING.

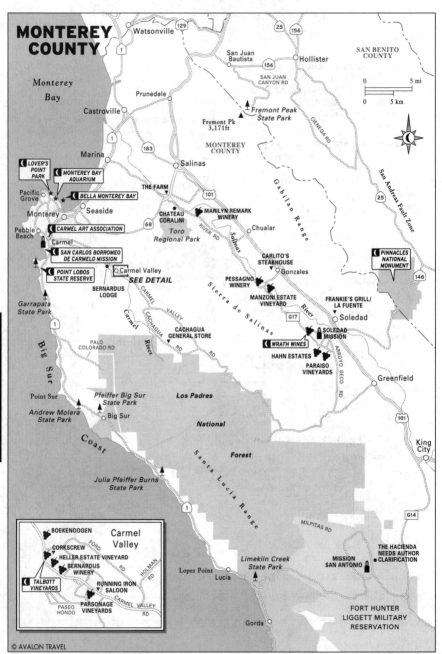

Santa Lucia's pinot noirs and chardonnays have become signature wines, bringing the Monterey county wine region to national and even international attention. The area is still growing—there are few restaurants, few shops, and few lodgings—but there are vineyards and tasting rooms. What more could you ask for?

HISTORY

As is true throughout most of California, the first grapes were brought to this area in the 1800s by Spanish missionaries, who used them for sacramental wines and the occasional indulgence on lonely California evenings. These cuttings had migrated from Europe into South America up to Mexico and into California. Years later, more cuttings arrived with the Italian and Swiss immigrants to the Salinas Valley and Monterey Bay. As early as 1919, pinot blanc grapes were planted in the remote hill location of Chalone, 15 miles east of Highway 101 near Soledad, an out of the way area where growing grapes is difficult at best. The first viable commercial plantings in Monterey County appeared in 1968 with 40 acres of cabernet sauvignon in the Cachagua (pronounced ca-shaw-wa) area of Carmel Valley. In the 1970s, Monterey became an attractive option for people looking for an alternative to skyrocketing Napa and Sonoma land prices, leading to aggressive growth of the local wine industry. Today, there are over 40,000 planted acres in the county, and nine distinct American Viticultural Areas (AVA). Monterey is known predominately for chardonnay and pinot noir, though there are pockets of Rhône grapes, like syrah and viognier, and cabernet sauvignon and merlot in the Carmel Valley. A sizeable amount of juice is still sold to other producers in and out of the county.

PLANNING YOUR TIME

Most visitors use Monterey or Carmel as a base to explore the coastal and inland areas. Since Monterey and Carmel are only five miles apart, choose the town that better suits your personality. The Carmel Valley and Santa Lucia

---

ONE-DAY WINE TOUR: MONTEREY, CARMEL, AND THE SANTA LUCIA HIGHLANDS

Heading up Highway 101, swing west to River Road near Soledad in the Santa Lucia Highlands and make your way to **Pessagno Winery** for terrific pinot noir and chardonnay. A bit farther north you'll reach **Marilyn Remark Winery** for Rhône wines. You'll be right near Highway 68 and **The Farm:** grab farm fresh fruits to snack on the way.

Take Highway 1 South and drive to the **Carmel Valley** for a Wine Country-inspired lunch at **Corkscrew. Talbott Vineyards** is right next door; sample the pinot noirs here and then visit **Boekenoogen** for terrific chardonnay.

Head back to Monterey and **Cannery Row.** Visit **A Taste of Monterey** for killer views of the Pacific and a wide diversity of Monterey wines. On Cannery Row, amble down the street to the **Monterey Bay Aquarium,** then feast on seafood at **C Restaurant.** Wrap up the day by listening to live music at **Sly Mcfly's.** End up at the **Old Monterey Inn** for the night and relax and recount your day in the hot tub.

Highlands, where most of the wineries are located, are both about a 20-minute drive from Monterey Bay, depending on traffic. You could cover the region in a single day, but would be better off taking your time and planning on two. Keep in mind that traffic congestion, especially during the peak summer months and along some of the mountain roads, can make even the brief drive from Monterey south to Carmel Valley or east to the Santa Lucia Highlands arduous.

The Monterey Peninsula is cooler than many people think, therefore planning your visit to factor in the weather is important.

Summer temperatures are usually in the low 60s. That doesn't mean there aren't days of warm sunshine; but Monterey weather has much in common with San Francisco's. Often the marine influence of low clouds doesn't burn off until late morning. The Santa Lucia Highlands are warmer during the day as the mountain range blocks the marine fog. The valley can get windy, with ocean breezes funneled from the bay. Evenings can see as much as a 30-degree drop in temperature. Typically, rains hit Monterey and Carmel October–May; December–March are the wettest, coldest, and foggiest months.

Monterey

The best days in Monterey are picture perfect: It's no wonder that so many artists have been inspired to paint this land- and seascape. The Kashmir blue of the ocean beckons you to wander the twisting coastline, taking in the boats, kayaks, and otters playing along the bay. Nearly four million people heed this call annually.

There are two distinct sections to Monterey, separated by about a mile: the waterfront area around Cannery Row, and downtown. The six blocks of Cannery Row retain much of the sardine-cannery look described in Steinbeck's novel, though the buildings have been spruced up a bit (and in some cases, completely rebuilt) since the 1940s. The canneries are long gone, and today the Row is packed with businesses, including the must-see Monterey Bay Aquarium, terrific seafood restaurants, shops, galleries, and wine-tasting rooms. As you walk the street, you have direct access to the beach and the ocean. Downtown Monterey is somewhat neglected by tourists, but it offers more unique stores, some historic buildings, and fewer crowds. With the exception of a few streets, it's laid out on a grid, with new buildings plopped next to historic structures from the 1850s. Slightly east is Pacific Grove, a quiet community that receives its share of overflow traffic.

WINE-TASTING

There are no wineries along the Monterey Bay, but tasting rooms punctuate the streets, so you can sample wine while watching sea lions playing in the ocean. That's a pretty good trade-off.

PIERCE RANCH

You won't find Monterey's signature pinot noir or chardonnay at Pierce Ranch (499 Wave St., 831/372-8900, www.piercevineyards.com, noon–6:30 P.M. Sun.–Mon., 1–6:30 P.M. Tues.–Wed., noon–8 P.M. Thurs.–Sat., tasting $5). Instead there are mainly Spanish varietals: They produce an excellent petite sirah and very nice, super mellow cabernet sauvignon, as well as albariño, tempranillo, and verdelho. They are also making a port, using traditional grapes like tinta cao, nacional, and touriga, and making the brandy to fortify the port from their own tempranillo. Overall, the wines show a nice acidity. The grapes come from 33 acres in the

the tasting room at Pierce Ranch

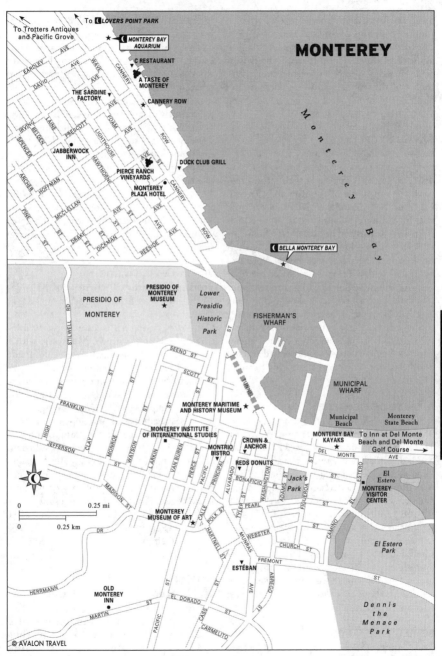

MONTEREY

To Trotters Antiques and Pacific Grove

To **LOVERS POINT PARK**

★ **MONTEREY BAY AQUARIUM**

C RESTAURANT

A TASTE OF MONTEREY

THE SARDINE FACTORY

★ CANNERY ROW

JABBERWOCK INN

DUCK CLUB GRILL

PIERCE RANCH VINEYARDS

MONTEREY PLAZA HOTEL

Monterey Bay

BELLA MONTEREY BAY ★

PRESIDIO OF MONTEREY

PRESIDIO OF MONTEREY MUSEUM ★

Lower Presidio Historic Park

FISHERMAN'S WHARF

MUNICIPAL WHARF

MONTEREY MARITIME AND HISTORY MUSEUM ★

MONTEREY INSTITUTE OF INTERNATIONAL STUDIES

CROWN & ANCHOR

MONTRIO BISTRO

REDS DONUTS

Jack's Park

Municipal Beach

Monterey State Beach

MONTEREY BAY KAYAKS ★

To Inn at Del Monte Beach and Del Monte Golf Course →

El Estero

MONTEREY VISITOR CENTER

MONTEREY MUSEUM OF ART ★

El Estero Park

ESTÉBAN ▼

OLD MONTEREY INN ●

0   0.25 mi

0   0.25 km

Dennis the Menace Park

© AVALON TRAVEL

MONTEREY

San Antonio AVA in the southernmost portion in Monterey County, which nets them about 1,700 cases of wine. Pierce Ranch is open later than all of the other tasting rooms in the Cannery Row area. The small space was converted from a 1915 residence; the original hardwood floors are still in an unfinished state. It can get crowded and loud. Wines by the glass are $7.

BAYWOOD CELLARS

Baywood Cellars (381 Cannery Row, 800/214-0445, www.baywood-cellars.com, noon–6 P.M. daily, tasting $5) has been at their location toward the south end of the Row for 15 years. Much of the fruit for their wines comes from within Monterey County, but some comes from Paso Robles and Lodi. Of their Monterey wines, their merlot is excellent, as is their smoky and unusual Rosso de Tavola, a blend of pinot noir with a little malbec tossed in. They carry chardonnay and gewürztraminer. They also make and sell grappa (although they can't legally allow you to taste it). Non-Monterey county wines include petite verdot, syrah, and cabernet sauvignon. The room has a Thomas Kincade feel; it's a little over-decorated and too polished. Four chairs near the tasting bar offer a bit of relaxation.

A TASTE OF MONTEREY

A Taste of Monterey (700 Cannery Row, 888/646-5449, www.tastemonterey.com, 11 A.M.–6 P.M. daily, tasting $10–20) has, hands down, the best views of any tasting room in Monterey. Standing at the tasting bar, you look directly at Monterey Bay through the expansive second story windows. Twelve tables fill the 4,000-square-foot space. This co-op is dedicated to a variety of Monterey County wines, from both well-known producers and small boutique winemakers. The wines rotate every Friday, so there's always something new to try. They also offer cheese and cracker plates for $8. The large retail section includes a vast selection wine, posters, and gifts.

SCHIED VINEYARDS

The Cannery Row tasting room of Schied Vineyards (751 Cannery Row, 831/656-9463, www.scheidvineyards.com, 11 A.M.–8 P.M. daily, tasting $10–15) is sophisticated: Four leather club chairs flank the fireplace, dark wood tones complement the tasting bar, and tables offer views of the Row. They offer two wine lists, with the more expensive reserve list poured on weekends only. Though they produce whites like sauvignon blanc, chardonnay, and Riesling, their best efforts are the reds: compelling pinot noirs, syrah, and cabernet sauvignon blends, and an excellent merlot. Schied began as a grape grower, planting its first acreage in 1972. Today, the vineyards grow over 5,000 acres of grapes, selling most of them to other wineries, almost exclusively within Monterey County. Though they don't advertise it, you can get wines by the glass for $7–20.

VENTANA VINEYARDS

Ventana Vineyards (2999 Hwy. 68, 831/375-7415, www.ventanawines.com, daily 11 A.M.–6 P.M. June–Sept., 11 A.M.–5 P.M. Oct.–May, tasting $5) is located just 10 minutes outside of downtown Monterey, with a convenient location on the right-hand side of Highway 68 as you enter town. They are best known for their white wines, including chardonnay, sauvignon blanc, and their very popular, simple yet effective Riesling. Their red wines are more fully developed wines than the whites, and include tempranillo and two blended wines: Rudystone (Grenache and syrah) and due Amici (tempranillo and cabernet sauvignon). All of their wines are estate grown; they pour everything they have as they do not have a reserve list. The tasting room is a stone house built in 1919, covered by foliage, and looks like it might belong in the English countryside. The interior is dimly lit with a hand-carved table. There's also an outdoor patio.

SIGHTS
◖ Monterey Bay Aquarium

There is no better aquarium on the West Coast, possibly even in the entire United States, than the **Monterey Bay Aquarium** (886 Cannery Row, 831/648-4800, www.montereybayaquarium.org, 10 A.M.–6 P.M. daily, adults $29.95, students and seniors $27.95, children 3–12 $17.95), located right on the bay. Don't miss the Outer Bay section to see the beautifully lit jellyfish, their graceful movements like a ballet. The penguin exhibit is another popular show, more so when they dive into the water and you can see the agility these birds have. Other must-see exhibits include the kelp forest, a two-story high view into an ethereal underwater world. Divers feed the fish and give informative talks at 11:30 A.M. and 4 P.M. daily. Other exhibits showcase sharks, sheepshead, and schools of anchovies that move as a single unit. But the otter exhibit is often the most crowded, especially at the 11 A.M. feeding time. More often than not they are playing and acting up for the crowds; everyone loves otters. There's also the Splash Zone, a series of open rooms with touch tanks and moving exhibits that keep kids entertained and, hopefully, informed. With so many wonderful exhibits, not to mention the crowds, the aquarium will take more time than you may anticipate; plan at least 2–3 hours to explore. Facilities include a rather pricey on-site restaurant and gift shop, as well as outdoor decks with views of the bay.

Cannery Row

The fishing canneries and warehouses that lined Cannery Row (www.canneryrow.com) were successful in the 1930s and 1940s, and were made famous by John Steinbeck's novel. But as overfishing took its toll on the bay and the fishing industry, they fell into disrepair. By the late 1950s, Cannery Row was deserted; some buildings actually fell into the ocean. A slow renaissance began in the 1960s, driven by new interest in preserving the historic integrity of the area, as well as a few savvy entrepreneurs who understood the value of beachfront property. Today, the fabled street, similar architecturally to its fishing days, is one of the most popular destinations in California. The corrugated metal siding of the canneries is still here, as are the squared block industrial buildings and crossovers that connected them to the nearby railway. Now there's a bike and

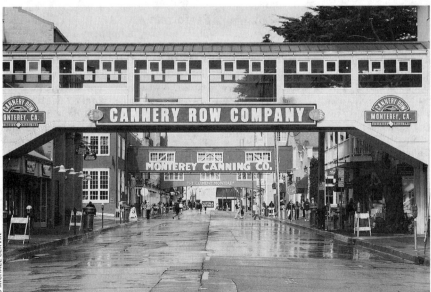

© MICHAEL CERVIN

historic Cannery Row

walking path where the trains once stopped to load up sardines for transport across the state. The smells of fish and a hard day's work are gone, and everything's been painted and clean, ready to show off for the tourists. In addition to the Monterey Bay Aquarium, the Row is home to dozens of shops and restaurants, with easy access to the water.

ENTERTAINMENT AND EVENTS
Nightlife

If live piano is your gig, then **The Lounge** (701 Wave St., 831/373-3775, www.sardine factory.com, 7:30–11 P.M. Tues.–Sat.) tucked into a corner of the bar at the Sardine Factory is your best bet. Expect to hear ballads and renditions of current popular songs. Say hi to Big Mike the bartender—he's been slinging drinks there for 36 years. Specialty cocktails include the Blue Sardine, the Pink Sardine, and Misty's Kiss, inspired by the Clint Eastwood movie *Play Misty for Me,* which was filmed here. Tapas and fish sandwiches are also on the bar menu.

Six nights a week you can find live music at **Cibo** (301 Alvarado St., 831/649-8151, www .cibo.com, 7–10:30 P.M. Tues.–Sun.). On Sunday nights, dinner is accompanied by light jazz music. Things heat up the rest of the week, with dancing to Latin jazz, R&B, salsa, soul, funk, and swing. Both the decor and menu are Italian, with soft Tuscan yellow walls creating a nice environment for enjoying pizza, pastas, and scampi along with the music.

Shoot some pool at **Blue Fin Café & Billiards** (685 Cannery Row, 831/717-4280, www.bluefinbilliards.com, noon–2 A.M. daily, table rates $12/hr), which offers 11 tournament-size pool tables as well as arcade games, darts, and even a small dance floor. They also have 16 draft beers on tap.

Sly McFly's (700 Cannery Row, 831/649-8050, www.slymcflys.net, 11:30 A.M.–2 A.M. daily, no cover charge) is the best venue for live music on Cannery Row, bringing in a wide variety of artists, some very well-known, to play rock, blues, and soul, seven nights a week.

The stage is small and the ambience is a little tired, but the music and the crowds spill out into the streets. Forget the food; just come for the tunes.

If you want a late-night brew, the **Cannery Row Brewing Company** (95 Prescott Ave., 831/643-2722, www.canneryrowbrewing company.com, 11 A.M.–11 P.M. Mon.–Thurs., 11 A.M.–midnight Fri.–Sun.) is a choice spot, with nearly 75 beers on tap and 25 beers in bottle. The industrial decor and concrete floors give it a bit of a rough feel—and can also make it quite loud.

If old school bars are your thing, it's worth stopping in at **Segovia's** (650 Lighthouse Ave., 831/372-9981, 10 A.M.–2 A.M. daily), the oldest bar in Monterey, started in 1937. Located away from downtown up a few blocks from Cannery Row, it's populated mostly by locals. The interior is dated, with a padded bar and stools and 1960s decor that now make it feel retro. There's no food, just drinks; the most popular concoction is the Tennis Ball: orange vodka, melon schnapps, pineapple juice, and sweet and sour mixed together.

Performing Arts

The **Monterey Symphony** (831/646-8511, www.montereysymphony.org) has provided a wealth of concerts for 65 years, focusing on traditional classical music, with works by Bach and Mozart, as well as a few operatic offerings.

The **Bruce Ariss Wharf Theatre** (Old Fisherman's Wharf #1, 831/649-2332, www .mctaweb.org, adults $25, children 12 and under $10) has been putting on light-hearted shows and musicals for 35 years, with occasional dramas and Broadway reviews. Community-based shows run Thursday–Friday evenings with a Sunday matinee.

Cinema

Living large in Monterey means seeing movies at the **IMAX** (640 Wave St., 831/372-4629, adults $9.95, children $7.95), with three big screens a block up from Cannery Row. The **Central Coast Cinemas** (350 Alvarado St., 831/644-8171, adults $9, seniors and children $6.25) offers three screens downtown. For a larger selection of films, **Century Cinemas** (1700 Del Monte Center, 800/373-8051, adults $9.75, seniors and children $6.75) has 14 screens with the latest in Hollywood entertainment.

Festivals and Events
The **Great Wine Escape Weekend** (831/375-9400, www.montereywines.org, $25–150) held each November mixes wine pairings with food and cooking demonstrations from chefs like Robert Bleifer, the executive chef at the Food Network. There are also multiple wine tastings around the county, such as pinot noir tastings investigating the diverse soil and growing conditions from the different Monterey AVAs. The grand finale tasting, held at the InterContinental Hotel overlooking the Monterey Bay, is probably the best part with more than 30 wineries represented. It's a great chance to get a full view of the wine and food that the Monterey Peninsula has to offer.

The **Winemaker's Celebration** (One Custom House Plaza, 831/375-9400, www.montereywines.org, 1–5 P.M., $50) held one day each August is an inexpensive tasting event that remains true to its humble roots, making it the best gateway to over 40 Monterey County wineries. There's live music, dancing, food, and of course, wine, including reserve tastings. But the celebration is small enough to make it easy to chat—not only with the people pouring the wines but also the many winemakers and winery owners in attendance.

For over half a century, the **Monterey Jazz Festival** (Monterey Fairgrounds, 831/373-3366, www.montereyjazzfestival.org, weekend in Sept., tickets start at $35) has brought together a who's who of jazz greats, both singers and musicians. If you are a jazz fan, this is heaven. This is the biggest event in Monterey, drawing in some 40,000 people. Plan ahead as tickets go quickly.

SHOPPING
If you're looking for antiques, you'll find anything that suits your fancy at the **Cannery Row Antique Mall** (471 Wave St., Monterey,

831/655-0264, 10 A.M.–5:30 P.M. Mon.–Fri., 10 A.M.–6 P.M. Sat., 10 A.M.–5 P.M. Sun.), which combines 150 vendors in a massive two-story warehouse, filled with sterling silver, vintage dolls, china, and furniture in mission, country, and deco styles.

You'll find a treasure trove of antiques—Tiffany lamps, 18th and 19th Century furniture, porcelain dolls—at **Trotters Antiques** (590 Lighthouse Ave., Pacific Grove, 831/373-3505, 11 A.M.–5 P.M. Mon.–Sat.). Owner Lee Trotter has been in the business for 46 years; her reputation is unquestionable.

Housed in an old green shingle-covered home, the **Monterey Peninsula Art Foundation** (425 Cannery Row, Monterey, 831/655-1267, 11 A.M.–5 P.M. daily) is a cooperative of about 30 local artists working in watercolor, acrylics, ceramics, jewelry, and sculpture. It's one of the few Monterey galleries that exhibit exclusively local art. They also have a good selection of greeting cards featuring the works of their artists.

At **Boatworks** (400 Cannery Row, Monterey, 831/643-9482, 10 A.M.–7 P.M. daily) you can find men's and women's clothes with a nautical bent, mainly nice, fairly conservative resort wear from names like Tommy Bahama and Bugatchi, with some more touristy clothes mixed in. There are also hats, sweaters, books, and gifts.

California Classics (750 Cannery Row, Monterey, 831/324-0528, 9 A.M.–9 P.M. daily) sells men's, women's, and kid's clothing with Monterey and California motifs. You can buy tourist sweatshirts and t-shirts to remind yourself or your friends that you were indeed on Cannery Row.

As the name suggests, **Carried Away** (612 Lighthouse Ave., Pacific Grove, 831/656-9063, www.carriedawayboutique.com, 10 A.M.–5 P.M. daily) is the place for bright colorful hand bags from designers like Vera Bradley. There are hats and outerwear as well.

Book Buyers (600 Lighthouse Ave., Monterey, 831/375-4208, www.bookbuyers.com, 11 A.M.–5 P.M. daily) is, sadly, one of the last independent used bookstores in the area. They have over 30,000 titles, an even mix of hardbacks and paperbacks. The tight maze of books is surprisingly well organized, with a diverse selection, including a large children's section.

RECREATION
◖ *Bella Monterey Bay*

To be near Monterey Bay is a treat, to be on it is a delight. Because the 47-foot sailboat *Bella Monterey Bay* (32 Cannery Row, 818/822-2390, www.bellamontereybay.com, rates start at $69 for 2-hour cruise) only seats six people, it offers more of a relaxed, intimate cruise than an organized tour. The quiet of the boat under sail will take you far from the crowds on Cannery Row: You'll feel like the bay is yours. Captain Christian is happy to tailor the experience to your interests. Once in a while, he'll pull up his crab traps out at sea and grill his catch up fresh on the boat. You can also ask him to put up the hammock on the bow so you can sway with the waves. Or bring your own picnic if you like. Typical

cruises last 2–4 hours. The shorter cruises put out for just 4–5 miles from shore, then return along the Cannery Row coast. Of course, since this is a sailboat, speed depends on the weather, sometimes reaching 25 knots when the wind is up.

Other Water Activities

Yes it's cold to scuba dive in the bay, but with the wealth of sea life present, it's worth it. Explore the bay and all it has to offer with **Monterey Bay Dive Charters** (250 Figueroa St., 831/383-9276, www.mbdcscuba.com, $49 and up), which offers guided beach diving right off Cannery Row. They also offer scuba lessons.

The **Monterey Bay Whale Watch Center** (84 Fisherman's Wharf, 888/469-4253, www.gowhales.com, $36 and up) offers whale-watching year-round. But December–March is the best time to see some of the 7,000 grey whales that make their annual migration to Baja California. You may also see dolphins, sea lions, seals, and otters, as well as a few other whales such as humpbacks and blues. A marine

relaxing in the hammock on the *Bella Monterey Bay*

© MICHAEL CERVIN

biologist is on board to answer questions about the sea life. Because the bay is protected, the water usually doesn't get too rough.

Monterey Bay Kayaks (693 Del Monte Ave., 800/649-5357, www.montereybaykayaks .com, 9 A.M.–7 P.M. daily) will rent you a kayak, or take you on a two- to three-hour guided tour of the bay. Kayak rentals start at $30 and include wetsuits, life vests, and a quick intro if you've never kayaked before. Single, double, or triple-seat kayaks are available. Guided kayak tours start at $50. They also sell new kayaks, clothing, sunglasses, and flip-flops.

Since 1966, family-owned **El Estero Boating** (831/375-1484, 10 A.M.–5 P.M. Mon.– Fri., 10 A.M.–7 P.M. Sat.–Sun., rates start at $15 for 30 min.) has rented colorful paddle boats on the U-shaped El Estero Lake around Dennis the Menace Park. The water on the lake is typically calmer than on the bay, which makes for a relaxing experience. Your legs will thank you.

Dennis the Menace Park

Originally envisioned by Hank Ketcham, the creator of the comic strip, **Dennis the Menace Park** (777 Pearl St., 831/646-3860, 10 A.M.–dusk daily) opened in 1956. Ketcham was heavily involved in the design process; he moved to the area after World War II, and lived here until his death in 2001. There's a nine-foot climbing wall, suspension bridge, long green curvy slide attached to brightly colored jungle gyms, real black locomotive, and a whole lot more, as well as a bronze sculpture of the little menace near the entrance.

◖ Lover's Point Park

Located near Cannery Row in Pacific Grove, Lover's Point Park (630 Ocean View Bl., Pacific Grove, dawn–dusk daily) juts out to offer views of Monterey to the right, Pacific Grove to the left, and Santa Cruz directly across the bay. It's one of the most beautiful spots on the Peninsula. There's access to sandy coves and stunning rock formations, like displaced shards of granite. Climb up for even more killer views of the coastline. It's a great spot for a picnic, with a large grassy area, tables, beach volleyball

MONTEREY

© MICHAEL CERVIN

The views from Lover's Point Park showcase the rugged coastline.

court, and restrooms just above the water. It's also a popular location for weddings.

Golf

Known locally as the Navy course because a lot of military personnel use it, the **Monterey Pines Golf Course** (1250 Garden Rd., Monterey, 831/656-2167, www.thegolfcourses.net, dawn–dusk daily, green fees $18–37) is a short and sweet 18-hole, par-69 course. Redesigned in 2009, it's the most inexpensive course in the area, ideal for beginners or for someone who wants to work on their short game. **Del Monte Golf Course** (1300 Sylvan Rd., Pebble Beach, 800/654-4944, www.pebble beach.com, dawn–dusk daily, green fees $135) is one of the oldest courses on the West Coast, originally designed in 1897. This uncrowded 18-hole, par-72 course is less difficult than more modern courses, but its fairways are studded with mature trees, making them a little challenging to negotiate.

Spas

The **Spa on the Plaza** (Two Portola Plaza, Monterey, 831/647-9000, www.spaontheplaza.com, 9 A.M.–9 P.M. daily) has seven treatment rooms, including two couple's massage rooms with whirlpool tubs. The spa also offers body wraps, Japanese soaking tubs, wet steam rooms with rock-lined walls, and a large relaxation room for de-toxing prior to your treatment. If you choose to make it a daylong adventure, you can order food from the Portola Plaza Hotel across the street.

Vista Blue Spa (400 Cannery Row, Monterey, 800/334-3999, 10 A.M.–4 P.M. Sun.–Thurs., 10 A.M.–7 P.M. Fri.–Sat.) performs massages on their fourth-floor sun deck overlooking the bay—not a bad way to relax. But it's the bath rituals that are the big draw: They last 25–45 minutes, with four different essential oils and minerals in the water, including arnica, rosemary, and basil.

ACCOMMODATIONS
$100-200

The **Best Western De Anza** (2141 Freemont St., Monterey, 831/646-8300, www.bestwestern california.com, $120–135 d) is in driving distance from Cannery Row and downtown, but it's one of the least expensive and nicest of the chain hotels in the Monterey area. Off-season rates drop to under $100, which can't be beat—not in Monterey. Forty-three rooms include microwaves, fridges, and coffee makers, and there's an outdoor heated pool and hot tub.

Closer to the ocean, the **Inn at Del Monte Beach** (1110 Del Monte Blvd., Monterey, 831/655-0515, www.theinnatdelmontebeach.com, $155–195 d) offers 15 rooms in a unique, boutique property with a 1960s meets beaux arts feel. Amenities include Wi-Fi in the rooms, DVD players, electric fireplaces, a full breakfast in the communal dining room, afternoon tea, and wine and cheese in the early evenings on the deck overlooking the Pacific (all included in the price). You can park on the street, or pay a small fee for the valet. A nice rooftop deck offers great views to the bay and downtown, which is just a five-block walk.

Designed by architect Julia Morgan of Hearst Castle fame, **(Asilomar** (800 Asilomar Ave., Pacific Grove, 888/635-5310, www.visit asilomar.com, $130–165 d) was originally commissioned as a YWCA by Hearst's mother. The original 65 rooms, built between 1913 and 1928, are true to their historic roots: They're small—quaint really—and face an outdoor courtyard. Built separately from the original building, 259 larger, more modern rooms are spartan, with no telephones or TVs. They have an outdoor pool and Wi-Fi in the communal areas and a business center. The overall vibe is log-cabin rustic: A park ranger offers talks around a campfire in the early evenings. It's a very short walk across the dunes to the beach in Pacific Grove, so it's not unusual to see deer wandering among the pines that grow throughout the property.

$200-300

Built as a private residence in 1911, **Jabberwock Inn** (598 Laine St., Pacific Grove, 888/428-7253, www.jabberwockinn.com, $169–299) was used as a convent for 50 years. Now it's the B&B with the best views of the bay, as they are perched up on the hills, a 10-minute walk (downhill) to Cannery Row. Breakfasts are served in the dining room, 8:30–9:30 A.M., which looks out a large window to the views, just above the bocce ball court. Wine and hors d'oeuvres are served 5–7 P.M. and every afternoon milk and home-baked cookies appear, and there is always homemade limoncello available. There is Wi-Fi on the property.

The woodwork is spectacular at the **Inn at 213 Seventeen Mile Drive** (213 Seventeen Mile Dr., Pacific Grove, 800/526-5666, www .innat17.com, $200–280 d), a classic craftsman home built in 1925. There are 4 upstairs rooms in the house, with an additional 10 in the separate coach house. Breakfast is served at 9 A.M. and each evening wine and hors d'oeuvres are served at 5 P.M., all prepared by a Cordon Blu–trained chef. The rooms are large, each with its own theme. There is also off street parking, Wi-Fi, and a small hot tub in the garden.

If you're looking for a traditional high-end hotel, this is it: The **Monterey Plaza Hotel & Spa** (400 Cannery Row, Monterey, 800/334-3999, www.montereyplazahotel .com, $239–359 d) has a prime location at the end of Cannery Row, with the Monterey Bay and beach access in its front yard. Many of the large, nicely appointed rooms face the bay with private balconies. Other amenities include in-room coffee makers, refrigerators, and turndown service. The service is first rate and it's far enough away from the center of Cannery Row to avoid the noise that accompanies the usual goings-on.

Although the **Portola Hotel** (Two Portola Plaza, Monterey, 831/649-4511, www.portola hotel.com, $270–330 d) is a big hotel it feels smaller than it is. About 40 percent of its 379 rooms offer prime views of the bay. There is also an on-site fitness room (daily 5 A.M.–11 P.M.), large round outdoor pool, and hot tub. The hotel is conveniently located between downtown Monterey and Cannery Row: The walk to downtown is 5 minutes, while the walk to Cannery Row is about 20 minutes along the coast (more if you stop and watch the sea lions).

The rooms and bathrooms are large and comfortable, with in-room coffee makers, and fridges upon request. Many packages include local restaurants and attractions, but you will need to pay extra for parking and Wi-Fi.

Over $300

The **❰ Old Monterey Inn** (500 Martin St., Monterey, 800/350-2344, www.oldmonterey inn.com, $330–390 d) is a delightful spot, perfect for a romantic getaway. It was the original residence built by the first mayor of Monterey in 1929. Thick vines cling to the entrance of this beautiful Tudor-style property with an oak tree shading the front. There are extensive gardens on the side and in the back. Breakfasts start with parfait and an entrée such as orange blossom French toast, and are served at 9 A.M. in the formal dining room (with a beautiful coffered ceiling) or in your room at 9:15 A.M. Wine and cheese is provided 4–6 P.M., but coffee, tea, sodas, and water are available all the time. The rooms are large, with comfortable beds, hot tubs, and carpeting throughout, which adds to the quiet atmosphere. Choose from over 100 DVDs to watch in your room. There is Wi-Fi but the signal is weak, therefore use the communal computer in the living room.

The **❰ Intercontinental Clement Monterey** (750 Cannery Row, Monterey, 831/375-4500, www.ichotelsgroup.com, $320–370 d) is a comfortable, minimalist hideaway. The modernist, Asian-inspired interior belies the pragmatic Cannery Row exterior. Tiles and woods are blended with woven fabric and inset rugs to create a dynamic play of materials and surfaces that honors its cannery past. Every guest room has its own orchids, and the furnishings are clean and sleek. There are 110 rooms on the bayside of Cannery Row and another 98 on the inland side, connected by a covered walking bridge. The hotel includes a full-service spa, a Kids Club with supervised daycare so parents can slip away for a while, and a 350-car covered garage. This is the newest and probably last oceanfront hotel that will be built on Cannery Row, due to stringent building regulations.

Al fresco dining on Cannery Row is a must.

© MICHAEL CERVIN

MONTEREY

FOOD
Breakfast
For 60 years people have been flooding into **Reds Donuts** (433 Alvarado St., Monterey, 831/372-9761, 6:30 A.M.–1:30 P.M. daily, $2) in downtown Monterey to grab an old fashioned, bear claw, or any of 20 different varieties. This is a local classic, with old yellow Formica counter tops, simple stools, and walls lined with old photos and paintings of clowns. There are no fancy coffee drinks or French pastries, nothing but donuts and basic coffee. Sometimes all you need is a glazed donut to go.

Around the corner is the **East Village Coffee Lounge** (498 Washington St., Monterey, 831/373-5601, 7 A.M.–9 P.M. daily, $5), which has a comfortable lounge vibe, as well as outdoor seating. There are plenty of coffee and tea drinks and they use organic milk. Pastry options include a tasty and moist chocolate scone and organic peach coffeecake. Parfaits, ham and cheese croissants, and tomato and basil panini are also available. Free Wi-Fi means lots of people hunker down with laptops.

Cheap Eats
On the far south end of Cannery Row, the **Cannery Row Deli** (101 Drake St., Monterey, 831/645-9549, 7 A.M.–5 P.M. daily, $8) offers massive breakfast burritos stuffed with eggs, chorizo and potatoes, and pancakes, lunch options like tuna melts and tofu pita, as well as hot and iced coffee drinks. The space is tiny with just three small tables, but the wood deck outside facing the bike path surrounded by ivy makes for a nice respite.

Pino's Café (211 Alvarado St., Monterey, 831/649-1930, 6:30 A.M.–9 P.M. daily, $8) offers daily pasta dishes and traditional salads like chicken and tuna, as well as Italian meatball sandwiches, salami, and turkey. They also have 16 different gelatos. The simple interior makes it a great spot for kids or for a grab-and-go breakfast. You're right near Cannery Row for a waterside stroll.

Seafood
◖ **The Sardine Factory** (701 Wave St., Monterey, 831/373-3775, www.sardinefactory

© MICHAEL CERVIN

The Sardine Factory

.com, 5 P.M.–midnight daily, $30) kicked off the resurgence of Cannery Row over four decades ago and remains a must-stop restaurant. There are several dining rooms. The Captain's Room pays tribute to the brave sailors who ruled the sea. The Conservancy is a glass room surrounded by greenery. The Wine Cellar is the more exclusive private dining room downstairs. The abalone bisque, served at both of President Reagan's inaugural dinners, is a must, and the fish entrées are tremendous: Consider Alaskan salmon topped with artichoke hearts and hollandaise sauce. Wine enthusiasts won't be disappointed: The Sardine Factory has received many awards for its impressive wine list, and the wine collection consists of over 35,000 bottles. The cellar below the dining room includes the only vertical collection of Inglenook cabernet sauvignons from 1949 to 1958 (No, you can't buy them, but you can take a peek). Nearby are the private wine lockers of Clint Eastwood and Arnold Schwarzenegger, among others, who can pull their wines when they dine there.

Desserts are simple: Leave the ice cream, take the cannoli.

The newest addition to the Cannery Row dining scene is also one of the best: **(C Restaurant** (750 Cannery Row, Monterey, 831/375-4500, www.the crestaurant-monterey.com, 6:30 A.M.–10 P.M. daily, $25). The sleek, minimalist interior offers unencumbered views to the bay. The clean lines also extend to the menu, which is heavy on seafood, but also includes rack of lamb, or pasta mixed with local sardines. Their lobster bisque is the best and the creamiest you'll find in the county. Also worthwhile is the local red abalone with angel hair pasta, harvested just steps away from the restaurant. All of their fish is sustainable in concert with the Monterey Bay Aquarium's seafood watch list, and fresh local ingredients rotate seasonally. Finish off with their staggeringly large sundae: a concoction of pistachio and chocolate gelato, and caramelized banana. You'll need multiple spoons.

Located in one of the original sardine cannery buildings, **The Fish Hopper** (700 Cannery Row,

Monterey, 831/372-8543, www.fishhopper .com, 10:30 A.M.–9 P.M. daily, $25) resides right over the bay, with a great deck, which gets crowded quickly. Fifteen daily specials include fresh fish, pasta, and steaks. Dishes worth sampling include their crab ravioli, seafood Louie salad, and maple soy marinated skirt steak. They also have a good-size kids menu.

Located away from the tourist haunts, **Monterey's Fish House** (2114 Del Monte Ave., Monterey, 831/373-4647, 11:30 A.M.– 2:30 P.M. Mon.–Fri., 5–9:30 P.M. daily, $20) has long been a locals favorite. They serve up all manner of seafood, from sole to oysters, calamari, and swordfish. The best versions of any of their fish are oak-grilled, with a delicate smoky note. Reservations are a good idea.

If sushi is more to your liking, then **Crystal Fish** (514 Lighthouse Ave., Monterey, 831/649-3474, 11:30 A.M.–2 P.M. Mon.–Fri., 5–9 P.M. daily, $25) is your place. From rolls to nigiri and sashimi, the fish is fresh and artfully prepared and served, and they have a selection of vegetarian rolls. There are noodles and tempura as well, but stick with the sushi and you won't go wrong.

French

At **Bistro Moulin** (867 Wave St., Monterey, 831/333-1200, www.bistromoulin.com, 5–9 P.M. daily, $20) you'll think you're in France, even though you're just steps away from the Monterey Bay Aquarium. It's a true European bistro with intimate tables, a casual environment, and a menu that includes classics like Coq au Vin, crepes, and pâté. Their wine list showcases the local wineries, but has a good selection of French wines too.

Fusion

◖ **The Duck Club Grill** (400 Cannery Row, Monterey, 831/646-1706, 6:30 A.M.–9:30 P.M. daily, $30) feels like a comfortable club where you want to become a member. Low back wood chairs and wood accents don't distract from the views of the bay. The menu is limited, with mainly fish and meat entrées. Start with the tuna poki tacos with a wasabi mayo dipping sauce; it comes with avocado and ginger in a crispy sesame taco, which has a nice kick to it. Their clam chowder, made with heavy cream and sherry, is terrific. Follow that with their flagship roast duck, glazed with a soy, ginger, and yuzu sauce four times before it arrives at your table. Consider a cocktail like the Patio Boss, their powerful signature margarita (voted "Best on the Bay" by the local reader's poll).

American

Montrio Bistro (411 Calle Principal, Monterey, 831/648-8880, 5–10 P.M. Sun.– Thurs., 5–11 P.M. Fri.–Sat., $25) is housed in an old firehouse, but you'd never know it once you walk inside, thanks to the high ceilings, graceful curved walls, and custom lighting. The menu emphasizes local and organic foods in dishes like the artichoke ravioli, seared diver scallops on parsnip puree, and the rosemary roasted portabella mushroom. It gets very busy, so the noise level can get high. Reservations are recommended.

Spanish and Mexican

Though **Estéban** (700 Munras Ave., Monterey, 831/375-0176, 5–10 P.M. daily, $15) focuses on small plates or tapas, there is still plenty to choose from. Traditional Spanish Serrano hams share the spotlight with crab cakes, chorizo dishes, and paella. Outdoor dining in the large wood chairs near the fire pit is the best, but the interior, all sleek and sophisticated, offers views to the kitchen.

The colorful cafeteria-style eatery **Turtle Bay Taqueria** (431 Tyler St., Monterey, 831/333-1500, 11 A.M.–9 P.M. daily, $10) focuses on foods and flavors of coastal Mexico. You'll find Yucatán-style soups, charbroiled tilapia, carnitas, tacos, and burritos. Their very good salsa, as well as the Mayan chocolate mousse, are made in-house.

Mediterranean

Petra (477 Lighthouse Ave., Pacific Grove, 831/649-2530, 11 A.M.–9 P.M. Mon.–Thurs., 11 A.M.–9:30 P.M. Fri.–Sat., $15) has been making kabobs, gyros, lentil soup, and stuffed grape leaves since 1984. The interior isn't much, with an upscale cafeteria vibe, but the Mediterranean menu is packed with flavor. They have a separate entrance, just to the left of the main door, for take-away orders.

The **Persian Grill** (675 Lighthouse Ave., Monterey, 831/372-3720, www.persiangril .com, 11:30 A.M.–2 P.M. and 5:30–9:30 P.M. Wed.–Mon., $20) smells amazing as soon as you walk in the door. The potent flavors of Persia are well represented with kabobs, lamb, walnut stew, feta cheese and herbs, and stuffed vine leaves. Traditional belly dancing every Friday and Saturday night at 7 and 8 P.M. add to the authentic atmosphere.

British
The **Crown and Anchor** (150 W. Franklin St., Monterey, 831/649-6496, www.crownand anchor.net, 11 A.M.–2 A.M. daily, $12) is about as British as you'll get, at least in downtown Monterey. It's located below street level; as you walk downstairs you'll see walls lined with images of kings and queens, lords and guns. Twenty British and international beers on tap complement lamb shanks, cottage pie, corned beef and cabbage, and, of course, fish and chips. It's very popular with the locals, mainly an older crowd.

Farmers Market
The often crowded **Monterey Farmers Market** (930 Freemont St., www.montereybay farmers.org, 10 A.M.–2 P.M. Fri.) is located at the Monterey Peninsula College and includes a very large selection of fruits, veggies, honey, meats, and flowers, as well as cheeses, many of them organically farmed or produced from within the region.

INFORMATION AND SERVICES
Housed in the old French Consulate building from the mid-1800s, the **Lake El Estero Visitors Center** (401 Camino El Estero, Monterey, 877/666-8373, www.seemonterey .com, summer: 9 A.M.–6 P.M. Mon.–Sat., 9 A.M.–5 P.M. Sun.; winter: 9 A.M.–5 P.M.

Mon.–Sat., 10 A.M.–4 P.M. Sun.) has a wealth of information on every conceivable thing to do in the county, even things you may not have considered.

The **Monterey County Herald** (www .montereyherald.com) is the daily newspaper. **Monterey County Weekly** (www.monterey countyweekly.com) is a free arts and entertainment paper. Both offer information on local activities and events.

In case of **emergency,** call 911 immediately. The **Community Hospital of the Monterey Peninsula** (23625 Holman Hwy., 888/452-4667, www.chomp.org) has 233 beds and every service imaginable. The **Monterey Police Department** (351 Madison St., Monterey, 831/646-3830, www.monterey.org) is located near downtown.

GETTING THERE AND AROUND
Like many attractive towns, Monterey, has retained its identity in part because it's difficult to reach. There are only two direct routes: Highway 1 from the coastal north or south, and Highway 68 which streams in from Highway 101 and Salinas heading west. Either way, it tends to be slow going during peak seasons.

The only bus service via **Greyhound** (19 W. Gabilan St., Salinas, 831/424-4418, www .greyhound.com) runs into Salinas. From there, you'll need to take a connecting bus into Monterey.

Amtrak stops in Salinas and to reach Monterey, you'll need to take the bus to the Aquarium Bus Stop, a curbside-only stop, though right on Cannery Row. **Monterey-Salinas Transit** (888/678-2871, www.mst .org) covers the Monterey Peninsula including Carmel Valley to the south and east to Salinas. One-way fares start at $2.50.

Cab 33 (1056 Seventh St., 831/373-8294) and **Yellow Cab** (831/646-1234) are two of the best cab companies serving Monterey.

The Monterey Peninsula Airport (MRY) has non-stop flights from Los Angeles (LAX), San Diego (SAN), Phoenix (PHX), Denver (DEN), Las Vegas (LAS), and San Francisco (SFO). All this is good and well, but prices are still high just to get there. Other options might be to fly into Salinas (SNS), which is close, or San Jose (SJC), which is still an hour's drive away. Then rent a car and drive in to Monterey.

Parking is constantly an issue in Monterey due to the large crowds. Expect to pay, no matter where you go. There are eight parking lots near Cannery Row, and all day fees run $15–20. The streets closest to Cannery Row have 12-hour metered parking. The farther away you go, the cheaper it gets. If you cross Lighthouse Avenue, and are willing to walk six blocks to the Row, you can find free residential parking. When you're downtown, there is free two-hour street parking and a handful of lots as well, though most charge about $1 per 30 minutes.

Carmel and Carmel Valley

There are no addresses in the City of Carmel. There are lots of trees and no street lights, and street signs are wooden posts with names written perpendicularly, to be read while walking along the sidewalk, rather than driving down the street. There's little to do at night and as little as five years ago, live music was outlawed in the evenings. These are a few clues as to how this village facing the Pacific Ocean maintains its lost-in-time charm.

It may also have something to do with the architectural diversity of the town, technically named Carmel-by-the-Sea, where it's not unusual to find English cottages, Spanish motifs, and other European accents. It's worth a visit just to walk the streets, see the creative homes, meander in and out of galleries housing local and international art, and enjoy the relaxed, nearly Bohemian vibe. Carmel is also dog lover's central: Many hotels, shops, and even some restaurants allow them inside.

The old world charms of Carmel don't make it seem very tourist-friendly. For example, without any addresses, directions are always given as: on 7th between San Carlos and Delores; or the northwest corner of Ocean Avenue. It takes some getting used to. But the town is immensely walkable and compact, laid out on a plain grid system, which makes it reasonably easy to get around, once you know the street names. The lack of streetlights makes driving at night a challenge, but since there's not really any nightlife, if you want to go out in the evening, you're better off heading back to Monterey.

Separated from Carmel-by-the-Sea by 13 miles, Carmel Valley is vastly different. It's accessed from Carmel by Carmel Valley Road, which is, for much of the stretch, a two-lane road; so at times it can be slow going. The landscape changes quickly as you leave the coast, with the mountains rising above you. You'll start to see horse farms, ranches, and orchards. It is rural and wants to stay that way. The Valley is far enough inland to benefit from diurnal swings, with much warmer and consistent daytime temperatures. While it's still foggy in Carmel, the fog will probably have burned off in the Carmel Valley, which will be basking in sunshine. That sunshine explains one of Carmel Valley's greatest advantages over Carmel-by-the-Sea: wine. It's in Carmel Valley that you'll find all of the tasting rooms; most of them scattered along Carmel Valley Road.

WINE-TASTING

The majority of tasting rooms are located in Carmel Valley; however, you can start with downtown Carmel and work your way east.

Carmel-by-the-Sea
CIMA COLLINA
Cima Collina (San Carlos between Ocean and 7th, Carmel, 831/620-0645, www.cimacollina.com, 11 A.M.–6 P.M. Thurs.–Mon., tasting $5) is located back in a courtyard, which makes it a little hard to find. A beautiful curved wooden bar takes up most of the small tasting room.

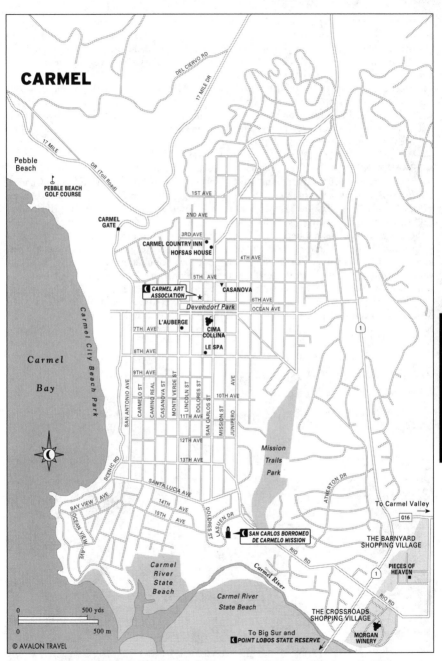

CARMEL

DEL CIERVO RD

17 MILE DR

Pebble
Beach

17 MILE

DR (Toll Road)

PEBBLE BEACH
GOLF COURSE

CARMEL
GATE

1ST AVE

2ND AVE

3RD AVE

CARMEL COUNTRY INN
HOFSAS HOUSE

4TH AVE

5TH AVE

CARMEL ART
ASSOCIATION

CASANOVA

6TH AVE

Devendorf Park

OCEAN AVE

7TH AVE

L'AUBERGE

CIMA
COLLINA

8TH AVE

LE SPA

*Carmel
Bay*

Carmel City Beach Park

9TH AVE

SAN ANTONIO AVE

CARMELO ST

CAMINO REAL

CASANOVA ST

MONTE VERDE ST

LINCOLN ST

11TH AVE

SAN CARLOS ST

MISSION ST

DOLORES ST

JUNIPERO
AVE

10TH AVE

12TH AVE

*Mission
Trails
Park*

13TH AVE

SCENIC RD

SANTA LUCIA AVE

BAY VIEW AVE

14TH
AVE

15TH
AVE

OCEAN VIEW AVE

DOLORES ST

LASUEN DR

SAN CARLOS BORROMEO
DE CARMELO MISSION

ATHERTON DR

To Carmel Valley

G16

THE BARNYARD
SHOPPING VILLAGE

PIECES OF
HEAVEN

*Carmel
River State
Beach*

Carmel River

RIO RD

*Carmel River
State Beach*

To Big Sur and
POINT LOBOS STATE RESERVE

THE CROSSROADS
SHOPPING VILLAGE

RIO RD

MORGAN
WINERY

0   500 yds

0   500 m

© AVALON TRAVEL

MONTEREY

Wines include a light crisp sauvignon blanc and a semi-sweet Riesling. But they excel at reds: Their pinot noirs are loaded with bright raspberry fruit, and a surprisingly good Meritage blend and Bordeaux blend prove that you can get excellent cabernet sauvignon fruit from this area. Also worthwhile is their Howling Good Red, a kitchen-sink blend of whatever red grapes might be available. This is a non-vintage wine, but very good.

MORGAN WINERY

Morgan Winery (204 Crossroads Blvd., 831/626-3700, www.morganwinery.com, 11 A.M.–6 P.M. daily, tasting $5) is a beautiful tasting room, surprising given that it's in a shopping center. Located between Carmel proper and Carmel Valley, it's a great stop to combine with lunch since nearby lunch options abound. The dark amber walls and warm woods, along with the leather couches and chairs, make it very inviting. Owner Dan Morgan has been part of the Monterey wine scene for a number of years; his pinot noirs

and chardonnays, all made with local grapes, are top notch. The first two tastes are free, then they charge for the next five. However, if you divide it up, make sure you try the Hat Trick chardonnay and pinot. These wines are taken from Morgan's best three barrels of each wine and his best grapes. Also sample the sauvignon blanc and his Rio Tinto, a table wine made from port grapes.

Carmel Valley
CHATEAU JULIEN

Winemaker Bill Anderson has been at Chateau Julien (8940 Carmel Valley Rd., Carmel Valley, 831/624-2600, www.chateaujulian.com, 8 A.M.–5 P.M. Mon.–Fri., 11:30 A.M.–5 P.M. Sat.–Sun., tasting $5) since it first started in 1982. The chateau-style tasting room, the first one you encounter in Carmel Valley, has a huge reception area. The central tasting table allows people to mingle freely. Notable wines include chardonnay and a merlot/malbec blend called Connivance, as well as their port and Carmel cream sherry, blended from palomino, Madera,

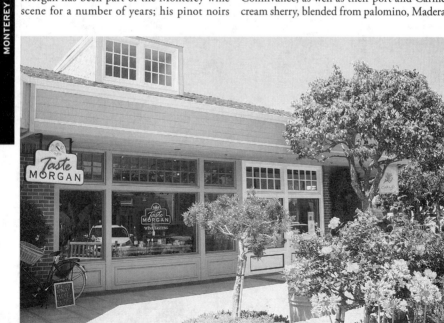

the Morgan Winery tasting room in Carmel

© MICHAEL CERVIN

MONTEREY

Chateau Julien in the Carmel Valley

and tokay grapes. This is one of the few tasting rooms located right on vineyard property; they offer twice daily tours of the 16-acre estate at 10:30 A.M. and 2:30 P.M.

TALBOTT VINEYARDS

You will not go wrong at Talbott Vineyards (53 W. Carmel Valley Rd., Carmel Valley, 831/659-3500, www.talbottvineyards.com, 11 A.M.–5 P.M. daily, tasting $8.50), which showcases some of the best of what the land in Monterey County can produce. The pinot noirs and chardonnays are universally excellent. The vineyards produce wines under the Talbott label, and although the top-end wines are very expensive, their very good secondary label, Kali Hart, offers pinot noir and chardonnay for about $20. They sell wines by the glass for $6–15. There are two tasting bars and shelves of bottled wine in what looks more like a nice hotel lobby than a tasting room. It's a bit formal and lacks much identity. Fortunately the wine takes center stage. There is a small, dog-friendly outdoor patio.

BERNARDUS WINERY

Bernardus Winery (5 W. Carmel Valley Rd., Carmel Valley, 800/223-2533, www .bernardus.com, 11 A.M.–5 P.M. daily, tasting $5–10) makes an astounding 55,000 cases, and manages to do it well. Though there are two lists, standard and reserve, the best choice is to sample both; that way you can compare the sauvignon blanc, chardonnay, pinot noir, and Bordeaux blends side by side. Local Monterey County grapes are used to produce these uniformly excellent wines, though the reserve wines are not inexpensive. The tasting room is small and proper, though a little boring, catering mainly to guests at Bernardus Lodge.

BOEKENOOGEN

The property at Boekenoogen (24 W. Carmel Valley Rd., Carmel Valley, 831/659-4215, www.boekenoogenwines.com, 11 A.M.–5 P.M. daily, tasting $5–9) began as cattle farming land in the late 1880s. These days the family sells most of their grapes to about eight other wineries and makes less than 3,000 cases of wine. But what they do make is excellent. Their chardonnays and pinot noirs are very impressive, and the syrah and petite sirah are coming along. The tasting room is completely unadorned (better to focus on the wines, they'll tell you). The tiled space can get terribly loud when more than four people are tasting. There's also a small outdoor patio with half a dozen tables and a fire pit. Wines by the glass are $10–12.

PARSONAGE VINEYARDS

Family-owned and operated, Parsonage Vineyards (19 E. Carmel Valley Rd., Carmel Valley, 831/659-7322, www.parsonagewine .com, 11 A.M.–5 P.M. daily, tasting $3–8) is part tasting room and part art gallery. The tasting room is simple and low-key, with a brightly polished copper-topped bar. All of the labels on the wine bottles are photographs of quilts made by Mary Ellen Parsons, and some of these are available for sale, along with other art. Most of their wines are minimal case production, usually under 500 cases. The pinot noir and chardonnay are nice, but their syrah, merlot, and Bordeaux blends are their stand-outs.

HELLER ESTATE VINEYARDS

Heller Estate Vineyards (69 W. Carmel Valley Rd., Carmel Valley, 800/625-8466, www .hellerestate.com, 11 A.M.–5:30 P.M. Mon.–Thurs., 11 A.M.–6 P.M. Fri.–Sun., tasting $7–15) is the only local winery growing organically certified grapes. Some wine drinkers are prejudiced against organic wines; the uninitiated seem uncertain of the quality. Everything is estate-grown on 120 acres and dry farmed: The stressed roots dip 30 feet into the earth searching for water, which ultimately creates more flavorful wines. They produce about 18,000 cases annually. Heller's red wines are nicely balanced and hefty. They carry Chenin Blanc and chardonnay, but their estate cabernet sauvignons and Meritage blends are their best wines. Wines by the glass are $5–10. The tasting room is located in a former ranch house, along with a series of restaurants and a small art gallery. Owner Toby Heller is a noted sculptor; a sculpture garden alongside the tasting room features her work.

SIGHTS
17 Mile Drive

You can't come to Carmel and not succumb to 17 Mile Drive (www.pebblebeach.com, daily sunrise–sunset, $10), the private road of luxury homes that hugs the rugged coastline. This road offers the only access to Pebble Beach and the Lone Cypress, the landmark so often depicted in paintings, photos, and postcards. From Highway 1 take Highway 68 West to Pacific Grove/Pebble Beach. At the exit, go straight through the light to the Pebble Beach gate. After you pay the admission fee you will bear to the right as you begin your drive.

The best time to view this scenic seascape is at dusk, when the pinks of the fading sun accent the blues of the ocean. This quintessential Carmel experience comes with a cost: It's a toll road. (It's also worth noting that motorcycles are not allowed.) A map at the entry gate will lead you through the area; if you take your time and bring a picnic, it will take you about two hours. The best picnic spots are between Point Joe and Seal Rock. There are also golf courses, hotels, and restaurants along the way, so you won't be stranded without services.

◖ Point Lobos State Reserve

Five miles south of Carmel is Point Lobos State Reserve (Hwy. 1 at Riley Ranch Rd., 831/624-4909, www.pointlobos.org, 8 A.M.–sunset daily, day-use fee $10), a stunning piece of land abutting the sea. The rugged, ragged cliffs and rocks, beautiful and malformed, are dotted with pine and cypress trees, so the scent of pine is as strong as the fresh ocean breeze. Spanish moss hangs languidly from many of the branches. You can access the water, or climb into the hills on wide dirt paths (it's important to stay on the paths to avoid the plentiful poison oak). This is a prime picnic spot.

The Carmel Mission is one of the most picturesque of the California missions.

The Carmel Art Association is the best spot for local art.

◖ San Carlos Borromeo de Carmelo Mission

More popularly known as Carmel Mission, the San Carlos Borromeo de Carmelo Mission (3080 Rio Rd., 831/624-1271, www.carmel mission.org, 9:30 A.M.–5 P.M. Mon.–Sat., 10:30 A.M.–5 P.M. Sun., adults $6.50, seniors $4, children $2) is still an active parish. The large compound includes an extensive museum, with the first known library in California still on display, along with exhibits of early Native American culture, building materials from the mission period, vestments, and displays on how the friars lived and cooked. The chapel is more ornate than the other California missions and it's clear that money has been spent on upkeep, as the place looks nearly pristine. It can get crowded, making parking out front difficult.

◖ Carmel Art Association

There are many galleries in Carmel, but none that have the breadth of local talent you'll find at the Carmel Art Association (Delores between 5th and 6th, Carmel, 831624-2176,

SACRED JUICE: MISSION WINE

Much is made of what is loosely called "mission wine" and at nearly every California mission, from Santa Barbara to San Luis Obispo to Carmel and Sonoma, the Spanish missionaries planted grapes on their property. **Mission San Antonio** had acres of vine, though they are all gone, and **Mission Soledad** still has a few old weathered vines. Biologically, mission grapes are similar to pais from Chile and criolla from Spain, though no true identification of what they exactly are has been made. It is believed that Jesuit missionaries transported the vines from Spain to Mexico somewhere in the mid-1500s. By the 1620s the mission grape had appeared in present-day Texas and New Mexico and the first known planting in California was 1769 in Southern California. By 1880 there were about 4,000 acres of mission grapes in the Napa Valley alone. The mission vines developed thick trunks and sturdy canes and thrived in warmer areas like the Sierra Foothills, in spite of being weak in acidity, bland in flavor, and pale in color. But they were disease-resistant and hardy.

The padres made wine for sacramental rituals in the church ceremonies, including a wine known as Angelica, a fortified wine (usually fortified with brandy) made from mission grapes. It is known that the padres at some of the missions sold their wine and Angelica to travelers throughout California, since, at the time, the missions were, in essence, centralized trading posts. It's also known that the padres sold and traded raisins, a portable food anyone could take on their journey without worrying about the food spoiling. Angelica is still made from producers like **Gypsy Canyon** in Santa Barbara and **Bonny Doon** in Santa Cruz. It is estimated that there are fewer than 100 acres of old mission vines still planted throughout California. If you get the chance to try it however, you should, and you can literally taste history.

www.carmelart.org, 10 A.M.–5 P.M. daily), a co-op of over 120 talented artists, all of whom live within a 30-mile radius of Carmel. The association was founded in 1927 and bought this space in 1933. The majority of the pieces are oil and pastel paintings, but there are other media too, such as wood and sculpture. Artists bring in new works on the first Wednesday of each month, ensuring a constant rotation.

ENTERTAINMENT AND EVENTS
Nightlife

Even though live music after dark is no longer against the law (as it was in Carmel for many years), the village still closes down after sunset. But there are a few places to hear live performances, with everything wrapping up by 10 P.M.

Terry's (at the Cypress Inn, Lincoln and 7th, 831624-3871, 6–9 P.M. Thurs. and Sun., 7–10 P.M. Fri.–Sat.) offers a variety of vocals, guitar, piano, and soft jazz. The fireplace and wood trusses give the small space an intimate feel, but during the summer the doors to the patio are opened and the crowds swell.

Jack London's (Delores between 5th and 6th, 831/624-2336, www.jacklondons.com, 8–10 P.M. Thurs.–Sat.) offers live guitar in their wood-toned bar. The spot is popular and the bar is small enough that seating is at a premium. On warmer nights the crowds spill into the courtyard.

With boots, saddles, and other Western paraphernalia hanging from the ceiling, the **Running Iron Saloon** (24 E. Carmel Valley Rd., 831/659-4633, 11 A.M.–10 P.M. Mon.–Fri., 10 A.M.–10 P.M. Sat.–Sun.) is true to its name, even if it's rather out of place for the ritzy Carmel Valley. (Of course, that's partly the point.) They present local live music on Fridays and karaoke on Tuesdays.

Performing Arts

The outdoor **Forest Theatre** (Verde and 8th, 831/626-1681, www.foresttheatreguild.org) was started in 1910. Productions include musicals by traveling off-Broadway troupes and the Films in the Forest series, with a variety of movies to enjoy under the stars. The indoor **Sunset Theatre** (San Carlos between 8th and 9th, 831/620-2048, www.sunsetcenter .org) hosts the Monterey Symphony, as well as other live performers and comedians.

Festivals and Events

Held in mid-April the **Pebble Beach Wine & Food Classic** (26364 Carmel Rancho Ln., Pebble Beach, 800/907-3663, www.pebble beachfoodandwine.com) has become in its short life the predominant culinary event between Los Angeles and San Francisco. Master chefs and high-end winemakers from across the nation converge on Pebble Beach for a three-day celebration of eating and drinking. There are cooking demonstrations, wine symposiums, and special vertical tastings of rare vintages, all against the gorgeous backdrop of Pebble Beach and the Pacific Ocean.

Each May the **Carmel Art Festival** (www .carmelartfestival.org, free) showcases the talent of local artists at Devendorf Park. Competitions and exhibitions focus on plein air paintings, watercolors, and sculpture garden. There are also live and silent auctions, live music, and painting demonstrations for the kids.

During the first two weeks of August, the **Concours d'Elegance** (www.pebblebeach concours.net) celebrates the automobile. Hundreds of cars—vintage, unusual, and just plain beautiful—congregate on the 18th green at Pebble Beach, while others line the streets in Carmel. Cars are judged for their historical accuracy; you'll see some stunning, expensive, mint-condition vehicles. Some sell at auction for nearly half a million dollars. This is one of the largest events in the area, second only to the Monterey Jazz Festival, with nearly 10,000 people swamping the tiny hamlet of Carmel. Getting reservations anywhere during this time is nearly impossible unless you plan well in advance.

Each October, the **Carmel Art and Film Festival** (www.carmelartandfilm.com, tickets $30–175) contrasts the quiet sophistication of Carmel with cutting-edge art and film through

© MICHAEL CERVIN

classic cars during the Concours d'Elegance

MONTEREY

five days of film, exhibitions, panel discussions, and tech expos. Of course, there's also food and wine (this is Carmel!). Some 50 independent films are presented.

SHOPPING

Carmel is a shopper's heaven. Fashionable people stroll quaint streets ripe with high-end stores. In contrast, shopping in Carmel Valley is geared to the practical needs of valley residents.

Founded in 1969, **Pilgrim's Way** (Delores between 5th and 6th, 800/549-9922, www .pilgramsway.com, 11 A.M.–6 P.M. Mon.–Thurs., 11 A.M.–7 P.M. Fri.–Sat.) is the only remaining bookstore in Carmel. It's a small store with a good selection of books with a spiritual theme, along with current bestsellers and biographies. The shop will gladly special order anything you might need. Be sure to take a peek at the secret garden in back, which is filled with water fountains, wind chimes, and plants—as well as peace and quiet.

You'll find two floors of furniture for sale at **Carmel Antiques** (Ocean and Delores, 831/624-6100, www.carmelantiques.net, 10 A.M.–6 P.M. daily), including wardrobes, desks and sideboards, many of them French and English pieces from the 1930s. Lamps and other small items round out an overall good selection.

The focus at **Robertson's Antiques & Art** (Delores and 7th, 831/624-7517, 10 A.M.–5 P.M. Mon.–Sat., 11 A.M.–5 P.M. Sun.) is on mid-19th- to mid-20th-century pieces. You'll find lots of porcelain and silver plates; but they also carry some more unusual items, including Asian pieces, small sterling silver tea sets, and even a small collection of swords. They have a strong reputation, having been in business for nearly 20 years.

"Clean sportswear" is the motto at **Pacific Tweed** (129 Crossroads Blvd., 831625-9100, www.pacifictweed.com, 10 A.M.–6 P.M. daily), one of the best-known clothing stores in Carmel. The clothes are slightly traditional, slightly trendy, casual, and subdued—aimed more toward the locals than the tourist crowd.

Conversely, **Carmel Forecast** (Ocean and Delores, 831/626-1735, 8 A.M.–10 P.M. daily) is all about casual tourist-wear, the best place to buy a gift for someone who wants the word "Carmel" emblazoned on their hat. There are two floors of clothes: hats, sweatshirts, flip flops, and jeans, along with mugs and knick-knacks. This is the place to go if your goal is comfort, affordability, or finding something to toss on your back when the weather turns.

Cow, goat, sheep, and triple crème: it's all here under one roof. For 35 years, **The Cheese Shop** (Ocean and Junipero, 800/828-9463, www.thecheeseshopinc.com, 10 A.M.–6 P.M. Mon.–Sat., 11 A.M.–5:30 P.M. Sun.) has offered some 300 cheeses for sale, with selections from France, Italy, Norway, Greece, Belgium, and the United States. They also carry a small section of wines to go with all that beautiful cheese.

And now for something completely different: Check out **Fine H2O** (San Carlos between Ocean and 7th, 831/625-6800, www.fineh2o .com, 10 A.M.–6 P.M. daily), the only place to taste and buy bottled waters from across the globe—from places like Switzerland, England, Norway, and Hawaii—about 20 different varieties in all. You can sample the various waters to try to distinguish the subtle differences in taste, and perhaps find something unique. Bottle prices range $2–9. It's tucked in the back of a narrow courtyard, in a space that's white and clean, and feels a little sanitized (although that's appropriate for water, isn't it?).

RECREATION
Parks

The wide, white sand and low waves at **Carmel City Beach** (Ocean Ave., dawn–dusk daily) are immensely popular; the small parking lot fills up quickly. It's also an easy walk of about eight blocks from the center of Carmel. Dogs are allowed to roam off leash; you'll see many happy dogs running freely along the water's edge. The view to the north is Pebble Beach; to the south is Point Lobos.

In contrast, **Devendorf Park** (Ocean Ave. and Junipero St., dawn–dusk daily) is one of

MONTEREY

the few spots in Carmel where dogs are not allowed; of course, you're not allowed to toss a football either. It occupies a full block, shielded from view by hedges and trees. The verdant grass, benches, and stone pathways that line the perimeter make it a pretty little refuge. There are restrooms, but no picnic tables.

Golf

Located in Carmel Valley, **Rancho Canada Golf Course** (4860 Carmel Valley Rd., 800/536-9459, www.ranchocanada.com, green fees $40–70) consists of two 18-hole courses, known as the East Course and the West Course. The East Course is longer, but both have wide and narrow fairways that cross the Carmel River. Starting at 2:30 P.M., Twilight Thursdays offer the least expensive rounds available at a mere $39. There's a pro shop, dining, and bunkered chipping greens.

Quail Lodge (8205 Valley Greens Dr., 831/620-8866 www.quaillodge.com, $100–$185) is a par-71 course tucked between the hills of Carmel Valley. The verdant greens

meander languidly between the mountains rising up on either side. It's quiet, despite being close to Highway 1. This is a traditional course, with three sets of tees at each hole and a seven-acre driving range. The presence of ten lakes and the Carmel River on the property provide some challenge. PGA-certified pros are available to help improve your game.

Spas

Le Spa (Delores between 7th and 8th, 831/620-0935, www.lespacarmelbythesea.com, 10 A.M.–6 P.M. Tues.–Sun.) offers not only traditional and deep tissue massage (which you might need after a round of golf), but also pomegranate and fig body scrubs and paraffin dips for your hands and feet. Reservations are a good idea, although they will accommodate walk-ins if they can.

At **Bernardus Spa** (415 W. Carmel Valley Rd., 831/658-3560, www.bernardus.com), you'll find all kinds of services from the traditional—massages and wraps, pedicures and manicures—to the exotic—such as the rosemary-cabernet

© MICHAEL CERVIN

Quail Lodge golf course

body wrap and the aqua float, where you are stretched as you float in 101-degree water. All treatments include complimentary visits to the eucalyptus steam sauna.

ACCOMMODATIONS

Carmel has an eclectic collection of places to stay. Most are smaller properties, without amenities like pools or exercise rooms. Another thing you won't find are parking lots; street parking is common, so beware of parking time limits. Since Carmel is so dog-friendly, it's a good idea to check to see which lodgings allow pets. During peak season, rooms go fast, so booking more than six weeks out is a smart idea.

$100-200

Family-owned and operated, 【 **Hofsas House** (San Carlos and 4th, Carmel, 831/624-2745, www.hofsashouse.com, $170–205 d) is a large, pink hotel. The Hofsas' Bavarian heritage is evident in the hand-painted mural near the front of the hotel. The third floor rooms have nice views to the ocean. The lodging options are some of the most diverse in Carmel: There are king, queen, and suite rooms to accommodate families and groups, some with full kitchens, kitchenettes, fridges, and microwaves. They also offer a heated pool and a men's and women's dry sauna. There's even a large meeting room with a full dedicated kitchen, which is often used for family reunions. Some rooms are pet friendly. There is a continental breakfast 8–10 A.M., and free Wi-Fi throughout property. There's a convenient trolley stop in front of the hotel.

Edgemere Cottages (San Antonio between 13th and Santa Lucia, 866/241-4575, www.edgemerecottages.com, $149–199 d) is removed from the hustle of downtown Carmel, and only two minutes to the beach. There are three cottages located in the back of a private residence and one room inside the house; all rooms are reasonably large, with comfortable everyday furnishings. The three cottages all have kitchenettes and all four rooms have Wi-Fi. Breakfasts are served 8:30–10 A.M. in the dining room. They are pet-friendly, but the two house cats, Riff-Raff and Magenta, rule the backyard (dogs beware!).

$200-300

The casual country feel of **Carmel Country Inn** (Delores and 3rd Ave., Carmel, 800/215-6343, www.carmelcountryinn.com, $225–295 d) makes it a comfortable, everyday spot, and people like it that way. Most guests leave the top portion of their Dutch doors open, creating a neighborly atmosphere. All the rooms include fridge, in-room coffee, tea, cream sherry, and DVD players (with 250 movies available). Breakfasts are available 8–10 A.M. There's a communal microwave in the lobby, along with a communal computer, though Wi-Fi is available throughout the property. This is another pet-friendly spot: Tescher, the 14 year-old black and white cat is such a fixture, that people send him cards! The parking lot, rare in Carmel, is another plus.

Over $300

Set amid seven acres of grapes, the 【 **Bernardus Lodge** (415 W. Carmel Valley Rd., 888/648-9463, www.bernardus.com, $545–745 d) is one of the nicest properties in Carmel Valley, with first-rate service and furnishings. Small bottles of Bernardus wines welcome you to your room, along with complimentary bottled water, a small fridge, and a spacious bed. Some rooms look out over the pool; others face the bocce ball and croquet lawn. There are two restaurants onsite; go for the Chef's Table, a small half booth right in the kitchen, where the chef will prepare your meal in front of you. The walls have been signed by well-known guests, including Julia Child. This is one of those places you just don't want to leave.

Built in 1929, **L'Auberge** (Monte Verde and 7th, 831/624-8578, www.laubergecarmel.com, $350–700 d) defines luxury. This is the place to come if you like to be pampered: Virtually anything you want will be provided. The brick courtyard where the horses were once brought in after a ride is the best feature of this European-style hotel. The furnishings

The relaxing Bernardus Lodge is one of the best places to stay in the Carmel Valley.

are beautiful but not stuffy. All 29 rooms have fridges and Wi-Fi. Pets are not allowed.

Doris Day is one of the owners of the **Cypress Inn** (Lincoln at 7th, 831624-3871, www.cypress-inn.com, $355–490 d), one of the oldest and classiest places to stay in Carmel. Her Hollywood memorabilia is on display throughout the property. Given Day's love of animals, it's no surprise that the inn is very pet friendly. The mid-sized rooms are well appointed, with fresh flowers, fruit, and cream sherry to welcome you. Many rooms have whirlpool tubs, and all have Wi-Fi. You can hear the ocean (four blocks away) from the charming outdoor patio.

FOOD
Breakfast
From Scratch (3626 The Barnyard Shopping Center , 831/625-2448, 7:30 A.M.–2:30 P.M. daily, $10) makes their breakfasts—including corned beef and hash, cheese blintzes, and crab eggs Benedict, granola, and oatmeal—well, from scratch. There's a country feel to the small

dining room, tucked downstairs from street level, but the best seats are out front, under the vine-covered arbor.

American
The funky 【 **Cachagua General Store** (18840 Cachagua Rd., 831/659-1857, dinner Mon., $20) defies description. The location is a run-down old general store, a piecemeal building that you wouldn't notice if you drove by. Not that you would drive by it, since it's out in the middle of nowhere—it will take you at least 45 minutes to drive from Carmel, past Carmel Valley up and down winding roads. Dinner is served only on Monday nights and reservations need to be made three weeks in advance. Menus are printed as guests show up and are sometimes incomplete. There are two seatings: 6:30 P.M. and 8:30 P.M., but those are only approximate. If the kitchen isn't ready to serve at 6:30, you wait. It's like an occasionally oiled, makeshift machine. So why is it worth all the trouble? Because Michael Jones' food is superb. The ever-changing menu offers dishes

like rabbit five ways, pumpkin basil ravioli, or local sardines. Many of the ingredients come from the surrounding farms. Sometimes there's live music. There's no decor to speak of, the chairs are mismatched, and the servers wear whatever suits their mood, but that's all part of the charm. Don't fight it, just go with the flow.

The outdoor patio at **Corkscrew Café** (55 W. Carmel Valley Rd., 831/659-8888, Wed.– Mon. 11:30 A.M.– 3:00 P.M., Wed.– Sun. 5 P.M.–9 P.M., $12), with its brightly colored chairs and umbrellas, is perfect on spring days. The interior has a soft Tuscan feel, with tiled floors and ochre walls. The menu is limited but good: Meals begin with hummus and toasted bread, and continue with items like calamari, halibut tostadas, sandwiches, and salads. They make a terrific croque monsieur, dished up on a hearty nut bread. They also carry a decent list of Monterey County wines.

Em Le's (Delores between 5th and 6th, 831/625-6780, www.em-les.com, 7 A.M.–3 P.M. Mon.–Tues., 7 A.M.–3 P.M. and 4:30–8 P.M. Wed.–Sun., $20) focuses on comfort foods like meatloaf, Caesar salad, pasta dishes, triple decker clubs, and patty melts. The food is simple but fresh, and fairly inexpensive compared to surrounding restaurants. Unfortunately, their wine list doesn't match their food. The decor is country comfortable and the service attentive. This is one of the older restaurants in Carmel, having opened its doors in 1955.

Italian

The King of Jordan has dined at **Casanova** (5th between San Carlos and Mission, 831/625-0501, www.casanovarestaurant .com, 11:30 A.M.–3 P.M. and 5–10 P.M. daily, $25), a Carmel fixture. It's deceptively small from the outside; the restaurant unfolds into several dining areas, including a fine dining section, a large arbor-covered outdoor patio, several small intimate spaces, and the Van Gough room—where you eat your meal at a table that once belonged to artist Vincent Van Gough. An excellent wine list complements the country French and Italian menu,

with options like Nicoise salad, linguini with lobster, bacon-wrapped rabbit and house-made cannelloni.

Mexican

The walls and ceilings at **Baja Cantina** (7166 Carmel Valley Rd., 831/625-2252, 11:30 A.M.–10 P.M. Mon.–Fri., 11 A.M.–9 P.M. Sat.–Sun., $15) are decorated with everything imaginable, as if you just walked into a very festive yard sale. It's an upbeat environment, with an outside deck that's perfect for sunny days and a fireplace near the bar that's perfect when the fog rolls in. The tequila selection will also keep you warmed up; most shots are in the $10 range. Menu favorites include the rosemary chicken burrito, mango chicken enchiladas, and halibut fish tacos. The chips and salsa are excellent.

Cheap Eats

When you just want a good burger, go for **r.g. Burgers** (201 Crossroads, 831/626-8054, 11 A.M.–8:30 P.M. daily, $10). All their burgers can be made with beef, bison, turkey, chicken or veggie falafel, with variations like the black and bleu, the jalapeno cheddar, and even a Reuben, so no one gets left out. They also offer over 20 varieties of milkshakes (including mint chip, strawberry, banana, or mocha); while they aren't thick, they are flavorful. Since it gets loud inside, the few tables outside are a better choice.

Brophy's Tavern (4th and San Carlos, 831/624-2476, 11:30 A.M.–11 P.M. daily, $10) serves basic pub food like potato skins, sliders, BLTs, French dip sandwiches, and hot dogs smothered with sauerkraut, all in a golf-themed, wood-paneled environment. There's a good selection of beers as well as tequilas, and they're open late—unusual for Carmel.

Sweets

People gather at the storefront window of **Pieces of Heaven** (3686 The Barnyard Shopping Center , Carmel, 831625-3368, 10 A.M.–6 P.M. Sun.–Thurs., 10 A.M.–8 P.M. Fri.–Sat., $3) to watch owners Peg and Bob

Whitted make candy and pull taffy. Peg and Bob are that rare breed of chocolatier that actually makes almost everything on site. They've been turning out two dozen kinds of truffles, English toffee, caramel-covered marshmallows, and plenty of other candies since 1995. Real cream and butter make the taste far superior to factory-manufactured chocolates.

Farmers Markets

You'll find fruits, veggies, honey, meats, cheeses, and flowers—many of them organically farmed or produced at the **Carmel Certified Market** (3690 The Barnyard Shopping Center, Carmel, www.montereybayfarmers.org, 9 A.M.–1 P.M. Tues., May–Sept.). A second farmers market held at City Hall (1 Civic Square, Carmel, www.carmelfarmersmarket.com, 8–11:30 A.M. Sat., May–Oct. 2) focuses on local products including orchids, pastries, beeswax, poultry, and a whole lot more.

INFORMATION AND SERVICES

The **Carmel Visitor Center** (San Carlos between 5th and 6th, 800/550-4333, www.carmelcalifornia.com) has maps and brochures of the area and of the greater Central Coast. There is two-hour street parking throughout Carmel and they keep tabs on it so don't overstay. Parking can get cramped; there are long-term lots, but they aren't cheap.

In case of **emergency,** call 911 immediately. The **Carmel Police Department** (Juniper and 4th Sts., 831/624-6403) is centrally located. The **Community Hospital of the Monterey Peninsula** (23625 Holman Hwy., 888/452-4667, www.chomp.org) has 233 beds and every service imaginable.

GETTING THERE AND AROUND

The much preferred coastal routes into Carmel are via Highway 1, which runs north-south. You can access Carmel from Highway 1 from San Francisco or Santa Barbara, though these are slow but incredibly beautiful routes. Most people travel north-south on Highway 101 then connect with Carmel through Monterey via State Route 68 at Salinas. This too can be a slow road, heavily congested during weekends and peak summer times.

The **Monterey Salinas Transit** (888/678-2871, www.mst.org) has service all around the peninsula and can transport you from Monterey to Carmel. They also operate a shuttle service running through Carmel: a green and wood shuttle that operates every 30 minutes. The **Carmel Valley Grapevine Express** (888/678-2871, www.mst.org, 11 A.M.–6 P.M.) shuttle picks up from Cannery Row, downtown Monterey, and The Barnyard Shopping Center in Carmel, and will get you to the Carmel Valley wineries for just $6 roundtrip. Buses run every hour, year-round. This is a great idea to avoid the hassle of driving and finding parking.

Carmel Taxi (26080 Carmel Ranch Blvd., 831/624-3885) will shuttle you all around the peninsula.

Amtrak (www.amtrak.com) stops in Salinas. To reach Carmel, you'll need to take the bus to the Aquarium Bus Stop in Monterey first, which is a curbside only stop. From there, switch to the Monterey Salinas Transit (MST) bus which will get you into Carmel.

The Monterey Peninsula Airport (MRY) has non-stop flights from Los Angeles (LAX), San Diego (SAN), Phoenix (PHX), Denver (DEN), Las Vegas (LAS), and San Francisco (SFO). All this is good and well, but prices are still high just to get to Monterey and Carmel. Other options might be to fly into Salinas (SNS), which is close, or San Jose (SJC) which is still an hour's drive away, rent a car and drive in to Carmel.

Santa Lucia Highlands

The Santa Lucia Highlands occupy a bench clinging to the sloped hillsides between the crop-heavy flatlands of the Salinas Valley and the stern Santa Lucia Mountain range. As kind of a netherworld between the valley and the mountains, the area receives less rain than both Monterey and Carmel Valley, and receives its share of wind and sunshine, making for interesting grape-growing conditions, which over the years has made the Santa Lucia AVA the most well-known and respected wine region in Monterey County. Pinot noir and chardonnay are the two dominant varietals, with Riesling a distant third. Visit the tasting rooms and vineyards along the River Road (the north-south line of demarcation between the Santa Lucia AVA and the rather generic Monterey County AVA on the valley floor), and you'll have the chance to try them all.

People travel to Monterey and Carmel for seaside charm and all of the tourist trappings that go with it. There's less of that here—you won't find world-class restaurants, exotic day spas, or high-end hotels. But increasingly, you will find world-class wines.

WINE-TASTING
MARILYN REMARK WINERY
They only produce about 1,500 cases at the unpretentious Marilyn Remark Winery (645 River Rd., Salinas, 861/455-9310, 11 A.M.–5 P.M. Sat.–Sun., tasting $5), but it's certainly worth a stop. Owners Marilyn Remark and Joel Burnstein pour wine themselves. The tasting room is utilitarian, with barrels stacked against the walls. Out of the norm for the area, you won't find any pinot noir or chardonnay here. They have a thing for Rhône-style wines. Their best are two different Grenache bottlings: syrah and petite sirah, all with a surprising acidity to support the structure of the wines. They also produce viognier, roussanne, and marsanne.

You'll find Rhône-style wines at Marilyn Remark Winery.

© MICHAEL CERVIN

© MICHAEL CERVIN

The Wrath tasting room has great views.

WRATH WINES

With a beautiful location overlooking a pond, surrounded by tall grasses and lavender, Wrath Wines (35801 Foothills Rd., Soledad, 831/678-2212, www.wrathwines.com, 11 A.M.–5 P.M. Thurs.–Mon., tasting $10) makes a wonderful spot for a picnic. And then there are the wines: Wrath uses indigenous yeasts and dry farms their fruit. The result is wonderful, though not inexpensive. Their sauvignon blanc is one of the best coming from Monterey, as is their chardonnay, pinot noir, and pinot noir saignee. In the cavernous tasting room, they also offer about half a dozen varieties of cheese for sale. This used to be called San Saba Winery, but a change in ownership (from father to son) has resulted in a different, even better experience. You can also purchase wines by the glass for $6–9. This is a highly recommended stop.

PESSAGNO WINERY

Among the 10,000 cases Pessagno Winery (1645 River Rd., Salinas, 831/675-9463, www.pessagnowines.com, 11 A.M.–5 P.M. daily, tasting $5) produces annually, they're turning out some excellent, though pricey, wines. The focus is single vineyard wines, with superb chardonnays and pinot noirs. Their Four Boys Vineyard pinot noir is an outstanding example of a ripe but balanced local pinot noir. Also worth checking out are their syrahs, which have a unique jammy quality, more zinfandel-like, but very interesting. Sauvignon blanc and a few different port wines are also available. Wine by the glass is $6–16. The tasting room is unremarkable, but there are three picnic tables outside, looking out on a small duck pond.

MANZONI ESTATE VINEYARD

The Swiss-Italian Manzoni family came here in 1920 as dairy workers and farmers. Today, their crops include several acres of wine grapes used at Manzoni Estate Vineyard (30982 River Rd., Soledad, 831/675-3398, www.manzoniwines.com, 11 A.M.–5 P.M. Sat.–Sun., tasting $5). They also buy some fruit in order to max out at 2,000 cases. Their white wines, including chardonnay and pinot gris, are nothing special; but their reserve pinot noir and syrah are terrific. Their Manzoni syrah, for example, a smoky and peppery wine, has a touch of viognier in it for a smoother mouth feel. The tasting room is small, with boards on top of barrels and Swiss flags decorating the walls.

HAHN ESTATES
There used to be a cattle farm on one side of this property and a horse ranch on the other; as you drive up the long driveway, you will still see the trees which demarcated the two. But for 30 years, Hahn Estates (3770 Foothills Rd., Soledad, 866/925-7994, www.hahnestates.com, 11 A.M.–4 P.M. Mon.–Fri., 11 A.M.–5 P.M. Sat.–Sun., no tasting fee) has focused on wine, even leading the charge in getting federal recognition for the Santa Lucia AVA. From their tasting room, perched in the Highlands, you can see all the Salinas Valley across to the Gavilan and Sierra de Salinas mountain ranges. The killer views make it a great spot for a picnic. Although their wines are universally inexpensive, not everything in their large portfolio is a winner. Stick with the SLH (Santa Lucia Highlands) label wines, where you will find a terrific creamy chardonnay and a very nice syrah. Their Smith & Hook cabernet is their best red.

PARAISO VINEYARDS
Paraiso Vineyards (37500 Foothill Rd., Soledad, 831/678-0300, www.paraiso vineyards.com, 11 A.M.–4 P.M. Mon.–Fri., 11 A.M.–5 P.M. Sat.–Sun., tasting $5) planted the area's first pinot noir and chardonnay grapes nearly four decades ago, so the grapes for today's wines have been on the property since the early 1970s. Today, with the exception of their zinfandel, all their fruit is estate grown. Their best wines are their Riesling and pinot noir. Their non-vintage Souzao port is nice, true to its Portuguese heritage, though it won't give Portuguese wines a run for their money. Their small wood patio offers views of the vineyards, which give way to the Salinas Valley below. They offer a decent selection of wine gifts as well, unusual for tasting rooms in this area.

SIGHTS
◖ Pinnacles National Monument
Fifteen miles off Highway 101 heading east, you'll find beautiful ancient volcanic

the Pinnacles

formations, spires of rock ascending from the earth. This is the often-overlooked Pinnacles National Monument (5000 Hwy. 146, Pacines, 831/389-4485, www.nps.gov, 9 A.M.–5 P.M. daily, day-use fee $5). The spectacular rock formations make it well worth a stop just for the photo op, or a longer visit to hike along some 30 miles of trails. In the summer months, Pinnacles temperatures routinely rise well over 100 degrees, so take the necessary precautions to avoid sunstroke and stay hydrated by taking sufficient water with you. Also be sure to pick up a trail map at the ranger station at the entrance. Pinnacles is a release site for the endangered California Condor (although you shouldn't expect to spot one) and home to more than 400 species of bees, who do not live in hives (go figure).

National Steinbeck Center

With a visit to the National Steinbeck Center (1 Main St., Salinas, 831/775-4721, www.steinbeck .org, 10 A.M.–5 P.M. daily, adults $10.95, seniors, students, and teachers $8.95, children

the National Steinbeck Center

13–17 $7.95, children 6–12 $5.95) you'll gain an appreciation not only for some classic works of literature, but for the era in American life that Steinbeck chronicled, from the dust bowl to Cannery Row. It's a worthy stop even if you've never read any of Steinbeck's work. Six separate small galleries showcase the author's life and the impact he had on American culture. In addition to exhibits that correlate to classic works like *Of Mice and Men, The Grapes of Wrath,* and *Travels with Charley,* there's also a section on local agriculture, which played a huge part in Steinbeck's life. An hour is probably all you'll need, unless you're a die-hard fan. The center is located in Salinas. From the Highlands it's about a 20-minute drive east on Highway 68.

Mission San Antonio de Padua

The third mission founded in California, Mission San Antonio de Padua (Mission Rd., Jolon, 831/385-4478, www.missionsanantonion .net, 10 A.M.–4 P.M. daily, admission $3) is commonly called the "mission that time forgot." After making the 25-mile drive off Highway 101 to find it, you realize why that might be true. The location is remote; currently it sits on the Fort Hunter Liggett military base. Look for the original brick wine vat, constructed between the late 1700s or early 1800s, which uses a gravity flow system. Several other rooms display artifacts like embroidered vestments, mission era tools, and priests' quarters. There are also remnants of the old waterworks, and a beautiful large olive tree planted in the 1840s. The church itself is longer than most, but simply decorated, with painted wainscoting along the walls.

Mission Nuestra Señora de la Soledad

Founded in 1791, Mission Nuestra Señora de la Soledad (36641 Fort Romie Rd., Soledad, 831/678-2586, 10 A.M.–4 P.M. daily, admission $3), more commonly called Mission Soledad, was the 13th in the chain of 21 California missions. Today, it's probably the least visited mission. Although easily accessed on the way to the wineries in the Santa Lucia Highlands (take the Arroyo Seco exit off Highway

MONTEREY

STEINBECK AND THE GRAPES OF MATH

There's no escaping the fact that John Steinbeck, a product of the agricultural working class of the Salinas Valley and Monterey, loved the region he grew up in and understood it. But he could have never guessed how this sleepy area of blue-collar workers and farmers would transform into the destination it is. Regardless of Monterey's Cannery Row, which draws in nearly four million tourists each year, the farming aspect of the region has grown exponentially and become America's salad bowl. The county grows a stunning diversity of crops, nearly 50 in total: bok choy, strawberries, peas, carrots, broccoli, celery, kale, leeks, spinach, asparagus, avocados, not to mention barley, grain, and even honey. Additionally, Monterey is trading partners with Guatemala, Puerto Rico, Taiwan, Panama, Japan, and over a dozen other countries.

The development of the **Santa Lucia Highlands** as a wine region would surely take Steinbeck by surprise. Yes, it is still home to small farming operations and high-end pinot noir and chardonnay, but it has also attracted big names to the area; large commercial wineries who want in on the action. One of the largest is Constellation, which, when it purchased the Robert Mondavi Winery, also took ownership of the Bianchi Vineyard, at 750 acres, the single largest in the Highlands. Constellation also owns the 82-acre Stonewall Vineyard, and E. and J. Gallo owns the 576-acre Olson Ranch Vineyard. The Wagner Family, of Caymus fame from Napa, owns the 495-acre Mer Soleil Vineyard. All told, these wine companies own well over one-third of all vineyard acreage in the Highlands. But the real numbers are in the selling of grapes. Chardonnay is planted on about 17,000 acres in the county, which fetches on average $1,200 per ton; the total value of chardonnay grapes has a value of about $92 million each year. Pinot noir, the top red, planted on over 7,000 acres fetches, on average, $2,000 per ton of grapes, worth nearly $50 million. Riesling, the second most widely planted white grape, brings in nearly $12 million and cabernet sauvignon hauls in about $25 million. Grapes coupled with fruits, nuts, veggies, and everything else have a production value of close to $4 billion! The math is simple: Monterey County is a place to be reckoned with.

---

101), it's small and not as postcard-pretty as California's other missions. The original mission was badly damaged in the floods of 1828, and wasn't reconstructed until the early 1950s. But the original adobe walls can still be seen, looking like mounds of rounded earth. In its day, the mission hosted a vineyard, fruit trees, and herds of cattle.

ACCOMMODATIONS

There are not yet abundant hotel choices in the Santa Lucia Highlands. There are two very cool lodgings at the north and south end of the Highlands and a few chain hotels in Salinas, which offer a less-expensive alternative to staying in Monterey and Carmel.

Under $100

The Hacienda Lodge (at Fort Hunter Liggett,

101 Infantry Rd., 831/386-2900, $50–95) sits on what was once the eastern boundary of William Randolph Hearst's estate, a day's ride on horseback from Hearst Castle on the coast. Hearst needed a place to stay when he took guests like Clark Gable and Errol Flynn on long horse rides; the Hacienda also served as the ranch house for his holdings. The building is Spanish Colonial Revival with its red tiled roof, long arched walkways, and open courtyards. Like Hearst Castle, it was designed by architect Julia Morgan. Located at the southern end of the Highlands, it makes an ideal stop if you've finished your wine tour of Monterey and are heading toward Paso Robles.

Today, the property is part of the military training base at Fort Hunter Liggett, but the lodge is also open to civilians. A valid driver's license, proof of vehicle registration, and proof

© MICHAEL CERVIN

The Julia Morgan-designed Hacienda Lodge at Fort Hunter Liggett.

of insurance are necessary to get on base. The twelve rooms range from simple cowboy rooms, with shared bathrooms, to very large garden rooms, to suites that combine two full-size rooms. The furnishings are sparse, with simple amenities (in-room coffee, microwave, and fridge). The walls are all reinforced concrete (material Morgan also used at Hearst Castle), so the rooms stay reasonably cool in the summer; few of the rooms have air-conditioners. Simple breakfast is served in the dining hall.

Guests can also use the pool and the six-lane bowling alley while on base, just down the road from the lodge. There's also a bar (5–11 P.M. Wed.–Fri., 5 P.M.–2 A.M. Sat.), which has a pool table and karaoke every Saturday night. Civilians can access the bar, which is located next to the rooms. Food options are limited on the base: There are burgers and sandwiches at the bowling alley.

$100-200

The **Holiday Inn Express** (195 Kern St., Salinas, 877/859-5095, www.hiesalinas.com, $145–175 d) may be a chain, but it does lodging right, for a fraction of the price of hotels in Monterey. The hotel has a heated indoor pool and hot tub; complimentary, though minimal breakfast; Wi-Fi in public areas; small fitness room; and fridges, microwaves, and coffee makers in the rooms.

The 107-room **Residence Inn** (17215 El Rancho Way, Salinas, 831/775-0410, www .marriot.com, $160–200 d), just north of downtown Salinas, offers similar amenities: complimentary breakfast, in-room coffee, a fitness room, and an indoor pool.

Over $200

There's really no way to prepare you for the plush surroundings you'll find at **C Chateau Coralini Retreat and Spa** (100 River Rd., Salinas, 831/455-2100, www.chateaucoralini .com, $250–425 d), which offers nine guest rooms in an opulent setting. Located at the north end of the Highlands, where Highway 68 heads toward Monterey, this 1891 home has been masterfully renovated into a French-style

Chateau Coralini is the best place to stay in the Santa Lucia Highlands.

retreat. Each room is furnished with one-of-a-kind antiques. This is high-end pampering, removed from the crowds of Monterey and Carmel, though just a 15-minute drive will get you there. Everything here is personalized and customized and that's the point. Breakfasts include soft, warm scones and their signature chilled oatmeal served in a glass. They also have a small day spa on site. This secluded spot makes an ideal romantic getaway.

FOOD
Since you'll be traveling the Santa Lucia Highlands along a lonely road with a few wineries, meals can be a challenge. It's a good idea to bring a picnic lunch with you and stop at whatever tasting room suits your fancy (consider Hahn Estates or Wrath Wines). Otherwise you'll need to drive east toward Salinas, Soledad, or Gonzales to find a restaurant.

Breakfast
Located in historic downtown Salinas, **First**

Awakenings (171 Main St., Salinas, 831/784-1125, www.firstawakenings.net, 7 A.M.–2 P.M. daily, $11) is perfect for a hearty breakfast prior to a day of wine-tasting. Their breakfasts are all large and a great value, served quickly and without pretense. Abundant egg dishes include the Pope John eggs, with Polish sausage, Swiss cheese, and yellow mustard. Or try their signature pancakes: literally the size of a Frisbee but soft and flavorful, with flavors like traditional blueberry and raspberry coconut. Like its sister restaurant in Monterey, it gets packed quickly on weekends.

Barbecue
If you are a vegetarian, don't bother showing up at **Smalley's Roundup Restaurant** (1190 S. Main St., Salinas, 831/758-0511, www.smalleysroundup.com, 11 A.M.–9 P.M. Tues.–Fri., 4–9 P.M. Sat.–Sun., $20), which serves large portions of sloppy, spicy barbecue like ribs, chicken, and shrimp. This place is for carnivores willing to wear bibs. You get a lot for your money: Entrées include soup or salad,

First Awakenings offers discus-sized pancakes to start your day.

garlic bread, chili, and some kind of starch like potato or French fries.

American

You can find **Growers Pub** (117 Monterey St., Salinas, 831/745-1488, www.growerspub.com, 11 A.M.–9 P.M. Mon.–Fri., 5–9 P.M. Sat., $20) by looking for the old neon sign that reads "Pub's Prime Rib." Inside, the wood paneling and circular brown leather booths will make you feel like you've stepped back into the 1940s. There are a few fish and pasta dishes, but Growers retains its identity as an old-school steakhouse with a menu long on grilled meats and vegetables from the surrounding farms.

Carlito's Steakhouse (148 Alta St., Gonzales, 831/675-3401, 11:30 A.M.–9 P.M. daily, $12) is nothing impressive from the outside. Or the inside, for that matter. But you're here for meat: The oak-grilled Porterhouse, T-bone, or rib eye steaks are the reason for visiting this hole-in-the-wall. Spaghetti, scampi, and chicken strips are also on the menu.

Interested in lunch at author John Steinbeck's

actual home? The **Steinbeck House** (132 Central Ave., Salinas, 831/424-2735, www .steinbeckhouse.com, 11:30 A.M.–2 P.M. Tues.– Sat., $12) is open for lunch only and comes complete with historical Steinbeck artifacts. Menus rotate weekly: dining choices include sandwiches and salads, and entrées like manicotti and quiche. They also feature some very nice soups, all made on the premises. They will gladly prepare to-go orders so you can take a picnic to one of the wineries in the Highlands.

Mexican

Many of the patrons at **La Fuente** (101 Oak St., Soledad, 831/678-3130, 11 A.M.–9 P.M. Mon.–Sat., 10 A.M.–8 P.M. Sun., $15) are local field workers. The service is a little slow, but the menu is authentic, with chorizo sopes, fajitas, and burritos with more flavor than you'll ever find at a Mexican chain restaurant.

The interior of **Frankie's Grill** (185 Kidder St., Soledad, 831/678-3499, 9 A.M.– 8 P.M. Tues.– Thurs., 9 A.M.–8:30 P.M. Fri.–Sat., 9 A.M.–3 P.M.

Sun., $10) is short on charm and the service is a little slow. But the food is good and all made from scratch. You'll find leguna (beef tongue), enchiladas, chili rellenos, and chicken flautas topped with an avocado and tomatillo sauce. The salsa is super spicy; you've been warned.

Farmers Markets

Not exactly a farmers market, **The Farm** (7 Foster Rd., 831/455-2575, www.the farm-salinasvalley.com, 9 A.M.–6 P.M. Mon.–Sat., $5) is easy to find because there are 20-foot-high painted cut-outs of workers in the field. It's where River Road joins Highway 68 between Monterey and Salinas. There is a patio area, demonstration farm, and you can get fresh organic produce and veggies grown on their 15 acres, like green beans, strawberries, tomatoes, and leafy greens. They also buy other local fruits, veggies, candy, cookies, and honey.

The **Marketplace** (1 Main St., Salinas, 831/905-1407, 9 A.M.–2 P.M. Sat.) is both certified farmers market and marketplace with family activities, flowers, foods, arts and crafts, and jewelry, located in Salinas in the same plaza with the Steinbeck Center and the Maya Cinemas.

INFORMATION AND SERVICES

Winery information is best derived from the **Monterey Vintners Association** (www.montereywines.org) who have a comprehensive website where you can download their latest tasting room map.

In case of **emergency,** call 911 immediately. Help is also available at the **Salinas Valley Memorial Hospital** (450 E. Romie, Salinas, 831/757-4333) or the **Salinas Police Department** (222 Lincoln Ave., Salinas, 831/758-7090).

GETTING THERE AND AROUND

Highway 101 is the corridor by which all things are accessed. If you are traveling north from the Paso Robles area, take the Arroyo Seco exit in Soledad, and turn west to begin your River Road journey. Once on River Road you can take that north all the way to Highway 68, which will get you either east to Salinas or west to Monterey.

Amtrak (www.amtrak.com) stops in Salinas. However, there is no bus service from there to the Highlands area or River Road.

SAN LUIS OBISPO AND PASO ROBLES

Locals call San Luis Obispo by its nickname, SLO, and a visit to the city will immediately impress upon anyone that slow is the order of the day. But the secret is out, and a bourgeoning wine industry and excellent quality of life means that SLO is starting to speed up. With a beautiful downtown fronted by Higuera Street and the accompanying river walk, San Luis Obispo is beginning to receive attention for its idyllic way of life, proximity to the ocean and mountains, wide-open tracts of land, and nearly ideal weather.

Paso Robles, 30 minutes north of San Luis Obispo off Highway 101, is the heart of the wine industry in San Luis Obispo county, and this cowboy town, home to fewer than 30,000 people, is garnering worldwide acclaim for its wines. Paso Robles is also a hop, skip, and a jump from the coast, where nearly a million people flock to the tiny hamlet of San Simeon on the rugged Pacific Coast to visit Hearst Castle. But El Paso de Robles, known simply as Paso by locals, is slowly eking its way out of its Western roots and embracing a more cosmopolitan vibe. Artisanal cheese makers, abalone farmers, high-end restaurants and wineries, and a thriving (if competitive) olive oil industry share the downtown with renegade dive bars and local mom-and-pop venues. You're just as likely to see a tractor heading through town as you are a limo packed with eager wine tasters.

PLANNING YOUR TIME

Since San Luis Obispo is called SLO, that's really how it should be explored, slowly. You can get the feel of SLO in a weekend, but a long three-day weekend is even better to explore

HIGHLIGHTS

◖ Higuera Street: Many of the original turn-of-the-20th-century buildings are still in operation on this main boulevard in San Luis Obispo. Creek-side restaurants and shops make this the ideal Central Coast street (page 447).

◖ Bubblegum Alley: To some, this alley covered with used chewing gum that's been there since the 1960s is urban pop art. Make a statement and add your chew to the collection (page 449).

◖ Madonna Inn: The flamboyant decor is the highlight at the Madonna Inn, which is overrun with pink kitsch. It's a unique place to stay, but also a fun spot for lunch, dinner, or even just a photo op (page 450).

◖ Hunt Cellars: Hunt Cellars owner David Hunt is legally blind, which has aided in his winemaking and blending abilities. His lavish, textured wines are not to be missed (page 469).

◖ Denner Vineyards: Stellar architecture and wines come together at Denner Vineyards. A gracefully modulated tasting room complements the layered and inviting wines, all with beautiful views of rolling hills of vines (page 471).

◖ Eberle Winery: Eberle Winery was the harbinger to the Paso Robles wine industry when it opened its doors in 1973. The most-awarded winery in the nation, it continues to produce wines that showcase the best of the region (page 473).

◖ Ancient Peaks Winery: Their vineyard was planted in an upraised ancient ocean-floor bed, where the ocean's inherent minerals and nutrients aid the complexity of their wines, providing nuanced flavors (page 476).

◖ Paso Robles Downtown Square and City Park: This Norman Rockwell-esque grassy one-block town park and square complete with mature trees, picnic tables, horseshoes, a gazebo, and a 1910 historic museum at its center is ground zero for all things social in Paso Robles (page 477).

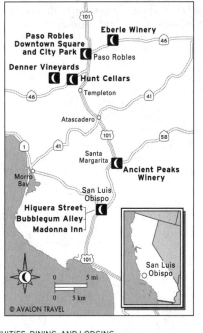

LOOK FOR ◖ TO FIND RECOMMENDED SIGHTS, ACTIVITIES, DINING, AND LODGING.

SAN LUIS OBISPO

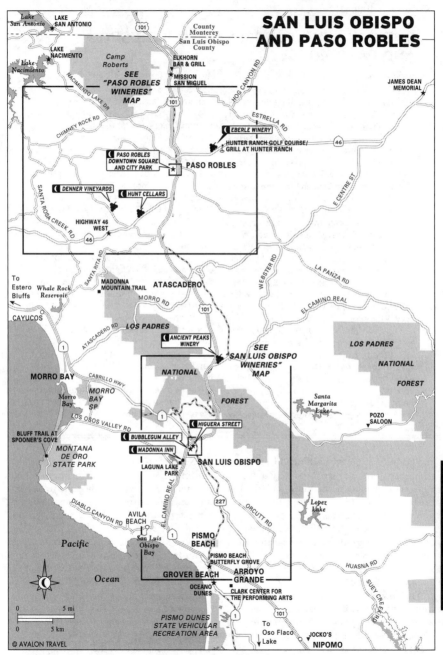

SAN LUIS OBISPO AND PASO ROBLES

Lake San Antonio
LAKE SAN ANTONIO
LAKE NACIMIENTO
Lake Nacimiento
NACIMIENTO LAKE DR
Camp Roberts
SEE "PASO ROBLES WINERIES" MAP
County Monterey
San Luis Obispo County
ELKHORN BAR & GRILL
MISSION SAN MIGUEL
HOG CANYON RD
JAMES DEAN MEMORIAL
CHIMNEY ROCK RD
ESTRELLA RD
EBERLE WINERY
HUNTER RANCH GOLF COURSE/ GRILL AT HUNTER RANCH
46
E CENTRE ST
SANTA ROSA CREEK RD
PASO ROBLES DOWNTOWN SQUARE AND CITY PARK
PASO ROBLES
DENNER VINEYARDS
HUNT CELLARS
HIGHWAY 46 WEST
46
SANTA RITA RD
WEBSTER RD
LA PANZA RD
To Estero Bluffs
Whale Rock Reservoir
MADONNA MOUNTAIN TRAIL
ATASCADERO
MORRO RD
EL CAMINO REAL
CAYUCOS
ATASCADERO RD
LOS PADRES
101
LOS PADRES
ANCIENT PEAKS WINERY
SEE "SAN LUIS OBISPO WINERIES" MAP
NATIONAL
FOREST
MORRO BAY
CABRILLO HWY
MORRO BAY SP
NATIONAL
Morro Bay
MORRO BAY SP
LOS OSOS VALLEY RD
1
Santa Margarita Lake
POZO SALOON
BLUFF TRAIL AT SPOONER'S COVE
HIGUERA STREET
BUBBLEGUM ALLEY
MADONNA INN
SAN LUIS OBISPO
MONTANA DE ORO STATE PARK
LAGUNA LAKE PARK
DIABLO CANYON RD
AVILA BEACH
227
ORCUTT RD
Lopez Lake
EL CAMINO REAL
Pacific
San Luis Obispo Bay
1
PISMO BEACH
Ocean
GROVER BEACH
PISMO BEACH BUTTERFLY GROVE
ARROYO GRANDE
HUASNA RD
OCEANO DUNES
CLARK CENTER FOR THE PERFORMING ARTS
0   5 mi
0   5 km
PISMO DUNES STATE VEHICULAR RECREATION AREA
To Oso Flaco Lake
JOCKO'S
NIPOMO
SUEY CREEK RD
101
© AVALON TRAVEL

SAN LUIS OBISPO

ONE-DAY WINE TOURS: SAN LUIS OBISPO AND PASO ROBLES

SAN LUIS OBISPO

This day is laid out as a big loop. Starting from downtown, drive out to the Edna Valley via Tank Farm Road, which turns into Orcutt Road. This is a little longer back-roads route past the dormant volcanoes, but is a preferred drive over Highway 227 because you see more of the valley as the road rises and falls, with views of the impressive vineyards.

Stop at **Saucelito Canyon Vineyard** to start your day of tasting with old-vine zinfandel, sourced from their historic 1880 vineyard. You'll also pass **Edna Valley Vineyards;** stop in if you have time. Otherwise, head west through Price Canyon, which will place you in **Pismo Beach.** Explore the waterfront and the surfers and try **Pismo Beach Winery** for their broad portfolio of wines. Lunch at **Splash Cafe** and order their award-winning clam chowder. Head back up Highway 101 and stop at **Salisbury Vineyards**' historic old schoolhouse tasting room, then visit **Per Bacco Cellars** for exceptional pinot noir and petite sirah.

End the day with a sloppy rack of ribs at **Mo's Smokehouse BBQ,** then crash at **The Apple Farm.**

PASO ROBLES

This is a vast region, separated geographically by Highway 101. There are differences in temperature, soil, and growing conditions on Highway 46 East and 46 West. A well-planned trip allows you to taste these differences. Head to **Hunt Cellars** on Highway 46 West, talk with Uncle Willie in the tasting room, and try their plush, velvety wines, specifically sangiovese and zinfandel.

Take Vineyard Drive up to the exceptionally sleek and cool-looking **Denner Vineyards** to enjoy their exquisite Rhône wine with views to the vineyards. Then drive back down Vineyard Drive (the way you came), which will place you at the **Donati Vineyard** for Meritage blends.

Head into downtown Paso Robles for lunch at **Villa Creek,** then hop across Highway 46 East to **Eberle Winery** and take one of their tours, which include the caves and winery. Then head west to see the mammoth art sculptures and wines at **Sculpterra Winery.** While you are there, taste the pistachios they grow on the property.   Once you circle back to downtown Paso Robles it will be time for dinner: For Wine Country cuisine, dine at **Artisan.** If you still want to try more local wines, walk the three blocks to the **Pony Club Bar** at the **Hotel Cheval** and see what local wines they are pouring that night.

---

and get into the groove of this laid-back town, stroll the streets, and see the variety of sights. The summer months see more tourists, but because the two local colleges aren't in session then there are actually fewer people. Ideal times to visit are March–May and September–November due to the moderate weather that allows you to play outdoors, hiking, biking, and just hanging out at the beach.

Paso Robles is further inland, making the area much warmer during the summer months; triple-digit weather is common. Conversely, the winter months dip down toward the freezing point. The best times to visit, unless you prefer the heat of summer, are also around March–May

and September–November. Keep in mind that September in Paso Robles is harvest time for the wineries. It's still usually quite warm, and oftentimes you can be where the winemaking action is as the wineries are busy crushing grapes. Paso Robles can best be explored over a weekend. If wine is a focal point, however, you'll want to visit for at least three or four days—or do a one-day wine tour for a quick overview of the wineries in the area. Weekends are the most crowded at the tasting rooms, so you may want to visit wineries on a weekday since many tasting rooms are open seven days a week. If you have a particular winery you're especially eager to visit, plan ahead and find out their hours.

San Luis Obispo

San Luis Obispo is not a coastal town, though the water is less than 10 minutes away. The beauty of its location is that it offers everything within a 15-minute drive: great restaurants, access to hiking and biking trails, wineries, wide-open space, and an ideal climate. Since it is inland, if it's foggy at the beach, more often than not San Luis is warmer and sunny. If it's in the triple digits in Paso Robles, San Luis tends to be cooler. It's just one of those spots with great weather.

WINE-TASTING

Though Paso Robles is the undisputed leading wine region in the county, the San Luis area, which includes the Edna Valley and Arroyo Grande, has a diverse number of wineries. Don't dismiss this region, thinking that Paso is the end all, be all. There are some excellent wines coming out of this area, and any exploration of the wine region needs to include San Luis Obispo.

WOOD WINERY

Taste wine and watch the sunset at the Wood Winery (480 Front St., Avila Beach, 805/595-9663, www.wildwoodwine.com, daily 10:30 A.M.–6 P.M., tasting fee $5) on Avila Beach boardwalk. They are licensed to sell wines by the glass, and they offer cheese plates and patio seating. There's a love of syrah here, but also a wide selection of sangiovese, cabernet sauvignon, chardonnay, and zinfandel. The vineyards are at the foot of the Cuesta Grade, just north of downtown San Luis. The tasting room is one of the few oceanfront tasting rooms in the entire state, and from the tasting bar you can simply turn around to enjoy the views. The room is decorated in soft aquatic tones and local artwork hangs on the walls. It's so relaxing here you may not want to leave.

PER BACCO CELLARS

The Per Bacco Cellars (1850 Calle Joaquin, 805/787-0485, www.perbaccocellars.com, daily 11 A.M.–5 P.M., tasting fee $5) tasting room, located on a historic ranch property, sits a stone's throw off the 101 freeway near San Luis Obispo. It isn't your typical well-appointed tasting room. In fact, it's not really a tasting room at all, but is the actual winery, filled with barrels and fermentation equipment. They have added a small bar area to serve guests and tacked a few paintings on the walls, but the surroundings are still very industrial. The focus is on a restrained style of winemaking, one that allows the nuances of the grape to shine through. Small batches of pinot noir, chardonnay, syrah, petite sirah, and pinot grigio come out of this well-regarded winery.

EDNA VALLEY VINEYARDS

A stalwart of the area, Edna Valley Vineyards (2585 Biddle Ranch Rd., 805/544-5855, www.ednavalleyvineyard.com, daily 10 A.M.–5 P.M., tasting fee $5–10) benefits from its namesake region. The large tasting room and panoramic views to the hills (dormant volcanoes known as the Nine Sisters) in the distance with near views to the vineyards are stunning. They have a sizable number of gift items for sale in the large tasting room. There's also a demonstration vineyard out front, a place to examine different trellising techniques and how those methods affect how the grapes grow. Zinfandel, chardonnay, syrah, and pinot noir are the main wines produced here.

TALLEY VINEYARDS

The name Talley has been associated with farming in San Luis Obispo County since 1948. As you drive towards Lopez Lake you'll immediately notice Talley Vineyards (3031 Lopez Dr., 805/489-0446, www.talleyvineyards.com, daily 10:30 A.M.–4:30 P.M., tasting fee $8–15) on your left. The Mediterranean/Tuscan-style tasting room sits squarely in the middle of flat cropland, the surrounding hillsides covered in vines. A three-tiered fountain stands like a

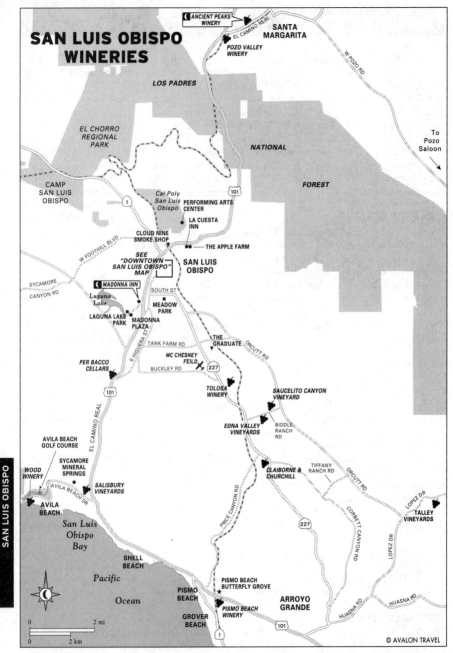

SAN LUIS OBISPO WINERIES

ANCIENT PEAKS WINERY

EL CAMINO REAL

SANTA MARGARITA

POZO VALLEY WINERY

W POZO RD

LOS PADRES

EL CHORRO REGIONAL PARK

NATIONAL

To Pozo Saloon

CAMP SAN LUIS OBISPO

FOREST

Cal Poly San Luis Obispo

PERFORMING ARTS CENTER

LA CUESTA INN

CLOUD NINE SMOKE SHOP

THE APPLE FARM

W FOOTHILL BLVD

SEE "DOWNTOWN SAN LUIS OBISPO" MAP

SAN LUIS OBISPO

SYCAMORE CANYON RD

MADONNA INN

Luguna Lake

LAGUNA LAKE PARK

MADONNA PLAZA

SOUTH ST

MEADOW PARK

TANK FARM RD

THE GRADUATE

ORCUTT RD

PER BACCO CELLARS

MC CHESNEY FEILD

BUCKLEY RD

227

TOLOSA WINERY

SAUCELITO CANYON VINEYARD

AVILA BEACH GOLF COURSE

EL CAMINO REAL

EDNA VALLEY VINEYARDS

BIDDLE RANCH RD

WOOD WINERY

SYCAMORE MINERAL SPRINGS

SALISBURY VINEYARDS

CLAIBORNE & CHURCHILL

TIFFANY RANCH RD

ORCUTT RD

AVILA BEACH DR

AVILA BEACH

San Luis Obispo Bay

PRICE CANYON RD

227

CORBETT CANYON RD

LOPEZ DR

TALLEY VINEYARDS

SHELL BEACH

Pacific

Ocean

PISMO BEACH BUTTERFLY GROVE

PISMO BEACH

PISMO BEACH WINERY

ARROYO GRANDE

HUASNA RD

HUASNA RD

GROVER BEACH

1

101

LOPEZ DR

0   2 mi
0   2 km

© AVALON TRAVEL

SAN LUIS OBISPO

Saucelito Canyon Vineyard

sentinel in the courtyard. The interior of the spacious tasting room features floor-to-ceiling glass, a horseshoe-shaped tasting bar, and high vaulted ceilings. You can often purchase some of the fruit and vegetables that grow on the property, including bell peppers, zucchini, tomatoes, and spinach. Pinot noir, chardonnay, syrah, cabernet sauvignon, and pinot gris are the main wines here, but they are most well known for producing excellent chardonnay and pinot noir. Talley also has a second label, Bishop's Peak, a line of very good-value wines for under 20 bucks.

SAUCELITO CANYON VINEYARD
Saucelito Canyon Vineyard (3080 Biddle Ranch Rd., 805/543-2111, www.saucelito canyon.com, daily 10 A.M.–5 P.M., tasting fee $6) has one of those unique stories better suited to the History Channel than the pages of a guidebook. The parcel of land, located past Lake Lopez down a three-mile gated road, is so far removed from anything, that during Prohibition federal agents could

never shut the winery down simply because they couldn't find it. The three acres of zinfandel originally planted in 1880 are still producing fruit to this day. The tasting room is small, and though it's not made for more than 15 people, it has the necessary ingredients for a good time, namely a friendly staff, very good wine, and a relaxed, intimate environment. There are even old photos from the turn-of-the-20th-century showing the old vine zinfandel and homestead. Outside there are a few tables for relaxing. Zinfandel is king here, though they are making other varieties such as sauvignon blanc, tempranillo, merlot, and cabernet sauvignon. They open their historic vineyard property about once a year for the public to view the centuries-old vines. The canyon is remote, beautiful, and serene, and pulsates with the history of men and women working the land.

TOLOSA WINERY
Imagine James Bond creating a tasting room, and you'll get an idea of what the interior of

Tolosa Winery (4910 Edna Rd., 805/782-0500, www.tolosawinery.com, daily 11 A.M.–5 P.M., tasting fee $5) is like: cork floors, stainless steel ceilings, glass bar, wood panels, and back lighting, all sleek and sophisticated. A plasma screen displays pictures of recent events and the winemaking process, while the LCD screen displays up-to-date specials and wine club information. There's even ambient music playing throughout the tasting room, patio, halls, and bathroom. The tasting room looks out over the fermentation tanks of gleaming polished stainless steel. Guests can take a self-guided tour through the facility as well. Stay and picnic at their tranquil outdoor picnic area, or play a round of bocce ball as you soak in the peaceful surroundings. The focus is on chardonnay and pinot noir, but you'll also find merlot, syrah, viognier, and even grenache blanc.

SALISBURY VINEYARDS

This 103-year-old schoolhouse, now a tasting room and art gallery, underwent a historic interior renovation and opened in the spring of 2005 with a new lease on life. As you enter the tasting room at Salisbury Vineyards (6985 Ontario Rd., 805/595-9463, www.salisbury vineyards.com, daily 11 A.M.–6 P.M., tasting fee $5), you're immediately struck by the openness of the space and the copious amount of wood, most notably the original hardwood floors. A sign by the front door warns that stiletto heels can have a detrimental effect on their old floors, and to walk gently, but that everyone is still welcome. Salisbury is aiming for the schoolhouse to serve a multitude of diverse functions, not simply as a tasting room. It's also part art gallery, presenting artwork from around the globe that rotates every 8–10 weeks. Chardonnay, syrah, zinfandel, and cabernet sauvignon are the main wines produced here.

CLAIBORNE & CHURCHILL

Claiborne & Churchill (2649 Carpenter Canyon Rd., Edna Valley, 805/544-4066, www.claibornechurchill.com, daily

Claiborne & Churchill

11 A.M.–5 P.M., tasting fee $5) winery was started in 1983, inspired by the wines of Alsace, France, even though these types of wine were not often made in California, let alone San Luis Obispo County. Claiborne & Churchill decided to specialize in premium dry wines made from Riesling, gewürztraminer, and pinot gris grapes, as well as pinot noir from nearby vineyards. Not wanting to limit their portfolio, they also produce small lots of other wines, including a dry muscat, chardonnay, syrah, cabernet sauvignon, sparkling rosé, and a port-style wine. Claiborne & Churchill is still a small family-owned winery, and their facility is constructed out of straw bales and covered in plaster, making it unique among wineries in the United States. Using these sustainable materials has greatly reduced their cooling costs. However, when you visit the winery, you won't notice, as it looks like any interior. They do have a small section of part of a wall that shows how the bales fit together and gives more information about this unique architectural approach.

PISMO BEACH WINERY

It took nearly 10 years for the dream of two brothers to become a reality when Pismo Beach Winery (271B Five Cities Dr., 805/773-9463, www.pismobeachwinery.com, daily noon–5 P.M., tasting fee $10) finally opened its doors. Located across from the outlet mall, this urban winery is making about 1,500 cases of wine; their portfolio consists of chardonnay, cabernet sauvignon, zinfandel, barbera, pinot noir, and petite syrah. This is a small, family-owned operation, and the corrugated metal exterior belies what's inside. The tasting room is bright and open, with soft yellow walls and wood door trim and tasting bar, and views into the barrel room. There's a low-key vibe here, and usually someone from the family is behind the counter pouring their wines.

SIGHTS
◖ Higuera Street

Higuera Street is the defining street in San Luis Obispo, and pretty much everything revolves around it. Mature trees flank the charming street, and many of the historic turn-of-the-20th-century storefronts are still in place. There are no large buildings on Higuera Street, which creates a very open and walkable space. It's also a one-way street, which means traffic and congestion is reduced. The street follows the same path as San Luis Creek, making Higuera Street an ideal spot for dining and strolling. Shops and restaurants overlook the creek, and during the spring and summer months these are the best spots to be. The creek is accessible from several points and kids often play in the freshwater. Bubblegum Alley is on the 700 block, and just across the creek is the mission. Higuera itself even has a book written about it, *San Luis Obispo: 100 Years of Downtown Business: Higuera Street*, which was published in 2007. It shows how much the surroundings have changed, but how little the storefronts have changed.

Mission San Luis Obispo de Tolosa

The Mission San Luis Obispo de Tolosa (751 Palm St., 805/781-8220, www.missionsan luisobospo.org, daily 10 A.M.–4 P.M., suggested donation $3) was founded in 1769. On September 7–8 of that year Gaspar de Portolá and his expedition party traveled through the San Luis Obispo area on the way to rediscover the Monterey Bay. The expedition's diarist, Padre Juan Crespi, recorded the name given to this area by the soldiers as Llano de los Osos, or "the bear plain," as there used to be a preponderance of bears in the area. In fact, Los Osos, just west of San Luis Obispo, still holds that name. In 1770, Father Serra founded the second mission, San Carlos Borromeo, in Monterey, which was moved to Carmel the following year. As supplies dwindled in 1772 at the four missions in existence at the time, the people faced starvation. Remembering the bear plain, a hunting expedition was sent to San Luis Obispo to bring back food in the summer of 1772, and over 25 mule loads of bear meat was sent up coast to the waiting mission. It was after this that Father Serra

Mission San Luis Obispo de Tolosa

decided that San Luis Obispo would be the ideal place for a fifth mission. The region had abundant supplies of food and water, the climate was mild, and the local Chumash were very friendly. Given these conditions, Serra set out on a journey to reach the bear plain and on September 1, 1772, he celebrated the first mass with a simple cross erected near San Luis Creek.

After Father Serra left, the task remained to actually build the mission, which was accomplished primarily by the hard work of the local Chumash. The church and priest's residence were built by 1794, and other structures made up the primitive mission in the early days, namely storerooms, residences for single women, barracks, and mills. The mission also used the land for farming and raising livestock, since the mission padres, soldiers, and indigenous people depended upon any and all produced goods, including vegetables, fruits, nuts, and meats, for their survival. Expansion proceeded for a few years due to the prosperity of the mission, but

those days were numbered and Mission San Luis, like all the other missions, gradually fell into disrepair. When Mexico won her independence from Spain in 1821, the missions were secularized and often mission lands were sold off. Governor Pio Pico sold the San Luis Obispo Mission to Captain John Wilson for a mere $510 in 1845. The building served multiple functions, including jail and first county courthouse.

Today the mission fronts Mission Square, facing the creek, and Higuera Street. The courtyard is a popular place for small gatherings and festivals. The interior of the mission is minimally decorated, mainly hand painted, and is long and tall. Still an active church, it holds mass each day. While the church itself is modest looking, the interior grounds, also rather simple, are quite pretty, with flowers and hedges and a small arbor. The museum portion includes black-and-white photographs and a limited collection of furniture and accessories from mission life.

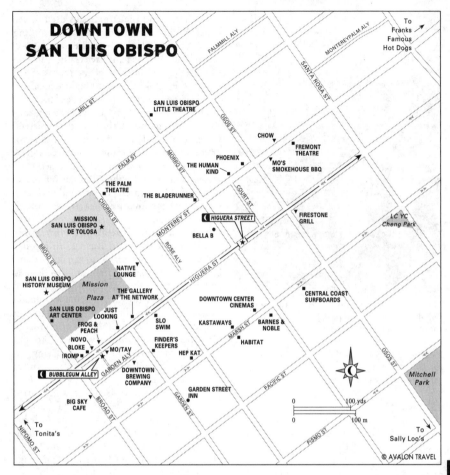

❰ Bubblegum Alley

Bubblegum started mysteriously appearing on the walls of Garden Alley, on the 700 block of Higuera Street, in the 1960s, with a few people defacing the exposed brick with their chewed-up bubblegum. Some assumed it was college kids disposing of their used-up wads. Fast forward to today, and Bubblegum Alley is a sticky and unusual landmark in San Luis Obispo.

It doesn't resemble anything but what it is: tens of thousands of wads of multicolored chewing gum squished one on top of another in a masticated mosaic some 70 feet long and 15 feet high. At the top of the brick-walled alley, the gobs have been blackened by age and weather. This might be sickening to some, to others it is urban pop art, a unique expression of individuality. Some people seek to make a statement, spelling out their love or their hopes, while others merely press tasteless gum onto the wall. It's not uncommon to hear people walk by and use adjectives like "disgusting" and "gross" to describe the alley. There are gum

"Look, but don't touch!" – words to live by when enjoying the funky delights of infamous Bubblegum Alley

dispensers on either side of the alley; for a mere 25 cents, you can get a piece of gum to add your own chewed-up message.

Madonna Inn

The Madonna Inn (100 Madonna Rd., 805/543-3000, www.madonnainn.com) is a one-of-a-kind sight. It would be considered kitschy if it was planned today, but it wasn't: The first 12 rooms were completed in December 1958. An additional 28 rooms were quickly built, making a total of 40 rooms available to travelers. Pink was the color of choice when the inn was built.

Today there are 110 unique rooms, each decorated wildly differently to suit many individual tastes. There are rock rooms, waterfall showers, rock fireplaces, European fixtures, and fine furnishings, to name a few features. It's truly an experience to stay here and shouldn't be missed, in part because the service is routinely excellent.

The Madonna Inn sits on approximately 2,200 acres, and the large rocks used in the construction came from these surrounding acres. Some of the larger rocks weigh in excess of 200 tons each and are clearly visible on the exterior and in some of the rooms. Then there is the well-known men's bathroom downstairs, where the urinal is built out of rock and a waterfall flushes away the waste. Men routinely stand guard so their mothers, sisters, wives, and female friends can go in to gawk at the unusual bathroom. The leaded glass work throughout the inn and the etched-glass windows in the coffee shop were custom made. The leaded-glass inserts in the windowed area facing the large fireplace illustrate each of the various Madonna enterprises of construction, lumber, and cattle. The hand-carved marble balustrade in the Gold Rush dining room came from Hearst Castle. All the copper and brass items were etched from original designs and fabricated on-site. The 28-foot gold tree fixture in the main dining room was made from electrical conduit left over from building projects, as well as from left-over remnants of copper. Several wood carvers were brought in for the specialty work of hand carving the doors, beams, railings, and the many other carved adornments you see everywhere.

And then there is the pink, pink everywhere—it was Alex Madonna's favorite color. The gregarious Alex Madonna made his money in the construction business, something he learned when he served in the Army Corps of Engineers. After he left the service he built much of Highway 101 along the Central Coast. He was known to be flamboyant, effervescent, and larger than life, and he never shied away from the bold use of pink. Nowhere is this more robustly expressed than the beyond Vegas-style dining room. Of course it's crazy, but it's also unique, and has been a landmark since the day it opened. Most people who visit the Madonna don't stay here, which is a shame, since it's a really cool place to stay. But they stop by to marvel at the over-the-top decor, maybe have lunch or dinner, get their photos taken, and head on their way. It's worthy of a stop, however brief, and you won't soon forget it.

San Luis Obispo History Museum

The San Luis Obispo History Museum (696 Monterey St., 805/543-0638, www.slochs.org, Wed.–Sun. 10 A.M.–4 P.M., free) is housed in a Carnegie Library from 1904, and was designed by the same architect who designed the Carnegie Library in Paso Robles. The museum itself is pretty simple, with a few artifacts and lots of photographs detailing the visual history of the area. Just behind the building on Broad Street is a small portion of wall, the only remaining original wall from the mission dated to 1793. It's covered with moss now, but gives an idea of how the original buildings were made.

Pismo Beach Butterfly Grove

The Monarch butterfly grove in Pismo (Hwy. 1 just south of North Pismo State Beach Campground, 805/473-7220, www.monarch butterfly.org, daily 24 hours, docents available 10 A.M.–4 P.M.) sees the return of butterflies each November–February, when tens of thousands of Monarch butterflies migrate to this small grove of eucalyptus trees near the beach to mate. On average there are about 30,000 of these silent winged creatures, and the trees are often transformed into brilliant shades of orange after their 2,000-mile journey to get here. This is the largest of the four gathering spots for the Monarchs in California. Docents staff the area between 10 A.M. and 4 P.M. and give brief and fascinating talks about the butterflies and their very unique but short lives. Talks are given daily at 11 A.M. and 2 P.M. during season. It's free to walk into the grove and free to hear the docents, and there's a short boardwalk that leads to the beach near a large picnic area near the low sand dunes and cypress trees near the water's edge. Parking is along the side of the road, so use caution when crossing the busy street.

BEACHES
Avila Beach

Avila Beach (San Miguel and Front Sts.) has a nice pier and large wide, flat beaches, and tends to have a more family vibe, probably because of the swing sets right on the sand facing the ocean. There are restroom facilities on the

Avila Beach

beach side of the street and plenty of food and coffee options in the sherbet-colored buildings on the other of the boardwalk. The bay is protected, therefore the water tends to be warmer and gentler, and the weather here is almost always nicer than any other place on the Central Coast.

Pismo Beach

Pismo Beach (Pomeroy and Cypress Sts.) is how we imagine classic 1960s California: friendly people, great waves, low-key and easygoing. Pismo still has that allure and the beaches, best accessed by heading down Pomeroy straight towards the pier, are flat, long, and wide stretches of sand. There are plenty of restrooms, food, and parking nearby, and the pier is the focal point of this beach.

Oceano Dunes

Just south of San Luis Obispo and Pismo Beach are the Oceano Dunes (928 Pacific

THE PISMO CLAM

Pismo Beach was once nearly synonymous with the word *clam,* as there used to be a thriving clam industry here. Even before the arrival of the Europeans, the Chumash Indians made use of the clams, using the meat for food and the shells for decorative arts.

From the turn of the 20th century until about World War II, the clam industry as defined by Pismo Beach, part of Morro Bay, and into Monterey was substantial. And though the clam population is smaller these days, due to over-fishing and natural predators like otters, the Pismo clam still has good years and bad years. But clamming isn't what it used to be, and though Pismo Beach has its share of clam chowder, few people recall the association between Pismo Beach and its clams.

Enjoy dramatic views of the ocean waves from the bluffs above Pismo Beach.

Blvd., 805/473-7220, www.parks.ca.gov), vast sand dunes that stretch for 18 miles from Pismo Beach south to Guadalupe in Santa Barbara County. This is one of the few places left in America with this amount of dunes covering so great a distance. And some of these are not small dunes, but large and domineering, reaching 20 feet or more. The benefit to visiting Oceano Dunes is that it's relatively uncrowded and there are flat, wide beaches. It can be breezier here at times, but there is also a moonscape beauty to the beaches.

The Oceano Dunes are also home to a vehicular recreation area, meaning you can actually drive on the beach in certain parts, though you do need a State of California license for an Off-Highway Vehicle. There are very specific rules and regulations for this section of beach, and it's best to visit www.parks.ca.gov for detailed information.

ENTERTAINMENT AND EVENTS
Nightlife
BARS AND CLUBS

San Luis is a college town, and the college bar is **Frog & Peach** (728 Higuera St., 805/595-3764, daily noon–2 A.M.), a narrow, small space that's usually packed on the weekends. When the bands start playing it gets warm, but the outside patio overlooking the creek is a way to cool down and escape the throngs. Though they call themselves a pub, it's more a pure bar, with basic worn wood and booths that face the long bar. Tuesday evenings are pint nights. If you're looking for a younger crowd, this is the spot.

Koberl at Blue (998 Monterey St., 805/783-1135, www.epkoberl.com, daily 4–11 P.M.) has white tablecloths, exposed brick walls, and more sophisticated flair than Frog & Peach. There are still beers—a wide variety of European brews, in fact—and a stellar wine list. But they are most well known for their martini options—locals know it's one of the best places to grab a signature martini after work.

Mo/Tav (725 Higuera St., 805/541-8733, www.motherstavern.com, daily 11:30 A.M.–1:30 A.M.) used to be called Mother's Tavern, but this is not your mother's tavern. In addition to bottle service and a dance floor, they have karaoke every Sunday and Monday and DJs spinning dance tunes the rest of the week. The long wood bar with a massive round mirror echoes the upscale saloon feel of this very popular place.

Native Lounge (1023 Chorro, 805/547-5544, www.nativelounge.com, Tues.–Sun. 10 P.M.–2 A.M.) is one of the hippest looking places in SLO, with sleek lines and minimalist furnishings. It's the trendy place for the younger crowd. DJs spin nightly and the place crackles with bottle service and cool drinks. The patio fronts the creek, for those needing some air or just wanting to be seen.

LIVE MUSIC

The Graduate (900 Industrial Way, 805/541-0969, www.slograd.com, cover $5–10) is aimed, as the name implies, at the college and post-college crowd. There's College night on Wednesday, salsa and merengue on Friday, country on Thursday and various other events in between, and a large dance floor with a bar and restaurant. Live bands as well as DJs provide a a cool place to hang out.

The **Pozo Saloon** (90 W. Pozo Rd., 805/438-4225, www.pozosaloon.com) is one of the best venues for live music on the entire Central Coast. The problem is, it's not near anything—seriously. Seventeen miles off the highway in the all but forgotten town of Pozo, you'll come across this 3,000-seat outdoor venue. It may seem unknown to most, but many big-name acts have performed in Pozo, like the Black Crowes, Ziggy Marley, and Merle Haggard. If you decide to go with general admission, you need to bring your own chair or blanket. Cell phones don't work out here and there's only one restaurant. It gets packed, in part because it's such a cool venue, away from everything, out among low hills and oak trees. Always check the schedule, as you don't want to head all the way out there on the wrong day.

For a step back in time, the Madonna Inn's

Gold Rush Steakhouse (100 Madonna Rd., 805/784-2433, www.madonnainn.com) has live music and dancing Thursday–Monday beginning about 7:30 P.M. There is no cover, and they have mainly swing and ballroom music. There's an older crowd here, but it's festive and everyone's in a good mood, in part because it's hard to be unhappy in the vibrant pink interior. You don't have to dance, of course—just watch and listen if you like.

At the **Downtown Brewing Company** (1119 Garden St., 805/543-1843, www.dtbrew.com) there is an actual stage, with the best acoustics in town. They showcase a diverse range of music here, including acoustic, rock, country, and blues. They serve food in the upstairs portion, and there are pool tables, while the downstairs acts like a true entertainment venue; it holds 300 people. Shows begin at 8 P.M. and run most nights of the week. When they do have cover charges, which is dependent on the band, they run about $5.

Festivals and Events
SPRING
Each March in Pismo Beach, the **World of Pinot Noir** (805/489-1758, www.worldof pinotnoir.com), an all pinot noir event, is held on the bluffs overlooking the ocean. This three-day event is filled with seminars about growing conditions and regions, and there's a vintage tasting and a chef's challenge. The pinot noirs are not exclusive to California; every year pinot producers come from Oregon and Europe as well. It's a great focused time on one varietal and there are plenty of tastings in which to educate your palate.

If wine is not your thing, there is the **California Festival of Beers** (www.hospice slo.org, tickets $75–200) held each May at the Avila Beach Resort. For over two decades, this collection of nearly 50 brewers from the West Coast and beyond has gathered near the ocean in Avila Beach to celebrate all things beer. Get your pretzel necklace, enjoy the live music and the golf tournament, and know that the proceeds from the event support Hospice of San Luis Obispo. This event always sells out.

SUMMER
Similar to its cousin in Santa Barbara, the **I Madonnari** (805/541-6294, www.aiacentral coast.org) festival appears each year in September at the plaza of the Old Mission downtown, which is transformed with colorful large-scale street paintings. The 200 squares are divvied up and the labor-intensive work of chalk painting commences. Festival hours are daily 10 A.M.–6 P.M., and admission is free. Street painting has a long tradition in cities in Western Europe and probably started in Italy in the 16th century. The artists who use chalk to draw on the street are known as *madonnari*, or "Madonna painters," because they originally reproduced icons of the Madonna.

FALL
It's no time to clam up at the annual **Pismo Beach Clam Festival** (195 Pomeroy St. at the Pismo Beach pier, 805/773-4382, www.pismo chamber.com) each October. The parade comes first, then clam digging in the sand, and, of course, the clam chowder cook-off, where local restaurants strenuously attempt to defeat whoever was top clam the year before. There's live music and vendors with arts and crafts and wine-tasting. This has been going on for over six decades, and the Pismo namesake is both celebrated and eaten.

The **City to the Sea Half Marathon** (www .citytothesea.org) is still the best running event in SLO. It starts in downtown SLO and heads all the way to the ocean in Pismo Beach each October when the weather is just about perfect for a long run. This is one of the largest races in the area and draws all manner of runners, from experienced to novice, to attempt the 13-mile route.

The Central Coast is home to lots of writers, and once a year they get to showcase all things literary at the **Central Coast Book and Author Festival** (805/546-1392, www .ccbookfestival.org). This festival is by no means just local writers, however. In addition to public readings for kids and adults, the one-day fall event takes over Mission Plaza with dance performances and even cooking demonstrations. There are seminars by authors and illustrators, used and new books for sale, and booths to browse and meet your new favorite writer. It's free to attend.

WINTER
Restaurant Month (800/634-1414, www.san luisobispocounty.com) is a month-long culinary celebration in which about 40 restaurants throughout the county participate in showing off their styles. For 30 days, each restaurant serves a three-course meal for just 30 bucks. It's a great way to explore new dining options and has been a huge success. If you're visiting in January and you happen to like food, you'll have a breadth of options to explore at reasonable prices.

SHOPPING
Bookstores
Many bookstores in San Luis Obispo have closed, but **Phoenix** (990 Monterey St., 805/543-3591, Mon–Sat. 10 A.M.–9 P.M., Sun. 11 A.M.–9 P.M.) still has a large selection of used books. It's actually two stores joined by a doorway, with wall-to-wall books, and some just stacked on the floor. The upstairs section has world histories like Ireland and Wales, suggesting a good selection in any category. There is one small case of rare books, and you're more likely to hear NPR than music on the radio.

Other than the Phoenix bookstore, the only other options in the area for your literary needs are large blockbusters like **Borders** (243 Madonna Rd., 805/544-8222, www.borders .com, Sun.–Thurs. 10 A.M.–9 P.M., Fri.–Sat. 10 A.M.–10 P.M.) at the Madonna shopping center, or downtown's **Barnes & Noble** (894 Marsh St., 805/781-8334, www.barnesand noble.com, daily 9 A.M.–11 P.M.).

Clothing and Shoes
Bella B (1023 Morro St., 805/547-8700, www .bellab.com, Sun.–Thurs. 10 A.M.–6 P.M., Fri.–Sat. 10 A.M.–8 P.M.) sells comfortable dresses, sandals, and active wear that reflect the San Luis Obispo casual lifestyle in loose fitting, free-flowing fabrics that are easy to care for and colorful enough that they're simple to accessorize.

Head to **!Romp** (714 Higuera St., 805/545-7667, www.rompshoes.com, Mon.–Sat. 11 A.M.–6 P.M., Sun. 11 A.M.–5 P.M.) for hand selected, handmade Italian footwear that isn't carried most places. Owner Karen English offers an exclusive collection of fashionable footwear for women that's worth seeking out. There are also handbags, belts, and some jewelry. The stylish store also carries some styles for men, including boots, sneakers, and loafers.

Hep Kat (778 Marsh St., 805/596-0360, www.hepkatclothing.com, daily 11 A.M.–8 P.M.) has a focus on 1950s clothes, hats, and accessories, but these retro Rat Pack–style looks are not true vintage but brand-new modern renditions of men's and women's fashions from that period. Though the store is small, there's a lot to look at here, including Bettie Page–style dresses and hair pomade.

Decades (785 Higuera St., 805/546-0901, daily 11 A.M.–5:30 P.M.) is a large thrift shop crammed with used, mostly vintage, clothes for men and women. There's also a good selection of Hawaiian shirts for men plus kitschy memorabilia like a giant Homer Simpson doll, shark heads, lunch boxes, and other oddball items. But they predominantly sell clothes, shoes, and hats.

Finder's Keepers (1124 Garden St., 805/545-9879, Mon.–Sat. 10 A.M.–5 P.M.) is a high-end women's consignment store carrying mostly name-brand items from some of the bigger names in fashion like Gucci, Donna Karan, Prada, True Religion, and many others. The stock rotates often in this small space and since it works on consignment, you can sell your fancy shoes or purses to the shop and then choose something else in exchange.

SLO Swim (795 Higuera St., 805/781-9604, daily 10 A.M.–5:30 P.M.) sells bathing suits and swimwear with an emphasis on full-figured women. There's a tiny selection of suits for men, but not much. Shopping for swimwear can be taxing as it is, but here they'll find something that actually fits your body type, especially if you're a hard to fit type.

Kastaways (778 Marsh St., 805/610-3153, Tues.–Sun. 10 A.M.–5 P.M.) is an upscale re-sale store featuring men's and women's clothes, some vintage, but most just older items. There are accessories as well, such as jewelry, belts, and hats, even a few shoes. Books and house-wares round out the offerings.

Bloke (716 Higuera St., 805/542-0526, daily 11 A.M.–5:30 P.M.) is a men's store that caters to gents the way most clothing stores cater to women. Designed to be an attractive interior with soft green walls and leather chairs, it feels more like a salon. A few animal heads dot the walls, overseeing trendy urban clothes and name-brand designers.

Specialty Stores

The SLO life can be best summed up at these cool stores. **Cloud 9 Smoke Shop & Hookah Lounge** (584 California Blvd., 805/593-0420, www.cloud9slo.com, Mon.–Wed. noon–10 A.M., Thurs.–Sat. noon–2 A.M., Sun. noon–8 P.M.) has two parts. The first is the smoke shop, with beautiful high-end water pipes and accessories, and next door, through the black curtain, is a surprisingly nice hoo-kah lounge with black leather couches and chairs and interesting artwork on the walls. Though it's near campus, it's not child's play here, and they have strict regulations about ev-erything. There's a great diversity of flavored tobacco for the hookahs but minimal snack items, mainly candy and chips. It's one of the few hookah lounges between Los Angeles and San Francisco, and they do a nice job keeping it clean and inviting. Hookah prices start at $6 per person.

At **Central Coast Surfboards** (855 Marsh St., 805/541-1129, www.ccsurf.com, daily 10 A.M.–7 P.M.) you'll find the classic surfboards and boogie boards with which this 30-plus-year institution originally made a name for itself. There are wet suits upstairs, and downstairs are swimsuits, skate shoes, and a wide selection of clothing including backpacks for the skater, surfer, or wannabe. They have a huge selection of Ugg boots.

Habitat (777 Marsh St., 805/541-4275, Mon.–Sat. 10 A.M.–6 P.M., Sun. 11 A.M.–5 P.M.) sells furniture and home accessories, and they use lots of recycled wood and old roots polished into beautiful tables, some capped with metal. There is a Polynesian and Balinese theme and a few antiques mixed in, and all in all some re-ally cool and unique pieces you may not have seen before.

The Human Kind (982 Monterey St., 805/594-1220, www.humankindslo.org, Mon.–Sat. 10 A.M.–6 P.M.) is a nonprofit store that deals with fair-trade products like clothing, home accessories, books, toys, and jewelry. It's all certified as fair trade, so you can shop with confidence knowing that your purchase will directly benefit the person who made the item.

Art Galleries

It's no surprise that this area inspires artists to create, and more galleries are turning up all the time. The choices here will give you a great overview of the art scene in town; check out www.sanluisobispogalleries.com for more in-formation on SLO galleries.

Group and solo exhibitions feature Central Coast artists at **San Luis Obispo Art Center** (1010 Broad St., 805/543-8562, www.slo artcenter.org, Wed.–Mon. 11 A.M.–5 P.M., closed July 4–Labor Day), but they also oc-casionally feature artists from across the United States. Four small galleries show new exhibits each month. They also offer lectures and art workshops, including stained glass, working with silks, printmaking, and a va-riety of other media. Plans are in the works to eventually turn this into a museum, but that's years away. For now they continue to occupy their space near Mission Plaza and the river walk.

Just Looking (746 Higuera St., 805/541-6663, www.justlookinggallery.com, daily 10 A.M.–5:30 P.M.) is the oldest gallery in SLO, having opened its doors in 1984. They repre-sent well-known artists from across the globe and do not have a focus on local artists, which is unusual for the area. Also unusual is that many of their clients are tourists to the city, who "discover" these international artists while visiting downtown. That's not to suggest that locals are not interested in what is currently hanging on the walls. In fact, it's a great way to be exposed to artists from around the United States and Europe. You just won't find anything made in the county.

The Gallery at The Network (778 Higuera St., Ste. B, 805/788-0886, www.galleryatthe network.com, daily 11 A.M.–6 P.M.) features about 35 artists, some local and some regional, that work with glass, pottery, oil and pastel, wood, and ceramics. The gallery is inside a small indoor mall, which can be easy to miss since there's no storefront on Higuera Street. If you're looking for local art, this is a good stop.

RECREATION
Golf
The **Avila Beach Golf Course** (6464 Ana Bay Dr., Avila Beach, 805/595-4000, www .avilabeachresort.com, green fees $56–70) is an 18-hole, par-71 public course. The front nine holes are situated within oak-lined valleys, peaceful and serene. The back nine traverse a tidal estuary. Try not to let the views distract you from the task at hand. There are elevated tees and the course is a little tight, but certainly readable. Just don't underestimate it. There's a pro shop and a very good grill on-site.

Monarch Dunes (1606 Trilogy Pkwy., Nipomo, 805/343-9459, www.monarch dunes.com, green fees $30–78) is an 18-hole, par-71 public course, fairly new to the Central Coast. Their 12-hole challenge course is becoming a favorite because you can play a little more after the regular course, or just this one if you're short on time. But it's tough, as in some cases you're hitting directly into the wind, and there are five lakes that actually serve as storage water for the nearby housing development. The layout of the course uses the natural sand dunes as a road map to create a rugged and raw course.

Hiking
With so many hills in close proximity, there are great hiking trails to try out. The **Oso Flaco Lake** two-mile round-trip trail (Oso Flaco Rd. off Hwy. 1, north of Guadalupe, www.dunescenter.org) is more of a walk than a hike. The trail is on a boardwalk that crosses the lake and reaches the top of the dunes overlooking the ocean, with killer views of the coast. It has a very large number of birds, best seen in the morning hours. White pelicans, cormorants, herons, snowy plovers, and California least terns are a few of the birds using the lake. In all, about 200 species have been spotted. Parking is $5; walk down the tree-shaded causeway and turn left onto the boardwalk. There are benches on the boardwalk over the lake.

Walk the **Bluff Trail at Spooner's Cove** (Montana de Oro, Pecho Valley Rd.), where you will get excellent views of the ocean and back to Montana de Oro State Park. Spooner's Cove is on the right about four miles from the official park entrance. There's a parking lot at Spooner's Cove, which is clearly labeled. The trail hugs the blufftop and cliffs and the low, flat vegetation allows killer views of the ragged short cliffs and rock. Out and back is about two miles, but there are inland trails that connect to Rattlesnake Flats Trail, so you can be out much longer if you wish.

The **Estero Bluffs** (Hwy. 1 at San Geronimo Rd.) is a four-mile stretch of relatively new state park coastline just north of Cayucos. Access the trail by any of several pullouts on the west side of Highway 1. A trail follows the bluff the entire way, and you can often find short scrambles down to the rocky beaches. It's a great place for seeing sea otters and is mainly level except for heading down to and back from the beach areas. The northern half has better access to beaches and good tide-pooling at low tide. Reach the area just one half mile past North Ocean Avenue as you leave Cayucos on Highway 1. Park at any of the pullouts and head towards the bluff. There you'll find the trails and low sparse vegetation.

Bike Trails

There's no shortage of cyclists in SLO. The **San Luis Obispo Bicycle Club** (805/543-5973, www.slobc.org) organizes weekly rides and has a wealth of information on local routes.

Bob Jones City to the Sea (Hwy. 101, exit at Avila Beach Dr.) is undoubtedly one of the most popular and well-traveled routes, in part because it's separate from the main road and is fully paved, wandering through pretty trees and shrub-lined areas until it terminates at the ocean. It follows an old railroad line, and this out-and-back three-mile course also follows San Luis Obispo Creek. From Highway 101, exit at Avila Beach Drive and take that a quarter of a mile, then turn right on Ontario. About another quarter mile up you'll see the dirt parking lot. The trailhead is across the street.

Barranca Trail Loop (access via Pecho Valley Rd.) is part of the Hazard Peak Trail in Montana de Oro Sate Park and has ocean views and some elevation gain depending on how far you ride. This is a dirt single-track. Access the trail off Pecho Valley Road, and turn left towards Horse Camp, which puts you on the Hazard Canyon multiuse road. The road is gated, so you'll need your bikes at this point. You'll ride about a half mile on the road, then it turns dirt and becomes the Manzanita Trail for another half mile before you pick up Barranca Trail, which if you take it to the end is a little over two miles one-way. If you're feeling frisky, you can access the Hazard Trail through the interior portion of Montana de Oro to elevation gains of a thousand feet.

In town there is **Madonna Mountain** (Maino Open Space at Marsh St.), also known as San Luis Mountain, which has short steep trails that are great for a fast, hard bike workout. The wide fire road is two miles to the top of the hill, which gives you great views back toward San Luis and of the surrounding hills. The trailhead is accessed at the Maino Open Space at the termination of Marsh Street at Fernandez Lane on the west side of Highway 101.

Spas

Sycamore Mineral Springs (1215 Avila Beach

Every time of year provides great biking opportunities in San Luis Obispo County.

Dr., 805/595-7302, www.sycamoresprings .com, daily 8:45 A.M.–8:45 P.M.) is best known for its private hot tubs built into the hillside and fed by natural mineral waters. The spa, located near the tubs, is a Tuscan-looking building with treatment rooms facing a central pool. You can get a massage, facial, body wrap, anything you want—and incorporate a mineral soak as well. Or take a yoga class, or simply stroll the grounds and use the labyrinth to detox. This is a one-stop place to find something to soothe you.

The Bladerunner (894 Monterey St., 805/541-5131, www.thebladerunner.com, Mon.–Sat. 9 A.M.–6 P.M., Sun. 11 A.M.–4 P.M.) is a spacious full-service salon and spa with tranquil green walls and a very competent staff. You can have everything done here, from facials to waxing to a cut and color. They also offer chair massage in 15-minute increments if you need a quick de-stress. They are right downtown for easy access and have a little waiting area should someone come with you.

ACCOMMODATIONS

In spite of being so close to the beach, there are still relatively inexpensive places to stay in town. Prices are higher at places near the water.

Under $150

Inn at Avila Beach (256 Front St., 805/595-2300, www.hotelsavilabeach.com, $115–130 d) is known locally as the pink hotel because of its faded pink walls. A Mexican theme runs throughout this 32-room property, with tiled walkways and decent-sized rooms, some of which face the beach. The rooms are a little older looking, and some are more decorated than others. The beach is right out the front door of the hotel, and even if you're not at the beach you can hear the surf. The sun deck is a favorite hangout with semi-private cabanas with couches, TVs, and hammocks overlooking everything. There is no air-conditioning here, but chances are you won't need it. They also have a collection of 300 movies you can rent for in-room entertainment for those nights

when you might be wondering what to do since Avila shuts down early.

La Cuesta Inn (2075 Monterey St., 805/543-2777, www.lacuestainn.com, $90–120 d) offers great pricing, and although the place is average in appearance, it hardly matters since you'll be spending most of your time outside anyhow. This 72-room property is set near the hills and in the afternoons they serve tea, coffee, and cookies. The rooms are comfortable and nicely decorated, but nothing out of the ordinary, and a great choice if you're not picky about views. It's a mile to downtown, with a heated outdoor pool and hot tub and free Wi-Fi.

$150-250

Embassy Suites (333 Madonna Rd., 805/549-0800, www.embassysuites.com, $200–240 d) offers comfortable rooms, standard in size and decor; the suites provide more room for a longer stay. They offer a wide range of packages, including golf, wine, and Hearst Castle. There is a nice indoor pool and hot tub, and next door is the fitness room. The lobby is a central courtyard with rooms facing the voluminous space. The restaurant is there, as well as a coffee bar, and they provide a cooked-to-order complimentary breakfast. Pets are welcome. It's at the south end of the shopping mall and near Laguna Lake Park, though you'll need to drive to downtown.

The Apple Farm (2015 Monterey St., 800/255-2040, www.applefarm.com, $150–180 d) has 104 rooms spread out over a large area, and the Victorian-country theme and dainty decor draws big crowds because it feels like a hotel your grandmother might run. There tends to be an older clientele here, and the service is very focused. Fireplaces, large shower tubs, and the daily newspaper are available, and they also have an extensive gift shop and in-house restaurant with early-bird dinner specials for seniors. They are right off the highway just north of downtown and near the site of the very first motel in California. Though it's near the freeway, it's relatively quiet here.

Best Western Royal Oak Hotel (214

Madonna Rd., 800/545-4410, www.royal oakhotel.com, $150–190 d) has 99 rooms that are larger than most hotel chain rooms and thoughtfully decorated. There is the usual and customary continental breakfast, pool, and hot tub, and it's close to downtown (though you'll need to drive); you can walk to Laguna Lake Park. This is an independently owned property and there is a level of service here that exceeds many Best Westerns.

Garden Street Inn (1212 Garden St., 805/545-9802, www.gardenstreetinn.com, $179–199 d) is a 13-room bed-and-breakfast right downtown, so you can walk anywhere. It was built in 1887, and though the kitchen has been remodeled, the rest remains pretty much original. The floor-to-ceiling wood-paneled library on the 1st floor has lots of books to read, and a full breakfast is served each morning. Every evening the inn offers a wine and cheese reception. The rooms are very nicely furnished, all with an eye toward creating a sense of authenticity, even if the room phones are push-button models.

$250-350

The **[** **Dolphin Bay Resort and Spa** (2727 Shell Beach Rd., Pismo Beach, 805/773-4300, www.dolphinbay.com, $270–320 d) has undoubtedly one of the best locations on the entire Central Coast, perched just yards from the cliffs that drop dramatically down to the Pacific Ocean. From oceanview suites to their well -nown Lido Restaurant, the resort not only boasts magnificent views, but has proximity to much of what the Central Coast offers. You can bike (bikes are provided for all guests), kayak, fish, shop, or simply bask in the golden hues of sunsets. The one-bedroom suites, at nearly 1,000 square feet, have full kitchens, fireplaces, and flat-screen plasma TVs. All guests have access to the pool and 24-hour workout room. Cooking classes are available throughout the year, and on Tuesday nights there's a wine-tasting featuring local wineries. If you are traveling with little tykes, they offer a Saturday afternoon educational exploration of the beach's tide pools and sealife,

along with lunch, so the adults can have some time off to play.

The **[** **Avila La Fonda** (101 San Miguel St., Avila Beach, 805/595-1700, www.avilalafonda .com, $280–320) has a Spanish hacienda feel. A walled waterfall greets guests as they enter. The lobby was patterned after Mission San Miguel in both size and height. If you look at the front of the hotel you'll see it's meant to resemble a Mexican village, with the mission set in the center. A hospitality suite to the right of the lobby always has chocolate chip cookies, coffee, and tea, and a full spread of cheeses and wine 5 to 6:30 P.M. And there is the chocolate pantry, open 24 hours, if you get a craving for something sweet, all at cost to guests. The 28 rooms feature large, deep whirlpool tubs, towel warmers, fireplaces, and wide flat-screen TVs. Some rooms have tiled floors and some are carpeted; the colorful walls and Mexican accents like pottery and paintings do a good job of creating a modern hacienda interpretation. Some rooms are spa rooms, some are studio rooms with a kitchen, and they can be opened to each other to form a full-size master suite. There is covered parking. Costco members can save 30 percent off their bill.

Each of seven rooms at **The Sanitarium** (1716 Osos St., San Luis Obispo, 805/544-4124, www.thesanitariumspa.com, $290–350 d) is different, though each has a deck, a wood-burning stove, and a Moroccan tub. This bed-and-breakfast in a residential neighborhood of well-tended Craftsman houses was founded in the 1880s as an actual sanitarium. The owner whitewashed the wood-sided building inside and out and filled it with paintings and sculptures. Breakfasts are made from local produce and include basics like pancakes, French toast, and scrambled eggs served with fresh organic fruit, unusual jams, fresh-squeezed juice, and coffee.

SeaVenture Resort (100 Ocean View Ave., Pismo Beach, 800/662-5545, www.seaventure .com, $290–320 d) has oceanview and mountain-view rooms, all just steps from the sand. There's covered parking, and an in-house restaurant on the 2nd floor with uninterrupted views to the ocean. There are fireplaces in the rooms, and some have private balconies, and a continental breakfast is delivered to your room when you want it. The rooms are intimate and very comfortable, with dark green walls accented by white beach-type furniture with a country flair. You're within walking distance to the center of Pismo Beach and the pier, but you'll need to drive 10 minutes to reach San Luis. But with these views, you may not want to leave.

FOOD
Steakhouses
Jocko's (125 N. Thompson, Nipomo, 805/929-3565, daily 8 A.M.–10 P.M., $25) is out of the way in Nipomo, and off to the east several miles in an unremarkable building, something like a 1950s Elks lodge that never caught up to the present day. They're known for their oak-grilled steaks and their decor, which is comprised of stackable banquet-type chairs, inexpensive tables, and frankly rather cheap silverware—it's all part of the experience. The steaks and grilled meats are all prime quality, cooked and seasoned by people who know how to grill. On weekends, and often on weeknights as well, there are notoriously long waits. Make reservations, though that doesn't mean you won't still wait.

The **(** **Gold Rush Steakhouse** (100 Madonna Rd., 805/543-3000, www.madonna inn.com, daily 5–10 P.M., $25), located inside the Madonna Inn, is an old-school steakhouse with over-the-top decor. There aren't too many places like this around: The pink booths, surrounded by golden cherub angels hanging from the ceiling and red velvet wallpaper, might make you feel like you're in a David Lynch movie. Dine on prime beef grilled over red oak, with salad and a baked potato wrapped in gold foil. They do offer chicken and fish as well. The service is attentive, and the blue cheese dressing is dynamite. Finish the meal with a slice of pink champagne cake and you'll be close to heaven.

Just down from the Madonna Inn is **Tahoe Joe's** (485 Madonna Rd., 805/543-8383, www.tahoejoes.com, Mon.–Thurs.

11 A.M.–10 P.M., Fri.–Sat. 11 A.M.–11 P.M., Sun. 11 A.M.–9 P.M., $20), where big booths and big portions are the name of the game. It is a small chain, but this is the only coastal location, and they serve excellent prime rib and steaks, not to mention some of the best garlic mashers. It's a hugely popular spot and you may have to wait on weekends, but if you're hungry, this is your stop.

American
(**Mo's Smokehouse BBQ** (1005 Monterey St., 805/544-6193, www.smokinmosbbq .com, Sun.–Wed. 11 A.M.–9 P.M., Thurs.–Sat. 11 A.M.–10 P.M., $18) is the spot for barbecue. Forgo the salads and sandwiches, and go for the pork and beef ribs with their special barbecue sauce, which you can purchase on-site (and you'll want to), and get a side of onion rings. All their meats are smoked on-site and they use hickory wood. The walls are covered with photos of barbecue joints all across the country, an homage to those unsung heroes who create mouthwatering barbecue each and every day.

The **Custom House** (404 Front St., Avila Beach, 805/595-7555, www.oldcustomhouse .com, Sun.–Thurs. 8 A.M.–9 P.M., Fri.–Sat. 8 A.M.–10 P.M., $15), situated on the boardwalk, provides copious seating, both indoors and out, with views to the beach. It's certainly popular, and there is often a wait on weekends. The interior has a nautical theme, with dark wood and large wide windows. For breakfast, they have excellent eggs Benedict with a large slab of ham and creamy hollandaise sauce. For lunch their mahi mahi fish-and-chips can be served either tempura style or breaded. Dinner has six different steaks, fresh fish, and barbecue dishes with their house-made sauce.

At the **Firestone Grill** (1001 Higuera St., 805/783-1001, Mon.–Wed. 11 A.M.–10 P.M., Thurs.–Sat. 11 A.M.–11 P.M., Sun. 11 A.M.–10 P.M., $12), it's all about the tri-tip sandwich. There's a heavy college contingency, and game days can be cumbersome and loud. Most any weekend means lines out the door that may move quickly, but seating is at a premium.

Don't be alarmed by the wait, but do be prepared for it.

At **Franks Hot Dogs** (950 California Ave., 805/541-3488, daily 6 A.M.–9 P.M., $5), the real highlights are the chicken strips and breakfast burritos, not the hot dogs. Crowded because it's pretty cheap, it's also not an overly attractive place, but hey—it's a hot dog stand. For something slightly different, order what the owner calls the pigpen, a hot dog and bun chopped up then doused with chili, cheese, and onions.

Gardens of Avila (1215 Avila Beach Dr., 805/595-7365, www.sycamoresprings.com, Thurs.–Sun. 5–9 P.M., $25) is tucked into the Sycamore Mineral Springs. The small space has a large glass wall that looks onto the stone wall holding up the back hill, so it's feels intimate, almost cave-like. The best spot, however, is a one-table balcony overlooking the dining room. The menu is limited, but the selections cover a wide range of flavors from Niçoise tuna tartar and local snapper to duck confit and traditional steaks. They also always provide a vegetarian option. For breakfast, the sour cream banana pancakes are terrific. They provide complimentary corkage on local wines.

International Fusion

Novo (726 Higuera St., 805/543-3986, www.novorestaurant.com, daily 11 A.M.–2:30 P.M. and 5 P.M.–close, $20) was originally a cigar factory in the 1890s. Their brick building is located downtown across from the Mission Plaza and has a fully heated terraced patio overlooking the creek. In the center of the deck an oak tree provides shade and a bit of tranquility. Downstairs, the Cellar is truly a unique subterranean room; once home to the Old Cigar Factory safe it's now a must-see wine cellar. Novo specializes in international cuisine, pulling spices and flavors from Brazil, Asia, and the Mediterranean with entrées like lavender lamb chops with sea salt and roasted spring onions, and *sopes* with slow-roasted carnitas.

Italian

Café Roma (1020 Railroad Ave., 805/541-6800, www.caferomaslo.com, lunch Mon.–Fri. 11:30 A.M.–2 P.M., dinner Mon.–Sat. 5–9 P.M., $20) offers a casual dining experience with upscale decor featuring yellow mottled walls with red accented carpet and drapes and white tablecloths. There's a separate bar and a large outdoor patio for those slow summer evenings, with views to the trains just across the way. Stick with the pasta dishes, like the pumpkin ravioli with sage sauce or the orecchiette with Hearst Ranch beef Bolognese, which is what they do best, and everything will be all right. If pasta isn't quite your thing, they offer fish, chicken, and beef dishes, all with an Italian flair.

Asian

Chow (1009 Monterey St., 805/540-5243, Mon.–Sat. 11 A.M.–3 P.M. and 5 P.M.–close, Sun. 5 P.M.–close, $20) specializes in California-Asian cuisine featuring house-made noodles, farmers market produce, and fresh fish specials. Try the Chinese chili crab or the five-spice roast duck breast. The duck is served with fresh crepes for rolling the duck medallions with scallions and hoisin sauce. Located next to the historic Fremont Theater in downtown San Luis Obispo, Chow's hip sky-lit bistro interior highlights all the bamboo and Asian furniture. It's bright and open, with red booths hugging the walls.

Organic and Farm Fresh

It's not all vegetarian at homey **Sally Loo's** (1804 Osos St., 805/545-5895, Tues.–Sun. 6:30 A.M.–6:30 P.M., $12), but they certainly focus on healthy natural organic ingredients in dishes like strawberry and black pepper scones or goat cheese and asparagus quiche. They occasionally feature live music and even tango lessons. The venue feels like it belongs in San Francisco and has a community vibe, with communal tables, worn couches, and funky art on the walls. You'll see Sally Loo there too: Just keep your eyes peeled for the content pit bull.

Big Sky Cafe (1121 Broad St., 805/545-5401, www.bigskycafe.com, Mon.–Fri.

7 A.M.–9 P.M., Sat.–Sun. 8 A.M.–10 P.M., $15) supports a farm-to-table mentality and offers organic-only dishes like roasted eggplant lasagna, as well as dishes like marinated catfish, braised lamb, and a full selection of salads. The ambience is pleasant and service is very friendly. The wood tables and chairs can be a bit uncomfortable after a while, but after a salad and some organic bread you really don't mind.

Mexican

Tonita's (1024 Nipomo St., 805/541-9006, daily 9 A.M.–3 A.M., $7) is very small with only four tables inside and a tiny counter for ordering. They have a basic menu with flavorful Mexican favorites like burritos, albóndigas soup, and carnitas. Expect to pay extra for chips and salsa. The restaurant sits over a creek and features an outdoor patio. It usually gets packed with the late-night crowd on weekends, looking for something to do after the bars close.

Seafood

Steamers of Pismo (1601 Price St., 805/773-4711, www.steamerspismobeach.com, daily 11:30 A.M.–3 P.M. and 4:30–9 P.M., $25) is all about seafood, with dishes like cioppino, Chilean sea bass, and a very good clam chowder. They are also well known for their cocktails, including the (local) award-winning apple-coconut mojito martini. Their small bar area with great views of the water is available during lunch and for early dinners. If you want a table that looks directly to the Pacific, make reservations. This is a popular spot for tourists because of the excellent views, and the service and food are equally good.

Splash Cafe (197 Pomeroy, Pismo Beach, 805/773-4653, www.splashcafe.com, daily 8 A.M.–9 P.M., $10) is the place to go for cheap eats by the beach. This is classic Pismo—bright, airy, and rambunctious, with plastic chairs and tables and crudely painted walls with old surfing photos and other surfing paraphernalia. They are best known for

their thick, chunky, and creamy clam chowder, which has recently been picked up by Costco. The fish-and-chips and fish tacos are also worth trying. Burgers and shakes are also served. It does get crowded, so plan to get there early.

The oft-crowded **Cracked Crab** (751 Price St., Pismo Beach, 805/773-2722, www.crackedcrab.com, Sun.–Thurs. 11 A.M.–9 P.M., Fri.–Sat. 11 A.M.–10 P.M., $25) is *the* place to crack open crab, lobster, and other shellfish in a cafeteria-style environment. Old black-and-white photos of fishing days gone by line the walls. Perhaps it's the plastic bibs that give it away, but this is a hands-on joint. They will dump the shellfish right on your table so you can get to work.

Farmers Market

Every Thursday night year-round, a great farmers market kick-starts the weekend. Around 5 P.M. local farmers set up stands along the four blocks of Higuera Street downtown to sell seasonal fruits, specialty herbs, organic vegetables, fresh flowers, and barbecue tri-tip sandwiches. Local musicians provide much of the entertainment, setting up concerts on adjoining streets, and many of the stores and shops extend their hours for the evening. It's more than a farmers market, it's a social and cultural event that has drawn tourists, college kids, and locals for years.

INFORMATION AND SERVICES

The **tourist center** (1037 Mill St., 800/634-1414) is located right in downtown. They have maps and specific guides for restaurants, wineries, and the like, but nothing authoritative of the area, unless you purchase a guide for about four bucks.

The *San Luis Obispo Tribune* is the second largest daily paper on the Central Coast and is widely distributed. The *New Times* is the free alternative weekly, which appears every Thursday. *Central Coast Magazine* (www.centralcoastmag.com) makes a monthly appearance and covers a variety of subjects including entertainment and events, with an emphasis on San Luis Obispo.

In an **emergency,** call 911 immediately. Two hospitals serve San Luis Obispo: **French Hospital Medical Center** (1911 Johnson Ave., 805/543-5353, www.frenchmedicalcenter .org) and rhe smaller **Sierra Vista Regional Medical Center** (1010 Murray Ave., 805/546-7600, www.sierravistaregional.com). For Police services can be found at the City of San Luis Obispo Police Department (1042 Walnut St., 805/781-7317) and the San Luis Obispo County Sherriff's office (1585 Kansas Ave., 805/781-4550).

GETTING THERE AND AROUND
By Car

As with most towns on the Central Coast, Highway 101 cuts through the town, and access is off this main artery. Traveling north or south, the main exits are Broad and California Streets. You can also reach town by driving south from Morro Bay via Highway 1, which will place you right in downtown. San Luis Obispo is on a grid system with its main street, Higuera, a southbound one-way street; Marsh is one-way heading north. Two-hour parking is the norm except on Sundays, when there is free parking all day on city streets.

If you need to move about on someone else's wheels, **234-Taxi** (872 Morro St., 805/234-8294, www.234taxi.com) is a good bet. They serve the area and take all major credit cards. There's also the **SLO Cab Company** (202 Tank Farm Rd., 805/544-1222).

The **Pacific Surfliner** (www.amtrak.com), one of Amtrak's coastal trains, travels between San Luis Obispo in the north and San Diego in the south, with stops in Los Angeles, Goleta, Santa Barbara, Grover Beach, and smaller towns in between, while the **Coast Starlight** (www.amtrak.com) travels between Seattle in the north and Los Angeles in the south, with local stops in Paso Robles, San Luis Obispo, and Grover Beach. This has sleeper cars and can be a great way to reach the area from the Pacific Northwest.

Amtrak Thruway Motorcoach Service (www.amtrak.com) travels between Oakland in the north and Santa Barbara in the south, with stops in Paso Robles, San Luis Obispo, and Grover Beach. The specific bus routes are 17, 21, and 36, and one can connect to the Pacific Surfliner as well. The San Luis Obispo Regional Transit Authority (179 Cross St., 805/781-4472, www.slorta.org, Mon.–Fri. 6 A.M.–9:45 P.M., $1.25–2.75) covers all of the county. All the buses are wheelchair accessible and have bike racks. As a general rule they do not operate on major holiday, so it's best to contact them for specific schedules. Exact change only.

The brown and green **Downtown Trolley** costs a mere $0.25 to ride. The loop goes from the hotels on the north end of Monterey Street, near Highway 101, to Mission Plaza, down Higuera Street, back up Marsh Street, and back to Monterey at Osos Street. It runs every 15–20 minutes on Thursday 3:30–9 P.M., Friday–Saturday noon–9 P.M., and Sunday 10 A.M.–3 P.M.

Located just two miles south of the city of San Luis Obispo, the **San Luis Obispo County Regional Airport** (903-5 Airport Dr., 805/781-5205, www.sloairport.com) serves areas as far north as southern Monterey County and as far south as northern Santa Barbara County. The airport offers dozens of flights daily; it's currently served by four commercial airlines with flights to Las Vegas, Los Angeles, Phoenix, Salt Lake City, and San Francisco.

Paso Robles

El Paso de Robles, meaning "the pass of the oaks," is just called Paso around here. Part Western outpost, part sleepy town, it's emerging as a destination for wine and food lovers. Though it's still a small town, with a population under 30,000, there are many who believe it will grow to become larger than the county seat, San Luis Obispo. That may or may not happen, but Paso still has an easygoing charm and its own unique feel. You'll still see farmers in cowboy boots and tractors driving along the roads, due to the area's very viable farmland. Though it's spread out, the downtown is on Spring Street, accessed right off Highway 101, and this is where most people find themselves.

To the west are the Paso Robles wineries, as well as Morro Bay, Cambria, and Hearst Castle, a 30-minute drive from downtown Paso Robles. San Luis Obispo is a 30-minute drive to the south. And heading north is undeveloped land stretching towards Monterey.

WINE-TASTING

That Paso Robles has become known for being an important wine region should not be surprising. That it's taken this long is the real stumper. Things are changing quickly, but there are still a number of small family-owned wineries with tasting rooms that are simple and unpretentious and perhaps even a little inglorious, and that's part of the charm. Often you'll find the winemaker pouring your wines. As the area has grown there are more of the large and flamboyant Napa-style tasting rooms, which might make you forget you're in a small farming town.

Downtown

Within the downtown area, meaning only a few blocks, you can walk to over a dozen tasting rooms, making wine almost as ubiquitous as food.

EDWARD SELLERS VINEYARDS

Edward Sellers wanted to make wine, in spite

© EDWARD SELLERS VINEYARDS & WINES

SAN LUIS OBISPO

Edward Sellers wines

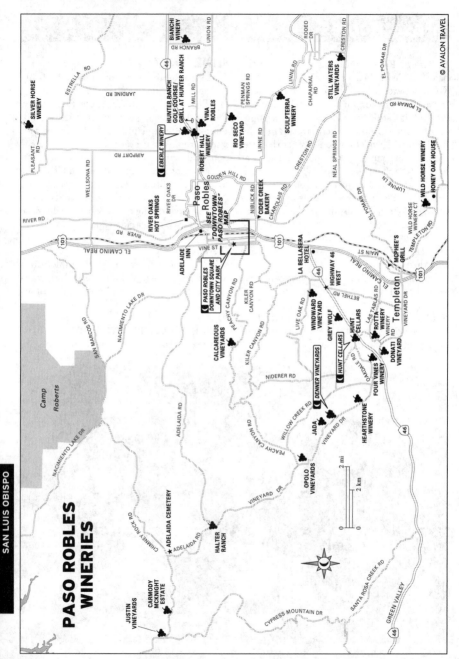

PASO ROBLES WINERIES

SAN LUIS OBISPO

BIANCHI WINERY

SILVER HORSE WINERY

HUNTER RANCH GOLF COURSE/ GRILL AT HUNTER RANCH

VINA ROBLES

EBERLE WINERY

ROBERT HALL WINERY

RIO SECO VINEYARD

SCULPTERRA WINERY

STILL WATERS VINEYARDS

WILD HORSE WINERY

HONEY OAK HOUSE

Paso Robles

RIVER OAKS HOT SPRINGS

SEE DOWNTOWN PASO ROBLES MAP

CIDER CREEK BAKERY

ADELAIDE INN

PASO ROBLES DOWNTOWN SQUARE AND CITY PARK

McPHEE'S GRILL

LA BELLASERA HOTEL

HIGHWAY 46 WEST

CALCAREOUS VINEYARDS

WINDWARD VINEYARD

GREY WOLF

HUNT CELLARS

ROTTA WINERY

Templeton

DONATI VINEYARD

DENNER VINEYARDS

HUNT CELLARS

FOUR VINES WINERY

JADA

HEARTHSTONE WINERY

OPOLO VINEYARDS

Camp Roberts

ADELAIDA CEMETERY

HALTER RANCH

CARMODY MCKNIGHT ESTATE

JUSTIN VINEYARDS

0 — 2 mi
0 — 2 km

© AVALON TRAVEL

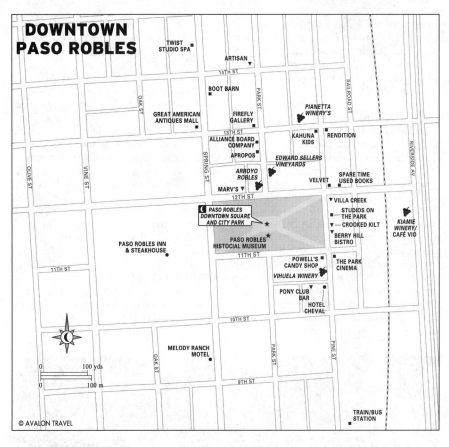

DOWNTOWN PASO ROBLES

TWIST STUDIO SPA

ARTISAN

14TH ST

BOOT BARN

PARK ST

RAILROAD ST

GREAT AMERICAN ANTIQUES MALL

FIREFLY GALLERY

PIANETTA WINERY'S

OAK ST

SPRING ST

13TH ST

ALLIANCE BOARD COMPANY

KAHUNA KIDS

RENDITION

APROPOS

EDWARD SELLERS VINEYARDS

RIVERSIDE AV

ARROYO ROBLES

SPARE TIME USED BOOKS

OLIVE ST

VINE ST

MARV'S ▼

VELVET

12TH ST

KIAMIE WINERY/ CAFÉ VIO

PASO ROBLES DOWNTOWN SQUARE AND CITY PARK

★

▼ VILLA CREEK

STUDIOS ON THE PARK

PASO ROBLES INN & STEAKHOUSE

PASO ROBLES HISTOCIAL MUSEUM

★

▼ CROOKED KILT

BERRY HILL BISTRO

11TH ST

11TH ST

POWELL'S CANDY SHOP

THE PARK CINEMA

VIHUELA WINERY

PONY CLUB BAR

PARK ST

PINE ST

HOTEL CHEVAL

10TH ST

MELODY RANCH MOTEL

OAK ST

0   100 yds
0   100 m

9TH ST

TRAIN/BUS STATION

© AVALON TRAVEL

of his moniker. (Yes, that's his real name, not a marketing gimmick.) With a production of 5,000 cases and using exclusively Paso Robles fruit, the Edward Sellers (1220 Park St., 805/239-8915, www.edwardsellers .com, daily 11 A.M.–6 P.M., tasting fee $6) winery specializes in viognier, rosé, syrah, and various blends, and these are uniformly some of the best Rhône-style wines coming out of Paso Robles. The tasting room is simple and uncluttered with minimal accessories. Winemaker Amy Butler possesses an uncanny ability to make her wines both lush and restrained. In fact she gets many compliments from fellow winemakers.

With wines like these you don't need much else.

VIHUELA WINERY

Vihuela (840 11th St., 805/226-2010, www .vihuelawinery.com, Sun.–Mon. 11 A.M.–4 P.M., Wed.–Sat. 11 A.M.–7 P.M., tasting fee $5) only makes one white wine so far, a chardonnay; they mainly focus on syrah and cabernet sauvignon. They plan a white Rhône blend of marsanne, roussanne, and viognier to round out their white offerings, but the two best friends who formed this winery still prefer big reds and Bordeaux varietals. Their signature blend, called Concierto del Rojo, meaning "concert of red," is an unorthodox blend of syrah, merlot, and petite verdot. The tasting room shares an unpretentious and frankly uninteresting space with Vivant Fine Cheese. But there is an outdoor patio in which to enjoy the wines and cheese.

PIANETTA WINERY

The tasting room for Pianetta Winery (829 13th St., 805/226-4005, www.pianettawinery.com, Wed.–Mon. noon–6 P.M., tasting fee $5) is charming, clean, and inviting. The theme is that of a ranch house, and there are wooden arbors set against the walls and old family farming photos hanging in close proximity. In keeping with the theme, and honoring tradition, at the front of the tasting room is the very pump that the owners' grandfather used when making his homemade wine. Wood tones dominate the space; the old hardwood floors remind you that this is one of the older buildings in Paso Robles, the Grangers Union Building, which dates to the late 1880s. Wines include sangiovese, syrah, cabernet sauvignon,

petite sirah, and several blends that will win you over with lots of up-front fruit and balance.

KIAMIE WINERY

Kiamie Winery (1111 Riverside Dr., 805/226-8333, www.kiamiewines.com, Thurs.–Mon. 11 A.M.–6 P.M., tasting fee $5) is a newer addition to the Paso Robles wine scene. Their tasting room is downtown, though just off the downtown square near the train tracks, and is simple and unpretentious. The salmon-colored walls hold a few pieces of artwork, but aside from that it's all about the wines. The emphasis is on Rhône and Bordeaux blends. Their grapes come from the Westside region, and all the vineyards they source are within close proximity to each other, lending to the balanced nature of their wines.

ARROYO ROBLES

Arroyo Robles (739 12th St., 877/759-9463, www.arroyorobles.com, daily 11 A.M.–7 P.M., tasting fee $5) is located directly across from Paso Robles' downtown historic City Park.

sorting grapes by hand at Kiamie Winery

Arroyo Robles offers wine, of course, but also a plethora of other items in their well-stocked tasting room, including books, gift items, and maple syrup and pancake mix, a sort of homage to a property they owned back in Vermont. Even now they offer a pancake breakfast before all the major wine festivals in town. A broad portfolio of wine is made here, including the standard offerings like chardonnay, zinfandel, and syrah, but they have also branched off into viognier, tempranillo, two rosés, and several

ports. Not willing to rest on their laurels, they also produce two sparkling wines, one of which is a sweet almond sparkler.

Highway 46 West
ℂ HUNT CELLARS

David Hunt was diagnosed at a young age with a degenerative retinal disorder; his sight has eroded over four decades and is now all but gone. For many people that may seem like a handicap, but for Hunt, it has honed his sense

JAMES DEAN: DEATH ON THE HIGHWAY

In the 1950s, James Dean was fast becoming a well-known movie star, and he loved making films. He also loved his car, a silver Porsche 550 Spyder that he nicknamed Little Bastard. In the early afternoon of September 30, 1955, Dean and Porsche factory mechanic Rolf Weutherich were on their way to an auto rally in Salinas, California. Dean was pulled over for speeding by a Bakersfield police officer, who issued a citation for driving 65 in a 55 zone and cautioned Dean to slow down and be careful. Dean and his companion continued on their way towards Paso Robles, with plans to spend the night, then leave the next morning for Salinas.

Around the same time, 23-year-old Cal Poly student Donald Turnupseed was heading home in his 1950 Ford Tutor. He made a left turn at the intersection of Highway 41 onto State Route 466 (later named State Route 46), unaware of the Spyder approaching. Contrary to reports that have since stated Dean's speed was in excess of 80 miles per hour, California Highway Patrol officer Ron Nelson, one of the first law enforcement officers on the scene, said the wreckage and the position of Dean's body "indicated his speed at the time of the accident was more like 55 mph." The two vehicles met nearly head on. Little Bastard crumpled and spun around, coming to rest near a telephone pole about 15 feet off the road. Rolf was thrown from the car and suffered a broken leg and serious head injuries, though he would survive. Amazingly, Donald Turnupseed escaped the accident with

only a gashed forehead and bruised nose. But James Dean suffered fatal injuries, including near decapitation. The coroner listed Dean's injuries as broken neck, multiple fractures of upper and lower jaw, multiple fractures of the left and right arm, and other internal injuries caused by the two-car collision. James Dean was 24 years old.

In 1977, a James Dean memorial was erected near the site of the crash. The stylized sculpture is composed of concrete and stainless steel around a tree in a place called Cholame. Today the Jack Ranch Café sits nearby, all that's left of the little town of Cholame. The sculpture was made in Japan and transported to Cholame, accompanied by the project's benefactor, Seita Ohnishi. Ohnishi chose the site after examining the location of the accident, now little more than a few road signs and flashing yellow signals. This is not the exact spot where the crash occurred; it was 900 feet northeast, before the highways were realigned. In September 2005, the intersection of Highways 41 and 46 in Cholame was dedicated as the James Dean Memorial Highway as part of the commemoration of the 50th anniversary of his death. Donald Turnupseed went on with his life, forming a fairly successful electrical contracting business and trying to avoid the spotlight, refusing all interview requests. He died in 1995. The site still draws visitors and curiosity seekers, though not as many as it used to. Dean only made three films, *Rebel Without a Cause, East of Eden,* and *Giant,* but his legacy lives on.

of taste and smell, and his wines benefit tremendously from his acute ability. "Blindness in some ways helps me in making wine," he says. He claims he can actually sense the weight and texture of a wine by its sound. The timbre changes as it pours into a glass, explains this ex-musician. A full line of wines, predominantly reds, all velvety and seductive, are available at Hunt Cellars (2875 Oakdale Rd., 805/237-1600, www.huntcellars.com, daily 10:30 A.M.–5 P.M., tasting fee $5–10), but they are not inexpensive. You'll find cabernet sauvignon, barbera, zinfandel, petite sirah, and tremendous ports and dessert wines.

HALTER RANCH

A long drive on curved roads under a canopy of oaks leads up to the old property known as Halter Ranch (8910 Adelaida Rd., 805/226-9455, www.halterranch.com, daily 11 A.M.–5 P.M., tasting fee $5). The 1880 Victorian house and old silo and barn seem perfectly suited to the spot. By contrast, the tasting room, built in 2005, is modern, with a curved bar, warm wood tones, and hip track lighting embedded in the wood beams. Halter Ranch is a 960-acre ranch with 150 acres of grapes, mostly dedicated to cabernet sauvignon. They also make rosé, sauvignon blanc, and syrah. A selection of cheeses, cured meats, dipping oils, and crackers are for sale and are perfect for a spontaneous picnic outside under the olive trees, or near the outdoor fireplace on the flagstone. Fresh bread is brought in on Fridays. Halter Ranch honey is also available.

JADA

Wines at Jada (5620 Vineyard Dr., 805/226-4200, www.jadavineyard.com, Thurs. noon–5 P.M., Fri.–Sun. 10 A.M.–5 P.M., tasting fee $10) go by unique names like XCV, a white blend of viognier, roussanne, and grenache blanc; Mirror, a mix of syrah and petit verdot; Hell's Kitchen, another blend of syrah, grenache, mourvedre, and tannat; and Jack of Hearts, a Bordeaux blend of cabernet sauvignon, petit verdot, and merlot. The stacked stone walls and arched iron gate that fronts

tasting room at Jada

the highway will lead you alongside a line of mature purple-leafed plum trees. Inside the tasting room, the ceiling narrows down, forcing the eyes to the windows behind the tasting bar with beautiful views to the vineyards. The viewing deck, an expansive area of tables and chairs, also provides views of the vines and nearby properties. The facility has a hip modern design, which juxtaposes the earthy, laid-back rolling hills.

DONATI VINEYARD

All of Donati Vineyard's (2720 Oak View Rd., 805/238-0676, www.donatifamilyvineyard.com, daily 11 A.M.–5 P.M., tasting fee $5–10) wines come from Paicines, a place most people have never heard of in a remote part of Monterey County. The majority of their production is red wine, especially cabernet sauvignon, which is made into a single varietal wine and which is also blended into their claret, Meritage, and merlot. There are also limited quantities of syrah, cabernet franc, and malbec. As for the white wines, they produce pinot blanc, chardonnay, and pinot grigio. The tasting room is housed in a European-looking white building off Highway 46 west. The interior is modern with a sleekly styled tasting bar, in contrast to the Old World feel of the exterior. They make some wonderful wines and it's a worthy stop.

GREY WOLF

Grey Wolf's (2174 Hwy. 46, 805/237-0771, www.greywolfcellars.com, daily 11 A.M.–5:30 P.M., tasting fee $5) tasting room is inside a restored 60-year-old farmhouse, a great backdrop for tasting their wines. Grey Wolf was established in 1994 with the goal of mainly red wine production. They use only French and American oak in their barrel program, which supports their big reds like zinfandel, syrah, petite sirah, cabernet sauvignon, and their excellent Meritage blend. They have one or two white wines, but those are produced in small quantities and usually sell out quickly.

(DENNER VINEYARDS

At Denner Vineyards (5414 Vineyard Dr., 805/239-4287, www.dennervineyards.com, daily 11 A.M.–5 P.M., tasting fee $10), it's all about Rhône-style wines, with the lone exception of zinfandel. Syrah, mourvedre, grenache, viognier, and roussanne are the grapes of choice, blended into seamless plush and sensuous wines. It's a state-of-the-art modern winery with a curvilinear design to match the rolling hillside. The tasting room, with expansive views to the surrounding vineyards, feels more like Napa Valley than Paso Robles. But it's all wonderfully executed, and from the wines to the building it is a sophisticated and beautiful experience.

CALCAREOUS VINEYARDS

Calcareous Vineyards (3430 Peachy Canyon Rd., 805/239-0289, www.calcareous.com, daily 11 A.M.–5 P.M., tasting fee $5) is named for the calcareous limestone soil that is rich with calcium and magnesium and pretty much defines this region's dirt. With over 400 acres they are able to make an impressive

array of wines, from cabernet sauvignon and petit verdot to pinot noir, chardonnay, viognier, and lots of blends. Their beautifully manicured lawn at the front and back of the tasting room gives nice views to the mild hills that surround them, and they have tables to relax at.

WINDWARD VINEYARD

Windward Vineyard (1380 Live Oak Rd., 805/239-2565, www.windwardvineyard.com, daily 10:30 A.M.–5 P.M., tasting fee $10) is something of an anomaly. Normally pinot noir grows better in cooler weather, often near coastal influences. Windward is in Paso Robles, which is hot in the summer and downright cold in the winter. But this small parcel of vines is situated down in a pocket of land that protects it. All they make is pinot noir, and they usually have several vintages out for tasting to compare and contrast. They sit among other vineyard neighbors, and their wood-paneled tasting room, though small, occasionally carries artwork tacked to the wall.

FOUR VINES WINERY

Four Vines Winery (3750 Hwy. 46, 805/227-0865, daily 11 A.M.–6 P.M., tasting fee $10) burst onto the wine scene in 2002 with an edgy attitude and wines like the Heretic, a petite syrah; the Biker, a zinfandel; and a Naked chardonnay, meaning it is fermented in stainless steel and therefore retains a crisp acidity. They also offer barbera, syrah, and dessert wines. Most of their grapes are sourced from Paso Robles, and some from the Sierra Foothills. They make a lot of wines, about 60,000 cases, so this ain't no small-town winery. It's popular and the small tasting room does get crowded, so arrive early.

ROTTA WINERY

Rotta Winery (250 Winery Rd., 805/237-0510, www.rottawinery.com, daily 10 A.M.–5 P.M., tasting fee $5) is a small tasting room with views into the fermentation and barrel room. The Rotta family goes back to the early 1900s in San Louis Obispo County and is the oldest family-operated winery on the Central Coast. Their wines are well priced, most under $20, including chardonnay, zinfandel, merlot, and their black monukka, a dessert wine from an obscure grape that's done tremendously well for them.

OPOLO VINEYARDS
Opolo is the name of a blended rosé-style wine found on the Dalmatian Coast bordering the Adriatic Sea. Yes, it's a far cry from Paso Robles, and Opolo Vineyards (7110 Vineyard Dr., 805/238-9593, www.opolo.com, daily 10 A.M.–5 P.M., tasting fee $10) doesn't even make the opolo wine. They do, however, make lots of other wine, nearly 40,000 cases of 30 different wines, including the standard offerings of zinfandel, cabernet sauvignon, chardonnay, merlot, and syrah. But they also produce lesser-known wines like roussanne, malbec, grenache, and petite verdot. There are also three walking trails that meander through the vineyards, so everyone can experience first hand the beauty and tranquility of the vines.

Tables are placed strategically along the trails for impromptu picnics.

HEARTHSTONE WINERY
At Hearthstone Winery (5070 Vineyard Dr., 805/260-1945, www.hearthstonevineyard .com, Thurs.–Mon. 11 A.M.–5 P.M., tasting fee $5), the tasting room, in a modest building in some of Paso's prime wine-growing region, has postcard views from the back deck of the verdant rolling hills the area is known for. The warm, earthy tones of the interior make you feel like you're safe and secure, like being protected by rock and earth, which is exactly what the name Hearthstone was meant to imply. The 40 planted acres have a shallow clay top layer, perfect for stressing the vines, and is dotted with chunks of limestone rocks everywhere. One particular wine called Slipstone, a blend of syrah and grenache, received its moniker when the earthquake that hit Paso Robles in 2003 dislodged a large limestone rock that tumbled down the mountain and hit up against the grenache vines. It's still there

vineyards at Hearthstone Winery

to this day. Cabernet sauvignon, sangiovese, syrah, pinot noir, roussanne, and rosé round out the offerings.

CARMODY McKNIGHT ESTATE

The Carmody McKnight Estate (11240 Chimney Rock Rd., 805/238-9392, www .carmodymcknight.com, daily 10 A.M.–5 P.M., tasting fee $10) is one of those spots you just don't want to leave. As you're tasting the wines, you look out onto a little pond with a small boat in it, and you know you could get in it and lounge away the day. And then there's the art gallery located inside the tasting room; much of the art finds its way onto the labels, and most of it is done by the owner himself. The wines are wonderful, restrained, balanced, and elegant. You will find pinot noir, cabernet franc, and four versions of chardonnay, among others.

JUSTIN VINEYARDS

Up the road from Carmody McKnight Estate is Justin Vineyards (11680 Chimney Rock Rd., 805/238-6932, www.justwine.com, daily 10 A.M.–6 P.M., tasting fee $10). Justin has become known as one of the best wineries in the area, crafting Bordeaux blends like Isosceles and Justification that almost always score well in the national wine press. Once inside the tasting room, the plush rich wood tones of the bar and remote setting make it hard to leave and drive back down the mountain.

Highway 46 East

Though the majority of wineries are concentrated on the west side of Highway 101, the east side has a number of wineries as well. Since the region is warmer, there are different expressions of the wines.

(EBERLE WINERY

Gary Eberle is the father of Paso Robles wine—that much is undisputed. He arrived from Pittsburgh and realized the potential of the area, and with a few investors bought 160 acres in 1973. Today his Eberle Winery (3810 Hwy. 46 East, 805/238-9607, www

.eberlewinery.com, daily 10 A.M.–5 P.M., free) is the single most-awarded winery in the United States. Rub the boar statue out front for good luck before you enter the tasting room. All money tossed into the fountain is collected and given to a local charity. Don't mind the friendly black poodles that will come up next to you as you sip the wines; they are part of the Eberle family. Once inside, the long wood bar allows plenty of space to see the countless ribbons they have won. There are gift items and views to the outside vineyards. Tours of the winery and their wine caves are offered free of charge. Eberle reserve cabernet sauvignons are top-notch. Other wines in the portfolio include viognier, sangiovese, barbera, zinfandel, chardonnay, and too many others to list. One of the reasons they are so good is that the wines are uniformly consistent. Bring a picnic and relax on the deck, as this is a great spot to soak up the visuals of the vine-covered hills. The majority of Eberle wines are priced under $25.

ROBERT HALL WINERY

Robert Hall Winery (3443 Mill Rd., 805/239-1616, www.roberthallwinery.com, daily 10 A.M.–5 P.M., tasting fee $10) is a massively large complex; as you enter the tasting room you realize how small you are by contrast. The chandelier alone is huge. The tasting bar sits in the center, and the perimeter is full of products and gift items. They offer a wide selection of wines, from everyday inexpensive wines like their chardonnay and sauvignon blancs, to their higher-end reserve syrah, cabernet sauvignon, and vintage ports. Robert Hall wines are widely distributed. Part of that is marketing, but part of that is due to the talent of winemaker and Texas native Don Brady. The grapes are sourced from the Paso Robles region in part to show off how wonderful a region like Paso Robles is. Robert Hall made enough money doing diverse entrepreneurial things to be able to secure a prime plot of land in the early 1990s. Today they are one of the largest wineries in Paso Robles and stalwart promoters of the area.

© BIANCHI WINERY & TASTING ROOM

Bianchi Winery's tasting room

VINA ROBLES

At Vina Robles (3700 Mill Rd., 805/227-4812, www.vinarobles.com, summer daily 10 A.M.–6 P.M., winter daily 10 A.M.–6 P.M., tasting fee $5–12), the centerpiece of the tasting room is the large fireplace surrounded by comfy sofas. This is a voluminous space with stone walls and eclectic artwork. The massive arched window looks out to the vineyards and small lake. The wines consist of cabernet sauvignon, petite sirah, zinfandel, petite verdot, and blends of these grapes as well. Their estate wines are well priced, most being under $20, and they source fruit from other counties as well, notably Monterey County. They also offer summer concerts held on their expansive lawn. They're becoming quite popular, as are weddings, due to their large location.

BIANCHI WINERY

The tasting room at Bianchi Winery (3380 Branch Rd., 805/226-9922, www.bianchi wine.com, daily 10 A.M.–5 P.M., tasting fee $10), off Highway 46 east, has a small lake that hugs the exterior patio, surrounded by vines. The interior is beautifully designed, a melding of natural stone, expansive windows, and an inviting fireplace. The curved bar has an etched glass countertop and the vibe inside is modern and hip, a juxtaposition to the rural surroundings. Bianchi produces about 15,000 cases and has the standard offerings of pinot noir, chardonnay, cabernet sauvignon, and others, with a nod to Bianchi's Italian heritage with wines like sangiovese, barbera, and refosco, an obscure oddball grape from Northern Italy.

STILL WATERS VINEYARDS

Still Waters Vineyards (2750 Old Grove Ln., 805/237-9321, www.stillwatersvineyards.com, Thurs.–Mon. 11 A.M.–5 P.M., tasting fee $5) produces very small lots of wine, at most 200 cases per wine of chardonnay, viognier, merlot, malbec, and cabernet sauvignon at their out-of-the-way property. Since there was a 100-year-old olive grove on the property, they naturally decided to make olive oil too, something becoming more common in the Paso

Robles area. A somewhat under-the-radar winery, they make some very nice wines.

SCULPTERRA WINERY

At first glance, Sculpterra Winery (5125 Linne Rd., 805/226-8881, www.sculpterra .com, Fri.–Sun. 10 A.M.–5 P.M., tasting fee $10) seems more like a gimmick than a serious winery. Huge sculptures like a 10-ton puma and an 8-ton mammoth, all designed by local Atascadero artist John Jagger, greet visitors. The gardens are great for picnicking near these pieces after you've sampled mourvedre, merlot, petite sirah, and chardonnay. While you're visiting, try the pistachios that grow on the property. Their wines are well balanced, achieving acidity with fruit ripeness, and their blends are quite nice.

RIO SECO VINEYARD

At Rio Seco Vineyard (4295 Union Rd., 805/237-8884, www.riosecowine.com, daily 11 A.M.–5 P.M., tasting fee $5), you'll realize that baseball has nothing in common with wine—unless you're owner Tom Hinkle. Tom was a baseball scout, visiting high school, college, and semi-pro games to find the best young talent throughout America. Then he retired and went into the wine business. The tasting room is unimpressive, a metal and wood building whose former owner was growing marijuana in the barn, but the wines Tom makes, like zinfandel, viognier, cabernet sauvignon, and syrah are inexpensive and unpretentious, just the sort of wine you'd have with pizza or burgers.

SILVER HORSE WINERY

The first thing you notice as you step out of your car onto the blufftop tasting room of Silver Horse Winery (2995 Pleasant Rd., San Miguel, 805/467-9463, Fri.–Mon. 11 A.M.–5 P.M., tasting fee $7) is how quiet it is. Then you notice the views of a vast sky with simple rolling hills that begin to dissipate in the distance. The Silver Horse portfolio includes only one white wine, albariño, as well as cabernet sauvignon, merlot, petite sirah, and several blended wines.

The interior of the Spanish-style tasting room is comfortable with a vaulted ceiling, wood-burning fireplace, and leather club chairs. Autumnal tones and Southwest art creates a warm, relaxed vibe. On either side of the tasting bar, window cutouts allow for views into the barrel room. Outside are bocce ball courts and, fittingly, horseshoes.

WILD HORSE WINERY

Wild Horse Winery (1437 Wild Horse Winery Ct., 805/788-6310, www.wildhorsewinery .com, daily 11 A.M.–5 P.M., tasting fee $5) has long been one of the leading wineries on the Central Coast. They produce nearly 200,000 cases each year, and few wineries in California source fruit from such a broad spectrum of vineyards, which has allowed Wild Horse to select grapes from the specific areas they feel best showcase a particular wine. For example, they produce a pinot noir from one growing region in San Luis Obispo and two distinct growing regions in Santa Barbara. Viognier, chardonnay, and their malvasia bianca, which

© WILD HORSE WINERY

Wild Horse Winery

SAN LUIS OBISPO

is a perennial favorite, are just some of their white wines. Syrah, sangiovese, cabernet sauvignon, merlot, and their flagship variety, pinot noir, are on tap for the reds. When you visit be certain to try the heirloom varietals they have become known for like negrette, blaufrankish, and grenache blanc. When in season, the grapes hanging from the arbor at the entrance are tantalizing fruit that you're encouraged to sample. There are plenty of picnic tables out front on the grass. The tasting room is small with a low bar on one side of the room, and frankly isn't interesting. Like many tasting rooms, the decor is not really the point, it's the wines. They are located near Templeton, and it's a quiet drive through rolling hills to get there.

POZO VALLEY WINERY

Pozo Valley Winery (2200 El Camino Real, Santa Margarita, 805/438-3375, www.pozo valley.com, Fri.–Sun. noon–5 P.M., tasting fee $5) is not located specifically in Pozo Valley, which might arguably be a good thing. The town of Pozo is 18 miles southeast of Santa Margarita, whereas the Pozo Valley Winery tasting room is merely a mile and a half off Highway 101 in Santa Margarita. The tasting room is rustic, much more of a cowboy feel than the flashy architecture of Napa Valley. An old wooden wine press sits in the corner, a reminder of earlier days. Viognier, zinfandel, cabernet sauvignon, and merlot are the inexpensive offerings, and they work well with food.

◖ ANCIENT PEAKS WINERY

Ancient Peaks Winery (22720 El Camino Real, Santa Margarita, 805/365-7045, www .ancientpeaks.com, Thurs.–Mon. 11 A.M.– 5:30 P.M., tasting fee $5) is located just a mile off Highway 101 in Santa Margarita. Their vineyards are located at the southernmost part of the Paso Robles growing area and their unique soils, comprised of ancient ocean floor, is what makes their wines different, as well as the talent of the winemaker. The nutrients found in this uplifted sea bed is like nothing else in the entire region. You really need to sample the wines yourself to understand their uniqueness. Their

vineyards at Ancient Peaks Winery

tasting room is all polished wood with a pleasing rustic charm, and they pour sauvignon blanc, merlot, cabernet sauvignon, syrah, and zinfandel with bottle prices usually under $20.

SIGHTS
◖ Paso Robles Downtown Square and City Park

Mature oaks and sycamore trees dot the interior of the one-block square and City Park in downtown Paso Robles, the focal point of the city. There is a gazebo, playground, horseshoe pit, and plenty of grass to stretch out on. Free concerts are offered, and a majority of festivals and the farmers market are held here. In the center is the old original Carnegie Library, which has a sister in San Luis Obispo. Between 1883 and 1919, philanthropist Andrew Carnegie spent a vast sum of his money to help fund libraries all across the globe, nearly half located in American towns. Now the library has new life as a fully restored and beautiful history museum. Most everything fans out from the City Park: wine-tasting rooms, restaurants, lodging, bars, a movie theater, antiques stores, and clothing stores. It's easy to spend an entire day within the few blocks that make up this downtown area.

Mission San Miguel

Founded on July 25, 1797, as a stop between San Luis Obispo and Mission San Antonio, Mission San Miguel (775 Mission St., San Miguel, 805/467-2131, www.mission sanmiguel.org, daily 10 A.M.–4:30 P.M.) is one of those missions that's not near a major city and therefore became something of an outcast. Like many of the other missions on the Central Coast, it went through periods of disrepair and secularization, but it retains a stark beauty. Though not on most people's radar, it is worth a visit if you're in Paso Robles.

Just after 11 A.M. on December 22, 2003, the Central Coast was rocked by a 6.5-magnitude earthquake, the largest to strike the region in over 50 years. Though the mission was located 35 miles from the epicenter, it was especially hard hit. Numerous cracks appeared in many of the old walls, and entire

Mission San Miguel bell tower

© SAN LUIS OBISPO COUNTY

sections of plaster fell apart, exposing the vulnerable adobe. The entire mission complex was closed to the public for a three-year renovation costing nearly $15 million.

Today the church looks much the way it has for hundreds of years, in fact the inside of the church has never been repainted, and you can still see the handiwork of the early Salinan Indians who painted it. The interior is long and narrow, as was common at the time it was built, and the hand-carved beam ceiling is actually the most interesting part of the simple structure. The extravagantly painted church is a contrast from the subdued interiors of other missions of the Central Coast. The exterior has been shored up and kept true to its original design of multiple arches fronting a quadrangle. It's located directly off Highway 101, the most accessible of all of the missions in Central California.

The Paso Robles Historical Museum

Dead center in City Park, the Paso Robles Historical Museum (Spring St. btwn. 11th

SAN LUIS OBISPO

GHOSTS OF THE COAST

You may be a believer, or you may not be. Either way, most everyone loves a good ghost story. In and around Paso Robles are three long-standing ghost stories. You can visit these spots and decide for yourself. At the **Adelaida Cemetery** (near the intersection of Chimney Rock and Adelaida Rds.) there is apparently a woman in white who stands by a grave. The woman is believed to be Charlotte Sitton, a Mennonite woman who took her life at age 19 after her two children died from diphtheria. Allegedly she has been seen laying flowers on the grave sites of her children, buried next to her own grave, and. Many people have reported seeing other paranormal activity at the old cemetery, including apparitions of boys playing.

Just south of Paso Robles in Arroyo Grande, the old **Rose Victorian Inn** (789 Valley Rd.) was believed to be the death site of a young girl named Alice. There was apparently no foul play relating to her death – some say it was pneumonia, some say an adverse reaction to a bee sting. Regardless, a little girl's laughter is said to be heard coming from the nursery of the building, which is no longer an inn. These days the property is used for weddings and special events. Perhaps you might hear her too as you pass by.

At **Mission San Miguel,** just north of Paso Robles, there was a bloody killing rampage in 1848. John Reed, who bought the mission after secularization, turned the church into a tavern. Apparently Reed had amassed quite a fortune and liked to brag about his hidden wealth. One night a group of men, some say pirates, came into the tavern and heard Reed boasting of his buried treasure. They left the tavern and doubled back and went on a killing spree, murdering everyone in the mission, 11 people in all, to find the loot. They didn't find anything, and the law eventually caught up with the killers in Santa Barbara. Cold spots have been reported in the chapel, and there have been many reports of ghosts wandering the mission grounds, ghosts who may resemble John Reed and his wife. No one knows if the treasure was for real, or if it was ever found.

---

and 12th Sts., 805/238-4996, www.pasorobles historicalsociety.org, Thurs.–Tues. 10 A.M.–4 P.M.) is housed in a former library built in 1907 that underwent a long renovation and seismic upgrade in order to become the historical museum. It's been worth the wait, as the interior is beautiful, with wood column supports and cases, old books and photographs, memorabilia, and period furniture. There's even an 1810 harmonium, an early reed organ from Wales. You don't need a lot of time to explore the exhibits here, so it's easy to add this sight to your itinerary. There is also a small gift shop as well as maps of the downtown area and wineries.

ENTERTAINMENT AND EVENTS
Nightlife

This is still a growing area, and there are not very many nightlife options yet. The **Pony**

Club Bar (1021 Pine St., 866/522-6999, Sun.–Thurs. 5–9 P.M., Fri.–Sat. 4–11 P.M.) at Hotel Cheval is like an old-school clubhouse: wood toned, sophisticated, and centered around a zinc-topped horseshoe bar. They serve light appetizers and many local wines. You don't need to stay at the hotel to pony up to the bar and sample Central Coast wines.

Crooked Kilt (1122 Pine St., 805/238-7070, www.thecrookedkilt.com, daily 11 A.M.–9 P.M.) offers live music Thursday–Sunday, with Tuesday night always devoted to Irish music, at their courtyard stage in their back patio with a blarney stone at the foot of the stage. Times vary, so you'll need to call ahead. A classic neighborhood tavern, it has a new section through the small doorway at the back that loses the woody bar atmosphere and has a more upscale feel. From either place, however, you can hear the music. Local bands with a rock sensibility perform here, as well as out-of-county bands.

Café Vio (1111 Riverside Dr., 805/237-2722, www.cafe-vio.com, daily 6:30 A.M.–6 P.M.) is a cozy coffee shop, Internet café, art gallery, and live music joint, where people like hanging out because it's just so comfortable with stuffed chairs and relaxing wood tones. Every Friday they have live music, and every Saturday evening is open mic night. The first and third Wednesday of each month is devoted to jazz with a local band.

Just up the road from Café Vio in San Miguel is one of the oldest operating bars in the entire state of California, originally started in 1853. **Elkhorn Bar & Grill** (1263 Mission, San Miguel, 805/467-3909, Mon.–Thurs. 10 A.M.–midnight, Fri.–Sat. 9 A.M.–2 A.M., Sun. 9 A.M.–midnight) has friendly bartenders and a rowdy but enjoyable local crowd. Animal heads share the walls with beer signs and sports paraphernalia without covering up the old walls. There are pool tables, a jukebox, free Wi-Fi, and large-screen TVs, and Pabst Blue Ribbon is always on tap.

Festivals and Events
SUMMER
The Western spirit is alive at the **California Mid-State Fair** (2198 Riverside Ave., 805/239-0655, www.midstatefair.com, $8 adults, $5 children 6–12) held each July–August. In addition to big-name musical talent performing at one of the multiple stages, the Western-themed fair has horse events, pig races, and of course a carnival. But as this is now wine country, there are special winemaker dinners around town, the Central Coast Wine Challenge judged by professional wine judges to find the best wines, and an olive oil competition. A state-of-the-art culinary center hosts cooking demonstrations to show off the many local farmers and growers. This is a great family event at a great price.

The **Winemakers' Cook-Off** (800 Clubhouse Dr., 805/238-4600, www.winemakerscookoff.com, $75), which began in 1998, and is held each August, raises money for local charities. The event, open to the public, pulls in 30 winemakers, all of whom personally grill up their best dishes to match their wines. It's a feast for the senses, and more food than you can possibly consume. The live band adds to the festive environment as the public chooses their favorite wine and food pairing too. The event has raised over a quarter of a million dollars and has become one of the must-attend events in the region. Don't be surprised to see people sneaking around with beers and tequilas—after all, with that much wine, you might want something different.

SPRING
Not very family oriented, but nonetheless fun, the **Zinfandel Festival** (2198 Riverside Ave., 805/239-8463, www.pasowine.com, $60–85), held the third weekend in March, is all about California's signature grape. About a dozen local restaurants pair foods to match the big jammy zinfandel characteristics of this area. The main draw is the all-zinfandel tasting held on Saturday night, when four dozen wineries pour their zins and zin blends and a dozen local restaurants showcase food to match. There's a silent auction, live music, and all weekend long local wineries offer special deals at their tasting rooms.

If you enjoy wine and food but are concerned about the toll on the environment, then the **Earth Day Wine & Food Festival** (held the weekend closest to Earth Day, 805/369-2288, www.earthdayfoodandwine.com, $75) is right up your alley. About a thousand people attend this very fun event. Recyclable and compostable plates, bowls, forks, and spoons are used, and a team of volunteers manages a constant effort of both recycling and composting. Event programs and information guides are produced using only post-consumer recycled materials, and even the entertainment stage is solar powered. About 200 producers of sustainably grown food and wine gather to let you sample dishes sourced from locally grown fruits, vegetables, meats, cheeses, olive oils, and wine. There is live music, a silent auction, and the chance to kick back and meet farmers and vintners who are committed to sustainability.

FALL
Oaktoberfest (held at River Oaks, 800 Clubhouse Dr., 805/238-2556,

SAN LUIS OBISPO

www.firestonewalker.com, $35)—no, that's not a misspelling—is sponsored by Firestone Walker Brewery. This version of Oktoberfest is given a California twist and is held outside near the oaks. In addition to the beer Olympics, which include a keg-tossing contest (they actually use what's called a firkin, an empty 11-gallon stainless steel keg), the barrel roll, and stein racing, there's lots of German food and music, horse-drawn carriages, and people dressed up as beer maidens, with most of the guys wearing silly hats. The mayor taps the first keg and though this is about beer, there are a few wines present too. The proceeds benefit Hospice of San Luis Obispo.

SHOPPING
Clothing

Alliance Board Company (1233 Park St., 805/238-2600, Mon.–Sat. 10 A.M.–6 P.M., Sun. 10 A.M.–5 P.M.) is the place to buy surf, skate, and snow accessories and gear. It's a large shop, comprehensive in its inventory, with plenty of street clothes. Wet suits, ski gear, sports watches, and footwear like Vans and flip-flops round out the offerings. The staff is young, and very helpful and nice.

Apropos (1229 Park St., 805/239-8282, Mon.–Thurs. 10 A.M.–6 P.M., Fri.–Sat. 10 A.M.–8 P.M., Sun. noon–4 P.M.) caters to an older clientele for women's retail clothing, with predominantly dresses, pant suits, wraps, and jewelry. The clothes are a bit more traditional, though within that context they have some pieces with an urban flair.

By contrast, **Velvet** (801 12th St., 805/237-7372, Mon.–Sat. 10 A.M.–6 P.M., Sun. noon–4 P.M.) has hip boutique clothing with a wide selection of styles, from sleek and sexy dresses to coats, tops, shoes, and even a few hats, all set in a relaxed but fun environment looking out to the park.

As soon as you walk into **Boot Barn** (1340 Spring St., 805/238-3453, Mon.–Fri. 9 A.M.–7 P.M., Sat. 9 A.M.–6 P.M., Sun. 11 A.M.–5 P.M.), the heady scents of leather greet you. Boots, hats, belt buckles, and all types of jeans, shirts, and coats are ready for

trying on to get into the cowboy mentality. Paso is still a Western town at its heart, and there are plenty of boot-wearing farmers walking around. This has been a staple outfitter for the area for a long time. You can't miss the store—just look for the faded plastic horse high atop the sign.

For the latest and hippest fashions for the cool little one in your life, drop by **Kahuna Kids** (840 13th St., 805/237-9497, www .kahunakidspasorobles.com, Mon.–Sat. 10 A.M.–6 P.M., Sun. 11 A.M.–5 P.M.), which has clothes for toddlers and infants. The owners come from a surf background, so there's a lot of skater-type baby clothing, as well as baby carriers and blankets.

Art Galleries

Studios on the Park (1130 Pine St., 805/238-9800, Thurs. noon–6 P.M., Fri.–Sat. noon–7 P.M., Sun. noon–6 P.M.) is a warehouse-sized space with a series of studios that are home to two artists each. There's a silversmith, pottery throwers, and others that create right in front of your eyes. You can watch, ask questions, and get intimately involved with the two dozen local artists. Their finished works are presented for sale.

The **Firefly Gallery** (1301 Park St., 805/237-9265, daily 11 A.M.–5 P.M.) is a mother-daughter team who left the constraints of Los Angeles to open this unique space. Downstairs is jewelry, clothing, crafts, handmade dishes, and accessories, and upstairs is an art gallery. There are a number of local artists represented, not just with the upstairs art, but with the crafts downstairs as well. Most of the items are handmade, some from recycled materials.

Specialty Stores

The **Great American Antiques Mall** (1305 Spring St., 805/239-1203, daily 10 A.M.–5 P.M.) has 40 vendors who are ready to buy sell and trade. Virtually everything is here—kitchen furniture, kitsch, glassware, silver, collectibles, and both new and vintage in a comfortable 9,000-square-foot space. It's well organized and makes intuitive sense as you walk around.

This isn't high-end antiques, but a very good selection of well-priced items.

Powell's Candy Shop (840 11th St., 805/239-1544, Mon.–Sat. 10 A.M.–9 P.M., Sun. 10 A.M.–8 P.M.) has all sweet things vintage. From the pressed-tin ceilings to the candy you assumed they stopped making years ago, it's all here, including a lot of novelty candy like bacon-flavored mints. They also carry gelato and hand-dipped truffles, jelly beans, and bulk candy. If you are looking for that gum you always chewed as a kid, chances are you will find it here.

Rendition (1244 Pine St., 805/238-2433, www.renditioninterior.com, Mon.–Sat. 10 A.M.–6 P.M., Sun. 11 A.M.–4 P.M.) sells lots of big furniture. They have a plethora of wrought-iron sconces, chandeliers, and beautiful hefty wood pieces for the dining room, kitchen, and bedroom. Not afraid to be bold, these are pretty masculine works with a hand-crafted feel.

Spare Time Used Books (805/237-1140, Mon.–Sat. 10:30 A.M.–5 P.M.) sells predominantly paperback books with only a small fraction of hardbacks. As you enter you can clearly smell the paper and print of old books. The prices for most of the paperbacks are $2–5.

RECREATION
Lakes

Even though Paso is located about 30 miles from the coast, you can still get a water fix nearby. **Lake Nacimiento** (10625 Nacimiento Lake Dr., 805/238-3256, www.nacimiento resort.com), or "Nassi" as it's called locally, is 165 miles of shoreline, with a year-round general store, a full-service marina, over 350 campsites, and basketball courts, volleyball, rentals of water skis, wake boards, kayaks, and pontoon boats, and 120 rental boat slips, all just 15 miles from Paso Robles. Kayak rentals start at just $5 per hour and you can move up to a 24-foot pontoon boat. Semi-rustic lodge accommodations are available as well. It's only 20 minutes up a curvy road to reach the lake; the area looks like a small village. There's a housing community called Heritage Ranch here as well, so the infrastructure is good.

Lake San Antonio (74255 San Antonio Rd., 805/472-2311, www.lakesanantonioresort .com) is the smaller sister lake with just 65 miles of shoreline on its 17-mile length, but with over 2,000 campsites. It's further north from Paso Robles and Lake Nacimiento. For fishing, the lake is stocked with largemouth and smallmouth bass, striped bass, crappie, catfish, bluegill, and squawfish, as well as other varieties. If you bring your own boat, the slip fees are just $15 each night, much less expensive than the cabins, which range $160–250 nightly. The south shore general store is open year-round, but leans towards expensive. There is water skiing and boat rentals as well. The lake is accessed from Highway 101 north or south by taking the Jolon exit west to New Pleyto Road, then following signs to the lake.

Water Park

Considering it gets into the triple digits in Paso during the summer, a cooling ride in some clean pure water might be just the thing. At **The Ravine Waterpark** (2301 Airport Rd., 805/237-8500, www.ravinewaterpark .com, summer daily 10:30 A.M.–6 P.M., hours can vary—phone ahead, from $19.95 adults, $14.95 under 48", $10 seniors) you can take a 325-foot flume ride into a bed of water, grab an inner tube and simply let the current take you leisurely around the water creek, or splash in the wave pool. It's great for younger kids, but the truth is there are a lot of adults here too. It's probably the best way to cool off and have fun at the same time.

Golf

Hunter Ranch Golf Course (4041 Hwy. 36 East, 805/237-7444, www.hunterranchgolf .com, daily 6:30 A.M.–dusk, green fees $50–100) is surrounded by oak trees with views to vineyards. It's directly off the highway and this 18-hole, par-71 course might lull you into a false sense of security. You earn each shot here, and familiarity with the course beforehand will definitely help you. They have a full-service restaurant, pro shop, and three tee boxes and driving range.

THE SULPHUR SPRINGS

Paso Robles used to be considered a health resort, much like Santa Barbara. In 1864 the *San Francisco Bulletin* commented that Paso Robles was the spot for natural springs and mud baths, and by 1868 people were coming from as far away as Oregon, Nevada, Idaho, and even Alabama to take the waters. Besides the well-known mud baths, there were the Iron Spring and the Sand Spring, which bubbled through the sands.

In 1882, Drury James and the Blackburn brothers issued a pamphlet advertising "El Paso de Robles Hot and Cold Sulphur Springs and the Only Natural Mud Baths in the World." By then there were first-class accommodations in Paso Robles, a reading room, a barber shop, a general store, a top-of-the-line livery stable, and comfortably furnished cottages for the tourists. Visitors could stay in touch with the rest of the world since mail was delivered twice each day. There was also a Western Union telegraph office and a Wells Fargo agency. As the springs became more and more a destination

of the well-to-do as a place to socialize and be seen, the original purpose of the springs, to heal, became peripheral.

A bathhouse was erected over the sulphur spring in 1888, with 37 bath rooms, and a plunge where water is piped in from the springs. The following year, work began on the large Hot Springs Hotel, which was completed in 1900 but burned down 40 years later before being rebuilt as the Paso Robles Inn. Since the privileges of using the baths were restricted to guests of the hotel, and many people who desperately needed its healing powers couldn't afford the rates of the fashionable hotel, a few businessmen in Paso Robles made arrangements for the right to bore for sulphur water on a private lot. A sulphur well was reached, a bath house built, and baths offered at an affordable rate of 25 cents. The establishment was later offered to the City, and is currently the site of the Municipal Pool. The main spring was originally located at 10th and Spring Streets.

River Oaks (700 Clubhouse Dr., 805/226-7170, www.riveroaksgolfcourse.com, daily 8:30 A.M.–dusk, green fees $10–12) is a six-hole course, so three go-rounds gets you to 18. It was designed in part as an instructional course, and there are plenty of ways to utilize it, either with a golf pro, or if you simply want to get in a quick short round. It's a par 19 with three tees for each hole providing different approaches for each shot.

Bike Trails

Highway 46 West to the Coast is not an official route or anything like that, it's just a very popular stretch of road. Assuming you pick up the route near Highway 101, it's about 24 miles one-way. But the best parts are at the back end, closer to the coast, for sweeping vistas of beautiful multiple rolling hills. About 13 miles in you can park off York Mountain or Apple Roads and unload your bike there.

The elevation at the top of the pass, before it drops down towards Cambria and Highway 1, is about 1,700 feet, and on clear days the views extend all along the lush green hills, looking like so much carpeting, to Morro Rock and the Pacific Ocean.

Vineyard Drive can be accessed directly off Highway 46 or further south off Highway 101. This is a two-lane road with moderate climbs and lots of twists and turns taking you by old vineyards, farms, and moss-covered oaks that hang languidly over the road. You can even plan to stop by a winery as part of your ride. You do need to keep an eye on the traffic, as chances are they've been visiting the area wineries, and with little wiggle room on this road it's always best to be vigilant.

Spas

Service with a twist is what **Twist Studio Spa** (1421 Spring St., 805/239-3222, daily

9 A.M.–5 P.M.) is impressive from the moment you walk in, with its dark wood tones, slate-tile floors, and open feel. You can get a haircut or color in the front, then head to the back where there is a narrow café serving sandwiches and salads. They also have a mini–wine bar that features a different winery each week. Spa packages can be up to five hours for full-day treatment. There are private massage and esthetician rooms and the dark woods, exposed trusses, and earthy-looking environment makes this feel more like a really cool cabin.

For a more traditional approach, the **River Oaks Hot Springs** (800 Clubhouse Dr., 805/238-4600, www.riveroakshotsprings .com, Tues.–Sun. 9 A.M.–9 P.M.) has massage and the usual list of services like waxing and facials, but the best part of their offerings is the outdoor hot tubs with Paso Robles' natural water being fed into them at 102 degrees. Each tub is surrounded by wood latticework for privacy, and the serene environment lets you view the oaks on the low sloping hillsides. You can even bring your own bottle of wine for a $10 corkage fee. If that's too outdoorsy, you can experience the same waters inside in a private room. The outdoor tubs start at $16 per hour, but the views to trees and the pastoral scents of the short grasses are all free.

ACCOMMODATIONS
$100-200
The **Melody Ranch Motel** (939 Spring St., 805/238-3911, $80–90) is a classic California motor court with all rooms facing the center. It's easy to miss the low building as you drive by it. It's close to downtown and is kept well cleaned, but remember this is not a new property. There is an outdoor pool and though not fancy, it's probably the best bargain in town. From here it's a five-block flat walk to the City Park, the hub of the action.

The **Best Western Black Oak Motor Lodge** (1135 24th St., 805/238-0726, www .bestwestern.com, $129–140 d) has 100 rooms that are larger than those at most hotels, and three dedicated for folks with disabilities. They have a heated pool, hot tub, sauna, and free Wi-Fi. Each of the renovated rooms is decorated differently, but certainly in a traditional style. They don't provide breakfast, but do provide a $5 voucher for breakfast at the nearby diner. Downtown is a 10-block walk from here, otherwise a very brief drive is inevitable.

The rooms at **La Quinta** (2615 Buena Vista, 805/239-3004, www.lq.com, $139–150 d) are all a pretty standard size, but the main features are the fitness room, their 5:30–7 P.M. wine reception, the in-room 32-inch flat-screen TVs, and the outdoor pool and hot tub. Since it is just on the west side of Highway 101 there's less traffic noise and plenty of privacy. This also makes for a closer drive if you're spending time over at Cambria or Morro Bay.

At the **Holiday Inn Express** (2455 Riverside Dr., 805/238-6500, www.hixpaso.com, $150–170 d) there are 91 very nicely appointed guest rooms with in-room coffeemakers, free Wi-Fi, free local phone calls. A hot breakfast is also included, and you are reasonably close to downtown, though you will need to make a short drive to get there. There's a small fitness room too, and the rooms, while nothing spectacular, are comfortable and spacious.

The **Hampton Inn** (212 Alexa Ct., 805/226-9988, www.hamptoninn.com, $160–180 d) is right off Highway 101 just south of the Spring Street exit, which makes it very convenient. The 81 rooms are garden variety, but they are clean. There's a lovely lobby with a sofa and a fireplace and they have a gift shop, safety deposit boxes, and a coin laundry. Located on the west side of Highway 46, it's also next door to a shopping mall with a few food places and coffee outlets.

◖ **Adelaide Inn** (1215 Ysabel, 805/238-2770, www.adelaideinn.com, $99–119 d) has been family-owned and -operated for 45 years. The rooms are very spacious and well appointed, and the staff is very friendly. There's an outdoor pool and hot tub. For the price, this is an exceptional value. Rooms include a work desk, refrigerator, coffeemaker, microwave, free high-speed DSL, and large bathroom and dressing area. Frankly, many places in the area charge more for less than you get here. You have quick access to Highway 101 and though you're not near downtown, there are restaurants and coffee places within walking distance.

At **Seven Quails B&B** (805/237-2598, www.sevenquails.com, $160–200 d), four rooms are tucked into the middle of nowhere, except that you have views to the vineyards from each room. Quiet and serene, it's removed from downtown and the noise, and with so few rooms you won't see too many people. The owners make their own wine, which they will share with you; their hospitality is excellent. You're already near many of the wineries on the Westside and only a 20-minute drive to the coast.

$200-300

Paso Robles Inn (1103 Spring St., 805/238-2660, www.pasoroblesinn.com, $230–250 d) is the brick building on Spring Street across from the park and has been an institution for years. The interior portion is beautifully landscaped with brick walkways, a koi pond, and a heated outdoor pool. The rooms are a bit small since this is an older property, but you can walk to the majority of downtown shops and restaurants from the hotel. They offer in-room coffeemakers and double-vanity bathrooms, and the attached restaurant serves breakfast, lunch, and dinner.

(Honey Oak House (2602 Templeton Rd., Templeton, 805/434-5091, www.laraneta .com, $200–250 d) is located at Laraneta Winery, where owners Bill and Melinda Laraneta have opened up two rooms in their home and a freestanding room off the main house as a bed-and-breakfast. The owners are nice, friendly people, and they make excellent wine. The added bonus of staying here is that it's not a corporate hotel, nor a hotel at all. All three rooms have their own bathrooms, and the upstairs unit has a balcony with serene, peaceful views of the vineyards right below. The separate cottage is so peaceful you might think you're the only one left on earth. All rooms feature queen beds and there are no visible street

lights from the property. This accommodation is a bit remote, yet not that far from downtown; it is a good place to relax.

The **Courtyard by Marriott** (120 S. Vine, 805/239-9700, www.courtyardpasorobles.com, $200–230 d) has 130 rooms, with an on-site restaurant and fitness center. One of the newer hotels to be built in Paso, it has great views of the city from the top floors. It's not in downtown, but it is within walking distance to the Woodland Shopping Mall. They have a 24-hour business center and outdoor heated pool and hot tub, as well as same-day laundry service and large in-room flat-screen TVs. The rooms are a bit small, but the suites are more spacious. Since you're on the west side of the freeway, it offers faster access to the Westside wineries and the coast.

$300-400

(Hotel Cheval (1021 Pine St., 805/226-9995, www.hotelcheval.com, $300–450 d) is hands down the nicest place to stay in Paso Robles. There are 16 large rooms with wood-burning fireplaces and private balconies or patios, depending on which floor you are on. The interior courtyard is hewn stone with fireplaces for an intimate setting and umbrellas to shield the heat. You're close enough to walk to the City Park, shopping, restaurants, and downtown wineries, and they have a horse-drawn carriage to take you about if you don't feel like walking. It's a classy place with service to match, and their bathrooms and showers are quite large. A continental breakfast is served to your room and there's in-room free Wi-Fi and CD/mp3 players, plus a complimentary morning paper. This is one of those pampered getaways that's plush enough you just don't want to leave.

At the **La Bellasera Hotel and Suites** (206 Alexa Ct., 805/238-2834, www.labellasera .com, $199–399 d), many of the rooms start at over 400 square feet, so space is not even an issue. The 60 rooms, some with whirlpool tubs, are all nicely appointed and comfortable, with a hint of an Italian theme running throughout. The place doesn't feel large and that's part of its success—that and the exceptional attention to service. There's a pool, a fitness room, an on-site restaurant, and free Wi-Fi, and you're right at Highway 46 for easy winery or coastal access.

FOOD
Breakfast and Bakeries

If you want a filling, tasty meal that's not complex, try **House of Bagels** (630 1st St., 805/237-1818, www.centralcoastbagels.com, Mon.–Fri. 6:30 A.M.–3:30 P.M., Sat. 7 A.M.–3 P.M., Sun. 7 A.M.–2 P.M., $6). The beauty of a bagel sandwich is the large selection of bagels to choose from: whole wheat, plain, sesame seed, and plenty of others. They add turkey for lunch, or egg and ham for breakfast. The service is quick and efficient, and this is a great to-go stop, right off Highway 101 where Spring Street exits, so you can grab and go. They do have a few tables inside and a few outside should you decide to stay.

Across Highway 101 is **Cider Creek Bakery** (205 Oak Hill Rd., 805/238-4144, Mon.–Fri. 7 A.M.–6 P.M., Sat.–Sun. 7 A.M.–3 P.M., $6), which started out as a small bakery on the Westside of Paso Robles. Then they started making wine—just one wine actually, a zinfandel. Then they expanded to the Eastside and added sandwiches and soups. But it's still a bakery at heart, and their store is packed with muffins, cookies, breads, pastries, and the best snickerdoodles in town. They also have their own line of preserves like peach amaretto and plum butter, and make their own salsas. There are a few tables inside for when that heady sugar rush makes you weak in the knees.

American

When you enter the **Good Times Café** (1104 Pine St., 805/238-3288, Sun.–Thurs. 11 A.M.–8 P.M., Fri.–Sat. 11 A.M.–9:30 P.M., $10), you walk into the 1950s. Photos of Elvis, James Dean, old license plates, and 45s cover the walls, and music from the 1950s and 1960s fills the air. They serve milk shakes and cook up old-fashioned burgers like the Duke, with bacon, onion rings, and melted cheese and

slathered with barbecue sauce, which is no frills but very satisfying.

The Grill at Hunter Ranch (4041 E. Hwy. 46, 805/237-7440, daily 7 A.M.–4 P.M., $12) has great views to the Hunter Ranch golf course, set in a beautiful Craftsman-style restaurant with ample outdoor seating. The food here is basic grilled food, perfect whether you golf or not. Their BLT is a great choice for lunch, as is the chicken-fried steak for breakfast. Pleasant and away from the rush of most restaurants, it's a nice deviation from the norm.

◖ McPhee's Grill (416 S. Main St., Templeton, 805/434-3204, www.mcphees.com, daily 11:30 A.M.–2 P.M. and 5 P.M.– close, $20) is consistently rated as one of the top restaurants in the area, and Ian McPhee has created a true dining destination in little Templeton. Locals love it, tourists keep coming back for more, and the food and service have not suffered because of it. Best known for their Kobe beef burger, duck and cheese quesadilla, and spicy Kung Fu ribs, the modest tavern exceeds expectations in its upscale yet rustic ambience with wood-paneled walls.

Artisanal Cheeses

Vivant Fine Cheese (840 11th St., 805/226-5530, www.vivantfinecheese.com, Sun.–Thurs. 11 A.M.–5 P.M., Fri.–Sat. 11 A.M.–7 P.M., $11) does offer a few sandwiches and flatbread pizza, as well as an organic soup each day, with produce farmed at Cal Poly. But it's the cheese that brings people here. There are local artisanal cheeses made in Paso Robles, like Rinconada Dairy, as well as cheese from places across the globe such as France, Spain, and Italy. This tiny spot smells absolutely heady as you walk in. They offer large and small cheese plates that include delectable Marcona almonds and other items. They are right off the City Park, so you don't have to go too far.

Pizza

It's all about the pie at long-standing pizza joint **Marv's** (729 12th St., 805/238-1851, daily 11 A.M.–9 P.M., $15). Located just across from the City Park, they turn out excellent

THE NEW GOLD: PASO ROBLES OLIVE OIL

In 1849 the gold rush brought thousands of people to California. These days, wine has replaced gold nuggets to draw people in. But there is a new gold that is actually close to gold in color – olive oil – and Paso Robles has become a huge producer of estate olive oils. As the Franciscans marched north establishing missions in California in the late 1700s, they also planted olive groves. Southern California probably saw the very first olive trees at Mission San Fernando. The olive is native to Asia Minor and spread from Iran, Syria, and Palestine to the rest of the Mediterranean basin about 6,000 years ago. It is among the oldest known cultivated trees in the world. It was being grown on Crete by 3,000 B.C. and the Phoenicians spread the olive to the Mediterranean shores of Africa and Southern Europe. Olives have been found in Egyptian tombs from 2,000 B.C. The olive culture was spread to the early Greeks then Romans. As the Romans extended their domain they brought the olive with them. These days local wineries like **Laraneta, Carmody McKnight, Jada,** and **Halter Ranch** are turning out small batches of olive oil along with dedicated producers like **Pasolivo,** who has its own press. The gold is still in the hills, only now it's hanging from the trees.

traditional crust pizzas like their vegetarian, or meat combination, both of which are loaded with toppings. The interior is exactly what you'd expect a pizza place to be, basic and utilitarian with TVs bolted to the walls and clunky furniture as well as a few arcade games. If you're staying locally, they will deliver to your hotel room.

Organic and Local
◀ **Artisan** (1401 Park St., 805/237-8084, www.artisanpasorobles.com, Sun. brunch 10 A.M.–2:30 P.M., lunch Mon.–Sat. 11 A.M.–2:30 P.M., dinner Sun.–Thurs. 5–9 P.M., Fri.–Sat. 5–10 P.M., $28) showcases locally grown organic produce and foods that are seasonally grown, wild caught, or sustainably farmed, with no growth hormones or antibiotics. That's been part of their success. The other part is that they serve excellent food. You'll find organic chicken, Arctic char, lamb, and Hearst Ranch grass-fed beef, all artfully prepared and executed. This is a destination restaurant for most visitors to the area, and it does Paso Robles proud. The feel is upscale with its white linens, but still comfortable and not pretentious. It's also immensely crowded, so make reservations.

Villa Creek (1144 Pine St., 805/238-3000, www.villacreek.com, nightly 5:30–10 P.M., $20) excels with natural and organic ingredients in their dishes, be that their butternut squash enchilada or their poblano chile stuffed with oxtail. They have an extensive wine list and separate bar area, and when the windows are opened to the City Park it has an expansive feel. There's a small back patio for something a little more intimate.

Eclectic
Berry Hill Bistro (1114 Pine St., 805/238-3929, Sun.–Thurs. 11 A.M.–8:30 P.M., Fri.–Sat. 11 A.M.–9:30 P.M., $15) is located right off the City Park. This friendly spot is Mediterranean in its feel with mottled walls, colorful accents, and plants, and it gets loud when crowded. But the food shines, and their seasonal menu has dishes like raspberry chipotle chicken panini and crab wontons. There are a few outdoor seats, prime in summer, when you can watch everyone in the park.

INFORMATION AND SERVICES
A visit to the **Paso Robles Visitor's Center** (1225 Park St., 805/238-0506, Mon.–Fri. 8:30 A.M.–5 P.M., Sat.–Sun. 10 A.M.–2 P.M.) will provide you with all the necessary materials to make your stay perfect.

In case of **emergency,** call 911 immediately.

Twin Cities Community Hospital (1100 Las Tablas Rd., Templeton, 805/434-3500) is the nearest hospital to Paso. The **Paso Robles Police Department** is located right downtown at 1220 Paso Robles Street (805/237-6464).

GETTING THERE AND AROUND

Paso Robles is directly off Highway 101 as you traverse a north–south route. Additionally, from the central valley (Fresno and Bakersfield), Paso Robles is accessed via Highway 46, which leads directly into the city. It's a two-lane road with a few passing lanes; if you get stuck behind a camper, RV, or someone towing a boat, which is very common, simply enjoy the ride and pass when it's safe to do so.

Amtrak's Coast Starliner makes northbound and southbound stops at 800 Pine Street, but only two stops daily. There are no ticket sales here; you'll need to buy in advance from Amtrak (800/872-7245, www.amtrak.com).

Paso Robles Cab (805/237-2615) has rates at about $3 per pickup and $2 per mile.

Amtrak's Coast Starliner makes northbound and southbound stops at 800 Pine Street, but only two stops daily. There are no ticket sales here; you'll need to buy in advance from Amtrak (800/872-7245, www.amtrak.com).

The City of Paso Robles is the official agent for the Greyhound depot (805/238-1242, www.greyhound.com), which is located within the Transit Center Facility at 800 Pine Street along with other modes of transportation. Greyhound operates Monday–Saturday 8:30 A.M.–4:30 P.M.

The local bus, the **Paso Express** (805/239-8747, www.pasoexpress.com), is a fixed-route bus operating along designated routes within the city. It's available to the general public and provides low-cost transportation. Paso Express can be picked up at any designated bus stop in the city and the buses are lift equipped to serve those with disabilities; they also feature bicycle racks. Then there is **Dial-A-Ride** (805/239-8747, www.pasoexpress.com), an on-demand public transit service that provides curb-to-curb service anywhere within city limits. These too are lift equipped. One-way fares for both buses are $1.50, but they offer a variety of passes that will save money in the long run.

The Wine Line (805/610-8267, www.hoponthewineline.com) is one of the few companies to offer a hop on, hop off option. For about $50 they'll pick you up at your hotel, then you can use three vans that operate on essentially a figure-eight route between downtown and both east and west wineries, running about every 40 minutes. They provide water and small bags of chips; you'll need to get more substantial food on your own. This is not a tour, but merely a shuttle service operating to and from some of the wineries. The best part? At the end of the day, they'll drop you back at your hotel.

Breakaway Tours (179 Nibblick Rd., 800/799-7657, www.breakaway-tours.com), on the other hand, is a full-service operation that will cover wine-tasting, basic ground transportation, airport shuttle, groups—virtually anything. They'll even head all the way down to Los Angeles to get you from the airport. They've been operating for 15 years and know the area well. They're happy to customize a day or weekend event for you. Frankly, anything you throw at them they can handle. They also operate out of San Luis Obispo and Santa Barbara.

Amtrak's Coast Starliner makes northbound and southbound stops at 800 Pine Street, but only two stops daily. There are no ticket sales here; you'll need to buy in advance from Amtrak (800/872-7245, www.amtrak.com).

The **Paso Robles Airport** (4912 Wing Way, 805/237-3877, www.prcity.com) sits just on the outskirts of town. There is no scheduled commercial airline service at Paso Robles, but there are charter services available.

SANTA BARBARA WINE COUNTRY

Santa Barbara's laid-back vibe, inspired by endless waves and eternal sunshine, is complemented by great shopping and recreational opportunities, world-class wine-tasting, and breathtaking Spanish architecture. The city has been referred to as "America's Riviera"—and with good reason. It has an enviable setting, nestled between the Pacific Ocean and the mountains, and incredible views of both—plus fantastic weather. It's an idyllic spot—so much so that if you stay long enough, you probably won't want to leave.

Santa Barbara inspires physical activity and healthy living: With copious sunshine, wide roads, lots of warm sandy beaches, and challenging mountain trails, it's the kind of environment where getting outside is so easy that simply being in Santa Barbara is equated with being out-of-doors. There are no excuses not to walk, jog, hike, surf, run, bike, dive, or play. Surfing is a favorite activity here, with eager surfers dotting most of the coastline. And along the waterfront, a paved path allows anyone on two feet, two wheels, or anything else that moves to enjoy the coastline alongside grassy areas with palm trees gently tottering in the breeze. At least five farmers markets held every week make healthy produce abundant and accessible to all residents.

To both residents and visitors, Santa Barbara seems almost like a dream. Its natural beauty and great weather, plus stunning geography, creative restaurants, local culture, rich history, a thriving wine industry, and unique festivals, all bookended by the mountains and ocean, make this prime spot enviable beyond belief.

HIGHLIGHTS

(**The Santa Barbara County Courthouse:** This building offers the definitive Santa Barbara experience, with Spanish and Moorish architecture, California history, and views of the city, mountains, oceans, and islands from a stunning building rightly called the most beautiful public building in America (page 500).

(**Old Mission Santa Barbara:** Known as the Queen of the California missions, this intricately painted church has some of the most lush grounds and landscaping of any mission, making it a routine stopping point (page 504).

(**Lotusland:** The sheer diversity and immaculate arrangement of the plants, trees, and every other form of flora and fauna at this estate creates a botanical wonderland (page 506).

(**Casa del Herrero:** This 11-acre estate is an incredible example of Spanish Colonial Revival architecture from the early 20th century. The building is in its original pristine condition, with mesmerizing interior detail (page 506).

(**Knapp's Castle:** A magnificent 1920s seven-building estate burned to the ground, leaving only forlorn stone outcroppings above the Santa Ynez Valley. The stark beauty compels locals, tourists, and photographers to visit and imagine what once was (page 507).

(**Leadbetter Beach:** There's no better beach in all of Santa Barbara. Others are larger, but this cove-like beach, flanked by a point and the harbor, has everything you could want, including great views (page 508).

(**Solvang:** Long before thematic towns came into vogue, the town of Solvang decided to stay true to its Danish heritage. With Danish bakeries and restaurants, a Danish history museum, and excellent wineries, Solvang is completely unlike any other town on the Central Coast (page 546).

(**Beckmen Vineyards:** Having set the standard for sustainable farming using biodynamic methods, Beckmen Vineyards is one of those places where not only are the wines terrific, but the planet is better off for it (page 559).

(**Foxen Canyon:** Whether you drive with the top down or ride your bike, Santa Barbara wine country has beautiful scenic back roads. Foxen Canyon Road, beginning in Los Olivos and ending in Santa Maria, is one of the most popular routes, passing rolling hills, farms, and vineyards (page 561).

(**Flying Goat Cellars:** Pinot noir lovers should not miss a chance to taste the seductive wines at this simple, industrial-like tasting room, where the dedication and focus on the grape is evident in each sip (page 565).

(**Kenneth Volk Vineyards:** Taste award-winning wines, with a focus on chardonnay, pinot noir, and "heirloom" varietals, on 12 acres of serene land along the Tepusquet Creek (page 569).

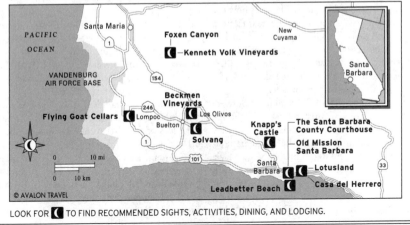

LOOK FOR (TO FIND RECOMMENDED SIGHTS, ACTIVITIES, DINING, AND LODGING.

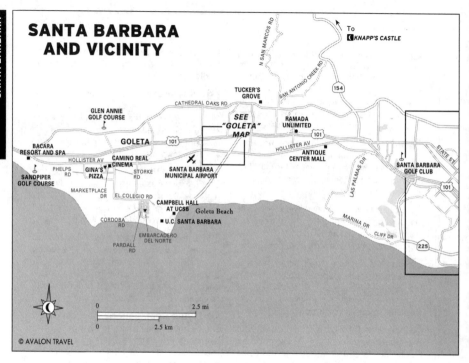

PLANNING YOUR TIME

Santa Barbara is fairly compact and can easily be enjoyed in a weekend, but to fully explore the city you'll need at least three or four days, especially if you want to enjoy water activities, hiking, or cycling. If you're the meandering type, the waterfront and State Street will suit you fine and can be explored in a weekend.

At the heart of Santa Barbara's wine country are the towns of Santa Ynez, Los Olivos, Solvang, and Santa Maria. Santa Ynez has always been a laid-back horse and farming community, unaffected by time. That it is now the gateway to the wine region does not detract from its agrarian roots. Los Olivos is an artist's enclave and a wine taster's dream. Unpretentious and simple, it's a perfect one-day getaway—unless you also use it as a base to explore Lake Cachuma, Figueroa Mountain, or the broader wine region, in which case you'll need several days. Solvang started in 1911 as a Danish retreat. It is still ripe with Scandinavian heritage as well as a new modern sensibility, though the theme park atmosphere is not lacking in kitsch. Santa Maria is the workhorse of the agricultural area within Santa Barbara County. Its wineries that produce some of the top-scoring and top-selling wine in the country, and the Santa Maria Valley Strawberry Festival.

The ideal time to visit is from March to May, when everything is pristine after the mild winter rains. The temperatures are still moderate, the views are crystal clear, and the air is fresh and crisp. The June gloom kicks off summer, with lots of fog that sometimes doesn't burn off until early afternoon. October through December is also a great time. There are more chances of rain then, but it's not unusual to be able to spend Thanksgiving weekend at the beach, playing in the water and burning off all those calories.

The city's grid layout makes sightseeing

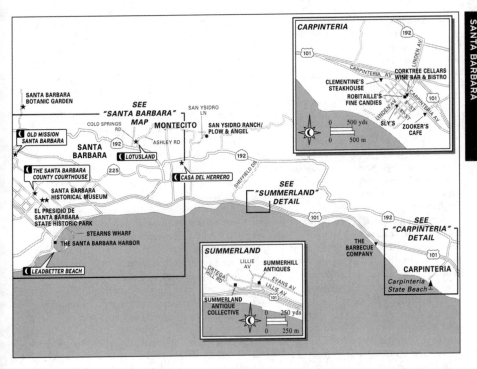

easy; the majority of sights are within 12 blocks downtown, so walking is often preferable to constantly having to find parking. If you are an early riser, it's recommended to get to sights when they first open in order to avoid crowds. Everything gets progressively more crowded as the day wears on, but the early mornings, and even as late as 10–11 A.M., are reasonably crowd free. Many visitors stay downtown or by the waterfront, and the city is an easy base for the sights you'll need to drive to, such as the mission, Montecito, and Carpinteria. Even the Santa Ynez Valley is only a 30-to-40-minute drive, and is a great day trip.

Santa Ynez and Los Olivos can both easily be visited within a day from Santa Barbara. Solvang is a five-minute drive from Santa Ynez and Los Olivos, but it is suggested that visitors reserve an entire day for this town. Santa Maria is a 15-minute drive north of Solvang, and because it has a lot more outdoor recreational opportunities, it is best to reserve an entire day for a visit to this area as well. In a weekend, you can get a feel for all of the towns in the Santa Barbara Wine Country, but as always, more time is necessary if you want to really explore these areas in depth.

If you head to the valley for the day, drive up via the San Marcos Pass (Highway 154) over the mountains and return to the city via Highway 101 along the coast, or vice versa. That way you get the best of everything—mountains with killer views, and lots of ocean and ranch land.

HISTORY

Today we call it wine country, but this vast expanse in Northern Santa Barbara County is really two valleys—the Santa Ynez Valley and the Santa Maria Valley—and they were not originally known for grapes or wines. Santa Maria was originally farmland, and still is, producing strawberries and broccoli, among many other crops. Between 1869 and 1874, four of the valley's prominent settlers were farming on 40 acres of land where their properties met to form a four-square-mile city that became known as Grangerville, centered on Main Street and Broadway today. It was renamed Santa Maria in 1905; it is the agricultural heart and soul of the county.

The Santa Ynez Valley is made up of Solvang, Santa Ynez, and Los Olivos; these towns were formed more out of necessity, as Los Olivos and Santa Ynez were stagecoach and rail stops. In the late 1800s the stagecoach from Santa Barbara stopped twice a day in Santa Ynez at the College Hotel, then proceeded down Edison Street toward the main stagecoach stop at Mattei's Tavern in Los Olivos, which eventually became a railroad stop. Solvang, which means "sunny fields," developed as a settlement for the Danish who migrated to these sunny fields in 1910. The town fathers bought 10,000 acres and the town was created in 1911. The goal was to create a home away from Denmark; the first building was the Lutheran Church, the second building to be built was a Danish folk school, which still stands today as the Bit O' Denmark restaurant.

The Wines

The first documented viticulture in California dates from 1779 at Mission San Gabriel Arcángel in Southern California, and eventually grapes were grown throughout the mission system. The so-called "mission grape," a hybrid of different types, was high in sugar content, low in acid, and produced a thin sweet wine that by many accounts of the times, wasn't all that good. But this grape dominated the industry until the end of California's

Mexican era in the late 1840s. By that time, wine and brandy production was a significant source of income for some of the missions. Mission Santa Barbara established a vineyard and winery around the 1830s. Grapes were used not only to make wine, but also raisins, which were handy food for travelers. But grape production was not limited to the missions. About 1820, San Antonio winery was built in what is now Goleta. The lonely historic adobe winery is still standing nearly 200 years later, though on private property. Another commercial winery, the Packard Winery, was built in 1865, also in Santa Barbara, and in the late 1890s about 200 acres of grapes were being turned into wine on Santa Cruz Island. Near Mission La Purisima grapes were planted in the 1880s as well, and a few of those vines still survive today, though they are now on private property.

When the first commercial grapevine plantings were made after prohibition in the 1960s and 1970s in the Santa Maria Valley, grape growers and vintners planted anything and everything, without regard to the end product. It has taken Santa Barbara nearly 20 years to understand its soil, its climate, and what is best suited for their diverse growing regions and the American Viticultural Area's (AVA) federally recognized grape growing regions. Currently there are 64 different varieties of grapes planted throughout the county on 21,000 acres. Pinot noir and chardonnay are the most widely planted varieties, with chardonnay commanding an astounding 40 percent of that acreage; pinot noir comes in at 25 percent. The wine industry in Santa Barbara County is thriving, in spite of the fluctuations of the economy, transitional markets, fickle consumers, and inconsistent harvests.

Santa Barbara

Most tourists enjoy Santa Barbara's idyllic setting and mellow mood along the city's popular waterfront and State Street, but this city of roughly 120,000 people also offers a wealth of cultural, architectural, and historical treasures. Fiercely proud of its heritage, Santa Barbara has a history that extends back to the Chumash Indians' habitation of the area more than 10,000 years ago. The city is also committed to maintaining a unifying architectural theme of whitewashed authentic adobe and adobe-looking buildings capped with red-tile roofs that stand out against the blue skies—it's no surprise that the National Trust for Historic Preservation named Santa Barbara a Distinctive Destination in 2009. The mission, superb Moorish-influenced county courthouse, historic Spanish and Mexican adobes, and the handsome State Street corridor with its vine-covered walls and mature trees shading brick sidewalks all combine to give you a unique experience among American cities.

Santa Barbara is defined by State Street, the main drag, which runs from the beach through the downtown area. There is only one major artery into and out of Santa Barbara, Highway 101. Aside from the San Marcos Pass (Highway 154), which heads from Santa Barbara over the mountains and into the Santa Ynez Valley, no other roads lead here. This can be a problem every once in a while: Fires can shut down Highway 101, leaving Santa Barbara isolated from its neighbors. If there is a major traffic accident, there simply are no alternate routes.

Aside from that, getting around Santa Barbara is easy, as the city is laid out in a classic grid pattern. State Street does get congested during summer months; unless you enjoy sitting in your car and inching your way along, it's best to use other arteries on the weekends. The first street east of State Street is Anacapa, which runs one way to the ocean. Chapala, the first street west of State Street,

runs one way towards the mountains. These two streets allow for quick travel through the city.

Though State Street is not a lengthy street, the 400–600 blocks have become known as "Lower State" and you will hear people refer to this often.

WINE-TASTING

The wines in Santa Barbara County have been receiving very favorable scores and write-ups in the national press. The area is predominately known for pinot noir and chardonnay, but with so many diverse microclimates, there are over 50 different types of grapes planted here. This means you can find traditional varieties like cabernet sauvignon, merlot, sauvignon blanc, and syrah, but you will also find sangiovese, dolcetto, viognier, cabernet franc, malbec, and many others.

Not all wine-tasting is done surrounded by vineyards. On the Urban Wine Trail (www .urbanwinetrailsb.com) you can sample some of the county's best wines without even seeing a vine. Near Lower State Street, a block from the beach, you can walk to six tasting rooms. Visiting others that are part of the trail will require a little driving. Recently passed legislation means that some, but not all, wineries now offer wines by the glass in addition to wine-tasting, so if you sample something you like, you can purchase a glass to enjoy on the spot or a bottle to take with you.

KALYRA WINERY

Kalyra Winery (212 State St., 805/965-8606, www.kalyrawinery.com, daily noon–7 P.M.) is famous for having been featured in the movie *Sideways*. This tasting room, their second, wasn't in the film, but you can still sample their California and Australian wines made by Mike Brown, an avid surfer and Aussie. There's a tribal feel to the interior, with a thatched roof over the tasting bar, and the vibe is relaxed. They started out making sweet wines, of which

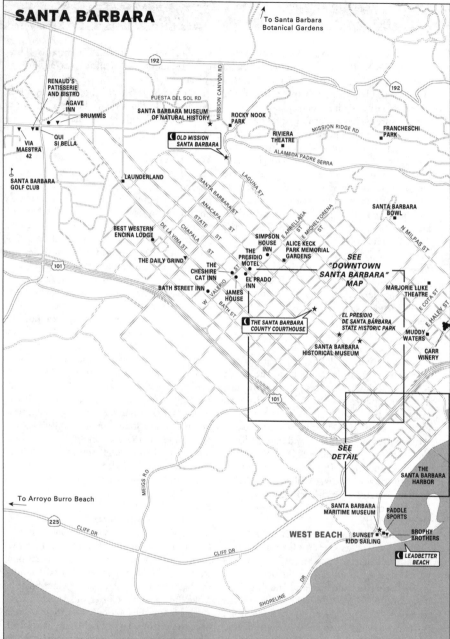

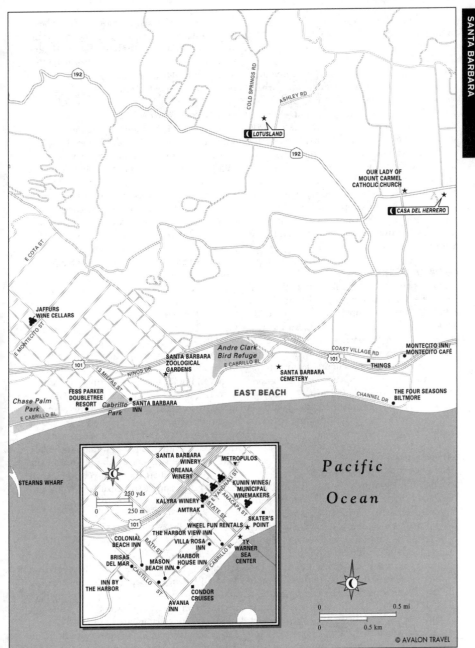

© AVALON TRAVEL

they still offer quite a few, but Kalyra has a broad portfolio.

SANTA BARBARA WINERY

Once you're done at Kalyra Winery, walk a block down Yannonali Street to Santa Barbara Winery (202 Anacapa St., 805/963-3633, www.sbwinery.com, daily 10 A.M.–5 P.M.), which is the oldest winery in the county, started in 1962. Their chardonnay is delightful and truly expresses a Santa Barbara character with its bright citrus notes. They produce a lot of wine in varieties including pinot noir, sangiovese, sauvignon blanc, and many others. If you are looking to sample a diverse array of wines, this is your best stop. The tasting bar is just a few feet from the barrel room, and there's a good-sized gift shop too.

OREANA WINERY

Across the street from Santa Barbara Winery is Oreana Winery (205 Anacapa St., 805/962-5857, www.oreanawinery.com, daily 11 A.M.–5 P.M., tasting fee $10), an old tire store converted for use as a winery. The interior retains its warehouse feel with a tasting bar up front and the production facility in the back. You'll find syrah, cabernet sauvignon, chardonnay, verdelho, and others. Many of the wines are priced under $20. It's a laid-back vibe here, with lots of light coming in and a friendly staff.

KUNIN WINES
AND WESTERLY VINEYARDS

Another block towards the beach you'll find the shared space of Kunin Wines and Westerly Vineyards (28 Anacapa St., 805/963-9696, www.kuninwines.com and www.westerly wineyards.com, daily 11 A.M.–6 P.M., Kunin tasting fee $10, Westerly tasting fee $8). Seth Kunin, a surfer, styles his wines after the Rhône Valley varieties from southern France, like syrah and viognier. The tasting room, a sleek interior with a minimalist approach, is a small space within eyesight of the beach; it can get crowded on summer days—and for good reason. His wines are smooth and very

drinkable, and it's easy to enjoy your time here. The Westerly lineup consists of merlot, syrah, and sauvignon blanc. The beauty of this double whammy is that you can get a very good understanding of Santa Barbara wines as you visit two wineries in one place.

MUNICIPAL WINEMAKERS

Located just behind Kunin Wines and Westerly Vineyards is the newest addition to the scene, Municipal Winemakers (28 Anacapa St., 805/931-6864, www.municipalwinemakers .com, Sat.–Sun. 11 A.M.–6 P.M., tasting fee $10), in an unpretentious small space with an even smaller deck. The inside is all rough wood ceilings and plain walls, with a four-top table and standing room at the bar. This is a weekend venture for owner Dave Potter, who will be there to answer your questions and pour his wines. The offerings are Rhône wines including grenache, syrah, and a sparkling shiraz.

CARR WINERY

Carr Winery (414 N. Salsipuedes St., 805/965-7985, www.carrwinery.com, daily 11 A.M.–5 P.M., tasting fee $10) has a focus on small lots of syrah, grenache, cabernet franc, and pinot noir. The tasting room is in a WWII Quonset hut, with a bar up front and tables in the back. Thursday–Saturday 5 P.M.–midnight they open their wine bar, which features live music and appetizers and wines by the glass. It's run by another surfer-winemaker, and you'll see surfboards placed around the tasting room. There's a much younger crowd here, eager to sample some excellent wines and enjoy life.

JAFFURS WINE CELLARS

Craig Jaffurs of Jaffurs Wine Cellars (819 E. Montecito St., 805/962-7003, www.jaffurs wine.com, Fri.–Mon. 11 A.M.–5 P.M., tasting fee $10) has been an avid surfer for decades, and he equates wine to surfing. "The joy I get surfing is the same joy I get walking through a vineyard, or tasting barrel samples," he says. His seven different syrah and petite sirah are excellent, and his downtown location is all

more than enough places to grab a bite, get more cash at a bank, or step inside a store to find something of interest. There are even plenty of combination trash cans and recycle bins (the dark green ones). What are lacking, however, are restrooms. Surprisingly, there is only one public facility (914 State St., next to Borders), and many businesses will not allow non-customers to use theirs.

EL PRESIDIO DE SANTA BÁRBARA STATE HISTORIC PARK

El Presidio de Santa Bárbara State Historic Park (123 E. Canon Perdido St., 805/965-0093, www.sbthp.org, daily 10:30 A.M.–4:30 P.M., closed major holidays, $5 adults, $4 seniors, admission includes Casa de la Guerra) can rightfully be called the birthplace of Santa Barbara. The presidio, as it's referred to, was founded on April 21, 1782, and was the last in a chain of four military fortresses built by the Spanish along the coast of California. The whitewashed buildings were constructed of sun-dried adobe bricks laid upon foundations of sandstone boulders. Timbers from the Los Padres forest supported roofs of red tile. The buildings of the presidio form a quadrangle enclosing a central parade ground, and the whole structure is surrounded by an outer defense wall with two cannon bastions. The most prominent building was and still is the chapel, Santa Barbara's first church for its townspeople (the Christianized Chumash Indian population worshipped at the mission). Today, only two sections of the original presidio quadrangle remain, and both are within the state park: El Cuartel, the family residence of the soldier assigned to guard the western gate into the Plaza de Armas, and the Canedo Adobe, named after the presidio soldier to whom it was deeded when the presidio became inactive.

Though much has been reconstructed at the presidio, El Cuartel (the second oldest building in California, dating from 1782), right across the street from the chapel, is a great example of living architecture; it's the type of historic building that can be accessed by the public, touched, and experienced. The massively thick

© MELISSA FARGO
Jaffur Wine Cellars

by itself on a small street. Once the doors are rolled up, the public comes in eagerly to taste beautiful wines.

WINE CASK TASTING ROOM

The Wine Cask Tasting Room (813 Anacapa St., 805/966-9463, www.winecask.com, daily noon–6 P.M., tasting fee $12) is a consortium of sorts. It used to be a wine shop and now hosts wine-tastings each day. The various winemakers are all producers who make small amounts of wine and who may not have their own tasting room. It's an eclectic offering, featuring the wine of Doug Margerum, the co-owner of the Wine Cask, who makes wines under his own name as well as consults for many smaller producers in the area. These tend to be whites like sauvignon blanc and high-end reds like cabernet sauvignon, merlot, and syrah.

SIGHTS
Downtown

Downtown Santa Barbara covers about 12 blocks. It is a pedestrian-friendly area with

BUILDING A BETTER BRICK: ADOBE CONSTRUCTION

Santa Barbara's early Spanish settlers found a landscape devoid of trees, where lumber was almost non-existent–hard to believe considering the incredible population of trees in the area today. The settlers' answer for building the new town was the very earth beneath their feet. They made adobe bricks by digging a pit, into which clay-like soil and water were added. Once the mixture was smooth, straw and sand were added to bind and strengthen the adobe.

Obtaining the correct proportions of soil, water, straw, and sand was crucial to prevent the bricks from crumbling. The mixture was poured into wooden forms to create bricks, then set aside to dry in the sun. Depending on the size of the bricks, which averaged 50–60 pounds, they could take as many as 30 days to thoroughly dry. As many as 5,000 bricks would typically be used to create even a modest one-room structure. Adobe walls were thick by modern standards, usually about two feet for smaller buildings. To give the walls greater strength they were covered with a coating of sand and mud. The walls were then sealed with a plaster made of lime mixed with sand and water. As the mixture dried it hardened, forming a protective coating. The finished adobe was cool in the summer, warm in the winter, and proved to be quite durable.

Santa Barbara's historic adobes have survived most of the earthquakes over the last 200 years. But the influx of Americans predominately from the east coast to Santa Barbara after 1850 caused a decline in the popularity of adobe construction, as the new residents wanted houses that reminded them of their wood-framed homes they had recently abandoned. In some cases the adobe structures were covered with wood siding, or they were simply torn down. There are some 300 adobe structures still standing in the county, proving that the original construction methods were sound.

walls still stand as they have for more than two hundred years, with only cosmetic touch-ups to the plaster that covers the original adobe bricks. El Cuartel is small, with tiny doors and windows reflective of the time, but it's awesome to stand in the spot where Santa Barbara was first formed, and feel the connection to history. The presidio is just a block off State Street downtown and can easily be worked into your downtown sightseeing plans.

SANTA BARBARA HISTORICAL MUSEUM

The Santa Barbara Historical Museum (136 E. De La Guerra, 805/966-1601, www.santabarbara museum.com, Tues.–Sat. 10 A.M.–5 P.M., Sun. noon–5 P.M., free, donations accepted) houses a beautiful and comprehensive collection of historical artifacts covering the last 600 years of local history, including an 1813 Peruvian mission bell, a three-foot tall hand-painted wood carving of Saint Barbara, and an exquisitely carved ornate 15-foot Tong shrine from the days when Santa Barbara had a thriving Chinatown. There are also Chumash, Spanish, and Mexican period garments on display, as well as guns, swords, and working tools.

The entry foyer hosts rotating exhibits that feature anything from important local artists to designer Kem Weber's industrial work and furnishings from his time spent teaching art and design in Santa Barbara at a his own small studio. The museum, which also has a small gift store, is one of the great jewels of the city, and a visit is nearly mandatory for anyone who desires an understanding of the multilayered history of this area.

CASA DE LA GUERRA

Casa de la Guerra (15 E. De La Guerra St., 805/965-0093, www.sbthp.org, Sat.–Sun. noon–4 P.M., $5 adults, $4 seniors, includes admission to Presidio) has been at the heart of Santa Barbara's history since its construction

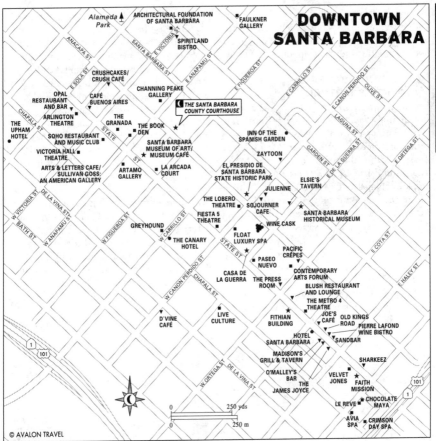

DOWNTOWN SANTA BARBARA

Alameda Park

ARCHITECTURAL FOUNDATION OF SANTA BARBARA

FAULKNER GALLERY

SPIRITLAND BISTRO

CRUSHCAKES/ CRUSH CAFÉ

CHANNING PEAKE GALLERY

OPAL RESTAURANT AND BAR

CAFÉ BUENOS AIRES

THE SANTA BARBARA COUNTY COURTHOUSE

ARLINGTON THEATRE

THE GRANADA

THE BOOK DEN

THE UPHAM HOTEL

SOHO RESTAURANT AND MUSIC CLUB

SANTA BARBARA MUSEUM OF ART/ MUSEUM CAFÉ

INN OF THE SPANISH GARDEN

ZAYTOON

VICTORIA HALL THEATRE

ARTS & LETTERS CAFE/ SULLIVAN-GOSS: AN AMERICAN GALLERY

ARTAMO GALLERY

LA ARCADA COURT

EL PRESIDIO DE SANTA BARBARA STATE HISTORIC PARK

ELSIE'S TAVERN

JULIENNE

THE LOBERO THEATRE

SOJOURNER CAFÉ

SANTA BARBARA HISTORICAL MUSEUM

FIESTA 5 THEATRE

GREYHOUND

WINE CASK

THE CANARY HOTEL

FLOAT LUXURY SPA

PASEO NUEVO

PACIFIC CRÊPES

CASA DE LA GUERRA

THE PRESS ROOM

CONTEMPORARY ARTS FORUM

BLUSH RESTAURANT AND LOUNGE

THE METRO 4 THEATRE

D'VINE CAFÉ

LIVE CULTURE

FITHIAN BUILDING

JOE'S CAFÉ

OLD KINGS ROAD

PIERRE LAFOND WINE BISTRO

HOTEL SANTA BARBARA

SANDBAR

MADISON'S GRILL & TAVERN

O'MALLEY'S BAR

THE JAMES JOYCE

VELVET JONES

FAITH MISSION

SHARKEEZ

LE REVE

CHOCOLATE MAYA

AVIA SPA

CRIMSON DAY SPA

0   250 yds
0   250 m

© AVALON TRAVEL

1819–1827 by the fifth presidio commandant, Don Jose de la Guerra. Among Santa Barbara's wealthiest and most influential citizens, the Spanish-born commandant stood out as the patriarchal figure to whom the entire community looked for protection and assistance. Casa de la Guerra was the social, political, and cultural center of the pueblo of Santa Barbara. That legacy survived with the political activity of de la Guerra's son, Pablo, during the early years of California's statehood. Don Pablo served as a state senator and as lieutenant governor of the state; prior to statehood he was a local judge. In 1874 the first city hall was constructed opposite the Casa in Plaza de la Guerra. In 1922 El Paseo was designed and built around the Casa. When the first Old Spanish Days Fiesta was held in 1924, parties, dances, and teas in honor of the members of the early families were held at Casa de la Guerra in the large courtyard where you can walk today. Following the devastating 1925 earthquake, the Casa and El Paseo served as models for rebuilding parts of downtown. It may seem a simple structure, but it serves as a reminder of the vast importance of Santa Barbara's heritage. A visit lets you see the rooms that were, at the time, some of the nicest and most ornate around, though by today's standards they seem a little crude. Unless you're a history buff, a self-guided tour of the site is sufficient, though they do offer hour-long guided tours by appointment only.

◖ THE SANTA BARBARA COUNTY COURTHOUSE

Covering an entire city block, the still-functioning Santa Barbara County Courthouse (1100 Anacapa St., 805/962-6464, www.sb courts.org, free docent-led tours Mon.–Sat. at 2 P.M., additional free docent-led tours Mon., Tues., and Fri. at 10:30 A.M.) is a stunning example of Spanish and Moorish design. William Mooser designed this courthouse to replace the earlier 1872 version, a colonial-looking thing with a massive domed cupola. When the courthouse was completed in 1929, it was unlike anything in the city. Lush grounds including the copious lawn and Sunken Gardens lay the foundation for the sandstone building with arabesque windows, archways, hand-painted wood ceilings, walls with intricate designs, and pueblo tile inlays nearly everywhere flashing brilliant colors and native designs. Of particular note is the Mural Room, once used by the county board of supervisors. The huge room is covered in a mural depicting the early Chumash Indians and following the history of the area leading up to California statehood. All tours of the building meet in the Mural Room and are approximately one hour.

The clock tower, known as **El Mirador,** juts out of the top of the courthouse, making it one of the tallest structures in the city, though the tower is a mere 85 feet tall. But it is here that you'll get the best views of downtown, the mountains, and the ocean from a downtown perspective—it's a must for photo ops. Take the elevator to the 4th floor. Once there, a dozen steps lead up and out to the platform. You'll be thrilled at the red-tile roofs splayed out in front of you on the nearby buildings. There are placards describing points of interest in each direction so you can easily get your bearings. You don't need the formal tour to appreciate the sheer beauty and craftsmanship of the building, but it will give you more specific

the Spanish-Moorish architecture of the Santa Barbara County Courthouse

information. Ironically, the courthouse doesn't meet the county's current building codes and standards, and could never be approved for construction today.

SANTA BARBARA MUSEUM OF ART

See the power of the visual arts at the Santa Barbara Museum of Art (1130 State St., 805/963-4364, www.sbmuseart.org, Tues.–Sun. 11 A.M.–5 P.M., $9 adults, $6 seniors and students, free children under 6, free Sun.). Santa Barbara has one of the most impressive art museums and best collections for a community of its size. Two stories of rotating exhibits always keep the public intrigued; the museum showcases abstract, post-modern, and much more in a large diversity of media, from print to photography. Of particular note is their collection of Asian art. At the museum's inception in 1941, 19 Chinese robes were donated to the museum, which encouraged the donation of more Asian works. Today the Asian collection consists of over 2,600 objects spanning a period of 4,000 years, including 19th-century Japanese woodblock prints. Admission is free to everyone on Sunday, though a donation is suggested.

Oceanfront

Santa Barbara's oceanfront is defined by Cabrillo Boulevard, which follows the shore line and includes Stearns Wharf and the harbor. With the exception of the wharf and harbor there are no business or shops on the beach side of the street. This undeveloped sandy, grassy area lined with palm trees has helped to create an idyllic setting that people find intoxicating and typically Californian. On clear days the islands hug the horizon and the sounds of the crashing surf, the gulls, and people milling about create a relaxing experience.

This four-mile stretch incorporates Stearns Wharf, the harbor, hotels, and shops; the concrete bike path stretches past a number of beaches and is the main access route to the area besides Cabrillo Boulevard. Rent a bike, a tandem bike, or a four-person surrey at **Wheel Fun Rentals** (23 E. Cabrillo Blvd., 805/966-2282, www.wheelfunrentalssb.com, daily

© JAY SINCLAIR

Santa Barbara Museum of Art

SANTA BARBARA

8 A.M.–8 P.M., $8–35 per hour depending on vehicle) and meander the path from Leadbetter Beach at the west end to the zoo in the east. It's actually a lot of fun, even though the surreys seem to have a mind of their own and steering is sometimes challenging. Or use the path as many other people do to stroll, run, or in-line skate while basking in the sunshine.

STEARNS WHARF

Stearns Wharf (intersection of State St. and Cabrillo Blvd., www.stearnswharf.org, parking $2.50/hr, first 90 mins free with validation) is Santa Barbara's most visited landmark. Santa Barbara has no natural harbor and the shifting sands prohibited large ships from docking here; the wharf was built in 1871 to allow ships to off-load supplies for the bourgeoning town. The wharf, which used to extend much further into

the ocean than it does currently, has burned completely twice and has been destroyed by storms. The current iteration, scaled back in size, is a favorite for tourists. Frankly, there are a lot of typical tourist shops selling seashells, small personalized license plates, and gift items you can find most anywhere, which has nothing to do with Santa Barbara in the least, but if you walk to the end you get some of the best views back to the city. There are no railings at the end of the wharf, so keep an eye on little ones.

In addition to the views, there are a few restaurants, an ice cream store, and the **Ty Warner Sea Center** (211 Stearns Wharf, 805/962-2526, www.sbnature.org, daily 10 A.M.–5 P.M., $8 adults, $7 seniors and teens 13–17, $5 children 2–12), which is a two-story building devoted to giving you a better understanding of how our oceans work. When you first enter you'll

---

SANTA BARBARA: AN ARCHITECT'S CANVAS

It's no wonder that many prominent architects have used Santa Barbara's stunningly beautiful topography as a backdrop for their own inspired creations. Julia Morgan, best known as the sanity behind Hearst Castle, designed several buildings in town, two of which survive today. Her first commission was for a 3,000-square-foot ballroom for the Montecito estate The Peppers, completed in 1917, which made use of redwood, mahogany, and oak, and featured a magnificent fireplace. In 1918, she designed a tuberculosis clinic for children on North San Antonio Road. In 1925, she was hired to design the Margaret Baylor Inn (924 Anacapa St.). Today, as the **Lobero Building**, it holds a variety of offices. The **City Gymnasium** (102 E. Carrillo St.) was badly damaged in the 1925 earthquake, and Morgan was retained to design a new one. She placed handball and tennis courts on the roof, and her Spanish Colonial Revival concept fitted in nicely with the city's new architectural guidelines for the downtown area. The building is a City Structure of Merit.

Other prominent architects were also active in the area. Frank Lloyd Wright built two

residential homes here. Kem Weber, the post-WWI industrial designer, created the **Church of Religious Science Reading Room** (1301 State St.). Myron Hunt, best known for his Rose Bowl and Huntington Gardens, both in Pasadena, was the creative brains behind La Arcada Court (1114 State St.) and the Santa Barbara Public Library (40 E. Anapamu), whose beautifully detailed original entrance facing Anapamu is, sadly, no longer used.

Greene and Greene, the ultimate Craftsman designers, also from Pasadena, designed a gorgeous dark shingled residence, the **Nathan Benz Residence** (1741 Prospect Ave.), near the Mission in 1911. Local legendary architect George Washington Smith designed over 80 residences and commercial buildings in the city, not to mention other buildings across the nation. Undoubtedly Smith, more than anyone else, is associated with the Spanish Colonial Revival architecture that has made Santa Barbara famous. Most notably, Smith worked on **Casa del Herrero** (1387 E. Valley Rd.), which is a National Historic Landmark, and the redesign of the **Lobero Theatre** (33 E. Canon Perdido).

view from Stearns Wharf

notice the full-size replica of a blue whale hanging from the ceiling. There are touch tanks on the lower level and staff to answer questions and discuss why you should pet the starfish, how sealife coexists with humans, and other educational ideas. As you move upstairs you come eye to eye with the blue whale, giving you an idea of how massive these creatures really are. There's also a very beautiful little exhibit, nicely backlit, showing jellyfish and how these supple, graceful creatures impact our oceans.

THE SANTA BARBARA HARBOR

The Santa Barbara harbor (the intersection of Cabrillo and Harbor Way) is home to about 1,100 sailing vessels, a few stores and restaurants, and a museum. It's a short walk from Stearns Wharf and is the eye candy most people expect to see when visiting. One of the best parts of the harbor is the long breakwater wall, often with colorful flags flying in the wind. It's a great walk and terminates on a sand spit, which you can access at low tide. At high tide and during storms the breakwater is constantly hit by crashing waves that splash over the wall; half the fun is trying to outrun them. There's minimal shopping at the harbor, but you can buy fresh fish every day of the week and smell the catch as it's hauled in.

Interestingly, the area where the harbor is positioned today is not a natural harbor at all, but was built in the 1920s when millionaire Max Fleischmann (of Fleischmann's yeast) wanted a protected place to moor his yacht and ponied up a lot of money to build the breakwater. Unfortunately, the shifting sands under the water need to be constantly dredged, at a huge cost to taxpayers, to allow boats to enter the harbor, and you'll usually see the rather unsightly dredging equipment sitting near the sand spit.

While at the harbor, stop in to the **Santa Barbara Maritime Museum** (113 Harbor Way, 805/962-8404, www.sbmm.org, Thurs.–Tues. 10 A.M.–5 P.M., $7 adults, $4 seniors, students, and active military, free active military in uniform, free to all third Thurs. of month), which is housed in a 1940s naval building. Inside the two-story structure are exhibits on surfing and shipwrecks and a full-length *tomol,* a wood canoe the Chumash used to cross between the mainland and the islands. There are rotating exhibits with the sea as a common theme as well as lectures and special screenings in their upstairs theater.

The Mission and the Riviera

One of the older parts of the city, the Riviera sits in the foothills where the mountains cascade down to the lowlands. The area is studded with oak trees and natural waterways and was obviously chosen as a place to build homes because of the views. The main draw of the area is the Mission Santa Barbara, but it is also home to the Santa Barbara Botanic Garden, great hiking opportunities such as the popular Rattlesnake Canyon trail, secluded parks like Franceschi Park, and estates from the 1920s. Some of the estates here, including Lotusland and Casa del Herrero, can be accessed by the public.

◖ OLD MISSION SANTA BARBARA

More closely associated with Santa Barbara than

any other landmark, Old Mission Santa Barbara (2201 Laguna St., 805/682-4713, www.santabarbaramission.org, daily 9 A.M.–5 P.M., self-guided tours $5 adults, $4 seniors, $1 children 6–15) was founded on December 4, 1786 (the Feast of Saint Barbara). Originally there were no plans to place the mission on this spot, but after considering the proximity to a fresh water source, namely Mission Creek, and the defensible position of being able to view the ocean in time to spot unfriendly ships approaching, it was decided the area was ideal. As you stand on the church steps you immediately understand the importance of this location. Still an active church, this has been a gathering spot for over 225 years.

Though visually striking, it is one of the least authentic looking of the missions, and what you see today is the culmination of decades of restorative efforts. The original adobe church was a simple structure that was enlarged two times to accommodate the growth of the Chumash Indian population and the settlers in the area. The fourth and current iteration was built in 1820. The 1925 earthquake inflicted major damage on the mission, and the east bell tower was almost completely destroyed while its twin tower sustained serious injury. Restoration efforts began in May 1926, but within 10 years signs of further problems began to appear. Cracks emerged in the mission towers and facade, and the conditions continued to worsen so that by 1949 it was apparent that something desperately needed to be done. Studies revealed that chemical reactions inside the concrete were fatally weakening the material, rendering the building unsafe. Drastic action—nothing less than a total reconstruction of both towers and the church facade—was called for. Work began early in 1950 and continued until the summer of 1953.

Around back of the mission is the Huerta Project, where about 10 acres of *huertas,* or gardens, were originally established so that there would be food for everyone living at the mission and presidio. Considered a living museum, the garden today has a variety of fruit trees, grapevines, herbs, and edible plants, all consistent

Old Mission Santa Barbara

© MELISSA FARGO

with what would have been grown in mission times. Across the lawn is the rose garden, where over 1,000 different varieties are growing. As you walk across the street, consider that this is where some of the grapevines were planted.

The **Mission Museum** offers a docent-guided tour Thursday–Friday at 11 A.M. and Saturday at 10:30 A.M. Admission is $8 and the 90-minute tour allows a maximum of 15 people. You cannot see the church unless you pay for a guided or self-guided tour. Should you decide on a self-guided tour, you'll first come across the interior courtyard, where a center fountain is encircled by palm trees. Following the signs you then come upon the cemetery with a handful of headstones and crypts and a beautiful Moreton Bay fig tree planted about 1890. From there it is a few steps into the church. This is the most decorated of the mission interiors, with lots of vibrant stenciling surrounding the doors and altar and a complete painted wainscoting. Large paintings flank both walls; near the formal entrance is a small gated room wherein is the only original altar and tabernacle in the entire mission chain, dating from 1786. After leaving the church you'll enter the museum section, which houses old photographs of the mission from the 1880s and a few vestments and artifacts from the early services. There's also a side room that shows how a typical kitchen looked during the mission's heyday as well as other exhibits dealing with how they constructed the mission and the tools of the times.

SANTA BARBARA BOTANIC GARDEN

Santa Barbara Botanic Garden (1212 Mission Canyon Rd., 805/682-4726, www.sbbg.org, daily 9 A.M.–6 P.M., closed major holidays, $8 adults, $6 seniors and teens, $4 children 2–12, guided tours weekdays at 2 P.M., weekends at 11 A.M. and 2 P.M.), or the Garden as it is simply known, is 78 acres of pristine wilderness where redwood trees grow in a shaded creek, and oaks fan out everywhere. The garden was founded in 1926 to showcase the rich diversity of western plants. By 1936 this emphasis had narrowed to plants native to the state of California, and now includes northwestern Baja California and

PEARL CHASE: A WOMAN WITH VISION

It seems in every town, there's someone who makes it their mission to force the idea of preserving history while everyone else is in a hurry towards the future – and it's a good thing. It is impossible to overstate the contribution Pearl Chase has made to Santa Barbara; simply put, she is one of the reasons that the city looks the way it does. She also founded the local chapter of the American Red Cross, the Community Arts Association, and the Santa Barbara Trust for Historic Preservation. She was selected Woman of the Year by the *Los Angeles Times* in 1952, and was chosen Santa Barbara's first Woman of the Year in 1956. Her reputation as a preservationist was acknowledged by the National Trust for Historic Preservation, which awarded her their highest honor in 1973. It is because of Chase that the **Moreton Bay Fig Tree** (Chapala and W. Montecito Streets at the train station) was never cut down and remains the single largest of its kind in the United States, measuring a whopping 38 feet in circumference.

Today her fierce determination has taken shape as the **Pearl Chase Society** (www.pearlchasesociety.org), an all-volunteer organization that continues her legacy of preservation and historical and cultural awareness by sponsoring lectures, trips to various historically significant sites around town, and a continuing education agenda to remind people that it's because of people like Pearl Chase that Santa Barbara has the identity it does.

southwestern Oregon, which are part of the California Floristic Province. There is a rich diversity represented here, including part of the original mission aqueduct that fed the mission with clean water from the mountains. Today there are nearly six miles of walking trails and

The Santa Barbara Botanic Garden is set on 65 acres in the foothills.

© GREG PETERSON

over 1,000 species of plants, and their library contains over 15,000 volumes of works related to the disciplines of botany and horticulture. They have a gift shop and you can purchase plants directly from them.

LOTUSLAND

To enjoy the beauty of nature, albeit in a methodically constructed way, visit Lotusland (695 Ashley Rd., 805/969-9990, www.lotusland .org, tours Wed.–Sat. at 10 A.M. and 1:30 P.M. mid-February–mid-November, $35 adults, $10 children 5–18), 37 acres of the most well-manicured and lovingly tended gardens you will probably ever see. Given that Lotusland is a public garden operating in a residential neighborhood, reservations are mandatory; tours are docent-led and average just under two hours. There was a commercial nursery on the land in the 1880s, and the garden was last owned by Madame Ganna Walska, a Polish opera singer in the 1920s, who routinely arranged her vast collections of plants into bold color schemes and unusual shapes. For over four decades she

constantly tinkered with her gardens. After Walska's death in 1984 her estate, Lotusland, so named because of the lotus flowers on the property, became a nonprofit.

It is one thing to visit a botanical garden, and yet another to wander here, through the moonscape barrenness of the cactus gardens, to the topiary garden, to the serenity of the Japanese garden, to the olive allée and the formal English-styled gardens. Lotusland is that rare stop where you feel you could stay forever—in fact, one of the staff gardeners has been there for over 30 years. It is truly an awe-inspiring place and is nearly overwhelming in its botanical diversity and beauty. Bring a jacket, as it can get brisk in the many areas that are so heavily wooded that you can't see the sun. The wide walking paths easily accommodate wheelchairs.

CASA DEL HERRERO

At first glance the entrance to Casa del Herrero (1387 E. Valley Rd., 805/565-5653, www.casadelherrero.com, docent-led 90-min. tours Wed. and Sat. 10 A.M. and 2 P.M., $20 adults and children 10 and up, reservations mandatory), the "house of the blacksmith," seems like just another Spanish facade in a town overrun with seemingly thousands of Spanish-style houses. But the moment you cross the threshold and enter the lobby, you'll see the Tibetan 18th-century wood ceiling and know you're in another world. Designed by owner George Fox Steedman and architect George Washington Smith, it was completed in 1925. The estate, essentially unchanged from its original state, is Spanish Colonial Revival architecture at its best. The house is included on the National Register of Historic Places and is a National Historic Landmark. The amount of detail is overwhelming: From intricate tile work and hand-carved door surrounds to authentic Spanish antiques, it is a precise expression of interior design. Steedman traveled throughout parts of Europe searching for interiors to embellish his home, and in fact he had the house altered to fit the doors and windows he purchased. Though it is ornate and elaborate, the amazing thing is the sense of proportion throughout the home. Steedman also commissioned local artist Channing Peak to provide a western flair to some of the original art.

◀ KNAPP'S CASTLE

The lonely burned remnants of a seven-building complex sit on a precipice overlooking the Santa Ynez Valley. In 1916 George Owen Knapp, founder of Union Carbide company, which has become a behemoth chemical monopoly, purchased a 160-acre parcel including this ridgeline. He set out to construct what he called the Lodge at San Marcos, not really a castle at all. He wanted a more rustic home in contrast to his manicured and immaculate 70-acre Arcady estate in the tony Montecito area. The laborious efforts to build the lodge took many years, given the relative isolation of the property and the difficulty in hauling materials into the mountains. In 1940, Frances Holden bought the property from Knapp, no doubt looking forward to many years of peace and quiet in the remote home, but just five weeks later the entire property was destroyed by a forest fire. Today only the massive

sandstone foundations, fireplace pillars, walls, and arches looking out to the valley remain intact. It is hauntingly beautiful and rugged, and often only the whisper of the wind through the trees can be heard. The parcel is still privately owned but open to the public. To access it, turn onto East Camino Cielo at the top of the San Marcos Pass and drive exactly three miles. On your left will be a rusted gate. From there it's about a 10-minute walk to the property. As you slowly descend off the road you'll begin to see the tops of the chimneys, standing guard like sentinels in the distance. Knapp's Castle is a popular place for photo shoots (especially for weddings) and picnics, and has amazing views. It's impossible to get a bad photo here—good news for any shutterbug.

BEACHES

People flock to Santa Barbara's beaches, which are generally long and flat. Water temperatures in the summer are generally about 61 degrees, and cool down to about 58 degrees in the winter months. At low tide you can clearly see the rocks hidden under the waves, which makes for great tide pooling. Due to several creeks running into the ocean, and the inability to keep the creeks clean and free from debris and waste, there are occasional closures at some beaches. These are posted on the beaches should they occur. Aside from that, swimming in Santa Barbara is a safe endeavor. There are lifeguards during peak summer hours, but they disappear once the crowds do. At Goleta Beach in particular, and occasionally at West, East, and Leadbetter Beaches, you might see bulldozers scooping sand back into the ocean. It's a peculiar sight, but they do this to keep the beaches from eroding too much.

East Beach

East Beach (Cabrillo Blvd. at Milpas, daily sunrise–10 p.m.) is so named because it is east of Stearns Wharf. It's all soft sand and wide beach. There are a dozen volleyball nets in the sand close to the zoo (if you look closely you can see the giraffes and lions), and it has all the amenities a sun worshipper could wish for, like a full beach house, snack bar, play area for children, and a path for biking and in-line skating. The beachfront has picnic facilities and a full-service restaurant at the East Beach Grill. The **Cabrillo Pavilion Bathhouse** (1119 East Cabrillo Blvd.), built in 1927, offers showers, lockers, a weight room, a single rentable beach wheelchair, and volleyball rental.

West Beach

West Beach (Cabrillo Blvd. and Chapala St. btwn. Stearns Wharf and the harbor, daily sunrise–10 P.M.) is an 11-acre beach offering a picturesque sandy area for sunbathing, swimming, kayaking, windsurfing, and beach volleyball. Large palm trees and a wide walkway and bike path make this beachfront area a popular tourist spot. Outrigger canoes also launch from this beach.

◀ Leadbetter Beach

Leadbetter Beach (Shoreline Dr. and Loma Alta, daily sunrise–10 P.M.) is the best beach in Santa Barbara. There's a long, flat beach and a large grassy area; Leadbetter Point is the demarcation line for the area's south- and west-facing beaches. The nearly sheer cliffs suddenly rise up from the sand and trees dot the point. The beach, which is also bounded by the harbor and breakwater, is ideal for swimming because it's fairly protected, unlike the other flat ocean-facing beaches.

Many catamaran sailors and windsurfers launch from this beach, and you'll see occasional surfers riding the waves. The grassy picnic areas have barbecue sites that can be reserved for more privacy, but otherwise there is a lot of room. The beach and park can get packed during any of the many races and sporting events held here. There are restrooms, a small restaurant, and outdoor showers. Directly across the street is Santa Barbara City College. If you enter the stadium and walk up the many steps, you'll get some terrific views of the harbor, plus a mini-workout.

Arroyo Burro Beach

Arroyo Burro (at Cliff Dr. and Las Positas, daily sunrise–10 P.M.), which is known locally

Arroyo Burro Beach, known to locals as Hendry's Beach

© GREG PETERSON

as Hendry's, sits at the mouth of Arroyo Burro Creek. This dog-friendly beach is a popular spot for surfers and the occasional kayaker or scuba diver. With a restaurant on-site and a small grassy area for picnics, plus restrooms and outdoor showers, it's very popular with locals and far removed from the downtown beaches, though it can still become very crowded on summer days. At peak times when the parking lot is full, there's no other parking around. It's flanked by large cliffs, one of which holds the **Douglas Family Preserve,** still known locally as the Wilcox Property. The 70-acre eucalyptus-studded dog-friendly preserve is popular with locals, but few tourists even know about it. The parcel was to be a planned housing development, but this concept was thwarted when a grassroots campaign raised awareness of the property and the potentially destructive development. Money to purchase the property was limited until actor Michael Douglas gave a substantial gift, enabling the parcel to remain undeveloped. He then named it after his father, actor Kirk Douglas.

Butterfly Beach

Butterfly Beach (Channel Dr. across from the Four Seasons Hotel, Montecito, daily sunrise–10 P.M.) is accessed by a handful of steps leading to the narrow beach. Many people come here hoping to catch a glimpse of a celebrity from nearby Montecito, but chances are that won't happen. Butterfly is the most west-facing beach in Santa Barbara, meaning that you can actually see the sun set over the Pacific here. To find it, take Highway 101 to Olive Mill Road in Montecito (a few minutes south of Santa Barbara). At the stop sign, turn towards the ocean (away from the mountains) and follow it a quarter of a mile along the coast. Butterfly Beach is on your left. The beach is packed on most weekends and often on weekdays too, and parking is limited. Park on either side of the street along the beach or drive up Butterfly Road and park in the nearby neighborhoods. Bring your lunch, water, and sunscreen—there are no public facilities at this beach. Dogs roam freely here.

© JAY SINCLAIR

Butterfly Beach

Carpinteria State Beach

Carpinteria State Beach (5361 6th St., Carpinteria, 805/684-2811, daily 7 A.M.–sunset, no day-use fees, camping fees $20–100 per night) has designated itself the "world's safest beach." Whether that's an understatement or not, this beautiful wide, flat beach is definitely a favorite for locals and tourists. With plenty of campgrounds, picnic tables, outdoor showers, RV hookups, telephones, and a short walk to Linden Avenue, where there are lots of restaurants, shops, and a grocery store, you'll have everything you need, all within walking distance. Parts of the campgrounds are tree lined but right next to the train tracks; passing trains might wake up light sleepers. Aside from that, there is a great sense of community with the campers here.

Goleta Beach

At the base of the University of California, Santa Barbara, campus, Goleta Beach (5986 Sandspit Rd., daily sunrise–10 P.M.) is popular for its picnic tables, barbecue pits, horseshoes, multiple restrooms, and fishing opportunities. The grassy area is partially shaded by trees and there's also a small jungle gym for the kids. The pier is popular for fishing and the low breaks make this an easy entry for kayakers. You can also launch small boats from the pier on weekends only, when they have a crane that lowers boats into the water (there is no launch ramp directly into the water). On the mountain-facing side along the bike path are a few platforms for viewing birds in the slough that runs behind the beach.

Refugio State Beach

Refugio State Beach (10 Refugio Beach Rd., Goleta, 805/968-1033, www.parks.ca.gov, daily 8 A.M.–sunset) is a state park with a small strip of grass that abuts the water. It offers excellent coastal fishing, snorkeling, and scuba as well as hiking, biking trails, and picnic sites. Palm trees planted near Refugio Creek give a distinctive look to the beach and camping area. With one and a half miles of flat shoreline, Refugio is located 20 miles west of Santa Barbara on Highway 101 at Refugio Road.

El Capitán State Beach

Near Refugio State Beach is El Capitán State Beach (off Hwy. 101, 17 miles west of Santa Barbara, 805/968-1033, www.parks.ca.gov, daily 8 A.M.–sunset); if you take Highway 101 north about 15 minutes from downtown you will see the El Capitán signs. At the bottom of the exit, turn left and go under the bridge. The road will take you right into the park. El Capitán State Beach offers visitors a sandy beach, rocky tide pools, and stands of sycamore and oak trees along El Capitán Creek. It's a perfect setting for swimming, fishing, surfing, picnicking, and camping. A stairway provides access from the bluffs to the beach area. Amenities include RV hookups, pay showers, restrooms, hiking and bike trails, a fabulous beach, a seasonal general store, and an outdoor arena. Many of the camping sites offer an ocean view.

ENTERTAINMENT AND EVENTS

Though people flock to Santa Barbara to be outside, there's plenty to do inside as well. In bars, clubs, and theaters, Santa Barbara has its own brand of action when the sun goes down. The area is also home to a lively roster of festivals and events year-round.

Nightlife

Every city needs its watering holes, and Santa Barbara is no different. Plenty of bars clog a two-block-long section of State Street; a few more hug the side streets. But this is nothing new: Of the very first 50 business licenses issued by the city in 1850, 32 were for saloons.

BARS

In the 400–600 blocks of State Street you'll find the majority of Santa Barbara's bars. Frequented mainly by college students, the area has become a hot spot on weekends for flitting in and out of as many bars as possible, while taking advantage of cheap drink specials. This has become known as the State Street Crawl, that slow, methodical negotiating of bars and clubs. It's worth remembering that any bar in Santa Barbara leans towards mellow on the weeknights and rowdier on the weekends. All bars close at 2 A.M. and this is often when trouble occurs, especially on weekend nights; fights are common enough as far too many intoxicated people converge on the streets at the same time. It's best to be back at your hotel long before that.

At **Madison's Grill & Tavern** (525 State St., 805/882-1182, www.madisonssb.com, Mon.–Sat. noon–2 A.M., Sun. 11 A.M.–2 A.M.), the food is typical bar fare, and the fact that it's served by a sexy all-girl waitstaff in umpire uniforms won't make it taste any better. But this spot is packed during playoff games, and over 20 flat screens means you won't miss a second of your favorite team's action. The drinks are inexpensive and they offer lots of two-for-one specials to keep you in your seats.

Joe's Café (536 State St., 805/966-4638, Thurs.–Sat. 11 A.M.–1:30 A.M., Sun.–Wed. 11 A.M.–11 P.M.) undeniably serves the stiffest drinks in town. A renovation to the interior has produced an old-school feel to the place, harkening back to its 1920s origins. It gets packed here on weekends, and the bar and restaurant has found new life. It's also the only place on State Street where you'll see a neon sign advertising the joint.

The James Joyce (513 State St., 805/962-2688, daily 10 A.M.–2 A.M.) offers free darts and free peanuts, and the Guinness comes quickly from the tap. There is a great selection of other beers and whiskey as well. The walls are lined with photos of, we assume, Irishmen, and the tin ceiling and rugged feel of the place, not to mention the nice fireplace, means that there's usually an older crowd here. A small dance floor in the back doesn't get much use, but the wood bar is a classic drinking spot.

Old Kings Road (532 State St., 805/884-4085, www.oldkingsroad.com, daily noon–2 A.M.) is as close as you'll get to a British tavern on the Central Coast. It's not filled with as many college-age kids and tends to be less rowdy, but that should not suggest a quaint, quiet gentlemen's tavern. Wednesday is quiz night, a very popular trivia time, and when

darts are flying, it's boisterous. The look and feel is fairly authentic inside this small bar.

O'Malley's Bar (523 State St., 805/564-8904, daily noon–2 A.M.) has a giant-screen TV and draws big crowds for fight nights. There are plenty of other smaller screens ringing the perimeter of the bar. The only drawback is that no food is served, but they have no problem with patrons bringing in their own grub from one of the many establishments that line State Street. The antique bar at O'Malley's looks like a bar should look—wooden, thick, substantial, and well-worn.

The **Sandbar** (514 State St., 805/966-1388, www.sandbarsb.com, Mon. 3 P.M.–close, Tues.–Fri. 11:30 A.M.–close, Sat.–Sun. 11 A.M.–close) is a kind of rustic tequila bar with big cushioned love seats and chairs and 20 different tequilas available by the shot. The interior is small and most people crave the patio fronting State Street, as that's where the action is. But you also might want to stay inside with the 20 plasma TVs and chow down on south-of-the-border food.

Sharkeez (416 State St., 805/963-9680, Mon.–Fri. 11 A.M.–2 A.M., Sat.–Sun. 9 A.M.–2 A.M.) is a sports bar on steroids, with plenty of energy and testosterone. Their cluttered, hyperactive decor includes every kind of plastic pennant there is, plus flags, jerseys, and any other sports paraphernalia under the sun tacked to the wall. It's a loud, crazy place, with people drinking far too early in the morning, but if that's your thing, it's one of the only bars open before noon.

Elsie's Tavern (117 E. De La Guerra, 805/963-4503, Mon.–Thurs. noon–2 A.M., Fri.–Sun. 4 P.M.–2 A.M.) is an old garage that was turned into a tavern. There is a funky room with abandoned couches as you first enter, and as you make your way to the back the space opens up with a bar and pool table. It's low-key here: No one is trying to really impress anyone, and the place has an almost lonely feel to it. Rotating shows of local art hang on the walls, and though this is close to downtown, it's a world away.

Located behind the *Santa Barbara News-Press*

building is **The Press Room** (15 E. Ortega, 805/963-8121, daily 9 A.M.–6 A.M.), a little English bar with a great jukebox, stiff drinks, British pints, and a fine selection of whiskies. Game nights get noisy and crowded, like at any bar, but this spot is usually chill enough for conversation and without the typical on-the-prowl types who make some bars uncomfortable. Posters of British bands like The Who cling to the old walls, and it's also still on the inexpensive side.

LIVE MUSIC

Though Santa Barbara is home to a handful of well-known musicians, live music here is a small scene. Yes, there is always some guy with a guitar playing in a corner somewhere, but we're talking actual bands here. One of the better spots is **Velvet Jones** (423 State St., 805/965-8676, www.velvet-jones.com, daily 8 P.M.–close), which offers live music seven nights a week, much of it up-and-comers from the Los Angeles area. The space isn't going for looks, but it does go for hard rock, ska, hip-hop, and anything other than popular and middle-of-the-road music. They have a tiny kitchen and you can get hot dogs and pizza, but that's it. A small interior balcony and medium-sized dance floor gives you space so you're not crammed in, and a small gated front patio lets you cool down before you heat up again.

Live Culture (11 W. De La Guerra, inside Paseo Nuevo Mall, 805/845-8800, www.liveculturelounge.com, Sun.–Thurs. 11 A.M.–10:30 P.M., Fri.–Sat. 11 A.M.–midnight) is a wine bar, restaurant, yogurt stop, and yes, live music venue. The musicians, usually just one to three people, perform on a small, elevated stage near the bar, which makes more room for patrons. You won't hear many full bands—there just isn't space—but this is a great place for the wine crowd on a weekend night.

Muddy Waters (508 E. Haley, 805/966-9328, Mon.–Sat. 6 A.M.–6 P.M.) has the distinct look of an unsupervised dorm room; it's unkempt and laid-back, but it works. Local musicians, mostly playing alternative music, use this as a spot to work out their new songs,

and local art hangs on the walls. The have open mic nights as well. Coffee drinks, a few brews, and simple sandwiches and Wi-Fi are on offer, but note that they only take cash. On scheduled performance nights the venue will stay open later, so call ahead for extended hours.

SOhO Restaurant and Music Club (1221 State St., 805/962-7776, www.sohosb.com, daily 6–10 P.M.) is the premier midsized venue in town. There's live music seven nights a week, and every Monday is jazz night. SOhO has seen its share of well-known performers, including David Crosby, Kenny Loggins, Rickie Lee Jones, Jimmy Cliff, the Mad Caddies, Acoustic Alchemy, and many others. The 2nd-floor outdoor patio is a prime spring and summer location to enjoy tunes under the stars. They also have a full bar and restaurant.

The outdoor **Santa Barbara Bowl** (1122 N. Milpas, 805/962-7411, www.sbbowl.org), with just over 4,500 seats, is an intimate venue that brings in big A-list talent. It was originally built in the 1930s, but a renovation has greatly expanded the facilities. From its hillside location you can see the ocean and dance away under the stars. There is no larger or more preeminent music venue in town, and certainly for live music, this is the most beautiful.

Festivals and Events
YEAR-ROUND

Once a month, **First Thursday** (downtown, www.downtownsantabarbara.com for downloadable map, first Thurs. of each month 5–8 P.M.) provides an evening of art and culture in downtown Santa Barbara. Nearly a dozen galleries and art-related venues offer free access to visual and performing art and feature attractions such as art openings, live music, artist receptions, lectures, wine-tasting, hands-on activities, and even mobile poetry, where local poets spontaneously recite their works. It's become quite the social scene.

Nite Moves (www.runsantabarbara.com) is a weekly 5K race held each Wednesday May–September. For a small fee anyone can race, as well as participate in the open-water swim. There's food, music, and awards. It starts at

Leadbetter Beach as the sun begins to set, climbs for a mile and a half, then returns the same way. It's not flat, but it's also not difficult, and with so many people participating, you probably won't be the slowest in your age group.

SPRING

I Madonnari Italian Street Painting Festival

(www.imadonnarifestival.com, free) is held at the Santa Barbara Mission every Memorial Day weekend. Adults aren't even encouraged to use chalk to draw on the sidewalk—except at the I Madonnari Festival. The parking lot in front of the mission is transformed from bleak black to more than 200 chalk paintings as artists, many local and some from across the globe, take chalk to asphalt and create beautiful reproductions of classic works as well as original art. The mission comes alive and the lawn is crowded with food vendors, live music, picnics, and the chance to watch surprisingly beautiful art in action. Going for over 20 years, it's the perfect weekend stop if you're in town. Bring a picnic and munch on the lawn or buy food there—either way it's a day well spent.

The stars of **The International Orchid Show** (805/687-0766, www.sborchidshow .org, $12) may seem like just a bunch of flowers, but ask any lover of orchids and they will tell you passionate stories of these plants. Santa Barbara enjoys a mild, Mediterranean climate with temperate nights and soft, ocean breezes, and orchids first took root in Santa Barbara at the turn of the 20th century when wealthy industrialists came to the area's burgeoning spas and resorts to escape harsh, eastern winters. Many of them stayed, building estates and commissioning world-class horticulturists and landscape architects to design elaborate gardens. Exotic orchids became the rage, with mass plantings of Cymbidiums and other unusual species adding prestige to Montecito and Hope Ranch estates. Held since 1945, and with current attendance in excess of 5,000 people, the March orchid festival is most certainly worth a visit. Thousands of unique and in some cases bizarre-looking plants are displayed at the Earl Warren Showgrounds. Experts are on hand to discuss the unusual flowers and there are a large number for sale.

SUMMER

The **French Festival** (www.frenchfestival .com, free) is a yearly tradition held at Oak Park (at Juniper and Alamar Sts.) each Bastille Day weekend, which for us Americans means mid-July. The festival runs 11 A.M.–7 P.M. and over 20,000 people attend to sample escargots, French onion soup, crepes, and baguettes; watch cancan dancers; and line up to see the poodle parade, where poodles are dressed in berets and scarves, perhaps even Hermès. There are jugglers, mimes, and more accordion music than you thought possible. Dozens of chefs also attend to showcase their food, French wine, and French water. It's almost like going to France without paying for the airfare. Local French restaurants are here as well. C'est magnifique!

The **California Wine Festival** (www .californiawinefestival.com) is held across from the beach at Chase Palm Park and pulls in some 3,000 folks to sample wines from across California. Local wines are here, yes, but Napa and Sonoma are also well represented, as well as about a dozen breweries. There's plenty of food and live music, and you can't beat wine-tasting near the ocean. It does get crowded and warm during this July event, which translates into a rowdier crowd.

Woodies at the Beach (www.national woodieclub.com, free) is one of the coolest festivals, held in mid-August. About 100 woodies (wood-bodied vehicles), from cars to trucks to campers and a handful of hot rods, grace the grassy bluffs at Santa Barbara City College overlooking Leadbetter Beach. There's live music, a surfboard raffle, and the chance to examine up close some beautifully restored classic cars. It's all free, and even if it's not your thing it's worth a stop to admire a piece of the past. Plus everyone's wearing Hawaiian shirts and seems so relaxed that you'll easily end up making friends.

The **Solstice Parade** (www.solsticeparade .com, free) started in 1974 as an homage to local artists and a pseudocelebration of the summer solstice and has exploded into a free-for-all of color, costume, political incorrectness, dance, music, and just plain summertime revelry. Think of this as a family-oriented Mardi Gras and you get the idea. Nearly 100,000 people cram the streets to celebrate the longest day of the year with the parade of funky floats and dancing in the streets, and a thousand people end up volunteering in the effort. The after party at Alameda Park is sometimes more fun than the parade itself, with drumming circles, more dancing, food, vendors, two live bands, and people wearing the bare minimum in the July sun. Grab your tie-dyed T-shirt and join in.

Also known as Old Spanish Days, **Fiesta** (www.oldspanishdays-fiesta.org, some events free) is a five-day extravaganza held the first weekend of August, and is Santa Barbara's oldest and best-known festival. Started in 1924 to honor the Spanish and Mexican heritage of the city, Fiesta has blossomed into the second largest equestrian parade in the United States, plus a feast of Mexican food and margaritas, and an opportunity to see lots of dance. There are three *mercados* (marketplaces) around town with tortillas, burritos, tamales, tacos, and more Mexican food. There are also activities for the kids at the *mercados,* like climbing walls, mariachi bands, and carnival rides. During Fiesta the Sunken Gardens at the county courthouse is transformed for a three-night free event known as Las Noches de Ronda (meaning "nights of gaiety"), with a stage where performers from across the globe dance *folklórico,* flamenco, and ballet, and belt out hip-hop and traditional Mexican songs, all under the beautiful evening skies of an August moon. The courthouse, lit up and shining in her magnificence, is a beautiful venue for the free concerts; all you need to do is grab a blanket or chair and a picnic and you're set.

But Fiesta officially kicks off with La Fiesta Pequeña (the "little fiesta"), held at the mission, with dance, local political figures, and a blessing of the mission fathers. It also now includes tribal dances by native Chumash people. There are a number of additional festivities during Fiesta, many of which you need to pay to attend, but the parade, Las Noches de Ronda, and the *mercados* are all free. During the Fiesta festivities, you'll see people walking all over town with baskets of hollowed-out eggs that are painted and filled with confetti; it's typical to crack them over the heads of friends and loved ones and shout out, "Viva la Fiesta!" Many locals flee town during Fiesta, as everything in town changes during the event. Hotel room rates increase, parking is at a premium, and there are cover charges at bars and clubs and lines at restaurants.

FALL

Pier to Peak (www.runsantabarbara.com), a 13.1-mile race, starts at Stearns Wharf and takes you on a point-to-point course up nearly 4,000 feet to La Cumbre Peak in September. Yes, you see much of Santa Barbara, the ocean, the mountains, and the mission, but you may not care as you gasp for air. This is a tough race, but an extraordinarily satisfying one, and the views are part of your reward.

It's fitting that Santa Barbara should have a seafood festival. After all, the Santa Barbara Channel is one of the nation's richest sources of bountiful, sustainable seafood. Lobster, ridgeback shrimp, rock crab, white sea bass, California halibut, yellowtail, salmon, swordfish, thresher shark, spot prawns, and sea urchin all thrive here, and about 100 local anglers catch between 6 and 10 million pounds of seafood annually. Held each October, the **Harbor and Seafood Festival** (805/897-1962, 10 A.M.–5 P.M., free) is a one-day event that brings out local fishermen, food vendors, and craftspeople together with cooking demonstrations and coast guard vessels, all to edify the public about the fish they consume, the water they play in, and the men and women who hit the ocean each day to bring in fresh fish and shellfish. It's all to celebrate the sea and our relationship with it.

The **Avocado Festival** (www.avofest .com, Fri. 4–10 P.M., Sat. 10 A.M.–9 P.M., Sun. 10 A.M.–6 P.M., free) is held each October in Carpinteria. Between 40 and 60 bands perform over the three-day event, and there are arts and crafts, lots of food purveyors, and yes, a guacamole contest. Since the region is the third largest producer of avocados, it only makes sense to celebrate it. This is a family event, free to everyone, and draws in massive numbers of people to bask in the sun and enjoy one of the Central Coast's best fruits.

The *Santa Barbara News-Press Half-Marathon* (www.newspress.com/half marathon) is the granddaddy of half marathons, having been held for over three decades. The half-marathon course hugs much of the coast, while the 5K race is all flat and all by the water. The early November race offers cooler temperatures. Several thousand people sign up for this, the city's premier race event.

SHOPPING
Antiques

As the old saying goes, one person's trash is another's treasure, and antiques shopping is more treasure hunt than anything else.

Old Town Antiques (5799 Hollister, Goleta, 805/967-2528, www.antiquesoldtown.com, Mon.–Sat. 10 A.M.–6 P.M., Sun. 11 A.M.–5 P.M.) in Goleta is a collective of 15 dealers and over 5,000 square feet of eclectic items, especially furniture. The pieces here are clean, unusual, and well priced, since it is way off State Street. The inventory rotates regularly, with new merchandise coming in frequently.

Also off State Street is the **Antique Center Mall** (4434 Hollister, 805/967-5700, Mon.–Sat. 11 A.M.–6 P.M., Sun. noon–5 P.M.), with nine rooms packed full of everything you can imagine. Of particular note is a very good selection of mid-century modern by a local dealer who knows her stuff; it's located right at the entrance. There is also a lot of wrought-iron outdoor pieces and statuary, plus furniture, jewelry, and accessories.

Summerland, just south of Santa Barbara, has become a centralized location for antiques and furnishings. There are a dozen places on or just off Lillie Avenue, Summerland's main drag. The best, and oldest, is the **Summerland Antique Collective** (2192 Ortega Hill Rd., Summerland, 805/565-3189, daily 10 A.M.–5 P.M.). Over 30 years they've amassed over 45,000 square feet of everything you can imagine: Mid-century modern, jewelry, retro, artworks, and garden furnishings, it's all here under one roof.

More expensive, but with some amazing museum-quality items, **Summerhill Antiques** (2280 Lillie Ave., Summerland, 805/969-3366, daily 11 A.M.–5 P.M.) has a lot of French and Asian furniture, accent pieces, tables, and unusual pieces like 17th-century statuary. This is a place for the serious antiques lover.

The aptly named **Things** (1187 Coast Village Rd., 805/845-8411, www.thingsof montecito.com, Tues.–Sun. 11 A.M.–5 P.M.) is a high-end consignment store with antique furnishings and decorative items like wall sconces and ornamental iron work. The intriguing and visually appealing selection varies, as the store sells merchandise quickly.

Art Galleries

Santa Barbara has long been a draw for artists hoping to capture the stunning terrain, landscapes, seascapes, and whitewashed buildings with red-tile roofs. There is a focus in town on plein air, but it is by no means the only form of art represented. Most galleries are bunched in the downtown core and have great accessibility, while a few other galleries dot the outer edges of the city. Beyond that, you're likely to see art hanging, and even artist receptions taking place, in restaurants, salons, offices, and other businesses.

The **Santa Barbara Art Dealers Association** (www.sbada.org) is the ideal place to start. Their map gives the locations of the galleries in town and can help you in your search for a specific style.

Sullivan Goss: An American Gallery (7 E. Anapamu, 805/730-1460, www.sullivangoss .com, daily 10 A.M.–5:30 P.M.) is the most well-known art gallery in town. Owner Frank Goss knows his stuff and hosts constant exhibitions showcasing top talent from across the United States, with an emphasis on the 19th through 21st centuries. Two side-by-side galleries create a large enough space to show oversized works. Sullivan Goss has a number of local artists on its large roster of clients, and also looks to acquire new works.

Decidedly smaller, **Artamo Gallery** (11 W. Anapamu, 805/568-1400, www.artamo gallery.com, Wed.–Sun. noon–5 P.M.) has a clear and aggressive focus on abstract expressionism. Shows rotate every 2–3 months, with artists both well known and under the radar from around the globe. Artamo represents an excellent selection of artists working in mixed media, found media, paint, sculpture, and photography.

The **Contemporary Arts Forum** (653 Paseo Nuevo, inside and upstairs at Paseo Nuevo Mall, 805/966-5373, www.sbcaf.org, Tues.–Sat. 11 A.M.–5 P.M., Sun. noon–5 P.M., $5) is, as the name suggests, devoted to contemporary arts, be that visual, media, or performing arts, representing a wide range of artistic attitudes. CAF shows new works of local, regional, national, and international artists in a warehouse-sized space and pushes the envelope with many of their exhibitions. Multimedia

exhibits and performance art is common, perhaps confusing, but CAF gives Santa Barbara much-needed exposure to diverse expressions.

The **Faulkner Gallery** (401 E. Anapamu, 805/564-5608, Mon.–Thurs. 10 A.M.–8 P.M., Fri.–Sat. 10 A.M.–5:30 P.M., Sun. 1– 5 P.M., free) is one of those places you'd rarely think about going into, and if you didn't know it was there you would walk right past it. Located in a separate room inside the main branch of the public library, there is a large space with art exhibits rotating every few months, and two small side rooms with even more art. There's always something interesting, and everything is for sale at prices lower than those of traditional galleries. Mainly local artists exhibit here, and you just might make a very cool discovery.

The **Channing Peake Gallery** (105 E Anapamu St., 1st fl., 805/568-3990, www .sbartscommission.org, Mon.–Fri. 9 A.M.–5 P.M., free) is located on the ground floor of the County Administration building, which seems odd until one learns that the Arts Commission, which runs the gallery and other

Even shopping is scenic in Santa Barbara.

© JAY SINCLAIR

artistic endeavors around town, is supported by the county government. There are significant works presented on the ground floor, from photography exhibits to art, poetry, and more. And who knows, you might just bump into a county supervisor while you're admiring the work.

The **Architectural Foundation of Santa Barbara** (229 E. Victoria, 805/965-6307, www.afsb.org, Tues.–Fri. 9 A.M.–2 P.M.) is housed in an old Victorian residence and has an attached gallery that showcases the work of local architects and artists. The works tend to have an abstract bent. One exhibit featured all the things that architects use to sketch out ideas when they are not in their offices: napkin, matchbook cover, tablecloth, menu, and other unusual spur-of-the-moment idea pads. In 1989, the Architectural Foundation started the highly successful Kids Draw Architecture program, which provides an opportunity for children to sketch Santa Barbara's famous landmark buildings. The result is a yearly show featuring some excellent works by children. This is one of the few venues where local architects can present not only images of their architectural work, but their artistic side as well.

Sweets

Everyone loves something sweet, and Santa Barbara has offers a small share of confections made right here.

Chocolate Maya (15 W. Gutierrez, 805/965-5956, www.chocolatemaya.com, Mon.–Fri. 11 A.M.–6 P.M., Sat. 10 A.M.–5 P.M.) has an assortment of chocolates from across the globe, including some they make on-site. High-quality playful molded chocolates make great gifts. They'll put together a special chocolate tasting on request.

When you enter **Chocolats du CaliBressan** (4193 Carpinteria Ave., Carpinteria, 805/684-6900, www.choco calibressan.com, Mon.–Fri. 10 A.M.–6:30 P.M., Sat. 10 A.M.–5:30 P.M.) you're hit with a heady aroma of chocolate. The shop is run by a French chocolatier, so you're pretty much guaranteed to get fabulous bonbons and truffles to satisfy your sweet tooth. They offer

© JAY SINCLAIR

confections on display at Chocolate Maya

State Street

samples and tours of the chocolate-making process; contact them for details.

Robitaille's Candies (900 Linden Ave., Carpinteria, 805/684-9340, www.robitailles candies.com, Mon.–Sat. 10 A.M.–5:30 P.M., Sun. 10 A.M.–3 P.M.) has been making and selling chocolates for 40 years, and has been at their Linden Avenue location for over 25 years. Though they carry a of lot of prepackaged items, including sugar-free candies, they are best known for their original thin mints, small multicolored minty discs.

RECREATION
Parks

Rocky Nook Park (610 Mission Canyon Rd., 805/568-2461, daily 8 A.M.–sunset) is a great spot for watching Mission Creek wander towards the mission and is covered with, well, rocks. This 19-acre park is a wonderful respite or place for a picnic. It offers barbecue grills, picnic tables, hiking trails, horseshoes, a small playground, and restrooms.

From there you can head up Alameda Padre Serra to **Francheschi Park** (1510 Mission Ridge Rd., daily sunrise–sunset), home to an old dilapidated estate. The house, named for Italian horticulturist Francesco Franceschi, is closed to the public, but the 18-acre grounds are open and offer some of the absolute best views of the city, harbor, and coast, especially at sunset. There's a small parking lot and a few picnic tables, and even a disturbingly dirty bathroom. The view corridor is narrowed by the eucalyptus trees, but it makes a perfect frame for photos.

Elings Park (on Los Positas between Cliff Dr. and Modoc Rd., 805/969-5611, www .elingspark.org, daily 7 A.M.–sunset) is a former landfill and now a 230-acre park that offers activities such as a BMX course, radio-controlled car racing, and paragliding, as well as a soccer field, wedding venues, hiking trails, picnic grounds, and perfect views of the harbor, mountains, and ocean. A number of large events take advantage of the grounds, including the **Santa Barbara Beer Festival** (www .sbbeerfestival.com), held each October, and the **Santa Barbara Bicycle Festival** (www .santabarbarabikefest.com) held in June with cross-country, BMX, and downhill courses and races. This is a wonderful gem of a spot. The hiking on moderate hills will take you to some great vistas of both the ocean and mountains.

Skater's Point (Cabrillo Blvd. at Garden St., daily 9 A.M.–sunset) was one of those concepts that people decried when the idea was first floated: A concrete skate park at the beach? Over $800,000 later, it's proved a great success. Skateboards and bikes swoop up and down the ramps covering nearly 15,000 square feet of concrete in full view of anyone who cares to watch. Skater's Point is located just east of Stearns Wharf in Chase Palm Park, and it's fun just to hang out there and imagine yourself doing some of the tricks.

Alameda Park (1400 Santa Barbara St., daily 8 A.M.–sunset) is a wonderful two-block family-oriented picnic and playground spot that hosts the 8,000-square-foot Kids Zone playground, a medieval-looking fort with swings, slides, and climbing equipment. It's close to downtown, and you can usually find plenty of parking and a picnic table if you come early. Don't expect sunbathing here, though, as the trees provide plenty of shade. There are restrooms, a small gazebo, and plenty of open spaces for Frisbee. This park is a centerpiece for many citywide celebrations, such as on the summer solstice.

Just across the street is the **Alice Keck Park Memorial Gardens** (1500 Santa Barbara St. at Arrellaga, daily dawn–dusk), which is one of the city's most beautiful spots. The site used to hold a grand hotel, and Alice Keck Park (that's her name, not the name of the park) deeded the plot of land to the city. Well-tended gardens surround a man-made pond with koi and turtles. Of special note is that the 75 different plant and tree species can be enjoyed by guests with vision or hearing difficulties, as there are Braille signs and audio posts at specific spots to identify what has been planted. The walkway meanders around specialized planting beds that feature low-use water species. It is a labor of love with a message: Beautiful plants don't

have to consume lots of precious resources. The park is popular with both student and professional photographers, and every Saturday and Sunday you will find brides vying for position in front of the most beautiful flowers or splash of unique foliage to immortalize their big day. There are no facilities here; you'll have to head across the street to Alameda Park.

Tucker's Grove (805 San Antonio Creek Rd. at Cathedral Oaks, 805/967-1112, www .sbparks.com, daily 8 A.M.–sunset) is officially called San Antonio Canyon Park, as San Antonio Creek runs through it, but it's known locally as Tucker's Grove (which is actually the lower section where the entrance to the park is located). Tucker's Grove is open and sunny, and the lower park is great for families because of its wide-open spaces and relatively flat grounds right next to a large playground. There are lots of picnic tables here, even a vending machine with cold drinks. The upper section of the park, called the Kiwanis Meadow, as the look and feel of a completely different park. From Kiwanis Meadow you can access hiking and riding trails that go all the way to San Marcos Road. For all of Tucker's Grove, there are picnic and barbecue facilities for up to 400 people, playgrounds, volleyball, horseshoe pits, ball fields, hiking, lots of free parking, and restrooms.

Shoreline Park (Shoreline Dr. at La Marina, daily sunrise–10 P.M.) is a long, narrow oceanside park that offers fabulous views of the harbor, the islands, and the mountains. Scattered parking and picnic facilities, as well as a small playground, make this a popular spot for family gatherings. This is a great park for walking, skating, playing Frisbee, and flying kites as well. Follow the narrow wooden stairs near the restrooms to discover a local secret: a beach and tidal pool area (when the tide is low) that is both private (sort of) and beautiful. You will often see dolphins skimming the surface from here. There is a stationary metal binocular by the bronze whale tail at the west end of the park.

Golf

There are only six 18-hole golf courses in Santa Barbara, and a few nine-hole courses.

Rancho San Marcos (4600 Hwy. 154, 805/683-6334, www.rsm1804.com, green fees $79–104), built on the site of the historic 1804 Rancho San Marcos, is a Robert Trent Jones Jr.–designed gem that gracefully saddles the natural topography, meandering amidst a plethora of ancient oaks and preserved traces of 19th-century adobe structures. This par-70 course sits off the San Marcos Pass, just 15 miles from both Santa Barbara and Solvang. It's a course for business types, with a small pro shop and restaurant, but plenty of privacy to close a deal. No denim clothing is allowed.

Forgo the inland for the breathtaking views at **Sandpiper Gold Course** (7925 Hollister Ave., 805/968-1541, www.sandpipergolf .com, daily dawn–dusk, green fees $139–159), one of the most beautiful courses anywhere. Sandpiper is a par 71, which provides expert-level play and terrific views from the bluffs above the ocean. The only oceanfront course between Los Angeles and Pebble Beach, this is a must-play for visitors.

Tucked into the hills with views to ocean is **Glen Annie Golf Course** (405 Glen Annie Rd., 805/968-6400, www.glenanniegolf.com, daily dawn–dusk, green fees $59–74). Part of what makes this par-72 course so beautiful is its natural setting, away from it all in the low hills facing the ocean. In conjunction with Audubon International, this course is one of six in California that supports an Environmental Enhancement Program. Three different habitats provide homes to numerous wild animals that call the golf course home, so if you go looking for that lost ball, you won't be alone. There is a pro shop and restaurant on-site.

The **Santa Barbara Golf Club** (3500 McCaw Ave., 805/687-7087, www.santabarbara ca.gov, daily dawn–dusk, green fees $40–50) is a par-70 public course sitting on what used to be an airstrip. The course is dotted with eucalyptus trees, and there are peek-a-boo views to the islands. It's a beautiful course and you may forget you're next to the freeway. The greens are a little slow for the avid golfer, but for a municipal course it's one of the best in the region (and priced accordingly).

Hiking

Santa Barbara offers hikes for all difficulty levels in a variety of settings. The best place to start to plan a hike is www.santabarbarahikes .com. Here are some suggestions that will get you outside for some of the city's best views.

Rattlesnake Canyon is one of the more popular hikes and is fairly easy—and no, you probably won't come across any rattlesnakes; it was named for its winding canyon location. It's close to downtown, well marked, and less than four miles long. You'll pass pools and streams and eventually come out at the top of a small hill with panoramic views to the ocean. From the mission, take Mission Canyon Road north to Foothill Road. Turn right and make a quick left onto the continuation of Mission Canyon Road. After about half a mile, make a sharp right at Los Conoas, which will take you just over a mile to Rattlesnake Bridge, an old stone bridge over the creek. Park in one of the pull-outs. The trailhead is here, clearly marked.

Seven Falls has an elevation gain of 600 feet over a two-and-a-half-mile path that follows Mission Creek through a gorge and across small waterfalls and deep pools, over boulders and sandstone rocks. It's a moderate hike, and in season when the creek flows unabated the trail is alive with the sounds of water. To access the trail, from the mission take Mission Canyon Road north to Foothill Road. Turn right and make a quick left onto the continuation of Mission Canyon Road. The road divides—veer left up the hill; you'll be on Tunnel Road at this point. It's about a mile drive before the road ends. Park there and walk to the end of Tunnel Road, staying on the pavement. You'll pass a gate and the road splits off about a half mile up—stay left. You'll cross a wooden bridge over Mission Creek, with Fern Canyon Falls right below you. At just under a mile the road ends at a trail split. The right fork is a fire road, so take the left fork, the Jesusita Trail, which drops into Mission Canyon. Once you cross the next creek you'll take the narrow path to the right, which runs up the west side of the canyon. This is not a very well-maintained trail and requires scampering over boulders, but you'll soon come upon the waterfalls and pools.

Bike Trails

Off road, on major streets, by the beach—anywhere you go in town you'll see someone on a bike. From flat beachfront rides to tough mountain roads, there is something for every skill level. Lance Armstrong used to train in the mountains here, and there are hard-core cyclists everywhere. Regardless of your skill level, when you come up behind another cyclist always call out "on your left" to alert him or her to move over to the right. Contact Traffic Solutions (805/963-7283, www.traffic solutions.info) to obtain a copy of the free and most excellent Santa Barbara County bike map. If renting, consider a mountain bike over a touring bike; the slightly beefy tires are perfect for getting off road and even riding on the sand. Yes, you'll have a slower pace, but you'll be able to go anywhere the mood strikes you.

The Foothill Route, also known as Highway 192 or Cathedral Oaks, alternates between narrow stretches of road around Mission Canyon to flat wide streets near Winchester Canyon and the beach in Goleta. It's very popular because of its many hills, and you can ride from the beach in Goleta all the way into Ojai. There is a lot of traffic around the Mission Canyon area; as the road climbs it twists and turns and cyclists need to be on the lookout for cars coming around blind curves. Between Mission Canyon and Goleta, the road widens and takes you past avocado orchards and citrus ranches until it leads into Winchester Canyon by the water.

For the most part, the **Coast Route** bike path hugs the coast near the waterfront, then climbs into a residential area and drops you down near Arroyo Burro Beach. From there the road climbs into Hope Ranch, a beautiful and well-to-do section of Santa Barbara with a stunning number of mature trees. Eventually you hit the Atascadero Bike Path, which shuttles you through low marsh lands before arriving at UCSB. You can continue on through campus to hook up with the Foothill route and make a wide loop, but it's a taxing ride.

Water Activities
WHALE-WATCHING AND SUNSET CRUISES

There is nothing like the thrill of seeing a whale, a pod of dolphins ripping through the surf, or the tranquil simplicity of a sunset cruise. These boats offer a variety of excursions. Most places will offer you another trip if you don't see any whales. But remember, a small break in the water as one of these magnificent creatures takes in air might count as a sighting.

Sunset Kidd Sailing (12 Harbor Way, 805/962-8222, www.sunsetkidd.com, daily 8 A.M.–7 P.M., $40 and up) offers private charters and morning, afternoon, evening, and full-moon cruises on their 41-foot sailing yacht. They can accommodate about 20 people, so it's not a crowded outing, and you're not fighting to get to the sides to see anything. It's a great ship in that on the return to the harbor they generally cut the motor and rig the sails for a quiet return. But remember, this is a sailboat, so there's a lot of up and down movement.

© JAY SINCLAIR

beach biker

In contrast, **Condor Cruises** (301 W. Cabrillo Blvd., 805/882-0088, www.condor cruises.com, whale-watching $48 adults, $12 children under 12, cruises $25–35) is a 75-foot high-speed catamaran, which means you're tooling across the water quickly, not sailing. This is a more stable ride for those prone to motion sickness. Whale-watching cruises run about two and a half hours. They too offer a full roster of cruises and excursions, including bird-watching trips. Those trips are usually about two hours and have an open bar and light food.

KAYAKING

Sitting low in a kayak allows you to really experience the water. Kayaking need not be a strenuous activity, and paddling is not difficult. You can rent kayaks for an hour or longer and explore the coast easily and up close—pack food with you and you can choose a beach for a picnic. All rental places will train you in the simple forms of safety. If you do launch from the harbor and choose to pass the breakwater,

a half mile straight out is a green buoy that is usually packed with seals basking in the sun. Make a slow approach, and you can easily get within five feet. Otherwise, just enjoy the coast, but remember that it's easy to paddle out and it's always longer to come back. Winds, currents, and fatigue could mean it ends up being a longer day than you had planned. Always take water and sun protection with you.

There are also companies offering guided tours of the Channel Islands, including some of the sea caves on Anacapa and Santa Cruz Islands. Some of the caves go several hundred feet into the islands and are simply spectacular with their soft color palettes of ochers, blues, and greens. Please note: Do not ever attempt to kayak into a sea cave without a knowledgeable person with you. The surges can easily lift your kayak up and smash you into the roof or sides of the caves. Yes, the caves are enticing, but if you don't know the area and how the surges affect the caves, you're asking for problems.

Paddle Sports (117 Harbor Way, 850/899-4925, www.kayaksb.com, basic kayak rental

paddleboarding

© JAY SINCLAIR

$25 for 2-hour minimum) has been around for 20 years and has a great staff. You can rent and get trained in both kayaking and paddle surfing. They also rent pedal kayaks so you can save your arms.

The **Santa Barbara Sailing Center** (at the harbor, 800/350-9090, www.sbsail.com, basic kayak rental $10–15/hr) will also take you to the islands or just along the coast. They provide single and tandem kayaks and can provide extensive kayak instruction if you want to get really serious.

Spas

Healing Circle Massage (805/680-1984, www.healingcirclemassage.com, by appointment only, basic one-hour massage $80) is where you go to get the kinks worked out. This isn't fluffy pampering with hot stones while sipping cocktails; this is serious deep-tissue and trigger-point work. Owner Kathy Gruver works on hard-core athletes and anyone with chronic pain–related problems, and specializes in medical and therapeutic massage—not for the faint of heart. In addition to returning range of motion to stressed-out individuals, she also does pre-natal massage, health consultations, Reiki, and Bach flower essences. While many places actually give you a 50-minute massage and call it an hour, at Healing Circle you get a full hour.

Acupuncture, aromatherapy, spa parties, warm seaweed wraps, and waxing are just some of the offerings from **Crimson Day Spa** (31 Parker Way, 805/563-7546, www.crimson dayspa.com, Mon. noon–4 P.M., Tues.–Sat. 10 A.M.–5 P.M., and by appointment, basic one-hour massage $80). The space is uncluttered, with nice touches of decor to suggest relaxation, and they are very professional and have developed a loyal following.

Avia Spa (350 Chapala St., 805/730-7303, www.aviaspa.com, Mon.–Wed. and Fri. 10 A.M.–6 P.M., Thurs. 10 A.M.–8 P.M., Sun. 11 A.M.–6 P.M., basic one-hour massage $100) offers a wealth of services, including tanning beds (both sunless and UV), massage, and salon and spa services like nail and foot care,

all housed in a bamboo-accented interior with wood floors and an Asian-inspired decor. They also have their own line of skin-care products.

Float Luxury Spa (18 E. Canon Perdido, 805/845-7777, www.floatluxuryspa.com, Mon.–Sat. 9 A.M.–7 P.M., Sun. 10 A.M.–6 P.M., basic one-hour massage $100) is one of the newest additions to the spa scene, aiming for a day-spa concept, where you can stay for hours. Located downtown, their space is surprisingly large, sleek, and uncluttered. They offer the usual treatments like massage, facials, and the rest, but out back is a beautiful rectangular tiled reflecting pool, a great spot to get lunch or to take a deep breath. Upstairs they have a quiet space, a nearly solid white room with chairs fronting a fireplace; here you can sit and detox.

Le Reve (21 W. Guttierez, 805/564-2977, www.le-reve.com, Mon.–Tues. 10 A.M.–3 P.M., Wed. 10 A.M.–6 P.M., Thurs.–Fri. 10 A.M.–7 P.M., Sat. 9 A.M.–5 P.M., Sun. 10 A.M.–5 P.M., basic one-hour massage $95) is the only green-certified spa in town. If you love lavender, Le Reve ("the dream") offers an aromatherapy massage or body wrap. Located downtown near the freeway, this spa uses Jurlique products, which have plant-based and herbal ingredients such as lavender. They also offer Girls Night Out every Wednesday from 6 to 8 P.M., which starts off with a glass of champagne and chocolate, then it's off to relaxation. They also offer waxing and tinting and a host of other services.

Qui Si Bella (3311 State St., 805/682-0003, www.quisibella.com, Mon. noon–5 P.M., Tues.–Sat. 10 A.M.–7 P.M., Sun. 10 A.M.–5 P.M., basic one-hour massage $80) handles manicures and pedicures, scrubs and facials, in an Italian-designed spa on Upper State Street. They also perform massages and microdermabrasion, and bath soaks in coconut milk. Or, get an ion-cleanse foot bath before your walks on the beach.

ACCOMMODATIONS

Santa Barbara has never been an inexpensive place to stay. Regardless of time of year, weather, even economic downturns, people continue to flock to the area—and they pay for the privilege of hanging out here. Be prepared to spend some cash, and don't expect much negotiating. The bed tax is currently at 12 percent; make sure to factor that into your travel plans and budget. Most properties will require a two-night minimum stay during the peak summer season.

Downtown

The great thing about staying downtown is that you don't need a car. You walk out your door and you're close to shopping, restaurants, galleries, and bars. On the flip side, weekend evenings can get noisy, and there's a lot of foot traffic on State Street.

UNDER $200

The Presidio Motel (1620 State St., 805/963-1355, www.thepresidiomotel.com, $150–175 d) is several blocks up State and is a very cool motel. The 16 rooms are minimalist, but each one has unique designs created by UCSB students, like abstract stars or a girl holding a parasol as she walks a tightrope above the gaping jaws of an alligator. It's not in the thick of things, but you can still easily access many activities by walking a little farther. They have complimentary beach cruisers so you can explore on two wheels, and an upstairs sun deck from which to watch the happenings on State. A continental breakfast and free Wi-Fi add to the allure. The young owners are dedicated to making the motel a must-stop for those who want something different.

At the **Best Western Encina Lodge** (2220 Bath St., 805/682-7277, www.encinalodge.com, $175–195 d), 122 good-sized rooms are decorated with a country motif; the suites are great for an extended stay. Located on a residential street near a hospital, it's an out-of-the-way place and fairly quiet. They have a heated pool, small aviary, free Wi-Fi, and free shuttle service to the airport and train station. It's not really within walking distance to much, so you will probably need a car if you stay here.

$200-300

The super-under-the-radar **(** **Inn of the Spanish Garden** (915 Garden St., 805/564-4700, www.spanishgardeninn.com, $265–285) is so unknown that most locals don't even know where it is. Tucked off of State Street, this Spanish-style full-service hotel aims for stellar service while keeping a low profile. All 23 rooms are beautifully appointed and have either balconies or patios facing a central courtyard. They have high-end linens and French press coffeemakers, plus generous bathrooms. It's an easy three-block walk to the action, but you'll love returning to the luxurious beds and deep baths and large showers. It's something of a secret that many celebrities stay here because it's so low-key.

(**The Upham Hotel** (1404 De La Vina St., 805/962-0058, www.uphamhotel.com, $220–325 d) is the oldest continuously operating hotel in Santa Barbara, having opened its doors as the Lincoln House in 1871. A Historic Hotel of America, the property has seven buildings, though it feels much more intimate, and is predominantly centered about a garden courtyard. There are smaller rooms, ideal for a busy weekend, or larger rooms with fireplaces for a stay-in weekend. The Upham has an attached restaurant, Louie's, but you're also within walking distance of State Street or a cab ride from the beach. There are varying degrees of antiquity within the hotel, with some rooms from the 1800s and 1920s.

Similar in style is the **Cheshire Cat Inn** (36 W. Valerio, 805/569-1610, www.cheshirecat.com, $159–299 d), which has adopted an Alice in Wonderland theme. The 17 rooms and cottages in this Queen Anne 1894 building are decorated, though not with the wild, goofy colors you'd expect—there's a more restrained English country feel to the rooms, some of which have fireplaces, hot tubs, and balconies. Full breakfasts are included, as is an evening wine and cheese reception; there's free Wi-Fi and off-street parking. It's quiet here, in spite of being just a few blocks from the action on State Street.

Also quiet is the remarkable **James House** (1632 Chapala St., 805/569-5853, www

.jameshousesantabarbara.com, $259 d), a historic 1894 Queen Anne property with only five rooms, nicely appointed with period-style furnishings and hardwood floors. The bathrooms have all been upgraded to more modern amenities, but the rooms will remind you of time gone by. Breakfast cooked by the owner herself is served each morning. People return here again and again for the hospitality, the small number of rooms, the walking distance to much of State Street, and just the thrill of being in a property where time slows down as it does here.

If being right downtown is what you want, the **Hotel Santa Barbara** (533 State St., 805/957-9300, www.hotelsantabarbara.com, $229–249 d) is a good choice—it's directly on State Street, right where the action is. You walk out your door and everything is within walking distance. The 75 rooms are nicely appointed and comfortable, if a tad small for the standard rooms. Copious amounts of tile work inside will give you that Santa Barbara feel. The pillows are either down, feather, or hypoallergenic. There are in-room coffeemakers, but there's also a Starbucks on the premises. There is no on-site gym, but they offer a package with a local gym (that you would need to drive to). They offer a basic continental breakfast.

OVER $300

The best selling point of **The Canary Hotel** (31 W. Carrillo, 805/884-0300, www.canary santabarbara.com, $430–445 d), other than its dead-center location in town, is the rooftop deck with a pool and fireplace. On summer nights you can lounge here for hours under the stars with some pretty excellent views. The smartly designed interiors have a Moroccan feel with Spanish undertones and hardwood floors—it's kind of like a modern-day Casablanca. They have the best access to State Street and all that it offers. The 97 rooms and suites are a little small for the money, but beautifully done. The drawback is that it's across the street from the bus terminal and a gas station, but if you don't look out your window you'll never notice.

The **Simpson House Inn** (121 E. Arrellaga, 805/963-7067, www.simpsonhouseinn.com, $255–475 d) bed-and-breakfast features a total of 16 opulent rooms on an 1874 estate with a well-manicured and formal English garden—you'll feel like you're in another world. A vegetarian breakfast starts the day, afternoon tea and desserts are available mid-day, and an evening wine-tasting brings it to a close. They offer croquet and a day pass to a local fitness club, and they boast gratuity-free services. Situated on a corner lot in a residential section, it's a short walk to State Street.

Oceanfront
$150-200

The **Harbor House Inn** (104 Bath St., 805/962-9745, www.harborhouseinn.com, $149–209 d) is a great little property a half block from the water. They'll loan you beach towels, chairs, and umbrellas for lounging at West Beach, and bikes to ride there. The 17 rooms and studios are surprisingly well appointed, with a more home-like feel than most hotels, and they have a respectable amount of furnishings—the kind you'd find in someone's house. Best of all, you won't break the bank.

With a pseudo-1950 retro flair to their interiors, the **Avania Inn** (128 Castillo St., 805/963-4471, www.avaniainnsantabarbara .com, $175–195 d) is just a block up from the beach in an unremarkable two-story motel building. But the rooms are cool and hip, and you're saving some clams at this 46-room, five-suite pad. Perhaps the best thing they offer, in addition to standard fare like a simple breakfast and proximity to the beach, is the small redwood spa and heated outdoor pool. They will give you a free morning paper so you can plan your day.

$200-300

Santa Barbara Inn (901 E. Cabrillo Blvd., 800/231-0431, www.santbarbarainn.com, $279–299) is prime oceanfront property. The 69 spacious rooms all have a palm motif, from the bedding to the furniture to actual palm trees inside. Most rooms face the water, with private balconies and sliding glass doors; some face the mountains. There's an outdoor pool and hot tub, and you're literally steps from the beach with unfettered views. The trolley stops directly in front of the hotel, so you can go carless with ease. They provide a continental breakfast each morning and offer free Wi-Fi.

The **Villa Rosa Inn** (15 Chapala St., 805/966-0851, www.villarosainnsb.com, $229–279 d) is deceptive from the outside. The small door in what looks like someone's house a half block from the beach seems nearly hidden, except for the sign. But beyond the door is a beautiful hideaway with a Mediterranean feel and luxurious antiques. The 18 rooms are all vastly different, and it's intimate and very comfortable. All rooms have views—of the ocean, mountains, harbor, or courtyard—though some are constrained and the bathrooms are a little small. They claim they are only 84 steps to the beach. They offer evening port or sherry by the fire and a continental breakfast.

(**Brisas del Mar** (223 Castillo, 805/966-2219, www.brisasdelmarinn.com, $267–297 d) is located just two blocks from the beach. Half of their rooms are larger suites with full kitchens, making this 31-room hotel great for a longer getaway. Though the exterior is Mediterranean, the interiors have knotty pine furnishings and soft tones. There's covered parking, something unusual for most hotels in town, as well as a collection of over 800 DVD, Wi-Fi, an exercise room, continental breakfast, and a gracious staff. There's an outdoor shower by the pool.

The 42 guest rooms at the **Inn by the Harbor** (433 W. Montecito St., 805/963-7851, www.innbytheharbor.com, $225–269 d) are decorated with Spanish Mediterranean–style furnishings, all slightly different. Many rooms feature full-sized kitchens, ideal for budget vacations or extended stays. In addition to a deluxe continental breakfast and afternoon wine and cheese, they serve evening milk and cookies. Bud Bottoms, a local artist who created the bronze dolphins that are at the entrance to Stearns Wharf, created the dolphin sculpture in front of the inn.

The **Mason Beach Inn** (324 W. Mason, 805/962-3203, www.masonbeachinn.com, $239–269 d) is a pretty simple whitewashed hotel with 45 rooms that feature standard furnishings. But it's clean, close to the beach and harbor, and right across from the Carriage Museum. It's not fancy, but it is a fine base for accessing the beach and downtown while saving some cash. They offer a heated outdoor pool and hot tub, basic continental breakfast, and free Wi-Fi.

OVER $300

The Harbor View Inn (28 W. Cabrillo Blvd., 800/755-0222, www.harborviewinnsb .com, $325–375 d) has a plum spot at the intersection of State Street and Stearns Wharf. Of course, you pay for such proximity. But this high-end amenity-filled property, wrapped in red-tile roofs and Mexican-tiled stairways and fountains, is classic Santa Barbara. There are 102 rooms and 13 suites, an in-house restaurant, a pool, a spa, and, frankly, all you'd need to make your stay in town wonderful. There are in-room safes, free Wi-Fi, and quick access to the beach and activities.

Not too far down the beach is the **Fess Parker's DoubleTree Resort** (633 E. Cabrillo Blvd., 805/564-4333, www.fessparkersanta barbarahotel.com, $410–455 d), a Mission-style spread with four restaurants, an exercise facility, three tennis courts, shuffle board, and a putting green, all just across from the beach. The 360 rooms face either the mountain or the beach; a few face the interior courtyard. Even their small rooms are pretty large, and you can't beat the location if you like being close to the water. They offer a free shuttle to the airport and train station, but charge a fee for parking.

Upper State Street

Staying just outside the money zone is not necessarily a bad idea. Sure, you don't have the ocean views and are not close to downtown, but if you save some cash on your room you can spend it elsewhere.

Fess Parker's DoubleTree Resort

UNDER $200

Agave Inn (3222 State St., 805/687-6009, www.agaveinnsb.com, $169–189 d) uses the Spanish theme a little differently: Spanish movie posters and brightly colored throws as well as various brightly painted walls are the accents that set this place apart. It's like a bit of modern pop was tossed into each of the 13 rooms, where you'll also find iPod docks. Agave Inn is directly across from a small park and near Loreto Plaza, a small shopping center with a grocery store and restaurants. The freeway is close, as is downtown. Some rooms come with full kitchens, and the inn is a delightful spot, very cool, hip, and simple.

$200-300

Amid the visually unappealing architecture on Upper State Street is the **Best Western Pepper Tree Inn** (3850 State St., 805/687-5511, www.bestwesternpeppertreeinn.com, $225–255), a five-acre locally owned property. The 150-room building is large by Santa Barbara standards, but you're close to the freeway and right across the street from La Cumbre Mall. The private decks and balconies look over a central courtyard where the pool is located. Though the style is somewhat Spanish, it's a more classic hotel interior with standard furnishings. The rooms are large enough but a little dark, as the one window faces the courtyard and you may not want your sliding door open. There are two pools, two hot tubs, and a fitness center. They offer shuttle service to the airport and train station.

Goleta
UNDER $200

Ramada Unlimited (4770 Calle Real, Goleta, 805/964-3511, www.sbramada.com, $149–189 d) is a locally owned and operated Ramada, about a 10-minute drive from downtown. The best rooms and suites face the mountains, and every one of the 126 rooms has a small refrigerator, a microwave, and a coffeemaker. Dead center in the hotel, near the outdoor pool, is an amazing tropical lagoon with water lilies, palms, and koi. The

GOLETA

© AVALON TRAVEL

rooms are standard, but also less expensive than downtown.

OVER $300

If money is no object and you want a luxury lodging close to the beach, the **Bacara Resort and Spa** (8310 Hollister Ave., Goleta, 877/422-4245, www.bacararesort.com, from $475) is ideal. It is a 360 room Andalusian-style village of suites and rooms just steps from the crashing surf. Perched on 80 acres of prime Pacific coast shoreline it is also exclusive and expensive, but that is the point. The rooms are large, with sliding doors to views of the ocean. It's all five-star here, and with the multiple restaurants, spa, and even a little shopping on-site, you may not spend a million bucks, but you're sure to feel like a million bucks when you stay here. Amenities include 24-hour in-room dining, personalized voice mail, and free Wi-Fi.

Montecito
$200-300

That Charlie Chaplin founded the **⟨** **Montecito Inn** (1295 Coast Village Rd., 805/969-7854, www.montecitoinn.com, $265–285 d) is of no small importance. In the late 1920s Chaplin wanted a getaway from the hectic Hollywood crowd, and so built the inn, more so his friends could escape with him than as an actual inn. These days it's still as charming as it was intended.

The 61 rooms are small, the halls even smaller, but that's how life was back then. This is a wonderful historic property; vintage Chaplin posters line the walls, and there's a collection of Chaplin's DVDs to watch in your room. Visitors also have free use of the beach cruisers, or jump into the heated pool or sweat in the exercise room. The hotel is only two blocks from the beach and on Coast Village Road, the heart of the tony Montecito shopping district.

OVER $300

There's no place quite like **The Four Seasons Biltmore** (1260 Channel Dr., 805/969-2742, www.fourseasons.com, from $425), which sits just above Butterfly Beach in Montecito and has long held its ground as one of the best places to stay. It's laid out like a small Spanish village, with lush landscaping including ferns and bright red bougainvillea set against the whitewashed hand-troweled walls creating an almost tropical feel. The rooms continue the Spanish theme with large ornate furniture. You can walk to shopping and restaurants on Coast Village Road, or drive into downtown. In addition to tennis courts and exercise rooms, guests are able to access the exclusive Cabana Club next door, a private club for members and guests only. The Cabana Club's historic 1937 structure was renovated 2005–2008 and now has a postmodern interior. There's a large pool, cabanas, and a play room for the kids, and it has an excellent restaurant where sliding doors on the 2nd floor open up to expansive views of the ocean.

If a mountain retreat is more your style, the **San Ysidro Ranch** (900 San Ysidro Ln., 805/565-1700, www.sanysidroranch.com, from $795) has 41 individually and lushly appointed rustic cottages and suites tucked neatly into the mountains with exceptional ocean views. Rooms range from small and intimate to the 1,300-square-foot Kennedy Cottage, where John Kennedy and his new bride, Jackie, honeymooned in 1953. There are two restaurants on the property and 17 miles of hiking trails. In-room spa services are available, and pets are welcome.

© MELISSA FARGO

Montecito Inn

FOOD

There's a long-standing claim that Santa Barbara has more restaurants per capita than any other place in the United States. That's never been proven, nor disproven, but with everything from taco stands to five-star restaurants, you will definitely find something you like. Touristy places are not always the best choice. There's a lot of average food in town, so seek out the exceptional.

Downtown

Many restaurants in downtown Santa Barbara have outdoor seating, and it's not unusual to see long waits on summer nights. Not all places take reservations, but many do—make reservations if you can. Many of the restaurants serve what is loosely labeled "wine country cuisine," which is to say local fresh foods and ingredients used in lighter dishes, not heavily laden with sauces, that pair well with local wines. Specifically, this means fresh fish from the harbor, fresh veggies and fruits from the many local farmers, and locally sourced meats—not

processed foods, but foods that are inherently, naturally flavorful.

WINE COUNTRY CUISINE

Opal Restaurant and Bar (1325 State St., 805/966-9676, www.opalrestaurantandbar .com, Mon.–Thurs. 11:30 A.M.–2:30 P.M. and 5–10 P.M., Fri.–Sat. 11:30 A.M.–2:30 P.M. and 5–11 P.M., Sun. 5–10 P.M., $20) is eternally popular with locals. With fresh pastas, seafood, salads, and steaks, plus a well-rounded wine list with over 300 selections, Opal succeeds every time. The owners have been part of the Santa Barbara dining scene for over two decades, and some of their staff have been with them for nearly as long. The interior is soft yellow tones and dark hardwoods, and the place is noisy, lively, and energetic.

At **⬤ Julienne** (138 E. Canon Perdido, 805/845-6488, www.restaurantjulienne.com, Wed.–Sat. 5–10 P.M., Sun. 5–9 P.M., $25), chef Jason West uses vegetables pulled from the ground that day and seafood that's arrived on the dock that morning. The small space with

MARKET FORAYS

Market Forays (805/259-7229, www
.marketforays.com, Tues. 3-8:30 P.M., Sat.
8 A.M.-3:30 P.M., $145) is a unique hands-
on cooking class – the very cool idea was
started by the founder of the local slow-
food movement. You spend the day meeting with local fishermen, then spend time
at the farmers market, all while obtaining
fresh food you will then use to cook an
ideal Santa Barbara meal. The point is
to get people in touch with farmers and
local suppliers, to get to know them and
gain an understanding and appreciation
for one's food.

only 12 tables has a bistro feel to it, and the menu rotates as often as every few days, so you often can't come back and order the same thing. The menu is limited, and at first you might think you want more options. But the food (and service) is excellent; be adventurous and let the thoughtfully prepared food work its magic. Things you may have thought you didn't like are masterpieces in the chef's hands.

(**Arts & Letters Café** (7 E. Anapamu St., 805/730-1463, www.sullivangoss.com, lunch Mon.–Sun. 11 A.M.–3 P.M., dinner Wed.–Sun. 5–9 P.M., $18) is sequestered behind the Sullivan Goss Art Gallery, and you need to walk through the gallery to reach the secluded back patio. Once there you'll feel like you're a world away. Try their excellent pumpkin soup, which was written up in the *New York Times,* the smoked-salmon pot stickers, or their very best salad, with warm lamb on top of baby spinach with feta cheese. You'll be looking at beautiful art on the walls, and beautiful food on your plate. You needn't buy any art, but you might be so pleased with your meal that a new painting could be the perfect ending.

Bouchon (9 W. Victoria, 805/730-1160, www.bouchonsantabarbara.com, Sun.–Thurs. 5:30–9 P.M., Fri.–Sat. 5:30–10 P.M., $30) is classic farm-fresh Santa Barbara cuisine, paired with local wines. The small space, with

simple country furnishings that belie the complex food, also has an outdoor covered patio. The kitchen excels at most everything it does, including foie gras, venison, and stellar duck breast. You pay dearly for this kind of food and service, but the fresh, flavorful food will leave you hankering for more. The staff knows what Santa Barbara wines pair well with your food.

Blush Restaurant and Lounge (630 State St., 805/957-1300, www.blushsb.com, daily 11 A.M.–10 P.M., late-night menu Mon.–Sat. 10 P.M.–midnight, $25) is hip, sleek, and very cool inside. Big comfy booths line up against exposed brick walls, and glass balls of light suspended by thin wire give the illusion of stars hanging in mid-air. The long outdoor area has couches and three fireplaces. Fortunately, the food matches the cool ambience. Juniper chicken and a surprisingly excellent and unusual beet carpaccio are some of the creative dishes they have come up with. There's a crowded bar and it gets loud inside, but dining outside on a couch near the fireplace while watching people amble down State Street is a fine experience.

The **Wine Cask** (813 Anacapa St., 805/966-9463, nightly 5:30–9 P.M., $30) has been one of the most influential restaurants in town for over 25 years; it was one of the first to create wine pairings with food. Several years back it was sold to an out-of-town interest who fouled it up tremendously. It was then taken back by the original owner and a new partner, and now it's the flagship restaurant for wine country cuisine that people have always expected, with attentive service and well-executed innovative dishes like pistachio and watercress soup, cassoulet of duck leg confit, pork cheeks and rabbit sausage, and pan-seared salmon.

One of the single best spots for alfresco dining is **Pierre Lafond Wine Bistro** (516 State St., 805/962-6607, www.pierrelafond .com, Mon.–Fri. 9 A.M.–9 P.M., Sat.–Sun. 8 A.M.–9 P.M., $20). The interior, with its large plate-glass windows fronting State Street, feels somewhat industrial and lacks a motif, but that doesn't belie the quality of the food. The exterior gated patio allows all kinds of people-watching and is the prime place to be. The food choices are creative, like the grilled Hawaiian escolar, a goat cheese and onion tart, or the chicken chorizo omelet. Since this is owned by the Santa Barbara Winery, you'll see plenty of their wines offered along with a wide selection from around the globe.

ARGENTINIAN

Café Buenos Aires (1316 State St., 805/963-0242, www.cafebuenosaires.com, Mon.–Fri. 11:30 A.M.–2:30 P.M. and 5:30 P.M.–close, Sat.–Sun. 11:30 A.M.–3:30 P.M. and 5 P.M.–close, $20) offers food from the owners' home country of Argentina. A central fountain is surrounded by tables on a patio that allows for fresh air and people-watching. On Wednesday evenings, live tango music and dancing fills the patio for those who want to burn a few calories. On weekend nights, Latin jazz takes center stage. The menu offers traditional South American dishes of beef, pork, and fish, as well as vegetarian options. Keeping with the theme, they pour Argentina's most well-known wine, malbec, by the glass and bottle.

FRENCH

Often overlooked, **Pacific Crêpes** (705 Anacapa St., 805/882-1123, www.pacificcrepe.com, Mon. 10 A.M.–3 P.M., Tues.–Fri. 10 A.M.–3 P.M. and 5:30–9 P.M., Sat. 9 A.M.–9 P.M., Sun. 9 A.M.–3 P.M., $18) is a delightful spot. The interior is laden with French posters, and books line the walls. It's an intimate space, with simple French country decor and indoor and outdoor seating. They use buckwheat as their main ingredient—traditional for crepes in Brittany where the owners are from—hence the brown color. The fillings are as diverse as you could want, and the crepes are surprisingly large. Also be sure to try the french onion soup, escargot, and the wonderful profiteroles. Each Wednesday conversational French classes are held 5:30–7:30 P.M.

MIDDLE EASTERN

Zaytoon (209 E. Canon Perdido, 805/963-1293, www.cafezaytoon.com, Mon.–Sat. 11:30 A.M.–9 P.M., Sun. 5–9 P.M., $25) is an amalgam of Middle Eastern foods, from Lebanese wine to Turkish coffee and immensely flavorful tabbouli, hummus, and lamb, all spicy and earthy. This is a lounging spot with plenty of outdoor tables, belly dancers, and hookah. This is not a place for a quick bite to eat, however, as the service can be pretty slow, especially on weekend nights, but it's a great overall experience. There's very little in the way of Middle Eastern food in town; fortunately Zaytoon does it well.

HEALTHY FARE

Don't be alarmed by the word *vegetarian* if you're a carnivore. The **◖ Sojourner Cafe** (134 E. Canon Perdido, 805/965-7922, www.sojournercafe.com, Mon.–Sat. 11 A.M.–11 P.M., Sun. 11 A.M.–10 P.M., $10), or The Soj, as it's called, will make you rethink how good vegetarian can be. Celebrating 30 years in business, they turn out some of the best food in town, with amazingly flavorful smoothies, fresh-baked cookies, and daily specials. The interior needs a face-lift, but that doesn't detract from the polenta royale, their Cobb salad using hominy, or their cornbread supreme, doused with pinto beans, veggies, garlic butter, and cheese.

Spiritland Bistro (230 E. Victoria, 805/966-7759, www.spiritlandbistro.com, Wed.–Sun. 5:30–9 P.M., $25) is more high-end vegetarian, in an intimate dimly lit environment with booths and freestanding tables. They do have some chicken and fish dishes, but their menu identifies which dishes are gluten-, wheat-, and/or dairy-free. The bistro of a dozen tables manages to stay quiet even with lots of guests. They serve dinner only, and the food—like falafel salad, Thai coconut curry, and the very tasty artichoke purée—will make you realize how wonderful healthy can taste. A favorite dessert is the lavender and organic honey crème brûlée.

CHEAP EATS

Quick and easy is always a good option, especially when it's coupled with good prices.

D'Vine Café (205 W. Canon Perdido St.,

805/963-9591, www.dvinecafe.com, Mon.–Fri. 8 A.M.–4 P.M., Sat. 11 A.M.–3 P.M., $8) has been crafting sandwiches and salads for years, creating inexpensive, portable food that does not shock your wallet nor offend your taste buds. Insanely popular is their grilled salmon salad, and the chicken salad sandwich is great. They make wraps, and you can customize you sandwich in either a whole or half size. The place is basic to look at—indoor and outdoor seating with lots of plastic chairs. But for made-to-order food at these prices, you won't go wrong.

BREAKFAST AND BRUNCH
At **Crush Café** (1315 Anacapa St., 805/963-3752, www.crushcakes.com, daily 8 A.M.–5 P.M., $10) the cupcakery has expanded into a full-service restaurant. The old hardwood floors give way to a European country feel (a wood pitchfork is clamped against one wall, for example). It's not elaborately decorated; instead the place prefers simple wood tones. It feels homey, undoubtedly because the 100-year-old place was once a residence. They bake a lot here, including strawberry scones and cinnamon rolls. If you've been out too late the night before, try their Hangover Helper: a grilled breakfast sandwich of eggs, tomato, cheddar cheese, and bacon on sourdough, with a side of fresh fruit. Another favorite is Peace, Love, and Granola: chunky house-made granola over house-made vanilla bean yogurt and drizzled with honey.

COFFEE AND TEA
There are always the ubiquitous national coffee chains, but since you're in Santa Barbara, go local. At **The Daily Grind** (2001 De La Vina, 805/687-4966, Mon.–Sun. 5:30 A.M.–10 P.M.), which is one of the most popular places for early morning, the prime seats on the outside deck always seem to be taken, but there is an indoor seating area near the counter as well. This place is so full of locals that you might feel intimidated. Teas, smoothies, and an abundance of coffee drinks and 11 regular coffees are at the ready. They serve a variety of pastries made on-site and breakfast and lunch options. It's cash only.

DESSERTS
There has been a surge of cupcake joints in recent years, but **Crushcakes** (1315 Anacapa St., 805/963-9353, www.crushcakes.com, Mon.–Sat. 9 A.M.–6 P.M., Sun. 10 A.M.–5 P.M.) takes the cake. They produce a dozen different varieties of these minicakes each day; their red velvet cake is the most popular. They also bake up a vegan cupcake. At $3 a pop they aren't cheap, but one is all you really need.

Oceanfront
For better or worse, the oceanfront offers a collection of average restaurants with great views. The food is standard and the service is usually hit and miss. Most visitors want ocean views, understandably. But you may find it's best to search out better food to avoid being frustrated by a bad experience. The ocean is visible from much of Santa Barbara, so save your hard-earned cash and spend it on quality food, then go walk on the beach. Listed here are some of the oceanfront places that shine.

SEAFOOD
◖ **Brophy Brothers** (119 Harbor Way, 805/966-4418, www.brophybros.com, Sun.–Thurs. 11 A.M.–10 P.M., Fri.–Sat. 11 A.M.–11 P.M., $25) is the exception to the oceanfront rule. Located at the harbor, it is eternally busy serving fresh local seafood in a hectic, loud environment. The prime seats are outside on a narrow strip of balcony crowded with people standing at their outdoor bar. A sunset dinner of fresh seafood here overlooking the boats is killer. Their side dishes like salad, coleslaw, and rice seem like afterthoughts, but the entrées are exceptional. They offer a raw oyster bar and the staff, while busy, are efficient. They don't take reservations, so if you arrive late, you'll find yourself in their downstairs bar waiting to be called.

SANDWICHES AND BURGERS
Metropulos (216 E. Yanonali, 805/899-2300, www.metrofinefoods.com, Mon.–Fri. 8:30 A.M.–6 P.M., Sat. 10 A.M.–4 P.M., $10) is a

mere block from the beach and is the best place to stop to gather picnic supplies. Get a sandwich or salad to go, or some of the many olives from Africa, Spain, and Italy. Their sandwiches are wonderful, such as their apple ham brie panini on multi-grain sourdough. Ortry a cranberry goat cheese salad with spinach and organic mixed greens. They also have a small wine shop, colorful and creative pastas to cook at home, and a really moist chocolate biscotti. There are a handful of prime outdoor seats.

Upper State Street

Far from the madding crowds—well, not too far—State Street as everyone knows it turns into Upper State, a decidedly different place than what most tourists ever see. It's mainly residential, with some restaurants worth checking out.

ITALIAN

⟨ **Via Maestra 42** (3343 State St., 805/569-6522, Mon.–Sat. 8:30 A.M.–9 P.M., Sun. 11 A.M.–5 P.M., $15), so named for the owner's address in his hometown in Alba, Italy, is located in an unremarkable strip mall right next to the post office. But this place turns out delicious, authentic Italian food, including a wide variety of pastas and cured meats. The space is small, with a few outside seats. It gets crowded and the service is a tad slow, but it's worth the wait. You can also buy Italian cheeses, meats, and gelato to go. During truffle season, they import both white and black truffles from Italy for sale to the public can buy, several restaurants in town also purchase their truffles here.

GERMAN

Brummis (3130 State St., 805/687-5916, Mon.–Fri. 11:30 A.M.–1:30 P.M. and 5–9 P.M., Sat. 5–9 P.M., $20) has an inside decor as simple as spaetzle; all bare bones, with a few posters hanging loosely on the walls. But the restaurant, run by a mother and daughter team from Germany, is as authentic as you can get. A few German beers are available to complement your meal, and it's not uncommon to hear conversations in German taking place around you.

Schnitzel, sauerbraten, and kasslerbraten will put the oompah in you if you have a hankering for German food.

STEAKHOUSE

Tee-Off (3627 State St., 805/687-1616, www .teeoffsb.com, Mon.–Thurs. 5–10 P.M., Fri.–Sat. 5–11 P.M., Sun. 5–9 P.M., $25) is old school meets, well, old school. Tee-Off has been around for 40 years, and very little has changed. It's the kind of place where when you walk in, people immediately know if you're a local or not. (But don't worry, they're still friendly.) This is the place where the waitress will call you "hon" and mean it. Get there early for a choice seat in the red booths that face the bar and pig out on way too much food. Forget the fish or anything else and get the prime rib—that's what the locals do.

SUSHI

Kyoto (3232 State St., 805/687-1252, www.kyoto sb.com, lunch Mon.–Fri. 11:30 A.M.–2 P.M., Sat. noon–2:30 P.M., dinner Sun.–Thurs. 5–10 P.M., Fri.–Sat. 5–10:30 P.M., $20) is on the opposite end of Upper State Street, in a spot that has been a sushi restaurant for 30 years. Eight booths face the four tatami rooms; a separate sushi bar is sequestered behind a pony wall. There's a great price-to-value ratio here, enhanced by their nightly sushi happy hour from 5 to 6 P.M. when the small space gets crowded and 40 rolls and nigiri are half off. For those who don't like sushi there's plenty of tempura and hibachi, served by a family who is genuinely glad you're there.

BREAKFAST AND BRUNCH

If you've ever been to Paris and eaten a fresh baguette, you know heaven can look like a loaf of bread. Classic French pastries and breads are loaded with real butter, cream, and plenty of calories at **Renaud's Patisserie and Bistro** (3315 State St., 805/569-2400, Mon.–Sat. 7 A.M.–6 P.M., Sun. 7 A.M.–3 P.M., $15), which also has the best croissants in the city. Their classic European breakfast basket containing a croissant and toasted baguette with butter and jam, plus coffee or tea, will transport you to Paris. For those who need something more, quiche lorraine, *pain bagnat,* and cheese ravioletis will satisfy you. Save room for any of their sweets. It's run by a Frenchman, so you know you're getting authentic French food.

Goleta

Goleta, no longer Santa Barbara's unincorporated sister, became an incorporated city in 2002. Though the area is predominantly residential, there are more and more restaurants coming in to serve the residents who don't want to make the trek downtown.

PIZZA

Pizza may be ubiquitous, but it's not all the same. And **Gina's Pizza** (7038 Marketplace Dr., 805/571-6300, daily 11 A.M.–10 P.M., $15) serves some of the best in the city. Whether you order a Hawaiian style or a meat lovers or even a vegetarian pizza, what sets this place apart is the copious use of fresh ingredients and an exceptional crust. You can order thick or thin crust, and the sauce is kept to a minimum instead of using ridiculous amounts to cover up faulty ingredients like many other pizza places do. The ingredients are well spaced throughout the pizza so each bite gives you comprehensive flavors. They also have pasta dishes like lasagna, and minestrone soup.

CHINESE

Red Pepper (282 Orange Ave., 805/964-0995, Mon.–Sat. 11 A.M.–2:30 P.M. and 5–9 P.M., $15) is a wonderful local Chinese restaurant in Goleta, sitting incongruously right next to a plumber and a locksmith. Though the ambience is sparse and frankly uninteresting—unless you consider the nine-pound koi in the fish tank an intriguing sight—the food makes up for the decor. Their onion pancakes are a great start to any vegetarian or meat dishes, and their hot and sour soup lives up to its name. As you leave you'll get a hug from the owner, but that's nothing unusual.

DESSERTS

The idea of an organic pie or cheesecake might not turn some people on, but **Simply Pies** (5392 Hollister Ave., 805/845-2200, www.simplypiessb.blogspot.com, Tues.–Sat. 11 A.M.–3 P.M.) makes extremely excellent pies that are, in a sense, almost good for you. They offer the option of gluten- and sugar-free crusts as well as a vegan option, and frankly, they taste fantastic—especially the pumpkin cheesecake. Or pick up a strawberry rhubarb pie or chocolate cream. You will be amazed.

The Mesa and Milpas

As is true anywhere, once you veer off Santa Barbara's main drag you'll still find good eats, but oftentimes cheaper and certainly with fewer crowds. Areas like Mesa and Milpas offer very nice food without the hassle of long waits, as is typical on State Street during the summer season. That's not to say off-the-beaten-track restaurants don't get busy, only that if you go, you'll be surrounded by locals and you'll discover terrific food.

THAI

Meun Fan Thai (1819 Cliff Dr., 805/882-9422, Mon.–Thurs. 11 A.M.–9:30 P.M., Fri.–Sat. 11 A.M.–10 P.M., Sun. 4–9:30 P.M., $15) makes no apologies for the very flavorful and spicy foods served in their spot on the Mesa—let them know if you need a restrained version of your meal. There is a terrific selection here: pineapple fried rice with a bit of curry, drunken noodles with deftly prepared pan-fried noodles, *nam* salad with mint, ginger, red onions, and peanuts on top of rice and lettuce with a healthy dash of lime juice. The service is well meaning but a little slow, but the food is worth the wait.

Carpinteria

Just south of Santa Barbara, Carpinteria is attempting to assert itself as a dining destination along Linden Avenue, and they are doing quite well.

AMERICAN

The absolute best spot in all of Carpinteria is **Sly's** (686 Linden Ave., Carpinteria,

805/684-6666, www.slysonline.com, lunch Mon.–Fri. 11:30 A.M.–2:30 P.M., dinner Sun.–Thurs. 5–9 P.M., Fri.–Sat. 5–10 P.M., brunch Sat.–Sun. 9 A.M.–3 P.M., $25) for classic American fare, such as beautifully tender steaks and fresh local abalone and pastas. Chef James Sly built a huge following while he was the head chef at Lucky's in Montecito before starting his own venture—and the people have followed. The interior is high-end retro, with gorgeous wood tones, exposed brickwork, and white tablecloths. And the food is nearly perfect, as long as James is in the kitchen. Order any steak and you'll be happy, or try the spaghetti carbonara. Everything is à la carte here, therefore the amazing creamed corn is an additional charge. Sly's is pricey but worth it.

For a throwback to a long gone dining era, **Clementine's Steakhouse** (4631 Carpinteria Ave., 805/684-5119, Wed.–Sun. 5–9 P.M., $22) is your place. Schmaltzy music plays over the speakers, the older clientele talks quietly, the decor is 1960s country—and you can't help but smile. Burgundy tablecloths are contrasted with pink scalloped napkins, and nearly everyone leaves with leftovers. All entrées come with a crudités plate, house-baked bread, soup, and salad, along with a choice of side dish and finally home-baked pie. It's a tremendous amount of food, and they haven't changed their formula in over 30 years. Steaks, fresh fish, chicken, and pastas plus all those sides will keep you very full.

WINE COUNTRY CUISINE

At **Corktree Cellars Wine Bar & Bistro** (910 Linden Ave., 805/684-1400, www.corktree cellars.com, daily 11 A.M.–10 P.M., $15) you can order a full meal, an appetizer, a glass of wine, or a flight of wine. The interior is decked out with wood tables and chairs, a curved bar, comfy leather chairs, and yellow walls with rotating artwork. It's warm and inviting—and yes, they actually have a cork tree. The food is creative and uses diverse ingredients; try the lobster and white truffle macaroni and cheese, the corn bisque, or New England lobster melt

© JAY SINCLAIR

fresh vegetables from the local farmers market

panini. Wines can be ordered by the glass or in flights—three different tastes of a particular varietal, like Hailing a Cab with three cabernet sauvignons, or Drawing a Blanc with three sauvignon blancs. All the wine flights show a diversity of places: Santa Ynez, Napa, Argentina, New Zealand, and more.

BARBECUE
Santa Barbara has long had a dearth of dependable barbecue joints, so it's great that **The Barbecue Company** (3807 Santa Claus Ln., 805/684-2209, Wed.–Sun. noon–9 P.M., $15) is around. Two flat-screen TVs flanking the faux rustic interior play an endless supply of concert footage, and a musical motif continues in the artwork. All their meats are slow smoked, then finished on the grill and "mopped" with an amalgam of all the sauces they make on-site. Whether you order baby-back ribs, pulled chicken, or pork, you can get a side of cornbread or mac 'n' cheese and feel like you're down home.

Farmers Markets
Santa Barbara County hosts 11 farmers markets each week. The markets are just as much for socializing as getting lemon basil or torpedo onions. Strolling musicians entertain while local chefs scour the stalls for what they'll serve that evening. Check out www.sbfarmersmarket .org for a complete schedule. The markets occur all over the county, including Goleta, Montecito, and Carpinteria, but the biggest and best are the Saturday-morning **downtown market** (Santa Barbara and Cota Sts., Sat. 8:30 A.M.–1:30 P.M.), which is the largest and most social, and the Tuesday-afternoon **State Street market** (500–600 blocks of State St., Tues. 3–6:30 P.M.). Be advised that the Tuesday market shuts down parts of State Street, and drivers are re-routed through the area.

INFORMATION AND SERVICES
The **Santa Barbara Chamber of Commerce Visitors Center** (1 Garden St., 805/965-3021, www.sbchamber.org, Mon.–Sat.

9 A.M.–4 P.M., Sun. 10 A.M.–4 P.M.) is located directly across from the beach and offers discounted tickets to many restaurants and sights in town.

John Dickson has put together a most comprehensive website, www.santabarbara.com, which includes things to do, and reviews of hotels and restaurant by locals. Though some of the information is out of date, it's still a valuable resource. And www.santabarbaraca.com is the official website for the visitors center, with an up-to-date section of maps you can download, and the latest specials and deals.

Many local retailers offer the **Axxess Book** (www.sbaxxess.com), a coupon book which costs $30, but allows a number of two-for-one wine tastings, discounts at area restaurants, golf and local sights.

In case of **emergency,** call 911 immediately. **Cottage Hospital** (at Bath and Pueblo Sts.) is the only hospital in town, and has the only emergency room. The **Santa Barbara Police Department** is located at 215 East Figueroa Street (805/897-2335).

GETTING THERE
The **Santa Barbara Municipal Airport** (601 Firestone Rd., Goleta, 805/967-7111, www .flysba.com) is a small airport that currently serves only regional flights from 10 destinations on five airlines. There is an expansion underway to enlarge the runways to accommodate more and larger planes, and the airport will be expanded from two terminals to four, losing some of the charm of the small-town red-tile-roofed airport.

Chances are you'll fly into Los Angeles or San Francisco and then connect to Santa Barbara. If you're coming in from L.A. and not connecting to Santa Barbara by air, the 90-mile drive takes about two hours. There are commercial shuttle vans and buses from L.A., but keep in mind these will also take two-plus hours, depending on traffic. **Santa Barbara Air Bus** (805/964-7759, www.santa barbaraairbus.com) runs between LAX and Santa Barbara every day and will deliver you in comfort.

Santa Barbara Municipal Airport

By car, the only entrance to Santa Barbara north or south is Highway 101, a two-lane highway that is reasonably traffic free—at least so far. Exits and off-ramps are clearly marked, and you'll know you are getting close when you see the ocean out your window.

Greyhound (34 W. Carrillo, 805/965-7551, www.greyhound.com) has a somewhat dingy terminal a block off State Street. It's convenient, though, as this is the main hub. **Amtrak** (209 State St., 805/963-1015, www.amtrak.com) pulls into Santa Barbara's 1905 depot right on State Street, one block from the beach.

GETTING AROUND
A great resource for bike trails, walking paths, train info, taxi cabs, water excursions, and all manner of transportation is www.santa barbaracarfree.com, which offers downloadable maps and ways to experience Santa Barbara while reducing your carbon footprint.

It's important to make a note about the unusual orientation of Santa Barbara. As you stand at the water's edge near the harbor, it would be easy to assume you are facing west—but you are actually looking southeast. It's a geographical oddity, but it's important to know in order to get your bearings. The city of Goleta is to the west (upcoast), and to the east (downcoast) are the unincorporated areas of Montecito, Summerland, and the City of Carpinteria, which abuts the county line with Ventura.

Driving and Parking
Laid out in a grid pattern, the city is very easy to navigate, at least the downtown core. Of particular note is that State Street, the defining street, travels from the oceanfront in a northwest direction and then makes a 90-degree bend to run east–west (where it's known as Upper State Street). Eventually State Street turns into Hollister, and by then you are entering Goleta. But all things fan out from State Street, and most directions are given in relationship to State.

The other thing to consider is that although most streets have unique names and there is little possibility of confusing them, three streets can cause a problem: Castillo, Carrillo, and Cabrillo. Here's all you need to know: Cabrillo (think of the *b* as in beach) runs the length of the waterfront. Carrillo (think of the *r* as in running right through town) bisects State Street in the center of downtown. And Castillo (think of the *s* for State) parallels State Street. If you keep that in mind, it should be easier to get around.

In general, parking is pretty easy. There are a number of parking lots in the downtown area and street parking is, mostly, 75 minutes for free. But be advised that parking enforcement is out and about, and they will ticket you should you go over your allotted time; parking tickets are $50.

Walking Tours

Seeing Santa Barbara on foot is the best way to experience the city. The **Red Tile Walking Tour** (www.santabarbaraca.com) is a condensed 12-block self-guided tour of all the important buildings in town. You can download either a map version to print, or a podcast version narrated by John O'Hurley (of TV's *Seinfeld*). You'll see Casa de la Guerra, the county courthouse, and the presidio, among other defining buildings.

Or for a more structured tour, **Santa Barbara Walking Tours** (805/687-9255, www.santabarbarawalkingtours.com, $23) has a 90-minute docent-led tour of the visual art and history in town. It combines parts of the Red Tile tour but also shows you some of the beautiful paseos, tile work, and public art that's almost everywhere.

Trolley Tours

If walking just isn't your thing, get an expanded overview of the city by riding through it. The best is the **Landshark** (805/683-7600, www

.out2seesb.com, Nov.–Apr. noon and 2 P.M., May–Oct. noon, 2, and 4 P.M., $25 adults, $10 children under 10), which is a live-narrated 90-minute tour on the Landshark, a 15-foot-high amphibious vehicle. You'll see most of the important buildings, though not the mission. On the plus side, in the last portion of the tour the Landshark plunges into the ocean and turns into a boat, going past the breakwater for great views of the coast. It's fun and informative, and you can ask all the questions you want. More likely than not you'll see dolphins and seals at the very least. All Landshark tours depart from the entrance to Stearns Wharf.

The **Santa Barbara Trolley Company** (805/965-0353, www.sbtrolley.com, daily 10 A.M.–5:30 P.M., $19 adults, $8 children under 12) offers another live narrated tour that includes the mission and other great locations like Butterfly Beach in Montecito. Tours pick up and drop off at 15 different locations every 60 minutes; see the website for a comprehensive schedule.

Taxi Cabs

Taxis are not abundant in town, nor are they in much of a rush; it's best to call for one. Assuming you do get a taxi, you're apt to get a leisurely cab ride to your destination. **Santa Barbara Checker Cab** (888/581-1110) is a safe bet.

State Street Trolley

For just 25 cents, you can ride the trolley the length of the waterfront, or the length of State Street. Two electric shuttle routes (www.sbmtd.gov) serve the downtown corridor (State St.) and the waterfront (Cabrillo Blvd.) daily every half hour. Children under 45 inches can ride free, and a free transfer is available between the Downtown Shuttle and the Waterfront Shuttle—just ask your driver.

Santa Ynez Valley

Santa Ynez has always been a laid-back horse and farming community, unaffected by time. That it is now the gateway to the wine region does not detract from its agrarian roots. The wine industry has dominated the region in the last 10 years, even though commercially planted grapes have been here for over four decades. With the success of the film *Sideways,* the area has received additional attention, helping to place a visit to this area on the list of wine lovers across the globe. Some areas, like Happy Canyon, have hotter temperatures and can produce cabernet sauvignon and sauvignon blanc. And cooler growing regions like the Santa Rita Hills benefit from close proximity to the coast. There are cool- and warm-climate plantings of syrah and chardonnay, providing different styles and acid levels, and the diversity of the area is astounding. Every winery is doing something different, and it is this attitude of experimentation that has contributed to its success. It also doesn't hurt that the valley is a beautiful place to spend time.

SANTA YNEZ AND VICINITY

Named The New Town when it was founded in 1882, Santa Ynez retains its historical Western flavor, with some of its old storefronts still intact. By 1889, the town had become the focal point both socially and economically of the entire Santa Ynez Valley, complete with mercantile stores, blacksmith shops, garages, grocery stores, a barber shop, harness shop, millinery shop, and several saloons. The College Hotel was once the area's main lodging establishment, complete with a Victorian design and 16 roof turrets. The hotel, which stood on Sagunto Street just south of Edison Street, hosted guests from all over the world. These days Santa Ynez is a shadow of its former self, no longer the important hub it was, a quiet spot with a handful of businesses. And yet people still come to the valley from the world over to explore the region.

Santa Ynez is a very small town. There are only two hotels here, not including the Chumash Casino resort, which is technically in Solvang in spite of being just down the road from Santa Ynez. One of the reasons people choose to stay here is that it makes a good base from which to explore, and it is quiet.

Wine-Tasting

There used to be a larger contingency of wineries in and near Santa Ynez, but the migration to Solvang and Los Olivos has left only a few. A short drive will get you to some wonderful area wineries.

IMAGINE

Imagine (3563 Numancia St., 805/688-1769, www.imaginewine.com, Mon.–Sat. 10 A.M.–5 P.M., tasting fee $10) is the only tasting room still in town, and it is staffed solely by the owners. The light wood-toned interior has a classic Victorian feel, and the room is spacious with lots of light. You'll get an average of six tasting samples to ponder, including viognier and chardonnay on the white side, and syrah, zinfandel, pinot noir, and merlot

SANTA YNEZ VALLEY

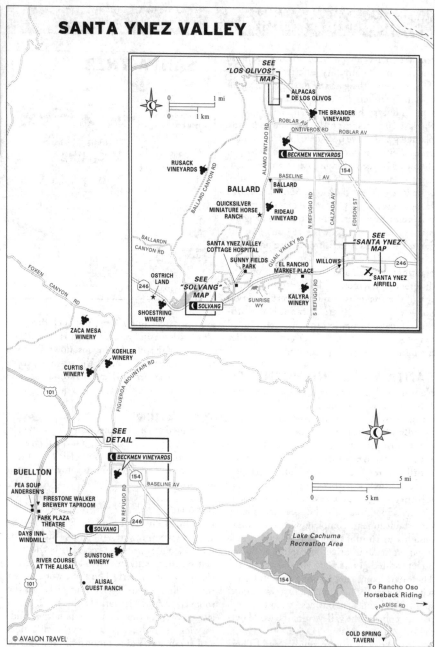

SEE
"LOS OLIVOS"
MAP

ALPACAS
DE LOS OLIVOS

THE BRANDER
VINEYARD

ROBLAR AV
ONTIVEROS RD   ROBLAR AV

BECKMEN VINEYARDS

154

RUSACK
VINEYARDS

BASELINE   AV

BALLARD

BALLARD
INN

QUICKSILVER
MINIATURE HORSE
RANCH

RIDEAU
VINEYARD

BALLARD N
CANYON RD

SEE
"SANTA YNEZ"
MAP

SANTA YNEZ VALLEY
COTTAGE HOSPITAL

SUNNY FIELDS
PARK

EL RANCHO
MARKET PLACE

WILLOWS

246

FOXEN

OSTRICH
LAND

246

SEE
"SOLVANG"
MAP

SANTA YNEZ
AIRFIELD

CANYON   RD

SOLVANG

SUNRISE
WY

KALYRA
WINERY

SHOESTRING
WINERY

ZACA MESA
WINERY

KOEHLER
WINERY

CURTIS
WINERY

101

FIGUEROA MOUNTAIN RD

SEE
DETAIL

BECKMEN VINEYARDS

BUELLTON

154

BASELINE AV

PEA SOUP
ANDERSEN'S

FIRESTONE WALKER
BREWERY TAPROOM

PARK PLAZA
THEATRE

DAYS INN-
WINDMILL

246

SOLVANG

Lake Cachuma
Recreation Area

RIVER COURSE
AT THE ALISAL

SUNSTONE
WINERY

101

ALISAL
GUEST RANCH

154

To Rancho Oso
Horseback Riding

PARDISE RD

COLD SPRING
TAVERN

0   1 mi

0   1 km

0   5 mi

0   5 km

© AVALON TRAVEL

on the red side. The winery is an easy walk from anywhere in town; the space doubles as an art gallery.

KALYRA WINERY

Kalyra Winery (343 N. Refugio, 805/693-8864, www.kalyrawinery.com, Mon.–Fri. 11 A.M.–5 P.M., Sat.–Sun. 10 A.M.–5 P.M., tasting fee $7) is famous for having been featured in the film *Sideways*. The building itself has been home to several other wineries prior to Kalyra moving in, such as the Santa Ynez Valley Winery and Lincourt Vineyards. The partial wraparound deck provides great views of the valley and mountains, and when the sun is setting and the golden hues hit the leafed-out vines, it's truly beautiful. The winery's interior gives a nod to brothers Mike and Martin Brown's Australian roots and love of surfing. They initially started out producing sweet wines but have since expanded their portfolio to include a large number of red and white wines, including some made from Australian grapes.

RIDEAU VINEYARD

Rideau Vineyard (1562 Alamo Pintado, 805/688-0717 www.rideauvineyard.com, daily 11 A.M.–4:30 P.M., tasting fee $10) is housed in an 1884 two-story adobe, one of the few remaining in the entire state. The emphasis here is on Rhône varieties, namely syrah, viognier, roussanne, and grenache, as well as blends and other wines like Riesling and grenache blanc. The small gift shop has some New Orleans–inspired items since owner Iris Rideau originally hails from Louisiana, and they have concerts several times each year where you'll find gumbo and other Creole foods being served. It's a beautiful spot to enjoy a picnic on their lush green back lawn and relax. Tastings are done both inside and outside.

BRIDLEWOOD WINERY

As you drive up the long driveway of Bridlewood Winery (3555 Roblar, 805/688-9000, www.bridlewoodwinery.com, daily 10 A.M.–5 P.M., tasting fee $10) you'll come upon a long structure that looks like a mission but is actually a former equestrian center; all Bridlewood's wines have a horse theme. The focus here is on Rhône varieties, such as eight different versions of syrah alone, as well as three different viogniers, which they do very well. Tossed in the mix is a bit of chardonnay, port, pinot noir, and zinfandel, from vineyards up and down the state. The tasting room is a large facility that can accommodate big crowds, but you can also head outside and enjoy the surroundings. Being removed from the main road, it's a peaceful spot, perfect for a picnic on their back veranda.

SUNSTONE WINERY

Just a mile from Kalyra Winery is Sunstone Winery (125 N. Refugio, 805/688-9463, www.sunstonewinery.com, daily 10 A.M.–4 P.M., tasting fee $10), which has a Spanish and Tuscan vibe with mottled yellow walls suggesting an old estate in the countryside in Europe—it's not actually an old building, but it feels like it. Since its inception in 1990, the focus at Sunstone has been growing grapes without any pesticides, and they are certified organic growers. Probably best known locally for their merlot, they also produce Bordeaux blends and syrah, and their white wines include viognier and sauvignon blanc. This is a very popular spot and sometimes gets downright crowded.

Sights and Drives
HAPPY CANYON

Directly off Highway 154 is an area known as Happy Canyon, which is the warmest grape-growing area in the entire valley. To get here, you can take Highway 246 toward Happy Canyon from Santa Ynez. Highway 246 eventually connects with Highway 154 and near the intersection of Highways 154 and 246 is Armor Ranch Road. If you follow Armor Ranch Road for about four miles Happy Canyon Road will be on your left. There are a lot of horses here, and if you take Happy Canyon Road towards the mountains there is some beautiful scenery as it heads deeper into the low, flat region before it begins climbing into the mountains. Or, simply stay on

© SUNSTONE WINERY

toasting the good life at the Sunstone Winery

Armor Ranch Road and make a loop back to Highway 154. You'll exit south of where you entered, so turn right back on to Highway 154, then to get back to Santa Ynez turn left onto Highway 246.

SANTA YNEZ VALLEY HISTORICAL MUSEUM AND PARKS-JANEWAY CARRIAGE HOUSE

Though Santa Ynez is small, the area does have some history to it, admirably presented at the Santa Ynez Valley Historical Museum and Parks-Janeway Carriage House (3596 Sagunto St., 805/688-7889, www.santaynez museum.org, Wed.–Sun. noon–4 P.M., suggested donation $2). There's a good-sized diorama with a narrow gauge train that shows how the train depot near Mattei's Tavern used to look back in the day. There are also small displays in the Valley Room showing the original five small towns of Solvang (founded 1911), Santa Ynez (1882), Los Olivos (1887), Ballard (1881), and Buellton (1920). The Pioneer Room is three rooms outfitted with turn-of-the-20th-century furnishings, many from local ranches.

The carriage house is an impressive collection of all types of carriages, surreys, and wagons, including an old popcorn wagon from 1909 that sold nuts and fresh popcorn, as well as an old fire wagon. These carriages are in fantastic shape; it is clear they have been well cared for. There is also a selection of tack and saddles.

Entertainment and Events

The land in Santa Ynez was home to the Chumash Indians long before grapes were ever planted. With the advent of the reservation system, the Indian community needed a source of viable revenue and a way to be self sustaining, so the **Chumash Casino** (3400 E. Hwy. 246, 800/248-6274, www.chumash casino.com, 24 hours) was created. For a long time it was housed in a tent structure, but they eventually petitioned the county to build a proper resort. This was met with local opposition, but they got their casino. Now it is

THE *SIDEWAYS* UP EFFECT

The movie *Sideways* was released in 2004; it was nominated for five Academy Awards, and won one for best adapted screenplay. In the 30 weeks the movie was in theaters, gross domestic ticket sales topped $70 million, with worldwide sales reaching more than $100 million, making it the 40th highest-grossing movie of that year.

In spite of the off-putting behavior of the two main characters, it showcased the Santa Barbara wine country like no film ever had, and soon visitors were showing up in the valley's towns toting *Sideways* maps, enamored with the wine country vibe and the images of lush leafy vines, clear blue skies, beautiful valleys, and soft rolling mountains, looking to re-create the film's experiences for themselves. And they kept coming. Many local businesses saw a net increase in business of 20-30 percent after the film came out.

In a well-known scene, one of the characters, Miles, tells his friend that he won't drink merlot (using more colorful language than is appropriate here), and also praised the virtues of pinot noir. That registered in the minds of a fickle public, and sales of pinot noir increased approximately 15 percent, while the maligned merlot dropped about 2 percent in sales. Was it just the result of a line in a movie? Well, yes and no. Merlot had been over-planted in California to begin with, and there was a surplus of inadequate merlot flooding the market. But pinot noir did see an impressive rise in sales as a direct result of the film. Merlot producers across California were frustrated by the merlot bashing, and wine writers only added fuel to the fire by dissing merlot. Rex Pickett, author of the novel *Sideways* on which the film was based, was the featured speaker at a "Merlot Fights Back" dinner. The success of the film even spawned a Japanese-language remake, changing the location to Napa from Santa Barbara.

Regardless, the film generated traffic for the wine country. In Santa Barbara County, wine is a $360 million industry that produces more than one million cases annually. More than a quarter of those bottles come from the Santa Ynez Valley, which is home to over 100 wineries and roughly 5,000 acres of vineyards. The county is best known for its pinot noir and chardonnay – and yes, there is merlot produced here too. In 2008, nearly 17 percent of the over eight million visitors to the county said they came for the wine. *Sideways* produced an up effect, and the ripples are still being felt.

one of the largest draws in the area and one of the few places in the county to draw big-name performers. Additionally, the Chumash have been actively involved in giving back to the community in various ways. The casino itself consists of 2,000 slots, a variety of poker options, including a 24-hour room, bingo large enough for 1,000 players, and blackjack. People are routinely bused in, so expect crowds. There are three restaurants within the casino, a 123-room hotel, a gift shop, and a 1,300-seat entertainment showroom bringing in a solid lineup of performers.

The **Maverick Saloon** (3687 Sagunto St., 805/686-4785, www.mavericksaloon.org, Mon.–Fri. noon–2 A.M., Sat. 10 A.M.–2 A.M.) has hardwood floors, dollar bills hanging from the ceiling, and every kind of sign you can imagine tacked to the walls. It gets loud and wild here, especially on nights and weekends when the bar is packed—in part because there's not much else to do in the area. The outdoor patio seating is taken first, then the bar becomes flooded with people. The stage area is a larger space for overflow, unless there's a band playing. Live bands from the region play on Friday and Saturday night 8:30–11:30 P.M., then a DJ spins tunes till closing. A $5 cover charge applies. There's also darts, pool, and a whole lot of that renegade, devil-may-care vibe.

Each May hundreds of people get ready for the **Wine Country Half Marathon** (starts on Sagunto St., www.runsantaynez.com), a 13.1-mile race through the wine country. Both individuals and teams can enter. If you enjoy running, this is a great way to see the valley, as it starts in Santa Ynez, winds through Los Olivos, traverses down Ballard Canyon, and ends in Solvang, passing vineyards and farms along the way. The plants are leafed out in May and the weather is nearly perfect. The post-race festival includes a wine- and beer-tasting, music, food, and awards.

Held at Live Oak Camp each October, the **Chumash Intertribal Pow Wow** (www .powwows.com) is open to the public to watch traditional tribal dances and drumming circles and learn about Native American culture via speakers and literature. There are also native arts and crafts for sale and the chance to expand your knowledge of Chumash and other Indian tribal culture by conversing with members of various tribes. It's free to attend but there is a small parking fee.

Recreation
GLIDER RIDES
Windhaven Glider Rides (at the Santa Ynez Airport, 900 Airport Rd., 805/688-2517, www .gliderrides.com, Sat.–Sun. 10 A.M.–5 P.M., $125–245) offers glider rides over the wine country. It's an amazing experience to float above the region and not only see the vineyards, but get a better understanding of the topography of the land. Windhaven has been operating for 20 years and takes any age, from 4–104 years old. Flights last 15–30 minutes. A plane tows the glider up along with you and a pilot, then drops the tow line so you're soaring above the earth without the noise of engines, making this a relatively quiet and very scenic experience. Of course, everything ultimately depends on the weather.

HORSEBACK RIDING
Sitting on 300 acres and a fair drive from anywhere, **Rancho Oso Horseback Riding** (3750 Paradise Rd., 805/683-5110, www.ranchooso .net) offers a variety of horseback riding options. The one-hour trail ride starts at $40, and though your horse isn't roaming free, it's still a nice, if predictable, ride through the

backcountry. You cross streams and will see a few Chumash Indian artifacts (this was a Chumash village site long ago) as you meander the lower canyons. There are longer rides that offer scenic vistas, but the lumbering pace can be annoying after a few hours.

Shopping
The few shops in Santa Ynez are all a stone's throw from each other, so you can browse all the shops in this area easily.

For 15 years **Dennee's** (3569 Sagunto St., 805/686-0842, Mon.–Sat. 9 A.M.–5 P.M., Sun. 11 A.M.–5 P.M.) has provided lots of interesting home furnishings with a country and equestrian motif. The place is packed with large and small items, some from local craftsmen in town, and there's a large diversity of things from leather couches to accent pieces, mirrors, and decorative pieces for your home. Think of it as high-end farm decor with a country twist.

Outpost Trading Company (1102 Edison St., 805/686-5588, Mon.–Fri. 10 A.M.– 5:30 P.M., Sat.–Sun. 11 A.M.–4 P.M.) is an eclectic shop that sells Western wear, art, and home furnishings, couture clothing, hand-crafted items, and custom-made furniture and woven tack.

Forever Posh (3583 Numancia, 805/688-1444, Tues.–Sat. 10 A.M.–5 P.M.) has trendy clothes and lounge wear for women, custom jewelry, sunglasses, and designer handbags, as well as bridal gifts. The shop is small but offers expert help and a nice assortment of items.

Sage (1095 Edison St., 805/688-0955, Mon.–Sat. 10 A.M.–5 P.M.) features a wide variety of home items and decor, including imported furnishings, table linens, Italian dishware, books, candles, unique lamps, bath products, Egyptian cotton towels, soaps from Provence, wind chimes, and CDs.

Accommodations
$200-300
Four rooms and a guest cottage make up the unique **Edison Street Inn** (1121 Edison St., 805/693-0303, www.edisonstreetinn.com, $230–305 d). It represents the best of the area

by combining Victorian and Western themes. The rooms are more home-like than inn-like, detailed, spacious, and comfortable, and all very romantic. A full breakfast at a local restaurant is included. Note that there are no in-room telephones, so make sure to bring your cell.

OVER $300

As you enter the elegant and opulent ▐ **Santa Ynez Inn** (3628 Sagunto St., 805/688-5588, www.santaynezinn.com, $345–495 d) you're transported into a Victorian era. Think of this as a high-end bed-and-breakfast and you get the idea. The average room is about 600 square feet and has a steam shower and heated tile floor. The rooms are large with beautiful antiques, and it's clear they have spent a good deal of time and money to make it all the highest quality they can. Breakfast is served each morning in the parlor, a lushly wood-rich Victorian room that feels more like a museum than an inn. In the evening they offer a wine and cheese reception. There are only 20 rooms here; it's a quiet place in a quiet town to enjoy a quiet experience.

Food
ITALIAN

The immensely popular Italian restaurant **Trattoria Grappolo** (3687 Sagunto St., 805/688-6899, www.trattoriagrappolo.com, lunch Tues.–Sun. 11 A.M.–3 P.M., dinner nightly 5–10 P.M., $25) serves pizzas, fresh fish, and tender roast chicken, all cooked in their wood-burning oven. Of course, there is also pasta, and a nice diverse selection of Californian and Italian wines is presented. The restaurant has a compact interior, so many people opt for the deck instead. It's not uncommon to see workers and winemakers from the vineyards show up in their cowboy boots and hats for authentic Italian cuisine in the sometimes loud space.

MEXICAN

Modern pueblo meets country at Mexican restaurant **Dos Carlitos** (3544 Sagunto St., 805/688-0033, www.doscarlitosrestaurant .com, daily 11 A.M.–10 P.M., $25), which boasts high vaulted ceilings and a nice outdoor patio. The furnishings were made in Mexico and there is an authentic feel to the place, though the authentic Mexican food comes with a steep price tag. Sit at the copper-topped bar and try one of 50 tequilas by the shot. Shots range $25–75.

AMERICAN

Inside the 1907 ▐ **Vineyard House** (3631 Sagunto St., 805/688-2886, www.thevineyard house.com, Mon.–Sat. 11:30 A.M.–3 P.M. and 5–9 P.M., Sun. 10 A.M.–3 P.M., $20), there is some magic at work. Creative flavorful food comes out of this kitchen on a regular basis. The baked brie is always a treat, as is the crispy buttermilk chicken and a hearty, thick venison chile verde. They make their own soups and salad dressings as well as desserts like the eternally decadent and gooey molten chocolate cake. The interior is homey and intimate, but the prime seating on nice days is the deck overlooking Sagunto Street, where the pepper trees hang languidly over the tables.

You can't miss **Red Barn** (3539 Sagunto St., 805/688-4142, daily 11 A.M.–2 P.M. and 5:30 P.M.–close, $20) since it actually is a red barn. Though the white unmarked door seems like an obscure entrance, once inside it's all down home. A small bar is off to one side and the country wood tables with red and white checkered tablecloths and chairs have the feel of a low-key country diner. People have been coming to Red Barn for its steaks and desserts since 1924. The portions are generous, if a little pricey.

Sequestered from the casino, **Willows** (3400 E. Hwy. 246, 805/686-0855, www.chumash casino.com, Sun.–Thurs. 5–10 P.M., Fri.–Sat. 5–11 P.M., $30) is unexpectedly elegant, with white tablecloth–clad tables between narrow arches. They have private dining rooms on the outdoor terrace as well. The emphasis here is seafood and beef entrées. Side dishes are extra, so be prepared to throw down some cash. The only drawback is that you have to walk through the casino to get here, but once inside the noise of clanging slot machines quickly fades away.

The no-frills **Burger Barn** (3621 Sagunto St., 805/688-2366, Mon.–Fri. 7 A.M.–3 P.M., Sat.–Sun. 8 A.M.–3 P.M., $8) is known for inexpensive but tasty burgers and salads. Very popular with tourists and locals, in part because of the price, it can get very crowded. The outdoor area has plastic tables and chairs and the interior doesn't fare much better, but it's all about quick and easy food.

(Cold Spring Tavern (5995 Stagecoach Rd., 805/967-0066, www.coldspringtavern .com, restaurant Mon.–Fri. 11 A.M.–3 P.M. and 5–9 P.M., Sat.–Sun. 8 A.M.–3 P.M. and 5–9 P.M., tavern daily noon–9 P.M., $20) was a former stagecoach stop when wagons and riders had to traverse the mountains from the valley to Santa Barbara. It was built in 1886 and hasn't changed much since. Rustic and secluded, it hosts live music every Friday– Sunday. A stream runs by the place, situated in a narrow canyon that can be cool even during the summer months. Motorcyclists, townies, and locals hang out in the bar area and there is often dancing both inside and outside the bar. The on-site restaurant, in a separate building, is the place to find tri-tip sandwiches during the summers months, grilled outdoors over an open flame, as well as wild game, rabbit, venison, boar, and very good chili. A visit to the tavern is as much about the food as it is about enjoying the charming space. There's also an old jail on-site, a one-room wood building that used to hold unruly customers.

Information and Services

Your only bet is the **Santa Ynez Valley Visitors Association** (www.syvva.com), which has a fairly comprehensive website covering much of the valley. Remember that many businesses here still don't have websites, only phone numbers, so getting specific information is often a challenge.

The *Santa Ynez Valley Journal* (www .syvjournal.com) publishes weekly and though small, usually about 30 pages, it has a broad scope. There is a calendar listing current and upcoming events and plenty of local stories and interviews.

In case of **emergency,** dial 911 immediately. The **Santa Ynez Valley Cottage Hospital** (2050 Viborg, Solvang, 805/688-6431) offers emergency services. Police services are contracted with the **County of Santa Barbara Sheriff's Department** (1745 Mission Dr., Solvang, 805/688-5000).

Getting There

Santa Ynez is accessed by Highway 246, which cuts through the area. If you're arriving by car from the north you can exit and drive through Solvang, or take Highway 154 exit and drive the back way. Each drive has its advantages. Driving through Solvang is great if you've never seen the town before, but on weekends the road is packed with slow-moving cars, buses and RVs. The back route with scenic rolling hills and a few vineyards can take you through Los Olivos or along Highway 154 until you turn right onto Highway 246. If you're driving from the south, take either Highway 101 up through the Gaviota Pass and exit through Solvang, or drive the San Marcos Pass, Highway 154, which can also be a long drive depending on traffic. Here you'll pass Lake Cachuma, where chances are you'll see deer and cattle strolling about the oak-studded hillsides.

Small craft can land at the **Santa Ynez Valley Airport** (900 Airport Rd., 805/688-8390, www.santaynezairport.com), a tiny airport right near town that serves the entire valley.

(SOLVANG

To some, Solvang might seem like Denmark on steroids, but the colorful and charming village-like town is unlike any other in the area—or the state for that matter; it's a great escape from the tedious mall architecture that dominates much of America.

Solvang started in 1911 as a Danish retreat. It is still ripe with Scandinavian heritage as well as a new modern sensibility, though the theme park atmosphere is not lacking in kitsch. In the 1950s, far earlier than other themed communities, Solvang decided to seal its fate by keeping

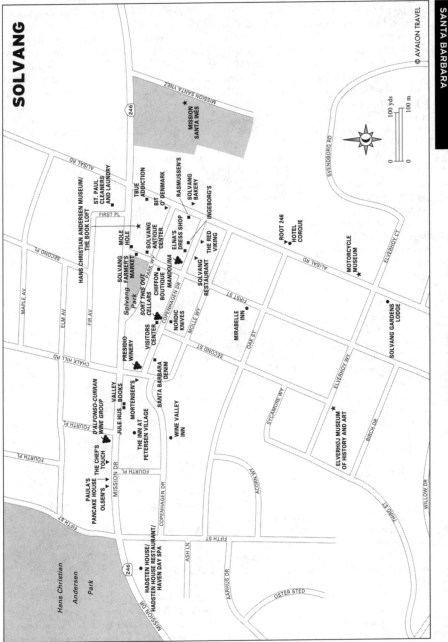

SOLVANG

MISSION SANTA YNEZ

MISSION SANTA INÉS

ST. PAUL CLEANERS AND LAUNDRY

HANS CHRISTIAN ANDERSEN MUSEUM/ THE BOOK LOFT

TRUE ADDICTION

BIT O' DENMARK

RASMUSSEN'S

SOLVANG BAKERY

INGEBORG'S

FIRST PL

MOLE HOLE

SOLVANG ANTIQUE CENTER

ELNA'S DRESS SHOP

ROOT 246

HOTEL CORQUE

SECOND PL

SOLVANG FARMER'S MARKET

Solvang Park

SORT THIS OUT CELLARS

CHIFFON BOUTIQUE

MANDOLINA

SOLVANG RESTAURANT

THE RED VIKING

MOTORCYCLE MUSEUM

MAPLE AV

ELM AV

FIR AV

PRESIDIO WINERY

VISITORS CENTER

NORDIC KNIVES

COPENHAGEN DR

MOLLE WY

FIRST ST

MIRABELLE INN

ALISAL RD

SOLVANG GARDENS LODGE

CHALK HILL RD

SANTA BARBARA DENIM

SECOND ST

OAK ST

D'ALFONSO-CURRAN WINE GROUP

VALLEY BOOKS

MORTENSEN'S

JULE HUS

WINE VALLEY INN

SYCAMORE WY

ELVERHOY WY

PAULA'S PANCAKE HOUSE

THE CHEF'S TOUCH

OLSEN'S

THE INN AT PETERSEN VILLAGE

COPENHAGEN DR

ACORN WY

ELVERHOJ MUSEUM OF HISTORY AND ART

BIRCH DR

FOURTH PL

MISSION DR

FOURTH PL

FIFTH ST

ASH LN

THIRD ST

WILLOW DR

Hans Christian Andersen Park

HADSTEN HOUSE/ HADSTEN HOUSE RESTAURANT/ HAVEN DAY SPA

MISSION DR

AARHUS DR

OSTER STED

SVENDBORG RD

ELVERHOJ CT

0 100 yds

0 100 m

© AVALON TRAVEL

a focus on Danish architecture, food, and style, which still holds an allure nearly 50 years after its conception.

Solvang originally looked like other towns of the day, with a Spanish theme punctuated by Western stores. The vision to create the Solvang we see today emerged post–World War II. Long before thematic towns or city centers were in vogue, Solvang agreed upon a unifying design theme, and that is part of the allure.

You'll notice storks displayed above many of the stores in town; they're a traditional symbol of good luck. Solvang draws nearly two million visitors each year, and you'll still hear the muted strains of Danish spoken on occasion. During peak summer times and holidays, Solvang can be congested, with people clogging the brick sidewalks, riding rented surreys through the streets, loitering in front of the bakeries and chocolate shops, and it feels uncharacteristic of a small town. Try to visit during off season, when the simple joys of meandering the lovely shops can still be enjoyed. It's at its best in the fall and early spring when the hills are verdant green and the trees in town are beautiful.

An easily walkable town, Solvang is close to the now-famous ostrich farm from the movie *Sideways*. Solvang is also home to Mission Santa Inés, bakeries, miles of rolling paved roads for bikers and cyclists (Lance Armstrong once trained here), oak-studded parks, and the well-known Solvang Theaterfest, an outdoor event and theater venue. The Chumash Casino is nearby if you need your one-armed-bandit fix.

Wine-Tasting

There are no actual vineyards in Solvang per se, but there are tasting rooms, and they're all within walking distance of each other. Many people overlook Solvang tasting rooms because they assume that since it's a tourist spot, the wineries located here might be, shall we say, not as serious. Well, that's definitely not so. There are some excellent wines represented locally, and you would do well to seek these out.

PRESIDIO WINERY

Presidio Winery (1603 Copenhagen Dr., Ste.

1, 805/693-8585, www.presidiowinery.com, daily 11 A.M.–6 P.M., tasting fee $8) is one of the few wineries in all of the Central Coast to be certified as a biodynamic winery. You'll see a small label on the back of the bottles that identifies the wine as having been approved by Demeter, the authoritative body that governs this farming method. Biodynamic is beyond organic and employs, ideally, a closed-loop farm system. Simply put, it's farming the best way to insure non-intrusive outside elements don't interfere with a healthy respect for the land. That aside, owner Doug Braun's wines are quite good, and his style of winemaking is more restrained than most others in the area. Chardonnay, pinot noir, syrah, and late-harvest wines are on offer at his tasting room on Copenhagen Drive at Mission Drive, in the heart of Solvang, a great place to begin your education about local wines and biodynamic farming methods.

MANDOLINA

Winemaker Megan McGrath-Gates produces some terrific white wines at Mandolina (1665 Copenhagen Dr., 805/686-5506, www .mandolinawines.com, daily 11 A.M.–5:30 P.M., tasting fee $8–12), a bright and airy tasting room with exposed beams on the ceiling and a copper-topped wood bar. The focus here is on Italian varietals including pinot grigio, barbera, nebbiolo, dolcetto, malvasia bianca, and sangiovese. There's a delicate touch to the wines due to Megan's sensibilities, and she's studied in Italy to understand their winemaking process—reflected in the wonderful wines she makes. The wines, especially the whites, are quite good and sold at very reasonable prices.

D'ALFONSO-CURRAN WINE GROUP

A merger between a husband and wife team, the D'Alfonso-Curran Wine Group (1557 Mission Dr., 805/688-3494, www.curran wines.com, Mon.–Fri. 11 A.M.–5 P.M., Sat.– Sun. 10 A.M.–5 P.M., tasting fee $15) now has their own tasting room. Both winemakers have long been well known in the local wine industry and have worked as winemakers for respected names like Sea Smoke and Sanford. They have always crafted their own wines as well, and this tasting room is dedicated to their own small-production labels. The zinc-topped bar and cool, minimalist interior belies the beauty of their wines, chardonnay and pinot noir on the D'Alfonso side, and grenache blanc, sangiovese, and syrah on the Curran side. The tasting fee is a little pricey, but it's a worthwhile stop.

SHOESTRING WINERY

Shoestring Winery (800 E. Hwy. 246, 805/693-8612, www.shoestringwinery.com, Fri.–Sun. 10 A.M.–4 P.M., tasting fee $10) is on the main road into Solvang, just before you reach the town. This winery started out when the owners migrated from Baltimore, Maryland, and bought 65 acres. Formerly adept at training racehorses, they still have a few on the property, but the focus is on wine. The early days were tight financially and a shoestring budget allowed them to plant more and more vines. They still have a small production, but they offer merlot, syrah, sangiovese, rosé, and pinot grigio. The tasting room, in an old barn with a really cool floor made from wood posts, is more farm feeling than polished and glitzy.

SORT THIS OUT CELLARS

Michael Cobb, owner of Sort This Out Cellars (1636 Copenhagen Dr., 805/688-1717, www.sortthisoutcellars.com, Sun.–Thurs. 10 A.M.–7 P.M., Fri.–Sat. 10 A.M.–10 P.M., tasting fee $5–15), decided to create a new type of winery that doesn't own any vineyards, land, or actual grapes, but instead simply buys the fruit. After all, you don't need a plot of land to make wine. The retro tasting room was inspired by an old photograph of the famed 1960s Rat Pack outside the Sands Hotel in Las Vegas. It has low-back bar stools at the tasting counter, lots of shiny chrome, and pin-up girls on the wine labels. The ambience just might make you feel cool enough to sample their cabernet sauvignon, merlot, syrah, sangiovese, sauvignon blanc, chardonnay, muscat, and a super Tuscan blend.

RUSACK VINEYARDS

Rusack Vineyards (1819 Ballard Canyon, 805/688-1278, www.rusackvineyards.com, daily 11 A.M.–5 P.M., tasting fee $9) is one of the best picnic spots in the valley. Bring your lunch and pick up a bottle of their sauvignon blanc, sangiovese, pinot noir, or their flagship Bordeaux wine called Anacapa, and lounge under the old oaks on the side deck. Ballard Canyon is, for the most part, a quiet canyon, and the views of the other vineyards from the outside patio are wonderful. Around Halloween the canyon is dotted with bright pumpkins, and you'll occasionally see bison roaming the hills.

Sights and Drives
BALLARD CANYON

Ballard Canyon is not only a great local drive, it's also popular with cyclists and even runners. Just off the main street in Solvang, you can ride, drive, or run the canyon past vineyards, bison, and cattle; the road will drop you out near Los Olivos. What makes this road so wonderful is the combination of straight parts mixed with gentle curves and occasional steep climbs, and of course the bucolic scenery from low in the canyon to high atop the ridge with views to the surrounding areas. To access Ballard Canyon from downtown Solvang, head north on Atterdag. The hill will climb for a while, then drop you down into the canyon. You'll veer right onto Ballard and take that all the way through the canyon to meet up with Highway 246. To your right is Los Olivos; straight ahead is Foxen Canyon Road.

SANTA ROSA ROAD

Santa Rosa Road winds its way through the Santa Rita Hills, the best-known pinot noir–growing region in the county. The two-lane road meanders past a few wineries, old ranch houses, and lots of gentle sloping hills. Both cars and cyclists share this road, which eventually connects with Highway 1 south of Lompoc. The hills rise to your left; to your right are vineyards and farmland. Early morning and late afternoon are great times to be here as the sun gently bathes the hills and vineyards in a soft golden hue.

OSTRICH LAND

Made popular by the film *Sideways,* the Ostrich Land (610 E. Hwy. 246, 805/686-9696, www.ostrichlandusa.com, daily 10 A.M.–dusk, $4 adults, $1 children under 12) farm is on Highway 246 two miles before you reach Solvang from Highway 101. At first glance it seems somewhat prehistoric; you'll see massive birds wandering through the shrubs in the distance, their thin necks sporting small heads and big eyes. They usually keep their distance and only approach when there is food to be had. Should you decided to feed them, you need to hold the food plate firmly in your hand as they don't eat gingerly, but attack the plate with a fierce determination to get food, so if you have a loose grip on the plate it will fly out of your hand with the first attack for food. Aside from feeding them you can shop for ostrich eggs and ostrich jerky as well as emu eggs and ostrich-feather accoutrements.

MISSION SANTA INÉS

Throughout its 200-plus-year history, Mission Santa Inés (1760 Mission Dr., 805/688-4815, www.missionsantaines.org, daily 9 A.M.–5 P.M., mass daily 8 A.M., $4) has overcome natural disasters, political turmoil, and financial hardships and remains a working church to this day. It is named after Saint Agnes, Santa Inés in Spanish. The town name is spelled Santa Ynez, an anglicization of the Spanish pronunciation. The interior is similar in size to the other missions. A long, tall narrow church, this one is more simply decorated with hand-painted interiors and without much architectural detail. Of note is the large collection of about 500 church vestments held here, dating from the 15th century to the early 1700s. Near the stations of the cross at the south end of the property, there are expansive views to the valley below, which used to be orchards for the mission. There is a back entrance few people seem to know about through a parking lot at Mission and Alisal Roads in Solvang. Behind the public restrooms,

a brick walkway leads into the backside of the mission grounds.

The mission, established in 1804, was designed to be a stopping point between the missions of Santa Barbara and La Purisima in Lompoc. It was devastated by the earthquake of 1812 but was rebuilt; what is visible today is not original, with the exception of part of the original arch toward the south end of the property. The Chumash population was reported to be close to 1,000 at its peak. After Mexican Independence from Spain in 1821, secularization caused the departure of the Spanish missionaries and most of the Chumash and the decline of the mission itself until it was rescued by much-needed attention and money.

ELVERHØJ MUSEUM OF HISTORY AND ART

To fully understand Solvang, it's important to visit the Elverhøj Museum (1624 Elverhoy Way, 805/686-1211, www.elverhoj.org, Wed.–Thurs. 1–4 P.M., Fri.–Sun. noon–4 P.M., $3) which is a delightful and surprisingly cool place. Not only do they offer tabletop and kitchen linens and local crafts, they have a comprehensive history of the area with nostalgic photos of the early settlers. Of particular note is the typical Danish kitchen, hand-painted in green with stenciled flowers everywhere and pine floors, countertops, and tables—it gives an idea of how creative the Danes made their homes, no doubt in an effort to brighten bleak winters. Those winters brightened considerably after arriving in the area, but it was a long journey. The museum also features exhibits of traditional folk art from Denmark like paper-cutting and lace-making, which is clearly evident throughout town. There are displays of wood clogs and the rustic tools used to create them, and they offer rotating exhibits throughout the year that focus on the valley. It would be easy to dismiss the museum as just a novelty, but clearly the passion of the original settlers and their willingness to come to America and continue their way of life from the old country is something we can all learn from.

HANS CHRISTIAN ANDERSEN MUSEUM

The small Hans Christian Andersen Museum (1680 Mission Dr., 805/688-2052, www .bookloftsolvang.com, daily Sun.–Mon. 9 A.M.–6 P.M., Tues.–Thurs. 9 A.M.–8 P.M., Fri.–Sat. 9 A.M.–9 P.M., free) has a few artifacts of Andersen including a bronze bust (a copy of which is in the park on Mission Dr.), first editions of his books from the 1830s in Danish and English, photographs, and a timeline chronicling his life and work and his impact on literature. It's easy to overlook Andersen as simply the writer of fairy tales, but Andersen also wrote novels, plays, and other works. Even a short visit will enlighten you about the prolific work of Andersen.

MOTORCYCLE MUSEUM

The Motorcycle Museum (320 Alisal Rd., 805/686-9522, www.motosolvang.com, Sat.–Sun. 11 A.M.–5 P.M., weekdays by appointment, $10) is truly a unique and interesting stop. Along the self-guided tour 95 motorcycles, vintage and new, are on display. Each bike has a description and some are downright beautiful, polished and lovingly restored. There are bikes from the 1930s and 1940s, the earliest from 1903, and some are so cool that you'll want to strap on a helmet and take a ride. After 10 years in this spot they have amassed quite the private collection with Ducati, Crocker, Matchless, Nimbus, and many more. Admission is not inexpensive compared to other things to do in town, but if motorcycles are your passion, you need to visit.

QUICKSILVER MINIATURE HORSE RANCH

It's free to stop by the Quicksilver Miniature Horse Ranch (1555 Alamo Pintado Rd., 805/686-4002, www.qsminis.com, daily 10 A.M.–3 P.M.), a ranch that specializes in miniature horses for a growing list of customers from across the globe who desire these horses as pets. If you drive by the farm on most any spring day, you may catch a glimpse of 25–30 newborn foals, measuring 20–21 inches tall, testing out their new legs as they attempt to leap and bound on the grass. Visitors can get up close with the newborns and the adults, but should remember that this is not a petting zoo, it's a working ranch. There are usually about 90 horses on the ranch at all times.

Entertainment and Events

It's important to understand that this part of the valley rolls up the sidewalks pretty early. There are events that take place, but bars and clubs are nearly nonexistent, unless you head to a restaurant bar. For a full-on bar and club scene, you'll need to either drive 30 minutes south to Santa Barbara, or 20 minutes north to Santa Maria. Businesses don't stay open late, and you'll be hard pressed for things to do when the sun goes down.

FESTIVALS AND EVENTS

The **Solvang Theaterfest** (420 2nd St., 805/688-1789, www.solvangtheaterfest.org) features semiprofessional theater, with both professional actors and local talent, at a beautiful outdoor venue. The Solvang group puts on four plays each year between June and October in a 700-seat venue originally built in 1974. There is a focus on musicals and lighter fare, and there has been great support for live theater in this small town. In a small compound of Danish-style architecture and beautiful old oak trees, this is a great summertime tradition.

Danish Days (www.solvangusa.com), held the third weekend in September, is a big draw. Started in 1936, it features clog-wearing Danes dancing in the streets, pastries and coffee everywhere, and even an *aebleskiver* (pancake)-eating contest. It's Solvang's annual salute to its cultural heritage and local women dress in traditional skirt, apron, and cap, despite the heat of the season. The men too wear their clogs and traditional outfits. The festival is also referred to as Aebleskiver Days on occasion, and it has been a tradition for locals to serve *aebleskiver* from pans set up in the streets.

The food and wine event **Taste of Solvang** (www.solvangusa.com), held the third weekend in March, has been in existence for 18 years and it keeps growing and becoming more sophisticated each year. It starts with a dessert reception, and considering the pastry and sweets history among the Danes, that's enough right there. Following that is the walking smorgaasbord, which features roughly 40 stops in town where you pop in and sample what they might be serving, usually Danish food, though some restaurants and stores offer non-Danish food samples. Ten tasting rooms pour their vintages into your souvenir glass, and there's live entertainment in the park where many people bring a picnic and relax. It's a three-day event that immerses you in the local culture and customs and the new crop of wineries.

The Solvang Century (562/690-9693, www.bikescor.com) is the best-known cycling race in the entire valley. Well, technically it's not a race, but a fundraiser, but you still can't help but compete. They added a half-century race to accommodate riders who prefer the shorter distances, but there is still some pretty serious elevation gain at a minimum of 2,000 feet, making this a challenging course. The money raised benefits heart-related diseases since the founder of the event used cycling as a way to promote health after his own heart surgery.

Shopping
BOOKSTORES
Valley Books (1582 Mission Dr., 805/688-7160, daily 9 A.M.–7:30 P.M.) sells predominantly used books with a small section of new books. There's an abundance of paperbacks, but also magazines, newspapers, and hardcovers. You can sit outside, or inside in comfy chairs, and read, sip coffee or tea, and enjoy a Danish pastry. This place is made to lounge. The have Wi-Fi and there's a small kids' section with little tables and chairs. It's a quiet respite from all the shopping.

The Book Loft (1680 Mission Dr., 805/688-6010, www.bookloftsolvang.com, Sun.–Mon. 9 A.M.–6 P.M., Tues.–Thurs. 9 A.M.–8 P.M., Fri.–Sat. 9 A.M.–9 P.M.) sells mostly new books, though there's a small section of used books as well. This 35-year-old two-story store has a vast very well-organized selection of authors, including locals. The wood stairs creak as you venture upstairs to see even more books. It has

the feel of an old bookstore, not sanitized with fancy shelves—in fact these shelves were all handmade. They also have a nice selection of antiquarian books, and upstairs is the Hans Christian Andersen Museum.

ANTIQUES
The **Solvang Antique Center** (486 1st St., 805/686-2322, www.solvangantiques.com, daily 10 A.M.–6 P.M.) is home to some incredible antiques. In addition to a stellar collection of magnificent gilded antique clocks, there are music boxes, jewelry, watches, and gorgeous vintage telephones from old candlestick models to the 1930s and 1940s models. They also have artfully restored antique furniture. The 7,000-square-foot showroom has over 65 specialty dealers from around the globe. It is an expensive place, but has such diversity that any antiques lover should stop in, even if just to browse one of the finest stores in the Central Coast.

CLOTHING
Elna's Dress Shop (1673 Copenhagen Dr., 805/688-4525, daily 9:30 A.M.–5:30 P.M.) is the place to go for handmade Danish dresses and costumes, as well as more contemporary but conservative and non-Danish-themed dresses for women. If you're searching for that perfect Danish outfit for a young one, you'll find it here. Aprons, caps, and brightly colored simple dresses, some with beautiful lace, are available off the rack, or they will make one for you. They have only a few Danish pieces for young boys, and they're pretty darn cute.

True Addiction (485 Alisal Rd., 805/686-2868, Thurs. 9:30 A.M.–6 P.M., Fri.–Mon. 9:30 A.M.–7 P.M.) sells hip and trendy clothing for a younger crowd including a large section of shoes, boots, and jewelry. Their stock rotates frequently and in spite of being situated in a tourist area, they have very reasonable prices and contemporary fashions.

Santa Barbara Denim (1608 Copenhagen Dr., 805/688-5458, daily 10 A.M.–6 P.M.) has fashions for both men and women at greatly reduced prices. The women's clothing is front and center while the men's is relegated to the back upstairs portion. The store was formerly called Beach Bumz, but the name change hasn't affected their focus on providing quality clothes at a discount. The fashions lean toward modern and hip, and there are a lot of silk shirts for men. Their stock rotates with the seasons.

SPECIALTY STORES

Mole Hole (1656 Mission Dr., 805/688-7669, www.moleholesolvang.com, daily 9:30 A.M.–5:30 P.M.) is a gift shop with an emphasis on miniature collectibles, as well as decidedly feminine and romantic items, many with a fairy theme or lots of lace. There is an upstairs humorous section of gifts for men—well, men heading over 50. They are extremely helpful here, which has contributed to their success.

You'll feel a little better from the moment you enter **Jule Hus** (1580 Mission Dr., 805/688-6601, www.solvangschristmashouse.com, daily 9 A.M.–5 P.M.), where it's the holiday season all year long. They offer hand-carved wood ornaments, blown-glass ornaments, traditional Scandinavian ornaments, and stand alone decorations, as well as a huge selection of nutcrackers. There are also traditional Danish quilts and lace items and plenty of trees fully decked out. Jule Hus has celebrated the Christmas spirit since 1967, and there are always people milling about searching for that ideal ornament. Other stores in town have small sections of Christmas items, but here it's all they have.

Rasmussen's (1697 Copenhagen Dr., 805/688-6636, www.rasmussenssolvang.com, daily 9 A.M.–5:30 P.M.), opened in 1921 and still going strong five generations later, is everything Scandinavian, a one-stop shop for gifts, books, souvenirs, Danish packaged food items, and kitchen items.

Nordic Knives (1634 Copenhagen Dr., 805/688-3612, www.nordicknives.com, daily 10 A.M.–5 P.M.) has more knives than you've probably ever seen in one place, including expensive high-end custom-made knives by well-known knife makers, and jeweled, engraved, and one-of-a-kind knives. Many of them are very impressive. There are also hunting and kitchen knives with prices that are much lower than the custom blades. The shop has been in Solvang nearly 40 years, and they know their knives. Whether you need a simple knife or a traditional Swiss Army knife, they'll have it. The display case on the right-hand side as you enter is worth a look, with beautiful knives of all types and pedigree.

Ingeborg's (1679 Copenhagen Dr., 805/688-5612, www.ingeborgs.com, daily 9:30 A.M.–5:30 P.M.) has been making traditional Danish chocolates for nearly half a century. Over 70 varieties of chocolates are here, handmade on the premises. It isn't cheap, but it is Danish chocolate made by Danes. They also carry hard-to-find Dutch chocolates. Grab a seat at one of the six round red barstools and enjoy their ice cream.

Every Wednesday year-round, rain or shine, fresh fruits, veggies, flowers, and local items from surrounding farms make an appearance at the **Solvang Farmer's Market** (Mission Dr. and 1st St., 805/962-5354, summer 4–7 P.M., winter 3–6 P.M.). This is not a major farmers market and takes up only two blocks, but they close off the street next to the park and you can find fresh food harvested from local farms, many of which are within a mile of town. It's hard to get much fresher than that.

Sports and Recreation
PARKS

At 15 acres, **Hans Christian Andersen Park** (500 Chalk Hill Rd.) is the largest park in the area. Enter through a castle gate and you're amidst pine and oak trees. Then you come to the skate park, which has cavernous half pipes and is actually well designed, though there are more bikers who use it than boarders. There is a small wooden playground behind the skate park for the younger ones. If you continue driving through the park you'll come to another playground with tall chute slides embedded in the sand. There are plenty of trees and picnic tables, all well groomed. If you drive all the way to the end, there are four tennis courts right next to a beautiful gnarled old oak tree. There are restroom facilities and drinking fountains.

Sunny Fields Park (900 Alamo Pintado, 805/688-7529) is almost a pint-sized Solvang. There's a Viking ship, swings and slides, and monkey bars, plus a gingerbread house, a faux windmill, and plenty of things to climb around on. Trees offer shade, as it gets hot during the summer. This is a great spot for little kids and it's reasonably quiet, being just outside of town. There are drinking fountains and restrooms, plenty of parking, and a large grassy flat ball field.

GOLF

The 18-hole, par-72 **River Course at the Alisal** (150 Alisal Rd., 805/688-6042, www .rivercourse.com, green fees $60–70) was featured in *Sideways*. It's a beautiful course on the banks of the Santa Ynez River, punctuated with magnificent oak trees. Challenging and beautiful, it features four lakes, open fairways, tricky hazards, and large, undulating greens accented by native sycamore trees. Elevated tees reveal some vistas and occasional vineyards, so bring your best game and your camera.

Accommodations
UNDER $100
Days Inn-Windmill (114 E. Hwy. 246, Buellton, 805/688-8448, www.daysinn.com, $70–90 d) was featured in the film *Sideways*—you can even stay in the same room where the main characters stayed in the film. The 108 rooms here are pretty standard and basic, with the best feature being the outdoor pool. It's right off Highway 101 and you can't miss its namesake windmill. It's best to avoid the rooms fronting the freeway and go for an interior room to cut down on the noise. There are no views to speak of, but the prices are good.

$100-200
Solvang Gardens Lodge (293 Alisal Rd., 805/688-4404, www.solvanggardens.com, $169–199 d) is a 24-room delight just on the edge of town. It feels like a small village. There are stone fireplaces and marble bathrooms, and each room is unique and different. Some are decorated with a more modern theme, some

have a traditional feel, but all are very well appointed. Beautiful gardens in both the front and center of the property give you a peaceful green space. The local owners will do everything they can to ensure your stay is the best it can be. It's quieter here since it's not on the main drag. In the morning you can walk into town or down to the dry riverbed.

$200-300
Wine Valley Inn (1465 Copenhagen Dr., 800/824-6444, www.winevalleyinn.com, $209–359 d), with 56 rooms and six cottages, is larger than it looks, and the rooms are spacious as well, with interiors bathed in soft tones. Some of the rooms have wood-burning or artificial fireplaces. The inn is right downtown, so you can get around without a car.

Hotel Corque (400 Alisal Rd., 800/624-5572, www.hotelcorque.com, $279–309 d) was originally a very Danish hotel, but an extensive renovation morphed it into a sleek and sophisticated hotel catering to a younger crowd. It feels like it belongs in a major city, not a rural area, and that's part of its appeal. Though the 100 rooms and 17 suites are a tad small and the amenities are nothing unique, there's no disliking the decor—if you're looking for cool digs, you've found them.

Hadsten House (1450 Mission Dr., 805/688-3210, www.hadstenhouse.com, $205–255 d) is a nonsmoking property, and one of the best places to stay in Solvang. French-style furnishings with custom mattresses, dark-toned furniture, and ample space pulls you out of the Danish mentality and into a contemporary and sophisticated setting. A full breakfast and nightly wine and cheese are offered, as well as a heated outdoor pool and hot tub. It's one of the closest hotels to the 101 and the first you come to as you enter Solvang. Set in a square horseshoe pattern, it offers no views, except across the street to another hotel. Regardless, these are comfortable, well-appointed rooms with a European flair.

The 42-room **The Inn at Petersen Village** (1576 Mission Dr., 805/688-3121, www .peterseninn.com, $265–295 d) is unusual in that the rates include dinner and breakfast at their in-house restaurant. The decor is traditional, maybe even a little stuffy, but it is also right on Mission Drive, so you simply walk outside into the thick of things. The inn has been around a long time, and it sees its share of return guests.

Mirabelle Inn (409 1st St., 805/688-1703, www.solvanginns.com, $250–295 d) is run by well-seasoned veterans of the hospitality industry. The 10 medium-sized rooms decorated with antiques and lace are much more Victorian bed-and-breakfast in their feel; many have four-poster beds and a few have sleigh beds. It's located in the heart of Solvang, so you can leave the vine-covered walls and go explore, then return to this other world. They have an in-house restaurant that serves wonderful food.

OVER $300

The **Alisal Guest Ranch** (1054 Alisal Rd., 805/688-6411, www.alisal.com, $495–650 d) dates back to 1946. The 73 rooms at this ranch retreat are all very large and have a strong Western and pueblo feel to them. Full breakfasts and dinners are included in the rates. And since this is considered a retreat, there are no TVs or telephones, but you do have access to Wi-Fi, tennis courts ($20 per hour), fishing in their lake (guided three-hour trip starts at $180), horseback riding ($50 per hour), and even archery ($35 per hour). The secluded and luxurious environment makes it possible for complete relaxation. But if you need to, you can walk into town.

Food

There are many places in town that serve traditional Danish food, which doesn't typically conjure up images of innovative global fare. But as Solvang is growing, with new hotels and wine-tasting rooms opening up, restaurants are looking to stand out from the traditional in what is becoming, albeit slowly, a true destination with farm-fresh food and innovative ways of preparing it. But if you are looking for the traditional, you'll find it here too, occasionally with an accordion player outside the front door, enticing you to come in.

AMERICAN

The Chef's Touch (1555 Mission Dr., 805/686-1040, www.thechefstouch.com, Mon. and Wed.–Sat. 11 A.M.–4 P.M., Sun. 9 A.M.–3 P.M., $12) is one of those hybrid places—restaurant, wine shop, kitchen store, and cooking class central. The outdoor seating gives you people-watching views to the main street in Solvang, but the interior lets you watch a variety of foods being prepared. The paninis are excellent, and their pizzas and salads are infused with fresh ingredients. The Roman artichoke is a deep-fried artichoke dusted with parmesan, garlic, salt, and pepper and is a great start to any meal. The prices are perfect for a quick bite or a cappuccino. If you're in town for a while, consider one of their cooking classes.

◀ **Hadsten House Restaurant** (1450 Mission Dr., 805/688-3210, www.hadstenhouse.com, Sun.–Thurs. 5–9 P.M., Fri.–Sat. 5–10 P.M., $25) entered the dining scene in 2008 but immediately elevated the local culinary perspective. Dark and moody inside, it has a central fireplace that creates a hip urban environment, more metropolitan than rural. The short ribs have a demi-glace that will send your mind reeling, and the warm spinach salad is perfectly balanced. Or go for the Hadsten burger, which is piled with everything—including an egg. It's best to make reservations for this small space producing some very fine food.

Sleek and sophisticated, **Root 246** (420 Alisal Rd., 805/686-8681, www.root-246.com, daily 5:30–10 P.M., $30), one of the newest additions to the dining scene, has upped the ante. It looks like it belongs in Hollywood, not in rural Solvang, but that's part of the evolution of Solvang and wine country cuisine. Chef and consultant Bradley Ogden has started over 10 restaurants and knows how to create exciting food. The menu rotates often depending on seasonal ingredients. You'll find oysters, organic mushroom flatbread, and a variety of fish and game dishes. The crowd is young and urban—you don't see a lot of old-school Danish residents here.

Firestone Walker Brewery Taproom (620

McMurray Rd., Buellton, 805/686-1557, www .firestonewalker.com, daily 11 A.M. to 9 P.M., tasting fee $6.50, food $20) features four Firestone Walker beers in addition to four alternating beers on tap. You can get it by the pint or mug, or try a sampler of four beers. They also offer food like pork chops, steaks, and burgers, and beer-battered fish-and-chips. Firestone Walker is the best brewery on the Central Coast and right off Highway 101, just north of Buellton. Grab a brew, and if your picky friend wants wine, well, they'll pour Firestone wines by the glass.

DANISH

Year after year, **Paula's Pancake House** (1531 Mission Dr., 805/688-2867, daily 6 A.M.–3 P.M., $10) is the top spot for Danish food. It can get very crowded, especially on the patio, so be prepared to wait during peak times. Their three-page breakfast menu is replete with huge plate-size pancakes of all types including the Danish apple. Or go Dutch and try the Dutch sausage omelet. They serve breakfast and lunch, but not dinner. Lunches include traditional Danish foods as well as some Americanized versions. The interior is casual, with more of a coffee shop feel, but it's also slightly Scandinavian.

Bit O' Denmark (473 Alisal Rd., 805/688-5426, daily 11 A.M.–9 P.M., $15) is known for their traditional smorgaasbord as well as roasted duck and Monte Cristo sandwiches. It is the oldest restaurant in Solvang, housed in one of the very first buildings the original settlers built in 1911. It became a restaurant in 1929 and continues to cook up Danish ham, Danish pork, roast beef open-faced sandwiches, and their extensive smorgaasbord, which includes *medisterpolse* (Danish sausage), *frikadeller* (meatballs), *rodkaal* (red cabbage), *spegesild* (picked herring), and an array of cold salads. The room to the left as you enter is the best, with large curved booths.

Solvang Restaurant (1672 Copenhagen Dr., 805/688-4645, www.solvangrestaurant .com, daily 6 A.M.–3 P.M., $10) is well known for their *aebleskivers*, round doughy concoctions

topped with jam; don't be surprised to see a line out the door. This little diner also dishes up breakfasts in a quaint environment. The overhead wood beams are decorated with Danish proverbs.

◖ **The Red Viking** (1684 Copenhagen Dr., 805/688-6610, daily 8 A.M.–8 P.M., $10) rolls out Danish dishes such as *hakkebof* (chopped sirloin and onion topped with a fried egg), Weiner schnitzel (veal cutlet), and authentic Danish smorgaasbord, and a line of Danish cheeses, hams, and beers. They are one of the top Danish food stops.

Pea Soup Andersen's (376 Avenue of the Flags, Buellton, 805/688-5881, www .peasoupandersens.net, daily 7 A.M.–10 P.M., $15) is the granddaddy of Danish restaurants, first opened in 1924. They serve American food, like burgers and milkshakes, and of course, pea soup in a bread bowl. There's a small gift shop, a bakery with fresh daily sweets and fudge, a small art gallery upstairs, and best of all, a mini-museum about Rufus T. Buell (as in Buellton), how he started the town, and how Andersen's came into being. It also chronicles some of the changes in the dining scene locally. It's just outside of Solvang proper, located right off Highway 101, and has the feel of a coffee shop. And there are plenty of cans of soup for sale.

BAKERIES

Mortensen's (1588 Mission Dr., 805/688-8373, Mon.–Fri. 8 A.M.–5:30 P.M., Sat.–Sun. 7:30 A.M.–6:30 P.M.) is one of the stalwarts of the Danish bakeries. It's best to visit the low-key interior for a strudel or éclair and a pot of tea or coffee and relax in the subdued environment. The Danish decor is not over the top, but it's still good Danish, and this is a great place to start your day.

Olsen's (1529 Mission Dr., 805/688-6314, www.olsensdanishbakery.com, Mon.–Fri. 7:30 A.M.–6 P.M., Sat.–Sun. 7:30 A.M.–7 P.M.) was established in Denmark way back in 1890, though this location isn't quite that old. They've been turning out homemade breads like grain pumpernickel, sunflower seed pumpernickel, and Swedish cardamom, as well as cookies and all manner of sweets, for three decades.

Solvang Bakery (460 Alisal Rd., 805/688-4939, www.solvangbakery.com, Sun.–Fri. 7 A.M.–5 P.M., Sat. 7 A.M.–6 P.M.) is a bright open space in a blue and white shop with an eye-catching array of gingerbread houses, Danish waffles, almond butter rings, and plenty more. They have been baking in Solvang for 30 years. Their onion cheese bread is a signature loaf.

GROCERIES

El Rancho Market Place (2886 Mission Dr., 805/688-4300, www.elranchomarket.com, daily 6 A.M.–10 P.M.) is an upscale supermarket and features an old-fashioned full-service meat counter, fresh local organic produce, and a complete selection of local and international wines, champagnes, and spirits. They have very good hot and cold entrées, salads, and fresh baked bread and pies—perfect for putting together a picnic. If you want something quick and easy, they have a great selection. There's some outdoor seating near the entrance and on occasion they grill tri-tip outside.

Information and Services

The **Solvang Visitors Center** (1639 Copenhagen, 800/468-6765, www.solvangusa.com) is staffed by locals wearing red vests. They have comprehensive information on not just Solvang, but the entire valley as well.

The *Santa Ynez Valley News* covers the local angle and is published each Thursday. For more countywide coverage, the *Santa Barbara News-Press* and the *Santa Maria Times* are both dailies available for purchase.

Should you have an **emergency,** dial 911 immediately.The **Santa Ynez Valley Cottage Hospital** (2050 Viborg, Solvang, 805/688-6431) offers emergency services. Police services are contracted with the **County of Santa Barbara Sheriff's Department** (1745 Mission Dr., Solvang, 805/688-5000).

Getting There

Highway 246 bisects the town. Known as Mission Drive while it runs through town, Highway 246 connects to Highway 101, which is the primary freeway on the Central Coast, and the small but still well-traveled Route 154, which connects to Santa Barbara in the south and Highway 101 further north. It's important to note that Solvang gets crowded on weekends, and getting in and out can be a slow proposition. But, since you have little choice but to wait it out, just remind yourself of how good a Danish cookie will taste when you finally arrive.

The **MTD Valley Express** (805/683-3702) is a regional commuter line running Monday–Friday between Santa Barbara, Buellton, and Solvang.

Amtrak will connect to the valley via motorcoach. The bus stop is located at 1630 Mission Drive in Solvang, but trains stop only in Santa Barbara and San Luis Obispo. Travel times for the coaches is approximately one hour.

Getting Around

Solvang, while the largest of the small towns in the area, is still a very navigable town and can easily be explored on foot in less than a day. A horse-drawn trolley traverses the streets of Solvang, taking willing participants on a narrated tour on the Honen Streetcar, which is a replica of either a late 1800s or 1915 streetcar, depending on whom you choose to believe. Two large horses will pull you around town as you learn the history and noteworthy spots of Solvang. The tours last about 25 minutes and run every 35 minutes Thursday–Monday noon–6 P.M. Board at the visitors center at Copenhagen and 2nd Streets. Cost is $9 adults, $7 seniors, $5 children.

The Santa Ynez Valley Transit (805/688-5452, www.cityofsolvang.com) is a scheduled minibus serving Ballard, Buellton, Los Olivos, Santa Ynez, and Solvang, operating Monday–Saturday starting at 7 A.M. The Chumash Casino also offers a shuttle service serving Solvang, Buellton, Santa Barbara, Goleta, Santa Maria, and Lompoc (800/248-6274). Riders with a Club Chumash gaming card get preferred seating.

Solvang Taxi (805/688-0069) operates 24 hours a day. You'll need to call them, however, as you rarely see a taxi in town. They also offer, like everyone else, wine transportation. **Promenade Cab Company** (805/717-8400) also operates in Solvang.

LOS OLIVOS

Los Olivos is an artist's enclave and a wine taster's dream. The central flagpole, sitting boldly on Grand Avenue, is the de facto rallying point for tourists, since there are still no stoplights in the area. Within a two-block radius of the flagpole are a dozen tasting rooms, half a dozen excellent restaurants, and a few art galleries representing some of the best local artists. Unpretentious and simple, it's a perfect one-day getaway—unless you also use it as a base to explore Lake Cachuma, Figueroa Mountain, or the broader wine region, in which case you'll need several days.

Los Olivos began as a town in 1861 with the establishment of the Overland/Coast Line Stage Station at Ballard. Actually, at the time it was more a loose aggregate of residences; it wasn't until 1887 when Swiss-Italian immigrant Felix Mattei, anticipating the arrival of the Pacific Coast Railway, opened a hotel to accommodate rail and stage passengers making both north and south connections in Los Olivos that a semblance of an actual town began to form. The local streets were leveled by Chinese workers from the railroads, and following the first whistle of the engine in November 1887, Los Olivos, while still small, was finally placed on the map. Though the town is reasonably new, the Keenan-Hartley home from 1882 is the oldest wooden home in Los Olivos and is a Santa Barbara County landmark. The house has undergone several additions and is now the Wildling Art Museum.

Wine-Tasting

Los Olivos has become a hub of wine-tasting rooms. Not long ago the area was mainly full of art galleries and just a few wineries. Now with 20 wine-tasting rooms, Los Olivos has become a convenient stop to taste and shop

A message board touts the possibilities of wine tasting in Los Olivos.

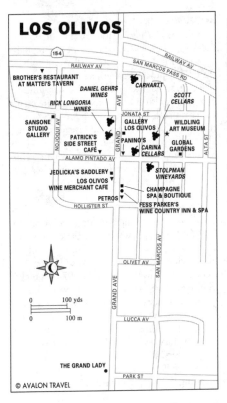

grapes are biodynamically farmed, using no chemicals whatsoever, on a plot of land called Purisima Mountain. You'll see this name at many wineries in the valley; the Beckmen fruit is very popular and sold to other wineries. Sauvignon blanc, cabernet sauvignon, marsanne, a killer grenache, and a variety of syrahs are available to taste. This is one of the best wineries in the area, and they excel at most every wine they make.

CARHARTT

Carhartt (2990 Grand Ave., 805/693-5100, www.carharttvineyard.com, daily 11 A.M.–5 P.M., tasting fee $10) is the smallest tasting room in the entire valley, but the winery makes big wines. Their tasting room, which looks like a wood shack, can comfortably hold maybe six people, but it does have an outdoor area allowing for some elbow room—though people seem to like crowding themselves inside. Their signature wines, merlot and syrah, come from their very own 10-acre estate, a former cattle ranch, and they buy fruit to produce sauvignon blanc, sangiovese, and petite sirah from both Santa Barbara and Paso Robles.

CARINA CELLARS

Carina Cellars (2900 Grand, 805/688-2459, www.carinacellars.com, daily 11 A.M.–5 P.M., tasting fee $10) has made a name for themselves with syrah, specifically syrah coming from the well-regarded Colsen Canyon vineyard. But they also have a blend, Iconoclast, that merges Napa Valley cabernet sauvignon with Santa Barbara syrah. Other wines in their portfolio include viognier, petite sirah, and red Rhône blends. Their tasting room also features rotating art on the rustic-looking walls. They have expanded to two tasting bars inside to handle the influx of people. Located right in downtown Los Olivos, this is one of the best and most consistent wineries.

STOLPMAN VINEYARDS

Stolpman's (2434 Alamo Pintado Ave., 805/688-0400, www.stolpmanvineyards .com, daily 11 A.M.–5 P.M., tasting fee $15)

for all things wine. This tiny hamlet can become quite packed during the high season: Parking is at a premium, tasting rooms can be full to overflowing, and there are often waits at the few restaurants in town. Plan your trip to avoid the high season and you'll have a much better time.

◖ BECKMEN VINEYARDS

You'll need to drive to Beckmen Vineyards (2670 Ontiveros Rd., 805/688-8664, daily 11 A.M.–5 P.M., tasting fee $10–15), since it is located in the middle of a residential district. The tasting room is small, plain, and uneventful, but there are several lattice-walled picnic booths that overlook a small pond and the surrounding soft hills covered with vines. It's peaceful out here, and that's the point. Their tasting room, in a late-1800s building with a red-painted board-and-batten exterior with white trim, was originally a private residence. The tasting room's interior was designed using recycled materials and features two tasting bars. These days, lawyer turned vintner Tom Stolpman remains steadfastly focused on syrah and syrah blends as their flagship wines, but also includes sangiovese, malbec, and white Rhône blends. The tasting room also has a selection of crystal decanters and their very own estate olive oil. They produce outstanding wines, though a little on the pricey side.

DANIEL GEHRS WINES

Housed in a 100-year-old home, Daniel Gehrs Wines (2939 Grand Ave., 805/693-9686, www .danielgehrswines.com, daily 11 A.M.–6 P.M., tasting fee $10) was a residence, then a doctor's office, long before it became a wine-tasting room. There are several rooms packed with gift items, a small tasting bar in the front, and a nice patio in the back where they conduct wine-tastings during the summer months. Dan Gehrs has long been a fixture in the wine scene and was one of the first winemakers in the valley. Among their offerings are Riesling, pinot noir, ports made with traditional Portuguese grapes, sangiovese, gewürztraminer, and a few of Dan's daughter's wines under the Vixen label.

RICK LONGORIA WINES

Like Daniel Gehrs, Rick Longoria has been involved in the wine industry for decades, and his winery (2935 Grand Ave., 805/688-0305, www. longoriawine.com, daily 11 A.M.–4:30 P.M., tasting fee $10) is right next door to Daniel Gehrs Wines. The small, narrow tasting room, originally a machine shop from the turn of the 20th century, carries chardonnay, pinot noir, and tempranillo, and Rick's locally well-known Blues Cuvée, a blend of predominantly cabernet franc with the addition of merlot and cabernet sauvignon. Their Blues series of wines features labels portraying famous blues artists. The winery has a little partially shaded side patio with a few tables, and you can hear the two water fountains on the patio as you sample the wines.

KOEHLER WINERY

The Koehler Winery (5360 Foxen Canyon Rd., 805/693-8384, www.koehlerwinery.com, daily 10 A.M.–5 P.M., tasting fee $10) seems to have it all: They produce cabernet sauvignon, syrah, viognier, sauvignon blanc, and other wines in a very pretty hillside location. There are picnic tables outside, and since it's pulled back from the main road, it's quiet and serene here. They also make pinot noir, which they don't grow on-site but source from the Santa Rita Hills. Koehler wines have received outstanding scores from the national press.

ZACA MESA WINERY

The Zaca Mesa Winery (6905 Foxen Canyon, 805/688-9339, www.zacamesa.com, daily 10 A.M.–4 P.M., tasting fee $10) is one of the oldest wineries in the county and the very first to plant syrah way backing the 1970s, long before anyone even knew what syrah was. This has given them a leg up on working with the variety. Viognier, chardonnay, roussanne, grenache, and mourvedre round out the offerings at this winery, which has a very cool large-scale chess set on the property. It's a great spot to picnic, as it's off the beaten path. The tasting room is midsized, meaning it can get crowded at peak times.

SCOTT CELLARS

Owner Peter Scott does almost everything himself at Scott Cellars (2933 San Marcos Ave., 805/686-5450, www.scottcellars.com, Wed.–Mon. 11 A.M.–5 P.M., tasting fee $7), including building his own tasting bar. With production of less than a thousand cases, this is a small operation, but a dream come true for Scott, a self-taught winemaker who started out with a tiny winery in Ventura before it shut down. His wines include sangiovese, pinot noir, syrah, pinot gris, and chardonnay. He's usually there, brimming with enthusiasm, and will talk as along as you stay at the tasting bar. The interior is simple and uncluttered and there is one table off to the side.

CURTIS WINERY

Curtis Winery (5249 Foxen Canyon, 805/686-

8999, daily 10 A.M.–5 P.M., tasting fee $10) has a thing for Hawaiian shirts, and that's pretty much the vibe here: low-key and fun. The emphasis is solely on Rhône-style wines like grenache, mourvedre, syrah, roussanne, and viognier. They were actually one of the first wineries to focus on these grapes. They routinely turn out some very fine wines that showcase the area, which leans toward bright expressive fruit. They also have a lot of gift items and books, and a grassy area fronting the main road with picnic tables and views to the vineyards across the street.

THE BRANDER VINEYARD

The Brander Vineyard (2401 N. Refugio Rd., 805/688-2455, daily 10 A.M.–5 P.M., tasting fee $10) facility looks like a small wine château in Europe—well, except for the pink walls. Surrounded by flowers and poplar, cottonwood, and redwood trees, and a rustic courtyard with picnic tables, this is a place known for sauvignon blanc. Brander is the undisputed king of that varietal in this area, having been making it since the 1970s. Equally impressive is a cabernet sauvignon—remarkable considering that this is not the prime growing area for it. Chardonnay, syrah, and merlot round out the offerings.

Sights and Drives

◖ FOXEN CANYON

If there is any drive or ride that's important to Los Olivos, it's Foxen Canyon. It's the site of a wine trail but worth checking out even if you're not into wine; Foxen Canyon is a beautiful, meandering road, immensely popular with cyclists and perfect for tooling about with the top down. Where Alamo Pintado Road ends and turns into Highway 154 at the northern end of Los Olivos, Foxen Canyon Road Begins. You can take Foxen Canyon Road just south to Los Alamos or continue all the way into Santa Maria. Typical of these areas, there are wineries, ranches, and farms populated with oak trees, cattle, deer, and hawks.

FIGUEROA MOUNTAIN

Figueroa's 4,528 foot crest is one of the shortest drives you can take to get the furthest away from what is the typical valley topography of chaparral-covered hills and lots of oak trees. Yes, this is also where Michael Jackson's Neverland Ranch is located, but you can't see anything, just a rather nondescript gate. As Figueroa Mountain Drive peels off from Route 154 near Los Olivos and you make your way toward the foothills, the oak trees begin to be replaced by pine trees, wildflowers, and more pronounced rock formations. From the lookout tower located on top of the mountain, 360-degree views of much of the county greet you. The Santa Ynez Mountains are to the south, appearing as a sheer mountain wall from this perspective. On a clear day, typically between February and April, the Channel Islands shimmer on the horizon.

The foreground of this view is the Santa Ynez Valley. Above and to the west is Point Conception, a land revered by the Chumash, the place of the setting sun, where these Native Americans believed they would travel to in the life that comes after death. You can descend the way you came, or if you're adventurous (and depending on the type of car you have), you can continue on some bumpy roads and over streams to eventually merge with Happy Canyon Road, making this a 30-plus-mile loop. This is not a short drive, but offers some spectacular scenery.

WILDLING ART MUSEUM

The genesis of the Wildling Art Museum (2928 San Marcos Ave., 805/688-1082, www.wildling museum.org, Wed.–Sun. 11 A.M.–5 P.M., $3) was a desire to showcase the West and its expansive beauty in landscapes, flora, and fauna. There's an educational center, research library, and a large museum gift shop where the books and other items feature wilderness art. Each year they mount four large exhibitions, which include lectures on art but also the preservation of the diminishing western lands. Once a month they offer a free Friday night movie, again with the theme of the wilderness and the inherent beauty it possesses. The museum is housed in the 1882 Keenan-Hartley house, the oldest frame-constructed house in the area, which was moved to its present location in 2000. The house, a Santa Barbara County Historical Landmark, is the perfect backdrop for an arts museum whose views are to the very mountains from which it draws inspiration.

CLAIRMONT FARMS

Clairmont Farms (2480 Roblar, 805/688-7505, www.clairmontfarms.com, daily 10 A.M.–6 P.M., suggested donation $3) is a family-owned and -operated working organic lavender farm that has five acres of lavender, as well as 175-year-old olive trees originally planted by the Catholic fathers (it's part of the grove that gave Los Olivos its name). Visitors can observe the process of distilling lavender and learn all the ways this herb is being used, in essential oils or as a cooking herb. They sell oils, teas, honey, soaps, and more, all infused with lavender; there's even lavender shampoo for your dog. Not only is it informative, but you'll leave feeling totally relaxed.

Festivals and Events

The annual **Quick Draw and Art Auction** (805/688-1222, www.judithhalegallery.com) is held right across from the flagpole each August. Local artists race against the clock to complete a drawing, painting, or sculpture within 45 minutes. The works are then auctioned off in a live auction, and you can walk home with something hot off the press. There's also a silent auction and a barbecue in the park, and artists have demonstrations as all the local galleries stay open late. They've been doing this for over a quarter of a century.

Shopping

CLOTHING

Jedlicka's Saddlery (2883 Grand Ave., 805/688-2626, www.jedlickas.com, Mon.–Sat. 9 A.M.–5:30 P.M., Sun. 10 A.M.–4:30 P.M.) is all cowboy, all the time. Jeans, hats, boots—whatever you might need for actual cowboy work or pretend cowboy work is all here. Jedlickas's first opened in 1932 on the site of the town's turn-of-the-20th-century blacksmith shop. Western and English clothing,

gear, and tack and a large selection of clothing for kids keeps people coming back.

SPECIALTY AND GIFTS

Global Gardens (2477 Alamo Pintado Ave., 805/693-1600, www.oliverevolution.com, daily 11 A.M.–5 P.M., tasting fee $3) uses mainly organic pesticide-free ingredients in their line of extra virgin olive oils, fruit vinegars, appetizer spreads, glazes, snacks, and sweets. They import Greek oils as well, and a tasting at the small wood-framed store will open your eyes to the vast differences in oils. If you've had enough wine, opt for olive oil.

Alpacas de Los Olivos (2786 Corral de Quati, 805/688-5748, www.whyalpacas.com, Sat. 11 A.M.–3 P.M., or by appointment) is a private ranch dedicated to alpaca, the smaller cousins of llamas and camels. Their rustic gift shop is stocked with items made from the soft, durable alpaca fibers, including sweaters, vests, ponchos, blankets, and even dresses. Additionally they'll give you a brief education about the animals, which are pretty darn cute, and you can see them up close.

ART GALLERIES

What once was an art destination with a dozen galleries has dwindled down to just two galleries now, and the Wildling Art Museum.

The largest gallery in town these days is **Gallery Los Olivos** (2920 Grand Ave., 805/688-7517, www.gallerylosolivos.com, daily 10 A.M.–5 P.M.), which acts as an artists' co-op, with the artists themselves running the show. They present regional artists from within Santa Barbara County working with wood, acrylic, ceramic, and pastels to create original traditional and abstract works of art. They rotate monthly solo shows. The space is larger than you'd expect, with a lot of first rate work.

At **Sansone Studio Gallery** (2948 Nojoqui Ave., 805/693-9769, www.sansonestudio.com, daily 11 A.M.–5 P.M.), Joel and Pamela Sansone use the medium of vitreous enamel on copper to create vibrant work. Vitreous enamel is applied to a copper surface, then kiln fired. The powdered glass becomes molten and fuses to the copper, making the colors extremely rich and deep. Their work is abstract in theme and their small off-the-beaten-path studio is worth seeking out just to see their unique pieces.

Accommodations

$200-300

It's easy to pass by **The Grand Lady** (2715 Grand Ave., 805/686-5762, kspurbeck@verizon .net, $250), which bills itself as a cottage and vacation rental. But they also rent out a 700-square-foot space located above the garage next to the beautiful Victorian home for single-night guests. There are two rooms that can sleep up to four people, a full kitchen, a washer and dryer, and you can easily walk the one block into Los Olivos. This is an upstairs unit private deck, and you have access to owner Kathy and Gerry Spurbeck's lovely back garden. The decor is simple, but it's a nice change from a hotel and you'll feel like you're a world away. They do not provide any amenities like food or morning coffee, but that's easy to find in town. Should you consider this option it's best to contact them in advance, as they sometimes rent the space for as long as several months.

OVER $300

Fess Parker's Wine Country Inn & Spa (2860 Grand Ave., 805/688-7788, www.fess parker.com, $395–520 d) was built by Fess Parker (who played Davy Crockett and Daniel Boone in the early TV shows), whose mini-empire included his own winery. Parker, who passed away in March 2010, was smart enough to get into land and real estate after his television days, and he was long a fixture of the valley. There's a wine store and a restaurant on the premises, and the feel of this traditional inn is changing to adopt a more modern feel, letting go of the older Victorian decor and replacing it with hipper and sleeker decor. But it still retains the elements people come here for: small-town hospitality, easy access to the wine country, and a Victorian and Western motif. The rooms are comfortable and large, and they surround a garden courtyard. This

is the only hotel in Los Olivos, but Santa Ynez and Solvang are a short drive away.

Food

At **Patrick's Side Street Café** (2375 Alamo Pintado, 805/686-4004, Wed.–Fri. 11:30 A.M.–4 P.M. and 5–9 P.M., Sat.–Sun. 11:30 A.M.–3 P.M. and 5–9 P.M., $25), owner Patrick is something of a prickly pear. If he doesn't like you, you're out. If you want a meal cooked a certain way and he doesn't agree, he'll let you know. But the man knows how to cook—trust him. The rustic, unpretentious space has artwork adorning the walls, local wines, a dedicated clientele, and fierce food. The warm duck salad is worth having, as is the paella. Be advised that it is a pet-friendly restaurant, meaning any and all animals are welcome, both inside and on their outdoor deck.

Panino's (2900 Grand Ave., 805/688-9304, daily 10 A.M.–4 P.M., $10) is all about sandwiches and salads. A small chain in the county, this outpost does very well. It's the perfect choice when you don't want a full sit-down meal but a quick bite to eat, maybe something to take on the road. Their sandwiches and salads are made to order, and there is a good selection of vegetarian options. The roast turkey and brie sandwich is a favorite, as is the avocado and provolone with fresh basil and honey mustard.

Ballard Inn (2436 Baseline, Ballard, 805/688-7770, Wed.–Sun. 5:30–9 P.M., $28) is one of those restaurants where you keep thinking, How did they end up here, of all places? Chef-owner Budi Kazali has transformed Ballard into a destination—well, actually, it's the only reason to stop in Ballard, which is sandwiched between Solvang and Los Olivos. There are only a dozen tables in this intimate space, and on busy nights (most any weekend), it can get loud. The menu rotates often to take advantage of the freshest ingredients Kazali can find. Most all the vegetables come from local farms, and the seafood from Santa Barbara. On any given night you might find crispy barramundi, truffled cauliflower soup, or a beef dish. Whatever is presented on the small menu, you can be sure it will be artfully prepared and exceptionally good.

Brother's Restaurant at Mattei's Tavern (2350 Railroad Ave., 805/688-4820, www .matteistavern.com, daily 5–10 P.M., $30) is part history lesson, part restaurant. It was built in 1886 right across from the railroad, which was where the highway is now. The narrow gauge would stop here and folks would head to Mattei's for food and rest—and they still do. With prime rib, lots of beef and fish entrées, it's a wonderful stop, and the old wood interior is lined with photos of times gone by and original paintings done by the original owner's son. Eternally popular with locals and tourists, Mattei's offers a well-priced and versatile wine list to complement their food. The current restaurant is run by actual brothers Jeff and Matt Nichols, who have been creating fine dining in the valley since 1996.

Los Olivos Wine Merchant Cafe (2879 Grand Ave., 805/688-7265, www.los olivoscafe.com, Mon.–Fri. 11:30 A.M.–9 P.M., Sat.–Sun. 11 A.M.–9 P.M., $20) has been plying their trade since 1995, and always did well. But *Sideways* really cemented their popularity, and now it's nearly always packed. You can sit outside on the deck, inside at the tables, or at the bar. They have a wall of wine as part of their offering, so if you find something you'd like to have with your lunch or dinner you can buy a bottle, or take one home with you. It gets noisy and the service is usually strained because of capacity crowds, but they prepare wonderful food like cage pot roast, and their excellent housemade bread dipping oil is sold by the bottle.

Petros (2860 Grand Ave., 805/686-5455, www.petrosrestaurant.com, Sun.–Thurs. 7 A.M.–10 P.M., Fri.–Sat. 7 A.M.–11 P.M., $25) is located inside the Fess Parker Inn. The Greek restaurant has a stunningly modern and hip decor in contrast to the conservative inn and the town, and is a culinary change of pace unlike anything in the valley. They bake their own pita, make fresh yogurt, and serve predominantly small plates, which is perfect since there is an abundance of things to try like the sesame-crusted feta and spanakopita. There are

full entrées as well, and many of the seasonings used are imported from Greece.

Los Olivos Grocery (2621 W. Hwy. 154, 805/688-5115, www.losolivosgrocery.com, daily 7 A.M.–9 P.M.) is part grocery store and part deli. With an impressive selection of cheeses and a decent wine department, they also have a full deli for picnic foods or will assemble one for you. Get the red-pepper hummus or their Happy Canyon club, or grab a breakfast burrito to go. All their produce in sourced from the area, and they have terrific sandwiches and salads to eat there on the covered patio, or to take with you as you explore wine country.

Information and Services

The website www.losolivosca.com is the best source of information about the town, though it is by no means comprehensive.

The *Santa Ynez Valley News* covers the local angle and is published each Thursday. For more countywide coverage, the *Santa Barbara News-Press* and the *Santa Maria Times* are both dailies available for purchase.

Should you have an **emergency,** dial 911. **The Santa Ynez Valley Cottage Hospital** (2050 Viborg, Solvang, 805/688-6431) offers emergency services. Police services are contracted with the County of Santa Barbara Sheriff's Department (1745 Mission Dr., Solvang, 805/688-5000).

Getting There

Los Olivos is best accessed off Highway 154 near the 101, as it sits directly off the highway. The Santa Ynez Airport accepts small craft, and the Santa Maria Airport is within a 20-minute drive.

Getting Around

Just like Santa Ynez, Los Olivos is a walking town. Only three blocks by two blocks, it is simple to get around. Some of the side streets don't have sidewalks, so be careful. It's also a small enough town that people simply wander the streets and cross whenever they feel like it, which is not a good idea—peak times get busy with traffic, and it's important to obey the traffic rules.

Santa Maria Valley

The Santa Maria Valley used to be a stretch of lonely land populated with sagebrush, deer, bears, and rabbits stretching from the Santa Lucia Mountains toward the Pacific Ocean. Today, Santa Maria is agriculture central. As you pass through on Highway 101, you see fields and vineyards coupled with new housing developments. Most people readily assume this is all farming, but Santa Maria has a strong Western history, and its namesake food, the Santa Maria–style tri-tip. Though it doesn't have the idyllic charm of other towns along the Central Coast, it is the gateway to the wine industry, beaches, and some fabulous under-the-radar restaurants.

The Chumash Indians made their homes here, and in 1769 the Portolá exploration party came through the Santa Maria Valley, signaling the advent of Mission San Luis Obispo in 1772 and Mission La Purisima in 1787. Settlers soon followed, looking for the possibility of free land. By the time of California statehood in 1850, the Santa Maria River Valley was one of the most productive agricultural areas in California, and it's still a key component of the economy.

The Santa Maria Valley saw its share of oil exploration beginning in 1888, leading to large oil discoveries by the turn of the 20th century. In 1901, William Orcutt urged his company, Union Oil, to lease more than 70,000 acres. For the next eight decades, thousands of oil wells were drilled and put into production, facilitating growth for the city. By 1957 there were almost 1,800 oil wells in operation in the Santa Maria Valley, producing $60 million worth of oil. The city remained just four square miles until 1954, when annexations increased the city's size to about 22 square miles. You can still see some of the old wells, but more than likely you'll see vineyards and row crops, and chances are you'll eat and drink the bounty of Santa Maria wherever you dine.

WINE-TASTING

The wineries in the Santa Maria area are spread out, requiring a car to visit even a few of them. Some are in industrial sections of the city, and some are among vineyards. Unlike Solvang, Los Olivos, and Santa Ynez, where it's easy to find several wineries along one road or right in the middle of the town, you have to plan your trips to these wineries. A great initial resource is www.santamariawines.com.

◖ FLYING GOAT CELLARS

The focus is on pinot noir at Flying Goat (1520 E. Chestnut, Unit A, Lompoc, 805/736-9032, www.flyinggoat.com, Thurs.–Sat. 11 A.M.–4 P.M., tasting fee $10). In addition to several iterations of beautifully seductive pinot noir, they are locally well known for Goat Bubbles, a light, delicate pinot noir sparkling wine. Owner Norm Yost goes for an uncommon restrained style with his wines, allowing the lush cherry and raspberry elements of the pinot noir grapes to express themselves and not be overwhelmed with too much oak. These are consistently excellent wines and avoid the bombastic and overripe characteristics that many pinot noirs tend to exhibit. As Norm has said, Why spend $4,000 a ton buying pinot noir fruit only to mask it behind oak? Ultimately he makes wine he would like to drink, and Norm steadfastly adheres to his principles. His tasting room is nothing more than a table at his small winery. This is a working facility and not a spot to lounge and look at pretty vineyards. In fact the only wildlife you'll see will probably be Norm's dog.

FOXEN WINERY

Foxen Winery (7600 Foxen Canyon Rd., 805/937-4251 daily 11 A.M.–4 P.M., tasting fee $10) is known for its rustic wood tasting room that looks like a run-down shed. But the wines are a far cry from that image. In addition to chardonnay, syrah, cabernet sauvignon, and pinot noir, the winery is one of the few to produce chenin blanc, an underappreciated grape.

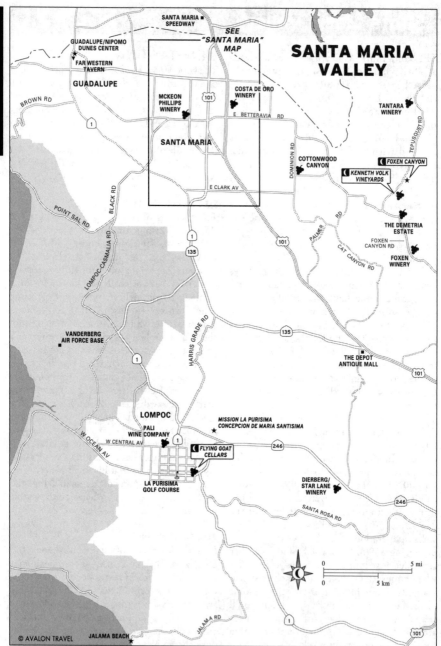

Foxen has a long-standing reputation of producing some of the finest wines in the area, and the Foxen name goes back six generations. Their 10-acre vineyard is the only dry-farmed vineyard in the area, meaning that there is no irrigation, they simply rely on what Mother Nature provides.

COTTONWOOD CANYON

Cottonwood Canyon (3940 Dominion Rd., 805/937-8463, daily 10 A.M.–5:30 P.M., tasting fee $10) started in 1988, and though it's just 10 minutes from downtown Santa Maria, this winery has managed to keep under the radar, though after trying their wines you'll wonder why you haven't heard of them. With a standard portfolio of wines including six iterations of chardonnay, they also include a couple of sparkling wines and a dessert-style syrah as well as several pinot noirs. They farm 78 acres with the San Rafael Mountains as a backdrop. Winemaker Norm Beko also loves food, and many weekends he's grilling up something to share.

MCKEON PHILLIPS WINERY

McKeon Phillips Winery (2115 S. Blosser Rd., 805/928-3025, daily 11 A.M.–6 P.M., tasting fee $8–13) is part tasting room and part art gallery and studio, where you can sip wines while examining rotating works of art including the winemaker's own impressionistic creations. Chardonnay, nebbiolo, cabernet sauvignon, and some delicious thick ports come out of here. This is another winery that has a low profile; when you drive to their tasting room located in a small industrial warehouse you may initially think that you might be in the wrong spot. There are no pretty views here, but a broad portfolio of wines and good conversation.

TANTARA WINERY

A dozen different pinot noirs are the flagship wines at Tantara Winery (2900 Rancho Tepusquet Rd., 805/938-5051, www.tantara winery.com, by appointment only). There is also chardonnay, but that's it. These wines are sold directly at the winery since they have no tasting room, which is located at Bien Nacido

Vineyards. The winemaking team of Jeff Fink and Bill Cates is focused on small lots of exceptional fruit, and they source pinot noir from some diverse growing areas along the Central Coast and Monterey and produce various expressions of those spots. Often they will pull barrel samples for visitors to taste. Their wines are not on the cheap side, but this is the place if you're looking for beautiful high-end pinot noir.

DEMETRIA ESTATE

The Demetria Estate (6701 Foxen Canyon Rd., 805/686-2345, www.demetriaestate. com, by appointment only) features stellar beautifully crafted pinot noir, syrah, pinot blanc, chardonnay, and a Rhône white blend, though these are not inexpensive wines. They biodynamically farm their vineyard, which was formerly the site of a vineyard that made merely average wines—apparently the farming techniques make all the difference. The care given the vines is expressed in these wines. Their facility is a yellow mottled Tuscan-looking building set on a hill overlooking the vines and is impressive enough, but even more so coupled with the wines. Bring some food and relax.

DIERBERG/STAR LANE WINERY

Dierberg/Star Lane Winery (1280 Drum Canyon Rd., Lompoc, 805/739-0757, www .starlanevineyard.com, daily 11 A.M.–5 P.M., tasting fee $10) has vineyards located in Happy Canyon, one of the warmest spots in the valley, hence the reason they can make exceptional cabernet sauvignon. Their green and red barn tasting room is on the opposite side of the valley, however, and a little off the beaten path, but worth the drive for any serious wine lover. The Dierbergs operate three wine labels: Star Lane, their estate wines called Dierberg, and Three Saints. All of these wines, at various price points, are excellent. The Star Lane sauvignon blanc is terrific, and the value-priced Three Saints wines, including merlot, cabernet sauvignon, and pinot noir, are best bets.

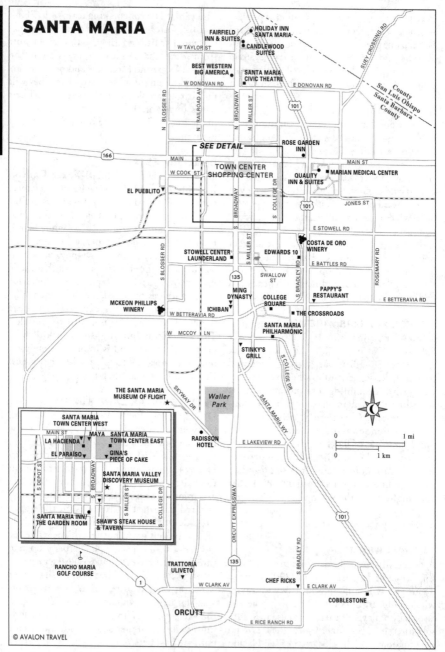

SANTA MARIA

FAIRFIELD INN & SUITES
HOLIDAY INN SANTA MARIA
CANDLEWOOD SUITES
W TAYLOR ST
BEST WESTERN BIG AMERICA
SANTA MARIA CIVIC THEATRE
W DONOVAN RD
E DONOVAN RD
N BLOSSER RD
RAILROAD AVE
BROADWAY
MILLER ST
101
SUEY CROSSING RD
County San Luis Obispo County Santa Barbara

SEE DETAIL
ROSE GARDEN INN
166
MAIN ST
MAIN ST
TOWN CENTER SHOPPING CENTER
W COOK ST
QUALITY INN & SUITES
MARIAN MEDICAL CENTER
EL PUEBLITO
BROADWAY
S COLLEGE DR
101
JONES ST

E STOWELL RD
STOWELL CENTER LAUNDERLAND
S MILLER ST
EDWARDS 10
COSTA DE ORO WINERY
S BLOSSER RD
135
SWALLOW ST
E BATTLES RD
ROSEMARY RD
MCKEON PHILLIPS WINERY
MING DYNASTY
ICHIBAN
W BETTERAVIA RD
COLLEGE SQUARE
PAPPY'S RESTAURANT
E BETTERAVIA RD
THE CROSSROADS
S BRADLEY RD

W MCCOY LN
SANTA MARIA PHILHARMONIC

STINKY'S GRILL
S COLLEGE DR

THE SANTA MARIA MUSEUM OF FLIGHT
SKYWAY DR
Waller Park
SANTA MARIA WY

[Inset detail map]

SANTA MARIA TOWN CENTER WEST
MAIN ST
MAYA
SANTA MARIA TOWN CENTER EAST
LA HACIENDA
EL PARAÍSO
GINA'S PIECE OF CAKE
S DEPOT ST
BROADWAY
SANTA MARIA VALLEY DISCOVERY MUSEUM
S MILLER ST
S COLLEGE DR
SANTA MARIA INN/ THE GARDEN ROOM
SHAW'S STEAK HOUSE & TAVERN

RADISSON HOTEL
E LAKEVIEW RD
ORCUTT EXPRESSWAY

0   1 mi
0   1 km

RANCHO MARIA GOLF COURSE
1
TRATTORIA ULIVETO
135
W CLARK AV
CHEF RICKS
E CLARK AV
S BRADLEY RD
101
COBBLESTONE
ORCUTT
E RICE RANCH RD

© AVALON TRAVEL

WHAT'S IN A NAME? THE STORY BEHIND SOME WACKY WINERY NAMES

A quick glance at the wine industry reveals that the majority of wineries are named after people. There's certainly nothing wrong with naming a winery after yourself: Foley, Babcock, Melville, Rusack, Beckmen, Mosby, Huber, and many other wineries are named after their owners. But some winery names go beyond a mere surname.

Mike Brown named his winery Kalyra, which loosely translated from Australian Aboriginal means "a wild and pleasant place." Sea Smoke in the Santa Rita Hills sounds seductive, through most folks don't realize that the name refers to the ocean fog climbing over the mountains. Lincourt Winery refers to the names of two daughters of the owner, Lindsey and Courtney.

Bill Cates, co-owner of Tantara Winery, owned a horse named Tantara when he lived in Virginia, and she led a charmed life. When Tantara got on in years, Bill sent her to live out her days with other mares. But after a while Bill realized she wasn't getting around very well, and made the difficult decision to put her down, and arranged for a vet to euthanize her. About a month later he went back to visit Tantara's grave site. As he stood there, tears in his eyes for the loss of his beloved horse, something bumped him from behind. It was Tantara. The vet had put down the wrong horse! After that, Bill says, he let Tantara live out her days on her own terms.

Kathy Joseph, owner of Fiddlehead Cellars, already had two different vintages aging in barrels, but still had no idea what to call her new winery. One day, while working in her fern bed, it struck her — she'd call the project Fiddlehead, the word for the coiled tip of a fern frond. The fiddlehead emerges once a year into a very elegant leaf, just like her vintages, and is considered a delicacy; the name was perfectly playful, matching her approach to making wine.

You may have never seen a goat fly, but Norm Yost, owner of Flying Goat Cellars, has. Apparently he had pygmy goats on his property, and he built a little house for them. A few of the goats would climb on top of the house and jump off the roof. A perfect name for his pinot noirs, he thought. In fact, many people try his wines based solely on the label and name. Norm says, "Names are powerful and I wanted to create some levity in the wine business."

PALI WINE COMPANY

Pali Wine Company (1036 W. Aviation Dr., Lompoc, 805/736-7200, www.paliwineco .com, Fri.–Sat. 11 A.M.–4 P.M., Sun.–Thurs. by appointment, tasting fee $10) is located out in a warehouse-looking building in Lompoc, where you taste the wines next to the barrels, stacked cases of wine, and stainless steel fermentation tanks. Pinot noir from multiple vineyard sites across California is their specialty, showcasing how a single grape type can be so different depending on where it was grown. They also make a killer grenache, chardonnay, and cabernet sauvignon. It's a younger winery, but they have produced impressive wines in part because they are dedicated to not taking shortcuts with their wines.

K KENNETH VOLK VINEYARDS

The owner of Kenneth Volk Vineyards (5230 Tepusquet Rd., 805/938-7896, www.volk wines.com, daily 10:30 A.M.–4:30 P.M., tasting fee $5) was not initially into wine. At college in San Luis Obispo he pursued a degree in fruit science, imagining a future in an orchard or greenhouse. But in 1981 he established Wild Horse Winery & Vineyard in Templeton, and over the next two decades production soared from 600 to 150,000 cases. In 2003, Ken sold Wild Horse, and in 2004 he formed Kenneth Volk Vineyards in Santa Maria. He wins countless awards, and makes damn good wines using as many diverse aspects of winemaking as possible. "Just as a rich stew or curry creates a more vivid culinary experience when it includes a complex combination of ingredients that harmonize, we seek to bring together complementary flavors for a richer wine experience," he says. In addition to the standard offerings like chardonnay, pinot noir, viognier, cabernet sauvignon, and merlot, he's been a champion of what are called heirloom varieties, funky, wonderfully oddball wines like cabernet pfeffer, négrette, verdelho, and Aglianico. You won't regret the long trek to get to the tranquil 12-acre property along the Tepusquet Creek, surrounded by oak and sycamore trees.

COSTA DE ORO WINERY

Costa de Oro Winery (1331 S. Nicholson Ave., 805/922-1468, www.cdowinery.com, daily 10 A.M.–6 P.M., tasting fee $7) started off as a farming operation with row crops; they then decided to plant grapes on a patch of land that wasn't working right. Well, the grapes thrived, and now pinot noir and chardonnay are the main wines they produce from their 20 acres. Friday nights and Sundays there's usually something musical happening at the tasting room, which is also the outlet for their produce operation. Today the tasting room, which opened in 2006, sits on the site of the Gold Coast strawberry stand, where you can also pick up fresh veggies and fruits in season. The wines offered at Costa de Oro include sauvignon blanc, three different versions of chardonnay, and three different versions of pinot noirs, among others.

RANCHO SISQUOC

Rancho Sisquoc (6600 Foxen Canyon Rd., 805/934-4332, www.ranchosisquoc.com, Mon.–Thurs. 10 A.M.–4 P.M., Fri.–Sun. 10 A.M.–5 P.M., tasting fee $8) is one of those spots where you really have to want to go there. Located out in the boonies, it's a beautiful spot, and is probably best enjoyed by bringing a picnic. Their wood-sided tasting room is rustic but comfortable, more like an upscale barn. Grab a bottle of their sylvaner, chardonnay, sangiovese, or merlot and sit outside with some food and enjoy wine country, looking out to a vast field with low hills in the distance. This is definitely a quiet place!

SIGHTS
Santa Maria Museum of Flight

The Santa Maria Museum of Flight (3015 Airpark Dr., 805/922-8758, www.smmof.org, Fri.–Sun. 10 A.M.–4 P.M., $5 adults, $4 seniors, $3 children 12–18, $1 children 6–12) features displays of WWII and present-day aircraft and artifacts. The small but interesting museum is presided over by an all-volunteer staff. There are two hangars and a few old planes, as well as a 3,000-volume library on aviation. Their yearly air show, Thunder Over the Valley, is a huge draw each August. This is not a large museum, but the dedication of a few individuals makes this a great visit for aviation lovers.

Santa Maria Valley Discovery Museum

Santa Maria Valley Discovery Museum (705 S. McClelland St., 805/928-8414, www.smvdiscoverymuseum.org, Mon.–Sat. 10 A.M.–5 P.M., $8) is a place for kids, and the emphasis is on education. They have a lot of small hands-on exhibits such as how a tractor works, and information about agriculture, how saddles are made, a boat and its terminology, and a 3,000-gallon tank with—you guessed it—sharks! If you're traveling with younger kids, this is a great stop. They do an admirable job at this museum, with a diversity of things for kids to be involved in. The interior is brightly colored, allowing for a lot of stimulation.

Guadalupe-Nipomo Dunes Center

Guadalupe-Nipomo Dunes Center (1055 Guadalupe St., Guadalupe, 805/343-2455, www.dunescenter.org, Thurs.–Sun. noon–4 P.M.) is housed in a 1910 Craftsman house, still beautiful inside with built-in bookshelves that hold the research library. Staff can guide you as to how best to explore the 18 miles of coastline and the 22,000 acres that broadly encompass the dunes complex, whether you're a bird-watcher or an off-roader, or you just want to walk the beach. Upstairs is a small exhibit space including a vertebrae from a whale, a brief history of the area and dunes, and most visited of all, the history of the set of the 1923 film *The Ten Commandments,* which was filmed at the dunes.

Mission La Purisima Concepcion de Maria Santisima

Mission La Purisima Concepcion de Maria Santisima (2295 Purisima Rd., Lompoc, 805/733-3713, www.lapurisimamission.org, self-guided tours daily 9 A.M.–5 P.M., free one-hour guided tours daily at 1 P.M., $6 adults, $5 seniors) was founded on December 8, 1787, but the first mission was destroyed in the earthquake of 1812. The fathers then rebuilt the mission in a different spot, and it is that mission that a quarter of a million visitors enjoy today as a state historic park. Sitting inside 2,000 acres are trails for simple hikes and walks, and many people bring a picnic. When you visit you can examine the five-acre garden that shows native and domestic plants typical of a mission garden, including fig and olive trees and a wide variety of plants like sage and Spanish dagger. There are also

mission animals typical of the times, such as burros, horses, longhorn cattle, sheep, goats, and turkeys, which are displayed in a corral located in the main compound.

The mission is actually three buildings and there are well over a dozen rooms to explore, including sleeping quarters of the soldiers, the weaving shop, the candle-making room, the simple church, chapel, priest's quarters, and a lot more. Many of the rooms still have their original dirt floors, and this is the best mission to visit to truly get a feel for daily life back then. There are also a few conical huts that the Chumash used to live in. This is one of the only missions that does not have church services, now that it's a state park.

In 1785, Sergeant Pablo de Cota, stationed at Mission San Buenaventura in present-day Ventura, was ordered to find a location for a new mission, which was to be roughly equidistant between the missions at San Luis Obispo and Santa Barbara. The Mission of the Immaculate Conception of Most Holy Mary was dedicated and construction began in the spring of 1788,

© GREG PETERSON

La Purisma mission

after the winter rains. It was constructed in the traditional quadrangle shape, and the converted Chumash lived outside the mission walls in their traditional huts.

On the morning of December 21, 1812, a major temblor stuck the coast. Two shock waves virtually destroyed the mission, and what was left of the shattered adobe walls dissolved in the heavy winter rains. When they decided to rebuild the traditional design was abandoned and the new mission was built in a linear design, making it unique among California missions.

But this mission, too, would fall into ruin, a victim of the passage of time and simple neglect. In 1824, La Purisima was at the center of a failed Chumash revolt. Soldiers guarding the mission were poorly paid, and the mission was waiting to receive monies owed them from Spain. Spain didn't pay, and the soldiers turned their frustrations out on the Indian population. The friction between the military and the missions exploded as the Chumash Indians of the three Santa Barbara missions rose up in armed revolt. Soldiers from the presidio at Monterey took the La Purisima mission by force; the attack left 16 Chumash Indians dead and several wounded. One of the fathers negotiated surrender terms for the Chumash Indians, but seven Chumash Indians who surrendered were executed, and 12 others were sentenced to hard labor at the Santa Barbara presidio.

Secularization in 1834 was the final nail in the coffin for La Purisima. Church services ceased in 1836, and buildings fell into disrepair. By 1845 the mission was sold for a little more than $1,000, and the church was stripped of its roof tiles and timbers. The walls, exposed to the elements, crumbled. Eventually, the building was used as a stable. It was rescued in 1934, when the site was deeded to the State of California. A resulting restoration project became one of the largest of its kind in the nation.

Vandenberg Air Force Base

The tours at Vandenberg Air Force Base (Hwy. 1 at Black Rd., 805/606-3595, www .vandenberg.af.mil) take visitors by bus through the base and include a tour of the Heritage Museum, which provides mock-ups of missile silos, an old missile control station, and decommissioned rocket engines, as well as a visit to Space Launch Complex 10, an old still-intact launch area for missiles from the 1960s to the 1980s. They do offer private tours for 15 or more people. Tours last nearly three hours, in part because the drive time around this massive military installation will consume over an hour of that. Remember that this is an active military base and joking about national security is seriously frowned upon. Public base tours are offered through the Public Affairs office the second Wednesday of each month. Reservations are required at least two weeks in advance.

Information on **Vandenberg rocket launches** is available by calling the Launch Update and Rumor Control Hotline at 805/606-1857. Launch days and times are released three to five days in advance. The public viewing site for Vandenberg launches is off Corral Road near Vandenberg's main gate. To access the area, take Highway 1 to the Santa Maria Gate and proceed on Casmalia Road. At the barriers, turn right onto Corral Road and bear left to the top. Most launches are held in the very early morning hours. Due to weather, visibility might be hindered.

Originally called Camp Cooke, this base was a training center for armored and infantry troops during World War II. It was then transformed into the nation's first space and ballistic missile training base in 1957 and renamed Vandenberg Air Force Base after General Hoyt S. Vandenberg. The base is the only military base in the United States from which unmanned government and commercial satellites are launched into polar orbit. It is also the only site from which intercontinental ballistic missiles are test fired into the Pacific Ocean; they land at the Kwajalein Atoll near the Marshall Islands. The base's coastal location, in addition to its size, remoteness from heavily populated areas, and moderate climate that afforded year-round operations, allows these missiles to be launched without any negative impact over populated areas. Today, Vandenberg is the third largest air force base in California.

Jalama Beach

This 23-acre Santa Barbara County park (9999 Jalama Rd., Lompoc, 805/736-3504, www.jalamabeach.com, day-use fee $8) near Jalama Creek, once a Chumash Indian settlement called Halama, maintains 98 campsites, all overlooking the ocean. Each site has a picnic table and barbecue pit, with hot showers, restrooms, and potable water nearby; 29 sites offer electrical hookups, and dump stations are available. It's easy to think that since Jalama is so remote it would be off the radar, but it can actually be a busy place on holiday weekends. From Highway 101, take Highway 1 toward Lompoc. After 14 miles you'll see the sign for Jalama. This road is another 14 miles to the beach. It's a stunning drive.

Once you reach Jalama Beach you'll see so many RV and tents you'll think you've arrived at a camping convention. Thankfully the campsites, which fill very fast, are well spaced apart. Groceries, sundries, firewood, fishing bait and tackle, ice, and beer and wine can be purchased at the Jalama Store. Other services include mail and video rentals. The store and its popular grill are open daily starting at 8 A.M. Day-use picnic areas provide tables and raised fire boxes. Additional activities include surfing, horseshoes, whale-watching, bird-watching, nature photography, and fishing the surf or rock outcroppings for perch, cabezon, kelp, bass, or halibut, and there's a play area for the kids. You probably won't get cell service out here. Many protected California native plants like sand verbena, saltbush, and sea rocket grow within the park. There's a lot of powerful surf at Jalama, so be careful if you get in the water. It also tends to be blustery, but the views to the coastline, all green cliffs and blue water, are fantastic.

ENTERTAINMENT AND EVENTS
Festivals and Events

Strawberries are a big crop here, and for over two decades they have celebrated the berry with more strawberries than you've ever seen at the **Santa Maria Valley Strawberry Festival** (Santa Maria Fair Park, 937 S. Thornburg, 805/925-8824, www.santamariafairpark.com, $6 adults, $4 seniors and children 6–11, $5 parking), held over three days in April each year. There are food booths, rides, live bands, an old-fashioned carnival, and the chance to sample different strawberry varieties and strawberry desserts while you learn about the strawberry industry, the valley's number one crop. This is one of the most attended festivals in the county.

The **Celebration of Harvest** (Rancho Sisquoc Winery, 6600 Foxen Canyon Rd., www.sbcountywines.com, 1–4 P.M., $75) is an annual event held each October. In fact the Chumash also had a harvest ceremony, known as the Hutash, which lasted for several days. Now, it's a time to drink wine, listen to bands, bid on silent auction items, see local artists, sample local food, and bask in the outdoor beauty of Rancho Sisquoc. The winery itself is located here, but it's also one of the few fields around that's large enough to accommodate 3,000 people. Most every winery shows up and frankly there's no way to sample everything. But if you're on the hunt for certain wines or varieties, this is a great place to get a feel for all of Santa Barbara County's wines.

RECREATION
Golf

La Purisima Golf Course (3455 E. Hwy. 246, Lompoc, 805/735-8395, www.lapurisimagolf.com, daily 6:30 A.M.–dusk, green fees $40–91) is an 18-hole, par-72 course designed by Robert Graves, who also designed Sandpiper in Santa Barbara and Hunter Ranch in Paso Robles. It's moderately priced and there is a small grill for food and a pro shop. This is a tough course, with more hills than most any course, and brisk, cool winds in the afternoon—in other words, "challenging" is an understatement. But if you're up for it, it will be worth your effort, in spite of its rather remote location. Like many courses on the Central Coast, there is an abundance of oak trees to contend with.

Rancho Maria Golf Course (1950 Casmalia Rd., 805/937-2019, www.ranchomariagolf.com, daily 6:30 A.M.–dusk, green fees $22–35) is a rather unknown 18-hole, par-72 course even more secluded than Purisima. Though there are no parallel fairways and no houses to be seen on this remote course, there are a lot of trees and a short elevation gain. They have a small coffee shop, putting green, and practice bunkers. The pricing is quite good for a municipal course.

ACCOMMODATIONS
Under $100

The **Rose Garden Inn** (1007 E. Main St., 805/922-4505, $70–85 d) is for the budget conscious. The place is a little worn but offers a great value compared to most hotels in Santa Maria. You won't find too many amenities here—but then if you don't need them, why pay for them? Coffee is located in the lobby, as is Wi-Fi. They are a little further from the shopping malls so you'll need to drive to them, or most anywhere else.

At the **Quality Inn & Suites** (210 S. Nicholson, 805/922-5891, www.qualityinn.com, $90–105 d), a complimentary breakfast is served each morning. In addition to an outdoor pool they provide a spa tub and a children's pool, Wi-Fi, a coffee shop, and outdoor barbecue grills. There are 64 guest rooms in this two-story property, and the standard rooms feature refrigerators and coffee- and tea-makers.

$100-200

Santa Maria Inn (801 S. Broadway, 805/928-7777, www.santamariainn.com, $139–169 d), constructed in 1917, now has 164 good-sized rooms and 18 suites. You can choose to stay in the historic part of the hotel, or one of their newer rooms. Either way they keep the feeling of the turn of the 20th century in the decor and Victorian-style furnishings. Located centrally in Santa Maria, the pet-friendly inn has an in-house restaurant and an old tavern on the premises. The rooms have coffeemakers and hairdryers, and there are five acres of grounds for you to walk with your pet.

Candlewood Suites (2079 Roemer Ct., 805/928-4155, www.candlewoodsuites.com, $135–164 d) is a newer 72-room hotel located on the outskirts on town, which means you'll need your car to get around. Located in a more industrial area next to a few other hotels, it does benefit from close freeway access north of town. There's a fitness area and laundry facility, as well as a small business center. It's clean, comfortable good-value accommodations.

Radisson Hotel (3455 Skyway Dr., 805/928-8000, www.radisson.com/santamariaca, $135–195 d) is located near the airport and the southern portion of town. It's another standard hotel, though the rooms have been given a face-lift with brighter colors. There's an outdoor pool and an in-house restaurant, which looks to the airstrip. Basic amenities and good pricing make this a worthwhile choice if you're searching for a reliable name.

The **Holiday Inn Santa Maria** (2100 N. Broadway, 877/859-5095, www.holidayinn.com, $135–195 d) offers some rooms with kitchenettes, which is why it's big with business travelers and for extended stays. The four-story hotel was renovated in 2008 and has 415 rooms and suites, which are the standard rooms you'd expect from Holiday Inn—nice, but nothing out of the ordinary. They have free Wi-Fi, a fitness room, and a swimming pool on the premises.

Fairfield Inn & Suites (2061 Roemer Ct., 805/925-8500, www.marriott.com, $129–209 d) is a four-story newer hotel that has 89 rooms from a trustworthy name. The rooms are nicely decorated, going for an upscale corporate feel. There's an indoor pool and continental breakfast, but it's a pretty basic hotel. It does not accept pets, but is completely smoke free. The entire hotel is wired for Internet as well as Wi-Fi.

With an eye toward what they call early-American furnishings, **Best Western Big America** (1725 N. Broadway, 805/922-5200, www.bigamerica.com, $125–145 d) is one of the top-rated places to stay in Santa Maria. The 106 rooms, while a little dull and of the standard hotel type, are still large and clean, and there are a lot of amenities, including a 24-hour pool and hot tub and a continental breakfast each morning. It is located downtown right in the thick of things. They have an on-site restaurant, and provide shuttle service to the airport.

FOOD
American
Chef Ricks (4869 S. Bradley Rd., 805/937-9512, www.chefricks.com, Mon.–Sat. 11 A.M.–9 P.M., $25) has long been regarded as Santa Maria's best restaurant, certainly its most dependable. There's a low-key approach to the menu, which is filled with salads, sandwiches, and entrées. There is a Southern influence to much of the food, like the Louisiana blackened halibut salad. But there are also straightforward dishes like the smoked turkey burrito or Black Angus steaks. Decorated with brightly colored paintings, it's festive without being pretentious.

Stinky's Grill (2430 S. Broadway, 805/614-9366, www.stinkysgrill.com, daily 11 A.M.–10 P.M., $15) is your loud, noisy sports bar, stuffed with all kinds of sports decorations and way too much testosterone. But if you like a true sports bar that serves food, here it is. There are 15 different beers on tap and the garlic fries, sliders, and St. Louis ribs are all home runs here. They also have a great happy hour with inexpensive drinks and food.

The Garden Room at the Santa Maria Inn (801 S. Broadway, 805/928-7777, www.santamariainn.com, daily 6 A.M.–2 P.M. and 5–10 P.M., $25) is located on the 1st floor of the hotel. White tablecloths, lots of old wood, and a proper environment—like your grandparents' house, it's a little stuffy inside but worth a stop, if only for the ridiculously decadent Vermont french toast. Tri-tip is on the menu, as is their very good signature tortilla soup. On nice days they serve on the back patio, a sunny little spot away from the noise on the main street.

Pappy's Restaurant (1275 E. Betteravia, 805/922-3553, Mon.–Thurs. 6 A.M.–11 P.M., Fri.–Sat. 6 A.M.–1 A.M., Sun. 6 A.M.–10 P.M., $15) is more truck stop than sit-down formal.

It opened in 1959 and, frankly, not much has changed with the place. Old cowboy photos line the walls, and it's very casual, with a counter facing the kitchen and basic booths and furniture. It's also one of the few places open late. They make a great trip-tip and their home fries are terrific. It's right off the freeway, and the large parking lot is convenient if you're towing something.

Steakhouses
The ◖ **Far Western Tavern** (899 Guadalupe St., Guadalupe, 805/343-2211, www.farwesterntavern.com, Mon.–Sat. 11 A.M.–close, Sun. 9 A.M.–close, $25), out in Guadalupe, is one of those places where you can scarcely believe it hasn't changed since it was originally built as the Palace Hotel in 1912. Modern restaurants can only try and emulate the authenticity of this very cool place. Old leather booths, animal heads on the walls including a massive bull moose, red velvet wallpaper, and hides acting as drapes—this is classic old-school steakhouse dining. They grill their meats over red oak, which lends a beautiful smokiness to them. Best known for a 14-ounce bull's-eye steak, this is a great throwback.

At **Shaw's Steak House & Tavern** (714 S. Broadway, 805/925-5862, lunch Mon.–Fri. 11:30 A.M.–4 P.M., dinner nightly 5–9 P.M., $20) old black-and-white photos line the walls of the heavy wood interior. Your main courses are prepared in plain sight, meaning the oak-wood grill sits behind a window and is visible from just about every table. Best known for their tri-tip, this is the kind of comfortable place where you're tempted to kick off your shoes and get totally relaxed. Shaw's has been a locals' spot for years, in part because the portions are large, and the tavern is often packed.

Italian
Housed in a little cottage, **Trattoria Uliveto** (285 S. Broadway, Orcutt, 805/934-4546, www.trattoriauliveto.com, Tues.–Sun. 11:30 A.M.–2:30 P.M. and 5–10 P.M., $18) has warmth

TRUE TRI-TIP

Everyone seems to have heard of tri-tip, but most people don't know exactly what tri-tip is. Santa Maria barbecue has its roots in the mid-19th century, when the rancheros gathered to help each other brand their calves each spring. The host would then prepare a Spanish-style barbecue as a thank you. The meal included barbecued sirloin, salsa, Pinquito beans (which are native to the area), toasted French bread, and green salad. The present Santa Maria-style barbecue grew out of this tradition, and further developed about 60 years ago when locals began to string their beef on skewers and cook it over the hot coals of a red-oak fire. The meat, either top block sirloin or the triangular-shaped bottom sirloin known as a tri-tip cut, is rolled in a mixture of salt, pepper, and garlic just prior to cooking. It is then barbecued over red-oak wood, giving the meat a hearty, smoky flavor. The only condiment used is fresh salsa. Barbecue, however needs to be understood in its proper context, which in this case means that the meat is grilled low and slow, close to the flame for an extended period of time – this does not refer to a sweet barbecue sauce, as real tri-tip has no sauce. Tri-tip is everywhere these days, even for sale in supermarkets across the country, but if you want the real deal, you need to stop in Santa Maria and try authentic tri-tip for yourself at a place like **The Garden Room at the Santa Maria Inn** (801 S. Broadway, 805/928-7777, daily 6 A.M.–1 P.M. and 5-10 P.M., www.santamaria inn.com, $25) or **Shaw's Steak House & Tavern** (714 S. Broadway, 805/925-5862, lunch Mon.-Fri. 11:30 A.M.-4 P.M., dinner nightly 5-9 P.M., $20).

Chinese

Ming Dynasty (2011 S. Broadway, 805/928-6881, Mon.–Thurs. 11 A.M.–9 P.M., Fri.–Sat. 11 A.M.–10 P.M., Sun. 11 A.M.–9 P.M., $12) is a hugely popular restaurant most notable for its buffet. Yes, it's kind of Americanized and has that usual Chinese decor that seems just slightly old, but it is great value, fresh and flavorful food, and it gets crowded. They do have à la carte options, but most everyone heads for the all-you-can-eat lunchtime buffet.

Sushi

It seems stunning to most everyone that in the midst of steaks and tacos is **Ichiban** (2011 S. Broadway, 805/614-9808, daily 11:30 A.M.–2 P.M. and 5–9 P.M., $20), a very good, though pricey, Japanese restaurant in the middle of Santa Maria. They offer attentive service, and the quality of the fish is uniformly very high. They survive because they serve some of the best sushi on the Central Coast.

Mexican

El Pueblito (603 S. Blosser, 805/349-1088, daily 6 A.M.–10 P.M., $10) has solid, dependable Mexican food, made with real ingredients. Sometimes the food can be a little greasy, but the shrimp fajitas are excellent. The restaurant is small but spacious enough, and the prices are lower than most other spots.

The hefty wood tables and chairs at **La Hacienda** (312 W. Main St., 805/349-8820, daily 10 A.M.–8 P.M., $12) are spaced out so they seem like they fit inside this spacious restaurant. The food here is so authentic that you see lots of Mexicans, some wearing boots and cowboy hats. They have a few breakfast items like the Chilaquiles Don Jose, a mix of fried tortilla chips, eggs, onion, rice, beans, chicken, and salsa that will get your morning started off right. They also serve burgers and fries for those who don't like Mexican food—yes, there are a few!

Maya (110 S. Lincoln, 805/925-2841,

and charm from its hardwood floors to its soft wood and exposed-beam ceilings. Yet it still feels slightly sophisticated. The food is dependable and authentic, and it's one of the few Italian places in the area.

Mon.–Thurs. 7 A.M.–9 P.M., Fri.–Sun. 7 A.M.–10 P.M., $12) has been faithfully serving Mexican food since 1966. The brightly painted wood chairs and tiled floors make it feel festive as well as intimate. In addition to the standard Mexican fare they offer a lot of fish dishes like the *pescado a la diabla,* a fillet with a bacon, ham, and onion sauce. They also have a great senior menu—a typical Mexican item, which includes rice and beans, for about six bucks.

Bakery

Voted the best in the area, **Gina's Piece of Cake** (307 Town Center East, 805/922-7866, www.ginaspieceofcake.com, Tues.–Fri. 7:30 A.M.–7 P.M., Sat. 7:30 A.M.–6 P.M., Sun. 11 A.M.–5 P.M., $3) is that great bakery where you can smell the sweet icing used for all the cakes they make. But more than just beautiful custom cakes, they bake brownies, cookies, muffins, éclairs, bagels, and breads in their little pink shop.

Farmers Markets

There are two farmers markets in Santa Maria. On Wednesday from 12:30 to 4:30 P.M. at 100 South Broadway at Main Street (location of the original town site), there are the usual veggies and breads, pastries, plants, flowers, and lots of bee products including pollen and honey. In Orcutt there is a market on Tuesday from 10 A.M. to 1 P.M. at the corner of Clark and Bradley.

INFORMATION AND SERVICES

The **Santa Maria Valley Chamber of Commerce and Visitor & Convention Bureau** is located at 614 South Broadway (800/331-3779, www.santamariavisitor.com). There are two newspapers that compete for attention. The *Santa Maria Times* (805/739-2200, www.santamariatimes.com) is the daily paper available throughout Santa Maria. The *Santa Maria Sun* (805/347-1968, www.santa mariasun.com) is the free alternative weekly, which publishes on Thursdays.

Should you have an **emergency,** dial 911. The **Marian Medical Center** (1400 E. Church St., 805/739-3000) offers emergency services. The **Santa Maria Police** are located at 222 East Cook Street (805/925-0951).

GETTING THERE

If you're driving, Santa Maria is located directly off Highway 101. The major streets that have access from both north- and southbound Highway 101 are Betteravia, Main, and Stowell.

An unstaffed stop for Amtrak motor coaches connecting to Amtrak trains in Santa Barbara and Hanford is located in Santa Maria at the International House of Pancakes (205 Nicholson Ave. at Main St.), just off Highway 101. Neither tickets, nor baggage, nor package express shipments are handled here. The nearest stations to Santa Maria offering these services are either north in San Luis Obispo or south in Santa Barbara.

The Amtrak Surfliner does not stop in Santa Maria. The closest train stops are 10 miles south in Guadalupe, or 10 miles north in Grover Beach in San Luis Obispo County.

The Santa Maria Airport (SMX, 805/922-1726, www.santamariaairport.com) is quite small, but a few airlines do fly here. It might be worth looking into if you can get a commuter connection from Los Angeles or Las Vegas.

GETTING AROUND

Bus services are provided by the **Santa Maria Area Transit** (805/928-5624), which can accommodate both bikes and wheelchairs. For a complete schedule visit www.santa-maria .ca.us. Basic one-way fares are $1.25 and exact change is required.

Santa Maria Yellow Cab Co. (1125 E. Clark Ave., 805/937-7121), the **Yellow Cab Company of Santa Maria** (805/939-5454), and **Santa Maria Valley Taxi** (805/937-1121) are all available on short notice.

BACKGROUND

The Land

CLIMATE

For a winemaker, different climates are measured using a method called heat summation (also known as the Winkler Scale), which categorizes climates into regions on a scale from 1 to 5 depending on how hot the average daily temperature is during a vine's main growing season from April to October. Different grapes grow and ripen best in each climate region.

If California were a country, it would be one of the few on earth that have areas corresponding to all five growing regions. Napa and Sonoma alone contains four of the five regions, which means there's an ideal climate for almost any type of grape.

Winemakers also have an easier job here than their colleagues in many other parts of the world, particularly in Europe, because rainfall is almost nonexistent for much of the summer, so grapes can ripen in the plentiful sun and avoid damp-related fungal disease like mildew. Similarly, hail and damaging winds are almost unheard of here during the summer. Most rain falls between November and April, and apart from the rare summer thunderstorm or late spring showers, it is generally dry from late May through October.

Fog

One of the defining aspects of the weather along the California coast is the fog. Damp, chilly marine fog creeps—sometimes charges—inland from the cold Pacific Ocean during the summer through every gap it can find in the mountains.

Perhaps no aspect of the weather here is more important. It takes the edge off the sometimes vicious summer heat and sun, keeps the nights cool, and slows the ripening of grapes in many places to a perfect tempo. It also generates the damp conditions in which California's famous coastal redwoods thrive, from Santa Cruz to Mendocino and nowhere more so than in the Russian River Valley, which is essentially a fog freeway, providing a direct channel from the ocean through the coastal hills and inland.

The factors that generate the fog, however, actually start hundreds of miles away in the sun-baked Central Valley of California. As the temperature there rises on summer days, so does the hot air, lowering the atmospheric pressure near the ground. Something has to replace all that rising air and even out the pressure. Imagine, then, a giant sucking noise as cool air is pulled in from the ocean to do just that.

Because the ocean is so cold, thanks to some chilly Alaskan currents, it actually condenses water from the air (much like cold air does to your breath), forming a deep bank of fog that sits, menacingly, just off the coast. The onshore winds generated by the inland sun drag that fog onto the coast.

How far inland it gets depends on all sorts of factors, from the time of year to the prevailing atmospheric pressure. During summer days it usually hugs the coast. At night it can advance inland, burning off rapidly as the sun heats things up.

Many additional factors have recently been found to influence fog formation, from weather over the Rocky Mountains to the currents in the South Pacific. But all the winemakers care about is that the fog helps make a great bottle of wine.

UNIQUE VINEYARD CONDITIONS

The combination of diverse soils and diverse microclimates offers just about everything a winemaker could want. There are very few grapes that have not been able to grow somewhere in California, and the current diversity of grape varietals (or lack thereof) has more to do with marketing than weather.

The French have a term for the unique conditions of a place that a grape is grown: *terroir*. It describes the combination of geological, geographical, and climate-related aspects of the land, including the soil, the slope, elevation, sun exposure, wind levels, and temperature patterns. California has a vast number of distinct *terroirs*.

Terroir explains why grapes grown in one vineyard will make a wine that tastes different from that made from grapes in a neighboring vineyard. So-called vineyard-designate wines sourced from one specific vineyard rather than multiple vineyards take advantage of that difference. There can even be a difference in the wine made from different sections, or blocks, of an individual vineyard.

It explains why the Napa Valley's Stag's Leap Wine Cellars can make very different wines from different blocks of one of its vineyards, for example, and why Stags Leap District cabernets as a whole taste different from those produced in the Rutherford District just a few miles up the road.

Best Soils and Climate

Almost without exception, the best soils for growing wine grapes are well drained and relatively infertile. Drainage is important to prevent the vines and grapes from getting too damp and potentially rotting, and also to encourage the vines to grow deep roots in search of a stable source of water. Some of the oldest vines have been known to send roots down as deep as 100 feet.

Drip irrigation systems are common sights in Californian vineyards, but they often have more to do with producing a financially viable quantity of grapes per acre than keeping the vines alive. Without some artificial water the vines might well survive but would not look nearly so lush with leaves and plump grapes by the end of the summer.

Fertility (or the lack of it) is a less important factor, although it's not by chance that some of the world's most distinctive and flavorful wines come from vineyards that thrive on fairly barren, rocky land, including steep mountainsides where even native plants struggle to grow.

Ultimately, grape growers are trying to produce a stressed vine—one that has to relentlessly search for water and survive on meager nutrients. This is not exactly the aim of most gardeners, who water and feed their plants to make them as big and lush as possible.

The theory goes that a stressed vine will produce fewer and smaller grapes but they will have a far more concentrated flavor. The same principle (taken to an extreme) explains why a shriveled raisin has a far more concentrated and powerful flavor than a plump Thompson seedless grape grown with the aid of plenty of watering and fertilizer.

Climate plays an equally important role in how a wine turns out, determining how quickly a grape ripens and the level of ripeness it is ultimately able to reach as measured by its sugar content. Temperatures during the day and night are affected by sun exposure, wind patterns, and countless other factors. Climate helps explain why a cabernet produced from vineyards on the west-facing slopes of a valley side that gets sun much of the warmest part of the day will taste slightly different from that made from a vineyard on an east-facing slope that might get less sun due to morning fog.

Appellation or AVA?

The diversity of grape growing conditions is recognized around the world in various national systems of defining geographical regions based on their specific soils and climate. Such systems have given rise to the names of famous types of wine all over the world, from Bordeaux to Burgundy, Chianti to Barolo. In the United States, such regions are called **American Viticultural Areas,** or AVAs, though many

people simply call them appellations, after the French word meaning almost, but not quite, the same thing.

An appellation describes a geographical area, like an entire state or even a country. An AVA is based on a unique growing region only, one that can be shown to have conditions (soils, climate etc.) that make it stand apart from other areas around it. An appellation can be an AVA, but not all are. If wine were an appellation, then specific types of wine would be the viticultural areas. In the same vein, California is an appellation, and the Napa Valley is an AVA.

The federal Bureau of Alcohol, Tobacco, and Firearms (ATF) is the arbiter of AVAs and dishes them out only when wineries in a specific area have been able to prove that theirs is a unique place to grow grapes. Such proof usually comes in the form of an analysis of soils, climate, and physical features of the land. The petitioning and granting of an AVA takes many years, as is typical of most federal government processes, and is usually led by one or a group of wineries. Wine-making politics often complicates matters, especially when some wineries don't want to be included in an AVA for some marketing reason or another, leading to some very drawn out application processes and sometimes arbitrary AVA boundaries.

The first AVA was established in 1980 in, of all places, Augusta, Georgia, and they are still being established today. The biggest in the country in terms of area is the Ohio River Valley, covering 26,000 square miles in parts of four different states. The smallest is Cole Ranch in Mendocino County, California, covering about a quarter square mile.

In California there was a rush to get AVA status in the early 1980s by most of the major wine regions, and by 2009 there were 108 AVAs in California, a figure that is constantly growing. The first AVA in Northern California's Wine Country was the Santa Cruz Mountains, created in early 1982, followed shortly thereafter by the Sonoma Valley in the same month and Livermore Valley later that year. In 1983 the Napa Valley and Dry Creek Valley gained their AVA status, and since then there has been a steady stream of applications.

There can also be AVAs within AVAs, often called subappellations (again a technically incorrect term in some cases, but often used anyway). The Napa Valley AVA, for example, contains a patchwork of 15 smaller AVAs, each producing its own distinctive style of wine. The appellation of Sonoma County contains 11 AVAs, some of which overlap. If defining the land is so complicated, it's no wonder that the wines are so varied.

One interesting pattern exists in the Napa Valley. Since 1989, thanks to an arcane labeling law designed to protect the exclusivity of the Napa Valley name, no Napa County viticultural areas can fall outside the Napa Valley AVA. That's why many of the smaller AVAs in the Napa Valley, such as Mount Veeder and Spring Mountain, end abruptly at the county border. The one exception is the Los Carneros AVA, which sprawls across the southern portion of the Napa Valley and west into Sonoma County. It defies Napa Valley borders only because it was created before the 1989 law was enacted.

History

Spanish Missions

California's missions played a crucial, though controversial, role in California's history, including its wine-making history. Their inexorable march northward from Mexico through California introduced important wine-making skills thanks to the demand for sacramental wines. The missions also marked the beginning of the end for the lifestyles and cultures of the region's Native Americans, who had lived off the land for thousands of years.

The last mission built in California was

Mission Santa Barbara against the Santa Ynez Mountains

the 21st—Mission San Francisco de Solano in present day Sonoma. It was established by Father Jose Altimira, who arrived in the Sonoma Valley in 1819. Once the mission had been dedicated in 1824, the missionaries quickly set about their religious purpose. With the aid of the Mexican army, Native Americans were converted to Christianity whether they wanted to be or not. Within six years the mission had also established a big farming operation in the Sonoma Valley, with thousands of head of sheep and cattle, and had planted some of the region's first vines.

The new mission was founded not only to continue the spread of Christianity but also to provide food for the ailing missions in present-day San Francisco and San Rafael, which were struggling to sustain themselves. It was also the first and only mission in California created under Mexican rule, and it's likely that part of its purpose was to help prevent any expansion of a trading outpost established by Russian hunters nearby on the Sonoma coast at Fort Ross.

Just three years later, trouble rode into town in the form of a 25-year-old Mexican army lieutenant, Mariano Guadalupe Vallejo, who was sent north from the Presidio in San Francisco to rattle some sabers at the Russians and establish a military post at Sonoma. Vallejo would remain in Sonoma for the next half century and play a pivotal role in the creation of modern California.

When the missions were secularized by the Mexican government in 1835, Vallejo's garrison at Sonoma was well established and had created a Mexican-style plaza (present-day Sonoma Plaza) as a parade ground. He was ordered to take over the mission, and he promptly started to divide the buildings and land between friends and relatives. Meanwhile, the garrison and the town started to grow in importance, and Vallejo was promoted to colonel, the highest rank he ever achieved (despite this, he somehow became commonly known as "General Vallejo," a title that sticks to this day). As the military importance of his garrison in peaceful California slowly dwindled, he started living the good life, amassing land and planting vineyards.

The Land Grants

As the military commander and later Director of Colonization in Mexico's Northern Frontier, Vallejo controlled much of the land in today's Napa and Sonoma Counties and was under orders to dole it out to Mexican citizens for development. In reality he doled it out to friends, relatives, and business associates.

The land was snatched up by names that would eventually become a big part of modern wine history, including Agoston Haraszthy, a Hungarian immigrant who planted some of the earliest European vineyard cuttings and is credited with dragging the California wine industry from its missionary roots into the modern era through his Buena Vista Winery in the Sonoma Valley.

Over in the Napa Valley, Edward Bale was granted a huge swath of land in 1844 near present-day St. Helena by way of marriage to Vallejo's niece. He planted some vines, and friend Charles Krug, a Napa wine pioneer, made wine for him. Another Napa valley pioneer, George Yount, was granted the 18-square-mile Rancho Caymus in the Napa Valley in 1836, an area that today includes Yountville. He built up a huge agricultural business and is credited with planting the first grapes in the Napa Valley. He made small quantities of wine but never became one of the valley's big early producers.

Up at the northern end of the Sonoma Valley, in 1859, Scotsman Charles Stuart bought some of Vallejo's land and named his home and ranch Glen Ellen, after Ellen, his wife. The name was eventually adopted by the town that developed in the area, and Stuart's ranch was renamed Glen Oaks. It still exists today. Captain Henry Boyes was another beneficiary of Vallejo's land and would go on to establish his mineral baths, Boyes Hot Springs, another name that eventually became a town.

Also in northern Sonoma, Captain Henry Fitch was granted 48,000 acres of land around present-day Healdsburg, about a quarter of which he later gave to Cyrus Alexander (after whom Alexander Valley is named) in recognition of the help that the former mountain man had been in managing Fitch's huge acreage.

As the early agricultural pioneers got started on these vast new swaths of land, the stage was set for an even bigger catalyst for change in California's early history—gold. The gold rush that started in 1848 brought a tidal wave of European immigrants to California, many of whom made their fortunes not from gold but by supplying the massive new economy with agricultural products.

The sheer scope of the immigrant influx is staggering. The nonnative population of California was believed to have been around 15,000 people in 1848 when gold was first discovered in the Sierra Nevada Mountains. Five years later it was an estimated 300,000, and most of those people were under age 40.

The Bear Flag Revolt

It was around this time that more American settlers were crossing the mountains to California and letting everyone know about it. The Mexican government became apoplectic and tried to round up these American illegals and dissuade others from coming to California, an ironic reversal of roles compared to today's flow of Mexican migrant workers into California. Near Sacramento, Captain John Sutter was welcoming the new immigrants at his fort, riling the Mexican government even more. Not helping matters was the arrival of U.S. Army captain John C. Frémont in California on a mapping expedition.

As the tensions rose, Vallejo tried to stay neutral, walking a fine line between supporting various parties in the increasingly fragmented Mexican government and remaining friendly with the new American immigrants.

Soon tensions boiled over. In 1846, word came that Mexican general Castro was planning to drive out the Americans at Sutter's fort. Some of the settlers believed that Vallejo, who had met with Castro several times, was part of the plan to re-exert Mexican authority, and

THE "BARE" FLAG

The flag of the great State of California, symbol of strength, courage, and freedom, started out as a crudely painted rectangle of fabric incorporating a woman's red petticoat. At least, that's one version of events back in 1846 when it was first raised over Sonoma Plaza.

The ragtag group of men behind the short-lived Bear Flag Republic needed something for their symbol. A loose committee finally decided that it should incorporate a bear, symbolizing strength and courage, and a star, inspired by the newly minted flag of Texas. So the saddle-stitchers and painters in the group set about making their new flag.

One member supplied the red fabric that some say was part of his wife's petticoat, although others maintain it was actually a flannel shirt. This was sewn to some bleached fabric onto which was painted the bear, the star, and the words "California Republic," the bear apparently looking more like a squat pig.

When it was finally done, the paint still wet, the flag was raised and flew for the 25 days it took the U.S. Army to march into town. The handmade Bear Flag was replaced by the Stars and Stripes on July 9, 1846. The flag was destroyed in the San Francisco earthquake and fire in 1906, but in 1911 the design was adopted as the official state flag, and today it flies above almost every public building in the state.

they launched a preemptive attack on Vallejo's small garrison at Sonoma.

A ragtag group of about 30 men rode the 120 miles from Sacramento to Sonoma on the night of June 13, 1846, and barged into Vallejo's unprotected residence, La Casa Grande, to arrest him. He was taken the next day to Sacramento, where he remained under arrest until August. That day the members of the raiding party made a flag for their newly declared California

Republic, and that Bear Flag replaced the Mexican emblem over Sonoma Plaza.

The U.S. Navy, which had a ship off the coast, soon stepped into the power vacuum created by the Bear Flaggers and raised the Stars and Stripes over Sonoma Plaza on July 9, 1846, claiming California for the United States with little in the way of a fight. Coincidentally, a few months earlier, U.S. president James Polk had declared war on Mexico after his request to buy Texas and California had been rejected. News of the war didn't reach California until mid-July. Two years later when the war was over, California and other Southwest states were officially ceded by Mexico.

The Early Wine Boom

When Vallejo was released, he returned to Sonoma and, over the next decade, became a big player in the region's politics. As Northern California's importance and wealth grew during that period, helped by the Gold Rush, the entrepreneurs and immigrants that would shape the region for the next 100 years arrived by the boatload.

By now, the missionaries, General Vallejo, and the early wine pioneers had shown that the region was well suited to growing just about everything, including grapes. The twin catalysts of the Mexican land grants and the Gold Rush had just given a huge boost to California's agricultural industry. The next few decades would see wine production surge as all the newly arrived Europeans put their wine making and wine drinking experience to use.

By 1876, the Sonoma Valley alone was producing 2.3 million gallons of wine a year, and Northern California had overtaken Southern California as the biggest wine-producing region in the state. Around this time many of the immigrants that would shape the Napa and Sonoma wine industry had started to arrive from Europe, lured by the early successes of pioneering winemakers in the Napa and Sonoma Valleys like Charles Krug, Jacob Gundlach, and the Beringer brothers.

Outlying areas like the Alexander Valley and Dry Creek Valley were being planted

with vines; the Italian-Swiss Colony, a wine-making cooperative, was established near Cloverdale; and down in Santa Cruz the first vines were planted on land freshly cleared of redwood forests.

Then the scourge of phylloxera struck. It is a devastating disease caused by a small aphid-like insect that attacks the roots of vines and slowly kills them by preventing the plant from absorbing water and nutrients. Phylloxera wiped out many vineyards in Europe in the late 1800s but is actually native to the United States. In fact, California's wine industry was doing so well in the late 1800s in part because the devastation in Europe wiped out exports and left Americans on the East Coast gasping for wine from other sources.

It would only be years later, after most Californian vineyards had themselves been decimated, that vines with resistant rootstock were replanted in Northern California by Gundlach, one of the Sonoma Valley's early wine pioneers.

Not long after Northern California's wine industry had started to recover from phylloxera and was once again booming, it took another economic hit, one from which it barely recovered.

Prohibition

The 18th Amendment of the United States Constitution, which ushered in the era of Prohibition in 1919, was born not out of government meddling but of an increasingly powerful temperance movement that had its roots in the puritanical beliefs of the country's founding fathers. Not helping matters was the increasing drunkenness of American society during the 1800s, which resulted in widespread public disgust and calls for change.

By some estimates, average Americans were drinking almost three times the amount of whiskey and other spirits in the mid-1800s as they do today. The more people drank, the more temperance movements tended to spring up all over the country in response. Eventually, the so-called "Drys" gained the political clout to pass laws in many states that banned public drinking, finally getting the Volstead Act, and with it Prohibition, passed in Congress. Winemakers had hoped that, being an upper-class drink, wine would be exempt from the legislation. In the end, the commercial production, sale, and transportation of any form of alcoholic drink was banned.

As with any piece of legislation, it doesn't take long for people to find the loopholes and to take advantage of weak enforcement. Bootleggers and gangsters set up a huge underground liquor network, and the wine industry got in on the act. Despite all commercial wine being banned, there were more acres of vineyards in existence during Prohibition than before it, and the price of grapes actually increased even as the quality of the grapes generally declined. Grape juice concentrate or bricks of compressed grapes were shipped all over the country, sometimes even accompanied by yeast tablets, for individuals to make their own wine behind closed doors, which was perfectly legal.

Although many grape growers flourished, wineries did not, and many closed. The few that remained open did so by making sacramental wine, which was still legal (as wine historians like to say, a lot of people found religion during Prohibition) or wine for government functions, also legal. After all, leaders still had to be able to entertain foreign dignitaries with fine wine even when the rest of the country had to do without.

In many ways, Prohibition marked the end of one chapter of California's wine-making history. In some areas, like the Santa Cruz Mountains and Livermore Valley, virtually all the wineries closed, never to reopen. Fruit trees replaced vines in many of today's wine-making valleys and held sway until relatively recently.

In Napa and Sonoma, a handful of wineries continued to operate during Prohibition, making sacramental wines, including Beringer Vineyards (the oldest continuously operating winery in the Napa Valley), Beaulieu Vineyard, Buena Vista Winery (its Carneros facility is the oldest continuously operating winery in California), and Sebastiani Vineyards. Still others turned to farming or supplying grapes until Prohibition was repealed, then resumed wine-making, while a few wineries continued to make wine and store it in the hope that Prohibition would soon end.

It took 14 years for Prohibition to come to an end; it was finally repealed in 1933, when the 21st Amendment was passed by Congress. In those 14 years, California's wine industry had been gutted. Most wineries had closed, important wine-making skills had been lost, and the public had lost the taste for fine wines, instead preferring homemade hooch. Making matters worse, the few remaining wine producers emerged from the shadow of Prohibition and into the gloom of the deepest economic crisis in American history, the Great Depression.

Picking Up the Pieces

Following repeal, winemakers were left with broken wineries, vineyards that had been planted with grapes that shipped well rather than grapes that made good wine, and a non-existent domestic market for wine. For an industry in such a dire state, recovery was surprisingly fast.

In some ways the wine industry took several steps back after repeal, turning out bulk and fortified wines of far lower quality than the world-class wines made by the new European immigrants some 30 years earlier. The few big wineries that did survive, especially those in the Napa, Sonoma, and Livermore Valleys, continued to make some high-quality wines, but they too joined the bulk bandwagon.

They were joined by former grape growers who made a tidy profit during Prohibition, including the Gallo brothers who, in 1933, established a winery that would morph into the world's largest wine producer half a century later. Other new wineries prospered from the sale of massive quantities of cheap wines. Fine-wine production remained a rarity and the preserve of the modest number of old-school wineries that had largely been left behind in the new wine-making environment, where size mattered.

After all booms come busts, and it was no

different for the booming Californian wine industry. By the end of the 1930s the industry was suffering a monumental postrepeal party hangover as the market imploded under the weight of too much bad wine. Prices crashed and the number of wineries dramatically declined, but there was a silver lining. The formation of two important marketing organizations in the 1930s, the Wine Institute and the Wine Advisory Board (the board has long since been disbanded), would give California's wine industry some much-needed strategic direction as it once again picked itself up after the war.

The Modern Era

The Californian wine industry emerged from the frugal war years as production of cheap wines sourced from cheap grapes once again soared as it had after Prohibition The difference this time was that improved marketing had created more buyers of cheap wine than in the 1930s, but important figures in the industry still recognized the need to improve quality and wean the public onto finer wines. This was the period when the pioneers of California's modern wine industry would start to appear—figures like Martin Ray in the Santa Cruz Mountains region, André Tchelistcheff at Beaulieu Vineyards in the Napa Valley, Herman Wente in the Livermore Valley, and perhaps most importantly, the Mondavi family.

One of the key figures in the start of the modern age of fine wine making was Robert Mondavi in the Napa Valley. His father, Cesare Mondavi, was one of the many producers of bulk wine in the Napa Valley after Prohibition, and his two sons, Robert and Peter, were already getting some experience helping run the bulk business. When Cesare bought the old Charles Krug winery in 1943, the family's attention increasingly turned to fine wines, but following a family feud after Cesare's death, Robert was forced out of the family business.

With wine already in his blood, he started his own Robert Mondavi Winery in 1966, the first new winery to be built in Napa since the repeal of Prohibition. It proved to be one of the most important symbols for growth in the fine wine industry in the region, and Mondavi is often cited as one of the figures who proved that a dream of starting a great winery from scratch could become reality. Whether by luck or by design, Mondavi's venture coincided with a surge in the popularity of fine wines, and in the following decade hundreds more wineries were established by dreamers hoping to catch the same wave, including many of today's biggest wine-making names.

From the 1940s to the 1970s the number of wineries in California steadily declined as production of fine wine slowly replaced massive output of cheap wine. In 1945 there were just over 400 wineries in the state. By 1970 that number had dwindled to about 240 wineries. The industry had reached another nadir by 1970, but it would rise yet again, this time with a strategy that would last. By the end of the 1970s the number of wineries had more than doubled to more than 500.

There was no single person or event that helped usher in this modern wine era in California. Instead, it has been linked to the more general growth in modern technology. The world became smaller as air travel and television introduced millions to previously unknown cultures and ideas. There was a population boom in the United States and an economic boom that introduced the modern consumer age. And, it seems, the wine industry's marketing efforts finally started to click.

The Judgments of Paris

The reputation of California's modern wines was cemented at an international wine-tasting event in Paris in 1976. British wine writer and critic Stephen Spurrier, already familiar with the rising quality of California's wines, suggested a taste-off between what he regarded as the best Californian and best French wines in an event to celebrate the American bicentennial.

Five Californian chardonnays and five cabernet sauvignons were pitted against the same number of French white Burgundies and red

Bordeaux wines. The all-French panel of esteemed judges had to taste blind in case the French national disdain for New World wines at the time influenced their conclusions. Having set all this up, Spurrier must have been pretty confident the Californian wines would do well, but he reportedly did not expect them to win.

The tasting panel placed a 1973 cabernet sauvignon from Stag's Leap Wine Cellars in the Napa Valley at the top of the reds, followed by the three Bordeaux wines and a cabernet from Ridge Vineyards. The Californian whites did even better. A 1973 Chateau Montelena chardonnay was judged to be the best white wine, and two other Californian chardonnays were placed in the top five (from Chalone Vineyard and Spring Mountain Vineyards).

The shockwave of the French being beaten at their own game reverberated around the wine world. The French were gutted. California winemakers never looked back.

The French tried to salvage some pride, suggesting that Californian wines might well taste better upon release but they would not age as well as their French counterparts. That theory was disproven when the tasting was recreated 30 years later. The so-called Judgment of Paris was retried in 2006, when the same 1970s vintage wines were pulled from cellars and tasted again. Once again the Californian wines trounced the French, perhaps more decisively so than in the original tasting. The top five reds were all from California, led by the 1971 Ridge Monte Bello cabernet sauvignon and the 1973 Stag's Leap cabernet.

Marketing types proclaimed that this proves Californian wines can age as well as the best Bordeaux. Critics suggested it was simply a gimmick, and the wines of 30 years ago bear no resemblance to wines made today. It was a fun exercise nonetheless, even if it only proves that California can indeed make good wines (as judged by the French).

The events leading up to the 1976 tasting were recounted in the 2008 movie *Bottle Shock*. The producers of the film were accused by Stephen Spurrier of taking too much artistic license in the name of entertainment, and he was particularly annoyed at his depiction in the film, but it nonetheless provided an entertaining portrayal of an important turning point in California's wine-making history.

CALIFORNIA'S MODERN WINE INDUSTRY
Economy

The wine industry is an integral part of the cultural and social fabric of California. Everyone seems to have some link to the wine business, whether directly or indirectly, and given the industry's sheer size it's hardly surprising.

If California were a country, it would be the fourth-largest producer of wine in the world after Italy, France, and Spain. The state's wine industry made 620 million gallons of wine in 2008, according to the Wine Institute, or more than 90 percent of all the wine produced in the United States. That makes California's wine industry about an $18 billion industry in terms of U.S. retail sales, but it brings a lot more money to the state in other ways.

An estimated 20 million tourists visit many of the state's almost 3,000 bonded wineries each year, and the wine industry accounts for more than 300,000 jobs in California directly and indirectly. All told, the value of the wine industry to California's overall economy was estimated at more than $60 billion in 2008, and the economic impact on the U.S. economy was more than $120 billion, according to one research report.

Napa and Sonoma dominate California's wine industry, though not by sheer size. Together the two counties contain almost half of all the wineries in the state, even though they account for less than one-fifth of the state's total acreage of wine-grape vineyards. The important factor is quality. Huge quantities of cheaper wines are churned out in the Central Valley of California, but Napa, Sonoma, and other important Northern California wine regions produce a big proportion of the state's premium wines, the fastest-growing category of wines that sell for premium prices.

UNSUNG HEROES

They pick the grapes, prune the vines, and help manage the vineyards, but the workers toiling away during the long hot summers in Northern California are largely the unsung heroes of the wine industry, ensuring winemakers have the best vines and grapes to work with but rarely remembered when the cork is pulled.

As is the case in much of the rest of the state's agricultural sector, most of these workers are migrants from Latin America. They do the work that locals usually won't touch for the money offered, which in many cases is barely above the state's minimum hourly wage.

The political debate continues over their legal status – it's a thorny issue that will probably never be fully resolved. But without question, the migrant labor pool is a valuable competitive asset for California's winemakers and the state's agriculture industry as a whole.

Despite the low wages paid to workers, it still costs almost double the amount per ton to harvest grapes and maintain vines by hand than by machines. Increasing mechanization has drastically reduced the number of vineyard workers in the past few decades, but they remain a critical part of the wine industry, particularly in the premium growing areas like Napa and Sonoma, where hand-picking of the valuable grapes is much preferred over letting a machine bludgeon its way through the vines. Steep mountain vineyards in Northern California also pose problems for machines and require the human touch to manage and harvest them.

By some estimates, 98 percent of the vineyard workers in California are from Mexico, so it's no surprise that after decades of toiling in the vineyards, an increasing number of Mexican American families are cashing in on the skills, knowledge, and contacts they have developed.

Since the early 1990s, more than a dozen Mexican families have started their own wineries in Sonoma and Napa. Former migrant worker Reynaldo Robledo, for example, started working in California's vineyards in the 1960s, later established his own vineyard management company, and finally realized his dream to make his own wine. He founded the Robledo Family Winery in Carneros, which became the first Mexican American winery to open a public tasting room in 2003.

His story and those of the numerous other newly minted Mexican American wine-making families are just part of the latest chapter in California's wine industry, which owes a historical debt to immigrants from all over the world, from the Victorian pioneers like Charles Krug and Samuele Sebastiani to the Gallo and Mondavi families, who helped put California's wine industry on the international map after Prohibition.

Consumption Trends

Luckily, the rest of the world likes to drink wine, because Americans apparently don't. Although an impressive 750 million gallons of all types of wine were consumed in the United States in 2008, much of it made in California, consumption per person is only about 2.4 gallons, or about 11 bottles, per year.

Per capita consumption in the United States is actually about the same today as it was in the mid-1980s, but it has been increasing at quite a pace. Still, by 2006 people in the United Kingdom were drinking about twice as much wine on average as their U.S. counterparts, the Germans almost three times more, and the French a whopping six times more. Even Slovaks, Finns, and Swedes drink more wine than the average American. And the top per-capita wine consumer in 2006? Vatican City.

It's not that Americans in general don't drink much wine, just that most Americans don't drink any at all. Nearly all the wine consumed is drunk by less than one-fifth of the population (and Californians drink about a fifth of all the wine consumed in the United States). A wide range of factors might explain the country's low rate of wine consumption, including its puritanical roots, the legacy of Prohibition, and even the climate.

One important factor is simply that the U.S. population does not have a great wine-making legacy. Wines have only been made in California in commercial quantities for 150 years, which might seem like a long time but is the blink of an eye when you consider that the Romans fueled their orgies with the stuff some 2,000 years ago. Moreover, the waves of recent American immigrants from Central America and Asia also tend to have little previous exposure to wines.

Europeans have been making wine for thousands of years, and it is as much a part of the culinary culture in many European countries there as, say, apple pie is in the United States. American consumers tend to view wine as a special-occasion drink, something to be enjoyed once in a while rather than every day.

While it's true that high-quality wine might be a little too expensive for most people to open a bottle every day, consider that wine in an open bottle can remain fresh for 4–5 days if stored correctly. If you prefer to save an expensive wine for a special occasion, consider stocking up with "house wine," which still tastes good but at a price far more inviting for an everyday drink.

Chardonnay remains the most popular wine, even though that popularity has waned slightly in recent years. Merlot, cabernet sauvignon, and white zinfandel are not far behind in popularity. Those four varietals together accounted for just over half the wines sold in U.S. food stores in 2006, and overall sales of red wines were about the same as sales of white.

The Power of Marketing

Take a trip to wineries in Napa and Sonoma and you'd be lucky to find any wine for sale under $30, which might give the impression that wine is generally an expensive drink. But those pricey wines account for only a fraction of the wine made in California. A trip to the local supermarket or liquor store will confirm that most wine sold in the United States is of the cheap and cheerful kind, usually in big

1.5-liter bottles or casks. In fact, about two-thirds of the wine sold in the United States in 2004 cost less than $7 per bottle, according to the Wine Institute. That represents about the same alcoholic bang for the buck as beer.

So-called premium wine, costing over $7 per bottle, is where the big money is for the wineries, however, so that's where the marketing dollars tend to get spent. It's also the fastest-growing segment of the wine industry in the United States, although there are signs that the 2009 recession has slowed the growth in sales of the most expensive wines.

Wineries in the best wine-making regions of California have high costs to recoup. Land for vineyards in the Napa Valley costs about $120,000 per acre. It then costs $25,000–50,000 per acre to prepare and plant it with vines. Add the costs of managing that vineyard and actually making, bottling, and distributing the wine, and some wine prices start to seem justified.

But it's also in a winery's best interests to try to wean consumers onto the expensive stuff because then they'll probably be consumers for life. Research shows that once your palate is used to a $50 cabernet, you're highly unlikely ever again to choose a jumbo bottle of $5 generic red wine to go with dinner. You'll buy as much of the $50 wine as you can afford.

Gaining and retaining consumers is a tough balancing act for the wineries from a marketing point of view. On the one hand they want to lure new premium wine consumers into the fold by promoting their wines as an easy entry into some sort of elite Wine Country lifestyle. But as wineries push pricey wines and all the pretensions that go along with them onto non–wine drinkers, they risk scaring the uninitiated away altogether. Just visiting the Napa Valley, with its $25 tasting fees, can be enough to scare some people off.

The industry sometimes doesn't seem to help itself either. One new winemaker in Sonoma recounted asking some industry colleagues how he should price his new wine. He was told not to price it too low or no one would take it seriously. It goes to show that price is not necessarily a firm measure of quality but is just one of many indicators.

Fortunately, the wine industry sometimes gets some marketing help from unlikely places. Touting the health benefits of moderate amounts of wine has always been a surefire, if temporary, way to get more Americans to drink the stuff. The increasing marketing of food and wine together is also helping to push up consumption—cooking shows now routinely feature advice from wine experts.

More recently, the Oscar-winning 2004 movie *Sideways,* a comedy-drama that follows two aging bachelors on a voyage of self-discovery through the Santa Barbara Wine Country, did wonders for sales of pinot noir. As the movie's characters waxed lyrical about the joys of a good pinot, American consumers apparently decided to discover the joys themselves, and sales of pinot noir in California jumped by a third in the year leading up to the 2005 Academy Awards compared to the previous year, according to statistics from A. C. Nielson, which monitors sales at retail outlets.

The 2008 movie *Bottle Shock,* about the famous 1976 Judgment of Paris, had less of an effect on overall wine sales, but did reportedly bring more tourists to the already-popular Napa Valley and reminded the world how good California wine can be.

Wine and Health

In 1991, CBS aired a *60 Minutes* program titled "The French Paradox," which reported that the French population has a far lower incidence of heart attacks than the American population despite getting less exercise, eating more fatty foods, and smoking more. According to some medical experts, this apparent health paradox could be explained by the fact that the average French person drinks a lot of wine.

The American wine industry could not have asked for better publicity. In the month following the broadcast, wine sales reportedly jumped by 44 percent compared to the same period a year earlier. Although the sales spurt didn't last, and research has since suggested that the French paradox is far more complex

than can be explained simply by higher wine consumption, the wine industry gained a new marketing angle for its wines.

Wine and some other alcoholic beverages have been shown to indeed have health benefits. In the case of the French paradox, however, it is thought that the health benefits have as much to do with overall lifestyle and food consumption patterns as they do with drinking wine.

Low stress (the French take far more vacations than most Americans) and a Mediterranean diet rich in fish, fresh vegetables, and oils, for example, could be factors. Regular wine drinkers also tend not to be binge drinkers, avoiding all the potential health hazards associated with overconsumption of alcohol.

The jury is still out on whether alcoholic beverages, and wine in particular, have direct effects on long-term health. Statistical studies performed all over the world suggest that moderate wine drinkers (those that drink 1–2 glasses a day) seem to suffer from lower rates of heart diseases and certain cancers, but no one yet knows exactly why or what other factors might be involved.

Some research has focused on a family of chemicals found in the skins of red grapes (and therefore only in red wines) called polyphenols, which are believed to be natural antioxidants. Some polyphenols have specifically been shown to reduce the likelihood of arteries getting clogged in laboratory tests.

As is the case with many health-related issues, there seems to be a new study done every year that in some way contradicts results from the last. It's enough to give anyone a headache even before drinking too much wine.

In one study published in the science journal *Nature* in 2005, for example, researchers in Denmark reported that levels of "good" cholesterol increased in test subjects who drank red wine and not in those who drank grape-skin extract rich in polyphenols or water. That seemed to suggest lifestyle or simply alcohol content are more important factors than chemicals in the wine. Then, in 2006, a Harvard Medical School study found that another naturally occurring substance in red wine called resveratrol could offset the bad effects of high-calorie diets in mice.

Yet another study published in 2006, this time in the United Kingdom, suggested another family of chemicals found in wine, procyanidins, could help lower the risk of heart attacks by blocking a chemical signal in the body that normally constricts blood vessels. Moreover, wines from southwest France and southern Italy were found to contain higher levels of procyanidins, perhaps lending credence to the supposed benefits of the Mediterranean diet.

Whether research will ever be able to discover the secrets behind the French paradox, if indeed there are any, is anyone's guess. While much of the media focus has been on the supposed beneficial effects of drinking wine, there are some less-well-publicized downsides to drinking wine, even in moderate amounts, aside from the headaches, impaired driving ability, and worse things that everyone knows about.

As anyone who has drunk several glasses of a cabernet with dinner will probably have discovered, red wine stains the teeth. But it does more than just this temporary cosmetic damage; the acids in both red and white wines wear away the protective enamel on teeth (white wines are the worst offenders), making them more susceptible to decay. For wine tasters who often swill hundreds of wines around in their mouths each week, it is a very significant problem, and regular fluoride treatment is often recommended to replace minerals lost from the teeth.

But even for the occasional wine drinker there can be an effect, not least because wine is consumed over several hours, giving those acids plenty of time to start working on the teeth. Recommendations to prevent damage range from drinking plenty of water to help dilute the acidity and get your saliva flowing to eating cheese at the end of the meal. Cheese neutralizes acids, and it has been suggested the calcium in cheese might even harden the enamel weakened by the wine's acid.

Wine 101

CALIFORNIA GRAPE VARIETALS

The diversity of California's wine industry and the multitude of growing conditions are illustrated by the vast number of grape varietals grown in the state. There are more than 30 types of red wine grapes grown in almost 300,000 acres of vineyards, and 25 types of white wine grapes grown in almost 200,000 acres of vineyards. It's a dizzying array of varietals but is dominated by just a handful.

Certain grapes will only grow in certain conditions, while others will grow anywhere. Chardonnay, for example, is the everyman's grape, able to grow happily almost anywhere in the Wine Country. Pinot noir is fussy and will only grow in a narrow range of cooler climates—and makes good wine in an even narrower range.

Red Wine Grapes

Cabernet sauvignon is by far the most important red wine grape in California, accounting for about a quarter of all red grapes grown in the state. It is easy to ripen in the Californian sun and capable of making both powerful, tannic wines in hotter climates and lighter, more austere wines in cooler mountain regions, all of them usually capable of long-term aging if they are well-made and all having the telltale aromas of cassis (blackcurrant), blackberry, green bell pepper, cedar wood, and leather.

Merlot is the second most widely planted red wine grape in California, though its popularity peaked in the 1990s and is now waning. It is usually blended with cabernet sauvignon in Bordeaux wines, but in California is often made into an easy-drinking wine that is less tannic and more plump than most cabernet sauvignons. Sometimes its more subtle flavors can be lost, resulting in a bland wine, but a well-made merlot has just as much structure as other reds.

Zinfandel is not far behind merlot in terms of total acreage planted and is often considered a California native, though recent genetic studies have shown it probably originally came from southern Europe. Zinfandel can come in many styles, from intense, jammy, and tannic wine to a more subtle, spicy wine with cherry and berry flavors and nice structure—typical of cooler-climate styles. A characteristic of zinfandel vines is that individual grapes can vary dramatically in size within bunches, so they ripen at different speeds. This can result in some being overripe when picked, leading to high sugar levels and even higher alcohol levels in the wines, together with an almost raisiny flavor. Old vines tend to have a smaller crop with more uniform grape size and are favored by winemakers—some zinfandel vines are over a century old.

Pinot noir is a distant fourth in terms of acreage due to its finicky nature, which limits the areas where it can be successfully grown. It is said to have the most complex flavors and be able to communicate the unique properties of the *terroir* like no other grape, but only if grown in the right conditions—not too hot, yet just warm enough to ripen the grapes sufficiently. Classic pinot flavors and aromas include cherry, raspberry, strawberry, violet, and any number of earthy overtones. Cooler parts of California are some of the few areas of the world where great pinot noirs are made, the most famous being the Burgundy region of France. It is also one of the most important grapes for making champagne.

Syrah is the rising star of California's red wines and the fifth-most-planted red grape in the state. Its traditional home is the Rhône region of France, and it is often made into Rhône-style wines in cooler parts of California, exhibiting telltale black pepper and chocolate flavors and an almost purple color. It makes a much denser, more powerful wine when grown in hotter climates, including parts of California

and in Australia, where it is commonly known as **shiraz.**

Petite sirah is normally used as a blending grape, particularly in zinfandels, but it is also increasingly bottled on its own. The resulting wine is one of the darkest colored you'll see and has a trademark intensity with plenty of dark fruit and peppery flavors that can (and often do) support some fairly robust tannins. It can age well but is at its best when blended with Rhône varietals to give it a little more complexity. Despite the different spelling, petite sirah is genetically related to syrah, although most of the petite sirah grown in California has actually been found to be a varietal called durif, which is itself a cross between petite sirah and another varietal called peloursin. The confusion is yet another example of how California's pioneer winemakers were often a little too casual or simply inaccurate when documenting newly planted grapes.

White Wine Grapes

Chardonnay is the king of white grapes in California. It accounts for almost 100,000 acres, or more than half the total acreage planted with white varietals, and about a quarter of all wine made in California in 2005. It grows almost anywhere and can be made into wines of a multitude of styles to suit almost every palate, depending on the wine-making process. Over-oaking is a common fault of Californian chardonnays, as is an over-reliance on high levels of malolactic fermentation, which give the wines a sweet, buttery, and slightly generic flavor. Chardonnay is also one of the most important champagne grapes.

Chenin blanc is the grape that chardonnay eclipsed, and the acreage planted to this varietal in California has been declining steadily since the 1980s. It makes an equally easy-drinking (some say plain) wine as chardonnay, full of fruity flavors, but it is most commonly used as a blending grape.

Sauvignon blanc is one of the most important white grape varietals in Bordeaux, where it is usually blended with semillon, and it is growing in popularity in California. In cool climates like its home in France and parts of California it makes a refreshingly crisp, aromatic wine, often with unusual aromas of grass and herbs. In warmer climates it makes a more intense style of wine from which winemakers sometimes coax richer, more tropical fruit flavors. These richer styles are often called **fumé blanc** but are still made from the same sauvignon blanc grape.

Viognier is an increasingly fashionable white varietal originally from the Rhône region of France that exploded onto the California wine scene in the 1990s. In 1992 there were just 100 acres planted of this varietal; by 2002 there were 2,000 acres. It does well in California's warm climate, where it ripens enough to create full-bodied, elegant wines with a distinctive exotic, floral aroma and rich texture. It is sometimes used in small quantities as a blending grape in red wines. Watch out for sometimes excessive levels of alcohol (often over 15 percent) that can give the wine a "hot," or overly alcoholic, taste.

Riesling is regarded as the king of white wines on its home turf in Germany and is increasingly popular in California thanks to its ability to make different styles of wine depending on the climate and wine-making process. Some rieslings are too sweet and lack structure, but the best wines from places like the Anderson Valley in Mendocino have a unique balance of acidity, tropical fruit flavors, powerful aromas, and a lightness that makes them some of the most complex in the white wine world. Also look for a delicious dessert wine made from so-called botrytized grapes, which have been infected by the botrytis mold either naturally on the vine or artificially after harvest. The mold has the effect of dehydrating the grape, concentrating the sugars and flavors into an uncommon intensity.

Gewürztraminer is another Alsatian grape that has found a home in the cooler parts of California, most notably the Anderson Valley in Mendocino, and produces wonderfully complex wine with a telltale floral aromas and a refreshing acidity that makes them great with food. Most gewürztraminer is made in a dry

white wine grapes

© PHILIP GOLDSMITH

style, but grapes are also often harvested later than usual to make a rich and equally complex dessert wine.

HOW WINE IS MADE

For thousands of years civilizations have made wine, and the chemical process of fermentation that turns the sugar in grape juice into alcohol in wine is the same as it's always been. The actual process of making wine has changed drastically, however, particularly since the science behind fermentation was first discovered in the mid-1800s. Since then, wine making has become ever more refined to get the best out of particular grapes and to make different styles of wine, some for aging and others for mass consumption.

The year that appears on a wine bottle, known as the wine's vintage, is the year that the grapes are harvested and wine making begins. The processes used to make red and white wines are similar but with a few important differences. One of the most important is that red wines are made by fermenting the juice in

© GEORGE ROSE

harvesting grapes

contact with the skins of the grapes. The skins contain the pigments that make red wine red; juice from virtually all grapes, whether red or white, is relatively colorless. Cut a red grape in half, scoop out the flesh, and it will be almost identical in color to flesh from a white grape.

Grapes are brought from the vineyards to the crush pad at the winery, where they are unloaded onto a conveyor and fed into a **crusher-destemmer,** a machine that chops off the stems but lets the grapes through, gently crushing them in the process so the juice can seep out. In the case of the best grapes destined for more expensive wines, human sorters often pull out withered, unripe, or otherwise unworthy grapes and stems from the conveyor so only the best get through. Once grapes are crushed and destemmed, the wine-making process begins.

Although red and white wine-making techniques differ in many ways, they both involve a fermentation stage during which naturally occurring yeasts on the skins of the grapes, often supplemented by the addition of other yeast

strains for certain flavor characteristics, get to work on the grape juice and turn the naturally occurring sugar into alcohol. Fermentation can be carried out in giant wooden tanks (the old fashioned way), temperature-controlled stainless steel tanks (the modern way), or even open-top concrete tanks (old-fashioned but still widely used in California for some wines, like pinot noir).

Almost as important as the type of fermentation vessel used is how the wine gets in and out of it. A lot of modern wineries use standard food-grade pumps and pipes to move the wine between each stage of wine making. The more traditional method of moving the liquid around is gravity flow—literally letting gravity do the work. This is how it used to be done before the age of modern pumps and electricity. Many old (and an increasing number of modern) wineries are designed around the gravity flow principle, whereby each stage of the winemaking process is at a progressively lower level of the winery. Purists argue that gravity-flow wine making minimizes the amount of contact the wine has with processing equipment and the heat it generates. It also saves a considerable amount of power.

Californian wine making differs from that in some other parts of the world in that winemakers cannot add any sugar to the wine (known as chaptalization). Luckily, the weather is hot enough and the sun strong enough that ripening grapes to their necessary sweetness is generally not a problem in California. Very little else can be added to wines during fermentation either, except for yeast and clarifying agents, but winemakers have plenty of ways to manipulate wines after fermentation. More sugar can be added in the form of additional grape juice, acid levels can be increased with the addition of tartaric or citric acid, and alcohol levels can be lowered if necessary using a process called reverse osmosis. Such manipulation of the finished product is more common than wineries and winemakers want you to believe.

Alcohol and many naturally occurring chemicals act as preservatives in bottled wine, but a chemical that is usually added for its additional preservative action is sulfur dioxide, and this is responsible for the statement on wine labels that a wine "contains sulfites." Sulfur dioxide is added to wines before bottling to prevent the growth of bacteria that could spoil the wine, and it is also sometimes added at the beginning of the wine-making process to kill naturally occurring yeasts, some of which might impart slightly funky flavors to a wine. In most cases, however, natural yeasts are an important part of the wine-making process, though often supplemented by other strains of yeast, all of which create wines with slightly different characteristics.

The headaches that some people claim are caused by sulfites in wine, particularly cheap wine, could also be due to naturally occurring histamines. Some people experiment with taking an antihistamine before drinking wine.

Making Red Wine

After destemming and crushing, the grapes are either pumped or flow by gravity into the fermentation vessel, where fermentation begins and usually continues for a couple of weeks.

During fermentation, the grape skins, seeds, and remaining small pieces of stem float to the top and form a thick crust that has to be constantly broken and remixed with the fermenting wine to ensure all the pigments in the grape skins and the other desirable chemicals like tannins are leached out of this "cap" of crud. These days the wine from the bottom of the fermentation tank is usually pumped over the cap and filters back down through it, or a giant mixer-like system keeps all the skins and

HOW MANY GRAPES IN A GLASS?

Understanding the wine-making process is a bit easier if it's brought down to a personal scale – how many grapes go into the bottle of wine you're drinking. The Sonoma County Grape Growers Association has helpfully worked it out for us.

An average vineyard yields about 5 tons, or 10,000 pounds, of grapes per acre (it's actually far less for the best vineyards and most expensive wines). All those grapes make about 13.5 barrels of wine, which is 797 gallons, or 3,985 bottles.

Do the math and it turns out that one bottle of wine is made using about 2.4 pounds of grapes, so one glass comes from just under 10 ounces of grapes.

This is little more than a back-of-an-envelope calculation, however, and will depend on all sorts of factors, from the type of grape to the style of wine being made.

The Napa Valley Vintners Association has slightly different figures. It says a ton of grapes makes on average 720 bottles of wine, so each bottle contains about 2.8 pounds of grapes. It also helpfully calculates that one average vine plant produces enough grapes to make 4-6 bottles of wine each year.

stems constantly circulating through the fermenting wine.

Traditionally, the cap was broken up and pushed back down into the wine by hand using a big wooden paddle, and this punching-down technique is still used in some smaller wineries today, especially to produce pinot noir—a wine that requires more work to extract the color from the grape skins.

Once the winemaker determines that enough pigment and tannins have been extracted from the skins and fermentation has gone on long enough, the liquid is transferred into barrels or stainless steel storage tanks. This is known as the free-run juice and goes into the best wine. Sometimes the free run is blended with some of the more concentrated and tannic press wine, generated when the leftover skins and other mulch in the cap are pressed to extract all the remaining juice, which is then stored separately. In some cases fermentation is stopped by chilling the wine and filtering out the yeast, but fermentation will also stop naturally when alcohol levels rise high enough to kill the yeast—usually about 15 percent by volume.

The blending of the free-run wine and the press wine is just part of the important **blending** process. Wines from different vineyards, sometimes from different parts, or blocks, of the same vineyard, are usually made and stored separately and will have slightly different characteristics. They are blended together at a later stage by the winemaker, often together with small quantities of wines made from different grapes, to make the final product. Labeling laws determine how the final wine is described on the bottle.

Most of the premium wines made in California are aged in oak barrels once they have been blended—the barrels you often see stacked on giant racks in caves or cool storage rooms of wineries. This barrel aging not only lets the wine continue to develop its taste and aroma through ongoing chemical reactions but also imparts new flavors and aromas that come from the barrels themselves. It is also when most red wines undergo **malolactic**

fermentation, which is not fermentation at all but a bacterial reaction that converts the tart malic acid in a wine to the softer lactic acid.

Buying the barrels and storing them is expensive and reserved for the best wines that can command premium prices. Cheaper wines made to be drunk right away are bottled straight from the stainless steel tanks in which they were blended. Sometimes oak chips are added to those tanks to impart some of the important oaky flavors, a method still frowned upon by European winemakers.

Before wines are bottled or left to age in barrels, they are purified using a process called **fining,** which uses a coagulant to remove all the particles of dead yeast, excess tannins, and other crud suspended in the liquid. The coagulant can be anything from types of clay to egg whites or gelatin and is simply dropped into the wine, where it attaches itself to particles and pulls them down to the bottom of the barrel or tank. In fine wines that need to age further, the freshly cleaned wine is siphoned off into clean barrels to ensure this gunk does not interfere with the aging process, a process known as **racking.** After usually six months or a year (longer for the very best age-worthy wines) the wine from barrels will be bottled, often after being filtered to remove the last of the sediment. Cheaper wines stored in stainless steel tanks are usually bottled soon after fining.

Some more expensive red wines are made without the crusher-destemmer step; instead, whole bunches of grapes with the biggest stems removed are left to ferment using the yeasts naturally occurring on the skins. The grapes eventually burst and the fermented juice escapes.

Making White Wine

White wine production leaves out many of the steps involved in making red wines and is an altogether quicker process. The speed of the wine making and the fact that most Californian white wines are not aged for long (if at all) before bottling explain why a bottle of white wine often has a much more recent vintage date on the label than a red.

Winemakers don't want white grape juice to sit in contact with grape skins and stems for long because that would introduce all sorts of bitter flavors, so the grapes often go through not only the crusher-destemmer but also a press, which gently squeezes the juice out. The first juice out of the grapes is the best and is often reserved for the best wines, much like the best olive oils are the "first cold-pressed." The last juice to be squeezed out picks up some of the bitterness from the skins, seeds, and stems and is destined for cheaper wines.

Most Californian white wines are fermented in giant stainless steel vessels, and fermentation is carefully controlled using giant refrigeration jackets incorporated into the outside of the tanks to ensure a wine retains some sweetness—white wines, even dry whites, generally contain more residual sugar and have less alcohol than most reds. Because of this extra refrigeration the fermentation time for white wines is usually longer than that of reds.

During fermentation, dead yeasts and other particles, known as the **lees,** will slowly drop to the bottom and are sometimes left in contact with the fermented wine to add distinct yeasty, toasty aromas. This is often the case with more expensive white wines that are fermented and aged in barrels.

Once fermentation is complete, the wine is fined and filtered and either bottled or transferred to barrels for aging, which adds the oakiness that Californian chardonnays are so famous for. White wines often undergo some degree of malolactic fermentation, which turns a crisp white wine into a rich, buttery-tasting one. If a winemaker does not want malolactic fermentation to occur, the wine undergoes some additional filtering and might also be treated with sulfur dioxide to kill the bacteria responsible for the reaction.

Making Champagne

The cool climate of Carneros and the Russian River Valley is ideally suited for growing the two most important champagne grape varietals, chardonnay and pinot noir. A few other grapes are also often used, including small amounts of pinot blanc and pinot meunier (producers of the Spanish sparkling wine, cava, use totally different grapes more suited to the local Spanish climate).

Most Californian champagne-style wines are blends of both pinot noir and chardonnay, with some exceptions. A blanc de blancs champagne is made only from chardonnay grapes and has the lightest, most delicate style. A blanc de noirs is still a white wine but made exclusively from dark-skinned grapes like pinot noir, giving it a fuller body. Somewhere in between the two is rosé, or pink, champagne, which is made by adding a small amount of red wine to the white blend.

The key to making champagne is to bottle the wine while it is still fermenting so the yeast will continue to do its work and generate both alcohol and the all-important gas that creates the fizz, carbon dioxide.

The fizziness was likely discovered by accident when the cold winters of the Champagne region stopped barrel fermentation in its tracks before the wine was bottled. Once the wine was bottled and the weather warmed up, fermentation started again, only this time inside the sealed bottle, where the carbon dioxide (dissolved in the liquid as carbonic acid) had nowhere to go. As pressure built up the corks popped off (and the fizzy wine was immediately drunk by people assuming it had gone bad) or the bottles simply exploded from the immense pressure.

English merchants taking delivery of barrels of French wine were probably the first to experience this peculiar phenomenon of exploding wine. At the time, back in the late 1700s, England was also home to a state-of-the-art glass-blowing industry, so once the wine sellers understood what was going on with the wine, they were able to develop bottles thick enough to contain it.

The full potential of this new style of fizzy wine was quickly realized, and modern champagne production began. The biggest challenge for the early champagne houses was to remove the sediment of dead yeast and other by-products of fermentation from the bottle

FIVE FIZZY FACTS

- **Champagne making is a high-pressure business.** The pressure inside a champagne bottle created by the dissolved carbon dioxide gas (carbonic acid) is about 90 pounds per square inch, or about three times the pressure in a car tire. That's why the glass of champagne bottles is so thick and the cork can shoot so far.

- **Champagne isn't just for celebration.** More than 80 percent of sparkling wine sales occur between November and January, but it is a style of wine that can be enjoyed at any time of year and with a wide range of foods. Try it as an aperitif or instead of chardonnay at the beginning of a meal.

- **Not all bubbles are created equal.** The more expensive the champagne, the smaller the bubbles and the smoother and creamier it feels in your mouth. The priciest French champagnes barely taste fizzy at all. The cheapest supermarket sparklers feel like fizzy water or soda in your mouth.

- **Champagne gets you tipsy more quickly.** The carbonation in sparkling wine is thought to relax the valve between your stomach and small intestine, where alcohol is absorbed by the blood more quickly. So while still wines stay in the stomach longer, champagne enters the small intestine more quickly and really does go to your head faster.

- **Better champagne glasses make for better bubbles.** The tall, slender champagne glasses, known as flutes, help keep the wine sparkling for longer and show off the bubbles better. Most good-quality flutes have a small etching at the bottom that encourages the bubbles to form. That's why you'll usually see a long, straight line of bubbles rising from the very bottom of the glass.

without losing the fizz; otherwise the champagne would end up murky.

The process developed in 1805, known as *méthode champenoise*, is still largely unchanged today. Bottles of half-fermented champagne are stored neck-down in large racks and were traditionally turned on an exact schedule over many months to get the sediment to work its way down to the cork, a process known as riddling. Today, of course, the riddling is all done by computer-controlled machines (despite what many champagne houses would have you believe).

Then comes the process of disgorging, during which the sediment is carefully removed. In today's automated version, the neck of the bottle is frozen, the cork is removed, and the compressed gas in the wine shoots the frozen plug of muck out. Finally comes dosing, when the bottle is topped off with wine and some sugar (more sugar for the sweeter wines, less for the dry styles) before being recorked and allowed to continue fermenting in peace.

It's a precise and expensive process, which is why it's reserved for the high-end champagnes. Cheaper sparkling wines are today more likely to be made in large stainless steel tanks that are pressurized to keep the carbon dioxide dissolved in the wine before it is filtered and bottled.

Making Port

Dark, juicy ports have become increasingly popular in recent years, and some sort of port can now be found at most wineries. Not all of it is good, however. Some is nothing more than an overly sweet red dessert wine that has about as much complexity as concentrated, alcoholic grape juice. Others approach (though don't yet reach) the sophistication of the best ports made in the country where they were invented—Portugal. The name is derived from the Portuguese coastal city of Oporto from where the wines were shipped to their main market, England.

Traditional ports are made using the Portuguese grape varietals tinta barroca, tinta roriz, tinto cao, and touriga, though a lot of

Californian ports use more common regional varietals, particularly zinfandel and syrah.

The process starts out similar to the red wine–making process, but the fermentation is stopped in its tracks when the wine is poured into a fortified spirit like brandy, which has enough alcohol to kill the yeast that was turning the wine's sugar into alcohol. The result is a half-fermented wine still containing plenty of unfermented sugar but with a high alcohol level (usually around 20 percent) thanks to the addition of the brandy.

Because fermentation of red wine is stopped halfway, the winemaker has to work hard to ensure that enough color has been extracted from the grape skins before the wine is poured off into the brandy. In Portugal that is still often achieved by the age-old custom of crushing the grapes with bare feet to thoroughly grind up the skins. Not many Californian wineries will admit to that.

The best ports in the world are aged for many years in barrels, sometimes many decades, and eventually attain a pale, tawny color. These are the most expensive tawny ports. Most Californian ports are made to be drunk relatively young, although they can also be aged in the bottle just like regular wines.

Wine Barrels

Oak was traditionally used for making barrels because it was strong, had a fine grain and so was watertight, and was plentiful in the forests of Europe. Early winemakers also discovered that wines picked up some pleasant flavors and smells when stored in oak barrels, which is why oak has remained the most desirable wood to use when aging wines.

Most barrels used in wine making today are made of oak, but not all oak is the same when it comes to making wine. Just as different varietals of grape have different flavors and smells, different types of oak also have different characteristics that a winemaker can incorporate into the wine-making process. Even oak from different forests can have distinct properties.

French oak is the most highly prized because of the soft, subtle flavors it gives a wine. It is

oak wine barrels

also the most expensive. A typical French oak barrel costs a winery $600–800, compared to about $300–500 for a barrel made from American oak, which tends to add more pronounced flavors to a wine. As French oak is priced out of the market, the oak from Eastern Europe, particularly Hungary and Slovakia, is becoming more popular and has some of the same characteristics as its French cousin but at far less cost to the winery.

Some of the most distinctive flavors and smells added to a wine by aging it in oak barrels include vanilla, leather, tobacco, cloves, and cedar. Those flavors will be stronger the newer the barrel is. Wineries often age wine in a mixture of new and old barrels, both to save money and to get the right mixture of strong and mellow flavors from the oak. They will also often use a mixture of American and European oak to get the right balance of flavors and aromas.

When barrels are made by a cooper (an art in itself) they are usually **toasted** by lighting a fire inside the half-finished barrel to create a thin layer of burnt wood. This toasted wood imparts its own set of flavors and smells to the wine, including the rich, chocolate, caramel, and nutty characteristics typical in barrel-aged wines, particularly reds.

The Wine-Making Year

A winegrower's year is a busy one, and January is about the only time they can take significant time off for a well-earned vacation. Most of us have more flexible vacation time and can choose when to visit Wine Country based on all sorts of factors, including the weather, the scenery, events, and where the winegrowers are in their year-long process of creating great wines.

January: The vineyards are bare, the weather is cool and wet, and the Wine Country is at its quietest. This is also the time of year that the vines are pruned. Straggly bare stems are cut back to the thick branches and trunks of the vine. In the cellar, racking of the red wines is underway.

February: More vineyard maintenance and pruning are carried out, but the wet weather has by now started all the wildflowers blooming, including cover crops like the bright yellow wild mustard that fills the rows between vines in many parts of the Wine Country between now and April. Racking and blending the wines for barrel ageing continues.

March: New vines are planted, and bottling lines at wineries spring into action, bottling wines designed to be drunk young (like many whites) that were made the previous year.

April: Buds are open on the vines and the new growing season begins in the vineyard as the weather finally starts to dry out and warm up. The danger of late frosts often gets the giant wind machines going to keep the air moving and prevent ice from forming on the delicate shoots.

May: Vines are now growing vigorously, and wineries are gearing up for the summer rush of tourists.

June: The vines are tied to the wires and posts of the trellises to make sure the grapes get as much sun as possible later in the year. The vines also start flowering, so rain is an unwelcome, though rare, disruption. Bottling of older wines begins before the heat of summer sets in.

July: Flowering is over, and grapes are starting to form. Spraying with organic or other chemicals starts to safeguard the developing grapes from pests and diseases.

August: This is the first month that red grapes will really start to look red as they continue to grow. Pruning of excess leaves sometimes takes place to ensure grapes are not shaded and can fully ripen. Smaller, less-developed clusters of grapes might also be cut off so the vine can concentrate all its energy and nutrients into the remaining grapes. Wineries start to clear space for the imminent harvest.

September: The first harvesting begins, with the earliest-ripening grapes in the hottest areas picked first (in particularly hot years or those with an early summer, harvesting sometimes starts in August). Most grapes in Northern California's premium growing regions are picked by hand, usually by migrant workers. This is the best time to surreptitiously taste just how sweet wine grapes are if you see any dangling over the shoulder of country roads. Wineries themselves are hives of activity as tons of grapes start to be brought in by truck.

October: Harvesting finishes, and the vineyards start to look a little more bare, though the vines will keep their leaves for another month or so. The crush is well underway at wineries, and steel tanks rapidly fill up with wine.

November: The vineyards start to turn shades of red and yellow as the weather starts to cool, and the leaves finally drop when the nights get cold enough. In wineries, the wine is starting to be transferred from the fermentation vats into barrels to begin aging.

December: Many wineries offer barrel tasting of new wines, and the winemaker will start to plan the blends that will ultimately be bottled.

Reading Wine Labels

Thanks to strict labeling regulations overseen by the federal Bureau of Alcohol, Tobacco, and Firearms it is tough for wineries to mislead consumers about what goes into a bottle of wine, but there is a little more to a wine's content than might meet the eye.

The year on the bottle is the **vintage date** and indicates the year in which at least 95 percent of the grapes that went into the wine were harvested.

Usually underneath the vintage is the **appellation of origin,** which is where the dominant grapes in the wine were grown. It is usually a geographical area (appellation) like California or Sonoma County or a specific American Viticultural Area (AVA) such as Rutherford, Napa Valley, or Dry Creek Valley. In the case of an appellation, at least 75 percent of the grapes in the wine must have come from that area. In the case of an AVA, at least 85 percent of the grapes must be from the area identified on the bottle.

The type of grape the wine is made from, or **varietal designation,** is usually displayed above or below the appellation of origin. If a specific grape varietal is identified (cabernet sauvignon or sauvignon blanc, for example), then at least 75 percent of the grapes the wine is made of must be that named varietal. That leaves a lot of leeway for winemakers to blend small quantities of other grapes into a wine to add to its character; sometimes these blending grapes will be identified elsewhere on the label, other times not.

If less than 75 percent of the grapes in a wine are one varietal, then a winery will either simply call it red or white wine or will come up with a snappy and unique name to describe the blend. Such a wine is known as a **proprietary wine** or blend. Meritage (rhymes with heritage) is a name unique to the United States that is sometimes used to describe a blend of Bordeaux varietals, either red or white.

The final words to look for on labels are **estate bottled,** which means that all of the grapes in a wine came from land owned or controlled by the winery, and the wine was made and bottled on the winery premises. So-called estate wines tend to be among a winery's best and most expensive. Sometimes a wine is made using grapes from only one vineyard, in which case the vineyard is identified on the label (although it doesn't have to be) and the wine is known as a single-vineyard or vineyard-designate wine.

HOW TO TASTE WINE

The involved process of thoroughly smelling and tasting a wine is one reason why aficionados love the stuff and a big reason that novices tend to be intimidated. Some people seem to regard wine almost as an intellectual pursuit. Others just like the taste or want to get drunk.

On one level, it seems ludicrous to spend so long detecting every nuance of flavor in a wine. After all, when a plate of food arrives in a restaurant we don't sit for five minutes smelling it to try to detect every ingredient and how they were cooked. Then again, there is probably no other drinkable liquid on earth that can pack as many complex aromas and flavors into a glass as wine can, and certainly no other

wine tasters

food product that can reflect so completely the place that it came from.

With the magic worked by winemakers, simple grape juice can be transformed into wines that mimic the smells and tastes of a remarkable range of fruits, vegetables, and countless other substances. From a scientific point of view, however, there's no magic involved—grapes actually contain many of the same chemicals that give other fruits and vegetables their distinctive smells. Wine reviews often read like a shopping list for the produce department at a local supermarket.

Wine appreciation cannot be taught. It has to be learned by experience. One reason that many people are confused by those slightly pretentious-sounding reviews is that they cannot actually recognize many of the smells or tastes being referred to. Someone who has never smoked a cigar, for example, is not gong to understand what a reviewer is referring to when he describes a cabernet sauvignon as having an aroma of "cigar box." Everyone knows what chocolate tastes and smells like, though,

so a "chocolaty" cabernet will instantly ring a bell in most people's minds.

The sort of diverse smell and flavor database that critics use takes time (and an extremely varied diet) to develop. Patience is the best way to learn—it takes a while to develop a palate that can detect the subtle nuances of wine and years to build up a useful tasting memory that you can draw on to recognize and describe wines or their aromas.

When in doubt, simply listen to how everyone else describes the wine, or just ask whoever is pouring the wine at a winery what exactly you are supposed to be smelling or tasting. On a few occasions you might not get much help from a harried staffer, but usually they are happy to give a quick description.

Alternatively, an intensive wine-tasting course can shorten the process of learning all the smells and tastes by setting out every imaginable fruit, vegetable, and other organic substance in dishes, allowing students to directly match aromas from the foods to the aromas in wines (something you can

BOTTLE SIZE MATTERS

If you're wondering how the regular wine bottle came to be the size it is (750 milliliters – and one of the few beverages in the United States measured in metric units), it is because this was the approximate size a Victorian glassblower could blow with one deep breath. The size was then standardized by European winemakers. There are some bottles smaller – the half-bottle and the split or quarter bottle handed out on some airlines – but most people tend to notice the bigger bottles on display at some wineries.

Bigger bottles are actually better when it comes to aging fine wine. Aging is directly affected by how much of the liquid is exposed to the small gap between the wine and the cork, known as the ullage. The lower the proportion of wine there is in contact with the ullage, the longer the aging process will be. Since even giant bottles generally have necks almost as narrow as regular bottles, they also have a proportionately smaller ullage. Big bottles don't stop at the common magnum size either. There are some true giants that hold enough wine to keep a big party going all night long.

Bottle sizes are named after ancient, mythical kings. No one really knows why, but the theory is that such names convey greatness, grandeur, and longevity. They increase in size as follows:

- **Magnum:** 2 standard bottles (1.5 liters)
- **Jeroboam:** 4 bottles (3 liters)
- **Methuselah:** 8 bottles (6 liters)
- **Salamanazar:** 12 bottles (9 liters)
- **Balthazar:** 16 bottles (12 liters)
- **Nebuchadnezzar:** 20 bottles (15 liters)

And the biggest bottle ever? It was a one-time-only creation that held 130 liters of wine, the equivalent of 173 regular bottles or 1,200 glasses of wine, commissioned by the Morton's Steakhouse chain in 2004 to celebrate its 25th anniversary. That giant bottle was 4.5 feet tall and filled with Beringer Private Reserve cabernet sauvignon, a quintessential steak wine that is also a quintessentially expensive Napa Valley wine. The retail value of the wine in that bottle was a staggering $17,000, and the bottle eventually sold at auction in late 2004 for almost $56,000, giant corkscrew not included.

---

also do at home with whatever you have in your kitchen).

Of course, the world of smells and tastes is unique to each individual. There are some fairly standard categories of the basic flavors and aromas of wines. Beyond them, it's fine to make up your own comparisons and the more recognizable they are the better. For fun, make up your own personal wine descriptions every day—pinot noir can sometimes smell a little like a traffic jam on a hot summer afternoon, for example. Alternatively, just ignore all the fancy words and simply say "it smells and tastes good." Just never use the word "Yummy."

The fact that critics don't always agree with each other illustrates just how subjective the art of describing wines really is. Take these three excerpts from reviews in three major wine magazines of a 2001 merlot from Pride Mountain Vineyards. All three have a few common threads, but they could equally be describing totally different wines:

Possesses gorgeous aromas of creosote, damp earth, sweet black cherry as well as currant fruit, and a chocolaty aftertaste.

Rich in spicy currant, exotic spice, and ripe blackberry fruit, turning spicy and exhibiting pretty mocha-scented oak.

Smoky aromas of black raspberry, coffee, and nutty oak. Lush, fat, and sweet, with layered flavors of black raspberry and sweet oak.

Looking at Wine

There's no denying it: wine looks inviting. Whether it's the pale yellow of a sauvignon blanc, the golden hue of chardonnay, or the deep purple of a syrah, the purity of color in wines is striking. How a wine looks in the glass can also give some clues about what you're about to drink. Try to look at it against a white background (the tasting room menu, for example). Overall the wine should be crystal clear and a bright, vivid color. Any hint of cloudiness is generally not a good sign.

White wines range from a pale yellow in young and light wines like sauvignon blanc to a darker gold in some heavier whites like some styles of chardonnay that have been aged in oak. White wines darken as they age; a hint of brown might be a sign of a well-aged wine, but for most Californian whites it's usually the sign of a wine that's past its prime.

Red wines have a much wider range of colors, ranging from deep red in the case of cabernet sauvignon to deep purple in a young syrah and a paler brick red in pinot noir. The color of red wines fades as they age and the pigment molecules react with other chemical components of the wine, so the deeper the color, the younger the wine.

Smelling the Wine

There's no other drink that can match the array of aromas in a wine, and experiencing all those smells is one of the great pleasures of tasting wine. Trying to identify and describe them is one of the great challenges. Wine glasses are designed to concentrate the aroma of a wine and channel it straight to your nose. Most of what we taste is actually what we smell, so smelling a wine is the key to enjoying it and discovering its complexities.

Professionals smell the wine to learn more about it, such as the main grape varietals it contains and the region it came from, especially in blind tastings that are designed to be as objective as possible. Most people smell wine just to enjoy and appreciate the glorious aromas before drinking it. Identifying those aromas is really nothing more than a bit of fun that

might one day be useful if someone asks you to identify a wine with no label.

Swirl the glass two or three times to help release the aromas, and then take a deep sniff and try to identify all the aromas. Take as many sniffs as you want. Some wines have an intense smell, others more subtle ones.

Most of the up-front smells are the aromas that come directly from the fruit in the wine, and such fruity smells are the biggest category of aromas in the world of wine tasting. Another big category of aromas is vegetative, or anything that smells like it came from a plant, whether grass, bell pepper, or tobacco. Some of the most enticing aromas are those of exotic flowers.

Classic aromas for white wines include apple and pear, citrus fruits, tropical and stone fruits, grass, bell pepper, honey, and melon. For red wines there might be aromas of any number of berries, cherries, raisins, plums, licorice, and black pepper. The lists are almost endless. Some of the more subtle, underlying smells come from the barrel, yeasts, and other wine-making factors. They include vanilla, oak, nuts, butterscotch, and chocolate.

Wine aromas are supposed to be pleasant, but sometimes bad smells creep in and are an indicator of a wine gone bad. Most are pretty obviously bad, like the rotten egg smell of hydrogen sulfide, the vinegary smell of oxidized wine, or the sherry-like smell of cooked, or maderized, wine.

A corked wine—one that has been contaminated by mold on the cork—can sometimes be harder to detect. Often the characteristic musty or mildewed smell is so fleeting that it might be missed and quickly overpowered by other aromas. Another indicator of mold contamination is a strong smell of wet cardboard.

Tasting the Wine

Taking a sip of wine will be the ultimate test of whether to buy it or not. Most wine smells pleasant enough (unless you have an aversion to fruit or the wine is bad), but not all wines will taste good to everyone. This is where subjectivity becomes most evident.

More aromas than you initially smelled might be detectable once a wine is in your mouth as the body's heat vaporizes chemicals that you could not previously smell. The "flavors" of fruit are actually aromas hitting the back of your nose—most of what we think we taste is actually an aroma.

Our taste buds can only detect four fundamental tastes—sweet, sour, bitter, and salty—but those four are enough to determine whether a wine is in balance and ultimately good to drink. There's also a fifth element that taste buds can detect, known as umami, which can best be described as a savory character. What complicates matters is that everyone has a different threshold for those five tastes. Sweet to one person might be sour to another—it all depends on the structure of our mouths and the wiring of our brains.

The amounts of alcohol, tannin, residual sugar, and acid in a wine can all be detected by swirling it around in your mouth for about 10 seconds, making sure it coats every part of your mouth to hit all the different taste buds.

The sum of these tastes is more important than each one individually. How they all interact together is a reflection of a wine's balance, yet another highly subjective measurement of overall quality. Some people prefer sweeter wines; others prefer a little more acidity to make their mouths water. Some don't like the astringency of tannins, while others like the solid taste they can give to a powerful wine. Generally, however, people describe a wine as balanced when all these tastes are about equal to each other.

Aftertaste (the pleasant kind) is almost as important as the main taste. Poor wines have no aftertaste, and once the wine is swallowed, that's it. Good wines leave your taste buds tingling for anywhere from a few seconds to almost a minute, and aromas will waft around in your mouth almost as long.

Another aspect of a wine that is worth noting is its body. Much like water will feel lighter in your mouth than milk, a light-bodied white wine will have a different presence in your mouth than a full-bodied red like a zinfandel.

The Aroma Wheel

Recognizing smells is always easier than naming them, which is why tasting wine is more fun when you know what you're supposed to be smelling. The wine's label or a winery's description will often include a list of aromas the winemaker has identified in the wine, which can be useful, but the ultimate tool to train yourself to recognize aromas is the Aroma Wheel.

An educator at the University of California at Davis created the Aroma Wheel, and even professionals use it when describing wines. It broadly categorizes aromas and bouquets, then subcategorizes them and gives specific examples. If you smell something fruity, for example, the wheel will break down fruity smells into categories such as citrus, berry, and tropical fruit, then break each of those subcategories down further into examples of specific fruits.

Aroma Wheels are often sold among the wine paraphernalia in the tasting rooms of large wineries or can be bought online (along with Aroma Wheel T-shirts for those who live for wine) at www.winearomawheel.com. The website also includes information on how to use the wheel.

WINE AND FOOD

Probably as intimidating to many people as the smelling and tasting wine is the question of how to match a wine with food, or vice versa. Like everything else to do with wine it ultimately boils down to personal taste and personal experience, but there are some underlying principles worth knowing about.

Learning from scratch how your favorite wine interacts on your palate with your favorite foods will increase your appreciation for both the wine and the food. Along the way you'll probably discover the few combinations that really are best avoided and a few others that make your taste buds sing.

There really are no rules to pairing food and wine, despite what some connoisseurs might say. Instead, think of any advice you are given as merely guidelines that will help make the voyage of discovering your favorite food and wine combinations quicker and easier.

These guidelines are constantly in flux. Cuisine trends change and so do wine-making trends. The old adage of white wine with fish and red wine with red meat is somewhat irrelevant. It all depends on the style of a particular wine, how the meat or fish is prepared, and what goes into the accompanying sauces and dishes.

One guideline to pairing food and wine is based on sensory adaptation. An acidic wine will taste less acidic if paired with a fairly acidic food. Vinaigrette dressing on a salad, for example, will mellow out a wine that would otherwise taste too tart. Similarly, a sweet wine will taste less sweet if drunk with a dessert, which is why dessert wines taste far too sweet if drunk on their own.

Some food and wine interactions are more confusing. Saltiness of food has a profound effect on how a wine tastes, for example. A salty dish will give the impression of neutralizing some of the acidity of a particularly tart wine, making it taste smoother and fruiter. Foods with some inherent bitterness, such as green vegetables, can actually enhance the bitterness of some wines.

Perhaps one of the classic pairings is a bold red wine with steak, and for good reason. The concentrated protein in red meat serves to soften the taste of tannins in wine, taming what would normally be an astringent, tannic monster into a softer and fruiter beast altogether. A barrel-aged Napa cabernet, for example, would be perfectly balanced with a steak but would taste like a hunk of wood if you still have some left over when the crème brûlée arrives as the sugar in the dessert overpowers the fruit in the wine, leaving just those woody tannins to dominate.

For a thoroughly educational experience, try drinking just one wine, white or red, with a multiple-course meal to see how its taste dramatically changes with each course. It might not be fun for some courses, but the basics of food and wine interaction very quickly become evident.

Some of the simplest foods can prove to be the hardest to find a good wine match. Cheese, for example, does not (as many people believe) go terribly well with many red wines. Try port for rich cheeses like Stilton or a dry white wine like sauvignon blanc for sharper cheeses like goat cheese.

Wine in Restaurants

If you've ever wondered how restaurants can justify charging more than $40 for a wine that you just bought in a tasting room for $20, the answer is fairly simple, even if it's hard to swallow.

The markup helps restaurants cover their overhead costs, especially those related to the wine. It pays for the salary of a sommelier (so make sure you use his services), some of the salaries of the waitstaff, spoilage of wine (by some estimates, about 5 percent of all restaurant wines go bad before being opened), the cost of storing wine (wine cellars cost a lot of money), and all sorts of other costs of doing business, from the electricity bill to broken wine glasses that can cost a restaurant thousands of dollars a year to replace.

In general, cheap wines have higher markups, percentage-wise, than expensive wines. Those from well-known regions or made from popular grape varietals also tend to have higher markups because they're guaranteed sellers. The pricing ploys can be cynical, but there is a way to beat them.

One way to save money on wine in restaurants is to bring your own. Corkage fees (the fee charged by the restaurant for you to bring and open your own wine) vary but are generally about $15 in Napa and Sonoma restaurants. It sounds pricey, but it's worth considering if you plan to drink an expensive wine. Some places offer free corkage on certain days of the week, however, and many others offer free corkage on one bottle of your own wine for every bottle you buy from their wine list. Ask about the corkage policy of the restaurant when making a reservation.

Having ordered a bottle in a restaurant, there is yet another wine ritual to go through. The smelling and tasting ritual is all about finding those wines you like; this restaurant ritual is all about finding those wines that you don't want to drink.

When a server brings a bottle of wine to the table and shows it to you like some trophy, double-check that it is in fact the wine you ordered. Take note of the vintage because it's not uncommon for a restaurant to receive new vintages and forget to update its wine list.

When the wine is opened, the cork will often be handed to you or placed gingerly on the table. It might make a nice souvenir but is actually given to you to check whether it's in good condition. A good cork should feel springy and soft. A dried out and hard cork suggests that the wine was not stored well and should be a warning to pay close attention when you taste the wine. Don't bother smelling the cork—it will just smell of cork. And don't bother doing anything at all with synthetic corks, other than perhaps bouncing them off the ceiling for fun.

Finally, the server will pour a tasting-room quantity of wine into your glass. The idea is to check that the wine is the right temperature and that it is not oxidized or corked. If you simply don't like it, you're stuck with it, though many wines will sometimes taste a bit rough when first opened. Always give the wine a few minutes in the glass before drinking to let it open up and show off its full range of aromas and tastes.

Restaurants are usually pretty good about chilling white wines before serving, but red wines can sometimes feel like they have been stored above a hot oven in the kitchen. In those cases it's fine to ask for an ice bucket to cool the bottle down. After all, red wine is generally best drunk at 60–70°F, not 85°F.

AGING WINE

The whole point of aging wine for some people is to make it more valuable. For most of us, however, aging wine is all about making it taste better after a few years of development.

Youthful wine is like a youthful person—brash, unsure of itself, and a bit awkward. Like us, a wine mellows, gets more complex, and becomes a more well-rounded individual the older it gets. At least that's the theory.

As wine ages it undergoes a complex chemical process that only scientists fully understand. For the rest of us, the aging of wine is a process full of mystery and myths. One common myth is that all wine gets better as it ages. Sadly, that's not true, so don't start stocking a cellar with $10 bottles of cabernet. A poorly made wine that is not in balance when young will not turn into a finely balanced masterpiece after a few years.

A wine almost has to be designed to be aged by the winemaker. Moreover, a wine capable of aging for a decade or more might taste a little unappealing when young. A wine made to be drunk young will probably taste flat and generally awful after 10 years.

Another myth is that age-worthy wine gets better and better as it gets older. While that's almost true for some of the most famous Bordeaux wines, most modern wines are created to be drunk relatively young and will reach a peak after a certain number of years, then go downhill fast. Wineries don't help matters by making sweeping statements that a wine will "continue to improve for 10–15 years." It all depends on how it's stored. In many cases that wine will be barely drinkable after 10 years unless stored under almost perfect aging conditions.

Unfortunately, winemakers and wineries are the only sources of information on how a wine might age, because there are no hard and fast rules. One way to get a fairly good idea of how a particular wine will age is to taste some so-called library wines, those from previous vintages that are kept by wineries in part so they themselves know how their wines change with age. Most good wineries either offer library tasting to the public for a fee or will happily oblige if it will likely result in the sale of a case of expensive wine.

In California, virtually no white wines are made to be aged, and they should be consumed within a couple of years. Some that are more age-worthy tend to be chardonnays from mountain vineyards like those on Mount Veeder in the Napa Valley, and those in the Santa Cruz Mountains.

It's harder to determine which Californian red wines will age well. In very general terms, good quality red port will happily age for the longest, followed by a decent cabernet sauvignon, syrah, zinfandel, merlot, and finally pinot noir, which is often at its peak after a couple of years.

Price can also offer a hint at a wine's aging potential, though this test sometimes falls foul of marketing and overpricing. A $100 bottle of Napa Valley cabernet will probably only be bought by serious collectors, for example, who are unlikely to crack it open that night but will instead cellar it for years to either enjoy themselves or sell for a profit to another collector. Winemakers and wineries often have that sort of buyer in mind when they craft the style of wine.

STORING WINE

Research has shown that most American consumers drink wine very soon after buying it, so storage is not a big issue. Aging wines, even for a few years, however, requires a little care to ensure it does not spoil. A pretty iron wine rack on top of a fridge opposite a sunny kitchen window will be useless for anything but short-term storage.

Wine likes to be dark, still, and kept at a fairly constant temperature somewhere from 50–70°F, conditions found in most basements or even a dark interior closet in many homes. The most ideal storage conditions will also be cool (below 60°F) and damp (over 60 percent relative humidity), though these last two requirements can be tough to achieve without digging your own cave or buying some sort of specially designed storage cellar.

Although excessive heat makes wines age a little too fast to achieve their full potential, a constantly fluctuating temperature is the biggest enemy. As the temperature goes up and down during the day, the wine will expand and contract in the bottle, causing the cork to move in the bottle neck by a fraction and potentially suck in air. That air will gradually oxidize the wine and spoil it.

If a wine is stored in very low humidity, the cork might also dry out and expose the wine to air. Keeping the cork moist so it retains a good seal with the neck of the bottle is the main reason for storing wine sideways.

SHIPPING WINE

The 21st Amendment to the U.S. Constitution ended Prohibition in 1933 but still plagues the wine industry today because it allows states to continue to regulate the sale and distribution of all types of alcoholic beverages.

Since repeal, a patchwork of rules and regulations unique to almost every state has evolved. If you plan to buy wine at a Californian winery or on the Internet and have it shipped to your home state, you might be out of luck, although an important U.S. Supreme Court decision in May 2005 on interstate shipping laws is slowly reshaping the archaic laws all across the country.

Before May 2005, there were 23 states that banned any direct shipping of wine and other alcoholic drinks from out of state to consumers (Alabama, Arkansas, Connecticut, Delaware, Florida, Indiana, Kansas, Kentucky, Maine, Maryland, Massachusetts, Michigan, Mississippi, Montana, New Jersey, New York, Ohio, Oklahoma, Pennsylvania, South Dakota, Tennessee, Utah, and Vermont). Even buying the wine yourself and sending it home in a FedEx box to avoid having to carry it was illegal. Many of those states allow shipments from producers within the state, however, and some allowed wine shipments from out of state as long as it came through designated in-state distributors.

That discrimination between in-state and out-of-state wineries was the basis of the May 2005 Supreme Court decision that struck down such shipping laws in both New York and Michigan. The court ruled that such discrimination against out-of-state businesses was in violation of the Commerce Clause of the

U.S. Constitution, which ensures free trade between states. Although the ruling only affected two states, by definition it called into question the laws in the other states that similarly ban out-of-state wine shipments.

Importantly, however, the Supreme Court left the 21st Amendment untouched in its ruling, so many of those states are still free to enact legislation to either ban or put restrictions on all distribution of alcoholic beverages, whether from within or outside the state.

They could go the route of the 13 states (Alaska, Arizona, Georgia, Louisiana, Nebraska, Nevada, New Hampshire, North Carolina, North Dakota, Rhode Island, South Carolina, Texas, Virginia, and Wyoming) that, along with the District of Columbia, allow direct shipping but with restrictions. Though all stop short of an outright ban, the restrictions vary state by state and can be complex. Some allow shipment of only limited quantities of wine, others leave the rules up to each individual county within the state, and still others limit shipments from individual wineries. These rules also change regularly. Texas, for example, lifted many restrictions on shipments in May 2005 as a result of an earlier lawsuit.

The remaining states allow wine shipments from out of state but only on a reciprocal basis, meaning that shipments are only allowed from states that in turn allow shipments to be made to them.

Luckily, California wineries are on top of the ever-changing situation, and as of 2009 they will generally be able to ship wine for personal consumption to all states except Alabama, Arkansas, Delaware, Iowa, Kentucky, Maryland, Massachusetts, Mississippi, Montana, New Jersey, New Mexico, Oklahoma, Pennsylvania, South Dakota, and Utah. Be sure to ask your favorite winery about the latest laws, because everything might well have changed again by the time this book is published.

International shipping tends to be prohibitively expensive and involves considerable taxes, though some wineries will oblige. If you plan to take wine overseas yourself, be sure to check the liquor import laws of the countries in question. Unfortunately, taking wine on a plane yourself became much harder when airlines banned carriage of liquids in cabin baggage. Packing a few bottles of wine in checked luggage is an option, but make sure the bottles are well protected from the sometimes rough baggage handlers. Most wineries will sell shipping boxes with plenty of padding.

WINE CLUBS

Chances are that you will be told about a winery's wine club while at the tasting room bar. Every winery has a wine club of some sort, and many dream up fancy names to make them sound more exclusive (some actually are exclusive and have long waiting lists to join).

Wine clubs are an important marketing tool for wineries and can be one of the only distribution channels for small boutique wineries. They can also be a great way for visitors to the Wine Country to get discounts on their favorite wines even if they live hundreds of miles away or when the wines are not widely distributed. Make sure you read the rules carefully, however. The small print sometimes commits new members to buying far more than they anticipate.

When new members sign up to a wine club and hand over a credit card number, they often get an on-the-spot discount on wines (this club discount varies, but it's generally 10–20 percent). More importantly for the winery, the new club members have also agreed to buy at least one (sometimes more) wine club shipment in the future before they are able to cancel their membership. Those shipments contain wines that the winery chooses, not the customer, and are subject to often sizable shipping fees that can more than offset the club discount (if you live near the winery, you can usually avoid shipping fees by collecting the wine yourself).

Wine club shipments are usually made once every three or four months, and there's often a choice of different tiers of membership, offering different styles (red or white) or quantities of wine in each shipment. There are also plenty of other "exclusive" membership privileges, from discounts on gifts to free reserve wine tastings, some more worthwhile than others, depending on how far you live from the winery.

OPPORTUNITIES FOR STUDY

Where better to get some professional wine training than in the heart of Wine Country? It's easy to learn a lot just by visiting wineries and talking to the staff, but to really come to grips with wine it might be worth taking one of the short courses at the Culinary Institute of America, just north of St. Helena.

They don't come cheap and last several days, but these courses will quickly get your wine knowledge up to professional levels. The best introductory courses are **Mastering Wine** (level 1), a five-day crash course in everything wine for $1,000, and **Sensory Analysis,** a two-day course for $450 that focuses only on developing your sensory skills to appreciate wine. For a full catalog of these and other courses, together with schedules, contact the Culinary Institute at 707/967-2568 or browse the Professional Wine Studies Program online at www.ciaprochef.com.

A less formal crash course in wine making and wine appreciation is offered through the popular **Wine Boot Camp** program organized by Affairs of the Vine. The one-day courses ($400) take place at one or more wineries in a different wine region each month, with much of the education provided by winemakers and other experts. Students even get to try their hand at making a wine blend. For more information and a calendar, contact Affairs of the Vine at 707/874-1975 or www.winebootcamp.com.

ESSENTIALS

Getting There and Around

BY AIR

If you're focusing your Wine Country travels in Northern California, the biggest airport by far is **San Francisco International** (650/821-8211, www.flysfo.org), known locally as SFO. It is served by 28 airlines at last count, about two-thirds of which are international carriers. All major domestic U.S. airlines serve SFO (United Airlines has by far the largest number of flights), as do a number of low-cost carriers, including Southwest Airlines, ATA, JetBlue, and Virgin America.

The Oakland and San Jose airports get their "international" tag from just a handful of international flights, and most of the airlines serving them are domestic. Flying into either can often be cheaper than going to SFO, but the drawback is that direct flights from major U.S. cities tend to be less common and connections might be necessary.

Oakland International Airport (510/563-3300, www.flyoakland.com) is just across the bay from San Francisco and is served by three of the big domestic airlines (United, American, and Delta) as well as major low-cost carriers (JetBlue, Southwest, and America West) and a handful of charter airlines.

San Jose's **Norman Y. Mineta International Airport** (408/277-4759, www.sjc.org) is served by the six major domestic airlines and low-cost carriers including Southwest and ATA.

Sacramento International Airport is smaller than the three Bay Area airports and is really only an option for those visiting Napa, about a 1.5-hour drive.

In 2007, Horizon Air started service to the tiny **Sonoma County Airport** in Santa Rosa (800/547-9308, www.sonomacountyairport.org) and now offers daily or twice daily flights to and from Seattle, Portland, Los Angeles, and Las Vegas.

If you're beginning your wine country travels in Southern California, you might consider flying into **Los Angeles International Airport** (LAX, 310/646-5252, www.airport-la.com). The current expansion of the **Santa Barbara Airport** (SBA, 805/681-4803, www.flysba.com) will allow the airport to receive more commercial traffic, and San Luis Obispo is slowly adding more flights to its limited and small airport.

BY BUS

Greyhound (800/231-2222, www.greyhound.com) is the most common way of arriving by bus. There are major stops in Santa Maria, downtown Santa Barbara, downtown San Luis Obispo, and Paso Robles. Further north, Greyhound serves the major Bay Area cities of San Francisco, Oakland, and San Jose, plus Santa Rosa in Sonoma.

The bus systems on the Central Coast are well designed and help you move around within a given city. In Santa Barbara, you can ride the length of the waterfront, or the length of State Street, for just 25 cents, on two daily electric shuttle routes (www.sbmtd.gov). The Santa Ynez Valley Transit (805/688-5452, www.syvt.com) is a scheduled mini-bus serving Ballard, Buellton, Los Olivos, Santa Ynez, and Solvang. The San Luis Obispo Regional Transit Authority (805/781-4472, www.slorta.org) covers the entire county.

Local bus service from Santa Rosa on the **Sonoma County Transit** bus network connects to Guerneville, Healdsburg, Glen Ellen, and Sonoma. San Francisco is the best place to head for using Greyhound Lines for connections to Napa via the Vallejo ferry and local **Vine** bus service.

BY CAR

Almost everyone gets around by car in California. With so many people in cars, congestion is a constant problem. In the Wine Country, the roads are smaller but are also often congested during rush hour, and especially on summer weekends when visitors from local cities flock to their favorite wineries.

You can help the traffic flow by making sure you know where you're going and driving at the same clip as other drivers. If you're being tailgated by more than one car on a narrow, winding road, pull over at the nearest turnout or turnoff to let the faster traffic pass. And on two-lane roads with a center turn lane, use that lane both for turning left to avoid holding up traffic behind you and also to merge into traffic when turning left onto that main road.

Car Rentals

Renting a car is easy. All the major car-rental companies are represented at the major airports. It's always best to compare rates of course. If you do rent a car, make certain it includes unlimited mileage.

For current prices and availability contact **Alamo** (800/462-5266, www.alamo.com), **Avis** (800/831-2847, www.avis.com), **Budget** (800/527-0700, www.budget.com), **Dollar** (800/800-3665, www.dollar.com), **Enterprise** (800/736-8222, www.enterprise.com), **Hertz** (800/654-3131, www.hertz.com), and **Thrifty** (800/847-4389, www.thrifty.com). You can also get some good deals and make reservations through major online travel agencies, including **Orbitz** (www.orbitz.com), **Travelocity** (www.travelocity.com), and **Expedia** (www.expedia.com). Check whether there are any discounts from your airline too.

Always check what your own car-insurance

policy, credit cards, or travel insurance will cover before renting a car so you don't buy unnecessary (and often pricey) car, medical, or personal possession insurance at the rental counter. Liability insurance is required by law for all drivers in California, so if you have no car insurance of your own, you'll have to buy it from the rental company. Credit cards will generally not cover it.

BY BIKE

Biking is a potentially fun way of seeing parts of Wine Country but one that few people seem to try, if the lack of bicycles on the roads is anything to go by. Choose your location well, however, and the rewards of experiencing the warm air and all the unique smells of Wine Country are many. Plan badly and you'll be cursing all day long.

The roads in much of Wine Country can make biking more exciting than you'd like.

Small roads tend to be winding and narrow, with the ever-present danger of inattentive (or drunk) drivers failing to see cyclists or give them enough clearance. While accidents seem to be few, close shaves are more common, so be well aware of approaching cars and always cycle in single file as close to the edge of the road as possible.

Make sure you wear a helmet, and don't plan on drinking much. Biking drunk is illegal, and it increases your risk of having an accident, whether from being hit by a car or running off the road down a ravine.

Drinking and strenuous exercise is also a recipe for dehydration and heatstroke. If you do go in the summer, plan on taking a picnic and whiling away the hottest mid- and late-afternoon hours somewhere off the bike. Spring and fall are the best times to venture out on two wheels.

Tips for Travelers

SMOKING

Smokers will find California's environment far from tolerant. Smoking is banned in all bars and restaurants in the state and is usually not allowed in or near public buildings either. That includes many hotels and inns, which either have a property-wide no-smoking policy or will only allow smoking in outdoor areas.

Despite the rather stringent ban, there are a few bars where you might see people light up, probably because the bar owner tacitly approves (and risks a fine). In such cases, offended nonsmokers would do well to keep quiet, because any outsiders complaining may quickly find the wrath of the bar's local patrons bearing down on them.

TIPPING

As is the case in the rest of the nation, tipping is a voluntary but necessary practice in restaurants, bars, taxis, and for services given by valets or hotel concierges. A 15 percent tip is average, though more is normal in this land

where money talks. Most restaurants will automatically add a standard 18 percent gratuity to the bill for parties of more than six or eight people. If that's the case, you have no obligation to add any further tip when signing the credit card slip, even though there will still be a spot for one.

Tipping is definitely not necessary in winery tasting rooms. In fact, you risk offending the generally well-paid staff if you do try to slip them a fiver, however helpful they have been. If you feel a strong urge to return a favor, simply buy a bottle or two of wine.

TRAVELERS WITH DISABILITIES

California is one of the most progressive states in the country when it comes to access for people with disabilities, and its state laws often go beyond the requirements of the federal Americans with Disabilities Act, which requires that all new public buildings must be disabled-accessible and older ones must be retrofitted if readily achievable.

Major wineries that are open to the public without an appointment, together with museums and other sights, all generally have wheelchair access ramps and restrooms for disabled people. Appointment-only wineries often stay appointment-only partly because of the prohibitive cost of meeting the various building and safety codes required for commercial public buildings, including access for disabled people. Small B&Bs and inns often

do not have to comply with the strict laws because their historic buildings cannot easily be made disabled-accessible.

Many wineries are in rural areas, so access for disabled people is always going to be far from universal. One organization that can help people with disabilities plan visits within Northern California is **Access Northern California** (1427 Grant St., Berkeley, 510/524-2026, www.accessnca.com). It has specific information on accommodations and sights with access for the disabled. Also contact local chambers of commerce or visitors centers for more specific information. The Braille Institute (www.brailleinstitute.org) has great programs in the Central Coast; in Santa Barbara and Ventura Counties, contact the local field services coordinator at 805/682-6222, and in San Luis Obispo County phone 805/462-1225. Accessible Journeys (www.disabilitytravel .com) has great pointers and information about traveling with a disability and can put you in touch, through their network of resources, with the right help to fit your needs.

TRAVELING WITH CHILDREN

Most, but not all, winery activities are geared toward adults. Wineries generally allow children onto the premises, but anyone under 21, California's legal minimum drinking age, cannot taste any wines. And wineries without wine tasting tend to be pretty boring places, especially for kids.

If there are children in tow, careful planning can avoid tears of boredom and frustration. Some wineries offer educational tours that can be fun for kids and adults alike. Others have other attractions, ranging from art to historic cars. In all cases double-check that children are welcome because some wineries, such as the Castello di Amorosa castle, that might seem to offer plenty of entertainment for kids have an age limit.

Also worth noting is that a lot of higher-priced B&Bs and resorts do not allow children under a certain age, and some do not allow children at all. The reasons vary—in some cases the policy is to protect precious

---

ETHICAL TRAVEL

There are basic principles that apply no matter where you travel, and wine country is no exception.

- **Minimize your environmental impact:** Travel and camp on durable surfaces, dispose of waste properly, and recycle. Make sure your hotel recycles too.

- **Respect wildlife:** Don't feed animals. Feeding wildlife damages their health, alters natural behaviors, and exposes them to predators and other dangers. Always follow designated trails. Do not disturb animals, plants, or their natural habitats. **Leave what you find:** Take only photographs. Leave only footprints. The impact of one person may seem minimal, but the global effect of removing items from their native place can be decimating.

- **Support the local economy:** Be aware of where your money is going by supporting locally owned businesses. To avoid buying products made from endangered plants or animals, see Know Before You Go at www.cbp.gov for the U.S. Customs list of restricted items.

This copyrighted information has been reprinted with permission from the Leave No Trace Center for Outdoor Ethics. For more information or materials, please visit www.lnt.org or call 303/442-8222.

There is plenty to keep the kids entertained.

antiques, in other cases simply to ensure that the peace and tranquility that guests are paying top dollar for is not shattered by kids being kids. Always check the policy on young guests when booking a room.

WOMEN TRAVELING ALONE

For both males and females, traveling alone has its perks and its downsides. Women traveling by themselves will find a helpful public. The website Journeywoman (www.journeywoman .com) is a site devoted to women traveling solo, and offers some great advice.

Of course, it's always best to use common sense and to listen to your gut reaction if something or someone seems amiss. There have been reported at area clubs and bars cases of dosings (the act of slipping some kind of drug, such as the "date rape" drug, into your drink when you're not looking), so it's always important to be alert and never, ever leave your purse or drink unattended. If there is a problem, ask for help.

SENIOR TRAVELERS

The website Senior Journal (www.seniorjournal .com) offers senior travel tips, suggestions, and even itineraries. The locally based website Silver Years (805/405-3164, www.silveryears .net) also provides more detailed regional information. There are often senior discounts available at sights and events; fewer hotels and restaurants offer senior discounts, but it never hurts to ask.

TRAVELING WITH PETS

Most wineries are not dog-friendly. Dogs are actively discouraged or banned, even in those wineries that have their own resident winery pooch.

Worse still (from the dog's point of view), the hot summer weather makes cars thoroughly uncomfortable places to be even for short periods of time. Dogs should never be left for long periods in a car in the California sun, even with the windows slightly cracked.

If you are traveling with your dog, pet-friendly hotels and restaurants do exist. *The*

Dog Lover's Companion to California by Maria Goodavage is a great resource to help you find them.

MAPS

Beware the cartoonish maps in many of the free magazines that blanket the Wine Country. Many of them are highly inaccurate for anything other than determining the approximate location of wineries and other major sights. Even for that purpose they can sometimes be unreliable, putting wineries on the wrong side of the road, for example, or giving little idea of distances involved. As road maps they should certainly not be relied on. Many small roads are missing from them, and other roads turn out to be dead ends or are misnamed.

The most reliable road maps for planning a trip are published by the veteran map companies. Most of these maps don't have wineries or other sights marked on them but are good for general navigation, especially when used in conjunction with this book or the winery maps published by local wine associations in each region.

The **American Automobile Association** (AAA) publishes a specific *Sonoma and Napa Wine Country* map as well as more detailed road maps for the various wine regions. They are available from your local AAA office and are free for members. Check www.aaa.com for your local office and to order maps online.

Rand McNally also publishes several excellent road maps covering California Wine Country, usually available at bookstores and can also be ordered online at www.rand mcnally.com.

Health and Safety

DRINKING AND DRIVING

Driving (and even cycling) under the influence of alcohol is a serious offense in California. Both state and local police are well aware that visitors to Wine Country might have overindulged, and they will often be on the lookout for erratic driving in popular wine-tasting areas on busy weekends.

The blood alcohol limit for driving in the state is 0.08 percent, a level you can reach very quickly in a tasting room. Most wineries will pour about one ounce of wine per taste, which means that by visiting one winery and tasting (and swallowing) four wines, you will already be well on the way to that limit.

People weighing less than 150 pounds who taste another flight of four wines at another winery in a two-hour period will likely be at their legal limit already. Those over 150 pounds will have a little more leeway, but not much.

Trying to calculate how much can be drunk before reaching the limit is a notoriously inexact science. It depends not only on how much alcohol is consumed but also the person's weight, gender, metabolism, and how much food he or she has eaten over the previous few hours. Drinking a lot of water while tasting might ward off headaches but will do little to lower the blood alcohol level.

The penalties for a DUI conviction are severe, including a fine ranging from $200–7,000 and time in jail, not to mention the potential loss of your drivers license and a big jump in insurance premiums if you are able to get it back. If you are a driver involved in an accident that causes bodily harm while your blood alcohol is over the legal limit, the penalties are even stiffer.

The only way to guarantee you are safe to drive is not to drink at all. Instead, use a designated driver, or if that's not an option, learn to spit wine out after smelling the aromas and swirling it around your mouth. If you really want to experience the lingering aftertaste of a $100 cabernet, then swallow just one wine out of all those you taste. There are usually plenty of spitting containers on tasting room counters. Just double-check that it's not the water jug you're about to empty your wine into.

OUTDOOR SAFETY
Lyme Disease

Potentially the most dangerous animal for outdoor hikers in many parts of California is also one of the smallest. The diminutive deer tick, which thrives in most lowland hills and meadows, can transmit Lyme disease, one of the most common vector-transmitted diseases in the United States.

The good news is that Lyme disease is easily treated with antibiotics if caught early. The bad news is that it can be difficult to detect early, with many of the early symptoms (including fever, aches and pains, headaches, and fatigue) often mistaken for other ailments. If left untreated, Lyme disease can develop into a serious degenerative illness, and the longer it goes untreated the harder it is to cure with antibiotics.

The best protection is to wear long pants and sleeves to avoid picking the ticks up in the first place. Plenty of insect repellent also helps. If you are bitten by a tick and it is still attached, do not try to pull it off with your fingers because the head will likely stay embedded. Remove ticks with tweezers by grasping the tick's head parts as close to your skin as possible and applying slow steady traction. Do not attempt to get ticks out of your skin by burning them or coating them with nail polish remover or petroleum jelly.

Always check for ticks after being outdoors in woodland or grassy meadows and watch for the telltale circular rash that usually appears around tick bites from three days to a month after being bitten. Also be aware that any flu-like symptoms might be a sign of Lyme disease. If in any doubt, see a doctor.

Mountain Lions

Mountain lions, also known as pumas or cougars, do live in many of the hills and forests around urban areas, especially those where deer (their favorite prey) are common, but they are rarely seen and usually stay well away from humans, especially big groups of noisy humans (another reason never to hike alone).

Attacks by mountain lions are extremely rare. In fact, you're more likely to get struck by lightning. Sightings are more common, though still relatively rare. If you do happen across a lion on a hiking trail and it doesn't instinctively run the other way, try to make yourself look as large as possible to scare it, then slowly back away. Mountain lions are big cats—males can weight up to 150 pounds and grow up to eight feet long from head to the tip of the tail—but they'd rather not pick a fight with something their own size. In the rare instance a lion does attack, fight it with whatever comes to hand, like rocks and sticks. It's a strategy that has saved plenty of victims.

One thing you should not do is turn and run—mountain lions can run faster. Dogs should be kept on a leash (it's the law in most wilderness areas) to avoid agitating mountain lions, and also for the well-being of the dog, which would be easy prey. If you see a big cat in the brush next to the trail, do not try to approach it. Remember that you are trespassing on their territory, so if you let them get on with their lives, you'll likely be left alone.

Rattlesnakes

Another animal that can do some damage to humans but is rarely seen is the western diamondback rattlesnake, the most common of the eight varieties of rattler found in California. The snakes are brown with a triangular head and a dark diamond pattern running down their backs. They also have that distinctive rattle that should be a warning to walk the other way if you hear it.

Rattlesnakes live throughout California, preferring hot rocky or grassy areas. When tromping through such areas, always be aware of where you're stepping, and if climbing on rocky ledges, make sure you can see where you're putting your hands. If you are bitten, the venom is rarely fatal but can lead to a few days of discomfort and requires a visit to the local hospital.

Snakes will usually head the other way when they hear anyone approaching, but if you do see one and it refuses to budge, back off and give it a wide berth. Also be especially alert for rattlers in the spring when the snakes are just emerging from hibernation and tend to be groggy, hungry, and mean.

Poison Oak

Poison oak is a deciduous shrub, usually 2–4 feet tall, with glossy leaves resembling those of a real oak tree. The leaves are arranged in clusters of three and are tinged a rusty red color in the late summer and fall. Those leaves and stems contain an oil, similar to that in poison ivy, called urushiol, that causes an allergic skin reaction in an estimated three-quarters of the population, even after only brief exposure.

Even in the winter the bare stems remain just as dangerous to passing skin and can be hard to spot. Even burning a small amount of poison oak on a campfire generates dangerous smoke that, if inhaled, can lead to a potentially fatal inflammation of the lungs.

The plant is common all over California, particularly in shady lowland woods and meadows. You will almost certainly encounter it alongside hiking trails, and it's particularly abundant after wet winters. Learn to identify it and avoid it if at all possible.

Wear long pants and sleeves and wash both clothes and skin as soon as possible if you even *think* you have been in contact with poison oak. Rashes can take a few days to appear, but once they do there's little you can do to get rid of them, and they'll likely spread as your body's immune system battles to neutralize the poisons and becomes even more sensitized in the process. The oil stays active for months, sometimes years, on surfaces like hiking boots and clothes (and dogs) and can rub off on skin at any time and cause a rash, so wash these too if you think they have been contaminated. Any regular laundry detergent will remove the oil.

If you do get a rash, do not scratch it, and make sure it is covered to prevent infection. Contrary to popular belief, the ooze from the rashes cannot spread the toxins, but it can attract bacteria that will further irritate the skin. Mild rashes will usually go away in a few days. The more seriously afflicted could be driven mad for many weeks by a growing rash, and some might require treatment with anti-inflammatory steroids, though the application of readily available hydrocortisone cream is the usual treatment.

Some specialized cleansing products that will neutralize the toxic oils are worth using if you're highly allergic. They are sold under the Tecnu brand name and are available at most pharmacies.

Dehydration and Heatstroke

Dehydration is a perennial enemy in Wine Country, whether from tasting too much wine or from any sort of exertion in the heat. Be aware that many trails might start off in cool, damp woods but will often climb up to scrubland with little shade and often searing heat in the summer. Sunscreen, sunglasses, and a hat are mandatory in California during the summer. Luckily, most large wineries sell baseball caps should your bare head be overheating.

Drink plenty of water, especially if hiking but even when frolicking on or in the water on a hot day. For serious hiking in hot weather, at least a half-quart of water per hour is recommended (in small doses, not all at once). eatstroke, a potentially fatal condition created when the body is no longer able to cool itself sufficiently, causing symptoms including headache, confusion, and muscle cramps.

The water you do drink should always come from a bottle or a tap. Most of California's rivers and lakes contain parasites and bacteria that, although not fatal, can play havoc with digestive systems for several days and might require treatment. If camping at a primitive site near a stream or lake, consider taking a water filter so you don't have to carry all your water in with you.

WATER SAFETY

On the water, take the usual water-safety precautions. Don't jump in unless you know

HEALTH AND SAFETY **619**

what's under the water. Always wear a life-jacket when in a boat, and avoid doing anything on or in the water when you've had too much to drink.

Remember that the ocean is a force greater than yourself, and there are occasional riptides and undercurrents even along the most serene beaches. Signs are posted when weather conditions warrant it. It's always best to swim with a buddy, or at the very least have someone waiting on shore for you.

When boating on the ocean, be aware that many tankers and cargo ships move briskly through the waters. They have the right of way. They are huge, but they move fast, over 20 knots. So if you see a tanker in the water, know they probably can't see you—and even if they can, it's impossible for them to change course; they'll be near you faster than you can imagine. Never try and outrun one of them.

Also be on the lookout for dive flags. Divers are required to post a flag that sits atop a buoy; it is a red block with a white line through it. If you see one, avoid the area, as you could inadvertently cut an oxygen supply line. Also keep in mind that in the water, boats under sail have the right of way over motorboats.

EARTHQUAKES

Should a temblor occur while you are visiting, remain calm and follow these instructions.

If you are inside, take cover by getting under a sturdy table or other piece of furniture, and wait until the shaking stops. If there isn't a table or desk near you, cover your face and head with your arms and crouch in an inside corner of the building where the building supports are the greatest (freestanding walls fall easily). Stay away from glass, windows, outside doors and walls, and anything that could fall, such as light fixtures or furniture. Use a doorway for shelter only if it is in close proximity to you and you know that it's a strongly supported, load-bearing doorway. Stay inside until the shaking stops and it's safe to go outside. Research has shown that most injuries occur when people inside buildings attempt to move to a different location inside the building or try to leave altogether. Be aware that the electricity may go out or the sprinkler systems or fire alarms may turn on. Do not use the elevators!

If you are outside, stay there, move away from buildings, streetlights, and utility wires, and wait until the shaking stops. The greatest danger exists directly outside of buildings. Many of the 120 fatalities from the 1933 Long Beach earthquake occurred when people ran outside, only to be killed by falling debris from collapsing walls. Ground movement during an earthquake is seldom the direct cause of death or injury.

If you're driving, stop as quickly as safety permits and stay in the vehicle. Avoid stopping near or under buildings, trees, overpasses, and utility wires. Proceed cautiously once the earthquake has stopped. Avoid roads, bridges, or ramps that might have been damaged by the earthquake.

RESOURCES

Glossary

acetic acid All wines contain a minuscule amount of acetic acid (vinegar), but bad wine will have enough (over about 0.1 percent) to actually start smelling of vinegar – not a good thing.

acid/acidity The natural acids (citric, malic, tartaric, and lactic) in a wine create a tartness that is supposed to act as a counterpoint to sugary sweetness, balancing the wine.

aftertaste The flavors that linger on your palate after swallowing the wine. The longer the aftertaste, the better – sometimes you can still taste wines almost a minute after swallowing.

aging The process of storing a wine in barrels or bottles for a few months to many decades so it develops character and more desirable flavors. White wines tend to turn from a greenish hue in young wines to a yellowish caste/tone to a gold/amber color as they age. Reds usually have a purple tone when young, turning to a deep red (bordeaux wines and cabernet, for example) or a brick red color (burgundy wines and pinot noir, for example), detectable at the surface edge in a wineglass as they age.

alcohol The colorless and flavorless chemical created as a byproduct of fermentation that gets you drunk but also acts as a preservative for the wine. The higher the sugar content of the grape when picked, the higher the alcohol content of the wine. Californian red wines tend to have alcohol content of over 13 percent, sometimes as high as 16 percent in the case of some zinfandels.

angular Describes a tart wine with a sharp edge to its taste. The opposite of a round, soft, or supple wine.

appellation or AVA The specific area a wine comes from. Technically, appellation is a term simply to describe a geographic area. To be classified as an American Viticultural Area, or AVA, by the federal Bureau of Alcohol, Tobacco, and Firearms (ATF), an area must be shown to have unique soil, climate, or other growing conditions that will distinguish its wines from those grown in other areas. When an AVA, such as Napa Valley or Carneros, is named on the label, at least 85 percent of the grapes must have come from there (100 percent in Washington and Oregon). There can also be AVAs within AVAs. The Napa Valley, for example, is a single AVA that contains 13 other AVAs, commonly referred to as subappellations.

approachable An approachable wine is easy to enjoy and generally made to be drunk without aging.

aroma The smell of a wine that comes from the fruit or smells like fruit. As wine ages, some of the fruit-related smells dwindle and are replaced by more complex smells from chemicals created during the aging process, referred to as the bouquet.

aromatic Describes wines that have a strong flowery or spicy character.

astringent The rough, puckery taste that most people describe as sour and that often comes from a high tannin content. Astringent wines normally mellow with age.

austere Slightly hard and acidic wines that seem to lack depth of flavor. Such wines may soften a bit with age and develop more subtle complexity than fuller wines. Austere wines are often from cool growing regions, especially mountain areas.

Bacchus The Roman god of wine and a name sometimes seen in jokey marketing material.

balance A balanced wine is what winemakers strive to make, one in which no flavor or aroma overpowers another. Acid balances the sweetness, fruit against oak and tannin. You'll know a balanced wine when you taste one.

barrel A wooden vessel used to store wine before it is bottled, made of oak and charred (toasted) on the inside to impart specific flavors and color to the wine. On any winery tour you'll likely pass racks of oak barrels (sometimes called *barriques*) that are usually the standard size of 59 gallons or about 225 liters. American oak barrels cost more than $200 new. Highly prized French oak barrels cost more than $500 each. Barrels are usually used and reused for several vintages, then end up as planters or are discarded.

barrel fermenting The fermentation of wine in barrels to impart specific flavors and texture. It often gives a richer flavor to white wines, though is sometimes overused and will make a wine "over-oaked." In red wines, barrel fermenting will impart more tannins to the wine so it can age for longer. The increasingly common alternative is to age wines in stainless steel or concrete vats.

big Wine with a big, robust, and full-bodied character, usually because of high alcohol content. Dry Creek Valley zinfandel is an example of a "big" wine.

bitter One of the four basic tastes that your taste buds can detect. Some wines are supposed to have slight bitterness, but too much is a bad thing. It comes from unripe grapes or from too many stems being crushed with the grapes (that's why many wineries destem grapes first).

blanc de blancs Sparkling wine or champagne made purely from white grapes like chardonnay. Other white sparklers might contain the juice from the dark-skinned pinot noir grape and are called blanc de noirs.

blending The mixing of different types of wine (cabernet, merlot, or syrah, for example) or of wines made from the same grape but from different vineyards. Blending different wines is part of the winemaker's art and is done to create a wine of particular character, much like different shades of paint are blended to create the desired tone.

body How heavy the wine feels in your mouth, a perception created by the alcohol, glycerin, and sugar content of a wine. An Alexander Valley cabernet sauvignon is a full-bodied wine, while a Santa Cruz chardonnay is lighter bodied.

Bordeaux blend A wine (usually red) made from a blend of some or all of the main grape varietals used to make wine in the French region of Bordeaux – cabernet sauvignon, merlot, cabernet franc, malbec, petit verdot, and carmenère in the case of red wine; sauvignon blanc, semillon, and muscadelle in the case of white. See also *meritage*.

botrytis A gray fungus (also known at noble rot) that attacks grapes in humid conditions, shriveling them up like raisins and concentrating the sugar and acid content. Wines made from affected grapes are sweet and complex, often sold as dessert wines.

bouquet Often confused with the aroma, the bouquet refers specifically to the scent in a wine that comes from the aging process in either the barrel or bottle, rather than from the fruit.

brawny Term used mainly to describe young red wines (especially in California) with high alcohol and tannin levels.

briary An aggressive, prickly taste in young wines, sometimes described as peppery.

brix A measure of the sugar content in a grape, used to determine when grapes should be harvested. The final alcohol content of a wine is often related to the brix reading of the grapes when harvested.

brut Refers to a dry (but not the driest) champagne or sparkling wine with less than 1.5 percent residual sugar.

burgundy A catch-all term to describe red and white wine from the Burgundy region in France. Real red burgundies are usually pinot noir. Cheap Californian burgundies are usually misusing the term for totally unrelated wine.

buttery An obvious taste often found in good white wines, particularly Californian chardonnay.

cava A sparkling wine from Spain made in a similar style to champagne but using different grapes.

Champagne A region in northern France best known for production of sparkling wine by a very specific method, known as the *méthode champenoise*, using chardonnay, pinot noir, and pinot meunier. Since 2006, American wineries are no longer allowed to call sparkling wines made this way "champagne."

chaptalization The addition of sugar to wine before or during fermentation to increase the final alcohol content. It is legal in France, where cooler weather often means grapes do not have enough sugar when harvested, but not legal (and not necessary) in California.

charmat method The process of making cheaper sparkling wines by carrying out the secondary fermentation (the one that creates the bubbles) in large steel vats under pressure rather than in the bottle like the more expensive *méthode champenoise* used to make fine champagnes.

chewy Usually used to describe powerful tannins in red wines like cabernet that give it an almost viscous mouthfeel, making you almost want to chew it before swallowing.

citrus An aroma and flavor reminiscent of citrus fruits, especially grapefruit, in many white wines, particularly those from cooler growing regions like Carneros and the Russian River Valley.

claret An old English term used to describe red wines from Bordeaux. In France, "clairet" is a particular bordeaux that is produced like red wine, but the wine must stay in contact with the skins for the first 24 hours during its making.

clone A genetic variation of a grapevine. In a wine and vineyard context, usually the specific genetic type of vine picked to match the local growing conditions or the desired style of wine.

cloudy Used to describe a wine that is a little hazy when viewed through the glass rather than crystal clear. Except in some rare occasions, a cloudy wine is not a good thing and might also have an unpleasant smell.

complex The ultimate flattery for winemakers is to call their wines complex. Everything from the aroma to the long aftertaste is in balance and harmony.

cooked Leave wine in a hot car for a day, open it, and it will probably taste odd. It has been cooked (see *maderized*).

cooperage All the containers a winery uses to store and age wine, including barrels, vats, and tanks. They are made by coopers.

corked The most common fault of restaurant wine, it is the brief taste or smell of wet cardboard in a wine that is caused by bacteria in a contaminated cork interacting with chemicals in the wine. It can often be very subtle, so many people might not realize a wine is corked, and it is harmless to drink.

creamy The silky taste and texture of a white wine that has undergone malolactic fermentation. Often accompanied by the faintest smell of creamy foods like crème brûlée.

crisp A definite but not undesirable tartness and acidity usually used to describe white wines and often accompanied by the aroma of citrus fruits. White wines from cool climates like Carneros are often crisp.

crush Literally the crushing of the grape skins to release the juice and start the fermentation process. Crush is the term also used to describe the process of harvesting and transporting the grapes of a particular year prior to making the wine.

cuvée A French term to describe the blend of wines from different grapes and different years that is used to make champagne and sparkling wines.

decanting The slow and careful pouring of aged red wine into a broad, shallow glass container to ensure the sediment from aging stays in the bottle and to then allow the wine to breathe, or start to release its aromas, before drinking.

demi-sec A slightly sweet sparkling wine

or champagne containing 3.5–5 percent residual sugar.

dessert wine A sweet red or white wine usually drunk in small amounts with dessert. The sweetness of desserts would mask the much smaller amount of sugar in a normal wine and make it taste bitter or acidic. Sweet dessert wines are often made from late-harvest grapes, picked when they are riper and their sugar content is higher. The botrytis fungus can also be used to make these sweeter wines.

dry Describes a red or white wine that has been fermented until less than 0.2 percent of the natural sugars remain. Although a dry wine will not taste sweet, it might still taste fruity.

dumb My favorite wine term — it means, literally, a wine with nothing to say. Flavors and aroma might have been muted by overchilling a white wine or simply because a red wine is at a certain stage of aging when it is in between youthfulness and adulthood (often when about 5–6 years old).

earthy Fine pinot noir is always earthy, possessing an aroma and/or flavor that could have come straight from the ground. Think of what a handful of damp soil smells like, and that's the earthiness. Different soil smells a different way, and the pros can often detect the type of soil or region a wine comes from simply by recognizing the smell of that earth. Or so they say. A lot of wines have the potential to be earthy, but other aromas and flavors often mask the distinctive smell.

elegant How to praise a well-balanced and graceful wine. The opposite would be "rustic."

enology The science and study of wine making, often spelled *oenology* outside the United States. An *oenophile* is someone who loves wine.

estate bottled Refers to wine made from vineyards that are both owned by the winery and in the same appellation or AVA as the winery. In addition, the entire wine-making process from fermentation to bottling has to occur at that winery. Nonestate wines are made from grapes bought from other growers or grown in another appellation.

fat Describes the texture of a full-bodied wine with lots of fruit. A full-bodied wine without enough acidity to balance the fruit is often called flabby.

fermentation The process that turns grape juice into wine. A biochemical process in yeast cells converts the sugar in grape juice into alcohol and carbon dioxide. Usually that gas is simply allowed to escape, but in the secondary fermentation process used to make sparkling wines it is retained in the wine under pressure and released as the bubbles when a bottle is opened.

filtering The easy way to remove particles from a wine to ensure it is clear before being bottled. Pumping wine through filters can, however, damage the flavor of a wine. Fining is a more laborious but better way to clarify wine.

fining The process of adding a natural, non-reactive substance like gelatin or crushed eggshell to a tank of wine to slowly remove suspended particles as it falls to the bottom. It takes longer than simple filtering.

finish Also sometimes called the aftertaste, this is the lingering impression of the wine on your palate after swallowing. It might be long or short (or absent), acidic or sweet. Generally, a longer finish denotes a better wine.

firm A wine that has some acidic astringency, much like firm unripe fruit. Like unripe fruit, a firm wine is usually young and will ripen with age, mellowing its acidity. But sometimes it won't.

flat Wines with too little acidity are said to be flat and uninteresting.

flowery A white wine that has an aroma reminiscent of flowers.

forward A forward wine is one that has all its best aromas and flavors right up front and screams "drink me now." You'll usually hear the term *fruit forward* used to describe cheap red wines in which the fruity flavors overpower all others (if there are even others present).

fruity A generic term used to describe whatever aroma and flavor comes from the grape itself. Strangely enough, wine does not usually smell of the one fruit used to make it but of everything from grapefruit to honeydew melon, depending on the type of grape and how the wine was made. Fruity wines are not necessarily sweet wines.

funky Believe it or not, this is a real wine-tasting term used to describe a certain unidentifiable yeasty aroma that some wines have. You'll have to be a professional wine critic to recognize the smell. Most people simply call any unidentifiable smell or taste "funky." Just don't say it in front of a winemaker.

grassy Sauvignon blanc is often described as grassy. Imagine the smell of freshly cut grass. Too much grassiness is not a good trait.

green A term often applied to sauvignon blanc. It describes the slightly leafy taste of a wine made with underripe fruit.

hollow When there's really nothing between the first initial taste of a wine and the aftertaste. Something's missing in the middle for any number of reasons.

horizontal tasting No, not drinking wine while lying down, but tasting the same type of wine from the same year but from different wineries. It's fun to line up a horizontal tasting of, say, cabernets from different Napa Valley appellations to learn how different growing conditions affect wine.

hot You'll know a hot wine when the back of your throat burns after swallowing, as though you just downed a shot of vodka. It's caused by too much alcohol in the wine and not enough of everything else. This is a normal character of fortified wines like port and sherry but a no-no in regular wines like cabernet sauvignon. Cheap, high-alcohol zinfandels are often hot.

jammy Word most often used to describe Californian zinfandel. Imagine the taste of a spoonful of blackberry jam.

late harvest Picking grapes as late as possible so their sugar content is as high as possible to make a sweeter wine, usually a dessert wine.

lean More body would be good, sort of thin in the mouth, often too much astringency; sometimes a compliment for certain styles.

lees The leftover yeast and other crud that falls to the bottom of barrels or fermentation tanks or is removed by fining. It is also sometimes called mud. Makers of white and sparkling wines sometimes leave it in the bottle so it can impart a yeasty, toasty flavor and smell to aged wines. That technique is called fermenting wine *sur lies.*

legs Spot the novice wine taster cracking jokes about "great legs." Swirl wine around the glass, then stop and watch clear rivulets cling to the side of the glass. They are the legs, and how fat or long they are actually has nothing to do with the quality of the wine. Instead they have everything to do with how much alcohol and glycerin there is in the wine, what the temperature is, and even how clean the glass is.

length Pretty much the same as finish, namely how long the flavors and aromas of a wine last on the back of your throat after swallowing; the longer, the better.

maderized What might happen to your wine if you leave it in a hot car for too long. It is a distinctive brown color and smell caused by exposure of wine to excessive heat and oxygen. Also sometimes called "oxidized." Even if you haven't smelled the Portuguese fortified wine madeira, you'll know when a wine has maderized. It doesn't smell like wine anymore.

malolactic fermentation A secondary chemical process (not technical fermentation at all) that nearly all red wines undergo and white wines are sometimes put through to give them a smoother, less acidic flavor (often described as creamy or buttery). It converts the harsh-tasting malic acid that naturally occurs in wine into the softer lactic acid plus carbon dioxide. Wineries often use the process to make a more popular style of easy-drinking chardonnay, though sometimes they overdo it and create a wine that lacks any sort of acidity at all and is just flat.

meritage Californian wines have to contain at least 75 percent of one grape varietal to be labeled as such, but some of the best red wines are blends of some of the five varietals used in bordeaux wine with no grape in the majority. Californian winemakers, not wanting to use the term *bordeaux blend,* instead came up with a new term to describe blended red wines: meritage. It remains an uncommon term, however, and most wineries instead come up with their own proprietary names for their blends.

mouthfeel How a wine feels rather than tastes in your mouth. Use any description you want. Ones I use too much include "velvety" and "soft."

musty A flaw that makes a wine smell like your grandmother's dank old attic. It is caused by mold getting into the wine sometime during the wine-making or bottling process.

nonvintage Most wines are made with grapes harvested in a single year (vintage). Nonvintage wines are made by blending wines made in different years, and they have no year on their label. Some cheap red wines are nonvintage and made by using up surplus wine from different years. The best champagnes are also nonvintage so the winemakers can make sure the wine is of consistent high quality every year.

nose The most important tool for wine tasting, but in most cases used to describe the overall smell of a wine, a combination of the aroma and bouquet.

oaky The taste or smell of freshly sawn oak, toast, or vanilla that comes from aging wine in oak barrels that have usually been charred, or toasted, on the inside. A hint of oakiness in red wines is considered a good thing and is a matter of taste in white wines. Oak aromas and flavors should never overpower the fruit in a wine, as they do in some "over-oaked" chardonnays. There's an entire vocabulary used to describe oak smells and tastes, all of which depend on factors ranging from where the oak tree was grown to the size of the wood's grain.

open up/opening up Some bottled cellar-aged red wines possess the peculiarity that, when the cork is first pulled and the wine poured, the full flavors do not immediately make an appearance. However, after the passage of several minutes in an open glass goblet, the wine develops unsuspected flavor characteristics that can verge on the sublime. This phenomenon is referred to as "opening up." These flavors can disappear just as fast in just 30 minutes, leaving a subsequent impression of a flat, stale, over-the-hill, or mediocre wine.

overripe A grape precondition necessary for making certain styles of Californian zinfandel wines. Left on the vine to dry in the sun, certain grape varietals will develop the desirable raisiny character and concentrated sugar necessary for making specialty wines such as the Hungarian tokay.

oxidized As soon as a bottle of wine is opened, it is exposed to the oxygen in the air and starts to oxidize, usually a good thing for an hour or two. If it has been exposed to air for too long, however, either due to a leaky cork during storage or from being left open on a kitchen counter for a week, it will start to smell like cheap sherry and turn brown. At that point it is oxidized. With excessive heat as well it will become maderized.

peppery A term that usually goes hand-in-hand with *spicy* to describe the slightly pungent quality of wines like gewürztraminer and some styles of syrah.

phylloxera A small aphid-like insect that attacks the roots of vines and slowly kills them by preventing the plant from absorbing water and nutrients. It wiped out many vineyards in Europe in the late 1800s but is actually native to the United States, where it has periodically ravaged California vines, particularly in the early 1900s. Most vines are now grafted onto resistant rootstock, though some are not, and limited outbreaks still periodically occur.

Pierce's disease A virus that infects grapevines and kills them in 1-5 years. It is spread by a leafhopper-type insect called the glassy-winged sharpshooter. Though the disease is not yet endemic in Northern California's vineyards, authorities are worried it could soon be and have imposed strict plant quarantine laws to prevent its spread.

plump Almost a fat wine but not quite.

pomace The mashed-up residue of skin, seeds, stems, and pulp left after grapes are pressed to release the juice. In California it's often used as fertilizer. In Italy they distill it to make grappa.

racking A traditional method of wine

clarification that involves transferring wine from one barrel to another to leave sediment and other deposits behind.

reserve wine The term *reserve wine* actually means nothing in California thanks to the total lack of official definition. In general, a reserve wine is made from the best grapes (they are reserved specially) and often aged for longer to create a higher quality wine than a winery's normal offerings. In practice the term is often as much about marketing as good wine. Some wineries give their best-of-the-best wines other labels like "special selection."

residual sugar The percentage, by weight or volume, of the unfermented grape sugar that remains in wine when it is bottled. The driest wines have less than 0.5 percent residual sugar, though many have slightly more to give them a fuller flavor.

rootstock The roots of a grapevine, which often come from a different species than the leaves. Many vines are a combination of two different plants. The stems and leaves might come from one, and they are grafted, or grown onto, roots from another chosen either for its suitability for certain growing conditions or resistance to disease.

rough If a wine feels like it's taking the lining off your throat with its tannins, it's described as rough. Some rough wines smooth and mellow with age.

Rutherford dust A slightly mineral flavor said to be present in some of the classic cabernets grown in the Rutherford appellation of Napa Valley.

sediment The small quantity of particulate matter often found at the bottom of well-aged red wines, generated during the aging process. Sediment includes a lot of the phenols that give wine its color, so as a wine gets really old the color literally starts dropping out of it. Sediment is harmless but best left in the bottle for presentation's sake.

soft A wine that has low acid or tannin content that has little impact on your taste buds.

sommelier The person responsible for the wine cellar, wine service, and wine list in a restaurant. If you have no clue which wine to order, ask to speak to the sommelier, and he or she can usually help.

sour Almost a synonym for acidic. Implies the presence of acetic acid plus excess acid component. (It is also one of the four basic taste sensations detected by the human tongue.)

spicy Almost a synonym for peppery, but it implies a more nuanced flavor suggesting delicate Indian spices rather than those that get up your nose.

supple A red wine with a mouthfeel that lies somewhere between lean and fat; usually an easy drinker.

tannin The reason many people don't like red wines. Tannin is a naturally occurring chemical (a phenol) in grape skins, seeds, and stems as well as the wood of barrels. It gives red wines their backbone, helps preserve them, and has an astringent taste. Young wines, particularly those meant for aging, can be highly tannic but will mellow and soften with age. Other overly tannic wines taste rough or harsh and might never mellow. White wines generally contain very little tannin.

tartaric acid If you ever see what looks like small shards of glass in a bottle of white wine, they are probably crystals of tartaric acid, a harmless acid that is in all white wines and can crystallize under certain conditions.

terroir A French term for all the environmental characteristics of a vineyard, including every conceivable nuance of the soils, climate, and geography. The *terroir* is said to give the grapes grown there a unique flavor profile, and the best wine experts in the world can identify (allegedly) the exact vineyard that the grapes in a wine came from.

tobacco A common description of a flavor often found in cabernet sauvignon that refers to the smell of fresh tobacco leaves. *Cigar box* is a common term often used in its place. Like all those flavor descriptions, it's easier to identify if you have actually experienced the smell firsthand by smelling and smoking a cigar.

ullage The small gap between the wine in the bottle and the cork. It should be almost nonexistent and is formed by the evaporation of wine through the cork or cork leakage. If the ullage gets too big, it will contain enough oxygen to start oxidizing the wine.

vanilla A desirable aroma and taste component of many red wines that comes from the compound vanillin in oak barrels. Newer barrels have more vanillin than older barrels. Smell a bottle of vanilla essence used in cooking to help identify the subtle equivalent in a wine.

varietal A wine made from a particular type of grape, such as pinot noir, chardonnay, cabernet sauvignon, and so on, that shows the distinct characteristics of that type of grape. A varietal wine must contain more than 75 percent of the grape variety identified on the label. Blended wines made from more than one type of grape, such as many European wines identified more by their region than the grape (bordeaux and chianti, for example), are not varietal wines.

vertical tasting Tasting a number of different vintages of one varietal of wine from the same winery, starting from the youngest and working to the oldest. Vertical tasting can help identify the best years for a particular wine and show how it changes as it ages.

vineyard-designate Describes a wine that is made using grapes from a single, named vineyard only. These wines are usually more expensive and higher quality than those made with grapes from multiple vineyards.

vintage The year grapes are harvested, which is the year on the bottle label. Making the wine and bottling it often takes several more years, so a 2003 wine might not be released until 2005 or beyond.

Vitis vinifera The main grapevine species behind all the great wines of the world, and one that is often grafted onto rootstock from other *Vitis* species. All the major varietal grapes are members of the *Vitis vinifera* species, including chardonnay, cabernet sauvignon, pinot noir, sauvignon blanc, and so on.

yeast Single-celled fungi that use enzymes to turn the natural sugars in grape juice into alcohol and carbon dioxide gas (and energy for themselves) through a biochemical process called fermentation. Different wild and genetically modified yeasts are used by winemakers, each performing differently and imparting a slightly different flavor to the wine. Wild yeasts often live naturally on grape skins, and winemakers will simply rely on them. A few wild yeasts can, however, give an undesirable yeasty odor to wines.

Suggested Reading

CUISINE

Bernstein, Sondra. *The Girl & the Fig Cookbook.* New York: Simon & Schuster, 2004. Simple recipes that reflect the culinary fun to be had in the Sonoma restaurant, from liquid meals of martinis through to full French-inspired bistro meals, not all requiring the trademark figs.

Brown, Carrie, and John Werner. *The Jimtown Store Cookbook.* New York: HarperCollins, 2002. The Jimtown Store is the little store that could, hidden away in the heart of the Alexander Valley but still managing to compile a no-nonsense collection of classically stylish yet simple Wine Country recipes that cross all culinary borders.

Chiarello, Michael, and Penelope Wisner. *The Tra Vigne Cookbook: Seasons in the California Wine Country.* San Francisco: Chronicle Books, 1999. The landmark St. Helena Italian restaurant is beautiful to look at and so is this book, though some of the recipes might have you out in the woods hunting for a particular wild mushroom that happens to be in season.

Fisher, M. F. K. *The Art of Eating,* 5th edition. New York: Wiley, 2004. One of the Sonoma and Napa Valleys' most famous writers, who ended up living in Glen Ellen, Fisher was also one of the best-known food writers in the United States in her later years. This compilation of five of her books is a collection of autobiographical information and musings on food preparation, consumption, and nutrition. She was described by John Updike as "the poet of appetites."

Jordan, Michele Anna, and Faith Echtermeyer. *The New Cook's Tour of Sonoma: 150 Recipes and the Best of the Region's Food and Wine*. Seattle: Sasquatch Books, 2000. A sort of greatest hits of Wine Country cooking, with recipes from all over Northern California and profiles of the people behind the famous produce of the region that defines the cuisine.

Keller, Thomas. *Bouchon*. New York: Artisan Press, 2004. If you can't afford to eat at French Laundry or would rather spend $200 on a case of wine, then buy this giant cookbook from the little bistro opened by the same owners just down the street in Yountville and learn how to make some simple yet sophisticated bistro-style food to go with your new wine purchase.

Pawlcyn, Cindy. *Mustards Grill Napa Valley Cookbook*. Berkeley, CA: Ten Speed Press, 2001. One of the more digestible Wine Country cookbooks from this famous Yountville restaurant, with plenty of relatively simple recipes based on hearty American fare with twists of sophistication. This is the restaurant credited with starting the Wine Country food scene.

Sone, Hiro, and Lissa Doumani. *Terra: Cooking from the Heart of Napa Valley*. Berkeley, CA: Ten Speed Press, 2001. This cookbook, from one of St. Helena's best restaurants, contains often sophisticated and tricky recipes drawing on French, Italian, and Japanese cuisine, but it helps makes their preparation as simple as possible with plenty of handy kitchen tips.

WINE REFERENCE

Kolpan, Steven, Brian Smith, and Michael Weiss. *Exploring Wine: The Culinary Institute of America's Guide to Wines of the World*, 2nd edition. New York: Wiley, 2001. This giant tome is a crash course in wine making, wine appreciation, and the wines of the world, with the added authority of being from the Culinary Institute of America, which offers some of the most highly regarded wine and food education courses in the country. That probably explains the unbelievably comprehensive chapter on pairing food and wine that, like many chapters, tends to read more like a textbook.

Kramer, Matt. *Matt Kramer's New California Wine*. Philadelphia: Running Press, 2004. Opinionated food and wine writer Kramer explains what has shaped and continues to shape the modern Californian wine industry with plenty of facts and information about key wineries and wines from every California wine-making region, including Napa and Sonoma. A vital book for California wine enthusiasts.

MacNeil, Karen. *The Wine Bible*. New York: Workman Publishing, 2001. A book to be found on many winery office desks, not least because MacNeil and her husband are Napa Valley winemakers themselves. It has an altogether more chatty, approachable style than the CIA guide and contains information on just about every wine and wine-related term you will come across, although it sometimes lacks depth.

Pinney, Thomas. *A History of Wine in America from Prohibition to the Present*. Berkeley, CA: University of California Press, 2005. A followup to Pinney's out-of-print volume covering pre-Prohibition history, this exhaustive tome details the characters, trends, and policies that shaped both the West and East Coast wine industries from the 1930s to the turn of the century.

Robinson, Jancis. *The Oxford Companion to Wine,* 3rd edition. Berkeley, CA: University of California Press, 2006. A massive tome that is widely regarded as the most exhaustive and accurate encyclopedia of everything you ever wanted to know about wine, from a well-known British wine writer and master of wine.

Sullivan, Charles. *A Companion to California Wine: An Encyclopedia of Wine and Winemaking from the Mission Period to the Present.* Berkeley, CA: University of California Press, 1998. Learn just about everything there is to know about California's wine industry, from its history to key facts and figures, in this fascinating reference book.

Internet Resources

All the following Internet resources are either totally free or at least have some useful information that is free. They supplement the more specific regional Internet resources listed in each destination chapter. Most major magazines are not included in this list because they operate subscription-based websites.

Vines.org
www.vines.org
A free if slightly clunky-looking site that is a giant database of all things wine. Its encyclopedic format is not ideal for browsing, but it will likely have an answer to any specific question you can throw at it.

Vinography
www.vinography.com
An entertaining and sometimes brutally honest blog from a well-informed San Francisco wine enthusiast.

Wine Business Online
www.winebusiness.com
All the latest industry news, events, jobs, and other business-related wine information for industry insiders.

Winefiles
www.winefiles.org
An authoritative, searchable database of wine, wine making, wine history, and grape growing from the Sonoma County Wine Library.

The Wine Institute
www.wineinstitute.org
The main lobbying organization for the national wine industry, with all the background you could want on wine-related laws, regulations, and statistics.

Cervin It Straight
www.cervinitstraight.com
This book's co-author covers the wine country and beyond, offering his top picks for places to dine, where to stay, and suggestions for some of the best wines, beer, and spirits in the area.

Index

List of Maps

Acknowledgments

PHILIP GOLDSMITH

You've never heard gossip like the gossip in the Wine Country. That's one secret I learned while visiting hundreds of wineries, tasting hundreds of wines, and listening to entertaining stories from the folks that make, pour, or sell the stuff.

Those folks come from a tight-knit community of growers, winemakers, vineyard workers, and a cast of thousands working in tasting rooms and behind the scenes (winery dogs and cats included), who all seem to have a tale, a tip, some advice, or some gossip for this hapless writer with wine-stained teeth and a funny accent.

I'm grateful to all of the hundreds of people I met along the way who helped me tap into the sprawling Wine Country grapevine and taught me more than I ever thought I'd know about wine. In particular, Miryam Areas, Kate Jones, Michael Coates, and Monty Sander all introduced me to some fascinating wine-industry movers and shakers in Sonoma and Napa, and at the Culinary Institute of America John Buechsenstein tried his best to refine my belligerent palate.

I appreciate the time given by all my interviewees, including Steve Ledson, Bruce Cohn, Jeff Bundschu, Peter Marks, Daryl Sattui, and especially Bob Benziger, who redefined the term "Wine Country mover and shaker" with a white-knuckle ride through the Benziger vineyards in a golf cart, during which I miraculously managed to keep some wine in my glass.

Thanks also to the patient folks in Avalon's editorial, cartography, graphics, and marketing departments, who must have thought I was slumped in a wine-induced stupor as deadlines came and went without a word from me.

Closer to home, Nicole Phillips patiently listened to my frustrations, shared my dreams, endured my frantic all-night writing sessions, smiled gamely through endless winery visits, and managed to develop a wine palate more finely tuned than mine will ever be.

I should also mention the entertaining British wine critics, including Hugh Johnson, Jancis Robinson, and Malcolm Gluck, who helped pique my interest in wine decades ago in my home country. Their uniquely British combination of skepticism, humor, and bluntness helped demystify a subject that too many people still find intimidating. I hope their columns and books inspire many more people to explore the world of wine, and I hope my book encourages novices to explore California's colorful Wine Country.

MICHAEL CERVIN

Getting to write about California's best wine destinations is a treat, and the opportunity to support the state I grew up in and love dearly is really a dream come true. My hope is that the information from this book will enable you to have a terrific experience as you visit California's wineries.

But no writer is an island and thanks are in order to several key people for their help and support. First off, thanks to my editor, Kevin McLain, for his complete professionalism and diligence during the writing process. Thanks also to Ranee Ruble of Paper Moon Creative, who has been an invaluable resource, and to the California Association of Bed and Breakfast Inns (CABBI). Also lending much support for the Monterey section was Diane Mandeville of the Cannery Row Association who enthusiastically provided me with wonderful ideas. Generous nearly to a fault with the Sierra Foothills portion of the book was Maureen Funk, Jamie Lubenko and Jody Franklin, and the wine associations and visitors associations of El Dorado, Amador and Calaveras counties. They made my time in the Foothills seamless. Thanks also to Linda Parker Sanpei for help with the San Luis Obispo section. And lastly, thanks to my wonderful wife, Kathy, for her patience and understanding during my prolonged absences from home in order to make this book a reality.

www.moon.com

DESTINATIONS | ACTIVITIES | BLOGS | MAPS | BOOKS

MOON.COM is ready to help plan your next trip! Filled with fresh trip ideas and strategies, author interviews, informative travel blogs, a detailed map library, and descriptions of all the Moon guidebooks, Moon.com is all you need to get out and explore the world—or even places in your own backyard. While at Moon.com, sign up for our monthly e-newsletter for updates on new releases, travel tips, and expert advice from our on-the-go Moon authors. As always, when you travel with Moon, expect an experience that is uncommon and truly unique.

**MOON IS ON FACEBOOK—BECOME A FAN!
JOIN THE MOON PHOTO GROUP ON FLICKR**

MAP SYMBOLS

Expressway	(Highlight	✗ Airfield	⚑ Golf Course
Primary Road	○ City/Town	✈ Airport	ⓟ Parking Area
Secondary Road	⊙ State Capital	▲ Mountain	Archaeological Site
Unpaved Road	⊛ National Capital	✛ Unique Natural Feature	Church
Trail	★ Point of Interest		Gas Station
Ferry	• Accommodation	Waterfall	Glacier
Railroad	▼ Restaurant/Bar	▲ Park	Mangrove
Pedestrian Walkway	▪ Other Location	Trailhead	Reef
Stairs	ᴧ Campground	Skiing Area	Swamp

CONVERSION TABLES

°C = (°F - 32) / 1.8
°F = (°C x 1.8) + 32
1 inch = 2.54 centimeters (cm)
1 foot = 0.304 meters (m)
1 yard = 0.914 meters
1 mile = 1.6093 kilometers (km)
1 km = 0.6214 miles
1 fathom = 1.8288 m
1 chain = 20.1168 m
1 furlong = 201.168 m
1 acre = 0.4047 hectares
1 sq km = 100 hectares
1 sq mile = 2.59 square km
1 ounce = 28.35 grams
1 pound = 0.4536 kilograms
1 short ton = 0.90718 metric ton
1 short ton = 2,000 pounds
1 long ton = 1.016 metric tons
1 long ton = 2,240 pounds
1 metric ton = 1,000 kilograms
1 quart = 0.94635 liters
1 US gallon = 3.7854 liters
1 Imperial gallon = 4.5459 liters
1 nautical mile = 1.852 km

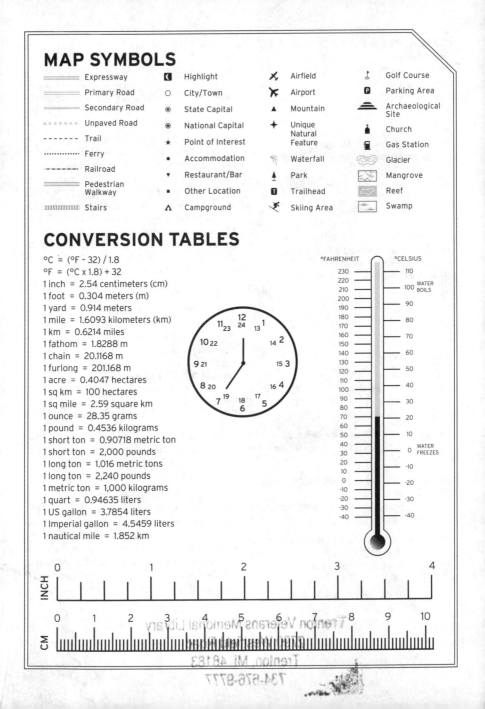

MOON CALIFORNIA WINE COUNTRY

Avalon Travel
a member of the Perseus Books Group
1700 Fourth Street
Berkeley, CA 94710, USA
www.moon.com

Editor: Kevin McLain
Series Manager: Kathryn Ettinger
Copy Editors: Naomi Adler Dancis, Amy Scott,
    Christopher Church
Graphics and Production Coordinators: Elizabeth Jang,
    Darren Alessi
Cover Designer: Elizabeth Jang
Map Editors: Brice Ticen, Albert Angulo
Cartographers: Kat Bennett, Chris L. Henrick,
    Andrea Butkovic, Bernadette Resero Dugtong
Proofreader: Kia Wang Nevarez
Indexer: Rachel Kuhn

ISBN: 978-1-59880-595-6
ISSN: 2160-4215

Printing History
1st Edition – 2006
3rd Edition – May 2011
5 4 3 2 1

Front cover photo: Vineyard in Napa Valley in Autumn
© Andy Z./shutterstock.com
Title page photo: Courtesy of Visit Mendocino
County, Inc.

Interior color photos: Pg. 4 ripe wine grapes ready
for harvest © Andy Dean/123rf.com; pg. 5 (top
left) Courtesy of Visit Mendocino County, Inc.,
(top center) vineyard in full bloom © Sonoma
County Tourism Bureau, (top right) 2009
harvest © George Rose, (bottom) © Sonoma
County Tourism Bureau; pg. 6 (thumbnail)
© Sonoma County Tourism Bureau, bottom Merlot
grapes ready for harvest at Ravenswood © Peter
Griffith, pg. 7 (top left) lavender plants in full bloom ©
Susan & Neil Silverman, (top right) cherryblock vines
© Foley Family Wines, (bottom left) It's hard to get
lost in the Sonoma Valley. © Philip Goldsmith, (bottom
right) Santa Barbara rooftops © Jay Sinclair; pg. 8
© Philip Goldsmith; pg. 9 © Robert Janover; pg. 10
© aspenrock/123rf.com; pg. 11 © Foley Family Wines;
pg. 13 © George Rose; pg. 15 © Thomas Barrat/123rf
.com; pg. 16 © Sonoma County Tourism Bureau; pg.
17 © Santa Barbara CVB; pg. 18 © Jay Sinclair; pg. 19
© Dylanwalker | Dreamstime.com; pg. 20 © Foley
Family Wines; pg. 21 © V. Sattui Winery; pg. 22
Courtesy of Domaine Chandon; pg. 23 © Auberge
Resorts; pg. 24 © The Ballard Inn

Printed in Canada by Friesens